The Muvipix.com Guide to DVD Architect Studio 5.0

Steve Grisetti

A guide to using Sony's powerful yet affordable software to create exciting, professional-looking DVDs and BluRay discs on your personal computer.

Dedication

This book is first and foremost dedicated to the wonderful people who have challenged, inspired and educated me with their questions, comments and insightful answers on the Sony and Muvipix.com forums. Without you, I'd just be talking to myself.

A special tip-of-the-hat to Danielle, who caught all those typos that not even a spellchecker and two previous proofreadings did not.

And to my family, Jeanne and Sarah, who once again allowed me to focus on this little obsession for several months and offered their unconditional support and constant patience, even when they weren't quite sure what the heck I was doing.

And to the wonderful, hard-working moderators at Muvipix.com, whose ideas, solutions and shared knowledge have often helped me to appear a lot smarter than I really am.

And, finally, to my friends and Muvipix.com co-founders, Chuck Engels and Ron Hoskins. To Chuck, whose dear friendship, support and efforts in helping me get this book together are beyond measure. And to webmaster extraordinaire Ron, for always quietly and diligently working in the background, without whom there couldn't be a Muvipix.com.

About Muvipix.com

Muvipix.com was created to offer support and community to amateur and semi-professional videomakers. Registration is free, and that gets you access to the world's friendliest, most helpful forum and lots of ad-free space for displaying your work. On the products page, you'll find dozens of free tips, tutorials, motion backgrounds, DVD templates, sound effects, royalty-free music and stock video clips. For a small annual subscription fee that we use to keep the site running, you'll have unlimited downloads from the ever-growing library of support materials and media.

We invite you to drop by and visit our thriving community. We'd love to have you join the neighborhood!

http://Muvipix.com

About the author

Steve Grisetti holds a master's degree in Telecommunications from Ohio University and spent several years working in the motion picture and television industry in Los Angeles. A veteran of several video editing programs and systems, Steve is the co-founder of Muvipix.com, a help and support site for amateur and semi-professional videomakers. A professional graphic designer and video freelancer, he has taught classes in Photoshop and lectured on design. He lives in suburban Milwaukee.

Other books by Steve Grisetti

The Muvipix.com Guide to DVD Architect Studio 4.5
Adobe Premiere Elements 2.0 In a Snap (with Chuck Engels)
The Muvipix.com Guide to Adobe Premiere Elements 7
The Muvipix.com Guide to Adobe Premiere Elements 8
The Muvipix.com Guide to Adobe Premiere Elements 9
The Muvipix.com Guide to Photoshop Elements & Premiere Elements 7
The Muvipix.com Guide to Photoshop Elements & Premiere Elements 8
The Muvipix.com Guide to Photoshop Elements & Premiere Elements 9
Cool Tricks & Hot Tips for Adobe Premiere Elements

An Introduction

To the book and DVD Architect Studio 5

What this program is

I can't tell you how happy I was to discover DVD Architect Studio.

In my quest to find the ideal PC-based video editing program, I'd sampled a wide variety. Many video editing apps came bundled with some sort of DVD and BluRay authoring system, though most of these were less than satisfying. They tended to compromise their disc authoring power in favor of video editing features.

That's understandable, but it also fueled my desire to find a good standalone disc authoring application to supplement my editor.

After all, what's the fun in creating an exciting, interesting video if you can't package it as part of an exciting, interesting DVD?

The authoring programs that included the features I was looking for tended to be geared more (and priced more) for the professional. Some of the higher-end applications were also only available bundled with a suite of video production applications – with prices from $500 to well over $1,000. And, for someone who, despite the occasional freelance gig, still considers himself predominantly a hobbyist, that was a bit out of my reach.

And then, a few years ago, Sony released DVD Architect Studio! At first it was only sold bundled with Sony's likewise excellent Vegas Movie Studio. But, eventually, Sony released it as a standalone application, and I was thrilled to get my hands on it!

Available for under $50 and yet loaded with great features, the program is only slightly scaled down from its professionally-geared big brother. Finally, I could add an introductory video clip before the main menu, develop intricate menu structures, create my own fully-customizable menu pages, complete with motion backgrounds and music, and even include bonus features, chapter menus and slideshows.

The program's interface may seem a bit daunting at first. Yet, once you learn a few basic moves, it quickly becomes extremely intuitive. And, as you dig deeper and deeper into the program, you'll find more and more customizable features and hidden gems.

My hope is that this book guides you to mastering this program – and that maybe it helps you find a few hidden gems yourself!

What this program is not

It's important to note that, although DVD Architect Studio 5 is a very powerful and versatile DVD and BluRay disc authoring system, it should be seen as a *supplement* to your video editing software – not a substitute for it.

You can do some very basic trims with the program, isolating a segment of a video clip so that only that segment is included on your final disc – but you can't cut segments out of the middle of a video, add transitions or special effects or even use it to capture video or output video in a format other than a DVD or BluRay disc. That's just not what the program is designed to do.

However, the program will interface beautifully with output from just about any PC- or Mac-based video editing program– from high-end programs like Sony Vegas, Adobe Premiere and Apple's Final Cut to lower end programs like iMovie and Windows MovieMaker. You can also create basic content, like slideshows and video compilations (assemblages of video clips) right in the program.

But the main purpose of the program is to take the video you've already created in your video editing program and package it with the kind of exciting and interesting disc menus and structures that are worthy of that video – and maybe impress the heck out of your friends, family and clients in the process!

Muvipix.com

Muvipix.com was created in 2006 as a community and a learning center for videomakers at a variety of levels. Our community includes everyone from amateurs and hobbyists to semi-pros, professionals and even people with broadcast experience. You won't find more knowledgeable, helpful people anywhere else on the Web. I very much encourage you to drop by our forums and say hello. At the very least, you'll make some new friends. And it's rare that there's a question posted there that isn't quickly, and enthusiastically, answered.

Our learning center consists of video tutorials, tips and, of course, books. But we also offer a wealth of support in the forms of motion background videos, licensed music and even stock footage. Much of it is absolutely free – and there's even more available for those who purchase one of our affordable site subscriptions.

Our goal has always been to help people get up to speed making great videos and, once they're there, provide them with the inspiration and means to get better and better at doing so. Why? Because we know making movies is a heck of a lot of fun – and we want to share that fun with everyone!

Our books, then, are a manifestation of that goal. And my hope for you is that this book helps *you* get up to speed. I think you'll find, once you get over the surprisingly small learning curve, making movies on your home computer is a lot more fun than you ever imagined! And you may even amaze yourself with the results in the process.

Thanks for supporting Muvipix.com, and happy moviemaking!

Steve
http://Muvipix.com

A Table of Contents

Table of Contents

What have I gotten myself into?

Some basic questions and answers about DVD Architect Studio 5 and how it works

What is DVD Architect Studio?

DVD Architect Studio is a DVD and BluRay disc authoring system. That means that it is designed as a tool for gathering your final video, building a menu system and ultimately creating the look and function of your disc – and, of course, burning this final product to a DVD or BluRay disc.

Can I edit my videos in DVD Architect Studio?

Not really. At least that's not what it is designed to do. DVD Architect Studio was created as a companion to a video editing system (primarily Vegas MovieStudio, although it can be used alongside virtually any video editing program). For the most part, you should do all of your editing in a dedicated video editor and then output the finished video or videos to DVD Architect Studio for final output to disc.

Why "Studio"?

The "Studio" designation indicates that the program was designed as consumer software, just as Vegas MovieStudio. Sony Creative Software also sells professional and pro-sumer versions of its programs, which include tools for, for instance, adding optional subtitles to your movies and including alternative language tracks. However, you will likely be surprised by how powerful even this consumer version of the program is, and how professional your projects will look!

The interfaces for the "Pro" and "Studio" versions of the program are, by the way, almost identical. And, if you can master one, you'll have little problem transitioning to the other.

How much video can I fit on a DVD or BluRay disc?

Because video discs use a variable form of file compression, you can squeeze nearly as much as you'd like a on a DVD or BluRay disc – however, the more you squeeze in, the lower the quality of the video will be.

As a rule of thumb, you can fit about 70 minutes of full-quality video on a single-layer DVD and about twice that on a dual-layer disc. A BluRay disc, however, will hold about two hours of high definition video while a dual-layer BluRay will hold about twice that. If you add more than this to your disc, the program can be set to automatically compress your video files and reduce the quality of this video for you.

My video is several gigabytes in size. How will it all fit on a disc?

Part of the process of creating a DVD or BluRay involves transcoding, or putting the video and audio into a more efficient format and reducing the file sizes so it all fits onto your disc.

The indicator in the lower right of the interface will display the size of your disc files, by default based on the actual size of your raw files.

However, if you go to the File menu and select Optimize Disc and, in the option screen that opens, click the Fit to Disc checkbox, this indicator will display the size of your final disc files *after* transcoding and compression.

What kinds of video can I load into DVD Architect Studio?

Although the program accepts a wide variety of formats, some formats work more efficiently and more reliably than others.

Most video editing applications (including Sony Vegas) include export options specifically for outputting DVD-ready or BluRay-ready video:

> For DVD projects, the best source video for DVD Architect Studio is the DVD-ready MPEG2, a 720x480 MPEG (720x576 if you're editing in PAL video) using non-square pixels and lower field first interlacing.
>
> For BluRay discs, the best source video is a BluRay-ready AVC file, a 1920x1080 60i video (50i if you are editing PAL video) MPEG/MTS file using the H.264 codec.

It is usually not a good idea to use video directly from a camera or camcorder or downloaded from online as source video in a DVD Architect Studio project. Whenever possible, you should load your raw video into a video editing program and then output one of the file formats above for use in you disc authoring program.

What's an Overlay?

An Overlay is an indicator, to your viewer, as to which button on your disc menu page is active. (Essentially, it is the highlight that appears over your button.) Overlays can be created in a number of colors and at a number of opacity levels and can appear over the entire button, just the thumbnail image, just the text or in a customized shape.

(Button Overlays should not be confused with Workspace Overlays, which we discuss on page 32.)

We show you how to create and customize your button Overlays in Chapter 4.

What are Color Sets?

Color Sets define the colors for your overlays and button highlights. They can be set to define the colors of overlays on your entire disc or can be customized for individual menu pages or individual buttons.

We discuss Color Sets and how to use them in Chapter 4.

How do I add chapters and buttons to launch specific scenes in my videos?

In DVD Architect Studio, you add the entire video to your disc as a single clip (with a button linking to it from one of your menu pages). In the Timeline panel, you then add Scene/Chapter Markers to your video. Once you've added these markers, you create a Scene Menu with buttons linking to each of your specific scenes.

We show you in detail how to do this in Chapter 6.

What is a Playlist?

A Playlist is a group of video clips launched by a single button. This clip group is created by gathering video clips that are already on your DVD or BluRay disc and making them playable, in the order you set, from a new button you add to a menu page.

For instance, your disc may include a number of short videos, each launchable from a button on a number of different menu pages. When you create a Playlist you set any or all of the videos to play, in the order you set, by clicking on a single button.

We show you how to create Playlists in Chapter 7.

What is a Compilation?

A Compilation is a video slideshow of sorts, a collection of video clips or slides that you gather and order in DVD Architect Studio. A Compilation can include your own custom music soundtrack.

Compilations are one of the few video projects you can actually create from scratch in DVD Architect Studio. However, remember that DVD Architect Studio is not a video editing program – so you'll likely find its composition, editing and customization features rather limited.

We show you how to create Compilations in Chapter 8.

Can I include a short video clip on my disc that plays before my main menu page appears?

Yes. And we show you to use this feature (Introduction Media) in Chapter 5.

Where can I get more help with DVD Architect Studio?

There are not a lot of online resources for DVD Architect and DVD Architect Studio. However, those that exist are very good.

Most notably, Sony Create Software (www.sonycreativesoftware/DVDAStudio) offers online tutorials as well as a helpful user-to-user forum.

Rob Strobbe also offers excellent help for DVD Architect and Sony Vegas users on his www.vegasvideohelp.com.

And, of course, Muvipix.com offers both an extremely helpful forum and a number of helpful tutorials for both basic and advanced functions with the program. You'll likely find me there, day or night, helping out where I can and answering questions.

I've even created a series of "Basic Training" tutorials to demonstrate the fundamental moves for creating a DVD or BluRay disc. You'll find them by going to the Muvipix.com home page and typing "DVD Architect" in the product search box.

Even if you're not finding the program challenging, I hope you'll drop by and say hello! We love to see our videomaker community grow!

Steve and the Muvipix team

Get to Know the Workspace

Basic Editing Moves

What's New in Version 9?

Chapter 1

Get to know DVD Architect Studio

What's what and what it does

The interface for DVD Architect Studio may seem intimidating at first. Where do you even begin?

But don't panic.

Once you know where things are, you'll find it a remarkably intuitive workspace.

In this first chapter, we'll take a tour of the various panels and show you how to find your way around. Then, in Chapter 2, we'll walk you through the process of creating a basic DVD or BluRay disc project.

The DVD Architect Studio 5 Interface

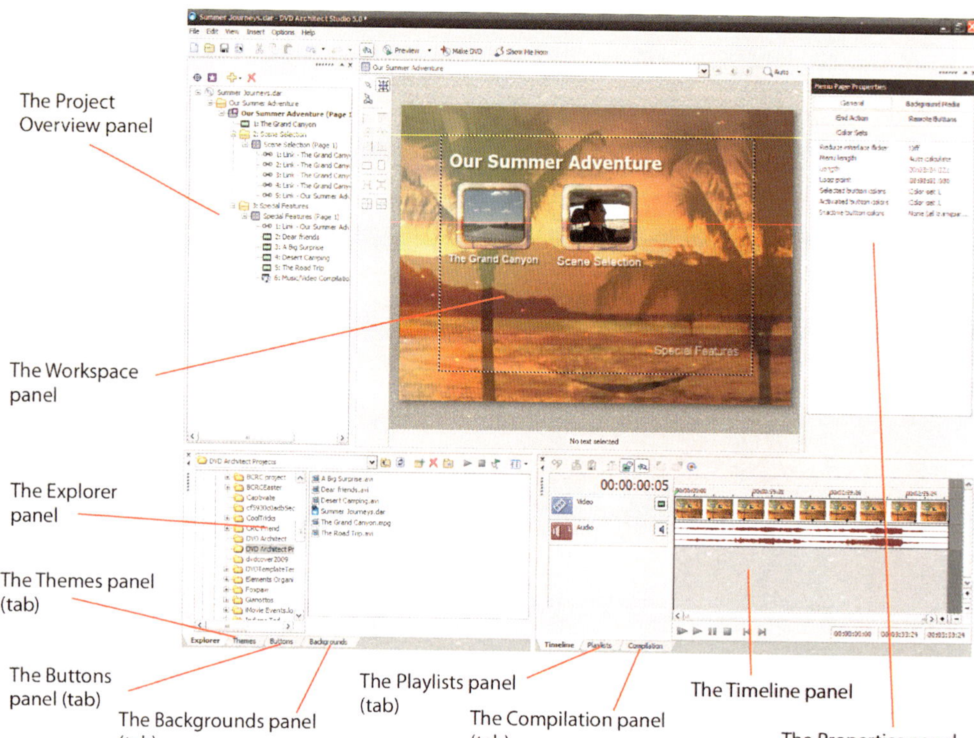

Sony Creative Software has done a terrific job of creating an efficient and easy-to-navigate interface for DVD Architect Studio. The default interface divides the work area into five panels, most of which include more than one tabbed workspace. (Though this interface can also be customized any way you'd like, as we discuss later in this chapter.)

The colorful central panel – by default, the largest panel in the interface – is the **Workspace** panel. This panel will display the menu page or media clip you're presently working on. It's likely where you'll do most of the assembling and designing of your individual menu pages.

As you add items to this panel and build out your disc menu system, you'll see the structure of your disc displayed in the **Project Overview** panel, to the left of the **Workspace** panel.

In the lower left of the interface is a tabbed, multi-purpose panel – which includes the **Explorer, Buttons, Backgrounds** and **Themes** – from which you'll gather media and templates to build your disc.

In the lower right of the interface, you'll find a **Timeline** and tabbed workspaces for assembling **Compilations** and **Playlists**.

And in the upper right is the **Properties** panel, a very powerful area in which you can customize the functions and look of your buttons, media and menu pages.

The Workspace panel

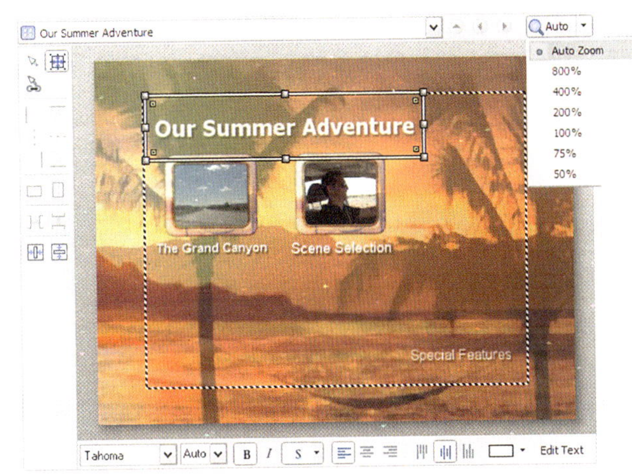

Dominating the interface, the **Workspace** is where you see your menu pages come together. This panel is amazingly intuitive in its function. To create a button linking to a video, for instance, you simply drag a video from the **Explorer** onto the menu page displayed in the **Workspace**.

Likewise, you can apply a custom DVD Architect Studio look to your menu page by simply dragging a **Theme**, **Background** or **Button** style from the collection included with the program – or you can create your own custom menu page by dragging a background image or music track from the **Explorer** panel.

Along the bottom of this panel are tools for customizing and editing the text on your menu pages or buttons.

Along the left side of this panel are tools for resizing and positioning the buttons and other elements on your menu page.

We'll discuss many of the functions of, and tools included on, this panel as we show you how to **Build a Menu Page** in **Chapter 4**.

The Project Overview panel

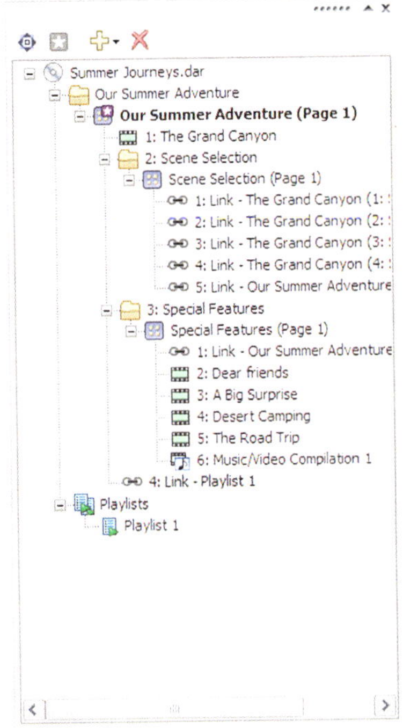

As you add text, graphics, scene buttons, media and menu pages to your disc project, the **Project Overview** panel will display the growing structure of your DVD or BluRay disc.

There are few limits to how many levels and branches your disc project can have in DVD Architect Studio. If you have a mind to, you can make your DVD menu structure every bit as complicated as a major web site!

But the **Project Overview** panel is not merely a passive display. It's also a dynamic workspace in which you can create items (like new menu pages), drag and re-arrange the order and locations of your menu pages and media, as we show you in **Build a Disc Menu Structure** in **Chapter 5**. We'll also show you some high level tricks, like adding a video clip that plays before your main menu appears and adding a transitional video that plays between your menu pages.

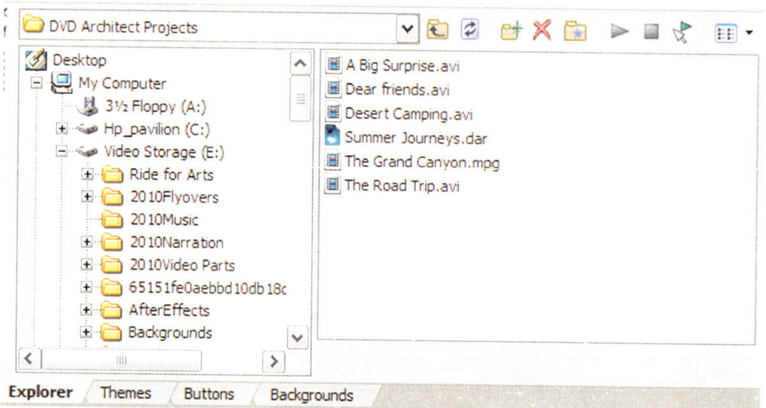

The Explorer

Similar in layout to Windows Explorer, the DVD Architect Studio **Explorer** panel provides a source for your media files. To add a link to your menu page, you need only browse to the video clip on your computer and then drag it to the menu page displayed in the **Workspace** panel. A button is automatically added to your menu page and the video itself is added to your DVD or BluRay disc's structure.

Additionally, you can use media from the **Explorer** panel to create **Picture** and **Music/Video Compilations**, features that you can include on your DVD in addition to – or in place of – your main videos.

By the way, you don't have to use this panel to get your media into you disc project. You can also open up Windows Explorer or My Documents on your computer, browse to video, stills or other media files and simply drag them from Windows Explorer directly into DVD Architect Studio's **Workspace** area.

We'll discuss the panel more closely in **Chapter 4, Create and Customize a Menu Button**.

Themes

Themes are style sets for your menu pages. As we discuss in more detail in **Chapter 9, Work with Themes, Backgrounds and Button Styles**, by dragging a theme onto a menu page in the **Workspace** panel, you can automatically apply a background, text style and button style to a menu page.

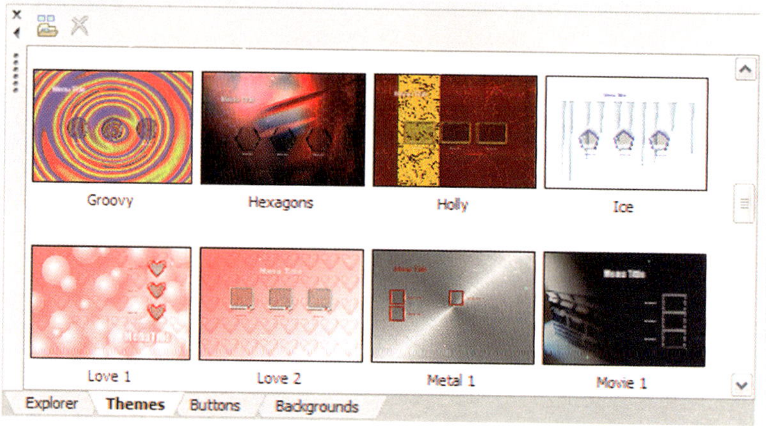

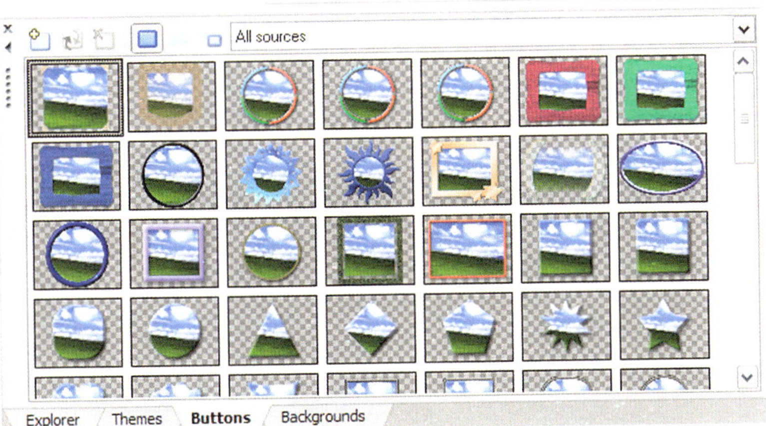

Buttons

Under this tab, you'll find a variety of button shapes, graphics and frames. By dragging a button style from here, you can apply these button styles to an individual button or to all the buttons on a given menu page. More on that in **Chapter 4, Create and Customize a Menu Button**.

We'll also show you how to create motion buttons, how to create a custom button frame and even how to replace your button completely with your own custom-created graphic.

Backgrounds

Like the button styles under the **Buttons** tab, many of the backgrounds under this tab are individual elements also used in the DVD Architect Studio **Themes** set. They are easily applied, just by dragging them onto a menu page displayed in your **Workspace** panel. And, as we'll show you in **Chapter 3, Build a Menu Page**, you can also swap in your own custom still photo or video backgrounds.

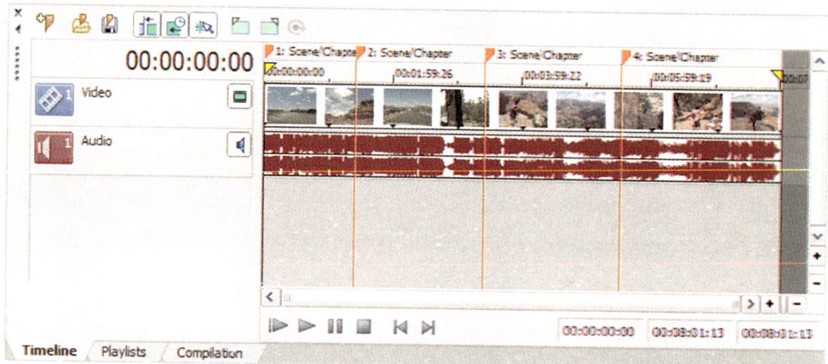

The Timeline panel

This panel displays a timeline of your selected media clip or menu page.

You can't do a lot of editing on this timeline or add transitions or effects. But you can trim from the end and beginning of your video clips so that their playback starts and ends at designated points.

You can also use the **Timeline** panel to add **Scene/Chapter Markers** to your video so that your viewer can jump from sequence to sequence or launch a scene from a scene selection menu. We'll show you how to do that in **Chapter 6, Add Scene/Chapter Markers and a Scene Menu**.

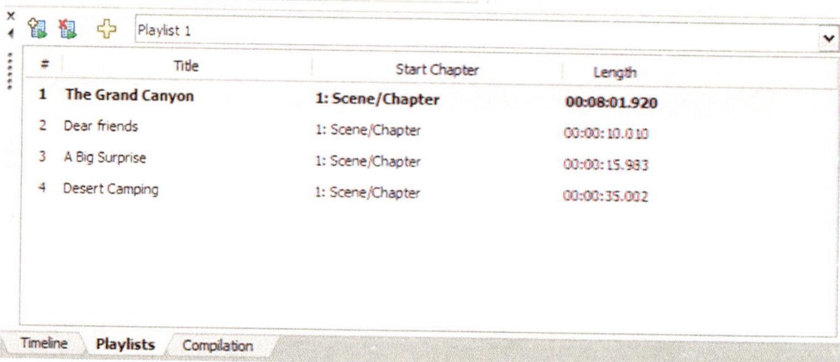

The Playlists panel

Playlists are mini-features, culled from existing media on your disc. In other words, when you build a Playlist, you gather video clips from other menu pages on your DVD or BluRay disc and set them up so that your viewer can view the entire set of clips with a single click. A nice thing about **Playlists** is that, since they merely link to existing video on your disc and don't include additional video footage, they don't increase the size of your disc file.

You'll find instructions for building and editing them in **Chapter 7, Create a Playlist**.

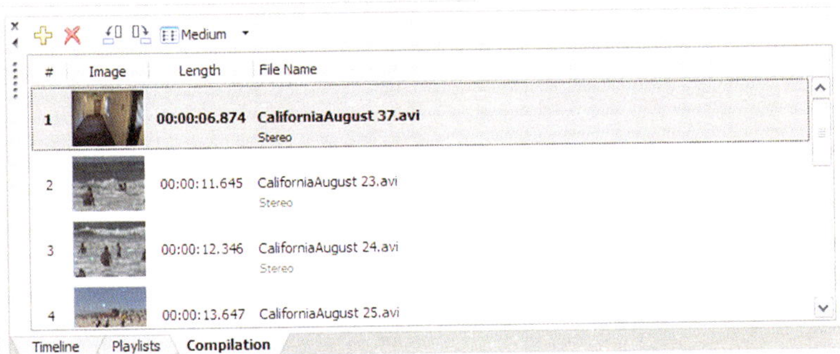

The Compilation panel

Like Playlists, **Compilations** are video features you create for your DVD or BluRay disc right in DVD Architect Studio. Unlike **Playlists, Compilations** are made up of *new media clips* you add to your disc from the **Explorer** panel. A **Compilation** can include video, stills and audio or music. We'll show you how to create one in **Chapter 8, Build a Picture or Music/ Video Compilation.**

The Properties panel

The **Properties** panel (to the right of the **Workspace** panel) is probably the deepest workspace in the whole DVD Architect Studio interface. It's here that every element of your menu pages and media is customized with any of dozens of options.

It's here that you can customize what your buttons and menu pages look and sound like.

It's here that you set how each button behaves and what color or highlight image appears over it when it is selected.

It's here that you add behaviors or end actions to your buttons, menu pages and your media.

It's here that you add custom-created button images and button frames.

We'll refer to the various **Properties** panels throughout the book, as we create the various elements for our disc. Like the program's interface itself, it may appear daunting at first. But, once you see how logically the designers have arranged the various properties in this panel, you'll find it surprisingly easy to use.

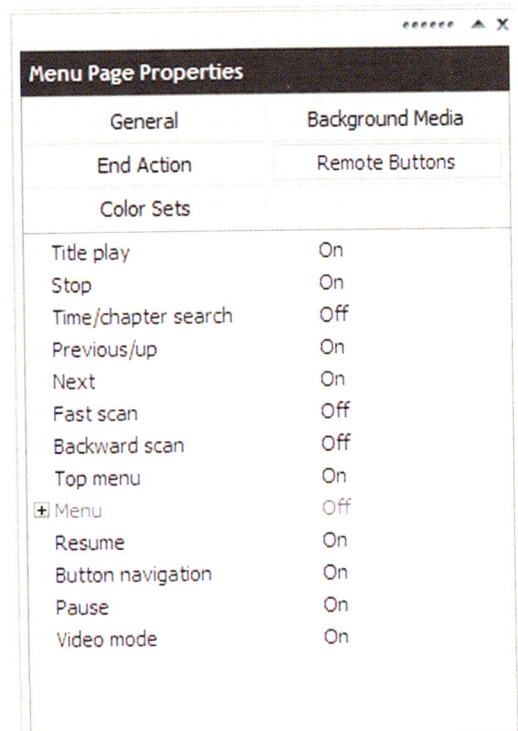

Menu Page Properties

General	Background Media
End Action	Remote Buttons
Color Sets	

Title play	On
Stop	On
Time/chapter search	Off
Previous/up	On
Next	On
Fast scan	Off
Backward scan	Off
Top menu	On
+ Menu	Off
Resume	On
Button navigation	On
Pause	On
Video mode	On

Customize your workspace

Although the default set-up for the interface makes fairly efficient use of your monitor space, you can easily customize it to take best advantage of your computer's desktop space or so that you can temporarily focus on one panel or two.

Resize the panels

To resize each of the panels, hover your mouse over the seams between them. When you see a double-headed arrow resizer indicator, click and drag. As you drag one panel larger, the other panels will resize to allow for it.

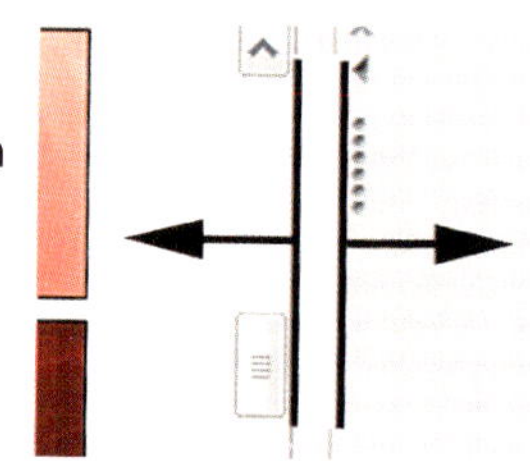

Maximize/Minimize the panels

The arrow buttons at the top left of each panel are single-click ways to minimize or maximize the panels.

Click on the arrow to the upper left of the **Explorer** panel, for instance, it snaps to the full width of the program's interface. Click again on the arrow and it snaps back to its original size.

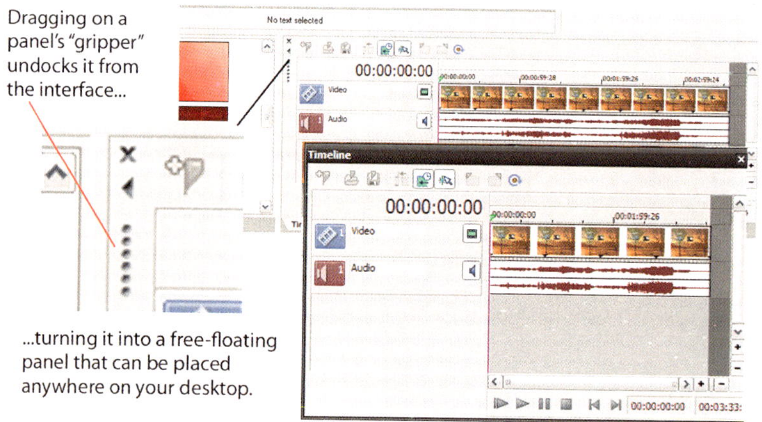

Dragging on a panel's "gripper" undocks it from the interface...

...turning it into a free-floating panel that can be placed anywhere on your desktop.

Undock the panels

If you click and hold on the "......" (officially the "**gripper**") at the top or left side of any panel, you can pull the panel completely free from the interface.

- Once you've dragged the panel free from the interface, you place it anywhere you'd like on your desktop. Particularly if you've got a dual-monitor set-up for your computer, this is a great way to leave several panels open at once for easy access.
- If you drag a panel into any of the "drop zones" in the program (areas of the interfaces in which panels already reside), when you release your mouse button the panel will drop right into this zone – becoming another tabbed panel in the set.

Starting a new project

Setups and Formatting

Basic Steps to Building Menus

Chapter 2

Create a DVD Architect Studio project

First steps

To demonstrate how each panel contributes to the process of designing a menu and creating a DVD or BluRay disc, let's create a basic menu structure.

Creating a complicated, highly-customized disc structure isn't much harder.

Once you understand what's going on in this exercise, you'll know pretty much all the necessary moves. Beyond this, it's just customizing, refining and adding a couple of optional flourishes.

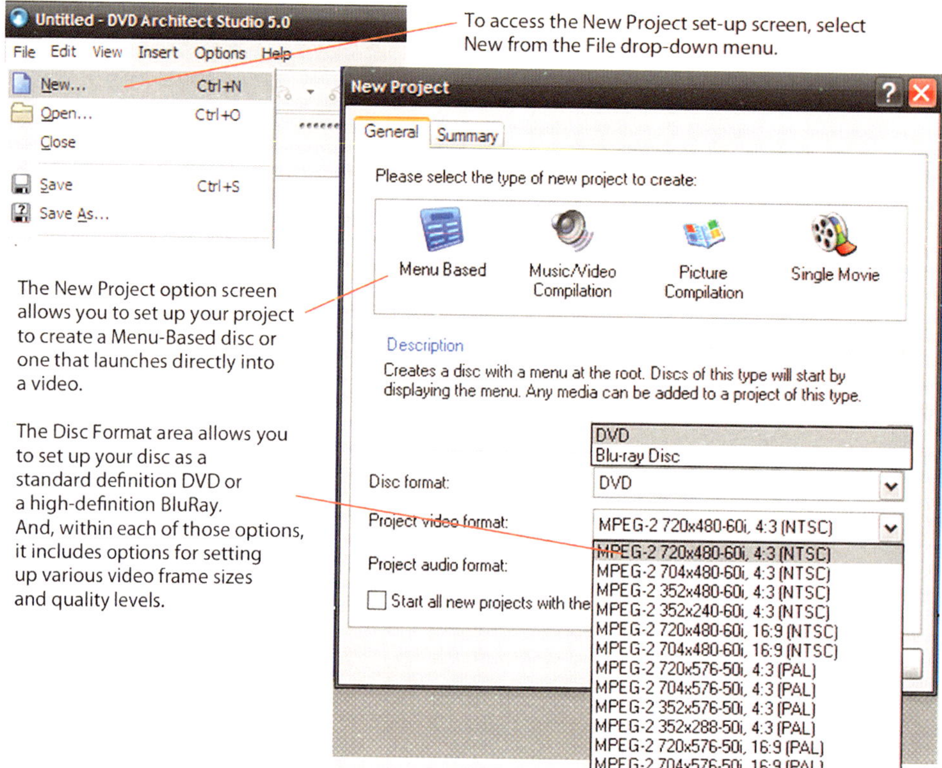

To access the New Project set-up screen, select New from the File drop-down menu.

The New Project option screen allows you to set up your project to create a Menu-Based disc or one that launches directly into a video.

The Disc Format area allows you to set up your disc as a standard definition DVD or a high-definition BluRay. And, within each of those options, it includes options for setting up various video frame sizes and quality levels.

A good start can take you a long way toward a successful project. Taking the time to ensure your disc project is set up right is always a smart move.

1 Start a new disc project

If you click on the blank "new menu" icon (the blank sheet of paper icon) in the upper left of the program's interface, you will get a new, empty disc menu.

However, if you go to the **File** drop-down menu and select the **New** option (or press **Ctrl+n** on your keyboard), the program will launch the **New Project** option screen.

As you can see in the illustration below, this screen offers a number of options for custom-designing your disc project. They are:

Menu Based. In most cases, if you plan to create a DVD or BluRay disc with a menu structure (which is what you bought the program for, right?) this is the option you will select.

Music/Video Compilation. This option will open a workspace for you to build a compilation or montage of video clips. By default, this type of disc will have no menu, but will go directly to your compilation.

Picture Compilation. Similar to a Music/Video Compilation, a Picture Compilation is a slideshow made of up still photos and can be accompanied by a music soundtrack.

Single Movie. This option creates a disc with no menus. Your disc will launch directly into your movie when it is loaded into a DVD or BluRay disc player.

More information on creating **Compilations** can be found in **Chapter 8, Build a Picture or Music/Video Compilation**.

Although the **Music/Video Compilation, Picture Compilation** and **Single Movie** options create a disc with no menu structures, you have the option to manually add a menu structure later. For more information on doing this, see **Chapter 5, Build a Menu Structure**.

2 Set up your disc's formatting

Once you've selected your disc's type, you can set up the disc's format.

The **Disc Format** drop-down menu allows you to designate whether your disc will produce a standard definition or high-definition video disc:

The **DVD** option creates a standard definition disc of up to 720x480 pixels (NTSC) or 720x576 pixels (PAL).

The **BluRay** option creates a high-definition disc up to 1920x1080 60i (NTSC) or 1920x1080 50i (PAL).

Once you have selected **Disc Format**, you will have the option of setting the **Project Video** Format. If you are planning to play your disc on a standard DVD or BluRay disc player, you'll most likely use the default or highest quality options.

For a DVD, the best Project Video Format is 720x480 (NTSC) or 720x576 (PAL). You can also designate whether your disc will be either 16:9 widescreen or 4:3 standard format, to match your source video.

For a BluRay disc, you can use either the standard MPEG2 1440x1080 60i (NTSC) or 50i (PAL) or the more advanced AVCHD 1440x1080 60i (NTSC) or 50i (PAL). (The program also includes a number of optional frame rates.) Your BluRay disc player can likely play both MPEG2 and AVCHD video, so either option is acceptable.

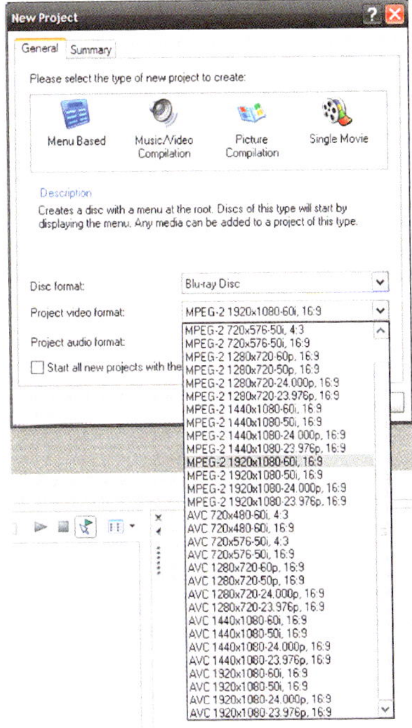

The wealth of BluRay video format options.

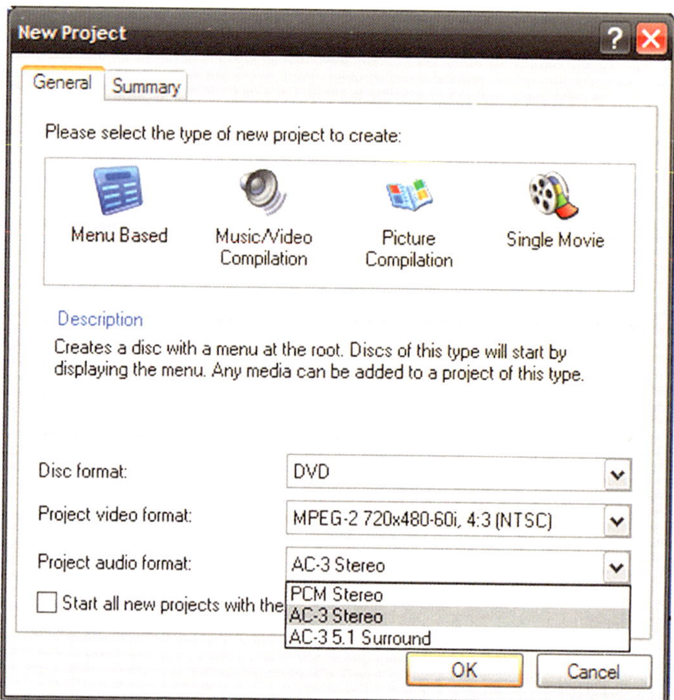

There are three settings for your disc's **Project Audio Format**:

> **PCM. Pulse code modulation** files are basic, uncompressed digital audio. (This is your only choice for BluRay discs.)
>
> **AC-3**. Audio Code 3 is another name for **Dolby Digital**. Because of its quality to size ratio, AC-3 is the most common audio format for stereo DVDs.
>
> **AC-3 5.1**. Also known as **Dolby Digital 5.1 Surround** is a compressed file that delivers audio over five channels – left and right, front and rear and center – surrounding the viewer with your DVD's audio. (Naturally, in order for it to provide a true surround sound experience, you will need to provide your DVD project with a five-channel audio source video.)

BluRay disc's can *only* be produced with PCM audio in DVD Architect Studio 5.

This panel also includes a checkbox option for setting the default format for your future projects. In other words, if you check this box, your next disc project will already be set up with this formatting, and you can skip this **New Project** screen in the future.

Click **OK** to close this window.

3 Set your disc's size

One other property worth setting or confirming for your disc's project is your disc project's size.

To access this setting, go to the **File** drop-down menu at the top of the interface and select **Properties**. The window that opens will display a summary of your disc properties, most of which you will have already set when you started your new disc project.

On the **Project Properties** screen, note the **Target Media Size** property.

If you are creating a DVD, this property is, by default, set to 4.7 gigabytes, the capacity of a standard, single-sided DVD.

If you are using a dual-layer DVD, click on the number 4.7 to the right of the **Target Media Size** listing and, from the drop-down menu that appears, select 8.5 gigabytes.

Likewise, if you are creating a BluRay, ensure that the **Target Media Size** is set up to the correct media size, whether you are burning to a standard (25 gigabyte disc) or a dual-layer BluRay (50 gigabyte). (You can also create a BluRay video for burning to a DVD as discussed in the sidebar at the top of page 22.)

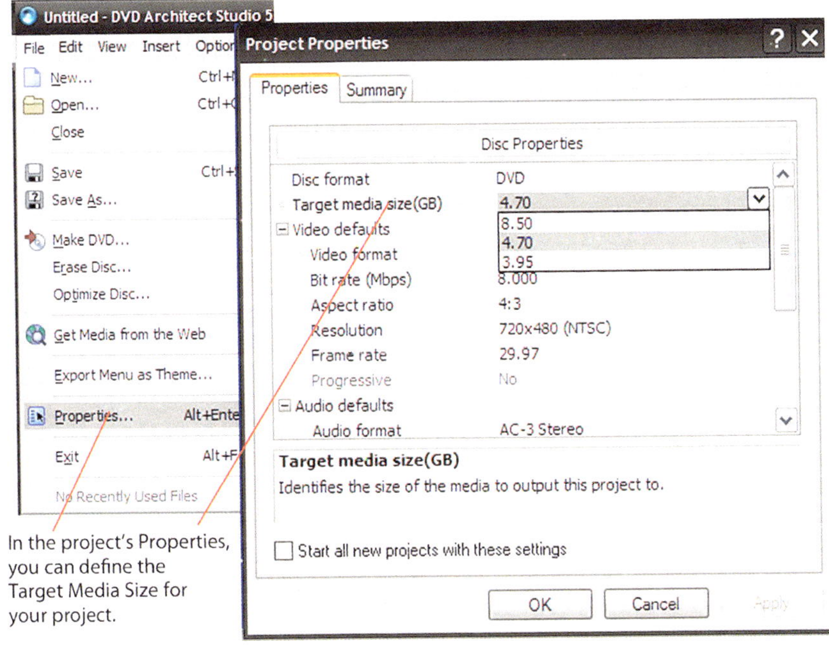

In the project's Properties, you can define the Target Media Size for your project.

Burn BluRay files to a DVD

If you plan to burn your high-definition BluRay files to a DVD, be sure to set your **Target Media Size** to either 8.5 gigabytes (for a dual-layer DVD) or 4.7 gigabytes. This will direct the program to ensure your video files do not exceed the capacity of your disc.

Two notes about BluRay on a DVD, however:

- You can not play these videos on a standard DVD player. The formatting of the video is still high definition BluRay, so these discs can only be played on a BluRay disc player.
- The capacity of a DVD is much less than that of a BluRay disc. You will likely only be able to fit 10-20 minutes of high definition video on a DVD at full quality.

This setting will become important as the programs tracks how much space your DVD or BluRay files will fill on your disc (as displayed in the lower right of the interface) and, more so, when you optimize your disc files for output, as discussed in **Chapter 10, Burn a DVD or BluRay disc**.

When you are satisfied with the settings in this panel, click **OK**.

The program will open into its default workspace and you can finally begin building your DVD or BluRay disc project!

4 Name your disc project

Save and name your disc's project by going to the **File** menu and selecting **Save** (or pressing **Ctrl+s** on your keyboard).

Your disc project's name will appear on the disc icon at the top of the structure tree in the **Project Overview** panel, as illustrated below.

You can save your project either by selecting the Save option under the File menu, pressing the Ctrl+s buttons on your keyboard or by clicking on the floppy disk icon on the upper left of the interface.

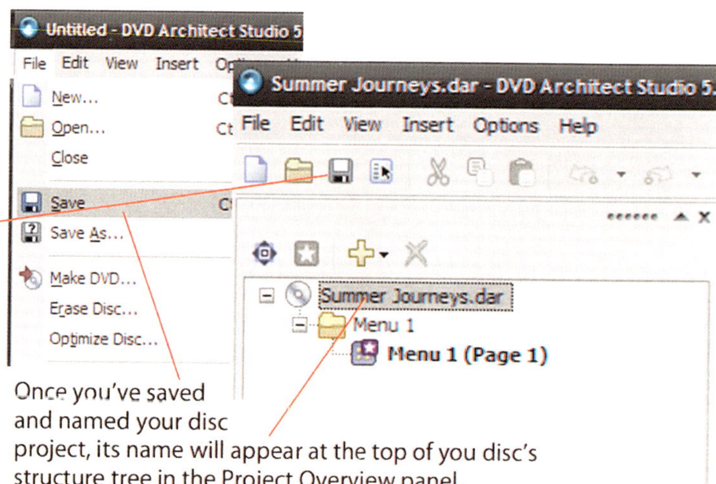

Once you've saved and named your disc project, its name will appear at the top of you disc's structure tree in the Project Overview panel.

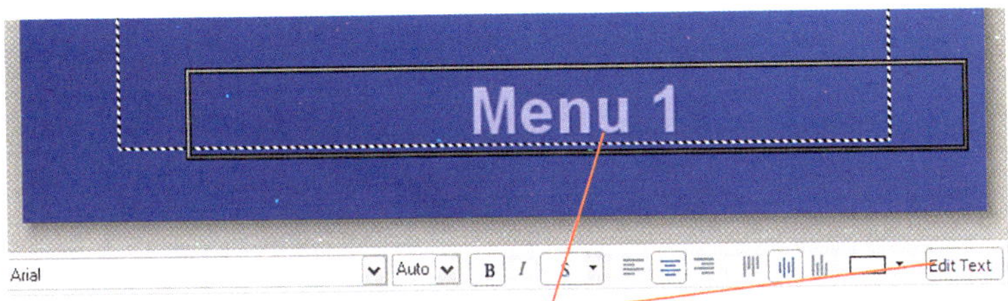

A text box will become editable if you select it in the Workspace panel and click the Edit Text button.

5 Give your menu page a title

Once you've created a new disc project, a generic menu page will be displayed in the **Workspace** panel.

Click on the text box containing the words "Menu 1" in the **Workspace** panel to select it. Now click on the **Edit Text** button in the lower right corner of the panel. The text in the box will become editable and you will be able to type over it.

This is your main menu, the first menu page your viewer will see when he launches your disc. Type in the text box the name you'd like to give to your DVD or BluRay disc.

The **Workspace** panel includes a number of options for customizing your text's font, size, characteristics and color. For more information on working with text, see **Edit or add text** in **Chapter 3, Build a Menu Page**.

6 Customize your page

There are a number of ways to customize the look and feel of your page:

For information on using a theme to stylize your entire page's look, see **Chapter 9, Work with Themes, Backgrounds and Button Styles**.

For information on adding a still photo or custom video loop as your menu background, see **Chapter 3, Build a Menu Page**.

Chapter 3 will also show you how to add a music or another audio loop to play in your menu's background as well as information on adding additional graphics and text.

The look of your entire menu page can be changed by applying a Theme.

A menu button is created on your menu page simply by dragging a video clip from the Explorer panel to the page displayed in the Workspace panel.

7 Add a video clip and create a button

Select the **Explorer** tab from the panel in the lower left of the interface.

Browse to a video clip on your computer and drag it onto your menu page in the **Workspace** panel. (You can also drag clips directly from Windows Explorer.)

The video will be added to your disc's structure and a button linking to it will be added to your menu page.

For information on applying a button frame style to your button, see **Chapter 4, Create and Customize a Menu Button**.

This chapter also includes information on manually customizing the look of this button (including making the button display a video loop rather than a still thumbnail), editing text on it and customizing the overlay (highlight) that appears over it when your viewer navigates the menu page.

At this point, you've created a basic disc with a menu! But beyond that, there are countless options you can apply.

Add "Extras" to your disc

In addition to the media items added to your DVD structure, you can also add non-video files to your disc, including photos, documentation and readme files. These added files will only be visible by browsing the disc on a computer and will not be visible while viewing the disc on a DVD or BluRay player. For more information on using this feature, see **Adding Extras** in **Chapter 11, An Appendix of Advanced DVD Architect Studio Tricks**.

In the Timeline panel, your video can be trimmed an Scene/Chapter Markers can be added.

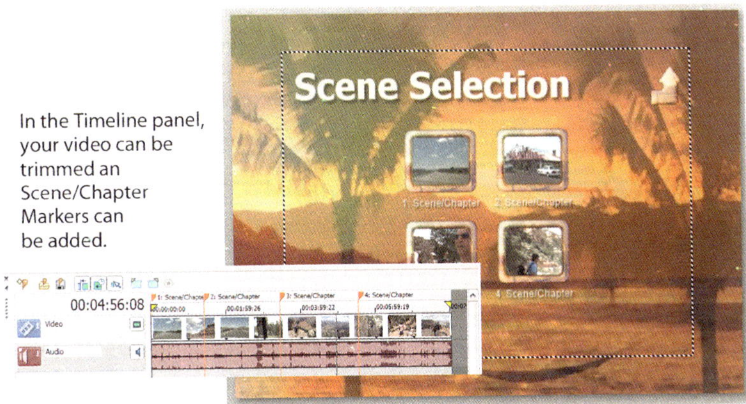

8 Trim and add scene/chapters to your video

Double-click on the button you've just created. Your video will display in the **Workspace** panel.

Select the **Timeline** tab in the lower right corner of the program's interface if this panel is not visible. The **Timeline** will display your video as a single clip.

On this **Timeline**, you can trim your clip (removing video from the beginning or end) as well as add **Scene/Chapter Markers** to it. Once **Scene/Chapter Markers** have been added to your video, you can create a **Scene Menu** with direct links to the scenes in your movie.

For information on working on your video on the **Timeline**, see **Chapter 6, Add Scene/Chapter Markers and a Scene Selection Menu**.

9 Add a sub-menu

There are actually a number of ways to create a new sub-menu page for your disc. The simplest is to click to select the menu page you want to add a sub-menu to in the **Project Overview** panel and then, from the **+** menu at the top of the interface, select **Menu**. The sub-menu is automatically added to your disc's menu structure in the **Project Overview** panel, and a button linking to it is automatically added to the menu page in the **Workspace** panel.

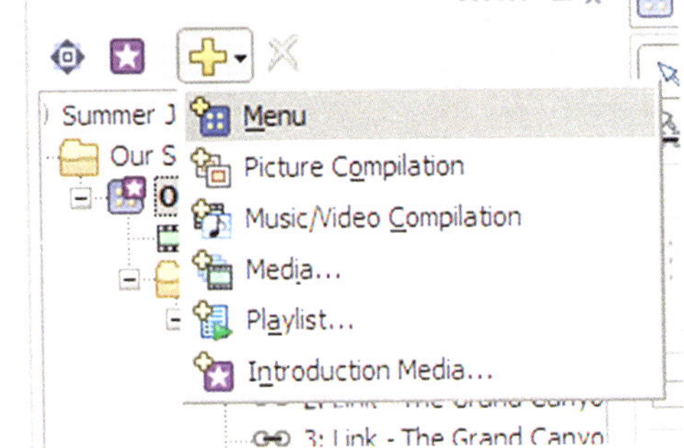

For more information on building out your disc's menu system, see **Chapter 5, Build a Disc Menu Structure**.

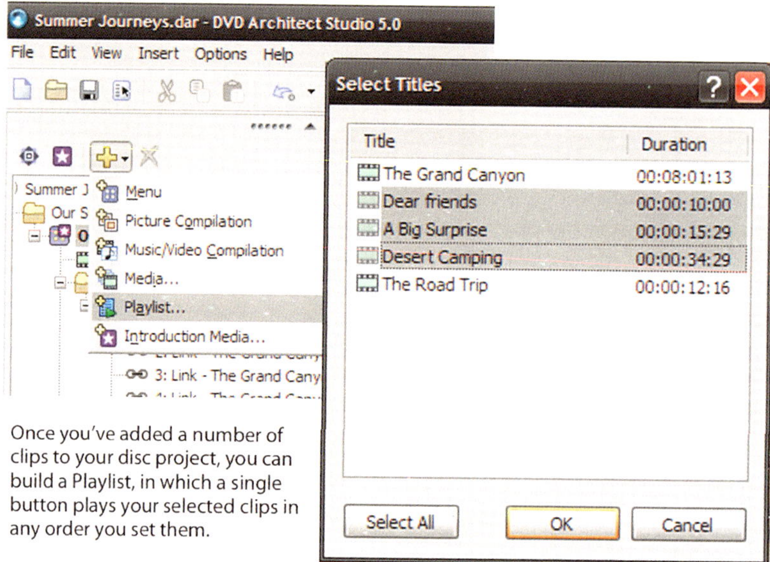

Once you've added a number of clips to your disc project, you can build a Playlist, in which a single button plays your selected clips in any order you set them.

10 Create a Playlist

Once you've added several clips or scenes to your disc project, you may want to create a link that allows your viewer to play several or all of these clips at once. To do this, you will create a **Playlist**.

A **Playlist** is created either by selecting the option under the **Insert** drop-down menu or by clicking on the option under the **+** menu on the **Project Overview** panel.

The **Playlist** option screen will list all of the video clips available on your disc. From this screen, you can select any video clips you would like added to your **Playlist**. Once you've selected your clips, you can arrange their playing order in the **Playlists** panel.

More information on building and editing **Playlists** can be found in **Chapter 7, Create a Playlist**.

11 Build a Compilation

As illustrated at the top of the facing page, DVD Architect Studio also includes tools for building **Compilations.**

There are two types of **Compilations.**

Picture Compilations are slideshows made up of stills.

Music/Video Compilations are montages of several video clips. Both types of **Compilations** can include a music or other audio background.

For more information on Compilations, see **Chapter 8, Build a Picture or Music/Video Compilation**.

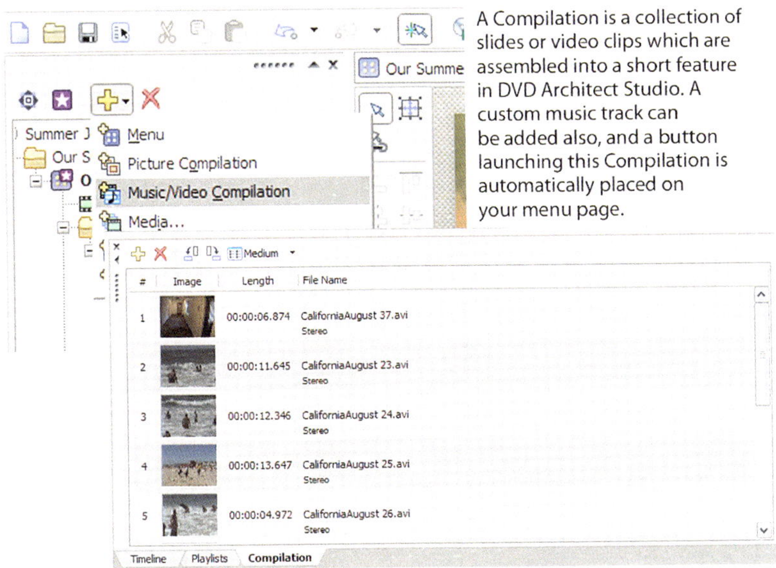

A Compilation is a collection of slides or video clips which are assembled into a short feature in DVD Architect Studio. A custom music track can be added also, and a button launching this Compilation is automatically placed on your menu page.

12 Check disc space used

As you add video and build menus for your disc project, DVD Architect Studio tracks how much space all of this media will take up. You can see this running total listed as **Disc Space Used** in the lower right corner of the interface, as seen below.

A standard DVD can hold 4.7 gigabytes of data. A dual-layer DVD will hold about 8.5 gigabytes. A standard BluRay disc holds 25 gigabytes of video while a dual-layer BluRay holds 50 gigabytes.

As DVD Architect Studio sees your project reaching its target media's capacity, it will change colors. As your disc fills, the **Disc Space Used** indicator will turn yellow. Once the program estimates that you're getting near a disc's capacity, it will turn red.

For more information on **Disc Space Used** and how this number is affected by settings elsewhere in the program, see **Pre-flight and optimize your disc** in **Chapter 10, Burn a DVD or BluRay Disc**.

As you work, DVD Architect Studio will display the amount of space your files will take up in the lower right of the program's interface. Once you have set up your disc on the Optimize Disc option screen, this area will display the *compressed* file size.

13 Preview your menu

At any point in your work, you can preview your disc project and give it a test drive! To do so, simply click the **Preview** button at the top center of the program's interface.

Your preview will begin on whatever menu page is displayed in the **Workspace** panel when you launch it.

14 Burn your disc!

Click the **Make DVD** or **Make BluRay Disc** button.

Simple, isn't?

But those are the basic moves.

You drag the media into the **Workspace** panel or insert elements in the **Project Overview** panel, and DVD Architect Studio builds your menu pages and buttons.

If you've got an idea for how you'd like your menu to look or behave, chances are there's a way to do it with this great, little program. It's relatively easy to create very interesting and dynamic menu systems.

But that, of course, is what the next 10 chapters are all about!

Understanding the Workspace panel

Placement and alignment tools

Adding a still or video background to your page

Adding a music background to your page

Setting a "Loop Point"

Chapter 3

Build a Menu Page

Creating a look and navigation for your page

A menu page serves two purposes – to serve as navigation for your viewer and to set the tone for your disc.

DVD Architect Studio includes simple tools for creating and designing a menu page. It also includes tools for customizing the look and feel of the page in almost any way imaginable!

When you open a new DVD Architect Studio project, a blank, generic, blue menu page will appear in **Workspace** panel.

This is your starting point. From here, you can go anywhere!

Building a menu system is like building a Web site. It can be simple, with a few links to your media, or it can be a massive networks of links, sub-menus and features.

But building each page is the same essential process: Adding descriptive text, adding links to media or other menu pages – and, of course, deciding how it all looks and behaves.

Since most of the work of designing and building your menu page will take place in the **Workspace** panel, it's important to know your way around this very powerful work area and understand its layout tools.

Get to know the Workspace panel

Most of the work you'll do building and designing your menu pages will likely be done in the Workspace panel, the large panel that dominates the center of the program's interface.

The **Workspace** is a very intuitive space to work in. Most of what you'll be doing in this panel involves simply dragging and dropping the elements you'd like to add to your design. Even creating buttons that link to your videos will done by simply dragging and dropping the clips from the **Explorer** panel. (We discuss this process in more detail in **Chapter 4, Create and Customize a Menu Button**.)

Zoom in or out with view controls

Along the top of the **Workspace** panel are controls for navigating and viewing your menu pages. The **Quick Select** drop-down menu lets you quickly select any menu page or link on your disc. The arrow buttons to the right of this menu can be used to navigate up to the main menu or to the next or previous menu page at your current menu page level.

At the magnifying glass icon on the upper right of the panel you'll find a drop-down menu for setting the **Workspace** zoom view of your menu page. In most cases, you'll likely leave this set to **Auto Zoom,** so that your menu is automatically sized to fit inside the panel. But, in the event you need to see a close-up of a particular area of your menu, you can set the zoom level at, say, 800%, using the scroll bars to adjust the view position so you can focus on a particular area of your menu page.

Turn on the Panel Overlays

No two televisions will display your video or your videos exactly alike. Because of something called overscan, all TVs cut off a bit of the edge of a video frame. This is less of an issue with modern flat-screen TVs than it

The Workspace panel

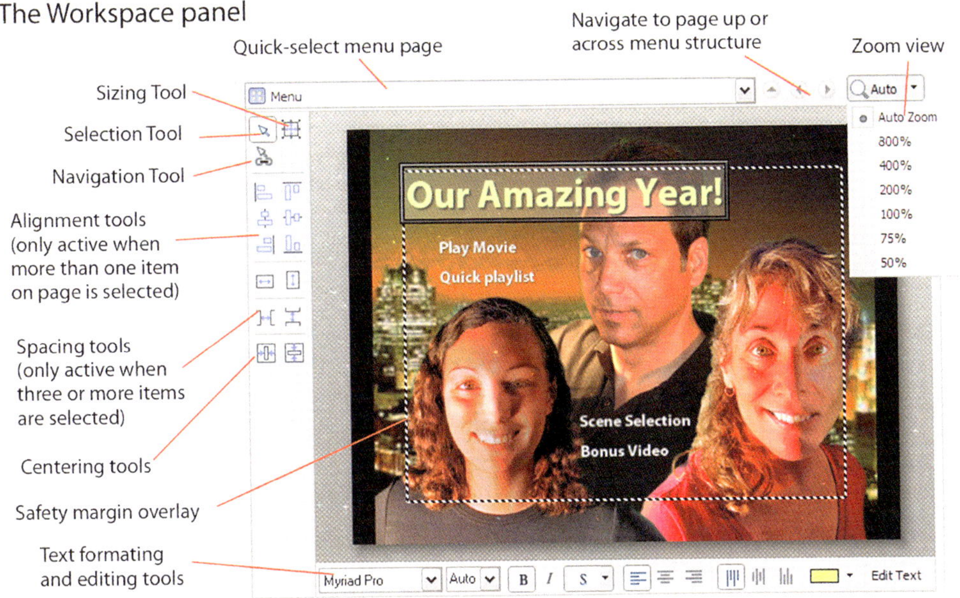

was with traditional CRTs, but it is still something to be aware of. There is always the risk that up to 10% around the edge of your video frame will not be displayed.

In most cases, this isn't that big of a deal. Usually what's around the edge of your video isn't vital information anyway. But, if you're creating a DVD or BluRay disc menu page, you certainly don't want the title of your menu or one of your buttons close enough to the edge of the frame that you risk *it* being cut off. (Otherwise your "Gone With the Wind" video might end up looking like "one With the Win" on some TVs!)

So, whenever you start a new video project, go to the **View** drop-down menu at the top of the program's interface, select **Workspace Overlays**, then **Title Safe Area**. This will place a dotted line box over the menu in your **Workspace**. The box doesn't show up in your final menu. It's just a guide for you to keep your menu navigation and text within in order to ensure that no vital information will be cut off when your menu is displayed on a TV.

Other **Workspace Overlays** will include:

- **Show Grid**, which displays a grid over your menu page, a guide for helping you compose your disc menu's layout, and options for displaying the order that the buttons will be selected when your viewer navigates the menu with his or her remote control.
- **Show Button Masks** displays a preview of the highlights that will appear over your buttons as your viewer navigates your menu.

Edit or add text

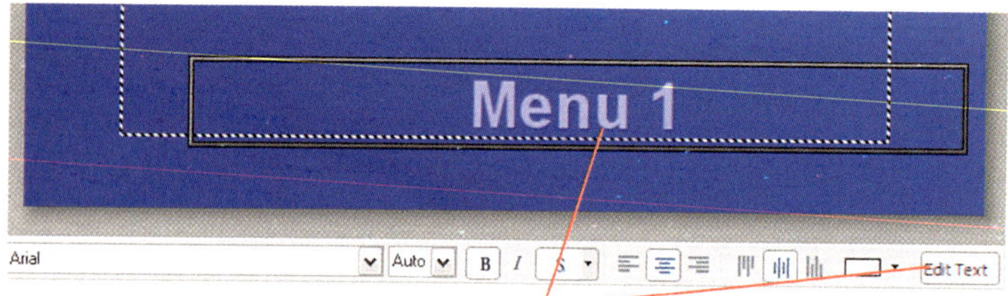

A text box will become editable if you select it in the Workspace panel and click the Edit Text button.

Edit a text box

Text boxes appear on menu pages with generic text (Usually "Menu 1", "Menu 2", etc. or simply the word "Text"). To edit the text in a text box:

1 **Select the text box**

Ensure that the **Selection Tool** (the arrow icon in the upper left of the **Workspace** panel) is activated and click on the text box to select it.

2 **Click the "Edit Text" button**

The **Edit Text** button is located in the lower right corner of the **Workspace** panel. (As a shortcut, you can click **F2** on your keyboard.)

The text box will become activated and the text inside will become editable.

3 **Customize the text**

Type over the generic text in the text box.

4 **Select your text's font, size and style**

When text is either selected in **Edit Text** mode or a the text box is selected with the **Selection Tool**, its font, size and style can be customized using the tools along the bottom of the panel, as discussed on the facing page.

Add new text

There are three ways to create a text box on a menu page:

- Right-click on a menu page in the **Workspace** panel and select "**Insert Text**" from the context menu.
- Go to the **Insert** drop-down menu at the top of the program's interface and select **Text**.
- Press **Ctrl+t** on your keyboard.

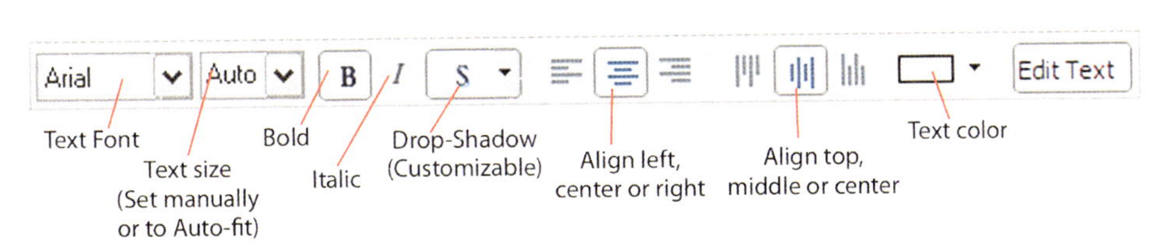

Set your text's style, size and formatting

When your text is selected (in **Edit Text** mode) or a text block is selected in the **Workspace** panel, the text's characteristics can be modified in a number of ways.

Font. The **Font** drop-down menu will display all of the fonts that have been installed on your computer. You can quickly jump to any font on this list by opening this drop-down menu and typing the first few letters of the font's name.

Font size. Font sizes range from 8 point (very small) to 90 point (huge!).

By default, the Font Size is set to **Auto** – which means that the size of the text changes when the text box is resized (with the **Resizing Tool**). Designating a specific font size locks the text to that size no matter how large – and to a point, how small – the text box is resized to.

The **B** and **I** buttons apply **Bold** and **Italic** styles to the text's font.

The **S** button applies a **Drop-Shadow** to the text. A drop-down menu on this button allows you to set the **X** and **Y offset** distance (how far the shadow falls above, below or to the side of the actual text) and to designate the color for the shadow.

Horizontal Alignment. The text in the box can be set to align left, center or right.

Vertical Alignment. The text can be set to align with the top, center or bottom of the text box.

Color. The color button will change the color of your text, which can be set using **RGB** (red, green and blue) values or **HSL** (hue, saturation and luminance) values. (You can toggle between the two color spaces by clicking the color box above the eyedropper.) Color can also be set by setting the crosshairs on the panel's rainbow palette or by clicking on the eyedropper icon and sampling a color from any place on your computer's desktop – even from the interface of another program you happen to have open!

In addition to color values, the panel includes options for setting the opacity – or alpha level (**A**) – of the text color. The alpha level determines how transparent the text color is.

Several text blocks on a menu page can be selected at once and stylized or colored at the same time.

Note that any settings you make – as far as your font, text size, color, etc. – will be overwritten if you later apply a **Theme** to your menu.

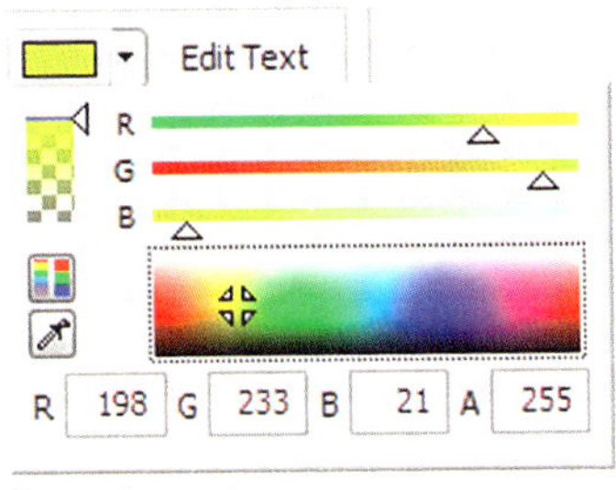

Text color options

The Workspace Tool Set

In the top left corner of the **Workspace** panel are three tools for manipulating the various elements on your menu page.

The Selection Tool

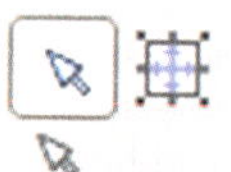

By default, the **Selection Tool** (the arrow icon) will be active. With this tool you can click on and drag any element – text box, graphic or button – and move it to to any position on your menu page.

Note that buttons, by the way, can not overlap each other even slightly. And, if you position a button so that it's live area overlaps another button's live area, a red box will appear between the buttons indicating the overlap.

The Sizing Tool

The **Sizing Tool** is used to resize any element on your menu page. When this tool is selected, any element can be resized by dragging on its handles – the little gray squares on the frame surrounding it.

When you drag on a corner handle, the element will resize, both horizontally and vertically equally. When you drag on a handle mid-way along a frame size, the element will resize either horizontally or vertically.

When the Sizing Tool is selected, elements on your menu page can be resized by dragging on the "handles" on its frame.

When the **Font Size** is set to **Auto**, the text will resize as its text box is resized. When it is set to a specific size, the text will remain the same size no matter how the text box is resized.

Additionally, when using the **Sizing Tool** to position elements on the menu page, a thumbnail image and text block for a button will move as two separate elements. This allows you to position the button's text so that it is to the side, above or even *overlayed onto* the thumbnail image for the button. However, you should note that your button's "live" area will stretch from wherever the thumbnail is located to wherever the text for that button is located!

The Navigation Tool

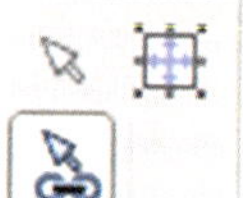

When you click on any buttons on your menu page with the **Navigation Tool** activated, an array of arrows will display around the button. These arrows illustrate the order the buttons will become active as your viewer navigates this menu page with his or her remote control.

Although, the selection order of these buttons will go from upper left to lower right of your menu page by default (and probably by preference), you can drag on the horns that appear on each side of your button with the **Navigation Tool** and arrange the buttons to activate in whatever order you'd like.

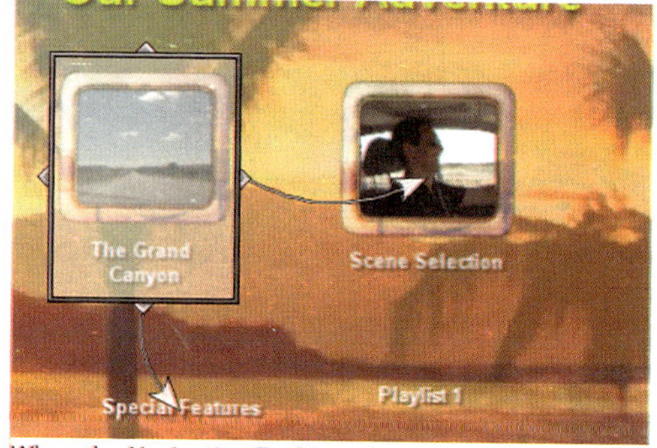

When the Navigation Tool is active, selected buttons will display arrows indicating the order of their navigation.

Automatic Alignment, Sizing and Spacing Tools

Along the left side of the **Workspace** panel are sets of tools for aligning the individual elements on your menu page.

Which tools are active and how they behave depends on which and how many elements are selected in the **Workspace** panel. (Most of these tools will only function when more than one element on a menu page is selected.) To select more than one element at a time, hold down the **Shift** or **Ctrl** key as you click to select.

Multiple element alignment tools

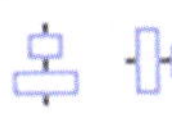

Horizontal Alignment Tools. Selected elements will all align to either the left, right or center on the same point.

Vertical Alignment Tools. Selected elements will all align to either the top, center or bottom on the same point.

"Make Same Size" Tools

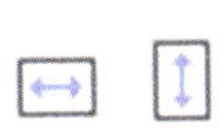

Make Same Height. Automatically sizes all selected elements to the same height.

Make Same Width. Automatically sizes all selected elements to the same width.

"Even Spacing" Tools

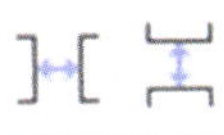

Evenly Space Down. Spaces three or more selected elements evenly between the top and bottom selected element.

Evenly Space Across. Spaces three or more selected elements evenly between the left and right selected elements.

Individual element alignment tools

Horizontal Centering. Positions the selected element in the horizontal center of the menu page.

Vertical Centering. Positions the selected element in the vertical center of the menu page.

Add a menu button to your page

A button is automatically added to your page as you add media or a new menu page link to it:

- For information on adding a video clip to your disc project and adding a menu button linking to it, see **Chapter 4, Create and Customize a Menu Button**.
- For information on adding buttons to your menu page that link to other menu pages, see **Chapter 5, Build a Disc Menu Structure**.

Apply a Theme to your menu page

A **Theme** adds a look to your page, complete with text styles, button frames and a background.

For information on using **Themes** to create a look for your menu page, see **Chapter 9, Work With Themes, Backgrounds and Button Styles**.

Add a graphic or animated video clip to your page

In addition to buttons and text on your menu, you can add purely decorative graphics to your menu page, including animated video clips.

To add a graphic or video clip to your menu page:

1 **Select Insert Graphic**

Go to the **Insert** drop-down menu at the top of the interface, or right-click on the menu page in the **Workspace** panel, and select **Insert Graphic** from the context menu.

This will open a screen in which you can browse to and select any still, graphic or video clip on your computer.

Click **OK**.

2 **Position the graphic**

Once you've placed the graphic on your menu, you can move it to any position or, using the **Sizing Tool** (see page 30), resize it.

If you'd like the graphic to go behind your buttons or layered with other graphics on your menu, right-click on it and select **Object Order**. Selecting the options to **Move Forward** or **Move Back** brings the graphic ahead or sends it back behind one item at a time on your menu page; Selecting **Move to Top** or **Move to Bottom** sends it directly to the front or directly behind all other items on your menu page.

If you are using a video clip as your graphic, you can set its looping **Start Time** in its **Graphics Properties**, on the **Media** pane.

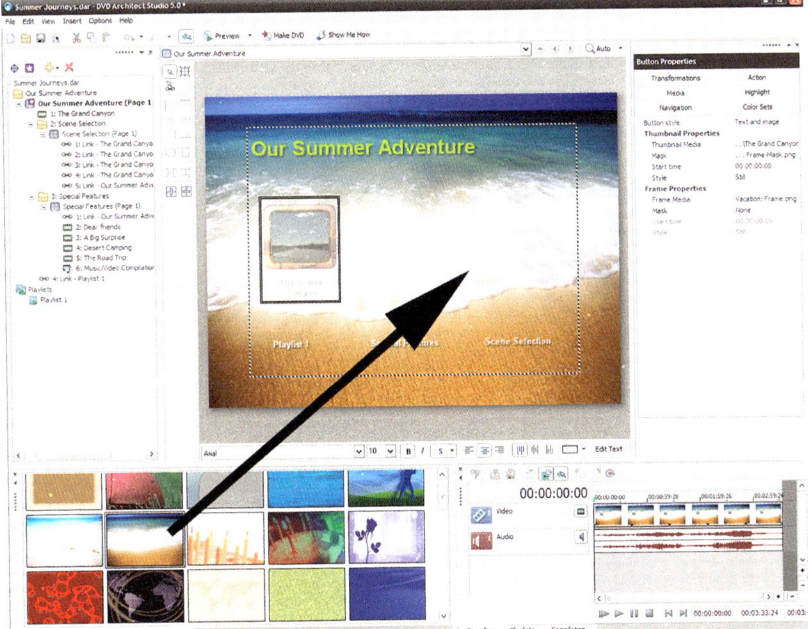

Adding a custom still image to a menu page's background is as simple as dragging an image from the Background or dragging a still photo from the Explorer panel.

Add a custom image background to your menu page

There are a number of ways to add a new background image to your menu page.

- **Drag a background from the Backgrounds panel.** DVD Architect Studio includes over 60 backgrounds, from realistic to thematic to abstract. To add one to a menu page displayed in your **Workspace** panel, drag it onto the page from the **Backgrounds** panel, or simply double-click on the image in the **Backgrounds** panel.
- **Drag a still photo from the Explorer panel.** You can also use any photo or graphic on your computer as a custom background image for your photo. To add it to the menu page displayed in your **Workspace** panel, drag it onto the page from the **Explorer** panel, or simply double-click on the image file's listing in the **Explorer** panel.
- **Browse to a photo from the Menu Page Properties panel.** When a menu page is displayed in your **Workspace** panel and no elements are selected, the **Properties** panel will display **Menu Page Properties**. On the **Background Media** page of this panel, click on the box to the right of the **Video** listing. This will open a browse screen in which you can locate and select a still image for your menu's background. (For more information on the **Menu Page Properties** panel, see **Chapter 11, An Appendix of Advanced DVD Architect Studio Tricks**.)

Note that you can *not* add video loop as a menu page background by dragging and dropping it from the **Explorer** panel. Dragging a video to a menu page will only create a button on the page.

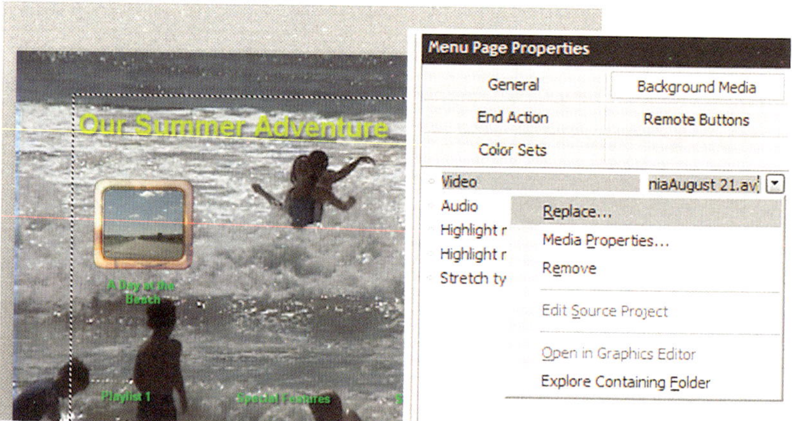

A video clip can be used as a menu background by setting it as your Background Media in the Menu Page Propertes panel.

Add a custom video background to your menu page

Adding a video background to a menu page is a little different than adding a still image. If you drag a video clip from the **Explorer** panel onto the menu page in the **Workspace** panel, a button will be added to the page.

A video clip, therefore, must be added as a background to your menu page through the **Menu Page Properties** panel.

1 **Go to the Menu Page Properties Background Media pane**

When your menu page is displayed in the **Workspace** panel and its background is selected (no page elements selected), **Menu Page Properties** will be displayed in the **Properties** panel.

Click on the **Background Media** button in this panel.

2 **Replace the current video.**

When you click on the box to the right of the **Video** listing on the **Background Media** page, a drop-down list will display several options.

Select **Replace**.

3 **Select a video clip**

Browse to and select a video clip on your computer.

Click **OK**.

Your video clip will become the menu's animated background.

By default, this clip will play in its entirety as a menu page background and then hold. (For information on setting your background to loop, see page 45.) Additionally, if you have included a music clip as well as a video background, the menu will continue to play for the duration of the *longer* of the two media clips! For information on setting this duration manually, see **Set the menu loop length for your background media** on page 42.

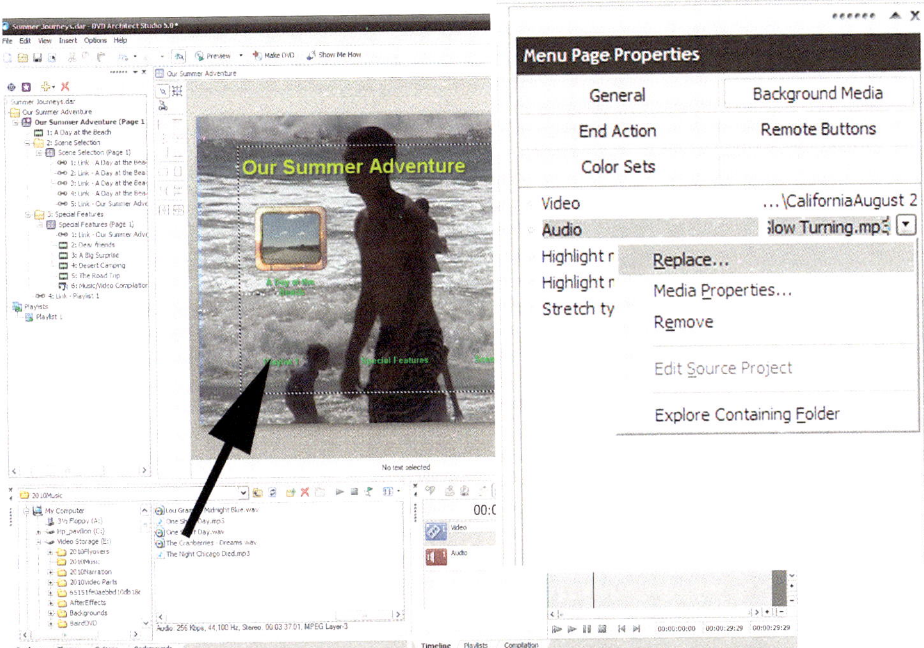

A musical or other custom audio background can be added to a menu by dragging the audio file from the Explorer panel onto the page in the Workspace panel or by browsing to the file from the Menu Page Properties panel.

Add a musical background to your menu page

As with adding a custom image as a menu background, there are a number of ways to add background music to your menu page.

- **Drag an audio file from the Explorer panel.** To add music or any audio clip background to the menu page displayed in your **Workspace** panel, drag it onto the page from the **Explorer** panel, or simply double-click on the audio file in the **Explorer** panel.
- **Browse to the photo from the Menu Page Properties panel.** When your menu page is displayed in the **Workspace** panel and its background is selected (no page elements selected), **Menu Page Properties** will be displayed in the **Properties** panel. On the **Background Media** pane, click on the box to the right of the **Video** listing. Selecting **Replace** from the drop-down menu that appears will open a browse screen in which you can locate and select your background image.

As with a video background, this music or audio will play, by default, in its entirety as a menu page background and then hold. (For information on setting your background to loop rather than hold, see page 45.) Additionally, if you have included a video clip as well as an audio background, the menu will continue to play for the duration of the *longer* of the two media clips! For information on setting this duration manually, see **Set the menu loop length for your background media** on page 42r.

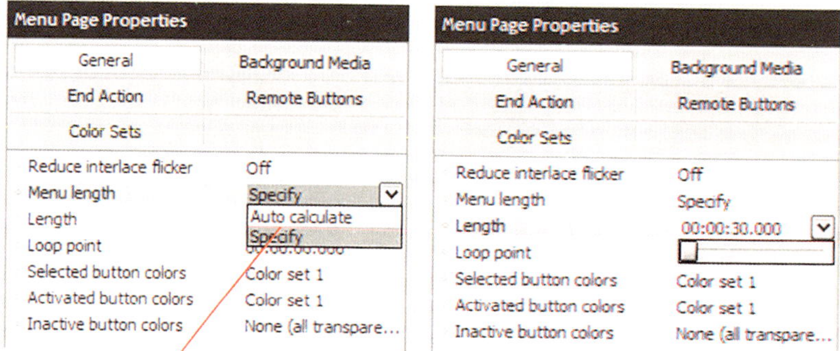

To change your menu background's playback length, you must change the Menu Length setting to Specify.

Set the menu "loop" length for your background media

By default, DVD Architect Studio use a menu length that is the longer of either the video or audio clip you have added as your menu page's background. This means, for instance, if you add a 45 second video clip and a 3-minute song as your menu page's backgrounds, the song will play in its entirety, even after the video ends– displaying a blank background as the audio continues!

It's best, then, to manually set a **Menu Length** for your page's media.

As a rule of thumb, most disc menu backgrounds are set to loop after about 30 seconds.

(By the way, you should note that, by default, your disc will *hold* rather than loop after your background has finished playing. For information on setting your menu background to loop or to replay continuously as long as the menu page remains onscreen, see page 45.)

To set your background to end its playback after 30 seconds:

1 **Open the Menu Page Properties General pane**

When your menu page is displayed in the **Workspace** panel and its background is selected (no page elements selected), **Menu Page Properties** will be displayed in the **Properties** panel.

Click on the **General** button.

2 **Specify Menu Length**

By default, the **Menu Length** property is set to **Auto Calculate**, which automatically allows the background media to play entirely through before looping.

Click on the box to the right of the **Menu Length** listing and select the **Specify** option.

3 Set the background media loop Length

Set the length of time you would like your menu background to play either by clicking on the numbers in the box to the right of the **Length** listing and manually typing in new values or by using the slider which appears as a drop-down when you click on this property's box.

Note that this length is displayed as **hours:minutes:seconds.fractions-of-a-second**. So, in order to change the media loop **Length** to 30 seconds, you will need to type in the value "30.0" (thirty and zero thousandths of a second).

Prior to reaching the Loop Point, your menu page will display the background video but won't show buttons or text.

Set a Loop Point for your background video

The **Loop Point** on your **Menu Page Properties** indicates two things:

- It is the point in your background video's playback in which your menu buttons appear over your menu page's background video. (By default, this is *immediately*, of course.)

  Prior to this **Loop Point**, the background video will display with no other elements over it. This is useful if you'd like to include some introductory video before the actual menu page's navigation appears. (Another way to add a video clip before your navigation pages is to **Add Introduction Media**, as we discuss in **Chapter 5, Build a Disc Menu Structure**.)

- Once your background media playback reaches its end, the menu page will loop back *only to this **Loop Point*** (It will not go all of the way back to the beginning of your background video) so that your menu buttons and other elements remain on screen continually after the initial video's play-through.

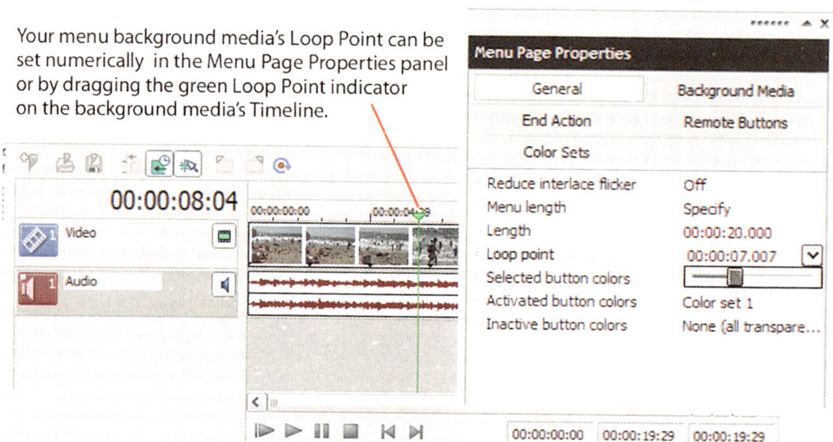

Your menu background media's Loop Point can be set numerically in the Menu Page Properties panel or by dragging the green Loop Point indicator on the background media's Timeline.

The menu page's **Loop Point** can be set in one of two ways: By setting it manually in **Menu Page Properties** or by positioning the green **Loop Point** indicator on the **Timeline** panel.

To set the **Loop Point** in the **Properties** panel:

1 **Open the Menu Page Properties General page**

When your menu page is displayed in the **Workspace** panel and its background is selected (no page elements selected), **Menu Page Properties** will be displayed in the **Properties** panel.

Click on the **General** button.

3 **Set the Loop Point**

Set the **Loop Point** of your video loop either by clicking on the numbers in the box to the right of the **Loop Point** listing and manually typing in new values or by using the slider which appears as a drop-down when you click on this property's box.

To set the **Loop Point** using the green **Loop Point** indicator on the **Timeline** panel:

1 **Locate the Loop Point indicator**

When a menu page is displayed in the **Workspace** panel, the page's **Audio** and **Video** (or still) will appear in the **Timeline** panel.

The **Loop Point** indicator is the fine green vertical line on this **Timeline**.

2 **Drag the Loop Point to a position on the Timeline**

This location will correspond with the settings in the **Menu Page Properties** panel, and you can use one tool to fine tune the location of the indicator in the other.

Set your menu background to loop

Whether you've added a musical background or a video background to your menu page, the background clip will, by default, play to the point you've specified and then hold.

To manually set your menu page background to replay continuously:

1 **Open the Menu Page Properties End Action pane**

When your menu page is displayed in the **Workspace** panel and its background is selected (no page elements selected), **Menu Page Properties** will be displayed in the **Properties** panel.

Click on the **End Action** button.

2 **Set Command to Loop**

By default, the **Command** property is set to **Hold**, which means that, after your background audio and/or video finishes playing, the menu will hold until your viewer clicks on a button.

To set the page background to repeat continuously, click on the box to the right of the **Command** property listing and select **Loop** from the drop-down menu.

The page background will then play, according to the loop length you've set (as on page 42) and then will repeat from either the beginning or from the **Loop Point** you've set (as on page 44).

Additional Menu Page Properties

Definitions for more **Menu Properties** and a reference sheet for the entire **Menu Page Properties** panel can be found in **Chapter 11, An Appendix of Advanced DVD Architect Studio Tricks**.

Creating a menu button

Setting your button as image or text only

Adding a button frame

Customizing a button's thumbnail image

Creating a video thumbnail image

Customizing your button's highlight

Customizing the button navigation order

Chapter 4

Create and Customize a Menu Button

Cool navigation

Menu buttons are links to your media as well as to other menu pages.

You can keep them simple – or give them lots of flash and dazzle.

DVD Architect Studio even includes tools for designing overlays, the highlights that appear over your buttons when your viewer navigates your menu pages.

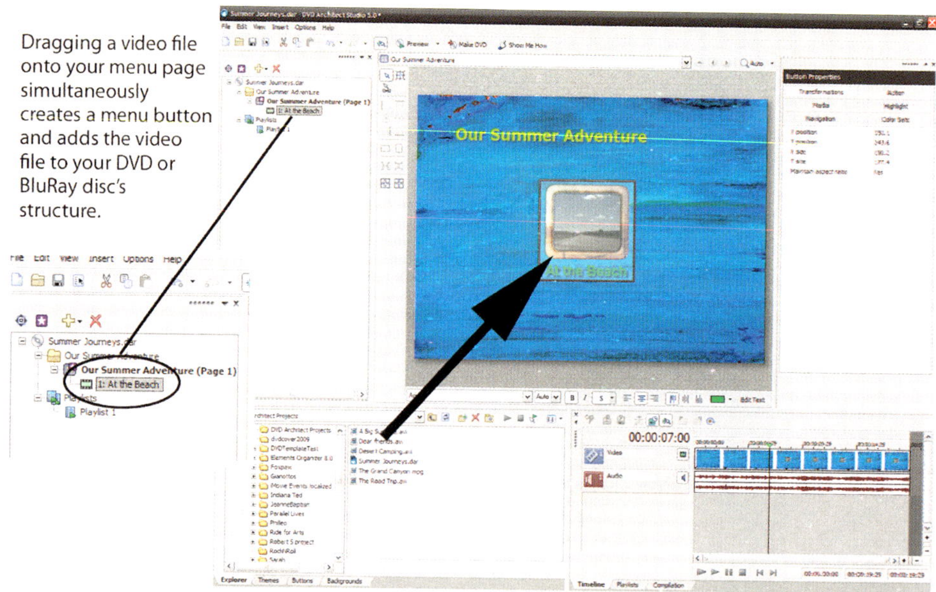

Dragging a video file onto your menu page simultaneously creates a menu button and adds the video file to your DVD or BluRay disc's structure.

Now that you've created a menu page, it's time to start adding your navigation – the links from this page to the media and other menu pages on your disc.

Buttons are easy to add – and can be modified in dozens of ways by adding images, frames, animation and custom overlays.

As with menu pages, most of the work you'll do in creating and designing your menu buttons will be done in the big **Workspace** panel in the center of the interface. And, as with menu pages, most of the work you'll do in building and designing these buttons will be done using fairly intuitive moves.

Add a video clip and create a button linking to it

Creating a menu button by adding a video file to the menu page displayed in your **Workspace** panel simultaneously adds the button to your menu page and adds the video itself to your disc's structure.

There are three ways to add a menu button to the menu page displayed in your **Workspace** panel:

- Drag a video file from the **Explorer** panel onto the menu page.
- Double-click on a video file in the **Explorer** panel. The button will automatically appear on the menu page.
- Drag a video file from a Windows Explorer browse screen onto the **Workspace** panel.

Although the program will work with a wide variety of video formats, some video formats work more efficiently in the program than others.

Use optimized video formats for your disc's source

Although the program accepts a wide variety of formats, some formats work more efficiently and more reliably than others. Using the optimal video format can, among other advantages, greatly reduce the program's rendering and transcoding time.

Most video editing applications (including Sony Vegas) include export options specifically for outputting DVD-ready or BluRay-ready video:

- **For DVD projects,** the best source video for DVD Architect Studio is the DVD-ready MPEG2, a 720x480 MPEG (720x576 if you're editing in PAL video) using non-square pixels and lower field first interlacing.
- **For BluRay discs**, the best source video is a BluRay-ready AVC file, a 1920x1080 60i video (50i if you are editing PAL video) MPEG/MTS file using the H.264 codec.

It is usually not a good idea to use video directly from a camera or camcorder or downloaded from online as source video in a DVD Architect Studio project. Whenever possible, you should load your raw video into a video editing program and then output to one of the file formats above for use in you disc authoring program.

(They also require less render time.) For more information on the optimal file formats to use as source files in DVD Architect Studio, see the sidebar above.

Trim your video clip and add scene markers

Once you've added a video to your disc project, you can do some modifications to it.

- You can trim footage from the beginning or the end of the clip.
- You can add **Scene/Chapter Markers** to your video and then create a **Scene Selection Menu** page linking to them.

We show you how to do both of these things in **Chapter 6, Add Scene/ Chapter Markers and a Scene Selection Menu**.

Add a button linking to another menu page

As with adding a button connecting to a media clip, creating a menu button for the menu page displayed in your **Workspace** panel simultaneously adds the button to your menu page and adds a new menu page to your disc's structure.

To learn more about adding menu pages and levels of menus to your disc project, see **Chapter 5, Build a Disc Menu Structure**.

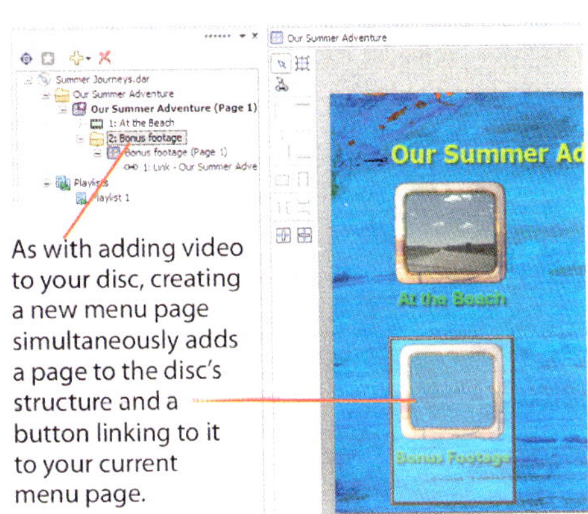

As with adding video to your disc, creating a new menu page simultaneously adds a page to the disc's structure and a button linking to it to your current menu page.

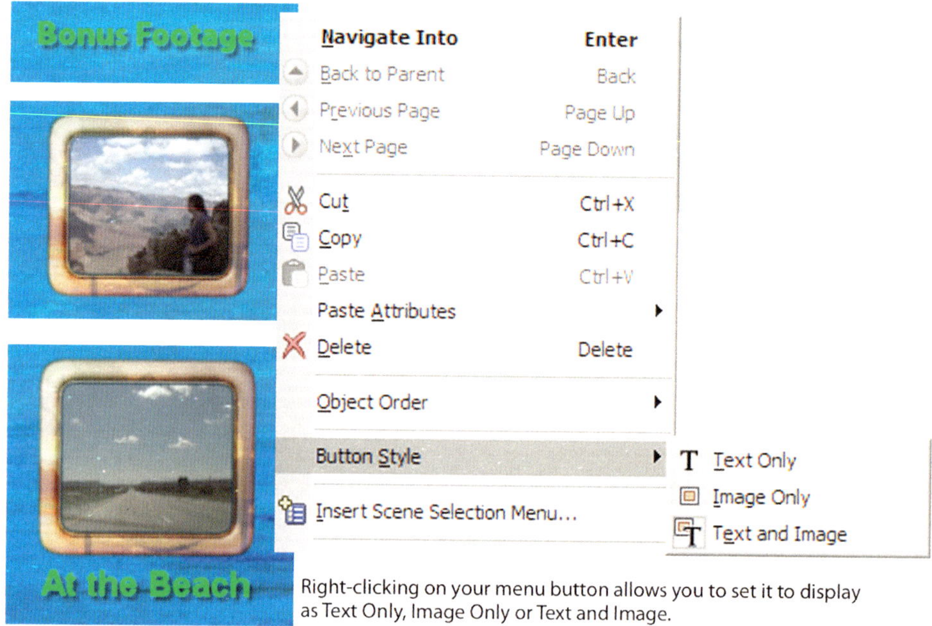

Right-clicking on your menu button allows you to set it to display as Text Only, Image Only or Text and Image.

Make your button display as text only or image only

Your menu buttons can be made to display as text and a thumbnail, text only, or a thumbnail or image only.

To select a display option for your menu button:

1 **Right-click on the menu button**

Right-click on the button on the menu page displayed in your **Workspace** panel.

2 **Select a Button Style**

From the context menu, select the **Button Style** option:

Text only
Image Only
Text and Image

When you select one of the **Image** options for your button, your button will display a thumbnail image representing the video it links to.

This image can be modified in a number of ways:

- By default, this image will be the first frame of your video clip. However, it can be set to display any frame from your video.
- This image can also be animated, to play the entirety of the clip it links to as a thumbnail image. For more information, see **Make your button's image animated** on page 52.

- This image, in fact, need not even be a still or animated clip from the video it links to! You can use any still or animated image or video on your computer as your button's thumbnail! For more information, see **Select a custom graphic or video as your button image** on page 52.

You can also modify the frame around this button. For more information on this option, see **Add a custom button frame** on page 54.

Set the thumbnail image for your button

By default, the thumbnail image that appears as your button will be the first frame of the video it links to. However, this image can be modified to display as any frame from the video you'd like.

1 **Select the button on your menu page**

The **Properties** panel will display **Button Properties**.

2 **Go to the Media page of the Button Properties panel**

Click on the **Media** button in this panel.

3 **Set the Start Time for the Thumbnail Property**

When you click on the box to the right of the **Start Time** listing under **Thumbnail Properties**, an adjustment bar will appear and the timecode will become editable.

Either by moving the adjustment bar or by typing over the timecode, set the thumbnail to the frame you would like to appear. Note that the timecode numbers represent hours:minutes:seconds: frames. In other words, in order to set the thumbnail to 25 and one-half seconds into your video, you would type 2:15 (since there are approximately 30 frames for every second of NTSC video).

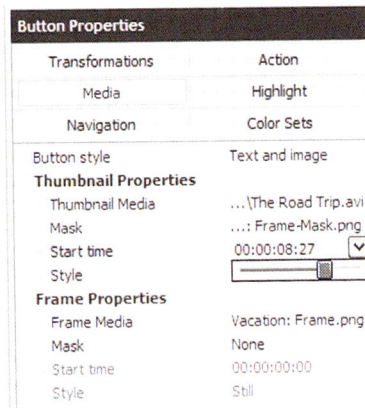

Button Properties

Transformations	Action
Media	Highlight
Navigation	Color Sets
Button style	Text and image
Thumbnail Properties	
Thumbnail Media	...\The Road Trip.avi
Mask	...: Frame-Mask.png
Start time	00:00:08:27
Style	
Frame Properties	
Frame Media	Vacation: Frame.png
Mask	None
Start time	00:00:00:00
Style	Still

Advancing the Start Time setting on the Media pane of Button Properties changes which frame of your video is displayed as your button's thumbnail image.

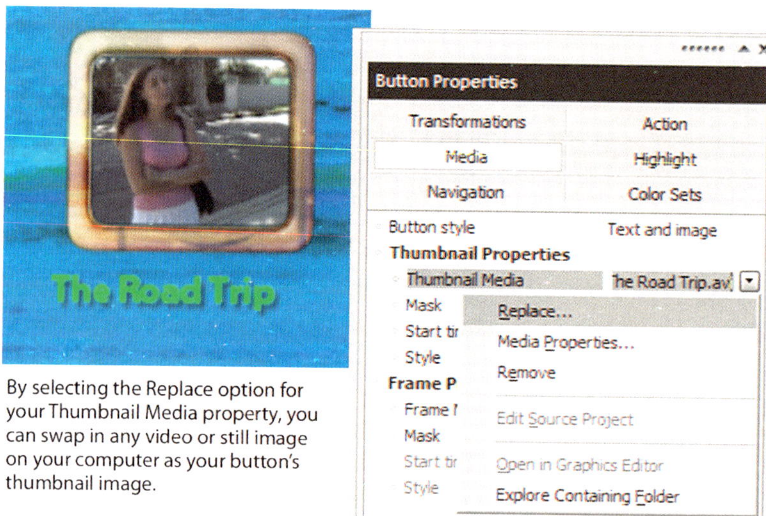

By selecting the Replace option for your Thumbnail Media property, you can swap in any video or still image on your computer as your button's thumbnail image.

Select a custom graphic or video as your button image

Your button's image need not display a thumbnail image or video from the video clip you're linking to. You can set your image to display as any graphic, photo or video on your computer.

Even button images for non-media links (such as links to other menu pages) can be set to display as images or video clips.

1 **Select a button on your menu page**

   The **Properties** panel will display **Button Properties**.

2 **Go to the Media page on the Button Properties panel**

   Click on the **Media** button in this panel.

3 **Browse and select new Thumbnail Media**

   Click on the box to the right of the **Thumbnail Media** listing under **Thumbnail Properties**.

   From the drop-down menu that appears, select **Replace**.

   Browse to select your button's new image or video clip.

If you select a video as your thumbnail, you can set it to display as a still image or an animated video.

Make your button's image animated

When your button links to a video, you can set its thumbnail image to display as a loop of the video itself.

1 **Select a button on your menu page**

   The **Properties** panel will display **Button Properties**.

2 **Go to the Media page on the Button Properties panel**

Click on the **Background Media** button in this panel.

3 **Set the Thumbnail Property's Style to animated**

Click on the box to the right of the **Style** listing, under **Thumbnail Properties**.

From the drop-down menu that appears, select **Animated**.

Once you've set the button's image to play a thumbnail of your video, you can also select where in your video this playback starts.

4 **Set the Start Time for the Thumbnail Property**

When you click on the box to the right of the **Start Time** listing under **Thumbnail Properties**, an adjustment bar will appear and the timecode will become editable.

Either by moving the adjustment bar or by typing over the timecode, set the **Start Time** to the frame you would like your thumbnail's playback to begin on.

Note that the timecode numbers represent hours:minutes:seconds: frames.

In other words, in order to set the thumbnail to 25 and one-half seconds into your video, you would type 2:15 (since there are approximately 30 frames for every second of NTSC video).

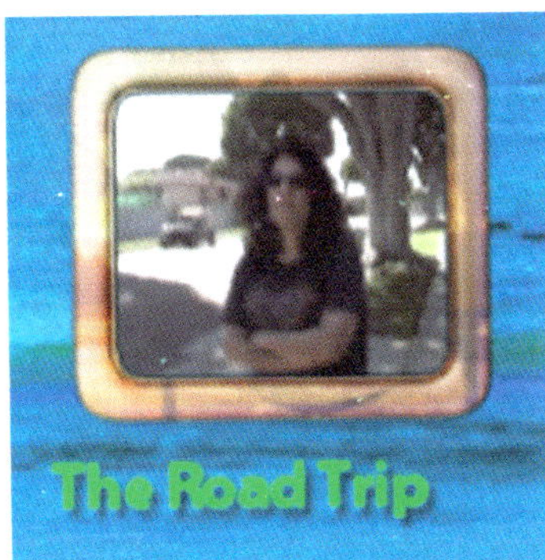

Setting the Thumbnail Properties' Style to Animated turns your button's image from a still into a video.

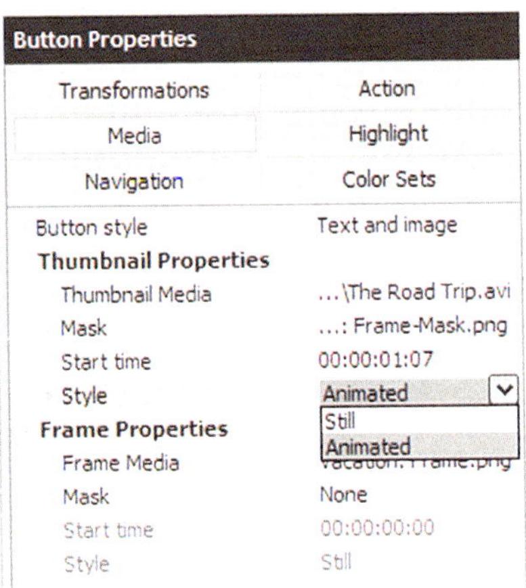

A button frame style can be dragged from the Buttons panel onto a selected button (or buttons) in the Workspace, or a Theme can be applied from the Themes panel – affecting the menu page background and all button and text styles.

Add a custom button frame

A button frame can be added or modified in a number of ways:

- A button frame will be added automatically to all buttons on a menu page when a **Theme** has been applied to that page.
- A custom button frame can be added by dragging a selected frame from the **Buttons** panel. (The panel also includes the option to use no frame at all.)
- A custom-created graphic or frame can be added from anywhere on your computer.

To add a frame or apply a theme from the DVD Architect Studio set:

1 **Open the Themes or Buttons panel**

Themes apply a style to your entire menu page and include styles for a background, all text and all button frames on the page.

Buttons apply custom frames only to the selected buttons on the menu page displayed in the **Workspace** panel.

2 **Select the button or buttons you want to frame**

By holding down the **Shift** or **Ctrl** key, you can select more than one button on the menu page displayed in the **Workspace** panel.

3 **Apply the frame or theme**

Drag the theme or button frame onto the menu page displayed in the **Workspace** panel, or simply double-click on your selection in the **Buttons** or **Themes** panel.

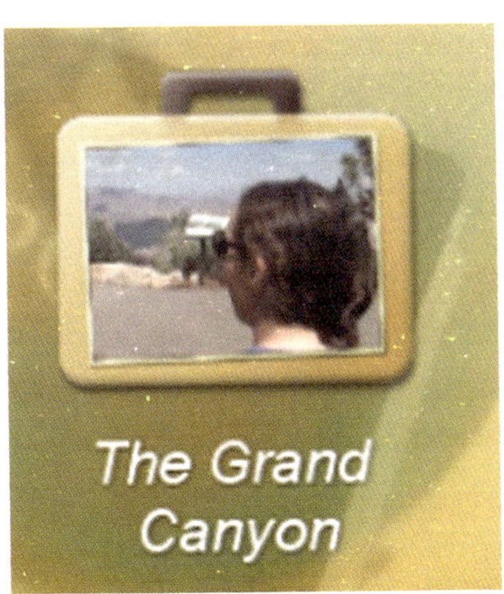

You can also use a custom-created graphic on your computer's hard drive as a custom button frame by browsing to it from the Button Properties panel.

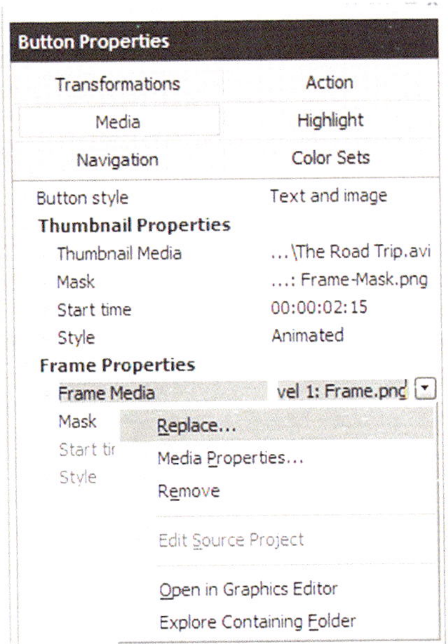

The frame(s) will be applied to the selected buttons in the Workspace panel. (For more information on **Themes**, see **Chapter 9, Work With Themes, Backgrounds and Button Styles**.)

As an alternative, you can add your own custom-created frame design to your button.

1 **Select a button on your menu page**

The **Properties** panel will display **Button Properties**.

2 **Go to the Media page of the Button Properties panel**

Click on the **Media** button in this panel.

3 **Browse and select new Frame Media**

Click on the box to the right of the **Frame Media** listing under **Frame Properties**.

From the drop-down menu that appears, select **Replace**.

Browse to select your button frame graphic.

Button frame graphics have some unique characteristics and must be saved to a specific file format. For information on how to create a button frame, see **Create a custom button frame** in **Chapter 11, An Appendix of Advanced DVD Architect Studio Tricks**.

Edit text on your button

The text on your button can be edited and stylized by selecting the button in the **Workspace** panel and clicking on the **Edit Text** button in the lower right of the panel.

More information on working with text and text boxes can be found in **Edit text and add text to a menu page** on pages 34 and 35 of **Chapter 3, Build a Menu Page**.

Position and size your button

Like text boxes or graphics placed on the menu page, your buttons can be easily resized and positioned using the **Selection Tool** and **Sizing Tool**.

More information on using these tools, as well as the **Workspace** panel's **Alignment** tools, can be found on pages 36 and 37 of **Chapter 3, Build a Menu Page.**

Select a button highlight's shape and color

Overlays are the **Highlights**, or colored shapes which appear over your menu buttons as your viewer navigates your menu pages, moving from button to button using his or her disc player's remote control.

When a viewer "mouses over" a particular button, a **Highlight** will appear over that button. This **Highlight's** shape, color and opacity (see **Color Sets**) are defined in the **Button Properties** panel, and can be set overall (for your entire disc project) or customized for individual pages or even individual buttons.

On the facing page is an illustration of the various **Highlight** styles available in DVD Architect Studio. Included in these is a **Custom** highlight option, in which this **Highlight's** shape is defined by your own custom design, using a process called **Mask Mapping**.

Highlight Styles define the shape of the color that appears over your buttons when your viewer "mouses over" them.

Menu Button Highlight Styles

Rectangle Mask

Mask Overlay

Text Rectangle

Image Rectangle

Text Mask

Image Mask

Underline

Custom
(Black dot)

The overlay shape options include:

- **Rectangle** overlays both text and image with a rectangle.
- **Mask Overlay** highlights the text and image only, without highlighting the surrounding area.
- **Text Rectangle** overlays a rectangle over your text only.
- **Image Rectangle** overlays a rectangle over your image only.
- **Text Mask Overlay** highlights only the button's text.
- **Image Mask Overlay** highlights the thumbnail image only, and in the shape of the thumbnail, if it is non-square.
- **Underline** highlights with a simple underline under your button.
- **Custom** allows you to apply any custom shape to your highlight, according to the settings below.

If you select the **Custom** option for your highlight, the shape of your overlay is defined by your own custom image. How that image defines this shape based on this image is a characteristic of **Mask Mapping**.

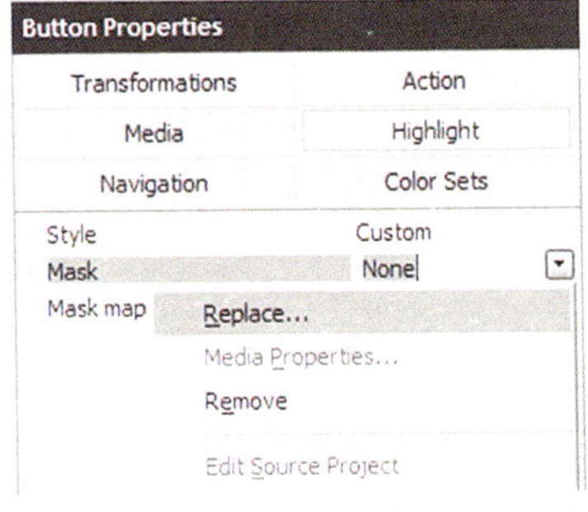

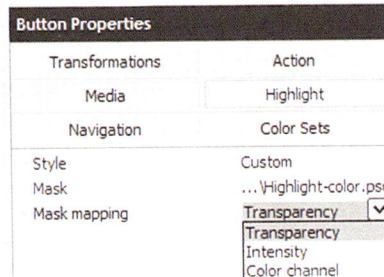

To create a custom shape for your overlay, browse to an image to use as your Mask and then define how DVD Architect Studio reads its shape and colors in Mask Mapping.

Mask Mapping Custom Button Style Highlights

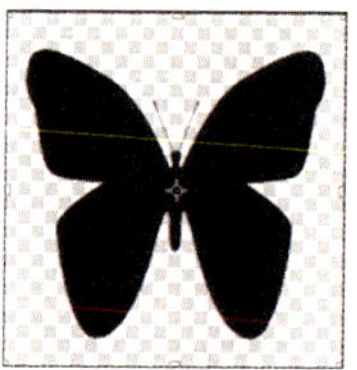

The **Transparency** setting creates a highlight, using your designated color set, based on your custom shape's black and transparent areas.

The **Intensity** setting creates a highlight, using your designated color set, based on your custom shape's black and white areas.

The **Color Channel** setting creates a highlight, using your designated color set, based on your custom shape's red, green, blue and black areas.

Setting this **Mask Mapping** property to **Transparency** maps the mask graphic so that the opaque (non-transparent) areas of the mask graphic become the **Fill Color** and the transparent become the **Transparent Color** (See **Color Sets**).

Setting this property to **Intensity** maps the mask graphic so that the lightest areas of the mask graphic become the **Fill Color** and the darkest become the **Transparent Color**.

Setting this property to **Color Channel** maps the mask graphic so that red areas of the graphic become the **Fill Color**, green areas become the **Anti-Alias** color, blue areas become the **Outline/Background Color** and black areas become the **Transparent** Color.

Color Sets

Color Sets are the customizable color schemes for the highlight masks that appear over your menu page's buttons as your viewer navigates your disc's menu pages.

A **Color Set** consists of four color definitions, each of which plays a role in a part of your button's **Highlight** overlay.

The definitions for each color include an opacity (or **alpha**) level, defined as "**a**" on the color selector panel. This level determines how transparent your overlay is.

A **Color Set** can be set to **Project Wide**, in which case the colors will be applied to all buttons on all menu pages on your disc, or it can set to **Custom**, in which case the colors will be applied only to your selected button. (Naturally, a **Custom** setting for any button overrides the **Project Wide Color Set** definition.)

Create and customize a menu button

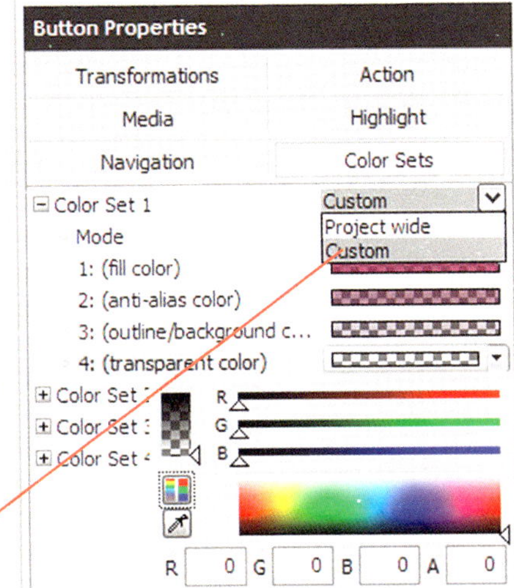

Color Sets are defined by red, green and blue levels or by hue, saturation and lightness, and include a setting for alpha, or transparency.

Color Sets can be custsomized for individual buttons or can be defined overall for a menu page or for your entire disc project.

Here's what each color in a set does. (By default – and probably for the best – the **Color Set** mode is set to **Blend Colors**, in which the three other colors are variations of the **Fill Color**):

Fill Color. Displays as a highlight over your button's text and thumbnail image.

Anti-Alias Color. Anti-aliasing smooths the edges of the menu highlight. It's generally a blend of the **Fill Color** and the **Outline/ Background Color.**

Outline/Background Color. Displays as the background or outline around the button as it is highlighted (usually defined by the button image's or text's black areas).

Transparent Color. This color setting designates which areas of a button display as transparent. As indicated in the illustration below, coloring this property fills the undefined, transparent area around a button's image and text. Most default color settings leave this as transparent.

Understanding how Color Sets affect button highlights

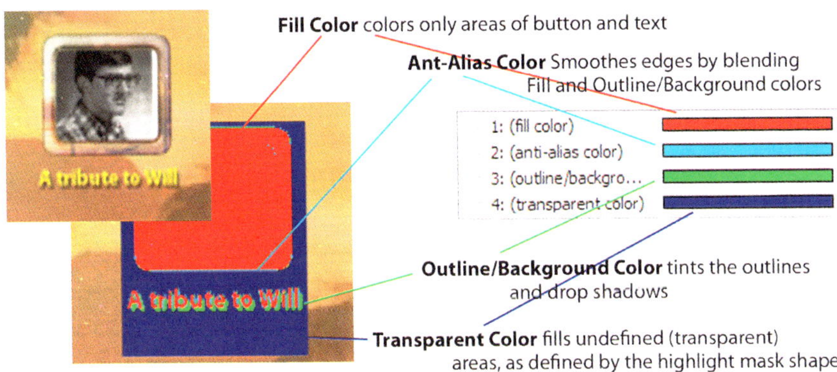

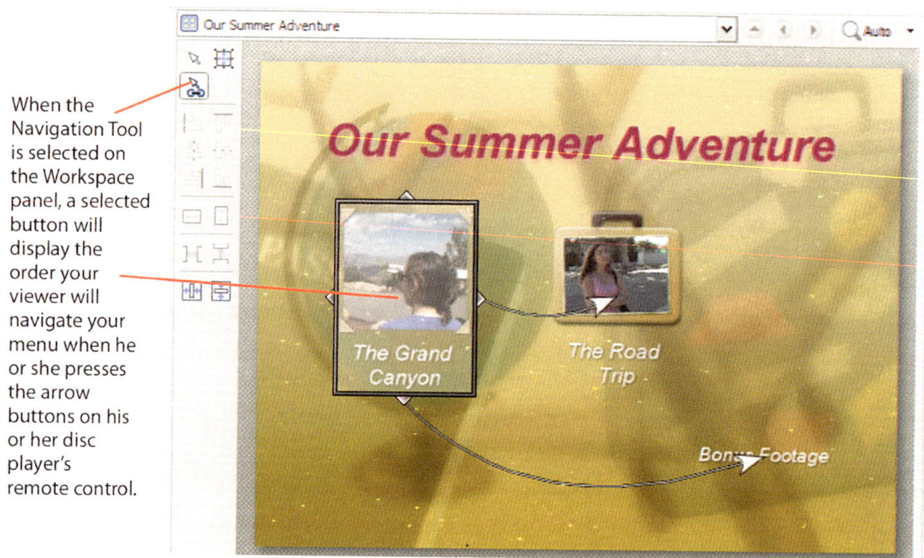

When the Navigation Tool is selected on the Workspace panel, a selected button will display the order your viewer will navigate your menu when he or she presses the arrow buttons on his or her disc player's remote control.

Modify your button navigation order

Navigation defines the order that the buttons are selected as your viewer navigates a menu page with his or her disc player's remote control.

By default (and probably most intuitively) this navigation moves from button to button from the upper left to the lower right of a menu page. However, this navigation order can be customized in one of two ways:

- Set the arrow connections from one button to another by dragging on the left, right, up or down "horns" surrounding the button in the **Workspace** panel.
- Select the navigation order from the drop-down options in the **Button Properties** panel.

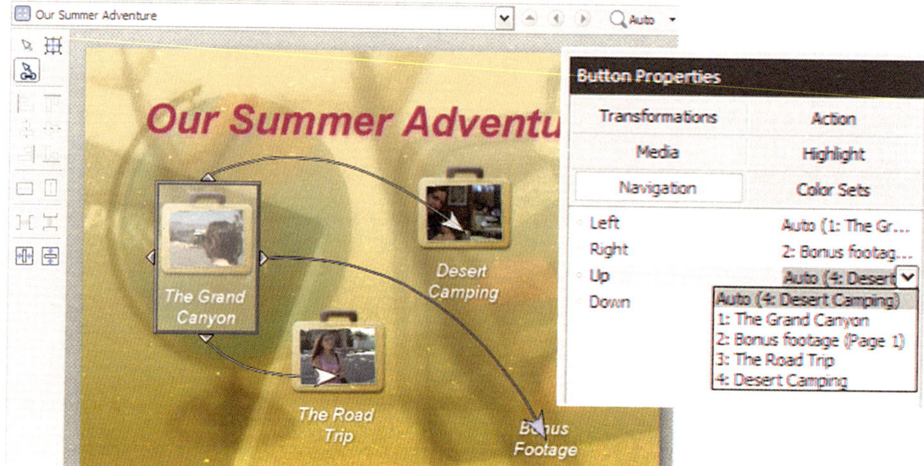

Navigation can be manually set by dragging connections from the "horns" around any button in the Workspace panel or by selecting from the options in the Button Properties panel.

Set a button to Auto-Activate

A button can also be set up to **Auto-Activate** – or to automatically link to a video or menu page when it is "moused-over" rather than when it is clicked on.

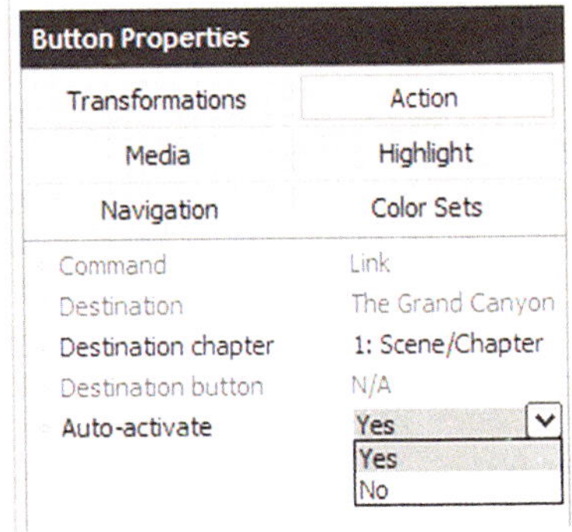

To set a button selected in the **Workspace** panel to **Auto-Activate**:

1. **Go to the Action pane properties**

   In the **Button Properties** panel, click on the **Action** button.

2. **Set Auto-Activate to Yes**

   Click on the box to the right of the **Auto-Activate** listing and select **Yes** from the drop-down menu.

Additional Button Properties

Definitions for more **Button Properties** and a reference sheet for the entire **Button Properties** panel can be found in **Chapter 11, An Appendix of Advanced DVD Architect Studio Tricks**.

Getting to know the Project Overview panel

Adding a new menu page or media clip

Rearranging your disc's structure

Adding video to play before your menu

Adding transitional video between your menus

Chapter 5

Build a Disc Menu Structure

Fleshing things out

A DVD or BluRay disc can be as simple as a single-page menu with a "play movie" button.

Or it can include sub-menus, scene selection menus, bonus features, outtakes and extras.

With DVD Architect Studio, you can flesh out a disc project as much as you'd like – adding many levels of menus and media links.

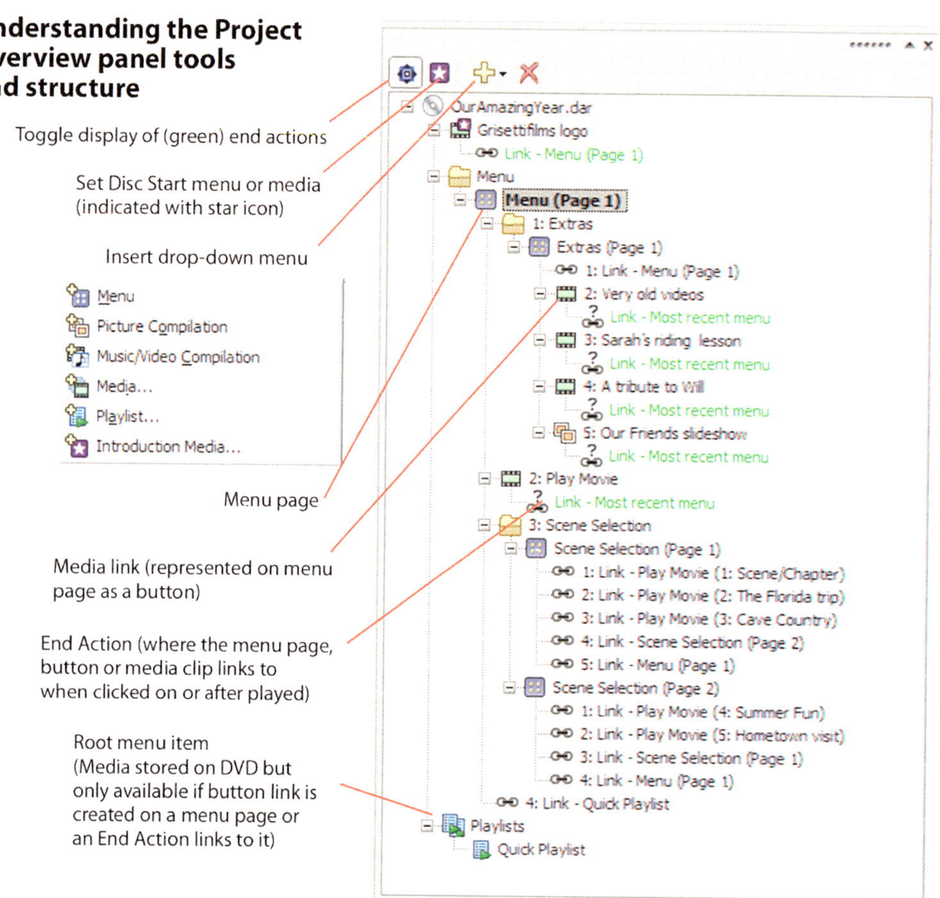

As you add menu pages, sub-menus and media clips, your DVD or BluRay disc's menu system will grow, like a tree, sprouting branches and growing from a single menu into as complicated a structure as you'd like. There's really no limit (other than the capacity of your disc, of course) to how complicated and deep your menu system can run.

Much of the work of building and modifying your disc's structure will likely be done in the **Project Overview** panel, on the left side of the interface, where the branches of menus and media are displayed and in which this structure can be easily modified.

Get to know the Project Overview panel

The **Project Overview** panel's layout may look familiar to those of you who have created a web site. Like a web site, your disc's structure will build, tree-like, a system of branches from its basic root, representing the various paths your viewer will have the option of taking as he or she navigates your disc.

Actions and End Actions

An **End Action** (usually a video clip property) indicates the page or media clip your video clip will link to automatically when it finishes playing. (**End Actions** are displayed as green "**Links**" in the **Project Overview** panel.) By default your video clips will link back to the **Most Recent Menu** – the menu page from which the clip was launched. In other words, once a clip finishes playing, your viewer is returned to the menu page that includes the button that launched the clip.

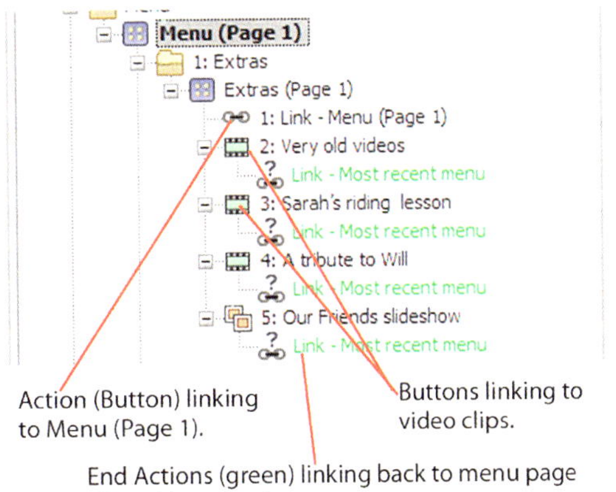

Actions (usually a button property) indicate the page or video clip that will be launched when your viewer clicks on a given button. (**Actions** are displayed as black **"Links"** in the **Project Overview** panel.) **Actions** are created automatically when you add a button to a menu page (as discussed in **Chapter 4, Create and Customize a Menu Button**).

Actions and End Actions can be modified and customized in the **Properties** panel. For more information on changing End Actions and Actions, see **Chapter 11, An Appendix of Advanced DVD Architect Studio Tricks**.

The option to display **Actions** and **End Actions** can be toggled on and off by clicking the button on the top left of the **Project Overview** panel.

At the top of the screen is an image of a **Disc**, representing, of course, your disc project's root. Once you've saved and named your project, that name will become the disc's name.

The next level down is your main menu page.

Each page of your menu will appear as a folder in this panel. To open a folder, click on + to the left of the folder in the **Project Overview** panel.

When a folder is open, it will display the menu page and all of its links. Closing a folder (by clicking –) simplifies the look of your disc project's structure.

As you add pages to your menu, they will appear as sub-folders, linked to this folder. As you add media, in the form of video clips, compilations or playlists, they will appear as icons mapped to the menu page by a dotted line.

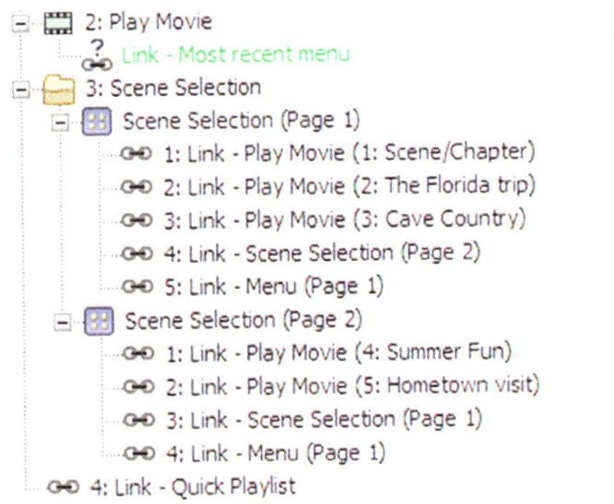

Menu pages are displayed as in the Project Overview panel, and the buttons as links from them. A link to a full media clip is displayed as , while a link to a scene or to another menu page is displayed as .

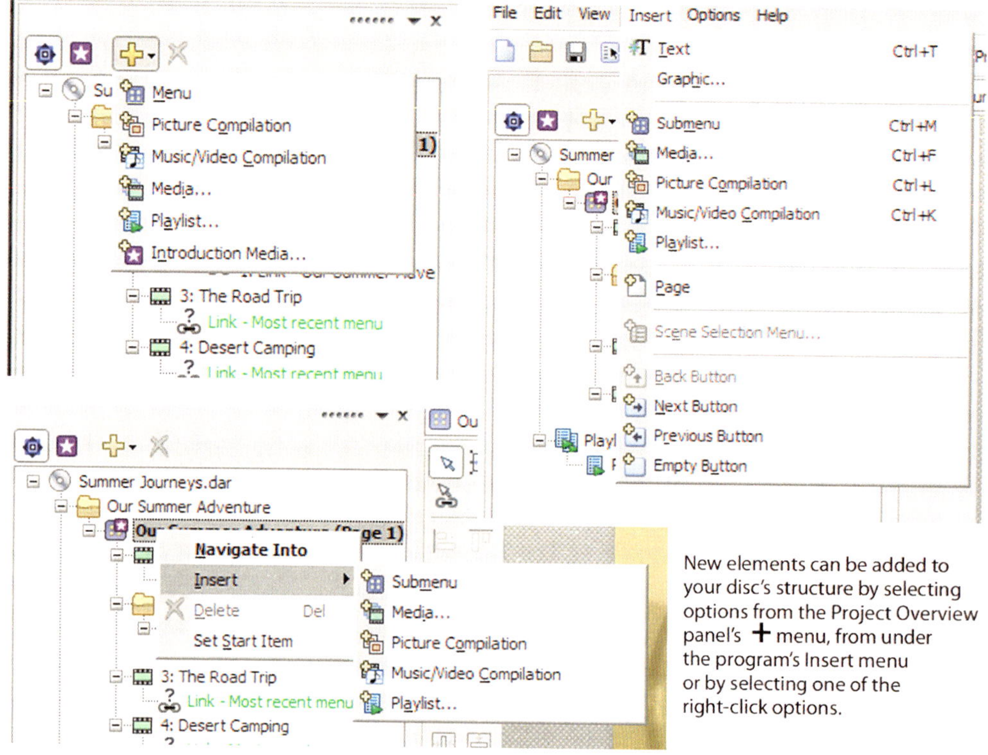

New elements can be added to your disc's structure by selecting options from the Project Overview panel's + menu, from under the program's Insert menu or by selecting one of the right-click options.

Insert a new menu page or media clip into your project

There are three ways to add a new menu page or media clip to your disc menu's structure. A link will be added to this new element on the page you currently have selected in the **Project Overview** panel.

- Select an option from the + menu at the top of the **Project Overview** panel.
- Select on option from the **Insert** menu at the top of the program's interface.
- Right-click on a page in the **Project Overview** panel and select an option from the **Insert** menu.

The options under all of these tools are virtually identical. (The + menu includes the option to set a page or media clip as **Introduction Media**, which we discuss on page 68.) They are:

Menu/Submenu. Adds a new menu page to your DVD or BluRay disc, linking it to the page selected in the **Project Overview** panel.

Picture Compilation. A **Picture Compilation** is a slideshow created in DVD Architect Studio and added as a video to your DVD or BluRay disc. More information on **Picture Compilations** can be found in **Chapter 8, Build a Picture or Music/Video Compilation**.

Jump to a menu page or media clip

You can quickly open any menu page in the **Workspace** panel for editing by double-clicking on it in the **Project Overview** panel.

Double-clicking on a video or other media clip in the **Project Overview** panel opens it in the **Workspace** panel so that you can set the clip's properties or add **Scene/Chapter Markers**, as discussed in **Chapter 6, Add Scene/Chapter Markers and a Scene Selection Menu.**

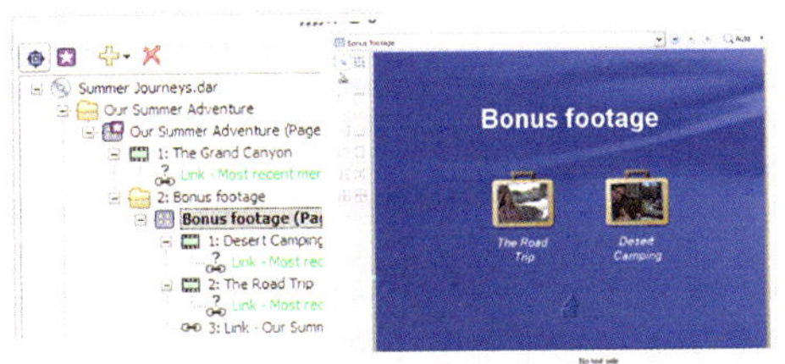

Double-clicking a menu page or video clip in the Project Overview panel opens it for editing in the Workspace panel.

Music/Video Compilation. A **Music/Video Compilation** is a collage of video clips created in DVD Architect Studio and added to your DVD or BluRay disc. More information on **Music/Video Compilations** can be found in **Chapter 8, Build a Picture or Music/Video Compilation**.

Media. Adds a media clip (usually video) to your DVD or BluRay disc, linking it to the page selected in the **Project Overview** panel. (For more information on working with menu buttons, see **Chapter 4, Create and Customize a Menu Button**.)

Playlist. A **Playlist** is a collection of video clips (gathered from media clips already added to your disc) which can be set to launch with a single button. More information on **Playlists** can be found in **Chapter 7, Build a Playlist**.

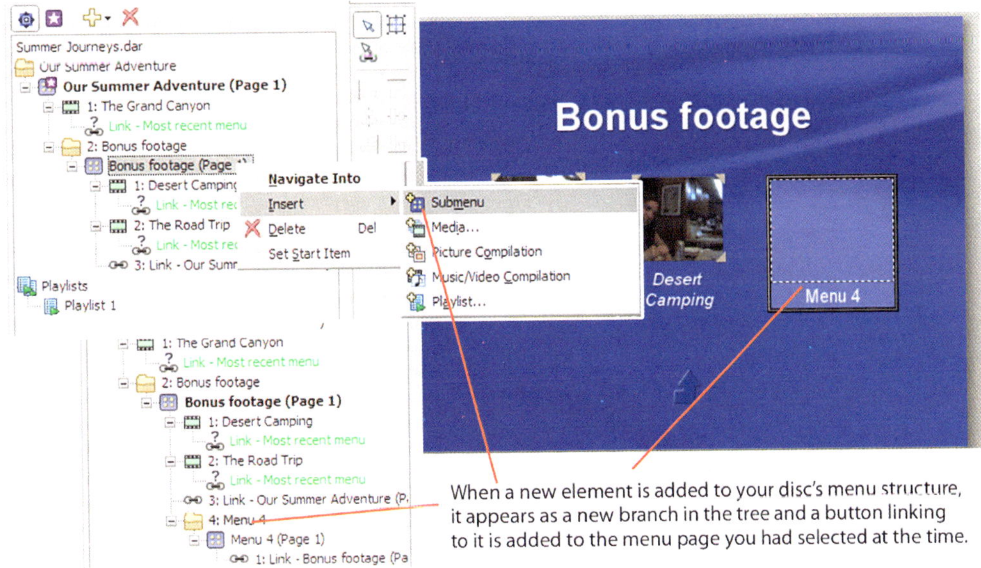

When a new element is added to your disc's menu structure, it appears as a new branch in the tree and a button linking to it is added to the menu page you had selected at the time.

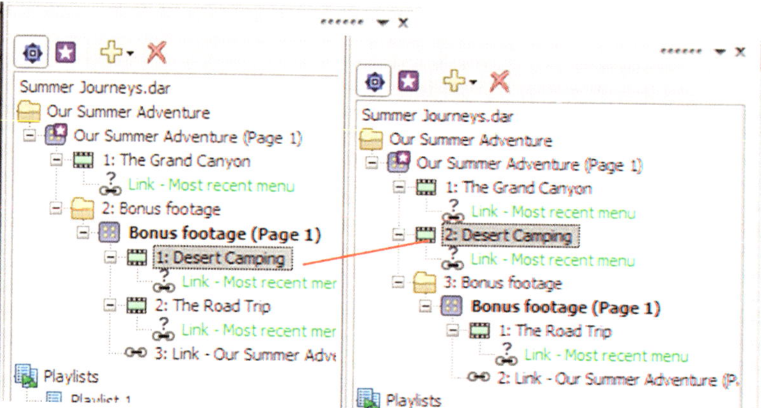

You can rearrange your disc's structure in the Project Overview panel simply by dragging the elements around. When a media clip is dragged from one menu page to another, the button is moved from menu to menu and all of the necessary links are automatically updated.

Rearrange your disc's structure

Although the primary function of the **Project Overview** panel is as a map for your disc's project's structure, it is by no means a passive workspace.

Your disc's structure can easily be rearranged by simply dragging the elements around in the panel.

For instance, when you drag a video clip from one menu page's structure to another, you move the button and its links from one menu page to the other.

Likewise, you can move entire pages from one area of your disc project to another, and the program will automatically update all links to it!

Add Introduction Media

Introduction Media is the first clip your viewer sees when your DVD or BluRay disc loads. In the **Project Overview** panel, the **Introduction Media** clip is indicated by the **Start Item** icon.

By default, your disc is set up to launch by displaying your first menu page.

However, it can be customized so that any menu page or media clip on your disc is the first element launched. This is particularly useful if you would like **add a clip (such as an animated logo or other video clip) to run before your first menu page appears.**

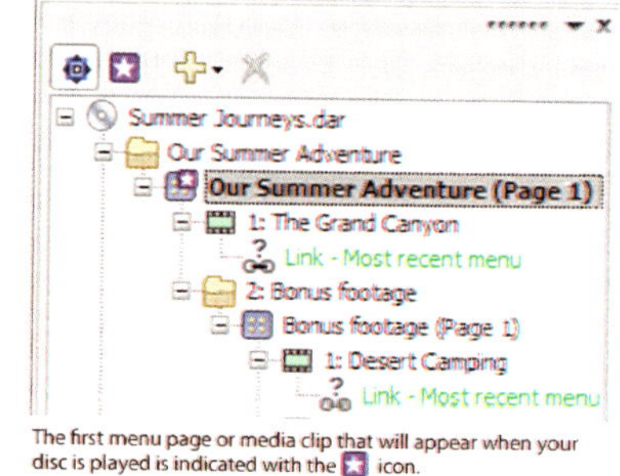

The first menu page or media clip that will appear when your disc is played is indicated with the icon.

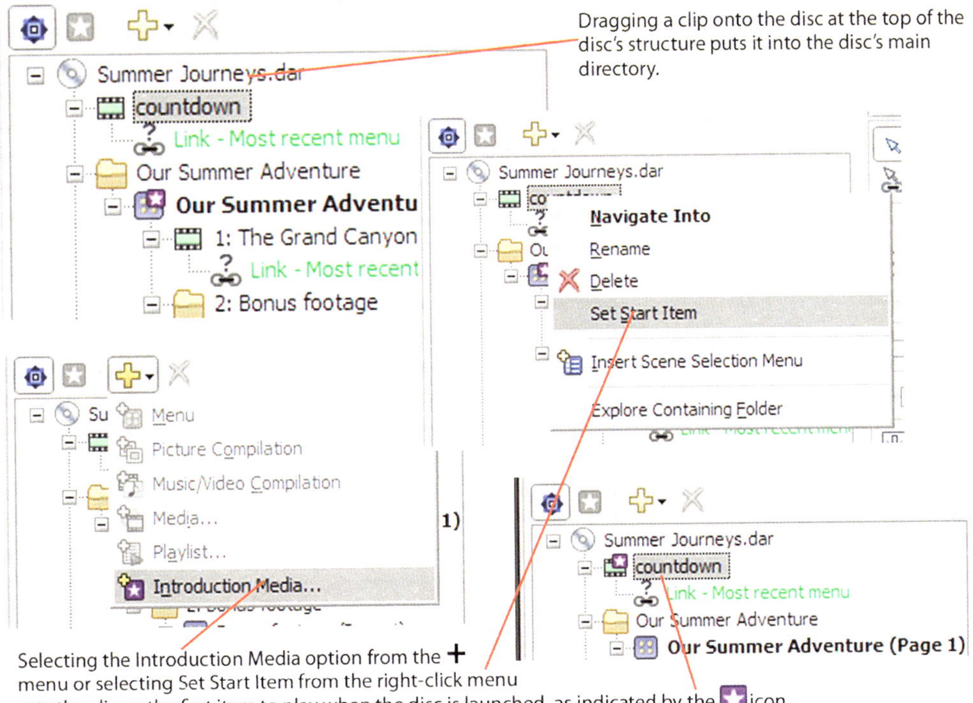

Dragging a clip onto the disc at the top of the disc's structure puts it into the disc's main directory.

Selecting the Introduction Media option from the + menu or selecting Set Start Item from the right-click menu sets the clip as the first item to play when the disc is launched, as indicated by the icon.

To add **Introduction Media** to your disc:

1. **Drag a media clip to the top of your disc's structure**

   Drag the video or other media clip you would like to use as your **Introduction Media** onto the **Disc** icon at the very top of your project's structure tree.

   It will appear as a clip right below the **Disc** icon, as in the illustration.

   You can use any kind of media clip as your **Introduction Media** – even a still photo. A still photo will appear for five seconds before automatically linking to your first menu page.

2. **Set your clip as the Introduction Media**

   With the clip selected in the **Project Media** panel:

   Right-click on the clip and select **Set Start Item**; or

   Click on the icon at the top of the **Project Media** panel and select **Introduction Media**.

   The icon will appear on the clip, indicating that it is the first element that will play when the disc is launched.

To preview this segment and its transition to your first menu page, click on the down arrow to the right of the **Preview** button and select **Preview Disc**. (Otherwise, the preview will launch from the page currently displayed in the **Workspace** panel.)

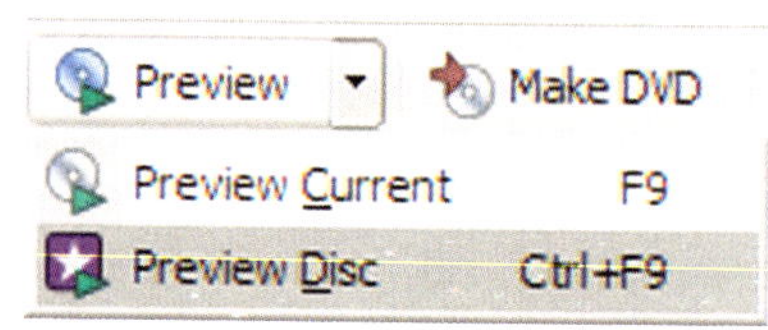

You can set any menu page or media clip on your disc as your **Disc Start** by selecting the element in the **Project Layout** panel and repeating **Step 2**, above.

Add a video transition between menu pages

This is a pretty advanced trick, but it can make for a pretty cool effect.

What we'll be doing is adding a short video clip between menus so that, when your viewer clicks on a button, rather than going directly from one menu page to another, there is a brief animated transition of your making between the menu pages.

Naturally, this transitional segment shouldn't be more than a few seconds long – since you don't want your viewer to fear he or she has pressed the wrong button. But a little animated transition between your pages can certainly make your disc more interesting.

For our purposes, we'll call our transitional clip "**Transition**".

"**Menu 1**" will be the menu page we'll be linking from, and "**Menu 2**" will be the menu page we're linking to.

Our goal, then, is to put **Transition** between **Menu 1** and **Menu 2**:

1 **Add a menu page to the main directory**

Rather than adding a sub-menu to an existing menu page , right-click on the **Disc** icon at the top of your disc's structure in the **Project Overview** panel and select **Insert Menu** (or select the **Menu** option from the menu at the top of the panel).

This creates a menu page outside the regular menu structure. In fact, at this point there won't even be a button on any menu page linking to it.

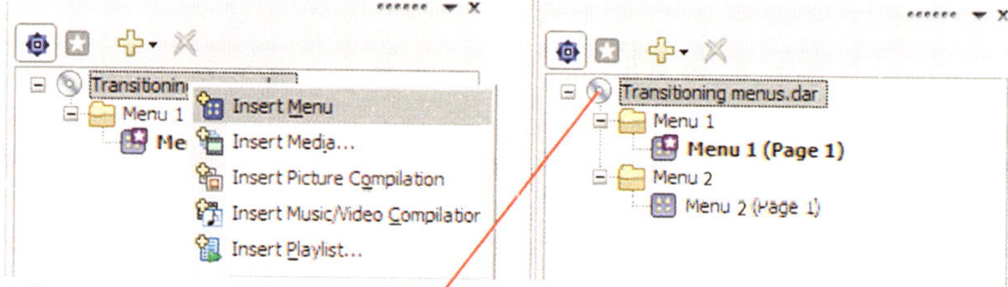

When you select the option to Insert Menu in the main directory, a menu page is created in "limbo" – fully functional but not linked to any other menu.

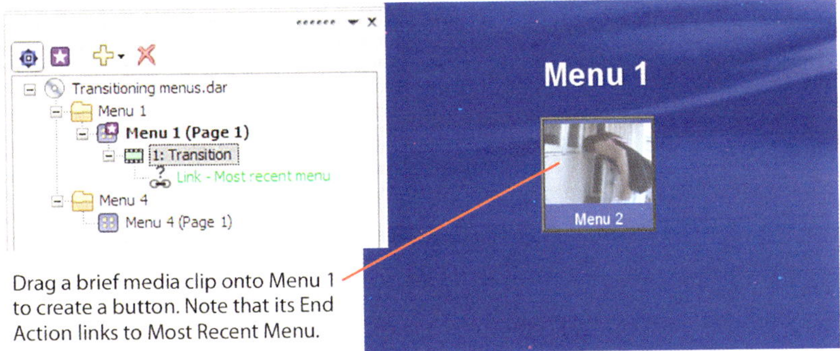

Drag a brief media clip onto Menu 1 to create a button. Note that its End Action links to Most Recent Menu.

You can treat this menu page just like a regular menu page. Customize it and add links to it, as we've described earlier in this book. The only difference between t his menu page and a "standard' menu page is that this one exists in limbo. It's on your disc, but right now it's "invisible" – outside your disc's menu structure.

2 **Add "Transition" to Menu 1**

Drag the video clip **Transition** from the **Explorer** panel onto **Menu 1** in the **Workspace** panel.

A menu button is added to this page, linking to the clip **Transition**.

In fact, at this point, we've pretty much just created a menu page with a button linking to a video, right? But here's where the magic happens.

3 **Open the Transition in the Workspace**

Double-click on the button linking to the **Transition** video clip in the **Workspace** panel.

The video clip will display in the **Workspace** panel and the **Properties** panel will display **Media Properties**.

Media Properties

General	Track Media
End Action	Remote Buttons

Command	Link
Destination	Most recent menu
Destination item	Start
Destination button	N/A

Double-click the button to open the video clip in the Workspace panel so that the clip's Media Properties are displayed in the Properties panel.

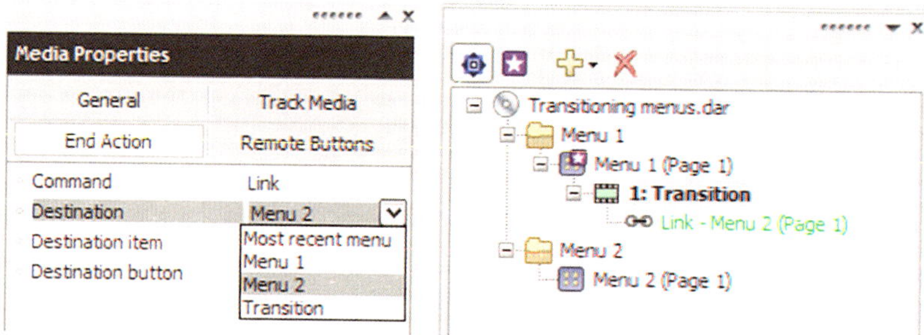

When the clip's End Action Destination is set to Menu 2, the clip will be launched by the button on Menu 1, then the disc will automatically go to Menu 2 – making the video serve as a transition between the two menu pages.

4 **Customize the clip's End Action**

Click the **End Action** button on the **Media Properties** panel.

End Action determine where the disc automatically links to once the video clip has played.

By default, the **End Action Destination** for a video clip is "**Most Recent Menu**." That means that, once the clip has played, the disc will automatically take the viewer back to the menu page it was launched from.

We will modify this **End Action** so that, once the clip has played, it will automatically link to **Menu 2**. In other words, when a viewer clicks the button we created on **Menu 1**, the **Transition** video clip will play, then **Menu 2** will open..

Click on the box to the right of the **Destination** listing on this panel.

A drop-down menu will appear, listing all of the media clips and menu pages on your disc project.

Select **Menu 2**.

Go back to **Menu 1** now and customize your button so that it looks like a link to **Menu 2**. (See **Chapter 4, Create and Customize a Menu Button**.)

Voila! When your viewer clicks on this button while playing your disc, he'll be taken to **Menu 2** by way of your **Transition** clip!

Trimming media in the Timeline panel

Adding Scene/Chapter Markers to your videos

Creating a Scene Selection Menu set

Chapter 6

Add Scene/Chapter Markers and a Scene Selection Menu

Linking to scenes in your video

When you've loaded a longer video into your DVD Architect Studio project, you may want to include scene and chapter markers.

Scene and chapter markers as well as scene selection menus allow your viewer to quickly jump to specific points in your video.

The Timeline panel

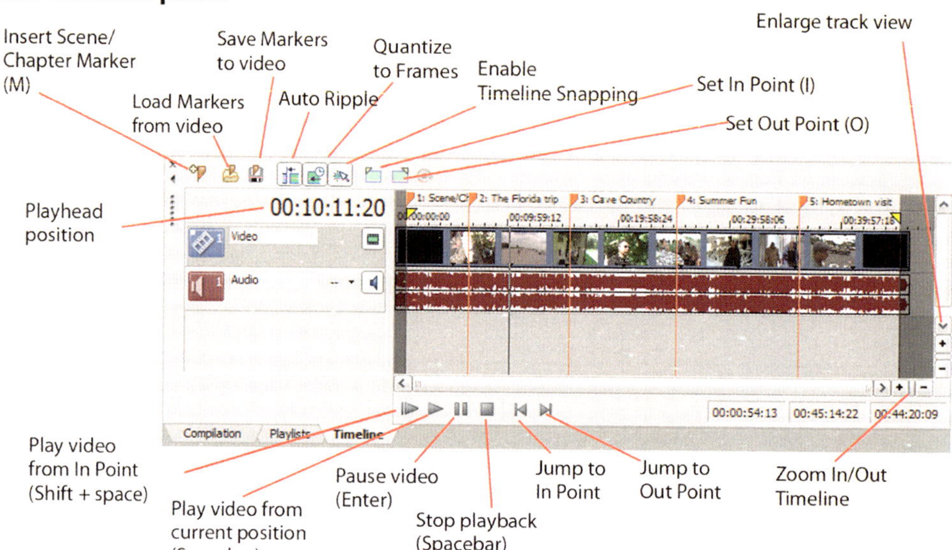

Building navigation to your video projects can not only involve building menu pages with links to your videos and other media, but can also include links to specific points in your videos.

DVD Architect Studio includes tools for adding **Scene/Chapter Markers** to your videos as well as tools for creating **Scene Selection Menus** that include buttons that link directly to those markers.

The main workspace for adding **Scene/Chapter Markers** is the **Timeline** panel. In the **Timeline** panel, you can also trim the media (setting a start point in a video clip, for instance, or setting a point at which this video will end and return your viewer to your menu).

Get to know the Timeline panel

To launch the timeline for any menu page or media clip (including a **Compilation**), double-click on the page or media clip in the **Project Overview** panel or double-click on the button linking to a video in the **Workspace** panel.

Timeline panel will display the timeline for whatever menu page or media file is displayed in your **Workspace** panel.

- If a menu page is displayed in your **Workspace** panel, the **Timeline** panel will display the video and audio that's being used as the page's background. (If you are using a still photo as your menu page's background, it will appear on the Video track.)
- If a video clip, playlist or compilation is displayed in your **Workspace** panel, the audio and video for that media or compilation of clips will be displayed in the **Timeline** panel.

Trim with In and Out Points

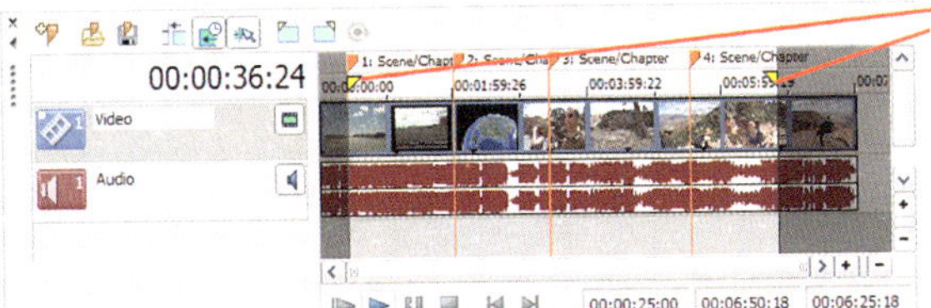

You can trim your video (removing frames from the beginning or end) by dragging on the yellow flags. Only the highlighted area between these flags will actually appear on your DVD or BluRay disc.

You may find that a song you'd like to use as a background for a menu page has too long a silence at the beginning. Or maybe you'd like this musical background loop to begin midway through the song. Or you might like to include only a segment from a longer video on your DVD or BluRay disc. To isolate the segment you'd like to include on your disc, you **trim** off the portions of the media clip you'd like to exclude by setting In and Out Points on the timeline.

Trimming a video is very easy, and it can be done in a couple of ways.

1. **Manually drag the yellow flags on either end of your video's timeline inward.** The highlighted portion of your video on the timeline is what will be displayed when your viewer clicks on the button to activate the clip. The darkened segments outside those In and Out Points will not be included on your final DVD or BluRay disc.
2. **To preview your video and set an in or out point based on the position of the timeline's playhead,** play your video using the playback controls – then pause it when you get to the spot at which you'd like to place your video's In Point.

   To move to a precise frame, advance or back the playhead one frame at a time using the left and right arrow keys on your keyboard. Once you've positioned the timeline cursor at the precise point you'd like to place an In or Out Point, click on the **Set In Point** or **Set Out Point** buttons along the top of the **Timeline** panel.

(DVD Architect Studio does *not* include tools for removing video from *within* a clip.)

Transport buttons for playing your media clips

As you can see in the illustration on the facing page, along the bottom of the **Timeline** panel are the timeline's playback buttons. You'll certainly recognize the play, pause and stop buttons.

In addition, the button to the left of the play button will play your video from its **In Point** (indicated by the yellow flag), a means of test driving it to see if it's a good starting point for your clip.

To the right of the playback buttons are a pair of buttons that will jump the timeline's playback head right to the video's **In** or **Out Point** – the beginning or end of your video, according to the positions you may have trimmed it.

In the lower right of the panel are two sets of **+** and **–** buttons for zooming into the timeline. The horizontal **+** and **–** buttons widen the timeline, so that you can zoom in more precisely to specific points. The vertical **+** and **–** buttons enlarge the view of the thumbnail images on the audio and video tracks.

When you add a new scene/chapter marker (by clicking the button or pressing the M key), you'll have the option of naming the marker point.

Scene/Chapter Markers are created at the playhead's position but can be dragged to any position on the timeline.

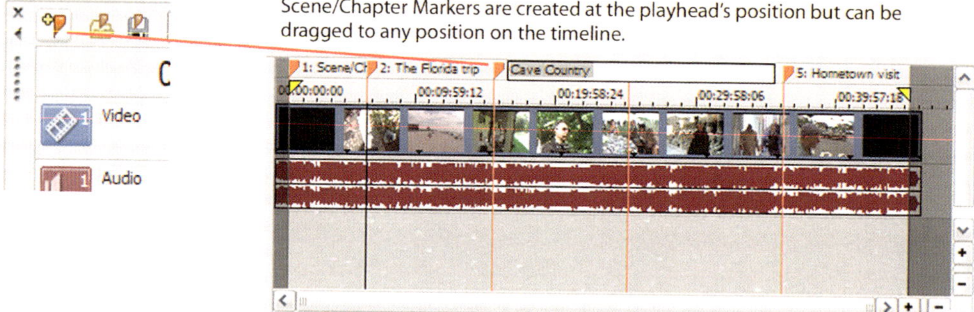

The name you give your scene/chapter marker will automatically generate a button with that same name if or when you create a scene selection menu.

Add scene/chapter markers

Scene/Chapter Markers add another level of navigation to your DVD and BluRay discs. Including **Scene/Chapter Markers** allows your viewer to jump to specific spots in your videos, either by using the controls on his or her remote control or by using a **Scene Selection Menu** that you've included on your disc.

To create a **Scene/Chapter Marker**, ensure that the video you want to mark is open in the **Workspace** panel and its video is displayed in the **Timeline** panel:

1 **Set the Timeline playhead to the point you want to mark**

Position the playhead on your timeline as near as possible to where you'd like to place a marker, either by dragging the playhead to a position, by using the playback controls along the bottom of the **Timeline** panel – or by using the left or right arrow keys on your keyboard to move the playhead backward or forward one frame at a time.

2 **Insert a Scene/Chapter Marker**

Click the **Insert Scene/Chapter Marker** button, on the top left of the panel, double-click on the tick marks along the top of the timeline or press the **M** key in your keyboard.

It doesn't matter if the marker is not in an exact position yet. You can adjust its position later by dragging on it.

3 **Name your Scene/Chapter Marker**

As you place your **Scene/Chapter Markers**, you may notice that the name of each markers opens as editable text. You can name each of your scenes either at this point or, later, by double-clicking on the orange flag representing an already placed marker.

Auto Ripple, Quantize to Frames, Timeline Snapping

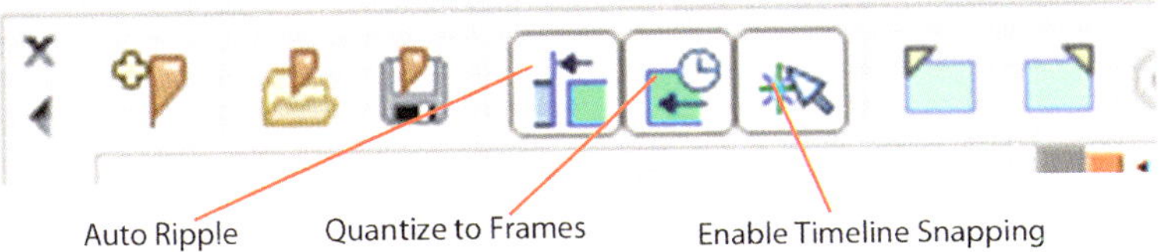

Along the top of the Timeline panel are three toggles that I recommend you leave activated – **Auto Ripple, Quantize to Frames** and **Timeline Snapping**. All three of these features are concerned with how the markers, trims or clips behave on your timeline.

Quantize to Frames, for instance, ensures that any markers you place or any trims you make are made at the beginning of a frame, rather than in the middle of one.

Timeline Snapping ensures that your scene markers are linked to I-frames

Auto-Ripple is related to the way **Compilations** or **Playlists** behave on the timeline as you add and remove segments. With this toggle activated, the clips will slide left to fill in the gap when a clip is removed. With **Auto-Ripple** turned off, the clips all remain in position when you remove a clip, leaving a big, empty gap in your timeline.

In fact, it's hard to imagine a situation in which you'd operate with these toggles turned off for any extended period of time. Activated, these features always work to your advantage.

The name that you give your marker will be, by the default, the name given to the button linking to it when you create a **Scene Selection Menu**.

I-frame warning

If you are using an MPEG video as a source file, you may also notice that occasionally, when you place a **Scene/Chapter Marker**, a yellow tag with an exclamation point on it will appear on your marker. This is a warning that your marker is not positioned on an I-frame.

MPEGs use a form of compression in which video information is reused over the course of several frames. This means, essentially, that only the master, or **I-frames**, contain a complete set of video information.

With **Timeline Snapping** enabled (as we discuss above) DVD Architect Studio will automatically help you locate an available I-frame as you drag your marker to a new position on the timeline.

An exclamation point on a marker indicates that it is between I-frames in a video. If this happens, ensure that Timeline Snapping is enabled and drag to adjust the position of the marker until the exclamation point disappears.

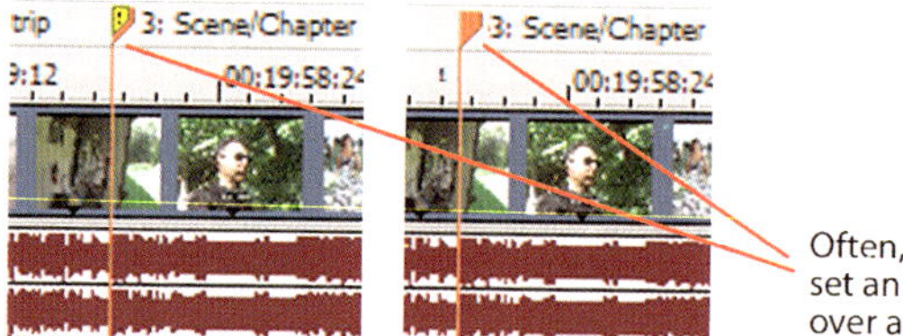

Often, it only takes a slight nudge to set an invalid Scene/Chapter Marker over a valid I-frame.

(To ensure that you are locating the nearest available I-frame in your video, zoom in to your timeline as far as you can using the **+** and **–** zoom buttons in the lower right corner of the **Timeline** panel.)

Drag your marker slightly on your timeline. When the marker no longer displays an exclamation point, you're in a valid marking position.

Other Scene/Chapter Marker limitations

In DVD Architect Studio, you can add up to 99 markers to a video.

Occasionally, you may get a warning if you place your markers too close together. **Scene/Chapter Markers** must be at least one second apart.

Remove a Scene/Chapter Marker

You can delete a **Scene/Chapter Marker** from the timeline by right-clicking on it and selecting the **Delete Marker** option.

Load Markers/Save Markers

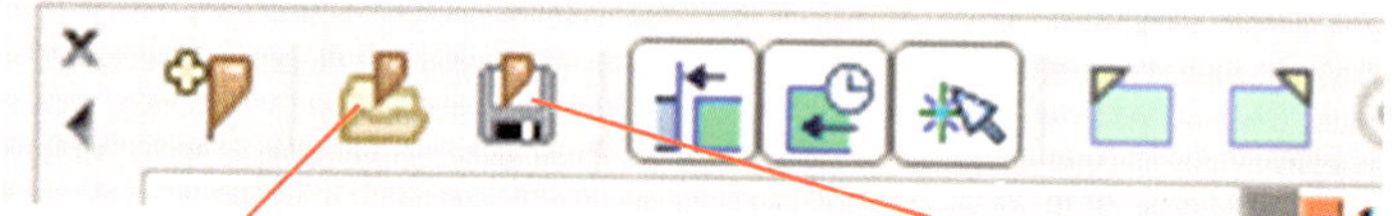

Load Scene/Chapter Markers saved to video file.

Save Markers to video file.

DVD Architect Studio is a companion program to Sony's Vegas and Vegas Movie Studio programs – both of which include the option to add **Scene/Chapter Markers** prior to exporting the video for disc authoring.

By clicking on the **Load Markers** button, the program will load any **Scene/Chapter Markers** which have been placed on your video clip in Vegas or Vegas Movie Studio. (This will also, by the way, overwrite any markers you've placed manually in DVD Architect Studio.)

Likewise, if you click the **Save Markers** button on the panel, the **Scene/Chapter Markers** that you've added to your video will be saved as metadata with the clip and can be recalled when the clip is opened in any of the Vegas or DVD Architect products.

Create a Scene Selection Menu

Once you've added **Scene/Chapter Markers** to your video sequence, you can create a **Scene Selection Menu** that automatically generates links to these marked scenes.

To create a scene selection menu:

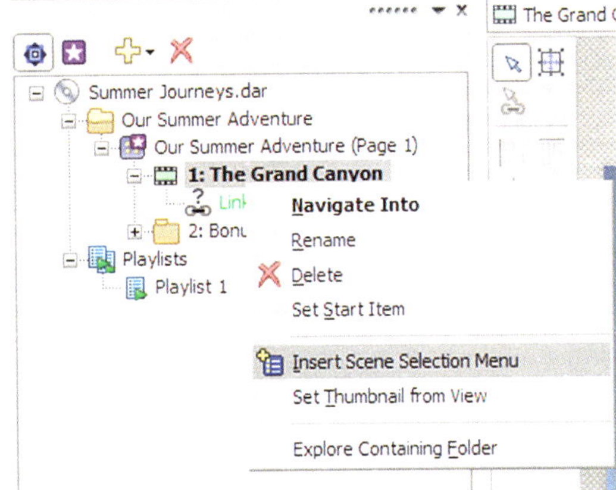

To create a Scene Selection Menu, right-click on the video clip you've added Scene/Chapter Markers to in the Project Overview panel.

1 **Right-click on the video clip in the Project Overview panel**

In the **Project Overview** panel, right-click on the video that you've added your **Scene/Chapter Markers** to.

It's very important that you click on *the video clip* – not the menu page. This option can only be accessed from the context menu on the video clip itself.

2 **Select Insert Scene Selection Menu**

Select the option to **Insert Scene Selection Menu** from the clip's right-click menu.

3 **Indicate the number of scenes per menu page**

Before generating the menu page(s), the program will display an option screen asking how many scene/chapter links you'd like to appear on each menu page.

Indicate the number of scene buttons you'd like to appear on each page and click **OK**.

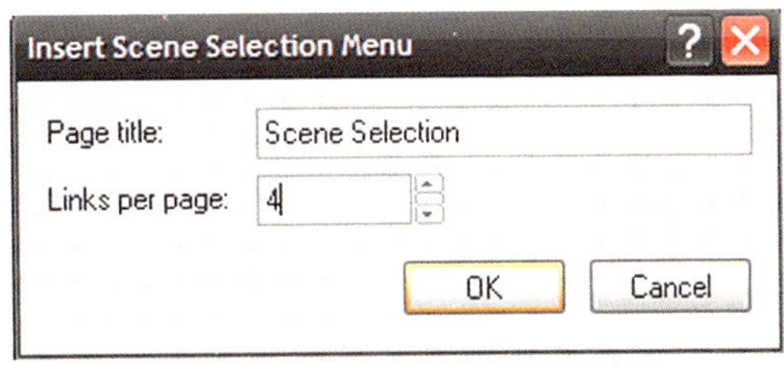

Indicate the number of scene buttons you'd like to appear on each page and, if you'd like, name your menu.

The program will create as many menu pages as necessary to accommodate all of the markers in your video.

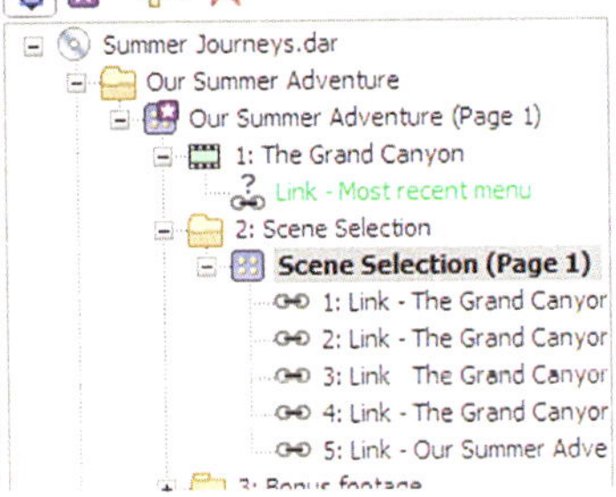

The program will create a set of as many menu pages as needed to accommodate your Scene/Chapters Markers, linking the set, by default, to a button on the same page that includes a link to the video itself.

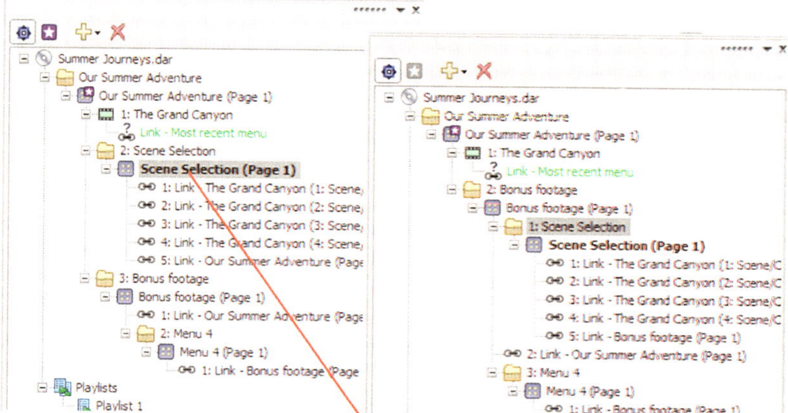

Although the program adds the Scene Selection Menu set to the same page as the main video by default, you can move the entire set of menus to any other menu page by dragging on the menu set's folder in the Project Overview panel.

4 Drag Scene/Selection Menu set to another menu

By default, this menu page set will be linked to the same menu page as the video itself. However, the button linking to them can easily be moved to another menu page by dragging the folder containing the scene selection menu(s) set to a new location in the **Project Overview** panel. When you rearrange your disc's elements by dragging them in this panel, the button links automatically update.

For more information on changing the locations of your disc's elements, see **Rearrange your disc's structure** in **Chapter 5, Build a Disc Menu Structure**.

Creating a Playlist

Editing a Playlist

Setting a clip's starting point

Chapter 7

Create a Playlist

Play many clips with a single button

Playlists are sequences of video clips that you assemble and order so that they can be played when your viewer clicks a single button.

Unlike Compilations (which we'll discuss in chapter 8), Playlists are composed of material already on your DVD or BluRay disc project – your main video, bonus features, outtakes, etc. Because of this, adding playlists to your disc does not increase your discs's size.

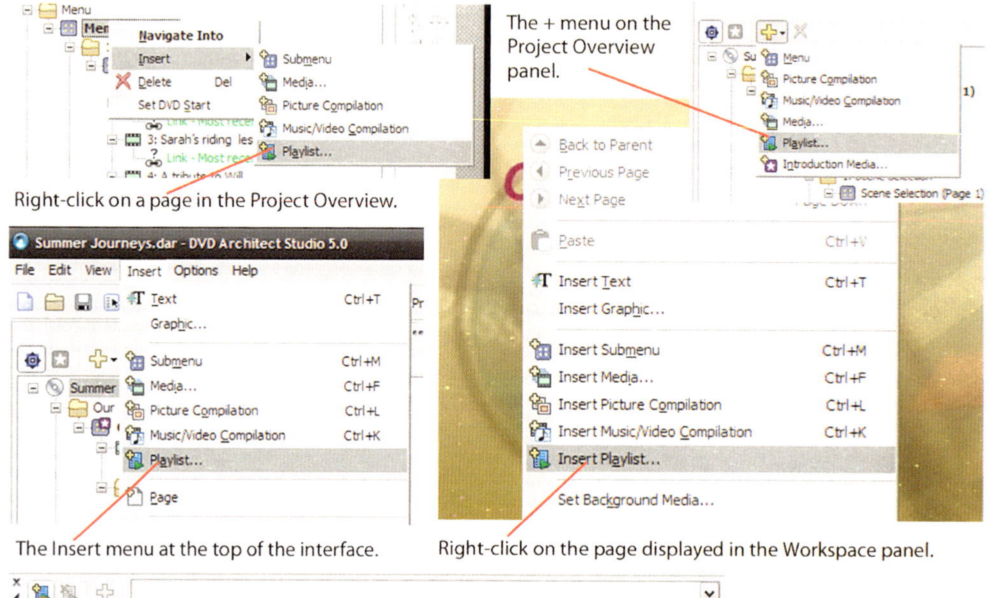

Right-click on a page in the Project Overview.

The + menu on the Project Overview panel.

The Insert menu at the top of the interface.

Right-click on the page displayed in the Workspace panel.

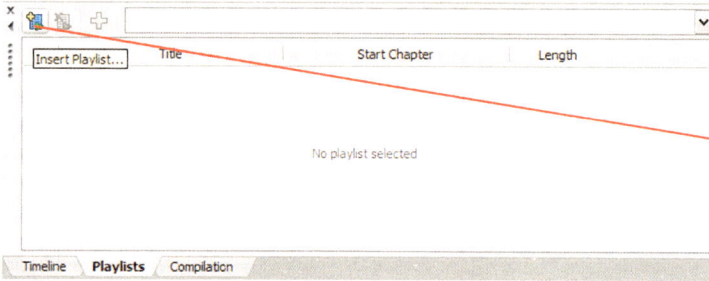

Insert Playlist... Title Start Chapter Length

No playlist selected

Timeline Playlists Compilation

The Insert Playlist button on the Playlists panel.

There are five ways to create a Playlists in DVD Architect Studio.

Create a Playlist

A Playlist is a sequence of clips on your disc that can be launched by a single click.

In other words, when you create a Playlist, you'll gather clips from existing video on your disc so that your viewer can view the entire sequence by clicking on a single button.

To create a Playlist:

1 Create the Playlist button

Select the menu page you'd like a playlist button created on in either the Workspace or in the **Project Overview** panel and then either:

- Click on the **+** (**Insert Object**) button at the top of the **Project** Overview panel and choose the Playlist option;
- Right-click on the selected location in the **Project Overview** panel and choosing **Insert Playlist**;

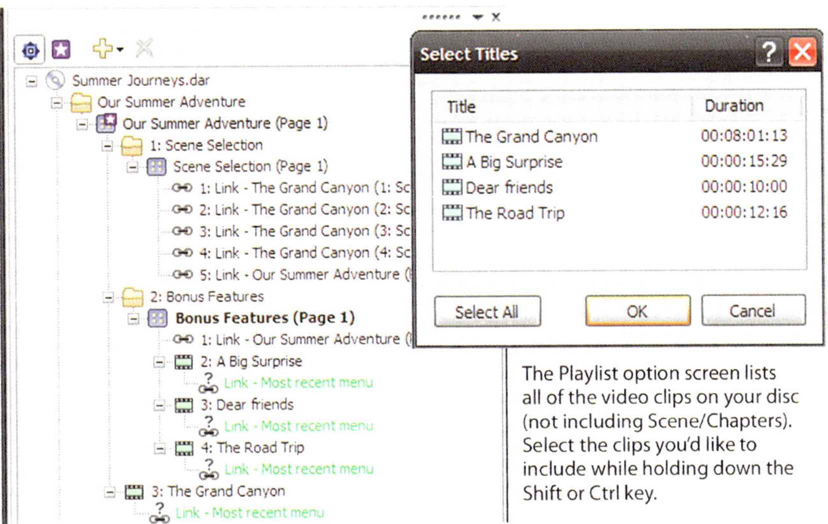

The Playlist option screen lists all of the video clips on your disc (not including Scene/Chapters). Select the clips you'd like to include while holding down the Shift or Ctrl key.

- Select the **Insert Playlist** option from the **Insert** drop-down menu at the top of the interface;
- Right-click on a menu page in the **Workspace** panel and select the **Insert Playlist** option; or
- Open the Playlists panel and click on the **Create New Playlist** button on the top left of the panel.

2 Select the clips you'd like to include in your playlist

Whichever method you use to create your Playlist, an option screen will appear listing all of the media clips on your disc.

Select the clips you'd like to add to your **Playlist** sequence by holding down the **Shift** key and selecting the first and last in a series or holding down the **Ctrl** key and selecting clips one at a time.

Click **OK**.

Playlists vs. Compilations

Playlists are collections of video clips that are already on your DVD or BluRay disc, set up by you to play in sequence from a single button.

Compilations are original slideshows or video compositions you create in DVD Architect Studio.

Because **Playlists** are composed of video already on your disc, they do not add to your disc's size. Because **Compilations** are made up of media added to your DVD or BluRay disc, they do increase your disc's file size. More information on **Compilations** can be found in **Chapter 8, Build a Picture or Music/Video Compilation.**

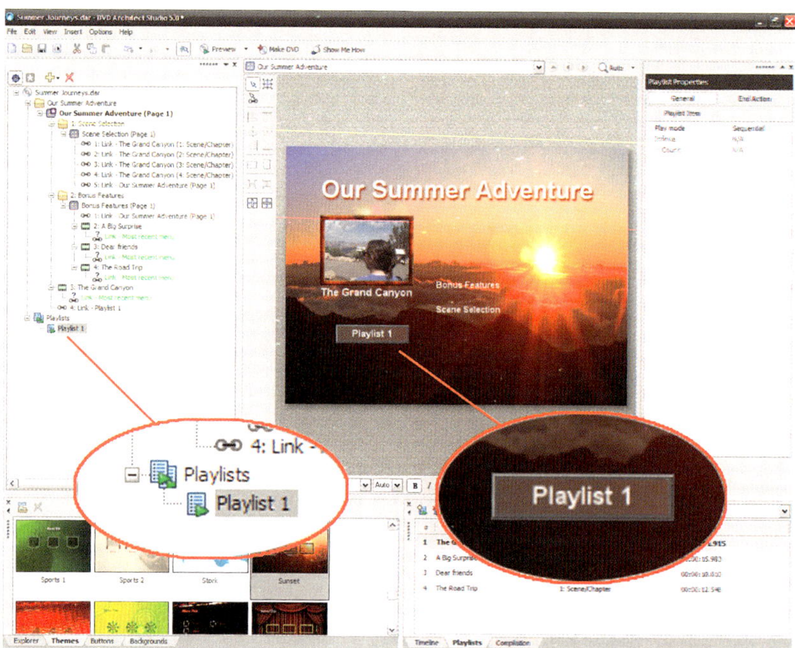

The Playlist file will be added to an area of your disc outside of your regular menu structure and a button linking to it will be added your menu page.

(Don't worry about committing to a list of clips at this point. You can always add or remove clips later.)

Your new **Playlist** will appear in a **Playlists** folder created in your disc's root directory, off to the left of the rest of your menu structure in the **Project Overview** panel.

Because of the nature of **Playlists**, they will always appear in this folder in the root directory, although links to them may appear on any menu page in your disc's structure.

If you had a menu page in the **Project Overview** panel selected when you created the **Playlist, a** button linking to this **Playlist** will automatically appear on that menu page.

A button may also be created manually on any menu page and a link to a playlist created by setting the **Destination** on the **Action** page of the **Button Properties**, as described in **Chapter 11, An Appendix of Advanced DVD Architect Studio Tricks**.

You can add as many **Playlists** as you'd like to your DVD or BluRay disc.

Because **Playlists** are only navigation instructions and do not add additional media to your disc project, they do not add to the file size of your disc.

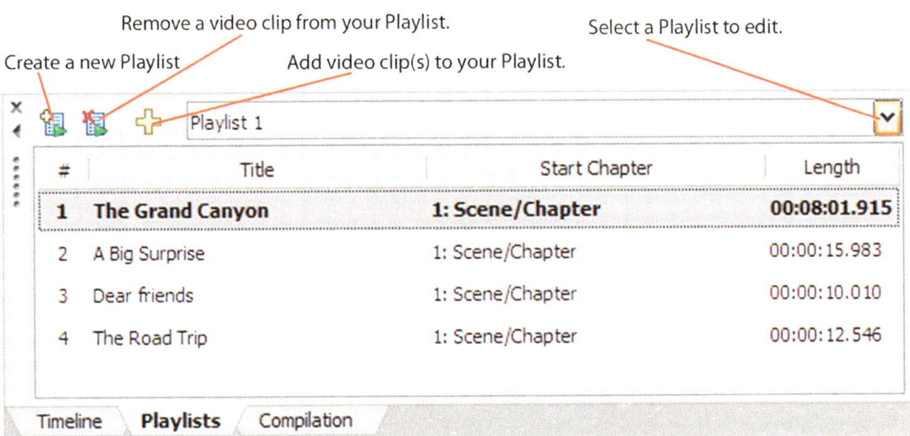

The Playlists panel shares a tabbed panel with the Timeline and Compilations panels.
The playing order of your clips can be rearranged by dragging them into order within this panel.

Edit your Playlist

Once you've created your **Playlist**, you can edit the list, and order, of the clips in the **Playlists** panel.

The **Playlists** panel is one of three tabbed panels in the lower right of the program's interface.

If you have more than one **Playlist** on your disc, the drop-down menu on the top right of the panel allows you to select which **Playlist** is displayed in the panel.

There are three ways to edit your **Playlist** in this panel:

- **Remove a video clip from your Playlist** by clicking the button or by selecting a clip and pressing the **Delete** button on your keyboard. (Removing a clip from your **Playlist,** by the way, does *not* remove it from your disc.)
- **Add a video clip to your Playlist by clicking the button.** This will re-open the **Playlist** option screen (as discussed on page 75), from which you can select additional video clips.
- **Rearrange your Playlist's playing order.** By dragging the clips up and down in this panel, you can change their playback order.

You can also create a new **Playlist** from this panel by using the button. However, if you do, you'll need to create a link from it to one of your menu pages. We show you how to do this in **Chapter 11, An Appendix of Advanced DVD Architect Studio Tricks**.

Finally, if a video clip in your **Playlist** has **Scene/Chapter Markers** assigned to it, you can set up your **Playlist** so that the clip plays from any **Scene/ Chapter** rather than from its beginning, as we discuss in the next section.

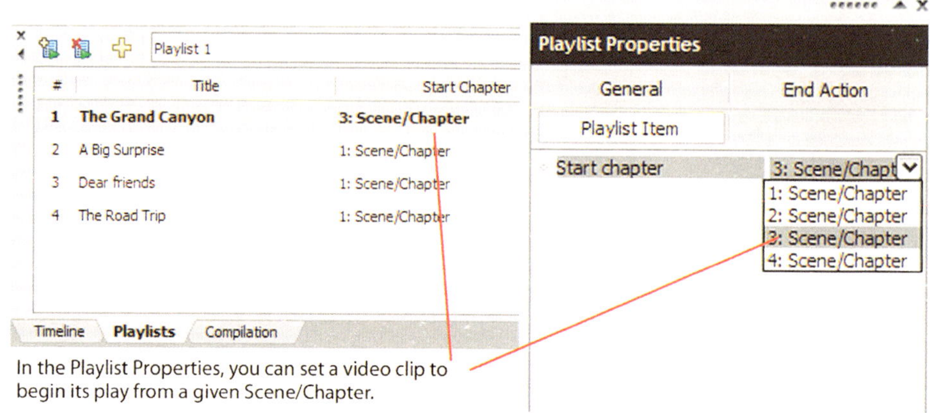

In the Playlist Properties, you can set a video clip to begin its play from a given Scene/Chapter.

Set a Playlist clip's Start Chapter

If a clip you've added to a **Playlist** has **Scene/Chapter Markers** applied to it (See **Chapter 6, Add Scene/Chapter Markers and a Scene Selection Menu**), you can set the clip up to play from one of these **Scene/Chapters** rather than from its beginning.

To set your video clip to play from a **Scene/Chapter**:

1 **Select the clip in the Playlists panel**

Click on the video clip's listing in the **Playlists** panel.

The **Properties** panel will display **Playlist Properties**.

2 **Select the Playlist Item page on the Playlist Properties panel**

Click on the **Playlist Item** button on the **Playlist Properties** panel.

3 **Set the Start Chapter**

Click on the box to the right of the **Start Chapter** listing.

A drop-down list will display the clip's **Scene/Chapters**.

Select the **Scene/Chapter** you'd like the clip's playback to begin on.

Note that this property only affects how the clip plays in this particular **Playlist**. It does *not* trim the actual clip or affect how it is played when the video is launched directly from a menu page.

Also note that setting up this property doesn't set the clip to play only the selected **Scene/Chapter**. This affects the *starting point* of the video clip only. The video will continue from this point through the end of the entire video.

Chapter 8

Build a Picture or Music/Video Compilation

Features created for your disc

Compilations are original features – slideshows, videos and/or music sequences – that you create for your DVDs or BluRay discs right in DVD Architect Studio.

Unlike playlists, compilations add media to your disc, and they will increase your disc's file size.

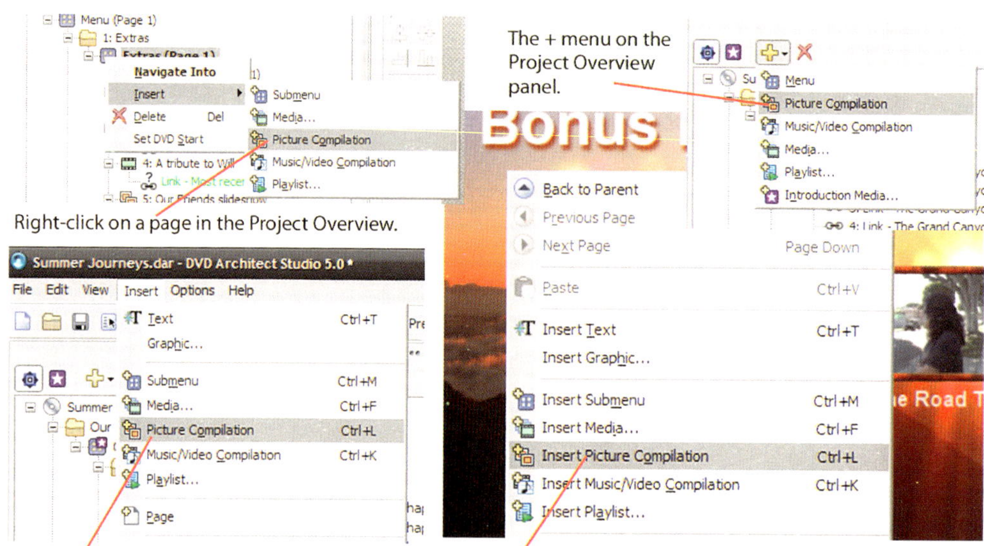

The + menu on the Project Overview panel.
Right-click on a page in the Project Overview.
The Insert menu at the top of the interface.
Right-click on the page displayed in the Workspace panel.

There are four ways to create a Picture or Music/Video Compilations in DVD Architect Studio.

Create a compilation

Compilations are photo slideshows (**Picture Compilations**) or video or music collages (**Music/Video Compilations**) that you create right in DVD Architect Studio. As with **Playlists**, there are number of ways to add a **Compilation** to your disc project.

Create a Compilation button

Select the menu page you'd like a **Compilation** button created on in either the **Workspace** or in the **Project Overview** panel and then either:

- Click on the **+** (**Insert Object**) button at the top of the **Project Overview** panel and choose the **Picture Compilation** or **Music/ Video Compilation** option;
- Right-click on a selected menu page location in the **Project Overview** panel and choose **Insert Picture Compilation** or **Music/Video Compilation**;
- Select the **Insert Picture Compilation** or **Insert Music/Video Compilation** option from the **Insert** drop-down menu at the top of the interface; or
- Right-click on a menu page in the **Workspace** panel and select either the **Insert Picture Compilation** or **Music/ Video Compilation** option.

A button linking to your **Compilation** will appear on the menu page you had selected when you created it.

Picture Compilations vs. Music/Video Compilations

Picture Compilations and **Music/Video Compilations** are assembled the same way and function similarly. However, there are subtle differences between them:

A **Picture Compilation** is basically a slideshow. It is composed of photo or still image files, and you may add a music track or other audio behind it.

You can not add video clips to a **Picture Compilation.**

A **Music/Video Compilation** can include music, video clips, stills or a combination of all three. Think of a **Music/Video Compilation** as a simple video project.

However, unlike a **Picture Compilation**, a **Music/Video Compilation** will not allow for an *audio track or a song to span across several slides or clips*. In other words, an audio track in a **Music/Video Compilation** can only be paired with one video clip or one still at a time – a single music clip can not be played as a background for your entire **Music/Video Compilations.**

This is one of the limitations that demonstrates why DVD Architect Studio works best as a *supplement to* rather than a *substitute for* your video editing software.

Compilations can be created as an added feature for your disc or they can compose the entirety of your DVD or BluRay project. As we discussed in **Start a new disc project** in **Chapter 2, Creating a DVD Architect Studio Project**, you can even create a disc with no menus at all that launches directly into a slideshow or video **Compilation.**

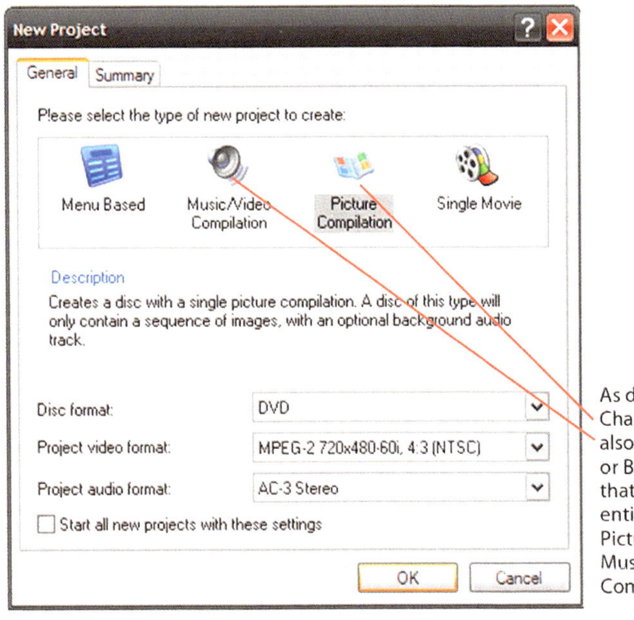

As discussed in Chapter 2, you can also create a DVD or BluRay disc that is composed entirely of a Picture or Music/Video Compilation.

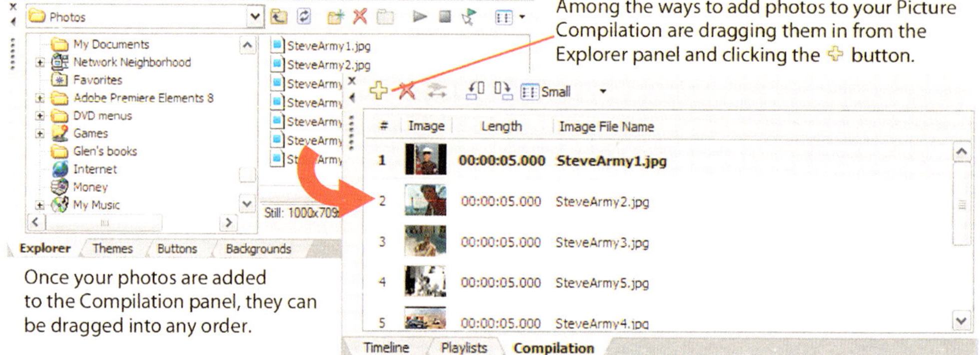

Among the ways to add photos to your Picture Compilation are dragging them in from the Explorer panel and clicking the ✚ button.

Once your photos are added to the Compilation panel, they can be dragged into any order.

Build a Picture Compilation

When you create a **Compilation**, you create an empty placeholder in your disc's structure. Your next step is to fill that placeholder with media.

Select the **Picture Compilation** you created (see page 94) in the **Project Overview** panel. If it is selected, you will see a gray box in the **Workspace** panel and the words "No Slides to Display."

1 Open the Compilation panel

Ensure that your **Picture Compilation** is selected in the **Project Overview** panel. Until you add media to it, it will be empty.

The **Compilation, Timeline** and **Playlists** panels share the tabbed panel set in the lower right of the program's interface.

Click on the tab to select the **Compilation** panel.

2 Add photos to your Picture Compilation

Add your still photos to the **Compilation** panel by either:

- Dragging photo files from the **Explorer** panel;
- Clicking the ✚ button on the top left of the **Compilation** panel and browsing to photos on your computer's hard drive; or
- Dragging photo files into the **Compilation** panel directly from Windows Explorer.

Only still photos can be added to a **Picture Compilation**. Video clips may not be included in this type of **Compilation**.

To delete photos from your **Picture Compilation**, select them in the **Compilation** panel and either click the ✖ button along the top of the panel or press your keyboard's **Delete** key.

3 Order and orient the slides in your Picture Compilation

You can easily re-arrange the order of your slides by dragging them to different positions within the **Compilation** panel.

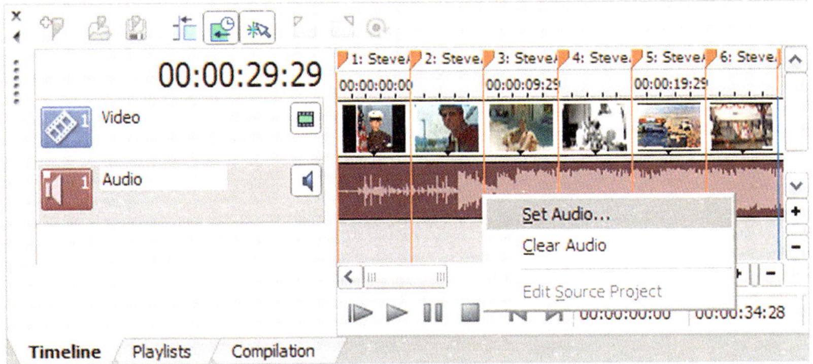

There are a number of ways to add music or other audio track to your slideshow, including right-clicking on the Audio track on the Timeline panel and selecting Set Audio.

If any of your photos need to be rotated 90 degrees left or right, you can change their orientation by selecting the photo and clicking either the or button along the tope of the **Compilation** panel.

Add music or an audio track to a Picture Compilation

When you add music or an audio track to your **Picture Compilation**, the music or audio will play in its entirety as your slides change.

As with adding photos to your **Picture Compilation**, you can add music or an audio track one of several ways:

- Dragging your music or audio clip from the **Explorer** panel;
- Clicking the button on the top left of the **Compilation** panel and browsing to the audio file on your computer's hard drive;
- Dragging the music or audio files into the **Compilation** panel directly from Windows Explorer. (Even though it won't appear in the panel, it's there – as you'll see when you switch to the **Timeline** panel.)
- Switching over to the **Timeline** panel for your **Picture Compilation** (by selecting the panel's tab), right-clicking on the audio track and selecting **Set Audio,** then browsing to the music or audio file you'd like to add; or
- Going to the **Track Media** pane of the **Picture Compilation Properties** panel and clicking the box to the right of the **Audio 1** listing, selecting **Replace** from the drop-down menu and browsing to your audio file.

DVD Architect Studio automatically ends your **Picture Compilation** slideshow after your last slide – no matter how long your music or audio track actually runs. However, the program does includes tools for setting the slideshow's length to match the length of your audio track.

For information on changing the duration of the slides, see the sidebar on page 98.

Adjust the duration of your Picture Compilation slides

There are three ways to adjust the length of time each slide or still image is displayed in your **Picture Compilation**.

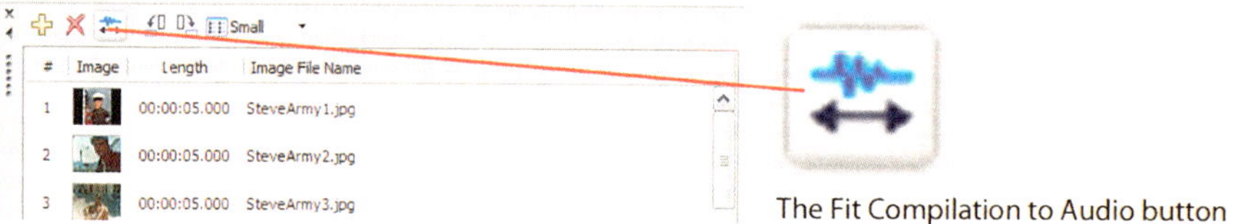

The Fit Compilation to Audio button

To set your slideshow to match the length of your music track:

Click the **Fit Compilation to Audio** button at the top of the **Compilation** panel. This will automatically expand your slideshow to the same length as your music track!

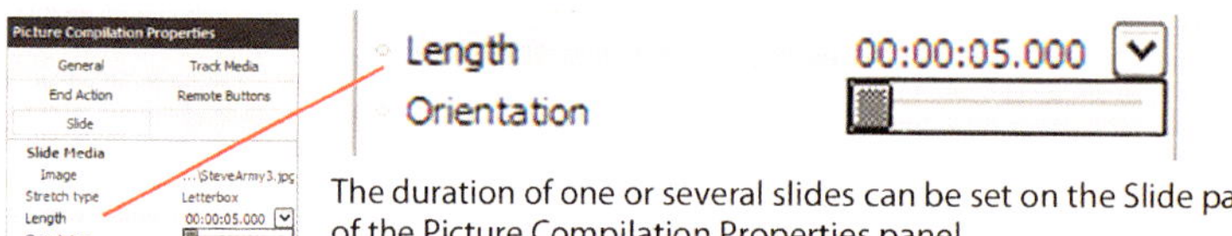

The duration of one or several slides can be set on the Slide page of the Picture Compilation Properties panel.

To set the duration property for one or several slides at once:

To set a specific duration for any or all of the slides in a **Picture Compilation**, select the slide or slides in the **Compilation** panel that you want to set the duration for. (To select more than one slide at once, hold down the **Shift** key and click the first and last in a series, or hold down the **Ctrl** key and click to select each slide one at a time.) When you've selected your set, go to the **Picture Compilation Properties** panel, click to select the **Slide** page and then click on the box to the right of the **Length** listing. You can set the duration by typing in the number of seconds (5.000 is five seconds) or by clicking the drop-down option and moving the slider. Your changes will affect the entire set of slides you have selected

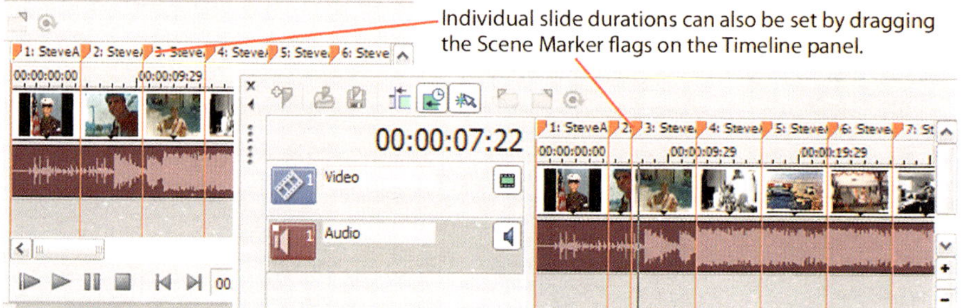

Individual slide durations can also be set by dragging the Scene Marker flags on the Timeline panel.

To manually adjust a slide's duration on the Timeline panel:

Finally, you can also change the duration of each slide by moving the orange **Scene Marker** flags on the **Timeline** panel. The nearer you drag these flags to each other, the shorter the slide's duration. (Note that, on the Timeline panel, DVD Architect Studio automatically trims the music to end after the last photo in your **Picture Compilation**, no matter how long your music track actually runs.)

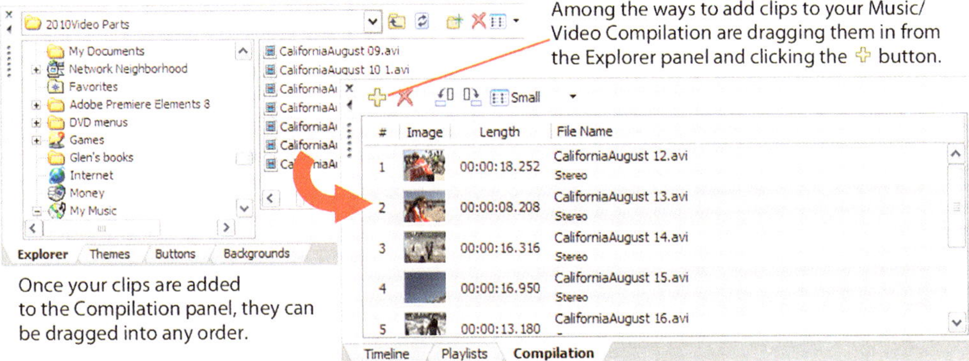

Among the ways to add clips to your Music/Video Compilation are dragging them in from the Explorer panel and clicking the button.

Once your clips are added to the Compilation panel, they can be dragged into any order.

Build a Music/Video Compilation

When you create a **Compilation**, you create an empty placeholder in your disc's structure. Your next step is to fill that placeholder with media.

Select the **Music/Video Compilation** you created (see page 94) in the **Project Overview** panel. If it is selected, you will see a gray box in the **Workspace** panel and the words "No Slides to Display."

1 Open the Compilation panel

Ensure that your **Music/Video Compilation** is selected in the **Project Overview** panel. Until you add media to it, it will be empty.

The **Compilation, Timeline** and **Playlists** panels share the tabbed panel set in the lower right of the program's interface.

Click on the tab to select the **Compilation** panel.

2 Add video clips and/or photos to your Music/Video Compilation

Add video clips or still photos to the **Compilation** panel by either:

- Dragging the files from the **Explorer** panel;
- Clicking the button on the top left of the **Compilation** panel and browsing to the files on your computer's hard drive; or
- Dragging photo or video files into the **Compilation** panel directly from Windows Explorer.

Unlike a **Picture Compilation**, you can add video or still photos to a **Music/Video Compilation.** But, also unlike a **Picture Compilation,** all photos display for five seconds and that duration *cannot be changed.*

You also can *not* trim or change the duration of the video clips in your **Music/Video Compilation**. Each clip must play in its entirety.

To delete photos or video clips from your **Music/Video Compilation**, select them in the **Compilation** panel and either click the button along the top of the panel or press your keyboard's **Delete** key.

3 Order and orient the clips in your Music/Video Compilation

You can re-arrange the order of your slides by dragging them to different positions within the **Compilation** panel.

Add music to your Music/Video Compilation (or not)

As with a **Picture Compilation**, you can add music or audio to a **Music/ Video Compilation**.

However, there are a couple of limitations to the music or audio tracks you can add to a **Music/Video Compilation** that you'll likely find rather frustrating:

- **Music or an audio track can only be added to replace audio on one video clip at a time.** It can not be added overall, behind the entire sequence of clips. In other words, you can only swap in one custom audio track per video segment. There is no way to have your music play continuously in the background as your **Music/Video Compilation** changes from clip to clip, as you can with a **Picture Compilation**.
- **Music or a custom audio clip can only be *swapped* in for existing audio. It can not be added to a clip that does not have any audio.** In other words, you can replace the audio on a video clip – but you cannot add music or audio to a still photo, which has no audio track.
- **If you do add music or a custom audio track to a video clip, the clip will extend to the longer of the video's or audio's duration.** In other words, if you add a 3-minute song to a 1-minute video clip, your **Compilation** will play as one minute of audio and video – followed by two minutes of blank screen as your music continues to play!

Because of these limitations, DVD Architect Studio is probably not the best place for you to build your video sequences or to create music/video combinations. You'll probably find a traditional video editor a much more powerful workspace for this kind of project.

In fact, a DVD Architect Studio **Music/Video Compilation** would probably more accurately be called *either* a music compilation or a video compilation. It doesn't make a good combination of both.

You can swap in music or custom audio for a video clip in your Music/Video Compilation by right-clicking on the audio waveform in the Compilation's Timeline or by replacing the Slide Media/Audio in the Music/Video Compilation Properties panel.

That said, there are two ways to swap in music or a custom audio track for a video clip in a **Music/Video Compilation**, as illustrated at the bottom of the previous page:

- In the **Timeline** panel for your **Music/Video Compilation**, right-click on the audio waveform under a video clip and select **Set Audio**. Browse to the music or audio file you would like to swap for the clip's existing audio.
- With the video clip you want work on selected in the **Timeline** panel, go to the **Slide** page on the **Music/Video Compilation Properties** panel. Click on the box to the right of the **Audio** listing and, from the drop-down menu that appears, select **Replace**. Browse to the music or audio file you would like to swap for the clip's existing.

Add titles to your Compilation's slides

Whether you've created a **Picture Compilation** or a **Music/Video Compilations**, you can add a title to each slide (or video clip) in your compilation. This title text can be added manually, by you, or the program can be set up to automatically add the text to your slides for you.

Option 1: Automatically add titles to your slides

The automatic titling tool will add text to your slides, based on the names of the photo or video files. This text can later be changed, and all titles can later be customized, in terms of font, color, size and location.

To automatically generate titles for each of the slides in your compilation:

1 **Open the Option drop-down menu**

Click on to the **Option** drop-down menu at the top of the program's interface.

2 **Select the Auto-Insert Track Title option**

From the **Option** drop-down menu select **Auto-Insert Track Title**.

Note that this preference will only affect items added to your compilation *after* it has been activated.

In other words, in order to apply it to slides already in a picture compilation, you will need to delete the slides or video clips from your Compilation and re-add them.

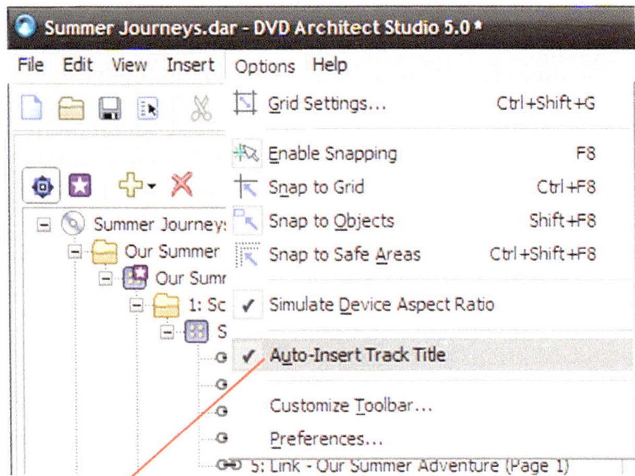

The Auto-Insert Track Title tool automatically generates titles for your slides, based on the file names of the original clips.

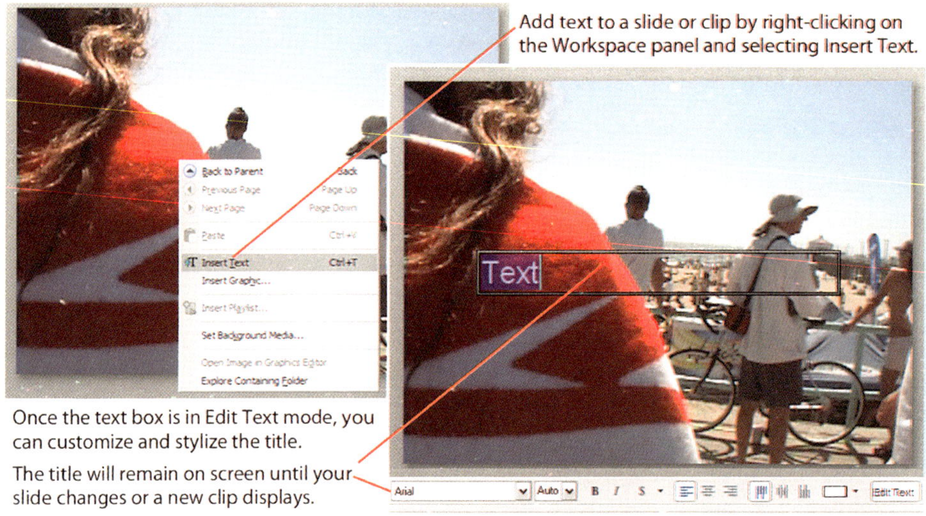

Add text to a slide or clip by right-clicking on the Workspace panel and selecting Insert Text.

Once the text box is in Edit Text mode, you can customize and stylize the title.

The title will remain on screen until your slide changes or a new clip displays.

Opton 2: Manually add titles to your slides

You can also manually add a text title to each slide or clip in your Compilation.

1 **Open a slide in the Workspace panel**

In the **Timeline** panel for your **Compilation**, double-click on the slide or video clip you want to title.

The photo or video clip will appear in the **Workspace** panel.

2 **Select Insert Text from the right-click menu**

Right-click on the clip displayed in the **Workspace** panel and select the option to **Insert Text.**

A text box will appear.

3 **Edit and customize your text**

Type in your title text and customize the text's font, size and style as in **Edit or add text**, on pages 34 and 35 of **Chapter 3, Build a Menu Page**.

The text you add to the slides or clips in a compilation will remain on-screen for the entire time the slide is on-screen – and it will change as your slides change or a new video clip appears.

Existing text added on a slide or video clip – even if added automatically by the **Auto-Insert Track Title** tool discussed on the previous page– can be edited or customized at any time.

To re-edit text, select the text box and click on the **Edit Text** button in the lower right of the **Workspace** panel.

Applying a Theme to your menu page

Adding a Background to your menu page

Customizing the look of your buttons

Adding and removing button frames

Chapter 9

Work with Themes, Backgrounds and Button Styles

Easy design tools for your menu pages

DVD Architect Studio comes loaded with a number of menu page themes, backgrounds, button styles and frames so that you can quickly apply a look to your disc menus.

Once applied, each theme or element is easily customizable.

The Themes panel

To apply a Theme to the menu page displayed in the Workspace panel:

1. Drag the Theme from the Themes panel onto the menu page in the Workspace or Project Overview panel.
2. Click the Apply Theme button on the top-left of the panel;
3. Select Apply Theme from a Theme's right-click menu; or
4. Double-click the Theme in the panel.

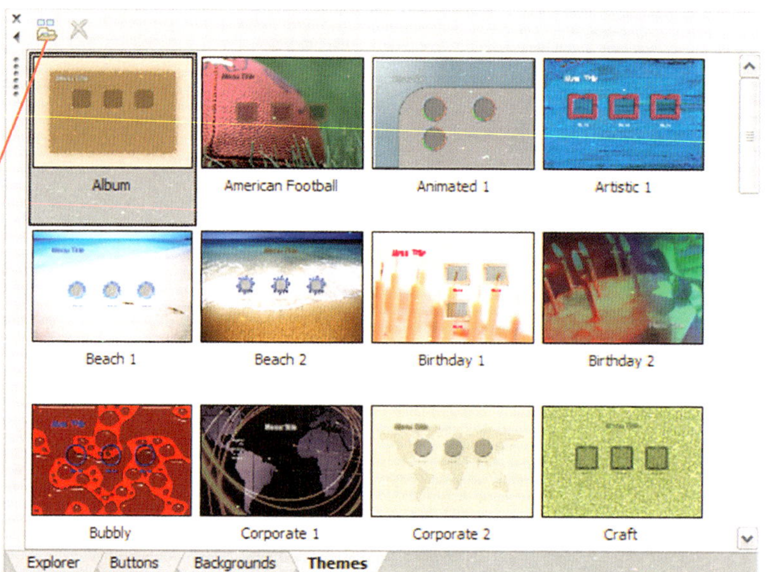

Creating a cool look for your disc menu pages is half the fun of building a DVD or BluRay disc project!

As we discussed in **Chapter 3, Build a Menu Page**, and **Chapter 4, Create and Customize a Menu Button**, there are a number of ways to design and customize your menus and buttons – both within the program and using your own custom-created elements.

Themes, Backgrounds and **Button** styles are easy-to-use tools for customizing the look of your disc menus and buttons.

The three libraries that include these themes, backgrounds and styles share a tabbed panel space with the **Explorer**, in the lower left of the program's default interface. Selecting a panel is as simple as clicking on its tab.

Apply a Theme

The **Themes** panel offers over fifty design styles for your DVD and BluRay disc menu pages – from abstract and artistic to simple and silly, from sports, event and holiday themes to birthdays, weddings and vacations.

A menu page **Theme** includes:

- A background image for your menu;
- Button styles and frames; and
- Text styles and text box alignments.

Once a theme has been applied to a menu page, any new buttons you add will automatically pick up the button style and button frame defined by that applied **Theme**.

Applying a **Theme** also *overwrites* whatever other styles, backgrounds, fonts and button frames you've already added to your page.

There are four ways to apply a **Theme** to a menu page:

- Drag your selected **Theme** from the **Themes** panel onto the menu page displayed in the **Workspace** panel.
- Select a **Theme** and click on the **Apply Theme** button in the upper left of the **Themes** panel;
- Right-click on a **Theme** in the **Themes** panel and select the **Apply Theme** option; or
- Double-click on a **Theme** in the **Themes** panel. It will be applied to the menu page displayed in the **Workspace** panel.

Themes can only be applied to one menu page at a time.

After a **Theme** has been applied, you can continue to customize the look of the background and other elements on the menu page.

Create your own Theme

If you create a menu page look that you're especially happy with, you can save it as your own custom **Theme**! It will then appear in the **Themes** panel so that you can easily apply it to any future menu pages, both in your current and in your future projects.

To create a **Theme** based on your current menu page's design:

1 Open the menu page in the Workspace panel

Ensure that the page whose look you want to save is selected in the **Project Overview** panel and displayed in the **Workspace** panel.

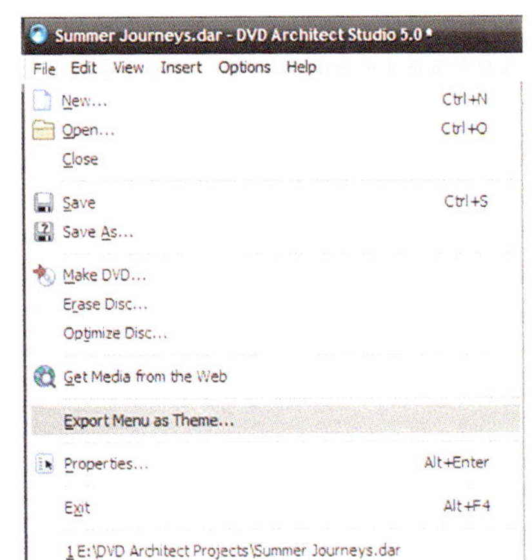

2 Select the Export Menu as Theme option

From the **File** drop-down menu at the top of the interface, select **Export Menu as Theme.**

You'll be prompted to name your **Theme**.

Name your **Theme** and then click **Save**.

If you later decide to remove this theme from your **Themes** panel, you can do so by selecting it and clicking the **Delete Theme** button on the top left of the panel. (Note that you can only remove *custom* themes you've added to this panel. You can not delete any of DVD Architect Studio's default **Themes**.)

The Backgrounds panel

To apply a Background to the menu page displayed in the Workspace:

1. Drag the Background from the panel onto the page in the Workspace panel; or
2. Double-click on a Background in this panel.

Add a Background

The **Backgrounds** panel includes over 60 **Background** images and designs for your menu pages. (You may recognize many of these **Backgrounds** as background elements from the program's **Themes** library.)

There are two ways to apply a DVD Architect Studio **Background** to a menu page displayed in your **Workspace** panel:

- Drag your selected **Background** from the **Backgrounds** panel onto the menu page displayed in the **Workspace** panel; or
- Double-click on a **Background** in the **Backgrounds** panel. It will be applied to the menu page displayed in the **Workspace** panel.

In addition to the **Backgrounds** included in this panel, you can use any still photo or video clip on your computer as a background for your a menu page. To use a custom still for your menu page background, just drag it from the **Explorer** panel onto your **Workspace** menu page.

A video clip can be added top a menu page as a motion background by selecting the option in the **Menu Page Properties** panel. We show you how to do that in **Add a custom video background to your menu page** in **Chapter 3, Build a Menu Page**.

Download additional Themes, Buttons and Backgrounds

As part of its continued support for its products, Sony regularly offers free backgrounds, themes and other items you can use in your DVD Architect Studio projects. You can download the latest from: http://www.sonycreativesoftware.com/download/freestuff

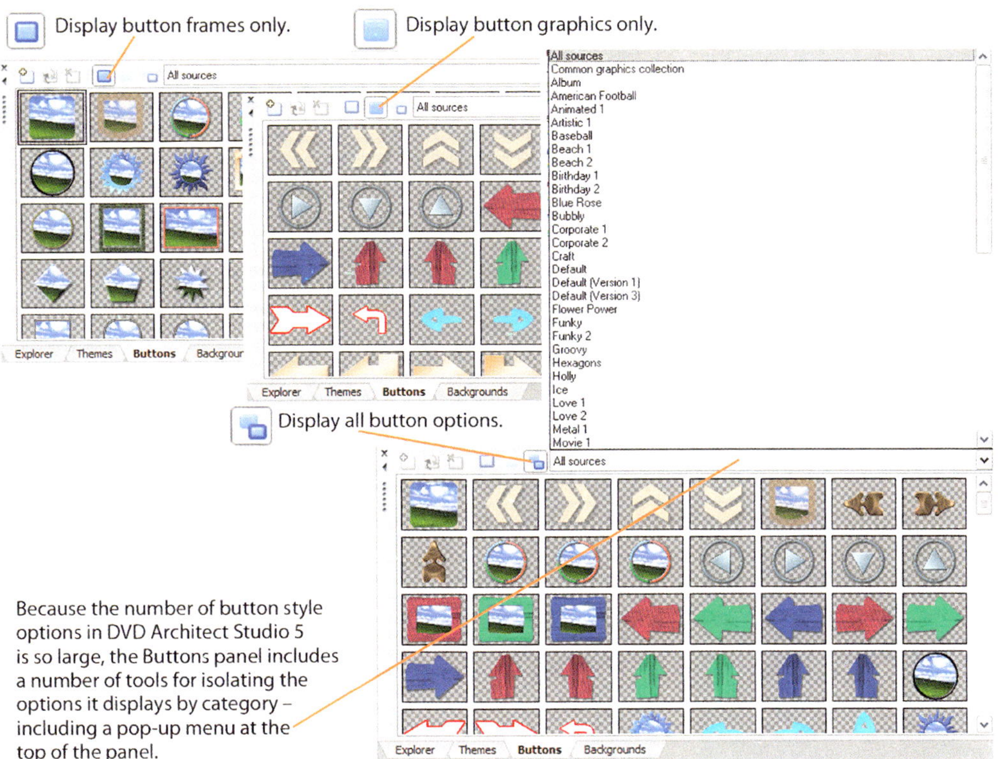

Display button frames only.
Display button graphics only.
Display all button options.
Because the number of button style options in DVD Architect Studio 5 is so large, the Buttons panel includes a number of tools for isolating the options it displays by category – including a pop-up menu at the top of the panel.

Navigate the Buttons panel

The **Buttons** panel offers over 350 different styles, graphics and frames for your menu buttons.

In this immense library, you'll find about 100 button frames, which place a graphic around your button's thumbnail image and, in some cases, change its shape.

You'll also find over 250 options for replacing your buttons' thumbnail image with a graphic.

Because this library includes so many buttons, frames, graphics and style options, the panel offers a number of tools for isolating which are displayed in the panel at any given time, as illustrated above.

- The panel can be set to display only button frames.
- The panel can be set to display only button graphics.
- The pop-up menu along the top of the panel lets your browse directly to a button frame or graphic in a certain category or style.

The Buttons panel

To apply a Button style to the button or buttons selcted in the Workspace panel:

1. Select a Button in the panel and click Replace Button;
2. Drag the Button from the panel onto the button(s) in the Workspace panel; or
3. Double-click on a Button in this panel.

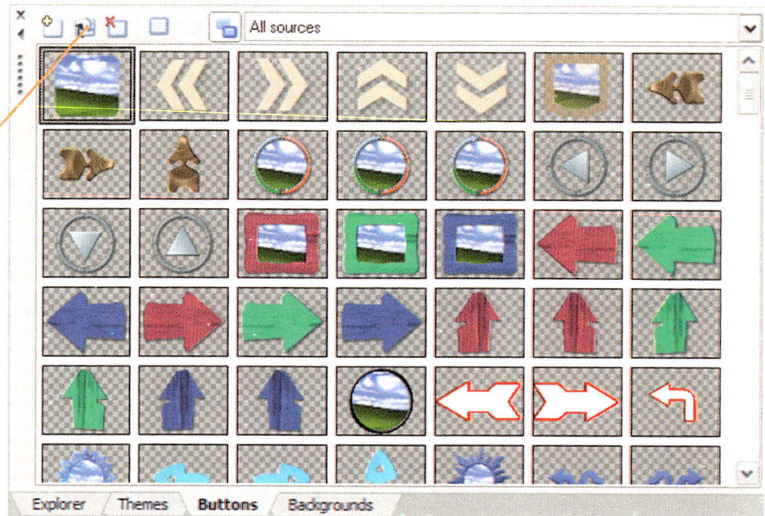

Add a frame to your button or replace it with a graphic

There are three ways to add a style, frame or graphic from the **Buttons** panel to the button or buttons selected on the menu page in the **Workspace** panel :

- Select a **Button** in the panel and click **Replace Button** on the top left of the panel;
- Drag your selected **Button** from the **Buttons** panel onto the button(s) selected in the **Workspace** panel; or
- Double-click on a **Button** in the **Buttons** panel. It will be applied to any or all of the buttons selected in the **Workspace** panel.

You can select several buttons at once and apply a button style to them all at the same time. To select several buttons at once, hold down the **Shift** or **Ctrl** key as you click to select the buttons on a menu page.

To remove a frame from a button, click the **Remove Frame** button, as described on the facing page.

Add a custom button frame

Applying a custom-created button frame to your menu buttons is as simple as selecting the **Replace** option on the **Button Properties** panel.

However, creating a button frame can be a bit of a challenge. Frames must be of a certain file format and must include transparency, which involves multi-layer graphic editing.

But if you'd like to give it a try, we'll show you how it's done in **Create a Custom Button Frame** (page 132) in **Chapter 11, An Appendix of Advanced DVD Architect Studio Tricks**.

Additional Button panel tools

The **Buttons** panel includes three special tools on the upper left of the panel.

Insert Button. Clicking this button adds a new button to the menu page displayed in your Workspace. This new button will *not be linked to anything,* however – and you will need to manually create a link from it to a menu page or media file in the **Button Properties** panel, as we describe on page 136 in **Chapter 11, An Appendix of Advanced DVD Architect Studio Tricks**.

Replace button. This option is available when you have an existing button selected in your **Workspace** panel and a **button style or frame** selected in the **Buttons** panel. Replacing a button will apply the selected button frame or graphic to the button you have selected. (You can also simply double-click your selection in the **Buttons** panel to apply the style to your selected button.)

Remove Frame. If you've applied a frame to your button and you decide you want to remove it, clicking **Remove Frame** will remove it. The frame will disappear and your thumbnail image will appear as a plain, unframed picture or video clip.

Note, however, that if you've replaced your thumbnail image with a *graphic* rather than merely adding a button frame, when you click **Remove Frame**, the graphic will be removed and you'll be left with *no* button graphic or thumbnail image at all! So this tool doesn't work in every case as a **Button** undo feature.

Burning your DVD or BluRay disc

Burning BluRay video to a DVD

Saving your "burned" files to your hard drive

Burning Prepared Files to a disc

Chapter 10

Burn a DVD or BluRay disc

Finishing your project

Now that you've assembled your media files and built your menu structure, it's time to enjoy the culmination of all your hard work! It's time to output your disc.

Yet, even at this point, DVD Architect Studio offers you a number of options.

Finally, we've come to the final step in the process.

Yet, even at this point, there are options. For instance, you can:

- **Burn a DVD or BluRay disc.** Naturally.
- **Burn high-definition BluRay files to a DVD disc.** Though you will only be able to play the disc, of course, on a BluRay player.
- **Save your DVD or BluRay files to your hard drive.** This is a great option if you plan to make several copies of your disc. You simply create a disc master on your hard drive and burn off copies as you need them.
- **Optimize your DVD or BluRay project.** Optimizing sets the compression and quality levels for your disc's videos and menus.

Pre-flight and optimize your disc

Before you output your DVD or BluRay project, it's wise to give it a "pre-flight" check on the **Optimize Disc** screen. **Optimize Disc** shows you all of the files on your disc (including your menus) and,if they are going to be re-compressed, how close to capacity your disc is and how much your files will need to be compromised in order to fit on your DVD or BluRay disc.

The amount the video in your disc project will need to be compressed or recompressed is a product of two things: How much video you have in your disc project (including in your menus) and what format your video is:

- **A standard 4.7 gigabyte DVD** can hold about 70 minutes of video at full quality. A dual-layer 8.5 gigabyte disc can hold about twice that.
- **A standard 25 gigabyte BluRay disc** can hold about two hours of high-definition video at full quality. A 50 gigabyte dual-layer BluRay can hold about twice that. The program includes the ability to burn high-definition BluRay video to a DVD (as we discuss later in this chapter). However a DVD disc can only hold about 20-30 minutes of high-definition video at full quality.

Once you've reached a disc's capacity, the program will automatically reduce the quality level (technically, the bitrate) of the video so that everything in your disc project will fit. This reduced quality, to a point, may not be immediately noticeable – so it's up to you if the reduction in quality is worth fitting a certain amount of video on a given disc.

The second factor that affects how much your video will need to be re-encoded is the format of the video you're using as your sources.

You'll get the best performance from DVD Architect Studio – and the fastest transcoding to DVD or BluRay disc files – if you use optimized video as all of your source files. Sony Vegas and Vegas MovieStudio (as well as most other video editing programs) include options for outputting video that optimized for DVDs and BluRay disc projects.

The ideal source formats for DVD Architect Studio projects are:

> **For DVD projects**, the best source video for DVD Architect Studio is the DVD-ready MPEG2, a 720x480 MPEG (720x576 if you're editing in PAL video) using non-square pixels and lower field first interlacing.
>
> **For BluRay discs**, the best source video is a BluRay-ready AVC file, a 1920x1080 60i video (50i if you are editing PAL video) MPEG/MTS file using the H.264 codec.

Although the program is capable of working with nearly all traditional video sources, it is usually not a good idea to use video directly from a camera or camcorder or from online as source video in a DVD Architect Studio project. Whenever possible, you should load your raw video into a video editing program and then output one of the file formats above for use in you disc authoring program.

To pre-flight your disc project, go to the **File** drop-down menu at the top of the program's interface and select **Optimize Disc**.

The **Optimize Disc** screen displays information about the menus and media you've assembled for your DVD or BluRay and allows you to change some settings to make the video and audio information encode to your disc more efficiently.

You'll note that some files are listed on this screen are followed by a green check mark while others are followed by an exclamation point.

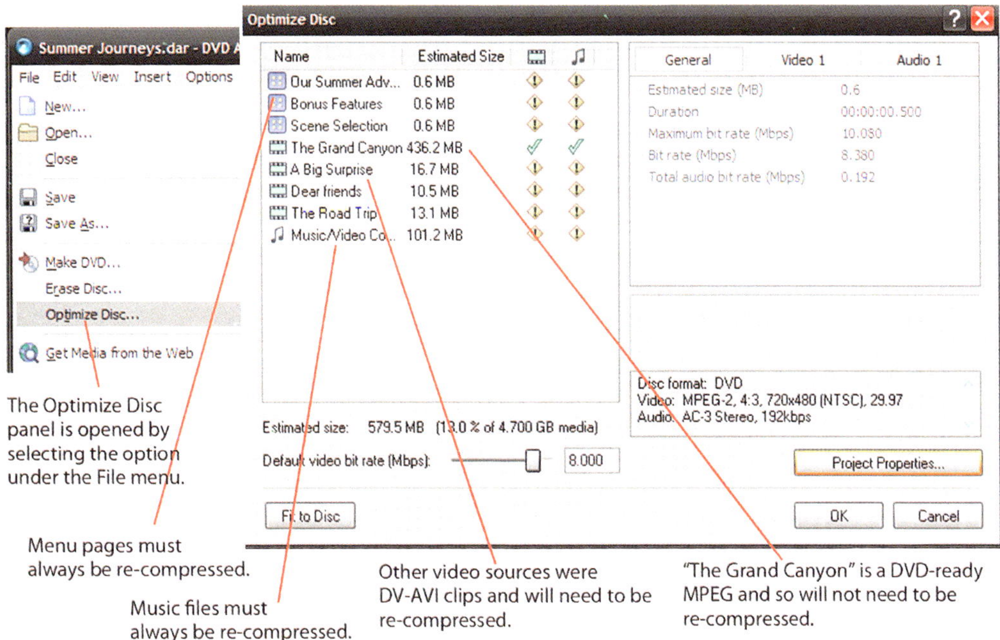

Optimized video files that do not have to be re-encoded are indicated with a green check mark.
Files that will need to be re-compressed are indicated with an exclamation point.

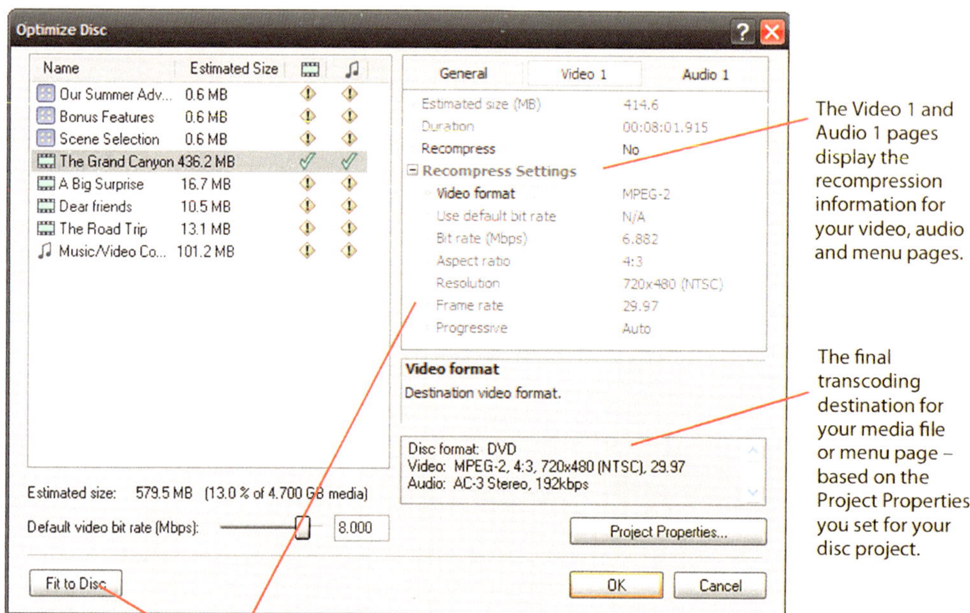

On the Optmize Disc screen, you can manually set the recompression settings for your individual media clips or menus – or you can simply click Fit to Disc and the program will do it for you.

Don't be alarmed by the exclamation points that appear to the right of your media and menu page listings! They don't indicate a problem. They merely indicate that this particular media or menu page will need to be rendered and encoded (transcoded) as DVD or BluRay files when DVD Architect Studio creates your disc. Menu pages, still photos, music and non-optimized video files will *always* need to be transcoded.

Green check marks indicate that the files are already in their final DVD or BluRay file format and will not need to be recompressed or re-encoded when you disc is created. This would be the case if you were using the optimized video formats we discussed on the previous page.

If your files fit within a disc's capacity in their current formats, you needn't do anything on this screen. Just click **OK** and continue outputting your disc files.

However, if your files exceed your disc's size (as indicated at **Estimated Size**, in the lower left of the panel), you will need to adjust the project's compression or quality settings.

If you select any media file or menu page listed on this panel, you can manually change the compression setting for that element on the **Video 1** or **Audio 1** pages of the panel, as in the illustration above.

But the easiest solution – and the best in nearly all situations – is to click the **Fit to Disc** button in the lower left of the panel. This will automatically adjust the **Bit Rate** for all of the transcoded files on your disc, essentially reducing your video's quality so that your entire project fits.

The highest **Bit Rate** setting (highest quality) for a DVD is 8 mbps. Top quality on a BluRay is a **Bit Rate** of 18 mbps. You may be able to reduce these **Bit Rates** by nearly half and still find your video looks acceptable. (Although you can also manually *increase* the **Bit Rate** for a BluRay disc, there's little to be gained by raising it above 18 mbps.)

As a general rule, if you're finding yourself setting your DVD **Bit Rate** below 4 or your BluRay disc's below 9, you're probably trying to squeeze too much video onto your disc.

Click the **OK** button to close the screen. If you've clicked the **Fit to Disc** button, the new *final, transcoded* disc size will be reflected in the **Disc Space Used** indicator in the lower right of the program's interface.

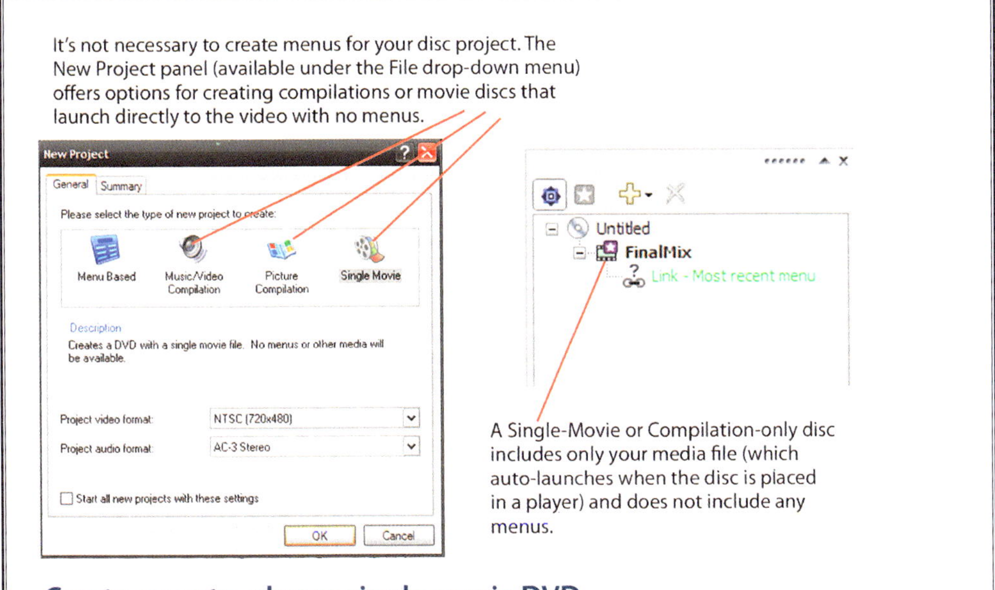

It's not necessary to create menus for your disc project. The New Project panel (available under the File drop-down menu) offers options for creating compilations or movie discs that launch directly to the video with no menus.

A Single-Movie or Compilation-only disc includes only your media file (which auto-launches when the disc is placed in a player) and does not include any menus.

Create an auto-play or single movie DVD

DVDs and BluRay disc don't have to include menus. You can create a disc with DVD Architect Studio that plays your video or compilation as soon as it's loaded into a DVD player. This type of disc is called an auto-play or **Single-Movie Disc**.

To create a **Single Movie Disc**, open a new DVD Architect Studio project by selecting **New** from the **File** drop-down menu at the top of the interface. In the **New Project** window that opens, select the option for a **Music/Video Compilation** (a music or video-based collection of clips), a **Picture Compilation** (a slideshow, with optional music track) or a **Single Movie** and click OK.

This option creates a disc whose structure consists solely of the media content you create or add. In the **Project Overview** panel, your project will be placed in the **Disc** icon's root directory, indicating that the media is the entirety of the disc's structure.

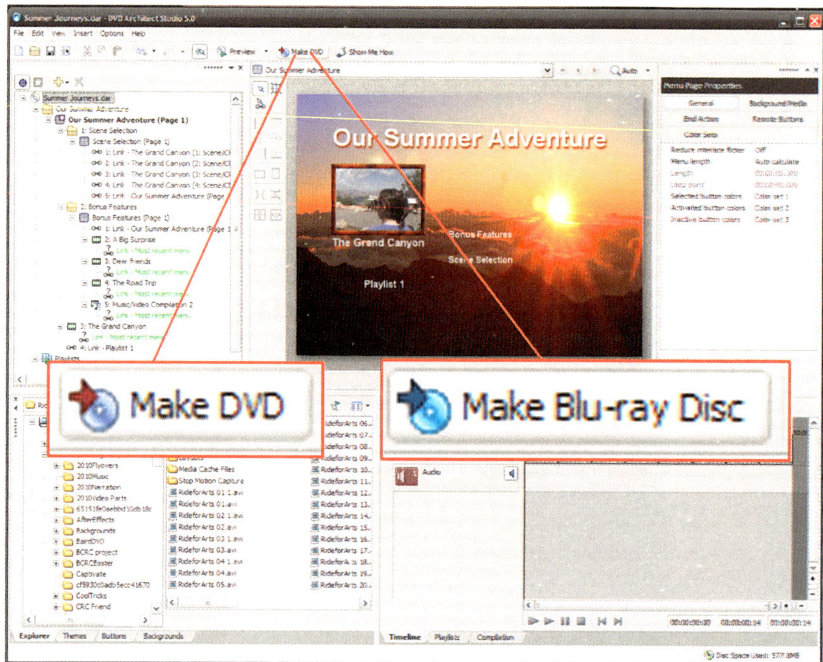

When your project is ready to go, click the Make DVD or Make Blu-Ray Disc button.

Burn a DVD or BluRay disc

Making a DVD or BluRay can mean burning your project directly to a disc – or, as we discuss later in the chapter, it can mean burning your disc files to a folder or files on your hard drive, from which you can later burn off as many copies as you'd like.

No matter which option you choose, DVD Architect Studio automatically creates **Prepared Files** on your hard drive. These **Prepared Files** are your disc's DVD or BluRay files.

To burn your DVD or BluRay project to a disc:

1 **Click Make DVD or Make BluRay Disc**

If your project is set up as a DVD, the button at the top center of your screen will read **Make DVD**. If your project is set up as a BluRay disc, this button will read **Make BluRay Disc**.

Click on the **Make DVD** or **Make BluRay Disc** button. (You can also select the option under the **File** drop-down menu.)

The **Select Operation to Perform** screen will open.

As we discuss in **Burn your disc files to your hard drive**, later in this chapter, this is the point at which you can elect either to burn your project directly to a disc or to set up your disc files to be saved to your hard drive for later burning to a disc.

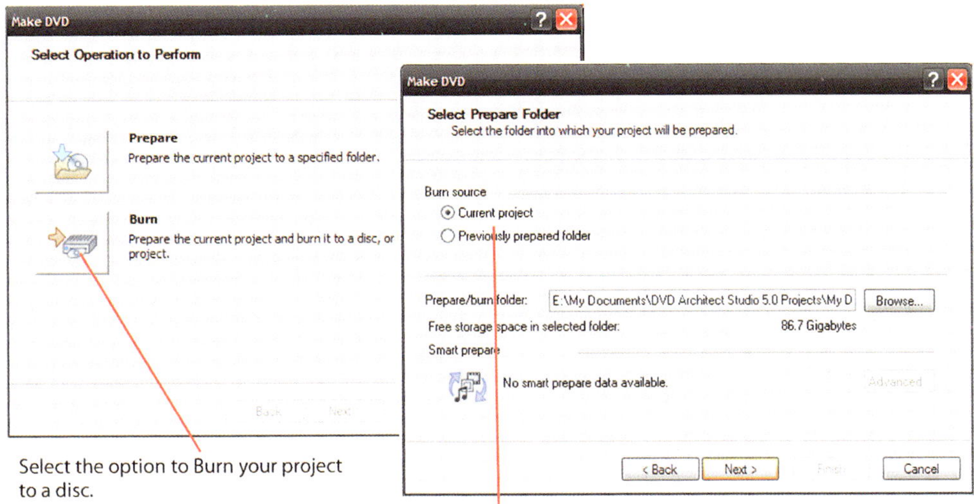

Select the option to Burn your project to a disc.

Set the Burn Source to your Current Project.

2 Select Burn

Click on the **Burn** button.

The **Select Prepare Folder** screen will open.

3 Select Current Project as your Burn Source

DVD Architect Studio's Burn tool can be used to burn your current disc project or it can be used to burn already created files from your computer to a DVD or BluRay disc, as we discuss in **Burn a previously prepared project** later in this chapter.

Leave the **Burn Source** set to your **Current Project**, then click **Next**.

4 Review Messages

The **Review Messages List** screen will open. This screen is a final "pre-flight" check for your disc project files.

It lists the media files and menu pages that will be compressed by the program and includes warnings about potential problems, such as one menu button overlapping another.

The screen will also warn you if there are any **orphans** in your project.

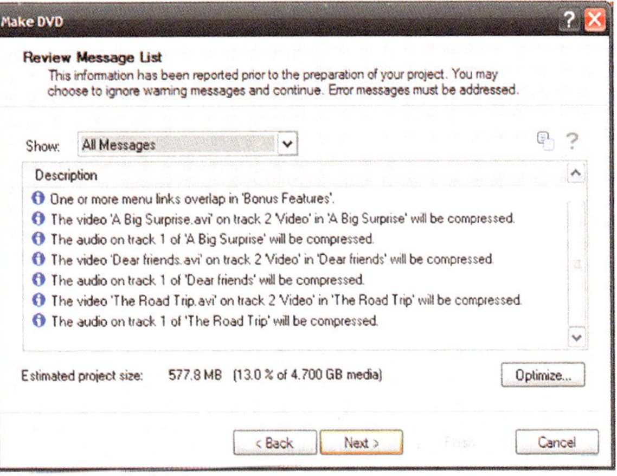

Orphans are files that have no links to any menus or media. Unless it is your intention to include these files, you will need to return to your disc project and create links for these files.

(You can, however, add material to your DVD that is not a part of the disc's structure. For more information on adding computer files that aren't a part of the DVD or BluRay to your disc, see **Create an Extras Folde**r in the **Chapter 11, An Appendix of Advanced DVD Architect Studio Tricks**.)

Unless this page posts something that you need to address, click the **Next** button.

The program will gather your files and prepare them for the burn and the **Select Burn Parameters** screen will open.

If you haven't done so already, place a blank disc in your drive.

5 **Select your Burn Parameters**

It's not necessary to name your disc **Volume Name**, but doing so can make your disc more easily identifiable on a computer.

Ensure that your disc burner is selected as your **Device.**

In most cases, the **Speed** will set automatically, based on the capacity of your drive and the speed rating of your disc.

Click **Finish**. Your burn will begin.

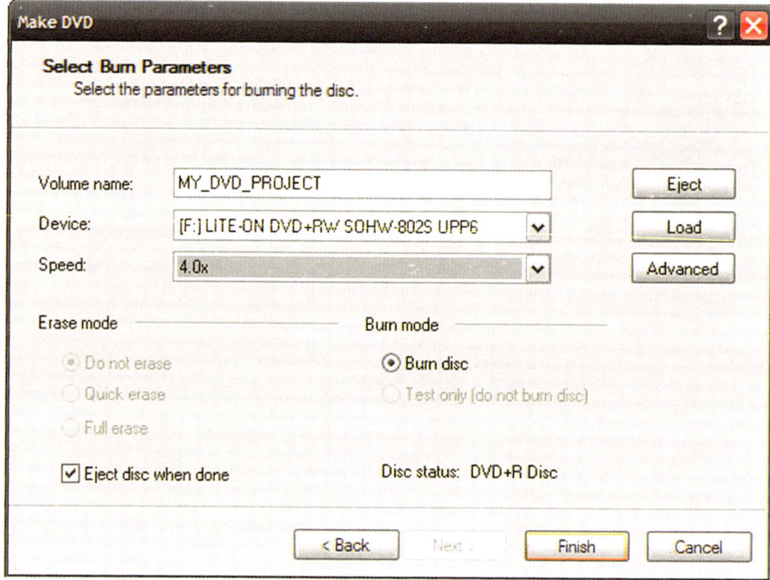

Finally, our project is committed to disc!

Burn your disc's Prepared Files to your hard drive

There are a number of advantages to "burning" your DVD or BluRay disc files to your computer's hard drive rather than directly to a disc.

For one thing, it eliminates a possible phase (the disc burning) where things can occasionally (if rarely) go awry. But, even greater, it allows you to keep an original copy of your finished disc files on your system – taking up relatively little space but easy to access if you ever need to burn off a fresh copy of your final DVD or BluRay disc.

DVD Architect Studio calls these final files **Prepared Files**. And, whether you set the program to burn your project directly to a disc or you set it to save your disc files to your hard drive, the program automatically saves **Prepared Files** as a back-up.

To burn your DVD or BluRay disc files to your hard drive:

1 **Click Make DVD or Make BluRay Disc**

If your project is set up as a DVD, the button at the top center of your screen will read **Make DVD.** If your project is set up as a BluRay disc, this button will read **Make BluRay Disc**.

Click on the **Make DVD** or **Make BluRay Disc** button. (You can also select the option under the **File** drop-down menu.)

The **Select Operation to Perform** screen will open.

2 **Select Prepare**

Click on the **Prepare** button.

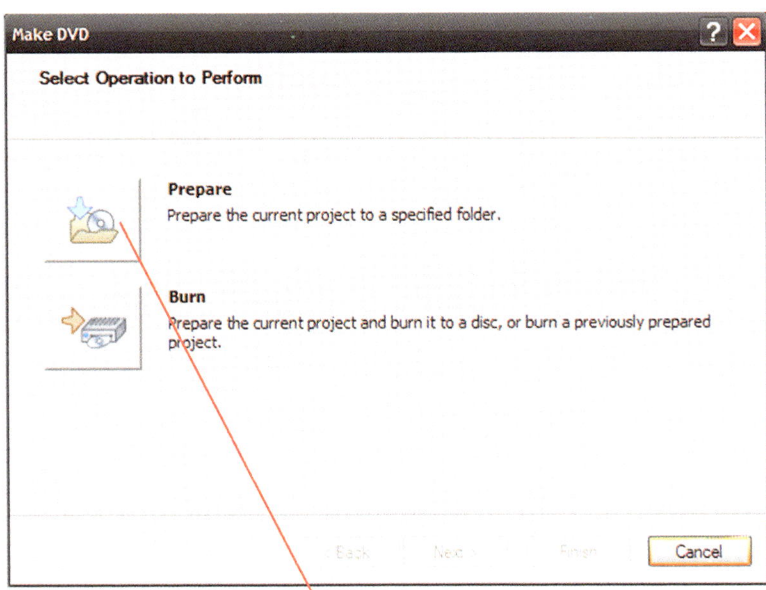

To "burn" your DVD or BluRay disc files to your hard drive rather than directly to a disc, click the Prepare button on the Select Operation to Perform screen.

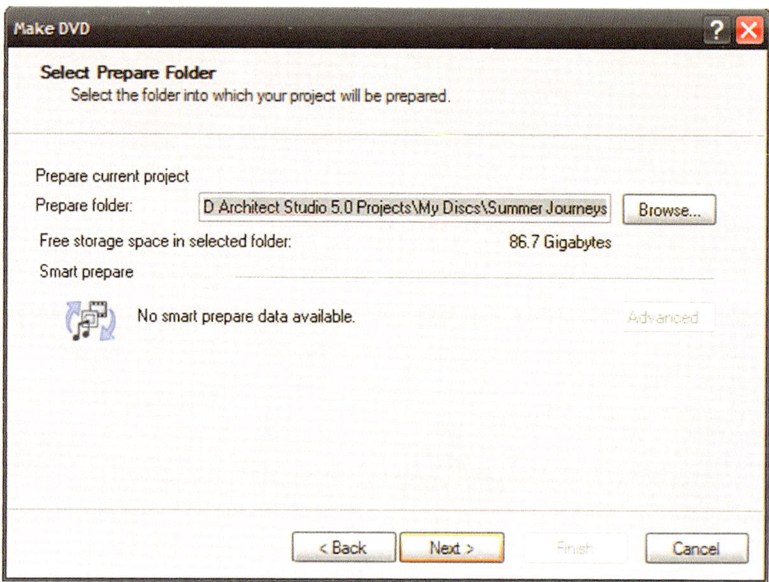

The **Select Prepare Folder** screen will open.

3 **Select a folder location**

By default the program will save your disc files to a DVD Architect Studio folder in your **Documents**.

Click the **Browse** button to select another location or to create a folder on your computer to send your DVD or BluRay files to.

You'll note that this screen also includes a **Smart Prepare** feature. If you have previously created DVD or BluRay files for this project, **Smart Prepare** will re-use as many of the old render files as possible – rebuilding only the changes files. This can save you significant transcoding time!

Once you've selected a destination folder for your files, click **Next**.

The **Review Messages List** screen will open.

4 **Review Messages**

The **Review Messages List** screen is a final "pre-flight" check for your disc project files.

It lists the media files and menu pages that will be compressed by the program and includes warnings about potential problems, such as one menu button overlapping another.

The screen will also warn you if there are any **orphans** in your project.

Orphans are files that have no links to any menus or media. Unless it is your intention to include these files, you will need to return to your disc project and create links for these files.

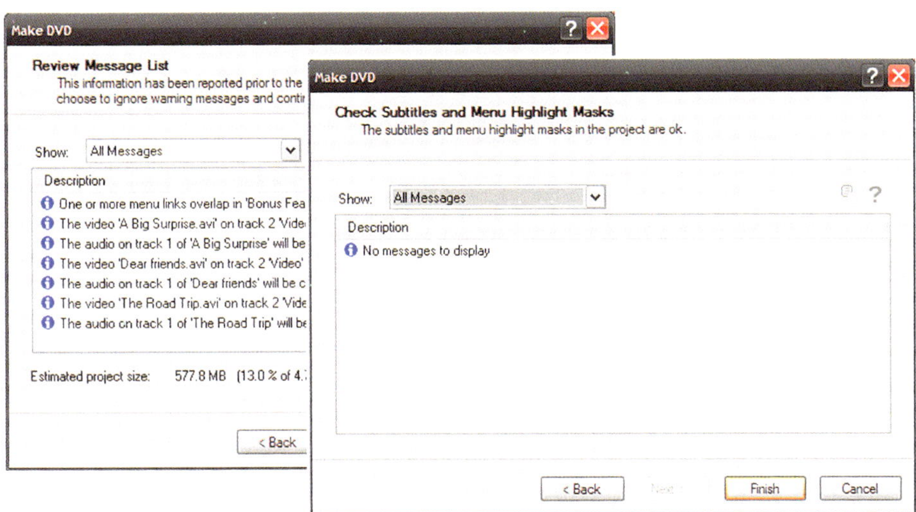

Two final "pre-flight" screens warn you of potential problems with your DVD or BluRay disc.

Unless this page posts something that you need to address, click the **Next** button.

The **Check Subtitles and Menu Highlight Masks** screen will open.

5 **Check Subtitles and Masks**

This screen will post warnings if there are problems with your subtitles or button overlay masks.

Unless this page posts something that you need to address, click the **Finish** button.

The program will create your **Prepared Files** – the finished files for your DVD or BluRay disc – and save them to the location you designated on your hard drive.

Burn BluRay video to a DVD

No special tricks here. You just put a DVD in your BluRay disc burner drive and click the **Make BluRay Disc** button, as discussed earlier in this chapter.

It is important, however, that you've properly set up your project file as a BluRay project for a 4.7 gigabyte or 8.5 gigabyte DVD, as discussed in **Chapter 2, Create a Basic DVD Architect Studio Project**.

In your **Project Properties** (page 21), select **BluRay Disc** as your **Disc Format**. Then set your **Target Disc Size** for the DVD size you will be using (either 4.70 or 8.50 gigabyte). This will ensure that the program knows the maximum file size your final disc can hold.

Burn Prepared Files to a DVD or BluRay disc

Once you've saved your DVD's **Prepared Files** to a folder or your BluRay's image file on your hard drive, generating a fresh copy of your DVD or BluRay disc is as simple as burning those files to a disc!

The **Prepared File** for your BluRay project will be an **.iso** (disc image) file named after your disc project.

The **Prepared Files** for your DVD project will be two folders (a VIDEO_TS folder and an AUDIO_TS folder) as well as an SPREPARE.SPSS file.

To burn a DVD or BluRay disc from these files:

1 **Click Make DVD or Make BluRay Disc**

If your current project is set up as a DVD, the button at the top center of your screen will read **Make DVD**. If your current project is set up as a BluRay disc, this button will read **Make BluRay Disc**.

Click on the **Make DVD** or **Make BluRay Disc** button. (You can also select the option under the **File** drop-down menu.)

The **Select Operation to Perform** screen will open.

2 **Select Burn**

Click on the **Burn** button.

The **Select Prepare Folder** screen will open.

3 **Select Previously Prepared Folder/Image as your Burn Source**

Set the **Burn Source** to either your **Previously Prepared *Folder*,** if you are burning a DVD from **Prepared Files**, or a **Previously Prepared *Image***, if you are burning a BluRay disc from a **Prepared File**.

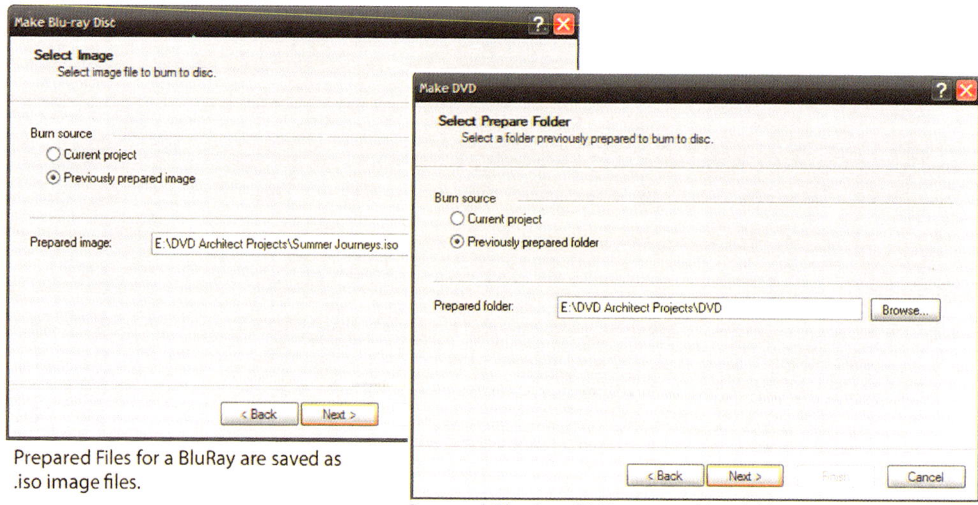

Prepared Files for a BluRay are saved as .iso image files.

Prepared Files for a DVD are saved in a folder.

4 Browse to your folder or file

If you are burning a DVD to a disc, click **Browse**, if necessary, and locate the folder that includes the prepared file folders. (In other words, do not select the VIDEO_TS or AUDIO TS folders. Select the *folder* that includes both of these folders.)

If you are burning prepared BluRay file to a disc, click **Browse**, to locate the project's .iso file.

Then click Next.

5 Select your Burn Parameters

Ensure that you have a blank disc in your drive and that this disc burner is selected as your **Device.**

In most cases, the **Speed** will set automatically, based on the capacity of your drive and the speed rating of your disc.

Click **Finish**. Your burn will begin.

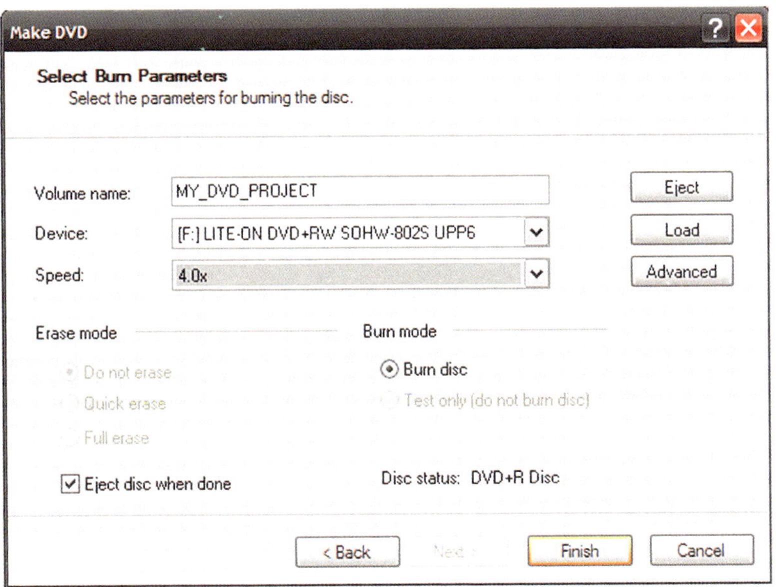

Seven great, not-so-obvious program features

Creating a custom button frame and mask

Building a button's link

A Properties panel reference manual

Chapter 11

An Appendix of Advanced DVD Architect Studio Tricks

Beyond the basics

DVD Architect Studio is, in my not so humble opinion, one of the best values on the market.

Rich with features and yet available for less than the cost of dinner for four at a typical family restaurant (not including tip), it's far and away one of the best under-$100 tools for anyone who wants to achieve professional results at an amazingly affordable price.

Here are a handful of non-essential-but-nice-to-know things that I hope will enhance your experience with this program.

Seven pretty great, not-so-obvious program features

In addition to its basic DVD and BluRay disc authoring tools, DVD Architect Studio offers some terrific bonus features.

Add Extras to your DVD

Extras are non-video files that you add to your DVD. (This feature is not available on BluRay discs.) These files might include full-resolution photos or ReadMe files or other documents – files that are only accessible when your viewer puts the disc in his computer's hard drive and browses to them.

To add **Extras** to your DVD:

1. **Create an "Extras" folder on your hard drive**

   This folder can reside anywhere on your hard drive and can be named whatever you'd like. But keep *only* the files you'd like added to your DVD in it. The tool will add the entire folder's files to your disc.

2. **Open Properties**

   Select **Properties** under the DVD Architect Studio's **File** menu.

3. **Set the Extras folder**

   Click on the box to the right of the **Extras Folder** listing under **DVD-Only Features** on the **Project Properties** panel.

   Browse to and select the **Extras** folder you created on your hard drive.

DVD Architect Studio saves these files in a separate "**Extras**" folder, outside of the regular menu structure of your DVD's menu system.

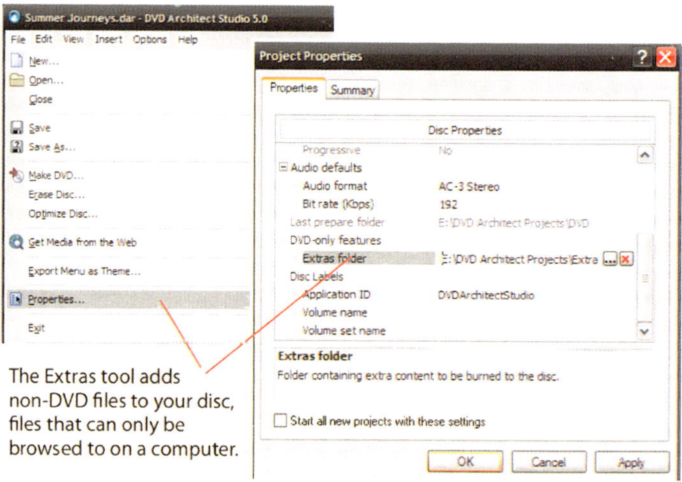

The Extras tool adds non-DVD files to your disc, files that can only be browsed to on a computer.

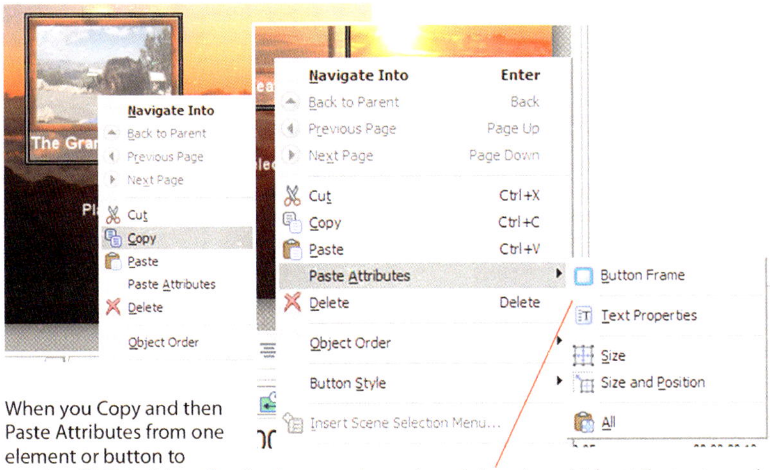

When you Copy and then Paste Attributes from one element or button to another, DVD Architect Studio gives you the option of choosing which attributes to apply.

Paste Attributes

Copying attributes is a great way to apply styles, colors and design settings you've applied to one graphic, button or text block to several others with just a few clicks.

To use this feature:

1 **Copy an element's Attributes**

Right-click on the menu item, button or text block you've customized in the **Workspace** panel and select **Copy** from the context menu.

2 **Paste the Attributes to another element**

Select one or several similar items, buttons or text blocks (by **Ctrl+clicking** or **Shift+clicking**) that you'd like to apply that same look to.

Right-click on these elements and select **Paste Attributes**.

Paste Attributes gives you the option of applying to your selected items the original element's button design, text properties, color, size and/or position.

Save your menu page design as a theme

If you're especially happy with a menu page you've created, you can save its look as a theme and then reuse the design in future menu pages – even in different projects.

To do so, ensure that the menu page is displayed in the **Workspace** panel. Then, from the **File** drop-down menu at the top of the interface, select **Export Menu as Theme**.

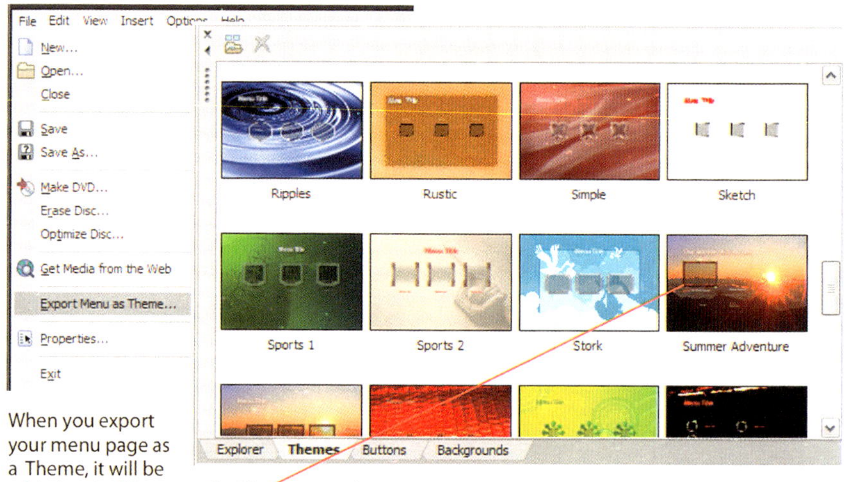

When you export your menu page as a Theme, it will be added to the library on the Themes panel.

Once you've created a theme, it will appear as an option in the **Themes** panel.

If you added a custom background to this menu page (a still photo, for instance) this background image will also appear as an option in the **Backgrounds** panel.

Burn any files to a disc

In addition to its functions as a disc authoring tool, DVD Architect Studio includes functions for burning data files to a disc and even erasing data from rewriteable DVD-RWs and BluRay discs.

To burn files to a DVD or BluRay using DVD Architect Studio:

1 Click Make DVD (or Make BluRay Disc)

Go to DVD Architect Studio's **File** menu and select **Make DVD.**

The **Select Operation to Perform** screen will open.

2 Select Burn

Click on the **Burn** button.

The **Select Prepare Folder** screen will open.

3 Select Previously Prepared Folder/Image as your Burn Source

Set the **Burn Source** set to **Previously Prepared Folder.**.

4 Browse to your folder or file

Click **Browse** and locate the folder that includes the files you'd like to burn to a disc.

Select the folder and click **Next**.

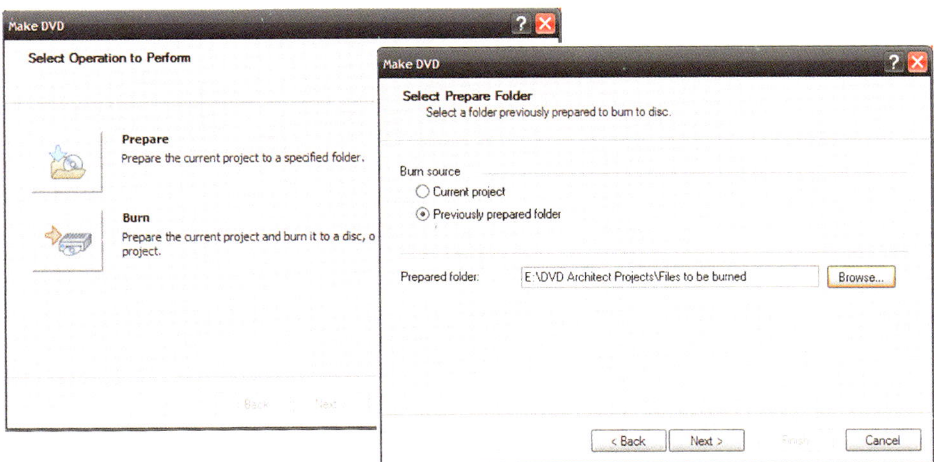

DVD Architect Studio can also be used as an all-purpose tool for burning files to disc.

5 **Select your Burn Parameters**

Ensure that you have a blank disc in your drive and that this disc burner is selected as your **Device.**

In most cases, the **Speed** will set automatically, based on the capacity of your drive and the speed rating of your disc.

This same process can be used to burn copies of a DVD you've previously prepared and saved to a folder in DVD Architect Studio, as discussed in **Burn your disc's Prepared Files to your hard drive** in **Chapter 10, Burn a DVD or BluRay Disc**.

Erase a rewriteable disc

The program includes functions for erasing rewritable DVD-RWs and BluRay RW discs.

The **Erase DVD** option can be found under the program's **File** menu.

The **Erase DVD** screen offers you the option of a **Quick Erase** or a **Full Erase**.

- A **Quick Erase** clears only the written area of a DVD; **Full Erase** clears the disc completely.
- A **Full Erase** takes significantly longer to perform. However, it also creates a "cleaner" disc, in the event you find that the former process doesn't produce a usable disc.

Download additional themes and media

As part of its continual support for its products, Sony regularly offers free backgrounds, themes and other items you can use in your projects. You can download the latest from:

http://www.sonycreativesoftware.com/download/freestuff

Get media from the web

In addition to the free content Sony offers regularly, the Sony store offers a variety of motion backgrounds and music packs. These items are all professionally produced and they're royalty-free, so you can use them legally in any of your amateur or professional productions. Prices start as low as $29.95, with specials sometimes offering packages for less than $10.

To access this store, go to DVD Architect Studio's **File** drop-down menu and select **Get Media from the Web**.

Create a custom button frame

A button frame is a graphic with a transparent area in the center (usually a PNG, although a PSD with no background layer will also work). Button frames overlay your button's thumbnail. Button frames are often rectangular, to fit the shape of a video frame. But, by adding a **mask**, you can even create a frame and button with non-square shapes.

To create a button frame, you'll need a graphics program like Photoshop, Photoshop Elements or Paint Shop Pro. The following are instructions for creating this button frame in Photoshop Elements – although other graphics programs function similarly:

1 **Create a 250x250 pixel file**

In Photoshop Elements, go to the **File** Menu and select **New/Blank File**.

On the **New File** option screen, set width and height both to 250 pixels and resolution to 72 pixels/inch, and set **Background Contents** to **Transparent**.

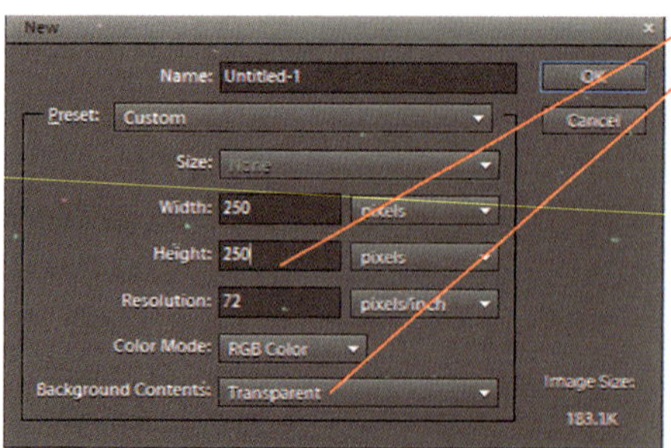

Create a 250px x 250px graphic file and set the Background Contents to Transparent.

Add your frame graphic to it as a new layer.

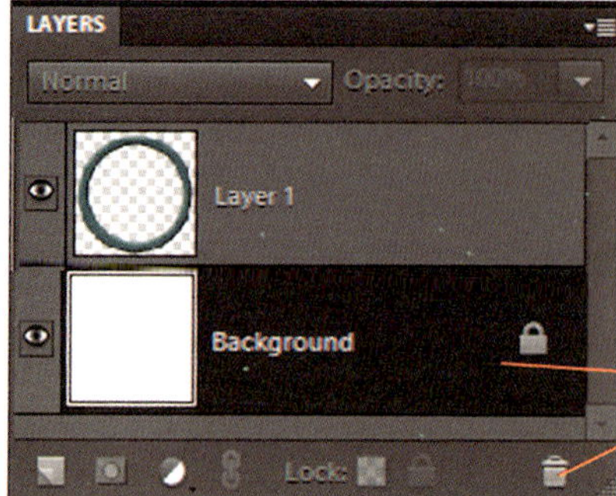

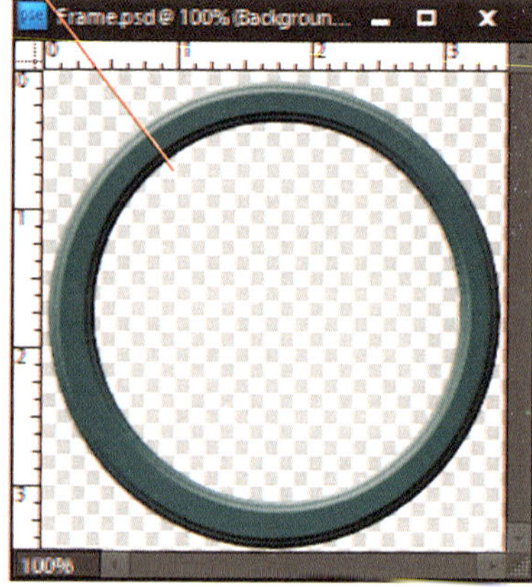

If you're working from a previously flat image or one that includes a Background layer, be sure to delete this Background.

2 Add your frame graphic on a new layer

Create or import the graphic you want to use as your frame into the file, resizing it as necessary to fit the file canvas. Make sure that this graphic is on a new layer and has a transparent center.

Photoshop Elements includes a number of frames in its **Custom Shapes** library. You can use any graphic or photo as a frame, as long as it includes a transparent center so that your video button's thumbnail image can show through.

3 Delete the background layer

If your frame image included a background layer, click to select the **Background** on the **Layers** palette and then click the little trash can icon on the panel to delete. When a graphic file has no background layer, any transparent areas on the other layers will be transparent completely through the file.

By default, transparent areas in a graphic file display as a gray checkerboard Photoshop Elements, as in the illustration.

4 Save the file as a transparent PNG

In Photoshop Elements, go to the **File** menu and select **Save for Web**.

On the **Save for Web** option screen, ensure that option to save the file's **Transparency** is checked.

Name and save the file as a PNG-24.

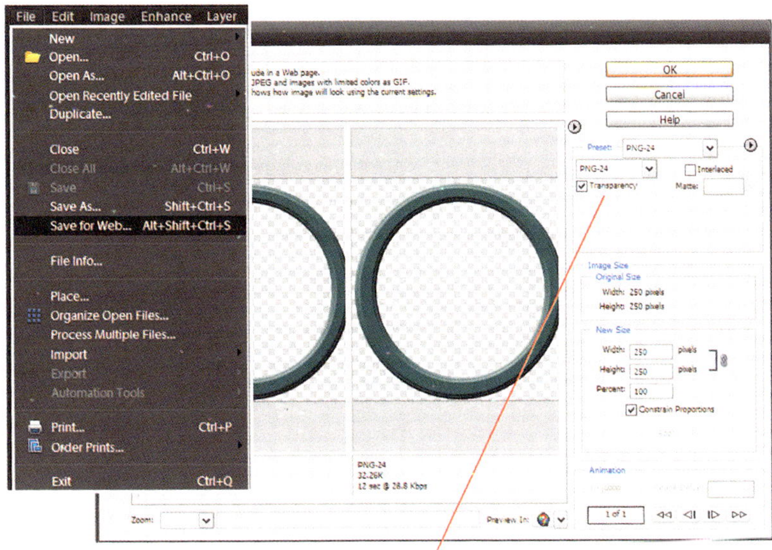

When you save your file as a GIF or PSD using Save for Web, ensure that the Transparency option is checked.

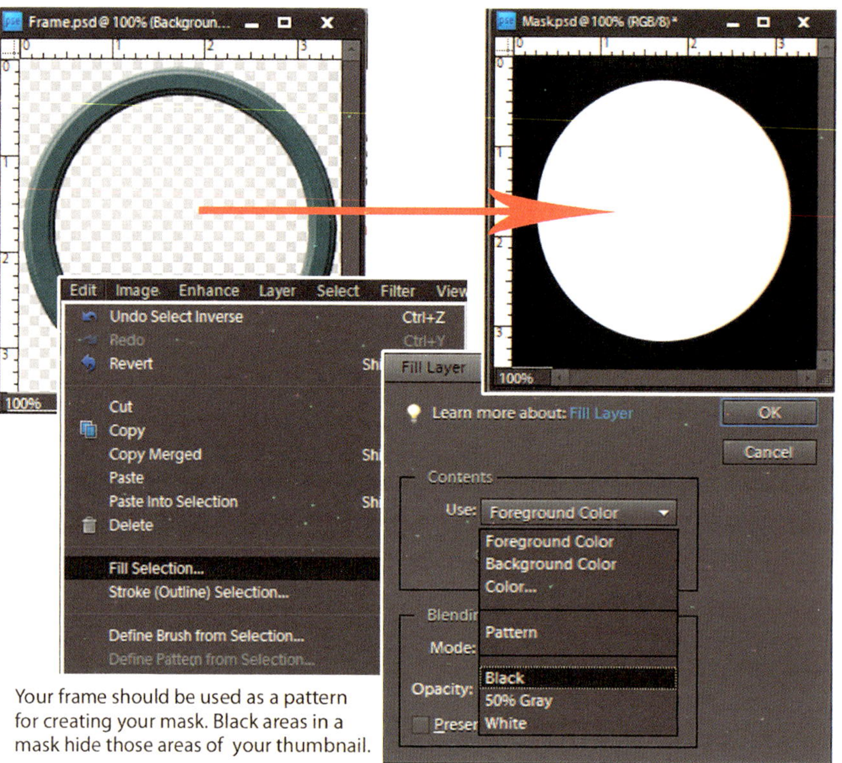

Your frame should be used as a pattern for creating your mask. Black areas in a mask hide those areas of your thumbnail.

Create a button frame mask

If your button frame has a non-rectangular shape, you'll need to also create a mask to hide the areas of your thumbnail that fall outside of this frame. Black areas on a mask file render those areas of your thumbnail invisible.

1 **Use your frame graphic as a guide for your mask**

If you open a copy of your frame graphic in Photoshop Elements, you can use it as a guide for creating your mask.

2 **Color the area outside of the frame black.**

In Photoshop Elements, use the **Magic Wand** tool or another selection tool to select the area outside of your frame. Go to the **Edit** menu and select **Edit/Fill Selected Area**.

On the **Selection** Screen, select **Black** as the fill color.

3 **Flatten and save your file**

Remove the frame or any other graphic you were using as a guide for drawing your mask so that only the black mask on a white background remains. From the **Layer** menu at the top of the interface, select **Flatten Image**.

Name and save the file it in any standard format.

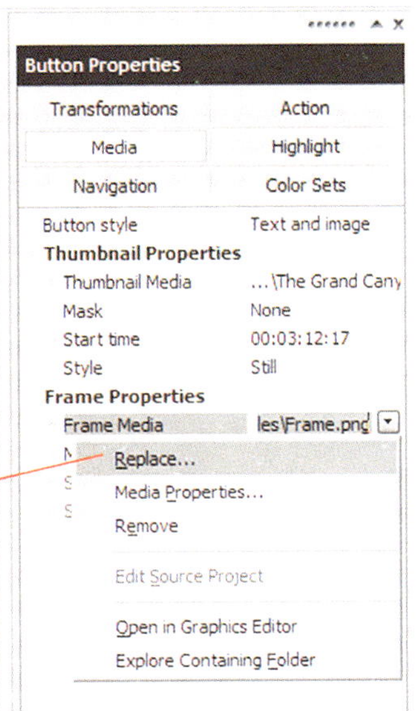

Adding your own transparent Frame Media overlays your thumbnail with your custom frame.

To shape the thumbnail image to fit in the frame, a corresponding mask must be applied to the button.

Apply a custom button frame and mask

Not every button frame you create will require an accompanying mask file.

Masks merely shape rectangular button thumbnail images into whatever shape fits inside your custom frame.

As we've discussed in the previous section, masks are merely black and white images – the black areas of which will hide (or make transparent) the corresponding areas of your button's thumbnail image while the white areas let the thumbnail show through.

Add a custom button frame

To add a custom frame to your button:

1 **Select a button on your menu page**

When you click on a button in the **Workspace** panel, the **Properties** panel will display **Button Properties**.

2 **Go to the Media page on the Button Properties panel**

Click on the **Media** button in this panel.

3 **Browse and select new Frame Media**

Click on the box to the right of the **Frame Media** listing under **Frame Properties**.

From the drop-down menu that appears, select **Replace**.

Browse to select your button frame graphic.

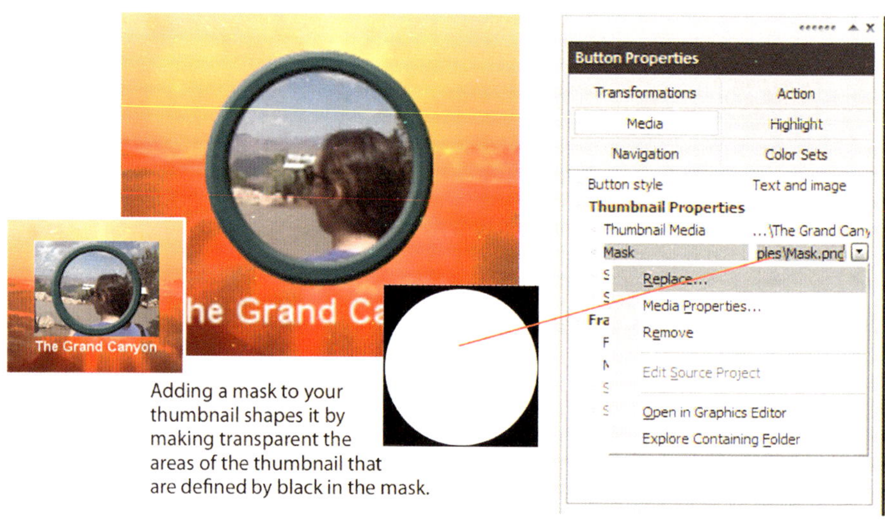

Adding a mask to your thumbnail shapes it by making transparent the areas of the thumbnail that are defined by black in the mask.

Apply a mask to your button's thumbnail image

To apply a mask to your button's thumbnail image:

1. **Select a button on your menu page**

   When you click on a button in the **Workspace** panel, the **Properties** panel will display **Button Properties**.

2. **Go to the Media page**

   Click on the **Media** button in this panel.

3. **Browse and select a Mask**

   Click on the box to the right of the **Mask** listing under **Thumbnail Properties**.

   From the drop-down menu that appears, select **Replace**.

   Browse to select your mask graphic.

Link a button to a page or clip manually

In most cases, you'll be adding a media clip or menu page to your disc project and simultaneously adding a button linking it to a menu page (as discussed in **Chapter 4, Create and Customize a Menu Button**).

However, it is possible to create a button manually and then build a link from it (or change a link from an existing button).

1. **Create a button**

   To create an unlinked button, click on the **Insert Button** icon on the top left of the **Buttons** panel.

   This creates an "orphaned" button – a button linking to nothing.

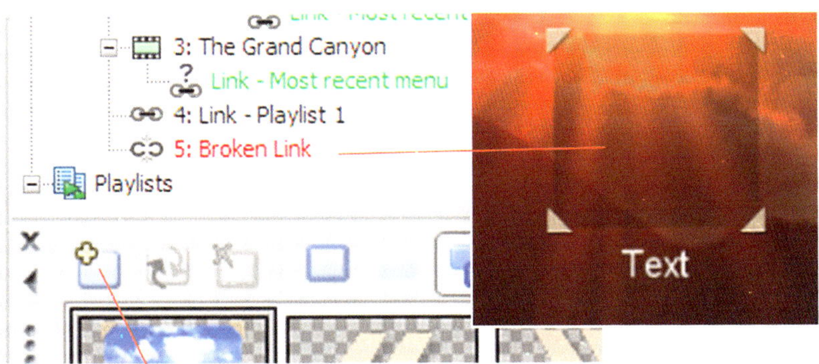

Clicking the Insert Button icon on the upper right of the Buttons panel creates an "orphaned" button on the menu page in your Worskpace. This button can be edited and designed, like any other button – however, until you define its Action, it will not be connected to any menu page or media clip.

The button is added to the menu page you have selected in the **Project Overview** panel and which appears in the **Workspace** panel. It will appear in the **Project Overview** panel with the red letter warning "**Broken Link**," as in the illustration above.

2 Select the button's Action Properties page

When the button is selected in your **Workspace** panel, the **Properties** panel will display **Button Properties**.

Click on **Action** to display the button's **Action Properties** page.

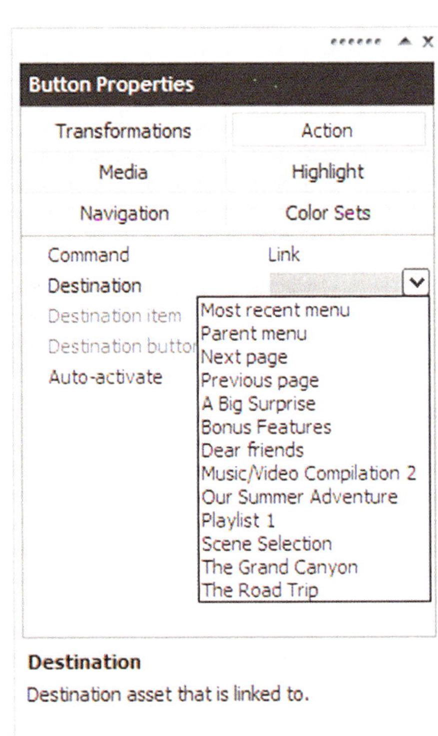

3 Set the button's destination

Click in the box to the right of the **Destination** listing.

A drop-down menu will display a list of every menu page and media clip on your disc.

Select the page or media clip you'd like the button to link to.

Other things worth knowing

Why your discs don't always play

Home-burned discs. They may look similar and behave similarly on a computer – but they're not quite the same as commercial discs.

Commercial DVDs and BluRay discs are produced on a press. Home-burned DVDs use a chemical process to save the data you write to them. That's why occasionally you'll find a DVD player that simply won't play a home-burned DVD!

This is the nature of the medium itself and of the DVD player's compatibility with it. It's not a short-coming on behalf of the program producing the DVD.

Because of the popularity of desktop DVD creation, most newer DVD and BluRay disc players will play home-burned discs as easily as they will commercial discs. But you can still improve the likelihood your disc will be readable (as well as increasing the odds that your DVD burn will go well) if you use high-quality DVD discs.

Quality discs don't need to be terribly expensive. Verbatim makes an excellent, consistent disc and Taiyo-Yuden, though harder to find, make some of the best.

But avoid store brand media and cheaper brands (including a popular product of notoriously inconsistent quality whose brand name begins with M and ends with x). This may not ensure every disc will work every time on every disc player. But spending a few extra cents for quality media will definitely improve your odds.

Widescreen vs. standard video

Believe it or not, a 16:9 widescreen DV video has *exactly the same number* of pixels as a 4:3 standard DV video. The pixels – the little square blocks of color that compose a video image – are just shaped differently.

In NTSC video, a standard DV pixel is only 90% as wide as it is tall. A widescreen NTSC video's pixels are 120% as wide as they are tall.

Why is this important to know? Because sometimes video programs, and even DVD players, become confused. They see 720x480 pixels and don't know whether it's supposed to be a widescreen or standard DV video and the image ends up stretched disportionately.

DVD Architect Studio usually does of great job of automatically interpreting your footage. If you put a standard DV video in a widescreen project, it will simply show up with black along the sides (or letterboxed, if you place a widescreen in a standard DV project). If, for some reason, you need to manually set this, however, you can usually do so under **Stretch Type** on the **Slide** page in the **Picture Playlist Properties** or **Music/Video Properties panel**, as ilustrated on page 161.

What's the ideal video format for importing into DVD Architect Studio?

Although the program accepts a wide variety of formats, some formats work more efficiently and more reliably than others.

Most video editing applications (including Sony Vegas) include export options specifically for outputting DVD-ready or BluRay-ready video:

> For DVD projects, the best source video for DVD Architect Studio is the DVD-ready MPEG2, a 720x480 MPEG (720x576 if you're editing in PAL video) using non-square pixels and lower field first interlacing.
>
> For BluRay discs, the best source video is a BluRay-ready AVC file, a 1920x1080 60i video (50i if you are editing PAL video) MPEG/MTS file using the H.264 codec.

It is usually not a good idea to use video directly from a camera or camcorder or from online as source video in a DVD Architect Studio project.

Whenever possible, you should load your raw video into a video editing program and then output one of the file formats above for use in you disc authoring program.

Maintain the program

Sony regularly releases patches and updates for its products.

These can be downloaded from the Sony Creative Software web site, or you can load them directly into the program by going to the program's **Help** drop-down menu and selecting **Sony on the Web** and then the **Latest Updates** option.

In addition, the function of the program requires the support of two other applications on your computer, and it's recommended that you regularly ensure that they are both up to date.

DirectX is Microsoft's collection of applications for handling tasks related to multimedia. Generally, if you keep your Windows operating system is up to date, you'll have the latest version.

Quicktime, on the other hand, is a multimedia framework developed by Apple Inc., and it plays a bigger role in the support of video and other media – even on a Windows computer – than you might imagine.

Apple updates this program extremely often, and it is highly recommended that you either check the Apple site regularly to ensure you have the latest version or that you install Apple's automatic updater so that you are notified when a new version is released.

Finally, remember that an emptier hard drive is a happier hard drive. For best performance, always keep your C drive at least 15% free and keep that free space as defragmented as possible.

What are the PCM, AC-3, 5.1 Surround audio formats?
DVD Architect Studio offers three options for encoding the audio for your DVDs and BluRay discs. Here is a brief description of each:

PCM. **Pulse code modulation** files are basic, uncompressed digital audio files on a DVD. They're universal – but not terribly efficient. This is, however, the only audio option available in DVD Architect Studio for BluRay discs.

AC-3. Audio Code 3 is another name for **Dolby Digital**, a compressed audio system developed by Dolby Laboratories that produces quality sound from smaller files than PCM. Because of its quality to size ratio, AC-3 is the standard choice for stereo DVDs.

AC-3 5.1. Also known as **Dolby Digital 5.1 Surround** is a compressed file that delivers audio over five channels – left and right, front and rear and center – surrounding the viewer with your disc's audio. Naturally, in order for it to provide a true surround sound experience, you will need to provide your disc project with five-channel audio as its source files in addition to selecting this option.

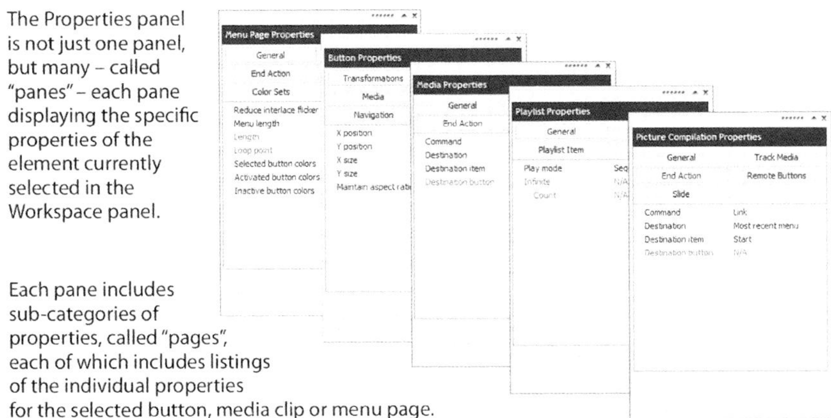

The Properties panel is not just one panel, but many – called "panes" – each pane displaying the specific properties of the element currently selected in the Workspace panel.

Each pane includes sub-categories of properties, called "pages", each of which includes listings of the individual properties for the selected button, media clip or menu page.

The Properties panel

A deep reference guide

Although each of the panels in DVD Architect Studio plays a role in the creation of your DVDs and BluRay discs, the **Properties** panel is in many ways the key to this program's deeper power.

In the **Properties** panel, you can build and modify links, swap in media and customize the behavior of pretty much any menu, button or media file you've added to your disc.

In fact, the **Properties** panel is not just one panel, but several – called "panes" by Sony – each of which displays the often unique properties of the menu item you are currently customizing.

There are **Menu Page Properties, Button Properties, Media Properties, Picture Compilation Properties, Music/Video Compilation Properties** and **Graphics Properties** panes. Each pane includes a number of sections, called "pages," accessed by clicking on one of the gray buttons at the top of the panel. In each of these pages are property listings in which you can modify your selected item's behaviors, actions or media.

To change a property, click on the box to the right of the property's listing. The property will become editable text or will display a drop-down a menu of selectable options or a slider that you can use to, for instance, change the duration of a still or audio or video clip.

In some cases, a property may be grayed out, indicating that it is unavailable to change. However, in many of these cases, even this property can be made editable by changing the setting of another property on that page.

For instance, you will not be able to change the length of a video loop background for a menu page in **Menu Page Properties** if the **Menu Length** property is set to **Auto-Calculate** (a setting which automatically makes the video loop the same length as the provided video clip). However, when you change the **Auto-Calculate** property to **Specify**, the option to set the **Length** becomes available.

Common Properties

There are a number of properties settings which are available in several or all of the **Properties** panes.

Reduce Interlace Flicker

A standard interlaced frame of television is created in two passes, each pass drawing every other horizontal line of pixels. This happens too fast for the eye to see (~30 times per second NTSC and 25 times per second in the PAL television system). However, some video formats create this interlacing by drawing the upper field of lines first and others by drawing the lower field first – and photos aren't interlaced at all. The result can mean that, occasionally (particularly when using photos that include very bright spots or detailed patterns), your image or menu background may look shaky or jiggly in your final disc. Turning **Reduce Interlace Flicker** on will nullify most such interlacing issues.

Color Sets

Color Sets are the customizable color schemes for the highlights that appear over your menu buttons as your viewer navigates your disc's menu pages. (See **Chapter 4, Create and Customize a Menu Button**.)

A **Color Set** consists of four color definitions, each of which plays a role in a part of your button's **Highlight** overlay.

The definitions for each color include an opacity (or **alpha**) level, defined as "**a**" on the color selector panel. This level determines how transparent your overlay is.

A **Color Set** can be set to **Project Wide**, in which case the colors will be applied to all buttons on all menu pages on your disc. Or it can set to **Custom**, in which case the colors will be applied only to your selected button(s). (Naturally, a **Custom** setting for any button overrides a **Project Wide** Color Set definition.)

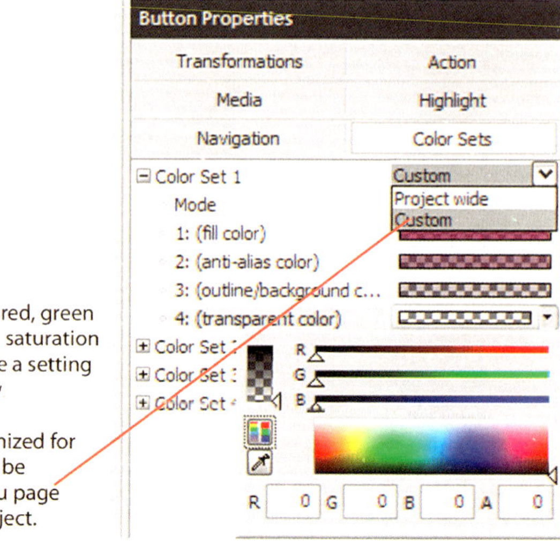

Color Sets are defined by red, green and blue levels or by hue, saturation and lightness, and include a setting for alpha, or transparency

Color Sets can be custsomized for individual buttons or can be defined overall for a menu page or for your entire disc project.

Understanding how Color Sets affect button highlights

A tribute to Will
A tribute to Will
Fill Color colors only areas of button and text
Ant-Alias Color Smoothes edges by blending Fill and Outline/Background colors
1: (fill color)
2: (anti-alias color)
3: (outline/backgro...
4: (transparent color)
Outline/Background Color tints the outlines and drop shadows
Transparent Color fills undefined (transparent) areas, as defined by the highlight mask shape

Here's what each color in a set does. (By default – and probably for the best – the **Color Set** mode is set to **Blend Colors**, in which the three other colors are variations of the **Fill Color**):

> **Fill Color.** Displays as a highlight over your button's text and thumbnail image.
>
> **Anti-Alias Color.** Anti-aliasing smooths the edges of the menu highlight. It's generally a blend of the **Fill Color** and the **Outline/ Background Color.**
>
> **Outline/Background Color.** Displays as the background or outline around the button as it is highlighted (usually defined by the button image's or text's black areas).
>
> **Transparent Color.** This color setting designates which areas of a button display as transparent. As indicated in the illustration below, coloring this property fills the undefined, transparent area around a button's image and text. Most default color settings leave this as transparent.

Exactly how each color in a set behaves as a button highlight is a combination of your **Color Sets** and the **Highlight Mask** and **Style** settings (as discussed in **Button Properties**, later in this chapter).

Setting duration times

When typing in a duration time for any media in the **Properties** panel, the numbers 00;00;00.000 represent hours; minutes; seconds.thousandths-of-a-second, such that five seconds is typed in as "5.000" or simply "5.0".

You must include this decimal point, or type the number of seconds with three zeroes behind it (as in "5000"). Otherwise, the program will assume you're setting the time to .005 seconds.

You can set the properties not only for the colors that appear as a button highlight but also the shape of this highlight. (See page 56.)

Additionally, in **Button Properties**, you'll see that you have the option of using one **Color Set** for **Selected Buttons** (the highlight color that displays as your viewer navigates around your menu page) and another set for **Activated Buttons** (so that the highlight changes color as your viewer clicks on the button).

You can adjust the different colors in your **Color Sets** from virtually any **Properties** pane. But which **Color Set** is ultimately applied to a particular menu page or button is entirely dependent on the settings applied in the **General** page of **Menu Page Properties** or set for the individual **Button Properties**.

Settings for **Color Sets** made on the **Menu Page Properties** override those made **Project Wide**. And **Color Sets** set up on a particular button's **Button Properties** supersede any other settings in your disc project.

End Actions

Virtually every **Properties** pane includes an **End Action** page. **End Actions** designate which menu page or media clip follows the item you are setting the properties for. You can see the **End Actions** path for any element in green text in the **Project Overview** panel. For media clips, the **End Actions** are displayed as links, usually back to the menu from which the media clip was launched.

In most cases, the **Command** property for a menu page's **End Action** will be set to **Hold**. This means that the page will remain displayed until your viewer clicks on a button or navigates away.

In **Button Properties**, the equivalent property is called an **Action**, since the link to the next item from a button is usually not automatic. (Since, by default, the button must be clicked on in order to follow its link.)

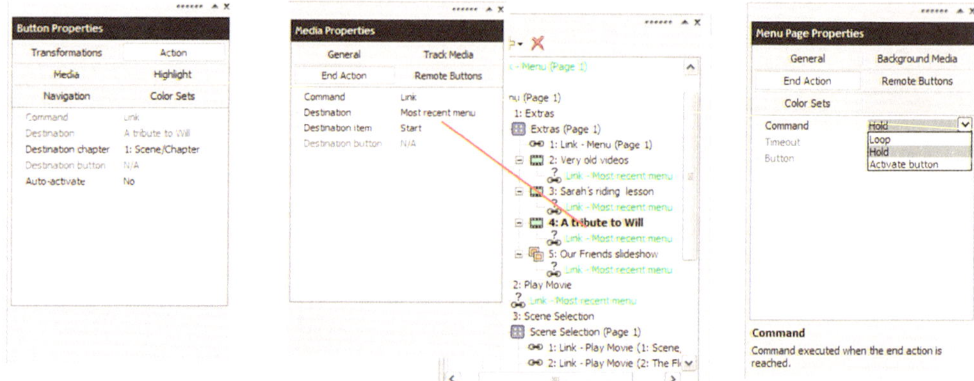

Actions or End Actions determine what the item will link to after it is displayed or activated. Button Actions link to media files or a menu page. Media End Actions determine the item that is launched when the media has finished playing – usually back to the menu page it was launched from. Menu Page End Actions are usually set to Hold until a button is activated. However, they can also be set to loop (if a video or music track is set to play in the background) or to automatically launch a designated button after a period of time (Timeout).

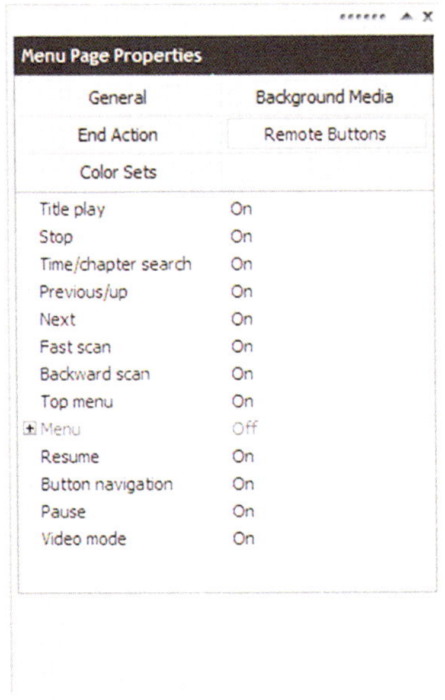

The Remote Buttons properties allow you to lock out certain of your viewer's DVD or BluRay disc player's remote control functions for a menu page or media clip – so that, for instance, your viewer can not fast forward through a copyright warning.

Remote Buttons properties

The toggle properties on the **Remote Buttons** page allow you to lock out or control the viewer's ability to use certain buttons on his or her remote control to navigate away from a menu page or media clip. These toggles would be useful if, for instance, you had a logo or a copyright warning for your DVD that you wanted to remain on screen for a certain amount of time and you wanted to disable your viewer's ability to navigate away from it.

The following are the functions of each button on this page:

Title Play. The ability for the viewer to skip to a specific menu page or media clip.

Stop. The ability to stop play of the DVD.

Time/Chapter Search. The ability to navigate to a specific chapter or spot in a video.

Previous/Up. The ability to navigate to a previous menu chapter or menu page.

Next. The ability to navigate to the next chapter or menu page.

Fast Scan. The ability to fast forward through a video clip.

Backward Scan. The ability to reverse through a video clip.

Top Menu. The ability to jump to the top-level menu on your DVD.

Menu/Command. Determines what happens when the viewer presses his Menu button. If **Link** is selected, pressing the Menu button takes the viewer to a **Destination**, as set in the property listing below it.

Menu/Destination. When the **Link** is set to **Command**, the Menu/ Destination designates the item that will launch when your viewer presses the Menu button.

Menu/Start. Sets a specific location in the **Destination**, set above, that the Menu button will take the viewer to. If a video with scene/ chapter markers is set as the **Destination**, the start point can be set to any of the scenes in the video.

Menu/Destination Button. If a menu page has been set as the **Destination**, a drop-down menu at this property will give you the option of choosing which button is highlighted on that menu page by default.

(Note that, due to the nature of their function, the **Menu's Command**, **Destination** and **Destination Button** toggle controls are not available in **Menu Page Properties** or **Button Properties**.)

Resume. The ability to return to a video clip (by pressing the **Menu** button) after exiting it (by pressing the **Menu** button).

Button Navigation. The ability to use the up/down/left/right buttons to navigate a menu page's buttons.

Pause. The ability to pause a video's playback.

Video Mode. The ability to be able to switch between widescreen, letterboxed and pan-and-scan modes for a widescreen video.

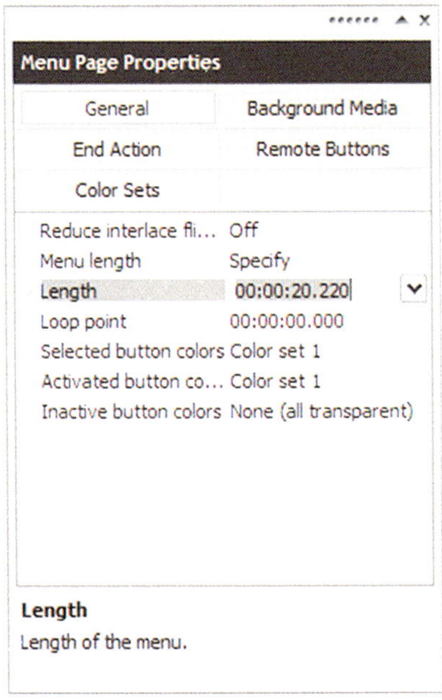

If you have set a video, music and/or audio clip as the background for a menu page, you can set the Menu Length property to Auto-Calculate, in which case the background loop will be as long as the longer of the audio or video background clip. If, however, you set Menu Length to Specify, you can set the Length of this background loop to any duration.

The Loop Point sets the point at which the buttons appear on your menu page, allowing you to include a video and/or audio introduction to any menu page.

Menu Page Properties

The **Properties** panel will display **Menu Page Properties** when you have selected a menu page in the **Project Overview** panel or you have a menu page displayed in the **Workspace** panel and no other item (button, text block, graphic) is selected.

For more information

For more information on **Menu Page Properties** and how they work see **Chapter 3, Build a Menu Page**.

General

The **General** page displays basic functions of the menu page.

Reduce Interlace Flicker. See the discussion in **Common Properties**, on page 142.

Menu Length. If your menu page includes an audio or video background and your Menu Length is set to **Auto-Calculate**, the loop length for the background will be the length of the longer of either the audio or video clip. In other words, if you use a 3-minute song as your menu background, **Auto-Calculate** will play the entire 3-minute song before looping. Setting the **Menu Length** property to **Specify** makes it available for you to designate a loop length for your menu background in the box below.

Length. If the **Menu Length** is set to **Specify**, you can set the length of the loop of your menu's video and/or audio background (as designated on the **Background Media** page). Loop length can be set by typing over the numbers displayed or by moving the slider at the drop-down.

Loop Point. Changing this setting, numerically or by using the slider, creates a segment, when the menu page first launches, in which your background audio or video clip plays but no other graphics, text or buttons appear on the page – a sort of introductory sequence for the menu page. Changes here will be reflected in the location of the green **Set Loop Point** indicator in the Timeline panel, and vice versa. For a more detailed discussion of how the Loop Point works, see **Set a Loop Point for your background video** in **Chapter 3, Build a Menu Page**.

Selected Button Colors. Indicates which **Color Set** appears as a highlight over your menu page's buttons as your viewer navigates this menu page. For more information on using **Color Sets**, see the discussion in **Common Properties** at the beginning of this chapter.

Activated Button Colors. Indicates which **Color Set** appears as a highlight over your menu page's buttons when your viewer clicks to select the button on your menu page. For more information on using **Color Sets**, see the discussion in **Common Properties** at the beginning of this chapter.

Inactive Button Colors. Indicates which **Color Set** appears as a highlight over your buttons when a button is *not* selected on your menu page. In most situations, unless you are creating an effect in which highlights on your buttons change colors as they are navigated over, this property is set to **None** to avoid confusing your disc's viewer.

Background Media

The **Background Media** page allows you to select and set the behavior of the background image, video and/or audio clip for your menu page. To set the duration of the loop of the video or audio background(s) for your menu page, go to the **General** properties, as discussed on the previous page.

Video. Indicates the still or video you've selected as your menu page's background. The drop-down menu gives you the options of replacing this image or video, by browsing to a new selection, or removing it completely. Browsing for an image or clip here accomplishes and reflects the same effect as dragging a still from the **Explorer** panel to the menu page displayed in your **Workspace** panel or selecting a clip using the **Set Video/Image** right-click option in the **Timeline** panel.

Audio. Indicates the music or audio clip selected for your menu page's background. The drop-down menu gives you the options of replacing this audio, by browsing to it, or removing it completely. Browsing for an audio clip here accomplishes and reflects the same effect as dragging a song or audio clip from the **Explorer** panel to the menu page displayed in your **Workspace** or selecting a clip using the **Set Audio** right-click option in the menu page's **Timeline** panel.

Highlight Mask. The **Highlight Mask** customizes the shape of the highlight displayed over your menu page's buttons as your viewer navigates the page. You can use any graphic file as a highlight mask, from a one-color graphic to a full-color photograph. How this mask behaves is determined by the **Highlight Mask Mapping** setting below as well as the **Color Sets** applied to your menu page's buttons.

Buttons also have their own individual settings for this mask, and they override the settings here in **Menu Page Properties**. For a more detailed discussion and illustrations of how the various masks and mask mapping settings work, see the **Highlight** section in the **Button Properties** sub-chapter.

Highlight Mask Mapping. This setting determines how the graphic selected as the **Highlight Mask** is read as a mask, and then applies that mask to the **Color Set** selected. Setting this feature to **Transparency** maps to the mask graphic so that the **Fill** color applies to opaque areas of the mask and the **Transparent** color applies to the transparent. Setting this feature to **Intensity** maps to the mask graphic so that the **Fill** color is area is set to the lightest areas of the mask graphic and the **Transparent** color is set to the darkest. Setting this feature to **Color Channel** maps to the mask graphic so that red areas of the graphic become the **Fill** color, blue areas become the **Anti-Alias** color, green areas become the **Outline/Background** color and black areas become the **Transparent** color.

Buttons also have their own individual settings for mask mapping, and they override the menu page settings. For a more detailed discussion and illustrations of how the various masks and mask mapping settings work, see the **Highlight** section in the **Button Properties** sub-chapter.

Stretch Type determines how your background image or video fills the menu background. **Letterbox** fits the image according to either width or height, leaving black above and below or left and right of the image if it does not fully fill the frame. **Zoom to Fit** fits the image so that it fills the frame both vertically and horizontally, even if a portion of the image extends beyond the frame and is trimmed off. **Stretch to Fit** stretches the image so that it fills the frame vertically and horizontally, even if this distorts the image unnaturally.

Illustrations of these various **Stretch** settings can be found in the **Picture Compilation Properties** sub-chapter.

End Action

End Actions determine what happens after your menu page is displayed. In most cases, you will want your menu page to hold until a button is activated – or at least until the menu times out. However, if the need arises for you to customize how your menu page behaves, this action can be customized here.

Command. This is the automatic action that occurs after the menu page is displayed. If it is set to **Hold**, the menu page will remain on-screen until the viewer takes an action, such as clicking on a button. If you select the option to **Activate Button**, the menu will automatically launch one of the button actions, according to the options you've chosen below. If you select the **Loop** option, the menu page will display with no buttons until it reaches the **Loop Point** you have set in the **General** page for the **Menu Page Properties**, as discussed in the **General** page section.

Timeout. When the **Command** property, above, is set to **Activate Button**, this property sets the amount of time the menu page displays before the button designated in the property below automatically activates.

Button. When the **Command** property, above, is set to **Activate Button**, this property designates which button on the menu page will be automatically selected after the **Timeout**, set above.

Remote Buttons

The toggles on the **Remote Buttons** page allow you to lock out or control the viewer's ability to use certain button's on his or her remote control to navigate away from the menu page. These toggles would be useful if, for instance, you had a copyright warning for your DVD that you wanted to remain onscreen for a certain amount of time and you wanted to disable your viewer's ability to navigate away from it. A discussion of each button's function can be found under **Common Properties** on page 145.

Color Sets

Color Sets are used to set the colors for highlights which appear over your buttons as your viewer navigates your disc menu page. You can create four **Color Sets** for your disc, which can be set to apply project-wide or customized for each menu page and/or for each individual button. A discussion of the functions of each color in a **Color Set** can be found under **Common Properties** on page 142.

Measuring in pixels
Positions and sizes of items on a menu page are measured in pixels, based on the center of the item.

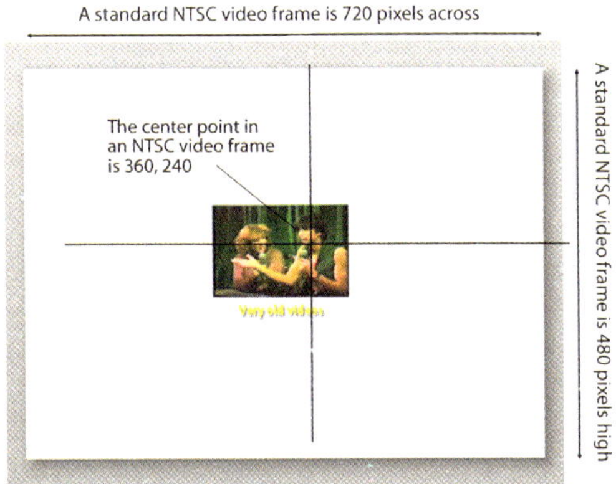

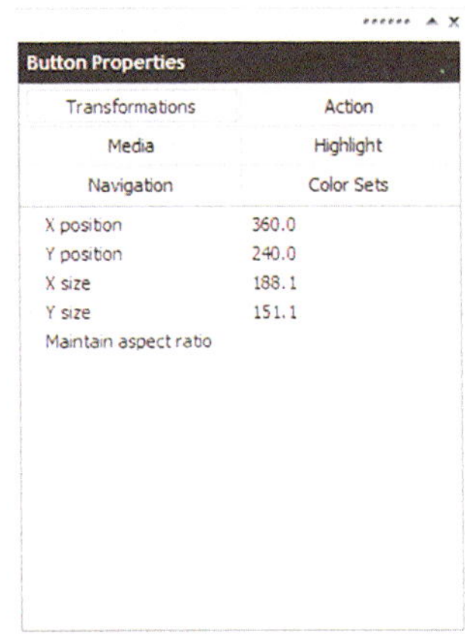

Button Properties

The **Properties** panel will display **Button Properties** when a button is selected in the **Workspace** panel. **Button Properties** control how your button is displayed and how it functions.

For more information

For more information on **Button Properties** and how they work see **Chapter 4, Create and Customize a Menu Button**.

Transformations

The **Transformations** page sets the properties for the size and position of your button.

X Position. This setting maps the location of the center of your button horizontally on your menu page, measured in pixels. A standard NTSC or PAL video frame is 720 pixels across, such that a button in the horizontal center of the frame would be at an X position of 360.

Y Position. This setting maps the location of the center of your button vertically on your menu page, measured in pixels. A standard NTSC video frame is 480 pixels tall, such that a button in the vertical center of the frame would be at a Y position of 240. (In the PAL television standard, the vertical measurement is 576 pixels.)

X size. This is the width of your button, measured in pixels.

Y size. This is the height of your button, measured in pixels.

Maintain Aspect Ratio. Set to **Yes** by default, this toggle keeps the aspect ratio of your button (or the text or thumbnail individually) constrained as you resize it. If this toggle is set to **No**, your button's thumbnail image or text will become distorted as you change the width or height independently.

Action

This page includes settings for controlling what actions are launched by your button. Buttons can be set to launch videos, compilations or playlists as well as other menu pages.

Command. A **Link** setting for this property links the button to a media clip's playback or another menu page. If your button was created as a link to media or to another menu page, **Link** will be your only option here.

If you manually created a generic button (by clicking on **Add Button** on the **Buttons** panel, as discussed on page 136), you will have two other options available for this button property: **Stop** terminates playback of the page and connects your viewer to the **Destination** you've designated below; **Resume** returns your viewer to the **Destination** set below, at the playback point at which he or she navigated to this menu.

Destination. If your button was created as a link to a movie or media clip or a menu page, this option will be grayed out because the destination for the button was inherent in its creation.

If you manually created a generic button (by clicking on **Add Button** on the **Buttons** panel, as discussed on page 136), a drop-down menu will be available, offering you the option of linking this button to any media clip or menu page on your disc.

Destination Item. If your button links to a video, playlist or composition, this property gives you the option of linking directly to a specific **Scene/Chapter Marker** within this media clip. **N/A** indicates that the property is not applicable to your designated link.

Destination Button. If your button's **Destination** is set to a menu page, this property allows you to designate which button on the destination menu is highlighted on that page by default. If you choose the **Default** option, the buttons will be highlighted as the viewer navigates them, in the order you set in the **Project Overview** or **Workspace** panel, using the **Navigation Tool**.

Auto-Activate. If a button is toggled to **Auto-Activate**, it will link to its destination as soon as the viewer highlights it, rather than after he or she clicks on it.

Media

The **Media** page of the **Button Properties** pane defines the look and behavior of your buttons' thumbnail, frame and highlight.

Button Style. Your selected button can be set to display as **Text Only**, **Image Only** or **Text and Image**.

Thumbnail Properties. These properties define the shape and behavior of the thumbnail image on your button.

Thumbnail Media. By default, the thumbnail of a button linking to a video or media clip will be the first frame of that clip. To set which

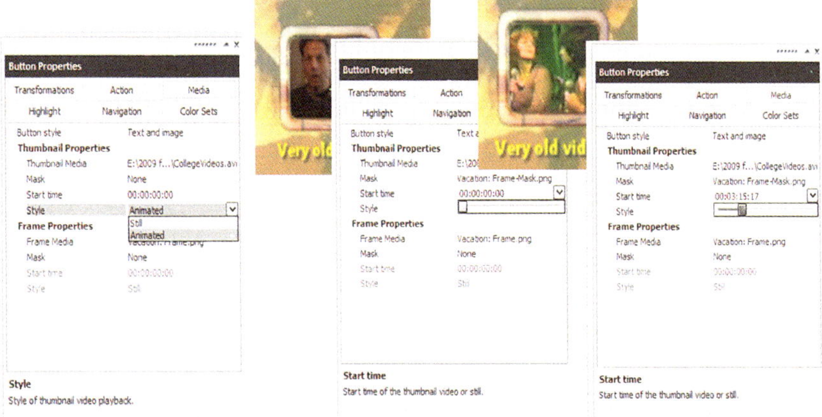

If the Thumbnail Media for your button image is a video clip, you can set the Style to play the button as a video loop. By adjusting the Start Time of this video loop, you can set at which point in the video the thumbnail motion menu begins its playback. The length of this video loop (30 seconds, by default) can be set in the Menu Length properties on the General page of the Menu Page Properties, and is set for the entire page's motion button set.

frame of the video is displayed or to make the button display a video loop, set **Start Time** and **Style** below.

To add or replace a button thumbnail image click on the property setting box to the right of this listing and, from the drop-down, select **Replace** (or **Remove** to delete it). If you are using a video clip and you'd like it to appear as a motion video loop, change the **Style** setting, as described below.

Mask. A mask (not to be confused with a **Highlight Mask**) makes certain areas of your thumbnail image transparent, so that your thumbnail can be a shape other than a rectangle. (Many of the button frames in the Buttons panel use masks to create different shapes.)

For information on creating and applying a mask, see **Apply a custom button frame and mask**, on pages 135-136.

Button frames can be any graphic but, because they include transparency, are usually PNGs, GIFs or PSDs.

Frames can even be animated GIFs, as seen in the Animated 1 frames in the Buttons panel. The animation will need to be toggled on, however, in the Frame Properties on the Media page.

Non-square frames, such as this round frame, must also include a companion mask, also linked to Frame Properties. Black areas in a mask render these areas of the button's thumbnail as transparent.

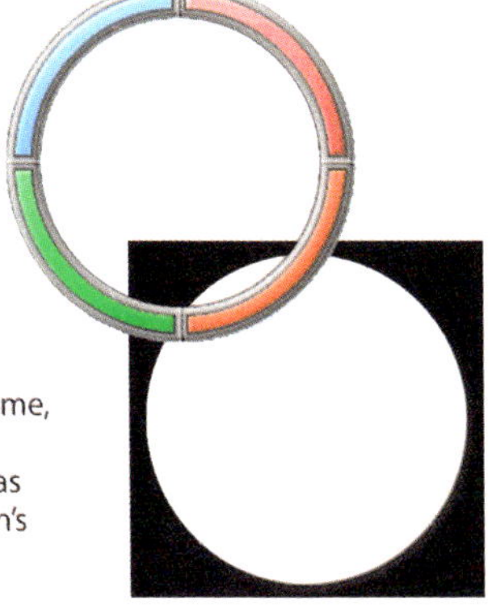

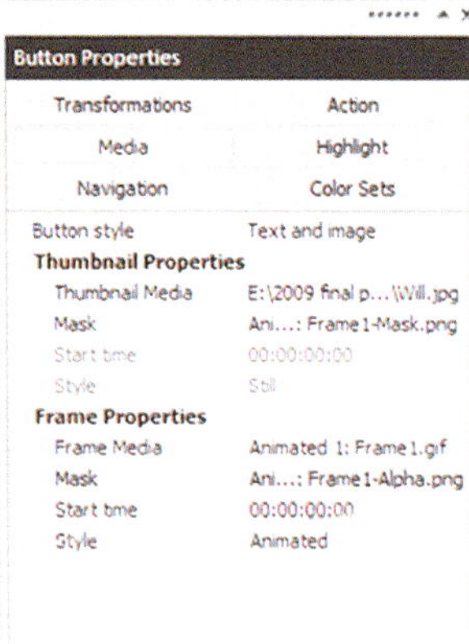

Start Time. Determines which frame of a video thumbnail is displayed as your button. If you have selected a video clip as your thumbnail and you have set the **Style** (below) to **Animated**, this property will determine where, in the linked or selected clip, the thumbnail's playback loop begins. The start point can be set using the slider from the drop-down menu or by manually typing in the timecode position.

Style. If you are using a video clip as your selected button's thumbnail, this toggle sets whether the thumbnail appears as a **Still** or **Animated** loop, according to the **Start Time** you've indicated above.

Frame Properties. These properties designate the frame, if any, for your button image as well as the frame's behavior, if animated.

Frame Media. In addition to the frames available in the **Buttons** panel, you can apply and create your own custom graphic or even animated video clip as your frame. (For information on creating your own button frame, see **Create a Custom Button Frame** on page 132.)

Mask. A mask makes certain areas of your frame transparent, so that your **Frame Media** can include, for instance, a transparent window for your thumbnail to be visible through. (Many of the button frames in the **Buttons** panel use masks to create different framed shapes.) To create your own custom mask (as discussed in **Create a button frame mask** on page 134), create a graphic of pure black and pure white. When applied (by selecting the **Replace** option for this property) the white areas of your graphic will determine which areas of your **Frame Media** are displayed; black areas will be rendered transparent.

Style. If you are using a video clip or other animated clip as your thumbnail's Frame Media, this toggle allows you the option of displaying the frame as a **Still** or **Animated** image.

Highlight

The **Highlight** page designates which highlight style appears over your selected button as your viewer navigates through your menu page and how these highlights behave. Your highlight's color is determined by the **Color Set** designated for your button.

Style. By default, your button will be highlighted with a **Rectangle** as your viewer navigates through your menu page. Setting this property to **Mask Overlay** highlights only the area of he button's thumbnail and text shape. An **Image Rectangle** highlights with a rectangle over your thumbnail image only. A **Text Mask Overlay** highlights only the button's text. An **Image Mask Overlay** highlights the thumbnail image only, doing so in the shape of the thumbnail if it is non-square. **Underline** highlights with a simple underline under your button. **Custom** allows you to apply any custom shape to your highlight, according to the settings below.

Menu Button Highlight Styles

Rectangle Mask

Mask Overlay

Text Rectangle

Image Rectangle

Text Mask

Image Mask

Underline

Custom
(Black dot)

Mask. If you have chosen the **Custom** option for your **Highlight Style**, above, selecting the **Replace** option from this property's drop-down menu allows you to select any custom graphic on which to base your button highlight. (The **Remove** option deletes the graphic from this property.) The button's highlight will be created, based on the options set below.

Mask Mapping. If you have chosen a custom graphic for your button highlight, the **Mask Mapping** setting will determine how that graphic's shape and color will be applied to your mask. Setting this property to **Transparency** maps the mask graphic so that the opaque (non-transparent) areas of the mask graphic become the Fill Color and the transparent become the Transparent Color. Setting

Mask Mapping Custom Button Style Highlights

The **Transparency** setting creates a highlight, using your designated color set, based on your custom shape's black and transparent areas.

The **Intensity** setting creates a highlight, using your designated color set, based on your custom shape's black and white areas.

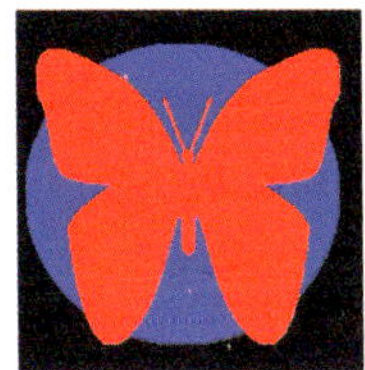

The **Color Channel** setting creates a highlight, using your designated color set, based on your custom shape's red, green, blue and black areas.

this property to **Intensity** maps the mask graphic so that the lightest areas of the mask graphic become the **Fill Color** and the darkest become the **Transparent Color**. Setting this property to **Color Channel** maps the mask graphic so that red areas of the graphic become the **Fill Color**, green areas become the **Anti-Alias** color, blue areas become the **Outline/Background Color** and black areas become the Transparent Color.

Navigation

Settings on the **Button Properties' Navigation** page determine which buttons on your menu page your viewer will navigate to as he or she moves from this button using his or her remote control's arrow keys. By default, these settings are generated automatically, based on the positions of the buttons on your menu page. However, this page does give you the option of overriding the **Auto** settings.

Color Sets

Color Sets are used to set the colors for highlights which appear over your buttons as your viewer navigates your disc menu page. You can create four color sets for your disc, which can set to apply project-wide or customized for each menu page and/or for each individual button. A discussion of the functions of each color in a **Color Set** can be found under **Common Properties** on page 142.

Note that, although the **Color Set** properties may be set for an entire menu page or even an entire project, the settings made for a specific button override any **Project Wide** settings.

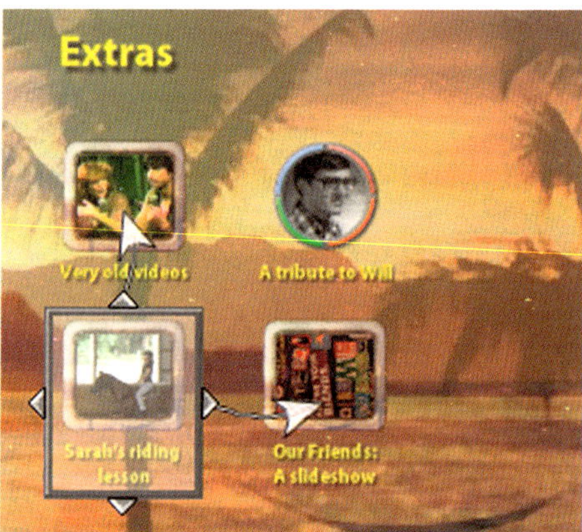

The Navigation properties of a button are the literal equivalent of the navigation arrows visible in the Workspace panel. When set to Auto, the navigation will generate the most intuitive order of button selection.

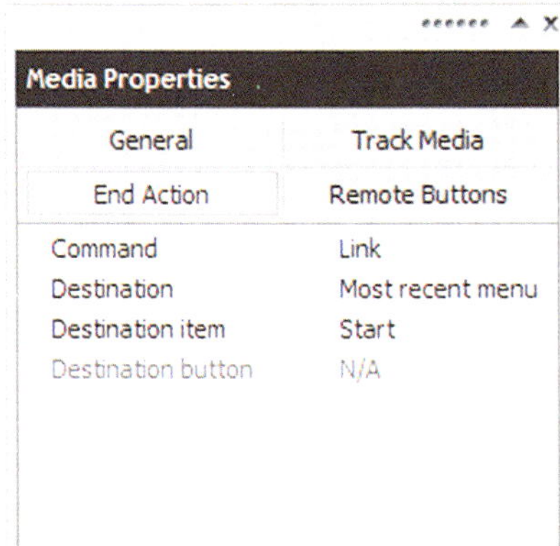

Media Properties define how your video and other media clips behave, and which page or other file they link to after they've finished playing.

Media Properties

The **Properties** panel will display **Media Properties** when a video (or other media clip) is selected by double-clicking on it in the **Project Overview** panel or by double-clicking on the button linking to it so that it is displayed in the **Workspace** panel. The properties in this pane define how this video is played and what menu page or other media clip launches when it has finished playing (**End Action**).

General

Because some video formats can have interlacing issues that may cause their images to flicker or play jiggly when encoded to disc, the sole property on this page, **Reduce Interlace Flicker**, can be used to reduce this effect. For more information on the **Reduce Interlace Flicker** property, see the discussion under **Common Properties** on page 142.

Track Media

The properties on the **Track Media** page designate the **Video** and **Audio** clips that make up this media selection. By clicking on the drop-down menus at each of these properties, you have the option of replacing or removing the video or audio for this selection. Replacing your media here is reflected, and creates the same effect, as right-clicking on the **Timeline** panel for this media and selecting the **Set Video/Image** or **Set Audio** options.

End Action

This page sets the properties for the media or menu page that this media clip links to after its playback is finished.

Command. The **Command** property sets the action that occurs when a viewer clicks a button on his or her remote control as the media clip is playing. If set to **Link**, the viewer will be linked automatically to the **Destination** designated below. If set to **Stop**, the disc will simply stop after the media playback.

Destination. This property sets where the media clip will link to after it has completed play or if playback is interrupted by the viewer. (It is set by default to the **Most Recent Menu**, the menu page the media was launched from.) The drop-down list allows you to set this to any menu page or media file on your disc. The setting here is reflected in the green **Link** displayed under the media clip in the **Project Overview** panel

Destination Item/Chapter. If your **Destination** is set to a menu page, this property (**Destination Item**) allows you link to the **Start** of the menu page or, if a **Loop Point** has been set (see the **General** settings under **Menu Page Properties**), the point at which the introductory segment has played and the menu buttons become available. If the **Destination** is set to a media clip, this property (**Destination Chapter**) allows you to link directly to a specific scene/chapter marker on video, compilation or playlist.

Destination Button. If the **Destination** is set to a menu page, this property allows you to designate which button on that menu is highlighted by default when that page is launched.

Remote Buttons

The toggles on this page allow you to lock out or control the viewer's ability to navigate away while this media clip is playing. For a further discussion of each button's function, see **Common Properties** on page 145.

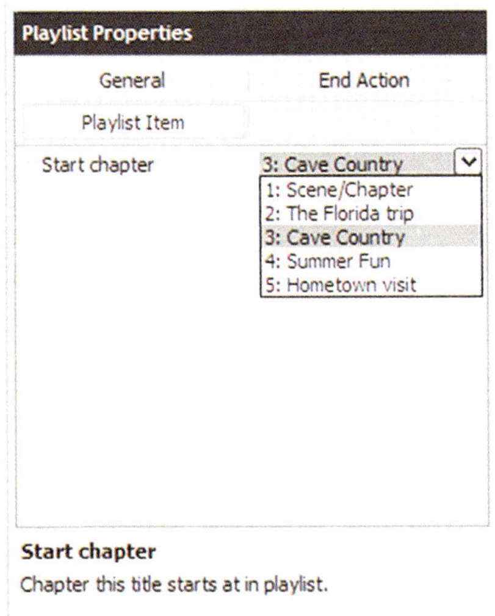

The Playlist Item page allows you to set start positions for each individual media clip in your playlist.

If a clip in your playlist has scene/chapter markers, your Playlist Properties can be set to start playback at a specific marker.

Playlist Properties

The **Properties** panel will display **Playlist Properties** when a playlist is selected (by double-clicking on it) in the **Project Overview** panel. The **Playlist** properties can be set for the entire playlist or for its individual video clips.

For more information

For more information on **Playlist Properties** and how they work see **Chapter 7, Create a Playlist**.

General

Since a playlist usually contains a number of media clips, most of the properties in this pane are concerned with how and in what order those clips play.

Play Mode. If the **Play Mode** is set to **Sequential**, your playlist will play in the order displayed within the **Playlists** panel. If set to **Random**, the clips will play in random order.

Infinite. If you have selected to have your playlist clips display in random order, you can choose to have them repeat indefinitely or play through only the number of times indicated in the **Count** property, below, before proceeding to the playlist's **End Action**.

End Action

This page sets the properties for the media or menu page the playlist links to after its playback is finished or is interrupted by the viewer.

Command. The **Command** property sets the action that occurs when a viewer clicks a button on his or her remote control during the playlist's play. If set to **Link**, the viewer will be linked to the **Destination** set below. If set to **Stop**, the playlist's, as well as the disc's, playback will stop.

Destination. This property sets where the playlist will link to after it has completed play or if playback is interrupted by the viewer. The drop-down list allows you to set this to any menu page or media file on your disc.

Destination Item/Chapter. If your **Destination** is set to a menu page, this property (**Destination Item**) allows you link to the **Start** of the menu page or, if a **Loop Point** has been set (see the **General** settings under **Menu Page Properties**), the point at which the introductory segment of the menu page has played and the menu buttons become available. If the **Destination** is set to a media clip, this property (which becomes **Destination Chapter**) allows you to link to a specific scene/ chapter marker on a video, compilation or playlist.

Destination Button. If the **Destination** is set to a menu page, this property allows you to designate which button on that menu is highlighted by default when the page is launched.

Playlist Item

The **Playlist Item** page gives you the option of setting the start point for the specific clip you have selected in the **Playlist** panel to specific a scene/ chapter marker point you have added to that media clip. By default, it is set to the beginning of the clip, **1:Scene/Chapter**.

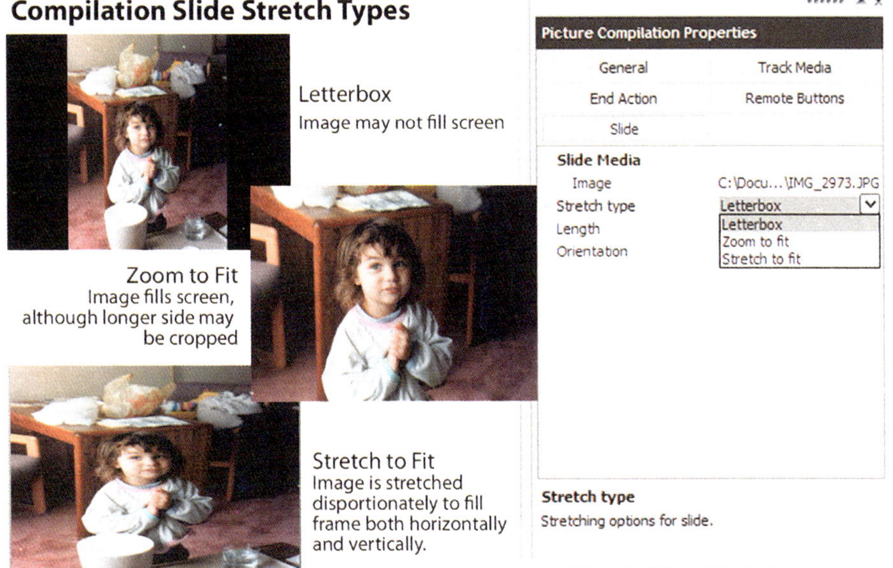

Picture Compilation Properties

The **Properties** panel will display **Picture Compilation Properties** when a Picture Compilation is selected (by double-clicking on it) in the **Project Overview** panel.

For more information

For more information on **Picture Compilation Properties** and how they work see **Chapter 8, Build a Picture or Music/Video Compilation**.

General

Because photographs can have interlacing issues that may cause their images to flicker when converted to video, the sole property on this page, **Reduce Interlace Flicker**, can be used to reduce this effect. For more information on the **Reduce Interlace Flicker** property, see the discussion under **Common Properties** on page 142.

Track Media

This page includes only one property in DVD Architect Studio, **Audio 1**, which designates the audio or music track that plays behind the slideshow in your picture compilation. This audio track may be replaced or removed by selecting the option in this property's drop-down menu.

End Action

This page sets the how the compilation links to menu page or media clip after its playback is finished or is interrupted by the viewer.

Command. The **Command** property sets the action that occurs when a viewer clicks a button on his or her remote control during the compilation's play. If set to **Link**, the viewer will be linked automatically to the **Destination** designated below. If set to **Stop**, the disc will simply stop after the compilation has played.

Destination. This property sets where the playlist will link to after it has completed play or if playback is interrupted by the viewer. The drop-down list allows you to set this to any menu page or media file on your disc. The setting here is reflected in the green link listed under the media clip in the **Project Overview** panel

Destination Item/Chapter. If your **Destination** is set to a menu page, this property (**Destination Item**) allows you link to the **Start** of the menu page or, if a **Loop Point** has been set (see the **General** settings under **Menu Page Properties**), the point at which the introductory segment has played and the menu buttons become available. If the **Destination** is set to a media clip, this property (**Destination Chapter**) allows you to link to a specific scene/chapter marker on a video, compilation or playlist.

Destination Button. If the **Destination** is set to a menu page, this property allows you to designate which button on that menu is highlighted by default when the page is launched.

Remote Buttons

The toggles on this page allow you to lock out or control the viewer's ability to navigate away while this compilation is playing. For a further discussion of each button's function, see **Common Properties** on page 145.

Slide

The **Slide** page allows you to set the properties for the individual pictures used in your slideshow. With the exception of the **Image** property, these properties can be applied to one picture at a time or, with several selected in the **Compilation** panel, to several slides at once.

Image. Designates the image selected in the **Compilation** panel. From the drop-down menu at this property, you can **Replace** or **Remove** this image.

Stretch Type determines how your slide image fills the video frame, as displayed in the illustration above. **Letterbox** fits the image according to either width or height, leaving black above and below or left and right of the image if it does not fully fill the frame. **Zoom to Fit** fits the image so that it fills the frame both vertically and horizontally, even if a portion of the image extends beyond the frame and is trimmed off. **Stretch to Fit** stretches the image so that it fills the frame vertically and horizontally, even if this distorts the image unnaturally.

Length. The duration of each slide in you picture compilation, which can be set numerically or, by clicking the drop-down menu, using a slider. When typing in a duration time, the numbers 00;00;00.000

represent hours; minutes; seconds.thousandths-of-a-second, such that five seconds is typed in as "5.000" or simply "5.0". (If you do not include the decimal point or type the number as "5000", the program will assume you're setting the time to .005 seconds.)

Orientation. The **Default** orientation is as the picture appears in the original photo file. Other options at the drop-down menu include rotation of the photo by **90, 180** or **270** degrees.

Picture and Music/Video Compilation Properties allow you to control how each clip or "slide" is displayed and how the audio track interacts with it.

Music/Video Compilation Properties

The **Properties** panel will display **Music/Video Compilation Properties** when a Music/Video Compilation is selected (by double-clicking on it) in the **Project Overview** panel.

For more information

For more information on **Music/Video Compilation Properties** and how they work see **Chapter 8, Build a Picture or Music/Video Compilation**.

General

Because some video formats can have interlacing issues that may cause their images to flicker or play jiggly when encoded to DVD, the sole property on this page, **Reduce Interlace Flicker**, can be used to reduce this effect. For more information on the **Reduce Interlace Flicker** property, see the discussion under **Common Properties** on page 142.

End Action

This page sets the how the compilation links to menu page or media clip after its playback is finished or is interrupted by the viewer.

> **Command**. The **Command** property sets the action that occurs when a viewer clicks a button on his or her remote control. If set to **Link**, the viewer will be linked automatically to the **Destination** designated below. If set to **Stop**, the disc will simply stop after the media playback.
>
> **Destination**. This property sets where the playlist will link to after it has completed play or if playback is interrupted by the viewer. The drop-down list allows you to set this to any menu page or media

file on your disc. The setting here is reflected in the green link listed under the media clip in the **Project Overview** panel

Destination Item/Chapter. If your **Destination** is set to a menu page, this property (**Destination Item**) allows you link to the **Start** of the menu page or, if a **Loop Point** has been set, the point at which the introductory segment has played and the menu buttons become available. If the **Destination** is set to a media clip, this property (**Destination Chapter**) allows you to link to a specific scene/chapter marker on a video, compilation or playlist.

Destination Button. If the **Destination** is set to a menu page, this property allows you to designate which button on that menu is highlighted by default when the page is launched.

Remote Buttons

The toggles on this page allow you to lock out or control the viewer's ability to navigate away while this compilation is playing. For a further discussion of each button's function, see **Common Properties** on page 145.

Slide

The **Slide** properties page allows you to set the properties of the video clips or stills used in music/video compilation. **Stretch Type** and **Orientation** can be applied to one video clip at a time or, with several selected in the **Compilation** panel, to several clips at once.

Slide Media/Video. Designates the video clip selected in the Compilation panel. From the drop-down menu at this property, you can **Replace** or **Remove** this video.

Slide Media/Audio. Designates the audio clip selected in the Compilation panel. From the drop-down menu at this property, you can replace or remove the audio.

Note, however, that, unlike in a Picture Compilation, *you can only replace audio for an individual clip in a Music/Video Compilation.* You can not, for instance, apply a single music track behind several video clips, as you can a picture compilation slideshow. Also, the shorter of the audio or video clip for each "slide" in your music/video compilation will automatically extend to the length of the longer, leaving black video or blank audio between its end and the end of the longer. For this reason, it is better to compose your music and video clip in a video editing program and import it into DVD Architect Studio complete rather than try to combine your music and your video in a music/video compilation.

Stretch Type determines how your background image or video fills the menu background. **Letterbox** fits the image according to either width or height, leaving black above and below or left and right of the image if it does not fully fill the frame. **Zoom to Fit** fits the image so that it fills the frame both vertically and horizontally, even if a portion of the image extends beyond the frame and is trimmed off. **Stretch to Fit** stretches the image so that it fills the frame vertically and horizontally, even if this distorts the image unnaturally.

Illustrations of these various **Stretch** settings can be found in the **Picture Compilation Properties** sub-chapter on page 161.

Length. The duration of each slide in you picture compilation, which can be set numerically or, by clicking the drop-down menu, using a slider. When typing in a duration time, the numbers 00;00;00.000 represent hours; minutes; seconds.thousandths-of-a-second, such that five seconds is typed in as "5.000" or simply "5.0" (If you do not include the decimal point or type the number as "5000", the program will assume you're setting the time to .005 seconds.)

Orientation. The **Default** orientation is as the video or photo appears in the original file. Other options at the drop-down menu include rotation of the clip by **90**, **180** or **270** degrees.

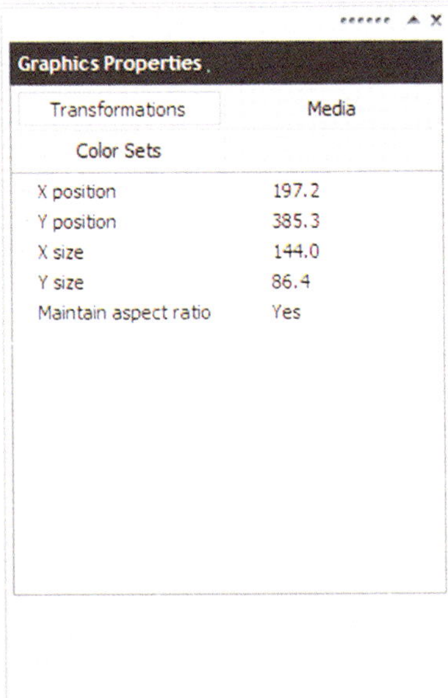

Graphics Properties define the location and media that you're using as a graphic over a menu page or media clip.

Graphics Properties

The **Properties** panel will display **Graphics Properties** when you have selected a graphic or video clip that you have placed (using **Insert Graphic**) on a menu page (as opposed to a button linking to a media clip). This properties pane is concerned with only the size and position of the graphic on the menu page and how the graphic behaves.

Transformations

The **Transformations** page sets the properties for the size and position of your button, as illustrated in the **Button Properties** sub-chapter.

X Position. This setting maps the location of the center of your button horizontally on your menu page, measured in pixels. A standard NTSC or PAL video frame is 720 pixels across, such that a button in the horizontal center of the frame would be at an X position of 360.

Y Position. This setting maps the location of the center of your button vertically on your menu page, measured in pixels. A standard NTSC video frame is 480 pixels tall, such that a button in the vertical center of the frame would be at a Y position of 240. (In the PAL television standard, the vertical measurement is 576 pixels.)

X size. This is the width of your button, measured in pixels.

Y size. This is the height of your button, measured in pixels.

Maintain Aspect Ratio. This toggle keeps the aspect ratio of your button (or the text or thumbnail individually) constrained as you resize it. If this toggle is set to **No**, your button's thumbnail image or text will become distorted as you change the width or height independently.

Media

The **Media** page on the **Graphics Properties** pane designates the graphic or media clip and how it behaves on your menu page.

Object Media. The **Object Media** is the image or video file which appears as the graphic. This file can be a graphic, photo or video clip, and can be replaced and removed using the drop-down menu at this property.

Start Time. If you have selected a video clip as your graphic, this property can be used to set the frame which is displayed as the graphic or, if you have set its **Style** as **Animation**, below, the point at which the playback of its video loop begins. This point can be set numerically or by using the slider available at the drop-down menu.

Style. If you have selected a video clip as your **Object Media**, this toggle allows you to set the graphic to display as a **Still** or to play as **Animation**.

Color Sets

Color Sets are used to set the colors for highlights which appear over your buttons as your viewer navigates your disc menu page. You can create four **Color Sets** for your disc, which can set to apply project-wide or customized for each menu page and/or for each individual button. A discussion of the functions of each color in a **Color Set** can be found under **Common Properties** on page 142.

Color Sets are not relevant to graphic files added to menu pages. They are a function of buttons and navigation highlights only.

Symbols

A

B

C

D

Index

Index

Made in the USA
Lexington, KY
15 April 2013

NEW DIRECTIONS
IN SCIENCE
FOR THE '90s
SCIENCE INTERACTIONS
GLENCOE

SCIENCE INTERACTIONS INVITES YOUR STUDENTS TO LOOK AT SCIENCE IN A WHOLE NEW WAY

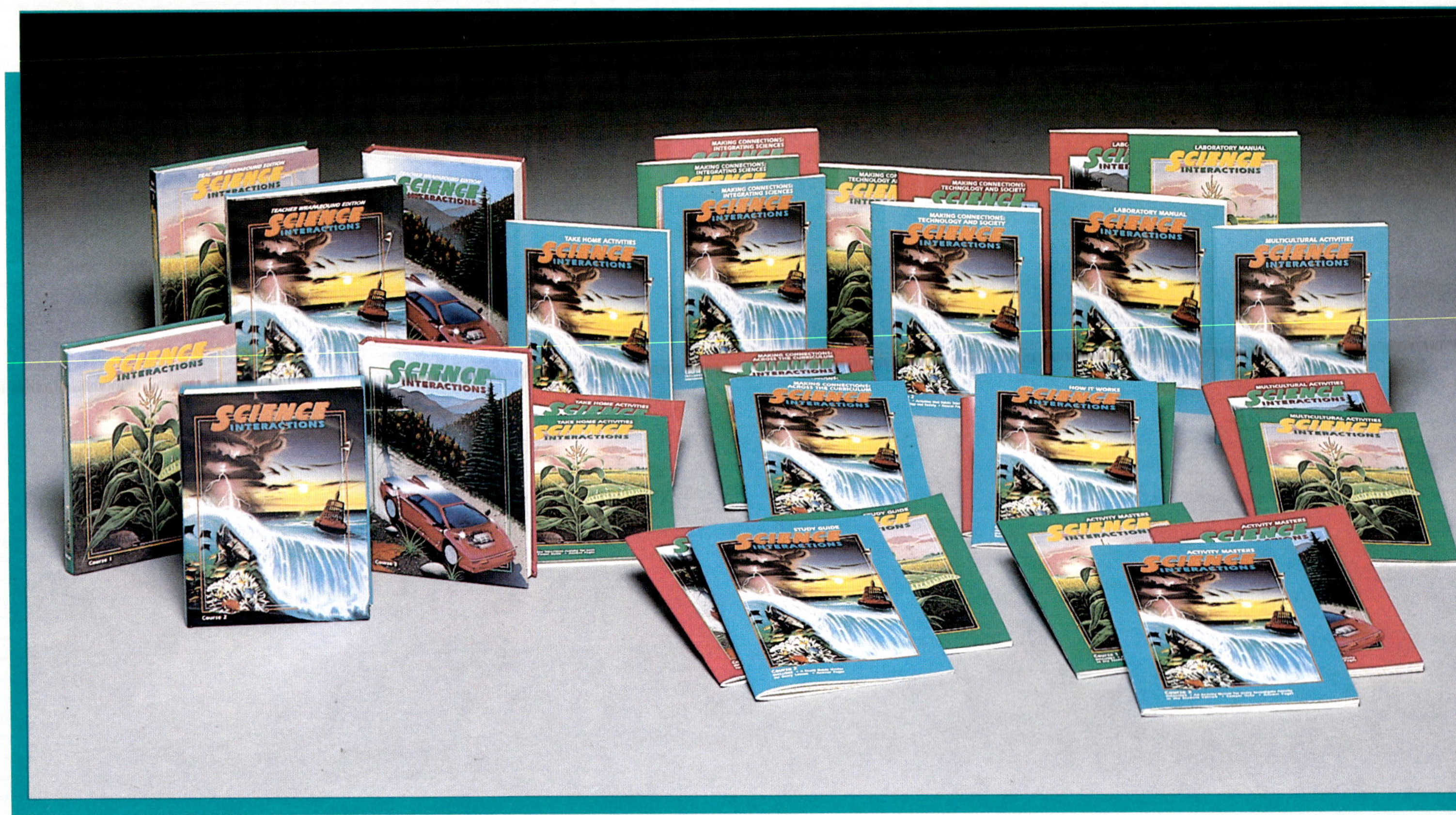

Responding to the recommendations of both Project 2061 (Science for all Americans) and Scope, Sequence and Coordination (SSC), Glencoe presents *Science Interactions*—a coordinated and integrated science program that offers your students a new way to learn science.

Science Interactions draws upon the students' own life experiences to engage them and to challenge their preconceptions. It places the "doing" of science before explanation and understanding before terminology.

An All-New Integrated Science Program That Connects All Areas of The Curriculum.

Senior author, Bill Aldridge, Executive Director of the National Science Teachers Association, and other leaders in the science reform movement developed this unique new series to help you meet the new challenges in science education and to improve your students' interest and performance in science. Unlike traditional science programs, *Science Interactions* stresses the interconnectedness of the sciences and the multifaceted connections between science and other disciplines, such as art, literature and history. Most important, it reflects a careful sequencing of content from all four science disciplines —chemistry, physics, biology and earth science—over a three-year period. Unifying science themes, such as energy and stability and change, help connect the major ideas presented throughout the series.

SCIENCE INTERACTIONS BRINGS NEW EXCITEMENT TO YOUR CLASSROOM

Science Interactions is a carefully designed sequence of units, chapters, and major teaching sections, with special features that guide students through the world of science. Core lessons within each chapter feature a variety of hands-on activities connected by an interesting narrative, enticing students to discover fundamental concepts on their own and to sharpen their critical thinking and problem-solving skills.

Course 1

1-1 Viewing Earth

OBJECTIVES

In this section, you will

- describe basic landforms such as mountains, plains, and plateaus;
- recognize the kind of landform on which you live.

KEY SCIENCE TERMS

landforms

OVER THE PLAINS, MOUNTAINS, AND PLATEAUS

Suppose you have tickets for an early morning flight from Washington, D.C., to California. You will be flying for about six hours. Thank goodness you were able to get a window seat! You want to see the land unfold beneath you. What will you observe as you fly over the United States? The Explore activity will give you some clues.

EXPLORE!

What does a profile of the United States look like?

You will need to borrow an atlas from the library for this activity. Find a physical map of the United States that shows its land features. Use the map to guide you as you draw a cross-section profile of the United States. Start with the west coast at the left, then move right to the east coast. Keep in mind that a profile shows the surface features as they would look if you cut the United States in half from the west to the east coast and looked at the surface from the cut edge. Some atlases contain profile maps. Use these as models for your own profile. Mark and label the different features. How do you think those features would look from the air?

Now that you have drawn a profile, you will see how your profile compares with the surface as seen from the air. The surface features you will see are called **landforms**. Mountains, plains, and plateaus are three common landforms in the United States.

The big day for your airplane trip arrives. You board the plane, settle yourself into your window seat, and fasten your seat belt. You're eager to compare your profile

4 CHAPTER 1 VIEWING EARTH AND SKY

EXPLORE are open-ended activities that allow students to observe, manipulate materials and discover things on their own.

CHAPTER OPENINGS introduce new scientific concepts with concrete, daily life examples students understand.

DID YOU EVER WONDER . . .

Why fire fighters put water on a fire?

Why water is called H_2O?

How a detergent gets your clothes clean?

You'll find the answers to these questions as you read this chapter.

Chapter 7

Combining Atoms

Did you ever dream of being a fire fighter? Fire fighters live exciting and dangerous lives. Every year they save many lives and protect valuable properties.

Today's fire fighters do more than just pour water on fires. If a tanker truck full of chemicals has an accident, the fire department may deal with it, spraying a special foam over the truck. If there is a gas leak, fire fighters may be first on the scene, deciding what precautions need to be taken until the leak is stopped. Perhaps they should be renamed "chemical reaction technicians."

Fire is a very rapid chemical reaction that releases heat and produces new compounds. Putting out a fire also involves chemical reactions. In this chapter, you'll learn more about the special language scientists use to describe such reactions.

EXPLORE!

What is in a fire extinguisher?

Put 20 grams of baking soda in a small test tube. Pour 50 mL of vinegar in a 500-mL flask. Carefully lower the test tube into the flask, making sure the baking soda does not contact the vinegar. Put a one-hole stopper containing a piece of tubing into the mouth of the flask. **CAUTION:** *If $C_3CO_2H + NaHCO_3$ react too fast, the stopper can blow out.*

While pointing the tubing into the sink, tilt the flask so that the vinegar wets the baking soda. Watch what happens.

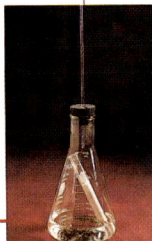

187

Course 3

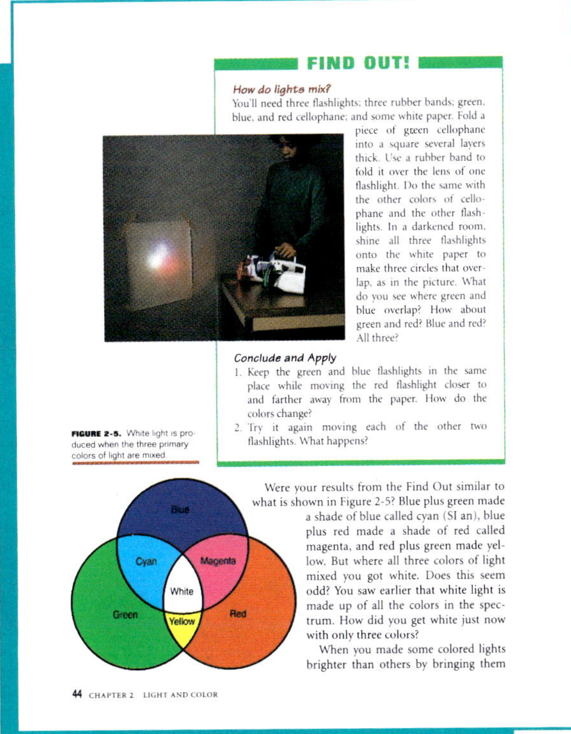

FIND OUT!

How do lights mix?

You'll need three flashlights; three rubber bands; green, blue, and red cellophane; and some white paper. Fold a piece of green cellophane into a square several layers thick. Use a rubber band to fold it over the lens of one flashlight. Do the same with the other colors of cellophane and the other flashlights. In a darkened room, shine all three flashlights onto the white paper to make three circles that overlap, as in the picture. What do you see where green and blue overlap? How about green and red? Blue and red? All three?

Conclude and Apply

1. Keep the green and blue flashlights in the same place while moving the red flashlight closer to and farther away from the paper. How do the colors change?
2. Try it again moving each of the other two flashlights. What happens?

FIGURE 2-5. White light is produced when the three primary colors of light are mixed.

Were your results from the Find Out similar to what is shown in Figure 2-5? Blue plus green made a shade of blue called cyan (SI an), blue plus red made a shade of red called magenta, and red plus green made yellow. But where all three colors of light mixed you got white. Does this seem odd? You saw earlier that white light is made up of all the colors in the spectrum. How did you get white light now with only three colors?

When you made some colored lights brighter than others by bringing them

44 CHAPTER 2 LIGHT AND COLOR

Course 1

FIND OUT! activities emphasize a specific concept, as students collect and analyze data.

I N V E S T I G A T E !

10-1 HOW ARE MINERALS IDENTIFIED?

In this activity, you will use tests for several mineral properties discussed in this chapter. You will use your test results to decide the identity of various mineral samples.

PROBLEM

How can mineral identities be determined from tests?

MATERIALS

mineral samples
hand lens
steel file
goggles
apron
streak plate
5% hydrochloric acid with dropper
Mohs' scale of hardness

PROCEDURE

1. Start a data table like the one shown below.
2. Use the hand lens to examine the mineral samples. **Observe** and record the luster and color for each sample.
3. Perform tests for hardness, streak, and fracture or cleavage. **Observe** and record the results.
4. Test the samples for other properties, such as reaction to hydrochloric acid. **CAUTION:** *Wear your goggles and apron. HCl may cause burns. If spills occur, rinse with water and notify your teacher.*

ANALYZE

1. **Analyze** the results you recorded in your table. **Compare** them with data in Appendices K and L. Then **infer** what each sample must be. Write the mineral's name in the appropriate space on your table.
2. Compare the usefulness of the different properties in identifying the given minerals. Which was most useful? Which property was least useful? Explain your answers.
3. **Compare and contrast** the ease of performing the various tests. Which test was the most difficult to do? Why?

CONCLUDE AND APPLY

4. How many tests should usually be performed before deciding what mineral a given sample is? Why?
5. **Going Further:** Pretend you are going on a geological expedition. Your purpose is to determine what minerals are abundant in the area of the expedition. What things will you pack to take along on your expedition? What activities will you be engaged in while you are on the expedition? How will you keep track of your observations? How might you share the data you obtain with others?

DATA AND OBSERVATIONS

MINERAL SAMPLE	COLOR	LUSTER	HARDNESS	STREAK	OTHER CHARACTERISTICS	THIS SAMPLE MUST BE:
A						
B						

298 CHAPTER 10 MINERALS AND THEIR USES

Course 2

Formal **INVESTIGATE!** activities teach your students to apply scientific methods and to manipulate quantitative data.

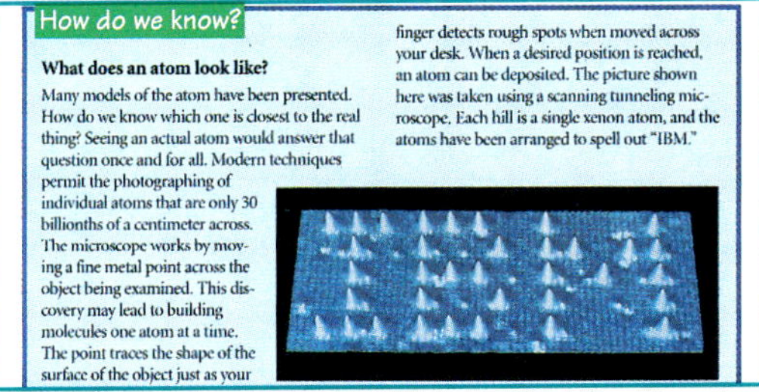

How do we know?

What does an atom look like?

Many models of the atom have been presented. How do we know which one is closest to the real thing? Seeing an actual atom would answer that question once and for all. Modern techniques permit the photographing of individual atoms that are only 30 billionths of a centimeter across. The microscope works by moving a fine metal point across the object being examined. This discovery may lead to building molecules one atom at a time. The point traces the shape of the surface of the object just as your finger detects rough spots when moved across your desk. When a desired position is reached, an atom can be deposited. The picture shown here was taken using a scanning tunneling microscope. Each hill is a single xenon atom, and the atoms have been arranged to spell out "IBM."

HOW DO WE KNOW? gives further insight into the discovery or development of important scientific ideas.

SKILLBUILDER

HYPOTHESIZING

When water waves pass through a thin gap the ones with a longer wavelength spread out more. Red light spreads more than blue light when passing through a thin slit. Form a hypothesis that would describe the difference between red and blue light using a wave model. If you need help, refer to the **Skill Handbook** on page 689.

SKILLBUILDER exercises offer students additional opportunities to practice skills and processes related to chapter content.

LOOKING BACK

UNIT 2 INTERACTIONS IN THE PHYSICAL WORLD

CONTENTS

UNIT FOCUS

In this unit, you investigated how substances on Earth differ. You observed how some materials dissolve in others, forming solutions, while others do not.

You can describe an iron nail using physical properties such as its size and mass, and chemical properties such as its ability to react with oxygen to form rust.

Physical and chemical properties can also be used to identify substances as acids, bases, and salts.

Try the exercises and activity that follow—they will challenge you to use and apply some of the ideas you learned in this unit.

CONNECTING IDEAS

1. Ocean water is very salty. You may have accidentally tasted some while swimming, or noticed that salt crystals formed on your body as you sat in the sun to dry after swimming. How does the salt appear on your skin?
2. **Analyzing Data:** Suppose you are trying to decide which vinegar to buy. One brand is much cheaper than the other brand. You wonder if the cheaper brand has been diluted with water. If this is true, the acidity of the cheaper, diluted vinegar should be lower than the more expensive brand. How could you design an experiment to see if the acidity was the same for both brands?

EXPLORING FURTHER

Make a card file of dangerous materials around your home. Identify acids, bases, and other toxic solutions and materials. Include the danger posed by each substance and the steps to be taken if the material is accidentally spilled or taken into your body. Use this activity to compile a first aid file for the home.

254

LOOKING AHEAD

UNIT 3 INTERACTIONS IN THE LIVING WORLD

CONTENTS

UNIT FOCUS

In Unit 2, you investigated materials of the physical world and observed how their physical and chemical properties allow you to identify materials. As you study Unit 3, you'll see how living things survive by interacting with the physical materials of our world. In addition, you will investigate how living organisms on Earth can be classified by their properties just as you classified physical materials in Unit 2. By looking at how plants, animals, and their environment interact, you will learn about the connections that link the biological and physical worlds together.

TRY IT

Look around your classroom. Can you think of ways to group the people in your class? The people in your classroom have many things in common. Everyone breathes, has a heartbeat, and eats. Grouping enables you to classify people based on similar characteristics. You can also observe differences among the people in your class. Perhaps you could group them using hair color or the color of their clothes. People share characteristics with other animals and plants as well. Make a drawing of a cactus plant, a bird, some weeds, and a person about your age. Show on your drawing some of the characteristics that are shared by all of these living things. You might show all of them obtaining energy. Also indicate in your picture some very obvious differences that would enable you to classify them as different organisms. After you've learned more about life forms on Earth, see how accurate your drawing is.

Course 1

LOOKING BACK and **LOOKING AHEAD** are unit opening and closing pages that focus on unifying themes and interactions among major topics in adjacent units.

SCIENCE INTERACTIONS ANSWERS THE QUESTION, "SO WHAT?"

Unique extension material at the end of each chapter provides in-depth exploration of the connections and applications of the science concepts discussed in the core lessons. EXPANDING YOUR VIEW, a six-page excursion through a variety of interesting articles, gives your students a wider perspective on the influence and relevance of science in their lives. Each article extends the science content of the chapter into another area of the curriculum or to society and technology.

EXPANDING YOUR VIEW

CONTENTS

A CLOSER LOOK

THE DENSITY OF A GAS

We move through a gas, air, all the time. Rarely are we aware of its presence. We know that gases exist and that they are made of atoms and molecules. How can we measure other properties of this generally invisible substance?

YOU TRY IT!

The purpose of this activity is to compare the density of dry ice, which is solid carbon dioxide (CO_2), with that of gaseous CO_2. Flatten a tall kitchen trash bag so there is no air in it. Use a cube-shaped piece of dry ice so you can measure its dimensions. **CAUTION:** *Dry ice is very cold and must be handled with extreme care because it could freeze your skin. Do not touch dry ice with your fingers. Always use tongs when handling the dry ice.* Quickly use a balance to find the mass of the dry ice cube. Then measure its dimensions, and immediately place the dry ice in a large plastic bag. Seal the bag tightly [illegible] you put the dry ice in. Try not to let any gaseous CO_2 escape.

Once the dry ice is sealed in the bag, you may begin your calculations of the volume and density of the dry ice. The volume is equal to the length times the width times the height, or $V = l \times w \times h$. The density is the mass divided by the volume, or $D = g/cm^3$.

While you are doing your calculations, the dry ice will be changing into a gas inside the plastic bag, so the bag will appear to be partially inflated. When you are sure there is no longer any solid dry ice in the bag, put the bag into a shape that is as boxlike as possible. When it is in this shape, measure its dimensions as well as you can. Then calculate the volume and the density. Since the bag is not perfectly boxlike, you will not be able to get measurements that are extremely accurate. However, with patience and care, you will get a close approximation. Because no CO_2 was allowed to escape, the mass of the dry ice will be about the same as the mass of the gaseous CO_2.

[illegible] the volume of the gaseous CO_2 compare with the volume of the dry ice? Is the number of molecules the same in the dry ice and in the gaseous CO_2? Why do the molecules in gaseous CO_2 take up more space?

CHAPTER 14 EXPANDING YOUR VIEW 431

A CLOSER LOOK examines a relevant chapter topic in more depth.

Course 2

EXPANDING YOUR VIEW

EARTH SCIENCE CONNECTION

RESEARCH GIANTS

Have you ever heard of an aerostat (AIR oh stat)? An aerostat is an aircraft that is supported by the buoyancy of a gas that is less dense than air.

Aerostats include blimps and dirigibles. The simplest kind is the balloon, because it has no means of propulsion or steering. In other words, a balloon just goes wherever the movement of the air takes it.

Basically, a balloon is a large bag that is filled with a gas that is lighter, or less dense, than air, for example, hot air or helium. This large bag displaces a lot of air, and has an upward force on it—called a buoyant force—that is equal to the weight of the displaced air.

These giant balloons can lift a load of instruments higher than a jetliner but lower than an orbiting satellite. The volume of helium needed to lift the load could be equal to the volume of a small house on the ground. Once the balloon reaches the altitude it's designed for, the volume of the gas could be the volume of 283 houses.

What kind of information can be obtained by balloons? Balloons carry many different kinds of instruments. Some have telescopes for viewing objects in space. Others collect and analyze the gases in space. Still others measure and record temperature, pressure, and the amounts and kinds of radiation from space. Ground-based radar can track balloons to find out about the speed and direction of high-altitude winds.

Information collected in these studies helps scientists understand the makeup and behavior of the gases in our atmosphere. As we learn more about this important part of the environment, we will be able to predict the atmosphere's behavior and to know how we can protect and preserve it.

WHAT DO YOU THINK?

What would be an advantage of taking pictures through telescopes on high-altitude balloons, rather than through ground-based telescopes? What are the disadvantages? In what ways are research balloons different from the multicolored balloon shown above?

432 CHAPTER 14 GASES, ATOMS, AND MOLECULES

EXPANDING YOUR VIEW

TECHNOLOGY CONNECTION

WHAT IS A VACUUM?

Vacuum cleaners, vacuum-sealed containers, vacuum-packed foods—just what is a vacuum?

A vacuum is a space that has no matter in it. There is no such thing as a complete vacuum because no one has ever been able to remove all the air molecules within a given space. Even in the near-vacuum of outer space, it is estimated that there are about 100 molecules of matter in every cubic meter of space.

Why would anyone want to create a vacuum in the first place? Have you ever used a straw to drink from a glass or can? When you draw on the straw, you remove some of the air inside the straw. This produces a lower pressure inside the straw than in the air outside—a partial vacuum. The greater air pressure of the air on the liquid pushes the liquid up the straw.

How else are partial vacuums used? A vacuum conducts heat poorly, so it's a good insulator. This property is used in devices such as insulating bottles. These bottles contain a double-walled glass container that has had the air removed from between the walls. Thermal energy can't pass through this space from either direction and so the liquid inside stays hot or cold.

You may recall when you studied sound that sound is a result of vibrations of molecules. Because there are no molecules—or atoms—in a vacuum, it does not conduct sound well.

Two of the most common uses for a vacuum are in your home and school. Light bulbs contain vacuums, which is why a light bulb will pop when it breaks. Since there is little air, or oxygen, in the light bulb, the burning filament lasts longer than it would if surrounded by air. You will learn more about this in a later chapter.

One of your favorite uses for a vacuum may be the television. The television tube works because there are very few air molecules in the tube. The beam inside the television tube would be too fuzzy and blurred to see if it had to travel through air molecules.

YOU TRY IT!

Roll a wax coated paper straw between your fingers a few times to remove the stiffness. Be sure to leave the straw open. Now press your finger tightly over one end so that no air can enter. Put the other end of the straw in your mouth and suck on it. What happens? Why did this happen?

CHAPTER 14 EXPANDING YOUR VIEW 433

Course 2

SCIENCE CONNECTION explores interconnections between one science field and another.

TECHNOLOGY and **SCIENCE AND SOCIETY CONNECTIONS** reveal the impact of science and technology on today's world.

Course 3

Course 2

TEENS IN SCIENCE shows real teenagers actively involved in various fields of science.

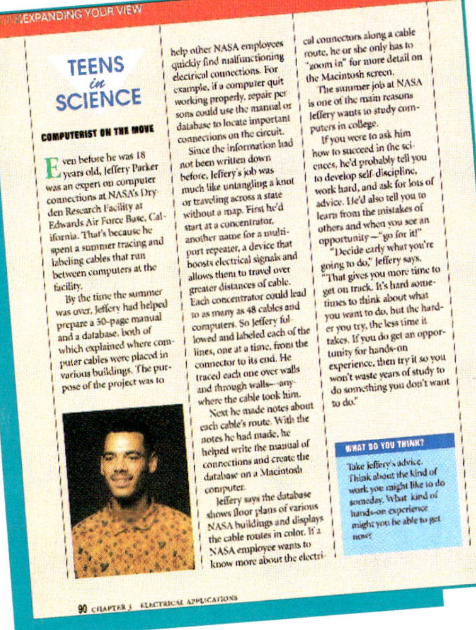

EXPANDING YOUR VIEW

TEENS *in* SCIENCE

COMPUTERIST ON THE MOVE

WHAT DO YOU THINK?

Take Jeffery's advice. Think about the kind of work you might like to do someday. What kind of hands-on experience might you be able to get now?

90 CHAPTER 3 ELECTRICAL APPLICATIONS

Course 3

EXPANDING YOUR VIEW

HOW IT WORKS

HOW DOES A MICROWAVE OVEN COOK FOOD?

YOU TRY IT!

380 CHAPTER 13 HEATING THE BODY

HOW IT WORKS applies scientific principles to the inner workings of everyday devices.

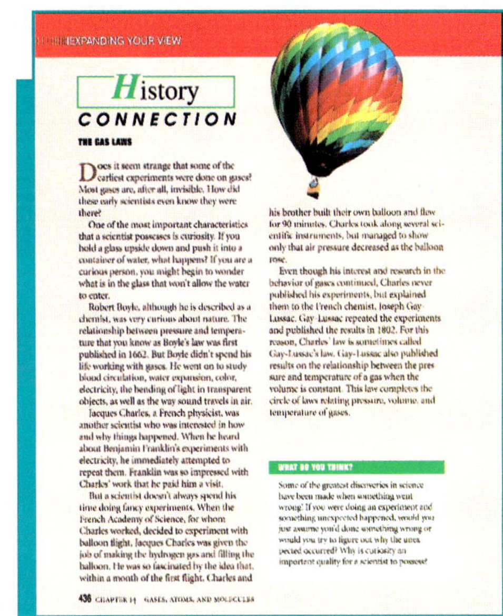

EXPANDING YOUR VIEW

History CONNECTION

THE GAS LAWS

WHAT DO YOU THINK?

436 CHAPTER 14 GASES, ATOMS, AND MOLECULES

CONNECTIONS to art, history, literature and other non-science subjects illustrate the relationships between science and these disciplines.

*T*hree pages of chapter-end material help students synthesize and review what they've learned.

REVIEWING MAIN IDEAS, with its combination of words and pictures, provides students with a unique summary of the chapter's main ideas, while the **Chapter Review** offers exercises to reinforce chapter content and to evaluate learning.

Chapter Review

USING KEY SCIENCE TERMS

UNDERSTANDING IDEAS

CRITICAL THINKING

PROBLEM SOLVING

CONNECTING IDEAS

2 CHAPTER REVIEW 61

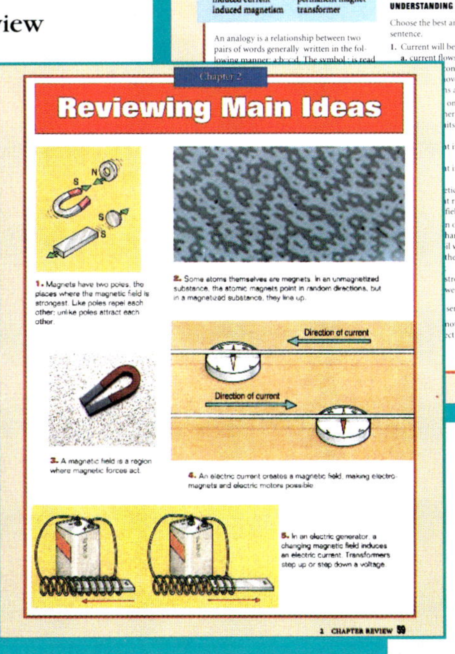

Reviewing Main Ideas

1. Magnets have two poles, the places where the magnetic field is strongest. Like poles repel each other; unlike poles attract each other.

2. Some atoms themselves are magnets. In an unmagnetized substance, the atomic magnets point in random directions, but in a magnetized substance, they line up.

3. A magnetic field is a region where magnetic forces act.

4. An electric current creates a magnetic field, making electromagnets and electric motors possible.

5. In an electric generator, a changing magnetic field induces an electric current. Transformers step up or step down a voltage.

2 CHAPTER REVIEW 59

Course 3

Teacher Wraparound Editions

ALL THE STRATEGIES AND RESOURCES YOU NEED, RIGHT AT YOUR FINGERTIPS

The Teacher Wraparound Editions are comprehensive resources for teaching *Science Interactions.* To put you at ease with the scope and content of the program's new curriculum, the Teacher Edition offers detailed explanations of the conceptual and thematic development of each chapter and section. It describes in detail not only *what* is being taught, but also *why,* and *how* it connects to themes, students' preconceptions and previously studied topics.

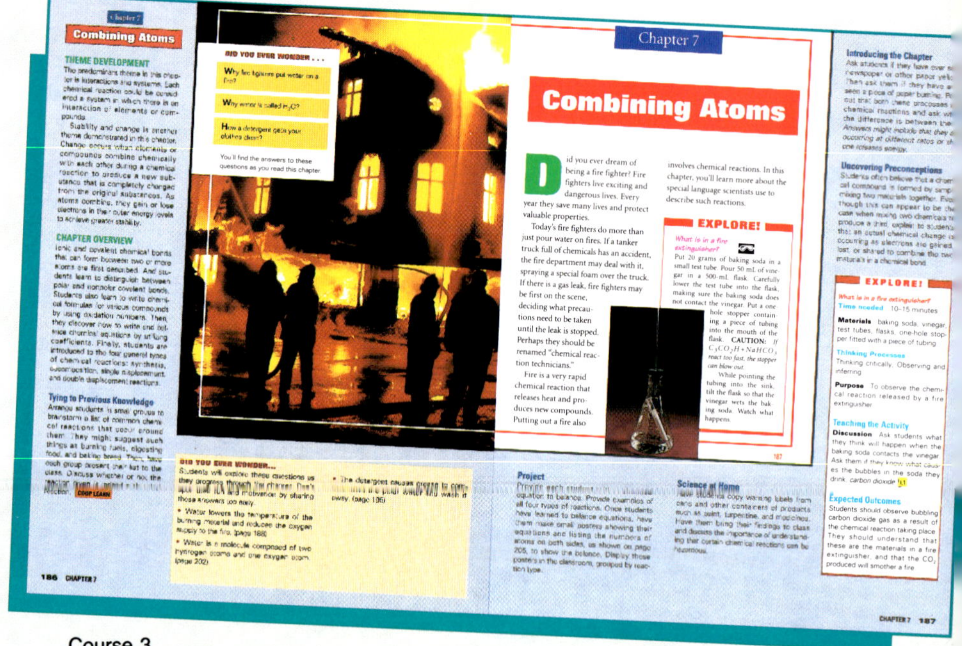
Chapter 7

Combining Atoms

THEME DEVELOPMENT

The predominant theme in this chapter is interactions and systems. Each chemical reaction could be considered a system in which there is an interaction of elements or compounds.

Stability and change is another theme demonstrated in this chapter. Change occurs when elements or compounds combine chemically with each other during a chemical reaction to produce a new substance that is completely changed from the original substances. As atoms combine, they gain or lose electrons in their outer energy levels to achieve greater stability.

CHAPTER OVERVIEW

Ionic and covalent chemical bonds that can form between two or more atoms are first described. And students learn to distinguish between polar and nonpolar covalent bonds. Students also learn to write chemical formulas for various compounds by using oxidation numbers. Then, they discover how to write and balance chemical equations by utilizing coefficients. Finally, students are introduced to the four general types of chemical reactions: synthesis, decomposition, single displacement, and double displacement reactions.

Tying to Previous Knowledge

Arrange students in small groups to brainstorm a list of common chemical reactions that occur around them. They might suggest such things as burning fuels, digesting food, and baking bread. Then, have each group present their list to the class. Discuss whether or not the reaction ... COOP LEARN

DID YOU EVER WONDER . . .

Why fire fighters put water on a fire?

Why water is called H_2O?

How a detergent gets your clothes clean?

You'll find the answers to these questions as you read this chapter.

DID YOU EVER WONDER...

Students will explore these questions as they progress through the chapter. ... those answers too early.

• Water lowers the temperature of the burning material and reduces the oxygen supply to the fire. (page 188)

• Water is a molecule composed of two hydrogen atoms and one oxygen atom. (page 202)

186 CHAPTER 7

Chapter 7

Combining Atoms

Did you ever dream of being a fire fighter? Fire fighters live exciting and dangerous lives. Every year they save many lives and protect valuable properties.

Today's fire fighters do more than just pour water on fires. If a tanker truck full of chemicals has an accident, the fire department may deal with it, spraying a special foam over the truck. If there is a gas leak, fire fighters may be first on the scene, deciding what precautions need to be taken until the leak is stopped. Perhaps they should be renamed "chemical reaction technicians."

Fire is a very rapid chemical reaction that releases heat and produces new compounds. Putting out a fire also involves chemical reactions. In this chapter, you'll learn more about the special language scientists use to describe such reactions.

EXPLORE!

What is in a fire extinguisher?

Put 20 grams of baking soda in a small test tube. Pour 50 mL of vinegar in a 500-mL flask. Carefully lower the test tube into the flask, making sure the baking soda does not contact the vinegar. Put a one-hole stopper containing a piece of tubing into the mouth of the flask. CAUTION: If $C_3CO_2H + NaHCO_3$ react too fast, the stopper can blow out.

While pointing the tubing into the sink, tilt the flask so that the vinegar wets the baking soda. Watch what happens.

187

Course 3

CHAPTER OPENING pages highlight concepts and themes to be developed.

Chapter 21
Simple Organisms

CHAPTER ORGANIZER

SECTION	OBJECTIVES	ACTIVITIES/FEATURES	TEACHER CLASSROOM RESOURCES	OTHER RESOURCES
Chapter Opener		**Explore!** What does yeast look like? p. 627		
21-1 Living Organisms (2 days)	1. **Classify** an organism as being one-celled or many-celled. 2. **Recognize** the difficulty of determining whether or not viruses are living. 3. **Conclude** that a one-celled organism is capable of carrying out the same life functions as a many-celled organism.	**Find Out!** How do two organisms compare to each other? p. 628 **Investigate 21-1:** Shapes of Viruses, p. 631	**Study Guide,** p. 72 **Activity Masters, Investigate 21-1,** pp. 85-88 **Multicultural Activities,** p. 45 **Making Connections: Integrating Sciences,** p. 45 **Making Connections: Technology & Sciences,** p. 45	**Laboratory Manual,** pp. 125-128, Monerans **Color Transparency and Master 42,** Virus Life Cycles ***STVS:** *Bacteriophage,* Plants and Simple Organisms (Disc 4, Side 1) *Mapping a Virus,* Plants and Simple Organisms (Disc 4, Side 1)
21-2 Classifying Simple Organisms (2 days)	1. **Identify** the general traits of three kingdoms—Monera, Protist, and Fungi. 2. **Learn** how scientists classify simple organisms.	**Explore!** In what ways can you classify organisms? p. 634	**Study Guide,** p. 73 **Take Home Activities,** p. 32 **Making Connections: Across the Curriculum,** p. 45 **Concept Mapping,** p. 29	**Laboratory Manual,** pp. 127-130, Life in Pond Water **Laboratory Manual,** pp. 131-132, Shapes of Bacteria **Color Transparency and Master 41,** Protists ***STVS:** *Bacterial Control of Mosquitos,* Plants and Simple Organisms (Disc 4, Side 1) *Fungal Collection for Research,* Plants and Simple Organisms (Disc 4, Side 1)
21-3 Simple Organisms Doing Their Jobs (4 days)	1. **Describe** the major characteristics and activities of monerans, protists, and fungi. 2. **Describe** the way monerans, protists, and fungi affect other living things.	**Find Out!** What causes milk to spoil? p. 637 **Skillbuilder:** Comparing and Contrasting, p. 639 **Skillbuilder:** Hypothesizing, p. 640 **Explore!** What organisms live in pond water? 641 **Explore!** What can you learn from a diatom? 642 **Find Out!** What characteristics do different protozoans have? p. 643 **Explore!** What can you learn about fungi by observing them? p. 645 **Skillbuilder:** Classifying, p. 646 **Investigate 21-2:** What is Needed for Molds to Grow? 647 **Explore!** How do fungi reproduce? 648	**Study Guide,** p. 74 **Critical Thinking/Problem Solving,** p. 29 **How It Works,** p. 19 **Multicultural Activities,** p. 46 **Flex Your Brain,** p. 8 **Activity Masters, Investigate 21-2,** pp. 87-88 **Review and Assessment,** pp. 85-88	***STVS:** *Disease Resistant Tomatoes,* Plants and Simple Organisms (Disc 4, Side 1) *Bacterial Digestion of Lignin,* Plants and Simple Organisms (Disc 4, Side 1) *New Uses for Algae,* Plants and Simple Organisms (Disc 4, Side 1) **Computer Test Bank**
Expanding Your View	A Closer Look **The Versatile Molds,** p. 649 Earth Science Connection **Bacteria that Solve Pollution Problems,** p. 650	Science/Society **Using Viruses to Fight Disease,** 651 History Connection **Louis Pasteur,** p. 653 Teens in Science **When are Gibberellins Too Much of a Good Thing?** p. 654		**Spanish Resources** **Cooperative Learning Resource Guide** **Lab and Safety Skills**

***Science and Technology Videodisc Series**

ACTIVITY MATERIALS

EXPLORE!	INVESTIGATE!	FIND OUT!
Page 627 dry yeast, warm tap water, microscope slide, microscope **Page 641** wet mount slide of pond water, microscope, wet mount slides of tap water **Page 642** diatomite, slide, coverslip, water, microscope, scrapings from the inside walls of a fishtank **Page 645** store-bought mushroom, hand lens **Page 648** bread mold, hand lens, slide, coverslip, water, microscope	**Page 631** 3.7 cm × 0.7 cm bolt; 2 nuts to fit bolt; 2 pieces #22-gauge wire, 14 cm long; polystyrene ball, 4.5 cm in diameter; pipe cleaners, cut in 2-cm lengths **Page 647** 8 small paper cups, sugarless dry cereal, dry macaroni, dry potato flakes, dry crackers without salt, water, hand lens, plastic wrap, labels, cotton swabs, mold source	**Page 628** wet mount slide of *Ulva,* wet mount slide of paramecium, flashlight, microscope **Page 637** spoiled milk, unspoiled milk, slide, microscope, methylene blue stain, coverslips **Page 643** wet mount slides of *amoeba* and *paramecium,* labels, microscope

KEY TO TEACHING STRATEGIES

Teaching strategies have been coded for varying learning styles and abilities. As you review teaching strategies in the margin, the following designations will help you decide which activities are appropriate for your students.

L1 Level 1 activities are basic activities and should be within the ability range of all students.

L2 Level 2 activities are average activities and should be within the ability range of the average to above-average student.

L3 Level 3 activities are challenging activities designed for the ability range of above-average students.

LEP LEP activities should be within the ability range of Limited English Proficiency students.

COOP LEARN Cooperative Learning activities are designed for small group work.

ADDITIONAL MATERIALS

SOFTWARE	AUDIOVISUAL
Cells, Educational Activities, Inc. *The Cell,* Queue. *Classification of Living Things,* Educational Activities, Inc. *The Taxonomy Game,* Queue.	*Microscopes and Modern Science,* filmstrip, National Geographic. *Cells: A First Film,* film, BFA. *The Cell: Structural Unit of Life,* film, Coronet/MTI. *The Living Cell: An Introduction,* film, EBEC. *Classifying Plants and Animals,* film, Coronet/MTI. *Bacteria—Friend and Foe,* film, EBEC. *Simple Organisms: Bacteria,* film, Coronet/MTI. *Classify—Classification Key Prog.,* film, Diversified Education Enterprise.

626A CHAPTER 21 · CHAPTER 21 626B

Course 2

CHAPTER ORGANIZER helps you plan effective lessons by identifying the objectives, activities and resources available for each section of every chapter.

Course 2

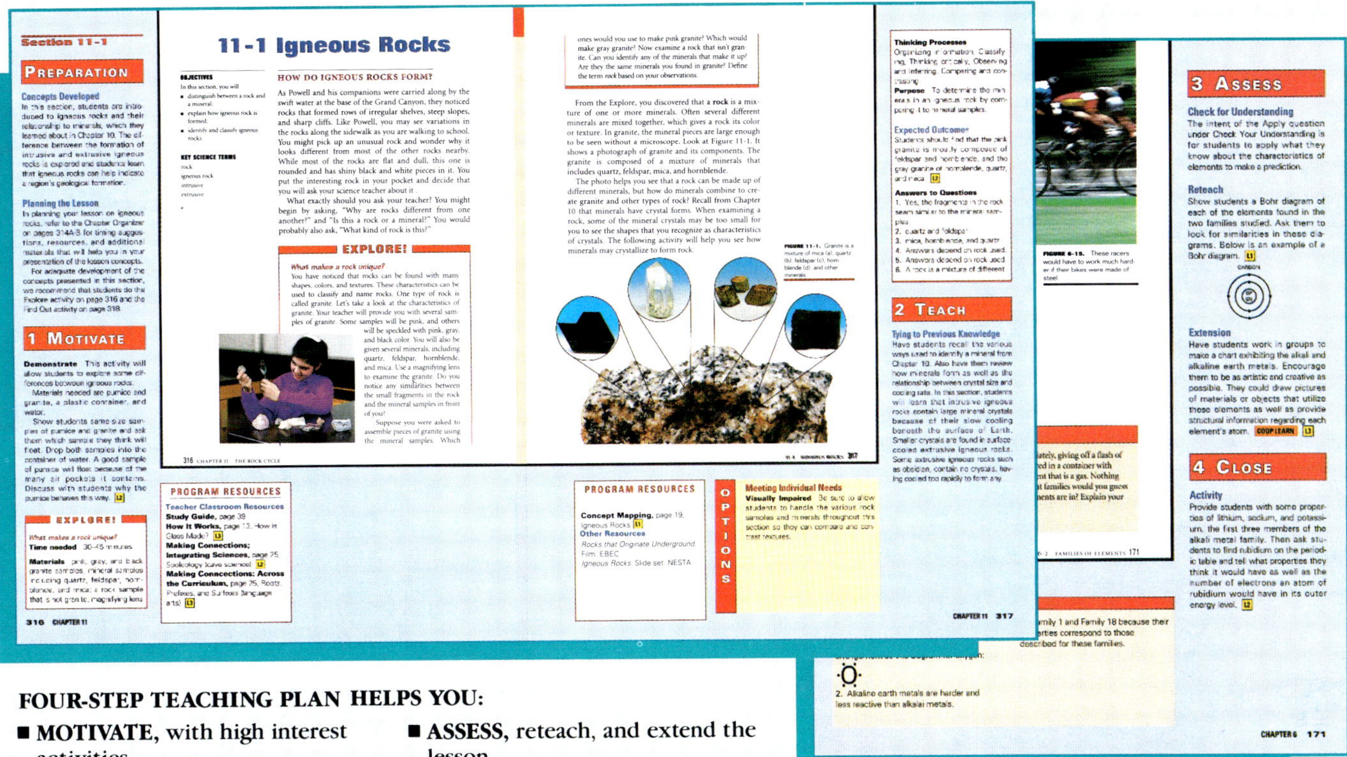

Course 3

FOUR-STEP TEACHING PLAN HELPS YOU:

- **MOTIVATE,** with high interest activities.
- **TEACH,** with a variety of active-learning strategies.
- **ASSESS,** reteach, and extend the lesson.
- **CLOSE,** with summarizing activities and discussions.

Uncovering Preconceptions

Students often believe that a chemical compound is formed by simply mixing two materials together. Even though this can appear to be the case when mixing two chemicals to produce a third, explain to students that an actual chemical change is occurring as electrons are gained, lost, or shared to combine the two

UNCOVERING PRECONCEPTIONS aids in dealing with students' common misconceptions about certain science principles and allows you to focus instruction on areas students find most difficult to grasp.

PROGRAM RESOURCES

Teacher Classroom Resources

Study Guide, page 21

Critical Thinking/Problem Solving, page 13, In the World of the Very Small L3

Multicultural Activities, page 14, Dr. Lloyd Quarterman L2

Other Resources

PROGRAM RESOURCES help you select the program's ancillary materials to reinforce, enrich, and assess student learning.

OPTIONS

Multicultural Perspectives

Meredith Gourdine, an African-American scientist, won a silver medal in track at the 1952 Olympics. His research into producing high-voltage electricity from natural gas has possible applications in preserving foods, burning coal more efficiently, and desalinization.

MULTICULTURAL PERSPECTIVES spotlights the contributions to science made by persons and societies from diverse cultures.

TYING TO PREVIOUS KNOWLEDGE explains how new chapter concepts relate to ideas previously covered.

MAKING CONNECTIONS helps you connect lesson concepts to non-science fields and to daily living.

MEETING INDIVIDUAL NEEDS offers you teaching strategies for students who present unique challenges.

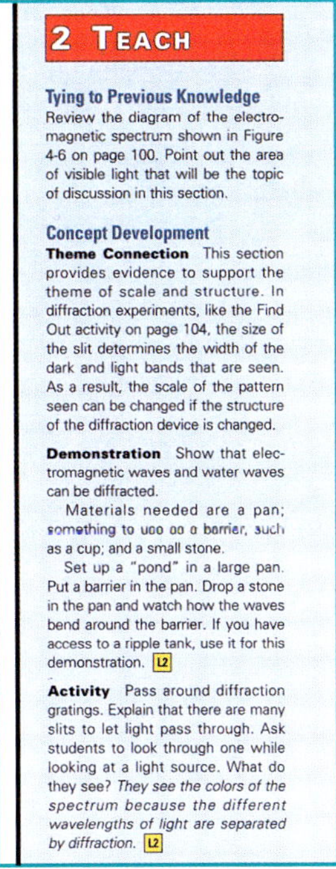

2 TEACH

Tying to Previous Knowledge
Review the diagram of the electromagnetic spectrum shown in Figure 4-6 on page 100. Point out the area of visible light that will be the topic of discussion in this section.

Concept Development
Theme Connection This section provides evidence to support the theme of scale and structure. In diffraction experiments, like the Find Out activity on page 104, the size of the slit determines the width of the dark and light bands that are seen. As a result, the scale of the pattern seen can be changed if the structure of the diffraction device is changed.

Demonstration Show that electromagnetic waves and water waves can be diffracted.

Materials needed are a pan; something to use as a barrier, such as a cup; and a small stone.

Set up a "pond" in a large pan. Put a barrier in the pan. Drop a stone in the pan and watch how the waves bend around the barrier. If you have access to a ripple tank, use it for this demonstration. L2

Activity Pass around diffraction gratings. Explain that there are many slits to let light pass through. Ask students to look through one while looking at a light source. What do they see? *They see the colors of the spectrum because the different wavelengths of light are separated by diffraction.* L2

TEACHING STRATEGIES are coded for individual student needs and ability levels, from those who require a little extra help to those who show exceptional aptitude.

UNSURPASSED TEACHER RESOURCES EXTEND AND ENRICH THE LEARNING EXPERIENCE

From hands-on activities to overhead transparencies to computer testbanks, *Science Interactions* program resources present you with an extensive array of options for dealing with the diverse needs of your students.

TAKE HOME ACTIVITIES: Safe activities for students to do at home with parents. Fun to do, they directly support your classroom instruction.

MAKING CONNECTIONS: Three unique booklets contain activities and exercises that allow your students to explore a wide variety of connections to science. They are **Making Connections: Integrating Sciences, Across the Curriculum,** and **Technology and Science.**

HOW IT WORKS: Students discover the science behind how everyday things work.

MULTICULTURAL ACTIVITIES: Biographies, readings, and activities address past and present contributions to science by persons and societies from various cultural backgrounds.

LABORATORY MANUAL: One or more additional labs for each chapter, complete with set-up diagrams, data tables, and space for student responses.

STUDY GUIDE: Section-by-section masters reinforce basic processes and content presented in the student text. Ideal for average to below-average ability students, it is also available in a consumable student edition.

ACTIVITY MASTERS: Copy masters of each INVESTIGATE activity in the student text.

CRITICAL THINKING/PROBLEM SOLVING: Readings and exercises that require students to apply critical thinking and problem-solving skills. Useful with average and above-average ability students.

CONCEPT MAPPING: One concept map for each chapter to reinforce relationships and connections between concepts and processes.

LESSON PLANS: Complete lesson plans for each major section in student text.

LAB AND SAFETY SKILLS: Reinforces basic laboratory and safety skills, including graphing and measurement.

VIDEODISC CORRELATION: By using bar code reader or key pad, you can access all images in Optical Data's life, earth, and physical science videodiscs that correlate with the content of *Science Interactions*.

COMPUTER TEST BANKS: A user-friendly and flexible tool for designing and generating your own tests. Available in IBM, Apple, and Macintosh versions.

REVIEW AND ASSESSMENT: Uses a variety of questioning strategies and formats to assess your students' understanding of concepts, processes and activities.

COLOR TRANSPARENCY PACKAGE: Two full-color transparencies per chapter and Transparency Masters Booklet, containing blackline masters of all color transparencies and student study sheets. Conveniently stored in a three-ring binder.

SPANISH RESOURCES BOOKLET: A complete Spanish-English glossary and translations of all objectives, key terms, INVESTIGATE activities and main ideas for every chapter.

COOPERATIVE LEARNING RESOURCE GUIDE: Contains strategies and practical tips for using cooperative learning techniques in teaching *Science Interactions*.

SCIENCE AND TECHNOLOGY VIDEODISC SERIES

Produced and narrated by Don Herbert, television's "Mr. Wizard," this program includes seven discs, with more than 280 full-motion 90-second reports on a wide spectrum of science topics, including current research, innovations in technology, science careers, and science and society issues. The series also provides reinforcement in science methods and laboratory techniques.

The Science Interactions Videodisc Teacher Guides shows you how to integrate the videoreports into your science lessons, identifies the science concepts supported, and suggests ways to use the series to introduce and extend lessons. Bar codes and a quick directory make access fast and simple.

THE SCIENCE CURRICULUM OF THE FUTURE IS HERE TODAY

Science Interactions brings science to life, with hands-on-learning and applications that are meaningful to students. With this series, you can demonstrate that science isn't simply something they study, it's something they live.

COMPONENTS

Title	Course 1	Course 2	Course 3
Student Edition	0-02-826032-5	0-02-826098-8	0-02-826106-2
Teacher Wraparound Edition	0-02-826033-3	0-02-826099-6	0-02-826107-0
Teacher Classroom Resource Package	0-02-826034-1	0-02-826100-3	0-02-826108-9
Laboratory Manual: Student Edition	0-02-826035-X	0-02-826087-2	0-02-826109-7
* Laboratory Manual: Teacher's Edition	0-02-826036-8	0-02-826088-0	0-02-826110-0
Study Guide: Student Edition	0-02-826037-6	0-02-826089-9	0-02-826111-9
* Study Guide: Teacher's Edition	0-02-826038-4	0-02-826090-2	0-02-826101-1
* Review and Assessment	0-02-826039-2	0-02-826091-0	0-02-826102-X
* Concept Mapping	0-02-826041-4	0-02-826092-9	0-02-826103-8
* Activity Worksheets	0-02-826042-2	0-02-826093-7	0-02-826104-6
* Critical Thinking/ Problem Solving	0-02-826043-0	0-02-826094-5	0-02-826105-4
* Multicultural Activities	0-02-826044-9	0-02-826076-7	0-02-826112-7
* Transparency Masters	0-02-826045-7	0-02-826077-5	0-02-826113-5
* Lesson Plans	0-02-826046-5	0-02-826078-3	0-02-826114-3
* Take Home Activities	0-02-826047-3	0-02-826079-1	0-02-826115-1
* How It Works	0-02-826048-1	0-02-826080-5	0-02-826116-X
* Making Connections: Integrating Sciences	0-02-826049-X	0-02-826081-3	0-02-826117-8
* Making Connections: Across the Curriculum	0-02-826050-3	0-02-826082-1	0-02-826118-6
* Making Connections: Technology & Society	0-02-826051-1	0-02-826083-X	0-02-826119-4
* Videodisc Correlation (Optical Data)	0-02-826054-6	0-02-826084-8	0-02-826121-6
* Science & Technology Videodisc Guide	0-02-826055-4	0-02-826085-6	0-02-826122-4
* Transparency Package	0-02-826058-9	0-02-826066-X	0-02-826125-9
Test Bank, IBM	0-02-826059-7	0-02-826067-8	0-02-826126-7
Test Bank, Apple	0-02-826060-0	0-02-826068-6	0-02-826127-5
Test Bank, Macintosh	0-02-826158-5	0-02-826162-3	0-02-826166-6
* Spanish Resources	0-02-826062-7	0-02-826070-8	0-02-826129-1
* Cooperative Learning Resource Guide	0-02-826052-X	0-02-826052-X	0-02-826052-X
* Lab and Safety Skills	0-02-826053-8	0-02-826053-8	0-02-826053 8

*Included in Teacher Classroom Package

Science and Technology Videodisc Series

Individual Disc Packages With Teacher Guide

Disc 1: Physics	0-02-826135-6
Disc 2: Chemistry	0-02-826136-4
Disc 3: Earth & Space	0-02-826137-2
Disc 4: Plants & Simple Organisms	0-02-826138-0
Disc 5: Animals	0-02-826139-9
Disc 6: Ecology	0-02-826140-2
Disc 7: Human Biology	0-02-826141-0

Series Package Contains 7 Discs With Teacher Guide

Series Package	0-02-826149-6

For more information contact your nearest regional office or call 1-800-334-7344.

1. Northeast Region
GLENCOE
17 Riverside Drive
Nashua, NH 03062
800-424-3451
603-880-4701

2. Mid-Atlantic Region
GLENCOE
5 Terri Lane
Suite 5
Burlington, NJ 08016
609-386-7353

3. Atlantic-Southeast Region
GLENCOE
Brookside Park
One Harbison Way, Suite 101
Columbia, SC 29212
803-732-2365

4. Southeast Region
GLENCOE
6510 Jimmy Carter Boulevard
Norcross, GA 30071
404-446-7493

5. Mid-America Region
GLENCOE
4635 Hilton Corporate Drive
Columbus, OH 43232
614-759-6600

6. Mid-Continent Region
GLENCOE
846 East Algonquin Road
Schaumburg, IL 60173
708-397-8448

7. Southwest Region
GLENCOE
320 Westway Place, Suite 550
Arlington, TX 76018
817-784-2100

8. Western Region
GLENCOE
610 East 42nd Street, #102
Boise, ID 83714
208-378-4002
Includes Alaska

9. California Region
GLENCOE
15319 Chatsworth Street
P. O. Box 9609
Mission Hills, CA 91346
818-898-1391

Canada
Maxwell Macmillan Canada
1200 Eglinton Avenue, East
Suite 200
Don Mills, Ontario M3C 3NI
Telephone: 416-449-6030
Telex: 069.59372
Telefax: 416-449-0068

Overseas and Hawaii
Macmillan/McGraw-Hill
International
866 Third Avenue
New York, NY 10022-6299
Telephone: 212-702-3276
Telex: 225925 MACM UR
Telefax: 212-605-9377

Glencoe Catholic School Region
GLENCOE
25 Crescent Street, 1st Floor
Stamford, CT 06906
203-964-9109

GLENCOE

Macmillan/McGraw-Hill
P.O. Box 508
Columbus, Ohio 43216

SC90592-3

Teacher Wraparound Edition

SCIENCE INTERACTIONS

Course 1

Bill Aldridge
Russell Aiuto
Jack Ballinger
Anne Barefoot
Linda Crow
Ralph M. Feather, Jr.
Albert Kaskel
Craig Kramer
Edward Ortleb
Susan Snyder
Paul W. Zitzewitz

Macmillan/McGraw–Hill

New York, New York   Columbus, Ohio   Mission Hills, California   Peoria, Illinois

A GLENCOE PROGRAM

Science Interactions

Student Edition
Teacher Wraparound Edition
Teacher Classroom Resource Package
Laboratory Manual: SE
Laboratory Manual: TE
Study Guide: SE
Study Guide: TE
Transparency Package
Computer Test Bank
Spanish Resources
Science and Technology Videodisc Series
Science and Technology Videodisc Teacher Guide

3T, 4T, Pictures Unlimited; **6T,** courtesy Bill Aldridge; **7T** (t), courtesy Russ Aiuto, (b), Tim Courlas; **8T,** courtesy Paul Zitzewitz; **9T,** courtesy Ralph Feather; **10T,** courtesy Jack Ballinger; **28T,** courtesy Susan Snyder; **29T** (t), courtesy Craig Kramer, (b), BLT Productions; **30T** (1), Kenji Kerins, (r), Studiohio, (b), Ken Ferguson; **31T,** courtesy Al Kaskel; **34T,** Ted Rice; **35T,** courtesy Ed Ortleb; **37T,** courtesy Linda Crow; **38T,** courtesy Anne Barefoot; **39T** (t,b), Doug Martin, (1), Cobalt Productions; **41T,** Crown Studios; **43T,** Doug Martin; **44T,** Studiohio; **45T,** Ken Frick; **46T,** Doug Martin; **47T,** Crown Studios; **48T,** Doug Martin; **49T,** Doug Martin; **50T,** Pictures Unlimited.

Send all inquiries to:

GLENCOE DIVISION
Macmillan/McGraw-Hill
936 Eastwind Drive
Westerville, OH 43081

ISBN 0-02-826033-3

Printed in the United States of America
3 4 5 6 7 8 9 V H 00 99 98 97 96 95 94 93

INTRODUCING THE AUTHOR TEAM

Bill Aldridge has been Executive Director of the National Science Teachers Association for the past 12 years. He came to NSTA after having served for 3 years in the Division of Science Education Development and Research, Science Education Directorate of the National Science Foundation. He received his B.S. degree in physics from the University of Kansas, where he also received M.S. degrees in both physics and educational evaluation. He also has an M.Ed. in science education from Harvard University. Mr. Aldridge taught high school physics and mathematics for 6 years, and physics at the college level for 17 years. He has authored numerous publications, including two textbooks, nine monographs, and articles in several journals and magazines. As Executive Director of NSTA, Mr. Aldridge has worked with the United States Congress and with government agencies in designing and producing support programs for science education. He is the recipient of awards and recognition from the National Science Foundation and the American Association of Physics Teachers and is a fellow of the American Association for the Advancement of Science. In addition to directing the National Science Teachers Association, he directs several national projects in science education.

Russell Aiuto is currently the Director of Research and Development for the National Science Teachers Association in Washington, DC. Throughout his career, Dr. Aiuto has held several prominent positions, including Director of the Division of Teacher Preparation and Enhancement of the National Science Foundation, President of Hiram College in Hiram, Ohio, and Provost of Albion College in Albion, Michigan. He also has 30 years experience teaching biology and genetics at the high school and college levels. Dr. Aiuto received his B.A. from Eastern Michigan University and his M.A. and Ph.D. degrees from the University of North Carolina. He has received numerous awards, including the Phi Beta Kappa Faculty Scholar Award, Campus Teaching Award, and Honors Program Faculty Award from Albion College. His professional memberships include Sigma Xi and the American Society of Human Genetics.

Jack Ballinger is a chemistry professor at St. Louis Community College in St. Louis, Missouri, where he has taught for 22 years. He received his B.S. degree in chemistry at Eastern Illinois University, his M.S. degree in organic chemistry at Southern Illinois University, and his Ed.D. at Southern Illinois University. He is a member of the American Chemical Society, the National Education Association, and the National Science Teachers Association. Dr. Ballinger has received the Manufacturing Chemists Association Award for Excellence in Chemistry Teaching.

Anne Barefoot is a veteran physics and chemistry teacher, with 35 years experience. She currently teaches at Whiteville High School in Whiteville, NC, and has served as department chair. A past recipient of the Presidential Award for Outstanding Science Teaching, Ms. Barefoot holds a B.S. and an M.S. from East Carolina University, and a Specialist Certificate from the University of South Carolina. Other awards include Whiteville City Schools Teacher of the Year, Sigma Xi Award, and the North Carolina Business Award for Science Teaching. Ms. Barefoot is the former District IV Director of the National Science Teachers Association, the former president of the Association of Presidential Awardees in Science Teaching, and is a member of the American Association of Physics Teachers, the American Chemical Society, and the National Science Teachers Association.

Linda Crow is an assistant professor in the Department of Community Medicine at Baylor College of Medicine. She is the project director of the Houston Scope, Sequence and Coordination (SS&C) Project. In addition to 21 years as an award-winning science teacher at college and high school levels, Dr. Crow is a recognized speaker at education workshops both in the United States and abroad. Dr. Crow received her B.S., M.Ed., and Ed.D. degrees from the University of Houston. She was named the 1989 OHAUS Winner for Innovations in College Science Teaching. Her professional memberships include the National Science Teachers Association, National Association of Geology Teachers, American Educational Research Association,

and the National Association for Research in Science Teaching.

Ralph M. Feather, Jr. teaches geology, astronomy, and Earth science, and serves as Science Department Chair in the Derry Area School District in Derry, PA. Mr. Feather has 21 years of teaching experience in secondary science. He holds a B.S. in geology and an M.Ed. in geoscience from Indiana University of Pennsylvania and is currently working on his Ph.D. at the University of Pittsburgh. Mr. Feather received the 1991 Presidential Award for Excellence in Science Teaching. He also received the 1991 Award for Excellence in Earth Science Teaching from the Geological Society of America. He is a member of the National Science Teachers Association, the American Association for the Advancement of Science, and the Association for Supervision and Curriculum Development.

Albert Kaskel has 31 years experience teaching science, the last 24 at Evanston Township High School, Evanston, Illinois. His teaching experience includes biology, A. P. biology, physical science, and chemistry. He holds a B.S. in biology from Roosevelt University in Chicago and an M.Ed. degree from DePaul University. Mr. Kaskel is a member of the National Science Teachers Association and the National Association of Biology Teachers. He received the Outstanding Biology Teacher Award for the State of Illinois in 1984 and the Teacher Excellence Award from Evanston Township High School in 1985.

Craig Kramer has been a physics teacher for 17 years. He is currently the Science Department Chairperson at Bexley High School in Bexley, Ohio. Mr. Kramer received a B.A. in physics and a B.S. in science and math education, and an M.A. in outdoor and science education from The Ohio State University. In addition to his teaching duties, Mr. Kramer is active in several professional organizations, including the National Science Teachers Association and the Science Education Council of Ohio. He has received numerous awards, including the Award for Outstanding Teaching in Science from Sigma Xi. In 1987, the National Science Teachers Association awarded Mr. Kramer a certificate for secondary physics, making him the first nationally certified teacher in physics.

Edward Ortleb is the Science Supervisor for the St. Louis, Missouri Board of Education and has 35 years teaching experience. He holds an A.B. in education from Harris Teachers College, an M.A. in education, and an Advanced Graduate Certificate in science education from Washington University, St. Louis. Mr. Ortleb is a lifetime member of the National Science Teachers Association, having served as its president in 1978-79. He has also served as Regional Director for the National Science Supervisors Association and has memberships in the Science Teachers of Missouri and Missouri Academy of Science. Mr. Ortleb is the recipient of several awards, including the Distinguished Service to Science Education Award (NSTA) in 1986 and the Outstanding Service to Science Education Award in 1987.

Susan Snyder is a teacher in Earth science at Jones Middle School, Upper Arlington School District, Columbus, Ohio. Ms. Snyder received a B.S. in comprehensive science from Miami University, Oxford, Ohio, and an M.S. in entomology from the University of Hawaii. She has 19 years teaching experience and is author of various educational materials. Ms. Snyder was the 1991 state recipient of the Presidential Award for Excellence in Science and Math Teaching, a 1987 finalist for National Teacher of the Year, and the 1987 Ohio Teacher of the Year. She won the Award for Excellence in Earth Science Teaching from the Geological Society of America in 1991. Ms. Snyder has memberships in several professional organizations, including the National Science Teachers Association and National Marine Educators Association.

Paul W. Zitzewitz is Professor of Physics at the University of Michigan-Dearborn. He received his B.A. from Carleton College and M.A. and Ph.D. from Harvard University, all in physics. Dr. Zitzewitz has taught physics to undergraduates for 21 years and is an active experimenter in the field of atomic physics with over 50 research papers. He is also Associate Dean of the College of Arts, Sciences, and Letters at the University of Michigan-Dearborn. He has memberships in several professional organizations, including the American Physical Society, American Association of Physics Teachers, and the National Science Teachers Association. Among his awards are the University of Michigan-Dearborn Distinguished Faculty Research Award, 1985.

Teacher Wraparound Edition

Student Edition

RESPONDING TO CHANGES IN SCIENCE EDUCATION

SCIENCE INTERACTIONS . . .
An Innovative Series Designed to Help You Prepare Your Junior High and Middle School Students For The FUTURE!

"What the future holds in store for individuals, the nation, and the world depends on the wisdom with which humans use science and technology.

—Project 2061

The concern for education reform comes from a realization that, as important as scientific literacy is, the need is no longer simply to grasp the fundamentals of biology, chemistry, physics and Earth science. Students must be able to deal with the processes of science in their daily lives—in their occupations, in their homes, and in their carrying out of citizenship duties.

THE NEED FOR NEW DIRECTIONS IN SCIENCE EDUCATION

By today's projections, seven out of every ten American jobs will be related to science, mathematics, or electronics by the year 2000. And according to the experts, if junior high and middle school students haven't grasped the fundamentals introduced in grades 6, 7, and 8—they probably won't go further in science and may not have a future in a global job market. Studies also reveal that high school students are avoiding taking "advanced" science classes.

America has learned that 70 percent of its third graders said they really like science. But by the seventh grade, the number who still enjoyed science dropped to below 30 percent. If you think those numbers are disturbing, even fewer and fewer students want to go on to classes in biology, chemistry, and physics.

THE TIME FOR ACTION IS NOW!

In the past decade, educators, public policy makers, corporate America, and parents have recognized the need for reform in science education. These groups have united in a call to action to solve this national problem. As a result, three important projects have published reports to point the way for America:

- **Project 2061** . . . by the American Association for the Advancement of Science.
- **Scope, Sequence, and Coordination of Secondary School Science** . . . by the National Science Teachers Association (NSTA).
- **Project on National Science Standards** . . . by the National Research Council.

Together, these reports spell out unified guiding principles for new directions in U.S. science education.

Glencoe's ***SCIENCE INTERACTIONS*** is based on these guiding principles. In fact, the leaders of the Scope, Sequence, and Coordination project were key participants in the writing and development of ***SCIENCE INTERACTIONS.***

SCIENCE INTERACTIONS ANSWERS THE CHALLENGE!

At Glencoe Publishing, we believe that ***SCIENCE INTERACTIONS*** will help you bring science reform to the front lines—the classrooms of America. But more important, we believe it will help students succeed in middle school and junior high science so that they will continue learning science through high school and into adulthood.

Glencoe knows that it's hard work getting teenagers interested in science because many of them think science is difficult . . . even boring. With ***SCIENCE INTERACTIONS,*** your middle school and junior high students will see that science is everywhere in their daily lives, that science can be fun and interesting, and that they need science to compete for the jobs of the future.

When you compare ***SCIENCE INTERACTIONS*** to a traditional science program, you'll see **fewer terms**. But you'll also see **more questions** and **more activities** to draw your students in. And you'll find broad themes repeated over and over, rather than hundreds of unrelated topics.

SCIENCE INTERACTIONS FITS YOUR CLASSROOM

SCIENCE INTERACTIONS has the right ingredients to help you ensure your students' future. But it also has to work in today's classroom. That's why, on first glance, ***SCIENCE INTERACTIONS*** may look like a traditional science textbook.

Glencoe knows you have local curriculum requirements. You teach a variety of students with varying ability levels. And you have limited time, space, or support for doing hands-on activities.

No matter. Unlike a purely hands-on program, ***SCIENCE INTERACTIONS*** lets you offer **the perfect balance of content and activities**. Your students will be eager to get their hands on science. But ***SCIENCE INTERACTIONS*** also gives you the **flexibility** to use only the activities you choose . . . without sacrificing anything.

SCIENCE INTERACTIONS IS LOADED WITH ACTIVITIES

You'll choose from hundreds of activities in all three courses. These easy to set-up and manage activities will allow you to teach using a hands-on, inquiry-based approach to learning.

The Find Out!, Explore!, and Investigate! activities are integrated with the text narrative, complete with transitions in and out of the activity. This aids comprehension for students by building continuity between text and activities.

Your teaching methods will include asking questions such as: *How do we know? Why do we believe? What does it mean?* Throughout both the narrative and activities, **you'll invite your students to relate what they learn to their own everyday experiences.**

"Science is built up with facts as a house is with stones, but a collection of facts is no more a science than a heap of stones is a house."

—Jules Henri Poincare

"Our task in science teaching is to be certain that not one child is turned off to science."

—MARGARET MEADE

SCIENCE INTERACTIONS TEACHES CONCEPTS IN A LOGICAL SEQUENCE FROM THE CONCRETE TO THE ABSTRACT

Research shows that students learn better when they deal with descriptive matters in science for a reasonable portion of their school years before proceeding to the more quantitative, and eventually the more theoretical, parts of science. Science Interactions helps your students learn in this manner.

Let's look at the way you'll teach the topic of light. In Course 1, students learn the nature of light by observing shadows, color, and the concept of reflected and refracted light. Learning to observe light gets students to think about it in a concrete way.

In Course 2, students learn more about the behavior and characteristics of light by observing how it interacts with mirrors and lenses. This study of mirrors and lenses also shows how light can be used to expand our senses to enable us to study very small and distant objects.

In Courses 1 and 2, students have learned a lot about light by observing it. But what is light? This theoretical explanation, which involves the electromagnetic spectrum and the wave theory of light, is found in Course 3.

SCIENCE INTERACTIONS INTEGRATES TOPICS FOR UNDERSTANDING

According to the experts, by using an integrated approacn like ***SCIENCE INTERACTIONS***, students will experience dramatic gains in comprehension and retention. For instance, the series helps you teach some of the basic concepts from physical science early on. This, in turn, makes it easier for your students to understand other concepts in life and Earth science.

But you'll be doing more than simply showing how the sciences interconnect. You'll also take numerous "side trips" with your students. Connect one area of science to another. Relate science to technology, society, issues, hobbies, and careers. **Show your students again and again how history, the arts, and literature can be part of science.** And help your students discover the science behind things they see every day.

Glencoe believes strongly that ***SCIENCE INTERACTIONS*** will help you arouse your students' natural curiosity and keep their innate love of science alive. With ***SCIENCE INTERACTIONS***, you will offer them more avenues for success, regardless of their abilities or interests. And that should give them fewer reasons to turn off science.

SCIENCE INTERACTIONS PROVIDES ALL THE SUPPORT YOU NEED TO PRESENT THE SERIES CONFIDENTLY AND EFFECTIVELY

To put you at ease with the scope and sequence of this innovative new series, ***SCIENCE INTERACTIONS'*** Teacher Editions offer detailed explanations of the conceptual and thematic development of each chapter and each section. You'll have every resource and all the support you need to present the series confidently and with ease.

IT'S TIME FOR NEW DIRECTIONS IN SCIENCE EDUCATION

The need for new directions in science education has been established by the experts. America's students must prepare themselves for the high-tech jobs of the future.

We at Glencoe believe that ***SCIENCE INTERACTIONS*** answers the challenge of the 1990s with it's new, innovative approach of "connecting" the sciences. We believe ***SCIENCE INTERACTIONS*** will assist you better in preparing your students for a lifetime of science learning.

YOUR QUESTIONS ANSWERED!

How is *SCIENCE INTERACTIONS* an integrated science program?

Although each chapter has a primary science emphasis, integration of other disciplines occurs throughout the program. Students are more likely to learn and remember a concept because they see it applied to other disciplines. This science integration is evident not only in the narrative of the core part of each chapter, but also in the "Expanding Your View" features at the end of each chapter, in the Teacher Wraparound Edition, and in the supplements.

How is *SCIENCE INTERACTIONS* different from general science?

There's really no comparing the ***SCIENCE INTERACTIONS*** program to a traditional general science text. In a general science program, the sequence of the topics and their relationship to one another is of little importance. For example, all the physics chapters in a general science text would be grouped together in a unit at the back of the book and probably have no relationship to the life, Earth, or chemistry units.

SCIENCE INTERACTIONS is different from general science in that chapters from different disciplines are intermixed and sequenced so that what is learned in one discipline can be applied to another.

In a general science program, students study each discipline in isolation from every other discipline. In ***SCIENCE INTERACTIONS***, students learn and retain more because its content sequence allows them to build knowledge and understanding progressively throughout the year.

How is *SCIENCE INTERACTIONS* different from the "layering" or "block" approach?

In a traditional three-year course, students study life science in sixth grade, Earth science in seventh, and physical science in eighth grade. *SCIENCE INTERACTIONS* is different because it contains all of these disciplines in each course. It is true integrated science, where life, Earth and physical science are integrated throughout the year.

Will *SCIENCE INTERACTIONS* prepare my students for high school science?

The national reform projects agree that the best preparation is a deep understanding of important science concepts. This, rather than requiring students to memorize facts and terms, will keep your students interested in science.

SCIENCE INTERACTIONS will help your students frame questions, derive concepts, and obtain evidence. When your students have mastered this language of science, they will be ready for further study.

In addition, ***SCIENCE INTERACTIONS*** offers your students plenty of reasons to stick with science—including unexpected career choices and examples of women and minorities achieving in science.

Does *SCIENCE INTERACTIONS* use a constructivist approach to learning?

Certainly. From chapter openers to activities to end-of-chapter questions, your students are actively involved in constructing their own understanding of concepts.

You'll begin every chapter with questions to trigger your students' curiosity. Short, informal activities let them explore on their own. And every activity is structured to help your students propose their own explanations and solutions. Finally, you'll find numerous suggestions for taking further action.

While ***SCIENCE INTERACTIONS*** is not a purely activity-based program, you'll see upon examination that even the writing style encourages your students to find out more.

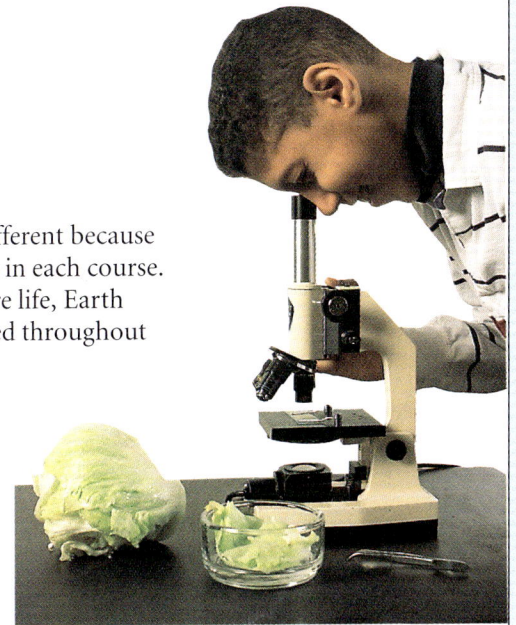

THEMES AND SCOPE AND SEQUENCE

The themes in SCIENCE INTERACTIONS are the threads that organize facts and concepts, and show the interrelationships among the disciplines.

SCIENCE INTERACTIONS, three science textbooks for middle school, is unique in that it integrates all the natural sciences, presenting them as a single area of study. As discussed in the previous section, "Integrating the Sciences," our society is becoming more aware of the interrelationship of the disciplines of science. It is also necessary to recognize the precarious nature of the stability of some systems and the ease with which this stability can be disturbed so that the system changes. For most people, then, the ideas that unify the sciences and make connections between them are the most important.

Themes are the constructs that unify the sciences. Woven throughout ***SCIENCE INTERACTIONS***, themes integrate facts and concepts. They are the "big ideas" that link the structures on which the science disciplines are built. While there are many possible themes around which to unify science, we have chosen four: Energy, Systems and Interactions, Scale and Structure, and Stability and Change.

Energy

Energy is a central concept of the physical sciences that pervades the biological and geological sciences. In physical terms, energy is the ability of an object to change itself or its surroundings, the capacity to do work. In chemical terms it forms the basis of reactions between compounds. In biological terms it gives living systems the ability to maintain themselves, to grow, and to reproduce. Energy sources are crucial in the interactions among science, technology and society.

Systems and Interactions

A system can be incredibly tiny, such as an atom's nucleus and electrons; extremely complex, such as an ecosystem; or unbelievably large, as the stars in a galaxy. By defining the boundaries of the system, one can study the interactions among its parts. The interactions may be a force of attraction between the positively charged nucleus and negatively charged electron. In an ecosystem, however, the interaction may be between the predator and its prey, or among the plants and animals. Animals in such a system have many subsystems (circulation, respiration, digestion, etc.) with interactions among them.

Scale and Structure

Used as a theme, "structure" emphasizes the relationship among different structures. "Scale" defines the focus of the relationship. As the focus is shifted from a system to its components, the properties of the structure may remain constant. In other systems, an ecosystem for example, which includes a change in scale from interactions between prey and predator to the interactions among systems inside an animal, the structure changes drastically. In ***SCIENCE INTERACTIONS***, the authors have tried to stress how we know what we know and why we believe it to be so. Thus, explanations remain on the macroscopic level until students have the background needed to understand how the microscopic structure was determined.

Stability and Change

A system that is stable is constant. Often the stability is the result of a system being in equilibrium. If a system is not stable, it undergoes change. Changes in an unstable system may be characterized as trends (position of falling objects), cycles (the motion of planets around the sun), or irregular changes (radioactive decay).

These four major themes, as well as several others, are developed within the student material and discussed throughout the **Teacher Wraparound Edition.** Each chapter of ***SCIENCE INTERACTIONS*** incorporates a primary and secondary theme. These themes are interwoven throughout each level and are developed as appropriate to the topic presented.

The **Teacher Wraparound Edition** includes a "Theme Development" section for each "Looking Ahead" feature. This section discusses the upcoming unit's key themes and explains how they are supported by the chapters in the unit. Each chapter opener includes a "Theme Development" section to explain the chapter's primary and secondary themes and to point out the major chapter concepts supporting those themes. Throughout the chapters, "Theme Connections" show specifically how a topic in the student edition relates to the themes.

Course 1 Chapters

Chapters	Scale and Structure	Energy	Stability and Change	Systems and Interactions
1: Viewing Earth and Sky	P			S
2: Light and Color		S		P
3: Sound		S	P	
4: Using Your Senses	S			P
5: Describing the Physical World	P		S	
6: Everyday Materials		P	S	
7: Matter in Solution			P	S
8: Acids, Bases, and Salts			S	P
9: Describing the Living World	S			P
10: Animal Life	P			S
11: Plant Life			S	P
12: Ecology			S	P
13: Motion			P	S
14: Motion Near Earth			S	P
15: Moving Water			S	P
16: Soil and Weathering		S	P	
17: Shaping the Land		S	P	
18: Waves		P		S
19: Earthquakes and Volcanoes		P	S	
20: The Earth-Moon System	S			P

Course 2 Chapters

Chapters	Scale and Structure	Energy	Stability and Change	Systems and Interactions
1: Forces and Pressure			S	P
2: Forces Inside Earth		P	S	
3: Circulation in Animals		S		P
4: Work and Energy		P		S
5: Machines		S		P
6: Thermal Energy		P		S
7: Moving the Body Machine		S		P
8: Controlling the Body Machine			S	P
9: Discovering Elements	P			S
10: Minerals and Their Uses	S			P
11: The Rock Cycle			P	S
12: The Ocean Floor and Shore Zones	P		S	
13: Energy Resources		P		S
14: Gases, Atoms, and Molecules	P			S
15: The Air Around You		P		S
16: Breathing		S		P
17: Mirrors and Lenses	S			P
18: Basic Units of Life	P	S		
19: Chemical Reactions		S		P
20: How Cells Do Their Jobs		S		P
21: Simple Organisms	P			S

Course 3 Chapters

Chapters	Scale and Structure	Energy	Stability and Change	Systems and Interactions
1: Electricity	S	P		
2: Magnetism		S	P	
3: Electrical Applications		S		P
4: Electromagnetic Waves	S	P		
5: Structure of the Atom	S	P		
6: The Periodic Table	P		S	
7: Combining Atoms			S	P
8: Molecules in Motion		P	S	
9: Weather			S	P
10: Ocean Water and Life		P		S
11: Organic Chemistry	P		S	
12: Fueling the Body	S	P		
13: Blood: Transport and Protection	P		S	
14: Reproduction	P		S	
15: Heredity	S		P	
16: Moving Continents		P		S
17: Geologic Time			P	S
18: Evolution of Life			P	S
19: Fission and Fusion		P	S	
20: The Solar System	P		S	
21: Stars and Galaxies	P		S	

P = PRIMARY THEME S = SECONDARY THEME

ORGANIZED FOR EFFECTIVE STUDY

*The network of units, chapters, sections, and features in **SCIENCE INTERACTIONS** guides students on an exciting journey through the world of science, from science as a body of knowledge to science as a process which they can directly experience.*

UNIT

Looking Ahead
Looking Back

These unit opening and closing pages bring focus to the themes and interactions that unify the chapters in the unit.

CHAPTER

Chapter Opening
Reviewing Main Ideas
Chapter Review

Each chapter starts with concrete experiences from the everyday lives of students and concludes with exercises that reinforce and extend chapter concepts.

SECTION

EXPLORE!
FIND OUT!
INVESTIGATE!
Skillbuilder
How Do We Know?
Check Your Understanding

Core lessons in each chapter feature a variety of hands-on activities connected by an interesting narration that allows students to discover fundamental science concepts for themselves.

EXPANDING YOUR VIEW

A Closer Look
Science Connection
Technology
Science & Society
How It Works
Teens in Science
Interdisciplinary

Presented in magazine format, these brief articles give students further insight into how core science concepts from the chapter relate to other science and "non-science" topics.

PUTS STUDENTS IN THE RIGHT FRAME OF MIND

SCIENCE INTERACTIONS, *whether starting a new unit or chapter, puts students in the right frame of mind to continue their exploration of science.*

LOOKING BACK
UNIT 2 INTERACTIONS IN THE PHYSICAL WORLD
CONTENTS
Chapter 5 Describing the Physical World
Chapter 6 Everyday Materials
Chapter 7 Matter in Solution
Chapter 8 Acids, Bases, and Salts
UNIT FOCUS
CONNECTING IDEAS
1. Ocean water is very salty. You may have accidentally tasted some while swimming, or noticed that salt crystals formed on your body as you sat in the sun to dry after swimming. How does the salt appear on your skin?
2. Analyzing Data:
EXPLORING FURTHER
Make a card file of dangerous materials around your home. Identify acids, bases, and other toxic solutions and materials. Include the danger posed by each substance and the steps to be taken if the material is accidentally spilled or taken into your body. Use this activity to compile a first aid file for the home.
LOOKING BACK concludes each unit with a Unit Focus, or reminder of some of the key ideas students studied in previous chapters. Use the activities in CONNECTING IDEAS and EXPLORING FURTHER to reinforce the connections among these ideas.
254
LOOKING AHEAD
UNIT 3 INTERACTIONS IN THE LIVING WORLD
CONTENTS
Chapter 9 Describing the Living World
Chapter 10 Animal Life
TRY IT
Look around your classroom. Can you think of ways to group the people in your class? The people in your classroom have many things in common. Everyone breathes, has a heartbeat, and eats. Grouping enables you to classify people based on similar characteristics. You can also observe differences among the people in your class. Perhaps you could group them using hair color or the color of their clothes. People share characteristics with other animals and plants as well. Make a drawing of a cactus plant, a bird, some weeds, and a person about your age. Show on your drawing some of the characteristics that are shared by all of these living things. You might show all of them obtaining energy. Also indicate in your picture some very obvious differences that would enable you to classify them as different organisms. After you've learned more about life forms on Earth, see how accurate your drawing is.
physical materials in Unit 2. By looking at how plants, animals, and their environment interact, you will learn about the connections that link the biological and physical worlds together.
LOOKING AHEAD begins each unit with a Unit Focus, or preview of upcoming chapters, and a simple TRY IT activity that challenges students to explore and think about some of the objects and events they will encounter later.
255

DID YOU EVER WONDER . . .
Why sometimes the waves in a swimming pool get so big?
Why a horn on a train seems to change pitch as it passes you?
How a radio speaker produces sound?
You'll find the answers to these questions as you read this chapter

Chapter 18

Waves

It's a beautiful day, and you're at the local pool. You are in the water with your friend Ladonna, who is basking on a float. Out of the corner of your eye you see Louie, the bodybuilder, launch himself off the diving board. SPLASH! Suddenly you are under the water, Ladonna bobs straight up, and water bursts over the sides of the pool. Louie has made a large wave in the pool.

After you get your hair out of your eyes, you think about what just happened. If someone had told you the wave was coming, you would have assumed it would knock you down. But the wave just flowed over and around you. You probably would have predicted that Ladonna would be thrown against the

EXPLORE

Can you make a wave on a rope?

Tie one end of a 4-m rope to a desk or a doorknob, as shown in the picture. Holding onto the other end of the rope with your hand, shake the rope up and down once. Observe the pulse, a single disturbance, as it travels away from your hand. Shake the rope up and down slowly and at a steady rate. This will form a wave—a continuous series of disturbances. Describe the motion of the wave on the rope. Does the wave seem to move from one end of the rope to the other?

The introductory narration draws from a common experience to help students see the science in everyday events. As the chapter unfolds, students are brought back to this example time after time.

Use the **DID YOU EVER WONDER** questions at the beginning of each chapter to explore what students may already know about the science in the upcoming lessons.

The **EXPLORE** activity gives students an open-ended opportunity to explore something that they will investigate more fully later on.

DEVELOPS BASIC CONCEPTS THROUGH OBSERVATION AND DIRECT EXPERIENCE

Each chapter is divided into two or more sections, or core lessons, which thoughtfully develop a few fundamental concepts through a sequence of hands-on activities connected by narrative.

1-1 Viewing Earth

OBJECTIVES

In this section, you will
- describe basic landforms such as mountains, plains, and plateaus;
- recognize the kind of landform on which you live.

KEY SCIENCE TERMS

landforms

OVER THE PLAINS, MOUNTAINS, AND PLATEAUS

Suppose you have tickets for an early morning flight from Washington, D.C., to California. You will be flying for about six hours. Thank goodness you were able to get a window seat! You want to see the land unfold beneath you. What will you observe as you fly over the United States? The Explore activity will give you some clues.

EXPLORE!

What does a profile of the United States look like?

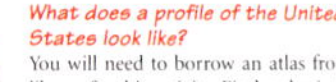

You will need to borrow an atlas from the library for this activity. Find a physical map of the United States that shows its land features. Use the map to guide you as you draw a cross-section profile of the United States. Start with the west coast at the left, then move right to the east coast. Keep in mind that a profile shows the surface features as they would look if you cut the United States in half from the west to the east coast and looked at the surface from the cut edge. Some atlases contain profile maps. Use these as models for your own ...e. Mark and label the different fea... How do you think those features ...d look from the air?

EXPLORE, one of three types of activities found in each chapter, is a simple, exploratory-type activity that promotes self-discovery and qualitative observation.

...drawn a profile, you will see how ... with the surface as seen from the ...s you will see are called **landforms**. ...d plateaus are three common land...ites.

...r airplane trip arrives. You board ...elf into your window seat, and fas...ten your seat belt. You're eager to compare your profile

FIGURE 1-1. East coast landforms include coastal plains.

with the landforms you see on the trip. The plane taxis down the runway, and soon you're in the air. Good-bye, Washington! California, here you come!

After taking off, you look down and see features on the surface. Study Figure 1-1. It shows an east coast landscape. You can see some buildings and roads, but what else do you see?

You begin to realize there are many landforms that may not be detailed on your profile. These natural features give shape and variety to the surface. Right after takeoff, you fly over flat lands. What are these landforms called?

ACROSS THE LOW PLAINS

What do you think of when you hear the word *plains*? You might think of endless flat fields of wheat or grass. That's often what plains look like because many of them are used to grow crops. Plains are large, low, mostly flat areas that cover much of the United States. In fact, about half of all the land in the United States is plains.

You will see plains along many of the coastlines and in the interior of the country. The lowland areas along the coastlines are called coastal plains. The Atlantic Coastal Plain stretches along the eastern coast of the United States. This area is characterized by low, rolling hills, swamps,

4 CHAPTER 1 VIEWING EARTH AND SKY

1-1 VIEWING EARTH 5

The narrative provides the story line and sets the stage for each activity as it comes up in the lesson.

Activities in ***SCIENCE INTERACTIONS,*** in addition to being effective in developing concepts, were selected because they are safe, utilize easily obtained materials, and address your concerns about classroom and time management.

FIND OUT!

How do lights mix?

You'll need three flashlights; three rubber bands; green, blue, and red cellophane; and some white paper. Fold a piece of green cellophane into a square several layers thick. Use a rubber band to fold it over the lens of one flashlight. Do the same with the other colors of cellophane and the other flashlights. In a darkened room, shine all three flashlights onto the white paper to make three circles that overlap, as in the picture. What do you see where green and blue overlap? How about green and red? Blue and red? All three?

Conclude and Apply

1. Keep the green and blue flashlights in the same place while moving the red flashlight closer to and farther away from the paper. How do the colors change?
2. Try it again moving each of the other two flashlights. What happens?

FIGURE 2-5. White light is produced when the three primary colors of light are mixed.

Blue
Cyan
Magenta
White
Green
Yellow
Red

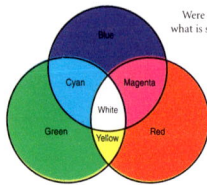

Were your results from the Find Out simila... what is shown in Figure 2-5? Blue plus green m... a shade of blue called cyan (SI an), ... plus red made a shade of red ca... magenta, and red plus green made ...low. But where all three colors of l... mixed you got white. Does this s... odd? You saw earlier that white light is made up of all the colors in the spectrum. How did you get white just now with only three colors?

When you made some colored lights brighter than others by bringing them

44 CHAPTER 2 LIGHT AND COLOR

FIND OUT activities tend to follow EXPLORE! activities, are more focused, and often ask students to collect and record a variety of data.

I N V E S T I G A T E !

5-1 MEASURING MASS

In this activity, you'll measure mass and use your results to make some estimates.

PROBLEM

How can you use mass to estimate an unknown number of paper clips?

MATERIALS

pan balance and set of masses
empty paper clip box
groups of 10, 20, and 50 paper clips
1 full box of paper clips, labeled *Full*
1 box of unknown number of paper clips labeled *X*

PROCEDURE

1. Copy the data table.
2. **Find the mass** of the empty box. Record it in your table.
3. **Find the mass** of 10 paper clips and record it. Calculate the average mass of one paper clip by dividing the mass by 10.
4. Find the mass of the full box of clips. Record the mass under the heading *Full box.* Subtract the mass of the empty box. Record this mass under the heading *Full box clips.* This is the mass of the paper clips.
5. Use your data to estimate the number of paper clips in the full box. Record your estimate.
6. Count the paper clips in the full box and record the actual number.
7. Find the mass of 20 paper clips and 50 paper clips. Record your data.
8. Find and record the mass of the paper clips in Box *X* using the procedure in Step 4.
9. Use the measurements from Step 7 to estimate the number of clips in Box *X*. Record your estimates, then count the clips in the box.

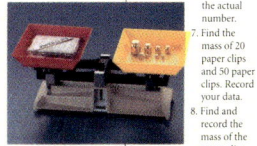

DATA AND OBSERVATIONS

ITEMS	MASS (g)	ESTIMATE	ACTUAL NUMBER
Empty box			
10 clips			
20 clips			
50 clips			
Full box			
Full box clips			
Box X			

ANALYZE

1. How did you estimate the number of paper clips in the full box?
2. How close was your estimate to the actual number?

CONCLUDE AND APPLY

3. How did you estimate the number of paper clips in Box *X*?
4. How close was your estimate?
5. **Going Further:** How would you estimate an unknown number of paper clips if the mass of the clips were less than the mass of 10 paper clips?

140 CHAPTER 5 DESCRIBING THE PHYSICAL WORLD

INVESTIGATE activities are more formal activities that usually require more materials and an entire class period to complete.

Safety symbols highlight appropriate cautions.

Probing questions and suggestions for further study conclude each **INVESTIGATE** activity.

Students typically have to collect and analyze quantitative data.

FIGURE 12-20. This alpaca is adapted to cold temperatures and less oxygen in the air.

there is less leaf surface area, less water is lost through the spines than would be with other types of leaves.

Plants in rain forests are adapted to different limiting factors. The lower levels of the rain forest receive very little light. Any nutrients in the topsoil are quickly absorbed by the roots of tall trees, so the soil has few nutrients. Plants called epiphytes (EHP uh fits) grow high up on the branches of the taller trees. They grow in the top layers of the forest and get water from the air and nutrients from decaying plant matter near their roots. Figure 12-19 shows you what an epiphyte looks like.

How do we know?

Earth's Warming

Scientists agree that average temperatures on Earth have risen 0.5°C over the last 100 years. They also agree that the amount of carbon dioxide in the atmosphere has increased over the last century. Measurements and observations have given us this information. However, scientists don't agree on how much this increase will affect Earth's climate or, if so, how soon a climate change will occur.

Models of climate changes can be made by computers. Scientists input data on past climate conditions. They also add data such as wind speed, air and water temperatures, land features, and precipitation patterns. All this information is analyzed by the computers, and models of climate changes are produced. Sometimes the models don't agree. You might ask why. Think about how often your local weather forecasts don't agree about tomorrow's weather. Now try to predict the climate for the

With the support of full-color photographs and illustrations, the narrative picks-up the story line after each activity and provides additional background, evidence, examples, and applications of the idea introduced or developed in the activity. It frequently reminds students of how science concepts from different science disciplines relate to one another.

HOW DO WE KNOW, a boxed feature set off from the narrative, gives students insight into additional evidence or experiments that support a particular theory or idea.

SKILLBUILDER

MAKING AND USING GRAPHS

Find the pH of the following substances: rainwater, apples, soda water, seawater, drain cleaner, distilled water, and milk of magnesia. Now use a bar graph to plot the pH of the substances against the pH scale in Figure 8-9. If you need help, refer to the **Skill Handbook** on page 650.

FIGURE 8-11. Lichens are the source of litmus.

INDICATORS AND pH

Acid-base indicators come in two varieties—a solution or an acid-base indicator paper. You used a solution indicator when you tested the pH of solutions in the Investigate activity. The paper can be an indicator itself or treated with an indicator. To use an indicator strip, just place a drop of the solution to be tested on the paper and watch for a color change. You already know about one of the most common indicators—litmus paper. Remember from the Investigate activity in Section 2 that litmus turns blue in the presence of a base and red in the presence of an acid. Would it change color in pure water? Why or why not?

Another common acid-base indicator is a chemical called phenolphthalein (feen ul THAY leen). Phenolphthalein is colorless in the presence of an acid, but it turns bright pink in the presence of a base. Phenolphthalein is also one of the indicators used to treat paper strips.

For living things to grow and be healthy, there must be a balance in the acids and bases in their bodies as well as in their environment. In this section, you've learned how to distinguish acids and bases and how to measure the strength of an acid or base. In the next section, you'll discover a way in which acid n damage might be temrarily repaired.

8.9
r, pH 14.0
er, pH 7.0
f the substances men-
tion 2 should have a

SKILLBUILDER

MAKING AND USING GRAPHS

Find the pH of the following sub stances: rainwater, apples, sod water, seawater, drain cleaner, distilled water, and milk of magr sia. Now use a bar graph to plo

SKILLBUILDER exercises in the margin provide students another opportunity to practice skills or processes relevant to the material they are studying.

REVEALS THE INTERDISCIPLINARY NATURE OF SCIENCE

A unique six-page section at the end of every chapter gives you and your students an opportunity to explore the diverse connections of science to other subjects. Each **EXPANDING YOUR VIEW** *article extends the science content of the chapter into another area of the curriculum or to society and technology.*

CONTENTS

The types of articles found in each **EXPANDING YOUR VIEW** section vary from chapter to chapter, but include several of the following:

* an in-depth look at some aspect of chapter content
* the relationship of science concepts from one science discipline to another
* connections to art, history, literature, and other non-science subjects
* applications of science to technology and society
* application of science principles to the inner workings of everyday devices
* true stories of teenagers actively involved in science
* career connections

EXPANDING YOUR VIEW

A CLOSER LOOK

CREATURE FEATURES

EARTH SCIENCE CONNECTION

A NATURAL DISASTER

WHAT DO YOU THINK?

What would happen to a seed-eating bird if a widespread drought caused no seeds to be produced in its habitat one year? This bird has a short, strong beak for cracking open and eating ... out? Would it move to ...

EXPANDING YOUR VIEW offers you many options for enriching the core content of the chapter. Cover all of them or select only those that interest you or your students. Assign them to individual students or to small groups of students as a cooperative learning activity.

Reinforce and extend the connections made in each article by assigning the **YOU TRY IT** or **WHAT DO YOU THINK?** questions.

REVIEWS, REINFORCES, AND EXTENDS

Three pages of chapter-end material help students synthesize ideas, review content, and think critically.

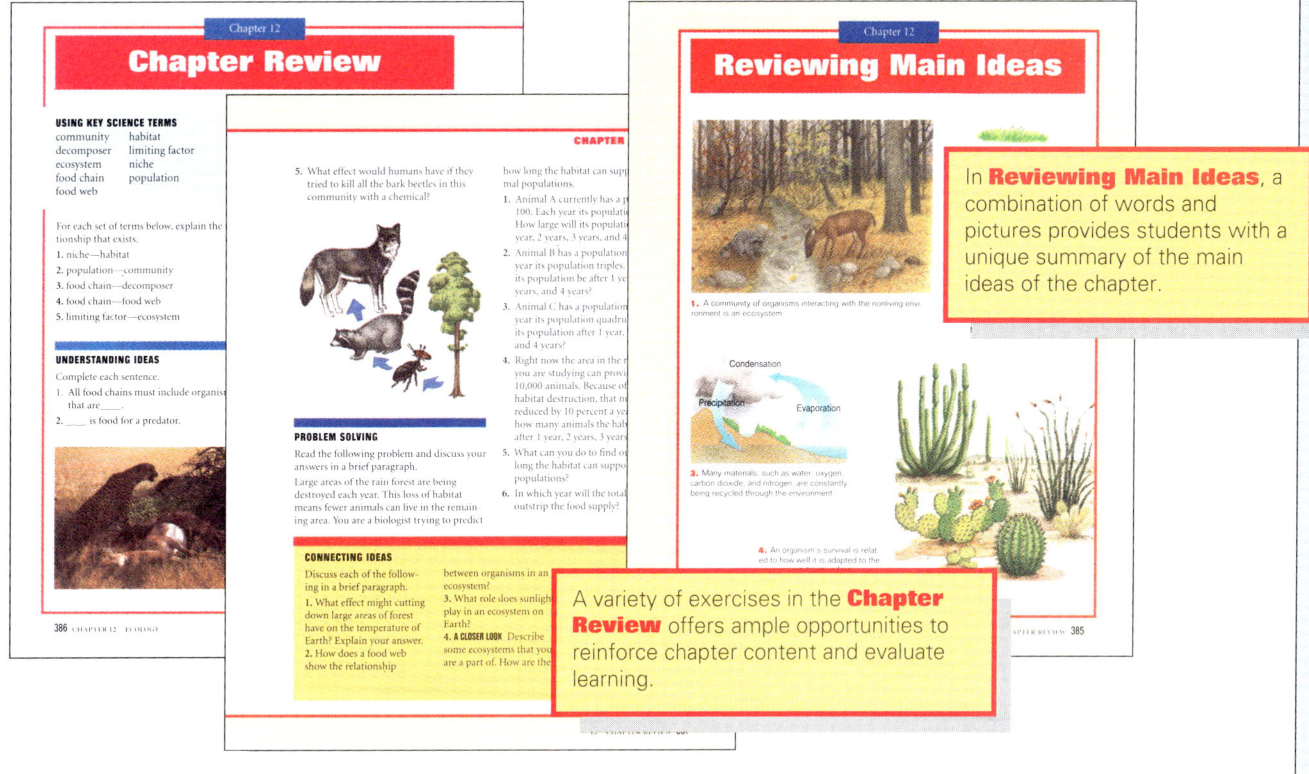

Chapter 12
Chapter Review
Chapter 12
Reviewing Main Ideas
In **Reviewing Main Ideas**, a combination of words and pictures provides students with a unique summary of the main ideas of the chapter.
A variety of exercises in the **Chapter Review** offers ample opportunities to reinforce chapter content and evaluate learning.

SKILL HANDBOOK

The **SKILL HANDBOOK** *contains 16 pages of information with examples on various science skills and processes. Students may refer to them as they do the* **SKILLBUILDER** *exercises in the student text or you may want to incorporate them into a lesson in which one or more of the skills may be used.*

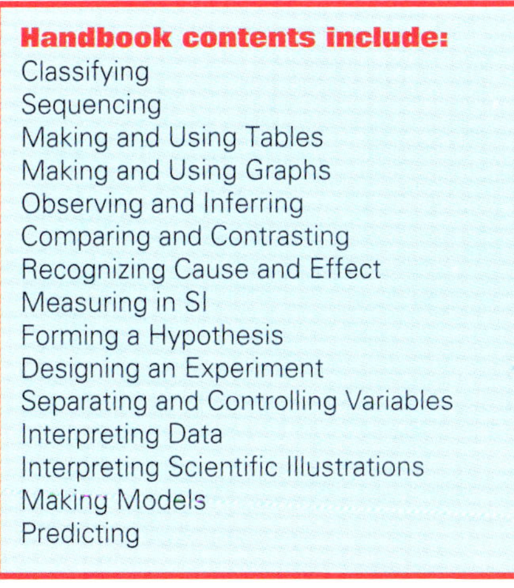

Handbook contents include:
Classifying
Sequencing
Making and Using Tables
Making and Using Graphs
Observing and Inferring
Comparing and Contrasting
Recognizing Cause and Effect
Measuring in SI
Forming a Hypothesis
Designing an Experiment
Separating and Controlling Variables
Interpreting Data
Interpreting Scientific Illustrations
Making Models
Predicting

DESIGNED TO KEEP YOU IN CONTROL

Recent demands for changes in the scope and sequence of curriculum, for more extensive integration of the sciences, and for greater emphasis on hands-on learning will make science teaching in the middle grades more challenging than ever. There will be more demands on your time, resources, and expertise. Consequently, we have developed the **Teacher Wraparound Edition** *for* ***SCIENCE INTERACTIONS*** *to help you meet these new challenges both efficiently and effectively. It is a comprehensive resource designed to keep you in control of the teaching and learning environment.*

CHAPTER RESOURCES AT YOUR FINGERTIPS

The **Chapter Organizer** *will help you plan effective science lessons by identifying on a section-by-section basis the objectives, activities, and resources available to you in the* ***SCIENCE INTERACTIONS*** *program.*

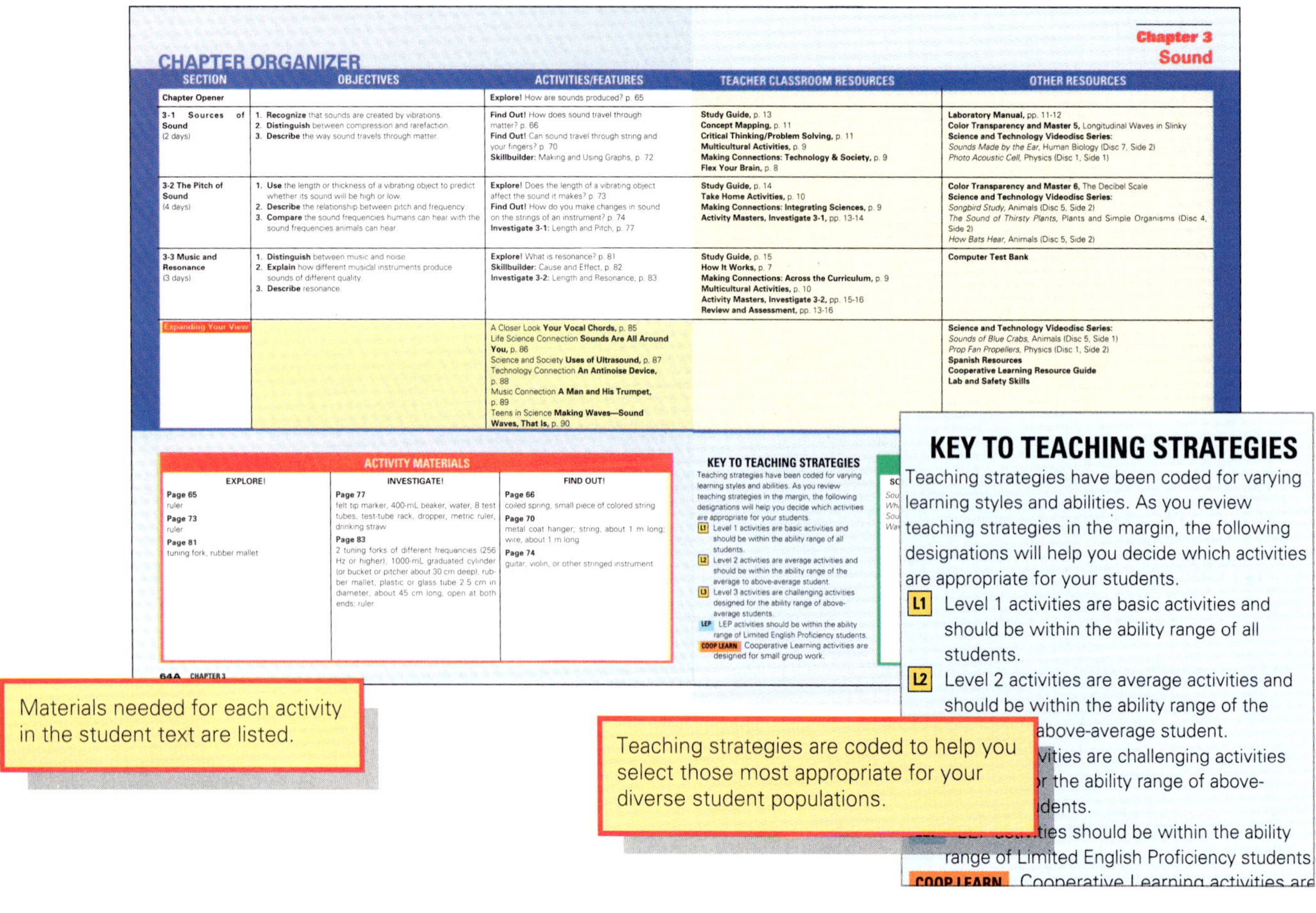

CHAPTER ORGANIZER

Chapter 3 Sound

SECTION	OBJECTIVES	ACTIVITIES/FEATURES	TEACHER CLASSROOM RESOURCES	OTHER RESOURCES
Chapter Opener		**Explore!** How are sounds produced? p. 65		
3-1 Sources of Sound (2 days)	1. **Recognize** that sounds are created by vibrations. 2. **Distinguish** between compression and rarefaction. 3. **Describe** the way sound travels through matter.	**Find Out!** How does sound travel through matter? p. 66 **Find Out!** Can sound travel through string and your fingers? p. 70 **Skillbuilder:** Making and Using Graphs, p. 72	**Study Guide,** p. 13 **Concept Mapping,** p. 11 **Critical Thinking/Problem Solving,** p. 11 **Multicultural Activities,** p. 9 **Making Connections: Technology & Society,** p. 9 **Flex Your Brain,** p. 8	**Laboratory Manual,** pp. 11-12 **Color Transparency and Master 5,** Longitudinal Waves in Slinky **Science and Technology Videodisc Series:** *Sounds Made by the Ear,* Human Biology (Disc 7, Side 2) *Photo Acoustic Cell,* Physics (Disc 1, Side 1)
3-2 The Pitch of Sound (4 days)	1. **Use** the length or thickness of a vibrating object to predict whether its sound will be high or low. 2. **Describe** the relationship between pitch and frequency. 3. **Compare** the sound frequencies humans can hear with the sound frequencies animals can hear.	**Explore!** Does the length of a vibrating object affect the sound it makes? p. 73 **Find Out!** How do you make changes in sound on the strings of an instrument? p. 74 **Investigate 3-1:** Length and Pitch, p. 77	**Study Guide,** p. 14 **Take Home Activities,** p. 10 **Making Connections: Integrating Sciences,** p. 9 **Activity Masters, Investigate 3-1,** pp. 13-14	**Color Transparency and Master 6,** The Decibel Scale **Science and Technology Videodisc Series:** *Songbird Study,* Animals (Disc 5, Side 2) *The Sound of Thirsty Plants,* Plants and Simple Organisms (Disc 4, Side 2) *How Bats Hear,* Animals (Disc 5, Side 2)
3-3 Music and Resonance (3 days)	1. **Distinguish** between music and noise. 2. **Explain** how different musical instruments produce sounds of different quality. 3. **Describe** resonance.	**Explore!** What is resonance? p. 81 **Skillbuilder:** Cause and Effect, p. 82 **Investigate 3-2:** Length and Resonance, p. 83	**Study Guide,** p. 15 **How It Works,** p. 7 **Making Connections: Across the Curriculum,** p. 9 **Multicultural Activities,** p. 10 **Activity Masters, Investigate 3-2,** pp. 15-16 **Review and Assessment,** pp. 13-16	**Computer Test Bank**
Expanding Your View		A Closer Look **Your Vocal Chords,** p. 85 Life Science Connection **Sounds Are All Around You,** p. 86 Science and Society **Uses of Ultrasound,** p. 87 Technology Connection **An Antinoise Device,** p. 88 Music Connection **A Man and His Trumpet,** p. 89 Teens in Science **Making Waves—Sound Waves, That Is,** p. 90		**Science and Technology Videodisc Series:** *Sounds of Blue Crabs,* Animals (Disc 5, Side 1) *Prop Fan Propellers,* Physics (Disc 1, Side 2) **Spanish Resources** **Cooperative Learning Resource Guide** **Lab and Safety Skills**

ACTIVITY MATERIALS

EXPLORE!	INVESTIGATE!	FIND OUT!
Page 65 ruler **Page 73** ruler **Page 81** tuning fork, rubber mallet	**Page 77** felt tip marker, 400-mL beaker, water, 8 test tubes, test-tube rack, dropper, metric ruler, drinking straw **Page 83** 2 tuning forks of different frequencies (256 Hz or higher); 1000-mL graduated cylinder (or bucket or pitcher about 30 cm deep), rubber mallet; plastic or glass tube 2.5 cm in diameter, about 45 cm long, open at both ends; ruler	**Page 66** coiled spring, small piece of colored string **Page 70** metal coat hanger; string, about 1 m long; wire, about 1 m long **Page 74** guitar, violin, or other stringed instrument

KEY TO TEACHING STRATEGIES

Teaching strategies have been coded for varying learning styles and abilities. As you review teaching strategies in the margin, the following designations will help you decide which activities are appropriate for your students.

L1 Level 1 activities are basic activities and should be within the ability range of all students.

L2 Level 2 activities are average activities and should be within the ability range of the average to above-average student.

L3 Level 3 activities are challenging activities designed for the ability range of above-average students.

LEP LEP activities should be within the ability range of Limited English Proficiency students.

COOP LEARN Cooperative Learning activities are designed for small group work.

64A CHAPTER 3

EMPHASIS ON THEMATIC AND CONCEPTUAL DEVELOPMENT

Because **SCIENCE INTERACTIONS** *is developmental, integrative, and thematic, the teacher editions place special emphasis on explaining the conceptual and thematic development that occurs in every section and chapter. In each section, we describe not only what is being taught, but why it's being taught, and how it connects to themes, student preconceptions, and previous sections and chapters.*

Chapter Opening *pages give you vital background information on the content and themes developed in the chapter.*

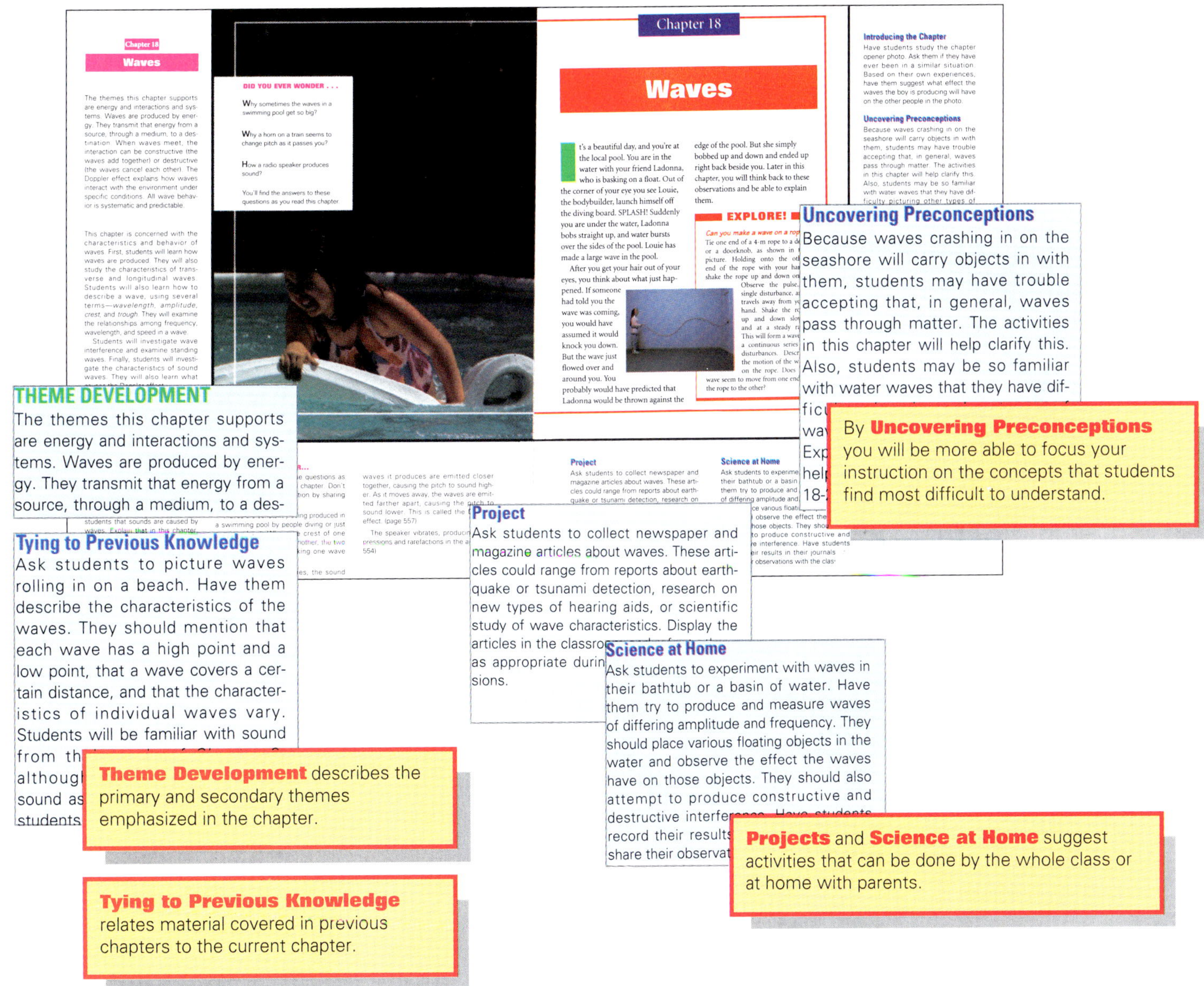

Chapter 18
Waves
THEME DEVELOPMENT
The themes this chapter supports are energy and interactions and systems. Waves are produced by energy. They transmit that energy from a source, through a medium, to a des-
Tying to Previous Knowledge
Ask students to picture waves rolling in on a beach. Have them describe the characteristics of the waves. They should mention that each wave has a high point and a low point, that a wave covers a certain distance, and that the characteristics of individual waves vary. Students will be familiar with sound
Uncovering Preconceptions
Because waves crashing in on the seashore will carry objects in with them, students may have trouble accepting that, in general, waves pass through matter. The activities in this chapter will help clarify this. Also, students may be so familiar with water waves that they have dif-
Project
Ask students to collect newspaper and magazine articles about waves. These articles could range from reports about earthquake or tsunami detection, research on new types of hearing aids, or scientific study of wave characteristics. Display the articles in the classro
Science at Home
Ask students to experiment with waves in their bathtub or a basin of water. Have them try to produce and measure waves of differing amplitude and frequency. They should place various floating objects in the water and observe the effect the waves have on those objects. They should also attempt to produce constructive and destructive interfe
By Uncovering Preconceptions you will be more able to focus your instruction on the concepts that students find most difficult to understand.
Theme Development describes the primary and secondary themes emphasized in the chapter.
Projects and Science at Home suggest activities that can be done by the whole class or at home with parents.
Tying to Previous Knowledge relates material covered in previous chapters to the current chapter.

TEACHING PLAN WITH PLENTY OF OPTIONS

The four-step teaching model in each lesson gives you direction when you want it and plenty of options to enrich the lesson or to meet the diverse needs of your students.

Preparation notes preview the lesson and help you select the activities that are most important to developing the lesson concepts.
1 MOTIVATE
Discussion Ask students to look closely at their own wrists and describe what they see.
Motivate with high interest "ice-breaker" activities.
2 TEACH
Tying to Previous Knowledge
Ask students to list ways water is distributed from a reservoir or from a well. Most students will suggest a system of pipes and conduits. Tell students that vascular plants also have systems to distribute water.
Concept Development
Teach students through a variety of active-learning strategies.
xylem, which is part of the structure of vascular plants. The theme of scale and structure is supported as students use the structure of seeds for classification.
Inquiry Question What conclusion can you draw about a part of a forest where the ground was thickly covered with moss? *Moss plants are nonvascular, thus they*
3 ASSESS
Check for Understanding
To help students with the Apply question, remind them that fast-flowing water tends to run in a fairly straight path. Ask students where fast-flowing water is usually found. *steep slopes*
Assess student progress, then reteach and extend the lesson as appropriate.
Reteach
Have students write a description of what they think the bed of a mountain stream looks like. They should picture it as narrow, with rocks and pebbles at its bottom.
stream
4 CLOSE
Activity
Have students draw an imaginary river system. They should link several fast-flowing streams
Close the lesson with a summarizing activity or discussion.

MEET THE NEEDS OF ALL YOUR STUDENTS

SCIENCE INTERACTIONS Teacher Editions provide you with an astounding array of features and options designed to make science learning a successful experience for all your students. Because hands-on experiences provide the most effective ways of teaching students with diverse needs, we devote special attention to the teaching notes and suggestions that accompany each activity in the student text.

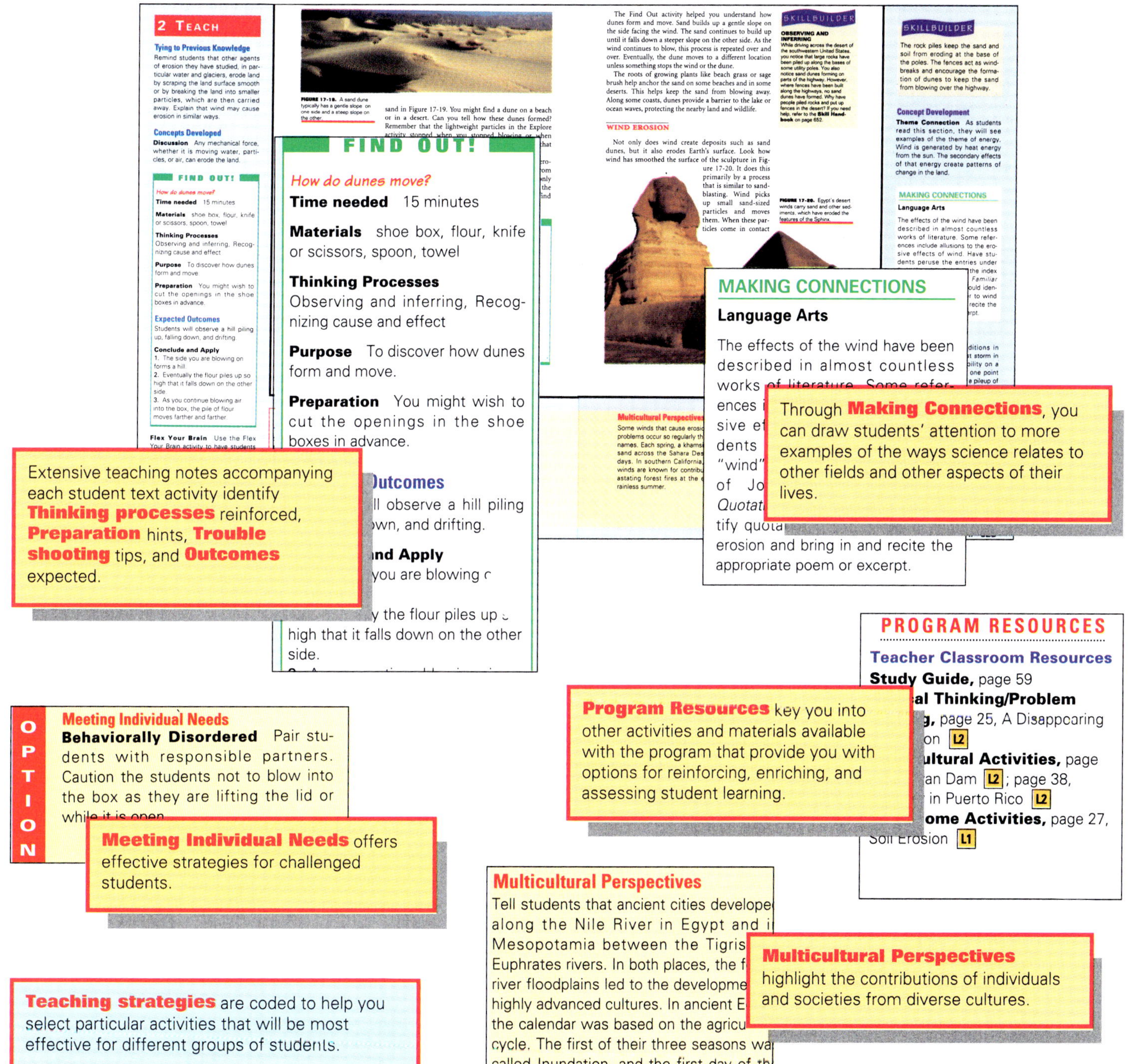

2 Teach
FIND OUT!
How do dunes move?
Time needed 15 minutes
Materials shoe box, flour, knife or scissors, spoon, towel
Thinking Processes Observing and inferring, Recognizing cause and effect
Purpose To discover how dunes form and move.
Preparation You might wish to cut the openings in the shoe boxes in advance.
Extensive teaching notes accompanying each student text activity identify Thinking processes reinforced, Preparation hints, Trouble shooting tips, and Outcomes expected.
SKILLBUILDER
WIND EROSION
MAKING CONNECTIONS
Language Arts
The effects of the wind have been described in almost countless
Through Making Connections, you can draw students' attention to more examples of the ways science relates to other fields and other aspects of their lives.
erosion and bring in and recite the appropriate poem or excerpt.
PROGRAM RESOURCES
Teacher Classroom Resources
Study Guide, page 59
Program Resources key you into other activities and materials available with the program that provide you with options for reinforcing, enriching, and assessing student learning.
OPTION
Meeting Individual Needs
Behaviorally Disordered Pair students with responsible partners. Caution the students not to blow into the box as they are lifting the lid or
Meeting Individual Needs offers effective strategies for challenged students.
Multicultural Perspectives
Tell students that ancient cities developed along the Nile River in Egypt and in Mesopotamia between the Tigris
Multicultural Perspectives highlight the contributions of individuals and societies from diverse cultures.
Teaching strategies are coded to help you select particular activities that will be most effective for different groups of students.

RESOURCES FOR DIFFERENT NEEDS

In addition to the wide array of instructional options provided in the student and teacher editions, ***SCIENCE INTERACTIONS*** *also offers an extensive list of support materials and program resources. Some of these materials offer alternative ways of enriching or extending your science program, others provide tools for reinforcing and evaluating student learning, while still others will help you directly in delivering instruction. You won't have time to use them all, but the ones you use will help you save the time you have.*

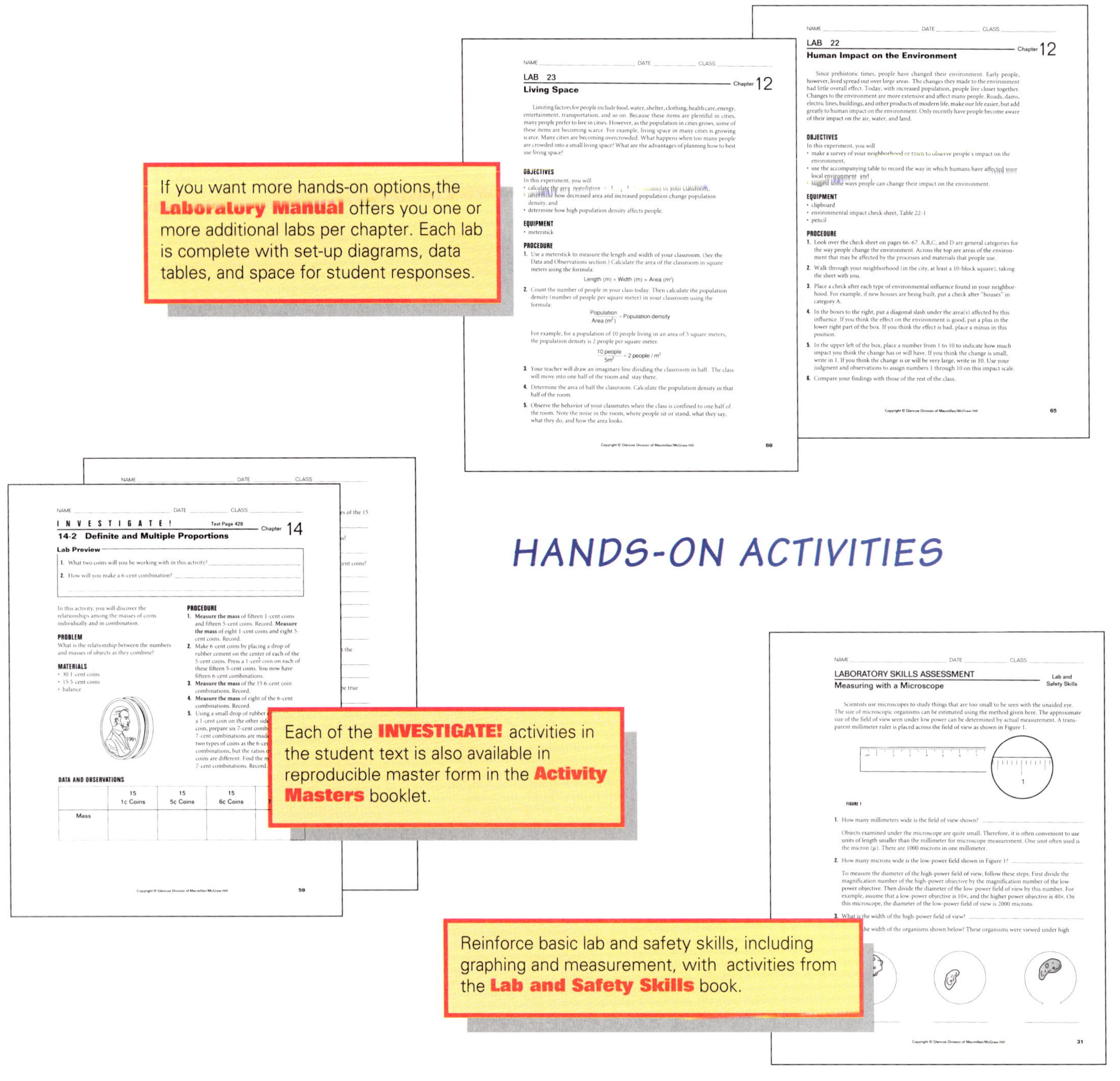
LAB 22 Human Impact on the Environment Chapter 12
LAB 23 Living Space Chapter 12
If you want more hands-on options, the **Laboratory Manual** offers you one or more additional labs per chapter. Each lab is complete with set-up diagrams, data tables, and space for student responses.
INVESTIGATE! 14-2 Definite and Multiple Proportions Chapter 14
HANDS-ON ACTIVITIES
Each of the **INVESTIGATE!** activities in the student text is also available in reproducible master form in the **Activity Masters** booklet.
LABORATORY SKILLS ASSESSMENT Measuring with a Microscope Lab and Safety Skills
Reinforce basic lab and safety skills, including graphing and measurement, with activities from the **Lab and Safety Skills** book.

Involve parents in your science program by sending your students home with easy-to-do, fun activities from the **Take Home Activities** book.

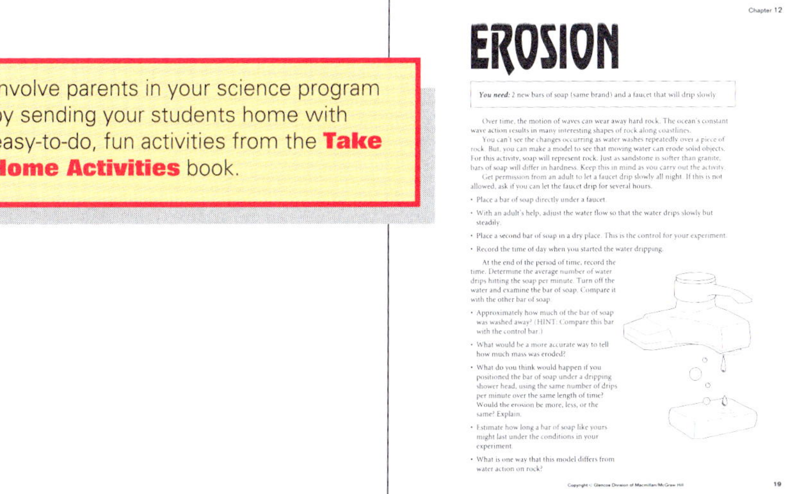

Chapter 12

EROSION

You need: 2 new bars of soap (same brand) and a faucet that will drip slowly

Over time, the motion of waves can wear away hard rock. The ocean's constant wave action results in many interesting shapes of rock along coastlines.

You can't see the changes occurring as water washes repeatedly over a piece of rock. But, you can make a model to see that moving water can erode solid objects. For this activity, soap will represent rock. Just as sandstone is softer than granite, bars of soap will differ in hardness. Keep this in mind as you carry out the activity.

Get permission from an adult to let a faucet drip slowly all night. If this is not allowed, ask if you can let the faucet drip for several hours.

- Place a bar of soap directly under a faucet.
- With an adult's help, adjust the water flow so that the water drips slowly but steadily.
- Place a second bar of soap in a dry place. This is the control for your experiment.
- Record the time of day when you started the water dripping.

At the end of the period of time, record the time. Determine the average number of water drips hitting the soap per minute. Turn off the water and examine the bar of soap. Compare it with the other bar of soap.

- Approximately how much of the bar of soap was washed away? (HINT: Compare this bar with the control bar.)
- What would be a more accurate way to tell how much mass was eroded?
- What do you think would happen if you positioned the bar of soap under a dripping shower head, using the same number of drips per minute over the same length of time? Would the erosion be more, less, or the same? Explain.
- Estimate how long a bar of soap like yours might last under the conditions in your experiment.
- What is one way that this model differs from water action on rock?

 19

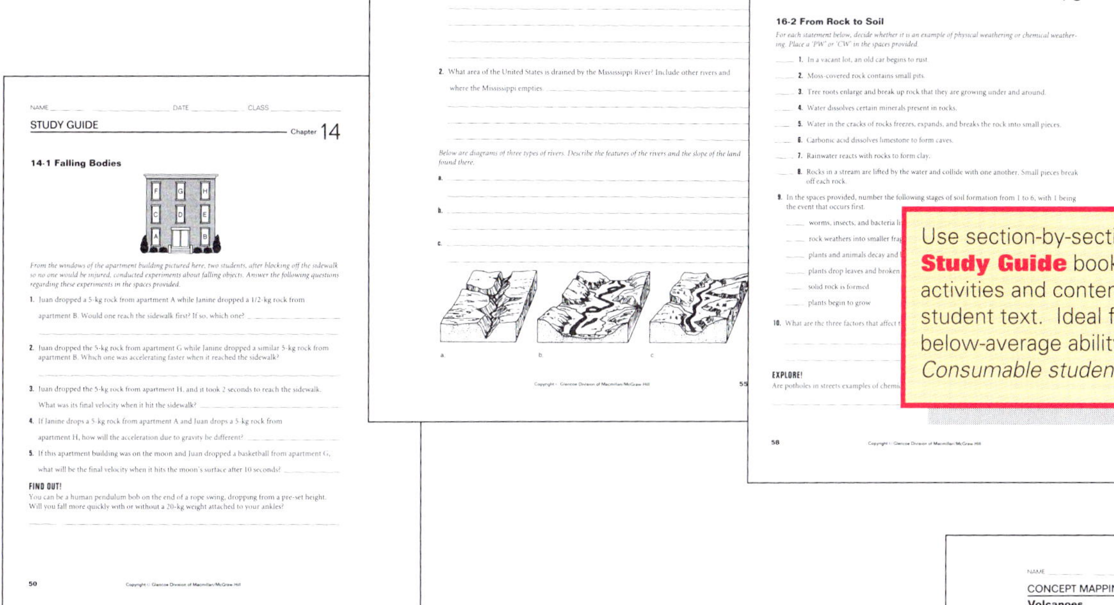

NAME ______ DATE ______ CLASS ______

STUDY GUIDE — Chapter 14

14-1 Falling Bodies

From the windows of the apartment building pictured here, two students, after blocking off the sidewalk so no one would be injured, conducted experiments about falling objects. Answer the following questions regarding these experiments in the spaces provided.

1. Juan dropped a 5-kg rock from apartment A while Janine dropped a 1/2-kg rock from apartment B. Would one reach the sidewalk first? If so, which one? ______
2. Juan dropped the 5-kg rock from apartment G while Janine dropped a similar 5-kg rock from apartment B. Which one was accelerating faster when it reached the sidewalk? ______
3. Juan dropped the 5-kg rock from apartment H, and it took 2 seconds to reach the sidewalk. What was its final velocity when it hit the sidewalk? ______
4. If Janine drops a 5-kg rock from apartment A and Juan drops a 5-kg rock from apartment H, how will the acceleration due to gravity be different? ______
5. If this apartment building was on the moon and Juan dropped a basketball from apartment G, what will be the final velocity when it hits the moon's surface after 10 seconds? ______

FIND OUT!
You can be a human pendulum bob on the end of a rope swing, dropping from a pre-set height. Will you fall more quickly with or without a 20-kg weight attached to your ankles?

50

NAME ______ DATE ______ CLASS ______

STUDY GUIDE — Chapter 15

15-2 Streams and Rivers

Answer each question, using complete sentences.

1. As rain begins to fall on Earth, trace how a drainage system is formed. ______
2. What area of the United States is drained by the Mississippi River? Include other rivers and where the Mississippi empties. ______

Below are diagrams of three types of rivers. Describe the features of the rivers and the slope of the land found there.

a. ______

b. ______

c. ______

 55

NAME ______ DATE ______ CLASS ______

STUDY GUIDE — Chapter 16

16-2 From Rock to Soil

For each statement below, decide whether it is an example of physical weathering or chemical weathering. Place a 'PW' or 'CW' in the spaces provided.

____ 1. In a vacant lot, an old car begins to rust.
____ 2. Moss-covered rock contains small pits.
____ 3. Tree roots enlarge and break up rock that they are growing under and around.
____ 4. Water dissolves certain minerals present in rocks.
____ 5. Water in the cracks of rocks freezes, expands, and breaks the rock into small pieces.
____ 6. Carbonic acid dissolves limestone to form caves.
____ 7. Rainwater reacts with rocks to form clay.
____ 8. Rocks in a stream are lifted by the water and collide with one another. Small pieces break off each rock.

9. In the spaces provided, number the following stages of soil formation from 1 to 6, with 1 being the event that occurs first.

____ worms, insects, and bacteria li…
____ rock weathers into smaller frag…
____ plants and animals decay and…
____ plants drop leaves and broken…
____ solid rock is formed
____ plants begin to grow

10. What are the three factors that affect t…

EXPLORE!
Are potholes in streets examples of chemi…

58

Use section-by-section masters from the **Study Guide** booklet to reinforce the activities and content presented in the student text. Ideal for average and below-average ability students. *Consumable student edition available.*

REINFORCEMENT

Reinforce relationships and connections within and among concepts and processes by using the **Concept Mapping** booklet.

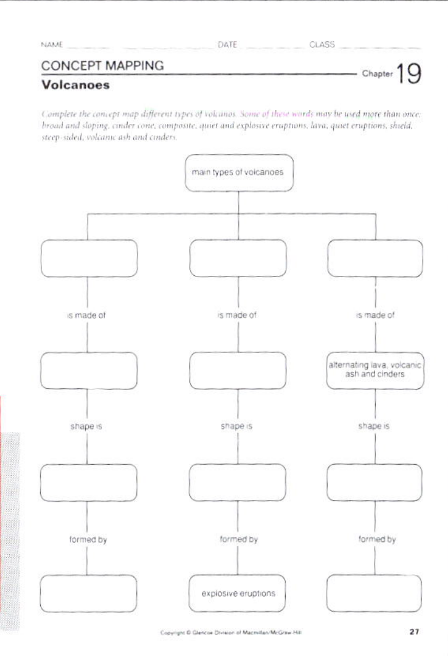

NAME ______ DATE ______ CLASS ______

CONCEPT MAPPING — Chapter 19

Volcanoes

Complete the concept map different types of volcanos. Some of these words may be used more than once: broad and sloping, cinder cone, composite, quiet and explosive eruptions, lava, quiet eruptions, shield, steep-sided, volcanic ash and cinders.

 27

ENRICHMENT

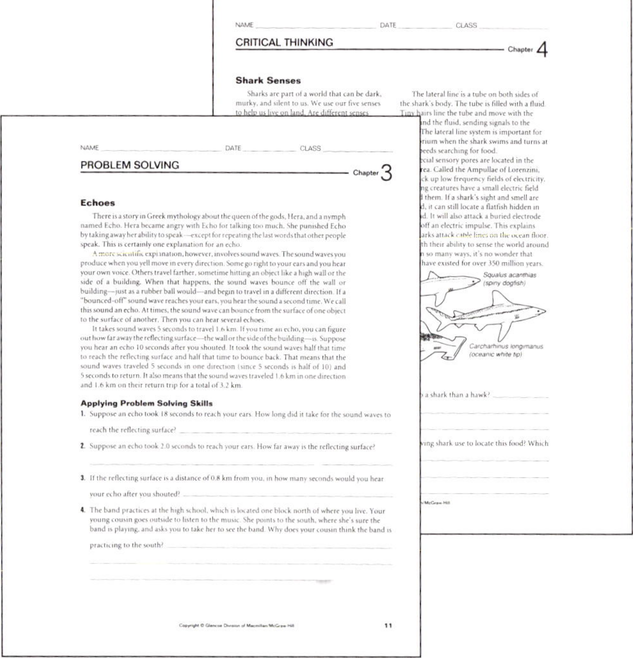

NAME ______ DATE ______ CLASS ______

CRITICAL THINKING Chapter 4

Shark Senses

Sharks are part of a world that can be dark, murky, and silent to us. We use our five senses to help us live on land. Are different senses ...

The lateral line is a tube on both sides of the shark's body. The tube is filled with a fluid. Tiny hairs line the tube and move with the ...

NAME ______ DATE ______ CLASS ______

PROBLEM SOLVING Chapter 3

Echoes

There is a story in Greek mythology about the queen of the gods, Hera, and a nymph named Echo. Hera became angry with Echo for talking too much. She punished Echo by taking away her ability to speak—except for repeating the last words that other people speak. This is certainly one explanation for an echo.

A more scientific explanation, however, involves sound waves. The sound waves you produce when you yell move in every direction. Some go right to your ears and you hear your own voice. Others travel farther, sometime hitting an object like a high wall or the side of a building. When that happens, the sound waves bounce off the wall or building—just as a rubber ball would—and begin to travel in a different direction. If a "bounced-off" sound wave reaches your ears, you hear the sound a second time. We call this sound an echo. At times, the sound wave can bounce from the surface of one object to the surface of another. Then you can hear several echoes.

It takes sound waves 5 seconds to travel 1.6 km. If you time an echo, you can figure out how far away the reflecting surface—the wall or the side of the building—is. Suppose you hear an echo 10 seconds after you shouted. It took the sound waves half that time to reach the reflecting surface and half that time to bounce back. That means that the sound waves traveled 5 seconds in one direction (since 5 seconds is half of 10) and 5 seconds to return. It also means that the sound waves traveled 1.6 km in one direction and 1.6 km on their return trip for a total of 3.2 km.

Applying Problem Solving Skills

1. Suppose an echo took 18 seconds to reach your ears. How long did it take for the sound waves to reach the reflecting surface? ______
2. Suppose an echo took 2.0 seconds to reach your ears. How far away is the reflecting surface? ______
3. If the reflecting surface is a distance of 0.8 km from you, in how many seconds would you hear your echo after you shouted? ______
4. The band practices at the high school, which is located one block north of where you live. Your young cousin goes outside to listen to the music. She points to the south, where she's sure the band is playing, and asks you to take her to see the band. Why does your cousin think the band is practicing to the south? ______

 11

Challenge students to apply their critical thinking and problem-solving abilities with the **Critical Thinking/Problem Solving** booklet. It is especially suitable for average and above-average ability students.

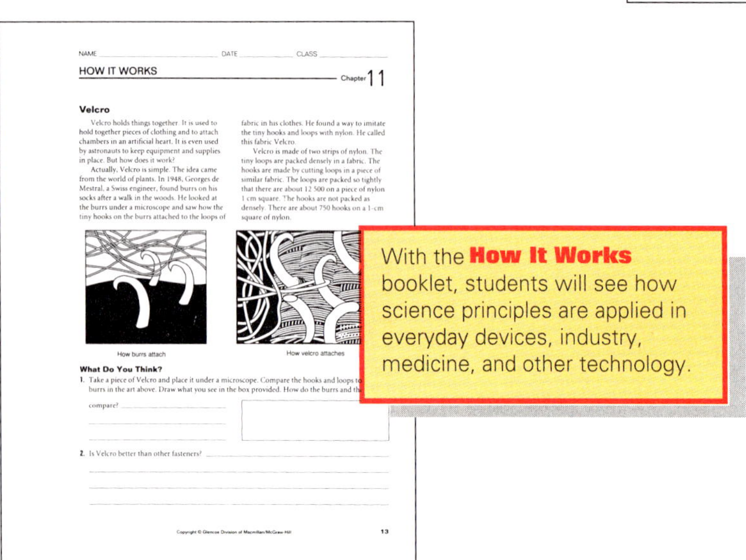

NAME ______ DATE ______ CLASS ______

HOW IT WORKS Chapter 11

Velcro

Velcro holds things together. It is used to hold together pieces of clothing and to attach chambers in an artificial heart. It is even used by astronauts to keep equipment and supplies in place. But how does it work?

Actually, Velcro is simple. The idea came from the world of plants. In 1948, Georges de Mestral, a Swiss engineer, found burrs on his socks after a walk in the woods. He looked at the burrs under a microscope and saw how the tiny hooks on the burrs attached to the loops of fabric in his clothes. He found a way to imitate the tiny hooks and loops with nylon. He called this fabric Velcro.

Velcro is made of two strips of nylon. The tiny loops are packed densely in a fabric. The hooks are made by cutting loops in a piece of similar fabric. The loops are packed so tightly that there are about 12 500 on a piece of nylon 1 cm square. The hooks are not packed as densely. There are about 750 hooks on a 1-cm square of nylon.

How burrs attach

How velcro attaches

What Do You Think?

1. Take a piece of Velcro and place it under a microscope. Compare the hooks and loops to burrs in the art above. Draw what you see in the box provided. How do the burrs and th... compare? ______
2. Is Velcro better than other fasteners? ______

 13

With the **How It Works** booklet, students will see how science principles are applied in everyday devices, industry, medicine, and other technology.

NAME ______ DATE ______ CLASS ______

MULTICULTURAL ACTIVITIES Use with Section 6:1 Chapter 6

Navajo Jewelry

When American and European traders went west, they traded silver to the Indians. The Navajo began working the silver into jewelry, bridles, and buckles. Today, the Navajo Indians are well known for making beautiful silver jewelry.

Pure silver is a very soft metal, too soft to use for jewelry. It is usually mixed with copper to produce a malleable alloy called sterling silver, which is 92.5 percent silver. Most of the Navajo work is made from sterling silver.

When Navajo silversmithing began, the tools were very simple: stone and adobe forges, sheepskin bellows, iron anvils, and clay crucibles. Modern Navajo Indians use sophisticated equipment to make their jewelry: diamond saws, hack saws, torches, and electric polishing equipment. They purchase silver from merchants in surrounding towns.

Some Navajo crafts are a family business, but this is not true of silversmithing. It is performed only by those skilled in the craft. The demand for silver Navajo jewelry is so great, silversmithing has become a full-time job. In some cases, the Navajo even produce jewelry by assembly line. This results in items produced by several Indians rather than just one craftsworker.

There are still many Navajo who create silver jewelry individually. They mark their work with their personal symbols, which often represents their family clan. Many people are still willing to pay higher prices for this fine, high-quality Navajo jewelry.

What Do You Think?

1. What are the qualities of silver that make it a good material for jewelry? ______
2. If you were given a small rectangular sheet of sterling silver, what tools would you use to make it into a bracelet? ______

16

Explore the past and present contributions to science of individuals and societies from various cultural backgrounds through the readings and activities in the **Multicultural Activities** booklet.

ENRICHMENT

Activities and readings in the **Making Connections** booklet series enable students to expand their understanding of the impact of science in other subjects and in different areas of their lives.

Integrating Sciences reinforces the interconnectedness of the science disciplines.

Technology and Society explores the relationship and consequences of the interaction among science, technology, and society.

Across the Curriculum relates science to a multitude of other disciplines, including art, literature, and social studies.

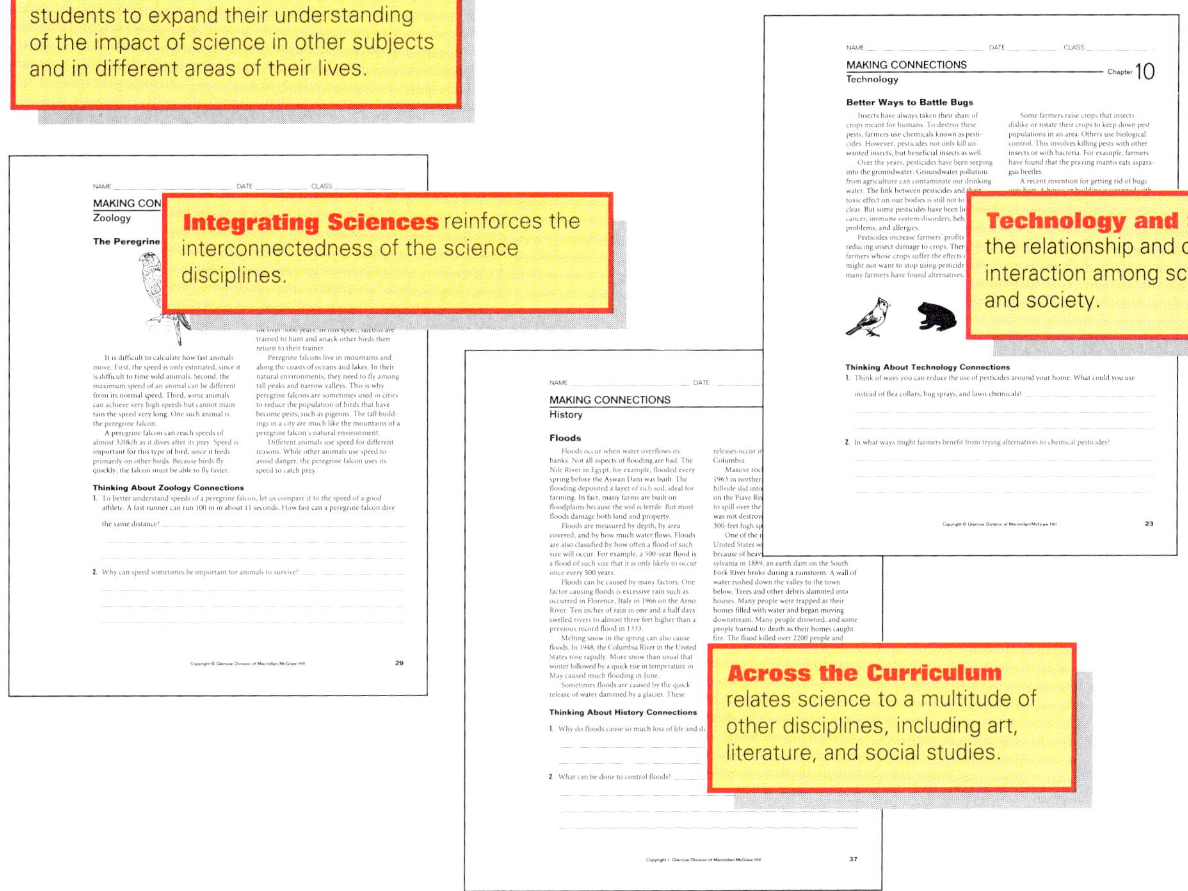

NAME ______ DATE ______ CLASS ______

MAKING CON
Zoology

The Peregrine

... trained to hunt and attack other birds then return to their trainer.

It is difficult to calculate how fast animals move. First, the speed is only estimated, since it is difficult to time wild animals. Second, the maximum speed of an animal can be different from its normal speed. Third, some animals can achieve very high speeds but cannot maintain the speed very long. One such animal is the peregrine falcon.

A peregrine falcon can reach speeds of almost 320k/h as it dives after its prey. Speed is important for this type of bird, since it feeds primarily on other birds. Because birds fly quickly, the falcon must be able to fly faster.

Peregrine falcons live in mountains and along the coasts of oceans and lakes. In their natural environments, they need to fly among tall peaks and narrow valleys. This is why peregrine falcons are sometimes used in cities to reduce the population of birds that have become pests, such as pigeons. The tall buildings in a city are much like the mountains of a peregrine falcon's natural environment.

Different animals use speed for different reasons. While other animals use speed to avoid danger, the peregrine falcon uses its speed to catch prey.

Thinking About Zoology Connections

1. To better understand speeds of a peregrine falcon, let us compare it to the speed of a good athlete. A fast runner can run 100 m in about 11 seconds. How fast can a peregrine falcon dive the same distance? ______
2. Why can speed sometimes be important for animals to survive? ______

Copyright © Glencoe Division of Macmillan/McGraw Hill 29

NAME ______ DATE ______

MAKING CONNECTIONS
History

Floods

Floods occur when water overflows its banks. Not all aspects of flooding are bad. The Nile River in Egypt, for example, flooded every spring before the Aswan Dam was built. The flooding deposited a layer of rich soil, ideal for farming. In fact, many farms are built on floodplains because the soil is fertile. But most floods damage both land and property.

Floods are measured by depth, by area covered, and by how much water flows. Floods are also classified by how often a flood of such size will occur. For example, a 500-year flood is a flood of such size that it is only likely to occur once every 500 years.

Floods can be caused by many factors. One factor causing floods is excessive rain such as occurred in Florence, Italy in 1966 on the Arno River. Ten inches of rain in one and a half days swelled rivers to almost three feet higher than a previous record flood in 1333.

Melting snow in the spring can also cause floods. In 1948, the Columbia River in the United States rose rapidly. More snow than usual that winter followed by a quick rise in temperature in May caused much flooding in June.

Sometimes floods are caused by the quick release of water dammed by a glacier. These releases occur i... Columbia.

Massive roc... 1963 in norther... hillside slid into... on the Piave Ri... to spill over the... was not destroy... 300-feet high sp...

One of the ... United States w... because of heav... sylvania in 1889, an earth dam on the South Fork River broke during a rainstorm. A wall of water rushed down the valley to the town below. Trees and other debris slammed into houses. Many people were trapped as their homes filled with water and began moving downstream. Many people drowned, and some people burned to death as their homes caught fire. The flood killed over 2200 people and

Thinking About History Connections

1. Why do floods cause so much loss of life and d... ______
2. What can be done to control floods? ______

Copyright © Glencoe Division of Macmillan/McGraw Hill 37

NAME ______ DATE ______ CLASS ______

MAKING CONNECTIONS Chapter 10
Technology

Better Ways to Battle Bugs

Insects have always taken their share of crops meant for humans. To destroy these pests, farmers use chemicals known as pesticides. However, pesticides not only kill unwanted insects, but beneficial insects as well.

Over the years, pesticides have been seeping into the groundwater. Groundwater pollution from agriculture can contaminate our drinking water. The link between pesticides and their toxic effect on our bodies is still not to... clear. But some pesticides have been li... cancer, immune system disorders, beh... problems, and allergies.

Pesticides increase farmers' profits ... reducing insect damage to crops. Ther... farmers whose crops suffer the effects ... might not want to stop using pesticide... many farmers have found alternatives.

Some farmers raise crops that insects dislike or rotate their crops to keep down pest populations in an area. Others use biological control. This involves killing pests with other insects or with bacteria. For example, farmers have found that the praying mantis eats asparagus beetles.

A recent invention for getting rid of bugs ...

Thinking About Technology Connections

1. Think of ways you can reduce the use of pesticides around your home. What could you use instead of flea collars, bug sprays, and lawn chemicals? ______
2. In what ways might farmers benefit from trying alternatives to chemical pesticides? ______

Copyright © Glencoe Division of Macmillan/McGraw Hill 23

ASSESSMENT

Assess student learning and performance through a variety of questioning strategies and formats in the **Review and Assessment** book. Test items cover activity procedures and analysis as well as science concepts within the four pages of reproducible masters available for each chapter.

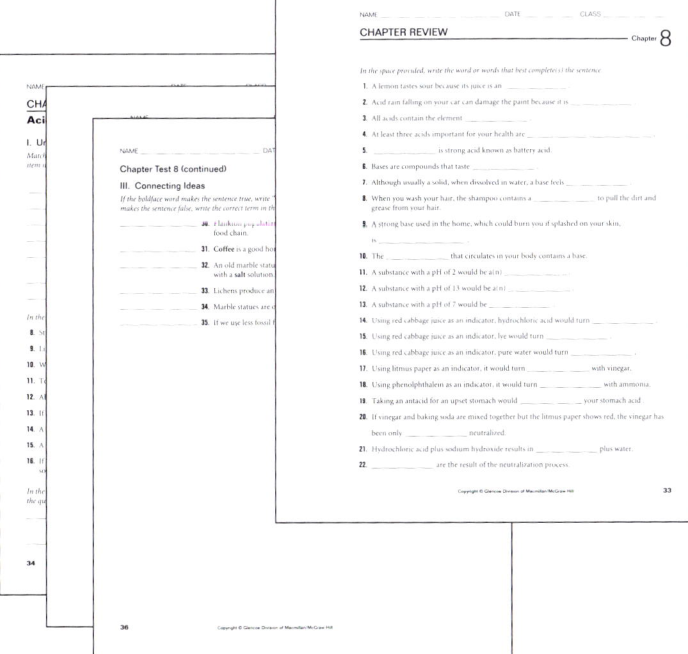

NAME ______ DATE ______

Chapter Test 8 (continued)

III. Connecting Ideas

If the boldface word makes the sentence true, write "... makes the sentence false, write the correct term in th...

______ 30. Plankton populati... food chain.
______ 31. **Coffee** is a good ho...
______ 32. An old marble statu... with a **salt** solution.
______ 33. Lichens produce an...
______ 34. Marble statues are ...
______ 35. If we use less fossil ...

36 Copyright © Glencoe Division of Macmillan/McGraw Hill

NAME ______ DATE ______ CLASS ______

CHAPTER REVIEW Chapter 8

In the space provided, write the word or words that best complete(s) the sentence.

1. A lemon tastes sour because its juice is an ______.
2. Acid rain falling on your car can damage the paint because it is ______.
3. All acids contain the element ______.
4. At least three acids important for your health are ______.
5. ______ is strong acid known as battery acid.
6. Bases are compounds that taste ______.
7. Although usually a solid, when dissolved in water, a base feels ______.
8. When you wash your hair, the shampoo contains a ______ to pull the dirt and grease from your hair.
9. A strong base used in the home, which could burn you if splashed on your skin, is ______.
10. The ______ that circulates in your body contains a base.
11. A substance with a pH of 2 would be a(n) ______.
12. A substance with a pH of 13 would be a(n) ______.
13. A substance with a pH of 7 would be ______.
14. Using red cabbage juice as an indicator, hydrochloric acid would turn ______.
15. Using red cabbage juice as an indicator, lye would turn ______.
16. Using red cabbage juice as an indicator, pure water would turn ______.
17. Using litmus paper as an indicator, it would turn ______ with vinegar.
18. Using phenolphthalein as an indicator, it would turn ______ with ammonia.
19. Taking an antacid for an upset stomach would ______ your stomach acid.
20. If vinegar and baking soda are mixed together but the litmus paper shows red, the vinegar has been only ______ neutralized.
21. Hydrochloric acid plus sodium hydroxide results in ______ plus water.
22. ______ are the result of the neutralization process.

Copyright © Glencoe Division of Macmillan/McGraw Hill 33

Computer Test Banks, available in Apple, IBM, and Macintosh versions, provide the ultimate flexibility in designing and creating your own test instruments. Select test items from two different levels of difficulty or write and edit your own.

TEACHING RESOURCES

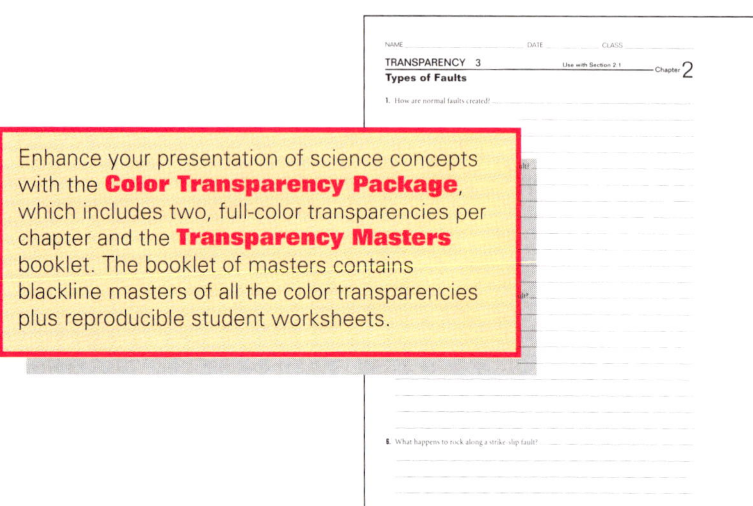

NAME DATE CLASS

TRANSPARENCY 3 Use with Section 2.1 Chapter 2

Types of Faults

1. How are normal faults created?

4. What happens to rock along a strike-slip fault?

10 Copyright © Glencoe Division of Macmillan/McGraw-Hill

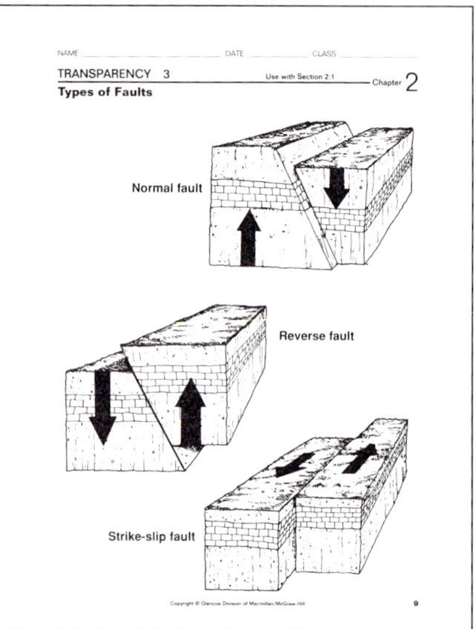

NAME DATE CLASS

TRANSPARENCY 3 Use with Section 2.1 Chapter 2

Types of Faults

Copyright © Glencoe Division of Macmillan/McGraw-Hill 9

Enhance your presentation of science concepts with the **Color Transparency Package**, which includes two, full-color transparencies per chapter and the **Transparency Masters** booklet. The booklet of masters contains blackline masters of all the color transparencies plus reproducible student worksheets.

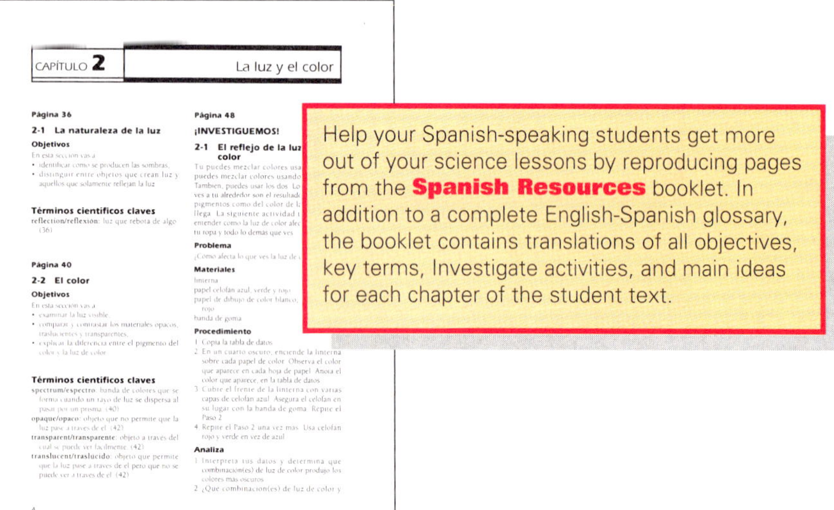

CAPÍTULO 2 La luz y el color

Página 36

2-1 La naturaleza de la luz

Objetivos

En esta sección vas a
- identificar cómo se producen las sombras.
- distinguir entre objetos que crean luz y aquellos que solamente reflejan la luz

Términos científicos claves

reflection/reflexión: luz que rebota de algo (36)

Página 40

2-2 El color

Objetivos

En esta sección vas a
- examinar la luz visible.
- comparar y contrastar los materiales opacos, traslucientes y transparentes.
- explicar la diferencia entre el pigmento del color y la luz de color

Términos científicos claves

spectrum/espectro: banda de colores que se forma cuando un rayo de luz se dispersa al pasar por un prisma (40)

opaque/opaco: objeto que no permite que la luz pase a través de el (42)

transparent/transparente: objeto a través del cual se puede ver fácilmente (42)

translucent/traslúcido: objeto que permite que la luz pase a través de el pero que no se puede ver a través de el (42)

Página 48

¡INVESTIGUEMOS!

2-1 El reflejo de la luz color

Tu puedes mezclar colores usa puedes mezclar colores usando Tambien, puedes usar los dos Lo ves a tu alrededor son el resultad pigmentos como del color de l llega La siguiente actividad t entender como la luz de color afe tu ropa y todo lo demas que ves

Problema

¿Como afecta lo que ves la luz de

Materiales

linterna
papel celofán azul, verde y rojo
papel de dibujo de color blanco, rojo
banda de goma

Procedimiento

1 Copia la tabla de datos
2 En un cuarto oscuro, enciende la linterna sobre cada papel de color Observa el color que aparece en cada hoja de papel Anota el color que aparece, en la tabla de datos
3 Cubre el frente de la linterna con varias capas de celofán azul Asegura el celofán en su lugar con la banda de goma Repite el Paso 2
4 Repite el Paso 2 una vez mas Usa celofán rojo y verde en vez de azul

Analiza

1 Interpreta tus datos y determina que combinación(es) de luz de color produjo los colores más oscuros
2 ¿Que combinación(es) de luz de color y

4

Help your Spanish-speaking students get more out of your science lessons by reproducing pages from the **Spanish Resources** booklet. In addition to a complete English-Spanish glossary, the booklet contains translations of all objectives, key terms, Investigate activities, and main ideas for each chapter of the student text.

COOPERATIVE LEARNING STRATEGIES

The **Cooperative Learning** Resource Guide contains background information, strategies, and practical tips for using cooperative learning techniques whenever you do activities from ***SCIENCE INTERACTIONS.***

13:1 LESSON PLAN

Chapter by chapter **Lesson Plans** will help you organize your lessons more efficiently.

Using the bar code directory in the **Videodisc Correlation** booklet, you can access with a bar code reader all the images in Optical Data's life, Earth, and physical science videodiscs that correlate to ***SCIENCE INTERACTIONS.***

SCIENCE AND TECHNOLOGY VIDEODISC SERIES

This seven-disc series contains more than 280 full-motion videoreports on a broad spectrum of topics relating to current research in various science fields, innovations in technology, and science and society issues. In addition to reinforcing science concepts, the videoreports are ideal for illustrating science methods, laboratory techniques, and careers in science.

Disc 1: PHYSICS
Disc 2: CHEMISTRY
Disc 3: EARTH AND SPACE
Disc 4: PLANTS AND SIMPLE ORGANISMS
Disc 5: ANIMALS
Disc 6: ECOLOGY
Disc 7: HUMAN BIOLOGY

Produced and narrated by Don Herbert, "Mr. Wizard".

Teaching Support

The teacher guides accompanying the videodisc series show you how to use the videoreports to enrich and add excitement to your science lessons.

Each **Videodisc Teacher Guide** includes a bar code directory plus teaching strategies, research updates, and complete narration for each videoreport.

The ***SCIENCE INTERACTIONS*** **Videodisc Teacher Guide** shows you how to integrate the videoreports into your daily science lessons. For each videoreport cited, the guide identifies the lesson concept or process it supports, suggests ways to use it to introduce or extend the lesson, and offers followup activities for students to do. Bar codes and a quick directory help you access the reports almost instantly.

THINKING PROCESSES

Science is not just a collection of facts for students to memorize. Rather it is a process of applying those observations and intuitions to situations and problems, formulating hypotheses and drawing conclusions. This interaction of the thinking process with the content of science is the core of science and should be the focus of science study. Students, much like scientists, will plan and conduct research or experiments based on observations, evaluate their findings, and draw conclusions to explain their results. This process then begins again, using the new information for further investigation.

SCIENCE INTERACTIONS provides the perfect balance of content and process so that students learn to apply the principles they learn through observation.

Observing

What are the thinking processes? The most basic process is *observing*. Through observation—seeing, hearing, touching, smelling, tasting—the student begins to acquire information about an object or event. Observation allows a student to gather information regarding size, shape, texture, or quantity of an object or event. The following statements and questions might be posed to students to focus their observations:

"Describe what the objects feel like."
"List the shapes that you see."
"What characteristics can you observe?"
"Give information about the size and quantity of the objects."

Organizing Information

Students can then begin to organize the information acquired through observation. This process of organizing information encompasses *ordering, organizing,* and *comparing.* How the objects or events are ordered, categorized, or compared is determined by the purpose for doing so. When ordering information, events are placed in a sequence that tells a logical story. To *classify* or *categorize* information, objects or ideas are compared in order to identify common features. By looking at similarities and differences, objects or ideas can be compared.

Communicating

Communicating information is an important part of science. Once all the information is gathered, it is necessary to organize the observations so that the findings can be considered and shared by others. Information can be presented in tables, charts, a variety of graphs, or models which make it easier to consider the facts. The following statements and questions may assist students in organizing the information so that it may be communicated to others.

"Compare these on the basis of color and shape."
"What information would you use to classify these objects?"
"Contrast the visible properties of these liquids."
"Order your data according to weight."
"Present your facts on a bar graph."

Inferring

This leads to another process—*inferring.* Inferences are logical conclusions based on observations and are made after careful evaluation of all the available facts or data. Inferences are a means to explain or interpret observations. They are a prediction or hypothesis that can be tested and evaluated. The teacher may pose the following questions to focus students on the process of inferring:

"What predictions can you make based on the outcome of this experiment?"
"What can you infer from the classification of this data?"
"Discuss the data that supports your prediction."

Relating

Another process to be discussed here is *relating* cause and effect. This process focuses on how events or objects interact with one another. It also involves examining dependencies and relationships between objects and events. Since not all relationships are directly observable, the process can also be based on logical conclusions drawn from all the available data. In science, experiments involve the process of cause and relating effect. The hypothesis states an inferred relationship between objects or events. Then, as the hypothesis is tested, each variable that may interact to effect the results must be carefully controlled.

Finally, the findings can be applied. *Applying* is a process that puts scientific information to use. Sometimes the findings can be applied in a practical sense or they can be used to tie together complex data. These statements and questions may be used to focus students on the process of applying:

"How does pollution affect vegetation?"
"Design a way to keep a drink cold without ice."

Interaction of Content and Process

SCIENCE INTERACTIONS encourages the interaction between science content and thinking processes. We've known for a long time that hands-on activities are a way of providing a bridge between science content and student comprehension. *SCIENCE INTERACTIONS* encourages the interaction between content and thinking processes by offering literally hundreds of hands-on activities that are easy to set up and do. In the student text, the EXPLORE! and FIND OUT! activities require students to make observations, and collect and record a variety of data. INVESTIGATE! activities connect the activity with the content information. The *Skillbuilder/Skill Handbook* provides the student with another opportunity to practice the thinking processes relevant to the material they are studying. The *Skill Handbook* provides examples of the processes which students may refer to as they do the *Skillbuilder* exercises.

Thinking Processes at Chapter End

At the end of each chapter, students use the thinking processes as they complete Apply (Check Your Understanding), Critical Thinking, Problem Solving, and Connecting (Relating) Ideas questions. *Expanding Your View* connects the science content to other disciplines.

Thinking Processes in the Teacher Wraparound Edition

These processes are also featured throughout the **Teacher Wraparound Edition.** In the margins are suggestions for students to write in a journal. Keeping a journal encourages students to communicate their ideas, a key process in science.

Flex Your Brain is a self-directed activity designed to assist students to develop thinking processes as they investigate content areas. Suggestions for using this decision-making matrix are in the margins of the **Teacher Wraparound Edition** whenever appropriate for the topic. Further discussion of Flex Your Brain can be found in the **Critical Thinking/Problem Solving** booklet of the **Teacher Classroom Resource Package.**

Concept Mapping

Concept mapping helps the student make abstract information more concrete and useful by visually representing relationships among concepts. Concept maps can show the interactions of a series of events, describe the stages of a process, or present a hierarchy of procedures. Further information on concept mapping and a concept map for each Chapter can be found in the front of the **Concept Mapping** booklet of the **Teacher Classroom Resource Package.**

More Process Skills

In each chapter opener, the **Teacher Wraparound Edition** provides Enrichment, Science at Home, and Project ideas. Each of these indicates a thinking process skill which students will use as they complete each activity.

On page 30T, you will find a Thinking Process Map which indicates how frequently thinking process skills are encouraged and developed in *SCIENCE INTERACTIONS.*

Hands-on activities are a way to bridge the gap between science content and student comprehension. *SCIENCE INTERACTIONS* encourages the interaction between content and thinking processes by offering literally hundreds of hands-on activities that are easy to set up and do.

Course 1 THINKING PROCESSES MAP

THINKING PROCESSES	Chapters																			
	1	2	3	4	5	6	7	8	9	10	11	12	13	14	15	16	17	18	19	20
Categorizing	1	1		2	1	4		2	5		2	2				1				
Ordering	1											1			1		2			
Communicating		1	3	2	1	2	3	3	3	3	2	1	3	3					2	2
Observing and Inferring	10	7	9	8	11	9	12	11	4	8	9	4	8	7	5	8	7	10	8	9
Comparing		6	6	4	5	6	10	4	3	3	7	3	1	4	2			6		1
Relating	1	4	7	1		3	3	2		1	3	1	1	2	3	2	2	6	5	4
Applying	3	2		2	1	1		1	2	2	1	3	1	1	2	2	4		7	3

The numbers in the map above indicate how many times the various processes are used in each chapter's activities (EXPLORE!; FIND OUT!; INVESTIGATE!) and *Skillbuilders.*

MEETING INDIVIDUAL NEEDS

Each student brings their own unique set of abilities, perceptions, and needs into the classroom. It is important that the teacher try to make the classroom environment as receptive to these differences as possible and to ensure a good learning environment for all students.

It is important to recognize that individual learning styles are different and that learning style does not reflect a student's ability level. While some students learn primarily through visual or auditory senses, others are kinesthetic learners and do best if they have hands-on exploratory interaction with materials. Some students work best alone and others learn best in a group environment. While some students seek to understand the "big picture" in order to deal with specifics, others need to understand the details first, in order to put the whole concept together.

In an effort to provide all students with a positive science experience, this text offers a variety of ways for students to interact with materials so that they can utilize their preferred method of learning the concepts. The variety of approaches allows students to become familiar with other learning approaches as well.

ABILITY LEVELS

The activities are broken down into three levels to accommodate all student ability levels. ***SCIENCE INTERACTIONS* Teacher Wraparound Edition** designates the activities as follows:

L1 activities are basic activities designed to be within the ability range of all students. These activities reinforce the concepts presented.

L1 activities are application activities designed for students who have mastered the concepts presented. These activities give students an opportunity for practical application of the concepts presented.

L1 activities are challenging activities designed for the students who are able to go beyond the basic concepts presented. These activities allow students to expand their perspectives on the basic concepts presented.

LIMITED ENGLISH PROFICIENCY

In providing for the student with limited English proficiency, the focus needs to be on overcoming a language barrier. Once again it is important not to confuse ability in speaking/reading English with academic ability or "intelligence." The following ideas may help you to structure learning for the LEP student:

1. Visual and experiential teaching is important. Use demonstrations to clarify ideas. For example, in discussing the "domino effect," do a demonstration using dominoes.
2. Make use of "independent" (especially small group) activities. Small group work allows for more participation and discussion by LEP students.
3. Concepts need to be presented and worked in a variety of ways. Try to relate the concepts to situations of relevance to the student. Provide examples, nonverbal strategies, and model the concept whenever possible.
4. Check for understanding frequently. Provide opportunities for students to do sample evaluation items similar to those on tests.

In general, the best method for dealing with LEP, variations in learning styles, and ability levels is to provide all students with a variety of ways to learn, apply, and be assessed on the concepts. Look for this symbol LEP in the teacher margin for specific strategies for students with limited English proficiency.

The chart on pages 32T-33T gives additional tips you may find useful in structuring the learning environment in your classroom to meet students' special needs. In the options margins of the **Teacher Wraparound Edition** there are two or more "Meeting Individual Needs" strategies for each chapter.

MEETING SPECIAL NEEDS

	DESCRIPTION	SOURCES OF HELP/INFORMATION
Learning Disabled	All learning-disabled students have problems in one or more areas, such as academic learning, language, perception, social-emotional adjustment, memory, or attention.	*Journal of Learning Disabilities* *Learning Disability Quarterly*
Behaviorally Disordered	Children with behavior disorders deviate from standards or expectations of behavior and impair the functioning of others and themselves. These children may also be gifted or learning disabled.	*Exceptional Children* *Journal of Special Education*
Physically Challenged	Children who are physically disabled fall into two categories—those with orthopedic impairments and those with other health impairments. Orthopedically-impaired children have the use of one or more limbs severely restricted, so the use of wheelchairs, crutches, or braces may be necessary. Children with other health impairments may require the use of respirators or have other medical equipment.	Batshaw, M.L. and M.Y. Perset. *Children with Handicaps: A Medical Primer*. Baltimore: Paul H. Brooks, 1981. Hale, G. (Ed.). *The Source Book for the Disabled*. NY: Holt, Rinehart & Winston, 1982. *Teaching Exceptional Children*
Visually Impaired	Children who are visually disabled have partial or total loss of sight. Individuals with visual impairments are not significantly different from their sighted peers in ability range or personality. However, blindness may affect cognitive, motor, and social development, especially if early intervention is lacking.	*Journal of Visual Impairment and Blindness* *Education of Visually Handicapped* American Foundation for the Blind
Hearing Impaired	Children who are hearing impaired have partial or total loss of hearing. Individuals with hearing impairments are not significantly different from their hearing peers in ability range or personality. However, the chronic condition of deafness may affect cognitive, motor, and social development if early intervention is lacking. Speech development also is often affected.	*American Annals of the Deaf* *Journal of Speech and Hearing Research* *Sign Language Studies*
Gifted	Although no formal definition exists, these students can be described as having above average ability, task commitment, and creativity. Gifted students rank in the top 5% of their class. They usually finish work more quickly than other students and are capable of divergent thinking.	*Journal for the Education of the Gifted* *Gifted Child Quarterly* *Gifted Creative/Talented*

TIPS FOR INSTRUCTION

1. Provide support and structure; clearly specify rules, assignments, and duties.
2. Establish situations that lead to success.
3. Practice skills frequently—use games and drills to help maintain student interest.
4. Allow students to record answers on tape and allow extra time to complete tests and assignments.
5. Provide outlines or tape lecture material.
6. Pair students with peer helpers, and provide classtime for pair interaction.

1. Provide a clearly structured environment with regard to scheduling, rules, room arrangement, and safety.
2. Clearly outline objectives and how you will help students obtain objectives. Seek input from them about their strengths, weaknesses, and goals.
3. Reinforce appropriate behavior and model it for students.
4. Do not expect immediate success. Instead, work for long term improvement.
5. Balance individual needs with group requirements.

1. Openly discuss with student any uncertainties you have about when to offer aid.
2. Ask parents or therapists and students what special devices or procedures are needed, and if any special safety precautions need to be taken.
3. Allow physically-disabled students to do everything their peers do, including participating in field trips, special events, and projects.
4. Help nondisabled students and adults understand physically-disabled students.

1. As with all students, help the student become independent. Some assignments may need to be modified.
2. Teach classmates how to serve as guides.
3. Limit unnecessary noise in the classroom.
4. Encourage students to use their sense of touch. Provide tactile models whenever possible.
5. Describe people and events as they occur in the classroom.
6. Provide taped lectures and reading assignments.
7. Team the student with a sighted peer for laboratory work.

1. Seat students where they can see your lip movements easily, and avoid visual distractions.
2. Avoid standing with your back to the window or light source.
3. Using an overhead projector allows you to maintain eyecontact while writing.
4. Seat students where they can see speakers.
5. Write all assignments on the board, or hand out written instructions.
6. If the student has a manual interpreter, allow both student and interpreter to select the most favorable seating arrangements.

1. Make arrangements for students to take selected subjects early and to work on independent projects.
2. Let students express themselves in art forms such as drawing, creative writing, or acting.
3. Make public services available through a catalog of resources, such as agencies providing free and inexpensive materials, community services and programs, and people in the community with specific expertise.
4. Ask "what if" questions to develop high-level thinking skills; establish an environment safe for risk taking.
5. Emphasize concepts, theories, ideas, relationships, and generalizations.

COOPERATIVE LEARNING

What is Cooperative Learning?

In cooperative learning, students work together in small groups to learn academic material and interpersonal skills. Group members learn that they are responsible for accomplishing an assigned group task as well as for each learning the material. Cooperative learning fosters academic, personal, and social success for all students.

Recent research shows that cooperative learning results in

- development of positive attitudes toward science and toward school
- lower drop-out rates for at-risk students.
- building respect for others regardless of race, ethnic origin, or sex.
- increased sensitivity to and tolerance of diverse perspectives.

Establishing a Cooperative Classroom

Cooperative groups in the middle school usually contain from two to five students. Heterogeneous groups that contain a mixture of abilities, genders, and ethnicity expose students to ideas different from their own and help them to learn to work with different people.

Initially, cooperative learning groups should only work together for a day or two. After the students are more experienced, they can work with a group for longer periods of time. It is important to keep groups together long enough for each group to experience success and to change groups often enough that students have the opportunity to work with a variety of students.

Students must understand that they are responsible for group members learning the material. Before beginning, discuss the basic rules for effective cooperative learning— (1) listen while others are speaking, (2) respect other people and their ideas, (3) stay on tasks, and (4) be responsible for your own actions.

Before teaching the lesson, decide on the academic task and the interpersonal skills students will learn or practice in groups. Prepare the students for the academic task by teaching any content they might need to know and by giving specific instructions for the task.

Explain your criteria for evaluating group and individual learning. Specify the interpersonal skills they will be working on and how these skills will be evaluated. Explain the sharing of materials and the roles assigned.

The **Teacher Wraparound Edition** uses the code COOP LEARN at the end of activities and teaching ideas where cooperative learning strategies are useful. For additional help refer again to these pages of background information on Cooperative Learning.

Using Cooperative Learning Strategies

The **Cooperative Learning Resource Guide** of the **Teacher Classroom Resource Package** provides help for selecting cooperative learning strategies, as well as methods for troubleshooting and evaluation.

During cooperative learning activities, monitor the functioning of groups. Praise group cooperation and good use of interpersonal skills. When students are having trouble with the task, clarify the assignment, reteach or provide background as needed. Only answer questions when no students in the group can.

Evaluating Cooperative Learning

At the close of the lesson, have groups share their products or summarize the assignment. Use the criteria discussed at the beginning of the lesson to evaluate and give feedback on how well the academic task was mastered by the groups. You can evaluate group performance during a lesson by frequently asking questions to group members picked at random or having each group take a quiz together. You might have all students write papers and then choose one at random to grade. Assess individual learning by your traditional methods.

To assess the learning of interpersonal skills, groups can list what they did well and what they could do to improve. Have groups share their analysis with the class and summarize the analysis of the whole class.

You can use study buddies to help students prepare for tests or create concept maps. After a chapter is completed, give study buddies one class period to master the materials in the Chapter Review before giving a chapter test. To have study buddies create concept maps, give each member a different colored pen. Buddies share the concept map, taking turns adding to the map with their colored pens.

MULTICULTURAL PERSPECTIVES

"Multicultural education is an idea stating that all students, regardless of the groups to which they belong, such as those related to gender, ethnicity, race, culture, social class, religion or exceptionality, should experience education equality in the schools."—James Banks

American classrooms reflect the rich and diverse cultural heritages of the American people. Students come from different ethnic backgrounds and different cultural experiences into a common classroom that must assist all of them to learn. The diversity itself is an important focus of learning experience.

Diversity can be repressed, creating a hostile environment; ignored, creating an indifferent environment; or appreciated, creating a receptive and productive environment. Responding to diversity and approaching it as a part of every curriculum is challenging to a teacher, experienced or not. The goal of science is understanding. The goal of multicultural education is to promote the understanding of how people from different cultures approach and solve the basic problems all humans have in living and learning. *SCIENCE INTERACTIONS* addresses this issue. In the Multicultural Perspectives sections of the **Teacher Wraparound Edition,** information is provided about people and groups who have traditionally been misrepresented or omitted. The intent is to build awareness and appreciation for the global community in which we all live.

The *SCIENCE INTERACTIONS* **Teacher Classroom Resource Package** also includes a **Multicultural Activities** booklet that offers additional opportunities to integrate multicultural materials into the curriculum. By providing these opportunities, *SCIENCE INTERACTIONS* is helping to meet the five major goals of multicultural education:

1. promoting the strength and value of cultural diversity
2. promoting the human rights and respect for those who are different from oneself
3. promoting alternative life choices for people
4. promoting social justice and equal opportunity for all people
5. promoting equity in the distribution of power among groups

Two books that provide additional information on multicultural education are:

Banks, James A. (with Cherry A. McGee Banks) *Multicultural Education: Issues and Perspectives.* Boston: Allyn and Bacon, 1989.

Banks, James A. (with others.) Curriculum Guidelines for Multiethnic Education. Washington D.C.: National Council for the Social Studies, 1977.

COMMUNITY INVOLVEMENT

There are a number of ways that teachers and schools can enlist the support of their community to enhance science education.

PARENTS. Continually inform parents about science classroom activities. Parents can encourage the students by asking questions about labs, following up on homework, and providing materials and support for projects.

In the **Take Home Activities** booklet of the **Teacher Classroom Resource Guide** are simple activities for parents to do with their children. The activities require readily available materials and relate directly to the chapter contents of *SCIENCE INTERACTIONS.*

CORPORATE PARTNERSHIPS. A business might provide students with visits to the industry, assistance with projects, speakers for career purposes, classroom demonstrations or exhibits, or assist with curriculum development.

SCIENTISTS IN THE CLASSROOM. You may recruit a local scientist to visit the classroom about once a month to provide lessons for the students, consult with you about curriculum or lab activities, or work with students on projects. Encourage the scientist to talk about how his or her work benefits the community.

INDUSTRIAL TUTORS. Encourage people with strong science backgrounds to volunteer their time to assist small groups of students who are having difficulty.

COMMUNITY SERVICE PROJECTS. Plan for students to study local problems such as recycling, land use, and conservation of resources. Students can then share their information with their community.

ASSESSMENT

What criteria do you use to assess your students as they progress through a course? Do you rely on formal tests and quizzes? To assess students' achievement in science, you need to measure not only their knowledge of the subject matter, but also their ability to handle apparatus, to organize, predict, record, and interpret data, to design experiments, and to communicate orally and in writing. ***SCIENCE INTERACTIONS*** *has been designed to provide you with a variety of assessment tools, both formal and informal, to help you develop a clearer picture of your students' progress.*

SCIENCE INTERACTIONS provides you with thorough and diverse assessment opportunities ranging from performance assessment to more traditional assessment.

Performance Assessment

Performance assessments are becoming more common in today's schools. Science curriculums are being revised to prepare students to cope with change and with futures that will depend on their abilities to think, learn, and solve problems. Although learning fundamental concepts will always be important in the science curriculum, the concepts alone are no longer sufficient in a student's scientific education. Performance assessments differ in formality and complexity, but in most cases, the teacher observes a pupil or group of pupils involved in an activity and rates the performance and/or the products that result from the activity. Background information and specific examples of performance assessment are included in Glencoe's *Alternate Assessment in the Science Classroom. SCIENCE INTERACTIONS*, Course 1, provides numerous opportunities to observe student behavior both in informal and formal settings. The laboratory activities present many instances where you can informally observe students and evaluate their understanding of both concepts and process skills. Each **INVESTIGATE!** activity contains suggestions for discussion or demonstration that will enable you to assess students' understanding of how the lab relates to the concepts presented in the text. A more formal assessment of student products is provided by the activity sheets found in the *Activity Masters* booklet. These sheets provide space for recording data and observations as students conduct activities and experiments.

Another approach for assessing student mastery of concepts and skills in the laboratory is provided in the *Science Interactions, Course 1, Performance Assessments.* It features one laboratory investigation per chapter that enables you to evaluate student skills in handling laboratory equipment and students' knowledge of laboratory processes. A generic method of evaluating the skills is also provided in the booklet.

Group Performance Assessment

Recent research has shown that cooperative learning structures produce improved student learning outcomes for students of all ability levels. *SCIENCE INTERACTIONS* provides many opportunities for cooperative learning and, as a result, many opportunities to observe group work processes and products. *SCIENCE INTERACTIONS*: Cooperative Learning Resource Guide provides strategies and resources for implementing and evaluating group activities. In cooperative group assessment, all members of the group contribute to the work process and the products it produces. For example, if a mixed ability, four-member laboratory work group conducts an activity, you can use a rating scale or checklist to assess the quality of both group interaction and work skills. An example, along with information about evaluating cooperative work, is provided in the booklet *Alternate Assessment in the Science Classroom.* All four members of the group are expected to review and agree on the data sheet produced by the group. You can require each member to certify the group results by signing the data sheet or lab report. In this approach, all members of the group receive the same grade on the work product. Research shows that cooperative group assessment is as valid as individual assessment. Additionally, it reduces the marking and grading workload of the teacher.

Portfolios: Putting It All Together

The purpose of a student or cooperative group portfolio is to present examples of the individual or group's work in a "non-testing" environment. A portfolio is simply a methodology for assembling and presenting selected examples of work products. The process of assembling the portfolio should be both integrative (of process and content) and reflective. The performance portfolio is *not* a complete collection of all worksheets and other assignments for a grading period. At its best, the portfolio should include integrated performance products that show growth in concept attainment and skill development. You can structure the portfolio development process by establishing categories and other limiting specifications. An essential component in portfolio development is the composition of a submission letter or reflective paper that lists the contents of the portfolio and discusses growth in knowledge, attitudes, and skills.

SCIENCE INTERACTIONS presents a wealth of opportunities for performance portfolio development. Each chapter in the student text contains projects, explorations, enrichment activities, investigations, skill builders, library research opportunities, and connections with life, society, and literature. Each of the student activities results in a product. A mixture of these products can be used to document student growth during the grading period. The *Science Interactions, Course 1 Performance Assessments* provides specific portfolio suggestions for each chapter, as well as a sample reflective paper for classroom use.

Finally, *SCIENCE INTERACTIONS* strongly suggests the use of student journals. Students are encouraged to write observations, descriptions, and reflections in their journals. They are also encouraged to include diagrams and drawings. Excerpts from the student journals can be included in the individual or group portfolio. Additionally, as many writers have discovered, the journal will be an excellent resource for developing the reflective submission letter or paper.

Content Assessment

While new and exciting performance skill assessments are emerging, paper-and-pencil tests are still a mainstay of student evaluation. Students must learn to conceptualize, process, and prepare for traditional content assessments. Presently and in the foreseeable future, students will be required to pass pencil-and-paper tests to exit high school, and to enter college, trade schools, and other training programs.

Traditional content assessment forms such as matching, multiple choice, and short essay items are effective in sampling content and can be quickly marked and scored. *SCIENCE INTERACTIONS* contains numerous strategies and formative checkpoints for evaluating student progress toward mastery of science concepts. Throughout the chapters in the student text, *Check Your Understanding* questions and application tasks are presented. This spaced review process helps build learning bridges that allow all students to confidently progress from one lesson to the next.

After instruction for the chapter is completed, a summation of the major concepts is presented. Here, a visual summary, *Reviewing Main Ideas*, enables students to check and reinforce their understanding of the broad picture presented in the chapter while participating in cooperative learning groups. Small groups of students can research the major concepts in the chapter and present restatements of their meaning in writing and as oral reports to the class.

After the main idea presentations, the formal review process for the written content assessment can begin. *SCIENCE INTERACTIONS* presents a three-page *Chapter Review* at the end of each chapter. Individual students or cooperative groups of three to five students can respond to these items to check their understanding of science terms, concepts, critical thinking skills, and problem solving techniques. By evaluating the student responses to this extensive review, you can determine if any substantial reteaching is needed.

For the formal content assessment, a one-page review and a three-page *Chapter Test* are provided for each chapter in the student text. The Review can be used to help you determine the students' grasp of the concepts and supporting facts presented in the chapter. Using the review in a whole class session, you can correct any misperceptions and provide closure for the text. On the *Chapter Test*, students document their mastery of the concepts developed in the chapter. The test includes multiple choice type items that test knowledge and numerous short answer and essay items that require students to apply and relate concepts. If your individual assessment plan requires a test that differs from the *Chapter Test* in the resource package, customized tests can be easily produced using the *Computer Test Bank*.

MANAGING ACTIVITIES IN THE MIDDLE SCHOOL CLASSROOM

The many hands-on activities throughout *SCIENCE INTERACTIONS* require simple, common materials, making them easy to set up and manage in the classroom.

SCIENCE INTERACTIONS engages students in a variety of hands-on experiences to provide all students with an opportunity to learn by doing. FIND OUT! and EXPLORE! activities are intended to be short and occur many times throughout the text. INVESTIGATE! activities are formal reinforcement exercises. These activities can be useful in a variety of ways:

Activities motivate. A demonstration can be set up in a specific place in the room with a light focused on it. Students begin to look for this as they come into the room. It invites them to learn.

Activities reinforce and check for true understanding. For example, after a lesson on pressure, do the egg in the bottle demonstration. Light a match and drop it into a bottle. Place a shelled hard-boiled egg on top of the bottle. When the match goes out, a partial vacuum is created, causing the egg to slip down into the bottle. Have students explain why the egg dropped into the bottle.

Activities enrich and extend.

Hands-on activities provide an opportunity for students to learn to work together. This is one of the best preparations for the job world since decisions today are often made by groups, not by individuals.

Preplanning and organization are important for successful use of hands-on activities in the classroom. Make copies of specific INVESTIGATE! worksheets ahead of time, from the **Activity Masters** booklet. Store materials for each activity in a box with a list of contents on the end. The boxes may be color-coded according to the unit of study. Place materials for each group of students in a plastic bag and label the bag with its contents. Students can be responsible for distributing the materials and checking the bag for its contents. Cleaning up and putting materials in their proper place is an essential part of the laboratory experience.

The materials used in *SCIENCE INTERACTIONS* are easily accessible. If the budget in your school is limited, have students bring in materials such as sugar, baking soda, etc. Parents may also be willing to donate materials and their time to help organize the materials.

It is important to remember that there is no such thing as a failure in science activities. If the experiment does not illustrate what you had intended, turn it into a question and hypothesis activity. Students evaluate their results and form hypotheses on how to alter the experiment. Students then test their hypotheses and draw conclusions. Activities can also end with a question or extension to encourage further exploration of concepts.

Laboratory Safety

Safety is of prime importance in every classroom. However, the need for safety is even greater when science is taught. Outlined on the next page are some considerations on laboratory safety.

In addition, *SCIENCE INTERACTIONS* **Lab and Safety Skills** booklet contains masters you can use to test students' lab and safety skills.

The activities in *SCIENCE INTERACTIONS* are designed to minimize dangers in the laboratory. Even so, there are no guarantees against accidents. However, careful planning and preparation as well as being aware of hazards can keep accidents to a minimum. Numerous books and pamphlets are available on laboratory safety with detailed instructions on preventing accidents. However, much of what they present can be summarized in the phrase: *Be prepared!* Know the rules and what common violations occur. Know the Safety Symbols used in this book (see p. 40T). Know where emergency equipment is stored and how to use it. Practice good laboratory housekeeping and management by observing these guidelines:

CLASSROOM/LABORATORY

1. Store chemicals properly. (For details see p. 42T.)
2. Store equipment properly.
   a. Clean and dry all equipment before storing.
   b. Protect electronic equipment and microscopes from dust, humidity, and extreme temperatures.
   c. Label and organize equipment so that it is accessible.
3. Provide adequate workspace.
4. Provide adequate room ventilation.
5. Post safety and evacuation guidelines.
6. Be sure safety equipment is accessible and works.
7. Provide containers for disposing of chemicals, waste products, and biological specimens. Disposal methods must meet local guidelines.
8. Use hot plates whenever possible as a heat source. If burners are used, a central shutoff valve for the gas supply should be available to the teacher. Never use open flames when a flammable solvent is in the same room.

FIRST DAY OF CLASS/LABS (with students)

1. Distribute and discuss safety rules, safety symbols, first aid guidelines, and safety contract found in the **Lab and Safety Skills** booklet of the **Teacher Classroom Resources.** Have students refer to Appendices C and D on pages 632-633 to review safety symbols and guidelines.
2. Review safe use of equipment and chemicals.
3. Review use and location of safety equipment.
4. Discuss safe disposal of materials and laboratory cleanup policy.
5. Discuss proper laboratory attitude and conduct.
6. Document students' understanding of above points.
   a. Have students sign the safety contract and return it.
   b. Administer the safety assessment found in the **Lab and Safety Skills** booklet. Reteach those points that students do not understand.

BEFORE EACH INVESTIGATION

1. Perform each investigation yourself before assigning it.
2. Arrange the lab in such a way that equipment and supplies are clearly labeled and easily accessible.
3. Have available only equipment and supplies needed to complete the assigned investigation.
4. Review the procedure with students, emphasizing any caution statements or safety symbols that appear.
5. Be sure all students know proper procedures to follow if an accident should occur.

DURING THE INVESTIGATION

1. Make sure the lab is clean and free of clutter.
2. Insist that students wear goggles and aprons.
3. Never allow a student to work alone in the lab.
4. Never allow students to use a cutting device with more than one edge.
5. Students should not point the open end of a heated test tube toward anyone.
6. Remove broken glassware or frayed cords from use. Also clean up any spills immediately. Dilute solutions with water before removing.
7. Be sure all glassware that is to be heated is of a heat-treated type that will not shatter.
8. Remind students that hot glassware looks cool.
9. Prohibit eating and drinking in the lab.

SAFETY SYMBOLS

	**DISPOSAL ALERT** This symbol appears when care must be taken to dispose of materials properly.		**ANIMAL SAFETY** This symbol appears whenever live animals are studied and the safety of the animals and the students must be ensured.
	**BIOLOGICAL HAZARD** This symbol appears when there is danger involving bacteria, fungi, or protists.		**RADIOACTIVE SAFETY** This symbol appears when radioactive materials are used.
	**OPEN FLAME ALERT** This symbol appears when use of an open flame could cause a fire or an explosion.		**CLOTHING PROTECTION SAFETY** This symbol appears when substances used could stain or burn clothing.
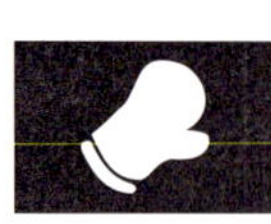	**THERMAL SAFETY** This symbol appears as a reminder to use caution when handling hot objects.		**FIRE SAFETY** This symbol appears when care should be taken around open flames.
	**SHARP OBJECT SAFETY** This symbol appears when a danger of cuts or punctures caused by the use of sharp objects exists.		**EXPLOSION SAFETY** This symbol appears when the misuse of chemicals could cause an explosion.
	**FUME SAFETY** This symbol appears when chemicals or chemical reactions could cause dangerous fumes.		**EYE SAFETY** This symbol appears when a danger to the eyes exists. Safety goggles should be worn when this symbol appears.
	**ELECTRICAL SAFETY** This symbol appears when care should be taken when using electrical equipment.		**POISON SAFETY** This symbol appears when poisonous substances are used.
	**PLANT SAFETY** This symbol appears when poisonous plants or plants with thorns are handled.		**CHEMICAL SAFETY** This symbol appears when chemicals used can cause burns or are poisonous if absorbed through the skin.

AFTER THE INVESTIGATION

1. Be sure that the lab is clean.
2. Be certain that students have returned all equipment and disposed of broken glassware and chemicals properly.
3. Be sure all hot plates and electrical connections are off.
4. Insist that each student wash his or her hands when lab work is completed.

The ***SCIENCE INTERACTIONS*** program uses safety symbols to alert you and your students to possible laboratory dangers. These symbols are explained on page 40T. Be sure your students understand each symbol before they begin an investigation or skill.

PREPARATION OF SOLUTIONS

The following text gives some general hints on solution preparation and some safety tips to keep in mind.

For best results, follow directions for preparing needed solutions as given in the margin of the **Teacher Wraparound Edition** adjacent to each activity. It is recommended that solutions be prepared fresh as needed.

Unless otherwise specified, solutions are prepared by adding the solid to a small amount of distilled water and then diluting with water to the volume listed. For example, to make a 0.1*M* solution of aluminum sulfate, dissolve 34.2 g of $Al_2(SO_4)_3$ in a small amount of distilled water and dilute to a liter with water. If you use a hydrate that is different from the one specified in a particular preparation, you will need to adjust the amount of the hydrate to obtain the required concentration.

It is most important to use safe laboratory techniques when handling all chemicals. Many substances may appear harmless but are, in fact, toxic, corrosive, or very reactive. Always check with the manufacturer or with Flinn Scientific Inc., (312) 879-6900. Chemicals should never be ingested. Be sure to use proper techniques to smell solutions or other agents. Always wear safety goggles and an apron. The following general cautions should be used.

1. Poisonous/corrosive liquid and/or vapor. Use in the fume hood. Examples: *acetic acid, hydrochloric acid, ammonia hydroxide, nitric acid.*
2. Poisonous and corrosive to eyes, lungs, and skin. Examples: *acids, limewater, iron (III) chloride, bases, silver nitrate, iodine, potassium permanganate.*
3. Poisonous if swallowed, inhaled, or absorbed through the skin. Examples: *acetic acid, glacial, copper compounds, barium chloride, lead compounds, chromium compounds, lithium compounds, cobalt (II) chloride, silver compounds.*
4. Always add acids to water, never the reverse.
5. When sulfuric acid and sodium hydroxide are added to water, a large amount of thermal energy is released. Sodium metal reacts violently with water. Use extra care if handling any of these substances.

CHEMICAL STORAGE AND DISPOSAL

General Guidelines

Be sure to store all chemicals properly. The following are guidelines commonly used. Your school, city, county, or state may have additional requirements for handling chemicals. It is the responsibility of each teacher to become informed as to what rules or guidelines are in effect in his or her area.

1. Separate chemicals by reaction type. Strong acids should be stored together. Likewise, strong bases should be stored together and should be separated from acids. Oxidants should be stored away from easily oxidized materials and so on.
2. Be sure all chemicals are stored in labeled containers indicating contents, concentration, source, date purchased (or prepared), any precautions for handling and storage, and expiration date.
3. Dispose of any outdated or waste chemicals properly according to accepted disposal procedures.
4. Do not store chemicals above eye level.
5. Wood shelving is preferable to metal. All shelving should be firmly attached to all walls and have anti-roll edges.
6. Store only those chemicals that you plan to use.
7. Hazardous chemicals require special storage containers and conditions. Be sure to know what those chemicals are and the accepted practices for your area. Some substances must even be stored outside the building.
8. When working with chemicals or preparing solutions, observe the same general safety precautions that you would expect from students. These include wearing an apron and goggles. Wear gloves and use the fume hood when necessary. Students will want to do as you do whether they admit it or not.
9. If you are a new teacher in a particular laboratory, it is your responsibility to survey the chemicals stored there and to be sure they are stored properly or disposed of. Consult the rules and laws in your area concerning what chemicals can be kept in your classroom. For disposal, consult up-to-date disposal information from the state and federal governments.

Disposal of Chemicals

Local, state, and federal laws regulate the proper disposal of chemicals. These laws should be consulted before chemical disposal is attempted. Although most substances encountered in science classes can be flushed down the drain with plenty of water, it is not safe to assume that is always true. It is recommended that teachers who use chemicals consult the following books from the National Research Council.

Prudent Practices for Handling Hazardous Chemicals in Laboratories, Washington, DC: National Academy Press, 1981.

Prudent Practices for Disposal of Chemicals from Laboratories, Washington, DC: National Academy Press, 1983.

These books are useful and still in print, although they are several years old. Current laws in your area would, of course, supersede the information in these books.

NONCONSUMABLES

ITEM	INVESTIGATE!	EXPLORE!	FIND OUT!
Apron (30)	8-2, p. 239		
Aquarium (1 or 2 per class)	12-1, p. 365		
Atlas (15)		4, 597	
Balance (15)	5-1, p. 140		226
	5-2, p. 142		
	7-2, p. 208		
	10-1, p. 295		
	16-2, p. 488		
Ball, polystyrene (15)	20-2, p. 613		
Ball, unmarked (15)		14	
Basketball (15)			598, 607
Beaker (15)	1-1, p. 13		
	4-2, p. 114		
	7-2, p. 208		
	10-2, p. 310		
Beaker, 250-mL (45)	16-1, p. 481		226
Beaker, 300-mL (15)			232
Beaker, 400-mL (30)	3-1, p. 77	205	195
Beaker, 500-mL (15)	15-2,p. 463	138	
Beaker, large (15)	7-1, p. 199		452
Beaker, small (30)	7-1, p. 199		452
Blindfold (15)		569	105
Bolts (15)			422
Books (30)		41, 576	37, 578
Bottle, plastic w/cap (15)	16-2, p. 488		
Bowl (15)	6-2, p. 181	323	
Bowl, transparent (15)		211	
Box, clear plastic (15)	1-1, p. 13		
Box, paper clip	5-1, p. 140		
Box, plastic storage (15)	10-1, p. 295		
Bronze, sheet (15)		170	
Burner (15)			144, 176
Button (15)	13-2, p. 405		
Can (45)	15-2, p. 463		144, 540, 554
Can opener (1)			540
Circle compass (15)	19-1, p. 573		
Clamps (30)	15-1, p. 458		195
	17-1, p. 512		
Clock, loudly ticking (10)			105
Coat hanger, metal (30)	19-2, p. 584		70
Coins (30)			429
Container (45)	10-2, p. 310	151	150, 200,
			518
Cookie sheet (15)			167
Copper, sheet (15)		170	168
Coverslip (several boxes)	9-1, p. 262		
	11-2, p. 344		
Cup, water	12-1,p. 365		
Dish (15)	11-2, p. 344	151, 491	144, 550
	18-2, p. 546		
Dish, evaporating (15)	6-1, p. 172		
Dishcloth (15)			194
Dropper (30)	3-1, p. 77	164	130, 194,
	4-2. p. 114		241, 330
	9-1, p. 262		
Dropping bottles (105)	8-2, p. 239		
Encyclopedia		604	
Feather (15)		149	
File (15)		164, 170	
File, triangular			168

Materials for *SCIENCE INTERACTIONS Course 1* are listed here according to categories as nonconsumables, chemical supplies, and living and preserved specimens. Use these lists as a ready reference for the materials you will need in planning activities for each chapter.

NONCONSUMABLES

ITEM	INVESTIGATE!	EXPLORE!	FIND OUT!
Flashlight (15)	2-1, p. 48 10-2, p. 310	40, 41, 129, 196, 211	44, 554
Flowerpot (60)	11-1, p. 340		258
Forceps (15)	11-2, p. 344		145
Fork (15)		149	
Freezer (1)	16-2, p. 488		144, 518
Funnel (30)			195
Glass (60)		53, 108, 193, 213	130, 202, 334
Glass, frosted (15)		41	
Glass, piece (15)		41	
Globe	20-2, p. 613	604	601
Goggles, safety (30)	5-2, p. 142 6-1, p. 172 6-2, p. 181 7-1, p. 199 7-2, p. 208 8-1, p. 235 8-2, p. 239 18-1, p. 541	505	145, 167, 176
Graduated cylinder (15)	4-2, p. 114 7-1, p. 199 7-2, p. 208 8-1, p. 235		150
Graduated cylinder, 1000-mL (15)	3-2, p. 83		
Graduated cylinder, 100-mL (15)	5-2, p. 142 8-2, p. 239		
Hammer (15)	6-2, p. 181		167
Hand lens (15)	10-1, p. 295 10-2, p. 310		337
Hole punch			578
Hot plate (15)	6-1, p. 172 7-2, p. 208		
Ice cube tray (15)			518
Iron, sheet (15)			168
Jar (15)		151	145, 234, 330
Jar, heat proof (30)		129	
Labels (as needed)			228, 232
Lamp (15)	17-2, p. 517 20-1, p. 603 20-2, p.613		103, 452, 601
Landform, model (15)	1-1, p. 13		
Lead, sheet (15)			168
Light bulb (15)		35, 38	37
Light, warming (15)	12-1, p. 365		
Limestone or shale chips (1500 g)	16-2, p. 488		
Magnet (15)			174
Magnifying glass (15)	16-1, p. 481	477	232
Marble, chips (100 g)			226
Marbles (15)	1-2, p. 20		452
Masses (15 sets)	5-1, p. 140 5-2, p. 142 10-1, p. 295		
Measuring cup (15)	6-2, p. 181		150
Metal, sample of (15)		164	
Meterstick (15)	13-1, p. 397 14-2, p. 439		429, 543
Microscope (15)	9-1, p. 262 11-2, p. 344		130, 174
Microscope slide (120)	9-1, p. 262 11-2, p. 344		130, 174

NONCONSUMABLES

ITEM	INVESTIGATE!	EXPLORE!	FIND OUT!
Mirror (15)	2-2, p.51	96, 151	554
Mortar and pestle (15)			174, 176, 194, 200
Oven			167
Oven mitt (15)	7-2, p. 208		
Pails (30)	15-1, p. 458 17-1, p. 512		
Pan (15)	1-2, p. 20 10-2, p. 310	570, 576	578
Paper clip (several boxes)	5-1, p. 140 6-2, p. 181	149	37
Paper, black (15)			337
Penny (15)	6-1, p. 172	149	145
Pictures, animal (15 sets)		273	
Ping pong ball (15)		570	
Pitcher, clear (15)		196	
Plastic foam (60 strips)	18-2, p. 546		
Plastic hose (30)	15-1, p. 458 17-1, p. 512		
Prism (15)		40	
Protractor (15)	13-2, p. 405 20-1, p. 603		407, 574
Radio (several)			540
Record turntable (1)		409	
Ring stand (30)	19-2, p. 584		195
Rocks (45)		138, 149	478
Rope (15-4m lengths)		537	543, 549
Rubber gloves (15 pairs)			111
Rubber mallet (15)	3-2, p. 83	81	
Ruler, metric (15)	1-1, p. 13 1-2, p. 20 2-2, p. 51 3-1, p. 77 3-2, p. 83 14-2 p. 439 15-2, p. 463 17-2, p. 517 18-2, p. 546 19-1, p. 573 19-2, p. 584	65, 73, 98, 409, 421, 456	37, 360, 522, 574, 578, 598
Scalpel (15)			330, 337
Scissors (15)	16-1, p. 481	521	522, 554, 598
Scoop (1)	7-2, p. 208		
Shoe box (15)			522
Spade (15)	15-2, p. 463		
Spoon (15)			232, 522
Spray bottle (15)		510	
Spring, coiled (15)	18-1, p. 541		66
Sprinkling can (15)		456	
Stirrer (90)	7-1 p. 199 8-1, p. 235	193, 196, 205, 213	194, 200, 202, 226, 232, 241
Stirrer, copper wire (15)	7-2,p. 208		
Stone, sample of (15 sets)		164	
Stones (as required)	12-1, p. 365		
Stopper (15)	7-2, p. 208	409	176
Stopwatch (15)	13-1, p. 397		200
Strainer, wire (15)	16-2, p. 488		
Stream table (2 per class)	15-1, p. 458 17-1, p. 512 17-2, p. 517	456, 461	
Stringed instrument (several)			74

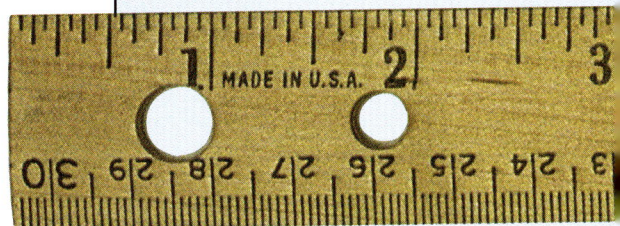

NONCONSUMABLES

ITEM	INVESTIGATE!	EXPLORE!	FIND OUT!
Sunglasses (15)		41	
Test tubes (120)	3-1, p. 77	409	174, 176, 241
	4-2, p. 114		
	7-2, p. 208		
	8-1, p 235		
	8-2,p. 239		
	9-1, p. 262		
Test-tube rack (15)	3-1, p. 77		176
	4-2, p. 114		
	7-2, p. 208		
	8-1, p. 235		
	8-2, p. 239		
Thermometer (15)	7-2, p. 208		
Thermometer, Celsius (15)	20-1, p. 603		
Timer, with second hand (1 large or 15 small)	14-2, p. 439		
	15-2,p. 463		
Tin, sheet (15)		170	168
Tongs (15)	6-1, p. 172		144
Toothbrush (15)			194
Towel (15)			226, 522
Toy car (battery-powered) (15)		401	
Tray, flat (15)		149	
Tube, plastic or glass (30)	3-2, p. 83		176
Tuning fork (15)	3-2, p. 83	81	
Washers (metal) (15)	14-2, p. 439		
Watch (15)	16-1, p. 481		
	20-1, p. 603		
Wire (15 pieces 1m long)			70
Wood (45 blocks)	15-1, p. 458	164, 456	422, 518
	17-1, p. 512		
World map (15)		604	
Zinc, sheet (15)			168

LIVING ORGANISMS

ITEM	INVESTIGATE!	EXPLORE!	FIND OUT!
Animals, or pictures of animals (15 sets)		273	
Anole (1 or 2)	12-1, p. 365		
Crickets (4)	12-1, p. 365		
Earthworms (15)	10-2, p. 310		
Flowers (15)			337
Fruit fly cultures (15)			103, 303
Leaves, variety of (15 sets)		257, 264	
Marigold plants (60)	12-2, p. 373		
Mealworms (200)	10-1, p. 295		
Philodendron			334
Plants (75)	12-1, p. 365		
	12-2, p. 373		
Seedlings in pots (30)		342	

CONSUMABLES

ITEM	INVESTIGATE!	EXPLORE!	FIND OUT!
Apple juice (1 bottle)			228
Aluminum foil (several rolls)	6-2, p.181	521	52, 167, 228
Balloon (90)		151	203, 554
Bird seed, wild mix (1 bag)			133
Box, pizza (15)		597	
Bran flakes (1 box)	10-1, p. 295		
Carrot (2)			330

CONSUMABLES

ITEM	INVESTIGATE!	EXPLORE!	FIND OUT!
Cinnamon, ground (1 can)		108	
Cardboard (30 pieces)		41, 151, 451	598
Cellophane (15 red, 15 blue, 15 green)	2-1, p. 48	41	44
Chalk dusk (sm. amount)		108	
Charcoal (1 bag)	12-1, p. 365		
Cheesecloth (several yards)	10-1, p. 295		
Clay (1 box)	16-1, p. 481	41, 164, 421	37, 167
Corn flakes (1 box)	10-1, p. 295		
Cornstarch (1 box)			232
Corn syrup (1 bottle)			194
Cotton (1 bag balls)		149, 193	105
Cotton swab (1 box)	10-2, p. 30		
Crackers, wheat (1 box)	10-1, p. 295		
Cup, paper (as needed)	4-2, p. 114		133
	11-1, p. 340		
	16-1, p. 481		
Cup, plastic, clear (75)	12-1, p. 365		232
Earplug, disposable (30)			105
Fertilizer (as needed)			478
Fish food, dried (1 box)			478
(Flour (1 bag)	1-2, p. 20	193	522
Food, vial of (15)			303
Gelatin dessert mix (several boxes)		211	
Glue (15 bottles)		597	
Gravel (as needed)	12-1, p. 365	505	
	16-1, p. 481		
Ice block containing sand, clay, and gravel	17-2, p. 517		
Ice cube (15)			144
Index cards (45)			37
Insects, dried (as needed)			478
Labels (several boxes)			228, 332
Lemon juice (1 bottle)	8-1, p. 235		228
Lemonade crystals (1 box)		196	
Lettuce (1 head)	11-2, p. 344		
Litmus paper (several vials)	8-1, p. 235		241
Marker (15)	3-1, p. 77	14, 342	
	12-2, p. 373		
	15-2, p. 463		
	19-2, p. 584		
Marker, transparency (15)	11-1, p. 13		
Oatmeal (dry) (1 box)	10-1, p 295		
	12-1, p. 365		
Paper (as needed)	2-2, p. 51	35, 38, 40, 391	44, 52, 66, 200
	4-1, p. 99	401, 597	232, 360, 433, 543
	9-2, p. 276		550
	11-2, p. 344		
	14-1, p. 425		
	16-1, p. 481		
	18-2, p. 546		
	19-1, p. 573		
	19-2, p. 584		
Paper, construction (as needed)	2-1, p. 48		
	20-1, p. 603		
Paper, lined (15)		391	
Paper, tissue (15)		41	
Paper, waxed (several rolls)		41, 451, 505	
Peanut, in shell (30)		332	
Peat moss (small bag)			478

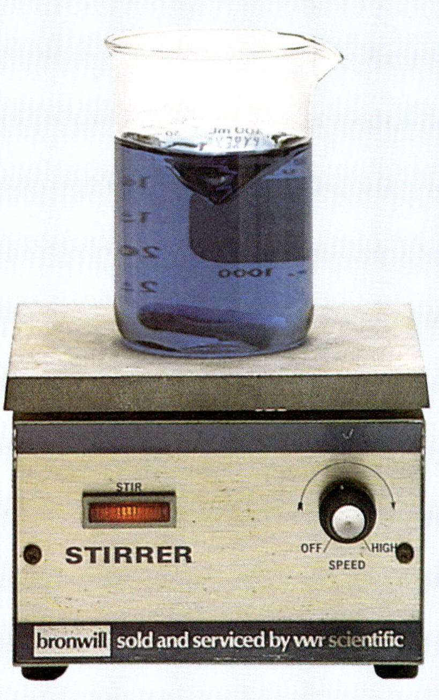

CONSUMABLES

ITEM	INVESTIGATE!	EXPLORE!	FIND OUT!
Pencil (30)	9-2, p. 276 11-2, p. 344 14-1, p. 425 16-1, p. 481 18-2, p. 546 19-1, p. 573 20-2, p. 613	53, 136, 421, 570	52, 66, 360 433, 543, 550
Pencil, grease (15)	4-2, p. 114 8-1, p. 235 8-2, p. 239		
Peppermint oil (1 bottle)			194
Plaster of Paris (5 kg)	6-2, p. 181		574
Plastic bag (30)		342	145
Plastic lids (45)	16-1, p. 481		578
Plastic wrap (several rolls)			452, 540
Plate, paper (120)		323, 510	133, 574
Rice, uncooked (1 box)		510	540
Rubber band (90)	2-1, p. 48 16-1, p. 481 19-2, p. 584		
Salad dressing (1 bottle)		323	
Sand (50 kg)	15-1, p. 458 16-1, p. 481 17-1, p. 512 17-2, p. 517	149, 456, 461, 505 576	195, 258, 518, 574 578
Seeds (several packets of 3 different types)	11-1, p. 340		258, 478
Sleeve, black paper (15)			103
Soil (2-10 lb bags)	11-1, p. 340 12-1, p. 365 16-1, p. 481	477	258
Steel wool (15 pads)		491	
Straw, drinking (30)	3-1, p. 77	196	
String (1 large ball)	13-2, p. 405 14-2, p. 439 19-2, p. 584		70, 422, 578
String, colored (1 large ball)	18-1, p. 541		66
String, thick, water-absorbent (1 ball)	7-1, p. 199		
String, white (1 ball)			543
Sugar (10 lbs)	7-2 p. 208 9-1, p. 262	193, 205	202, 232, 574
Sugar, cubes (1 box)			200
Sugar, powdered (1 bag)			176, 194
Tape (several rolls)	1-1, p. 13 12-2, p. 373 13-1, p. 397 14-2, p. 439 18-2, p. 546 19-2, p. 584 20-1, p. 603	409	203, 598, 607
Thumbtack (30)	16-1, p. 481		
Toothpicks (2 boxes)	9-1, p. 262 10-2, p. 310		
Towel, paper (several rolls)	6-2, p. 181 10-2, p. 310	451	145
Transparency (15)	1-1, p. 13		
Vegetables (as required)	11-2, p. 344	323	330
Wooden splint (15)		129	

CHEMICAL SUPPLIES

ITEM	INVESTIGATE	EXPLORE!	FIND OUT!
Alcohol (1 bottle)	5-2, p. 142	151	
Ammonia (1 bottle)	8-1, p. 235 8-2, p. 239		145, 234, 241
Baking soda (1 box)	8-1, p. 235 8-2, p. 239		232
Castile soap		213	194
Coffee, instant (1 jar)		510	
Cola (1 L)	8-1, p. 235		
Epsom salt (1 box)	7-1, p. 199		234
Food coloring (1 box)			150, 194, 330
Fruit juice (1 bottle)			194
Hydrochloric acid (100 ml)	8-2, p. 239		
Iron powder (1 bottle)			174
Laundry detergent (1 box)			232
Nitric acid (1 L)	6-1, p. 172		
Petroleum jelly (1 jar)		342	
Red cabbage juice indicator (120 ml)	8-2, p. 239		
Salt, solution (1 L)	5-2, p. 142 11-2, p. 344		
Salt, table (1 box)	1-2, p. 20 8-1, p. 235	193, 205, 510	195, 232
Soda water (1 L)			226
Sodium hydroxide (1 L)	6-1, p. 172 8-2, p. 239		
Soft drink (30)	8-2, p. 239		203
Starch (1 box)		193	
Sugar, solution (100 mL)	4-2, p. 114		
Sulfur powder (1 bottle)			174
Sulfuric acid (1 L)			226
Vinegar (1 gallon)	4-2, p. 114 8-1, p. 235 8-2, p. 239 10-2, p. 310		226, 228, 241
Water (as required)	1-1, p. 13 3-1, p. 77 4-2, p. 114 6-2, p. 181 7-1, p. 199 7-2, p. 208 9-1, p. 262 10-2, p. 310 11-1, p. 340 11-2, p. 344 12-1 p. 365 12-2, p. 373 15-2, p. 463 16-1, p. 481 16-2, p. 488 17-1, p. 512 18-2, p. 546	53, 108, 138, 164, 193, 196, 205, 342, 409, 451, 456, 461, 491, 510	111, 130, 144, 150, 194, 195, 202, 232, 258, 330, 334, 452, 478, 518, 550, 574, 578
Water, distilled (1 gallon)	7-2, p. 208 8-1, p. 235 8-2, p. 239		200
Water, muddy (1 L)		213	
Yeast (dry) (15 packages)	9-1, p. 262		
Zinc (30-mesh) (150g)	6-1, p. 172		

STUDENT BIBLIOGRAPHY

GENERAL SCIENCE CONTENT

Barr, George. *Science Tricks and Magic for Young People.* New York: Dover Publications, Inc., 1987.

Cash, Terry. *175 More Science Experiments To Amuse and Amaze Your Friends: Experiments! Tricks! Things to Make!* New York: Random House, 1991.

Churchill, E. Richard. *Amazing Science Experiments with Everyday Materials.* New York: Sterling Publishing Co., Inc., 1991.

Gold, Carol. *Science Express,* "50 Scientific Stunts for the Ontario Science Centre." New York: Addison-Wesley, 1991.

Herbert, Don. *Mr. Wizard's Supermarket Science.* New York: Random House, 1980.

Lewis, James. *Hocus Pocus Stir and Cook, The Kitchen Science-Magic Book.* New York: Meadowbrook Press, Division of Simon and Shuster, Inc., 1991.

Mandell, Muriel. *Simple Science Experiments with Everyday Materials.* New York: Sterling Publishing Co., Inc., 1989.

Roberts, Royston. *Serendipity Accidental Discoveries in Science.* New York: John Wiley and Sons, Inc., 1989.

Schultz, Robert F. *Selected Experiments and Projects.* Washington, D.C.: Thomas Alva Edison Foundation, 1988.

Strongin, Herb. *Science on a Shoestring.* Menlo Park, CA: Addison-Wesley Publishing Co., 1985.

Townsley, B.J. *Famous Scientists.* Los Angeles, CA: Enrich Education Division of Price Stern Sloan Inc., 1987.

PHYSICS

Aronson, Billy. "Water Ride Designers Are Making Waves," *3-2-1 Contact.* August, 1991. pp. 14-16

Asimov, Isaac. *How Did We Find Out the Speed of Light?* New York: Walker, 1986.

Berger, Melvin. *Light, Lenses, and Lasers.* New York: Putnam, 1987.

Cash, Terry. *Sound.* New York: Warwick Press, 1989.

Catherall, Ed. *Exploring Sound.* Austin, TX: Steck-Vaughn Library, 1989.

Heiligman, Deborah. "There's a Lot More to Color Than Meets the Eye," *3-2-1 Contact.* November, 1991. pp. 16-20.

McGrath, Susan. *Fun with Physics.* Washington, D.C.: National Geographic Society, 1986.

Myles, Douglas. *The Great Waves.* New York: McGraw-Hill Book Company, 1985.

Taylor, Barbara. *Light and Color.* New York: Franklin Watts, 1990.

Taylor, Barbara. *Sound and Music.* New York: Warwick Press, 1990.

Ward, Allen. *Experimenting with Batteries, Bulbs, and Wires.* New York: Chelsea House, 1991.

Ward, Alan. *Experimenting with Sound.* New York: Chelsea Juniors, 1991.

Wood, Nicholas. *Listen . . . What Do You Hear?* Mahwah, NJ: Troll Associates, 1991.

CHEMISTRY

Barber, Jacqueline. *Of Cabbage and Chemistry.* Washington, DC.: Lawrence Hall of Science, NSTA, 1989.

Barber, Jacqueline. *Chemical Reactions.* Washington, D.C.: Lawrence Hall of Science, NSTA, 1986.

Benrey, Ronald. *Alternative Energy Sources Experiments You Can Do...from Edison.* Washington, D.C.: Thomas Alva Edison Foundation, Edison Electric Institute, 1988.

Cornell, John. *Experiments with Mixtures.* New York: Wiley, John and Sons, Inc., 1990.

Matsubara, T. *The Structure and Properties of Matter.* New York: Springer-Verlag New York Inc., 1982.

Zubrewski, Bernie. *Messing Around with Baking Chemistry: A Children's Museum Activity Book.* Boston, MA: Little Brown and Co., 1981.

LIFE SCIENCE

Dewey, Jennifer Owings. *A Day and Night In the Desert.* Boston, MA: Little Brown, 1991.

Johnson, Cathy. *Local Wilderness.* New York: Prentice Hall, 1987.

Leslie, Clare Walker. *Nature All Year Long.* New York: Greenwillow, 1990.

McGrath, Susan. *The Amazing Things Animals Do.* Washington D.C.: National Geographic Society, 1989.

Markmann, Erika. *Grow It! An Indoor/Outdoor Gardening Guide for Kids.* New York: Random House, 1991.

Rand McNally. *Children's Atlas of the Environment.* Chicago, IL: Rand McNally, 1991.

VanCleave, Janice Pratt. *Biology for Every Kid: 101 Easy Experiments that Really Work.* New York: Wiley, 1990.

EARTH SCIENCE

Ardley. Neil. *The Science Book of Air.* New York: Gulliver Books, Harcourt, Brace, Jovanovich, Publishers, 1991.

Ardley, Neil. *The Science Book of Water.* New York: Gulliver Books, Harcourt, Brace, Jovanovich, Publishers, 1991.

Barrow, Lloyd H. *Adventures with Rocks and Minerals: Geology Experiments for Young People.* Hillsdale, NJ: Enslow, 1991.

Booth, Basil. *Volcanoes and Earthquakes.* Englewood Cliffs, NJ: Silver Burdett Press, 1991.

Javna, John. *50 Simple Things Kids Can Do to Save the Earth.* Kansas City: The Earth Works Group," Andrews and McMeel, a Universal Press Syndicate Co., 1990.

VanCleave, Janice. *Earth Science for Every Kid.* New York: John Wiley and Sons, Inc., 1991.

Wood, Robert W. *Science for Kids: 39 Easy Geology Activities.* Blue Ridge Summit, PA: Tab Books, 1992.

TEACHER BIBLIOGRAPHY

CURRICULUM

Aldridge, William G. "Scope, Sequence, and Coordination: A New Synthesis for Improving Science Education," *Journal of Science Education and Technology.*

Banks, James A. "Multicultural Education: For Freedom's Sake," *Educational Leadership.* December, 1991/January, 1992. pp. 32-35.

Beane, James A. "Middle School, The Natural Home of the Integrated Curriculum, *Educational Leadership.* October, 1991. pp. 9-13.

Chemistry of Life: 1988 Curriculum Module. Princeton, NJ: Woodrow Wilson National Fellowship Foundation, 1988.

Driver, R. *The Children's Learning in Science Project, Monographs on Preconceptions In Science.* England: Center for Studies in Science and Mathematics Education, Department of Education, University of Leeds, 1984-1989.

Hazen, Robert M. and James Trefil. *Science Matter, Achieving Scientific Literacy.* New York: Doubleday, 1991.

Philips, William. "Earth Science Misconceptions, *The Science Teacher.* October, 1991. pp. 21-23.

Piaget, J., *To Understand IS to Invent: The Future of Education.* New York: Grossman Publishers, 1973.

Rutherford, E. James and Andrew Ahlgren. *Science for All Americans.* New York: Oxford University Press, 1990.

TEACHING METHODS

Altshular, Kenneth. "The Interdisciplinary Classroom," *The Physics Teacher.* October, 1991. pp. 428-429.

Humphreys, David. *Demonstrating Chemistry.* Ontario, Canada: Chemistry Department, McMaster, University Hamilton, 1983.

Johnson, David W., Roger T. Johnson, and Edythe Johnson Holubec. *Circles of Learning.* Edina, MN: Interaction Book Company, 1990.

Johnson, David W., Roger T. Johnson, and Edythe Johnson Holubec. *Cooperation in the Classroom.* Edina, MN: Interaction Book Company, 1991.

Johnson, David W., Roger T. Johnson. *Cooperative Learning: Warm-Ups, Grouping Strategies, and Group Activities.* Edina, MN: Interaction Book Company, 1985.

Novak, Joseph. "Clarify with Concept Maps," *The Science Teacher.* October, 1991. pp. 44-49.

Penick, John. "Where's the Science?" *The Science Teacher.* May, 1991. pp. 27-29.

CONTENT AREA BOOKS

Physics

Arons, A. B. *A Guide to Introductory Physics Teaching.* New York: John Wiley and Sons, 1990.

Berman, Paul. *Light and Sound.* New York: Marshall Cavendish, 1988.

Gardner, Robert. *Experimenting with Light.* New York: Franklin Watts, 1991.

Urone, Paul Peter. *Physics with Health Science Applications.* New York: Harper and Row Publishers, 1986.

Walpole, Brenda. *175 Science Experiments to Amuse and Amaze Your Friends.* New York: Random House, 1988.

Chemistry

Element of the Week. Batavia, IL: Flinn Scientific, Inc., 1990.

Ground to Grits. Scientific Concepts in Nutrition/Agriculture . Columbia, SC: South Carolina Department of Education, 1982.

Joesten, Melvin. *World of Chemistry.* Philadelphia, PA: Saunders College Publishing, 1991.

Mitchell, Sharon and Juergens, Frederick. *Laboratory Solutions for the Science Classroom.* Batavia, IL: Flinn Scientific, Inc., 1991.

Solomon, Sally. "Qualitative Analysis of Eleven Household Compounds," *Journal of Chemical Education.* April, 1991. pp. 328-329.

Life Science

Hancock, Judith M. *Variety of Life: A Biology Teacher's Sourcebook.* Portland, OR: J. Weston Walch, 1987.

Middleton, James I. "Student-Generated Analogies in Biology," *American Biology Teacher.* January, 1991. pp. 42-46.

Vogel, Steven. *Life's Devices: The Physical World of Plants and Animals.* Princeton, NJ: Princeton University Press, 1989.

Earth Science

Callister, Jeffrey C., Lenny Coplestone, Gerald F. Consuegra, Sharon M. Stroud, and Warren E. Yasso. *Earthquakes.* Mary Liston Liepold, ed., Washington D.C.: NSTA/FEMA, 1988.

Lasca, Norman P. "Build Me a River," *Earth.* January, 1991. pp. 59-65.

Little, Jane Braxton. "California Town Unites to Save a Stream," *The Christian Science Monitor.* February 28, 1991.

Sae, Andy S. W. "Dynamic Demos," *The Science Teacher.* October, 1991. pp. 23-25.

SUPPLIER ADDRESSES

Software Distributors

(AIT) Agency for Instructional Technology
Box A
Bloomington, IN 47402-0120

Aquarium Instructional
P.O. Box 128
Indian Rocks Beach, FL 34635

Classroom Consortia Media Inc.
P.O. Box 050228
Staten Island, NY 10305

COMPress
P.O. Box 102
Wentworth, NH 03282

Compuware Corporation
1008 Abington Road
Cherry Hill, NJ 08034

Cross Educational Software
P.O. Box 1536
504 E. Kentucky Avenue
Ruston, LA 71270

Diversified Educational Enterprises, Inc.
725 Main Street
Lafayette, IN 47901

Educational Activities, Inc.
1937 Grand Avenue
Baldwin, NY 11510

Educational Coursewear
3 Nappa Lane
Westport, CT 06880

Educational Materials and Equipment Company (EME)
P.O. Box 2805
Danbury, CT 06813-2805

Focus Media, Inc.
839 Stewart Avenue
P.O. Box 865
Garden City, NY 11530

IBM Educational Systems
Department PC
4111 Northside Parkway
Atlanta, GA 30327

J & S Software
135 Haven Avenue
Port Washington, NY 11050

Minnesota Educational Computing Corporation (MECC)
3490 Lexington Avenue N.
Saint Paul, MN 55126

Micro-ED, Inc.
P.O. Box 24750
Edina, MN 55424

Micro Learningware
Route No. 1
Box 162
Amboy, MN 56010-9762

PH Media (Prentice Hall)
90 South Bedford Road
Mt. Kisco, NY 10549

Queue, Inc.
562 Boston Avenue
Bridgeport, CT 06610

Scott, Foresman, & Company
1900 E. Lake Avenue
Glenview, IL 60025

Sunburst Communications
39 Washington Avenue
Pleasantville, NY 10570

Ventura Educational System
3440 Brokenhill Street
Newbury Park, CA 91320

Audiovisual Distributors

Aims Media
9710 Desoto Avenue
Chatsworth, CA 91311-4409

BFA Educational Media
468 Park Avenue S.
New York, NY 10016

Churchill Films
662 N. Robertson Blvd.
Los Angeles, CA 90069

Coronet/MTI Film and Video Distributors of LCA
108 Wilmot Road
Deerfield, IL 60015

Encyclopedia Britannica Educational Corp. (EBEC)
310 S. Michigan Avenue
Chicago, IL 60604

(EME) Educational Materials and Equipment Company
P.O. Box 2805
Danbury, CT 06813-2805

Focus Media, Inc.
839 Stewart Avenue
P.O. Box 865
Garden City, NY 11530

Image Entertainment
9333 Oso Avenue
Chatsworth, CA 91311

Lumivision
1490 Lafayette
Suite 305
Denver, CO 80218

Macmillan/McGraw-Hill School Division
4635 Hilton Corporate Drive
Columbus, OH 43232

Modum Talking Picture Service
5000 Park Street N.
Saint Petersburg, FL 33709

National Geographic Society Educational Services
17th and "M" Streets, NW
Washington, DC 20036

Science Software Systems
11890 W. Pico Blvd.
Los Angeles, CA 90064

Singer Media Corporation
3164 Tyler Avenue
Anaheim, CA 92801

Society for Visual Education Inc. (SVE)
Dept. VM
1345 Diversey Parkway
Chicago, IL 60614-1299

SysCon Corporation
2686 Dean Drive
Virginia Beach, VA 23452

Time-Life Videos
Time and Life Building
1271 Avenue of the Americas
New York, NY 10020

Universal Education & Visual Arts (UEVA)
100 Universal City Plaza
Universal City, CA 91608

US Department of Energy
9800 S. Cass Avenue
Argonne, IL 60439

US Geological Survey (USGS)
National Center
Reston, VA 22092

TEACHER QUESTIONNAIRE

We at Glencoe Publishing feel that with ***SCIENCE INTERACTIONS: Course 1,*** we have produced a quality textbook program- but the final proof of that rests with you, the teachers who have had the opportunity to put our materials to use in your classrooms. That's why we would appreciate it if you would take the time to respond to any part of this questionnaire that is appropriate for you. In doing so, you will be letting us know how good a job we've done and where we can work to improve.

Please note: (1) you need not have used all of the program components to respond to this questionnaire; and (2) we encourage you to give us your honest and most candid opinions.

STUDENT TEXT

Excellent Poor

5 4 3 2 1 Organization
5 4 3 2 1 Narrative Style
5 4 3 2 1 Readability
5 4 3 2 1 Visual Impact
5 4 3 2 1 Usable Table of Contents
5 4 3 2 1 Accuracy of Content
5 4 3 2 1 Coverage of science principles
5 4 3 2 1 Reduced number of boldface terms
5 4 3 2 1 Skill Builders
5 4 3 2 1 Skill Handbook
5 4 3 2 1 EXPLORE! activities
5 4 3 2 1 FIND OUT! activities
5 4 3 2 1 Investigate activities

EXPANDING YOUR VIEW FEATURES

5 4 3 2 1 Connections to other sciences
5 4 3 2 1 Connections to nonscience disciplines
5 4 3 2 1 Science and Society
5 4 3 2 1 Teens in Science
5 4 3 2 1 How does It Work?
5 4 3 2 1 Technology
5 4 3 2 1 Glossary and Index
5 4 3 2 1 Appendices
5 4 3 2 1 Chapter Reviews
5 4 3 2 1 Looking Back and Looking Ahead Features

TEACHER EDITION

Excellent Poor

5 4 3 2 1 Organization
5 4 3 2 1 Teachability
5 4 3 2 1 Planning charts
5 4 3 2 1 Organization of teaching cycle
5 4 3 2 1 Performance Objectives

SUPPLEMENTS

5 4 3 2 1 Teacher Classroom Resources
5 4 3 2 1 Laboratory Manual
5 4 3 2 1 Color Transparency Package
5 4 3 2 1 Test Bank
5 4 3 2 1 Chapter Review Software
5 4 3 2 1 Lesson Plan Book

SCHOOL INFORMATION

1. What is the grade level of the students you teach?
   6 7 8 9
2. Total number of students in that grade?
   1-50 51-100 101-200 200+
3. Average class size?
   25 or less 26-30 31-40 41 or more
4. Total school enrollment?
   1-200 201-500 501-1000 1000+
5. Ability level of your average class?
   Basic Average Advanced
6. How appropriate is this text for your class?
   Too easy On level Too difficult
7. How many years have you used this text?
   5 4 3 2 1

Fold

Please feel free to include additional comments on a separate sheet.

Name ____________________ Date ____________________

School ____

Street ____

City ____________________ State __________ Zip __________

Fold

NO POSTAGE
NECESSARY
IF MAILED
IN THE
UNITED STATES

BUSINESS REPLY MAIL
FIRST CLASS PERMIT NO 284 COLUMBUS OHIO

POSTAGE WILL BE PAID BY ADDRESSEE

GLENCOE PUBLISHING
SCIENCE PRODUCT MANAGER
PO BOX 508
COLUMBUS OHIO 43272-6174

TEACHER WRAPAROUND EDITION

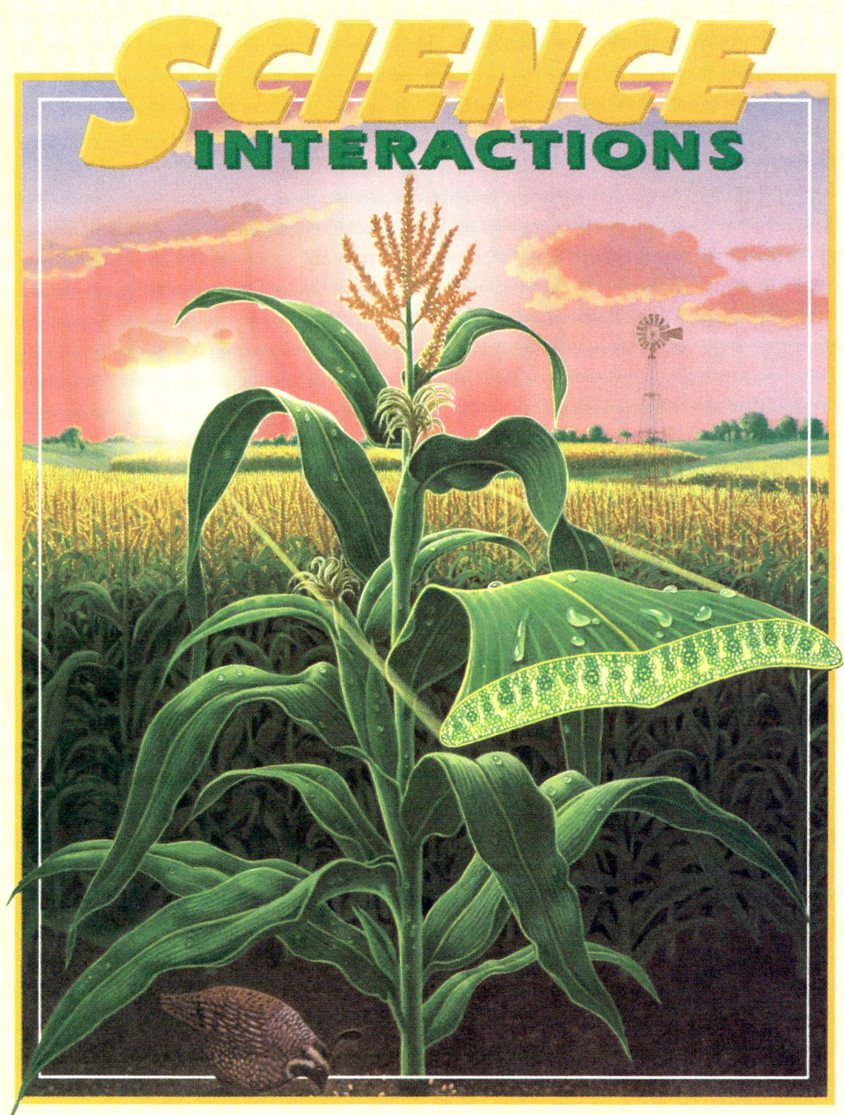

Science Interactions

Course 1

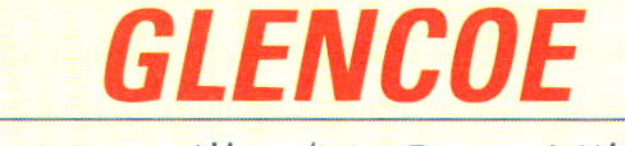

Macmillan/McGraw-Hill

Lake Forest, Illinois Columbus, Ohio Mission Hills, California Peoria, Illinois

Science Interactions

Student Edition
Teacher Wraparound Edition
Teacher Classroom Resource Package
Laboratory Manual: SE
Laboratory Manual: TE
Study Guide: SE
Study Guide: TE
Transparency Package
Computer Test Bank
Spanish Resources
Science and Technology Videodisc Series
Science and Technology Videodisc Teacher Guide

Send all inquiries to:

GLENCOE DIVISION
Macmillan/McGraw-Hill
936 Eastwind Drive
Westerville, OH 43081

ISBN 0-02-826032-5

Printed in the United States of America

3 4 5 6 7 8 9 - VH - 00 99 98 97 96 95 94 93

Authors

Bill Aldridge, M.S.
Executive Director
National Science Teachers Association
Washington, DC

Russell Aiuto, Ph.D.
Director of Research and Development
Scope, Sequence, and Coordination
National Science Teachers Association
Washington, DC

Jack Ballinger, Ed.D.
Professor of Chemistry
St. Louis Community College at Florissant Valley
St. Louis, MO

Anne Barefoot, A.G.C.
Physics and Chemistry Teacher
Whiteville High School
Whiteville, NC

Linda Crow, Ed.D.
Assistant Professor
Baylor College of Medicine
Houston, TX

Ralph M. Feather, Jr., M.Ed.
Science Department Chairperson
Derry Area School District
Derry, PA

Albert Kaskel, M.Ed.
Biology Teacher
Evanston Township High School
Evanston, IL

Craig Kramer, M.A.
Physics Teacher
Bexley High School
Bexley, OH

Edward Ortleb, A.G.C.
Science Lead Supervisor
St. Louis Board of Education
St. Louis, MO

Susan Snyder, M.S.
Earth Science Teacher
Jones Middle School
Upper Arlington, OH

Paul W. Zitzewitz, Ph.D.
Professor of Physics
University of Michigan-Dearborn
Dearborn, MI

Consultants

CHEMISTRY

Richard J. Merrill
Director, Project Physical Science
Associate Director, Institute for Chemical Education
University of California
Berkeley, California

Robert Walter Parry, Ph.D.
Dist. Professor of Chemistry
University of Utah
Salt Lake City, Utah

EARTH SCIENCE

Janifer Mayden
Aerospace Education Specialist
NASA
Washington, DC

James B. Phipps, Ph.D.
Professor of Geology and Oceanography
Gray's Harbor College
Aberdeen, Washington

LIFE SCIENCE

David M. Armstrong, Ph.D.
Director
University of Colorado Museum
Boulder, Colorado

Joe Wiliam Crim, Ph.D
Associate Professor of Zoology
University of Georgia
Athens, Georgia

John J. Just, Ph.D.
Associate Professor of Biology
University of Kentucky
Lexington, Kentucky

Richard D. Storey, Ph.D.
Associate Professor of Biology
Colorado College
Colorado Springs, Colorado

PHYSICS

Karen L. Johnston, Ph.D.
Professor of Physics
North Carolina State University
Raleigh, North Carolina

Eugen Merzbacher, Ph.D.
Kenan Professor of Physics, Emeritus
University of North Carolina
Chapel Hill, North Carolina

READING

Barbara Pettegrew, Ph.D.
Director of Reading/Study Center
Assistant Professor of Education
Otterbein College
Westerville, Ohio

SAFETY

Robert Tatz, Ph.D.
Instructional Lab Supervisor
Department of Chemistry
The Ohio State University
Columbus, Ohio

MIDDLE SCHOOL SCIENCE

Thomas Custer
Coordinator of Science
Anne Arundel County
Ellicot City, Maryland

Gerald Garner
LA Unified
Van Nuys, California

Garland E. Johnson
Science and Education Consultant
Fresno, California

MULTICULTURAL

Eileen Hiss
Lincoln Middle School
Santa Monica Malibu Unified School District
Santa Monica, California

Carol Mitchell
Science Supervisor
Omaha Public Schools
Omaha, Nebraska

Karen L. Muir, Ph.D.
Department of Social and Behavioral Sciences
Columbus State Community College
Columbus, Ohio

LEP

Harold Frederick Robertson, Jr.
Science Resource Teacher
LAUSD Science Materials Center
Van Nuys, California

Ross M. Arnold
Magnet School Coordinator
Van Nuys Junior High
Van Nuys, California

Linda E. Heckenberg
Director, Eisenhower Program
Van Nuys, California

Barbara Sitzman
Chatsworth High School
Tarzana, California

COOPERATIVE LEARNING

Linda Lundgren
Bear Creek High School
Lakewood, Colorado

SPECIAL FEATURES

Timothy Heron, Ph.D.
Professor
Department of Educational Services & Research
The Ohio State University
Columbus, Ohio

Reviewers

Assunta Black
Life Science Teacher
Lindenhurst Junior High
Lindenhurst, New York

Jayne Brown
7th Grade Science Teacher
Valley Springs Middle School
Arden, North Carolina

Mitchell Kyle Carver, Sr.
Science Department Chairperson
Reynolds Middle School
Asheville, North Carolina

James Cowden
Science Teacher Specialist
Chicago Public Schools
Chicago, Illinois

Gloria M. Dobry
Departmental Science Teacher
Gunsaulus Academy
Chicago, Illinois

Daniel H. Domenigoni
Science Department Chairperson
Milwaukie Junior High
Milwaukie, Oregon

Cheryl B. Domineau
Science Department Chairperson
Vero Beach Junior High
Vero Beach, Florida

Alex Domkowski
Physics Teacher
Saint Mary's Hall
San Antonio, Texas

Nancy Donohue
General Science Teacher
Emerson Junior High
Yonkers, New York

Nancy Ann Drain
Teacher
Bell Junior High School
San Diego, California

Nancy Prevatte Dunlap
7th Grade Science Teacher
Central Middle School
Whiteville, North Carolina

Laraine O. Franze
Life Science Teacher
Greenwood Lakes Middle School
Lake Mary, Florida

John A. George
Science Department Chairperson
Rivera Middle School
Miami, Florida

Corless Horne Goode
Teacher
New Hope School
Rutherfordton, North Carolina

Raymond Pat Hadd
Science Department Chairperson
Richbourg Middle School
Crestview, Florida

Karen Sue Hewitt
Teacher
Coldspring High School
Coldspring, Texas

Gordon N. Hopp
Environmental Science Teacher
Carmel Junior High School
Carmel, Indiana

Barbara D. Johnson
Life Science Teacher
Deep Creek Junior High School
Chesapeake, Virginia

Thomas E. Johnson
Life Science Teacher
Western Branch Junior High School
Chesapeake, Virginia

James R. Kimsey
Lead Science Instructor/Department Head
Plaza Park Middle School
Evansville, Indiana

Lonnie L. Lewis
Science Department Chairperson
Ramona Junior High School
Chino, California

William T. Martin
8th Grade General Science Teacher
Atkins Middle School
Winston-Salem, North Carolina

Vito Charles Mazzini, Jr.
Science Department Chairperson
H. D. McMillan Middle School
Miami, Florida

George Graham Ohmer
Teacher
Clay Junior High School
Carmel, Indiana

Thomas J. Pedersen
Graduate Research Assistant
North Carolina State University
Raleigh, North Carolina

Chuck Porrazzo
Science Department Chairperson
CJHS 145
New York City, New York

Allan G. Reisberg
6th Grade Teacher
Abraham Lincoln
Chicago, Illinois

Steven F. Rinck
Supervisor of Science
Pasco County School Board
Land O'Lakes, Florida

Ouida E. Thomas
Life Science Teacher
B. F. Terry High School
Rosenberg, Texas

Mary Coggins White
Science Department Chairperson
Sequoia Intermediate School
Newbury Park, California

Nedra A. Williams
Science Department Chairperson
Los Cerritos Intermediate School
Thousand Oaks, California

CONTENTS
An Overview

CONTENTS

In Depth

LESSONS		ACTIVITIES	
3–3 Music and Resonance	79	EXPLORE! What is resonance?	81
		INVESTIGATE! Length and Resonance	83

LESSONS		ACTIVITIES	
Chapter 4 Using Your Senses	**94**		
		EXPLORE! How do you experience space?	95
4–1 How Do You See?	96	EXPLORE! What is the function of your pupils?	96
		EXPLORE! How well do you think you see?	98
		INVESTIGATE! Testing Your Vision	99
		FIND OUT! How do fruit flies respond to light?	103
4–2 How Do You Hear?	105	FIND OUT! Are two ears better than one?	105
		EXPLORE! Why do you feel dizzy when you spin around, then stop suddenly?	108
4–3 Touch, Taste, and Smell	111	FIND OUT! How does your skin respond to different temperatures?	111
		INVESTIGATE! Tasting Solutions	114

UNIT 2 Interactions in the Physical World................127

UNIT 5 Wave Motion 535

LESSONS		ACTIVITIES	
20–3 Tides	615	FIND OUT! What is the relationship between the height of tides and the position of the moon?	616

EXPANDING YOUR VIEW

Appendices 629

Skill Handbook 647

Glossary 662

Index 666

INTRODUCTION

SCIENCE INTERACTIONS is a science program based on two core philosophies: (1) a study of all science disciplines contributes to an understanding of our natural world and its phenomena; and (2) students will understand science best by the "doing" of science. The text presents a variety of activities that engages the students to think about science in a different way. They become involved in the processes of science-questioning, observing, experimenting, and drawing conclusions. SCIENCE INTERACTIONS recognizes that this approach is different from most traditional science courses and designed the Teacher Wraparound Edition to guide you through the process of getting students to think scientifically–in an easy-to-follow format.

SCIENCE INTERACTIONS begins with an introductory chapter to acquaint you and the students with the fun of learning science. Students become involved in observing, formulating a hypothesis, and designing an experiment to test their hypothesis. In doing the experiment, students may find that their hypothesis was incorrect. Reassure them that making mistakes is part of the scientific process and that much can be learned from mistakes.

Introducing Science Interactions

What do you really know about yourself and your surroundings? Trying to make sense of the world is something that we struggle with from the very beginnings of our lives. Through our senses, we begin the process of gathering and sorting information, so that we can understand the world around us and our place in it. As you study Science Interactions, Course One, you'll use your senses to observe some everyday things and then collect and analyze your observations.

Mirror, Mirror, on the wall ...

Consider this problem. You want to buy a full-length mirror for your room to use as you get dressed each day. How tall does the mirror have to be for you to see your whole body from the top of your head to your feet? Does it have to be as tall as you? Do you have to stand in a certain place? If you stand further away, does the mirror have to be as tall? You can answer these questions yourself by looking at a mirror and finding out. Try it.

When you looked at yourself in a full length mirror and moved back and forth, what did you notice? Were you surprised that the mirror needed to be only half as tall as yourself? When you moved backward away from the mirror, what did you discover? You saw that it made no difference how close or how far away you were. The mirror could be the same height regardless of where you stood. This is an example of how observations can help you answer a question and make a decision. It also shows how our common ideas or beliefs are sometimes not correct. You are going to learn that there is a rather simple law in science that tells why you need a mirror only half your height to see yourself full-length.

xxiv

Mirror, Mirror

This activity will show students how observations can help them answer questions and make decisions. A full length mirror is needed.

Have students work in groups and try the activity described on the student page. Have one student hold the mirror still while others in the group experiment with their reflection in the mirror. Students should change roles so that each student has a chance to look in the mirror.

After completing this activity, students should conclude that the mirror needs to be half as tall as themselves in order to see their whole body in it. They should also conclude that the mirror could be the same height regardless of where they stood.

Did you ever wonder how your ears, eyes, and nose help your brain gather information? In Science Interactions, you will use your senses to observe such things as the sun and moon in Chapter 1, plants and animals in Chapters 10 and 11, and in Chapter 18, waves. And, you'll learn how your senses work in Chapter 4. Hopefully, you'll never again take your senses for granted! Let's look at another example where you must do more than just observe what your senses seem to be telling you.

The Upside Down Word Puzzle

First, get a glass stirring rod. Lay the stirring rod along the length of each of the following words. Adjust its position so that you can see the words clearly.

CARBON DIOXIDE   RAW HIDE   TIGHTLY BOXED

Looking through the rod at the words, what do you see? Do all the letters look the same? In what way are some letters different from others?

You probably noticed that the words do not all look the same. In fact, the words with red letters appear upside down, while the words with blue letters do not. These are the results of your observations.

A Look at the Table of Contents

Review the Table of Contents with your students for an overview of the subject areas to be studied during the course of the year. Point out that the twenty chapters are divided into five major units.

In Unit 1: Observing the World Around You, students use their senses to explore light, color, and sound.

The observational skills from the first unit are used in Unit 2: Interactions in the Physical World and Unit 3: Interactions in the Living World to describe both the physical and living worlds.

Unit 4: Systems in Motion describes motion and applies the description to soil, water, and shaping the land. Unit 5: Wave Motions continues to apply these descriptions to Earth and beyond.

As you continue to examine the table of contents, challenge students to explain how the subject areas in each chapter are related. Seeing the connections between the subject areas give students a more complete idea of the interrelated nature of science.

OPTIONS

Meeting Individual Needs

Visually Impaired Visually impaired students may have difficulty discerning color. If this is the case, avoid referring to the words by color. Instead, refer to them as the word on the left or right.

Learning Disabled Students with learning disabilities may have difficulty discerning letters that are upside down. If possible, have students work in groups of 2 or 3. After each student has looked at the words through the rod, have them compare their observations. You may also have them discuss their hypotheses and design an experiment as a group.

FIND OUT!

How can you solve the upside down puzzle?

Time needed 15 to 20 minutes

Materials glass stirring rod, student textbooks

Thinking Processes
Observing and Inferring, Thinking Critically, Comparing and Contrasting, Designing an Experiment to Test a Hypothesis

Purpose To formulate and test a hypothesis

Preparation Have a glass stirring rod available for each student.

Teaching Strategies

Troubleshooting Make sure students are holding the glass stirring rod correctly and are looking through the rod correctly.

Expected Outcome

Students should find that only mirror image words will appear right-side-up when viewed through the glass rod. Many students will find that they formulated a false hypothesis based on the color of the words. Encourage students to look for another pattern based on their observations to explain what affects how the words look through the rod. They should then formulate, and test their new hypothesis.

FIND OUT!

How can you solve the upside down puzzle?

Do you see any pattern in the results? Can you make up an explanation for these results? Design an experiment that would test your explanation. For example, maybe you think that the color of the words affects whether the words appeared upside down or not. How could you test this? Find words in your book printed in different colors. Use your rod and see how these words appear. Do only red words turn upside down? What about other colors? Do black words invert?

The results of this experiment will either agree with your explanation or won't agree. If the results are not in agreement, then you may need to make other observations, and perform further experiments to test your new observations. Make a new explanation and test it.

Acids help form caves in Earth and digest food in your stomach.

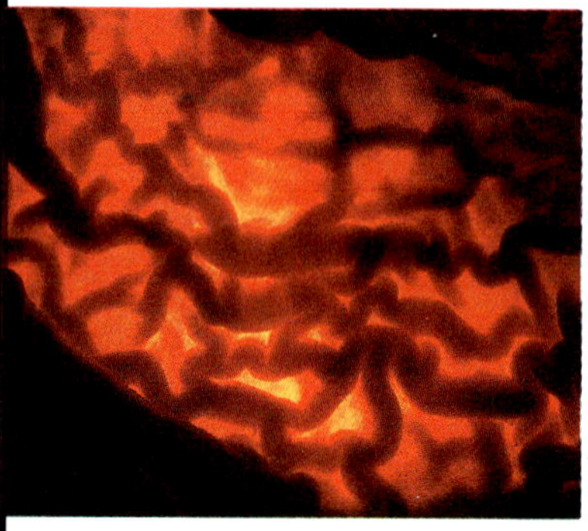

As you just saw, as much as we trust our senses, they often deceive us. Like you, scientists sometimes find that observations that they've made are not complete. Sometimes observations are measured. It is important to make careful and precise observations.

Solving the upside down word puzzle involved discovering a pattern and figuring out relationships. As you make observations during the activities in Science Interactions and as you read the text, you will learn about each topic from several perspectives. For example, you could memorize a definition that says an acid is a compound that contains hydrogen, tastes sour, and is corrosive. But if you study about acids and perform tests that help you find out the properties of acids in several different settings, you will have a better understanding of what an acid is. In Chapter 8, you'll discover how the structure of an acid is related to the way it acts on living and non-living things. In Chapter 16, you'll discover a connection to Earth science when you see how acids affect rocks to help produce soil. And in a Science and Society lesson on acid rain, you'll learn that acids may have a much larger impact on a global scale.

Activity What works better—memorizing or hands on?

This activity should show students that they will be able to remember science concepts more easily by doing hands-on activities rather than just memorizing. Prepare a box containing 10 to 15 cards with the name of one object on each. Students will have three minutes to look at the cards and try to remember as many objects as possible. When time is up they are to write down as many of the objects from the cards as they can remember. Next, give students a box containing 10 to 15 objects. Students should be given the same amount of time to see them, but they will be allowed to handle the objects. When time is up they should again write down as many of the objects as they can remember. What students should see is they are able to remember more of the objects that they handled.

By studying topics such as acids from the different perspectives of chemistry, Earth science, life science, and physics, you'll have a better, more complete idea of what an acid is. You will also see that, in many instances, you are already more familiar with the topic than you may have thought you were.

Science can help you find answers to all the marvelous, puzzling things you may have observed or wondered about. And as you complete the activities and study the chapters of this text, two things will happen for you. First, you will learn how to make observations that will lead you to gather useful scientific information. This skill will help you begin to make sense of the world. Second, you will begin to see and appreciate the patterns, the structure, and the amazing order of Earth.

Although they may look healthy, many lakes in the northeast have been affected by acid rain.

Fog over the Golden Gate Bridge, San Francisco

xxvii

Cooperative Learning Activity

This activity should result in students seeing the importance of integrating the sciences. Divide the class in half. Further, divide each half of the class into four groups. Assign one of the sciences: chemistry, biology, physics or Earth to each of the groups.

Give the groups the following problem. You are on a team whose job is to establish a new colony on an uninhabited island located in the middle of the ocean. The island is located near the equator and is not easily accessible due to surrounding waters that are essentially unnavigable and mountainous terrain that prevents the construction of an airstrip. Each group is to brainstorm the questions or problems they would be asked to solve as the biologist, chemist, physicist, or Earth scientist in helping to establish the new community on the island.

When the individual groups are finished, they should come together to pool information. Each of the two large groups should develop a presentation. The activity will end with the groups reviewing information presented to determine if all areas were covered. Pose the following question to the groups: "Could the colony be established without one of the sciences?"

Students should conclude that all sciences are needed, and sharing information between them necessary to establish the community.

Student responses will vary, but may include that the Earth scientist would be needed to explore possible natural sources for fuels and types of soil for plants and vegetation. The chemist would be needed to determine how to process the natural fuel efficiently without harm to the community. The biologist would provide insight to animal and plant life that could exist on the island. The physicist would help the community deal with environmental problems.

EXPERIENCE SCIENCE

HAVE FUN WHILE YOU LEARN SCIENCE

IN THE "EXPANDING YOUR VIEW" FEATURES, YOU'LL EXPLORE HOW SCIENCE CONNECTS TO ALL PARTS OF YOUR EVERYDAY WORLD

LOOKING AHEAD

TRY IT

In the world that we can see and hear, we rely on observations to gain information. The process of observing involves using one or more of our senses to learn about the world around us. What if you were limited to only one sense—the sense of touch? How do you think this would change your perception of the world around you? Find a partner to work with. Your teacher will provide each of you with a blindfold to wear and several objects. Can you determine what the objects are by touching only? Once you have examined your objects with the sense of touch, your teacher will place all the objects on a table. You can then remove your blindfold. Can you identify which objects you just studied? After you've learned more about observation skills, try this activity again and see whether you can identify the objects more easily than you did on your first attempt.

UNIT 1 OBSERVING THE WORLD AROUND YOU

CONTENTS

UNIT FOCUS

In Unit 1, you are starting on a journey of discovery and observations of the world around you. You'll observe Earth from above and up close as you use your senses of sight and hearing to study the light, color, and sounds of your world.

Try It

The purpose of this activity is for students to develop an understanding and appreciation of their senses—particularly sight. Students will rely on their sense of touch and attempt to identify objects through their texture and shape. Most students will have a difficult time identifying some objects since they are used to making observations using their sight.

LOOKING AHEAD 

UNIT 1
OBSERVING THE WORLD AROUND YOU

THEME DEVELOPMENT

The focus of this unit is discovery and observation using the themes of scale and structure, systems and interactions, change and stability and energy as the framework.

Scale and structure is developed in the treatment of landforms and their scale as viewed from a distance in an airplane. Earth is a part of the Earth-moon-sun system and interacts with the other members. The theme of energy is developed in the treatment of light and sound which are forms of energy. Senses are used to observe change and stability in the world around us.

Connections to Other Units

The concepts in this unit provide a foundation for developing observational experiences. These experiences will be used in describing materials, animals, and plants in the physical world in Unit 2 and in other units.

Getting Started

Discussion Some questions that you may want to ask your students are:

1. **What evidence is there that the Earth and the moon move?** Students may have a difficult time suggesting evidence for motion from their observations but rely on what they have been told.
2. **How can light "light up" objects?** Students may believe that light from a source such as the sun or a light shines on paper or another object and stays there.
3. **How can the color of light affect the color of an object?** Students may believe that the color of the object changes rather than the light illuminating the object.

The answers to these questions will help you establish misconceptions your students may have.

CHAPTER ORGANIZER

SECTION	OBJECTIVES	ACTIVITIES/FEATURES
Chapter Opener		**Explore!** What do the landscape and sky look like where you live? p. 3
1-1 Viewing the Earth (2 days)	1. **Describe** basic landforms such as mountains, plains, and plateaus. 2. **Recognize** the kind of landform on which you live.	**Explore!** What does a profile of the United States look like? p. 4
1-2 Using Maps of Earth (4 days)	1. **Identify** landforms using a topographic map. 2. **Demonstrate** how elevation is shown on a topographic map. 3. **Compare and contrast** latitude and longitude.	**Find Out!** Where is Central School located? p. 10 **Explore!** How can you identify a landform without actually seeing it? p. 12 **Investigate 1-1:** Using Contour Lines, p. 13 **Explore!** Can you describe the location of a dot on a ball? p. 14 **Skillbuilder:** Interpreting Scientific Illustrations, p. 16
1-3 Viewing the Sky (3 days)	1. **Describe** the position and appearance of the sun and the moon as viewed from Earth. 2. **Explain** the use of a star map in locating stars in the sky.	**Explore!** What can you find out by observing the moon? p. 18 **Investigate 1-2:** Making and Dating Moon Craters, p. 20 **Skillbuilder:** Sequencing, p. 22 **Explore!** What can you learn observing the sun? p. 24
Expanding Your View	A Closer Look **Irrigation on the Great Plains,** p. 25 Life Science Connection **Just the Right Conditions,** p. 26	Science and Society **What to Do with All That Garbage?,** p. 27 Technology Connection **Franklin Ramon Chang-Diaz,** p. 29 Teens in Science **Happy Trails to You,** p. 30

ACTIVITY MATERIALS

EXPLORE!	INVESTIGATE!	FIND OUT!
Page 4 atlas **Page 14** ball with no markings on it, felt tip marker	**Page 13** metric ruler, transparency marker, clear plastic box and lid, transparency, tape, plastic model landform, beaker, water **Page 20** flour, salt, pan (about 10x12 inches), marbles of different sizes, metric ruler	

Viewing Earth and Sky

TEACHER CLASSROOM RESOURCES	OTHER RESOURCES
	***STVS:** *Science of Bowling,* Physics (Disc 1, Side 1)
Study Guide, p. 7 **Flex Your Brain,** p. 8 **How It Works,** p. 5 **Making Connections: Across the Curriculum,** p. 5 **Making Connections: Technology and Society,** p. 5 **Multicultural Activities,** p. 5	***STVS:** *Charting Air Space,* Earth and Space (Disc 3, Side 2)
Study Guide, p. 8 **Activity Masters, Investigate 1-1,** pp. 5-6 **Critical Thinking/Problem Solving,** p. 9 **Take Home Activities,** p. 6 **Concept Mapping,** p. 9 **Multicultural Activities,** p. 6	**Laboratory Manual,** pp. 1-4, Determining Latitudes **Laboratory Manual,** pp. 5-6, Time Zones **Color Transparency and Master 1,** Latitude/Longitude **Color Transparency and Master 2,** U.S. Physiographic Regions ***STVS:** *Map Science,* Earth and Space (Disc 3, Side 2) *Mapping with a Rifle,* Earth and Space (Disc 3, Side 2)
Study Guide, p. 9 **Making Connections: Integrating Sciences,** p. 5 **Activity Masters, Investigate 1-2,** pp. 7-8 **Review and Assessment,** pp. 5-8	***STVS:** *Flying Observatory,* Earth and Space (Disc 3, Side 1) *Giant Meteorites,* Earth and Space (Disc 3, Side 1) **Computer Test Bank**
	Spanish Resources **Cooperative Learning Resource Guide** **Lab and Safety Skills**

***Science and Technology Videodisc Series**

KEY TO TEACHING STRATEGIES

Teaching strategies have been coded for varying learning styles and abilities. As you review teaching strategies in the margin, the following designations will help you decide which activities are appropriate for your students.

- **L1** Level 1 activities are basic activities and should be within the ability range of all students.
- **L2** Level 2 activities are average activities and should be within the ability range of the average to above-average student.
- **L3** Level 3 activities are challenging activities designed for the ability range of above-average students.
- **LEP** LEP activities should be within the ability range of Limited English Proficiency students.
- **COOP LEARN** Cooperative Learning activities are designed for small group work.

ADDITIONAL MATERIALS

SOFTWARE	AUDIOVISUAL
Mapping the Earth, Queue. *The Earth and Moon Simulator,* Focus. *Moonrise/Moonset,* Micro Learningware.	*Landforms on Earth's Crust,* slides, SVE. *Latitude/Longitude and Time Zones,* film, Coronet/MTI. *The Earth in Motion,* film, EBEC. *How We Know the Earth Moves,* film, BFA. *Moonwalk,* video, LCA.

Chapter 1

Viewing Earth and Sky

THEME DEVELOPMENT

The major theme of this chapter is scale and structure. Students learn how landform structures on Earth are related and how we can compare them to scale using maps. For example, students learn to find various elevations by reading contour lines on a topographic map in the Investigate activity on page 13. Students will work with a variety of maps in this chapter. Scales of different types play an important role in mapmaking and reading. Interactions and systems is another theme in this chapter. This chapter explores the interaction of the various landscapes and systems such as rivers, mountains, and plains.

CHAPTER OVERVIEW

Basic landforms such as mountains, plains, plateaus, and rivers are first described and students are guided to recognize the kind of landform on which they live. Students then use topographic maps to locate landforms and to define contour line, elevation, latitude, and longitude. Finally, structures in space, the sun and the moon, are described. The use of star maps to locate stars in the sky is also demonstrated.

Tying to Previous Knowledge

Arrange students in small groups to brainstorm different ways they can view Earth and sky. They might suggest viewing from above such as in an airplane or on a mountain and from the surface such as with a telescope standing on the ground.

DID YOU EVER WONDER . . .
How high the mountains are?
Why the moon seems to change shape?
What the Big Dipper is?
You'll find the answers to these questions as you read this chapter.

DID YOU EVER WONDER...

Students will explore these questions as they progress through the chapter. Don't spoil their fun and motivation by sharing these answers too early.

- The Rockies are over 4,000 meters above sea level; the highest mountain in the world, Mount Everest, towers 8,800 meters above sea level. (page 7)
- The moon seems to change shape because we see different portions of its lighted side. These changing images of the moon we see are called phases. (page 21)
- The Big Dipper is a group of stars shaped like a water dipper, called a constellation. (page 22)

Viewing Earth and Sky

Have you ever taken a long trip by car, bus, train, or plane? If so, then you know there's not much to do while actually traveling except look out the window. But when you do, what a view! You can see miles and miles of sweeping fields or desert areas; high, snowcapped mountains; green, rolling hills; gentle valleys; and deep canyons. You might ask yourself how so many different landscapes can exist!

Making observations and asking questions about them is an excellent way to learn about your world. When you are traveling, it's easy to sit back and observe the world going by you. But you don't have to travel to observe. You can start right where you are—at home, in your classroom, around your neighborhood. In this and future chapters, you will be looking up, down, and all around as you observe your physical surroundings—the land on which you live and the sky above. So let's get started—right now, right where you are.

EXPLORE!

What do the landscape and sky look like where you live?

Find a spot outdoors, and sit and make yourself comfortable. Facing west, draw what you see on the land and in the sky. Then face north and draw what you see. Continue on until you have drawn the east and south views as well. What features are in your drawings?

3

Introducing the Chapter

Have students look at the photograph on page 2 and discuss the landforms they see. Invite students to share memories of views they found impressive, especially unusual landscapes they recall vividly. The landforms they will probably name are explored in this chapter.

Uncovering Preconceptions

Students might think that to view Earth and sky, people must use scientific equipment. Use the following strategies to explore viewing from different vantage points. Have groups of students examine the same scene from close up, a middle distance, and far away. Have them assess what they learned in each instance.

EXPLORE!

What do the landscape and sky look like where you live?

Time needed 50–120 minutes

Materials No special materials are needed for this activity.

Thinking Processes Practicing scientific methods, Observing

Purpose To guide students to identify the landforms they live on and features of the sky above.

Preparation This activity is designed for a clear, mild day. Students should be situated so they can see all the landforms in the surrounding area.

It would be helpful if students could draw from the top of a hill on the school grounds or walk to a nearby park with hills.

Expected Outcomes

Answers will vary depending on where students live.

Teaching the Activity

Sketch one of the visible landforms to demonstrate to students the amount of detail they will need in their drawings. L1

Troubleshooting Be sure students know how to find west from the position of the sun.

Project

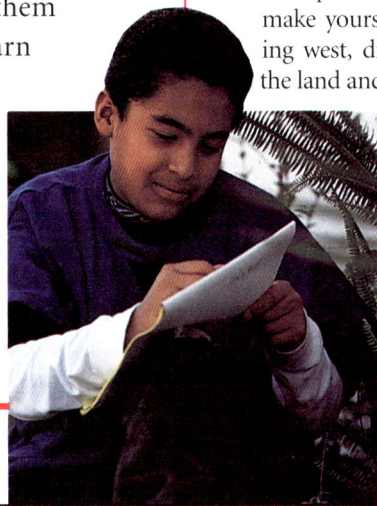

Have half the class chart the moon's position for a week at the same time every night. Have the other half record the tides in the nearest ocean for a week, using the newspaper, *Farmer's Almanac,* or direct observation. Have them correlate their findings to explain the relationship of the moon and tides. Students will discover that the moon is the main cause of tides and, most shores have two high tides and low tides each day.

Science at Home

Have students collect maps of their community, surrounding areas, their state, country, and the world. Have students find road maps, mass transit maps, hiking maps, atlases, and street maps. Have students describe what each map is used for in their homes. Then have students compare and contrast various types of maps. Sources may include travel brochures, chambers of commerce, sports stores, and gas stations.

Section 1-1

PREPARATION

Concepts Developed

Students will be able to identify various landforms and compare and contrast them. This topic relates indirectly to Chapters 15, 17 and 19 that deal with landforms and their causes.

Planning the Lesson

In planning your lesson on Earth's landforms, refer to the Chapter Organizer on pages 2A-B for timing suggestions, resources, and additional materials that will help you in your presentation of the lesson concepts.

For adequate development of the concepts presented in this section, it is recommended that students perform the Explore activity on this page.

1 MOTIVATE

Activity Display a relief map of the United States. Divide the class into groups of three students. Have each group list all of the different landforms they can find. Then lead a discussion comparing and contrasting various landforms. COOP LEARN L1

1-1 Viewing Earth

OBJECTIVES

In this section, you will

- describe basic landforms such as mountains, plains, and plateaus;
- recognize the kind of landform on which you live.

KEY SCIENCE TERMS

landforms

OVER THE PLAINS, MOUNTAINS, AND PLATEAUS

Suppose you have tickets for an early morning flight from Washington, D.C., to California. You will be flying for about six hours. Thank goodness you were able to get a window seat! You want to see the land unfold beneath you. What will you observe as you fly over the United States? The Explore activity will give you some clues.

EXPLORE!

What does a profile of the United States look like?

You will need to borrow an atlas from the library for this activity. Find a physical map of the United States that shows its land features. Use the map to guide you as you draw a cross-section profile of the United States. Start with the west coast at the left, then move right to the east coast. Keep in mind that a profile shows the surface features as they would look if you cut the United States in half from the west to the east coast and looked at the surface from the cut edge. Some atlases contain profile maps. Use these as models for your own profile. Mark and label the different features. How do you think those features would look from the air?

Now that you have drawn a profile, you will see how your profile compares with the surface as seen from the air. The surface features you will see are called **landforms**. Mountains, plains, and plateaus are three common landforms in the United States.

The big day for your airplane trip arrives. You board the plane, settle yourself into your window seat, and fasten your seat belt. You're eager to compare your profile

EXPLORE!

What does a profile of the United States look like?

Time needed 20 to 25 minutes

Materials atlases, pencil, paper, rulers

Thinking Processes Observing and inferring, Making models

Purpose To practice drawing cross-sectional features.

Preparation A world map and a map of the United States are provided in Appendices F-G, pages 638–641.

Teaching the Activity

Demonstration Shine a light at objects so that shadows fall on the chalkboard. Have students outline the shadows cast. The outline is a profile of the objects. L1 LEP

Expected Outcomes

Students will create a profile of landforms of the United States.

Answers to Question

Plains—flat and wide. Mountains—would look bumpy, round, and sharp. Plateaus—flat on top, with steep sides.

FIGURE 1-1. East coast landforms include coastal plains.

with the landforms you see on the trip. The plane taxis down the runway, and soon you're in the air. Good-bye, Washington! California, here you come!

After taking off, you look down and see features on the surface. Study Figure 1-1. It shows an east coast landscape. You can see some buildings and roads, but what else do you see?

You begin to realize there are many landforms that may not be detailed on your profile. These natural features give shape and variety to the surface. Right after takeoff, you fly over flat lands. What are these landforms called?

ACROSS THE LOW PLAINS

What do you think of when you hear the word *plains*? You might think of endless flat fields of wheat or grass. That's often what plains look like because many of them are used to grow crops. Plains are large, low, mostly flat areas that cover much of the United States. In fact, about half of all the land in the United States is plains.

You will see plains along many of the coastlines and in the interior of the country. The lowland areas along the coastlines are called coastal plains. The Atlantic Coastal Plain stretches along the eastern coast of the United States. This area is characterized by low, rolling hills, swamps,

2 TEACH

Tying To Previous Knowledge

Have students describe the most amazing landform feature they have seen or would like to see. Then have students leaf through the text to find a picture of a landform similar to the one they just described. Direct the class to turn to the page where the picture appears.

Concept Development

Using the Photo Direct students to look at the photo and read the caption for Figure 1-1. Based on their completion of the Explore activity, ask them to name another East Coast landform. *mountains*

Discussion Have students compare and contrast flat land, such as plains and beaches, to land that shows relief, such as hills and mountains. Major points of comparison are: All have rocks and/or soil, plants are capable of growing on all. Major points of contrast are: Plains and beaches are relatively flat, mountains and hills are "bumpy." L1

Flex Your Brain Have students use the Flex Your Brain master to write about LANDFORMS.

Teacher F.Y.I.

Point out that the highest mountain in the world, Mt. Everest, could fit in the Marianas Trench and still have about 2,000 meters of water above it. The Marianas Trench is the deepest point in the ocean.

PROGRAM RESOURCES

Teacher Classroom Resources

Study Guide, page 7

Critical Thinking/Problem Solving, page 8, Flex Your Brain

How It Works, page 5, Survey Equipment L3

Making Connections: Across the Curriculum, page 5, Photographing Landscapes (Photography) L2

OPTIONS

Meeting Individual Needs

Learning Disabled Have students bring in old magazines or obtain magazines to be discarded from the school or local library. Direct students to cut out and identify pictures of different landforms. Post the labeled landform pictures on the bulletin board.

Concept Development

Activity Have students use an atlas to count all the states that border on the Atlantic Ocean, Gulf of Mexico, and Pacific Ocean. *Atlantic—14, Gulf—5, Pacific—5* Which state borders an ocean and a gulf? *Florida* Which state borders on two oceans? *Alaska* What do the states bordering on the Atlantic Ocean or the Gulf of Mexico have in common other than the fact that they border on a large body of water? *All have coastal plains* L1

MAKING CONNECTIONS

Math

Have students use the answers from the activity above to write ratios to show: Atlantic states to the whole $\frac{14}{50}$; Gulf states to the whole $\frac{5}{50}$; Pacific states to the whole $\frac{5}{50}$. What is the ratio of states on the Coastal Plain to all states in the United States? $\frac{23}{50}$, *almost half*

Content Background

Due to farming and ranching, little natural and undisturbed prairie still exists. Much of the soil has been disturbed by constant plowing. The variety of species of grass and plant life are being replaced by uniform single-crop plantings. Have students write to the address below to find out more about prairie conservation. The Morton Arboretum, Route 53, Lisle, IL 60532.

FIGURE 1-2. The Florida Everglades are on a coastal plain.

and marshes. Another coastal plain is the Gulf Coastal Plain. It includes the lowlands surrounding the Gulf of Mexico. Look at Figure 1-2. Where do you think this area is? It's the coastal plain known as the Florida Everglades.

As you fly, you also see that a large part of the middle of the United States is made up of plains. They are called the interior plains. You may remember from the Explore activity that they extend from the Appalachian Mountains in the east, to the Rocky Mountains in the west, and to the Gulf Coastal Plain in the south. The first interior plains you see are the very low, rolling hills of the Great Lakes area and the lowlands around the Mississippi and Missouri rivers. Much of this area is rich farmland. As Figure 1-3 shows, you can even see the geometric patterns formed by the farmers' fields of grain.

To the west of the Mississippi lowlands, you see the Great Plains. This area has flat, grassy, dry plains with few trees. The Great Plains are covered with nearly horizontal layers of dirt and small rocks that were washed down into the plains during the last few million years. Where did these sediments come from? They washed down from the landform that you will fly over next on your trip.

FIGURE 1-3. Today much of the vast interior plains region is used for farming and ranching.

OPTIONS

Enrichment

Have students find information on two famous Americans—Meriwether Lewis and William Clark. Remind them that Lewis and Clark explored parts of the United States called the Louisiana Purchase and the Oregon Country. After students have identified the route taken by Lewis and Clark, ask them to draw the route on a map of the United States. Ask students the following questions: **Where did they begin their trip?** *St. Louis* **How long did it take them to get to the Pacific Ocean?** *more than a year* Using a physical map of the United States, ask students to identify the major rivers and other landforms that Lewis and Clark traveled on or across: Missouri and Columbia rivers, Central Plains, Rocky Mountains, Cascade and Coastal ranges. L3

MOUNTAINS

The dirt and rock that helped form the Great Plains washed down from the Rocky Mountains, pictured in Figure 1-4 (a) below. Mountains tower above the surrounding land, providing a spectacular view of Earth. The world's highest mountain peak, however, is not in the Rockies, or even in the United States. It is Mount Everest in the Himalayas, which rises more than 8800 meters above sea level. Mountain peaks in the part of the United States that you are traveling over reach just a little more than 4000 meters high.

As you might expect, mountains vary greatly in size and shape. Look at all the pictures of mountains in Figure 1-4, and you will see that they appear different. This is because they were formed in different ways. Also, some mountains are older than others. The older ones are often more like large hills, rounder and lower in

FIGURE 1-4. The Rocky Mountains (a), the Appalachian Mountains (b), the Cascade Mountains (c), and the California Coastal Mountains (d) are ranges in the United States. Each has a beauty all its own.

a

b

c

d

Concept Development

Using the Photo Direct students to compare and contrast the different mountain ranges shown in Figure 1-4 in terms of appearance.

Activity Have students locate the ranges on the U.S. map in Appendix G pages 640–641. Then have them name the closest and farthest mountain ranges to your area. L2

Demonstration This demonstration will help students understand the in-text question, where did these sediments come from? You will need a large rectangular aluminum or plastic pan, a large scoop of sand, a paper cup, and a sharp pencil.

Demonstrate the movements of sediment by rain and rivers. Moisten the sand so that it clumps together. Pile it up against one side of the pan, extending about 30 cm toward the center. Prop up the side of the pan about 5 cm. Have students form a semicircle to watch the demonstration. Poke a few dozen holes in the bottom of a waxed paper cup. Hold the cup over the sand and pour water into it. Continue pouring until all students have seen the sand move downhill. Ask **What will eventually happen to the sand in the dish?** *It will move to the lowest point. It will spread out.* **How does the demonstration show that the plains got sediment?** *Rain and rivers carried the sediment there.* L2

Student Journal Have students record their results in their journals. Your students will benefit from maintaining a small notebook or booklet as an ongoing Student Journal throughout the year. They can record their observations, results of activities, and impressions in words or diagrams. You may wish to review these journals for evaluation and assessment.

Multicultural Perspectives

The Anasazi built their homes directly into the sides of cliffs to utilize the natural shelter, protection, and cooling that canyon walls offer. Have students research the Southwestern Native Americans who were cliff dwellers and present reasons they chose to live in canyon walls.

Concept Development

Theme Connection Students are introduced to the concept of large-scale landforms. Students will learn to recognize and differentiate between the various Earth structures and their scale.

MAKING CONNECTIONS

Math

Students will need 12 meter sticks or 12 pieces of wood 1 meter long. Direct students to find the volume of material that was removed from the Bingham mine discussed in Did You Know on the next page. Use the formula: $l \times w \times h = V$. *4 km × 4 km × 0.8 km = 12.8 km*^{3}

Form a square of four meter sticks on the floor. Choose two students to hold four more meter sticks (two sticks each) perpendicular to the corners of the square. Choose two more students each to hold two sticks to form a square at the top of the perpendiculars. You now have one cubic meter. Ask students how many of those cubic meters would fit into 1 km^3. *1,000m × 1,000m × 1,000m = 1,000,000,000 m*^{3}*; 1 billion cubic meters* The material removed from the Bingham mine was almost 13 times this amount.

Teacher F.Y.I.

The Grand Canyon is not the deepest land canyon in the world. A gorge in the Andes mountain range in South America is more than 11 km deep!

comparison with younger mountains. They have been worn down to some degree by wind, rain, and running water. Which of the mountains shown in Figure 1-4 are older mountains?

ON THE FLAT PLATEAUS

As you continue your trip west, you see other highlands. These are the plateaus, raised areas of fairly flat land. Plateaus are made up of nearly horizontal rock layers. Unlike the plains, they rise steeply from the land around them.

Figure 1-5 shows the Colorado Plateau, which lies just west of the Rocky Mountains. The Colorado River has cut deep into the rock layers of this plateau, forming the Grand Canyon. Other rivers, such as the Green River and the San Juan River, have also created canyonlands on the vast Colorado Plateau.

FIGURE 1-5. The Colorado and other rivers have cut magnificent canyons into the Colorado Plateau.

PROGRAM RESOURCES

Teacher Classroom Resources

Multicultural Activities, page 5, Land-A Valuable Resource L1

Making Connections: Technology and Society, page 5, Northwest Passage Controversy 

OPTIONS

Meeting Individual Needs

Learning Disabled Some students have never traveled from their city or town. Therefore, they have never seen landforms other than the ones around their region. Obtain travel brochures or posters of various parts of this country and other countries from a local travel agency and share them with students. 

RIVERS

One feature that mountains and plains share with plateaus is rivers. Rivers cut through all different kinds of landforms. Look at Figure 1-6. Can you guess what river of the interior plains is shown? The Mississippi River is easily identified because it is so large and so long. It eventually empties into the Gulf of Mexico. Some rivers curve back and forth like snakes, while others flow fairly straight. Some run wildly down mountain slopes, while others move slowly along.

Now you hear the captain's voice. It's time to prepare for landing. Your flight is nearly over. It was great seeing landforms from the airplane, but such a view is not usually possible. You can't often observe land directly. Most of the time, you use maps to identify landforms. Can a map show how high a mountain is or how flat a plain is? You will find out that maps can do these things and even more.

DID YOU KNOW?

Some landforms are made by humans. The Bingham mine near Salt Lake City, Utah, is the largest hole ever made by humans. The Bingham mine is an open-pit copper mine that is almost 800 m deep and 4 km wide at the surface.

FIGURE 1-6. The mighty Mississippi River flows through the interior plains to the coastal plains of the Gulf of Mexico.

Check Your Understanding

1. How are plains and plateaus alike? How do they differ?
2. If you live near the Gulf Coast, on what landform would you live?
3. Why are the Rocky Mountains in the west higher than the Appalachian Mountains in the east?
4. **APPLY:** On which kind of landform do you live?

Answers to Check Your Understanding

1. Both plains and plateaus are relatively flat. Plains are large, low, mostly flat, areas that cover most of the United States. Plateaus are raised flat areas with steep sides.
2. If you live near the Gulf Coast, you live on a coastal plain.
3. The mountains are higher in the western U.S. than in the east because the eastern mountains are older and have been worn down.
4. The answer to the Apply question depends on location.

3 Assess

Check For Understanding

1. Have students name and list landform types from lowest to highest relief and give an example of each. *plains—Great Plains, Coastal Plains; plateaus—Colorado; mountains—Appalachian, Rockies, Cascade, Coastal*
2. Have students answer Check Your Understanding questions 1–3 individually and question 4 in groups.

Reteach

To understand the difference between a top view and a side view (which is how profile maps are constructed) ask students to look down at one of their shoes and draw a map of what they see. Then ask them to imagine they were to cut their shoe in half lengthwise from top to bottom and draw a profile map of what they would see if they looked at the cut side of the shoe. LEP L1

Extension

Students will need a U.S. map, Appendix G, pages 640 and 641; pencil and paper. Have students draw a cross section of the United States from the southern tip of Florida to the northwestern tip of Oregon. L3

4 Close

Activity

Divide the class into groups of four. Give each student 4 slips of paper so each group has 16 slips of paper. Have students write questions about landforms on one side of the slip and answers on the other. Have groups trade slips. Then have the groups play a question and answer game. One group member draws a question for the person seated to the right. If a student answers incorrectly then the student sitting to the left tries to answer. Have the groups trade slips. Repeat. COOP LEARN L1

Section 1-2

PREPARATION

Concepts Developed

Students will build on their knowledge of landforms. They will identify landforms on a topographic map, find elevations, and learn about the grid system of latitude and longitude. Students will also learn to locate points on a map using latitude and longitude.

Planning the Lesson

In planning your lesson on topographic maps, latitude, and longitude, refer to the Chapter Organizer on pages 2A-B for timing suggestions, resources, and additional materials that will help you in your presentation of the lesson concepts.

For adequate development of the concepts presented in this section, we recommend that students perform the Find Out activity on this page and the Explore activities on pages 12 and 14.

1 MOTIVATE

Activity Have students draw a map of the halls inside the school. Walk with students as they move from hall to hall on one floor. Have students sketch their journeys on paper. After they complete this task, have them redraw the diagrams on clean sheets of paper. Have them compare and contrast their maps. L1

1-2 Using Maps of Earth

OBJECTIVES

In this section, you will

- identify landforms using a topographic map;
- demonstrate how elevation is shown on a topographic map;
- compare and contrast latitude and longitude.

KEY SCIENCE TERMS

elevation
contour lines
latitude
longitude

CITY MAPS

Your plane has landed in California, where a good friend has moved, and you'd like to visit him at his school. You look around and observe that you're in a beautiful city park, but you wonder where your friend's school is. You know a map would be useful to you. Maps are useful for locating places, finding your way around, and getting a clearer picture of an area. Use the map in the Find Out activity to help you find your friend's school.

FIND OUT!

Where is Central School located?

You can find the school by studying the map. You're at the city park right now. How can you get to the school? Look at the different names of the streets and avenues. Now notice the location of the city park. How would you describe the location of the park?

Next, notice the location of Central School. How would you describe its location?

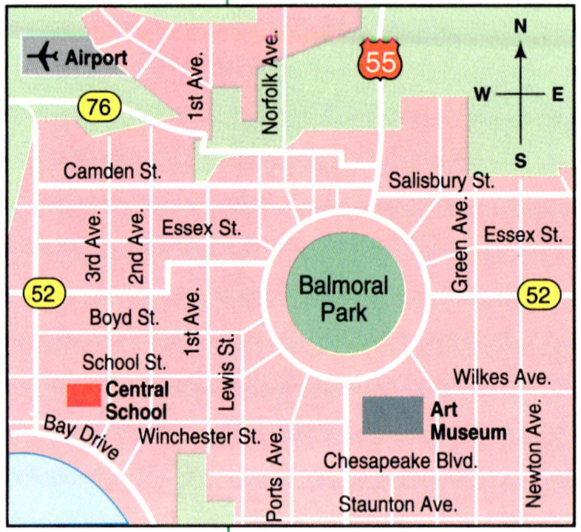

Conclude and Apply

Suppose you wanted to get from the park to the school. How would you do it?

With the city map, you were able to get from the park to the school. Does the map tell you anything about landforms in the area? Are you able to find the highest and lowest points in the city? No, you need a different kind of

FIND OUT!

Where is Central School located?

Time needed 10 to 15 minutes

Materials No special materials or preparation is required for this activity.

Thinking Processes
Interpreting data

Purpose To use a map to find locations and plot the route from one location to another.

Teaching the Activity

Ask a volunteer to describe the route. Ask students to agree or disagree and add comments. Point out that the route is in part dependent on where you are in the park. L3 COOP LEARN

Student Journal Have students write the correct route in their journals. Have them note any problems. L1

Expected Outcome

Most students will be able to find a correct route. Some will want to take the "scenic" route.

Answers to Conclude and Apply
See Teaching the Activity above

map to get this information. One kind of map that shows landforms as well as structures made by people is a topographic map.

TOPOGRAPHIC MAPS

As you can see, the topographic map in Figure 1-7 differs from the map in the Find Out activity. The topographic map shows the shape of the area by giving information about elevation. **Elevation** is the height above sea level or the depth below sea level. With a topographic map, you can tell how steep a mountain is or how deep a canyon is.

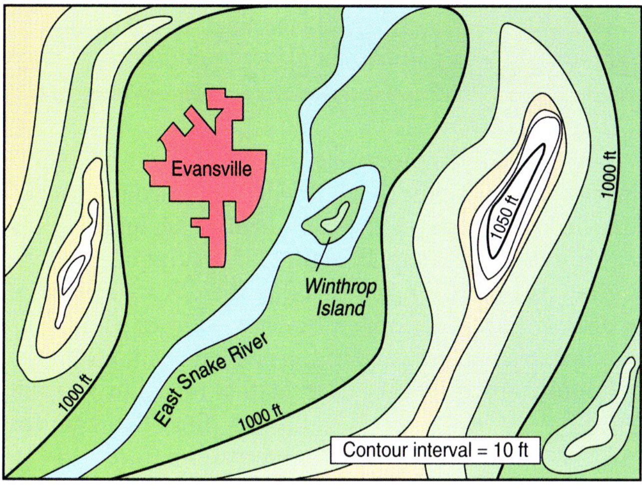

FIGURE 1-7. A topographic map has lines that show elevation of landforms and therefore their shape,

The thin lines on a topographic map are contour lines. **Contour lines** are lines of equal elevation that show the shapes, or contours, of landforms. The contour lines represent three-dimensional contours on a two-dimensional map. They show the vertical rise and fall of the land.

Look at Figure 1-8. As you can see, the artist used lines and shadows to suggest the curved contours of the face. Early mapmakers also used this artistic technique of shading to show the contours of a land surface.

Mapmakers today use contour lines to show differences in elevation on Earth's surface. Each contour line connects points of equal elevation. Between every two contour lines, the land is changing in elevation.

FIGURE 1-8. Artists use shading and contour lines to draw facial lines and shape. Early mapmakers often used the same techniques to show land features.

2 TEACH

Tying to Previous Knowledge

Ask students to think about times in their lives when they have used maps other than those they used in school, such as road maps, maps of a theme park, ski trail maps, subway maps, park maps, and campground maps. Lead into a discussion of a special kind of map called contour map, which they will be learning about in this section.

Concept Development

Inquiry Question How is a topographic map the same as a street map? How is it different? *Street maps and topographic maps show buildings, rivers, bridges, and railroads. Both have map scales for distances. Street maps show all the streets; topographic maps usually don't. Topographic maps show elevation and landforms; street maps don't.* L2

Teacher F.Y.I.

Cartography is the art of making maps. The word has two roots (*cart* means "chart" or "leaf of paper" and *ography* means "to write.") Relate this to students and ask them what the technical name for a mapmaker is. *cartographer*

OPTIONS

Meeting Individual Needs

Learning Disabled Draw a contour map with 5 to 10 contours, each spaced about 1 cm or more apart. Draw a straight reference line across the contours from the center of the page to any edge or corner. Photocopy the map and distribute it, cardboard, scissors, and paste to students. Have students cut out the outermost contour line and then trace the circular pattern on a piece of cardboard. Tell them to place an X where the reference line meets the cardboard. Direct students to cut out the cardboard along the traced line. Have them repeat the process, each time cutting out the next contour inward. Be sure they point the reference line to an X for each cut. When all the contours are cut out, students will paste the cardboard cutouts together, lining up all the X's. The stair-step result is a model of a hill landform. L1

EXPLORE!

How can you identify a landform without actually seeing it?

Time needed 5 to 10 minutes

Thinking Processes
Observing and inferring

Purpose To demonstrate how contour lines show steepness

Teaching the Activity

Have students create ficticious contour maps, exchange them and question each other on their maps. L1

Expected Outcomes

Students will interpret relative steepness of contour line spacing.

Answers to Questions
1. steep hills 2. plain 3. Larger distances between lines usually indicate gentle slope or nearly flat.

MAKING CONNECTIONS

Math

Students will need a string at least 7 m long, a nail, a penny, and 6 metersticks

To have students visualize how slope is determined mathematically, have them tie the end of the string to a nail 2 meters above the floor and let the string hang straight down. Place a penny where the string touches the floor directly under the nail. Ask students how far above the penny the nail is. *2 m* Ask them how far to the right of the nail the penny is. *0 m* Next have students use metersticks to move the penny 2 m to the right and draw the string tautly to the new penny position. Have them repeat the position. Have them repeat the move two more times. Students should observe the new slopes for the string and explain the change. *The slope decreases as the horizontal distance increases and the vertical distance remains the same.* See diagram at the right.

EXPLORE!

How can you identify a landform without actually seeing it?
Study the topographic map in Figure 1-9 and notice its contour interval. What kind of landform do you think occurs where the contour lines are close together? What kind of landform occurs where the lines are far apart? How do you know?

What is the difference in elevation between two contour lines on a topographic map? The difference from one contour line to the next is the contour interval, and it is the same on the entire map. In Figure 1-9 the contour interval is given as 10 feet. This means that there is a 10-foot rise or drop in elevation from a place crossed by one thin contour line to a place crossed by the next thin contour line.

Contour intervals vary from map to map, but you will always find the contour interval marked on a map. Maps of areas with steep slopes have a larger contour interval than maps of flatter areas because elevation changes so quickly. If small intervals were used, the lines would be so close together that you could not distinguish between them. Now that you know about contour lines on topographic maps, you can make your own topographic map.

FIGURE 1-9. Contour lines on a topographic map connect areas of equal elevation. The change in elevation between any two lines on the map is the same—in this case, 10 feet.

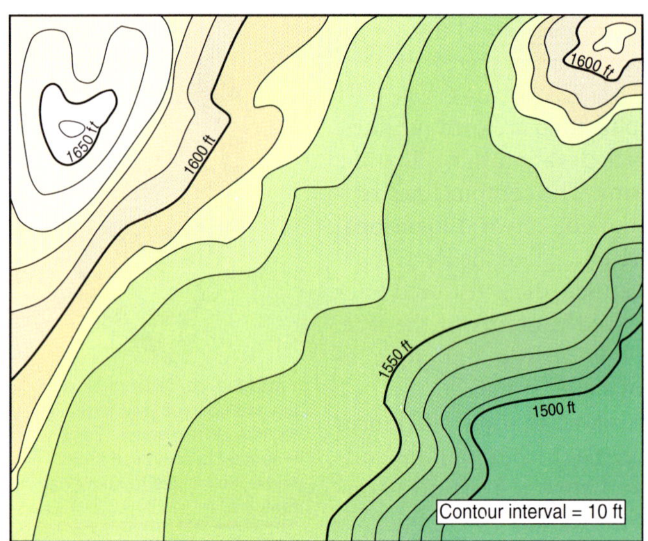

2m
2m
2m
2m
4m
2m
6m

PROGRAM RESOURCES

Teacher Classroom Resources
Study Guide, page 8
Take Home Activities, page 6, Making a Map L1
Critical Thinking/Problem Solving, page 9, A Change of Projection L2
Transparency Masters, page 5, and **Color Transparency,** number 1, Latitude/Longitude L1

INVESTIGATE!

1-1 USING CONTOUR LINES

You know that elevation can be shown by the contour lines on a topographic map. In the following activity, you will show the elevations of a landform by drawing contour lines on your own map.

PROBLEM

How can elevation of a landform be indicated on a map?

MATERIALS

metric ruler
transparency marker
clear plastic box and lid
transparency
tape
plastic model landform
beaker
water

PROCEDURE

1. Using the ruler and the transparency marker, **measure** and mark 2-cm lines up the side of the box.
2. Secure the transparency to the outside of the box lid with tape.
3. Place the plastic model in the box. The bottom of the box will be zero elevation.
4. Using the beaker, pour water into the box to a height of 2 cm. Place the lid on the box.
5. Looking down at the top of the box, use the transparency marker to trace the top of the water line on the transparency.
6. Using the scale 2 cm = 5 ft, mark the elevation on the line.
7. Remove the lid and add water to a height of 4 cm.
8. Trace and record this level on the transparency.
9. Repeat the process of adding water to the next 2-cm level and tracing until you have mapped the landform by means of contour lines.
10. Transfer the tracing of the contours of the landform onto paper.

ANALYZE

1. What is the contour interval of this contour map?
2. **Interpret** how the distance between contour lines on the map shows the steepness of the slope on the landform.
3. What can you **infer** about the total elevation of the landform?

CONCLUDE AND APPLY

4. How are elevations shown on topographic maps?
5. Explain whether all topographic maps must have a 0-ft elevation contour line.
6. **Going Further:** How would the contour interval of an area of steep mountains compare with the interval of an area of flat plains?

INVESTIGATE!

1-1 USING CONTOUR LINES

Time needed 30 minutes

Materials metric ruler, transparency marker, clear plastic box and lid, clear plastic, transparency, tape, plastic model landform, beaker, water

Thinking Processes
Observing and Inferring, Interpreting data

Purpose To learn how contour lines relate to height.

Teaching the Activity

Review the structure of a topographic map to be sure that all students see the relative steepness relationships shown by contour lines. Some students may need extra help. Have paper towels handy. A few drops of food coloring make it easier to see the water line on the model. Use the beakers to remove some of the water before moving the box when students finish.

Demonstration It may be a good idea to demonstrate the procedure to students. L1 LEP

Troubleshooting Circulate throughout the class to be sure that students are proceeding properly. Students should position themselves directly over the model while drawing the contour lines. Best results are obtained if students close one eye and look straight down. L1

Expected Outcomes

Students vill learn how height relates to contour lines on a topographic map. Students should be able to draw a simple topographic map.

Answers to Analyze/Conclude and Apply

1. 5 ft
2. The closer the contour lines, the steeper the slope. Increased distances between contour lines indicate relatively flat areas of the model.
3. Elevations will vary, but every 2 cm of the model are equal to 5 ft.
4. by contour lines
5. They do not, because all parts of the world aren't near sea level or 0 ft.
6. Maps with steep mountains will have a larger contour interval because the linear distance between contour lines is very small.

PROGRAM RESOURCES

Teacher Classroom Resources
Activity Masters, pages 5-6, Investigate 1-1

Concept Development

Theme Connection Maps are good examples of scale and structure. Students are introduced to scaled, map-sized versions of landforms. Students will learn to ascertain elevations by reading contour lines and locate reference points using a latitude and longitude grid. Both the scale and structure of land forms will be evident.

EXPLORE!

Can you describe the location of a dot on a ball?

Time needed 10 minutes

Materials ball, felt-tip marker

Thinking Processes
Observing and inferring

Purpose To show the usefulness of using longitude and latitude lines for locations on Earth

Preparation You might not want to use permanent markers on the ball. A small gummed dot is a possible alternative.

Teaching the Activity

Discussion Ask students to relate any methods they successfully used to describe the location of the dot. There will probably be none without the use of some reference point such as the seam on the ball, and even then, the location on the sphere will be unclear.

Troubleshooting Be sure that students do not show the ball to their partners.

Expected Outcomes

Students will understand how reference points are used to describe locations.

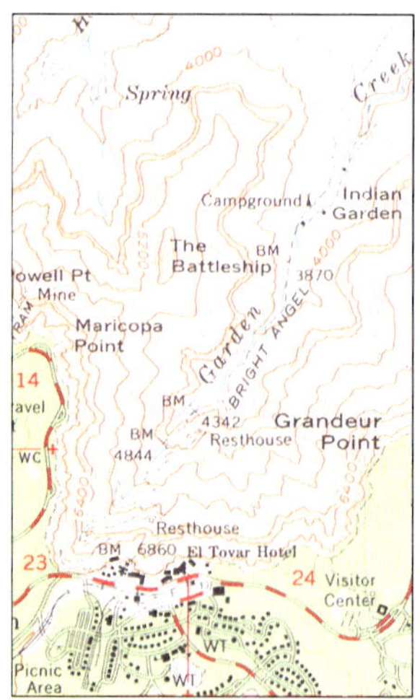

FIGURE 1-10. This section of a topographic map of the Grand Canyon in Arizona shows many closely spaced brown lines.

Look at the topographic map in Figure 1-10. Notice the different colors on the topographic map. Brown is usually used to indicate the contour lines. Green indicates vegetation, and all bodies of water are blue. Red usually indicates highways, and black is used to show all other structures made by people.

If you were visiting the Grand Canyon, a topographic map like the one in Figure 1-10 would come in handy. You could use it to plan a hike and identify features of the canyon.

As you can see, topographic maps can provide certain kinds of information. For example, you could find out how high the next stop on a hiking trail is. But the map wouldn't be useful for locating a specific place on Earth. For that purpose, other kinds of maps with different kinds of lines are made.

LATITUDE AND LONGITUDE

Recall how you reached your friend's school from the park. You used a city map. The city map gave you the reference points of streets and avenues to help you get to the school. But suppose you wanted to get from one place on Earth to another. What reference points would you use? Do the following activity to discover just how difficult it would be to describe a place without reference points.

EXPLORE!

Can you describe the location of a dot on a ball?

Work with a friend to do this activity. Obtain a ball that does not have any markings on it. Use a marker to place a black dot on the ball. Now, without showing the ball to your friend, try to describe the location of the dot. Can your friend tell you where the dot is located from your description?

PROGRAM RESOURCES

Teacher Classroom Resources

Concept Mapping, page 9, Maps L1

Multicultural Activities, page 6, The Incredible Shrinking Planet L1

Transparency Masters, page 7, and **Color Transparency,** number 2, U.S. Physiographic Regions L2

Laboratory Manual, pages 1-4, Determining Latitude L2; pages 5-6, Time Zones L2

OPTIONS

Enrichment

Activity Have students draw topographic maps that show these characteristics. It must show a hill or mountain with one steep side and one gentle slope. It must grade downward to a valley and back up to another mountain of any height. L3

As you have discovered, it is almost impossible to describe the location of a dot on a ball. Reference points are needed. Like the ball, Earth is a sphere. To provide reference points, mapmakers have given Earth a grid system that is something like the lines on graph paper.

Look at Figure 1-11. The North Pole is the northernmost point on Earth. The South Pole is the southernmost. The equator is an imaginary line that circles Earth exactly halfway between the North and South poles. It separates Earth into two equal halves called the Northern Hemisphere and the Southern Hemisphere.

The lines circling Earth parallel to the equator are lines of latitude. **Latitude** refers to distance in degrees either north or south of the equator. These degrees are not like the degrees of temperature. Instead, the degree value used for the latitude of a place is the measurement of the imaginary angle created by the equator, the center of Earth, and the location of that place.

Mapmakers decided to make the equator 0° latitude. They made each of the poles 90°. Therefore, latitude is measured from 0° at the equator to 90° at the poles. Locations north of the equator are referred to by degrees

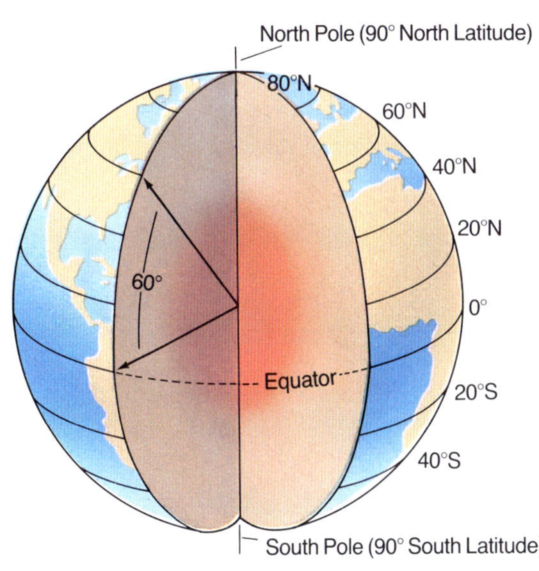

FIGURE 1-11. The reference points of latitude are used to locate places north and south of the equator.

Concept Development

Activity Tell students to think of a place in their city or town. The place must be specific, such as a particular restaurant, movie theater, shop, or the like. Have them write the name of the place on the slip of paper then fold it. Pair the students. One student has five minutes to try to explain the route to the chosen place to his or her partner without identifying the place. The student may not use any reference points, including outside appearances or street signs, to describe the route. The student must use only directions such as right, left 5 blocks or 3 miles. The partner must discover the name of the place from the directions. The first student should not tell if the answer is right or wrong at this point. The first student then gives directions using only reference points, such as, between the bakery and the video shop on Main Street. Have the student reveal the chosen place, then have students switch roles. Discuss with students the importance of reference points in getting from one place to another within their town. Introduce the concepts of latitude and longitude as reference points. COOP LEARN L2

Activity Students will need an $8\frac{1}{2}$" × 11" paper, a compass, a ruler marked in $\frac{1}{4}$" gradations, and scissors. Have students draw a bold horizontal line halfway down the paper. They should label the line *equator.* Next they should draw nine parallel lines above and below the equator line at intervals of $\frac{1}{4}$ inch. Ask students to count up one line from the equator and label it 10°N. Then have them count down one line from the equator and label it 10°S. Have them continue to do this until they have labeled all of the lines up to 90°N and down to 90°S. Have them put the point of the compass in the center of the equator line and open the compass so that the pencil end touches 90°N. Have them draw a circle and then cut it out. Which lines are shorter? *those near the North and South poles* Which is the longest line? *equator* L3

Enrichment

Research Have students interview a local geologist, hydrologist, city planner, or surveyor. Students should ask the person to bring topographic maps of the local area and explain how maps are made and what they show.

SKILLBUILDER

1. Moscow, Russia
2. Cape Town, South Africa
3. Havana, Cuba
4. Bangkok, Thailand
5. Lisbon, Portugal **L1**

Concept Development

Activity Have students draw a horizontal line across the center of a sheet of paper. This line represents the equator: Label this line *E.* Then have students draw a line that bisects the equator at a right angle. Have students sketch six longitude lines on either side of the line. The lines should run from pole to pole. The two outside lines should form a circle. Have students cut along those lines. Have them label the center line *Prime Meridian,* then continue numbering each line to the right in 15° increments to the edge. Have them repeat the procedure for the west longitudes. When they finish, they turn the model to the other side and draw a center line again. This time they label the center line 180°. Tell students to sketch the longitude lines this time—"W" longitudes go on the right side and "E" longitudes go on the left. Direct students to move outward from the center line and subtract 15° each time. Have them label the center line *International Date Line.* Then have them contrast the longitude lines on this model to the latitude lines of their earlier model. Lead students to see that longitude lines are not parallel, and that they intersect at the poles. **L2**

Content Background

Lines of latitude circle the earth and are parallel. Lines of longitude also circle Earth through the North Pole and the South Pole. To help students remember the difference between latitude and longitude, point out that longitude lines are *long.* The word *longitude* begins with *long.* Also point out that latitude lines are like steps in a ladder.

INTERPRETING SCIENTIFIC ILLUSTRATIONS
Use a world map that shows latitude and longitude to identify the cities that have the following coordinates:
1. 56° N; 38° E
2. 34° S; 18° E
3. 23° N; 82° W
4. 13° N; 101° E
5. 38° N; 9° W

Compare your answers with those of your classmates. If you need help, refer to the **Skill Handbook** on page 659.

north latitude. Locations south of the equator are referred to by degrees south latitude. For example, Minneapolis, Minnesota, is located at 43° north latitude.

Latitude lines are used for locations north and south of the equator, but what reference points do mapmakers use for directions east and west? Vertical lines called meridians indicate east and west directions.

Just as the equator is used as a reference point for north-south grid lines, there's also a reference point for east-west grid lines. This reference point is known as the prime meridian and is shown in Figure 1-12. In 1884, scientists agreed that the prime meridian should pass through the Greenwich (GREN itch) Observatory near London, England. This imaginary line represents 0° longitude.

Longitude refers to distance in degrees east or west of the prime meridian. The degree value used for the longitude of a place is the measurement of the imaginary angle created by the prime meridian, the center of Earth, and the location of that place. Locations west of the prime meridian have west longitude measured from 0° to 180°, while locations east of the prime meridian have east longitude measured from 0° to 180°. Often, meridians are called lines of longitude.

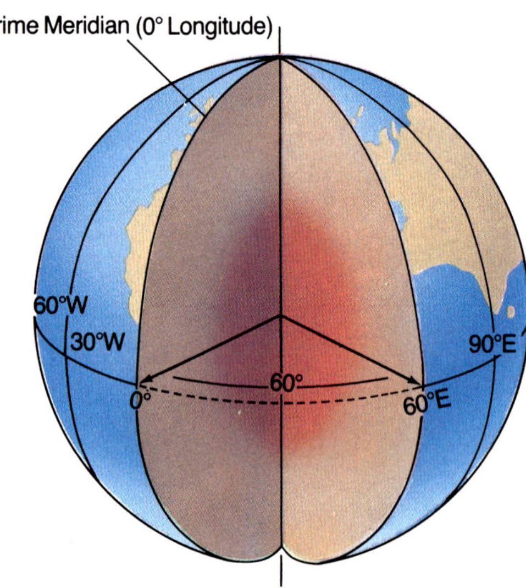

FIGURE 1-12. Meridians, also called lines of longitude, help locate places east and west of the prime meridian.

Look at Figure 1-12 again. Notice that the prime meridian does not circle Earth like the equator does. It runs from the North Pole through Greenwich, England, to the South Pole. The line of longitude on the opposite side of Earth from the prime meridian—where east lines of longitude meet west lines of longitude—is the 180° meridian.

Think about locating a spot on a ball again. Using the lines of latitude and longitude, you could locate that spot easily. Imagine that Hawaii is that spot to locate on Earth. Hawaii, shown in Figure 1-13, is located at 20° north latitude and about 155° west longitude.

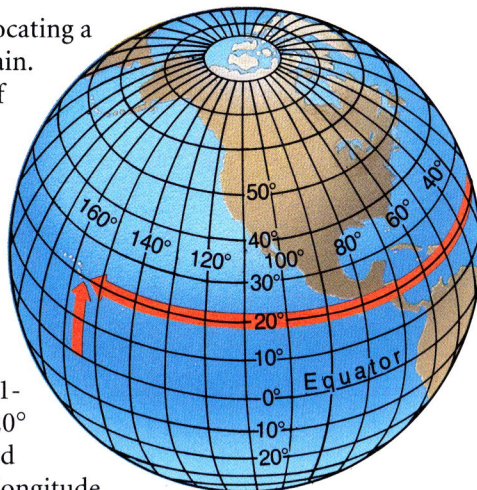

FIGURE 1-13. Hawaii, the fiftieth state, is located far out in the Pacific Ocean. How could you describe its location *without* lines of latitude and longitude?

As you found out, maps can be informative and helpful if you know how to use them. Maps are tools for observing the world at a distance. They are particularly helpful when you cannot visit or observe the locations directly. In this section, you have learned about city maps, topographic maps, and world maps with latitude and longitude. How do you think this information can be useful to you in the future?

Check Your Understanding

1. Suppose you are looking for an easy hiking route through a particular area. As you look at a topographic map, you notice the area has many closely spaced brown lines. How would you describe the area? Would it be a good place for an easy hike?
2. How would a plateau be represented on a topographic map?
3. Which lines are parallel to the equator?
4. **APPLY:** How can the approximate elevation of a place be obtained by looking at the contour lines on a topographic map?

Concept Development

Student Text Question (Figure 1-13) How could you describe its location *without* lines of latitude and longitude? *Possible answer: By indicating how far and in what direction Hawaii is from some point of reference.*

3 Assess

Check for Understanding

To help students answer the Apply question, have them draw a topographic map that shows a hill 900 m high and use a contour interval of 100 m. Make sure students add a sea level contour line.

Reteach

It may help students who do not understand latitude and longitude to try to locate points on a graph. Prepare a graph with a fake continent on it. Use letters to label the *x*-axis and numbers to label the *y*-axis. Label points on the graph with symbols and have students give the locations of the symbols. L1

Extension

Direct students to look on a world map and write the latitude and longitude of 10 to 15 capitals. Have them find the latitude and longitude of the city in which they live. L3

4 Close

Discussion

Discuss with students how flight and navigation of boats and planes would be different if there were no longitude and latitude grid system. What might people use instead? *stars, landmarks* L1

Answers to Check Your Understanding

1. The area is steep and not suitable for easy hiking.
2. A plateau would have very few contour lines crossing it because it is relatively flat. However, near the edge of the plateau, the lines would become close.
3. lines of latitude
4. by estimating the elevation in between the labeled contour lines

Section 1-3

PREPARATION

Concepts Developed

Students will learn about the relative positions of sun, moon, and Earth in space and discover the use of star maps. This section relates to Chapter 20, Earth-Moon System.

Planning the Lesson

In planning your lesson on the sky, refer to the Chapter Organizer on pages 2A-B for timing suggestions, resources, and additional materials that will help you in your presentation of the lesson concepts.

For adequate development of the concepts presented in this section, we recommend that students perform the Explore activity on page 18 and the Investigate activity on page 20.

1 MOTIVATE

Activity Tell students that the moon is an average distance of 386,000 km from Earth. To put this in perspective, have them figure out the time it would take to drive there at 88 km/h. *182 d, 18 h, 21 min, 49 sec* L1

1-3 Viewing the Sky

OBJECTIVES

In this section, you will

- describe the position and appearance of the sun and the moon as viewed from Earth;
- explain the use of a star map in locating stars in the sky.

KEY SCIENCE TERMS

phase
constellations

THE MOON

On your cross-country plane trip, you would probably notice the sky as well as the landforms below. What things in the sky do you notice? Perhaps you see white clouds or the bright sun. At nighttime, you might observe the stars twinkling in the sky. You might notice the position and shape of Earth's moon, too.

You've probably observed these objects in the sky before, but you may not have taken the time to notice how they change. Do the following activity to observe the changes in the moon.

EXPLORE!

What can you find out by observing the moon?

Observe the moon at the same time every night for a week. Record as many observations as you can about the moon. Here are some questions you should try to answer: What does the moon look like? Describe it in detail. In what general direction do you see the moon? How does the moon's position change? Does the shape of the moon appear to change? Describe this change.

Because the moon is easy to see, it has been observed by people for a very long time. These observations have led to many strange stories and superstitions about the moon. In past times, some people even thought that looking at the moon would cause insanity!

EXPLORE!

What can you find out by observing the moon?

Time needed 1 week

Thinking Processes
Observing and inferring

Purpose To watch and describe moon changes for a week

Preparation Have students prepare a data sheet. Tell them to write each question and leave eight spaces between questions.

Teaching the Activity

Students will need clear weather to view the moon.

Troubleshooting Students may wish to know why they can sometimes see the moon during the day. At certain distances and angles from Earth, the moon is sufficiently bright to be seen when the sun is up.

Expected Outcomes

Students will learn that the moon appears to change shape, rises at different times, and has light and dark areas.

Student Journal Have students record their observations in their journals.

What do you see when you look at the moon? Do you see a "man in the moon", as some people do? Look at the picture of the moon in Figure 1-14. You can see dark areas, which may sometimes create a pattern that looks like a face—the "man in the moon" that some people see. What are these dark spots, and what are some of the other features that people have discovered on the moon?

FIGURE 1-14. The "man in the moon" that people see is created by the presence of dark areas on the moon's surface.

Moon Features

The large dark areas on the moon, called maria (MAR ee uh), are very flat, low-lying areas. Such areas on Earth are covered by water. On the moon, however, the maria are basins that have been filled with lava. If water existed in great amounts on the moon, as it does on Earth, the maria would be covered by water.

If you could look through a telescope at the moon, you would also observe smaller depressions called craters. In fact, there are so many craters that some of them overlap. Figure 1-15 shows what these craters look like. How is a crater formed? Do the next activity to find out.

FIGURE 1-15. The moon's surface is marked by maria and by craters.

How do we know?

Lunar lava rocks

Earth astronauts began visiting the moon in 1969. They brought back rocks from the maria. These rocks have been analyzed and found to be similar to the lava rocks on Earth.

2 Teach

Tying to Previous Knowledge

Many students have already observed the moon. They may be familiar with the notion that the moon looks as if it has a face on it. Young children see various pictures of "the man in the moon." Have students describe the different shapes of the moon. Listen for terms like *crescent, full moon, half moon,* or *new moon.*

Concept Development

Using the Photo Have students look at Figure 1-14. Ask students what they think the dark spots on the moon are.

How do we know?

The moon is made of the same rock and mineral material as Earth. A relatively recent hypothesis about the formation of the moon states that the moon was part of Earth at one time. When Earth was still molten it collided with an asteroid. The collision blew material from the asteroid and Earth into space. The material began to orbit Earth.

Teacher F.Y.I.

Roman mythology tells of Luna, the goddess of the moon. A superstition held that people who went insane did so from staring at the moon. These people were called lunatics.

PROGRAM RESOURCES

Teacher Classroom Resources

Study Guide, page 9

Making Connections: Integrating Sciences, page 5, Looking to the Sky L2

Other Resources

How We Know the Earth Moves, film, BFA.

The Earth and Moon Simulator, software, Focus.

INVESTIGATE!

1-2 MAKING AND DATING MOON CRATERS

Time needed 30 minutes

Materials (per group) pan 10 in. × 12 in., marbles of different sizes, metric ruler, flour, salt

Thinking Processes Making models, Separating and controlling variables, Forming a hypothesis, Recognizing cause and effect, Observing and inferring

Purpose To create artificial moon craters.

Preparation Have students bring in old newspaper to cover the work areas.

Teaching the Activity

Discussion Tell students that the craters on the moon came from impacts with space debris like meteorites, comets, and asteroids.

Demonstration Demonstrate the procedure. Be sure to drop the marbles straight down. L1 LEP

Troubleshooting Be sure students are following the procedure step by step. Students must not overlap the craters until step 5.

Expected Outcomes

Students will learn how impact craters can be formed by collisions between space bodies.

Teacher F.Y.I.

The extinction of the dinosaurs may have been due to a large meteorite hitting Earth. The dust and vapor from the meteorite strike could have blanketed Earth, causing sunlight to be blocked out for years. As plants died, so did the plant-eating dinosaurs.

Answers to Analyze/Conclude and Apply

1. straight-sided craters
2. Answers will be different according to the actual sizes of the marbles. The larger marble will make a larger hole.
3. The higher the marble was dropped from, the deeper and larger its crater.
4. Overlapped craters will have material from one piled into the other.
5. The larger the marble, the larger the crater.
6. The higher the drop, the larger the crater.
7. Yes; the last crater made overlaps the first crater made.

I N V E S T I G A T E !

1-2 MAKING AND DATING MOON CRATERS

Craters are a common moon feature. In this activity, you will **observe** how craters form. You will also find out how you can tell which crater of two overlapping craters is the older and which is the younger.

PROBLEM

How do craters form?

MATERIALS

flour
salt
pan (about 10 x 12 inches)
marbles of different sizes
metric ruler

PROCEDURE

1. Mix the flour and salt together and fill the pan to a depth of about 3 cm.
2. Make some craters with the different sizes of marbles by just pushing them into the mixture.
3. Choose two marbles of different sizes and drop them from the same height. Be careful not to have the craters overlap. Use a ruler to **measure** the diameter of each crater.
4. Choose two marbles of the same size and drop them from different heights. Be careful not to have the craters overlap. **Measure** the diameters as before.
5. Choose two marbles of the same size. Drop them from the same height, but not at the same time. Also, drop them so that the craters will overlap. Sketch a drawing of the results.

ANALYZE

1. What kinds of craters are made by pushing marbles into the mixture?
2. What are the diameters of the two craters that were formed by dropping two marbles of different sizes from the same height?
3. What are the diameters of the two craters that were formed by dropping two marbles of the same size from different heights?
4. **Compare and contrast** the overlapping craters with the others you created. How can overlapping craters be distinguished from craters that do not overlap?

CONCLUDE AND APPLY

5. How does the size of a striking object affect the size of the crater it creates?
6. **Determine the effect** that the height from which the object falls has on the size of the crater that is formed.
7. **Going Further:** If you had not witnessed the marble dropping, could you **infer** which crater was formed first by looking at the resulting overlapping craters? Explain.

PROGRAM RESOURCES

Teacher Classroom Resources
Activity Masters, pages 7-8, Investigate 1-2

As you might guess, the craters on the moon were formed in much the same way as you formed craters in the Investigate activity. The craters were formed by large objects striking the surface of the moon. In space, rock fragments called meteorites sometimes hit other objects, such as the moon. Meteorites have even struck Earth.

Few craters remain visible on Earth because they are worn away by wind, rain, and water. Because these forces do not exist on the moon, craters remain for very long periods of time. Some of the moon's craters are also very large—one moon crater has a diameter of 226 kilometers.

Craters and maria are prominent features of the moon. Next, you'll read about one of the more interesting aspects of the moon—its phases.

DID YOU KNOW?

In the United States, the best-preserved meteor crater is found in Arizona. It is simply called Meteor Crater and is 174 meters deep and 1250 meters wide.

Moon Phases

Sometimes the moon looks like a thin wedge of melon. At other times it looks like a silver disc. If you have observed the moon over a period of time, you have noticed such changes in its shape. Why does the moon's shape change?

The moon does not really change its shape. Instead, we on Earth see the lighted side of the moon from different angles. Look at Figure 1-16. One half of the moon is illuminated by the sun at all times. The moon simply reflects the light that

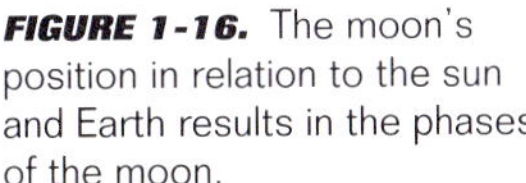

FIGURE 1-16. The moon's position in relation to the sun and Earth results in the phases of the moon.

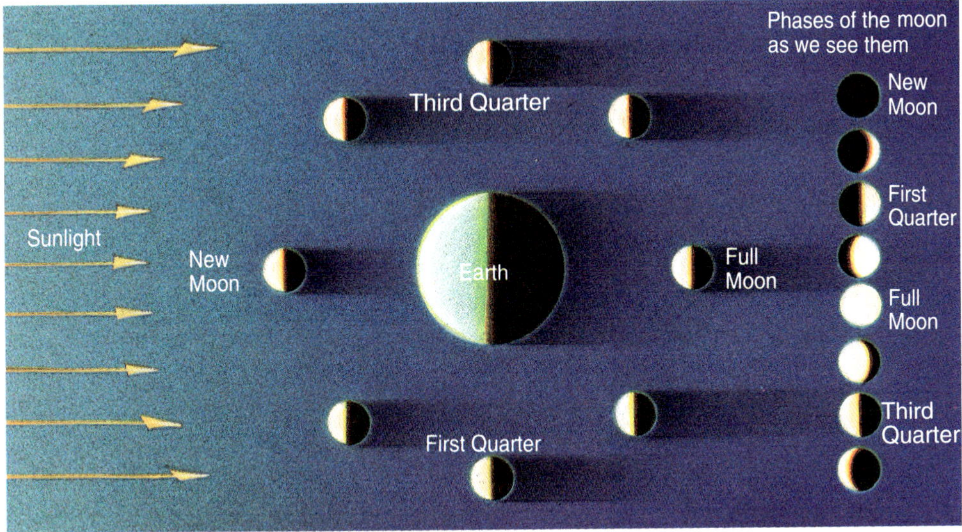

Concept Development

Using the Photo Have students observe the phase of the moon that evening. The next day have a volunteer hold up the textbook showing Figure 1-16. Have another student point to the phase in the photo that matches the previous night's phase of the moon.

Demonstration To show how the moon's position in relation to the sun determines its phases you will need a large Styrofoam ball or all-purpose ball, a flashlight, and aluminum foil.

Cover the ball with foil. Turn on the flashlight. Have a student hold the ball overhead. Turn off the lights and let students get accustomed to the darkness. Sit on a stool between the student and the class. Shine the flashlight directly on the ball. **What does the flashlight represent?** (*sun*) Adjust the distance so that the beam spot of the light and the circumference of the ball are the same. Ask students which phase of the moon this represents. (*full*) Have the student with the ball move around the "sun" while keeping the flashlight beam directly on the ball. Ask students to identify the phases they are seeing.

MAKING CONNECTIONS

History

In ancient times, people used the moon to mark the beginnings and ends of months. A calendar of months based on the moon's phases is called a lunar calendar. Native Americans even described the passage of time as "moons." Ask students what amount of time one moon would be. *about 1 month; 29 days, 12 h, 44.05 min*

OPTIONS

Multicultural Perspective

Some Middle Eastern and Far Eastern cultures use the lunar calendar. Obtain a calendar from one such culture and show it to students. Using the calendar, correlate the beginnings of the months to the new moon. Students will find that the beginnings of the lunar months coincide within two or three days of the new moon. They do not necessarily coincide with the months used in the United States. The students will also find that each month contains either 29 or 30 days and that there are 13 months.

Teacher F.Y.I.

In 1966, the Soviet *Luna 9* probe became the first spacecraft to land on the moon. Four months later, the American *Surveyor 1* spacecraft landed there.

Concept Development

Uncovering Preconceptions Some students may think that the far side of the moon is not seen because it is dark. Explain that the side of the moon facing away from Earth receives as much light as the side that faces Earth.

Inquiry Questions Is the far side of the moon ever completely lit? (*yes, during the new moon phase*) What causes moon phases? (*As the moon revolves around Earth, the relative positions of Earth, the moon, and the sun change. This causes the side of the moon visible from Earth to receive different amounts of solar radiation, changing the moon's appearance.*)

SKILLBUILDER

Lighted side not visible, small sliver visible, half the lighted side visible, almost all the lighted side visible, entire lighted side visible, almost all the lighted side visible, half the lighted side visible, small sliver visible. L1

MAKING CONNECTIONS

Literature

Constellations were named after mythological Greek or Roman gods. Have students name as many of the constellations as they can. Write the names of mythical characters or constellations on the chalkboard. Ask students to choose one character that became a constellation and research it. Have them present oral reports on their choices.

Concept Development

Inquiry Question What reference points could you use to navigate through space? *stars*

Uncovering Preconceptions Many people think that the stars "disappear" during the daytime. But they do not actually disappear, we just cannot see them. Radio telescopes are used even during the day to study stars.

DID YOU KNOW?

Has anyone ever said to you, "That happens only once in a blue moon"? Because there are a little more than four weeks in a month, once in a while there will be two full moons during a month. The second full moon is called a blue moon.

comes from the sun. The side of the moon that we see from Earth is not always completely or even partly lighted by the sun.

When we see the entire lighted side, we say we see a full moon. When no part of the moon that faces Earth is lighted by the sun, we call it a new moon. Between full moon and new moon, only part of the moon's lighted side is seen. Less and less of the lighted side is seen until there is a new moon. Then more and more of the lighted side is seen until there is a full moon again. Each stage in the cycle is known as a **phase.** Each cycle from full moon to new moon and back to full moon again takes a little over four weeks, or about a month.

CONSTELLATIONS

During your night observations of the moon, you probably noticed the stars, too. In ancient times, people looked into the sky and connected the stars with imaginary lines to create patterns. The patterns formed by groups of stars are called **constellations.** Many constellations were named for people or animals from Greek or Roman mythology. Other constellations were named for common objects that people used in their lives. The Big Dipper is a well-known grouping of stars that is actually a part of another constellation.

Constellations are used to organize the stars as reference points in the sky. Sailors even use the constellations for navigation. They relate the changing positions of their ship to the position of certain constellations.

To learn what some of the constellations are, you need a star map. Just as maps of Earth can be used to locate places on Earth, star maps can be used to locate stars in the sky. Star maps show the location of stars, constellations, and planets. For example, Figure 1-17 shows some of the constellations that you can see in July in the Northern Hemisphere. Suppose you are looking for a certain star and you know what constellation it is in. If you look at the star map, you can easily find the constellation. Since the stars are noted, you should then be able to find the star.

SKILLBUILDER

SEQUENCING

Arrange the following events in order. Use the last three phases twice.

lighted side not visible
entire lighted side visible
small sliver visible
half the lighted side visible
almost all the lighted side visible

If you need help, refer to the ***Skill Handbook*** on page 648.

OPTIONS

Enrichment

Research Have students explore the development of the U.S. space program. Direct them to write reports on a person or group who made special contributions to rocketry, satellites, space travel, or any aspect of the space program.

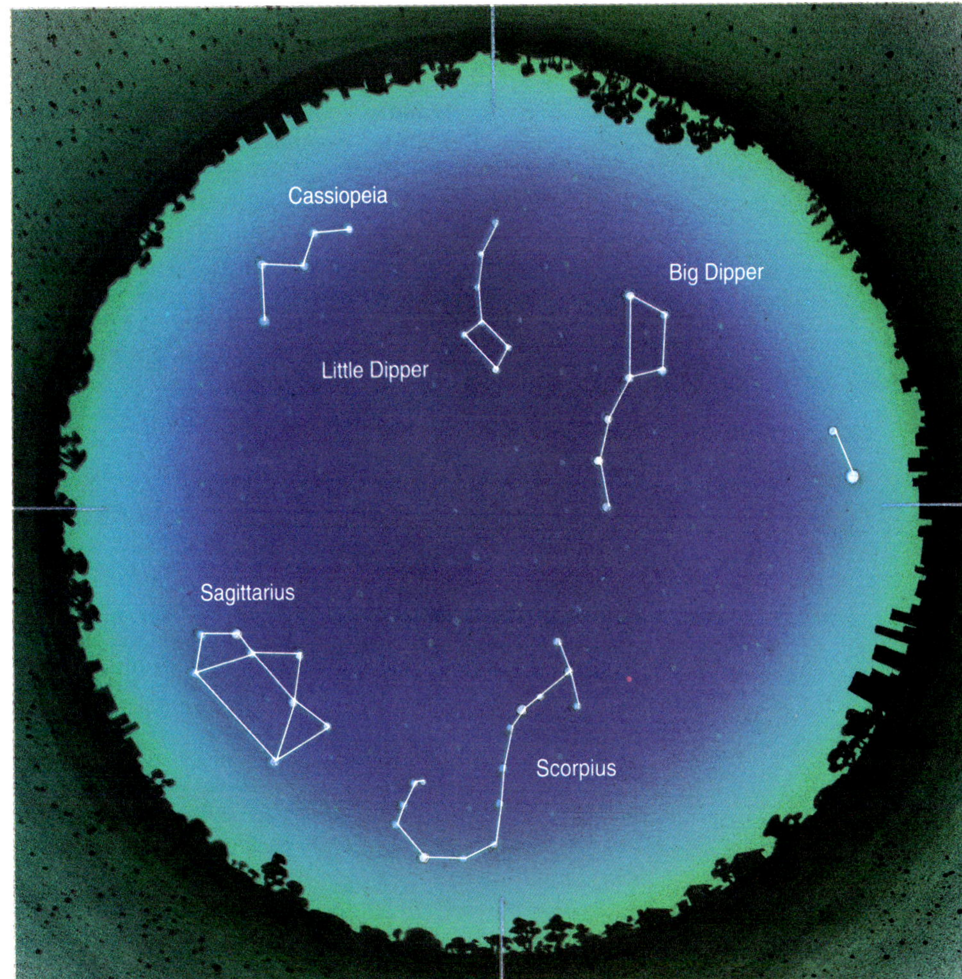

FIGURE 1-17. The star map shows the positions of some of the constellations in the sky during July in the Northern Hemisphere.

THE SUN'S APPARENT MOVEMENT

The stars and moon are visible in the night sky. What do you see in the daytime sky? You see the sun, of course. How does the sun move during the day? Do the following activity to find out.

DID YOU KNOW?

On a clear, dark night, you can see about 2000 stars. If you use binoculars, you can see about 50,000 stars.

Concept Development

Theme Connection Students move from identifiable Earth-sized objects such as landforms to the larger scale of bodies in the solar system and universe. Students will discover objects and star patterns in the sky using a star map and begin to recognize basic structures in the solar system and universe.

Activity Have students draw diagrams showing the phases of the moon. Have them make up, draw, and name a constellation. Then ask them to draw an actual constellation, either their zodiac sign or another that they may know. L1 LEP

3 Assess

Check for Understanding

Assign Check Your Understanding questions 1 to 4 to groups of students. Be sure students understand that from new moon to new moon is about 1 month and that from new moon to full moon is about half that time.

Reteach

The mechanics of the moon's phases may be difficult for some students. Direct students to perform the ball and flashlight demonstration. Work with them to increase their understanding. L1

Extension

Have students look at the moon with binoculars and describe the moon's surface. Tell them to sketch a crater or two and compare it to the craters they made in Investigate 1-2. L3

Student Journal Have students record their observations of the sun from the explore activity on page 24 in their journals. They may need to refer to these observations later in this course.

PROGRAM RESOURCES

Other Resources

The Earth in Motion, film, EBEC.
Moon Rise/Moonset, software, MicroLearningware.
Moonwalk, video, LCA.
Sneider, Cary I. *Earth, Moon and Stars*. Berkeley, CA: Laurence Hall of Science, 1986.

EXPLORE!

What can you learn observing the sun?

Time needed Little or no class time

Thinking Processes Observing and inferring

Purpose To make observations of the motions of the sun.

Preparation Tell students to heed the warning in the text—they must not look directly at the sun or even its reflection from a shiny surface.

Teaching the Activity

Discussion Ask students to describe the motion of the sun. Ask them if the sun really moves through the sky. Reinforce the fact that the sun does not move around Earth. L2 LCP

Demonstration Have a student sit on a revolving stool. Tell the student to hold a thumb up at arms length and look straight over the thumb. Tell the student to hold onto the stool with the other hand. Hold the student by the shoulders and slowly rotate him or her. Ask the student if the room looks as if it is moving. *it should*

Expected Outcomes

Students will be able to describe the apparent motion of the sun.

Answers to Questions

1. Shadows are larger in morning and afternoon, small around noon.
2. rising in the East in the morning and setting in the West in the evening
3. It seems to travel in a semicircle through the sky.

4 Close

Have students draw their zodiac constellation and connect the stars to form a "shape." Ask them to state whether they can see the shape described by ancient people. Plan a trip to a planetarium.

EXPLORE!

What can you learn observing the sun?

Observe the sun every hour or so from sunrise to sunset. **CAUTION:** *Do not look directly at the sun. You will damage your eyes if you do because the sun is too bright.* Make general observations of the sun based on shadows or reflections. Record as many observations as you can about the sun. Here are some questions you should try to answer. What are the shadows like at various times during the day? In what general direction do you see the sun? How does the sun's position change?

The sun appears to rise in the east and set in the west. It appears to move through the sky because Earth is spinning. The actual location of the sunset changes over time. As the seasons change in the Northern Hemisphere from summer, to autumn, and into winter, the sun appears to set farther south. Also, the sun doesn't get as high in the winter sky as it does in the summer, and the length of time that the sun is visible is shorter in the winter.

Viewing the sky, you now know that the moon is observed in different shapes called phases. You also know that the stars are found in patterns called constellations. You know, too, that the sun appears to move from east to west. These observations are just the beginning of your study of the world around you. In the next chapter, you will find out about the light from the sun—which helps you make your observations.

Check Your Understanding

1. Why does the moon appear to change its shape?
2. How is a star map useful in determining the location of a star?
3. What is the difference in the position of the sun in the sky between winter and summer?
4. **APPLY:** You've just received a telescope and you want to view the full moon to see as many maria and craters as possible. Tonight there will be a new moon. About how long will you have to wait to observe the full moon with your telescope?

Answers to Check Your Understanding

1. The moon's shape appears to change because we see different portions of its lighted side.
2. Constellations are shown on a star map. If you can find the constellation that includes or is near the star, you can find the star.
3. In winter, the sun is lower in the sky than in summer.
4. Since the time from new moon to new moon is about $29\frac{1}{2}$ days, the time from new moon to full moon is about 14 or 15 days.

EXPANDING YOUR VIEW

CONTENTS

A CLOSER LOOK

IRRIGATION ON THE GREAT PLAINS

Take a close look at the United States map in Appendix G. You can see that the great plains states—North Dakota, South Dakota, Nebraska, Kansas, Oklahoma, and Texas—are not near any obvious water sources. These states have hot dry summers, cold windy winters, arid conditions, and serious erosion problems. Yet most of the wheat used to make bread for Americans and much of the rest of the world is produced here in the "Bread Basket" of the world.

How does it happen? From the time agriculture began to be practiced in this region, there was also large-scale irrigation. Water was brought to the land from underground wells by different methods.

Early methods of irrigation involved pumping water up from a well and allowing it to flow along the crop rows. Later, pipes with adjustable water outlets along their lengths regulated the flow. Then aluminum pipes with sprinkler nozzles were used, but each method took a great deal of labor.

In 1949, the center-pivot irrigation system was patented. In this system, water is pumped into a vertical pipe, or tower, from a well in the center of a field. A horizontal pipe on a wheel is connected to the tower. The pipe pivots around the tower, or center pivot, carrying water that it sprays on the crops from holes along its length. The pipe is held about eight feet above the ground so that it will clear the tops of the rows of corn.

Center-pivot irrigation pumps allowed some Nebraska farmers to produce four times the amount of crops they could produce before this method was discovered.

WHAT DO YOU THINK?

If irrigation methods as efficient as the center-pivot system cannot be found, where can huge quantities of wheat and corn be grown? If you were a Nebraska farmer, how would you feel about having to control the amount of water used to raise your crops?

Going Further Have students imagine that they own a farm situated on a large plain. There is a large river within 40 kilometers of the region. The weather has been dry for several years, and crop production has fallen off drastically over an entire 6,400-square-kilometer region of 20 large farms. Divide the class into groups of four or five. Have them devise a plan to build irrigation systems with minimal damage to the environment. Have the groups present their plans to the class and have the class vote on the two best plans. Discuss the environmental implications of the two plans. COOP LEARN

Using Expanding Your View

Assign one or more of these excursions to expand students' understanding of features of Earth and the sky and how they apply to other sciences and other subjects. You may assign these as individual or small group activities.

A CLOSER LOOK

Purpose A Closer Look describes the type of irrigation system responsible for boosting grain production on the Great Plains, one of the landforms described in Section 1-1.

Content Background One of the best examples of the positive effects of irrigation can be found in Israel, where once-desert land has been converted to crop-bearing land.

Irrigation projects in the southwest United States and other areas of the world have resulted in salinization of the soil. Salinization occurs when irrigation water containing dissolved salts saturates the soil and then evaporates, leaving behind the salts. The effect is a buildup of salts, which impairs the growth of plants.

Debate When large amounts of water are diverted for irrigation purposes, the ecosystems of the areas from where this water is diverted are also affected. Conduct a debate in which one side represents Nebraska farmers and the other side environmentalists to address the issue raised in the What Do You Think activity.

Answers to

WHAT DO YOU THINK?

1. Large quantities of wheat and corn need large, moist areas on which to grow. Choices may be coastal plains, land around streams, river valleys, and deltas.
2. Answers will vary, from those who do not like the idea of limited control of "their" farm to those who view this as an issue of limited supply and voluntary self-control.

EXPANDING YOUR VIEW

LIFE SCIENCE CONNECTION

Purpose Section 1-1 describes the different landforms that occur throughout the United States. The Life Science Connection attributes the variety of crops grown in this country to its variety of landforms.

Content Background In a country as large as the United States, with its geographic and climatic diversity, it is easy to see why many different types of crops can be grown. Such an abundance of crops ultimately leads to overproduction and surpluses that can be sold to other countries or stored.

Developing nations are not as fortunate. American scientists have been crossbreeding plants for years in an effort to fight world hunger. Some plants have been developed to grow in areas where they are needed most. For example, in 1967, high-yield dwarf varieties of rice and wheat were introduced in Mexico, India, and other developing nations. Because of their shorter growing season, if they had enough water, they could be grown and harvested two or more times in a year. More plant nutrients also went into the growth of the grain than into the growth of leaves and stalks. Within ten years, however, nature had its way, and crop yields began to decrease due to floods, droughts, and the need for expensive fertilizers. When the plants became diseased, they had to be replaced with the old indigenous plant varieties. The crossbreeding research, though, continues in an effort to keep one step ahead of nature.

Teaching Strategies Have students decide which crops are essential for human needs. Write a list on the chalkboard of the crops they choose, the region of the U.S. where the crops are grown, and reasons the crops were chosen. From the list, have students rank the crops in order of most to least important for human needs.

LIFE SCIENCE CONNECTION

JUST THE RIGHT CONDITIONS

If you flew around the borders of our country, you would see many distinctly different farms growing a variety of crops in each area.

For instance, passing over North Carolina, you would notice a lot of tobacco farms. Farther up the coast, in New Jersey, farmers are growing vegetables such as tomatoes and green beans. Crossing the northern parts of the states, you see apple orchards on the interior plains around the Great Lakes, wheat on the Great Plains, potatoes in Idaho, and more (and different kinds of) apples in Washington State. In California, citrus fruit trees—grapefruit, oranges, lemons, and limes—would be

plentiful, while in Arizona and Texas, there would be cotton farms.

Why is there such diversity over the continental United States? Why are many crops grown in one place but not another? Crops need a growing season, a time free from frost. It takes a certain amount of time for an apple, an orange, or a cotton plant to grow. If the weather does not act as expected, something will probably happen to the crops. If it is too hot or too cold for too long, or if there is not enough rain or too much rain, crops will die.

Soil and land formation are as important as climate in growing crops. Mountains are rocky and steep, with a thin layer of soil. They are not good for growing food or grazing cattle. Desert plains or plateaus have little vegetation because of little rain, but they can often produce crops if water is provided through irrigation.

YOU TRY IT!

Choose a plant or crop and find out about its ideal growing conditions. For instance, corn needs a lot of water, tomatoes need sun, some vegetables need an acid soil, some grow in the shade. Would you start your farm in central Arizona, which has desert conditions, or in northern Ohio, bordering the Great Lakes? Back up your choice with details about the plants and the conditions in the area you choose.

Answers to YOU TRY IT

Students should choose appropriate soil, water, and sun conditions for plants of their choice. Be sure they consider possibilities such as irrigation in making their choices.

Going Further Direct students to work in pairs. Assign three to four neighboring states to each pair. Have students research the different agricultural resources for their states, including the production tonnage for each state. Make a master table for all states, listing the states on one axis and crops on the other. Have each pair enter the crop yield(s) for their states. Have students identify the states that are primarily producers and the states that are primarily consumers.

SCIENCE AND SOCIETY

WHAT TO DO WITH ALL THAT GARBAGE?

Until the mid-1960s, most communities disposed of waste in the town dump—an open, smelly place. The sanitary landfill has taken the place of the town dump. It's more than just a fancy new name for a familiar place. A sanitary landfill can cover acres of land. It changes the contours of the area it occupies and the land surrounding it. Engineering principles and construction techniques are used to confine wastes to the smallest possible space.

Pictured above are garbage barges waiting to be unloaded at the Fresh Kills Landfill in New York. The photo below shows only a small area of Fresh Kills. Wastes are covered daily with a layer of soil. For years, sanitary landfill was seen as a major advance.

Today we question whether landfills are safe. Although buried under layers of soil, garbage is far from harmless. Toxic chemicals and other hazardous wastes seep into the soil, eventually reaching underground water supplies. This is such a serious problem in much of the country that many states have ordered landfills closed. Many people do not want sanitary landfill sites in their communities. Therefore, it is more and more difficult to find space for new landfills.

Another problem is the production of hazardous gas. As garbage decomposes, gas by-products are released. As the oxygen in garbage is used up, these gases change in composition. Sometimes within six months to three years after garbage reaches the landfill site, the gas will be 50 to 70 percent methane and 30 to 50 percent carbon dioxide.

EXPANDING YOUR VIEW

SCIENCE AND SOCIETY

Purpose As an extension of the study of land contours in Section 1-2, this Science and Society excursion discusses sanitary landfills, an environmental problem that changes the contour of the land it occupies.

Content Background Students will probably not be familiar with open dumps that were common years ago. These dumps were infested with rats and insects, along with bad odors. Periodically, they would catch fire, some smoldering for months. Such fires caused air pollution containing hazardous fumes. Localities across the country wrestled with the problem of what to do with their solid waste.

Going Further Have students work in small groups to make a list of items they personally discard as garbage. Have them expand their lists to include items that are regularly disposed of as garbage by other members of their household, by stores, and by restaurants. Then hold a class discussion of the types of items that appear most often on the lists. Most will probably be packaging materials. Have students suggest alternative methods of garbage disposal for these items, which would not harm the environment.

COOP LEARN

Content Background Although it did solve some of the problems created by open dumps, landfill dumps may have been a shortsighted cure for solving solid-waste problems. Unfortunately, new environmental problems caused by sanitary landfills are just surfacing. Some materials in landfills may never completely decompose. Intact phone books and disposable diapers from twenty years ago can be dug up at some landfills. Hazardous materials leach into the soil below some landfills and permeate the groundwater.

Many municipalities are beginning to recycle materials like paper, plastics, metals, yard waste, and glass, cutting down on the volume of garbage dumped into landfills and preserving natural resources.

Teaching Strategies Try the mini-landfill activity with a variety of soil types ranging from acidic to alkaline and have students compare the relative decay rates. You may also have some students double, triple, or quadruple the suggested "decay" time to provide other comparisons. Have students keep careful daily observations of their mini-landfills. Be sure they are gathering information such as the required temperature and, in addition, appearance, odor, and volume decreases. Provide students with plastic gloves when they disassemble their mini-landfills.

Answers to

YOU TRY IT

The decomposition in the bottle stored in the warmer area will be greater.

Explosions and fires near landfill sites were often attributed to other causes. In the mid-1960s, the danger of sanitary landfill-generated gas was recognized. Highly combustible methane gas can move several hundred feet through soil and emerge above ground or in houses where a single spark may ignite it. To prevent this from happening, landfills can be lined with materials such as wet clay that methane can't get through. The gas can then be vented harmlessly through a pipe. In the 1970s, it became technically and economically possible to pipe methane out of landfills on a large scale. Once a garbage site has reached the stage where it is producing methane, it will go on doing so for years—even hundreds of years—depending upon such factors as the makeup of the refuse and its moisture content.

Some gas and oil companies have built gas plants on top of landfills. Raw gas, withdrawn from the landfill by a complex system of deep wells, is first sent to a purification plant. In one California plant, the purified gas, which like natural gas is 99 percent methane, provides enough fuel to meet the energy needs of 3500 homes.

YOU TRY IT!

To find out how long it takes various materials to decompose in a landfill, try this: Cut off the top of a 2-liter plastic soft drink bottle. Add soil to the halfway mark. Place various items (yard waste, plastic, food scraps, metal, foam cup, paper), one at a time, in the bottle after tracing their outlines on graph paper. Cover with soil. Add water to moisten the soil, place a thermometer in the bottle, and seal the bottle with plastic wrap and a rubber band. Store the bottle in a warm place. Repeat the procedure with a second bottle, but store it in a cold place.

Record the temperatures every day. After two weeks, remove all the items and trace their outlines next to the ones you made when you put them in the "landfill." Analyze the contents and see which items decomposed the most. Compare the results found in both bottles.

TECHNOLOGY CONNECTION

FRANKLIN RAMON CHANG-DIAZ

Franklin Chang-Diaz was born April 5, 1950, in San Jose, Costa Rica. As early as age seven he remembers wanting to go into space. In grade school, he wrote to Dr. Werner von Braun of the United States Space Program asking how to become an astronaut. Dr. von Braun wrote back that Franklin should come to the United States and study science. Franklin Chang-Diaz did just that in 1967. He moved in with distant relatives in Hartford, Connecticut, who were poor, but who opened their home to him. Chang-Diaz spoke no English when he arrived, and had no money, but he didn't let either of these things stop him. He attended public school to learn English. He studied hard in school to get a college scholarship and worked odd jobs to make extra money.

In 1973, Franklin Chang-Diaz received a degree in mechanical engineering from the University of Connecticut. Later, in 1977, he obtained a doctorate from the Massachusetts Institute of Technology (MIT) in applied plasma physics. After graduation, he worked on fusion reactor projects at a lab in Cambridge, Massachusetts. In addition to his research, he managed a rehabilitation center for chronic mental patients and drug users. In 1978, he applied for astronaut selection but did not even receive a response. But Dr. Chang-Diaz was not about to give up. In 1980, he was selected as one of 19 astronauts admitted to the NASA program. He completed his mission specialist training in 1981 and began working on various research projects. On January 12, 1986, Franklin Chang-Diaz finally journeyed into space on the Space Shuttle Columbia.

One of the missions of the shuttle voyage was to take light intensified pictures of Halley's Comet. Unfortunately the device to take these pictures malfunctioned. The Columbia did achieve a space shuttle first, however, when Dr. Chang-Diaz broadcast a commentary from space in Spanish.

Franklin Chang-Diaz considers himself a scientist-astronaut. He credits his mother for his interest in science and learning, and his father for his spirit of adventure. Dr. Chang-Diaz now designs plasma rockets. Plasma rockets use advanced propulsion systems that allow for greater speed than current systems. He hopes the plasma rockets will someday carry crews to Mars. He also designed a multi-purpose laboratory that has now been included in the plans for a space station. On the less serious side, Dr. Chang-Diaz has developed a coffee maker that works in zero gravity so that he can have fresh-brewed coffee, even in space.

Dr. Chang-Diaz believes there is a need for astronauts who can do their own research as well as carrying out someone else's experiments. He sees space as an opportunity for everyone. "...in 20 to 30 years, there will be all kinds of people in space and that makes a lot of sense.

WHAT DO YOU THINK?

If you could be included in the crew of a future shuttle flight or on the crew of a space station, what research problem would you like to help solve?

TECHNOLOGY CONNECTION

Purpose This Technology Connection examines a United States astronaut's goal to "view the sky", as is discussed in section 1-3.

Content Background During the space shuttle flight, Dr. Chang-Diaz helped launch the SATCOM KU communications satellite and conducted experiments in astrophysics to learn more about the physical nature and origin of the universe. He spent a total of 146 hours in space on this flight.

He flew a second mission in October 1989, on the shuttle orbiter Atlantis. He helped send the Galileo spacecraft on its way to Jupiter, took radiation measurements, mapped atmospheric ozone, conducted research on lightning, and performed an experiment on ice crystal growth in space.

Teaching Strategies Emphasize to students that Dr. Chang-Diaz accomplished what he set out to do in spite of many obstacles. Ask students to list what qualifications they consider important for an astronaut and why Dr. Chang-Diaz would meet these qualifications.

Answers to

WHAT DO YOU THINK?

Accept any reasonable answer.

Going Further Dr. Chang-Diaz has also helped develop closer links between the scientific community and the astronaut corps. Have students investigate the Astronaut Science Colloquium Program and the Astronaut Science Support Group, both of which were founded by Dr. Chang-Diaz.

TEENS IN SCIENCE

Purpose This excursion relates to Section 1-1, recognizing the landform type that you live on. Walking along a nature trail can give people a better view of the landform over which it runs.

Content Background Fossil dinosaur imprints in Texas show that trails were made long before people inhabited Earth. Trails usually follow the path of least effort across a landform or around a landform. Many Native-American trails through the plains and southwest United States were blazed by huge herds of bison. Tall vegetation was trampled regularly in a wide swath, leaving low grasses or bare soil. These trails led hunters to the bison, a major food source. Villages were moved to follow these trails, thus keeping the food source close at hand.

Teaching Strategies Prepare students to complete the What Do You Think? activity by reviewing local landforms. Encourage students to include these in their paths.

Discussion Tell students that the only way for early settlers in the United States to go from place to place was on trails made by animals or Native Americans. Have students discuss the need for trails in today's society.

TEENS *in* SCIENCE

HAPPY TRAILS TO YOU

Have you ever taken a walk on a nature trail? If so, you may remember seeing many plants and trees along the way. Have you ever wondered how a nature trail is made?

Nature trails are often made by employees or volunteers working in local, state, or federal parks. But in Chelsea, Michigan, there is a trail that was made by a 14-year-old naturalist. Jessica Flintoft began working on her trail when she was eight years old.

"I started the nature trail as a school project. It circles around my old elementary school. I'd always been interested in how plants grow and survive. I was especially interested in the plants that can be found in our everyday environment—plants that we take for granted. Since the school is on the edge of a marsh, there is some very interesting plant life there. But a lot of the time, people overlook things that are nearest them. I thought the nature trail would help point out how special our area is."

A local citizens' organization paid for a bulldozer to smooth the path. Jessica wanted to provide basic information about each of the 24 different varieties of plants found along the edge of the new trail. The first step was to carefully research each type of plant. Next, Jessica made small signs to identify and describe each type of plant. These signs serve as markers along the trail. So that more information could be provided, Jessica also wrote a detailed brochure people could read as they walked the trail.

"I still visit the trail and keep it in good shape. But now that it's done, it's not really *my* nature trail anymore. It belongs to anyone who walks along it. Recently, some senior citizens mentioned how much they enjoy the path. They didn't realize that I had made it. It's a good feeling to know that something I made is being enjoyed by others."

WHAT DO YOU THINK?

Jessica feels strongly about how important it is to notice things around you. Make a list of the types of things that you see each morning on your way to school. Be a pathfinder! Pretend that you are creating a path that leads from your house to your friend's house. Describe some of the signs you will place along the way.

Going Further Have students plan and make a nature trail similar to the one they read about in this excursion in a public area close to your school or on school property. First, obtain permission to create a nature trail in the selected area. Then assign a different section of the area to small groups. Have each group draw a map of its area and locate points of interest and flora for identification. Then direct students to use field guides to identify the trees, grasses, flowers, and other plants along their proposed trail and mark them on their maps. Provide materials for students to make weatherproof signs that identify each plant or landform in plain view. Finally, have the class choose a name for the trail and make a sign for its beginning, explaining the trail's purpose and an overview of what people will see along it. **COOP LEARN**

Reviewing Main Ideas

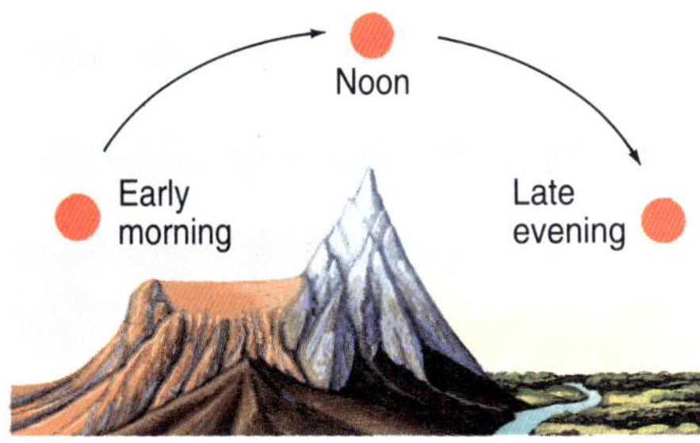

1. When we observe our surroundings, we see landforms such as mountains, plains, and plateaus. We also see the sun appear to move through the sky.

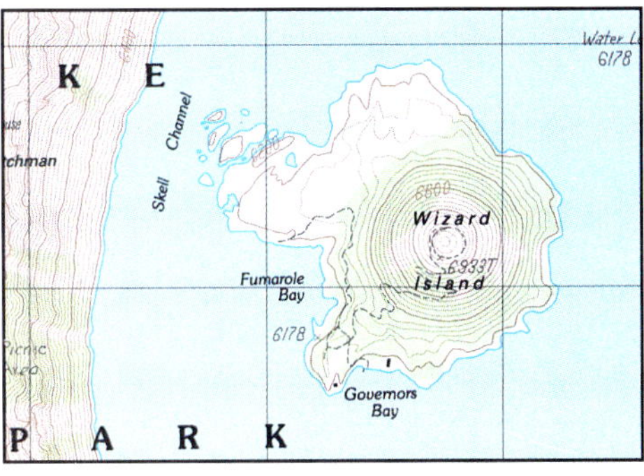

2. Topographic maps record our observations about landforms and their elevations through the use of contour lines.

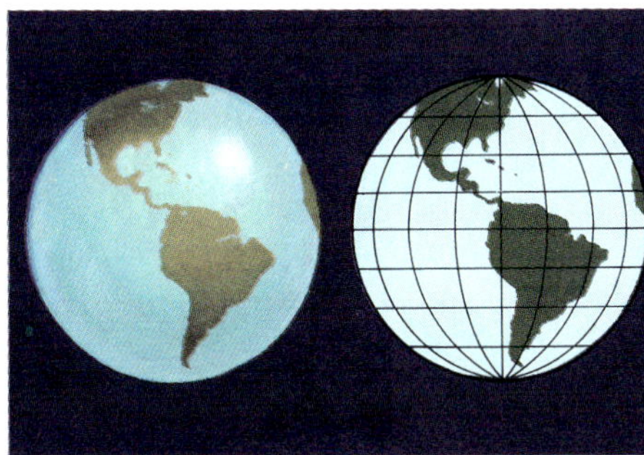

3. Lines of latitude and longitude were created as reference points to help people locate places on Earth.

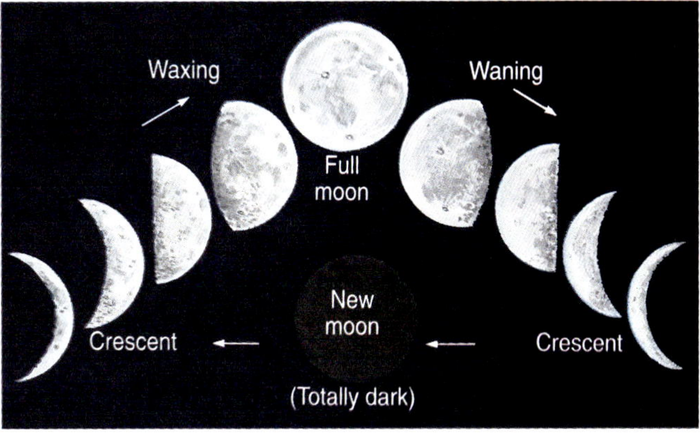

4. From Earth, we can observe large dark areas on the moon called maria. With a telescope, we can observe smaller depressions called craters. The moon's shape appears to change because we see different portions of its lighted side.

Reviewing Main Ideas

Have students look at the four pictures on this page. Direct them to read the statements to review the main ideas of this chapter.

Teaching Strategies

Divide the class into four equal groups and assign each group one of the illustrations. Have groups write a brief paragraph explaining what their photograph or diagram means. Students can read their paragraphs aloud or write them on the chalkboard. Sample responses include:

1. Earth and sky can be observed from the ground. During the day we see landforms like mountains, plateaus, plains, lakes, and streams on the ground and the sun in the sky.

2. Topographic maps give us a two-dimensional view of three-dimensional surfaces, such as landforms. Contour lines indicate elevations and show us the shapes of landforms.

3. Latitude and longitude lines form a grid over the surface of Earth. They intersect to make reference points that can be used to locate positions on Earth. Latitude lines are counted from north-south and run east-west. Longitude lines are counted from east-west and run north-south.

4. Maria are large flat areas of the moon's surface. Craters are formed when meteors crash into the surface of the moon.

Chapter 1

Chapter Review

USING KEY SCIENCE TERMS

Answers

1. constellations
2. latitude
3. landforms
4. elevation
5. phases
6. longitude
7. contour lines

UNDERSTANDING IDEAS

Answers

1. c
2. c
3. b
4. b
5. c
6. d
7. a
8. b

CRITICAL THINKING

Answers

1. Plains and plateaus are both relatively flat. Plateaus are generally raised flat areas surrounded by land of lower elevation. Plains can be at high elevations, but are not surrounded by land with lower elevation.

2. The night after a new moon, a thin wedge of the moon would be seen. The position of the moon in its revolution around Earth has changed so that a small part of its lighted side is visible.

3. 1040 feet and 1060 feet; With a 20 foot interval, the highest contour line on the map is at 1040. The small space in the center of the 1040 ft. contour line would then be under 1060 ft. in elevation because there is no 1060 ft. contour line.

4. The phases of the moon depend on how we view the moon from Earth in its orbit around Earth. As the moon revolves around Earth, its position constantly changes. Each week, the moon moves 90° in its orbit around Earth. The first week, the moon is between new and half lit. The second week, the moon is between half and full. The third week, the moon is between full and half, and the final week, the moon is between half and new.

Chapter 1

Chapter Review

USING KEY SCIENCE TERMS

constellations	latitude
contour lines	longitude
elevation	phases
landforms	

An analogy is a relationship between two pairs of words generally written in the following manner: a:b::c:d. The symbol : is read "is to," and the symbol :: is read "as." For example, cat:animal::rose:plant is read "cat is to animal as rose is to plant." In the analogies that follow, a word is missing. Complete each analogy by providing the missing word from the list above.

1. Big Dipper:____::Pacific:oceans
2. east:longitude::north: ____
3. houses:buildings::mountains: ____
4. degrees:temperature::meters: ____
5. innings:baseball game::____:moon cycle
6. equator:latitude::prime meridian: ____
7. latitude and longitude:direction:: ____: elevation

UNDERSTANDING IDEAS

Choose the best answer to complete each sentence.

1. If you lived on the coast in a relatively flat area, you would most likely be living on a landform called a coastal ____.
   a. plateau **c.** plain
   b. mountain **d.** crater
2. Imaginary lines west of the prime meridian are lines of ____.
   a. north latitude **c.** west longitude
   b. south latitude **d.** east longitude
3. The sun is highest in the sky in ____.
   a. early winter **c.** late fall
   b. early summer **d.** early spring
4. The large, dark areas on the moon are ____.
   a. craters **c.** mountains
   b. maria **d.** plateaus
5. Features found in all landforms are ____.
   a. plateaus **c.** rivers
   b. mountains **d.** plains
6. If you wanted to know the approximate elevation of a place, you would most likely look at a ____.
   a. city map **c.** globe
   b. star map **d.** topographic map
7. Suppose you wanted to locate a constellation. You would probably want to use a ____.
   a. star map **c.** topographic map
   b. globe **d.** phase illustration
8. The imaginary lines parallel to the equator are the lines of ____.
   a. contour **c.** longitude
   b. latitude **d.** elevation

CRITICAL THINKING

Use your understanding of the concepts developed in the chapter to answer each of the following questions.

1. How are plains and plateaus alike? How are they different?

PROGRAM RESOURCES

Teacher Classroom Resources

Review and Assessment, Chapter Review and Chapter Test, pages 5-8

Computer Test Bank, Chapter Test

OPTIONS

Cooperative Learning

Consider using Cooperative Learning in the Understanding Ideas, Critical Thinking, Problem Solving, and Connecting Ideas sections of the Chapter Review.

COOP LEARN

2. Suppose you knew there was a new moon last night. What kind of a moon would you expect to see tonight? Why?

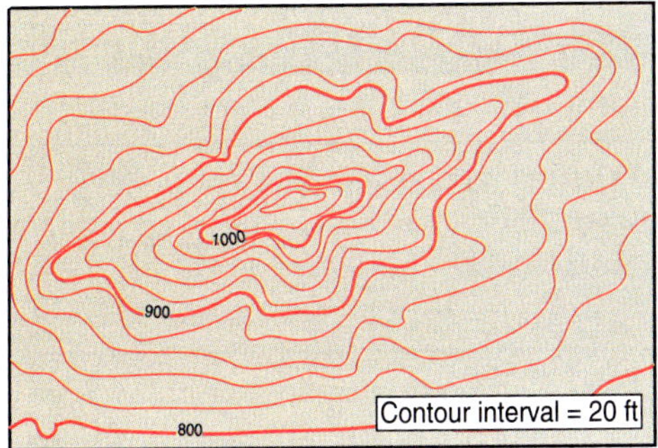

3. Study the topographic map of a hill above. Then fill in the blanks in this sentence: The elevation at the top of the hill is between ____ and ____. Explain your answers.
4. The moon takes about four weeks to move around Earth. Explain why the phases of the moon are also in a four-week cycle.

PROBLEM SOLVING

Read the following problem and discuss your answers in a brief paragraph.

The North Star can be seen from most places in the United States in the night sky when you look north. At different latitudes, the North Star appears at different heights in the sky. You can measure an angle between the surface of Earth at your location and the position of the North Star. This angle is equal to your latitude.

The latitude of any location can be found by using the North Star and an instrument called a sextant. You can make a sextant with a protractor and straw. Hold or pin the straw so that it pivots at the center point of the protractor. Hold the protractor up close to your eyes, so its base is parallel to the ground. Sight along the straw to find the North Star. Keep the base of the protractor parallel to the ground.

1. Why do you think the base has to be horizontal?
2. What is your latitude?

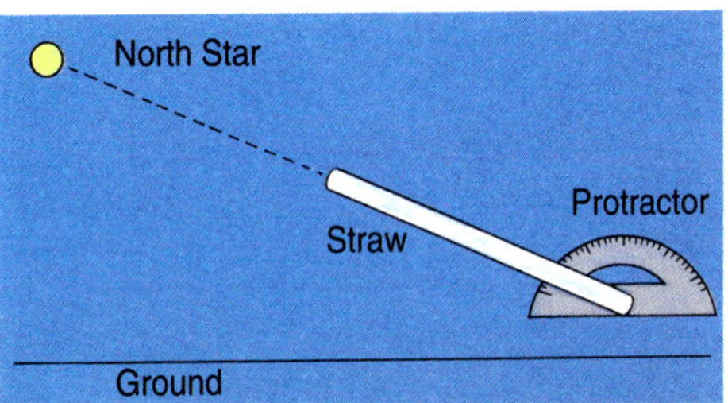

CONNECTING IDEAS

Discuss each of the following in a brief paragraph.

1. Suppose that you want to find the approximate elevation and location of a place. What kind of map would you use? Why?
2. How could all latitudes in the continental United States be north and all longitudes be west?
3. Two craters overlap. How can you determine which crater is the younger?
4. SCIENCE AND SOCIETY What are two environmental problems caused by sanitary landfills?
5. LIFE SCIENCE CONNECTION Name three factors that are important in determining where crops can be grown.

PROBLEM SOLVING

Answers

1. It has to be parallel to the ground because the angle to the North Star must be measured from a fixed reference line, in this case, the surface of Earth. If the measurement cannot be made on the ground, then it must be made from a parallel line somewhere above the ground.

2. Answers will vary with students' locations. Check a local map for the correct latitude of the area.

CONNECTING IDEAS

Answers

1. A topographic map would be used to find elevation and location. Topographic maps have both elevation as well as longitude and latitude shown on them, while other maps may only have longitude and latitude lines on them.

2. The equator, 0° latitude, is to the south of the continental United States, making all latitudes above it north latitude. The prime meridian, 0° longitude, is to the east, making all longitudes in the continental United States west.

3. The younger crater overlaps the older crater. The younger crater's rim would be in the older crater.

4. Toxic chemicals and other hazardous wastes may seep into soil and groundwater. Hazardous gases may be produced as garbage decomposes.

5. Answers may include growing season, climate, type of soil, landforms.

CHAPTER ORGANIZER

SECTION	OBJECTIVES	ACTIVITIES/FEATURES
Chapter Opener		**Explore!** How sharp is a shadow? p. 35
2-1 The Nature of Light (2 days)	1. **Identify** how shadows are produced. 2. **Distinguish** between objects that create light and those that only reflect light.	**Find Out!** How does light travel? p. 37 **Explore!** How does the source of light affect shadows? p. 38
2-2 Color (4 days)	1. **Examine** visible light. 2. **Compare and contrast** opaque, translucent, and transparent materials. 3. **Explain** the difference between pigment color and light color.	**Explore!** What colors are in sunlight or light from a light bulb? p. 40 **Explore!** What happens to light when it hits different objects? p. 41 **Find Out!** How do lights mix? p. 44 **Skillbuilder:** Comparing and Contrasting, p. 47 **Investigate 2-1:** Reflecting Colored Light, p. 48
2-3 Reflection and Refraction (3 days)	1. **Discuss** the different types of reflection. 2. **Describe** what happens to light during refraction. 3. **Examine** how refraction separates light into the colors of the spectrum.	**Investigate 2-2:** Mirror Reflections, p. 51 **Find Out!** How does light reflect on smooth and bumpy surfaces? p. 52 **Explore!** How does light refract? p. 53 **Skillbuilder:** Comparing and Contrasting, p. 53
Expanding Your View		A Closer Look **Why the Sky Is Blue and Sunsets Are Red,** p. 55 Life Science Connection **Natural Dyes,** p. 56 Science and Society **Light and Color in Our Lives,** p. 57 Art Connection **Seeing Things Differently,** p. 59 Technology Connection **Infrared Astronomy,** p. 60

ACTIVITY MATERIALS

EXPLORE!	INVESTIGATE!	FIND OUT!
Page 35 long clear light bulb, white paper **Page 38** long clear light bulb, white paper **Page 40** flashlight, prism, wall or sheet of white paper, sunlight or light from a film or slide projector **Page 41** flashlight, clay, white cardboard, piece of glass, piece of frosted glass, sheet of cellophane, book, waxed paper, sunglasses, tissue paper, piece of clothing, such as your jacket **Page 53** clear glass, water, pencil	**Page 48** flashlight; blue, green, and red cellophane; white, blue, green, and red construction paper; rubber band **Page 51** pocket mirror, ruler, unruled paper	**Page 37** 3 index cards, paper clip, light bulb or book, metric ruler, clay **Page 44** 3 flashlights; green, blue, and red cellophane; 3 rubber bands, white paper **Page 52** aluminum foil

Light and Color

TEACHER CLASSROOM RESOURCES	OTHER RESOURCES
Study Guide, p. 10 **Making Connections: Integrating Sciences,** p. 7 **Making Connections: Across the Curriculum,** p. 7 **Making Connections: Technology and Society,** p. 7	***STVS:** *Computerized Star Imaging,* Earth and Space (Disc 3, Side 1)
Study Guide, p. 11 **Flex Your Brain,** p. 8 **Activity Masters, Investigate 2-1,** pp. 9-10 **Multicultural Activities,** p. 7	**Color Transparency and Master 3,** Light Colors **Color Transparency and Master 4,** Pigment Colors ***STVS:** *Images of Heat,* Physics (Disc 1, Side 1) *Chroma Key,* Physics (Disc 1, Side 2) *Vision Diagnosis,* Human Biology (Disc 7, Side 1)
Study Guide, p. 12 **Concept Mapping,** p. 10 **Activity Masters, Investigate 2-2,** pp. 11-12 **Critical Thinking/Problem Solving,** p. 10 **Multicultural Activities,** p. 8 **Take Home Activities,** p. 7 **Review and Assessment,** pp. 9-12	**Laboratory Manual,** pp. 7-8, Producing a Spectrum **Laboratory Manual,** pp. 9-10, Refraction of Light ***STVS:** *Laser Identification of Fibers,* Physics (Disc 1, Side 2) **Computer Test Bank**
	Spanish Resources **Cooperative Learning Resource Guide** **Lab and Safety Skills**

***Science and Technology Videodisc Series**

KEY TO TEACHING STRATEGIES

Teaching strategies have been coded for varying learning styles and abilities. As you review teaching strategies in the margin, the following designations will help you decide which activities are appropriate for your students.

- **L1** Level 1 activities are basic activities and should be within the ability range of all students.
- **L2** Level 2 activities are average activities and should be within the ability range of the average to above-average student.
- **L3** Level 3 activities are challenging activities designed for the ability range of above-average students.
- **LEP** LEP activities should be within the ability range of Limited English Proficiency students.
- **COOP LEARN** Cooperative Learning activities are designed for small group work.

ADDITIONAL MATERIALS

SOFTWARE	AUDIOVISUAL
Reflection and Refraction, Queue.	*Learning About Light,* film, EBEC. *The World of Light Energy,* video, Focus. *Color From Light,* film, Churchill Films. *Mr. Wizard's World: Light Reflection; Light Refraction; Light Instruments,* videos, Macmillan/McGraw-Hill School Division.

Chapter 2

Light and Color

THEME DEVELOPMENT

One theme that this chapter supports is interactions and systems. Students learn how the properties of light interact with structures in our eyes so we see the world in a variety of ways. They also learn how light interacts with various objects to produce colors and reflections. Additionally, students conduct experiments that help them understand the nature of light and color. This becomes evident to students as they perform the Investigate activity on page 48. In terms of scale and structure, the Find Out activity on page 52 enables students see how various structures and surfaces affect the reflection of light.

CHAPTER OVERVIEW

First, students learn how light allows us to see a variety of images, including shadows. Students also learn to distinguish objects that produce light from those that reflect it. Then, students discover the properties of visible light and how it interacts with opaque, translucent, and transparent materials. Students also discover how colors are produced and perceived. Finally, students explore the principles of light refraction and reflection by observing how light rays bend and bounce in ways that help us see what is around us.

Tying to Previous Knowledge

Divide students into several groups. Have each group stand in different places in the room, with one group looking out the window. Ask each group to name the colors they see. Also ask them to describe which objects they see casting shadows. Then ask what makes the colors and shadows visible. They probably will have several explanations, such as the sunlight or lightbulb shining on them. They may also suggest that shadows are produced when objects block the path of light.

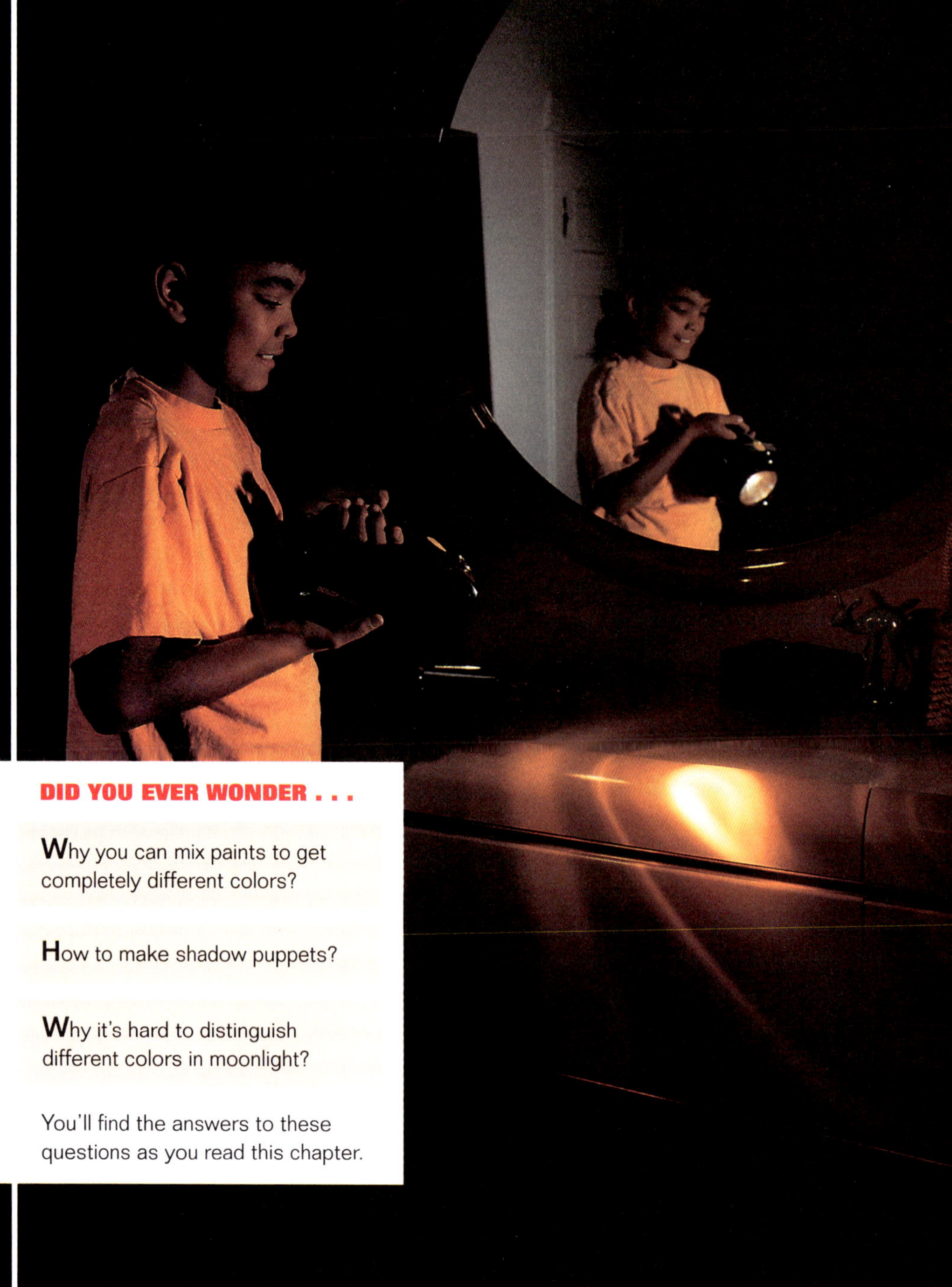

DID YOU EVER WONDER . . .

Why you can mix paints to get completely different colors?

How to make shadow puppets?

Why it's hard to distinguish different colors in moonlight?

You'll find the answers to these questions as you read this chapter.

DID YOU EVER WONDER...

Students will explore these questions as they progress through the chapter. Don't spoil their fun and motivation by sharing these answers too early.

- The pigments reflect some of the primary colors and absorb others in the white light that shines on them. When pigments are mixed, different colors are absorbed and reflected. (page 47)
- Shadow puppets are made by putting your hands in the path of a bright light shining on a white background. (page 39)
- There is not enough light to stimulate the cones that respond to the color. (page 45)

Light and Color

Do you ever want a drink of water in the middle of the night? Do you use a flashlight to find your way so you don't awaken your family? You grope for the flashlight with your hand in the dark room. When you find it and turn it on, you might point the flashlight beam first at the floor, then your dresser, and finally at the door to the hallway. You are able to see the dresser if you point the light beam at it, but as soon as you move the light toward the door, you can no longer see the dresser—it seems to disappear. The only objects you can see are the ones at which you point the flashlight.

Seeing any object requires light. Light may come from a flashlight, the light bulbs in your house, or from the sun. There are probably other sources of light in your home as well. Can you name them? What is light, and how does it allow you to see the world around you? In this chapter, you'll learn about light and how it affects what you see.

EXPLORE!

How sharp is a shadow?

Use a long, clear light bulb for this activity. Place the bulb so that the end of the long filament points toward some white paper several feet away. This will provide a point source of light. Hold your hand between the paper and the light, about an inch away from the bulb. Then, move your hand until it is about one foot from the paper. What changes? Does this give you any idea about the path light travels?

35

Introducing the Chapter

Have students look at the photograph on page 34. Ask students to describe what the student is doing. *Shining a flashlight.* Tell students that the chapter will explain light and color.

Uncovering Preconceptions

Many students think that black is a color. However, true black is an absence of color, since a truly black object absorbs the light that strikes it and reflects no light back to the eye. If we were to observe a truly black object all we would see is its outline or silhouette.

EXPLORE!

How sharp is a shadow?

Time needed 5 minutes

Materials long, clear light bulb, sheet of white paper

Thinking Processes Thinking critically, Observing and inferring

Purpose To discover how an object affects the path of light when placed in it.

Preparation A flashlight can be substituted for the light bulb.

Teaching the Activity

Discussion Explain to students that shadow images vary depending on the distance and angle of the light source from the object casting the shadow. Ask students what they think will happen to a shadow cast by an object as the distance between the object and the light source increases. L1

Expected Outcomes

Students should discover that the farther the object is moved from the light source, the fuzzier the shadow will become. They should also see that light travels in straight lines.

Project

Have students write a short play for a shadow puppet show. After they write the play, students can cut out figures from construction paper. They can also experiment with using their hands to form images. Have students plan to use a number of different color filter combinations on the light source to change the background color. The play can be put on for other classes.

Science at Home

In the early evening have students hold a dime at arm's length and slowly move it toward them until the dime blots out the moon and record the distance from the dime to the eye. Repeat the procedure later when the moon looks smaller. Now what distance is the dime from the eye? *The same distance as before.* What does this imply? *An optical illusion made the moon appear larger at the horizon.*

Section 2-1

PREPARATION

Concepts Developed

This section begins a study of the basic principles of light. Students will learn the difference between luminous and nonluminous objects and that shadows are caused by solid objects blocking the direct travel of light.

Planning the Lesson

In planning your lesson on the nature of light, refer to the Chapter Organizer on pages 34A-B for timing suggestions, resources, and additional materials that will help you in your presentation of the lesson concepts. For adequate development of the concepts presented in this section, we recommend that students do the Find Out and Explore activities on pages 37 and 38.

1 MOTIVATE

Demonstration The objective of this demonstration is to show that the intensity and amount of light affect visibility. You will need several flashlights.

Explain to students they can prove that how much they can see depends on how much light is available. Select one object in the room, such as a large map or wall chart. Have students look at it under ordinary lighting. Then pull the shades and have students look at the object as it is illuminated by the several flashlights. Have students discuss what they saw. Students should observe that the amount of the object visible changes with the amount of light available. L1

2-1 The Nature of Light

OBJECTIVES

In this section, you will

- identify how shadows are produced;
- distinguish between objects that create light and those that only reflect light.

KEY SCIENCE TERMS

reflection

LIGHT AND REFLECTION

Every day, all day long, light gives you information about the world around you. During the day, the sun is your primary source of light. You also receive light from light bulbs and fire, even from the television. These all create their own light. But most things you can see are visible because light from somewhere else bounces off them. You can read this page because light is reflecting off it to your eyes. The page is not making its own light. Light bouncing off something is **reflection**. You see your bedroom door when you shine a flashlight on it because the door reflects the light from the flashlight. You see your clothes in front of you in your closet because they reflect light from your bedroom lamp directly back to your eye. Notice that you can hear a friend call you from the next room, but you can't see her. It seems that sound can travel around corners but that light cannot. How exactly does light travel from its source to objects and then to your eye?

FIGURE 2-1. We can see objects that are not sources of light because light is reflected from them.

HOW LIGHT TRAVELS

You saw from the Explore that when an object blocks light, a shadow is produced. How dark that shadow is depends on the amount of light being blocked. When your hand was only an inch away from the light source, it blocked all the light from reaching the white paper, and the shadow was very black. When your hand was farther away from the light source, some of the light reached the

PROGRAM RESOURCES

Teacher Classroom Resources

Study Guide, page 10

Making Connections: Integrating Sciences, page 7, Bioluminescence L2

Making Connections: Across the Curriculum, page 7, In the Dark L2

Making Connections: Technology and Society, page 7, Flourescent Light L2

paper. The blocked light created a shadow with fuzzy edges. Are shadows with fuzzy edges proof enough for you that light travels in straight lines?

Let's try to gain some further evidence for this in the next Find Out.

FIND OUT!

How does light travel?

Lay three index cards together. Using an unbent paper clip, make a hole through all three cards. Stand each card upright, using small pieces of clay to hold them in a vertical position, as shown in the picture.

Place the cards about 2.5 centimeters apart, with the holes lined up. Place a light bulb about 5 centimeters behind the back index card.

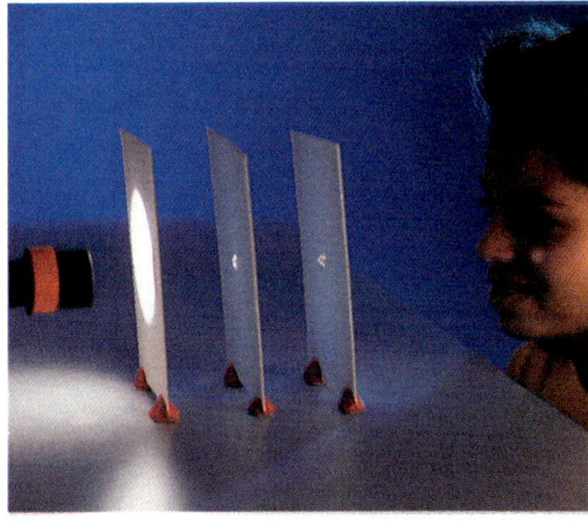

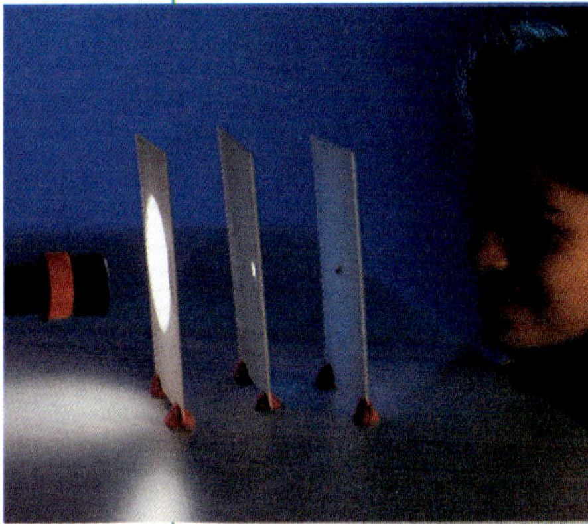

Conclude and Apply

1. Look through the holes in the index cards. Do you see the light?
2. Now move the center card slightly out of line, as shown in the next picture. Do you see the light now?
3. In what direction does light travel?

In the Find Out, you could not see the light through the first hole when the second hole was moved. Light was blocked. The light did not curve around the second

OPTIONS

Meeting Individual Needs

Visually Impaired For students who have difficulty perceiving images, use the related concept that light sources produce heat. You will need to supervise these students individually. Explain that the principle of reflection can be understood in another way. Guide a student's hand close enough to a light source to feel the warmth. That would be the equivalent of a reflection. Have the student place a heavy piece of paper between the source and the hand. That will demonstrate shadow because the heat is less.

2 TEACH

Tying to Previous Knowledge

Have students think about the difference between light and darkness. Ask them to discuss what they see when they turn on the lights in the morning and when they turn off the lights at night. Also ask them when they see shadows.

FIND OUT!

How does light travel?

Time needed 6–10 minutes

Materials (per student) three index cards, paper clip, lumps of clay, connected light bulb

Thinking Processes Thinking critically, Observing and Inferring, Comparing and contrasting, Recognizing cause and effect

Purpose To discover that light travels in what appears to be a straight line.

Preparation Have all the materials set out ahead of time. You may want to assign two students to each setup. Squares of construction paper can be substituted for the index cards. The clay can be replaced by anything that can hold a piece of paper upright. A flashlight can be substituted for the bulb. L1 LEP

Teaching the Activity

Troubleshooting Some students may have trouble lining up the cards. Have them use a ruler to keep the edges straight.

Expected Outcomes

When the cards are aligned, students should see the light bulb. When the center card is moved, the object should not be visible.

Conclude and Apply

1. yes
2. no
3. Light travels in a straight line through the holes in the index cards.

Concept Development

Theme Connection The experiments should show that light energy behaves in predictable ways. Point out that the basic nature of light rays is what makes our perception of color possible. It also accounts for the way mirrors work and the visual tricks of refraction. Stress that visible light, as well as other types of radiation, is actually a form of energy.

EXPLORE!

How does the source of light affect shadows?

Time needed 5 minutes

Materials an extended light source, white paper

Thinking Processes Interpreting scientific illustrations, Comparing and contrasting

Purpose To show that light rays travel in straight lines. The larger the light source, the more angles of light rays will meet, creating a fuzzy edge to a shadow.

Preparation Put an incandescent bulb over one sheet of paper on a desk. Use the overhead light of your classroom for the extended light source.

Teaching the Activity

Discussion Ask students to talk about what would happen if someone were to stand in front of a lighted flashlight. Have them speculate on what would happen to the path of the light if someone stood in front of a very large spotlight. Use answers to lead students to understand that the larger the light source, the more angles the light rays will be coming from. L1

Expected Outcomes

Students should see that the shadow from the smaller bulb is clearly defined. The shadow from the overhead light has gray edges.

Answer to Question

The shadows were fuzzier than those in the first experiment.

hole to allow you to see the light bulb. Let's go back to our first Explore and add one more test to determine how light travels.

EXPLORE!

How does the source of light affect shadows?

Set up an extended light source to shine on the white paper. You can use the long, clear bulb from this chapter's first Explore as an extended light source. This time turn the bulb so the long side of the filament faces the white paper. Make shadows. How do these shadows compare with the shadows from the first Explore?

A larger light can more easily send light rays past the hand. Examine the photographs closely. Use your finger to trace straight lines from anywhere on the small bulb to the paper. How easy is it to touch the paper without touching the hand? Now trace straight lines from anywhere on the long bulb to the paper. Isn't it easier to find ways past the hand? In the Explore, you saw that an extended light source makes fuzzier shadows than a point source. You can now explain this difference by assuming that light travels in straight lines.

THE SPEED OF LIGHT

Whichever type of light source you have, it seems that light zips instantly from it to the object and back to you.

PROGRAM RESOURCES

Other Resources

Learning About Light, film, EBEC.

The World of Light Energy, video, Focus.

Morris, Richard. *Light: From Genesis to Modern Physics.* New York: Macmillan Publishing Co., Inc., 1979.

Walker, Jearl. *The Flying Circus of Physics (With Answers).* New York: John Wiley & Sons, 1977.

OPTIONS

Enrichment

Activity Provide students with old magazines. Have them cut out photographs that use shadows. Have them create a collage showing the various ways shadows are used in photography. Have students explain where the light source is in each photograph.

You can see everything immediately. Light travels much faster than anything else we know of, but it does take some time for it to travel from place to place. How much time does it take light to travel?

Throughout history, many people have tried to measure how fast light travels, but it wasn't until the late 1800s that scientists found that light travels at about 300,000 kilometers per second. That's fast enough to go from the sun to you in about eight minutes. It's so fast that a beam of light can cross your bedroom several million times before you can let go of the light switch.

Whether you have the sun, a lamp, a flashlight, or a candle as your source of light, you can see the objects around you. You can see yourself in a mirror, find your way in the dark with a flashlight, or see your family sitting at the dinner table because all of these objects instantly reflect light back to your eyes. Light travels fast and in straight lines in all directions.

When a light source is interrupted, shadows are produced. Some are sharp and clear and look very much like the object that interrupts the light. Have you ever produced hand shadows on a wall or on a screen when your teacher showed filmstrips? Some were large and fuzzy and ghostlike. Using what you've learned in this section, look at your shadow on your bedroom wall tonight. Then try a few shadow experiments with the various lights available. Predict what you think would happen before you vary the light sources and the size and distances of the objects creating the shadows.

How do we know?

How was the speed of light first timed?

One of the most famous experiments to time light speed was performed in 1926 by an American, Albert Michelson, on Mount Wilson in California. Using two large mirrors 22 miles apart and a rotating mirror having eight sides, he was able to bounce light beams between the mirrors and make the most precise measurements of the speed of light ever made with mechanical methods.

Check Your Understanding

1. Name two items not discussed in this section that you could see without reflected light.
2. Would a candle flame at a distance of six meters produce a sharp or fuzzy shadow? Why?
3. The moon is about 387,000 kilometers from Earth. How long does it take light to get from the moon to Earth? Round your answer to the nearest quarter second.
4. **APPLY:** The closest star is four light-years away. That is, it takes four years for light from the star to reach us. Do we see the star as it is now or as it was?

3 Assess

To help students answer the Apply question in Check Your Understanding, ask them if the star exploded today, when would we see it? *in four years*

Reteach

For students who have problems understanding the relation between the path of light and shadows, have a student stand in front of the classroom window with one arm stretched out in front. Have another student stand touching the first student's arm. Have them both observe the shadow cast by the first student on the second. Then have the second student move away slowly step by step. Students should see that the shadow changes. L1 LEP

Extension

Have students who have mastered the concepts of light and shadow research how to set up a shadow theater. Then have them write and perform a short play using this technique. Allow students to write dialogue if they wish. L3

4 Close

Activity

Using your light bulbs, have students put their hands close to the light source and then move slowly away. They should be able to tell you that the closer the light source and the reflective object are, the brighter the object will appear. They will also notice a change in the shadow produced. LEP

Multicultural Perspectives

The Chinese used shadows for entertainment over two thousand years ago. Both royalty and villagers enjoyed shadow puppet shows made by silhouette figures cut from donkey skin that were illuminated by a torch from behind a translucent screen.

Answers to Check Your Understanding

Examples of answers are

1. fire in a fireplace, hot burners on a stove, luminous watch dials, or anything that creates its own light
2. sharp because it's a small source of light
3. 1.25 seconds
4. as it was four years ago

Section 2-2

Preparation

Concepts Developed

The previous section explored the basic nature of light. In this section the visible light spectrum is explained. Visible light reacts with three types of material: opaque, translucent, and transparent. Students will learn how each type reflects and absorbs colors differently.

Planning the Lesson

In planning your lesson on color, refer to the Chapter Organizer on pages 34A-B for timing suggestions, resources, and additional materials that will help you in your presentation of the lesson concepts. For adequate development of the concepts in this section, we recommend that students do the Explores on pages 40 and 41 and the Find Out on page 44.

1 Motivate

Discussion Ask students how colored objects appear to them in a dark room. They may suggest that the objects appear to be black. Can students figure out the reason? *Colored objects in a dark room appear black because there is so little light for the objects to reflect.* L1

2-2 Color

OBJECTIVES

In this section, you will

- examine visible light;
- compare and contrast opaque, translucent, and transparent materials;
- explain the difference between pigment color and light color.

KEY SCIENCE TERMS

spectrum
opaque
transparent
translucent

VISIBLE LIGHT

Sitting in your classroom, you notice that one of your classmates is wearing the brightest green shirt you've ever seen. You are sure that a shirt doesn't make its own light, so you must be seeing it by reflected light. Where does all that green come from? To get the clues you need to answer this question, try the following experiment.

EXPLORE!

What colors are in sunlight or light from a light bulb?

Use a flashlight to shine a beam of light through a prism—a triangular piece of glass—onto a wall or a sheet of white paper, as shown in the figure, or use sunlight or light from a slide or filmstrip projector. How does the light look after it has passed through the prism? Make a sketch of what you see. Label the colors that appear and the order in which they appear.

A MIXTURE OF LIGHTS

In the 1600s, Isaac Newton first observed and explained how a prism affects light in the way you've just seen. He proposed that white light is a mixture of all colors. He also showed that different colors of light bend differently as they pass through a prism, so they emerge as separate bands of color called a **spectrum**. We'll discuss the bending of light later. For now, let's see what the spectrum tells us about the makeup of light. When Newton

EXPLORE!

What colors are in sunlight or light from a light bulb?

Time needed 15 minutes

Materials triangular prism, movie or filmstrip projector, movie screen; paper and crayons for all students, flashlight.

Thinking Processes
Representing data, Making models

Purpose To show that the colors of the spectrum will bend and separate when white light is passed through a prism.

Preparation Before class have the prism and light source in position so that the spectrum will be displayed fully on the screen. A large white paper can be substituted for the screen.

Teaching the Activity

Discussion Ask students to describe what they see and have them suggest why light shows up as it does with a prism. *A prism breaks up white light into its basic components.* LEP L1

Expected Outcomes The seven basic colors of the spectrum should appear in the ROY G BIV pattern.

FIGURE 2-2. The colors of the spectrum are always in the same order. Their initials are ROY G BIV.

looked at the spectrum, as in Figure 2-2, he observed a pattern that had roughly seven colors: red, orange, yellow, green, blue, indigo (violet-blue), and violet. All white light contains these seven colors.

Now you know that light from the sun and most light bulbs contain green light because your classmate's shirt reflects that green light. Light also has blue light that is reflected by your jeans. But what happens to the blue light hitting the green shirt? Or to the green light hitting your blue jeans? When light hits an object, what happens to it depends on the nature of the object itself. Let's try shining light on different kinds of objects to see what happens to the light.

EXPLORE!

What happens to light when it hits different objects?

Obtain a flashlight, a piece of clay, and a piece of white cardboard. Using the clay, set the white cardboard on your desk vertically. Select a number of objects and place in front of the white cardboard, one at a time. Shine the flashlight on each object and record what you see on the white cardboard behind it. Shine the light on several different objects. You may wish to use a piece of glass, a piece of frosted glass, a sheet of cellophane, a book, a piece of waxed paper, a pair of sunglasses, a piece of tissue paper, a piece of clothing such as your jacket, your notebook, and a page from your

2 TEACH

Tying to Previous Knowledge

Ask students to describe sunlight. They will probably use the phrase *white light.* Point out that if you can see it, then it is part of the visible spectrum. Also point out that we do not really see sunlight. Instead we see the light reflected from objects on Earth. Ask students if sunlight behaves as the other light they have been investigating.

EXPLORE!

What happens to light when it hits different objects?

Time needed 10 minutes

Materials flashlight, lump of clay, and piece of white cardboard for each student

Have objects available, such as: piece of glass, piece of frosted glass, sheet of cellophane, piece of waxed paper, pair of sunglasses, piece of tissue paper

Thinking Processes
Thinking critically, Observing and inferring, Comparing and contrasting, Recognizing cause and effect

Purpose To discover the differences among opaque, translucent, and transparent materials.

Preparation If there are not enough materials for every student, have students work cooperatively in groups.

Teaching the Activity

Demonstration Shine a strong light, such as a movie projector, on a screen or large white paper. Hold up each object in front of the screen. You can substitute objects of the same materials. L1 LEP

Expected Outcomes Students should report that opaque materials block light entirely; translucent materials allow some light to pass through; and transparent materials block almost no light.

Answers to Questions

1. Almost all the light went through the glass and cellophane. Some went through the frosted glass, the waxed paper, and the sunglasses. None went through the other materials.
2. First: can see through the objects, and they allow light through. Second: can see through the objects, but not completely; some light goes through. Third: cannot see through objects, no light goes through.

Concept Development

Theme Connection The theme that this section supports is energy. The text and experiment in this lesson explain that all of the colors we perceive are a mixture of black and the three primary colors of red, blue, and green. The lesson also points out that the amount of light absorbed or reflected by different materials is important to how we see the world around us.

Using the Diagram Have students look at Figure 2-3. Point out that the arrow represents the color of light being reflected.

Inquiry Question Do transparent objects reflect light? *Transparent objects must reflect a little light in order to be seen.*

MAKING CONNECTIONS

Daily Life

Translucent material is used for restroom and office windows. Translucent material provides privacy by not allowing outsiders to see in, but light is allowed into the room. Have students make a list of places where translucent materials are used.

book. What happened to the light as it hit each object? Try sorting the objects into three groups depending on how the light behaved when it was directed at them. What can you say about the characteristics of the objects in each group? What can you say about how they affect light?

In the Explore, you saw that when light hits different objects, it behaves differently. When light hits an object, three things can happen. Light can pass through, be reflected, or be absorbed. What you see depends upon which of these three things occurs. Figure 2-3 shows what happens when light hits your classmate's green shirt. The shirt material reflects just the green light. It absorbs the other colors in the light. What do you suppose is happening right now as the light hits this page? Look at the paper. It reflects all colors, so you see it as white. The ink on the page absorbs all colors, reflecting none, so you see it as black.

FIGURE 2-3. The colors we see depend on the color of the light reflected from an object.

OPAQUE, TRANSPARENT, AND TRANSLUCENT

Most of the things you see around you reflect or absorb the light that hits them, allowing none to pass through. We say these objects are **opaque**.

This book is opaque. You can't see through it. What happens to light that passes through an object depends upon how the light passes through. Look at a clear window. You can see through it, almost as if nothing is there. When something allows enough light through so that you clearly see the other side, we call it **transparent**.

There are some materials that let light through, but bend it in many different directions. They are called **translucent**. When you look through translucent material,

OPTIONS

Meeting Individual Needs

Learning Disabled Some students may have difficulty with the Explore on page 41. Do the following project with them.

You will need a page from a newspaper, a sheet of clear cellophane, a sheet of waxed paper, and a meter-square piece of cardboard.

Place the newspaper in front of the student. Have the student put each of the other materials over it one at a time and tell how well the newspaper can be read through each one. Have the student label each item. The cellophane is transparent; the waxed paper is translucent; the cardboard is opaque. LEP

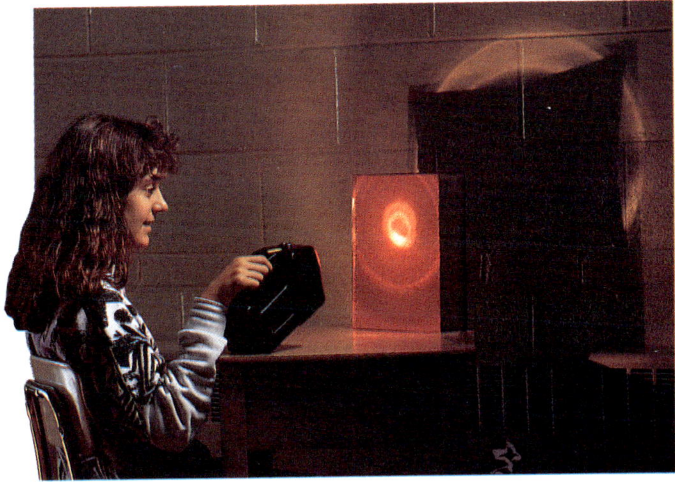

FIGURE 2-4. The book is opaque. Light can't pass through it, and you can't see through it.

you see a fuzzy image. Some lamp shades, frosted glass, and tissue paper are translucent.

Suppose during the lunch hour, you go outside. It's a sunny day, so you put on your green sunglasses. Now that you know about light, it occurs to you that everything that can happen when light hits an object happens when light hits your sunglasses. The lenses look green because they reflect green light. Green light also passes through the lenses. This is why you can see through the lenses. Because most other colors of light are absorbed, things seen through the sunglasses have a greenish tint.

MIXING COLORS WITH LIGHT

Your sunglasses are a type of transparent material called a filter. Filters may be transparent for one or more colors of light. These colors pass through the filters, but the other colors are absorbed. If you place a green filter over a flashlight, you'll get green light because the filter absorbs all the other colors except green. A red filter allows red light to pass through, and a blue filter allows blue light to pass. But what do you think might happen if you mixed the light coming from three flashlights—one with a green filter, one with a blue filter, and one with a red filter?

MAKING CONNECTIONS

Daily Life

Lighter colored materials absorb less light than darker materials. Ask students what color clothing they should wear on hot summer days if they want to be as cool as possible. *lighter colors* What color clothes should they wear on cold winter days in order to stay as warm as possible? *darker colors* What color clothes do students think would be best for people living in desert climates? *white*

Concept Development

Inquiry Question How can a colored light bulb be like a filter? *The color of the glass of the bulb is the same color as the light it gives off. The colored glass absorbs the other colors from the white light given off by the filament.*

Uncovering Preconceptions Ask students to name the three primary light colors. *red, blue, green* They may name the primary pigment colors—red, yellow, blue—instead. From their art education, students may have a working knowledge of color. Emphasize that the primary pigment colors are different from the primary light colors because light colors come from luminous objects, and pigment colors are reflected.

Teacher F.Y.I.

The phrase "looking at the world through rose-colored glasses" is based on reflection and transparency. It means that a person thinks about the world as if it were seen through a red filter. Everything would have a rosy or warm tint.

Student Journal Have students write a paragraph or make a chart in their student journals to show the differences between the primary colors of light and those of pigments.

Enrichment

Activity Color blindness is a common visual disorder. Chances are very high that some members of your class have a form of color blindness. Locate some color-blind tests in psychology books or encyclopedias and administer them to members of your class. Some color-blind students will not be able to distinguish between some of the colors.

Meeting Individual Needs

Learning Disabled Here is a way students can remember the difference between translucent and transparent materials. *Trans* means "through." *Translucent* means "to shine through." *Transparent* means "to appear through."

Have students bring in examples or pictures of translucent and transparent objects. Have students create a classroom display of each kind of material. LEP

FIND OUT!

How do lights mix?

Time needed 5–10 minutes

Materials three flashlights; three rubber bands; green, blue and red cellophane; white paper

Thinking Processes
Observe and infer, Compare and contrast, Recognize cause and effect

Purpose To show how the three primary colors of light combine to make other colors

Preparation Have the flashlights prepared ahead of time. Tape the sheet of white paper on the board. Practice arranging the lights so that the overlap works as seen in the diagram.

Teaching the Activity

You may wish to have students work in groups of three with each student holding a flashlight.

 COOP LEARN  L1

Expected Outcomes

Students should see that the overlap of green and blue results in cyan, the overlap of green and red results in yellow, blue and red result in magenta and white is the result of all three combined.

Answers to Conclude and Apply

1. The size and shape of the magenta, yellow, and white change. The intensity of the colors also changes, producing a variety of shades. The white may develop a pinkish tone.
2. The size, shape, and intensity of the other overlapping colors change as each light source moves closer or farther away.

FIND OUT!

How do lights mix?

You'll need three flashlights; three rubber bands; green, blue, and red cellophane; and some white paper. Fold a piece of green cellophane into a square several layers thick. Use a rubber band to fold it over the lens of one flashlight. Do the same with the other colors of cellophane and the other flashlights. In a darkened room, shine all three flashlights onto the white paper to make three circles that overlap, as in the picture. What do you see where green and blue overlap? How about green and red? Blue and red? All three?

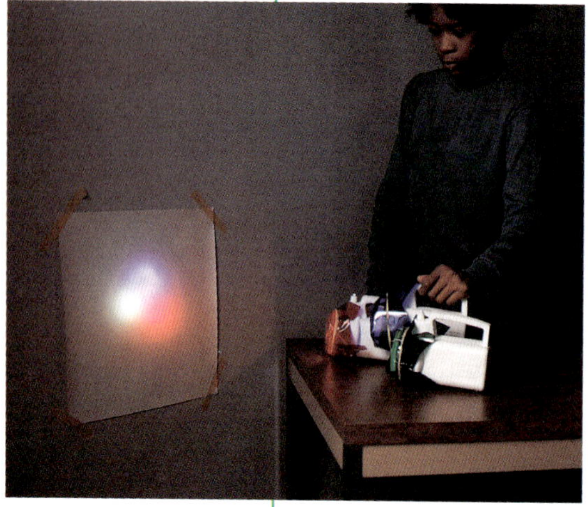

Conclude and Apply

1. Keep the green and blue flashlights in the same place while moving the red flashlight closer to and farther away from the paper. How do the colors change?
2. Try it again moving each of the other two flashlights. What happens?

FIGURE 2-5. White light is produced when the three primary colors of light are mixed.

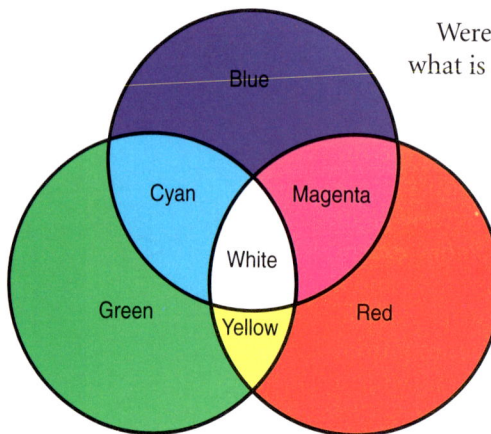

Were your results from the Find Out similar to what is shown in Figure 2-5? Blue plus green made a shade of blue called cyan (SI an), blue plus red made a shade of red called magenta, and red plus green made yellow. But where all three colors of light mixed you got white. Does this seem odd? You saw earlier that white light is made up of all the colors in the spectrum. How did you get white just now with only three colors?

When you made some colored lights brighter than others by bringing them

PROGRAM RESOURCES

Teacher Classroom Resources
Study Guide, page 11
Critical Thinking/Problem Solving, page 8, Flex Your Brain

closer to the paper, you saw different colors in place of the white. If you could combine the three colored lights, each with just the right brightness, you would be able to produce every color of the spectrum. Because you can create all the colors using only red, blue, and green light, these three colors are called the primary colors of light. How can they make all the colors?

Your results would be different if you were mixing paints rather than lights. In paints, the primary colors are different, as we'll soon see. But why are primary colors different in lights and paint? The answers to these questions have as much to do with how your eye sees light as they do with the nature of light itself.

HOW YOU SEE COLORS

Your eye contains two main types of light-detecting nerve cells. They're called cones and rods because of their shapes, as you can see in Figure 2-7. Rods are very sensitive to lights of all colors. Cones are sensitive to some colors of light more than to others.

You have three types of cones, referred to as red, green, and blue cones. Red cones respond primarily to red and yellow light. Green cones respond primarily to green and yellow light. Blue cones react primarily to blue and violet light. Different colors of light will cause different combinations of cones to respond to them, and some colors may

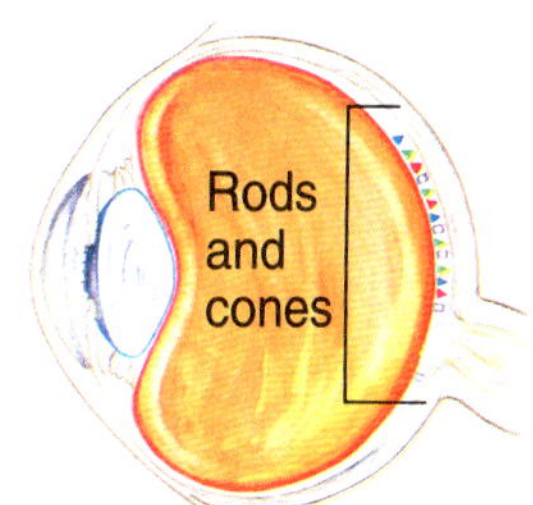

FIGURE 2-6. You can see where the rods and cones are located in your eyes.

FIGURE 2-7. Nerve cells in your eye help you to see light and color.

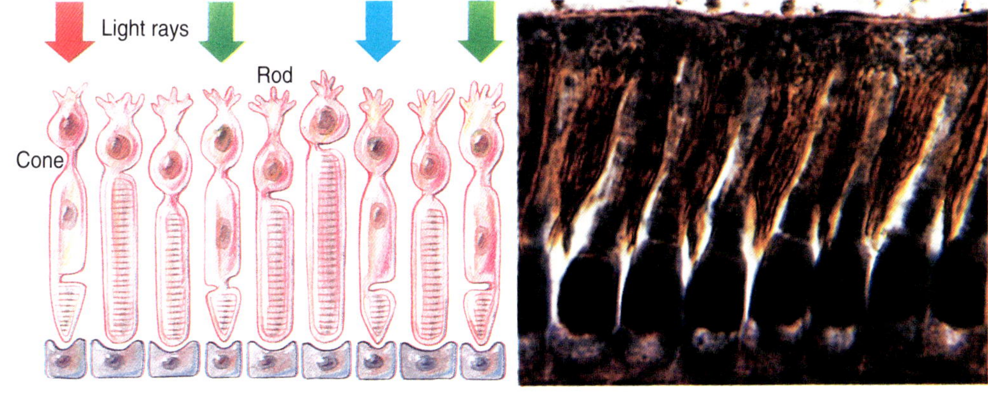

Concept Development

Using the Photo The image in Figure 2-7 is an electron photo micrograph of the cells in the retina of the eye that respond to different colors.

Student Text Questions How can they make all the colors? *All colors are achieved by adding and mixing the primary colors at various degrees of brightness.* Why are primary colors different in lights and paint? *Primary light colors are produced by light sources. Primary pigment colors are the result of reflection and absorption.*

Flex Your Brain Use the Flex Your Brain to have students explore COLORS.

Content Background

The light rays in the light spectrum are different lengths. The shortest rays are at the violet end of the spectrum. They bend the most when passed through a prism. The longest rays are at the red end of the spectrum; they bend the least.

Teacher F.Y.I.

Many people think that the color red will make a bull angry. But bulls are actually color blind. In a bullfight, the bull is charging at the movement of the cape or muleta, not its color.

OPTIONS

Multicultural Perspectives

Color is not only a part of the way people view the world. It also plays an important part in the way people think. Different colors have symbolic importance in many cultures. The Pueblo represent directions with color. White stands for the east, yellow usually stands for north, blue represents west, and red stands for south.

The Cherokee feel that colors represent important cultural ideas. Red means success, blue is trouble, black represents death, and white stands for happiness.

Concept Development

Theme Connection The theme that this section supports is energy. This lesson will develop an understanding of the relationship between the density of materials and the colors that we perceive. The point is made that without the color spectrum of light rays, we would see the world in black, white, and shades of black.

Student Text Question If persons can see yellow and blue but confuse red and green, which cones are they likely to be missing? *The missing cones are likely to be red and green.*

MAKING CONNECTIONS

Fine Arts

The Impressionist painters of the late 1800s took advantage of the way we see color. Instead of working with the outlines and details of objects, they made their images with rough patches of color. The Impressionists were especially interested in portraying different intensities of light. To do this, they developed a system of using complementary colors. Claude Monet and Pierre Renoir were two major Impressionists.

Postimpressionist Georges Seurat went even further. His technique was called pointillism. He used tiny dots of bright color instead of mixing colors on his palette. Up close to his painting, you can see each dot, but from a distance, the colors seem to merge.

How do we know?

Three kinds of cones

In the middle 1960s, George Wald and others showed for the first time that individual cone receptors of the eye react best to different light colors. Using a device that measures the amount of light absorbed by a tiny object, he found that single cone receptors absorbed more light of one color than light of other colors. He reasoned that if a cone absorbed light of a certain color, then that color would cause a reaction in the cone. By repeating his experiment on many different cones from the eye, he found that all cones can be classified into only three groups. One group absorbs blue light best, another absorbs green light best, and the third absorbs red. We now call these the blue, green, and red cones of the eye. These three kinds of cones are all we have and all we need to see all the colors of the spectrum.

TABLE 2-1. Types of Cones

Color Seen	Type of Cone Stimulated Most		
	Red	**Green**	**Blue**
Red	●		
Orange	●	•	
Yellow	●	●	
Green		●	
Blue			●
Violet	•	•	●

● = Heavy Stimulation • = Light Stimulation

cause one type of cone to respond more than another, as you can see in Table 2-1. Your brain receives the information from each type of cone and interprets this pattern of information in the nerve signals as colors. These three types of cones let you see the entire spectrum, from red through violet. Color-blind people lack one or more kinds of these cones. If a person can see yellow and blue but confuses red and green, which cones are they likely to be missing?

If the cones let you see everything in color, what's the purpose of the rods? Rods don't help you see color, but they're much more sensitive to light than cones are. Think about the way your room looks at night, with only a tiny bit of light coming in through the window. You can make out the shapes around you. But can you see colors? Your rods are at work, letting you see in light that's too dim for your cones.

MIXING COLORS WITH PIGMENTS

Colors appear the same to rods and cones whether they are produced from colored lights or colored paints. A blue that you see produced from mixing paints and a blue that you see from mixing lights may appear exactly the same. However, two very different processes produced the

Teacher F.Y.I.

The term *color blindness* was coined by Sir David Brewster in the early 1800s, but the problem was first described by John Dalton in 1794. Dalton's interest probably came from the fact that he himself was color blind.

PROGRAM RESOURCES

Teacher Classroom Resources

Transparency Masters, pages 9-12, and **Color Transparency,** number 3, Prism L2; number 4, Light Colors/Pigment Colors L2

Other Resources

Simon, Hilda. *The Magic of Color.* Wooster, OH: Lathrop, Norman Enterprises, 1981.

Color From Light, film, Churchill Films.

OPTIONS

Enrichment

Activity Divide the class into groups. Have each group pick an Impressionist or Postimpressionist artist. Have students research their chosen artist to find how that person used color. Have students find an example of the artist's work. Then have them try to imitate the artist's style using markers or watercolors. Suggest that they draw simple objects such as a piece of fruit or a flower.

same blue. Paints are examples of pigments—materials that absorb some colors and reflect others. You can make any pigment color by mixing different amounts of the three primary pigments of yellow, magenta, and cyan. A primary pigment's color depends on the color it reflects.

The key to understanding why mixing colored pigments is different from mixing colored lights lies in a very simple fact. When you mix lights, you are adding different light to the mixture. When you mix pigments, in a way, you are subtracting different colors from the mixture. More colors are actually being absorbed, and not reflected for you to see. Figure 2-5 shows what happens when you mix colored lights. Compare it with Figure 2-8, which shows what happens when you mix pigments. What do you see?

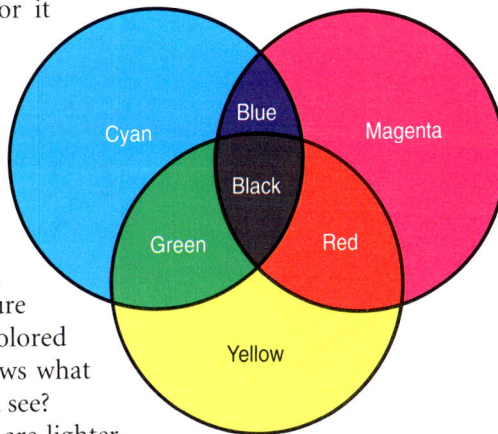

FIGURE 2-8. The three primary colors of pigment appear black when they are mixed.

Mix colored lights, and the resulting colors are lighter because they're closer to white—there are more different colors in the mix. If you mix pigments, the resulting colors are closer to black because they absorbed more colors—fewer different colors reach your eyes. But, just as you can dim and brighten three primary colored lights to produce any color, you can mix primary pigments in unequal amounts to produce any color. The results are the same—you can create the entire spectrum. Go to a hardware store that sells paint and look carefully at all the paint colors you can buy. All of these colors are produced by mixing only a small number of pigments.

LIGHT AND PIGMENTS TOGETHER

After school, you head for the mall to buy a sweater you want. You pay for it and hurry home. But when you pull it from the bag to show your family, it looks different. The colors are not quite the same. Then you realize that the store where you bought it had bright fluorescent lights. The room you're in now is lit by incandescent bulbs with more yellow light. You're relieved! When you wear the sweater at school tomorrow, it'll be seen under fluorescent light. It'll look just right.

SKILLBUILDER

COMPARING AND CONTRASTING

Cats have excellent vision in dim light and can see shapes very well. However, cats cannot distinguish one color from another very well, even in the brightest light. Describe how a cat's eye might be different from your eye. If you need help, refer to the **Skill Handbook** on page 653.

Concept Development

Using the Diagram The contrast of Figure 2-8 with Figure 2-5 should help students see the difference between colors from light sources and reflected colors. Especially point out the difference when all primary colors are mixed together.

Activity Making a color inertia disk helps students demonstrate the relationship between colors and how we see them. Each student should have a sheet of heavy white cardboard, crayons, a piece of 75-centimeter string or heavy thread, compass, scissors, and a ruler.

With a compass, draw a five-centimeter circle on the cardboard. Cut out the circle. Divide the circle into three equal pie-shaped wedges by drawing lines. Use the compass point to punch two holes about three–five millimeters off the center. Color one section blue, one red, and one green. Thread the string through one hole and back through the other and tie the ends together. Slide the circle to halfway between the ends. Holding each end of the string, twirl the disk.

Students should see the three colors blend into a grayish white. Their eyes are blending the colors.

Variations are to color one half one color and the other half another. Different colors will result. LEP L2

SKILLBUILDER

A cat's eyes probably have rods that are more sensitive to light but cones that do not perceive color as well as human eyes. L1

Enrichment

Activity The day before, tell students to wear colorful clothes. Set up a fluorescent light bulb and an incandescent bulb. Turn off the room lighting. Have students stand in front of one light and then the other. Discuss how each type of light affects the colors of their clothes. LEP

Meeting Individual Needs

Learning Disabled Students may not understand how our eyes combine individual colors into images. Locate a print or enlargement of a picture by Roy Lichtenstein. Lichtenstein created large-scale versions of comic book pictures by using many single dots of color. Have students examine the picture up close and then from a distance. Ask students to describe the appearance of the picture up close and from a distance. LEP

INVESTIGATE!

2-1 REFLECTING COLORED LIGHT

Time needed 10–15 minutes

Materials flashlight; blue, green, and red cellophane; white, blue, green, and red construction paper; scissors; rubber band

Thinking Processes
Organizing information, Making and using tables, Thinking critically, Observing and inferring, Practicing scientific methods, Forming a hypothesis

Purpose To show how both colored lights and pigments affect what we see.

Preparation Have materials out ahead of time. You may want to make sure all flashlights are in working order. If there are not enough flashlights, organize students into cooperative groups. You may want to have copies of the data table ready to save time.

Teaching the Activity

Troubleshooting Have students write on their data tables as they observe instead of waiting until the end of the activity. L1

Expected Outcomes

Students should see how colored light affects the colors they see.

Answers to Analyze/Conclude and Apply

1. The darkest colors are produced by the combinations of blue light on green paper, blue light on red, red light on green, green light on red.
2. The results closest to what was seen using white light are green on green, blue on blue, and red on red.
3. The combinations appear dark because the objects absorb the light and have little reflection.
4. the combination of blue on blue, for example, because most of the light is reflected
5. Red would be the worst for lighting a dinner. The green vegetables would appear almost black because a red filter absorbs green.

INVESTIGATE!

2-1 REFLECTING COLORED LIGHT

You can mix colors using lights, and you can mix colors using pigments. You can also use both. The colors you see around you are the result of both the pigments and the color of the light that hits them. The following activity will help you understand how colored light affects the color of your clothing—and everything else you see.

PROBLEM

How does colored light affect what you see?

MATERIALS

flashlight
blue, green, and red cellophane
white, blue, green, and red construction paper
rubber band

PROCEDURE

1. Copy the data table.
2. In a darkened room, shine the flashlight on each piece of colored paper. **Observe** the apparent color of each sheet of paper. Record the apparent color on the data table.

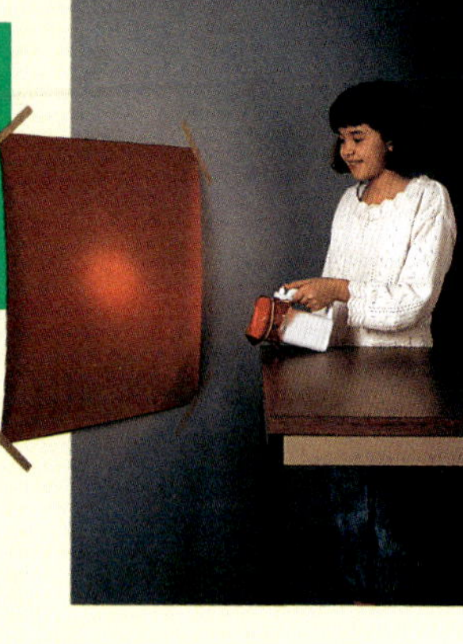

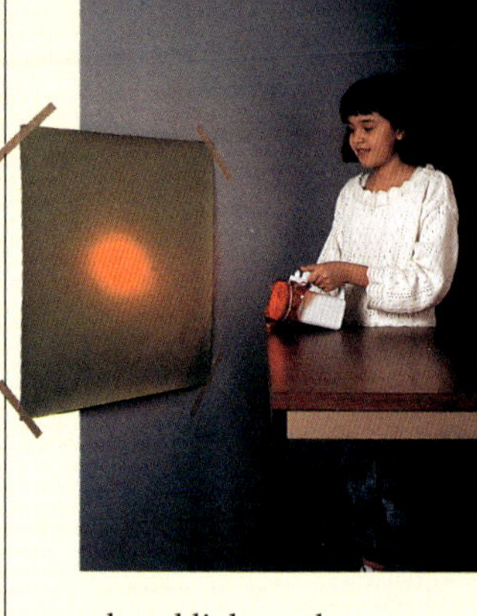

3. Cover the front of the flashlight with several layers of blue cellophane. Fasten the cellophane in place with the rubber band. Repeat Step 2.
4. Repeat Step 2 twice more, using red and green cellophane instead of blue.

ANALYZE

1. **Interpret** your data and determine what combination(s) of colored light and paper colors produced the darkest colors.
2. What combination(s) of colored light and paper color produced the results closest to what you saw using white light?

CONCLUDE AND APPLY

3. **Infer** why the combination(s) you noted for Question 1 might look darkest.
4. **Infer** why the combination(s) you noted for Question 2 might look most normal.
5. **Going Further**: What color of light in a dining room would make for the least appetizing dinner? Why?

DATA AND OBSERVATIONS

Sample data

	WHITE PAPER	BLUE PAPER	GREEN PAPER	RED PAPER
White light	white	blue	green	red
Blue light	blue	blue	black	black
Green light	green	black	green	black
Red light	red	black	black	red

PROGRAM RESOURCES

Teacher Classroom Resources

Activity Masters, pages 9-10, Investigate 2-1

Multicultural Activities, page 7, The Sun L1

OPTIONS

Enrichment

Activity Use a hand lens to examine some colored comics. You will see red areas made of red (magenta) dots, blue areas made of blue (cyan) dots and yellow areas, yellow dots. How are other colors made?
green—blue and yellow dots
orange—red and yellow dots
L1

The Investigate you just finished shows that the color of an object is determined by the light shining on it. Objects merely absorb or reflect certain colors of light or allow certain colors to pass through. Our idea of what something looks like depends upon the light we see it by. That shirt of your classmate's might be the greenest you've ever seen under white light. But how would it look under red light?

One of the applications of light and color is in theater and set design. Rather than designing two or three separate sets, set designers may change scenes by changing the lighting. In some cases, not only does the mood on stage change but the actual images change as the colors of the illuminating light changes. In this way, costume and set designers can obtain two entirely different scenes from one painted set and several different lights.

DID YOU KNOW?

Our eyes are most sensitive to the color yellow-green. That's why the preferred color for new emergency vehicles, such as fire trucks, is yellow-green.

FIGURE 2-9. Inventive use of lighting in theater can make one set look different from one scene to another.

Check Your Understanding

1. What colors make up white light?
2. How do transparent, opaque, and translucent objects differ? Give an example of each.
3. What is the difference between red pigment and a red light?
4. What color would you see if all types of cones in your eyes were strongly stimulated?
5. **APPLY:** What color would you see if you mixed yellow and blue light? Why? Yellow and blue pigments? Why?

3 Assess

Check for Understanding

To help students answer the Apply questions, review Figure 2-5 on page 44. Be sure students see the colors that result when primary colors of lights are combined. Then compare and contrast Figure 2-5 with Figure 2-8 on page 47.

Reteach

Obtain paper and some primary pigment paints from the art department. Have students work in groups and combine small amounts of various pigments to make other colors. For each color, have them describe which colors are reflected and which are absorbed. Be sure they mix all three primary pigments to produce black. Students should see that black pigment absorbs all light and reflects none. L1 LEP

Extension

Have students who have mastered this section try to describe a multicolored object without referring to the specific colors involved. L2

4 Close

Activity

Use the colored flashlights from Find Out. Have groups of students create their own light show by playing the lights in patterns around a darkened room. Give the groups five minutes to come up with a pattern to display to the class. LEP COOP LEARN

Answers to Check Your Understanding

1. all colors, but a minimum of green, blue, and red
2. Transparent objects allow at least one color to pass through window (glass), opaque objects allow no light to pass through (rocks), and translucent objects allow some through, but not enough to allow a clear view (stained glass window).
3. Red pigment has no "redness" of its own; it reflects red light. Red light is actually red.
4. white
5. White; yellow light is a mixture of red and green light. The three together make white; pigments: you see green because yellow absorbs mostly blue, and blue absorbs mostly red; they both reflect green.

Section 2-3

PREPARATION

Concepts Developed

The previous section focused on visible light and opaque, translucent, and transparent materials. This section illustrates how a mirror works. It also focuses on the relationship between light and the evenness (or unevenness) of surfaces. Finally, an understanding of the refraction of light is developed.

Planning the Lesson

In planning your lesson on reflection and refraction, refer to the Chapter Organizer on pages 34A-B for timing suggestions, resources, and additional materials that will help you in your presentation of the lesson concepts. For adequate development of the concepts presented in this section, we recommend that students do the Find Out on page 52, and Explore on page 53.

1 MOTIVATE

Demonstration Place a mirror on the bottom of an old fish tank, and add half a tank of water. Add a small amount of milk or fluorescent dye. Shine a narrow, intense beam of light on the mirror, and note the ray of reflected light. Move the beam to show different angles of incidence and reflection.

2 TEACH

Tying to Previous Knowledge

Ask students how portions of their bodies look when they are in a swimming pool. They probably will say that they look shorter and distorted. This is because the speed of light in water is different from the speed of light in air, causing light to refract and distort the image.

2-3 Reflection and Refraction

OBJECTIVES

In this section, you will

- discuss the different types of reflection;
- describe what happens to light during refraction;
- examine how refraction separates light into the colors of the spectrum.

KEY SCIENCE TERMS

refraction

WHEN LIGHT BOUNCES AND BENDS

We've seen a lot of reflected light so far—your reflection in the mirror, the light reflected off clothes, and the various colored lights you reflected off sheets of paper. In this section, you'll take a closer look at what happens when light bounces and when light is made to bend.

Light reflecting from your mirror isn't the same as light bouncing off a sheet of white paper. In both cases, all colors are reflected. But you can see yourself in a mirror. You can't see yourself in the paper.

If you were holding a mirror in place of this book, like the person in Figure 2-10(a), some of the light around you would reflect off you into the mirror, then reflect right back to you. Light reflected from your face hits the smooth, flat surface of the mirror and is bounced back in one direction. You receive a pretty accurate picture of yourself from a mirror. When a reflection is clearly defined and looks just like the object, it is called a regular reflection. Smooth surfaces, such as mirrors, produce regular reflections.

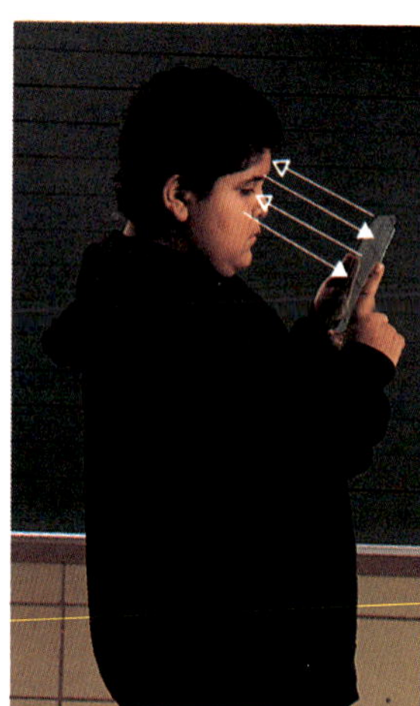

FIGURE 2-10. Light reflecting from a mirror reflects in one direction (a). As light reflects from an object such as a book, the light reflects in many directions (b).

What's happening now, as you read this page, is more like Figure 2-10 (b). Light is reflecting from your face into this page, just as it would into a mirror. But when the light hits the relatively rough paper, it scatters, bouncing every which way. When reflected light is scattered in many directions, it's called a diffuse reflection.

Let's take a closer look at regular reflections produced by mirrors.

PROGRAM RESOURCES

Teacher Classroom Resources

Study Guide, page 12

Concept Mapping, page 10, Light

Activity Masters, pages 11-12, Investigate 2-2

Critical Thinking/Problem Solving, page 10, Communication Innovations

Multicultural Activities, page 8, Light Phenomena 

INVESTIGATE!

2-2 MIRROR REFLECTIONS

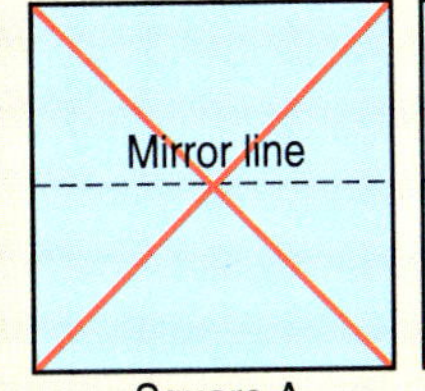

Square A

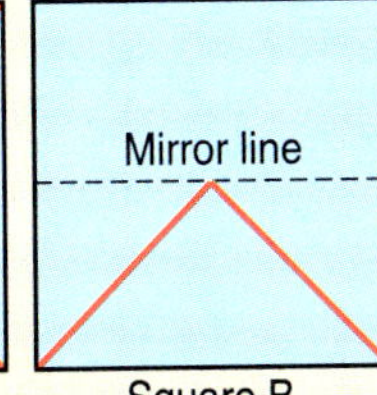

Square B

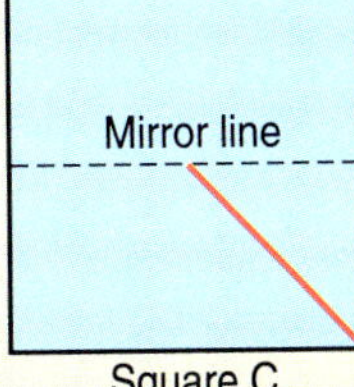

Square C

When you see light reflected from a mirror, you see an entire object—your head, a car, or a chair for example. You probably don't consider what happens to light coming from individual spots on the object or how that light reflects in a mirror. You can easily discover how mirrors reflect objects in this activity.

PROBLEM

How are objects reflected in a mirror?

MATERIALS

pocket mirror
ruler
unruled paper

PROCEDURE

Note: Always hold the mirror perpendicular to the mirror line in all of the following steps.

1. Hold the mirror on the mirror line in Square A. Where does the diagonal line that extends from the lower left-hand corner of Square A appear to be in the reflection? Write down your answer. Answer the same question for the diagonal line that extends from the lower right-hand corner.
2. Hold the mirror on the mirror line in Square B. Where do the diagonal lines that extend from the corners of the square appear to be in the reflection? Record your answer.
3. On paper, draw a copy of Square C. Draw a line in the upper half where you think the image of the line on the lower half of the square would appear. Now put the mirror on the mirror line. Where does the image of the diagonal line appear to be in the reflection? Record your observation.

ANALYZE

1. Did your **prediction** match what you **observed** in Step 3 by matching the mirror image of the diagonal line in Square C with your drawing? If it did not, why do you think you drew it another way?
2. How are lines reflected in a pocket mirror?

CONCLUDE AND APPLY

3. Would you **predict** the same kind of results if the mirror were not as smooth? If you used smooth aluminum foil? If you used crumpled foil?
4. **Going Further**: Have a friend sit next to you. Draw a red dot on the bottom right-hand diagonal line of your copy of Square C.

   Hold the mirror perpendicular to the mirror line. Use your pencil point to touch the surface of the mirror where the dot appears. Hold it there. Have your friend do the same with a pencil point. Are your pencil points on the same spot on the mirror? If not, try to explain why this is so.

INVESTIGATE!

2-2 MIRROR REFLECTIONS

Time needed 5–7 minutes

Materials pocket mirror, ruler, unruled paper, pencil

Thinking Processes Thinking critically, Observing and inferring, Predicting

Purpose To observe how mirrors reflect objects

Preparation Be sure to tell students to bring square or rectangular mirrors.

Teaching the Activity

Troubleshooting Students may not know what *perpendicular* means. Explain or draw a picture on the board of a right angle so that you may demonstrate perpendicular lines. L1 LEP

Expected Outcomes

Students will observe that objects appear in reverse or upside down in a mirror.

Answers to Procedure

1. Begins upper left-hand corner to lower center, begins upper right-hand corner to lower center.
2. Lines appear to begin at upper left-hand and upper right-hand corners and meet at the bottom left of center.
3. Extends from upper right-hand corner to lower center.

Answers to Analyze/Conclude and Apply

1. If the student was not correct, the answers will vary.
2. Lines are reflected in reverse.
3. If the mirror were not as smooth, the direction of reflection would remain the same but the line would be wavy. With smooth foil, the reflection would be fainter. With crumpled foil, the reflection would be dispersed.
4. The pencil points should be in different places. Each person is looking at the mirror from a different angle and so will perceive the reflection differently.

OPTIONS

Meeting Individual Needs

Learning Disabled Some students may not be able to distinguish left from right. A variation on Investigate may help them. This activity will probably require a helper.

First, make clear which hand is which. Have the helper hold up the mirror as directed. Have the student use the right index finger to touch the diagonal line on the right. (You may wish to mark the fingernail with a dot using a magic marker to further aid students.) Then have the student look at the mirror to see where the reflection of the index finger is. This will help him or her identify right in the reflection. Repeat the procedure with the left hand.

It may also help to have the student follow the diagonal lines with an index finger instead of simply by sight. LEP

FIND OUT!

How does light reflect on smooth and bumpy surfaces?

Time needed 3–4 minutes

Materials square of aluminum foil (about 13 cm × 13 cm), pencil

Thinking Processes Thinking critically, Observing and inferring

Purpose To demonstrate the difference between regular and diffuse reflection

Teaching Strategies

Discussion To help students understand what they see in the crumpled foil, use Figure 2-12. Point out the different directions the reflected light takes. Also remind students that the eye sees only light rays directed at it. You might want to draw an example on the board of how the eye perceives direct and diffused lines.  L1

Expected Outcomes

Students should be able to discover and explain the difference in reflection from a smooth and a bumpy surface.

Conclude and Apply

1. no
2. because the reflection is diffused by the rough surface

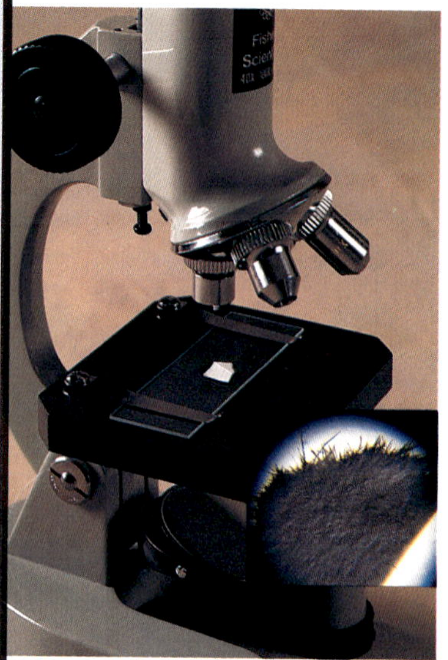

FIGURE 2-11. When light is reflected from a rough surface, the reflection is diffuse.

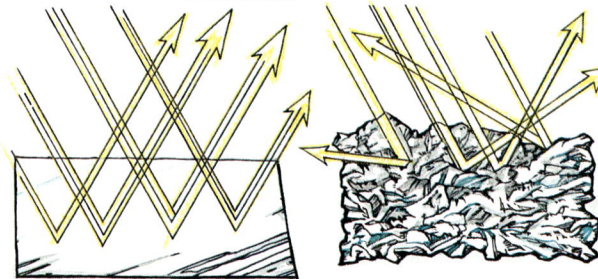

In the Investigate, you looked at the nature of the reflection from a mirror. You saw that the light from an object that reaches a mirror bounces off in a very orderly way. You see the reflected image as well as you see the object itself. The mirror reflects light this way because the surface of the mirror is very smooth. It reflects light back to your eye in orderly, straight lines. The page of this book appears to have a smooth surface. Why can't you see yourself? If you were to look at a piece of this page under a microscope, you would see that it's not really as smooth as it seems. The surface is actually quite bumpy, as shown in Figure 2-11. What happens when light hits a bumpy surface?

FIND OUT!

How does light reflect on smooth and bumpy surfaces?

You can see for yourself with this simple experiment. Make a piece of shiny aluminum foil as smooth as you can. Look into it. How well can you see yourself? Crumple the foil, then spread it out again. How well can you see yourself now?

Pick a spot on the crumpled aluminum foil that has a relatively large smooth area. Hold the point of your pen or pencil over that area.

Conclude and Apply

1. Can you see your pen or pencil point reflected?
2. Why or why not?

FIGURE 2-12. A flat metal foil can produce a regular reflection. Once the foil is crumpled, the reflection is different.

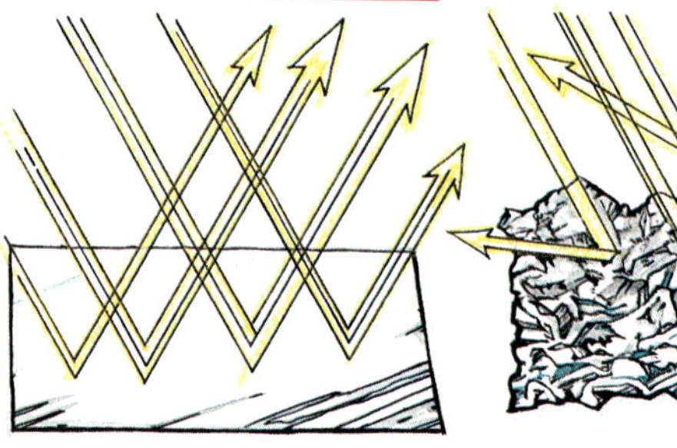

Your aluminum foil started out like a mirror—smooth enough to send back a reflection to your face. When you crumpled it, all the bumps and bends turned the foil from one mirror to thousands of tiny mirrors as shown in Figure 2-12. Each surface reflects, but light bounces off each tiny surface in straight lines in different directions. The foil first produced a regular reflection. After crumpling, it produced a diffuse reflection.

OPTIONS

Meeting Individual Needs

Visually Impaired Fill a glass of water almost full. Put in one straw to see when the bend in light takes place. Cut off the straw at the bottom so that the flex stands at the water line. Flex the straw so that a bend is evident. Cut off the second straw so that it will cap the first. The flex in the second straw should be level with the top of the glass. Bend the flex in the direction light will be refracted.

Explain to students that the straws will feel the way the pencil in water looks. Have students study the straw by touch in the water. Also have them compare by touch a straight straw and the bent straw.

REFRACTION

We started out this chapter by talking about how light always travels in straight lines. Now you've made light change direction by bouncing it off objects—by reflecting it. This doesn't mean that we were wrong. Light always does travel in straight lines, but you can make it change direction.

Are there other ways to make light change direction besides reflection? Find out for yourself in the next activity.

EXPLORE!

How does light refract?

Fill a clear glass with water. Place a pencil in the glass. The pencil should be long enough so that it isn't completely covered with water. Look at the glass from the side. Does the pencil look the same above and below the water line? Describe its appearance.

Do you think that the water is doing something to the light to make the pencil appear in a different location below the water? Do you think the glass may also have an effect on the light?

In the Explore, you saw that your view of a pencil changes when it is put in water. It appears that light can change as it moves from one substance, such as air, to another, such as water. In fact, you change light every time you pour yourself a glass of water. When the light ray moves from air to water, the light bends. When the light ray moves back from water to air, it bends back to its original angle. The result is that the light ray emerges in a different place than you'd expect it to be.

In the activity, the light rays carrying the pencil's likeness bent. That made the pencil appear broken. The process of bending light is called **refraction**. Keep in mind

SKILLBUILDER

COMPARING AND CONTRASTING

Compare and contrast reflection and refraction. Provide an example of each. If you need help, refer to the **Skill Handbook** on page 653.

Concept Development

Theme Connection Students have learned that light travels in straight lines and is reflected. The theme of stability and change is evident as students observe how different surfaces affect the direction in which light is reflected.

Discussion Have students name materials other than foil and mirrors that are examples of regular reflection. Examples may be various metals and water. Be sure students understand that the materials must be smooth in order to see the connection of a smooth surface and regular reflection.

EXPLORE!

How does light refract?

Time needed 3–5 minutes

Materials clear glass of water, pencil

Thinking Processes Thinking critically, Recognizing cause and effect

Purpose To show that light can change directions

Teaching the Activity

Troubleshooting Be sure that glasses are clean, to prevent other distortions. Do not fill the glass entirely. Allow students to see refraction caused by glass and refraction caused by water. L1

Expected Outcome

Students will see that the pencil appears broken at the water line.

Answers to Questions

The pencil looks different, as though in two parts. Yes. Yes.

Enrichment

Activity Students will need a shallow cup, a coin, and water. Place a coin in the bottom of a cup. Have one person hold the cup at about chest level of the other person. Move the cup until the coin is just hidden from view from the partner. Very slowly pour water into the cup. The coin will become visible. What happened? *The light reflected from the coin bends from the normal as it emerges from the water. Because the ray of light reaching the eye is lowered, the image of the coin appears higher in the water than the coin is.*

SKILLBUILDER

Both are ways that light changes direction. Reflection is light bouncing off surfaces. Example: a mirror. Refraction is light bending when it travels from one medium to another. Example: pencil in water in Explore. L1

3 Assess

Check for Understanding

To help students answer the Apply question, point out that a light ray from another room would bounce off several walls before arriving at your eye.

Reteach

Have students drop a washer into a glass of water. Then try to put a pencil through the hole in the washer. It is difficult to hit the hole. Explain that the light reflected from the washer bends away from the normal as it emerges from the water. Because the light ray that reaches your eye is lowered, the image of the washer appears higher in the water than the washer actually is. Students should see that refraction causes the washer to appear in a different place. LEP

Extension

Have students who have mastered this section research how the speed of light affects refraction. Have them look up the speed of light in air, water, and glass. Have students identify a pattern in the change in speed and direction of the light ray as it crosses a boundary. *an increase in speed; light bends away from the normal; a decrease in speed; light bends toward the normal* L2

4 Close

Activity

Ask students to hold their books up to a mirror and try to read them. Then ask them to describe the difference between how the photos and words are different when viewed in the mirror. Ask them to discuss what happens to the left/right orientation. What happens to the top/bottom orientation? Ask students to explain the differences in terms of what they have learned in this chapter. L1

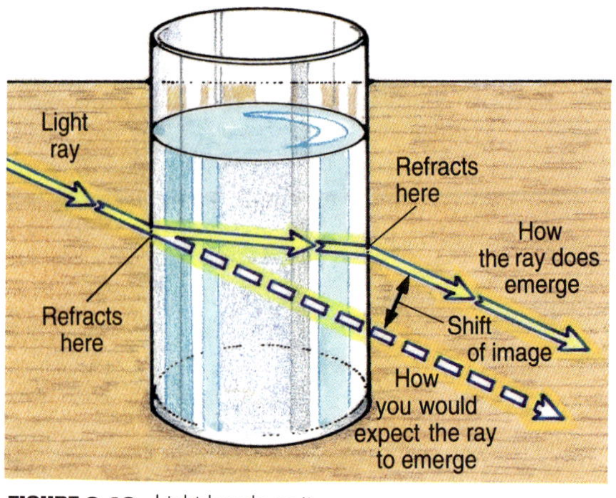

FIGURE 2-13. Light bends as it moves from air to water and again as it moves from water to air.

that light does not travel in curved pathways. Even though its direction may change, it does so by changing the angle of the straight line.

Remember how you used a prism to create a spectrum? That, too, was an example of refraction. Some colors of light bend more than others. As a result, the colors all spread out when they emerge from the glass prism.

The next time you see a rainbow you may think of a glass prism. Think also about how light bends as it moves through different materials. The way light reflects and bends helps us to see the world in mirrors and to observe the variety of color around us.

FIGURE 2-14. Light bends as it passes from one substance to another. Some colors bend more than others, as shown here.

Check Your Understanding

1. Draw diagrams showing how light is reflected from a smooth car bumper and from a crumpled bumper. Label the diagrams *diffuse reflection* and *regular reflection.*
2. Draw a diagram of light rays bending as they move from one material to another.
3. Draw diagrams of a beam of white light and a beam of red light striking a prism, traveling through the prism, and then falling on a sheet of paper. Explain the difference.
4. **APPLY:** Draw a diagram showing how you might be able to see light from a room around a corner.

Answers to Check Your Understanding

1, 2, 4. Drawings should follow information in the section.
3. Because white light consists of all colors, it will emerge as a spectrum. Red light will emerge only as a single beam of red light.

PROGRAM RESOURCES

Teacher Classroom Resources
Take Home Activities, page 7, Optic Fibers L1
Laboratory Manual, pages 7-8, Producing a Spectrum L2; pages 9-10, Refraction of Light
Other Resources
Cassidy, John. *Explorabook: A Kid's Science Museum in a Book.* Palo Alto, CA: The Exploratorium, Klutz Press, 1991.

EXPANDING YOUR VIEW

CONTENTS

A CLOSER LOOK

WHY THE SKY IS BLUE AND SUNSETS ARE RED

Reflection and refraction are responsible for many of the colorful effects we see around us. Some, such as rainbows, are rare enough to be a new delight each time we see one. Others, such as the blue of our sky, are things we're so familiar with that we don't often think about them.

Let's think for a moment about the blue sky you see outside. By now, you know that your blue jeans are blue because they reflect blue light. What accounts for the color of the sky?

Particles in the atmosphere scatter violet and blue light from the sun. Green and yellow light scatter little in the atmosphere. Orange and red scatter even less. The diagram shows more why we see blue during the day.

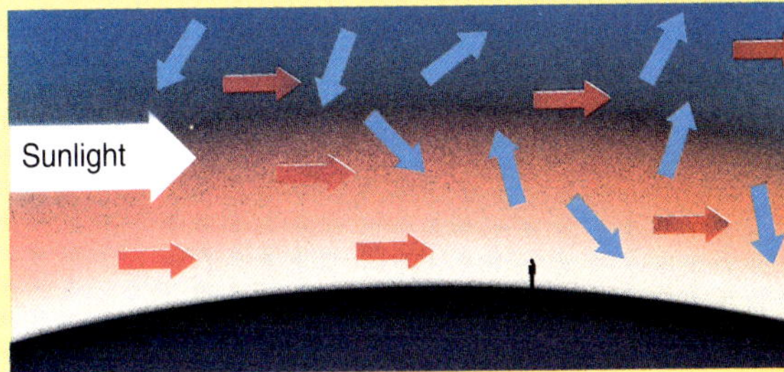

At sunrise and sunset, when the sun is low in the sky, its light passes through more of the atmosphere close to Earth's surface. This thicker layer of the lower atmosphere contains particles large enough to scatter some of the green and yellow light as well as the blue and violet. What reaches your eye? Right! Reds and oranges. That's why sunsets and sunrises look reddish.

YOU TRY IT!

Why is the sky blue? You can get some idea of why the sky is blue by making a simple model of the atmosphere. Fill a clear glass with water and add two to five drops of homogenized whole milk. Darken the room and shine a flashlight through the glass. What color do you see coming through the glass? Look at the light coming out of the top of the glass. It has been scattered (reflected away) by the milk particles. What color is it?

EXPANDING YOUR VIEW

Using Expanding Your View

Assign one or more of these excursions to expand students' understanding of light and color and how it applies to other sciences and other subjects. You may assign these as individual or small group activities.

A CLOSER LOOK

Purpose A Closer Look expands Section 2-3 by explaining how the refraction and reflection of light in the atmosphere account for different colors of the sky at different times.

Content Background Even though it is not visible, Earth's atmosphere is not empty. The two bottom layers, the troposphere and the stratosphere, are dense with molecules of air, primarily oxygen and nitrogen. As the white light of the sun beams down, it passes through this maze of molecules. The short wavelength of blue light is the right size to be reflected off air molecules, causing the scattering effect. Near the surface of Earth, water molecules and other large particles make the air more dense. The longer reddish wavelengths are reflected. The more water molecules and organic particles such as soot and dust that are present, the more long wavelengths will be reflected. Sunsets are red because the more slanted rays late in the day pass through more of the dusty lower atmosphere and are therefore scattered more.

Teaching Strategies Have pairs of students make enlarged diagrams of what the atmosphere looks like as it reflects short blue wavelengths and as it reflects long red wavelengths.

Going Further Students can work in small groups to find out how air pollution affects the colors seen in the sky. Have students make a list of types of air pollution. These should include auto exhaust and factory emissions. Have each group find color pictures that show these types of pollution. What effect does pollution have on the color of the sky? COOP LEARN

Have students brainstorm about the following questions.

- Why would scientists wonder what makes the sky blue or sunsets and sunrises reddish?
- Should people be concerned about major changes in what colors are seen in the sky? COOP LEARN

Answers to

YOU TRY IT

1. blue
2. red and orange

LIFE SCIENCE CONNECTION

Purpose The Life Science Connection further develops the concepts of color presented in Section 2-2 by explaining how people have used colors occurring in the plant world to enhance their lives.

Content Background A variety of chemical structures in plants react to the energy of light. These chemical structures result in the many colors seen in plants. A common chemical that reacts to sunlight is chlorophyll, which produces the greens in plants. Because natural dyes are made from vegetable solutions, the colors produced come from the interaction of plant chemicals and sunlight that occurred when the plant was alive. Unlike most paint pigments, which are made from minerals, natural dyes fade fairly quickly, especially if exposed to sunlight. Mordants are chemical compounds that prolong the life of the color.

Teaching Strategies Tell students that production of synthetic dyes began in 1855. Ask why a synthetic dye would be more useful than a natural dye for many purposes.

Troubleshooting When doing the You Try It activity, be sure students do not use their bare hands for crushing. The oil on their fingers will affect the solvency. Have students use mortars and pestles to grind the leaves or flowers. Plastic bags make a fine, even breakdown of the material difficult, especially if it is dried.

Answers to YOU TRY IT

6. The color will probably wash out.
7. The fabric dyed with the vinegar mordant will retain more of its color.

NATURAL DYES

The brightly colored fabrics that your clothes are made from are usually created by using synthetic dyes. Long before these dyes existed, however, people dyed fabrics with natural dyes that they made by boiling herbs, flowers, tea leaves, vegetable roots, and tree bark in water.

To dye natural fabrics such as cotton, linen, silk, and wool, you can use strong solutions made by boiling vegetables such as beets or spinach, parts of plants such as tea leaves or wildflowers, and barks of various trees. Many of these are pictured here. The hues will vary depending on several factors. These factors include the strength of the dye solution, the soil in which the plant grew, whether fresh or dried plant parts were used, and the way the fabric was treated before it was dyed.

The colors from natural dyes are not as bright as those from chemical dyes. They are much more subtle and muted—often described as "earth tones."

Here are some of the colors you can get from common plants:

- reds: oregano leaves, tea leaves, beet roots, fruits of the lipstick tree (shown here)
- yellow: barberry stems and roots, goldenrod blooms, saffron crocus blooms (shown here), onion skins
- violet: hibiscus flowers, oregano leaves
- blue: cornflowers, hollyhock flowers, wild indigo branches
- green: onion skins, sorrel leaves, spinach leaves, dyer's broom tops

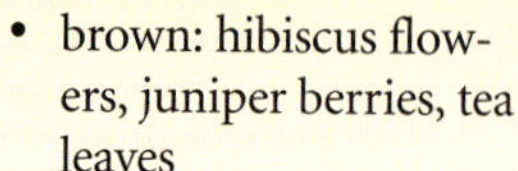

- brown: hibiscus flowers, juniper berries, tea leaves
- gray: blackberry shoots
- black: barberry leaves, yellow dock roots

Before dyeing a fabric, it must be treated with a dye-setting compound called a mordant. This makes the dye stay in the fabric. Without a mordant, the fabric's color would easily wash or fade away. Alum, ammonia, and vinegar are some mordants.

YOU TRY IT!

Make your own dye by following these directions.

1. Select one of the common plants listed. Use from one-half to one cup of leaves or flowers.
2. Place the plants in a plastic bag. Crush them by squeezing and rolling them between your fingers.
3. Place the crushed plants in one cup of water and heat the water to a gentle boil. Allow the mixture to simmer gently until most of the color has been removed from the leaves.
4. Remove from the heat and allow the mixture to cool. Then filter it through a strainer, collecting the liquid.
5. Place a piece of worn-out cotton sheet in the dye. Stir it until color absorbs evenly in the material.
6. Wring out the fabric and allow it to dry. Then try washing it. Does the color come out?
7. Soak another piece of fabric in vinegar, wring it out, and allow it to dry. Then repeat Steps 5 and 6. Is there a difference?

Going Further Students can work in groups to find out how synthetic dyes are made and how they are used. Divide the students into five groups and assign research into azo dyes, vat dyes, sulphur dyes, reactive dyes, and disperse dyes. Encourage students to find examples of each type of dye either in photographs or actual swatches of cloth. COOP LEARN

Tell students that during the 1960s, many young people wanted to go back to more natural ways of living. Part of their alternative life-styles involved weaving and dying their own cloth. Suggest that students find magazines from the late sixties and seventies such as Life and Time. What examples can students find of attempts to use natural cloths and dyes in a creative manner?

SCIENCE AND SOCIETY

LIGHT AND COLOR IN OUR LIVES

Most of the time, we just take light for granted. It may take the loss of electrical power for us to realize how important light is to our everyday life—and not just so that we can see. More and more, researchers are finding that light is necessary for our mental and physical well-being. Light can affect how we feel about our surroundings, how we feel about others, and how well we do our work.

While people respond differently, in general researchers have found that the brighter the room, the better the performance. Brightness generally seems to improve performance until the light reaches the point of glare. At this point, people tend to feel tired, irritable, or bored.

In meetings, people who want to be listened to tend to sit in the more brightly lit areas, while quieter people sit in shadowed areas. Our attraction to light has been demonstrated in various experiments. For example, people entering a cafeteria more often select seats in which they are facing the available light. When the light source was changed, even people who had a favorite seat changed it again to face the light.

The brightness of light also affects the sound level. The level of conversation in a brightly lit room or restaurant is greater by a factor of ten than that in a more dimly lit room.

EXPANDING YOUR VIEW

SCIENCE AND SOCIETY

Purpose Science and Society further develops Section 2-2 by giving examples of how the light and color we perceive affects the way we act.

Content Background Charles Fere conducted experiments that show that there is a physical response to color. Muscles become more active and blood circulation increases when a person is exposed to colored lights. The stimulus increases as the lights range from blue through green, yellow, and orange to red. Kurt Goldstein, a neurologist, also found that people react more excitedly to colors with long wavelengths than to colors with short wavelengths. These findings seem to support the associations most people have with various colors. Red is thought of as hot and lively. Orange is cheerful. Greens and blues are thought of as more peaceful and soothing. So experts suggest that certain colors should be used to fit the situation. Red surroundings are good for short-term stimulation. Green is good for calm concentration. For exercising, orange is best. A combination of blues and reds will make a soothing environment for students while also keeping them awake. A completely white environment is not recommended. It is too sterile. Bright light in a white room can make a person both physically and mentally tired.

Studies have shown that all animals, including humans, need sunlight in order to live healthy productive lives. Sunlight, especially ultraviolet light, affects both physical and emotional health. A group of Russian researchers discovered that workers who were exposed to doses of ultraviolet light performed better than workers who were not. People are more active and happy when they have sun in their lives.

EXPANDING YOUR VIEW

Content Background Sunlight stimulates the pineal gland, which produces melatonin. Lack of light impairs the control of the gland's function. Dr. Alfred Lewy was one of the first to treat the depression caused by SAD by using high levels of light to readjust the production of melatonin. Lewy suggests that all people would benefit by an early morning dose of sunlight.

Teaching Strategies Ask students how they feel about the color of the classroom. Does it make them comfortable and relaxed? Or does it make them tense? Ask students to explain their reactions.

Activity Have students work in pairs to examine various rooms in the school such as the study hall, cafeteria, library, and main office. Have them describe the color scheme in each room. Ask students to determine what effect the colors have on students, faculty, and staff. Then have each pair write a letter to the principal recommending changes and explaining how the changes could help the school.

Answers to WHAT DO YOU THINK?

Answers will vary depending on how students feel. Students should be able to relate colors to moods and emotions. They probably will say that the colors in a fast-food restaurant are intended to make people cheerful and eager to eat. The rooms they select will vary.

One reason for this is that when people enter a brightly lit room, they tend to gather in larger groups, while dimmer rooms lend themselves to smaller groups and quieter conversations.

Perhaps even more important is the effect of light on our health. Some people suffer from a form of depression that seems to get worse in the fall and winter. During the dark hours of the night, the brains of animals and humans secrete a chemical known as melatonin (mel uh TOH nuhn). This chemical affects many of the body's functions, including temperature and mood. At dawn, the brain stops producing this chemical. During the fall and winter, there are more hours of darkness and, therefore, more melatonin is produced. For some people, this causes them to feel very tired and sometimes depressed. One form of this condition is known as Seasonal Affective Disorder (SAD).

Physicians have had considerable success in treating the symptoms of SAD by having people extend their daylight hours. The patient sits under very bright light—about three times brighter than normal—for several hours early in the morning. This seems to change the body's rhythms and makes the patient feel better.

A new light-activated medication is also being used in the treatment of AIDS. Patients take the drug, which is absorbed into the body. Exposure to light changes the medication to an active form, which seems to produce improvement in some AIDS patients.

Babies with jaundice are treated by shining blue light on them. For some reason, this causes the chemicals that produce the jaundice to be broken down and washed out of their bodies.

Color also has important effects on the way that we feel and on our actions. Colors like orange tend to make us feel more active and may affect the amount that we eat. Blue is a more calming color. Research in gambling casinos shows that gamblers tend to bet more and select riskier bets when sitting under red light than under blue light.

WHAT DO YOU THINK?

Why is it important for you to understand the effect of color and light on your own actions and attitudes? The next time you're in a fast-food restaurant, take a look at the colors around you. What mood do you think the owners want you in? Are there rooms where you feel very comfortable or uncomfortable? Do you think that color or light might have something to do with how you feel or how much work you can get done in those rooms?

Going Further Have student groups make up lists of phrases and sentences in which people use color to express an emotion. For example, "I really feel blue today". Ask them to discuss the emotions that colors seem to represent.

Researchers have discovered that people who work at night tend to be less efficient than day workers. Night workers also have more accidents and more health problems than people who get more exposure to sunlight. For students who want to learn more about the physical and emotional problems night workers face, direct them to:

Dr. C. Czeizler
Harvard Medical School
Cambridge, MA 01021

Students interested in light as part of AIDS therapy can write to:

Damien Center
1350 N. Pennsylvania St.
Indianapolis, IN 46202

Art CONNECTION

SEEING THINGS DIFFERENTLY

If you look closely at a patch of grass or the trunk of a tree or the petals of a rose, you will see that what appears from a distance to be a solid color is actually made up of many colors. The patch of green grass may have specks of blue, yellow, white, or gray in it. The brown tree trunk probably has flecks of red, gray, or black in it. The pink rose petals may have specks of red, blue, white, or yellow in them.

Early painters tried to copy their subjects exactly. They wanted the pink rose in the painting to look exactly like the pink rose on the bush. During the 1870s and 1880s, a group of artists decided that they were more interested in the impression of a rose than its exact look. As a result, they were called *Impressionists.*

These artists used color to reach their goals. They did not give objects firm outlines or fill in large areas of their canvasses with solid colors as others had done. Instead, they noticed that when they looked at a rose or a person, there were not distinct outlines, but a gradual blending of colors as one shade touched another. They showed the light as it affected colors, so that sometimes the same pink rose was pale, other times very vivid.

Claude Monét was one of the best-known Impressionist painters. He is famous for his ability to show how light played among the flowers in his garden. He painted many pictures of the same flowers in the same place, but they were all different, depending on the angle of the sun, the time of day, and the season of the year. Each of these things affects the color of the light that we see and the color of the flowers in that light. One of Monet's paintings entitled *Water Lilies* is shown here.

The paintings of the Impressionists are very valuable today, and people consider them some of the most beautiful art ever created. Although they do not contain every detail of their subject, the paintings do give an "impression" of the subject that includes the feelings that the artist had about the subject.

YOU TRY IT!

1. Look out the window or go outside and look at an area of trees, grass, and flowers. Do you see every detail that makes up the landscape? Do you see every vein in the leaves or cracks in the tree bark? Or do you get an "impression" of the scene?
2. Look at books in the library that contain reproductions of paintings by Impressionists. Can you see how important color and light are to these painters?

EXPANDING YOUR VIEW

ART CONNECTION

Purpose Art Connection reinforces Sections 2-2 and 2-3 by describing how a certain group of artists, the Impressionists, used their perception of light to create paintings.

Content Background Impressionism is important in art history because it made a change from the traditional tonal mode of painting. In tonal painting, color was subordinated to light and dark patterns. Impressionist painters concentrated on chromatic richness and intensity, so shadows were portrayed as colors instead of shades of gray. The Impressionist painters were scientists in their own right because they realized how changes in light also affected a viewer's perception of an object. Although these artists lived long before many scientific discoveries about the nature of light, their work revealed a world of colored light. The artists' eyes discovered and their brushes proved that individual bits of color come together in the human brain to form a single image.

Teaching Strategies Have students work in pairs to paint the world. Assign each pair an object in the room. One student should try to render the object at one time of day. The partner should attempt it at another time. Have students use loose strokes of colored crayons to show what they see. Then compare the two drawings. COOP LEARN

Going Further Tell students the saying, "Beauty is in the eye of the beholder." Then tell them that the same is true for all that they see. The objects students see exist in whatever shape and color they take, but the way people perceive them can make a difference. Ask students to describe what they saw as they were coming to school. *Some may say they saw objects. Others might be able actually to describe the objects. Of these, some will probably describe some of the same objects in different ways.* COOP LEARN

Some students may want to know more about the Impressionist painters. They can write a letter of inquiry to art museums. One museum that has an excellent collection of Monet's paintings is:

The Museum of the Art Institute of Chicago
South Michigan Ave. and East Adams St.
Chicago, IL 62220

Answers to YOU TRY IT

1. Students should say they have a general impression, not a detailed view.
2. Answers should respond to the variety of colors and the intensity of light portrayed.

EXPANDING YOUR VIEW

TECHNOLOGY CONNECTION

Purpose This Technology Connection relates infrared radiation as a part of the electromagnetic spectrum to the nature of light, as is discussed in section 2-1.

Content Background Infrared radiation is used quite commonly in everyday life. For example, measurement of the body's emission of infrared radiation helps doctors make some medical diagnoses. A thermogram, which records varying amounts of infrared radiation as different colors, can be produced by measuring the infrared radiation given off by different body parts. Tumors can sometimes be detected in a thermogram because they are warmer than the healthy tissue around them.

Because infrared radiation raises the temperature of matter, it can be used to warm and dry objects. Infrared lamps are used in some restaurants to keep cooked food hot until it is served. Some auto paint shops use infrared radiation to dry car finishes.

Teaching Strategies Invite an insulation specialist to speak to the class about the use of thermograms to detect heat loss in the home. An optional activity would be to use the thermograms themselves and have students determine what colors represent large heat loss and what colors represent minimal heat loss.

Answers to

WHAT DO YOU THINK?

No; the money can be better spent on other programs. Yes; much of the knowledge gained cannot easily be gained elsewhere. Accept any reasonable answer and explanation.

TECHNOLOGY CONNECTION

INFRARED ASTRONOMY

One of the newer techniques for learning about the universe is infrared astronomy. Infrared radiation is radiation that has a shorter wavelength than visible red light, but a longer wavelength than radio waves. Most infrared radiation coming from space is absorbed by water vapor and carbon dioxide in Earth's atmosphere, but certain wavelengths pass through and can be detected.

One problem with studying infrared radiation on Earth is that Earth, and the instruments themselves, emit infrared radiation as well. Infrared telescopes such as those at the top of Mauna Kea on Hawaii are set up at high altitudes, to detect this radiation so that there is less interference from Earth's atmosphere. Using infrared detectors in space can solve problems with Earth's radiation and atmospheric intererence, and cooling the instruments to extremely low temperatures ends the problem of the equipment's own radiation. Dr. Adriana Ocampo, a scientist working at the Jet Propulsion Laboratory, has developed NIM, Near-Infrared Mapping Spectrometer, a remote sensing device used to detect infrared radiation from objects in space and to map the radiation using computer technology. Using the infrared range, scientists can observe the "cold bodies" (ranging from a few degrees to 3000 degrees Kelvin) of the universe. This includes the infrared radiation that is given off by dust clouds surrounding newly forming proto-stars, and dying red giants. Infrared detectors also allow astronomers to observe the central area of our own galaxy —an area that cannot be studied visually because of the interstellar dust that blocks it.

Dr. Ocampo's NIM is being used within our own solar system on Project Galileo. This project used a space shuttle to launch Galileo, a space probe in 1989. Galileo has already traveled by Venus and within 600 miles of the asteroid Gaspra. It is scheduled to enter its Jupiter orbit in December of 1995, where it will remain through 1997. NIM will be used to study the atmosphere and surface chemistry of Jupiter and its satellites.

Dr. Ocampo is a geologist as well as a planetary scientist. She analyzes infrared photographs using computers to produce computer models of geologic events and processes on Earth and, soon she hopes, on other planets.

WHAT DO YOU THINK?

American funding for space research is discussed each time a new national budget is proposed. Is it important for the United States to continue space research and exploration? Why or why not?

Going Further Have interested students further investigate infrared telescopes and compare them to optical telescopes. Students may discover that the infrared telescopes have shorter tubes and that its sensitive detectors are cooled by liquid helium.

Going Further Have students investigate how infrared-sensitive materials are used in certain types of binoculars, scopes, and home security systems. Students should find out that these materials detect objects giving off infrared radiation and are effective even in total darkness.

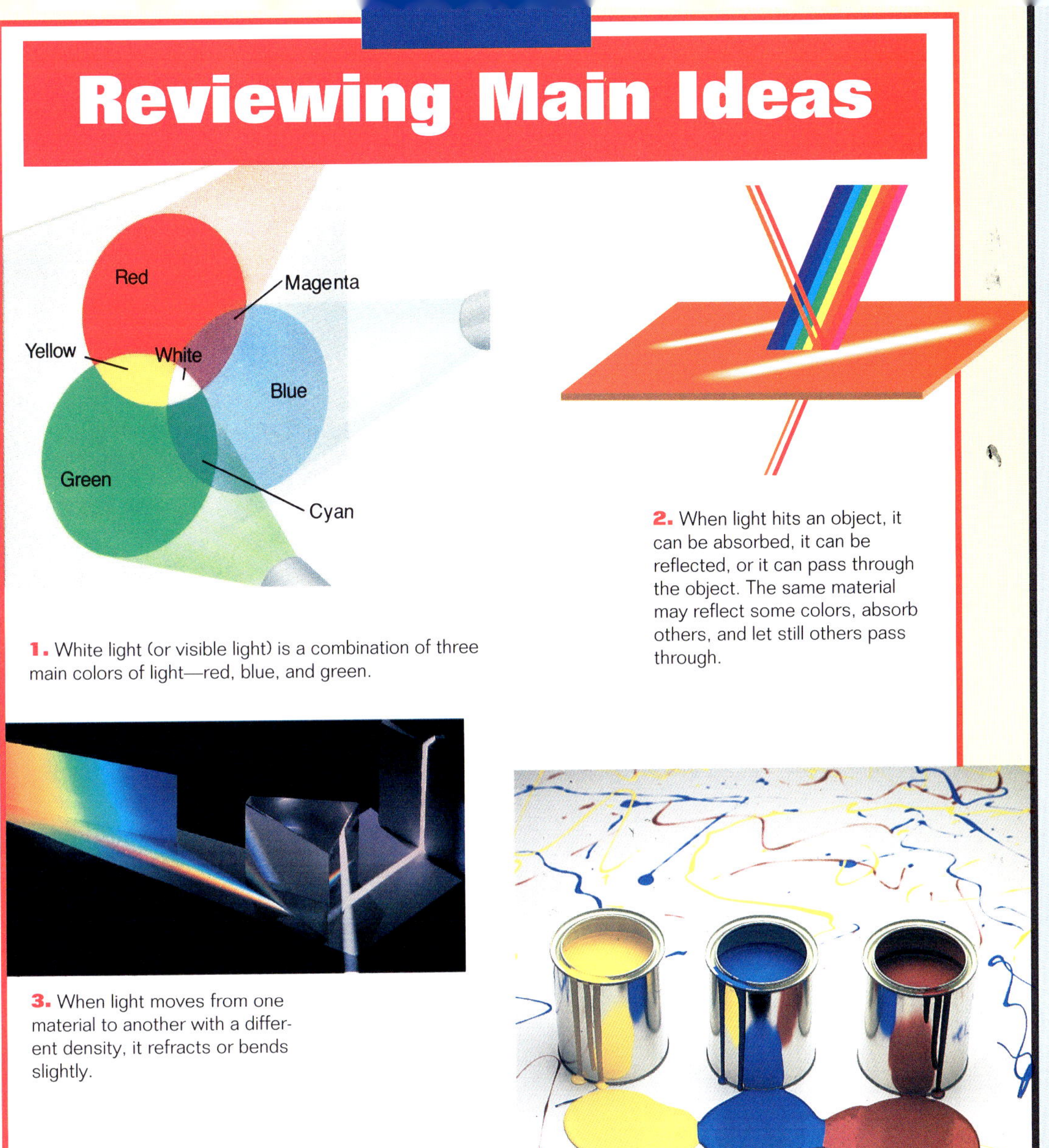

1. White light (or visible light) is a combination of three main colors of light—red, blue, and green.

2. When light hits an object, it can be absorbed, it can be reflected, or it can pass through the object. The same material may reflect some colors, absorb others, and let still others pass through.

3. When light moves from one material to another with a different density, it refracts or bends slightly.

4. All the colors in the world can be made from just three primary colors, although the three colors are different depending upon whether you're mixing lights or pigments.

Chapter 2

Reviewing Main Ideas

Although visible light is all around us, to many students it will seem like an abstraction because it doesn't occupy space like a desk or a chair or another person. To allow students to appreciate the reality of light, they should be given opportunities to manipulate it. The following strategies will give you some ideas of how this can be done. Prior to introducing the activities described below, have students study the illustrations and captions on the Reviewing Main Ideas page.

Teaching Strategies

We see objects because light is either reflected from them or produced by them. Students can appreciate the role of reflection by constructing a periscope. All they will need is a large piece of stiff cardboard, two flat mirrors of the same dimensions, and tape. Motivate students by telling them they can build a device to see around corners or over walls. Using illustrations from books on science projects, a "how it works" book, or an encyclopedia, show students what a simple periscope looks like. Then allow them to work in small groups to build and test their own periscopes. Ask students to make drawings of how images of objects they see through the periscope travel from the object, through the periscope, and to their eyes. **COOP LEARN**

To learn more about colors firsthand, ask students to write a description of a color, give it a name, and then invent it by mixing various paints. In effect, students will be using knowledge gained in the chapter to *predict* how various combinations of pigments produce new colors. Urge students to be very creative, but specific, in naming their colors. For example, they might name a color blue-jean-blue, or redhead-orange, or freckle-spot-tan, or dollar-bill-green. Using such real-life colors, students could match their invented color to the real thing.

Chapter 2

Chapter Review

USING KEY SCIENCE TERMS

Answers

1. opaque
2. spectrum
3. translucent
4. refraction

UNDERSTANDING IDEAS

Answers

1. d
2. b
3. b
4. b
5. b
6. a
7. d

Chapter Review

USING KEY SCIENCE TERMS

opaque, spectrum, reflection, translucent, refraction, transparent

An analogy is a relationship between two pairs of words generally written in the following manner: a:b::c:d. The symbol : is read "is to," and the symbol :: is read "as." For example, cat:animal::rose:plant is read "cat is to animal as rose is to plant." In the analogies that follow, a word is missing. Complete each analogy by providing the missing word from the list above.

1. window:wall:: transparent: ____
2. notes:musical scale::colors: ____
3. cellophane:transparent::waxed paper: ____
4. mirror:reflection::prism: ____

UNDERSTANDING IDEAS

Choose the best answer to complete each sentence.

1. Light travels in ____.
   a. slightly curved lines
   b. spirals about the earth
   c. erratic lines
   d. straight lines
2. Smaller lights create sharper shadows than larger lights because ____.
   a. their light is more spread out
   b. their light comes from a smaller region
   c. they emit more light
   d. they emit less light
3. A red shirt is red because ____.
   a. it absorbs red light and reflects the rest
   b. it reflects red light and absorbs the rest
   c. it's opaque to red light and transparent to the rest
   d. it's transparent to red light and opaque to the rest
4. A green light bulb is green because ____.
   a. it absorbs green light and is transparent to the rest
   b. it is transparent to green light and absorbs the rest
   c. it reflects green light from outside
   d. it is painted green
5. You can create all the colors in the spectrum with ____ lights.
   a. red, yellow, and green
   b. red, green, and blue
   c. cyan, yellow, and magenta
   d. blue, green, and yellow
6. The nerve cells in your eyes most sensitive at night are the ____.
   a. rods
   b. red cones
   c. blue cones
   d. optic cells
7. Diffuse reflections are caused by ___ _.
   a. highly opaque surfaces
   b. highly transparent surfaces
   c. smooth surfaces
   d. rough surfaces

PROGRAM RESOURCES

Teacher Classroom Resources

Review and Assessment, Chapter Review and Chapter Test, pages 9-12

Computer Test Bank, Chapter Test

OPTIONS

Cooperative Learning

Consider using Cooperative Learing in the Understanding Ideas, Critical Thinking, Problem Solving, and Connecting Ideas sections of the Chapter Review.

COOP LEARN

CRITICAL THINKING

Use your understanding of the concepts developed in the chapter to answer each of the following questions.

1. Imagine that you have one lamp with a small, bright bulb. You'd like to avoid harsh shadows. What might you do?
2. Sylvia did an experiment just like the first investigation in this chapter. Below are her data and observations. What color was the object? What else do you know about the object?

Color of light	Color of object	Cast a shadow
yellow	yellow	yes
green	green	yes
red	red	yes

3. Explain how a stained glass window absorbs light, reflects light, and/or lets light pass through. Based on your answer, tell if the window is opaque, translucent, or transparent.

PROBLEM SOLVING

Read the following problem and discuss your answers in a brief paragraph.

The new member of the drama club lighting crew was beside himself. The director of the upcoming play wanted two more spots of light on the set. He wanted more white light on the stage and a spot of yellow light on the backdrop. But only six lights were available. Two had permanent red filters in place, two had permanent blue filters, and two had permanent green filters. The crew member took his problem to the lighting chief. She told him an easy way to solve the problem. What was it?

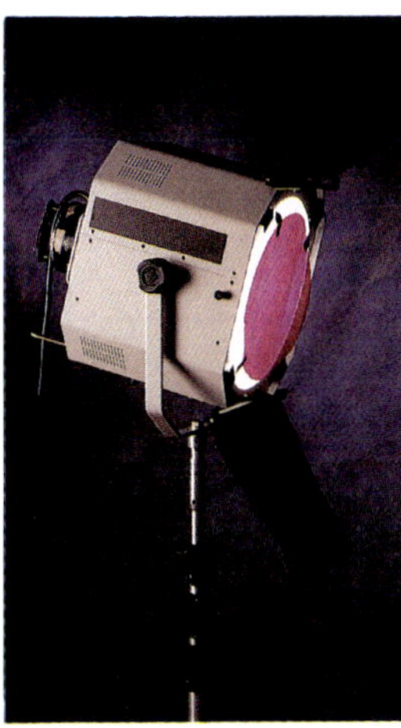

CONNECTING IDEAS

Discuss each of the following in a brief paragraph.

1. How does a flashlight use reflection? Look closely at the parts of a flashlight. You may want to take it apart and examine them.
2. Name two opaque things, two transparent things, and two translucent things in the room with you now.
3. What would absorb more sunlight—a white piece of plastic or a black piece of plastic?
4. A CLOSER LOOK Recall that a prism breaks up light into the colors of the spectrum. What do you think is acting like a prism in the case of a rainbow?
5. SCIENCE AND SOCIETY Auditoriums and theaters often dim the lights before a performance begins. Why do you think this is done?

CRITICAL THINKING

Answers

1. Use a translucent shade or a frosted bulb.

2. The object was white and opaque.

3. Colored glass reflects the colors it is stained. For example, red stained glass reflects red. Red-colored glass is also transparent to red light allowing red light to pass through. If the glass is clear, it would be transparent to all colors. Some glass is translucent, allowing some diffused light to pass through. The lead between pieces of glass is opaque, allowing no light to pass through.

PROBLEM SOLVING

Mix light from one red, one blue, and one green light to get white. Mix light from one red and one green to get yellow.

CONNECTING IDEAS

Answers

1. The light from the bulb is reflected from and focused by a curved mirror behind the bulb.

2. Possibilities include: opaque—notebook, pencil; translucent—fingernails, fluorescent fixture covers; transparent—window glass, glass on a clock

3. the black piece, because it absorbs all light rays

4. the rain drops

5. The dimly lit theater will tend to reduce the conversation level so the performers on stage can be heard when the curtain goes up.

CHAPTER ORGANIZER

SECTION	OBJECTIVES	ACTIVITIES/FEATURES
Chapter Opener		**Explore!** How are sounds produced? p. 65
3-1 Sources of Sound (2 days)	1. **Recognize** that sounds are created by vibrations. 2. **Distinguish** between compression and rarefaction. 3. **Describe** the way sound travels through matter.	**Find Out!** How does sound travel through matter? p. 66 **Find Out!** Can sound travel through string and your fingers? p. 70 **Skillbuilder:** Making and Using Graphs, p. 72
3-2 The Pitch of Sound (4 days)	1. **Use** the length or thickness of a vibrating object to predict whether its sound will be high or low. 2. **Describe** the relationship between pitch and frequency. 3. **Compare** the sound frequencies humans can hear with the sound frequencies animals can hear.	**Explore!** Does the length of a vibrating object affect the sound it makes? p. 73 **Find Out!** How do you make changes in sound on the strings of an instrument? p. 74 **Investigate 3-1:** Length and Pitch, p. 77
3-3 Music and Resonance (3 days)	1. **Distinguish** between music and noise. 2. **Explain** how different musical instruments produce sounds of different quality. 3. **Describe** resonance.	**Explore!** What is resonance? p. 81 **Skillbuilder:** Determining Cause and Effect, p. 82 **Investigate 3-2:** Length and Resonance, p. 83
Expanding Your View		A Closer Look **Your Vocal Chords,** p. 85 Life Science Connection **Sounds Are All Around You,** p. 86 Science and Society **Uses of Ultrasound,** p. 87 Technology Connection **An Antinoise Device,** p. 88 Music Connection **Heart and Soul,** p. 89 Teens in Science **Making Waves—Sound Waves, That Is,** p. 90

ACTIVITY MATERIALS

EXPLORE!	INVESTIGATE!	FIND OUT!
Page 65 ruler **Page 73** ruler **Page 81** tuning fork, rubber mallet	**Page 77** felt tip marker, 400-mL beaker, water, 8 test tubes, test-tube rack, dropper, metric ruler, drinking straw **Page 83** 2 tuning forks of different frequencies (256 Hz or higher); 1000-mL graduated cylinder (or bucket or pitcher about 30 cm deep); rubber mallet; plastic or glass tube 2.5 cm in diameter, about 45 cm long, open at both ends; ruler	**Page 66** coiled spring, small piece of colored string **Page 70** metal coat hanger; string, about 1 m long; wire, about 1 m long **Page 74** guitar, violin, or other stringed instrument

TEACHER CLASSROOM RESOURCES	OTHER RESOURCES
Study Guide, p. 13 **Concept Mapping,** p. 11 **Critical Thinking/Problem Solving,** p. 11 **Multicultural Activities,** p. 9 **Making Connections: Technology and Society,** p. 9 **Flex Your Brain,** p. 8	**Laboratory Manual,** pp. 11-12 **Color Transparency and Master 5,** Longitudinal Waves in a Slinky ***STVS:** *Sounds Made by the Ear,* Human Biology (Disc 7, Side 2) *Photo-Acoustic Cell,* Physics (Disc 1, Side 1)
Study Guide, p. 14 **Take Home Activities,** p. 8 **Making Connections: Integrating Sciences,** p. 9 **Activity Masters, Investigate 3-1,** pp. 13-14	**Color Transparency and Master 6,** Decibel Scale ***STVS:** *Songbird Study,* Animals (Disc 5, Side 2) *The Sound of Thirsty Plants,* Plants and Simple Organisms (Disc 4, Side 2) *How Bats Hear,* Animals (Disc 5, Side 2)
Study Guide, p. 15 **How It Works,** p. 6 **Making Connections: Across the Curriculum,** p. 9 **Multicultural Activities,** p. 10 **Activity Masters, Investigate 3-2,** pp. 15-16 **Review and Assessment,** pp. 13-16	**Computer Test Bank**
	***STVS:** *Sounds of Blue Crabs,* Animals (Disc 5, Side 1) *Prop Fan Propellers,* Physics (Disc 1, Side 2) **Spanish Resources** **Cooperative Learning Resource Guide** **Lab and Safety Skills**

***Science and Technology Videodisc Series**

KEY TO TEACHING STRATEGIES

Teaching strategies have been coded for varying learning styles and abilities. As you review teaching strategies in the margin, the following designations will help you decide which activities are appropriate for your students.

L1 Level 1 activities are basic activities and should be within the ability range of all students.

L2 Level 2 activities are average activities and should be within the ability range of the average to above-average student.

L3 Level 3 activities are challenging activities designed for the ability range of above-average students.

LEP LEP activities should be within the ability range of Limited English Proficiency students.

COOP LEARN Cooperative Learning activities are designed for small group work.

ADDITIONAL MATERIALS

SOFTWARE	AUDIOVISUAL
Sound, Cross Educational Software. *What Is a Wave?* Focus. *Sound Waves,* J & S Software. *Waves and Sound Energy,* Focus.	*A Look at Sound,* film, Time-Life. *Mr. Wizard's World: Sound Instruments,* Macmillan/McGraw-Hill School Division. *The World of Sound Energy,* video, Focus.

Chapter 3

Sound

THEME DEVELOPMENT

One theme of this chapter is energy. Students explore sound energy, the product of vibration carried to our ears by air or another medium. They observe how sound energy travels through matter in the Find Out activity on pages 66–67. The theme of stability and change is apparent as students use tuning forks for the Explore activity on page 81 and the Investigate on page 83 to see how sound energy can make a stable object resonate at the same frequency.

CHAPTER OVERVIEW

The chapter begins with students learning that vibrating objects produce sound through waves of compression and rarefaction. They also learn that sound only travels through a medium and that different media conduct sound differently.

Students then experiment with the length, width and tension of vibrating objects and conclude that the larger or looser the object, the lower the pitch. They define rate of vibration as frequency, and learn about the frequency ranges that human beings and other animals can hear. They distinguish between music and noise, learn how a musical instrument's construction affects its sound, and explore resonance.

Tying to Previous Knowledge

Show students a picture of a rainbow and a guitar. Point out that there are various colors on a rainbow as well as various notes on a guitar. Pluck each guitar string. Explain that the next chapter is about sound and lead a discussion about ways in which sound may be like light. Encourage them to see that both are energy and that the colors of the spectrum may be similar to the notes of the guitar. Colors of light are of different frequencies. Likewise, the notes on a guitar are of different frequencies.

DID YOU EVER WONDER . . .

If you could hear sounds on the moon?

Why you make a sound when you blow into a soft drink bottle?

Why covering different holes on a whistle or flute produces different sounds?

You'll find the answers to these questions as you read this chapter.

DID YOU EVER WONDER...

Students will explore these questions as they progress through the chapter. Don't spoil their fun and motivation by sharing these answers too soon.

- Sounds cannot be heard on the moon because there is no air to carry them. (page 70)
- The column of air in the bottle vibrates, producing sound. (page 73)
- Covering different holes changes the length of the vibrating air column inside, changing its frequency. (page 76)

Chapter 3

Sound

Today is moving day. Welcome to your new home! As you unpack, you hear a dog yapping next door. Someone turns a stereo up, and you hear your favorite song. A voice calls out, "Randy, please turn that down," and suddenly you can barely hear the music. Now you hear the whine of an electric saw, the pounding of a hammer, and the roar of traffic.

You've learned a bit about your new neighborhood before you've even had a chance to look around. You know that there is a dog next door, someone named Randy likes the same music you do, carpenters are working on your block, and a busy street is close by.

How did you discover all this? Simply by listening.

When you hear a sound, you are actually sensing the vibrations of your eardrums. Sound travels through the air to your ears and makes your eardrums vibrate. In this chapter, you'll find out what all sounds have in common, and how you are able to distinguish one sound from another.

EXPLORE!

How are sounds produced?

Place a ruler on a desk so that 6 inches of the ruler extends over the edge of the desk. Use one hand to hold the ruler firmly against the desk. With the other hand, snap the free end of the ruler so that it vibrates up and down. Describe what you see and hear. Shorten the length of ruler that extends out over the edge of the desk and snap the free end again. Has the sound changed? If so, how is it different?

Introducing the Chapter

Have students examine the photograph on page 64 and suggest what sounds might be heard in the scene. Write their suggestions on the chalkboard. Possible answers may include honking horns, engines, people talking.

Uncovering Preconceptions

Students may not connect sound with vibration. The Explore activity establishes this connection, and you may also want to ask students if they feel any vibrations when they are exposed to very loud music.

EXPLORE!

How are sounds produced?

Time needed 5 minutes

Materials ruler

Thinking Processes
Thinking critically, Observing and inferring, Comparing and contrasting

Purpose To observe the connection between sound and vibration and how the length of a ruler affects its pitch

Preparation Provide each student with a ruler.

Teaching Strategies

Troubleshooting Remind students to hold the ruler firmly to the desk. Students will find it easier to make the ruler vibrate if they snap it with an upward rather than downward motion. L1

Expected Outcomes

Students observe that the ruler's vibrations produce sound and that the pitch of the shortened section is higher.

Answers to Questions
Students hear a tone from the ruler. The shortened ruler produces a higher tone.

Project

Gather a wide range of materials, such as empty cans, plastic sheeting, rubber bands, cigar boxes, nails, pieces of plywood, dried beans, empty bottles, and spoons. Have students make musical instruments such as drums, rubber-band stringed instruments strung on cigar boxes or on nails hammered into plywood, maracas made of cans filled with dried beans, a bottle xylophone and spoons.

Science at home

Have students fill two large bottles of different sizes to the top with water. Then have them pour out the water into a measuring cup and record how much each bottle contains. They should then refill the bottles and pour equal amounts from each. The student then blows across the mouth of each bottle. Have them note whether the pitch is the same or different; it should be the same.

Section 3-1

PREPARATION

Concepts Developed

Chapter 2 described properties of light. In this section, students learn about sound. After learning that vibrations cause sound, students use Slinkies to visualize how sound travels through matter by compression and rarefaction. Students learn that sound travels only through a medium and they compare how well different media conduct sound. Students then contrast the speeds of sound and light.

Planning the Lesson

In planning your lesson on sources of sound, refer to the Chapter Organizer on pages 64A-B for timing suggestions, resources, and additional materials that will help you in your presentation of the lesson concepts.

For adequate development of the concepts presented in this section, we recommend that students do the Find Out activities on pages 66 and 70.

1 MOTIVATE

Activity Ask students to take out a pencil and paper. While they sit quietly for 60 seconds, they are to listen and write down whatever they hear. Typical sounds might include the scratching of pencils, the hum of fluorescent lights, voices in the hallway, and traffic noises. When the minute is over, make a list of the sounds on the chalkboard. Ask students if they heard any sounds that they could not identify. Have them guess what might have produced each sound. L1

3-1 Sources of Sound

OBJECTIVES

In this section, you will

- recognize that sounds are created by vibrations;
- distinguish between compression and rarefaction;
- describe the way sound travels through matter.

KEY SCIENCE TERMS

compression
rarefaction
medium

VIBRATIONS PRODUCE SOUND

What sounds did you hear on your way to school this morning? The growling engine and squeaking brakes of a school bus? The roar of traffic as you walked along the street? A radio blaring from a neighbor's open window? Did you notice the sound of your own footsteps or the wind blowing past your ears? We hear so many different sounds all the time that we aren't usually aware of all of them. Sit quietly for a minute and listen to the sounds around you. What do you hear right now?

Your ears allow you to recognize many different sounds, but do you know what these sounds have in common? All sounds are produced by vibrating objects. When you did the Explore activity at the beginning of this chapter, you created a sound by making the ruler vibrate up and down very rapidly. Vibrations are very quick, back-and-forth motions repeated over and over again. You could see the ruler vibrate, and those vibrations made a sound you could hear.

Vibrations produce sound. But what *is* sound? How does it reach your ears? Here is an activity that will give you some clues about what sound is and how it travels through matter to your ears.

FIND OUT!

How does sound travel through matter?

For this activity, you will need a partner, a coiled spring, and a small piece of colored string. With your partner holding one end of the coiled spring and you holding the other, put the coiled spring on the floor and stretch it out straight until it's at least 6 feet long. Make sure all of the coils are about the same distance apart. With one hand, squeeze together about 15 or 20 of the coils near your end.

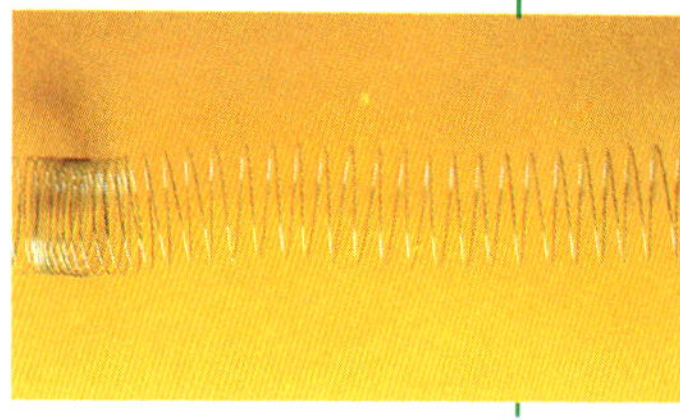

PROGRAM RESOURCES

Teacher Classroom Resources

Study Guide, page 13

Laboratory Manual, pages 11-12, How People Produce Sound COOP LEARN

Concept Mapping, page 11, Sound L1

Critical Thinking/Problem Solving, page 11, Echoes L2

Multicultural Activities, page 9, Linguistics L1

PROGRAM RESOURCES

Teacher Classroom Resources

Transparency Masters, page 13, and **Color Transparency,** number 5, Longitudinal Wave in a Slinky L2

Making Connections: Technology and Society, page 9, Telephones L2

Other Resources

Knight, David C. *All About Sound.* Mahwah, NJ: Troll Associates, 1983.

A Look at Sound, film, Time-Life.

These squeezed coils are bunched together. What happens to the unsqueezed coils? Make a drawing of what the coiled spring looks like when you squeeze together some of the coils. What happens when you let go of the bunched-up coils? All the coils move back to their original positions, about the same distance apart. Let your partner do the squeezing while you hold your end of the coiled spring steady.

Now ask your partner to keep a firm grasp on his or her end of the coiled spring, so that it can't move. Gently push your end of the coiled spring toward your partner a few inches, then pull it back to its original position. Do this several times. Try pushing at different speeds. Next, hold your end of the coiled spring steady and let your partner do the pushing.

Conclude and Apply

1. Can you describe what is happening?
2. Are there any similarities between what the coiled spring looks like now and what it looked like when you squeezed together some of the coils?

Now tie the piece of colored string to one of the coils. Repeat the pushing-and-pulling experiment, but this time keep your eyes on the string. How does the string move?

3. Does the coil with the string on it move all the way down the length of the coiled spring? Can you explain why it moves the way it does?

During the first part of this activity, you squeezed together some of the coils so that they were bunched up into a small space. What happened to the rest of the coils when you did this? They were stretched farther apart, so that there were fewer coils in the same amount of space. When you stopped squeezing, all the coils went back to their original positions, about the same distance apart.

FIND OUT!

How does sound travel through matter?

Time needed 20 minutes

Materials Slinky or Slinky Jr., 10–20 cm piece of colored string for each pair of students (Embroidery floss comes in numerous colors and is fairly thick.)

Thinking Processes
Thinking critically, Observing and inferring, Comparing and contrasting, Recognizing cause and effect

Purpose Students will use a Slinky to model how compression and rarefaction produce sound.

Preparation Each pair of students will need two to three meters of free floor space. Have students move their desks and chairs to the side of the room and arrange partners in rows.

Teaching the Activity

Troubleshooting If students are using Slinky Jr., they should stretch it only about one meter and, in the first part of the activity, squeeze fewer than 15 or 20 coils by hand. L1

Expected Outcomes

Students should observe the compression and rarefaction of the Slinky coils and how the band of compression travels the length of the Slinky without the coils themselves changing position.

Conclude and Apply

1. The pushing creates a pattern of bunched-together coils that travels down the length of the Slinky.
2. Yes; the bunched-together coils look like the part of the Slinky you squeezed together with your hand.
3. Since the coils are attached to one another, the coil with the string cannot move out of its place. But the bunched-together pattern does move down the length of the Slinky. The pattern can move, but the coil cannot.

OPTIONS

Meeting Individual Needs

Visually Impaired Many visually impaired people have made important contributions to music. Some people have suggested that a visual impairment can heighten a person's sensitivity to sound. Have students listen to the music of people such as Ray Charles, Stevie Wonder, and others.

2 TEACH

Tying to Previous Knowledge

Have students recall what they learned about making observations in Chapter 1 and the observations of light they made in Chapter 2. In this section students will use another of their senses, their sense of hearing, to make observations about how it travels.

Concept Development

Theme Connection In this section the students see that a vibrating ruler creates a pattern of compressions and rarefactions. This supports the theme of stability and change because the pattern causes a change in the surrounding environment. In this instance, the compressions and rarefactions travel through air particles, causing the eardrum to change by vibrating.

Student Journal Ask students to refer to Figures 3-2 and 3-3 and then try to visualize what it would be like if they could *see* sound. After students discuss the idea, have them write paragraphs in their journals in which they describe entering the classroom at the start of class. When they enter, the classroom is quiet but it fills rapidly with people and sound.

FIGURE 3-1. As the string shows, the pattern moves down the length of the coiled spring, but each coil moves back and forth.

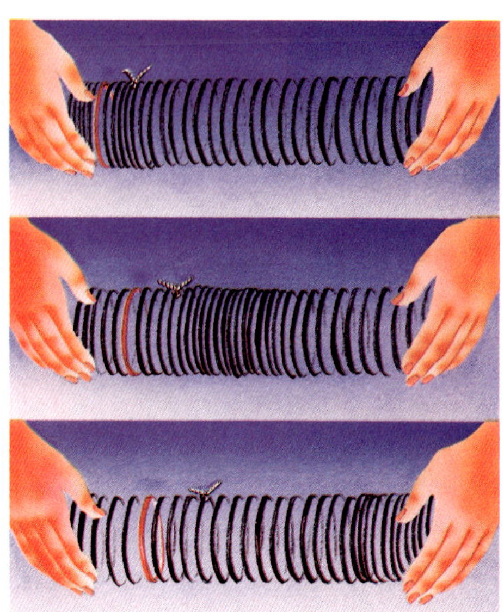

What happened when you pushed and pulled on your end of the coiled spring? The back-and-forth motion of the spring in your hand created a pattern of bunched-up and spread-out coils. This pattern traveled from your end of the coiled spring to your partner's end. Figure 3-1 shows how the pattern looks as it moves down the length of the coiled spring.

When you tied the colored string to one of the coils, did it keep moving forward? No. The coil with the string didn't move all the way down the coiled spring, even though the pattern did. One coil pushed the coil next to it. As the first coil pushed into the next one, the pattern was transmitted from coil to coil down the length of the spring. Each *coil* moved back and forth, but *the pattern* moved forward. How can this help you understand how sound travels?

The air that surrounds you is made up of particles so tiny you cannot see them. Even the space between this book and your eyes is filled with particles that are invisible to you. When everything is quiet, all these air particles are about the same distance from one another, just as the coils of the coiled spring were about the same distance apart when you first stretched it out.

A vibrating object pushes air particles just as your hand pushed the coiled spring. The vibrations create a pattern of bunched-up and spread-out particles that moves through the air just like the pattern that moved down the coiled spring. The pattern spreads out from the object in all directions, like the ripples that spread outward when you throw a stone into a pond. The pattern is invisible to us because we can't see the air. But you can imagine what it looks like. The part of the pattern with bunched-up particles is called the area of **compression.** The part with spread-out particles is called the area of **rarefaction.**

FIGURE 3-2. The ripples that spread out from a stone thrown into a pond are similar to the patterns created in the air by a vibrating object.

Examine Figure 3-3 and try to picture the pattern that a vibrating ruler makes in the air particles around it. Remember how the ruler vibrated up and down? In the split second when the ruler vibrated upward, it pushed

OPTIONS

Enrichment

Activity Use a finger or pen to tap on a desk, first very softly and then very loudly. Ask students what makes the difference between the soft and loud taps.

The difference in the amount of compression and rarefaction; the louder tap was made by striking the table with greater energy, which in turn produced a greater amount of compression. Have students model this difference using their Slinkies. Have students model loudness by pushing on one end to set up waves in the Slinky. Have students begin with a small push, which represents a soft, low-energy tap. Students should observe that this motion produces a small wave. Then have students use a large and sudden push, representing a loud, high-energy tap. They will observe that it produces a large wave.

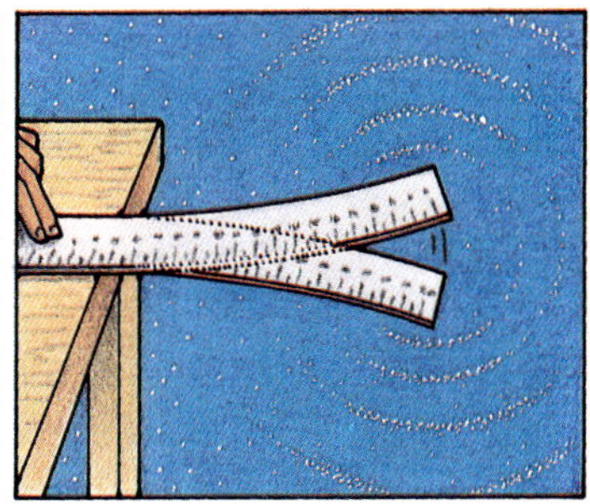

FIGURE 3-3. A vibrating ruler creates a pattern of compressions and rarefactions that spread out into the air.

the particles of air above it closer together. These bunched-up air particles formed an area of compression. At the same time, the air particles below the ruler spread farther apart. These spread-out air particles formed an area of rarefaction. A single motion of the ruler created one area of compression (bunched-up air particles) and one area of rarefaction (spread-out air particles). As the ruler continued to vibrate up and down, it created a pattern of compressions and rarefactions that traveled through the air. When this pattern reached your ear, it made your eardrum vibrate and you heard the sound.

When an object vibrates, whether it's a vibrating ruler, a guitar string, or your vocal cords, it creates a pattern of compressions and rarefactions in the air. The pattern travels through the air particles to your ear, causing your eardrum to vibrate. The sound you hear is really the air pushing on your eardrums. Figure 3-4 shows how sound travels to your ears.

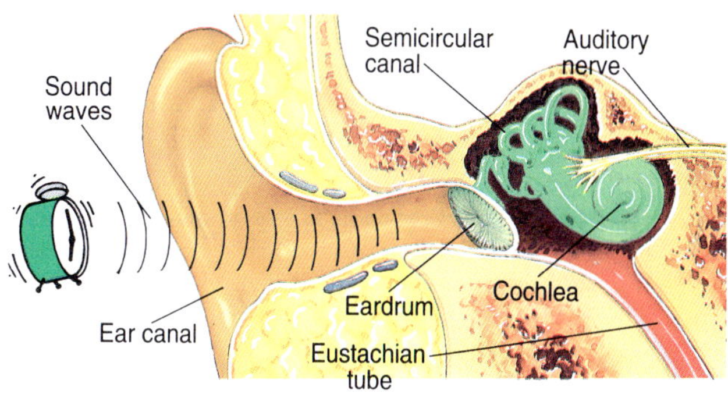

FIGURE 3-4. The sound patterns created by a vibrating object travel through the air to your ear and make your eardrum vibrate.

MAKING CONNECTIONS

Math

Tell students that sound travels through the air at about 330 m per second, while light crosses short distances almost instantaneously. Identify a location that is about 1 km away from your school. Ask students to tell how long it would take the sound of thunder to reach them if lightning struck that location. $\frac{330\ m/s}{1{,}000\ m} = 0.33$ *or* $\frac{1}{3}$ *second.* Repeat the question for a location that is about 2, 3, 4, and 5 km from your school.

Concept Development

Activity Have students line up and practice creating a "human wave" as seen at sports stadiums. Once they have perfected the wave, they can try creating waves of different speeds to simulate the different speeds at which sound moves through different types of matter. **LEP**

Discussion Grip one end of a plastic ruler and wiggle it, rotating your hand at the wrist, as fast as you can. Ask students why it is not producing sound even though it is vibrating. Encourage students to understand that not all vibrations produce sound that we can hear. Have students discuss what kinds of vibrations might produce sound and, if appropriate, lead students to understand that sound consists of much faster vibrations than the ruler produced.

Content Background

The speed of sound depends on the temperature and the medium through which the sound is traveling. Atoms are usually close together in solids, which is why solids transmit sound faster than air does.

Teacher F.Y.I.

When an object exceeds the speed of sound, it produces a sonic boom as shock waves reach your ear. Captain Chuck Yeager first broke the sound barrier in 1947.

Multicultural Perspective

There are over 3,000 languages spoken in the world today not including dialects. All of these languages have sound patterns made up of the 20 to 60 sounds that human speech organs can make. Have student volunteers say a few words or sentences in different languages. Have the students in the class listen for sounds they recognize.

If there are not any students in the class who speak a foreign language, videotape short excerpts from newscasts on foreign-language stations. Many cable television systems have stations broadcasting in other languages such as Spanish and Japanese.

FIGURE 3-5. Sound cannot be heard on the moon. There are no air particles to conduct the sound to your ear.

SOUND REQUIRES A MEDIUM

Vibrations produce sound by creating patterns of compression and rarefaction in the air. Would there be sound if there were no matter? In a vacuum, where there is no matter, there can be no sound. If you clapped your hands on the moon, it would make absolutely no sound. Why not? Because the moon has no atmosphere. There is no air through which sound can travel. There are no particles to carry the vibration patterns.

Have you ever listened to sounds under water or put your ear against a wall or the ground to try and hear something more clearly? Is air the only kind of matter that sound can travel through?

FIND OUT!

Can sound travel through string and your fingers?

You'll need a metal coat hanger, a piece of string about 1 m long, and a piece of wire 1 m long. Tie the middle of the string around the hook of the hanger. Wrap one end of the string around your left index finger and wrap the other end around your right index finger. Gently swing the hanger so that it taps against a table or chair. Listen for the sound it makes. Now, with the string still wrapped around your fingers, put your fingers in your ears and tap the hanger again. What do you notice about the sound? Which material makes a better conductor, the air or the string and your finger? Now do the same thing again, but use the wire instead of the string.

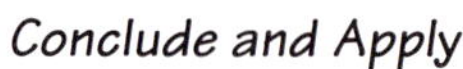

Conclude and Apply

1. Which is the better conductor, the string or the wire?
2. Why?

What do the air, the string, and the wire have in common? Do they all conduct sound? Do some materials conduct sound better than others?

FIND OUT!

Can sound travel through string and your fingers?

Time needed 15 minutes

Materials (per student) metal coat hanger or other light metal object, light string about 1 meter long, (thread or dental floss), flexible wire about 1 meter long

Thinking Processes
Thinking critically, Observing and inferring, Comparing and contrasting, Recognizing cause and effect

Purpose To compare the ability of air, string and wire to conduct sound.

Preparation Students can perform this activity standing at their desks and using the materials. You may wish to have students work in pairs.

Teaching the Activity

Discussion Ask students to keep quiet while performing this activity. They may wish to repeat it. Tell students to wrap the string and wire around their fingers to medium tightness, rather than knotting it. L1 LEP

Expected Outcomes

Students should observe that the solid objects are better conductors of sound than is air, and that wire is a better conductor than string.

Conclude and Apply

1. the wire
2. Sound travels better through the wire than through the string.

Concept Development

Student Text Question What do the air, the string, and the wire have in common? Do they all conduct sound? *yes* Do some materials conduct sound better than others? *yes*

OPTIONS

Meeting Individual Needs

Hearing Impaired Hearing-impaired students will not be able to respond to the Find Out activity above—involving listening to sounds made by metal objects—as presented. Students with limited hearing may be able to hear the sound with fingers in their ears. All hearing-impaired students should be able to feel in their fingers the vibrations conducted by the string or wire and they may be able to compare the abilities of the string and wire to conduct these vibrations. Encourage these students to conduct as many observations as they may require.

Any substance that carries the pattern of sound is called the **medium** for that sound. A medium is something that is between two or more other things. For sound, the medium is between the vibrating object and your eardrum. The medium conducts the sound to your ears.

The sounds you hear almost always come to your ears through the medium of air. But as you were able to see in the Find Out, air is not the only medium that conducts sound. Sound also travels through solids. Does sound travel through liquids? If you have ever swum under water, you know it does. In fact, liquids and solids are better conductors of sound than the air. You probably heard more of the sound of the coat hanger hitting the table when you listened through the string and your fingers than when you listened through the air. Why do you suppose the sound was even clearer through the wire?

Part of the reason liquids and solids conduct sound better than air is that sound travels through them much faster than it travels through air. Have you ever watched a passenger jet as it flies across the sky? That jet is traveling about 740 miles per hour, or about 1200 kilometers per hour. That is about the same speed that sound travels through the air. Sound travels through water almost five times faster, at 3350 miles per hour, or about 5200 kilometers per hour.

FIGURE 3-6. If all the air is pumped from this container, you cannot hear the clock's alarm. In a vacuum, there are no air particles to carry the sound.

How do we know?

Sound and a Vacuum

Here is a description of a famous experiment that proves sound cannot travel through a vacuum. Imagine you are a scientist in a laboratory. In front of you are four items needed for your experiment: an alarm clock, a glass cover that fits over the clock, a piece of thick felt to go under the clock, and a vacuum pump. You set the clock's alarm to go off in just a few minutes. You place the clock on the felt, put the glass cover over it, and wait until you hear the alarm ring. You hear it ring, even though the sound is muffled by the cloth and the glass cover.

Now you do the same experiment again, but this time you use the pump to remove all the air from inside the glass cover. This creates a vacuum inside the glass. This time, when the alarm goes off, you don't hear it. Why? Because there is no air inside the glass to carry the sound. Can you explain why you need the piece of felt for this experiment? You know that all kinds of matter, not just air, can carry sound. So you use the felt to muffle any sound that would be carried by the table. Can you use this information to solve a famous riddle? If a tree falls in a forest, and there is no one there to hear it, does it make a sound? How do you know?

How do we know?

Because air is invisible and always surrounds us, it is hard for students to think of it as a medium similar to metal or string. The experiment described here dramatizes the fact that air is a medium and demonstrates that sound does not travel in a vacuum. For more information, have students refer to

Knight, David C. *Sound: Space.* New York: New York University Press, 1978.

Concept Development

Student Text Question Why do you suppose the sound was even clearer through the wire? *The wire is a better conductor.*

Flex Your Brain Use the Flex Your Brain activity to have students explore compression and rarefaction.

Teacher F.Y.I.

One of the world's few solo percussionists is a hearing-impaired New Zealander who "hears" vibrations with her legs and feet.

PROGRAM RESOURCES

Teacher Classroom Resources

Critical Thinking/Problem Solving, page 8, Flex Your Brain

Other Resources

"Slowing Down the Speed of Sound," *Science News,* June 21, 1986, p. 395.

Sound, software, Cross Educational Software.

SKILLBUILDER

1. aluminum
2. oxygen
3. about 11,000 mph
4. The size of the bars for air is the same as the size of the bars for the gases contained in air. Sound travels at the same speed through air and the materials that make up air. L1

3 Assess

Check for Understanding

To help students answer the Apply question, ask them to describe sounds made in movie space battles. Ask them if they think the sounds are realistic and why they think so. Ask them why they think the filmmakers add these sounds.

Reteach

Set up a chain of dominoes and make the pieces fall, one after another. Explain that this is another way to visualize how sound travels. LEP

Extension

Have students who have already mastered the section concepts extend the Find Out activity on page 70 by tying different metal objects to the string and testing each one. They will see how lower-pitched sounds produced by larger objects are not easily heard through the air but travel well through the string. L3

4 Close

Tie two tin cans together with a long piece of string. Puncture a hole in the center of the bottom of the can and tie a knot so the string does not slip through the hole. Have one student talk into one end while another student listens at the other end. Ask students how the second student can hear the first student. The voice causes the string to vibrate.

DID YOU KNOW?

The ground is a better sound conductor than air. Native Americans knew that if they placed an ear to the ground they could hear the rumble of approaching horses long before they heard the same sound through the air.

Sound travels through metal 15 times faster—about 11,200 miles per hour, or 18,000 kilometers per hour. Figure 3-7 shows you the speed of sound through various materials.

When you made observations in Chapter 1, you were gathering information with your eyes. Most of us are aware that we depend on our sight to observe the world around us. But what you hear is also important. Your ears can even give you information about things you can't see. Remember moving day and how you found out about a possible new friend named Randy?

SKILLBUILDER

MAKING AND USING GRAPHS

Use the information in Figure 3-7 to answer these questions. If you need help, refer to the ***Skill Handbook*** on page 650.

1. Which material conducts sound fastest?
2. Which material conducts sound slowest?
3. What is the speed of sound through aluminum?
4. Air is made up of many gases, including oxygen and nitrogen. How can you relate this information to the sizes of the bars on the graph for these materials?

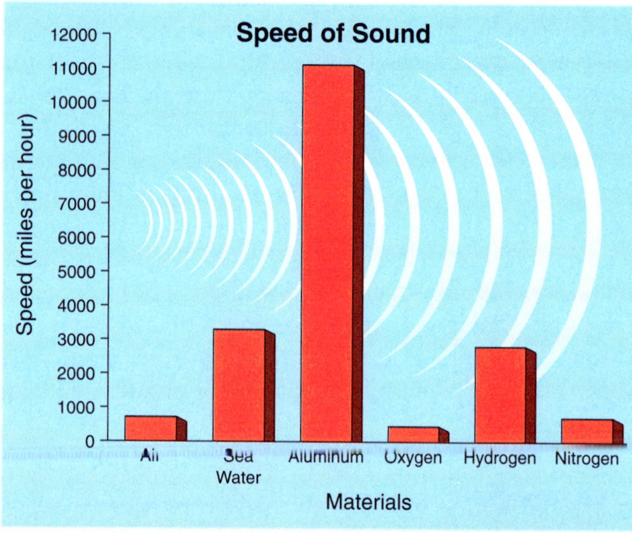

FIGURE 3-7. Sound travels at different speeds through different materials.

Check Your Understanding

1. Why doesn't a ruler that is sitting by itself on your desk make a sound? What must happen to an object before it can create a sound?
2. Explain how to use a coiled spring to show the compressions and rarefactions that are created by a vibrating object.
3. Explain how a vibrating object that is some distance away from you can cause your eardrums to vibrate.
4. **APPLY:** Imagine you are traveling in outer space. You see a nearby satellite explode when a large meteor crashes into it. Would you hear the boom? Why or why not?

Answers to Check Your Understanding

1. It is not vibrating. It must be set into vibration to create a sound.
2. When you push one end, you cause some of the Slinky's coils to bunch together into areas of compression and some to spread apart in areas of rarefaction. The pattern of compressions and rarefactions moves down the length of the Slinky.
3. It creates a pattern of compression and rarefaction in the particles of the air, which is carried to your ear.
4. No, because there are no air particles to provide a medium.

3-2 Frequency and Pitch

THE PITCH OF SOUND

Have you ever made a sound by blowing across the top of a soft drink bottle? Did you notice that the sound changes as you drink more and more of the liquid inside the bottle? As you drink, the liquid in the bottle is replaced with air. When you blow across the top, you make the air inside the bottle vibrate. The more air there is in the bottle, the lower the sound. The less air there is in the bottle, the higher the sound. In other words, the length of the air column inside the bottle determines the sound. What happens if you change the length of a vibrating solid? The next activity will help you answer that question.

OBJECTIVES

In this section, you will

- use the length or thickness of a vibrating object to predict whether its sound will be high or low;
- describe the relationship between pitch and frequency;
- compare the sound frequencies humans can hear with the sound frequencies animals can hear.

KEY SCIENCE TERMS

frequency
hertz (Hz)
pitch

EXPLORE!

Does the length of a vibrating object affect the sound it makes?

Use your ruler to create a sound, as you did at the beginning of this chapter. Extend exactly half the ruler's length beyond the edge of the desk. For example, if your ruler is 12 inches long, 6 inches will extend over the edge. Snap the free end and listen to the sound. Now move the ruler so that three fourths of its length extends beyond the edge of the desk. If you're using a 12-inch ruler, 9 inches will extend over the edge. Snap the ruler again and listen. Is the sound different? Does the vibration speed up or slow down? Does length affect the sound that is produced? What happens when you vibrate one fourth of the ruler's length?

Section 3-2

PREPARATION

Concepts Developed

In this section, students learn that the pitch of a sound depends on its frequency or the number of vibrations it makes per second. Through three experiments, they learn how the length or width of a vibrating object affects its pitch by determining how fast it vibrates. Finally, they learn that sound includes frequencies both lower and higher than humans can hear.

Planning the Lesson

In planning your lesson on frequency and pitch, refer to the Chapter Organizer on pages 64A-B for timing suggestions, resources, and additional materials that will help you in your presentation of the lesson concepts.

For adequate development of the concepts presented in this section, we recommend that students do the Explore on page 73 and the Find Out on page 74.

1 MOTIVATE

Demonstration Use different sized drums to demonstrate pitch.

You will need two plastic food containers with lids, one about half the size of the other.

Show students the containers and ask them to predict which one will make a lower sound when tapped with a pencil. Tap both containers and demonstrate that the larger one makes a lower sound. Ask students to suggest why the larger drum makes a lower sound.

EXPLORE!

Does the length of a vibrating object affect the sound it makes?

Time needed 5 minutes

Materials metal ruler

PROGRAM RESOURCES

Teacher Classroom Resources

Study Guide, page 14

Transparency Masters, page 15, and **Color Transparency,** number 6, Decibel Scale L1

Take Home Activities, page 8, Ear Trumpet L1

Making Connections: Integrating Sciences, page 9, Infrasound L2

PROGRAM RESOURCES

Other Resources

Mr. Wizard's World: Sound Instruments, Macmillan/McGraw-Hill School Division.

What Is a Wave?, software, Focus.

Sound Waves, software, J&S Software.

Waves and Sound Energy, software, Focus.

Thinking Processes
Thinking critically, Observing and inferring, Comparing and contrasting, Recognizing cause and effect

Purpose To demonstrate that the greater the length of ruler allowed to vibrate, the slower the vibrations and the lower the sound.

Preparation Students can perform the activity seated at their desks.

Teaching the Activity

Discussion After allowing students three to four minutes to experiment, ask them the text questions. If students grasp the concepts, extend the activity by having them slide the ruler inward and outward as they snap it, so that they hear the pitch changing.

Expected Outcomes

Students observe that a long section of ruler vibrates more slowly and produces a lower tone, while a short length vibrates faster, producing a higher tone.

Answers to Questions

1. yes
2. slow down
3. yes
4. It vibrates faster and sounds higher than the half length.

2 Teach

Tying to Previous Knowledge

Ask students to brainstorm concepts learned about light in Chapter 2. Tell them that this section will teach them properties of sound that will be familiar from their study of the properties of light.

FIGURE 3-8. The highness or lowness of the sound that is made when you blow across the top of a soft drink bottle depends on how much air is in the bottle.

In the Explore, you observed that a longer segment of ruler produces a lower sound than a shorter segment. In the same way, a longer air column in a soft drink bottle makes a lower sound than a shorter air column.

Examine the Explore illustration and try to imagine the compressions and rarefactions your vibrating ruler makes in the air around it. The longer the length of the ruler, the slower the vibrations. Slower vibrations create bands of compression and rarefaction that are farther apart, and the sound is lower. The shorter the length of the ruler, the faster the vibrations. Faster vibrations create compressions and rarefactions that are closer together, and the sound is higher.

Each back-and-forth vibration of the ruler's motion is one cycle. The faster the vibrations, the more cycles there are per second, and the higher the frequency of the sound. Frequency means how often something happens. A higher frequency means the vibrations are faster; there are more cycles per second. A lower frequency means the vibrations are slower; there are fewer cycles per second.

A **frequency** is the number of times an object vibrates in one second. We measure frequency with a unit called hertz, named after the German scientist Heinrich Hertz. One **hertz** (abbreviated Hz) is a frequency of one vibration per second or one cycle per second.

Is there another way to create high and low sounds? This next activity will show you.

FIND OUT!

How do you make changes in sound on the strings of an instrument?

Take a close look at a guitar, violin, or other stringed instrument. Are all the strings the same thickness, or are they different? Pluck the strings, one at a time. Does a thicker string have a higher or lower sound than a thinner string? Why?

Choose one string and pluck it. Now push the string firmly down onto the fretboard with your finger. Pluck the string again. What does your finger do to the length of the string? What happens to the sound?

OPTIONS

Meeting Individual Needs

Hearing Impaired As an alternative to the Find Out activity, have hearing-impaired students place a hand lightly across the front of their throats as they make a variety of sounds. Then have each student place a hand on the throat of a student who is humming at a very low frequency. Repeat by having each hearing-impaired student place a hand on the throat of a student who is humming at a very high frequency.

Choose one string and find the tuning peg it's attached to. Pluck the string. Turn the tuning peg so that the string becomes slightly loose. Pluck the string again. What happens to the sound? Pluck the string while turning the peg in the other direction. What happens to the sound as the string tightens?

Conclude and Apply

1. Can you name one way to make a string sound higher?
2. Can you name one way to make a string sound lower?

Your ears recognize differences in sound frequencies as differences in pitch. **Pitch** refers to the highness or lowness of the sound you hear. When you hum along with your favorite music, you raise and lower the pitch of your own voice. If you listen carefully, you can hear that the pitch of your voice rises and falls even when you're just talking with friends.

As you discovered in Find Out, changing the thickness of a string is one way to change its pitch. Can you explain why thicker strings produce lower-pitched sounds? Thicker strings are heavier than thinner strings, so they vibrate more slowly. And slower vibrations result in a lower pitch.

FIND OUT!

How do you make changes in sound on the strings of an instrument?

Time needed 10 minutes

Materials guitar or other non-electric stringed instrument

Try to get at least one instrument for each pair of students. If none is available, you can use a sturdy cardboard box with rubber bands of different thicknesses stretched across the opening.

Thinking Processes
Thinking critically, Observing and inferring, Comparing and contrasting, Recognizing cause and effect

Purpose To understand that the pitch of a vibrating string can be altered by varying its thickness, length, or tension

Preparation Have one student hold a guitar in a playing position where other students can all see.

Teaching the Activity

Troubleshooting Give the student with the guitar clear directions on when and how to pluck the strings. Allow time for all to see the strings being plucked, the movement on the fretboard, and the turning of the peg. Ask questions that guide students: comparing size of strings, pitches of an unfretted and fretted string, and the sound of a string when loosened and tightened. LEP

Expected Outcomes

Students observe three ways to change a string's pitch: by varying its size, length, and tension.

Answers to Questions

- Strings are different.
- Thick string has lower sound.
- lower frequency
- makes string shorter
- Sound gets higher pitch.
- becomes lower
- becomes higher

Conclude and Apply

1. Shorten or tighten it.
2. Lengthen or loosen it.

Multicultural Perspectives

Musical instruments from all over the world apply the principles outlined in this section. Examples include pan pipes from Greece and South America, African and Latin American drums, finger harps of southern Africa, and steel drums of the Caribbean. Pan pipes are played by blowing across tubes of different lengths. The pitch of drums varies with their sizes. The finger harp consists of different lengths of thin metal or wood that are flicked with the fingers to produce tones. It is the portable instrument of the nomadic Bush people of the Kalihari desert. The steel drum is a large metal bowl played with sticks. Striking it in the center produces a low note due to the large area being set into vibration. Striking it higher up toward the rim produces higher notes, as the area of vibration is more restricted.

MAKING CONNECTIONS

Music

When musical instruments are played together, they all have to be tuned to produce the same number of vibrations per second (Hz) when playing the same note. In 1859, the French government published a standard for musical notes, which made the A above middle C 435 Hz at 15°C. In the United States today, the same note is tuned to 440 Hz. Obtain several instruments and have students tune them at the same time.

Concept Development

Theme Connection Students learn ways to change the frequency of a stable vibrating system. In the Find Out activity the students changed the sound on the strings of an instrument. This supports the theme of stability and change.

Content Background

The electromagnetic spectrum is also defined in cycles per second (Hz). AM radio stations broadcast at 500,000 to 1.7 million Hz. Satellites broadcast at 4 million to 36 million Hz. By contrast, the U.S. Navy uses 30–300 Hz radio frequencies to reach submarines, because low frequencies penetrate deeply into water.

Changing the length of a string is another way to change its pitch. What happened when you held the string down onto the fretboard? You used your finger to shorten the string and make the pitch rise. This is the same thing that happened with the vibrating ruler. Length affects pitch. The shorter the vibrating object, the higher the pitch.

A third way to change the pitch is to change the tension on the string. Before guitarists begin playing, they tune their instrument by adjusting the tuning pegs until each string produces the correct pitch. The tuning peg controls the tension of the string. What happened to the guitar string when you loosened it? The pitch got lower, until the vibration was so slow it made almost no sound at all. What happened when you tightened it once again? The sound got higher. What does this tell you about tension and pitch? The greater the tension, the higher the pitch.

Many instruments besides the guitar create sound with vibrating strings. Can you name some of these stringed instruments?

FIGURE 3-9. Some musical instruments use vibrating strings to produce sounds (a). Other instruments use a vibrating column of air (b).

a

b

O P T I O N S

Enrichment

Discussion Have students recall the last time they heard a police car or fire engine pass by them. Ask them if the siren sounded different when the vehicle was approaching than when the vehicle was moving away. Let students identify the pitch of the siren as higher when the vehicle was approaching and lower when it was moving away. Explain that this is called the Doppler effect after Christian Johann Doppler (1803–53), the Austrian scientist who first described it. The Doppler effect occurs because as the siren moves toward you, the sound waves are emitted closer together so the observer hears a higher frequency. As the siren moves away, the sound waves are emitted farther apart, and the observer hears a lower frequency. The Doppler effect also happens when you pass by a stationary source of sound. L3

I N V E S T I G A T E !

3-1 LENGTH AND PITCH

Changing the length of a vibrating string changes the frequency. You will **determine the effect** on pitch when the length of an air column is changed.

PROBLEM

How does the length of an air column affect pitch?

MATERIALS

felt-tip marker
400 mL beaker
water
8 test tubes
test-tube rack
dropper
metric ruler
drinking straw

PROCEDURE

1. Copy the data table.
2. Number the test tubes and place in rack.
3. Leave test tube 1 empty.

DATA AND OBSERVATIONS SAMPLE DATA

TEST TUBE	LENGTH OF AIR COLUMN	INCREASED OR DERCEASED PITCH
1	As the length of the air column decreases (more water added), the pitch gets higher.	
2		
3		
4		
5		
6		
7		
8		

Add water to test tubes 2 through 8 so that each tube gets a little more water than the one before.

4. Blow across the top of each test tube with a straw and listen to the pitch. In the data table, record whether the pitch of each tube is higher or lower.
5. Use the dropper to adjust the level of water in the test tubes until each tube sounds higher than the one before.
6. Change the water in each tube until the tubes sound like a musical scale. Play the first few notes of "Three Blind Mice."
7. **Measure** the length of the air column above the water in each test tube. For test tube 1, this will be the entire length of the tube. Record these measurements in the data table.

ANALYZE

1. Which test tube produced the lowest pitch? How long was its air column?
2. Which test tube produced the highest pitch? How long was its air column?
3. **Compare and contrast** the pitches in the test tubes. Did the lengths of the air columns increase or decrease as you moved from tube 1 to tube 8? Did the pitches get higher or lower as you moved from test tubes 1 to 8?

CONCLUDE AND APPLY

4. Describe the relationship between pitch and air column length.
5. Imagine a test tube the same length as test tube 1, but bigger around, so that the air column inside it is thicker. **Predict** how its pitch would compare with test tube 1.
6. **Going Further:** Explain how the test tubes are like a pipe organ. What other musical instruments produce sound by vibrating the air in a tube?

PROGRAM RESOURCES

Teacher Classroom Resources

Activity Masters, pages 13–14, Investigate 3-1

INVESTIGATE!

3-1 LENGTH AND PITCH

Time needed 50 minutes

Materials (per pair) felt-tip marker, 400 mL beaker, water, 8 test tubes, test-tube rack, dropper, metric ruler, drinking straw

Thinking Processes
Organizing information, Making and using tables, Practicing scientific methods, Observing, Interpreting data

Purpose To determine how the length of an air column affects pitch

Preparation Provide each pair of students with the materials. Small bottles or other small-necked containers of identical size can be used instead of test tubes.

Teaching the Activity

Troubleshooting If there are not enough materials to go around, you may want to have students work in cooperative groups. COOP LEARN

Discussion It is not necessary to come up with a musical scale to make the needed observations. L2

Expected Outcome

Students will learn that smaller columns of vibrating air produce higher pitches than larger ones.

Answers to Analyze/Conclude and Apply

1. the tube with the longest air column, which is the full length of the tube
2. the tube with the shortest air column or the most water
3. The lengths decreased. The pitches got higher.
4. The shorter the column of air, the higher the pitch.
5. The pitch would be lower due to the larger air column.
6. The pipes of an organ contain vibrating air columns of different lengths. Instruments producing sound by air vibration include saxophones and trumpets.

3 Assess

Check for Understanding

To help students answer the Apply question, ask them to describe the three ways a guitarist can change pitch. Point out that guitarists do not change the tuning while playing.

Reteach

Ask students to make a percussion instrument by tightly stretching leather, chamois, heavy plastic, or canvas over a series of different-sized cans. By tapping each can with an instrument such as the eraser end of a pencil, they will detect the different sounds that are produced depending on the volume of air. An alternative activity is to place varying amounts of water in each of a half dozen same type and size glasses.

Extension

Have students who understand the concepts in this section fill three identical glasses with water to three levels: low, medium, and high. Have students tap each glass with a pencil. Ask them to explain why the glass with the longest column of air makes the highest tone. *The column of water, not air, is vibrating.*

4 Close

Demonstration

Show students a slide trombone or picture of one. Explain that the pitch is changed by moving the slide in and out. Ask students whether the trombone makes a high or low note with the slide out. *low, because the extended slide enlarges the column of air inside*

COMPARING SOUND FREQUENCIES

Have you ever seen a dog or cat perk up its ears as if it just heard something, when you didn't hear anything at all? Dogs, cats, and other animals can hear sounds that humans can't hear. Figure 3-10(a) shows the sound frequencies that humans and animals can hear.

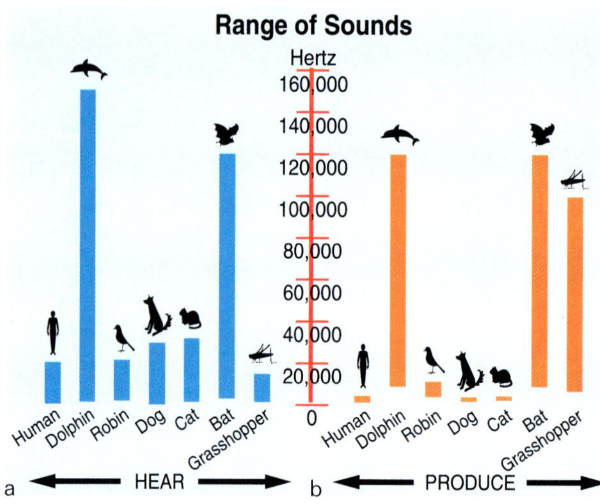

FIGURE 3-10. Graph (a) shows the range of frequencies humans and animals can *hear*. Graph (b) shows the range humans and animals can *produce*.

As the figure shows, many animals can hear a wider range of sound frequencies than humans can. Why do you suppose different animals hear different frequencies? An animal's ears are important for its survival. Many animals have a much better sense of hearing or smell than sight. Think about a mother wolf feeding and protecting her pups. She must have a keen sense of hearing to help her detect approaching danger and to find food for her family.

There are many more sounds around us than our ears can hear. You learned in Chapter 2 that the visible spectrum of light is just a small part of the radiation that exists in the universe. In the same way, there is a spectrum of sound frequencies that goes beyond what we are able to hear.

Check Your Understanding

1. If you stretched out a very thick rubber band and plucked it, how would the pitch of that sound compare with the pitch of a very thin rubber band? Why?
2. Would a whistle with a sound frequency of 3000 Hz have a higher or lower pitch than a whistle whose frequency was 5000 Hz? Explain your answer.
3. Use Figure 3-10 to compare the abilities of humans and dolphins to hear different frequencies.
4. **APPLY:** Explain how a guitarist can play all the pitches of a ballad with just six strings.

Answers to Check Your Understanding

1. The thick band makes a lower note. It vibrates more slowly.
2. A 3,000-Hz whistle has a lower pitch because there are fewer vibrations each second.
3. Dolphins can hear much higher pitches than humans.
4. Guitarists can produce many notes from a string by varying the thickness of the strings, as well as their length and tightness.

3-3 Music and Resonance

WHAT IS MUSIC?

You've just gotten home from school. You throw down your books, turn on some music, and dance around the room as you sing along with your favorite song. Has anyone ever called your favorite music a jumble of noise? Have you ever heard music that sounds noisy and confusing to you? What is the difference between music and noise?

Both music and noise are sounds. We sometimes think of noise as unpleasant or annoying. But some noisy sounds, like falling rain or ocean waves, can also be pleasant. What are some of the noises you hear during the school day? Lockers slamming, static on the public address system, brakes on school buses screeching, rain beating against the window, papers rustling, people laughing? Which do you think are pleasant and which are unpleasant?

You can make noise by tapping your pencil on the desk or speaking nonsense syllables. You can also use those sounds to create music. You could tap your pencil in rhythm or make up a melody for nonsense syllables.

OBJECTIVES

In this section, you will

- distinguish between music and noise;
- explain how different musical instruments produce sounds of different quality;
- describe resonance.

KEY SCIENCE TERMS

resonance

FIGURE 3-11. Music and noise are each sounds. What makes one more enjoyable than the other?

Section 3-3

PREPARATION

Concepts Developed

The previous lesson discussed pitch as the result of frequency. In this section, students learn the difference between music and noise, identify the factors that affect sound quality of musical instruments, and experiment with resonance, the tendency of objects to vibrate at the same frequency as a sound source.

Planning the Lesson

In planning your lesson on music and resonance, refer to the Chapter Organizer on pages 64A-B for timing suggestions, resources, and additional materials that will help you in your presentation of the lesson concepts.

For adequate development of the concepts presented in this section, we recommend that students do the Explore activity on page 81.

1 MOTIVATE

Discussion Ask students if they know what an electric guitar sounds like *without* electric power. Students should recognize that an electric guitar makes very little sound without power. Ask students to contrast this with an acoustic guitar, like the one used for the Find Out activity in the previous section. Students should recognize that the acoustic guitar makes much more sound than the powerless electric guitar. Ask students to brainstorm reasons the two differ. They should see that it has something to do with the acoustic guitar being hollow while the electric guitar is solid. L1

PROGRAM RESOURCES

Teacher Classroom Resources

Study Guide, page 15

How It Works, page 6, How a Record Player Works L1

Making Connections: Across the Curriculum, page 9, Synthesizer L1

Multicultural Activities, page 10, The Marimba

PROGRAM RESOURCES

Other Resources

The World of Sound Energy, video, Focus.

2 Teach

Tying to Previous Knowledge

In the previous lessons, students learned that sound is caused by the vibration of an object. In this lesson, students learn that the vibration of one object can set another object vibrating, whether or not the two objects are touching. For example, the vibrating loudspeaker will cause objects around it to vibrate.

Concept Development

Theme Connection The theme that this chapter supports is stability and change. Resonance causes a change in another object by causing it to vibrate at the same frequency. Resonance is at the heart of the study of sound. All acoustic musical instruments, including the human voice, depend on resonance for their loudness and sound quality. The theme of energy transfer is implied in the study of resonance where one object causes another to vibrate at the same frequency.

Using the Diagram When students examine Figure 3-12, ask them what specific features of the top wave makes it "organized," in the words of the text. If necessary, point out the repeated pattern of twin peaks, one much higher than the other. Ask students if they can see a similar pattern in the wave produced by noise. This wave has no such regular pattern.

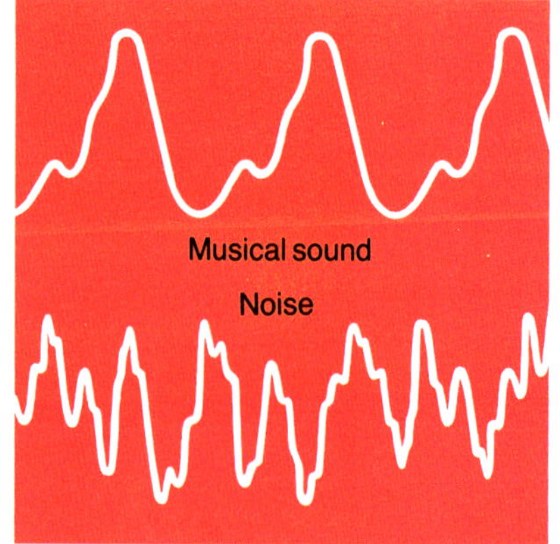

FIGURE 3-12. Musical sounds are organized. Noisy sounds are disorganized.

A sound that's considered noise in one situation might be music in another. The opposite is also true. A radio left on a music station overnight is noise to the person who's trying to sleep in the next room.

Imagine the sound of an electric saw cutting lumber. Now imagine the sound of a guitar. Why do we consider the saw noisy and the guitar musical? Examine the audiograms in Figure 3-12. Audiograms show a picture of sound vibrations. Using the audiograms, how would you describe the difference between the vibrations made by a noise, like an electric saw, and the vibrations made by a musical instrument, such as the guitar? Noisy sound looks messy and disorganized. But musical sound looks neatly organized into regular patterns. The organized guitar sound is pleasant to our ears. Disorganized, unpatterned sounds, like the noise of the saw, don't usually sound as good to us.

SOUND QUALITY

Think back to the activity where you played the guitar. The thinnest string on a guitar vibrates at about 330 Hz. You can play a note that has this same pitch on a clarinet, a cello, a piano, or a trumpet. You could even sing a note at this pitch with your voice. But, even though the pitch is the same, the quality of the sound will be different on each instrument. You can probably tell the difference between a note played on a piano and the same note played on a trumpet. You can hear the difference because each instrument has its own sound quality. This quality depends on a variety of things: whether the sound is made by a vibrating string or a vibrating column of air, the material the instrument is made of (wood, metal, plastic, or a singer's vocal cords), the size of the instrument, and its shape. The way the vibrations are set into motion can also have an effect on sound quality. For example, strumming guitar strings with your fingers and plucking them with a plastic guitar pick produces sounds with different qualities.

Here is an activity that shows how the quality and the loudness of a sound can be changed. The activity uses a

OPTIONS

Enrichment

Discussion Prepare for this discussion by obtaining a diagram of the nasal passages and sinuses. Ask students what happens to the sound of people's voices when they have a very stuffed-up nose. Students should enjoy imitating a person talking with a stuffed-up nose. Ask students to suggest reasons for this change in sound. After students have made several suggestions, display the diagram and ask students to explain how resonance might play a part in this change in sound. Students should identify the sinuses as chambers in which air resonates to the frequency of the vocal cords; when the sinuses are blocked, this resonance is lost.

tuning fork, which is a metal object designed to vibrate at a particular frequency. Musicians often use a tuning fork when tuning their instruments.

EXPLORE!

What is resonance?
Hold a tuning fork by the stem. Gently strike one of the fork's prongs with a rubber mallet. Listen to the sound.

Strike the tuning fork again. This time, hold the base of the stem against a table or desk top. What happens to the sound?

The tuning fork doesn't make a very loud sound. But what happens when you hold the stem of the tuning fork against the table? The sound gets louder. Can you explain why? You know that vibrating objects produce sound, and that sound can travel through solids such as the table as well as through air. Could the vibrating tuning fork have been making the entire table vibrate at the same frequency as the tuning fork?

a

b

FIGURE 3-13. A tuning fork vibrating alone (a) doesn't make a very loud sound. But if the tuning fork is placed against a table (b), the entire table vibrates, and the sound is louder. This is called resonance.

EXPLORE!

What is resonance?

Time needed 5 minutes

Materials tuning fork, rubber mallet

Thinking Processes
Thinking critically, Observing and inferring, Comparing and contrasting, Recognizing cause and effect

Purpose Students recognize that resonance can amplify sounds.

Preparation Make sure students stand near a wooden table or desk to perform the activity. If possible, have desks or tables with and without drawers available.

Teaching the Activity

Discussion The most effective resonance is obtained from hollow wooden objects. Have students place the tuning fork against the top of a desk or table with drawers or other space immediately beneath the top. Lead students to conclude that a table or desk with drawers results in the greatest resonance. L1

Expected Outcomes

Students should observe the difference between the loudness of the tuning fork alone and when touching the desk, and should infer that the vibrations of the tuning fork cause the desk to vibrate.

Answer to Question
The sound gets louder.

Enrichment

Activity Have students use tuning forks to test the resonance of different materials. Working in pairs, students should strike the tuning fork with a rubber mallet and touch the base to as many different kinds of materials as possible, including wood, plastic, glass, and metal. Ask students to prepare a bar graph of the relative resonance of the materials they test.

Content Background

For any object, the resonant frequency is the frequency at which it takes the least energy (loudness) to make the object vibrate. Bridges are designed so that wind or traffic vibrations will not match their resonant frequency. If strong vibrations match the bridge's resonant frequency, the bridge may vibrate enough literally to tear it to pieces.

SKILLBUILDER

The buzzing sound is resonance caused by the vibrating speaker. The vibrations of the speaker are causing another object to vibrate at the same frequency. L1

Concept Development

Activity Playing a kazoo demonstrates resonance in action in a fun way.

If possible, take apart a kazoo to show students the thin membrane inside. Ask for volunteers to form a "kazoo chorus." Have them begin by simply blowing through their kazoos. They might be surprised to discover that no sound is produced. Next have them hum a simple tune into the kazoo. Now they will notice that the kazoo gives a buzzing quality to their voices. Ask students if they can explain why there was an absence of sound when they blew into the kazoo but a musical sound was produced when they hummed into it. Lead them to discover that blowing air did not vibrate the membrane, but humming did. If you were not able to take apart a kazoo, it will probably be necessary to explain that there is a thin membrane inside of the instrument that resonates sound.

MAKING CONNECTIONS

Daily Life

Ask if any students have ever held a seashell (or water glass) to their ears and "heard the sea." Ask if any students know what the sound really is. Explain that the hissing sound they hear is blood moving through tiny veins in their ears. Resonance of the air within the shell helps amplify the sound so that it can be heard.

Teacher F.Y.I.

People with colds sometimes temporarily lose the ability to speak because their vocal cords swell up too much to vibrate and produce sound.

SKILLBUILDER

DETERMINING CAUSE AND EFFECT

When your stereo is playing, you occasionally hear a buzzing sound from another part of the room. What do you think might be causing this effect? If you need help, refer to the **Skill Handbook** on page 653.

RESONANCE

If you could take the low string off a guitar and stretch it tightly between two nails on a board, it would make a sound when plucked. But it wouldn't sound very much like the guitar pictured in Figure 3-14. A guitar's sound doesn't come just from the vibrating string making patterns of compression and rarefaction in the air. It also comes from the vibrations of the guitar body and the air inside it. When the string is attached to the guitar, the body of the instrument and the air inside it vibrate at the same frequency as the string. This tendency for an object to vibrate at the same frequency as another sound source is called **resonance** (REH suh nuns). Resonance means to resound, or to sound again.

Resonance is what caused the sound of the vibrating tuning fork to get louder when you placed it against the table. The vibrations of the tuning fork made the table vibrate at the same frequency. Since the table is much larger than the tuning fork, it set more particles of air into motion, and you heard a louder sound. The table resonated with the sound of the tuning fork. This is illustrated in the Explore figure.

FIGURE 3-14. When a guitarist plucks the strings on a guitar the strings make the wooden body of the instrument and the air inside it vibrate.

OPTIONS

Meeting Individual Needs

Visually Impaired Allow visually impaired students to make relative measurements in Investigate 3-2. Provide them with wide strips of non-corrugated cardboard at least 2.5 by 20 cm. Once the point of loudest resonance is determined, have the students grasp the tube gently between thumb and forefinger and slide their hand down until their fingers touch the water. (A partner or clamp must hold the tube motionless.) A cardboard strip should then be placed against the tube so that students feel its end just touching the water. With their free hand, students then grasp the top of the strip where it meets the end of the tube and bend it to mark its length. Repeat with the second tuning fork. Compare the two strips to draw conclusions about the length of the air column and its resonant frequency.

INVESTIGATE!

3-2 LENGTH AND RESONANCE

A tabletop resonates with the frequency of a vibrating tuning fork. The body of a guitar resonates with its vibrating strings. In this experiment, you will investigate the resonance of the air inside a glass tube.

PROBLEM

Can you find the length of a tube that will resonate with a given sound frequency?

MATERIALS

2 tuning forks of different frequencies (256 Hz or higher)
1 1000-mL graduated cylinder (or bucket or pitcher about 30 cm deep)
rubber mallet
plastic or glass tube, 2.5 cm in diameter, about 45 cm long, open at both ends
ruler

PROCEDURE

1. Copy the data table. Look at your tuning forks. You will see a number and the letters *Hz* etched into the metal. This is the tuning fork frequency in hertz. Record it under *Tuning Fork Frequency* in the data table.
2. Fill the graduated cylinder or bucket with water. While grasping one end of the plastic or glass tube with your hand, put the other end of the tube partway into the bucket of water as shown in the illustration. Hold it there.
3. Ask a partner to strike the tuning fork with the mallet and hold the fork over the tube, as shown.
4. Raise or lower the tube in the water until the loudest sound is produced. Without changing the tube's position, get your partner to **measure** the distance from the top of the tube to the water's surface. Record the length in the table. This is the length of tubing that resonates with the vibration of the tuning fork.
5. Repeat Steps 2–4 for the second tuning fork.

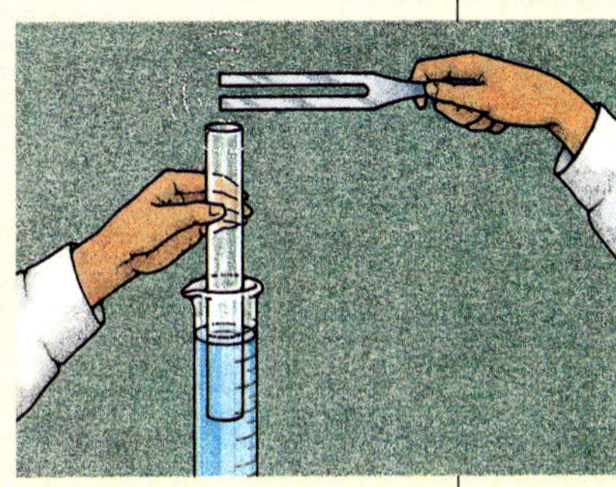

DATA AND OBSERVATIONS

TUNING FORK FREQUENCY	LENGTH OF THE TUBE OUT OF WATER (CM)

ANALYZE

1. **Interpret** your table to answer these questions. For which tuning fork is the length of tube out of the water longest? Which length of tube resonates at the lower frequency?
2. How does the length of a tube relate to its resonant frequency?

CONCLUDE AND APPLY

3. Obtain a different frequency tuning fork by trading with another group. Look at its frequency. **Predict** how the length of the tube that resonates with this tuning fork will compare with your earlier trials. Record your prediction. Try the experiment and see how your prediction compares with what you **observe**.
4. **Going Further:** Have you ever heard an object in a room buzz when a certain note is played loudly on the radio? What do you think causes this?

PROGRAM RESOURCES

Teacher Classroom Resources

Activity Masters, pages 15-16, Investigate 3-2

Answers to Analyze/Conclude and Apply

1. The greater length of tube resonates at the lower frequencies.
2. The longer the tube, the lower its resonant frequency.
3. Predictions should follow the rule that the greater the length of tube, the lower its resonant frequency.
4. The musical note was the resonant frequency for that object.

INVESTIGATE!

3-2 LENGTH AND RESONANCE

Time needed 30 minutes

Materials two tuning forks of different frequencies; 1,000-mL graduated cylinder; rubber mallet; plastic or glass tube 2.5 cm in diameter and about 45 cm long, open at both ends; ruler

Thinking Processes Organizing information, Making and using tables, Thinking critically, Observing and inferring, Recognizing cause and effect

Purpose Students learn that all sound media, whether air or an object, have a frequency at which they resonate most strongly, and that this resonance is directly related to the size of the medium.

Preparation Have students work in pairs. Any water container may be used so long as it is at least 30 cm deep and has a mouth wide enough to permit measurement with a ruler from the surface of the water upward. Distribute a higher-pitched and a lower-pitched tuning fork to each pair of students. If they are available, laboratory stands into which the pipes can be clamped will make the activity easier.

Teaching the Activity

Troubleshooting In raising and lowering the tube, students should be careful not to let the tube touch the container or the tuning fork. Tell students to study the illustration that shows the tips of the tuning fork being held close to the opening of the tube. Remind them to hold the tube as still as possible after determining the position of loudest resonance to allow accurate measurement. Students will produce the most accurate measurement if they test each tuning fork three times and average the measurements. L1

Expected Outcome

Students learn that a longer air column has a lower resonant frequency than a shorter one.

3 Assess

Check for Understanding

Remind students of your discussion of electric and acoustic guitars. Ask them to use what they now know about resonance to answer the Apply question completely.

Reteach

Provide the students with two tuning forks of the same frequency. Have one student strike a tuning fork. Have another student hold the second tuning fork near the first one. The second fork should start vibrating, too. Ask students why this happens. *the tuning forks have the same frequency* Have the students predict what would happen if the tuning forks were different frequencies. *the second one would not vibrate* COOP LEARN

Extension

For students who have already mastered these concepts play a note on a piano or acoustic guitar. (If a piano is used, press down on the right-hand pedal, which frees the strings to vibrate.) Have students sing the note you just played. Stifle the note as students continue to sing, then release that string. That string (and no others) should be vibrating by itself. Have students explain why the string continues to vibrate. LEP

4 Close

Obtain recordings of classical and hard rock music, and of noisy sound effects. Play selections and ask students to identify them as music or noise. LEP

DID YOU KNOW?

Cartoons and television commercials sometimes show a singer singing a long, loud, high note that causes a crystal glass to shatter. This can happen only if the singer produces a sound frequency the glass can resonate with. If you could sing a very loud note of the right frequency and hold the note long enough, you could make a glass vibrate so strongly that it would fall apart!

In the Investigate, you found that the length of an air column was related to its resonant frequency. There are many qualities of objects that affect the frequency at which they resonate. Thick plate glass windows will vibrate as heavy trucks rumble by on the street. You can see fine metal wire in a sculpture vibrate with sounds you can barely hear.

There are many sounds around us, with many different qualities. Sometimes people have different ideas about what makes a sound pleasant and what makes a sound unpleasant. What kinds of sounds do you like? Rain falling or rap music? What is your least favorite sound? Traffic noise or thunder? The next time you hear a sound that you really like, try to describe why you like it.

FIGURE 3-15. The deep, rich sound of an organ is the result of resonance.

Check Your Understanding

1. Compare and contrast music and noise.
2. Why can you identify different musical instruments just by listening, even when they are playing the same pitch?
3. Using a tuning fork and a table, how would you explain what resonance is?
4. **APPLY:** Explain why the body of an acoustic guitar is hollow, with an opening just under the strings. Hint: Remember that the strings are not the only part of the guitar that vibrates.

Answers to Check Your Understanding

1. Musical sound is neatly organized into regular patterns. Noise consists of disorganized, unpatterned sounds.
2. Instruments have different sound qualities depending on their shape, size, and material.
3. Strike the tuning fork with a rubber mallet to make it vibrate, then touch the base to the table. The table will resonate with the tuning fork to produce a louder sound than the fork alone.
4. The body of the guitar and the air inside the guitar resonate with the strings. The hole allows the sound to exit.

EXPANDING YOUR VIEW

CONTENTS

A CLOSER LOOK

YOUR VOCAL CORDS

What happens when you talk? How do you make those sounds? Just like other sounds, speech is produced by vibrations. When you speak or sing, the air you breathe out vibrates your vocal cords. The vocal cords are two thick folds of lip-shaped tissue that stretch across your larynx near the top of your windpipe.

When you make a high-pitched sound, your muscles in your larynx stretch your vocal cords, which tightens them and brings them closer together as shown in the illustration on the left. When you make a lower sound, your vocal cords relax a bit and move farther apart like the illustration on the right. You can control the pitch of your voice by tensing or relaxing your vocal cords. But changing the pitch of your voice rarely takes conscious effort because your brain adjusts your vocal cords automatically!

When you whisper, you form words with just your tongue and lips. Place your hand on your throat and say something out loud. Can you feel the vibrations? Now touch your throat and whisper. Your vocal cords should keep still.

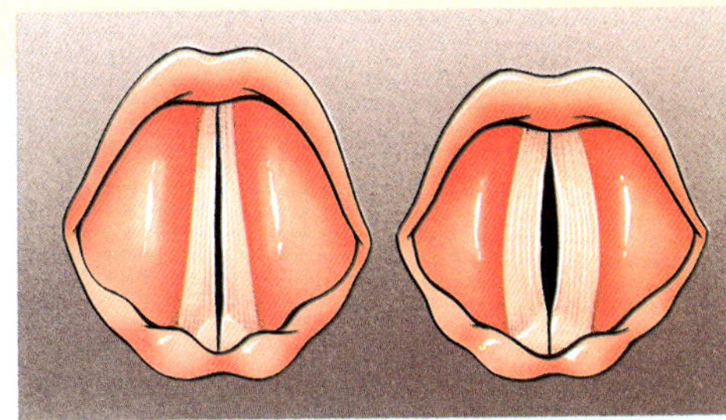

Ventriloquists make their voices seem to come from somewhere else—often from a puppet or dummy. The word *ventriloquist* comes from two Latin words meaning *belly* and *speak* (*venter* and *loqui*). Ventriloquists speak by moving only the tip of the tongue.

YOU TRY IT!

Practice these steps in front of a mirror, watching carefully for movement.

1. Bring your teeth together without tightening your jaw.
2. Part your lips slightly and smile a little.
3. Move your tongue to sound the vowels.
4. Next, try the consonants. Sounds like *f* and *v* may take longer because you usually touch your upper teeth to your lower lip to make them. *P*, *b*, and *m* sounds are tricky too because they're usually made by closing your lips. But, with practice, you can learn to imitate these sounds with just your tongue.

EXPANDING YOUR VIEW

Using Expanding Your View Assign one or more of these excursions to expand students' understanding of sound and how it applies to other sciences and other subjects. You may assign these as individual or small group activities.

A CLOSER LOOK

Purpose The role of vocal cords in producing speech is an example of some principles of sound presented in Chapter 3. Section 3-1 presented the concept that vibrations produce sound. In Section 3-2, students found that the pitch of a sound can be altered by changing the tension of the vibrating object. The pitch of people's voices is controlled by the tensing and relaxing of their vocal cords.

Content Background The tension of the vocal cords is the factor in voice production over which we have the least control. Adult men have vocal cords approximately one-third larger than adult women. This accounts for the deeper male voice. The other key factors in voice production are breath control and resonance in the nasal passages. This resonance is controlled by the position of the soft palette in the roof of the mouth. Providing a large, even volume of breath while lifting the soft palette provides the loudest, most resonant, and farthest-carrying sound.

Teaching Strategies The You Try It activity shows students how ventriloquists speak. Organize students into small groups to perform the activity. Ask each group to list the letters of the alphabet, noting whether each is easy or hard to produce with the teeth together and lips slightly apart. Then have students categorize the alphabet into two groups: those letters pronounced using the lips and those pronounced without them. COOP LEARN

Going Further Divide the class into small groups to conduct team library research into ventriloquism. Questions students should try to answer may include:

1. Do ventriloquists really "throw their voices" or is this an illusion?

2. What are the earliest known origins of ventriloquism and what purposes was it used for?

In addition to encyclopedias, students may wish to consult the following:

Richard, Dan. *Ventriloquism for the Total Dummy*. New York: Villard Books, 1987.

Winchell, Paul. *Ventriloquism for Fun and Profit*. Baltimore, MD: I & M Oppenheimer, 1954.

Have the groups present their findings as brief written reports. COOP LEARN

LIFE SCIENCE CONNECTION

Purpose The Chapter Opener focused on the variety of sounds surrounding us and the uses we make of them. The Life Science Connection describes the reticular activating system, a structure of the brain that filters these sounds.

Content Background Hearing involves a complex series of structures in the ear. When a compression wave strikes the eardrum, the eardrum bends inward, moving three linked bones in the middle ear that connect to a membrane at the entrance of the inner ear. The movement of this membrane sends waves through the spiral-shaped cochlea, causing tiny hairs in one of the cochlea's chambers to bend. This stimulates nerve fibers that carry signals to the brain. Approximately 27,000 nerve fibers and hairs run the length of the cochlea. High-frequency sounds vibrate only the front end of the cochlea. Medium frequencies vibrate the middle of the cochlea more than the front, while low frequencies make the strongest vibrations near the back end. Thus, our sense of pitch depends on which part of the cochlea vibrates most strongly.

Teaching Strategies Obtain a record or tape player and a recording of music likely to interest students. Play the recording at a fairly loud volume and read aloud the fourth paragraph describing the reticular activating system. Then ask students to explain what the RAS is and where it is located. Students will probably have trouble remembering, due to the music's interference. Point this out and ask them to describe their experience trying to pay attention to both things at the same time.

LIFE SCIENCE CONNECTION

SOUNDS ARE ALL AROUND YOU

Your ears are very sensitive instruments. They pick up many more sounds than you're aware of because your brain does such a good job of blocking out what you don't need to hear. Unless you make a conscious effort to listen to all the sounds around you, you may have no idea that many of them are there!

Take a moment just to listen. What do you hear? What about the sounds outside? Imagine how hard it would be to concentrate if you *always* noticed every sound around you!

Because your senses are constantly bombarded with all sorts of information, your brain needs a way to tune out some of it. Otherwise you couldn't concentrate.

An area in your brain called the reticular activating system (RAS) sorts out all the information your senses provide. The RAS is a network of nerve cells deep within your brainstem at the top of your spinal cord. It helps you focus your attention on specific sounds while tuning out all the others.

The RAS regulates your level of awareness by screening the messages from your senses and passing on only what seems important or unusual. For instance, your RAS helps you ignore the sound of lockers slamming in the hallway to concentrate on what your teacher says. And when a fire alarm goes off in that same hallway, your RAS automatically puts that message through.

Reticular Activating System

CAREER CONNECTION

Audiologists test people's hearing and work with those who have hearing disorders. Audiologists may work with schools, with business and industry, or with scientific or medical groups. Audiologists must have a master's degree from college to become practitioners. Many states also require them to be licensed.

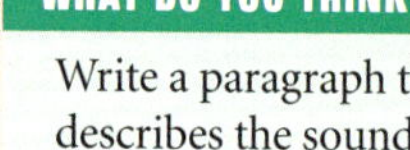

WHAT DO YOU THINK?

Write a paragraph that describes the sounds you hear in the morning when you wake up and the sounds you hear right before you fall asleep at night. What do these sounds tell you about your environment and the activities that are going on?

Going Further Divide the class into small groups to develop tests of what stimuli the RAS passes on and what it filters out. Each group's test may be different, but should present two stimuli and record which stimuli the subject perceived. For example, one test might ask the subject to read an interesting passage in a book or magazine while someone recites a list of 15–20 words. Immediately afterward, the subject would be asked to write down all of the words he or she recalls. The group can then discuss whether those words were important enough to pass through the RAS and why. Other tests might involve music and photos or a TV program and word list. After groups have conducted their own tests, have them exchange tests and compare the results. COOP LEARN

SCIENCE AND SOCIETY

USES OF ULTRASOUND

You already know that some animals—like cats and dogs—can hear sounds that humans cannot hear. Other animals—like bats and dolphins—can even make these high-pitched sounds themselves. Bats and dolphins use ultrasound—very high-pitched sound—to avoid obstacles and to find food. They produce these sounds and then listen for the echoes that reflect off animals and objects. The echoes help them navigate and find food.

Humans use ultrasound to navigate too, when we use sonar in the ocean. Sonar, which stands for SOund NAvigational Ranging, employs ultrasound echoes to measure depth and estimate the size and shape of underwater objects. This is done using a transducer, a device that first transmits the ultrasound and then converts the reflected echoes from sound waves into electronic signals. These signals are then used to produce video images or "sound maps."

We use ultrasound in many other ways, too. Because different substances reflect ultrasound in different ways, ultrasound has a number of medical uses. When ultrasound is sent into the body, the reflection from muscles, fat, and bones can be detected outside the body and converted into a video image. This lets doctors see inside the body without surgery or radiation.

Ultrasound provides a safe way to examine an unborn child inside its mother's uterus. Doctors can learn before delivery if there might be any problems. An ultrasound image, such as the one on the left, can also reveal the baby's sex as early as the third or fourth month of pregnancy.

Ultrasound is also used to study internal organs. Since it produces an immediate image, it can even show your beating heart! And because ultrasound images show subtle differences in tissue density, it might even help diagnose cancer.

Besides diagnosis, ultrasound has other medical applications. The man in the picture on the right is receiving a treatment called lithotripsy. The treatment employs ultrasound vibrations to shatter painful gallbladder stones and kidney stones, thus eliminating the need for surgery. Ultrasound is also used to treat muscle pain.

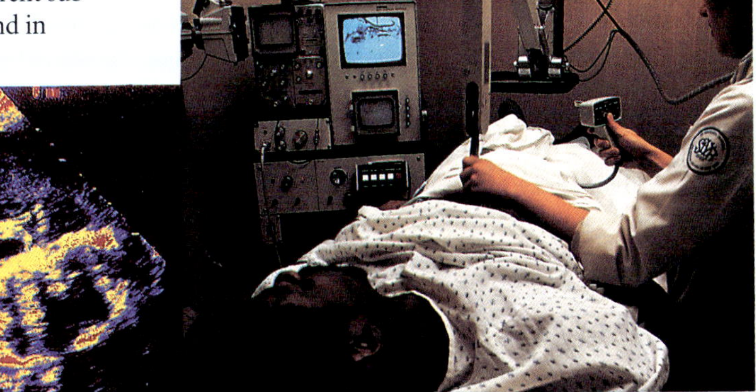

EXPANDING YOUR VIEW

SCIENCE AND SOCIETY

Purpose The pitch of sounds is a concept that was developed in Section 3-2. Science and Society describes the application of very high-pitched sounds, (ultrasound), and their echos in navigation, medicine, and industry.

Content Background Ultrasound is defined as sound vibrations above 20,000 hertz. Ultrasound technology is based on the fact that short sound waves tend to reflect from objects rather than bend around them, and that they can easily be focused into narrow beams. Transducers produce ultrasound through several methods. Magnetic systems apply a high-frequency electric current to a coil surrounding a metal rod, which contracts and expands slightly at the same frequency as the current. Piezoelectric systems apply an alternating electric current to a salt or quartz crystal, causing it to expand and contract. Other systems use high-velocity streams of gas or liquid resonating in a chamber filled with reflectors.

Teaching Strategies Have students working in groups create a table categorizing the uses of ultrasound described in the feature. Categories should include uses in nature (bats and dolphins), maritime uses (sonar), medical uses (internal diagnosis, stone and muscle treatment), and industrial uses (quality control, internal measurement, cleaning). After students have completed the You Try It activity on page 88, have them add these uses to their table, creating a consumer uses category to which the uses belong. COOP LEARN

Going Further Have students work either individually or in small groups to research specific aspects of ultrasound and present their findings as oral presentations accompanied by poster board text and illustrations. Topics for research may include:

1. The development of sonar and its importance in World War II
2. Medical applications not mentioned in the feature
3. Industrial uses not mentioned in the feature
4. How an ultrasound system works

In addition to encyclopedias, students may consult:

Knight, David C. *Silent Sound: The World of Ultrasonics.* New York: Morrow, 1980.

Windle, Eric. *Sounds You Cannot Hear.* Englewood Cliffs, NJ: Prentice-Hall, 1963.

EXPANDING YOUR VIEW

Answers to

YOU TRY IT

1. By breaking up fat globules into tiny droplets
2. An ultrasound system can detect when objects are approaching too closely and sound an alarm.
3. When invisible ultrasound beams set up across doorways are broken by an intruder, the burglar alarm is sounded.

TECHNOLOGY CONNECTION

Purpose The Technology Connection is a good follow-up to the discussion of noise in Section 3-3. Noise control methods based on the interaction of sounds that cancel each other out are being developed to cut unpleasant noises.

Content Background ANC is a new noise-control method. Traditional methods include sound absorption through carpets and porous materials that dissipate sound; sound isolation, preferably in an airtight enclosure; and the addition of white noise, pleasant, even noise which masks less pleasant sounds.

Teaching Strategies To help students understand ANC, draw a sound wave as a series of compressions and rarefactions. Draw a second wave overlapping it so that the peak of one wave is directly over the valley of another wave. Explain that the second wave represents the ANC sound, which balances the compression and rarefaction of the noise and cancels it out.

Answers to

WHAT DO YOU THINK?

Answers will vary but should note that only regular sounds can be canceled by ANC; not sudden, unexpected noise.

It carries energy into muscles deep inside the body. Such treatments provide relief for people suffering from arthritis or similar diseases.

Since ultrasound lets us see inside of objects, it is also useful in industry. Cracks, holes, and impurities can be detected in all sorts of materials without damaging the item or endangering the person running the test. Ultrasound helps us examine items made of metal, glass, concrete, ceramics, fiberglass, and rubber. It is even sensitive enough to measure the thickness of a tiny contact lens!

The automotive, aircraft, and electronics industries use ultrasound to clean and degrease parts. This is very helpful for hard-to-reach places and items that can't be cleaned safely with detergents.

It works like this—the dirty part is placed in a liquid solvent. Then when ultrasound is passed through the liquid, tiny bubbles are produced. When these tiny bubbles burst, they send out surprisingly powerful shock waves. These high-energy shock waves knock the dirt particles right off the part!

YOU TRY IT!

Find out about some other ways that ultrasound is used. Read about one of the following applications of ultrasound or interview people familiar with its use. Summarize what you learn in a brief report.

1. How is ultrasound used to pasteurize or homogenize milk?
2. How does ultrasound warn blind people about obstacles in their path?
3. How is ultrasound used in burglar alarms?

TECHNOLOGY CONNECTION

AN ANTINOISE DEVICE

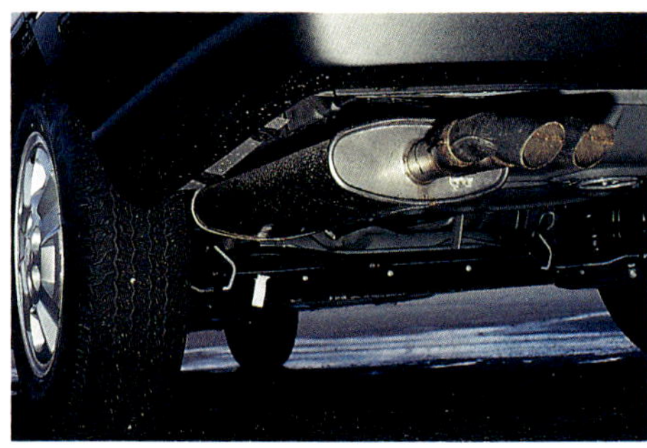

It may seem strange to fight noise with noise, but that's exactly what a new technology is doing! Active noise control (ANC) devices produce sound that matches the amplitude and frequency of noisy sound sources. But the sound in an ANC device vibrates in the opposite direction of the undesirable sound. The two sounds cancel each other out, and the result is silence.

ANC devices are already used in air conditioners, heaters, and fans. The devices will soon be added to refrigerators and car mufflers. The perceived noise from these machines will be cut to a noise almost as soft as a whisper. Thanks to innovations like ANC, it may soon be possible to cancel out troublesome noises before they even start!

WHAT DO YOU THINK?

1. Are there any noises in your school that ANC might silence?
2. In what household appliances do you think ANC could be useful?
3. What noises in your neighborhood might be reduced by ANC?

Going Further Ask students to assume that local government wants to build a new airport near their community. Organize the class into two teams to debate the pros and cons of the airport. Work with each team to help them brainstorm a list of reasons to support their position. The pro team should focus on economic benefits: new jobs, tax revenue, and improved transportation. The con team should focus on noise pollution and its consequences for the community. Have several representatives from each team present the team's position and arguments, then solicit responses from individual students on the issue. Interested students may wish to research actual airport projects and their encounters with local opposition. The construction of Tokyo's airport in Japan is one of the world's leading examples. COOP LEARN

Music CONNECTION

HEART AND SOUL

You've probably heard music before, but do you know how instruments make their own unique sounds? Like all sound, the sounds from instruments are the result of vibrations. In the case of a trumpet, a player blows into a mouthpiece, causing the air in the body of the trumpet to vibrate. The pitch and sound can be changed by varying the pressure of player's lips on the mouthpiece, and by opening or closing three valves that effectively lengthen or shorten the column of air in the trumpet body.

A violin player draws a bow across the strings of the violin to produce vibrations. The body of the violin amplifies these vibrations. The strings are different lengths and thicknesses, and therefore, produce different sounds. Pitch can be changed when the player presses the strings against the neck of the violin. This changes the length of the string that is vibrating.

Playing an instrument is more than using the science of sound. It also depends on the skill and heart of the player, together known as talent. Trumpeter Louis Armstrong and violinist Midori play different kinds of music on very different instruments, but both are recognized as musicians with very special talents. Louis Armstrong was known for playing jazz. Jazz has a strong rhythm and free-form melody where the musician is expected to improvise—or make notes up. Midori is known for playing classical music on her violin with tremendous vigor.

Louis Armstrong was born in 1900 in New Orleans—the city where jazz was born. He moved to Chicago, then on to New York where he became a major figure in jazz. In addition to playing the trumpet, he sometimes sang nonsense syllables, called scatting. Armstrong died in 1971, but he is still remembered worldwide by his nickname Satchmo and revered for what he could do with sound.

Midori was born into the world of music. As a youngster, she went to rehearsals with her mother, a professional violinist in Osaka, Japan, and was always trying to reach for the violin. On her third birthday, Midori was given a violin, half the size of an adult's. Midori practiced endlessly with her mother. An American music teacher heard a tape of Midori playing and invited the eight year old to play in a summer festival at Aspen, Colorado. Her power, technique, and skill amazed everyone. Midori and her mother moved to New York City in 1982 so that Midori could study at the Julliard Institute of Music. Since then, Midori has performed in many countries, including her native Japan. At one performance she played with violin masters Isaac Stern and Pinchas Zuckerman.

YOU TRY IT!

Listen to a recording of Louis Armstrong and to one of Midori. How does the music make you feel?

MUSIC CONNECTION

Purpose The beautiful tone of Louis Armstrong's trumpet or Midori's violin depends on the factors discussed in Section 3-3 that affect sound quality.

Content Background Louis Armstrong is recognized as the leading trumpeter in jazz history. As a child, he followed the brass bands through the streets of New Orleans and came to know many of the pioneers of jazz. Although early on he played the trumpet in marching bands and on Mississippi riverboats, it was not until 1922 when he came into his own. That year, his hero, Joe "King" Oliver, sent for him to play second trumpet in a Chicago band. This led to a series of recordings with Oliver's Creole Jazz Band, including such classics as "Dipper Mouth Blues" and "Canal Street Blues." The series of records he made from 1925-1928 with his Hot Five and Hot Seven bands established his pre-eminence. From the 1930s on, Armstrong also gained fame as a film star, comedian, and bandleader.

Teaching Strategies Have students help you develop a list of factors affecting the sound of a musical instrument, based on their reading of this feature. Point out that this list does not reflect the many possible variations that produce a particular sound.

Answers to YOU TRY IT

Answers will vary. Students may have different ideas of how Armstrong's and Midori's music makes them feel.

Going Further A number of your students probably play musical instruments. Have students bring in instruments and play them for the class, ensuring that there are as many different instruments as possible. For each instrument, ask the student to describe how it makes its sound and how the pitch and quality of the sound may be varied. Lead the discussion by reminding students what they learned in the chapter concerning vibration as the source of sound, the means for changing the pitch of sound, and the factors affecting sound quality. For example, a trumpet player may describe the vibrating column of air inside the trumpet as the source of sound, the valves as a means of changing the length of the column in order to change its pitch, and the metal as producing a hard, brassy sound.

EXPANDING YOUR VIEW

TEENS IN SCIENCE

Purpose Teens in Science discusses the importance of understanding concepts about sound for personal and career achievements. For example, a sound engineer decides what adjustments to make by understanding that a higher frequency results in a higher sound.

Content Background The development of digital recording systems has transformed the recording of music. Consumers are familiar with digital recording through compact discs and digital audiotape, but the real revolution is in the recording studio and is most evident in rock and roll, where studio special effects are given free reign. In conventional recording, the voices and instruments are recorded on separate tracks of recording tape. A final song is assembled by cutting and splicing the tape and controlling the volume and tone of each individual track. With advanced digital systems, the voices and instruments are fed directly into a computer in digital form. There the sound can be shaped, fed through synthesizers that drastically alter it, and reassembled in countless ways.

Teaching Strategies Borrow a portable electronic keyboard instrument from your school's music department, a staff member, or a student. If a student provides one, ask him or her to demonstrate the special effects the instrument can provide, or demonstrate them yourself for the class.

TEENS *in* SCIENCE

MAKING WAVES—SOUND WAVES, THAT IS

Your favorite musical group is coming to town, and you've got a ticket! On the day of the concert, you listen to every record the group has ever made. But that night you're surprised to find that the group sounds completely different. What's going on?

Eighteen-year-old West Virginian Torey Verts knows a lot about why things sound the way they do. She's a professional sound engineer. "When you listen to a record, you are hearing a lot more than your favorite band. Computers get a lot of use in the studio today. We can completely change a band's sound. For example, if the singer can't hit high notes, the engineer can turn a dial, and suddenly there's no problem. We can speed the music up or add special effects and synthesizers. Even though the sound engineer can do all these things, I don't think musicians have much to worry about. After all, who wants to see a computer in concert?"

Torey, like many sound engineers, is a musician herself. "If I could, I would be up on the stage playing my guitar. That's why I love to work live concerts. Engineering lets me be a part of the sound. Of course, live concerts can be tough. If something goes wrong with the sound, you've got to fix it fast. You can't ask the audience to take a break while you find a loose connection." Torey has found that a good understanding of scientific principles can really help when you need to solve a problem.

"If you want to get involved in music, you've got to learn as much as you can about the sciences," says Torey. "But you also need to know what sounds good. The best way to learn is to listen. Try and hear what it is you like about a song. What makes it sound good? What would make it sound better? And don't be afraid to listen to bad music either. Knowing what *doesn't* work is just as valuable as knowing what does."

YOU TRY IT!

Many radios, stereos, and CD players let you make adjustments to the sound that you hear. As you listen to a song, gently turn the treble knob as far to the right as it will go. Play the same song again and adjust the bass knob. What is the difference between these two adjustments? Reminder: When you have completed this assignment, be sure to return both knobs to their original positions.

Answer to YOU TRY IT

Turning down the treble control filters out the high notes; turning it up makes the high notes louder. Turning down the bass control filters out the low notes; turning it up makes the low notes louder.

Going Further Tell students that even though computers and electronic effects have become very popular in music, some people think that music loses more than it gains from them. Play two recordings in contrasting styles for students. One recording should be free of electronic effects. Classical or Folk, music will probably work best as music examples having few electronic modifications. The other recording should be contemporary rock or rap making heavy use of electronic effects. Organize the class into small groups. Have each group develop a list of things they like and do not like about each recording. Play each recording two to three times during the group discussions. Then lead a class discussion that pools the positive and negative comments on each recording and attempts to reach a consensus on the positive and negative impact of electronic effects. COOP LEARN

Reviewing Main Ideas

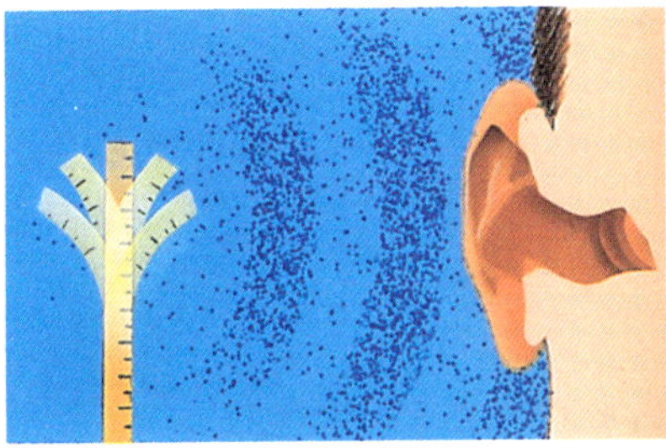

1. Sounds are created by vibrating objects. When an object vibrates, it creates a pattern of compressions and rarefactions in the particles of the air.

2. We usually hear sounds that travel to our ears through the air. But any kind of matter can conduct sound.

3. Your ears recognize differences in sound frequencies as differences in pitch. Pitch refers to the highness or lowness of a sound.

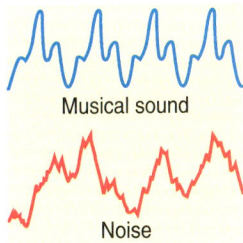

Musical sound

Noise

4. Both music and noise are sounds. We often think of noise as unpleasant or annoying. Musical sounds are organized in a pleasing way.

5. The tendency for any object to vibrate at the same frequency as another sound source is called resonance. Resonance means to re-sound, or to sound again.

Chapter 3

Reviewing Main Ideas

Have students read the page and look at the photos. The two teaching strategies below ask students to explain the basic mechanism of sound and media, and to explain the relationship among vibration, frequency, and resonant frequency. Have students use the terms *vibration, medium, frequency, music and noise,* and *resonance* as they review the photographs.

Teaching Strategies

Ask students to explain why their Find Out activity with the Slinky was a good model for how sound moves through the air. Help students as required to explain that vibrating objects alternately compress and rarefact the air and send out a series of compression and rarefaction waves, transmitting the vibration to your ear. Other than the vibrational motion, the air molecules do not change place. You may wish to raise the question of how solid materials can be compressed and rarefacted; the explanation has to do with the fact that solid objects still exhibit movement on the molecular level, and are elastic enough to be compressed and rarefacted by vibration. But because they are more solid, they transmit sound more efficiently.

Tell students that they performed two Investigate activities involving vibrating columns of air above water. Ask students to describe what they learned from each. One activity taught them that the frequency of a vibrating air column was determined by its size; the other taught them that the resonant frequency of an air column also varied with its size. Ask students to suggest what frequency of vibration and resonant frequency have to do with each other. Help them as required to see that the resonant frequency of an object is that frequency at which it vibrates most easily, and that this is naturally the frequency at which it vibrates when you blow across it.

Chapter 3

Chapter Review

USING KEY SCIENCE TERMS

Answers

1. rarefaction
2. compression
3. resonance
4. The number of times that a particle in a medium vibrates back and forth in one second is the frequency. We recognize changes in the frequency of vibration as changes in pitch.
5. As sound vibrations travel through a medium, they create rarefactions and compressions.
6. As the frequency increases, we hear a higher pitch.
7. Compressions in one medium can result in compressions in a second medium. Each medium produces the same pitch, and the result is resonance.

UNDERSTANDING IDEAS

Answers

1. frequency or pitch
2. compression and rarefaction
3. Hertz
4. medium
5. faster
6. lower
7. sound quality

CRITICAL THINKING

Answers

1. The trumpet was slightly larger, the air column in the trumpet is slightly longer and therefore the pitches were slightly lower.
2. In each instrument the length of the air column can be adjusted by depressing a key (which in turn moves a valve to lengthen or shorten the vibrating column of air.) The length of the air column determines the sound.
3. In outer space, there is little or no air. Therefore, the space between spaceships would probably be a poor conductor of sound and vibration and so the explosion of one spaceship is not likely to cause the explosion of another.

Chapter Review

USING KEY SCIENCE TERMS

compression	pitch
frequency	rarefraction
hertz	resonance
medium	

Give the science term with a meaning opposite to that of the following phrases.

1. a squeezed together area
2. a spread out area
3. two sound sources vibrating at different frequencies.

For each set of terms below, explain the relationship that exists.

4. pitch, frequency, vibration
5. compression, vibration, rarefaction
6. frequency, pitch
7. pitch, compression, resonance

UNDERSTANDING IDEAS

Complete each sentence.

1. You need to know how many times the sound source vibrates every second in order to determine the ____ or ____.
2. Vibrating objects create patterns of ____ and ____ that travel through the air to your ears.
3. Frequency is measured in ____.
4. The speed of sound depends on the ____ through which it travels.
5. Sound travels ____ through metal than it does through air.
6. The pitch of a 4-inch column of air is ____ than the pitch of a 3-inch column of air.
7. You can tell the difference between a guitar and a flute playing the same pitch because the ____ is different.

CRITICAL THINKING

Use your understanding of the concepts developed in the chapter to answer each of the following questions.

1. At the beginning of an outdoor band concert, Lee's trumpet was in tune. During intermission the trumpet was left out in the sun. The sun warmed up the metal, expanding it and actually making the trumpet slightly larger. When Lee began to play after intermission, the pitches weren't quite right. Were they too high or too low?

PROGRAM RESOURCES

Teacher Classroom Resources

Review and Assessment, Chapter Review and Chapter Test, pages 13–16

Computer Test Bank, Chapter Test

OPTIONS

Cooperative Learning

Consider using Cooperative Learning in the Understanding Ideas, Critical Thinking, Problem Solving, and Connecting Ideas sections of the Chapter Review.

COOP LEARN

2. Look at the photo. How are notes of different pitch produced in these musical instruments? Why do the instruments have different sounds?
3. In a science-fiction movie, when a spaceship explodes in outer space, the vibrations from the sound nearly destroy a nearby spaceship. If you were technical advisor for the movie, what would your advice be about this scene?

PROBLEM SOLVING

Read the following problem and discuss your answers in a brief paragraph.

Your class is putting on a variety show, and you've been assigned to put together a "kitchen" band. That is, you must come up with instruments made from ordinary household items like pots and pans, glasses, silverware, and other common articles.

1. Suggest at least five different types of instruments for your band. Remember that they must not only make noise, but they must also be able to produce differently pitched notes and play a melody.
2. For each kitchen instrument, describe how it is played and where the sound comes from. In other words, what is vibrating that produces the sound?

CONNECTING IDEAS

Discuss each of the following in a brief paragraph.

1. How are frequency and pitch related?
2. Can you explain how a stethoscope would help a doctor listen to a patient's heart?
3. Picture yourself at a party where everyone is drinking soft drinks out of 10-ounce bottles of the same shape and height. Every time you take a swallow, you blow across the top of your bottle to make a sound. Describe how the sound will change as everyone gets closer and closer to finishing his or her drink.
4. SCIENCE AND SOCIETY Some dentists use ultrasonic drills. Explain how an ultrasonic drill might work.
5. MUSIC CONNECTION A violin, a viola and a cello are about the same shape, but don't sound the same. What could cause this?

PROBLEM SOLVING

Students' answers will vary.

1. soda bottle filled with water, the sound would be made by blowing over the bottle and the air inside the bottle would vibrate
2. fork, the sound would be made by hitting the tines of the fork which would then vibrate
3. spoons make musical sounds when the bowls of the spoons are hit against one another, it is the spoons which vibrate
4. hitting a pan cover with a metal or a wooden spoon would vibrate the cover and the air around it
5. shaking a closed jar half full of beans would result in the beans vibrating against the glass and then the glass itself vibrating

CONNECTING IDEAS

Answers

1. Frequency describes how fast an object is vibrating, pitch is the sound a person hears. Greater or faster vibration produces higher sound or pitch.
2. The end of a stethoscope "collects" the sound and concentrates the vibrations. The air column in the stethoscope tubing vibrates at the same rate as the air. The air column conducts the sound to the doctor's ears.
3. As partygoers drink more soda, the air column in each bottle becomes longer and the sound from each bottle deepens.
4. An ultrasonic drill conducts vibrations into the decayed part of the tooth. This breaks up the decayed matter without breaking or damaging the healthy part of the tooth. After the decayed matter is loosened, it can be removed from the tooth cavity.
5. The size of the "box" used in each stringed instrument provides for a different resonance from the instrument. In addition, if the strings of the instruments vary in length, or thickness, the vibrations will sound different from one another.

CHAPTER ORGANIZER

SECTION	OBJECTIVES	ACTIVITIES/FEATURES
Chapter Opener		**Explore!** How do you experience space? p. 95
4-1 How Do You See? (4 days)	1. **Describe** the functions of the parts of the eye. 2. **Describe** how light and color are sensed. 3. **Compare** responses to light in humans and other animals.	**Explore!** What is the function of your pupils? p. 96 **Explore!** How well do you think you see? p. 98 **Investigate 4-1:** Testing Your Vision, p. 99 **Skillbuilder:** Interpreting Scientific Illustrations, p. 100 **Find Out!** How do fruit flies respond to light? p. 103
4-2 How Do You Hear? (3 days)	1. **Diagram** the pathway of sound in the ear. 2. **Explain** how you know where you are in space and how you keep your balance. 3. **Compare** hearing in humans with hearing in other animals.	**Find Out!** Are two ears better than one? p. 105 **Explore!** Why do you feel dizzy when you spin around, then stop suddenly? p. 108 **Skillbuilder:** Interpreting Scientific Illustrations, p. 108
4-3 Touch, Taste, and Smell (2 days)	1. **Describe** the mechanism of the sense of touch. 2. **Relate** the senses of taste and smell. 3. **Compare** touch, taste, and smell in humans and other animals.	**Find Out!** How does your skin respond to different temperatures? p. 111 **Investigate 4-2:** Tasting Solutions, p. 114
Expanding Your View	A Closer Look **Konrad Lorenz,** p. 117 Physics Connection **Sonar and Echolocation,** p. 118 Science and Society **Aiding the Hearing-**	**Impaired,** p. 119 Literature Connection **You Can Always Hear the Ocean,** p. 120 Art Connection **Perspective,** p. 121 How It Works **Cochlear Implants,** p. 122

ACTIVITY MATERIALS

EXPLORE!	INVESTIGATE!	FIND OUT!
Page 96 mirror **Page 98** ruler **Page 108** glass, water, chalk dust or ground cinnamon	**Page 99** blank sheet of white paper **Page 114** 1% vinegar solution, 1% sugar solution, 6 test tubes, test-tube rack, graduated cylinder, beaker or small pitcher, water, 2 eyedroppers, wax marking pencil, 1 cup for rinsing mouth	**Page 103** culture of fruit flies, black paper sleeve to fit over culture, desk lamp or microscope lamp **Page 105** loudly ticking clock, blindfold, disposable ear plug or cotton **Page 111** rubber gloves; 3 bowls of water (1 hot, 1 cold, 1 room temperature)

Chapter 4
Using Your Senses

TEACHER CLASSROOM RESOURCES	OTHER RESOURCES
Study Guide, p. 16 **Concept Mapping,** p. 12 **Activity Masters, Investigate 4-1,** pp. 17-18 **Flex Your Brain,** p. 8 **Multicultural Activities,** p. 11 **Making Connections: Integrating Sciences,** p. 11 **Making Connections: Technology and Society,** p. 11	**Laboratory Manual,** pp. 13-16, Parts of the Eye **Color Transparency and Master 7,** The Ear and the Eye ***STVS:** *Night Blindness Model,* Animals (Disc 5, Side 2) *Nearsightedness Surgery,* Human Biology (Disc 7, Side 2) *Low Vision Clinic,* Human Biology (Disc 7, Side 2)
Study Guide, p. 17 **Flex Your Brain,** p. 8	**Color Transparency and Master 8,** Echolocation
Study Guide, p. 18 **Critical Thinking/Problem Solving,** p. 12 **Take Home Activities,** p. 9 **Activity Masters, Investigate 4-2,** pp. 19-20 **How It Works,** p. 7 **Making Connections: Across the Curriculum,** p. 11 **Multicultural Activities,** p. 12 **Review and Assessment,** pp. 17-20	***STVS:** *Nerve Regeneration in Garfish,* Animals (Disc 5, Side 2) *Brain Development,* Human Biology (Disc 7, Side 1) **Computer Test Bank**
	***STVS:** *Hearing by Touch,* Human Biology (Disc 7, Side 2) *Ear Implants,* Human Biology (Disc 7, Side 2) **Spanish Resources** **Cooperative Learning Resource Guide** **Lab and Safety Skills**

***Science and Technology Videodisc Series**

KEY TO TEACHING STRATEGIES

Teaching strategies have been coded for varying learning styles and abilities. As you review teaching strategies in the margin, the following designations will help you decide which activities are appropriate for your students.

L1 Level 1 activities are basic activities and should be within the ability range of all students.

L2 Level 2 activities are average activities and should be within the ability range of the average to above-average student.

L3 Level 3 activities are challenging activities designed for the ability range of above-average students.

LEP LEP activities should be within the ability range of Limited English Proficiency students.

COOP LEARN Cooperative Learning activities are designed for small group work.

ADDITIONAL MATERIALS

SOFTWARE	AUDIOVISUAL
Senses, Ventura Educational System. *The Eye,* Queue. *The Ear,* Queue.	*Ears and Hearing/Eyes and Seeing,* laserdisc, EBEC.

Chapter 4

Using Your Senses

THEME DEVELOPMENT

The themes that this chapter supports are interactions and systems and scale and structure. Students learn how the structures of our sense organs enable them to collect information about the world. This chapter also discusses how the sense organs interact to form a sensory system. For example, the organs of taste and smell interact to provide information about food being eaten.

CHAPTER OVERVIEW

This chapter deals with the senses. First, students learn about the structure of the eye and how light and color are sensed. In addition, the vision of animals and humans is compared.

Students also learn how the various parts of the ear work together to allow us to sense sounds. The role of the ear in space perception and balance is discussed, as is the role of hearing in various animals.

Finally, the senses of touch, taste, and smell are explored. Students find out how the skin, nose, and tongue respond to stimuli. This section explains the importance of these senses to the survival of many animals.

Tying to Previous Knowledge

Ask students how they would learn about a new place if they had just arrived and found no one there to describe it. Lead students to realize that they would look around, listen to the sounds, smell the air, and touch objects. Divide the class into several small groups. Assign each group a type of place, such as a bakery, a wooded area, a zoo, and a science lab. Have each group describe their place in terms of what they could find out by using their senses. Have other groups try to identify the place being portrayed. COOP LEARN

DID YOU EVER WONDER . . .

What makes a cat's eyes shine in the dark?

Why you get dizzy when you stop spinning around?

How you can hear the sound of the ocean in a seashell?

You'll find the answers to these questions as you read this chapter.

DID YOU EVER WONDER...

Students will explore these questions as they progress through the chapter. Don't spoil their fun and motivation by sharing these answers too early.

- Cats have a mirrorlike area in the back of each eye that reflects light. (page 102)
- You get dizzy because the fluid in your semicircular canals keeps moving even though you have stopped. (page 108)
- The sound is really the sound of your own blood rushing through blood vessels in your ear. The shell focuses the sound. (page 109)

Chapter 4

Using Your Senses

Trying to make sense of the world is something you have struggled with since you were born. Through your sense organs—your eyes, ears, skin, tongue, and nose—you gather information about the world. Can your senses sometimes lead you to believe something that may not be true? Do you use information collected through your senses to train yourself to act in a certain way? The baby in the photograph is crawling out over a visual cliff with absolutely no fear. She hasn't learned yet that an edge is something to stay away from. In time, she may also learn to question some of the information her senses provide.

Finding out about your surroundings always begins with making observations. But your understanding of the world is limited by the information you are able to gather through your senses and how well-developed those senses are. Knowing how your senses operate and how to use them effectively helps you interpret your observations correctly.

EXPLORE!

How do you experience space?

Close your eyes. Move your hand from left to right in front of your face. Where does left change to right? Move your hand up and down. Where does up change to down? Move your hand from front to back next to your ear. Where do front and back meet? Where do the front/back, left/right, and up/down planes intersect? How do you locate yourself and other things in space?

Introducing the Chapter

Ask students what visual memories they have of an early event in their lives. Discuss the significance of the memories. You may also choose to discuss early memories of smells, tastes, sounds, and textures students recall and the significance of these memories.

Uncovering Preconceptions

Many people believe that reading in dim light can damage the eyes. Actually, there is no serious damage, just eyestrain, which can cause discomfort and headaches. Nevertheless, people should avoid straining their eyes.

EXPLORE!

How do you experience space?

Time needed 5 minutes

Materials No special preparation is required for this activity.

Thinking Process
Comparing and contrasting

Purpose To show how people sense their position in space.

Teaching the Activity

Demonstration Hold both arms out in front of you. Then hold your arms out at your sides. Ask students what areas you located. *Front and side.* L1

Expected Outcome

Students will see that they select reference points on the head to describe the motion of the hand.

Answers to Questions

1. Left changes to right in the middle of the face, near the nose.
2. Up changes to down in the center of the face.
3. Front and back meet in the middle, about where the ears are.
4. All planes intersect in the center of the head.
5. We compare our location with the location of other things. In this exercise, students located their hands in relation to their heads.

Project

Divide the class into five groups and assign each group one sense. Have each group read the newspaper and listen to the news every day. They should take note of any stories that relate to their assigned sense. Students can read about medical advances, restaurant reviews and recipes (taste, smell), movie reviews (sight, hearing), and any articles that are related to senses. Have each group report to the class.

Science at Home

Have students demonstrate how we rely on our senses. Tell students to fix a simple meal for a friend or relative and dye the food with food coloring. The person eating the meal should be blindfolded for the first taste. Then remove the blindfold and see how the person reacts to unusually colored food, such as green mashed potatoes. Ask how the color of food might be a danger sign. *Spoiled food may change color.*

Section 4-1

PREPARATION

Concepts Developed
Students have learned about the physics of light and color. In this section, students will discover how the eye allows us to see light and color. The primary detectors are specialized cells in the retina of each eye. One type, rods, are sensitive to light and dark, the other, cones, are sensitive to color.

Planning the Lesson
In planning your lesson on sight, refer to the Chapter Organizer on pages 94A-B for timing suggestions, resources, and additional materials that will help you in your presentation of the lesson concepts.

For adequate development of the concepts presented in this section, we recommend that students do the Explore, Investigate, and Find Out activities on pages 96, 99, and 103.

1 MOTIVATE

Discuss how information received from the eye is stored in the brain for later recall. Ask students how they recognize someone or something they have seen before. *They may say that images are like photographs or that the brain is like a camera, which records images on film, much like a memory.* L1

4-1 How Do You See?

OBJECTIVES

In this section, you will

- describe the functions of the parts of the eye;
- describe how light and color are sensed;
- compare responses to light in humans and other animals.

KEY SCIENCE TERMS

retina
receptors
rods
cones
phototaxis

LIGHTS, CAMERA, ACTION—YOUR EYES

When was the last time you had your picture taken or took someone else's picture? It may have been more recently than you think. In many ways, your eyes are like two cameras, always taking pictures. In a camera, light passes through an opening into a dark chamber. At the back of the chamber, the light strikes a light-sensitive material called film and produces an image. In a similar way, light enters your eye through an opening called the pupil. The pupil looks like a small black hole. It is really the entrance to a fluid-filled chamber inside your eye.

EXPLORE!

What is the function of your pupils?

Look at your eyes in a mirror. Notice your pupils, the dark circles at the center of each eye. Now stand in a dark closet for two or three minutes. Hold a mirror in front of your face, close to your eyes, and quickly open the closet door. Did your pupils change? How? Still holding the mirror close to your eyes, close the closet door almost all the way, until there is just enough light to allow you to see your eyes in the mirror. How did your pupils change this time? How does light affect your pupils?

FIGURE 4-1. The human eye sees color best during the light of day (a). In the dark of night, we see black and white best (b).

a

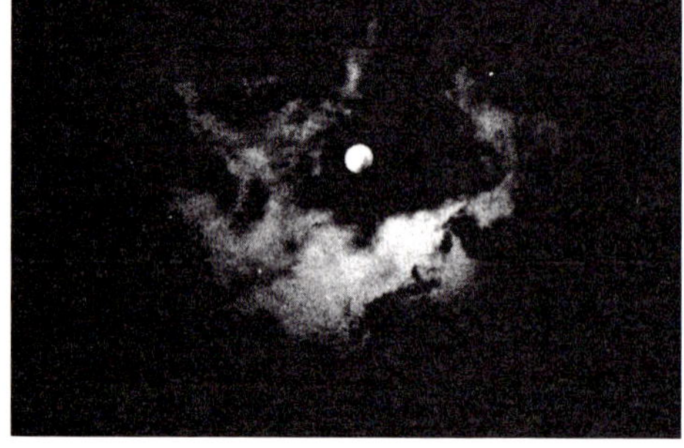

b

EXPLORE!

What is the function of your pupils?

Time needed 5 minutes

Materials No special materials or preparation are required for this activity, which can be done as an independent activity.

Thinking Process
Observing and inferring

Purpose To show that pupils react to the amount of light available

Teaching the Activity
Discussion Before assigning the activity, have students predict what will happen. Accept all predictions at this time. L1

Expected Outcome
The pupils get larger in darkness and smaller in light.

Answers to Questions
1. The pupils got smaller.
2. The pupils got larger.
3. The more light there is, the smaller the size of the pupils; the less light, the larger.

Did you notice the colored part of your eye when you looked at your pupil? This colored area is the iris, a ring of tiny muscles that surrounds the pupil. These muscles usually contain some blue or brown pigment. You can see these muscles in Figure 4-3. The iris muscles control the size of the pupil according to the amount of light available. What happened to your pupils in bright light and in dim light? What might be the reason for the changes you observed?

FIGURE 4-2. Light passes through the lens of a camera and strikes the film.

A camera can take pictures in color or black and white, depending on which kind of film is used. Did you ever hear of a camera that can take pictures in both color and black and white at the same time? Your eyes can. Look at all the different colors and shapes on this page. The light that enters your eye passes through the lens, a structure that focuses the light on the retina at the back of your eye. The **retina** is a tissue that is sensitive to light. It is similar to the film you put in a camera. Your eyes can detect all kinds of colors and shapes, light and shadows, without changing the "film" that is your retina.

FIGURE 4-3. The iris of your eye is a ring of tiny muscles that surrounds the pupil. These muscles control the amount of light that enters your eye.

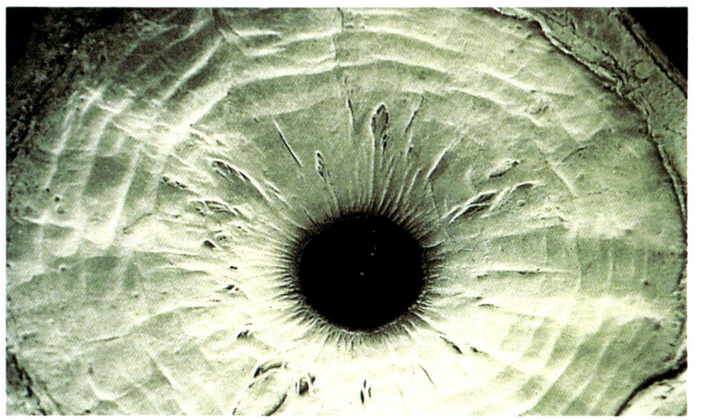

DID YOU KNOW?

The iris of the eye is named after Iris, the Greek goddess of the rainbow.

2 TEACH

Tying to Previous Knowledge

Ask students how they would describe themselves in a letter to a pen pal. Probably one of the first things they would describe is what they look like. Sight is the sense most often used to describe our environment.

Concept Development

Theme Connection As students do the Explore activity and learn about the function of the iris, they are exposed to the theme of interactions and systems. The nerves in the eye sense the amount of light. Interactions in the nervous system cause the iris to respond to changes in light level.

Student Text Questions What happened to your pupils in bright light and in dim light? *They got smaller in bright light and larger in dim light.* What might be the reason for the changes you observed? *To make sure the eye receives enough light to see by, but not so much light that the eye could be damaged*

Using the Photo You may want to compare the iris in Figure 4-3 to a camera diaphragm. The diaphragm is opened and closed so that the amount of light reaching the film (retina) is neither too bright nor too dim. If possible, borrow a camera and allow students to see the similarities.

OPTIONS

Meeting Individual Needs

Physically Challenged Some students may not be able to go in and out of closets. Students can sit at their desks in a darkened room. After they have observed their pupils, ask them to close their eyes and cover them with cupped palms. Then turn on the lights and have students uncover their eyes to observe any changes. Turn off the lights again while students are looking into their mirrors. Ask them to observe further changes. Some students may have trouble holding the mirror. Pair these students with students who can hold the mirror, or obtain a mirror on a stand.

EXPLORE!

How well do you think you see?

Time needed 5 minutes

Materials No special materials or preparation are required for this activity.

Thinking Processes
Observing and inferring, Comparing and contrasting

Teaching the Activity

Discussion Ask students whether they know what optical illusions are. Ask for examples. *Optical illusions are visual perceptions that lead a person to see something that does not look as it really is.* The "one line is longer" illusion is a misinterpretation of what is real. The crossties on a railroad track are all the same size. However, the parallel tracks appear to come together in the distance, which gives the impression that the more distant crossties are shorter than the closer ones. Based on this knowledge, the brain is fooled into thinking that the more "distant" bar is larger than the nearer one because the more distant bar overlaps the tracks while the closer one does not. L1

Expected Outcome

Students will believe that one bar is longer until they measure to find them the same.

Answers to Questions

1. They are the same length.
2. The position of the railroad tracks fooled the brain.

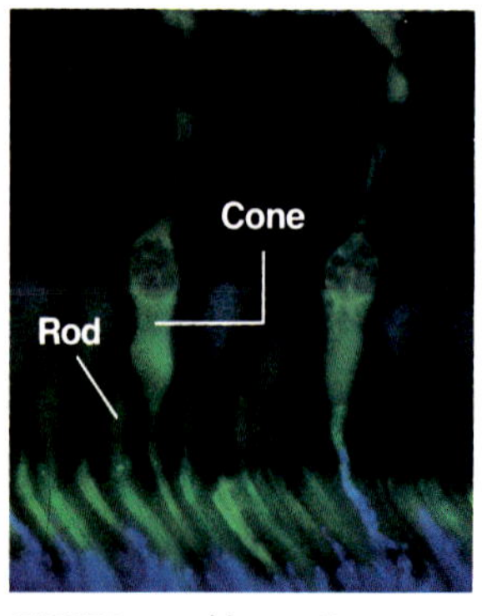

FIGURE 4-4. Your retina contains two types of light receptors. Black-and-white images are formed by receptors called rods. Color images are formed by receptors called cones.

Your eyes are similar to a camera that takes two pictures at the same time, one in black and white and one in color. This happens because there are two different kinds of light-sensitive structures, or light **receptors**, in the retina that respond to changes in light and color. These receptors are called rods and cones. **Rods** are receptors that are sensitive to light and dark. You see black-and-white images when the rods in your retina are stimulated. **Cones** are receptors that are sensitive to all the colors in the visible spectrum of light—red, blue, green, and so on. You see color images when the cones in your retina are stimulated.

Have you noticed that you don't see colors very well at night, or any time the light is dim? This is because cones, the color receptors in your retina, are not very sensitive to dim light. The light entering your eyes must be fairly bright before you can see colors. Rods are much more sensitive to dim light.

The rods and cones in the retinas of both your eyes send information to your brain through a large nerve at the back of the retina. Your brain works to combine all this information into a single image made up of both black-and-white and color images. Do you think it's possible that your brain might make mistakes in combining all that information to come up with just one image?

EXPLORE!

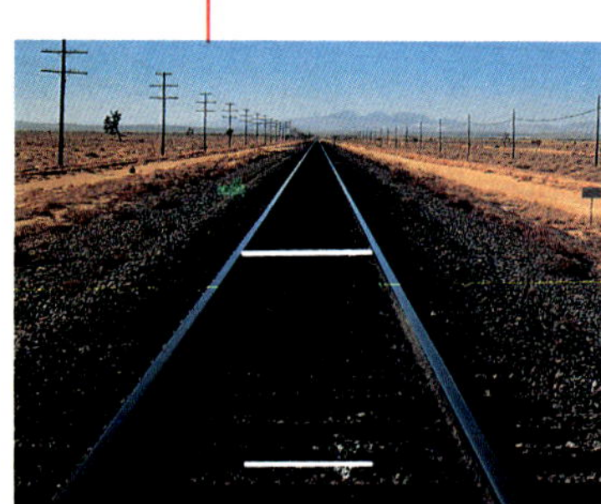

How well do you think you see?

Look at the railroad track in the photograph. Which white bar is longer? Did you pick the top one? Maybe you picked the bottom one. Measure both bars. How do their lengths compare? How do you explain your observation that one bar was longer than the other?

The railroad tracks in the photograph create an optical illusion. An optical illusion is a trick played on your eyes. It shows you that you can't always rely on what you see, or what you think you see. Let's find out why.

Teacher F.Y.I.

The color of the iris is caused by melanin, the same pigment that colors the skin.

PROGRAM RESOURCES

Teacher Classroom Resources

Activity Masters, pages 17-18, Investigate 4-1 L1

OPTIONS

Enrichment

Activity Have students keep a record of how they see from the time they get up until the time they go to bed. *They may record not being able to see well when entering a darkened theater or room on a bright day. They may also record that after a few minutes their vision seemed to improve.* Have students do research to discover how the eyes make this adjustment. L2

INVESTIGATE!

4-1 TESTING YOUR VISION

You probably rely on your vision more than your other senses for information about the world, but . . .

PROBLEM

Just how reliable is your sense of sight?

MATERIALS

blank sheet of white paper

PROCEDURE

1. Copy the data table.
2. With your left eye closed, stare at the cross on the left side of the figure for 10 seconds.
3. **Observe** the page as you move it slowly toward you. Does the dot on the right disappear at a certain spot? Record your observation in the data table.
4. Repeat Steps 2 and 3 with your right eye closed, but this time stare at the dot and see if the cross disappears. Record your observation in the data table.
5. Stare at the triangles for 30 seconds, then look at the blank sheet of white paper. You will still see two triangles. What colors are they? Record them in the table.

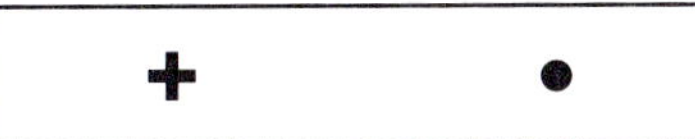

ANALYZE

1. Did the dot disappear when you stared at the cross with your right eye?
2. Did the cross disappear when you stared at the dot with your left eye?
3. What happened to the colors of the inner and outer triangles when you looked at the white paper?

CONCLUDE AND APPLY

4. **Compare and contrast** the receptors in your eyes that detected the cross and the dot with the receptors that detected the triangles.
5. **Going Further:** Form a **hypothesis** to explain why you aren't usually aware of having a blind spot in each eye.

DATA AND OBSERVATIONS

Sample data

TEST		OBSERVATIONS
Dot	Right eye open	disappears
Cross	Left eye open	disappears
Colors	Outer triangle	green
	Inner triangle	red/orange

INVESTIGATE!

4-1 TESTING YOUR VISION

Time needed 5 minutes

Materials blank sheet of white paper

Thinking Processes
Making and using tables, Observing and inferring, Comparing and contrasting, Forming a hypothesis

Purpose To show that the optic nerve produces a blind spot on the retina.

Preparation You may want to have the data tables prepared and copied in advance. Enlarge the table somewhat, to make it easier for students to fill in.

Teaching the Activity

Discussion Remind students that the sense of sight depends on the physical structure of the eye. Ask if they think that all parts of the eye function only to receive light. Suggest that there must be a way to relay information to the brain. L2

Student Journal Have students record their results in their journals.

Expected Outcomes

Students will discover a blind spot in their vision. The data tables should read down: disappears, disappears, red/orange, green.

Answers to Analyze/Conclude and Apply

1. yes
2. yes
3. They reversed. The green triangle became red-orange and the red-orange triangle became green.
4. Rods detected the black and white cross and dot; cones detected the colored triangles.
5. Since you usually have both eyes open, your brain receives enough information from the receptors to interpret what you are seeing. The part of the image that falls on the blind spot of one eye falls on a working area of the other eye.

Meeting Individual Needs

Visually Impaired Students who wear glasses or who should wear glasses may have difficulty with the Investigate activity in this section. Students with astigmatism will have the most trouble because of lack of focus. An alternative test for the blind spot follows. Have students extend both hands directly in front of them with the thumbs up. Then students should close the left eye, focus on the left thumb, and slowly move the right hand to the side. Students should be staring straight ahead at the left thumb during the activity. Students will find that the right thumb "disappears" when it is 8–10 inches from the left thumb. To make the activity easier, have students put small, colored sticky dots on their thumbs.

SKILLBUILDER

Students should list structures in the order that light strikes them: cornea, pupil, lens, retina. Light does not travel through the optic nerve. L1 LEP

Concept Development

Theme Connection One theme that this section supports is interactions and systems. The eye is a part of an animal's sensory system. The eye takes in information and passes it on to the brain. The brain interprets and acts on visual stimuli in coordination with other senses.

Discussion Discuss movie making with students. As mentioned in the text, movies are made from single frames of images shown so quickly that movement appears. Ask whether students have ever seen a demonstration of cartoon making. Explain that it is done with minute changes.

Activity Have students make a flip book to show how a series of drawings is interpreted by the brain as motion. On the bottom of the last page of a small notepad, have students make a simple line drawing. It could be a stick figure or a flower with a stem. On the sheet above it, students should make the same drawing in the same place. If the paper is thin enough, students can trace the figure. But one or two lines should be changed a little in succeeding drawings. For example, move an arm up bit by bit, or tilt the stem downward bit by bit. Students should continue doing this for 10 to 15 sheets. Their final drawing will look much different from their first. Now, students should flip the pages quickly front to back with a thumb. What do they see? *Students should discover that they have made a moving picture.* This is an example of how the brain fills in information that is not actually received.

Flex Your Brain Use the Flex Your Brain activity to have students explore nearsightedness and farsightedness.

SKILLBUILDER

INTERPRETING SCIENTIFIC ILLUSTRATIONS

Using Figure 4-5, list the structures that light travels through in the eye. If you need help, refer to the **Skill Handbook** on page 659.

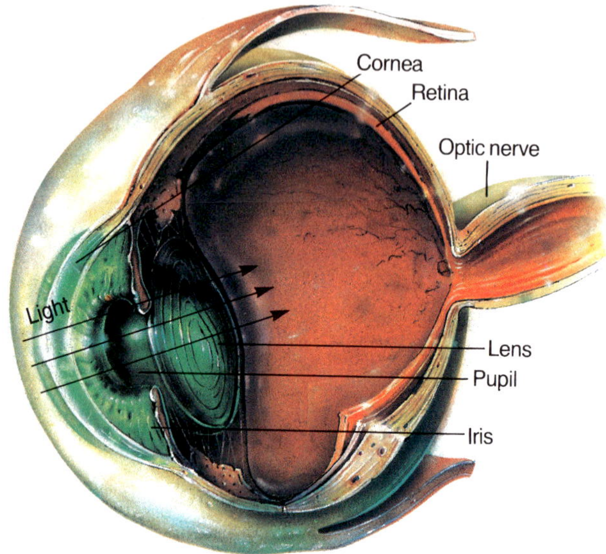

FIGURE 4-5. This diagram shows the parts of the human eye. The cornea is a clear covering that protects the iris and pupil.

In the Investigate, you demonstrated that you have a blind spot in each eye. The blind spot is an area on your retina where there are no rods or cones. Instead, this area is made up of fibers that form the optic nerve. You can see this area of the retina in Figure 4-5. The optic nerve carries information from the rods and cones to your brain. Normally, you don't notice your blind spots because your brain fills in these small gaps. Think about what happens when you watch a movie. Even though the movie is composed of separate photographs, or frames, that are shown one after the other, you see smooth, continuous action. This is because the frames of the film move by very quickly. Your brain fills in the gaps between frames. In a similar way, your eyes send a constant and very rapid series of pictures to your brain. You see your surroundings as smooth and continuous because your brain fills in the small gaps created by your blind spots.

FIGURE 4-6. Many times your brain will fill in missing visual information.

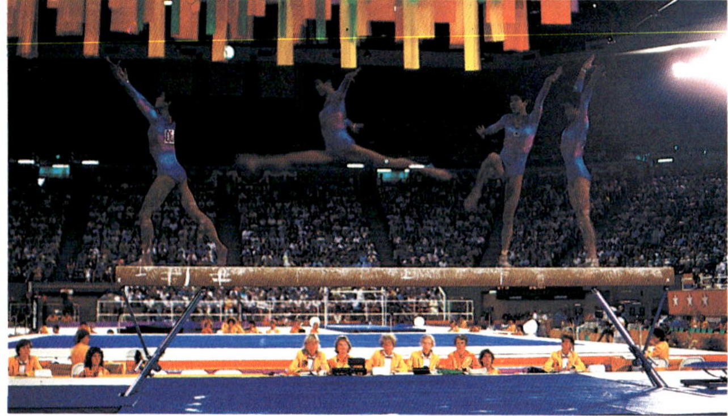

PROGRAM RESOURCES

Teacher Classroom Resources

Critical Thinking/Problem Solving, page 8, Flex Your Brain

Transparency Masters, page 17, and **Color Transparency,** number 7, The Ear and the Eye L1

Other Resources

Ears and Hearing/Eyes and Seeing, laserdisc, EBEC.

OPTIONS

Enrichment

Research Have students research the way the human lens turns images upside down. Ask students to draw a diagram illustrating how the image hits the retina. L3

FIGURE 4-7. Where is an eye in this photograph?

IT'S ALL IN HOW YOU SEE IT

Your brain often fills in missing visual information. Glance at Figure 4-7 quickly, then look away. What did you see? Now look at the photograph more carefully. What do you see this time? Did you first see the head of a large fish that, on closer inspection, was actually the whole fish? If you carefully examine the fish, you can see its real eyes. Do you think the large eyespot might fool a predator into thinking the fish is bigger and more dangerous than it really is?

Take a quick look at Figure 4-8. Did you see leaves? Look again. One "leaf"is really an insect. What would be the advantage to an insect looking like a leaf?

FIGURE 4-8. Is there an insect in this photograph?

ANIMAL EYES

Have you ever wondered whether animals see the world the same way humans do? Have you ever wondered what cats, dogs, birds, or bees see? One of the ways we can find out how an animal sees is by comparing the structure of that animal's eye to the structure of the human eye. Another way is to compare the behavior of that animal with our behavior or with the behavior of other animals.

Take the behavior of the cat, for example. We know that cats are more active at night than during the day. This is

Concept Development

Uncovering Preconceptions Because of cartoons such as *Superman,* students may believe that eyes send out light rays that bounce off objects and then back to our eyes. Actually, our eyes receive rays reflected from objects.

MAKING CONNECTIONS

History

When people first saw movies, they were terrified. The image of an approaching train appeared frighteningly real. Have students find out how the French brothers, Auguste and Louis Lumière, invented the first movie camera and projector. Also have students explore the reason Auguste refused to market their invention.

Content Background

A person's lens can be too curved, causing nearsightedness, or not curved enough, causing farsightedness. Eyeglasses help to correct defects in the shape of a person's eye. A concave lens corrects for nearsightedness by causing the image of an object falling in front of the retina to fall on the retina. A convex lens corrects farsightedness by causing the image of an object falling behind the retina to fall on it.

Teacher F.Y.I.

The image that forms on the retina is upside down, but the brain interprets the image as right side up. A Swiss scientist made glasses with special lens glasses that inverted the images as a camera does. People who wore these glasses received right-side-up images on their retinas. But their brains were used to reversing upside-down messages, so these images were inverted, too. These people saw everything upside down. But after a while, their brains started to reinterpret the images, because the brain knows the world is not upside down. Normal vision returned as the brain adjusted to the changed images.

Enrichment

Discussion Ask students to identify other examples of insects that look like objects. Students might have heard of walkingsticks and leafhoppers that look like thorns.

PROGRAM RESOURCES

Teacher Classroom Resources

Study Guide, page 16

Laboratory Manual, pages 13-16, Parts of the Eye L3

Concept Mapping, page 12, Sensing the World L1

Other Resources

Senses, software, Ventura Educational System.

The Eye, software, Queue.

Concept Development

Using the Photo In Figure 4–9, students may notice that the reflection from the cat's eyes is narrow at the top and bottom. This is because cats' irises contract in a vertical manner. Because of their hunting habits, cats need to be able to have excellent up-and-down focus. They use little peripheral vision.

Content Background

Students may want to know more about the structure of animals' eyes. Animals with backbones have eyes that are somewhat similar to humans' eyes. But their eyes often have different coverings. Cats have an extra membrane that acts as a mirror. Fish do not have tear glands. They do not need to wash the surface of their eyes. Even animals without backbones are sensitive to light. Planaria, a kind of flatworm, has light-sensitive cells. More-developed animals such as insects have compound eyes, which may consist of thousands of lenses joined together.

Teacher F.Y.I.

Because of the structure of a frog's eye, it responds only to motion. To find food, the frog looks for moving insects. A frog who had hundreds of freshly killed insects in front of it would starve to death. It would not recognize the insects as food.

How do we know?

A similar project was done by Dr. W. R. A. Muntz. His subjects were frogs. You or the students can read about his experiments and construct your own experiment. Refer to *The Brains of Animals and Man* by Russell Freedman and James E. Morriss (New York: Holiday House, 1972), pp. 29–31.

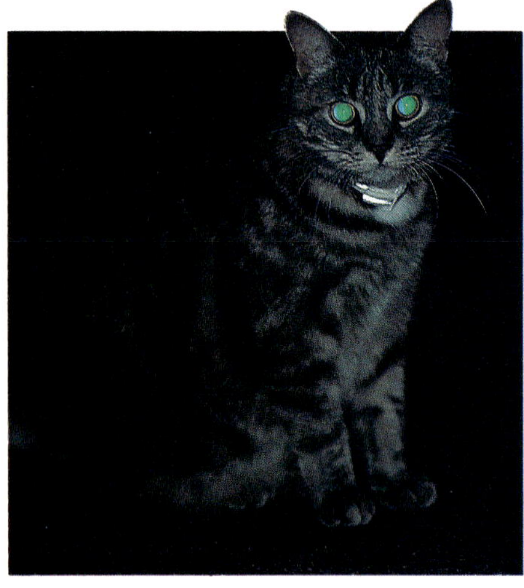

FIGURE 4-9. A cat's eyes sometimes seem to glow in the dark because they have a mirrorlike area in the back of each eye that reflects light.

one way that cat behavior differs from human behavior. We also know that cats are very good hunters, and can see well enough to catch mice, even in the dark. So we know cats must have better night vision than we do.

Look at the cat's eye pictured in Figure 4-9. By looking at the structure of the cat's eye, we can find some clues about why they can see so well in the dark. Have you ever watched a cat prowling at night? If it looked at you, perhaps you saw its eyes suddenly seem to glow in the dark. When you see this glow, you are actually seeing light reflected from a mirrorlike area at the back of the cat's eye. This mirror area reflects light onto the cat's retina, increasing the amount of light that reaches the retina. This is one of the reasons cats can see so well in the dark.

A second reason cats see well in the dark is that they have many more rods than cones in their retina. Can you

How do we know?

Do bees see color?

In 1913, Karl von Frisch determined that bees do indeed see the colorful world of flowers. He fed some bees sugar water on blue paper. Then he gave them a choice of blue paper without sugar water and papers of different shades of gray. The bees settled only on the blue paper, proving they had learned that blue was a color signal for food. They recognized the blue paper by its color, not just by its brightness.

Other scientists performed the same type of experiment, but they used lights of different colors and brightness in place of the blue-colored paper. In a different kind of experiment with bees, the colors of flowers were analyzed by measuring the light reflected by their petals. Combining the results of these two types of experiments gave scientists an idea of what colors bees are able to see. The scientists found that bees see red poorly, but they see violet so well that they can see markings on flowers (a) that we can't see (b). These markings may guide bees to the flower's nectar, like landing lights at an airport.

a 

b 

PROGRAM RESOURCES

Teacher Classroom Resources

Multicultural Activities, page 11, Percy Lavon Julian L1

Making Connections: Integrating Sciences, page 11, Machines and Mechanisms that Sense L2

Making Connections: Technology and Society, page 11, A New Vision L2

OPTIONS

Enrichment

Activity Have students write a story from the point of view of a cat. The images should be described primarily in black and white.

explain why having more rods would make it easier to see at night? Do you suppose cats see in color?

Light is important to the way an animal finds food, protects itself from other animals, and finds a mate. Look at the animals that are pictured in Figure 4-10. Can you tell anything about how they live or how well they can see by looking just at their eyes? The red-eyed tree frog lives in the dim light of thick tropical forests. Its large pupils let more light into the eye for better vision. The salamander is blind. It lives in a dark cave where there is no light. The bee, like many other insects, has compound eyes that can see in many directions at once. A bee's-eye view might look something like Figure 4-11. Let's find out whether another insect, the fruit fly, needs light.

FIGURE 4-10. What can you tell about these animals from their eyes?

FIND OUT!

How do fruit flies respond to light?

Your teacher will provide a culture of fruit flies and a black paper sleeve that fits over the culture. Leave the sleeve off the culture for the time being. Aim the light of a desk or microscope lamp so that one side of the culture is brighter than the other side. Where are most of the flies after 5 minutes? Are they on the side closer to the light source or farther away? Slip the paper sleeve over the culture so that the hole in the sleeve is on the side of the culture away from the lamp. After 5 minutes, carefully remove the sleeve and quickly oberve where most of the flies are.

Conclude and Apply

Do fruit flies move toward or away from light?

Concept Development

Student Text Questions Can you explain why having more rods would make it easier to see at night? *Rods are more sensitive to dim light than cones are.* Do you suppose cats see in color? *If there are cones in the retina of the cat's eyes, then a cat must be able to see color. But since cones require light, cats can see color best during the day.*

FIND OUT!

How do fruit flies respond to light?

Time needed 15 minutes

Materials culture of fruit flies with a black paper sleeve to cover the culture, lamp

Thinking Process
Observing and inferring

Purpose To investigate how fruit flies react to light.

Preparation Be sure your culture is alive and active. Prepare sleeves to cover culture. Use black paper to make a cover that slips over the culture. Cut a hole about the size of a dime in the paper.

Teaching the Activity

Discussion Ask students what insects they may have seen being attracted to artificial light sources. *Responses may include moths and other insects.* L1

Expected Outcomes

Students will see that fruit flies gather near the hole in the sleeve and will infer that they are attracted to light.

Conclude and Apply
Fruit flies move toward the light.

Enrichment

Field Trip Take a trip to your local zoo. Have students classify animals they see by the kind of eyes they have and the position of the eyes. Ask students to hypothesize what advantage the particular eyes of an animal may give it. To answer this question, students must be aware of the behavior of the animal. If a field trip cannot be arranged, borrow library books that have large photographs of animals.

Multicultural Perspectives

Owls have excellent night vision and hunt at night. Eagles and other predatory birds have keen vision. Many cultures believe that animals with keen senses can confer these abilities on people. Have students investigate the belief in totems and the special abilities they are supposed to give people.

Concept Development

Student Text Questions Can you conclude whether or not fruit flies exhibit positive or negative phototaxis? *yes, positive phototaxis* What does this tell you about these insects? *They need light to find food or mates.*

3 Assess

Check for Understanding

1. Have students make a list of animals that hunt at night. Ask students to discuss why these animals can see so well in the dark. *They should say the animals can see well because of having more rods than cones in their eyes.*
2. Have students answer and discuss the Check Your Understanding questions. With regard to question 4, discuss what might happen to the owl population if many owls were born with more cones than rods.

Reteach

Have students start a *Dictionary of the Senses*. Divide students into groups and have each group come up with a definition for one term in this section. For each term defined, have students provide a drawing or photograph from a magazine. L1

Extension

Have students who have mastered this section explore how sunglasses can protect the eyes from permanent damage. L3

4 Close

Have students observe objects in minimal light. Then tell them an old expression: "In the dark, all cats are gray." Ask them to explain this in terms of this section. *Students should refer to the fact that the human brain registers colors as shades of gray when light is minimal.* L1

FIGURE 4-11. The view through a bee's compound eyes might look something like this.

You have demonstrated that fruit flies are attracted to light. The movement of an animal in relation to light is called **phototaxis**. *Photo* means light, and *taxis* means movement. If an animal, such as a fruit fly, moves toward light, the movement is called positive phototaxis. If an animal moves away from light, the movement is called negative phototaxis. Using the results of the test you performed, can you conclude whether or not fruit flies exhibit positive or negative phototaxis? What does this tell you about these insects?

How important is light to your life? Think about the different things you look at every day. Imagine what your life would be like if you could not see. If you lost your vision, could you tell where you are, find out what is around you, or move from one place to another? Do you think you could learn to use your other senses to gather all the information you would need to survive? In the next section, you will learn about another one of your senses that would be difficult to live without.

Check Your Understanding

1. Name each part of the eye and describe its function in allowing you to read the words on this page.
2. Earthworms live in the soil. If you did an experiment with earthworms like the experiment you did with fruit flies, what would you expect your results to be? Explain in terms of phototaxis.
3. Write a comparison of how a bee and a cat respond to light and color. How do their responses help them locate food in their different environments?
4. **APPLY:** Owls hunt at night and sleep during the day. Would you infer that owls have more or fewer rods on their retinas than you do? More or fewer cones? Why?

Answers to Check Your Understanding

1. The pupil admits light into the eye. The lens focuses the images of the letters on the retina. The rods detect the dark print against the light background. This information is carried to the brain by the optic nerve.
2. Since earthworms live underground, they avoid sunlight. They would probably demonstrate negative phototaxis.
3. Bees are active in daylight. The colors they see lead them to flowers that contain nectar. Cats are active at night. Their night vision, not color, allows them to see the shapes of mice and other prey in the dark.
4. Owls probably have more rods than cones because rods are more sensitive to dim light.

4-2 How Do You Hear?

MUSIC AND DANCE--BOTH ARE IN YOUR EARS

You've come to a fallen tree in a forest. If no one was around when it fell, did it make a sound? This riddle kept philosophers guessing for hundreds of years. Vibrations moving through air, water, or earth, such as those started by a falling tree, are what we call sound. Sound, like light, exists whether or not a human or other animal is around to experience it.

You know that humans have two ears. Dogs, cats, birds, monkeys, elephants, and other animals also have two ears. Here's an activity that will show you one of the advantages of having two ears.

OBJECTIVES

In this section, you will

- diagram the pathway of sound in the ear;
- explain how you know where you are in space and how you keep your balance;
- compare hearing in humans with hearing in other animals.

KEY SCIENCE TERMS

eardrum
cochlea
semicircular canals

FIND OUT!

Are two ears better than one?

Work with two other students. Have one sit down, blindfolded, on a chair. Holding a clock that ticks loudly enough to hear it from a few feet away, move away from the blindfolded student until he or she can just barely hear the ticking. Stay this far away while you test the blindfolded student's ability to tell the location of the ticking. Change your position five or six times, remembering to be very quiet as you move. At each position, signal the third student to ask the blindfolded person where the ticking is coming from. For each position, the third student should record the location of the clock and where the blindfolded student said the ticking was coming from. He or she can either point in the direction he or she

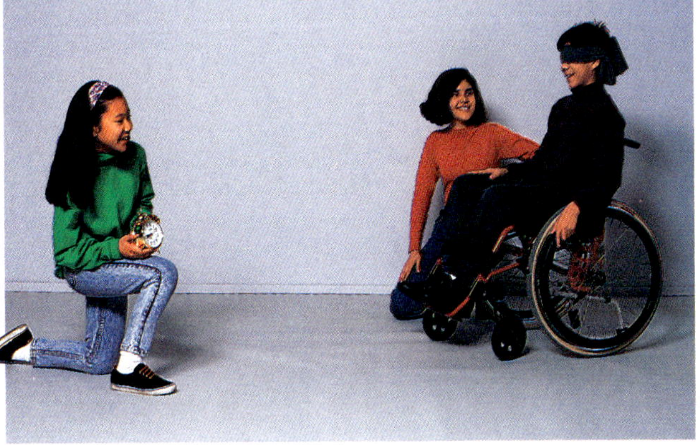

Section 4-2

PREPARATION

Concepts Developed

The sense organ that passes auditory information to the brain and maintains balance is the ear. Students have already read about how vision works. Now they will learn about the parts of the ear and what they do. Students will also compare how humans and other animals hear.

Planning the Lesson

In planning your lesson on hearing, refer to the Chapter Organizer on pages 94A-B for timing suggestions, resources, and additional materials that will help you in your presentation of the lesson concepts.

For adequate development of the concepts presented in this section, we recommend that students do the Find Out activity on pages 105–106.

1 MOTIVATE

Demonstration Use a whistle to show how the sense of hearing contributes to a person's awareness of his or her environment. Ask students if you could turn your back and still get their attention. They may say no. Let students talk quietly among themselves for 10 or 15 seconds. Turn your back and blow a whistle. You will have their attention. L1

FIND OUT!

Are two ears better than one?

Time needed 15 minutes

Materials loudly ticking clock, blindfold, disposable ear plug or cotton

Thinking Processes Observing and inferring, Comparing and contrasting, Recognizing cause and effect

Purpose To demonstrate that two ears locate sound better than one.

PROGRAM RESOURCES

Teacher Classroom Resources
Study Guide, page 17

Other Resources
The Ear, software, Queue.

OPTIONS

Meeting Individual Needs

Physically Challenged, Behaviorally Disordered For students who cannot walk around the room, or students for whom the movement would be a distraction, modify the activity by having students sit in a circle. The clock can be handed from student to student, and all can participate.

Teaching the Activity

Troubleshooting Show students how to indicate the location of sounds. Point out that they are to imagine themselves in the center of a clock. Have them point straight ahead and identify the direction as 12 o'clock. L1

Expected Outcomes

Students will find they can locate the clock better using both ears.

Conclude and Apply

1. The blindfolded student was often more correct when listening with both ears.
2. Using two ears makes sound location more accurate.

2 Teach

Tying to Previous Knowledge

Ask students whether they have to open their eyes to turn off the alarm clock in the morning. Most of them should say they can turn off the alarm without looking. The sound alerts them to the clock's position.

Concept Development

Student Text Question Before you get up to investigate, what would you do with your body to figure out where the sound is coming from? *You would turn your head, thus moving your ears around to help you identify the direction of the sound.*

hears the ticking coming, or use clock-face positions. For example, if the ticking is coming from directly in front of the blindfolded student, he or she would say it's coming from 12 o'clock. If the ticking is coming from directly behind, the position is 6 o'clock. If the ticking is on the right, the position is 3 o'clock. If it's on the left, the position is 9 o'clock, and so on.

Now have the blindfolded student plug one ear with a disposable ear plug or cotton. Repeat the same five or six trials, but do them in a different order. Again, record the position of the clock and whether the blindfolded student correctly identified where the sound was coming from.

Conclude and Apply

1. How do the results obtained with one ear compare with the results obtained with both ears?
2. What conclusion would you draw that could explain these results?

DID YOU KNOW?

The smallest muscle in the human body is found in the ear. It is a little over 0.01 inches long.

Imagine you've suddenly heard an unusual sound. Before you get up to go investigate, what would you do with your body to figure out where the sound is coming from? Unless a sound is straight in front of your nose, it arrives and is heard in one ear a split second before the other ear. Your brain uses this time difference to locate the direction the sound is coming from.

FIGURE 4-12. Does a tree make a sound when it falls, even if no one hears it?

OPTIONS

Enrichment

Activity Students may be interested in finding out how sharp their hearing is. Tell them they can learn to distinguish between the sounds of a penny, a nickel, a dime, and a quarter falling to the floor. A partner can drop one of each coin on a hard floor. The student can listen to each while watching, then listen with eyes closed as each coin is dropped. After a while, the student should be able to detect a difference in the sound each coin makes as it hits the floor. L1

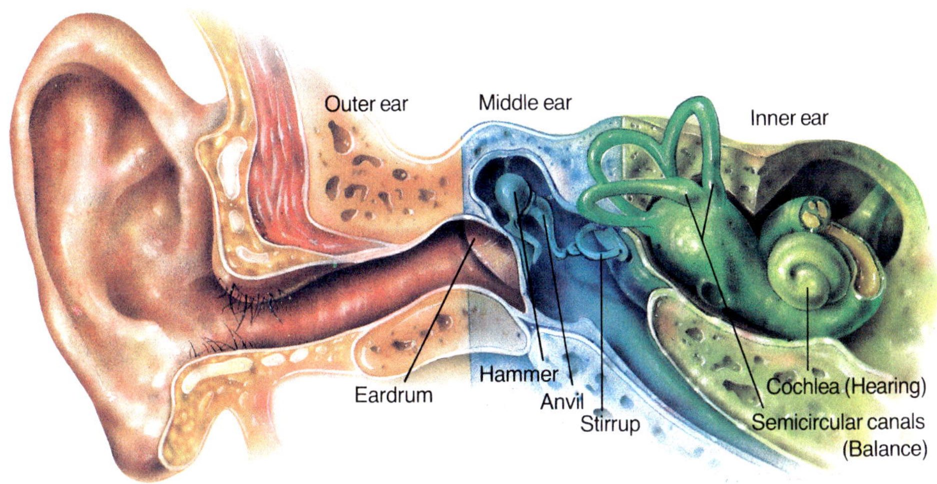

FIGURE 4-13. Your ear responds to sound and to changes in the position of your head.

What happens when sound vibrations enter your ear? In Chapter 3, you learned that when the vibrations reach your eardrum, they cause it to vibrate. The **eardrum** is a very thin tissue stretched across your ear canal. Sound vibrations make your eardrum vibrate in much the same way that the skin of a musical drum vibrates when you beat it. The vibrations pass from your eardrum to three tiny bones in your middle ear. Each tiny bone vibrates in turn. The vibrations pass from the third bone to the cochlea. The **cochlea** is a fluid-filled space in your skull bone that is similar in shape to a snail shell. The cochlea contains fluid and thousands of tiny receptor hairs. The bottom of each hair is attached to a nerve that sends messages to your brain. When sound vibrations reach the cochlea, they cause the fluid in it to vibrate. This makes the receptor hairs bend back and forth, much like wheat moves and bends in the wind. The way these hairs move depends on the sound vibrations. Different sounds cause the hairs to move differently, sending different sound messages to your brain.

FIGURE 4-14. Sound vibrations cause the tiny hairs inside the cochlea to move and bend, much like wind causes a field of wheat to move and bend.

Concept Development

Theme Connection Since the ears play an important part in the sensory system, which interacts with stimuli in the environment, the theme this section supports is interactions and systems. The ears not only transmit information about sound to the brain, they also interact with the environment to produce information about position in space, as demonstrated by the Find Out activity.

Inquiry Question What causes the feeling of pressure in your ears when you go up quickly in an elevator? *The feeling of pressure occurs because of the difference between the pressure outside and inside your ear. The outside pressure diminishes, but the inside pressure remains the same. The air in the middle ear pushes on the eardrum as a result. If you swallow or yawn, the tube connecting the middle ear to your throat opens and relieves the pressure.*

MAKING CONNECTIONS

Daily Life

Students use their sense of hearing to determine how far away objects are. Ask students to describe the sound of a car approaching, how it sounds as it passes, and how it sounds as it drives away.

Content Background

Damage to the ear can result in temporary or permanent deafness. The eardrum can be broken by a sharp object stuck into the ear. Then the eardrum cannot vibrate efficiently to transmit sounds to the middle ear. A very loud noise can damage the organ of Corti in the cochlea. That is why people who have been too near a fireworks display or attending a rock concert may experience a ringing in the ears or a period of deafness.

Meeting Individual Needs

Learning Disabled Some students may have trouble understanding how the three bones in the middle ear help to transmit sound. They may think that sound would travel better through open space. Explain that sound travels even better through solids than through air. Have them knock on their desks about 0.5m from an ear and listen to the sound. Then have them put one ear to the desk and knock about 0.5m away. The knock will sound much louder. Then have student look at and manipulate a model of the ear, and trace the path of vibrations. L1 LEP

Concept Development

Flex Your Brain Use the Flex Your Brain activity to have students explore BALANCE.

EXPLORE!

Why do you feel dizzy when you spin around, then stop suddenly?

Time needed 5 minutes

Materials glass, water, some kind of fine powder (cinnamon or chalk dust)

Thinking Processes Observing, Making a model

Purpose To illustrate the movement of fluid in the ear.

Teaching the Activity

Discussion Ask students whether they have ever been seasick or dizzy. Discuss possible causes for the sickness. *overstimulation of the inner ear by the motion of a ship or other vehicle* L1

Troubleshooting Students may notice some back-and-forth jiggling of the water while they are turning the glass. But once they stop they will see the water continue to swirl.

Expected Outcome

The water continues swirling after the glass has stopped being turned.

Answer to Question
The water continues to swirl.

SKILLBUILDER

Vibrations pass into the outer ear, which causes the eardrum to vibrate. These vibrations are passed through the middle ear from the hammer to the anvil to the stirrup. Finally, the vibrations reach semicircular canals and the cochlea in the inner ear. L1

FIGURE 4-15. The ballerina's ears are important to her ability to continue dancing once she has completed this spin.

How do the ears of the dancer in Figure 4-15 help her to dance? Hearing the music helps dancers with rhythm and beat. Do ears do anything besides hear? Think back to the Explore activity you did at the beginning of this chapter. You identified three planes, left/right, up/down, and forward/back, that you use to locate yourself in space. Look at that drawing again. Can you identify where these three planes meet? They meet near your inner ear, next to the cochlea, where the structures called semicircular canals are located. As their name suggests, the **semicircular canals** are tubes shaped like half circles. There are three semicircular canals in each ear. One canal corresponds to the left/right plane, one corresponds to the up/down plane, and the other corresponds to the forward/back plane. Each canal contains fluid and receptor hairs, like the cochlea. At the bottom of each hair is a nerve that carries messages to your brain. When you move your head, the fluid inside the semicircular canals also moves, bending the receptor hairs. Your brain analyzes the messages sent by the receptor hairs and signals your muscles to move your body in a way that will prevent or correct loss of balance. Without your sense of balance, you wouldn't be able to dance very gracefully. Here is an activity that will show you how the fluid in the semicircular canals moves when you move.

SKILLBUILDER

INTERPRETING SCIENTIFIC ILLUSTRATIONS
Using the illustration of the structure of the ear (Figure 4-13), explain the different steps involved in sensing sound. If you need help, refer to the **Skill Handbook** on page 659.

EXPLORE!

Why do you feel dizzy when you spin around, then stop suddenly?

Half fill a glass with water. Sprinkle a small amount of chalk dust or ground cinnamon onto the surface of the water. Without picking up the glass, use both hands to carefully turn it in circles so that the water begins swirling round and round. Now stop. What happens?

PROGRAM RESOURCES

Teacher Classroom Resources

Critical Thinking/Problem Solving, page 8, Flex Your Brain

Transparency Masters, page 19, and **Color Transparency,** number 8, Echolocation L2

OPTIONS

Multicultural Perspectives

The value of living in a quiet environment has been demonstrated by the Mabaan tribe. The Mabaan live in northeast Africa, in an area that is very quiet. Members of this tribe have excellent hearing. They hear much better than city dwellers, who are exposed to a lot of noise.

When you stopped turning the glass, the water kept swirling. In the same way, when you stop spinning around, the fluid in your semicircular canals continues moving for a few seconds. Because the fluid is still moving, the receptor hairs are still bending and sending messages that tell your brain you're still spinning. But you know you're not. It's this confusion that you feel as dizziness.

DID YOU KNOW?

The sound of the ocean that you hear when you hold a seashell to your ear is really the sound of your own blood rushing through blood vessels inside your ear. The seashell makes it easier for you to hear this sound, which you normally don't notice.

ANIMAL HEARING

You learned in Chapter 3 that many animals hear sounds that we can't hear. Dogs, cats, bats, dolphins, and even grasshoppers hear sound frequencies that are higher or lower than the frequencies the human ear is able to hear. Which of the animals in Figure 4-16 have ears? Some animals, such as the deer, bat, and elephant shown, have large outer ears that are very easy to see. The African elephant has very large outer ears, sometimes four feet wide. Can an elephant move its outer ears? Can you move yours? Can cats and dogs move their ears? How might a large, movable outer ear be useful to an animal?

What about the other animals in Figure 4-16? Do all of them have outer ears? How do insects and frogs hear? The frog doesn't have an outer ear. You can see its eardrum on the surface of the skin behind its eye. The cricket doesn't have an outer ear either. Its eardrums are on the first segment of its abdomen. Frogs' ears and crickets' ears don't

FIGURE 4-16. Can you identify the ears of each of these animals? Do all of them have ears?

Concept Development

Student Text Question How might a large, movable outer ear be useful to an animal? *A large outer ear picks up more vibrations than a small one. An animal with movable outer ears can move its ears around to locate where sounds are coming from without moving its head.*

Discussion Lead students to conclude that the brain can screen out sounds it does not perceive as important. Ask students how well they can understand a conversation in the school hallway with noise all around. Have students identify times when they do not notice noises; for example, the sounds on a busy street. Have students identify times when they suddenly notice small sounds; for example, hearing the refrigerator running at night.

Teacher F.Y.I.

- There are over 24,000 fibers to sense vibrations in the cochlea of the ear.
- It is easier to hear sounds over water than it is over land. Air over land heats more quickly than over water. This air rises. The coolness of the water's surface allows sound to travel more quickly and directly than over land. This is true because sound travels faster through more dense materials than less dense ones. And cool air is more dense than warm air.

Enrichment

Discussion Ludwig von Beethoven went on composing music and conducting even after he went deaf. Have students come up with explanations for how he was able to compose. *He could remember the sounds of various pitches.* Ask students how he could conduct. Remind students that the conductor sets the tempo, and vibrations in the floor could help him feel whether the orchestra was in time with him.

3 Assess

Check for Understanding

1. Have students list functions of the ear and an example of each. The list should include maintaining balance, being able to tell where sounds come from, and passing information about the world to the brain. *Examples might include: being able to turn when dancing without falling down, being able to locate a telephone just by its ringing, and being able to tell that it is raining just by the sound of the raindrops.*
2. Have students answer the Check Your Understanding questions. With regard to the Apply question, have students do research to find examples of animals that have poor vision and good hearing. Students should discuss how this helps the animal survive in its environment.

Reteach

Have students collect pictures of animals with different types of ears. For each picture, have students explain why the shape or size of the ear would help the animal. For example, bats have relatively large ears. They can fly safely and accurately only when they can hear sounds reflected off their surroundings. They also use their ears to locate food. L1

Extension

Have students who have mastered this section find out how hearing aids work. Students can do library research or interview a health care professional or special education teacher who specializes in hearing impairments. Students might also talk to someone they know who wears a hearing aid. They should give a class report. L2

4 Close

Have students make a list of noise pollution that could damage various parts of their ears, for example, jackhammers, loud music, honking in heavy traffic, jet engines. L1

look very much like yours, but they operate in a similar way. Sound vibrates the eardrums, and the vibrations start messages that are sent to the brain.

Hearing, like vision, helps animals gather information about their world. Animals that have poor vision and animals that live in environments with little light often have very good hearing. Their world is more one of sounds than of sights. In the next section, you will learn about animals that live in worlds of neither sight nor sound. They live in worlds of touch, taste, and smell.

FIGURE 4-17. Dolphins send out high-frequency sounds that bounce off the seafloor, fish, and other objects. By listening for the returning echoes, dolphins can judge the distance and direction of the objects.

Check Your Understanding

1. Describe what happens to sound as it travels through your ear to your brain, starting with your eardrum.
2. If you tripped over a crack in the sidewalk, what would happen in your ears and your brain to prevent you from falling?
3. Name at least three animals that can hear more sound frequencies than you can. Can you think of an animal that cannot hear as many sound frequencies as you can?
4. **APPLY:** Do you think it would be an advantage for an animal with poor vision to have a good sense of hearing? Why?

Answers to Check Your Understanding

1. Sound waves make the eardrum vibrate. These vibrations cause the three bones in the middle ear to vibrate, which causes the fluid in the cochlea to vibrate. The fluid moves tiny receptor hairs, which are connected to nerves that send the sound messages to the brain.
2. Fluid in your semicircular canals would bend receptor hairs, which are connected to nerves that would send messages to your brain. Your brain would signal your muscles to correct your body position.
3. Dog, bat, cat, dolphin, robin, and other animals can hear more sound frequencies than humans. Students may know that some fish, reptiles, and amphibians hear narrower frequency ranges.
4. Yes. It could use its ears. For example, it could hear a predator in time to hide.

4-3 Touch, Taste, and Smell

YOUR SKIN AS A SENSE ORGAN

Imagine you are the swimmer in Figure 4-18. While you swim and concentrate on the race, your brain is processing information from all of your senses. Your eyes tell you where the water is, where your opponent is, and how far you are from the end of the pool. Your ears pick up the splashing sounds of the water and the cheers of the crowd. Your nose and mouth smell and taste the water. How do you sense that the water is wet or warm? How do you sense where your body is in relation to the surface of the water without looking?

How would you describe your skin? It is a barrier between you and your surroundings, but is it just a bag you live in? What kinds of information come to you through your skin? Here is an activity that will help you identify some of the information you get from your skin.

OBJECTIVES

In this section, you will

- describe the mechanism of the sense of touch;
- relate the senses of taste and smell;
- compare touch, taste, and smell in humans and other animals.

KEY SCIENCE TERMS

taste bud

FIND OUT!

How does your skin respond to different temperatures?

You will need rubber gloves and three bowls of water, one hot, one cold, and one room temperature. Place the bowls on a desk or table. Put the room temperature water in the middle, the ice water on your left, and the hot water on your right. Put your left hand in the cold water and your right hand in the hot water and hold them there for about 30 seconds. Now plunge both hands into the bowl of room-temperature water. Does the water feel warm or cold on your left hand? Does the water feel warm or cold on your right hand?

Section 4-3

PREPARATION

Concepts Developed

This section explores how touch, taste, and smell work for both humans and animals. The sense of touch responds to stimuli of pressure, heat and cold, and pain, while the senses of taste and smell respond to chemical stimuli.

Planning the Lesson

In planning your lesson on touch, taste, and smell, refer to the Chapter Organizer on pages 94A-B for timing suggestions, resources, and additional materials that will help you in your presentation of the lesson concepts.

For adequate development of the concepts presented in this section, we recommend that students do the Investigate activity on page 114.

1 MOTIVATE

Discussion Ask students to imagine themselves at the dinner table. Is just looking at the food very interesting? Ask students to discuss what will make the meal more enjoyable. They will probably say eating it. Lead them to break their response down into experiences; for example, the smell of spaghetti, the taste of barbequed chicken, or the crispness of lettuce. L1

FIND OUT!

How does your skin respond to different temperatures?

Time needed 5 minutes

Materials bowl of cold water, bowl of very warm water, bowl of room-temperature water, rubber gloves

Thinking Process
Observing and inferring

Purpose To show that the sensing of heat and cold is relative.

PROGRAM RESOURCES

Teacher Classroom Resources

Study Guide, page 18

Critical Thinking/Problem Solving, page 12, Shark Senses L2

Take Home Activities, page 9, Touch Box L1

Teaching the Activity

Discussion Ask students to discuss whether they think that a sudden change in temperature can affect the way they sense heat or cold. Have them provide examples. L1

Expected Outcomes

The left hand will feel warm. The right hand will feel cold. Gloved hands in cold water will feel wet. In hot water they will feel pressure.

Conclude and Apply

The skin responds to changes in temperatures. The different sensations are the results of contrast.

2 TEACH

Tying to Previous Knowledge

Ask students whether the smell of cigars, baking cookies, or new leather makes them think of anything in particular. Smells are often associated with certain experiences. Cigar smoke might remind one student of a grandfather and another of being in a bus station. Some students may not be reminded of anything by the list. Ask if there are any special smells that make them feel happy or sad.

Concept Development

Theme Connection Since touch, smell, and taste often work together to provide the whole of a sensory experience, one theme of this section is interactions and systems. In this section, students will explore the interactions between the senses of taste and smell.

Inquiry Question How can we feel something that lightly touches our hair even though hair has no nerve cells? *The pressure on the hair is registered by the nerve cells at the bottom of each hair.*

Student Text Question Which sensors are involved in telling you that you've bitten your lip? *pressure and pain*

Dry your hands well and put on a pair of rubber gloves. Plunge both gloved hands into the cold water. What do you feel? Now plunge both hands into the bowl of hot water. What do you feel?

Conclude and Apply

How can one hand feel hot and the other hand feel cold when plunged into the same bowl of water?

FIGURE 4-18. This swimmer is gathering information with his skin.

You found that the room-temperature water felt warm to the hand that had been in cold water, and it felt cold to the hand that had been in hot water. In the same way, weather that feels cold to someone from a warm climate, such as Florida, might feel hot to someone who is from Alaska. You sense changes in temperature by comparing the change with the temperature you're used to.

By doing the Find Out, you showed that you feel hot and cold through your skin. What other sensations do you feel through your skin? Your skin responds to pressure and pain as well as hot and cold. There are four kinds of touch receptors that are located in your skin: pressure, pain, hot, and cold. Some sensations require only one kind of touch receptor. Other sensations require a combination of touch receptors.

Why did your dry, gloved hands feel wet when you put them in the bowl of cold water? When you feel wetness, you are actually sensing a combination of coldness and pressure. Coldness, pressure, heat, and pain combine in different ways to give you different skin feelings. These feelings are your sense of touch.

What is the baby in Figure 4-19 doing? Your lips are very sensitive to touch. As a baby, you learned a lot about the world by putting objects in your mouth. Even grown-ups learn a great deal this way. For example, pressure and heat sensors in your lips tell you what a warm spoonful of soup feels like. Which sensors are involved in telling you that you've bitten your lip? Where are you most ticklish? Your skin is more sensitive to touch in some areas than in others.

FIGURE 4-19. This baby is using its sense of touch to learn about its toy.

OPTIONS

Meeting Individual Needs

Learning Disabled Some students may think that all people feel pain in the same way. Explain that people can have different attitudes toward pain. Have them make the chart shown at the right. Students can compare and contrast the situations to see how their attitudes affect how they react to pain.

Person/Situation	Reaction
Football player falls in game.	Accepts pain as part of sport.
Businessman slips on ice and falls.	Unexpected pain hurts a lot.
Child afraid of needles gets a shot.	Fear makes pain worse than it would be without fear.

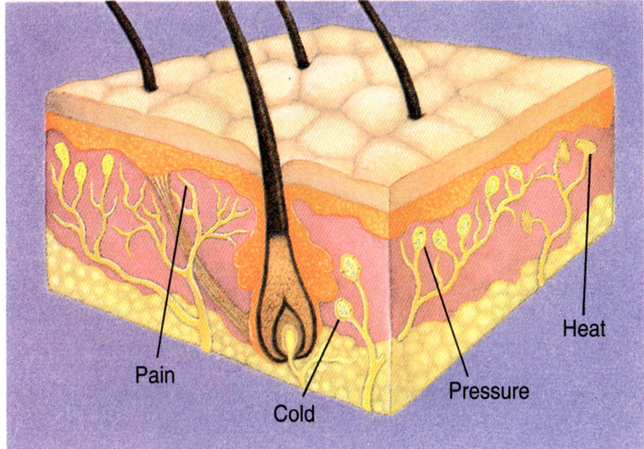

FIGURE 4-20. The skin has four kinds of touch receptors: heat, cold, pressure, and pain.

TASTE AND SMELL

What is your favorite taste? Sweet candy bars? Sour lemons? Salty potato chips? Bitter orange peels? How do you tell the difference between these flavors? There are four types of taste receptors, or **taste buds**, on your tongue. Each type of taste bud responds to one of the four basic tastes—sweet, sour, salty, and bitter. You can see what taste buds look like in Figure 4-21. Each type of taste bud is located on a different area of your tongue. Most foods are tasted as a combination of these four basic tastes. Although most of your taste buds are on your tongue, there are also taste buds on the roof of your mouth.

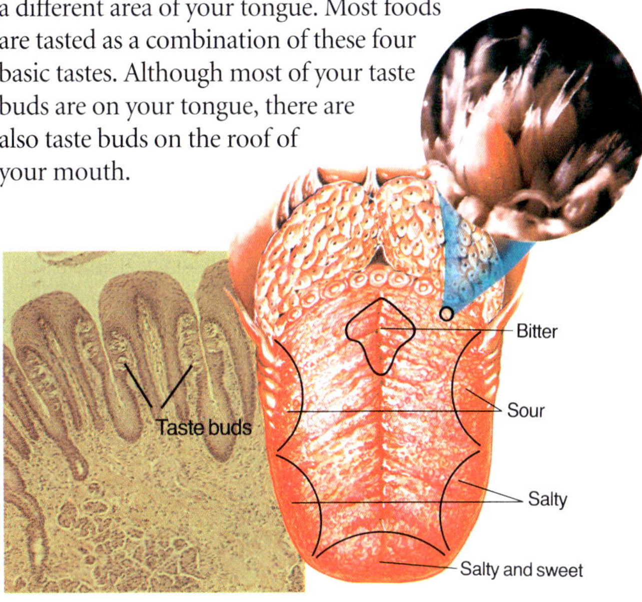

FIGURE 4-21. The taste buds are sense receptors located on your tongue. They contain nerve endings that react to chemicals in food. The endings are so small you need a microscope to see them.

Concept Development

Uncovering Preconceptions Many people believe that it is a sign of weakness to react to pain. Actually pain is usually a signal to the brain that something is wrong. The pain felt from touching a hot stove prevents a serious burn by causing a person to withdraw his or her hand. Pains caused by injury or disease alert a person to seek help.

MAKING CONNECTIONS

Literature

As a child, Helen Keller suffered a fever that left her deaf and blind. At first, the only way she could communicate with people was through the sense of touch. Students can read the story of how she learned to read, use sign language, and speak in her autobiography *Helen Keller: The Story of My Life.*

Using the Diagram Have students study Figure 4-21. Examine the way taste buds are arranged. Where do students think they might taste a few drops of lemon juice. *They will probably say at the back sides of the tongue because lemon juice is sour.* Ask students why licking a lollipop is better than holding it on the center of the tongue. *Sweet receptors are at the front of the tongue.*

Inquiry Question How can some people such as professional taste testers distinguish small differences among many varieties of a food such as coffee? *These people have very sensitive taste buds. They have learned to detect many subtle flavors other people are not aware of.*

Enrichment

Activity Have students set up their own taste test panels. Each panel should have four or five panelists. Have them select a type of product to test, such as orange juice or chocolate chip cookies. Then provide each panel with several brands of the product. Before tasting, the panel should agree on the tastes and textures they expect of the product. As they taste, have students make notes, such as too salty, too sweet, not crisp enough. Then have them compare notes and write a joint report evaluating each product. They may want to rank products as Good, Fair, and Poor. COOP LEARN L1

INVESTIGATE!

4-2 TASTING SOLUTIONS

Time needed 45 minutes

Materials See student activity.

Thinking Processes
Making and using tables, Observing and inferring, Comparing and contrasting, Measuring in SI, Predicting

Purpose To discover a threshold level for taste.

Preparation A 1 percent sugar solution can be prepared by mixing 1g of sucrose (table sugar) with 99mL of distilled water. Prepare the vinegar solution by mixing 1mL of vinegar with 99mL of distilled water.

Teaching the Activity

Troubleshooting Be sure students properly label test tubes and eyedroppers. You might want to have students practice using the eyedropper for measuring and transferring solutions. L1

Safety Be sure to use new eyedroppers, and to dispose of them after the activity. Straw-type coffee stirrers can be used for the tasting process. Give students a chance to practice using these to dispense small amounts of liquid.

Sample Data Some students will detect vinegar in tube C; all will detect vinegar in tube A. Some students will detect sugar in tube F; all will detect sugar in tube D.

Expected Outcome

Students will discover that the strength of the solution determines whether its taste is sensed.

Answers to Analyze/Conclude and Apply

1. the weakest solution, test tubes C and F
2. yes
3. yes, the vinegar
4. very sour; yes; the 2 percent solution
5. Yes, because there was no taste in the weak solutions, but they did contain sugar or vinegar.
6. They might think the taste was very weak.

INVESTIGATE!

4-2 TASTING SOLUTIONS

How strong does a stimulus have to be before your brain gets the message?

PROBLEM

How strong does a flavor have to be before you can taste it?

MATERIALS

1 percent vinegar solution
1 percent sugar solution
6 test tubes
test-tube rack
graduated cylinder
beaker or small pitcher of water
2 eyedroppers
wax marking pencil
1 cup for rinsing mouth

PROCEDURE

1. Copy the data table.
2. Use the wax pencil to label the six test tubes A, B, C, D, E, and F. Add 9 mL of water to each.
3. Label one eyedropper V and the other S. Fill one of the droppers with water from the beaker. Squeeze water from the dropper into the graduated cylinder. Count the number of drops it takes to deposit 1 mL of water in the graduated cylinder. Record this number.
4. Using the V dropper, add 1 mL of the 1 percent vinegar solution to tube A. Mix, then transfer 1 mL from tube A to tube B.
5. Mix the contents of tube B, then use the V dropper to transfer 1 mL from tube B to tube C. Mix the contents of tube C.
6. Using the S dropper, add 1 mL of 1 percent sugar solution to tube D. Mix, then transfer 1 mL from tube D to tube E.
7. Mix the contents of tube E. Using the S dropper, transfer 1 mL from tube E to tube F.
8. Place one drop from tube C on your tongue. **CAUTION:** *Do not touch the dropper to your tongue.* Record in the data table whether or not you detected a sour taste. Rinse your mouth with water before the next test. Rinse the dropper and shake it dry.
9. Repeat Step 8 with tube B, then tube A, then with the 1percent vinegar solution. Record your responses.
10. Repeat Steps 8 and 9 for tubes F, E, D, and the 1 percent sugar solution, in that order.

DATA AND OBSERVATIONS

SUBSTANCE	DILUTION AND RESPONSE			
Vinegar	1%	A	B	C
Sugar	1%	D	E	F

ANALYZE

1. With which sample could you not detect the presence of vinegar? Of sugar?
2. Each tube had 1/10 the amount of vinegar or sugar as the previous tube. Could you tell that the four vinegar solutions and the four sugar solutions were different strengths?
3. Did you **observe** any odors from either of the 1 percent solutions? Which smelled stronger?

CONCLUDE AND APPLY

4. **Predict** the taste you would expect if the strongest vinegar solution was 2 percent. Would it be twice as strong as the 1 percent solution? Which would smell stronger?
5. From your observations, can you **infer** whether there is a threshold, or point at which you can or cannot taste something?
6. **Going Further:** How might people react if you put in an extra can of water when mixing some juice?

PROGRAM RESOURCES

Teacher Classroom Resources
Activity Masters, pages 19-20, Investigate 4-2 L2
How It Works, page 7, Scratch-n-Sniff L2
Making Connections: Across the Curriculum, page 11, The Drug Debate L3
Multicultural Activities, page 12, Senses in the Future L1

OPTIONS

Enrichment

Activity Ask a reading specialist to demonstrate the use of Braille materials. Explain to students that this is a case where one sense is able to compensate in some way for the loss of another.

DO TASTE AND SMELL WORK TOGETHER?

Can you remember the last time you had a bad cold? Perhaps you were given a bowl of hot soup because someone thought it would make you feel better. You may not have been able to smell it very well with your nose all stopped up. Could you taste it?

FIGURE 4-22. How do you respond to the smell of pizza?

Think about the last time you ate a slice of pizza or a plate of spaghetti. When you eat, odors from the food float up through a passage that connects the back of your mouth with your nose. Your brain combines information from your taste buds and from smell receptors in your nose to identify the flavors of the food. The smell receptors in your nose respond to different kinds of smells. They are more sensitive than your taste buds. Without your sense of smell, your sense of taste doesn't work very well. When you have a bad cold, the smell receptors in your nose can't do their job very well. If you ate a bite of pizza, you might not be able to taste it. If you followed that bite of pizza with a bite of broccoli, you might not even taste the difference!

LIFE IN A CHEMICAL WORLD

You are bombarded with sights and sounds in your world, no matter where you live. Can you imagine a world without sights or sounds, but filled with touch, taste, and smell? What would it be like to find food, locate a safe place to sleep, or identify a friend by using those three senses? Catfish, like the one in Figure 4-23, live in just such a world. They live on the muddy bottom of murky waters, where visibility is poor. A catfish finds food by using its whiskers to feel around in the mud and taste what it finds.

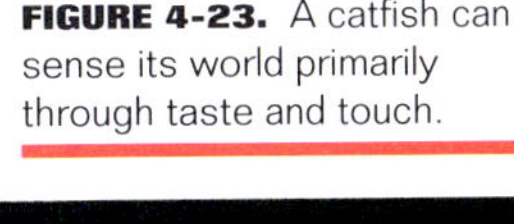

FIGURE 4-23. A catfish can sense its world primarily through taste and touch.

Taste and smell are very important to insects, fish, and other animals. Take the common housefly, for example. Have you ever watched a fly land on a surface, then rub its legs together? A fly has taste receptors on its feet and antennae as well as its

Concept Development

Discussion Have students make a list of foods whose taste they like or do not like. Divide the class into teams depending on their likes and dislikes. For example, some students might like liver, others will not. Some might like grapefruit juice, while others think it is awful. Have each team present "taste evidence" of why they preferred or did not prefer a particular food. Students should debate the merits of using the sense of taste to judge foods. For example, is there a relationship between taste and foods that are good or bad for health?

Inquiry Question Why do you enjoy a meal more when you eat it slowly? *By eating slowly, you have more time to inhale the aromas and become aware of the flavors of the food.*

MAKING CONNECTIONS

History

Since ancient times, humans have enhanced the way they smell to other people. Perfumes played an important part in the history of trade between the Orient and Europe. Have students write a short essay explaining why the perfume trade might have developed.

Content Background

The sense of smell is more important to animals than to humans. Many animals use their sense of smell to locate mates in addition to finding food. The females give off a special chemical that males are drawn to.

Teacher F.Y.I.

Some insecticides are treated with chemicals that smell like the odors insects use to attract mates. Thus, insect pests are drawn to the chemicals that will kill them. This technique is very useful when a particular insect is targeted. Other insects, such as bees, would not be attracted to the scents of pests such as certain moths.

Enrichment

Writing Have students write a smell travelogue. Have them observe and record the odors they encounter as they walk through the school, as they walk home, or as they walk around their homes. Students should try to describe the smells and explain what their sources might be.

Enrichment

Research Have each student select a different insect, fish, reptile or mammal. Ask students to write a short report about how their animal uses touch, taste, and smell to survive. L3

3 Assess

Check for Understanding

1. Set out a small pile of salt, a small pile of sugar, dill pickle slices, and squares of bitter chocolate on plates in front of the class. Ask students to describe each in terms of taste and touch. *salt—salty, hard and grainy; sugar—sweet, hard and grainy; pickle—sour, wet and squishy; chocolate—bitter, hard and smooth*
2. Have students answer the Check Your Understanding questions. With regard to the Apply question, have students identify animals whose primary senses are either touch, taste, or smell and explain how these senses help the animal survive.

Reteach

Ask a nutritionist or the school dietician to come to the class to explain or demonstrate how to make a meal appealing in addition to being healthful. Ask the nutritionist to stress the importance of variety in texture, aroma, and flavor. L1

Extension

Have students who have mastered this section find out how the physical structure of the nose assists smell, and report their findings to the class. L3

4 Close

Ask students which sense gives them the least experience of the world. They should say taste. Taste deals mainly with food. Smell and touch register many more things about the world. L1

FIGURE 4-24. The hammerhead shark can smell the blood of an injured fish a mile away.

mouth. This makes it possible for a fly to tell right away whether it's landed on food and, if so, what kind. A fly can even distinguish between sweet, salty, sour, and bitter flavors. Imagine for a moment what it might be like to be a fly. You would be able to taste whatever you walked on!

Can you smell odors when you're swimming under water? Some animals that live in water have poor eyesight but a very good sense of smell. The hammerhead shark pictured in Figure 4-24 can pinpoint the location of a wounded fish from a mile away by the smell of its blood. Can you think of any land animals that have a very keen sense of smell? Dogs have an excellent sense of smell, and we often use them to help us find things. Dogs can help find hikers who've gotten lost in the forest, or help hunters locate game. There are even beagles that have been trained to sniff out termites in buildings!

Our five senses—sight, hearing, touch, taste, and smell—are our means of gathering information about the world. The senses are a source of pleasure. We can see beautiful landscapes, hear music, cuddle a furry kitten, taste pizza, or smell the sweet odor of fresh flowers. Our senses warn us of danger. You can see the edge of a cliff, smell a dangerous gas leak, or feel that a stove is too hot to touch. The senses are our tools of observation. They are the tools we use when we make scientific observations, form hypotheses, or conduct experiments.

Check Your Understanding

1. Where is your sense of touch located? Be as specific as possible. How many different types of touch receptors are there? Name them.
2. How does your sense of smell affect your sense of taste?
3. What senses would you use if you were hungry and looking for food in the kitchen at home? What senses do you think a fly would use to find food in your kitchen?
4. **APPLY:** Describe how a cat might use its senses to catch a mouse at night. Compare this with how a catfish uses its senses to find food.

Answers to Check Your Understanding

1. Your sense of touch is located in touch receptors all over your skin and throughout your internal organs. There are four kinds of touch receptors: pain, pressure, hot, cold.
2. Your brain mixes signals from the taste buds in your mouth with the signals from the smell receptors in your nose. When you cannot smell, your sense of taste does not work very well.
3. You would probably use sight first, then smell. But you might smell cookies baking before you saw them. The fly would probably use smell first, then taste.
4. The cat uses sight, hearing and smell to catch a mouse. A catfish uses touch and taste to find food in the mud.

EXPANDING YOUR VIEW

CONTENTS

A CLOSER LOOK

KONRAD LORENZ

Konrad Lorenz was a famous scientist who used his sense of sight to observe animals. In fact, Lorenz was the founder of the science called ethology (ee THAWL uh jee)—the study of animal behavior.

Lorenz believed that in order to learn about animal behavior, an animal must be observed in its own environment. Before Lorenz, scientists had mainly studied animals in laboratories.

Lorenz devoted much of his time to observing colonies of birds, including geese. From these observations came one of his most important discoveries. In 1935, Lorenz concluded that if a mother goose is not present when her baby geese hatch, they will consider the first moving object they see to be their mother.

Lorenz found that if the moving object happened to be himself, the baby geese would follow him as if he were their mother. He found this to be true with ducks, too. Lorenz called this behavior *imprinting.* Imprinting is an animal instinct in which the animal becomes attached to another organism soon after birth or hatching. Imprinting is important because in order for baby animals to survive, they must recognize a mother who will feed and protect them.

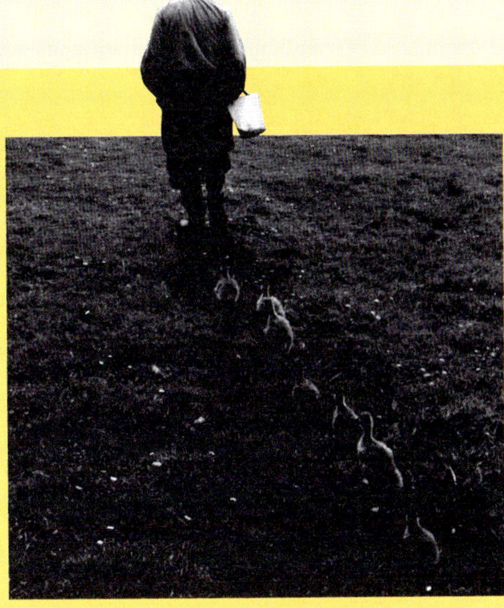

Lorenz continued his work in animal behavior and, in 1973, was awarded the Nobel Prize for his work. Lorenz died in 1989.

YOU TRY IT!

Choose an animal to observe for a week and keep a diary of the animal's activities. What conclusions can you make about the animal's behavior from your observations?

EXPANDING YOUR VIEW

Using Expanding Your View

Assign one of these excursions to expand students' understanding of senses and how they apply to other sciences and other subjects. You may assign these as individual or small group activities.

A CLOSER LOOK

Purpose A Closer Look explains how Lorenz gathered information about animals by observing how they learn, in particular, by imprinting. Section 4-1 pointed out that one way scientists learn about how animals see is to observe their behavior.

Content Background Lorenz's discovery of imprinting contributed to our understanding of how behavioral patterns evolve within a species. His findings were influential in the development of learning theory as well, as they suggest that animals are genetically programmed to learn specific information crucial for the survival of the species. Toward the end of his life, Lorenz applied his theories to humans as members of social groups. In his controversial book, *On Agression* (1966), Lorenz argued that aggression, like imprinting, is inborn and serves some useful functions. Unlike imprinting, however, aggression can be modified to play a more socially useful role.

Teaching Strategy Small groups of students can read the selection and debate whether animals are best observed in the laboratory or in their natural habitats. Have students list the advantages and disadvantages of each method.

Going Further Students can work in small groups to expand Lorenz's work with learning theory. Suggest that students create two lists of ten words each. The words in the first list should be random; those on the second list should be related to one another in a meaningful way. Have groups exchange lists and see which is easier to learn. Ask why the related words might be easier to memorize and what this suggests about the way we learn. **COOP LEARN**

Going Further Students might also want to write to zoos where animals live in approximations of natural habitats. Ask students to describe how Lorenz's belief that animals should be observed in their own habitats is applied in these zoos. Some possibilities for exploration are:

St. Louis Zoo
Education Dept.
Forest Park
St. Louis, MO

San Diego Zoo
Education Dept.
PO Box 551
San Diego, CA

Answers to YOU TRY IT

Accept all reasonable observations. Behavior will depend on the animal chosen.

PHYSICS CONNECTION

Purpose The Physics Connection reinforces Section 4-2 by exploring a special use of the sense of hearing—echolocation. Dolphins use this process to locate objects, and sonar works in much the same way.

Content Background Sonar, also called "echo-sounding," stands for *so*und *n*avigation *a*nd *r*anging. Sonar was first developed for the detection of submarines during World War II. The echo effect occurs because sound waves, like light waves, can be reflected off surfaces. The short pulses of sound are produced by a transducer, a machine that transforms electrical signals into another form and can also translate sound back into electrical signals. Because a transducer has a rotation of 360°, it can detect objects in the water both beneath and surrounding a vessel. At present, computer images are fairly rough black and white profiles. But scientists are working on ways to create clear pictures by using holograms generated by sound.

Teaching Strategies Ask students to brainstorm about the reasons sonar would be useful for ships. After all, they do not swim underwater like the dolphin. Lead students to consider the location of wrecks and the detection of submerged icebergs and other obstacles.

Activity You could expand the You Try It activity by having other students act as sonar for the blindfolded student. They could make short soft chirps when objects are far away and louder chirps when the student approaches an obstacle.

Answers to YOU TRY IT

The dolphin depends on sound, not sight, for navigation.

Physics Connection

SONAR AND ECHOLOCATION

Dolphins have a highly developed sense of hearing, even though their ears appear to be only tiny holes behind their eyes. The ears of a dolphin are only one part of a much more complicated system that they have. This is called echolocation (ek oh loh KAY shun).

Echolocation works very much like sonar systems that are used aboard boats and submarines. For example, if the captain of a ship wants to know how deep the water is, a ship equipped with sonar can send out a pulse of sound from an underwater loudspeaker. Sound travels at about 4800 feet per second in seawater. By clocking the time it takes from when the sound was sent to when it returns as an echo from the bottom of the ocean, the depth of the water can be calculated. Sonar might also be used to determine how far away an underwater object is or if there are any objects in the path of a ship or submarine.

How does all this translate to dolphins? Dolphins send out a series of high-pitched, rapid clicking noises made in their noses through a special fatty organ in their forehead called the melon. These noises bounce off objects, echo back, and are received in the melon and lower jaw. As echoes are received, the dolphin sends out different clicking noises until the object is finally located. This is the process called echolocation.

Using echolocation, a dolphin can locate a fish more than a half mile away or detect an object as small as a BB being dropped into a tank of water. A dolphin can also tell the shape, size, and texture of an object by using echolocation.

Experiments have been done to test the dolphin's echolocating skills. For example, a blindfolded dolphin can find its way through an underwater obstacle course without bumping into any objects.

The echolocation system of dolphins is very complex. Scientists continue their research to find out more about echolocation, but we don't know if humans will ever completely understand it.

YOU TRY IT!

Set up an obstacle course using desks and chairs and practice going through it several times. Then have someone blindfold you and try going through the obstacle course again without touching any of the objects. What does this tell you about a dolphin's ability to go through an obstacle course blindfolded?

Going Further Students can work in small groups to explore how humans can take advantage of what is known about animal hearing. Have students make a list of various forms of animal ears. Then have students brainstorm about how those forms could be applied to technological advances. Students can venture into fantasy if their basic facts are correct. COOP LEARN

Going Further Without hearing, it is difficult to learn how to speak. Students might want to find out how animal hearing systems are connected to communication. Some readings that discuss this question are:

Hahn, Emily. *Look Who's Talking.* New York: Crowell, 1978.

Lilly, John C. *Communication Between Man and Dolphin.* New York: Crown, 1978.

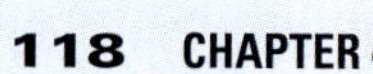

SCIENCE AND SOCIETY

AIDING THE HEARING IMPAIRED

In today's noisy world, nearly 21 million Americans suffer from either partial or total hearing loss, according to the Center for Assessment and Demographic Studies (CADS) at Gallaudet University. A very small percentage of the hearing impaired are born with the problem. Most hearing loss is the result of aging. People over age sixty-five are seven times more likely to be hearing impaired than those under age forty-five.

Products have been developed for hearing impaired people. For example, an alarm clock is now available which, when placed under the user's pillow, awakens the user with vibrations instead of noise. Also available is an electronic light system that can be programmed to flash when triggered by certain noises, such as a baby crying or a phone or doorbell ringing.

Closed-caption television is one of the greatest innovations for hearing-impaired people. With the help of a special decoder that connects to a television, the words spoken during a program that is closed-captioned are displayed in type at the bottom of the screen. Beginning in 1993, a federal law will require that all newly manufactured televisions be equipped with the ability to receive closed-captioning, making the use of a special decoder unnecessary.

CAREER CONNECTION

Audiologists test people's hearing and work with those who have hearing disorders. Audiologists may work with schools, with business and industry, or with scientific or medical groups. They must have a master's degree from college. Many states require them to be licensed.

Special telephones, called TDDs (telecommunications device for the deaf), are making it possible for the hearing impaired to make and receive phone calls. The latest TDD has a screen and a keyboard much like a personal computer. As the user types a message, it is sent over telephone lines to another TDD and appears on the screen. The receiver of the call, in turn, types a response that is sent back to the caller.

It is possible for people with TDDs to call people without TDDs through special phone company operators. These operators read to

Going Further Have students work in pairs to discover some of the problems a hearing-impaired or visually impaired student has. Have one of the pair cover the ears of the other. Then have the first student speak softly and with the head turned so that the second student cannot see lips moving. Have the second student cover the eyes of the first student and say, "Hey, look at that over there!" Have students discuss how they felt in each case. COOP LEARN

Going Further Some students might be interested in doing a science project about deafness or blindness. Or they might be interested in finding out more about careers working with communication systems for the deaf or blind.

EXPANDING YOUR VIEW

SCIENCE AND SOCIETY

Purpose Science and Society develops Sections 4-1 and 4-2 by explaining how the sense of sight can substitute in part for an impaired sense of hearing.

Content Background Computer technology is at the heart of advances in supplying assistance to hearing-impaired persons. Closed-caption television is possible because of computer graphics. The dialogue in a TV show is edited for content and entered into a computer program. The programmed text is recorded by an additional camera and superimposed by computer onto the projection of the program.

TDD would not have been available under the analogue system of telephone communication. The analogue system converted voice vibrations into electronic signals and back again. The new system is digital and transforms sound into a binary system. A binary system measures electric currents as sequences of 1 and 0, known as pulse-code measurement. The binary system is compatible with impulses from a keyboard, so both sound and keyboard impulses can now be transmitted through telephone lines. The TDD machines can both send and receive digital impulses that are input and received through the keyboard and computer screen.

Teaching Strategy Obtain a short film (about 5 minutes). Have a few students watch the movie with sound and prepare a closed-caption version of the dialogue and sound effects. They should use index cards or separate pieces of paper for each important part of dialogue. Then show the movie, without sound but with the closed-caption editors showing the cards to the class. Ask students whether knowing what was said made the experience more enjoyable.

EXPANDING YOUR VIEW

Discussion Ask students to reread the What Do You Think, substituting visually impaired for hearing-impaired. Ask the same questions. You might want to write all answers on the board and discuss them in detail.

Answers to

WHAT DO YOU THINK?

Students should find that they would be more sensitive to some things they now take for granted.

LITERATURE CONNECTION

Purpose The Literature Connection supports Section 4-2 by suggesting how important hearing is.

Content Background Sounds make sense only when they are associated with some action, person, or place. Jaime was able to hear the ocean when he put his ear to the shell because his uncle Osvaldo had told him what the sound would be. That sound then brought to mind images of his village and his friends. The sound helped him to remember what he missed. The sound he thought of as the ocean even reminded him of familiar smells he missed.

Teaching Strategy Have students work in pairs to list ten common sounds. Then have students list what those sounds remind them of. Have students exchange and compare lists to see how many sounds call up the same ideas.

Answers to

WHAT DO YOU THINK?

Some students will say that Jaime will not listen to the shell any more, because he has realized that he can be happy where he is and that he will always remember where he came from. Others will say that Jaime will continue to listen to remind him of where he came from.

the person receiving the call what the TDD caller types. Then they type the return message for the caller to read.

Still in development is a computer that will translate words typed on a keyboard into speech. The same computer will also recognize spoken language and translate it into print on a computer screen.

Every word must be spoken very clearly, however, otherwise the computer cannot tell the difference between words such as "I see" and "icy."

These products, as well as others that are either on the market now or are being developed, are allowing the hearing impaired to do things that they have never before been able to enjoy.

WHAT DO YOU THINK?

Think about what it would be like to not be able to hear. Are there any things that you might appreciate more as a hearing-impaired person than as a hearing person?

Literature CONNECTION

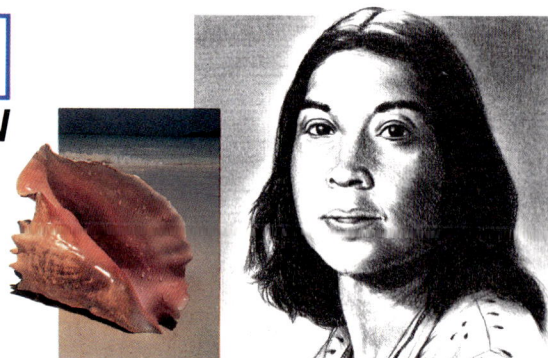

YOU CAN ALWAYS HEAR THE OCEAN

If you've ever walked along the seashore, you've probably seen seashells that were washed up onto the sand. They were once the coverings of live animals—snails, conchs, whelks, clams, oysters, or mussels—that live on the ocean floor.

Some shells form a single coiled cone. If you hold one of these against your ear, you can hear what sounds like the roar of the ocean. But, as you learned, what you're really hearing is the sound of your own blood rushing through the vessels inside your ear. You normally don't hear this sound. The seashell makes it easier for you to hear it.

The story "Jaime and the Conch Shell" was written by Nicholasa Mohr, an award-winning Latino author. It is about a young boy who leaves his small island country in the Caribbean Sea and moves with his family to New York City. As he is leaving the island, his uncle gives him a large pink conch shell.

Read the story to see how listening to the sound of the ocean in his conch shell helps Jaime when he moves to his city home.

WHAT DO YOU THINK?

How long do you think Jaime will continue to listen to his conch shell? Explain your answer.

Going Further Students can work in small groups to discuss how we use our hearing to make sense of the rest of the world. Have students make two lists of sounds, one they like and one they don't like. Then suggest that students try to explain why each sound is pleasant or unpleasant. What do the sounds make them think of? You will probably find that students think differently about certain sounds.

Going Further Some students might want to find other objects that distort or change sounds. Suggest they try to listen to sounds through common objects in the classroom, such as cups, paper coiled into a funnel, and their own hands.

Art CONNECTION

PERSPECTIVE

If everything in the world were flat, it would be easier for artists to draw realistic pictures. Since everything is not flat, artists must use something called perspective in their work. Perspective makes the subjects in a drawing appear lifelike. Perspective is also used to make objects that are close look close, and objects that are far away look far away.

Perspective can be a little tricky. For example, if you are standing in the middle of some railroad tracks, looking down them toward the horizon, the tracks will appear to come together as they get farther away. Your brain knows that railroad tracks always stay the same distance apart even though your eyes are telling you that the tracks come together.

To give a drawing perspective, an artist draws a line from left to right to represent the horizon. Then, the artist selects a point on the line, called the vanishing point. In the case of the railroad tracks, the vanishing point would be where the tracks appear to come together.

Let's say that there is a row of telephone poles running along each side of the railroad tracks. What do you think happens to the poles as they get closer to the vanishing point? If you said they appear to get shorter, you were right. In fact, if you were to draw a line connecting the tops of the poles together, the line would end at the vanishing point, too. In other words, all lines in the drawing will lead to the vanishing point if the perspective is correct.

Now that you know a little about perspective, look for horizons and vanishing points when you are looking at pictures in a book or when visiting an art museum.

YOU TRY IT!

Using perspective, draw a picture of a river flowing toward the horizon. Include trees along each side of the river.

ART CONNECTION

Purpose The Art Connection supports Section 4-1 by discussing how artists use their sense of sight to record a three-dimensional scene on a two-dimensional surface.

Content Background What the eye sees and what the brain knows about the structure of the world are not always the same. In modern perspective drawing, objects are not seen just as they are by themselves, but as how they are viewed in relation to other things. Perspective gives an impression of the world as three-dimensional wholes instead of as flat surfaces. A flat surface has only two dimensions, width and length. To create the illusion of depth on a flat surface, an artist uses both linear and aerial perspective. Aerial perspective uses the concept that distant objects are fainter and less colorful than close objects. Linear perspective uses the concept of foreshortening. This means that there is a decrease in size as an object or its parts get farther away from the viewer. If only one vanishing point results, the view is called one-point perspective. But artists also use two-point and multiple-point perspectives to represent the world as it can be seen.

Teaching Strategies Have students use rulers to trace the perspective line from the foreground of a picture to the vanishing point. Have students include a second river in their drawings. The two rivers should come from either side of the paper and meet at an off-center place on the horizon.

Going Further The idea of "proper" perspective drawings is both a learned and a cultural notion. Ancient Egyptians used only planes to portray objects. Chinese artists used aerial but not linear perspective. Children of all cultures draw differently than adults. Children draw in two dimensions instead of three. Have students work in small groups to find examples of each view of the world. Then have students debate which is better or more true to perception. **Do students think there is an absolute answer?** Have students look at examples of children's drawings. Ask students why they think children draw stick figures for people. **Why is a child's drawing of a box or a house square instead of three-dimensional?** Have students look at examples of Egyptian painting. **Do students think that ancient Egyptians might think that modern perspective means that objects are drawn wrong? Why or why not?**

EXPANDING YOUR VIEW

HOW IT WORKS

Purpose How It Works develops Section 4-2 by describing an invention that assists people who have lost the sense of hearing.

Content Background The cochlear implant is especially important to people who are deaf. Most hearing aids pick up sound waves and translate them into electrical signals. These signals are then amplified and changed again into sound waves that are fed into the ear. This process aids people who have trouble receiving or processing sound. Normally, it takes pressure of sound frequencies moving through the fluid of the snail-shaped cochlea to bend the hair cells in the organ of Corti. But without a functioning cochlea, sound vibrations cannot be transmitted. The cochlear implant permits direct transmission of electrical impulses to the nerve endings. These impulses can be picked up by the cochlear branch of the auditory nerve.

Teaching Strategies Ask students why they think it has taken so long for cochlear implants to be invented and used. Lead students to discuss how medical discoveries often cannot be made into practical items without proper materials or special surgical techniques.

For help in completing What Do You Think, suggest that students review the structure of the ear in Figure 4-13 of Section 4-2.

HOW IT WORKS

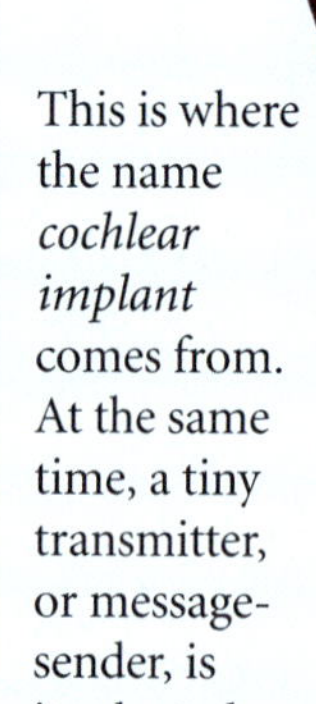

COCHLEAR IMPLANTS

Some people are hearing-impaired because the nerve cells in their cochlea are damaged. A device called a cochlear (KAWK lee er) implant, or electronic ear, can allow people with this problem to hear.

Inside the cochlea are tiny hair cells that are connected to the auditory nerve. In an undamaged ear, the hair cells vibrate faster or slower depending on what kind of sound they receive. These vibrations alert the auditory nerve to send the sound message to the brain.

For a cochlear implant to work, a person must have 22 special wires that take the place of the damaged hair cells in the cochlea implanted during an operation.

CAREER CONNECTION

A special education teacher is a teacher who works with children with physical and mental handicaps. A special education teacher may use sign language to teach deaf children.

This is where the name *cochlear implant* comes from. At the same time, a tiny transmitter, or message-sender, is implanted above and behind the person's ear.

How does the cochlear implant work? A tiny microphone fits behind the user's ear and "hears" sound. The microphone sends the sound to a pocket-sized computer that is worn on a belt or in a pocket. This computer changes the sound into an electrical signal and sends it up a wire to the transmitter. The transmitter sends the electrical signal to the 22 wires in the cochlea. The wires alert the auditory nerve to send the message to the brain.

Today, more than 3000 people have received cochlear implants. However, the results of the implants have not all been the same. At best, receivers of implants are able to hear people speak and can even enjoy music. At least, receivers can hear loud noises such as car horns and smoke alarms.

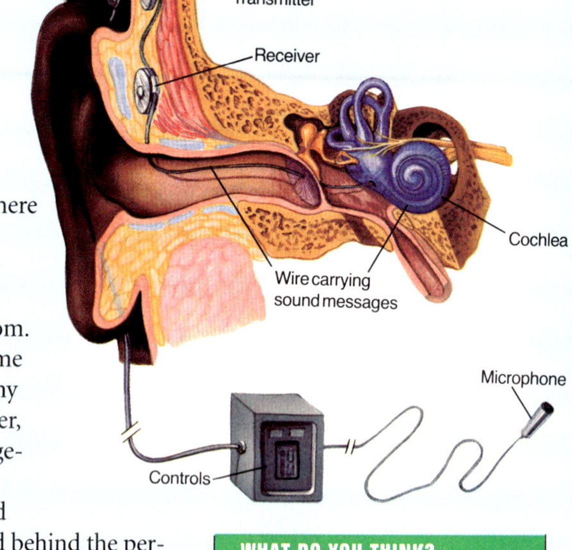

WHAT DO YOU THINK?

What steps do you think someone must take to develop something like a cochlear implant? How do you think that person feels when the successful invention is completed?

The reason for the wide range of results is that it is impossible for the small number of wires implanted into the cochlea to do the same thing as the many thousands of hair cells found in an undamaged cochlea. Research to improve cochlear implants is still in progress.

Answers to WHAT DO YOU THINK?

1. A scientist must understand how hearing works and what materials might take the place of natural fibers.
2. A person who made this successful invention would most likely feel proud and pleased that society has benefited.

Going Further Have students work in groups to discuss advances in hearing aids. Have them start with the old-fashioned ear trumpet. Encourage students to come up with reasons for each advance. Students should find pictures or drawings to illustrate ways that people have used to hear better. COOP LEARN

Going Further Ask students what special knowledge or skills a special education teacher might need to have. Have students make a list of activities they would do if they were special education teachers. Be sure to ask students if they are dealing with hearing-impaired or visually impaired students or both. **What activities would benefit both groups?**

Reviewing Main Ideas

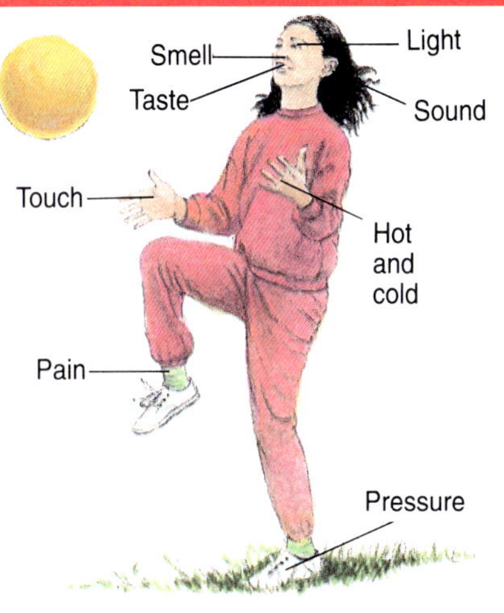

1. Your senses enable you to gather different kinds of information and make different kinds of observations about the world around you.

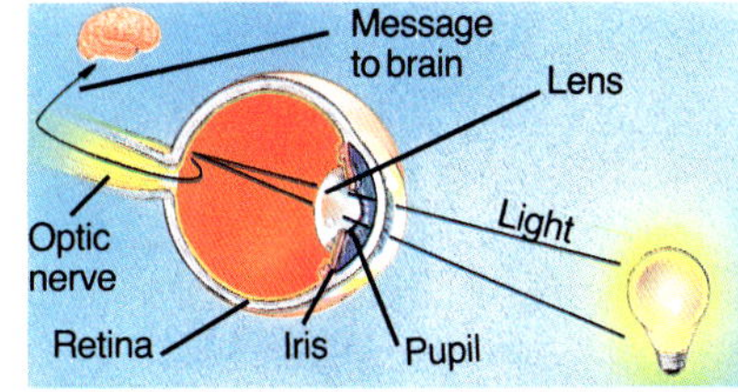

2. Light reflected from an object enters your eye and strikes the light-sensitive retina. Here rods react to light and dark and cones react to color. Your brain combines the information into one visual image of the object.

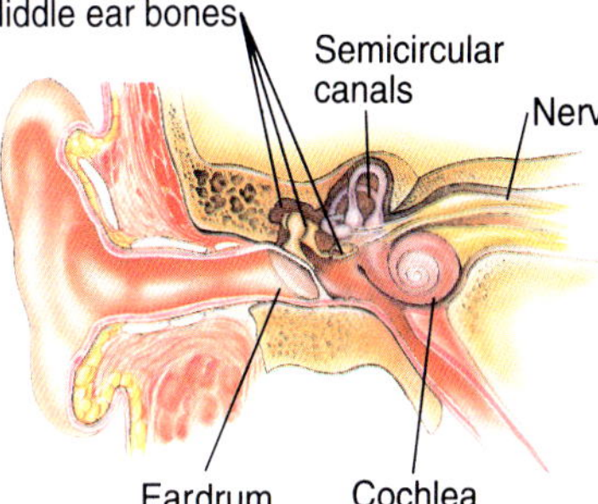

3. Sounds such as music and voices vibrate your eardrum. The vibrations are passed along to fluid in your inner ear. The bending of hairs in the cochlea by the fluid sends messages to your brain.

4. Your ear's semicircular canals signal your brain when your body is off balance.

5. The kinds of sense receptors an animal has can tell you something about the environment the animal lives in.

Chapter 4

Reviewing Main Ideas

Have students look at the five illustrations. Tell them to read the statements to review the main ideas in this chapter. The teaching strategy that follows will reveal to students how their senses working together link them to their environment and permit the development of uniquely human characteristics.

Teaching Strategies

Divide the class into five groups. Assign each group one of the photographs or diagrams. Have each group brainstorm about an important aspect of each illustration. Then have students write a short paragraph explaining their conclusions. These conclusions can be written on the board or read aloud to the class. Sample responses include: 1. Without information from the senses, people would have no way of learning about the world. 2. Our sense of sight allows us to take advantage of the natural occurrence of light. If we could not see colors, we would lack one way of describing the world around us. 3. Without being able to hear, people would not have developed the ability to speak. Hearing sounds allows humans to communicate in a special way. 4. Without a sense of balance, humans and other animals would be unable to get around well. 5. An animal's survival depends on how well it is adapted to its environment. For example, eagles have very good eyesight, which allows them to spot tiny animals on the ground from great heights.

Provide magazines for images that suggest the five main ideas. The pictures could be cut out and formed into collages that make a full picture of the concepts. Ask students to write a caption to fit their picture. Mat the collages and hang them around the room. **COOP LEARN**

Chapter 4

Chapter Review

USING KEY SCIENCE TERMS

Answers

1. phototaxis
2. semicircular canals
3. retina
4. cochlea
5. rods
6. eardrum
7. taste buds

UNDERSTANDING IDEAS

Answers

1. d
2. c
3. a
4. b, e, f
5. c
6. a
7. b, e, f

CRITICAL THINKING

Answers

1. If a frog can detect something only when the object is moving, the frog wouldn't notice the dead flies since they would not be moving.

Chapter Review

USING KEY SCIENCE TERMS

cochlea	retina
cone	rod
eardrum	semicircular canals
phototaxis	taste buds
receptor	

Using the list above, replace the underlined words with the correct key science term.

1. Movement in response to light can protect an animal from being caught and eaten.
2. The structures that sense loss of balance are located in your ears.
3. The light-sensitive area of your eye is like the film in a camera.
4. Sound vibrations bend receptor hairs in the fluid filled, snail shaped structure in your ears.
5. Your eyes contain color-sensitive and light and dark sensitive structures.
6. Sound waves cause vibration in the thin tissue that stretches across the ear canal.
7. Receptors on your tongue are sensitive to sour, sweet, salty, and bitter flavors.

UNDERSTANDING IDEAS

What kinds of information do the sensory structures numbered **1** through **7** gather? Match the information items labeled **a** through **f** with the appropriate sensory structure. In some cases, there may be more than one answer.

a. light	**1.** cochlea hairs
b. pressure	**2.** taste buds
c. chemical	**3.** rods
d. sound	**4.** skin
e. heat/cold	**5.** nose
f. pain	**6.** cones
	7. lips

CRITICAL THINKING

Use your understanding of the concepts developed in the chapter to answer each of the following questions.

1. The frog has a long, sticky tongue that it uses to catch insects, such as flies. The frog's retina contains receptors that can detect objects only if they are moving. How can you explain the fact that a frog can starve to death in a room full of dead flies?

OPTIONS

Cooperative Learning
Consider using Cooperative Learning in the Understanding Ideas, Critical Thinking, Problem Solving, and Connecting Ideas sections of the Chapter Review. COOP LEARN

2. Which animal pictured below probably lives in a dark or dim environment? Why do you think so? Which animal shown probably has a keen sense of hearing? Explain your reasoning. Which animal shown do you think must rely on touch, taste, or smell more than sight? Explain why you think so.

3. If you lost your vision, how could you learn to tell if you were about to walk into a wall?

PROBLEM SOLVING

Read the following problem and discuss your answers in a brief paragraph.

Imagine you have a beautiful flower garden. Along one side of the garden is a flower bed filled with petunias. Along the other side of the garden is a flower bed in which only zinnias are growing. Deer often come at night and eat the petunias, but they never eat the zinnias. Suggest a reason why deer would eat petunias but not zinnias. How could someone grow petunias without the deer eating them?

CONNECTING IDEAS

Discuss each of the following in a brief paragraph.

1. How could you tell you were at a zoo if you couldn't see? What if you could neither see nor hear?
2. How could you tell the difference between a bowl of creamy soup and a bowl of soft ice cream if you couldn't see or smell? Could you taste the difference?
3. In Chapter 1, you learned about landforms such as mountains and rivers, and sky objects such as the sun, moon, and stars. What sense receptors did you use when you read that chapter and discussed it in class?
4. **PHYSICS CONNECTION** Explain how the dolphin's echolocation system is similar to a ship's sonar system.
5. **SCIENCE AND SOCIETY** What is closed-caption television, and how does it aid the hearing-impaired?

2. The mole has very tiny eyes and is blind, and the earthworm has no eyes; accept either answer for first and last questions. The fox has large, well-developed ears.

3. You could learn to pay more attention to your sense of hearing and your sense of touch. You might learn to listen to the way sound in a room changes as you move closer to a wall. You could also learn to feel your way around with outstretched hands or with a cane.

PROBLEM SOLVING

Answers

A possible answer might be that the deer probably like the taste of petunias but dislike the taste of zinnias. If you grew the flowers together, instead of in separate flower beds, it would be more difficult for the deer to eat the petunias without also getting a taste of zinnias. Maybe then they would leave the flowers alone.

Connecting Ideas

Answers

1. by hearing the sounds of animals not normally found in your neighborhood; by the smells
2. Without your sense of smell, you might not be able to taste the difference. But you could sense the difference in temperatures with heat and cold sensors in your lips.
3. The rods in your retina sensed the light and dark of the words on the page, and the cones sensed the colors of the pictures. The sound receptors in your ears responded to the voices of your teacher and classmates when you discussed the chapter in class.
4. The dolphin's echolocation system and a ship's sonar both bounce sound waves off underwater objects to determine their location.
5. Closed-caption television is a broadcast system that provides written dialogue at the bottom of the screen. This allows the hearing-impaired to follow what is being said on regular TV programs.

PROGRAM RESOURCES

Teacher Classroom Resources

Review and Assessment, Chapter Review and Chapter Test, pages 17-20

Computer Test Bank, Chapter Test

LOOKING BACK

UNIT 1
OBSERVING THE WORLD AROUND YOU

THEME DEVELOPMENT

In Unit 1, the themes of scale and structure was used in observations of patterns of landforms and patterns of objects in the sky. The theme of energy was explored in emphasis on light and sound energy. Senses were used to observe both stability and change and to observe interactions within Earth and sky systems.

Connections to Other Units

The concepts developed in Unit 1 will help students better observe and understand natural phenomena in the physical world and their interactions as explored in Unit 2. The concepts will also be a foundation for the experiences and observations in the rest of the book.

Connecting Ideas

Answers

1. In flash photographs some people have eyes that appear normal while others have eyes that appear red because of the size of the pupil of the person's eyes at the time the photograph was taken. If the room is dark, the pupils will be large and light from the flash will reflect off the retina at the back of the eye.
2. You will have trouble locating the source of the tapping because although water conducts sound better than air, your ears hear the sound equally well. You might use interactions of your senses of touch and sight to located the tapped metal rail.

Exploring Further

The patterns of light you see in a kaleidoscope are made by reflection from mirrors. The patterns formed in your kaleidoscope are caused by reflections of reflections.

LOOKING BACK

UNIT 1 OBSERVING THE WORLD AROUND YOU

CONTENTS

UNIT FOCUS

In this unit, you investigated how your senses function and how they are used to obtain information about your world. Your senses were used to observe patterns and features on Earth and in the sky.

You used light and sound as two primary means of obtaining information about your world. The color of the light and whether it is reflected from a surface or refracted by it enabled you to identify characteristics of objects.

Try the exercises and activity that follow—they will challenge you to use and apply some of the ideas you learned in this unit.

CONNECTING IDEAS

1. You may have seen flash photographs showing several people. The flash is bright white, so why do some of the people have red eyes and other people have eyes that appear normal?
2. You and your friends are in a swimming pool. While underwater, one of your friends taps on a metal railing. Why do you have trouble locating the sound source while you are underwater? How might the interaction of your other senses help you determine where the metal railing is located?

EXPLORING FURTHER

What makes all the patterns of light you see inside of a kaleidoscope? Obtain three small identical mirrors. Tape them together to form a triangular shape with the reflective sides turned inward. Tape a triangular piece of paper to one end of your kaleidoscope, and drop pieces of colored paper into it. Look inside and describe what you see. What causes the pattern of color in your kaleidoscope?

LOOKING AHEAD

UNIT 2 INTERACTIONS IN THE PHYSICAL WORLD

CONTENTS

UNIT FOCUS

In Unit 1, you learned about how our senses of sight and hearing are used to observe patterns and features on Earth and in the sky. As you study Unit 2, you'll use these senses, as well as those of smell and taste, to describe materials that are part of our world. You can recall the taste of a salty chip and the strong odor that comes from certain materials, such as the sulfur in a burning match or a rotten egg. Using observations such as these, you can use your senses to identify various substances on Earth.

TRY IT

Do all substances interact in the same way? Salt, a substance necessary for us to survive, is a result of sodium and chlorine combining chemically. Not all substances, however, will react with each other. Some substances will not even mix together. What do you think will happen when powdered drink mix and water are placed together and shaken vigorously? Place some water into a jar and add some drink mix. What do you observe? Close the jar and shake it very rapidly. Stop shaking and observe what has happened to the drink mix and water. Now try the same thing, but substitute cooking oil for the water. After you've learned more about materials in the physical world, explain your observations.

Try It

The purpose of this activity is for students to observe that different substances interact differently. Drink mix and water are intended to mix and will. Cooking oil and drink mix will not mix. Have students describe other substances that they know of that mix and those that do not.

LOOKING AHEAD

UNIT 2
INTERACTIONS IN THE PHYSICAL WORLD

THEME DEVELOPMENT

The themes of stability and change and systems and interactions are evident in the descriptions of matter and its interactions in this unit. Many of the interactions within the systems in these chapters cause either physical or chemical change. However, not all the interactions cause changes. Some interactions with some kinds of matter are stable. Energy can cause change and energy is a result of certain changes. The theme of scale and structure allows students to distinguish between properties of matter.

Connections to Other Units

The concepts developed in this unit can be related to those in Unit 1 where the various physical properties of light and sound waves were shown to interact with the senses to create color, shadow, pitch, and volume. Students will learn the difference between physical and chemical properties and how they affect the interaction of one type of matter with another.

Getting Started

Discussion Some questions you may want to ask your students are:

1. **What properties can you use to describe a material?** Students may suggest color, size, shape and so on. Try to get students to continue naming physical or chemical properties, states of matter and so on.

2. **Name a common solution.** Students may name any liquid not understanding that a solution can be a liquid, gas or solid.

3. **Identify an acid, base and salt found at home.** Students may name acidic materials such as vinegar and a salt such as NaCl but most will have trouble naming a base.

The answers to these questions will help you establish misconceptions that your students may have.

CHAPTER ORGANIZER

SECTION	OBJECTIVES	ACTIVITIES/FEATURES
Chapter Opener		**Explore!** Can you make a model of smog? p. 129
5-1 Composition of Matter (2 days)	1. **Differentiate** between substances and mixtures. 2. **Give examples** of heterogeneous and homogeneous mixtures.	**Find Out!** What are some characteristics of water? p. 130 **Find Out!** Can you separate a mixture? p. 133
5-2 Describing Matter (3 days)	1. **Recognize** examples of physical properties. 2. **Measure** length, volume, and mass of different materials. 3. **Relate** density to mass and volume.	**Explore!** Can you measure without a ruler? p. 136 **Explore!** How can you measure the volume of a rock? p. 138 **Investigate 5-1:** Measuring Mass, p. 140 **Investigate 5-2:** Using Density, p. 142
5-3 Physical and Chemical Changes (2 days)	1. **Distinguish** between physical and chemical changes. 2. **Differentiate** between chemical and physical properties.	**Find Out!** Do changes in physical properties affect substances? p. 144 **Find Out!** Can the identity of a substance be changed? p. 145 **Skillbuilder:** Observing and Inferring, p. 147
5-4 States of Matter (2 days)	1. **Distinguish** among solids, liquids, and gases. 2. **Describe** physical changes relating to solids, liquids, and gases.	**Explore!** What do all solids have in common? p. 149 **Find Out!** What do all liquids have in common? p. 150 **Skillbuilder:** Making Tables, p. 150 **Explore!** What are some properties of gases? p. 151
Expanding Your View	A Closer Look **Separating Mixtures,** p. 153 Earth Science Connection **Are Tin and Oxygen Liquids?** p. 154 Science and Society **Metrics for All?** p. 155	How It Works **Taking a Spin,** p. 157 Art Connection **Alma Woodsey Thomas—Color Field Painter,** p. 158

ACTIVITY MATERIALS

EXPLORE!	INVESTIGATE!	FIND OUT!
Page 129 2 closed heat proof jars, a dark background to place them against, wooden splint, flashlight, matches **Page 136** pencil, button **Page 138** golf ball size rock, 500-mL beaker, water **Page 149** small rock, fork, penny, paper clip, cotton ball, feather, sand; flat tray, such as cookie pan; large mixing bowl **Page 151** 2 differently shaped balloons, clear glass jar with cap, rectangular container, rubbing alcohol, mirror, piece of cardboard, flat dish	**Page 140** pan balance and set of masses; empty paper clip box; groups of 10, 20, and 50 paper clips; 1 full box of paper clips, labelled *full;* 1 box of unknown number of paper clips, labelled *X* **Page 142** water, 3.5% saltwater mixture, rubbing alcohol, unknown (liquid) substance, 100-mL graduated cylinder, pan balance and set of masses, goggles	**Page 130** glass, water, microscope slide, microscope, dropper **Page 133** 1/2 cup wild bird seed, paper plates or cups **Page 144** empty can without label, freezer, ice cube, boiling water, tongs, small dish **Page 145** safety goggles, old copper penny, sealable plastic bag or small glass jar with a lid, household ammonia, forceps, paper towels **Page 150** several see-through containers of different shapes, food coloring, pitcher, water, measuring cup or graduated cylinder

Chapter 5
Describing the Physical World

TEACHER CLASSROOM RESOURCES	OTHER RESOURCES
Study Guide, p. 19 **Multicultural Activities,** p. 14 **Flex Your Brain,** p. 8	**Color Transparency and Master 9,** Classification of Matter
Study Guide, p. 20 **Concept Mapping,** p. 13 **Making Connections: Technology and Society,** p. 13 **Activity Masters, Investigate 5-1,** pp. 21-22 **Activity Masters, Investigate 5-2,** pp. 23-24	**Laboratory Manual,** pp. 17-20, Measurement and Graphing **Color Transparency and Master 10,** SI Units ***STVS:** *Measuring Body Fat,* Human Biology (Disc 7, Side 2)
Study Guide, p. 21 **Take Home Activities,** p. 11 **Multicultural Activities,** p. 13	***STVS:** *Fire Safety Tests,* Chemistry (Disc 2, Side 1) *Straw as Feed,* Chemistry (Disc 2, Side 1) *Oil Spill Identification,* Chemistry (Disc 2, Side 1)
Study Guide, p. 22 **How It Works,** p. 8 **Making Connections: Across the Curriculum,** p. 13 **Making Connections: Integrating Sciences,** p. 13 **Critical Thinking/Problem Solving,** p. 13 **Review and Assessment,** pp. 21-24	**Laboratory Manual,** pp. 21-24, Properties of Matter ***STVS:** *Radon Danger,* Chemistry (Disc 2, Side 2) *Droplets,* Physics (Disc 1, Side 2) **Computer Test Bank**
	Spanish Resources **Cooperative Learning Resource Guide** **Lab and Safety Skills**

***Science and Technology Videodisc Series**

KEY TO TEACHING STRATEGIES

Teaching strategies have been coded for varying learning styles and abilities. As you review teaching strategies in the margin, the following designations will help you decide which activities are appropriate for your students.

L1 Level 1 activities are basic activities and should be within the ability range of all students.

L2 Level 2 activities are average activities and should be within the ability range of the average to above-average student.

L3 Level 3 activities are challenging activities designed for the ability range of above-average students.

LEP LEP activities should be within the ability range of Limited English Proficiency students.

COOP LEARN Cooperative Learning activities are designed for small group work.

ADDITIONAL MATERIALS

SOFTWARE

The Metric System, Queue.
The Great Metrics Knowledge Race, Queue.
SI/Metric Literacy, EME.
Measurements: Length, Mass and Volume, Focus.
Physical or Chemical, EME.

AUDIOVISUAL

Mass and Density: Investigating Matter, laserdisc, AIMS Media.

Chapter 5

Describing the Physical World

THEME DEVELOPMENT

The themes supported by this chapter are scale and structure and stability and change. Students discover the size and structure of many materials and how these affect their interaction with one another. Students learn that apparently stable structures can change physically or chemically when acted on by outside factors.

CHAPTER OVERVIEW

This chapter is concerned with matter and its properties. First, students learn the difference between substances and mixtures. They differentiate between heterogeneous and homogeneous mixtures. Students also learn that all matter has certain physical properties. They discover how these properties are used to distinguish one material from another. Students are also introduced to the SI system of measurement.

Physical and chemical changes are explained and physical and chemical properties compared and contrasted. Finally, the three basic states of matter—solid, liquid, and gas—are described, and students learn how to identify each by its physical properties.

Tying to Previous Knowledge

Show students an unbroken egg. Ask students in what ways you can make the egg change. *They may mention cracking, mixing, boiling, or frying.* Then carefully break the egg so that it separates into yolk and white. Explain that you have produced a physical change. That is, the egg is still an egg. Use a fork to blend the yolk and white. This is also a physical change. The egg remains an egg. Ask students what happens to a fertilized egg that is incubated. *It develops into a chick.* Ask what kind of change this represents. *A chemical change; really a complex sequence of chemical changes that transforms the egg into something different.*

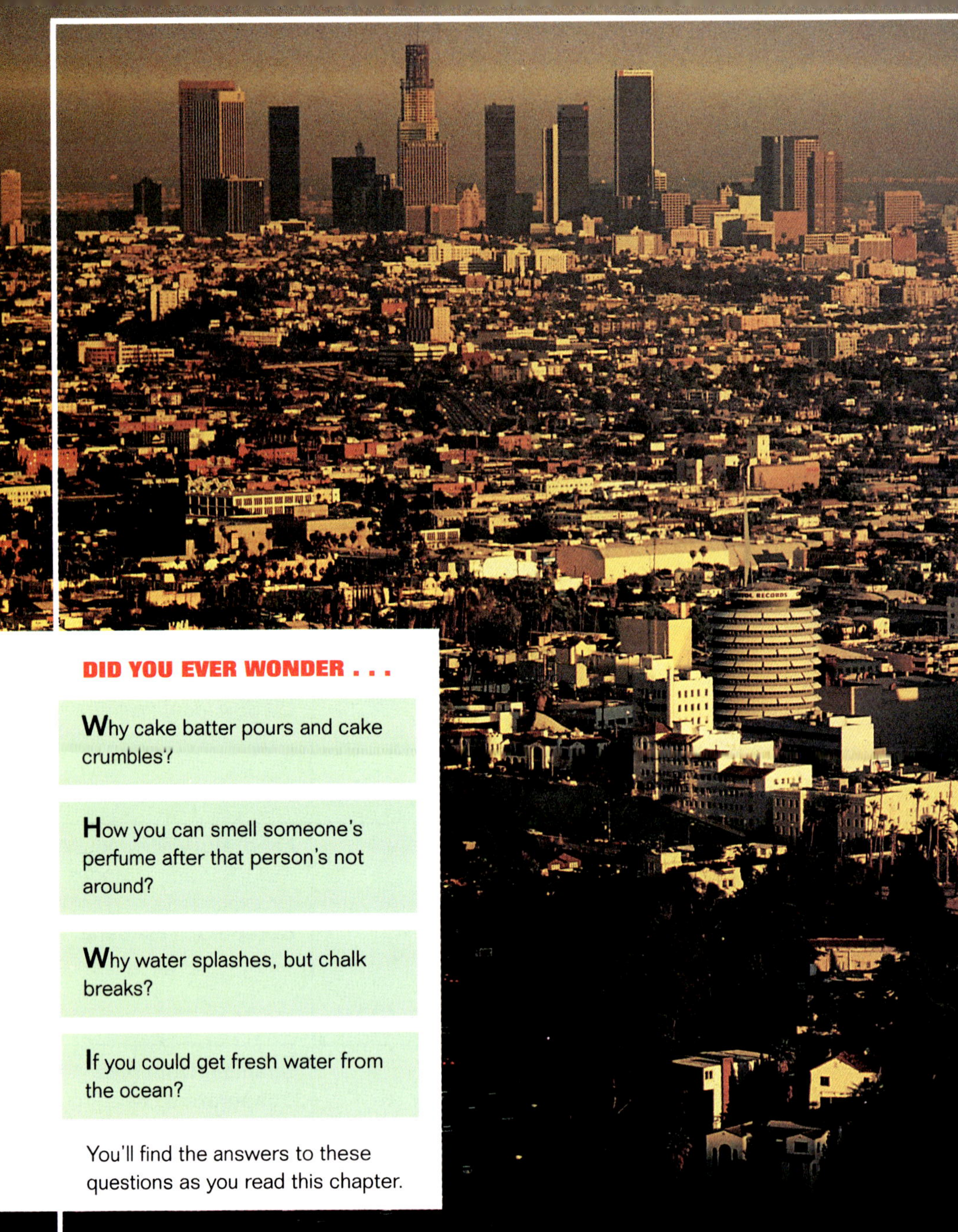

DID YOU EVER WONDER . . .

Why cake batter pours and cake crumbles?

How you can smell someone's perfume after that person's not around?

Why water splashes, but chalk breaks?

If you could get fresh water from the ocean?

You'll find the answers to these questions as you read this chapter.

DID YOU EVER WONDER...

Students will explore these questions as they progress through the chapter. Don't spoil their fun and motivation by sharing these answers too soon.

- Cake batter is a liquid. After the chemical changes brought about by baking, the cake becomes a solid. (pages 146)
- The particles of the perfume are dispersed in the air and remain a while before drifting away. (page 152)
- Water is a liquid and can easily change its shape when stressed. Chalk is a solid and cannot easily change its shape when stressed, so it breaks. (pages 149–150)
- Fresh water can be gotten from the ocean by evaporating salt water, leaving the salt behind, and then condensing the vapor back into fresh water. (page 134)

Describing the Physical World

Are there days when your eyes itch as you go to school? The air may smell funny or unpleasant. The sky may look brownish or yellowish. You might not be able to see as far as you usually can.

How the air feels, looks, and smells are clues as to what may be in the air that day. When the air is hazy and feels damp, it might mean that smoke, fog, and other matter are in the air. In and around some cities, those clues might mean that the air contains smog—a kind of air pollution.

Clues about how the air feels, looks, and smells, however, don't tell you exactly what air is. Is air the same all over the world? Is it made of one thing or a number of things? What does it mean to "clean up" the air? How do you begin to identify, describe, and classify the kinds of matter in the air around you?

You do some of these things already. This chapter will give you new ways of observing and classifying not only air, but many other materials in the physical world.

EXPLORE!

Can you make a model of smog? 

Place two closed, heat-proof jars in front of a dark background. Leave one jar alone. Open the other jar. With your teacher's help, drop a burning wooden splint into the open jar. Quickly close the lid so that the flame goes out and the jar fills with smoke. Shine a flashlight through both jars. What happens to the light?

129

Introducing the Chapter

Have students look at the photograph on page 128 and discuss how clearly they can see the buildings. Ask what they think might cause any changes in sharpness from front to back. They may be able to suggest air pollution as causing the blurring.

Uncovering Preconceptions

Students may think that in some physical changes one substance has been changed into another substance. A common misconception is that liquid, solid, and gaseous water are three different substance. Explain that ice, liquid water, and water vapor are chemically identical—they are each H_2O—but that temperature has a great effect on their physical appearance.

EXPLORE!

Can you make a model of smog?

Time needed 10 minutes

Materials two heatproof jars with lids, matches, wooden splints, flashlight

Thinking Processes Making models, Observing and inferring

Purpose To demonstrate that smog consists, in part, of smoke, or particles suspended in air

Teaching the Activity

Discussion Explain to students that smog is more than just smoke. It is a combination of smoke, particles given off by engines and factories, and tiny drops of moisture that trap smoke and particles in the air.

Expected Outcomes

Students should see that the beam of light goes straight through the empty jar but appears hazy in the smoke-filled jar.

Answer to Question
The light is partially blocked by the smoke, but is not blocked by the air.

Project

Have students keep a list of physical and chemical changes they see each day for several days. Make sure they distinguish between the two types of change. Have students check their lists to eliminate duplicates. Then divide the total number of changes by the number of days observed. This will give the number of physical and chemical changes that happen on an average day.

Science at Home

Have students observe and list the kinds of measuring devices used in their homes. What kind of units are used? Which are SI units? What materials are these devices used to measure? What units are used to measure larger materials?

5-1 Composition of Matter

OBJECTIVES

In this section, you will

- differentiate between substances and mixtures;
- give examples of heterogeneous and homogeneous mixtures.

KEY SCIENCE TERMS

substance
mixture
heterogeneous mixture
homogeneous mixture

HOW CAN YOU IDENTIFY SUBSTANCES?

The jars in the Explore weren't really empty. What was in the jars? The light that went through the jar containing only air came out in a clear beam. What was the appearance of the light in the jar containing smoky air? It would seem that something in the smoke affected how the light came out. Air and smoke are two different types or kinds of matter. They are two different kinds of materials. Examine another kind of material—water—to see what you can find out.

FIND OUT!

What are some characteristics of water?

Make some observations about a glass of plain water. What color is it? How does it smell? How does it feel? Place a drop of water from the top of the glass on a microscope slide. What color is it? Look at it under a microscope at low power. Compare it with a drop taken from the bottom of the glass. Try taking a smaller drop from the middle of the glass. Is there any difference in how each drop looks under the microscope? Compare drops of water from your glass with drops from a classmate's glass.

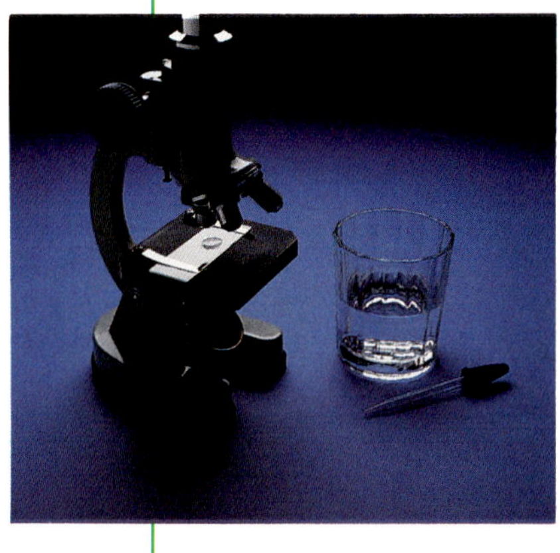

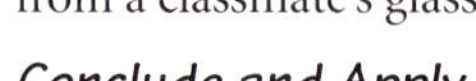

Conclude and Apply

1. What characteristics of water did you observe?
2. What can you conclude about the characteristics of all the drops of water in a glass of water?

Section 5-1

PREPARATION

Concepts Developed

Substances are made up of elements or compounds. These substances form the bases for all types of mixtures.

Planning the Lesson

In planning your lesson on matter, refer to the Chapter Organizer on pages 128A-B for timing suggestions, resources, and additional materials that will help you in your presentation of the lesson concepts. For adequate development of the concepts presented in this section, we recommend that students do the Find Out activity on page 133.

1 MOTIVATE

Discussion Ask students what they think matter is made of. How do they think it can be described? Accept all reasonable answers at this time.

FIND OUT!

What are some characteristics of water?

Time needed 5 to 10 minutes

Materials glass of water, microscope slide, microscope, dropper

Thinking Processes Observing and inferring, Comparing and contrasting

Purpose To observe and identify properties of matter.

Preparation If you do not have a microscope, use a magnifying glass and a small square of glass or plexiglass.

Teaching the Activity

Discussion Before the activity, ask students if they expect to find differences between various drops of water from the same source. L1

Troubleshooting Use distilled water if you can. Pollutants in tap water can give it color and odor.

Expected Outcomes

Students will notice that the water looks the same.

Conclude and Apply

1. Water is colorless, odorless, wet.
2. The characteristics of all drops are the same.

PROGRAM RESOURCES

Teacher Classroom Resources

Study Guide, page 19

Transparency Masters, page 21, and **Color Transparency,** number 9, Classification of Matter L1

Multicultural Activities, page 14, Luis Alvarez L1

Did you notice that one drop of water was exactly like every other drop of water, no matter how big or small the drops were? All the drops had no color, no odor, and felt wet. In fact, all water everywhere has the same characteristics. It is colorless, odorless, tasteless, feels wet, and is made of only one kind of material.

Another way to describe water is to say that water is a substance. A **substance** is anything that contains only one kind of material. You are familiar with other substances besides water. Sugar is a substance because it is made of only one kind of material. Sugar everywhere has the same characteristics. It tastes sweet, comes in small grains, and dissolves when mixed with water.

FIGURE 5-1. Sugar and water are both substances.

List some other everyday things you see or use. How many of them can be described or classified as substances?

IDENTIFYING MIXTURES

Is paper a substance? Look at a piece of paper through a hand lens. Do you think paper is made of only one kind of material? Look closely at the slice of bread shown in Figure 5-2. Would you say bread is a substance? Why or why not?

Both paper and bread contain tiny bits of other matter. So paper and bread are made of more than one substance. Any material made of two or more substances is called a **mixture**. Paper and bread are examples of mixtures. So are beef stew and many other foods you may eat.

Think back to the two jars you used in the Explore activity at the beginning of this chapter. Did either of the jars contain a substance? You might be tempted to say

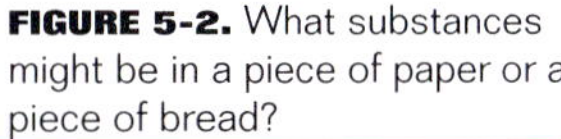

FIGURE 5-2. What substances might be in a piece of paper or a piece of bread?

2 TEACH

Tying to Previous Knowledge

Ask students whether they have ever watched a construction crew pour concrete for a building. Ask them to describe the concrete. Point out that fresh concrete is a mixture of solids—portland cement, sand, rocks—and a liquid, water.

Concept Development

Theme Connection In this section, students will see evidence of the theme of stability and change. They will see that substances can form mixtures without losing their identity.

Uncovering Preconceptions Students may use the word *substance* to describe any kind of matter. Remind students that a substance contains only one kind of material.

Activity This activity allows the students to make and observe a mixture that will form concrete.

Materials needed are 10 g of crushed calcium carbonate tablets, 20 g of sand, 30 g of small, clean gravel, 5 g of water, paper cup and stirrer.

Have students use a stirrer to mix the dry ingredients in the paper cup. Ask them to describe what they see. Then have them add the water and mix thoroughly with the stirrer. Caution students not to touch the wet concrete, as they could get chemical burns. Again ask them to describe the appearance of the mixture. Allow the mixture to dry overnight. Before they check the cups, ask students what they think might have happened overnight. They should find that they have made a form of concrete. L3

Student Text Question

What substances might be in a piece of paper or a piece of bread? *Answers may include cellulose for paper and salt, sugar, oil, and starch for bread.*

OPTIONS

Meeting Individual Needs

Visually Impaired Use this activity to help students understand how matter forms mixtures.

Materials needed are a shallow pan, 7 or 8 small marbles, and 7 or 8 large marbles.

Have students feel the marbles to note the different sizes. Put the marbles in the pan and shake the pan gently. Have students feel the marbles and note how they are jumbled together.

Concept Development

Demonstration This demonstration will show the effect that temperature has on a mixture.

Materials needed are sugar, glass of cold tea, heat-proof beaker and hot plate.

Place sugar in a glass of cold tea so that some sugar remains undissolved on the bottom of the glass. Transfer the mixture to a beaker and gently warm, stirring until the sugar dissolves. Ask students which mixture is heterogeneous (cold tea) and which is homogeneous (hot tea). Introduce the idea that temperature sometimes determines the characteristics of a mixture. L1

Student Journal Suggest that students record mixtures they find in their homes and determine whether they are heterogeneous or homogeneous.

MAKING CONNECTIONS

History

As early as 100 A.D., alchemists were trying to mix one substance with another to produce gold. What they did not realize was that gold was itself a substance and could not be the result of a mixture. But alchemists made an important contribution to modern science. Have students look up the instruments alchemists used in their research. Then have students find the same kinds of instruments in a modern laboratory. They should identify items such as flasks and beakers, condensers and receivers, and water baths. Other equipment used by alchemists included tripods, the mortar and pestle, and stirring rods.

Flex Your Brain Use the Flex Your Brain activity to have students explore MIXTURES.

FIGURE 5-3. The chunk of granite made of feldspar, mica, and quartz and the dry soup mix are heterogeneous mixtures.

DID YOU KNOW?

The bread you eat is a mixture of four materials—flour, water, salt, and yeast. It may also contain other foods, such as milk or eggs, in addition to vitamins, minerals, and chemicals added to improve its texture or keep it fresh longer. The list of ingredients on store-bought bread—and on almost every other food you buy—will tell you what materials make up the mixture.

that the jar with only air in it contained a substance and the smoke-filled jar contained a mixture of air and smoke. Actually, air itself is a mixture, although you can't see the different substances that make up air.

In Figure 5-2, were the different materials in bread mixed together evenly, or were they scattered throughout? Study the mixtures shown in Figure 5-3. How are the different materials distributed? A mixture in which the different substances are distributed unevenly is called a **heterogeneous** (het er oh JEEN ee uhs) **mixture.** Both bread and chocolate milk are heterogeneous mixtures. So is the mixture of smoke and air you observed in the Explore activity.

Suppose you make a mixture of salt and water. If you stirred the salt and water together thoroughly, would you be able to see the salt? Do you think that all parts of this mixture would taste the same? If you could look closely enough at a mixture of salt and water, you'd see that the salt is distributed evenly throughout the water. A mixture in which the different substances are distributed evenly throughout is called a **homogeneous** (hoh moh JEEN ee uhs) **mixture.** Salt water is a homogeneous mixture. What other homogeneous mixtures can you name?

SEPARATING MIXTURES

When you make smoky air, bread, chocolate milk, or salt water, you are putting substances together to make a mixture. Do you think you can take mixtures apart to separate the substances?

PROGRAM RESOURCES

Teacher Classroom Resources

Critical Thinking/Problem Solving, page 8, Flex Your Brain

OPTIONS

Enrichment

Research Have students explore ocean water as a mixture. Students should discover that salts and other minerals and substances are dissolved in ocean water. There are also many solids that are mixed with, but not dissolved in, ocean water. L2

FIND OUT!

Can you separate a mixture?

You will need about one half cup of wild bird food, which contains a mixture of different grains and seeds, such as millet, corn, safflower, and sunflower seeds. What kind of mixture is the bird food?

Count the number of different kinds of grains or seeds present. Set aside the same number of small paper cups or plates as there are different seeds in the bird food. Label each with the name of the seed or grain in the food. If you do not know the names, then write a description. There may be seeds or grains that look very similar. Be sure each description fits only one type of seed in the mixture.

Use your fingers to take all the corn or one type of seed out of the bird food. Is what remains a mixture? Why? Separate the different seeds from a tablespoon or two of the remaining bird food. How many kinds of seeds did your mixture contain?

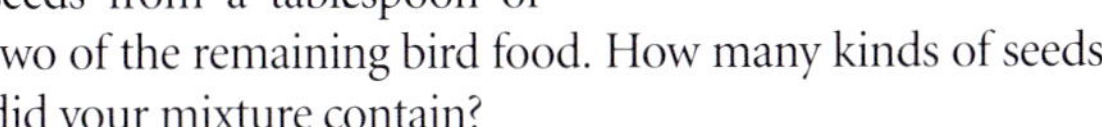

Conclude and Apply

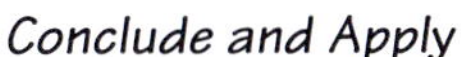

1. Is it possible to separate the different substances in a mixture?
2. Would it have been easier to make this mixture than to separate it?
3. What could you have used besides your fingers to help you separate this mixture?

Hand-separating the substances in some mixtures is one way to take them apart. What other ways are there to separate a mixture? Suppose you had a glass of sand and water. It would be difficult to separate the sand and water by hand. However, you could use a paper towel or a coffee filter. When you pour the mixture into the filter,

FIND OUT!

Can you separate a mixture?

Time needed 10 to 15 minutes

Materials half cup of bird seed per student, small paper cups or plates

Thinking Process
Classifying

Purpose To show that some mixtures can easily be separated by physical means

Preparation Paper napkins or towels can be substituted for the cups or plates. You might want to prepare examples of the seeds by taping each type to a labeled index card.

Teaching the Activity

Troubleshooting You might want to separate students into groups. One person in each group could look for a specific grain or seed. This would reduce both time and material needed. L1 COOP LEARN LEP

Student Journal Suggest that students write in their journals the conditions under which they might want to separate a mixture.

Expected Outcomes

Students should identify the mixture as heterogeneous. They should decide that, after removing only one substance, what remains is still a mixture.

Conclude and Apply

1. Yes
2. Yes
3. Forceps or tweezers; a strainer or other kind of sifter if the seeds are of different sizes

Enrichment

Activity Write the following words on the chalkboard: *air, gold, muddy water, salt water, ice, soil, granola, water, sugar, oxygen.* Have students make two lists, one for mixtures, another for substances. (Gold, ice, water, sugar, and oxygen are the substances.) Have students put each word in the proper list. Ask which mixtures, if any, can be separated easily. L2

Content Background

Another word for a homogeneous mixture is solution. The word *solution* makes people think of liquid mixtures. But air is a gaseous solution. Most alloys of metals are solid solutions.

3 Assess

Check for Understanding

Have students answer questions 1 through 3 and discuss the Apply question. Ask students to list some properties of salt and of sand. Point out that a property they share, such as particle size, is not a good basis for separation. Have students look for a property the two materials do not share.

Reteach

Demonstration Materials needed are a large jar of water, spoon, sugar, food coloring and sand.

Fill the jar with water and show it to the students. Then dissolve some sugar in the water.

Ask students if the materials are evenly mixed. Then add some food coloring and stir the mixture. Ask if the materials are evenly mixed. Students should recognize when the materials are evenly mixed. Remind students that this is a homogeneous mixture. Stir in some sand. As it settles, ask students if the materials are evenly mixed. (*No*) Remind students that this is a heterogeneous mixture. L1

Extension

Have students who have mastered this section look up and define *colloids* or *suspensions*. L2

4 Close

Ask students to identify examples of substances and heterogeneous and homogeneous mixtures in the classroom. In both cases, remind students that they should include themselves as objects in the classroom. In other words, they should consider their own body fluids in identifying substances and heterogeneous and homogeneous materials. L1

FIGURE 5-4. Salt is obtained from seawater by letting the water evaporate into the air.

the water slowly drips through the filter. The sand does not. It remains in the filter. Many heterogeneous mixtures can be separated this way.

Can a filter be used to separate salt and water? Usually not. The salt is small and too finely distributed throughout the water. It would pass through the filter with the water. Some other method of separation is needed for salt water and most other homogeneous mixtures. This method involves putting the mixture in a large, open container and leaving it uncovered. The water evaporates. The salt remains in the container. Figure 5-4 shows how this process can be used on a very large scale.

You've seen how substances and mixtures are related and how they are different. And you've seen that there are different kinds of mixtures. You know that there is more than one way to separate a mixture. This knowledge can help you classify materials.

Look again at the picture of smog that opened this chapter. When people in some places talk about smog, they are referring to a mixture of smoke and fog. Would that tell you about how much smoke or how much fog was in the air? Suppose you are told that smog is a heterogeneous mixture. Would you know any more about the smog?

In the next section, you will be introduced to other characteristics that will help you describe and identify materials.

Check Your Understanding

1. Differentiate between water and chocolate milk.
2. Give three examples of heterogeneous mixtures you use at school. Tell why they are heterogeneous.
3. Name three homogeneous mixtures you might eat, drink, or use at home. Explain your choices.
4. **APPLY:** How might you separate a mixture of salt and fine sand?

Answers to Check Your Understanding

1. Water is a substance; chocolate milk is a mixture of several substances.
2. Sample answers: paper, pen, and pencil; each consists of two or more substances that are not evenly distributed.
3. Sample answers: tea with sugar, salt water, liquid dishwashing soap: the substances that make up these mixtures are evenly distributed.
4. Add water and stir until the salt disappears; pour through a filter to separate the sand; evaporate the water to separate the salt.

5-2 Describing Matter

PHYSICAL PROPERTIES

In the last section, you separated the materials in some wild bird food. You observed the color, size, and shape of each type of grain or seed. You may have described some of the grains and seeds as flat, round, small, pointed, yellow, black, white, or striped. You used the characteristics of shape, size, and color to help you distinguish one kind of seed in the mixture from another. Notice that you can make this description without changing the grains in any way.

When you use characteristics such as color, shape, and brittleness to describe an object or a material, you are naming some of its physical properties. Any characteristic of a material that can be observed or measured is a **physical property**. When you describe physical properties, the substances that make up the material are not changed. How are the physical properties of chalk different from those of an aluminum can?

Later in your studies, you will observe the color, brittleness, and hardness of some materials. But first, familiarize yourself with some of the most common measurements related to physical properties.

OBJECTIVES

In this section, you will

- recognize examples of physical properties;
- measure length, volume, and mass of different materials;
- relate density to mass and volume.

KEY SCIENCE TERMS

physical property
density

FIGURE 5-5. The physical properties of a piece of chalk are different from those of an aluminum can.

Section 5-2

PREPARATION

Concepts Developed

This section explains how matter can be measured using the SI system. Recognizing and measuring physical properties contributes to the students' understanding of how matter varies.

Planning the Lesson

In planning your lesson on properties of matter, refer to the Chapter Organizer on pages 128A-B for timing suggestions, resources, and additional materials that will help you in your presentation of the lesson concepts. For adequate development of the concepts presented in this section, we recommend that students do the Explore activity on page 138, and the Investigate activities on pages 140 and 142.

1 MOTIVATE

Demonstration Show that mass and volume are not co-dependent.

You will need one kilogram each of five various items of varied densities, such as, feathers, cotton balls, paper, dry dog or cat food, sand and sugar, or flour.

Set out all five items. Do not tell students the mass of each item. Ask students which one they think is the heaviest, the lightest, and which ones fall in between. Ask students to explain how they arrived at their estimates. Explain that all the items have the same mass. The difference is in volume.

2 TEACH

Tying to Previous Knowledge

Ask students how they can tell an item of clothing will fit without trying it on. Or ask how they know how much taller they are this year than last. They will probably point to sizes and measurements.

PROGRAM RESOURCES

Teacher Classroom Resources

Laboratory Manual, pages 17–20, Measurement and Graphing L2
Study Guide, page 20
Concept Mapping, page 13, Matter L1
Transparency Masters, page 23, and **Color Transparency,** number 10, SI Units L2
Making Connections: Technology and Society, page 13, Institute of Standards and Technology L2

OPTIONS

Enrichment

Activity Ask students to list characteristics of clothes that are important to them. Responses might include shape, color, texture, weight, and size. Lead them to conclude they were listing physical properties and that all matter has physical properties that can be observed. L1

EXPLORE!

Can you measure without a ruler?

Time needed 10 minutes

No special materials or preparation are required for this activity, which can be done as an independent assignment.

Thinking Processes

Observing, Comparing and contrasting

Purpose To see how measurement techniques can vary.

Teaching the Activity

Student Journal Before students do this activity, have them estimate how many footsteps each measurement will equal. Then have students record their results and compare estimates with actual measurements. L1

Expected Outcomes

The number of footsteps will vary from student to student.

Answers to Question

Answers will vary, depending on the size of the student's foot and the distances to be measured.

Concept Development

Theme Connection The theme that is supported by this section is scale and structure. Any sample of matter has certain physical properties which can be measured. As students can see in Table 5-1, there are units for a variety of scales. Kilometers are used to express measurements of large distances. Millimeters are used to express measurements of small objects.

Debate There are two ways to measure physical properties of matter. One way is to do it directly, for example by using a ruler or scale. Another way is to measure indirectly, for example by using mathematical formulas. Divide students into two groups. Have one group argue the merits of direct measurement while the other group argues the merits of indirect measurement. Have both try to come up with examples to support their arguments. L3

EXPLORE!

Can you measure without a ruler?

Walk across the front of your classroom. As you walk, line up the heel of one foot with the toe of the other foot. How many footsteps did you take to walk across the classroom? Compare this number with the number of steps your classmates used. You'll probably find that the number of footsteps used to measure your classroom differs from one student to another. Now try to measure a pencil and a button using footsteps. How many footsteps do you think it is from your house to school?

In the Explore, you measured objects in "footstep" units. Maybe this type of unit works well enough for some measurements, but it has some problems. For example, the measurements are not the same from one person to the next. In addition, very large and very small measurements are not easy to make with this unit.

People around the world need to be certain that their measurements are understood by others. They also want to be sure that a bolt of cloth in Delhi, India, will be measured in the same way as a bolt of cloth in Paris, France. Therefore, most of the world's countries use standard units of measurement. The standard units they use were designed to multiply and divide easily, so they would be convenient for making very large or very small measurements. This standard measuring system is called the International System of Units, abbreviated SI, and is shown in Table 5-1.

DID YOU KNOW?

The ancient Romans used the width of the thumb as a unit of measurement. Twelve thumb widths were about equal to the length of a human foot. The units of length in the customary system that you know as the inch and the foot are based on these measurements.

Length

The students in Figure 5-6 are using metersticks to measure the length of objects. Just what does it mean to measure length? Is length the number of pages between the covers of a book? Or is it the number of minutes from

OPTIONS

Meeting Individual Needs

Physically Challenged Some students may not be able to measure with footsteps. Have them adapt the Explore activity by using a different standard of measurement. Measurements of a desk or book can be made by using either handwidth or fingerwidth. The pencil and button can also be measured using these units. Also have another student compare measurements using the same units.

FIGURE 5-6. What physical property are these students measuring?

the beginning to the end of a movie? In scientific measurement, length is the distance between two points. That distance could be the diameter of the period at the end of this sentence or the distance from Earth to the moon.

Study Table 5-1. What SI units of measure might the students use to measure the lengths of their objects? Will the book or the brick be changed when its length is measured? Is length a physical property of these objects? Explain.

TABLE 5-1. SI Units

Unit	Abbreviation	Size Comparison	Similar-sized Object
kilometer	km	1000 meters	ten football fields
meter	m	100 centimeters	guitar, baseball bat
decimeter	dm	1/10 meter	a little more than a new crayon
centimeter	cm	1/100 meter	staple
millimeter	mm	1/1000 meter	tooth on edge of stamp
kilogram	kg	1000 grams	your science textbook
gram	g	1/1000 kilogram	large paper clip

Concept Development

Using the Table Explain to students that meters and divisions and multiples of meters measure length or distance. Divisions and multiples of grams measure mass. So a book could be measured in both meters and grams.

Student Text Questions Figure 5-6: What physical property are the students measuring? *length* Will the book or the brick be changed when its length is measured? *No* Is length a physical property of these objects? Explain. *Yes. It can be observed and measured.*

MAKING CONNECTIONS

Astronomy

The stars are very far away from Earth. Scientists had to come up with a unit of measurement much larger than what is used to measure distances on Earth. They based this unit on the speed of light. A light-year is how far a ray of light travels in one year—about 9,400,000,000,000 km. The star Proxima Centauri is about 4.3 light-years away from Earth. Have students figure out how many kilometers that is. Then have them convert that into miles.

Content Background

The International Bureau of Weights and Measures has over thirty member countries. Its headquarters are located just outside Paris, France. Standards for metric measurements are kept there.

Enrichment

Activity Have students look up a measurement conversion chart in a dictionary or encyclopedia. Then ask them to convert the units in Table 5-1 to the English system. Ask which system seems to make more sense. L3

Enrichment

Research Some students might want to learn more about the metric system. Assign groups to look up metric measurements (such as the meter, the gram, or the Celsius degree), the history of the system, or the recent attempt of the United States government to convert to the metric system. L2

Concept Development

Student Text Question Would you say that volume is a physical property? Why? *Yes. It can be observed and measured.*

EXPLORE!

How can you measure the volume of a rock?

Time needed 5 minutes

Materials golfball-sized rock, 500 mL beaker, water

Thinking Processes Observing and inferring

Purpose Students will see that volume can be measured by water displacement.

Teaching the Activity

Discussion Ask students whether two objects can occupy the same space at the same time. They will probably say no. Remind students that the amount of space taken up by each object is its volume.

Expected Outcomes

The water level will rise. Students will infer that the rock took up space in the water.

Answers to Questions

1. The water level rises.
2. Yes

MAKING CONNECTIONS

Daily Life

Measurement of volume by water displacement can be used in cooking. For materials that are difficult to measure, such as peanut butter or solid shortening, this method is ideal. Half fill a large measuring cup with cold water and note the level. Add peanut butter (or shortening) until the water level rises by the amount indicated in the recipe.

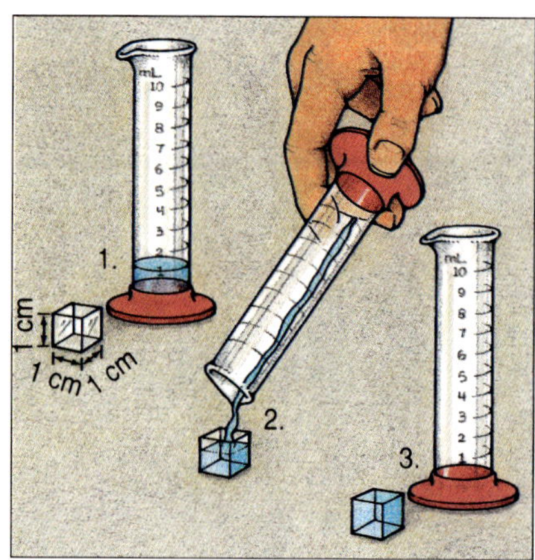

FIGURE 5-7. A milliliter and a cubic centimeter are equivalent measures of volume.

Volume

One of the teams in Figure 5-6 measured more than the length of the brick and the book. The team also measured the width and the height of each object. Then the students multiplied the three measurements for each object. They found out how much space each object occupied.

The students found the volume of the book and the brick. Volume is the amount of space an object or a material occupies. A small cube of sugar is about 1 cm long on each side. How much space does a cube of sugar occupy? Like the book and the brick, the volume of the sugar cube can be found by multiplying its length times its width times its height. So the cube's volume is 1 cm × 1 cm × 1 cm or 1 cubic centimeter, written 1 cm^3. Would you say that volume is a physical property? Why?

Can you measure the length, width, or height of a substance like water? Liters and milliliters are the most common units used to express the volume of water and similar substances. If you poured 1 mL of water into a 1-cm cube, it would fill up the cube. For this reason, it is said that 1 mL of water occupies 1 cm^3 of space. Although the liter and milliliter are not SI units, they are used with that system.

How much space do you think a small rock takes up? Can you use a ruler to help you find its volume?

EXPLORE!

How can you measure the volume of a rock?

Use a rock about the size of a golf ball. Add 250 mL of water to a 500-mL beaker. Carefully add the rock. What happens to the level of the water in the beaker? Is the change related to the volume of the rock?

PROGRAM RESOURCES

Other Resources

The Metric System, software, Queue.

The Great Metrics Knowledge Race, software, Queue.

SI/Metric Literacy, software, EME.

OPTIONS

Enrichment

Field Trip Have interested students visit the local supermarket. With the permission of the manager, have students inspect packaging that indicates volume. Have students make note of packages of different sizes or shapes that are supposed to contain the same volume. **Do the packages appear to have the right amount of mass? How can differences be accounted for?** *The density of the contents varies.*

When you put the rock in the beaker, the water level went up. The two materials in the beaker took up more space than the water alone. The amount the water level went up tells you the volume of the rock. You can find the volume of the rock by subtracting the volume before the rock was added from the final volume.

Mass

Although you can now find the volume of a book, a rock, or a glass of water, can you tell how much material is in each one?

Look at the table tennis ball and golf ball in Figure 5-8. They both seem to have about the same volume, but if you were to pick them up, you would notice a difference right away. The golf ball seems to contain more material than the table tennis ball. You might say the golf ball seems to have more matter. Mass is the amount of matter in an object or a material. The golf ball has more mass than the table tennis ball.

If you study Table 5-1, you'll notice that kilogram is the SI unit of mass. Masses of small objects are measured in grams. In the activity that follows, you will find the masses of some familiar items in grams.

FIGURE 5-8. Compare the mass of a golf ball to that of a table tennis ball.

DID YOU KNOW?

A newborn African elephant is about 91.4 cm high and has a mass of about 90.7 kg. By the time the elephant reaches full size (at about age 20), it is 365.8 cm high and has a mass of about 5805 kg.

MAKING CONNECTIONS

Art

The technique of perspective is the way artists represent volume on a flat surface. Have students look up perspective, or ask the art teacher to give a brief lecture and demonstration. Then set up a box or other object in front of the class. Have students draw the object in such a way that suggests that it has volume.

Concept Development

Discussion Ask students how moving companies use the idea of volume. In addition to knowing what items weigh, movers need to know how much space will be needed for a load. The size of the truck used often depends on the number of cubic feet needed to accommodate the load.

Content Background

The metric system acts as a universal language for scientists. It was developed in 1791 and has been used in most European countries since then. The English system was standardized in the 15th century, but its units are not based on a common factor. So the metric system, which uses a base of ten, allows more systematic conversions.

Multicultural Perspectives

Most societies develop ways to make measurements and record information. The Incas of South America kept accounts using a quipu, a knotted string. By tying knots at varying distances on different colored wool yarn, the Incas could count and transmit information to others. Counting with the quipu was apparently based on the decimal system and included the use of zero. Writing in 1549, the Spanish historian Pedro Cienza de León recorded the quipu's precision. Incas explained to him that the quipu kept accounts "with such accuracy that not so much as a pair of sandals would be missing."

INVESTIGATE!

5-1 MEASURING MASS

Time needed 30 minutes

Materials Pan balance and set of masses, empty paper clip box, groups of 10, 20, and 50 paper clips, one full box of paper clips, 1 box of unknown number of paper clips

Thinking Processes Organizing information, Making and using tables, Inferring, Thinking critically

Purpose Students will use the mass of a known object to estimate the number of objects in a larger group of the objects.

Teaching the Activity

Demonstration Using an object of known mass, show students how to determine mass with the pan balance. L1

Expected Outcomes

Students will find that mass can be measured and that the mass of groups of similar objects can be used to predict the mass of one object.

Answers to Analyze/Conclude and Apply

1. First, the mass of 1 paper clip was estimated. Second, the mass of the full box of clips was determined. Then the mass of the box was subtracted to get the total mass of the clips in the full box. Then the mass of the clips in the full box was divided by the estimated mass of 1 clip. The result equalled the approximate number of clips in the full box.
2. Because the mass of paper clips should not vary significantly, estimates should be fairly close to the actual count.
3. The mass of the clips in box *X* was divided by the estimated mass of one paper clip.
4. The estimate should be fairly close to the actual number.
5. Divide the total mass of paper clips by the average mass of one paper clip.

INVESTIGATE!

5-1 MEASURING MASS

In this activity, you'll measure mass and use your results to make some estimates.

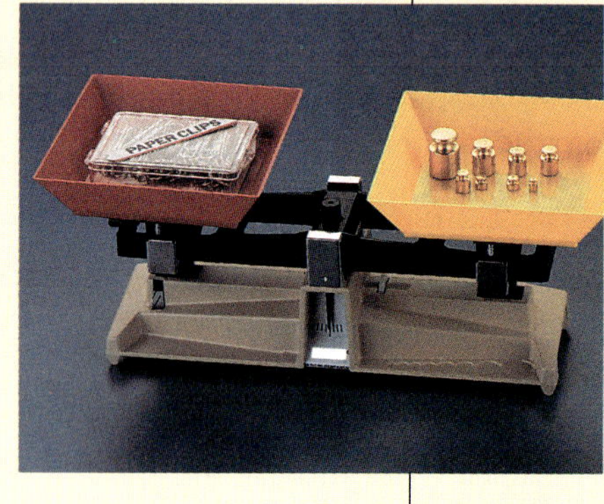

PROBLEM

How can you use mass to estimate an unknown number of paper clips?

MATERIALS

pan balance and set of masses
empty paper clip box
groups of 10, 20, and 50 paper clips
1 full box of paper clips, labeled *Full*
1 box of unknown number of paper clips labeled *X*

PROCEDURE

1. Copy the data table.
2. **Find the mass** of the empty box. Record it in your table.
3. **Find the mass** of 10 paper clips and record it. Calculate the average mass of one paper clip by dividing the mass by 10.
4. Find the mass of the full box of clips. Record the mass under the heading *Full box.* Subtract the mass of the empty box. Record this mass under the heading *Full box clips.* This is the mass of the paper clips.
5. Use your data to estimate the number of paper clips in the full box. Record your estimate.
6. Count the paper clips in the full box and record the actual number.
7. Find the mass of 20 paper clips and 50 paper clips. Record your data.
8. Find and record the mass of the paper clips in Box *X* using the procedure in Step 4.
9. Use the measurements from Step 7 to estimate the number of clips in Box *X.* Record your estimates, then count the clips in the box.

DATA AND OBSERVATIONS Sample data

ITEMS	MASS (g)	ESTIMATE	ACTUAL NUMBER
Empty box	4.0		
10 clips	6.6		
20 clips	13.2		
50 clips	33.0		
Full box	33.6		
Full box clips	29.6	45	45 or 44
Box X	Answer	will	vary.

ANALYZE

1. How did you estimate the number of paper clips in the full box?
2. How close was your estimate to the actual number?

CONCLUDE AND APPLY

3. How did you estimate the number of paper clips in Box *X*?
4. How close was your estimate?
5. **Going Further:** How would you estimate an unknown number of paper clips if the mass of the clips were less than the mass of 10 paper clips?

PROGRAM RESOURCES

Teacher Classroom Resources

Activity Masters, pages 21-22, Investigate 5-1 L1

Other Resources

Measurements: Length, Mass, and Volume, software, Focus.

Mass and Density. Investigating Matter, laserdisc, AIMS Media.

Density

Like length and volume, mass is a physical property that is used to describe materials. In the Investigate, you saw that knowing the mass of an object could be useful in gathering more information about the object. How might knowing the mass and the volume of an object be useful?

Which of the grocery bags shown in Figure 5-9 would you rather carry? The one that is filled with paper towels or the one that is filled with cans of soup? If you answered, "the one with paper towels," you already have an idea about density.

Density is another physical property used to describe materials. **Density** is the amount of mass an object or a material has compared to its volume. Density can be expressed as a certain mass per a certain volume. Recall that grams (g) are units of mass, and cubic centimeters (cm^3) are units of volume. So one way density can be measured is in grams per cubic centimeter, written g/cm^3.

FIGURE 5-9. These grocery bags are the same size and have exactly the same volume. Which would you rather carry? Why?

Suppose two identical bags were tightly closed, and you couldn't see inside them. Would you be able to tell which bag contained sand and which contained sugar? Surely you could determine the mass of the material in each bag. Perhaps you could guess the volume of each material. But suppose you knew the density of the material in each bag. Would you then be able to tell whether a particular bag contained sand or sugar?

Because sand and sugar have different densities, you could use this property to tell which material was in each bag. In the activity that follows, you will use density to identify a material.

Concept Development

Uncovering Preconceptions

Many people think that mass is the same as weight. Weight is a measure of the force of gravity on an object. A person standing on the moon has the same mass as when standing on Earth. But the person weighs only one sixth of his or her weight on Earth. This is because the force of gravity on the moon's surface is about one sixth of that on Earth.

Content Background

Most materials increase in density when they change from liquid to solid. But water doesn't. When water freezes, its volume expands because water molecules move farther apart. Even though the ice has the same mass as the liquid water that formed it, it is less dense than liquid water. This is why ice, which is a solid, floats on liquid water.

Teacher F.Y.I.

Some scientists believe that the densest object in the universe is a "black hole." A black hole is thought to be a tiny region in space, maybe several kilometers in diameter, with a mass of at least 2×10^{35} tons. A black hole the size of a pea would weigh more than Earth.

OPTIONS

Enrichment

Some students may be science fiction fans, especially fans of *Star Trek*. Have them read the Star Trek novel *Crisis on Centaurus*. Ask them to explain how Spock discovered that a black hole had caused the damage to the starship *Enterprise*. Spock discovered a tiny hole in the computer. Knowing the speed of the *Enterprise*, Spock was able to infer that the damage was caused by something with a very great density. Only a black hole could be that dense. L2

INVESTIGATE!

5-2 USING DENSITY

Time needed 30 minutes

Materials See student activity.

Thinking Processes
Making and using tables, Inferring, Drawing conclusions

Purpose To identify an unknown substance using density data

Preparation To prepare the 3.5% salt solution, dissolve 35 g of sodium chloride in 965 mL of distilled water. For the unknown, use any of the three known liquids. You may wish to give different unknowns to different students.

Teaching the Activity

Safety Students should wear goggles, which will prevent eye irritation. Be sure students do not ingest the alcohol or breathe its concentrated fumes. No open flames should be allowed during the activity.

You might want to do this as a group activity but challenge students to interpret data on their own.

COOP LEARN

Troubleshooting Students may ask if there is something wrong with the rubbing alcohol because its density is greater than the density listed for alcohol in Table 5-2. Rubbing alcohol is not pure alcohol. It is a mixture of alcohol and water.

Expected Outcomes

The unknown has a density that is equal to the density of one of the known solutions. Students will infer that the liquids are the same.

Answers to Analyze/Conclude and Apply

1. water, 1 g/cm³; rubbing alcohol, 0.89 g/mL; 3.5% salt water, 1.04 g/cm³.
2. salt water
3. Answers will vary depending on the unknown used.
4. The density of the unknown liquid was the same as the density of one of the known liquids.
5. Color, boiling point, melting point, odor

INVESTIGATE!

5-2 USING DENSITY

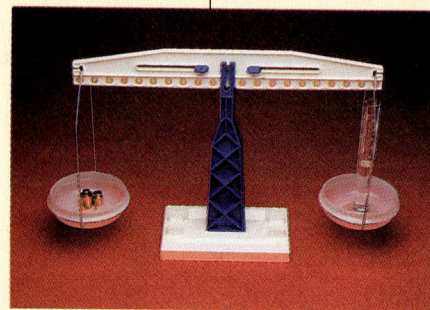

In this activity, you will find the density of three materials. You will use this information to help you identify an unknown material.

PROBLEM

How can density be used to identify an unknown material?

MATERIALS

water
3.5% saltwater mixture
rubbing alcohol
unknown (liquid) substance
100 mL graduated cylinder
pan balance and set of masses
goggles

PROCEDURE

1. Copy the data table.
2. Use the balance to **measure** the mass, in grams, of a clean, dry graduated cylinder. Record the mass in your table.
3. Fill the cylinder with water to the 50 mL mark.
4. **Measure** the mass of the filled cylinder and record it in your table under the heading *Total Mass.* Then discard the water as directed by your teacher.
5. Calculate the mass of the water by subtracting the mass of the empty cylinder from the total mass. Record the result under the heading *Actual Mass.*
6. Repeat Steps 3–5, first using the salt water, then the rubbing alcohol, and finally the unknown material.

CAUTION: *Alcohol burns readily, and its fumes can be irritating. Wear goggles. Be sure that the room is well-ventilated, and there are no open flames.*

7. Record the data for each material.

ANALYZE

1. **Calculate** the density for each material by dividing its actual mass by its volume. Round to two decimal places.
2. Which known material had the highest density?

CONCLUDE AND APPLY

3. What was the unknown material?
4. How did finding the density of the unknown material help you **identify** it?
5. **Going Further:** What other physical properties might you also look for and **measure** in identifying materials?

DATA AND OBSERVATIONS

Sample data

MATERIAL	MASS OF CYLINDER	TOTAL MASS	ACTUAL MASS	VOLUME	DENSITY (g/cm³)
water	117.59	168.31	50.72	50 mL	1.01
salt water	117.59	169.39	51.80	50 mL	1.04
alcohol	117.59	162.04	44.45	50 mL	0.89
unknown	117.59	167.60	50.01	50 mL	1.00

PROGRAM RESOURCES

Teacher Classroom Resources

Activity Masters, pages 23-24, Investigate 5-2

OPTIONS

Meeting Individual Needs

Learning Disabled Some students may be having difficulty understanding density. Have students blow up a balloon. Explain that the space in the balloon is its volume. Then have the student rest the balloon on a hand. The "feel" of the balloon is its mass. Put water into another balloon until it is the same size as the balloon blown up with air. Ask which balloon has more mass. *the water-filled balloon* L1

Like sand and sugar, the water, salt water, and alcohol you used in the Investigate have different densities. These differences helped you to identify an unknown substance. The densities of some materials that are probably familiar to you appear in Table 5-2. Notice that the densities of some materials, such as water and seawater, are almost the same. Why would it be harder to identify these substances using only density?

You already have many tools in your material identification kit. The physical properties of color, shape, length, volume, mass, and density are some of these tools or clues. Look at the piece of chalk and the iron nail in Figure 5-10. These objects have about the same length and volume. Is knowing just length and volume enough to identify these objects? The kilogram of chalk and the kilogram of salt have the same mass and are the same color. Is knowing just mass and color enough to tell these substances apart? When you are trying to identify materials, remember to use every clue or tool you have available. Using only one or two tools alone may not be completely reliable. As you continue with this chapter, you will be adding more tools to your identification kit.

FIGURE 5-10. Several physical properties may be needed to identify these materials.

TABLE 5-2. Densities of Common Materials

Material	Density (g/cm³)	Material	Density (g/cm³)
Aluminum	2.7	Alcohol	0.79
Brass	8.5	Blood	1.04
Copper	8.9	Coal	1.4 - 1.8
Gold	19.3	Gasoline	0.70
Iron	7.9	Mercury	13.6
Lead	11.4	Milk	1.03
Sand	2.6 - 2.65	Olive oil	0.92
Silver	10.5	Seawater	1.03
Sugar	1.6	Water	1.00

Check Your Understanding

1. Choose an object or a substance that you use at home or at school. Describe it using at least three of the physical properties you learned about in this section.
2. How do length, volume, and mass differ from one another? What units are used to measure each?
3. What physical properties of a wooden block is its density related to? How could density be used to identify another sample of wood?
4. **APPLY:** How might you use physical properties to identify and separate broken glass and water?

Student Text Question Why would it be harder to identify these materials using only density? *The densities are too similar. Even a small error in measuring volume or mass would affect one's ability to make a correct identification.*

3 Assess

Check for Understanding

1. Have students identify the two physical properties that determine density. (*mass and volume*) Remind students that materials that have different densities can sometimes be separated because of that difference.
2. Have students answer questions 1 through 3 and discuss the Apply question. Have volunteers suggest methods, and then ask students to critique the methods suggested.

Reteach

Have students prepare two sets of flash cards. Have students write on one set the definitions of words in this section. On the other set, write the words themselves. Students can then invent a card game based on matching words and definitions. L1

Extension

Have students who have mastered this section determine the identity of an object of unknown composition. The object has a mass of 57.0 g and a volume of 5.0 mL. Have students use Table 5-2 to identify the substance. (*Lead*). L3

4 Close

Have students pick out objects in the room and describe them using the physical properties discussed in this section. L1

Answers to Check Your Understanding

1. Example: a pencil is a solid, yellow, and 19 cm long.
2. Length is a measure of distance (meters); volume is a measure of space (liters); mass is a measure of matter (grams).
3. Its mass and its volume. Determine the density of an unknown sample of wood and compare it with the known densities of wood. The identity of the unknown sample can be determined, provided that two or more woods do not have the same density.
4. Although their colors may be similar, glass is a solid and won't pass through a filter; water will pass through a filter.

Section 5-3

PREPARATION

Concepts Developed

Chemical changes can produce new substances with new physical and chemical properties. Physical changes do not produce new substances.

Planning the Lesson

In planning your lesson on physical and chemical changes, refer to the Chapter Organizer on pages 128A-B for timing suggestions, resources, and additional materials that will help you in your presentation of the lesson concepts. For adequate development of the concepts presented in this section, we recommend that students do the Find Out activity on page 144.

1 MOTIVATE

Discussion Have students imagine and describe the smell of burnt toast. Do they think the smell is the result of materials that were not present before? Is the toast the same as it was earlier? (*New materials are present. The toast is now different than it was earlier.*) L1

FIND OUT!

Do changes in physical properties affect substances?

Time needed Several hours

Materials clean, empty can; tongs; hot plate or Bunsen burner; small dish; ice cubes; water; pan or heat-resistant glassware

Thinking Processes Observing and inferring, comparing and contrasting

Purpose To demonstrate that water remains the same substance in a physical change.

Preparation Prepare ice cubes ahead of time.

5-3 Physical and Chemical Changes

OBJECTIVES

In this section, you will

- distinguish between physical and chemical changes;
- differentiate between chemical and physical properties.

KEY SCIENCE TERMS

physical change
chemical change
chemical property

PHYSICAL CHANGES

Remember the properties of chalk described earlier? Length, color, and brittleness are some of those properties. What happens to a piece of chalk when you break it in two? Length and mass change compared with the original piece of chalk. But what about the substance that makes up the piece of chalk? Are each of the pieces still chalk? Even though you changed the chalk physically, the pieces keep the properties that identify them as chalk. Do substances change when you change their physical properties?

FIND OUT!

Do changes in physical properties affect substances?  

Put an empty can with no label on it into the freezer for use in a little while. Remove one ice cube from the freezer and place it on a small dish. Watch what happens. Is the substance that forms the same as the substance that made up the ice cube? Put the dish with this substance in it back in the freezer. Observe the dish after an hour. What changed? How does this new substance compare with an ice cube?

With your teacher's help, boil some water. Are the steam and the substance that goes into the air the same substance as the water you started with? Remove the can from the freezer. Using tongs, carefully hold the cold can near the steam. What happens?

Conclude and Apply

1. How are ice and steam the same as the water you drink?
2. How are they different?

Expected Outcomes

Students will discover that water can exist in three physically different phases, or states—liquid, solid, and gas. L1

Conclude and Apply

1. All are made of the same substance H_2O.
2. They have different physical properties, such as shape and volume.

PROGRAM RESOURCES

Teacher Classroom Resources

Take Home Activities, page 11, The Magic Card L1

Study Guide, page 21

Multicultural Activities, page 13, Walter E. Massey L1

Other Resources

Physical or Chemical, software, EME.

When an ice cube melts, its shape changes. But the water that made up the ice cube is the same substance as the water that forms in the dish. You know because the water in the dish turns back into ice in the freezer. When water changes to steam, its shape and its volume change, but it remains the same substance. You know because you collected some of this substance on the cold can.

In the Find Out, some of the physical properties of the substance water changed, but the water itself was not changed. Changes in physical properties caused by breaking, melting, or freezing, for example, are physical changes. In a **physical change**, the physical properties of a substance may change, but the kind of substance does not change.

You can change the physical properties of many substances by boiling, melting, and freezing. All of the changes will be physical changes. They will not change the identity of the substance.

FIGURE 5-11. The physical properties of wood, smoke, and ashes are different. Are they the same or different substances?

CHEMICAL CHANGES

When wood burns, are the ashes and smoke that result still wood? Let's find out.

FIND OUT!

Can the identity of a substance be changed?

Wear safety goggles while you or others are doing this activity. Observe the physical properties of an old, discolored copper penny. Then place the penny in a sealable plastic bag or small glass jar with a lid. Add about 2 tablespoons of household ammonia and close the bag or jar quickly. Observe the contents of the bag after one-half hour. With forceps, carefully remove the penny. Dry it with a paper towel and examine it. Do you think the penny will be old-looking again if you let it sit for awhile?

Conclude and Apply

1. In what ways did the properties of the penny and the ammonia change?
2. Do you think the substances changed?

FIND OUT!

Can the identity of a substance be changed?

Time needed 40 minutes

Materials ammonia, old, discolored penny, safety goggles, sealable plastic bag, forceps, paper towel

Thinking Processes Observing and inferring

Purpose To demonstrate a chemical change

Preparation You may want to do this as a general demonstration instead of an individual activity.

Teaching the Activity

Safety Caution students not to inhale the ammonia fumes, as they can damage the lining of the respiratory system. Explain that the goggles are necessary because ammonia fumes can cause eye irritation and forceps prevent chemical burns. L1

Expected Outcomes

The penny will become shinier. The ammonia changes to a bluish color.

Conclude and Apply

1. The color of the solution changed from colorless to blue. The penny became shinier.
2. Yes. A chemical reaction took place.

2 TEACH

Tying to Previous Knowledge

Have students identify changes that occur when a cake bakes. Ask them to discuss what clues (visual, tactile, olfactory) they use to determine what kind of changes have occurred. (*Some are chemical, while others are physical.*)

Concept Development

Student Text Question (Figure 5-11) Are they (wood, smoke, ashes) the same or different substances? *They are different.*

OPTIONS

Meeting Individual Needs

Physically Challenged This activity involves measuring, mixing, and observing on a scale that is easier for some students to work with. Materials needed are one cup of water, two teaspoons of sugar, one-quarter teaspoon of powdered dry yeast, one cup of flour, and two bowls.

Put a half cup of water in each bowl. To each bowl add a teaspoon of sugar and a half cup flour. Put the yeast in only one bowl. Stir the mixtures. Put the bowls in sunlight or over a radiator. After an hour, check the bowls. Students should be able to relate that the yeast bowl is bubbly due to chemical changes caused by the yeast. The other bowl will look the same as it did before the timing began.

Concept Development

Theme Connection This section gives examples of the theme of stability and change. As students do the Find Out activity on page 144, they will see that matter (water) can change state while its identity remains the same.

Uncovering Preconceptions Many students believe that when a substance boils or condenses, a chemical change has taken place. Melting, freezing, boiling, and condensing are physical changes. The substance remains unchanged.

Student Text Questions Do you think that a backyard grill or a fireplace has the property of flammability? *No.* Why do you think that fire doors are not made out of wood? *They would burn and would not stop the spread of a fire.*

MAKING CONNECTIONS

History

Chemical and physical changes usually involve the input or output of energy, often in the form of heat. James Prescott Joule, an English physicist, used the income from a brewery he owned to support his scientific investigations of heat. Have student volunteers research Joule's contribution to our understanding of heat and the concept of conservation of energy.

Content Background

Since Einstein discovered the concept expressed in the equation $E=mc^2$, mass and energy have been thought of as interchangeable; that is, mass can be changed into energy and energy can be changed into mass. However, the law of conservation of mass holds true for everyday physical and chemical changes. The law states that matter is neither created nor destroyed during a chemical change. The exception, which conforms to Einstein's equation, involves nuclear reactions.

FIGURE 5-12. Rusting is a chemical change.

In the Find Out, you saw that some of the copper in the penny was changed into a different substance. A change during which one of the substances in a material changes into a different substance is a **chemical change**. During a chemical change, the identity of a substance changes.

What clues did you have that a chemical change took place in the penny? Certainly, the change in the shiny copper color was one indication. What other clues can tell you that a chemical change has taken place? The smell of burnt toast or an automobile's exhaust fumes can be evidence that new substances have been formed. The smell is different from the smell of bread or gasoline. The foaming of fizzy tablets in a glass of water and the smell of ozone in the air after a thunderstorm are also signs that chemical changes have occurred. When a rocket blasts off, the light, sound, and smoke that accompany it are all clues that chemical changes are taking place.

FIGURE 5-13. A space shuttle takeoff involves many chemical changes.

CHEMICAL PROPERTIES

Look again at the picture of burning wood in Figure 5-11. The wood burns because there is something about it that makes it able to burn. The ability of wood to burn is a characteristic of wood. This characteristic, called flammability, is a chemical property of wood. A **chemical property** is any characteristic that gives a substance the ability to undergo a chemical change. Flammability is an important chemical property. Do you think a backyard grill or a fireplace has the property of flammability? Why do you think that fire doors are not made out of wood?

OPTIONS

Multicultural Perspectives

The Japanese developed a special pottery form for their Zen tea ceremonies. The process, of making this pottery, called raku, is at least 400 years old. Although the pottery was designed for ceremonial tea services, potters in many countries have learned the process and are using it in their own work. The raku process results in a glaze with a unique metallic luster. First, the tea pot is fired to the point where the glaze is smooth and glossy. Then the pot is immediately placed in a container of leaves, sawdust or grass. Chemical changes are induced by cooling the pot in this organic mixture. As a result, the clay body blackens and the glaze develops a metallic luster.

How do we know?

Tests for Chemical Change

Sometimes the usual clues for identifying a chemical change do not work. Perhaps there is no smell or maybe you missed the flash of light. There is one way you can be sure a chemical change has taken place. If the substances after the change are different from the substances before the change, you can be certain the change was chemical.

There are several tests that tell you what substances are present in a material. One such test is a little like looking at the colors of a rainbow formed when the sun shines through drops of rain. This test involves using an instrument called a spectroscope to look at the colors produced by glowing substances.

When viewed through a spectroscope, each glowing substance produces its own personal rainbow. Sodium, for instance, produces a particular yellow light. No other substance produces the same color light as sodium.

If the light produced by a glowing substance has the same colors in it before and after a change, then the substances have not been changed. You could conclude that the change was physical. What would you conclude if the colors of light produced before and after a change are different?

Some substances undergo chemical change when they are exposed to light. The next time you visit a drugstore, look around. Notice that some vitamins, drugs, and other products are stored in dark containers or containers that light can't get through. Such substances have the chemical property of light sensitivity. These substances are changed into other substances when light comes in contact with them. Hydrogen peroxide, sometimes used as a disinfectant, is one of these substances. When exposed to light, hydrogen peroxide changes chemically into water and oxygen gas and is no longer useful for cleaning wounds. Some medicines are labeled "Store in a cool, dark place." Why do you think this might be necessary?

SKILLBUILDER

OBSERVING AND INFERRING
Observe a burning candle and record your observations. For example, you might note how the candle changes over time. What evidence do you observe that physical and chemical changes are taking place as the candle burns? If you need help, refer to the **Skill Handbook** on page 652.

Check Your Understanding

1. When you mix sugar in water, the sugar disappears. Explain why this is an example of a physical change rather than a chemical change.
2. How is flammability different from burning?
3. Why is light sensitivity considered a chemical property rather than a physical property?
4. **APPLY:** Give one example of a physical change and one example of a chemical change that might occur when a meal is prepared.

Concept Development

Student Text Question Why Do you think this might be necessary? *Light causes chemical changes in some medicines.*

SKILLBUILDER

The candle's mass and length change. The wick shortens. The wax melts and hardens. The first two changes are due to chemical changes and reactions in the wax and wick. The melting and hardening of the wax is a physical change. L1

3 Assess

Check for Understanding

Have students discuss question 4 under Check Your Understanding. As students suggest examples, write each on the chalkboard. Arrange the ideas in two columns, one marked *Chemical Change* and one marked *Physical Change.*

Reteach

Write the following on the chalkboard: *drying clothes on a clothesline; producing light in an electric bulb; burning coal; digesting food.* Have students identify the changes as physical or chemical and give reasons for their classifications. L1

Extension

Have students who have mastered this section find out about the chemical changes that take place when photographic film is exposed to light. L3

4 Close

Show students some paper clips and a pile of sawdust. Ask whether water or heat would be more likely to produce a chemical change in each. *Heat could chemically change sawdust. Paper clips exposed to water would rust.* L1

Answers to Check Your Understanding

1. The sugar simply dissolves in the water but it is still sugar. If left in an open container, the water evaporates, leaving behind the sugar.
2. Flammability is a chemical property; it describes the ability of a substance to burn. Burning is a chemical change; it results in the formation of new substances.
3. Light sensitivity is the ability of a substance to change into another substance when exposed to light.
4. Physical: food is cut into pieces. Chemical: when food is cooked some substances in the food may react to form new substances.

Section 5-4

PREPARATION

Concept Development

Students have learned how matter changes physically and chemically. However, regardless of the type of change the matter assumes one of three basic states—solid, liquid, or gas. Students will discover how these three states of matter differ.

Planning the Lesson

In planning your lesson on states of matter, refer to the Chapter Organizer on pages 128A-B for timing suggestions, resources, and additional materials that will help you in your presentation of the lesson concepts. For adequate development of the concepts presented in this section, we recommend that students do the Explore and Find Out activities on pages 149 and 150.

1 MOTIVATE

Ask students whether they have ever heard of fuel line freeze-up or engine vapor lock. With vapor lock, fuel vaporizes at a hot spot, causing a fuel line to fill up partially with vapor, which is another term for a state of matter called gas. A car's fuel pump is designed to pump a liquid, not a gas, so the engine stalls. In summer, the gasoline can vaporize in the fuel line because of the heat. In winter, water condensation in the gas tank can freeze and block the fuel line. Again, the engine will stall. How many states of matter do students think are involved in the processes described above? Discuss with students how temperature affects the state of matter.

5-4 States of Matter

OBJECTIVES

In this section, you will

- distinguish among solids, liquids, and gases;
- describe physical changes relating to solids, liquids, and gases.

SOLIDS, LIQUIDS, AND GASES

Can you see a way to group some objects together in Figure 5-14? Perhaps you'd put the water, alcohol, and salt water in one group. What properties do sand, sugar, a penny, a book, and a rock have in common? In which group would you put the air inside the jar? Practically everything you are likely to see or use can be classified as a solid, a liquid, or a gas. These terms refer to the three basic states of matter. Clearly solids, liquids, and gases have different properties. What properties can you use to identify solids, liquids, and gases?

IDENTIFYING SOLIDS

You probably have a pretty clear idea of what a solid is. Certainly a rock is solid. But how would you describe a solid so that anyone would know what you mean? You might say that a solid is hard. Cotton balls and pillows are solids, too, yet they don't seem very hard, do they? Do all solids have some common property ?

FIGURE 5-14. You have observed or worked with these objects and materials throughout this chapter.

PROGRAM RESOURCES

Teacher Classroom Resources

Study Guide, page 22

Laboratory Manual, pages 21-24, Properties of Matter L3

How It Works, page 8, How to Make Dry Ice L2

Critical Thinking/Problem Solving, page 13, Hydraulics L2

OPTIONS

Enrichment

Research Have students prepare written reports explaining how gasoline manufacturers might solve the problems of fuel line freeze-up and vapor lock. Students will find that manufacturers use different gasoline blends for different seasons and different geographical locations. Have students discover how the blends are changed and how the changes affect the physical properties of the gasoline.

EXPLORE!

What do all solids have in common?

Examine a small rock, a fork, a penny, a paper clip, a cotton ball, a feather, a grain of sand, and any other solids you can find. List as many physical properties of each solid as you can. Do they seem to have any physical properties in common?

Place each solid into a flat tray, such as a cookie pan. Now, place each solid in a large mixing bowl. Did the shape or size of any solid change at any

Notice that none of the solids changed in size or shape when you held it or put it in different containers. Any matter that has a definite volume and a definite shape is a solid. This is the property that all solids have in common. Rocks, forks, pennies, cotton balls, feathers, sand, sugar, and all the other solids you've studied all share this property.

Recall that melting is a physical change. When a solid cube of ice melts, its shape changes. The cube turns into a runny puddle of liquid water. So melting is a physical change in which a solid becomes a liquid. Think about the difference between an ice cube and a copper penny. If you held an ice cube in one hand and a penny in the other, you know that the ice cube would melt, but the penny wouldn't. Why do these two solids act so differently?

FIGURE 5-15. Copper melts at 1083°C.

Perhaps you know that room temperature is about 20°C. Ice melts at a lower temperature than room temperature. The melting point of ice is 0°C. On the other hand, copper doesn't melt until its temperature reaches a little more than

2 TEACH

Tying to Previous Knowledge

Ask students what liquids are in their bodies and have them explain why they think these are liquids. Repeat the question with solid and gas. Accept all reasonable responses. Students will probably list blood and tears as liquids, bones as a solid, and air in their lungs as a gas.

EXPLORE!

What do all solids have in common?

Time needed 10 to 15 minutes

An assortment of solid materials is needed for this activity, which can be done as an independent assignment.

Thinking Processes
Observing, Comparing and contrasting, Drawing conclusions

Purpose To show that a solid has a definite shape.

Teaching the Activity

Discussion Ask students what changes they think happen to solids when they are moved from a container of one shape to a container of another shape. L1

Expected Outcomes

Students will see that the size and shape of the solids do not change.

Concept Development

Theme Connection The themes that are supported by this section are stability and change, and energy. Ask students what happens if you heat an ice cube and a piece of steel. Students may say that the ice melts and the steel gets hot. Point out that if the steel is heated further, it will melt. When sufficient amounts of heat energy are added or subtracted from a substance, the substance will change its state.

Uncovering Preconceptions Students tend to believe that ice is always at its freezing temperature. In reality, like any other solid, it can become colder after freezing.

Multicultural Perspectives

One solid that reacts to variations in temperature is rubber. South American natives played games using a ball made from a latex taken from trees. Although rubber keeps its shape, it turns soft and sticky when warm but stiff and brittle when cold. The Quechuans, Native Americans in what is now Peru, added sulfur to the rubber to make it more stable.

PROGRAM RESOURCES

Teacher Classroom Resources

Making Connections: Integrating Sciences, page 13, The Interior of Earth L2

Making Connections: Across the Curriculum, page 13, Killer Lakes L2

SKILLBUILDER

Three columns will be used to classify the substances as solids, liquids, and gases. Assume the substances are at room temperature. L1

FIND OUT!

What do all liquids have in common?

Time needed 10 minutes

Materials several transparent bottles of different shapes, pitcher of water, food coloring, measuring cup

Thinking Processes
Observing, Comparing and contrasting, Drawing conclusions

Purpose To demonstrate that a specific volume of liquid can take different shapes.

Teaching the Activity

Troubleshooting Be sure the volume of water poured into each container is the same. L1 LEP

Student Journal Have students indicate how the shape of the container affected the *perception* of volume. In what ways might the owners of a restaurant exploit such perceptions? *They might use glasses whose shape makes a small amount of beverage seem like more.*

Expected Outcomes

The volume measured will not change. The liquid will take on the shape of the container.

Conclude and Apply

1. Yes, whenever the water was put into a different container.
2. Yes, because the volume of a liquid doesn't change.

Teacher F.Y.I.

The pressure exerted by the blades of moving ice skates on ice melts a small amount of ice. This actually allows a skater to move on a thin film of water.

SKILLBUILDER

MAKING AND USING TABLES

Make a table to classify the following substances as usually solids, liquids, or gases: water, ice, milk, oxygen, gold, carbon dioxide, sugar, mercury, iron. Decide how many columns you will need for your table. Try to add two more substances under each heading in your table. If you need help, refer to the ***Skill Hand-***

1083°C. So, copper has a much higher melting point than ice. Each solid substance has its own melting point. Melting point is a physical property of solid substances.

IDENTIFYING LIQUIDS

You know that when a solid melts it forms a liquid. Yet the properties of liquids are clearly different from the properties of solids. What properties do all liquids share that could help you identify them?

FIND OUT!

What do all liquids have in common?

Find several see-through containers having different shapes. The more unusual the shape the better. Add some food coloring to a pitcher of water. Use a measuring cup or graduated cylinder to pour the same amount of colored water into each container. Observe what happens to the shape of the water in each container.

Pour the water from one container back into the graduated cylinder. Did the volume change?

Conclude and Apply

1. Did the shape of the colored water change? When?
2. Do liquids have a definite volume? How do you know?

You know that when you spill some milk or water on a table, the liquid flows and spreads out on the surface. Clearly, liquids do not have a definite shape the way solids do. However, as you observed in the Find Out activity, liquids can be poured, and can change shape to fit the container they are in. Any matter that has a definite volume, but takes the shape of its container is a liquid.

When you put liquid water in the freezer, it forms a solid shape like its container. Freezing is a physical change in which a liquid becomes a solid. Each liquid has its own freezing

OPTIONS

Enrichment

Activity Every day a certain volume of water passes through water systems in the students' homes. Have students look at pipes in their homes. Then have students draw the various shapes water takes as it waits in pipes, sits in the bathtub or sink, is poured into containers, and is poured down the drain.

Enrichment

Discussion Ask students if they know what to do if they are trapped in a fire. Students may know to feel the door to see if it is hot, or to stay close to the floor. If the latter strategy is not mentioned, tell students about it. The hot gases produced by the fire rise, and fresh air is close to the floor. This is why crawling is the safest way to move around during a fire. L1

point. Water, for example, freezes at 0°C. Mercury, which like water is a liquid at room temperature, won't freeze until the temperature is -38.87°C. Like the melting point of a solid, the freezing point of a liquid is a physical property.

IDENTIFYING GASES

Air is a mixture of gases. This mixture is all around you, but you can't see it. How do you know it's there? How can you tell when a substance is a gas?

DID YOU KNOW?

Solid carbon dioxide changes to carbon dioxide gas without first changing to a liquid. Because of this property, solid carbon dioxide, often called dry ice, is used to make smoke rise up from the stage in plays and concerts. The smoke is actually water vapor condensing as it comes into contact with cold carbon dioxide gas.

EXPLORE!

What are some properties of gases?

Blow up two differently shaped balloons. What happens? What takes up the space inside the balloon?

Cover a clear, glass jar with a cap. Cover a rectangular container with a piece of cardboard. What is the shape of the air occupying each container?

Put a drop or two of rubbing alcohol into a small, flat dish. What happens after a few minutes?

Hold a mirror close to your mouth and gently breathe out onto the mirror. What do you observe?

When you blow into a balloon, the gases you breathe out go into the balloon. These gases take up space inside the balloon, so they have volume. Could you measure the volume using a graduated cylinder? What did you conclude from the Explore activity about the shape of gases? Matter that has no definite shape and no definite volume is a gas. Oxygen is one of the gases in air that you can't live without. Another gas in air is carbon dioxide. You give off small amounts of carbon dioxide when you breathe. Carbon dioxide gas is also given off during burning.

A gas spreads out to fill a container it's in, no matter how large the container. Remember what happened to the alcohol in the dish in the Explore activity? After a few

Concept Development

Discussion Tell students that a description of a gas will include its volume, mass, pressure, and temperature. Ask students whether they can think of an example that proves that hot air rises. They should be able to think of hot air balloons or rooms in which the temperature is warmer near the ceiling than near the floor.

Inquiry Question Whether or not a sample of matter takes the shape of its container has to do with a property called fluidity. Compare the fluidity of solids, liquids, and gases. *Solids are not fluid. Liquids and gases are fluid.*

MAKING CONNECTIONS

Art and Design

As students visit shopping malls, have them observe how the states of matter are used to decorate and to make shopping more pleasant. Have them write about things they see, such as waterfalls, helium balloons, and marble floors.

Teacher F.Y.I.

Although glass is hard to the touch, it is not considered a solid. It is actually a liquid. The molecules in glass move very slowly over and around each other. Panes of glass in an old building are thicker at the bottom than at the top, because the glass "runs" down over the years.

EXPLORE!

What are some properties of gases?

Time needed 10 minutes

Materials two balloons of different shapes, clear jar with cap, cardboard, box, rubbing alcohol, mirror, small dish

Thinking Processes
Observing, Drawing conclusions

Purpose To show that gases take the shape of their containers but do not have a definite volume.

Teaching the Activity

Troubleshooting If students blow up their own balloons, warn students not to overinflate the balloons. They could burst. L1

Expected Outcomes

Students will notice that gases take the shape of their container and do not have definite volumes.

Answers to Questions

1. Air that fills the balloons takes the shape of the balloon.
2. Air takes up space.
3. Air takes the shape of its container.
4. Liquids can turn to gases through the process of evaporation.
5. Gases can turn to liquids.

Student Text Question How can what you've learned in this chapter help explain how smoke, fog, and other substances in the air can reach areas thousands of meters from their source? *Particles in the air are not limited to a particular space. They can drift as air moves.*

3 Assess

Check for Understanding

1. Have students list the physical properties that can describe the three states of matter. Ask students to explain how the three states differ from each other.
2. Have students answer questions 1 through 3 and discuss question 4 under Check Your Understanding. Have students make drawings of the situations they suggest as answers.

Reteach

Have students put together a bulletin board representing the three states of matter. They could use pictures from magazines or their own drawings. Be sure that the pictures are based on the properties discussed in this section. L1

Extension

Have students who have mastered this section look up *sublimation,* which is the change from a solid directly to a gas. L3

4 Close

Ask students what changes of state they could expect to see in the streets after a snowstorm. L1

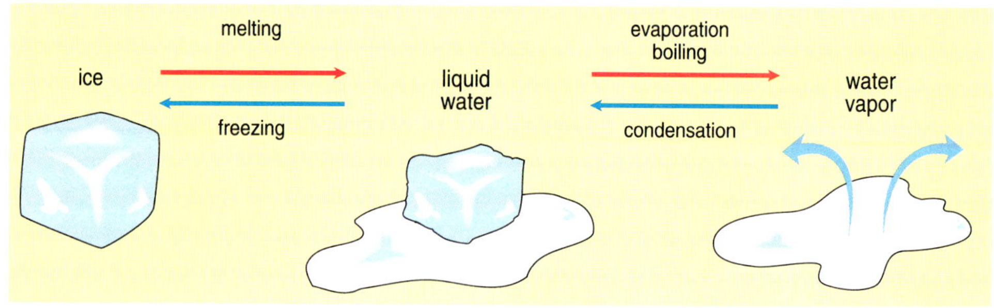

FIGURE 5-16. This diagram shows the relationship among the three states of water.

minutes, it disappeared into the air. The liquid alcohol quickly turned into a gas. The alcohol evaporated. When you open a bottle of perfume, which contains alcohol, the odor soon becomes noticeable. The gas given off does not stay in the opened container. It spreads out to occupy the entire space available to it.

Can a gas become a liquid? What happens when you bring a cold can near steam? Some of the boiling water goes into the air as water vapor. It forms liquid water when it touches the cold can. The water vapor condenses to form liquid water. Cooling speeds up condensation. Now think about what condensed on the mirror in the Explore activity. How do you know there is water vapor in the air you breathe out?

Like the other changes you've studied in this section, condensation is a physical change. Study the diagram in Figure 5-16 to see how evaporation and condensation are related to solids, liquids, and gases. How can what you've learned in this chapter help explain how smoke, fog, and other substances in the air can reach areas thousands of meters from their source?

Check Your Understanding

1. How are a brick, milk, and helium, which is sometimes used to fill balloons, different?
2. Is chocolate syrup a solid, a liquid, or a gas? Why do you say so?
3. What physical change occurs when you leave ice cream in a dish on the counter for a few minutes?
4. **APPLY:** Describe a place or a situation where you could find water as a solid, as a liquid, and a gas all at the same time.

Answers to Check Your Understanding

1. Brick is a solid, so it has a definite shape and definite volume. Milk is a liquid, so it has a definite volume but takes the shape of its container. Helium is a gas, so it has no definite volume and no definite shape.
2. Liquid, because it has definite volume but takes the shape of its container
3. It changes to a liquid by melting.
4. In a refrigerator/freezer; ice in the freezer, water in the refrigerator, water vapor in the air contained in the refrigerator

EXPANDING YOUR VIEW

CONTENTS

A CLOSER LOOK

SEPARATING MIXTURES

You know that you can use properties like size, color, or shape to separate substances in a mixture. You can use the property of boiling point by heating liquid mixtures and collecting each substance as it changes to a gas.

One property that is more difficult to observe is the attraction that the particles in a substance have for one another and for other substances. For example, when you place a drop of water on a piece of waxed paper, the water stays in a spherical shape. But when you drop the water onto newspaper or a paper towel, the water spreads out. How can this be explained? On the waxed paper, the particles in the water have a greater attraction for one another than they do for the waxed paper. On the paper towel, though, the water particles have a greater attraction for the paper.

YOU TRY IT!

Cut newspaper, paper towel, and filter paper into strips 2 cm wide by 8 cm long. Tape one end of each strip to the middle of a pencil as shown below. Dip a toothpick into green food coloring and make a line across the bottom of each paper strip about 2 cm from the bottom. Allow the lines to dry. Then, add 15 mL of water to a jar. Place the pencil across the top of the jar so that just the tips of the paper strips contact the water. The strips should not touch the sides of the jar. Wait 10 to 15 minutes and observe the strips.

How would you use your observations to describe the attraction of the colored pigments for themselves and the paper?

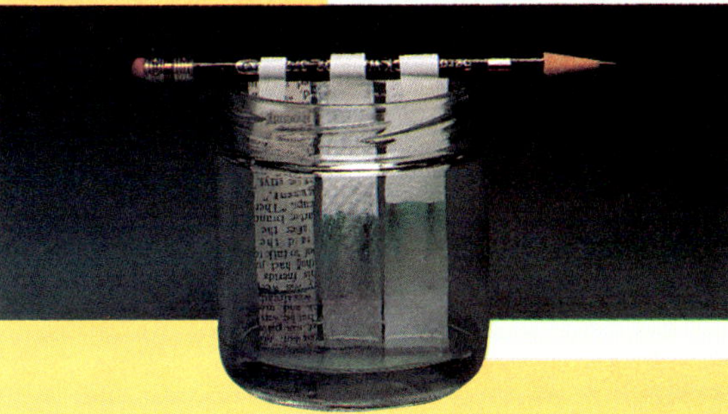

EXPANDING YOUR VIEW

Using Expanding Your View Assign one or more of these excursions to expand your student's understanding of the physical world and how it applies to other sciences and other subjects. You may assign these as individual or small group activities.

A CLOSER LOOK

Purpose A Closer Look provides an opportunity for students to contrast the attraction particles in water have for each other when they contact different surfaces. This extends the discussion of separating mixtures in Section 5-1 and the discussion of some properties of a liquid in Section 5-4.

Content Background When water is dropped on a non-porous surface it will bead, or form droplets, because the attraction of water molecules to each other is greater than their attraction to the material making up the surface. When water is in contact with a porous material such as paper, it will diffuse, or spread, through the porous material. As a result the water molecules will creep along the surface of the porous material.

Teaching Strategies Lay a paper towel over a sheet of waxed paper. Pour some water on the paper towel. Water will spread through the towel. Have students hypothesize what they will see when the paper towel is lifted up. Lift up the towel. Students should find that water has beaded on the waxed paper.

Discussion Before assigning the You Try It activity, ask students what they think will happen to the food coloring. Accept all predictions at this time.

Answers to YOU TRY IT

The different pigments in the coloring separate, which indicates that their attraction for the paper is greater than their attraction for each other.

Going Further Students can work in small groups to expand the idea that the properties of one substance allow it to interact in special ways with another substance. Have students make two lists of common materials such as paper, water, glue, wood, etc. Then have students decide what properties items on the first list might have that allow them to react to items on the second list. Students might want to revise their lists several times. COOP LEARN

Going Further Tell students that dead wood dries out after a while. A long-dead log floats in water much better than a log just cut from a tree. Why? Remind them about the pores no longer occupied by plant fluids. Also ask students to find out what physical property of water would allow a needle to float on it. Explain surface tension if you need to.

EXPANDING YOUR VIEW

EARTH SCIENCE CONNECTION

Purpose The Earth Science Connection reinforces Section 5-4 by relating the states in which certain substances naturally exist to the range of temperatures on Earth and other planets.

Content Background The differences between states of matter occur because of molecular arrangement. In solids, chemical bonds hold the molecules in relatively fixed positions. When the temperature of a solid increases, the atoms in its molecules move more quickly. This movement causes some solids to melt or change to liquid. The molecules in gases are far apart and so move quickly in that state. Then, as they are slowed by lower temperatures, some gases can change to liquids. The change in states of matter also depends on pressure. For example, water boils at 100°C at sea level. As the altitude increases, the air pressure decreases. At 90,000 ft above sea level, the pressure is so low that water boils without any increase in heat.

Teaching Strategy Based on the planet temperatures given in the table, have the students describe what the other planets might look like.

Answers to YOU TRY IT

1. Mercury
2. Neptune

EARTH SCIENCE CONNECTION

ARE TIN AND OXYGEN LIQUIDS?

The state of a substance depends upon its temperature. We classify a substance as solid, liquid, or gas according to which state it is in at "room temperature" on Earth—23°C.

You know that water freezes at 0°C and boils at 100°C. Water can exist naturally in the solid, liquid, and gaseous states on Earth. But what about other planets? What is "room temperature" on them? Of course there are no rooms on other planets, but the surface temperature of a planet would determine in what state a substance would be.

If you lived on Mercury, shown in the larger picture, or Neptune, shown in the smaller picture, would substances exist in the same states as they do on Earth? On Mercury, surface temperatures may range from -170°C to 450°C just from nighttime to daytime. If water existed on Mercury, it would constantly be changing states.

SUBSTANCE	MELTING POINT, °C	BOILING POINT, °C
Hydrogen		−253
Iron	1535	
Lead	327	
Oxygen		−183
Tin	231	

What about iron and lead? Look at the table. Is there anywhere on Earth where these substances would exist as liquids? How about on Mercury? As you can see, lead would be in the liquid state if it were found on Mercury.

What about gases? We just assume that oxygen and carbon dioxide are gases. That's because average temperatures on Earth are above the boiling points of these substances. Remember that the boiling point is simply the point at which a liquid changes to a gas. It doesn't have to be considered hot by humans living on Earth.

Weight is another property that might change from one planet to another. While one kilogram weighs 2.2 pounds on Earth, it weighs only 0.36 pounds on the moon. In contrast, the physical property of mass, the amount of matter in an object, would stay the same from place to place. As humans travel in space, they may need to express some properties of matter in terms of where the matter is observed.

PLANET	TEMPERATURE
Mercury	−170 to 450°C
Earth	−89 to 58°C
Mars	−140 to 20°C
Jupiter	−149°C
Neptune	−218°C

YOU TRY IT!

Look at the boiling points of the substances in the table above. Then look at the temperatures of the planets on the table below. On which planet(s) would tin be a liquid? On which planet(s) would oxygen be a liquid?

Going Further Assign a different metal to each small group of students. Have each group research how its metal can be used in various ways. Relate the physical properties of the metal to the uses they come up with. Have each group share its findings with the class accompanied by actual examples or pictures. Encourage students who want to learn more about liquid oxygen and the uses of liquid air to research experiments done by Louis Caillet who liquified oxygen in 1877 and Zygmunt Wroblewski who liquefied hydrogen in 1845. COOP LEARN

SCIENCE AND SOCIETY

METRICS FOR ALL?

In the United States, athletes compete on courses that are measured in meters, medicine is sold in milligrams and milliliters, and many automobile parts are measured in metric units. However, carpenters still buy lumber in feet and inches, and farmers measure their land in acres and their crops in bushels. Fabric is sold by the yard, and milk by the quart. Most highway signs give distances in miles and speed limits in miles per hour.

In 1975, the Metric Conversion Act became law. The law states that the federal government will coordinate and plan the increasing use of the metric system on a voluntary basis. So, for the time being, we are living with two different systems.

For nearly one hundred years, those favoring the metric system have argued for its widespread use in the United States, but opponents have argued just as vigorously against it. People from industry say that such a change would require them to replace or convert their machinery—a costly process. Those in favor say that machinery is often replaced anyway, and the cost would be a one-time expense that would produce lasting benefits. Trade would be easier with other countries, most of which use metrics.

Since the metric system is based on multiples of ten, calculations are much easier. Using metrics might reduce calculation errors and save time. Some people have estimated that up to two years could be cut out of traditional math courses in school because fractions and conversions would not be taught.

The metric system, called SI from the French "Le *S*ysteme *I*nternationale d'Unite's," is the standard system of measurement used worldwide. All SI units and their symbols are accepted and understood by the scientific community. In SI, each type of measurement has a base unit—meter (m) for length, kilogram (kg) for mass, etc. Look at the table on the following page to see these base units.

In the English system, you have to remember that there are 12 inches in one foot, three feet in one yard, and 5280 feet in one mile.

EXPANDING YOUR VIEW

SCIENCE AND SOCIETY

Purpose Science and Society expands the discussion of SI units in Section 5-2 by looking at the two systems of measurement used in the United States, English and SI (metric).

Content Background The history of metric use in the United States goes back over a century before the Metric Conversion Act. In 1866, the use of metric weights and measures was made legal. In 1875, the United States was the only English-speaking nation in the Diplomatic Conference on the Meter. The traditional measurements of the English system continued to be used for everyday purposes. But the metric system was favored by scientists.

The development of international trade led to an important discovery about the English system. The standards for many of the units such as pints, quarts, and gallons were not the same in the United States and Britain or Canada. In 1959, nations using the English system agreed to base their units on a uniform standard based on metric equivalents. An example of this is that the inch is equivalent to 2.54 centimeters.

International scientific advances led to a renewed debate about adopting the metric system. In the late sixties, the National Bureau of Standards carried out a study of metric use in the United States. The study showed that metrics were becoming more popular in the United States. Since the 1975 law, more and more industries have converted to metric use. Even though none of the 50 states have passed laws that require use of SI units, most of the states have laws that encourage it. Metric measures can now be seen side by side with English units. Road signs often give distances in kilometers. Gasoline pumps register in liters as well as gallons. Many soft drinks are packaged in liters.

Going Further Students can work in small groups to better understand the need for standards of measurement. Have each group devise a new system of length measurement. Units might include school supplies such as paper, pencils and erasers; and furniture parts such as desk tops, chair backs, and seats. Have groups exchange tables of measure for their systems and try to measure objects in the room with these systems. Discuss how confusing the measuring got. **COOP LEARN**

Going Further Have students write to their congressional representatives explaining why they would or would not support a complete conversion by the U.S. to the metric system. Letters to senators should be mailed to the Senate Office Building, Washington D.C. 20510, and letters to representatives, should be mailed to the Cannon House Office Building, Washington, D.C. 20510.

Content Background Some conversion factors in the English system are shown below. These conversions are good examples of the complicated relationships between English units.

1 fluid ounce = 1.805 cubic inches
16 ounces = 1 pound
63,360 inches = 1 mile
1 nautical mile (no longer in official U.S. use) = 6080 feet
1 statute mile = 5280 feet
43,560 square feet = 1 acre

Teaching Strategies Conduct a class debate of the questions posed in the last paragraph of this excursion.

Activity After students have selected the SI measurements for the You Try It activity, have them actually measure the items in SI units. You will need to provide students with a metric ruler, a metric scale, a large milk carton and a graduated beaker or graduated cylinder.

Answers to

YOU TRY IT

a. liter
b. meter
c. kilogram (here the measurement will be greater than ten for your students.)
d. centimeter
e. millimeter

In SI units, there are prefixes that indicate which multiple of ten should be used. You would say that there are 10 *milli*meters in a centimeter, 100 *centi*meters in a meter, and 1000 meters in a *kilo*meter—all multiples of ten.

SI BASE UNITS

Measurement	Unit	Symbol
Length	Meter	m
Mass	Kilogram	kg
Time	Second	s
Electric current	Ampere	A
Temperature	Kelvin	K
Amount of substance	Mole	mol
Light intensity	Candela	cd

Many people resist the switch to metrics because they are not very familiar with metric units. They have grown up using feet, pounds, and gallons and feel more comfortable continuing to use them. Most people, however, do not really know very much about these units, especially about how they relate to each other. Do you know how many cubic inches are in a fluid ounce? How many ounces are in a pound, or inches in a mile? For that matter, did you know that there are two kinds of miles—the nautical mile and the statute mile? How many feet are in each? How many square feet make one acre?

Knowing what you now know about the metric system, do you think the government should pass a law requiring that the United States convert completely to SI units by a given time? Would the advantages of adopting the metric system outweigh the possible disadvantages?

Comparing English and SI Units

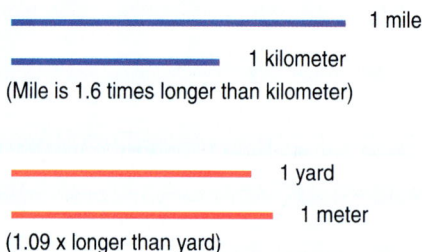

YOU TRY IT!

Look at the diagram comparing SI and English units. Which SI unit would you use to measure each of the following?

a. a large carton of milk
b. your height
c. your mass
d. the length of your arm
e. distance across a state

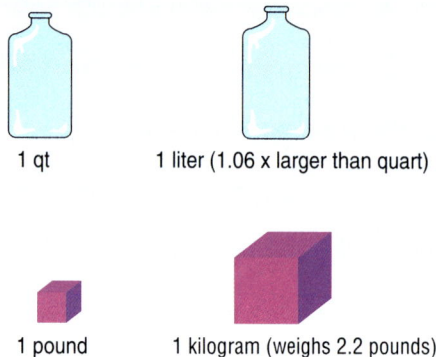

HOW IT WORKS

TAKING A SPIN

Did you ever go into an amusement park ride that looked like a large, round room, like the one in the picture? You and the other riders stand with your back against the wall. Then the room begins to rotate, and you are pressed against the wall. When the room is spinning fast enough, the floor drops, and you are held against the wall.

In scientific and technical work, machines that work very much like this amusement park ride are often used to separate substances from mixtures. These machines are called centrifuges, and they work by separating substances in mixtures according to the density of the substance. A centrifuge is pictured below.

A good example of the use of a centrifuge is for the separation of the materials in blood. Blood is a heterogeneous mixture containing plasma, blood cells, and other materials. Since plasma and blood cells are used for different purposes, it is necessary to separate them. Blood is placed in small tubes that hang down from the part of the machine that spins. The tubes are mounted so that, as the machine begins to spin, the tubes pivot upward into a horizontal position. As the machine spins around, sometimes at thousands of spins per minute, the denser materials move to the bottom of the tube, and the less dense materials stay toward the top of the tube. Because red and white corpuscles, plasma, platelets, and other materials in the blood have different densities, they will separate.

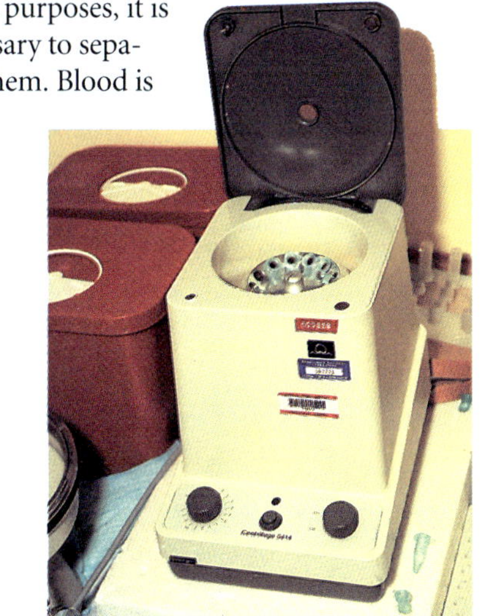

YOU TRY IT!

Other liquids can be separated by using the action of a centrifuge. For example, cream can be separated from milk. Which do you think has the greater density—cream or milk? Design an experiment to find out. You might be surprised.

EXPANDING YOUR VIEW

HOW IT WORKS

Purpose How It Works expands Section 5-1 by explaining a common method of separating mixtures into substances, using a centrifuge. This method works because substances in the mixture have different densities, a property discussed in Section 5-2.

Content Background Because the particles in mixtures vary in size, several types of centrifuges are needed for different purposes. The spin drier is a basic type of centrifuge that separates liquids from solids. Separative centifuges operate at high speeds and can separate cream from milk and impurites from oil and clarify wine and beer. Zonal centrifuges can separate particles into various levels and densities. These machines are used for separation of subcellular particles such as nuclei, RNA, and DNA. Ultra centrifuges operate at extremely high speeds and are used to separate solids from very fine suspensions.

Teaching Strategies After reading the selection, ask students to name other possible uses of centrifuges. Have the class discuss the applicability of a centrifuge for each suggestion.

Activity Students who have not ridden the amusement park ride described in the selection can feel the effect of centripetal force by riding on a playground merry-go-round while someone else makes it go around very fast.

Going Further Have students work in small groups to explore the importance of the centrifuge. Have students brainstorm about what things could **not** be done or would be done very slowly if the centrifuge had not been invented. COOP LEARN

Going Further Have students find out how centrifuges are used in their own towns or cities. Suggest that students work in pairs to write letters of inquiry to local doctors, hospitals, and industries asking what type of centrifuge is used, how it makes medical or industrial practice easier, and what separation process it replaces. Then have students share their information with the class. COOP LEARN

Answers to YOU TRY IT

milk

ART CONNECTION

Purpose Art Connection expands Section 5-2, in which students learn that color is a physical property. This excursion also shows how objects and movement can be represented in terms of color.

Content Background Alma Woodsey Thomas was the first African-American woman to have a solo exhibition at the Whitney Museum of American Art (1972). During her years of teaching, she was an important force in the Washington arts scene. She organized clubs and art lectures for her students, established art galleries in the public schools, and helped found the Barnett-Aden Gallery, one of the first galleries in Washington devoted to modern art. Thomas' use of color dominated the entire canvas. Her broad strokes of color suggested images instead of limiting them to specific forms.

Teaching Strategy Have pairs of students read the article together. Then ask students to discuss what Thomas probably felt about the use of color. They will probably say that she used mosaics of color patches to create abstract images of nature. She saw nature revealed as color. Students might also want to find examples of Alma Thomas's paintings so that they can better understand color field painting. Students could describe her use of color in each painting.

Art CONNECTION

ALMA WOODSEY THOMAS—COLOR FIELD PAINTER

Alma Thomas was an artist who achieved prominence in the mainstream art community. She worked in the modern tradition of Color Field painting.

She was born in 1892 in Columbus, Georgia. Because her aunts were teachers, she decided at an early age that teaching could be her way to a better life, too. Her family moved to Washington, D.C., in 1907. In 1924, she was the first graduate of the new art department at Howard University.

Thomas taught art in the Washington schools for 35 years. During that time, she earned an M.A. at Teachers College of Columbia University. During her teaching career, she exhibited realistic paintings in shows of African-American artists. In the 1950s, she took painting classes at American University and became interested in color and abstract art.

By 1959, Thomas's paintings had become abstract. By 1964, she had discovered a way to create an image through small dabs of paint laid edge to edge across the painting's surface. In *Iris, Tulips, Jonquils, and Crocuses*, the color bands move vertically and horizontally across the canvas to represent a breeze moving over a sunlit spring garden. In *Autumn Leaves Fluttering in the Wind*, rust-colored patches move in patterns like those of swirling autumn leaves. The spaces between the patches show glimpses of blue, yellow, and green—representing the sky and land.

Thomas's paintings are mosaic patches of color that she said, "represent my communion with nature." She wrote, "Color is life. Light reveals to us the spirit and living soul of the world through colors."

WHAT DO YOU THINK?

Alma Thomas wrote that she was "intrigued with the changing colors of nature as the seasons progress." Describe how you would paint a natural scene using the Color Field painting style.

Going Further Students can work in small groups to describe the visual impact of color field paintings. Suggest that students think of the painting as a detail of some larger image. Also suggest that students think of how color field painters are using the two dimensions of the canvas instead of trying to create an illusion of three dimensions. COOP LEARN

Going Further Students might also like to look at other color field painters. Suggest that they look at work by Nassos Daphis, Helen Frankenthaler, Ellsworth Kelly, and Frank Stella.

Reviewing Main Ideas

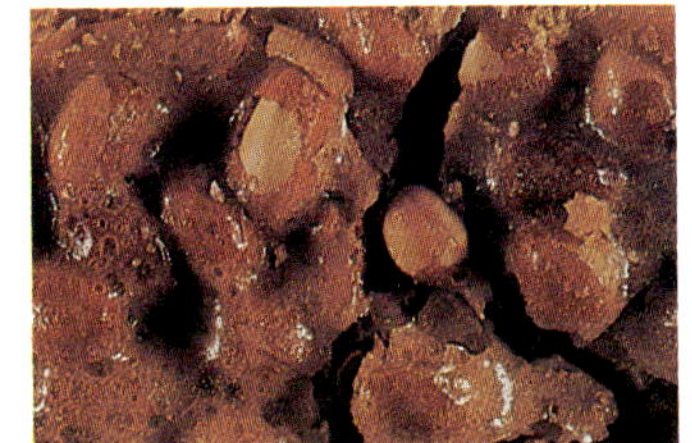

1. A substance is made of only one kind of material. A mixture consists of two or more substances.

2. Physical properties, such as, color, shape, hardness, length, mass, volume, and density, are used to describe and identify materials. So are chemical properties, such as flammability.

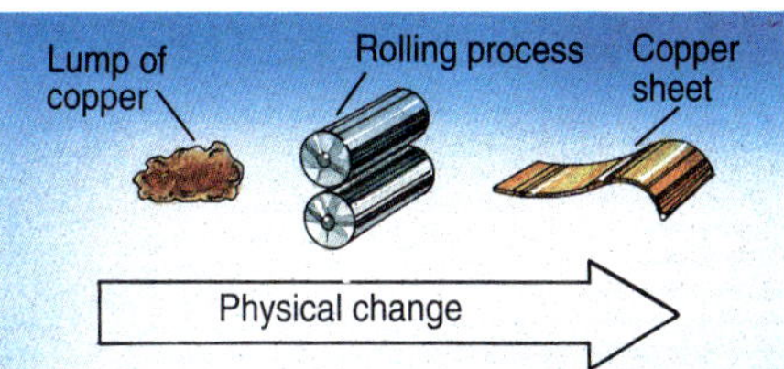

3. A substance is the same after a physical change.

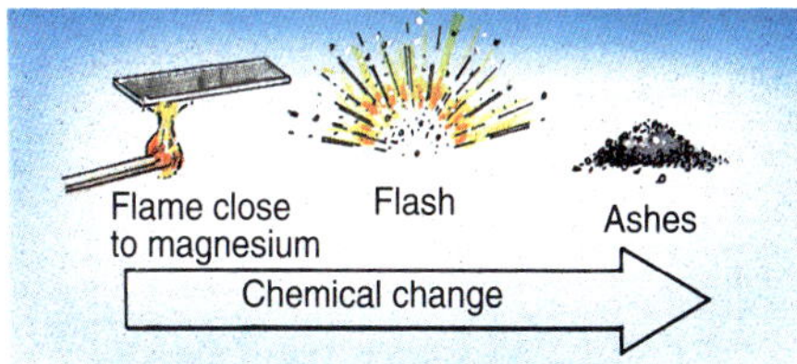

4. A substance is different after a chemical change.

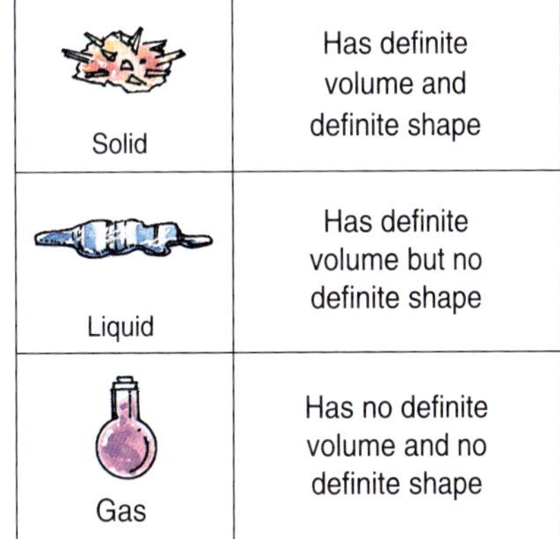

Solid	Has definite volume and definite shape
Liquid	Has definite volume but no definite shape
Gas	Has no definite volume and no definite shape

Chapter 5

Reviewing Main Ideas

Have students study the pictures and read the captions. Then have students expand their understanding of the main ideas by inventing or finding new examples of the ideas.

Teaching Strategies

Divide the class into four groups. Assign each group a photograph or diagram. Have each group come up with another idea that illustrates the concept involved. They should then draw a picture or find a photograph from a magazine that relates to their idea. They should write a caption that explains what is happening. These can be put together in book form or on a poster for display. Sample Ideas:

1. Raisin bran and milk form a mixture.
2. A person on a scale is measuring a physical property.
3. Snow or ice thaw to form puddles of water.
4. A nail left outside will rust.

Chapter Review

USING KEY SCIENCE TERMS

Answers

1. physical change
2. chemical change
3. mixture
4. physical property
5. physical change
6. density
7. homogeneous mixture

UNDERSTANDING IDEAS

Answers

1. evaporation
2. densities
3. physical
4. physical
5. chemical
6. physical
7. liquid
8. mixtures

CRITICAL THINKING

Answers

1. If the materials can be separated by mechanical means, the sample is a mixture.

Chapter 5

Chapter Review

USING KEY SCIENCE TERMS

chemical change
chemical property
density
heterogeneous mixture
homogeneous mixture
mixture
physical change
physical property
substance

An analogy is a relationship between two pairs of terms generally written in the following manner: a:b::c:d. The symbol : is read "is to," and the symbol :: is read "as." For example, cat:animal::rose:plant is read "cat is to animal as rose is to plant." In the analogies that follow, a term is missing. Complete each analogy by providing the missing term from the list above.

1. density:physical property::melting:____
2. breaking:physical change::burning:____
3. substance:oxygen::____:air
4. flammability:chemical property::length:____
5. a substance becomes a new kind of substance:chemical change::a substance stays the same substance:____
6. length, width, and height:volume::volume and mass:____
7. salt and pepper:heterogeneous mixture::sugar water:____

UNDERSTANDING IDEAS

Choose the word in parentheses that makes each sentence true.

1. Filtering and (rusting, evaporation) are two ways of separating mixtures.
2. The measurements: 10 g/cm^3, 1.5 g/mL, and 13.9 kg/L are all (densities, volumes).
3. The freezing point of mercury is a (physical, chemical) property.
4. Color, hardness, mass, and length are (physical, chemical) properties.
5. The burning of paper is a (physical, chemical) change.

6. When water vapor condenses, a (physical, chemical) change takes place.
7. A material that has a definite volume, could be a (gas, liquid).
8. Both air and salt water are (substances, mixtures).

CRITICAL THINKING

Use your understanding of the concepts developed in the chapter to answer each of the following questions.

1. How might you determine whether a sample of matter is a substance or a mixture?

PROGRAM RESOURCES

Teacher Classroom Resources

Review and Assessment, Chapter Review and Chapter Test, pages 21-24

Computer Test Bank, Chapter Test

OPTIONS

Cooperative Learning

Consider using Cooperative Learning in the Understanding Ideas, Critical Thinking, Problem Solving, and Connecting Ideas sections of the Chapter Review.

COOP LEARN

2. The density of steel is greater than the density of water, so a solid bar of steel sinks when it is placed in water. What can you infer about a steel ocean liner, knowing that it floats on water?
3. The following graph shows the mass of a given number of pebbles. Use the graph to: a) estimate the number of pebbles in a sample that has a mass of 20 g; b) estimate the mass of 110 pebbles.

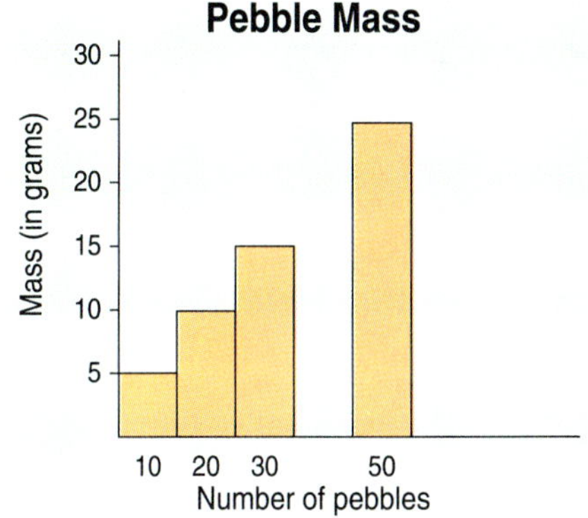

PROBLEM SOLVING

Read the following problem and discuss your answers in a brief paragraph.

You are walking along the beach, when you find a small, shiny chunk that looks like silver. You can use density to determine whether the chunk is actually pure silver or just some other silvery-colored material. Assume you have enough pure silver available to you that you can prepare a sample having the same mass as your chunk. Why would this be useful?

If you prepared a sample of pure silver with the same mass as the chunk, you could measure the volume of the sample by putting a small glass in a bowl, filling the glass to the rim with water, then putting the silver sample into the full glass. You could then measure the volume of the water that spilled into the bowl. Using this method, you measure the volume of the chunk you found. You find that the volume of the chunk is greater than the volume of the silver sample. What can you conclude about the material the chunk is made of? Why?

CONNECTING IDEAS

Discuss each of the following in a brief paragraph.

1. At the start of an activity, a material is transparent—light can pass through it. After the activity, the material is opaque—no light can pass through it. Did the activity include a chemical or a physical change? Support your view.
2. List at least two physical properties that can be observed using each of your five senses.
3. **SCIENCE AND SOCIETY** Give three arguments in favor of the United States converting completely to the SI system, and three arguments against it. Which arguments do you feel are stronger?
4. **EARTH SCIENCE CONNECTION** Imagine that a new planet has been discovered farther from the sun than Pluto. Would you expect the new planet to have an atmosphere in which you could breathe? Explain.
5. **HOW IT WORKS** Explain how centrifuges can be used to separate heterogeneous mixtures such as blood.

2. The ship has less mass per unit volume than a steel bar. Because it contains air, its total density is less than the density of water.
3. a) 40 pebbles; b) 55 g

PROBLEM SOLVING

Answers

If the chunk is pure silver, it will have the density of pure silver. Equal masses would have equal volumes. Because the volume of the chunk is greater than the volume of the silver sample, the density of the chunk is less than the density of the silver. Therefore, the chunk is not pure silver.

CONNECTING IDEAS

Answers

1. Because the same material was present before and after the activity, the change was physical.
2. Answers will vary but might include: sight, color and shape; hearing, pitch and loudness; touch, temperature and texture.
3. Suggested answers are as follows. For: 1. The U.S. would be using the same measurements as other countries. 2. SI measurements are easy to multiply and divide. 3. Measurements would not have to be converted. Against: 1. Many measuring devices would have to be changed. 2. People who grew up with the English system would have to learn the SI system. 3. Former measurements of everything would have to be converted.
4. No; being further from the sun, the temperature would be too cold for oxygen to exist as a gas.
5. The property of density allows centrifuges to separate heterogeneous mixtures, such as blood, by using the force of spinning motion to move denser materials to the bottom.

CHAPTER ORGANIZER

SECTION	OBJECTIVES	ACTIVITIES/FEATURES
Chapter Opener		**Explore!** What materials are around you? p. 163
6-1 Materials with a Past (4 days)	1. **Identify** common alloys and ceramics. 2. **Compare and contrast** alloys and ceramics.	**Explore!** How could you use age-old materials? p. 164 **Find Out!** How can you test a ceramic? p. 167 **Find Out!** What are some physical properties of metals? p. 168 **Explore!** How is bronze different from copper and tin? p. 170 **Skillbuilder:** Compare and Contrast, p. 170 **Investigate 6-1:** Making an Alloy, p. 172
6-2 Elements and Compounds (2 days)	1. **Distinguish** elements from mixtures. 2. **State** properties of a compound.	**Find Out!** How is an element different from a mixture? p. 174 **Find Out!** How can you break down a compound? p. 176
6-3 Modern Materials (3 days)	1. **Identify** plastics and their uses. 2. **Describe** a composite.	**Skillbuilder:** Making and Interpreting Tables, p. 178 **Investigate 6-2:** Making a Composite, p. 181
Expanding Your View		A Closer Look **All That Glitters Is Not Gold,** p. 183 Life Science Connection **Cloth from Worms,** p. 184 Science and Society **The Throwaway Society,** p. 185 Health Connection **Are Amalgam Fillings Safe?** p. 187 Technology Connection **Polymers,** p. 188

ACTIVITY MATERIALS

EXPLORE!	INVESTIGATE!	FIND OUT!
Page 164 samples of wood, clay, stone, and metal; water, file, dropper **Page 170** samples of copper, tin, and bronze cut into 10 cm × 10 cm sheets; file	**Page 172** copper penny, 30-mesh zinc, hot plate, dilute nitric acid, dilute sodium hydroxide solution, evaporating dishes, goggles, tongs **Page 181** plaster of Paris, paper clips, heavy-duty aluminum foil, water, measuring cup, bowl, beaker, hammer, safety goggles, paper towels, cardboard	**Page 167** clay, cookie sheet, aluminum foil, oven, hammer, safety goggles, oven mitt **Page 168** samples of copper, lead, tin, zinc, and iron cut into 10 cm × 10 cm sheets; triangular file **Page 174** 2 small test tubes, iron powder, sulfur powder, glass slides, microscope, small magnet, mortar and pestle **Page 176** safety goggles, 10 g powdered sugar, test tube, stopper with long piece of glass tubing, test-tube holder, mortar and pestle, burner

Everyday Materials

TEACHER CLASSROOM RESOURCES	OTHER RESOURCES
Study Guide, p. 23 **Concept Mapping,** p. 14 **Critical Thinking/Problem Solving,** p. 14 **Multicultural Activities,** p. 15 **Multicultural Activities,** p. 16 **How It Works,** p. 9 **Making Connections: Integrating Sciences,** p. 15 **Making Connections: Across the Curriculum,** p. 15 **Making Connections: Technology and Society,** p. 15 **Flex Your Brain,** p. 8 **Activity Masters, Investigate 6-1,** pp. 25-26	**Color Transparency and Master 12,** Steel Alloys ***STVS:** *High-Tech Ceramics,* Chemistry (Disc 2, Side 1) *Dating by Thermoluminescence,* Chemistry (Disc 2, Side 2)
Study Guide, p. 24 **Take Home Activities,** p. 13	**Laboratory Manual,** pp. 25-26, Mixtures and Compounds **Laboratory Manual,** pp. 27-30, Chromatography **STVS:** *Uses for Super Slurper,* Chemistry (Disc 2, Side 1)
Study Guide, p. 25 **Activity Masters, Investigate 6-2,** pp. 27-28 **Review and Assessment,** pp. 25-28	**Color Transparency and Master 11,** Production of Nylon ***STVS:** *Fibers from Rocks,* Earth and Space (Disc 3, Side 2) *Composite Materials,* Chemistry (Disc 2, Side 1) *Rubber from Guayule,* Plants and Simple Organisms (Disc 4, Side 2) **Computer Test Bank**
	***STVS:** *Garbage Science,* Ecology (Disc 6, Side 2) **Spanish Resources** **Cooperative Learning Resource Guide** **Lab and Safety Skills**

***Science and Technology Videodisc Series**

KEY TO TEACHING STRATEGIES

Teaching strategies have been coded for varying learning styles and abilities. As you review teaching strategies in the margin, the following designations will help you decide which activities are appropriate for your students.

- **L1** Level 1 activities are basic activities and should be within the ability range of all students.
- **L2** Level 2 activities are average activities and should be within the ability range of the average to above-average student.
- **L3** Level 3 activities are challenging activities designed for the ability range of above-average students.
- **LEP** LEP activities should be within the ability range of Limited English Proficiency students.
- **COOP LEARN** Cooperative Learning activities are designed for small group work.

ADDITIONAL MATERIALS

SOFTWARE

Chemaid: Introduction to the Periodic Table, Ventura Educational Systems.

Hydrogen Spectrum, Scott Foresman & Co.

AUDIOVISUAL

What Are Things Made of? film, Coronet/MTI

The Rock that Glowed: The Importance of Recycling, video, Focus.

Plastics, The World of Imagination, video, Modern Talking Picture Service.

Matter and Molecules: The Matter of Elements, filmstrip, Singer Media Corporation.

Chapter 6

Everyday Materials

THEME DEVELOPMENT

The predominant theme in this chapter is stability and change. Materials such as ceramics have great stability and are not easily changed even by intense heat. This stability enables them to have many uses with respect to industry, space exploration, and everyday life. Another theme presented in this chapter is energy. Energy is required to produce many synthetic materials and alloys. This energy is usually in the form of heat or electricity.

CHAPTER OVERVIEW

Students first explore the making and use of ceramics, metals, and alloys, materials that have long been used. Students then learn that elements are the purest form of matter and that compounds are produced when elements are chemically combined. Finally, students are introduced to synthetic materials such as plastics, synthetic fibers, and composites. Their manufacture and use are discussed.

Tying to Previous Knowledge

The last chapter was about describing the physical world. Have students describe the physical properties of the materials around them. Note how these properties determine their use. Have students write down as many different types of materials as they can find in the room and their uses. See if they can identify what these materials are made of. **COOP LEARN**

DID YOU EVER WONDER . . .

Why gold-colored jewelry sometimes turns green when it's worn?

What your dentist uses to fill cavities in teeth?

How something as light as plastic can be used in rockets?

You'll find the answers to these questions as you read this chapter.

DID YOU EVER WONDER...

Students will explore these questions as they progress through the chapter. Don't spoil their fun and motivation by sharing these answers too early.

- Gold jewelry is actually made of a copper-gold alloy. A cheaper alloy that contains a high percentage of copper can turn green when it is exposed to air or other materials. (page 171)
- an alloy of mercury called amalgam (page 171)
- Plastics can be light yet extremely durable. (page 178)

Chapter 6

Everyday Materials

On your way to school each morning, you are surrounded by materials. The clothes you put on are made of cotton or synthetic fibers. At breakfast, you may drink your milk from a glass and eat your cereal in a ceramic bowl. The car or bus you ride in has smooth vinyl seats, thick rubber tires, colorful plastic molding, and a shiny steel body. The streets you ride over contain asphalt and concrete. Even your school building holds an assortment of materials: wooden shelves, tile floors, aluminum lockers, and green or black chalkboards.

Steel, glass, and plastic are common materials you use every day. All of these materials are well-suited for the objects you use every day. The cotton fibers fit your body and keep you warm, but they wouldn't hold your morning cereal. The bus's rubber tires make the ride to school comfortable, but rubber bookshelves probably wouldn't be of much use, would they?

What are these materials made of? How are they put together? This chapter will help you answer these questions.

EXPLORE!

What materials are around you?

Sit quietly in your classroom and look around you. Try to list ten different materials in your room without leaving your seat. Make a list in your notebook. What are these materials made of? How are they different from each other?

163

Introducing the Chapter

Have students look at the photograph on page 162. Have them identify as many different types of materials as they can. List student responses on the chalkboard.

Uncovering Preconceptions

Students may think that all the materials discussed in this chapter are human-made materials. Explain to them that ceramics can actually be made from natural materials found in Earth such as clay. Even synthetic materials require some naturally occurring substance in their manufacture. Also point out that the discovery, use, and development of these materials took many years.

EXPLORE!

What materials are around you?

Time needed 10–15 minutes

Materials No special materials or preparation are required for this activity, which can be done as an independent assignment.

Thinking Processes
Organizing information, Classifying, Thinking critically, Comparing and contrasting, Practicing scientific methods, Observing

Purpose To become aware of the various materials that surround us in our everyday lives.

Teaching Strategies

Demonstration Ask students why they think that wood is a good material to make doors out of. Why might steel or another metal be better? *They are stronger.* L1

Expected Outcome

Students should be able to identify at least six different materials that are used for various things.

Answers to Questions

1. Answers will vary but should include things like metal, glass, stone, paper, wood.
2. Materials differ from each other by their luster, hardness, and general appearance.

Project

Many materials, especially plastics, are recyclable. Throughout the teaching of this chapter, have students become active in collecting plastic bottles, milk cartons, and other plastic containers from around the school. If your town already has a recycling program, encourage students to bring collected items from home also. Then organize a field trip to bring the collected items to a recycling center.

Science at Home

Have students keep a running list of materials that they find and use around their homes. The list should continue to grow as students learn about different materials from this chapter's lessons. Ask students to include in their lists the location of the material, its use, and, if possible, its origin.

Section 6-1

PREPARATION

Concepts Developed

This section will introduce students to ceramics, metals, and alloys. Properties and uses of each type of material are discussed. A ceramic is a material made from dried clay or claylike mixtures. It is lightweight and can withstand high temperatures. An alloy is a mixture of metals or nonmetals and has different properties from the material used to make it. Ceramics do not expand or contract due to temperature changes, have little flexibility, and will shatter on impact. Metals and alloys can bend and do not shatter.

Planning the Lesson

In planning your lesson on materials with a past, refer to the Chapter Organizer on pages 162A-B for timing suggestions, resources, and additional materials that will help you in your presentation of the lesson concepts. For adequate development of the concepts presented in this section, we recommend that students do the Explore activity on page 164 and the Find Out activity on page 168.

1 MOTIVATE

Discussion Show students some examples of ceramics such as a piece of tile, spark plug, glass, coffee cup, and trivet. Ask students to identify the function of each item. Then ask them why ceramic is a good material to use for each. L1

EXPLORE!

How could you use age-old materials?

Time needed 20–30 minutes

Materials samples of wood, Playdough or modeling clay, stone, and metal; medicine droppers; files; water

6-1 Materials with a Past

OBJECTIVES

In this section, you will

- identify common alloys and ceramics;
- compare and contrast alloys and ceramics.

KEY SCIENCE TERMS

ceramic
glass
alloy
amalgam

CERAMICS

When you sat and thought about the objects in your classroom, you were probably amazed at the variety of materials around you. Steel, brick, and glass are such an important part of our lives that it is difficult to imagine getting along without them. Try to picture highways without steel bridges, cities without brick buildings, and rooms without glass windows!

Suppose, though, that you were living 5000 years ago. What types of materials would you find around you then? How useful would those materials be for you?

EXPLORE!

How could you use age-old materials?

Carefully examine samples of wood, clay, stone, and metal. List some of their physical properties. Add a few drops of water to each. Test for hardness by scratching each with a file. Try to bend or shape each sample. What do you observe?

Which materials absorb water best? Which materials are easy to chip? Which ones are easy to bend or shape? Which appear strongest? Which is the shiniest? Can you think of practical uses for each of these materials?

Historians have divided early history into periods, based on the materials used to make tools in each period. You may have remembered reading about the Stone Age or

PROGRAM RESOURCES

Teacher Classroom Resources

Study Guide, page 23

Concept Mapping, page 14, Alloys L1

Critical Thinking/Problem Solving, page 14, How Much Is Your Penny Worth? L2

Multicultural Activities, page 15, Porcelain L1; page 16, Navajo Jewelry L1

Iron Age in your social studies class. Have you ever wondered why certain materials were used when they were?

Clay, earth, and mud were the first materials to be shaped by early humans. These materials were the ones easiest to find outdoors. As you saw in the last activity, clay is soft enough to be shaped by hand pressure, but firm enough to stay in a certain shape when you leave it alone. Archaeologists have dug up clay tablets and pottery from ancient times. Clay tablets tell the story of humankind before the era of writing. Old jugs, bowls, and figurines tell how earlier civilizations lived, what they ate, and what was important in their lives.

FIGURE 6-1. This ancient pottery is made of a mixture of clay and water.

These old pottery items, such as those in Figure 6-1, were made by mixing clay and water and allowing the mixture to harden. This process is still used today. Have you ever watched a potter making a bowl? If you have, you know the potter spins wet clay on a wheel while shaping it into a bowl by hand. When mixed with water, clay forms a paste that is easy to mold into various sizes and shapes. The bowl is then heated in a very hot oven to remove the water and to harden the clay, making it quite strong. The kind of material used to make the bowl is called a ceramic. A **ceramic** is a material made from dried clay or clay-like mixtures. Some common ceramics are shown in Figure 6-2.

FIGURE 6-2. Some common ceramics include tiles, sinks, and porcelain enamel kitchenware.

Thinking Processes
Classifying, Comparing and contrasting, Observing and inferring

Purpose To investigate some properties of metals, alloys, and ceramics.

Preparation Provide metal samples that can be bent, such as metal strips or wire.

Teaching the Activity

Discussion Have students discuss how the practical uses of wood, clay, stone, and metal are related to their physical properties.

Troubleshooting If the sample of wood is a two-by-four, students should find it won't bend. However, if the sample is a green twig, it will. L1

Expected Outcomes

Students should find that wood absorbs water, is easy to chip, and appears strong; that clay absorbs water and bends easily; that stone is easy to chip and is strong; and that metal is easy to bend and is strong and shiny.

Answers to Questions

1. clay, wood
2. wood, stone
3. clay, metal
4. wood, stone, metal
5. metal
6. Acceptable answers would include, metal may be useful for jewelry, clay for dishes, stone for building, and wood for shelving.

2 TEACH

Tying to Previous Knowledge

Have students recall the difference between physical and chemical changes from Chapter 5, Section 3. Be sure they understand that the drying or firing of ceramic materials is simply a physical change, not a chemical one. Showing students fresh clay and clay that has been dried will help students make the distinction between a physical and chemical change.

PROGRAM RESOURCES

Teacher Classroom Resources

Making Connections: Integrating Sciences, page 15, Biomaterials L2

Making Connections: Across the Curriculum, page 15, Glass L2

Making Connections: Technology and Society, page 15, Recycling L1

How It Works, page 9, How Does Cement Harden? L1

OPTIONS

Meeting Individual Needs

Learning Disabled, Visually Impaired Allow students to handle any of the items brought into the classroom to represent ceramics or any of the materials used in the Explore activity. Follow the Explore guidelines, but ask them to identify any differences in texture or density they can detect.

Concept Development

Theme Connection A theme that this section supports is energy. Ceramics are materials that can be used to absorb a form of energy—thermal energy. Thermal energy is a form of energy that can readily transfer from one material to another. However, ceramics are often used to intercept that energy before it moves to another material. For example, a ceramic trivet can absorb the thermal energy from a hot pot so the surface of a table is not damaged.

Student Journal Have students write their observations in their student journals.

Ceramics don't change in size when they are heated or cooled. Therefore, they can withstand high temperatures without cracking. Have you ever watched someone remove a hot pan from the stove and set it on a trivet to cool? The trivet may be made of a ceramic tile. The trivet absorbs the heat from the pan that might otherwise burn your kitchen counter.

Figure 6-3 shows workers placing ceramic tiles on the body of the space shuttle orbiter. When the shuttle returns from space, it has to pass through Earth's atmosphere at great speeds. The air friction that results heats the surface of the shuttle to extremely high temperatures. The ceramic tiles absorb the heat much like a trivet does, protecting the surface underneath. If the shuttle were not protected by ceramic tiles, it would be greatly damaged by the heat.

There are many other different uses of ceramics. Pottery, china dishes, cement, roofing tiles, and spark plugs in automobiles all contain ceramic materials. Ceramics are also used in electronic products such as radios and computers. Ceramics are lightweight and resistant to corrosion and wear. Many airplanes and missiles use ceramics because they weigh about half as much as the metal parts they are replacing.

FIGURE 6-3. Ceramic tiles are used to protect the space shuttle from high temperatures.

OPTIONS

Enrichment

Activity Have students conduct a survey of ceramic objects they find at home or at school. Have them bring their written lists to school. Arrange the students in groups to compare lists. Then have students speculate as to what these objects would be made of if there were no ceramics. COOP LEARN

Brick is an example of a type of ceramic known as a structural ceramic. Structural ceramics are used in construction because of their sturdiness, strength, and resistance to weather. The red color in bricks is due to iron that is added to the clay in order to make it stronger and less likely to crumble.

As you have seen, ceramics offer many advantages. Do ceramics involve any disadvantages?

FIND OUT!

How can you test a ceramic? 

Mold a small piece of clay into several thin pieces. Layer a cookie sheet with aluminum foil, and space three or four of these clay cookies on the pan. Place the pan in an oven at 400°F for one hour. Remove the pan and let it cool. When the clay pieces are cool, remove them from the pan and place them on a flat surface.

Conclude and Apply

1. Try to bend one clay piece with your hands. What happens?
2. Put on some safety goggles and use a hammer to hit one of the other pieces. What happens now?
3. How are these properties of clay a disadvantage?

Using ceramics has certain disadvantages. You discovered two of them in the last activity. Ceramics will not bend without cracking, and a sudden blow will shatter them entirely. Nevertheless, their strengths are greater than their weaknesses. The durability of ceramics is astonishing. Pieces of ancient pottery have been found in nearly perfect condition, long after other items from the same time have crumbled into dust!

FIND OUT!

How can you test a ceramic?

Time needed 1–2 hours

Materials clay, cookie sheet, aluminum foil, oven, oven mitt, safety goggles, hammer

Thinking Processes
Observing and inferring

Purpose To examine some properties of ceramics.

Preparation Prior to class, make arrangements to use an oven in your school.

Teaching the Activity

Troubleshooting Encourage students to mold uniform clay pieces so that they will dry the same and yield similar results. Have students press their initials into their own pieces of clay before placing them in an oven.

Student Journal Students may want to draw diagrams and describe their ceramic work and its properties in their student journals. LEP

Expected Outcomes

Students should find the heated clay impossible to bend. It should also crack and shatter when struck.

Answers to Conclude and Apply

1. The clay cracks or breaks.
2. The clay shatters.
3. A dried clay object is likely to break if someone drops it or hits it hard.

Flex Your Brain Have students use the Flex Your Brain activity to explore CERAMICS AND ALLOYS.

PROGRAM RESOURCES

Teacher Classroom Resources

Transparency Masters, page 27, and **Color Transparency,** number 12, Steel Alloys L2

Critical Thinking/Problem Solving, page 8, Flex Your Brain

Other Resources

Salmang, Hermann. *Ceramics: Physical and Chemical Fundamental.* Ann Arbor, MI: Books on Demand UMI.

FIND OUT!

What are some physical properties of metals?

Time needed 20–30 minutes

Materials 4-inch squares of copper, lead, tin, zinc, and iron; triangular files

Thinking Processes Classifying, Making and using tables, Observing and inferring

Purpose To investigate the properties of some representative metals.

Preparation Items that could be substituted for the metal squares include a wire of each of the metals.

Teaching the Activity

An alternate method for determining which metal is the hardest is to try to scratch each metal sample with each of the other samples. The metal that can scratch each of the other samples is the hardest.

Expected Outcomes

Students should be able to determine the physical properties of hardness, color, shine, and ease of bending for each metal sample.

Answers to Conclude and Apply

Answers may vary slightly based on student observations.

1. iron
2. lead
3. lead and iron
4. copper
5. copper and lead
6. iron and tin

FIGURE 6-4. Almost half of all ceramics produced today are glasses.

A **glass** is a ceramic that is usually transparent or translucent. Glass, like other ceramics, is a mixture. However, glass differs from other ceramics by being homogeneous. As you learned in Chapter 5, a homogeneous mixture has the same composition throughout.

The glass you are probably most familiar with is the type found in windows or drinking glasses. This glass is made from sand, which contains silicon and oxygen, along with boron, sodium, calcium, and a trace of aluminum. The sand is heated to a very high temperature until it melts. The melted glass can then be shaped into flowing sheets, or molded and blown into shape.

As with other ceramics, glasses can be made to have different uses by changing their chemical composition. Figure 6-4 shows an assortment of different types of glass, including stained glass and different thicknesses of safety and plate glass. Crystal pendants, vases, glasses, and chandeliers are made from glass that contains lead as well as sand. Food storage dishes you can use in an oven or place in a freezer are glasses made with boron and magnesium or lithium. Glass used in laboratories is made of sand, boron, sodium, and aluminum and can withstand very high temperatures.

DID YOU KNOW?

Your telephone wires contain a special kind of glass known as an optical fiber. Optical fibers are glass threads that conduct light the same way that copper wire conducts electricity. The best fibers carry more information than a standard metal cable.

METALS AND ALLOYS

If you have ever used a hammer, gone ice skating, or played pinball, you have relied on metals. From the start of civilization, metals have played an important role in our history. They are so important that whole periods of human history have been named after them—the Bronze Age and Iron Age, for example. Why are metals used so often?

FIND OUT!

What are some physical properties of metals?

Make a table like the one shown on the next page. Then obtain samples of copper, lead, tin, zinc, and iron, cut into thin 10 cm × 10 cm sheets. Determine the hardness by scratching each metal with a triangular file. Record your observations in the table as very soft, soft, somewhat hard, or very hard. Note the color of

OPTIONS

Meeting Individual Needs

Visually Impaired Pair visually-impaired students with a fully-sighted student to do the Find Out activity on this page. Check each piece of metal closely to make sure there are no sharp edges. Have the visually-impaired student (with assistance as needed) identify each metal. Have the fully-sighted student assist with the visual characteristics of color and brightness. The visually-impaired student should be able to determine hardness and ease of bending.

each metal. Describe the shine of each of the samples. Tell whether it is dull, bright, or very bright. Finally, try to bend each sample.

DATA AND OBSERVATIONS

Sample data

Substance	Hardness	Color	Shine	Ease of Bending
Copper	soft	reddish brown	very bright	bends
Lead	very soft	grey	dull	not easy
Tin	somewhat hard	silver-grey	bright	bends
Zinc	somewhat hard	grey-black	bright	bends
Sheet iron	very hard	silver-grey	bright	not easy

Conclude and Apply

1. Which metal is the hardest?
2. Which is the softest?
3. Which metals appear the dullest?
4. Which is the brightest?
5. Which samples are the easiest to twist into shape?
6. Which are the hardest to bend?

When you examined the samples in the activity, you discovered that not all metals are alike. Some are bright and shiny. Others are dull. Some are easy to bend, while others are more stiff and rigid. What uses could you imagine for each of the metals?

Unlike wood, flint, or stone, metals can be worked into a variety of shapes and forms. Unlike clay, dirt, or mud, metals resist breaking. Therefore, they can be used to make tools and machines. Steam engines, tractors, automobiles, and airplanes all exist because of the discovery of various metals. Can you imagine any of those machines built of wood, stone, or clay?

All naturally occurring metals are found in the upper rock layers of Earth. Figure 6-5 shows streaks of the metal silver in rock. The first metals discovered were gold, silver, and copper. Because of their bright shine, each was made into jewelry, death masks, and art objects. The earliest known jewelry dates back to about 5000 B.C.E.

Have you ever been awarded a plaque or trophy? It might have been made of bronze. Bronze is an example of

FIGURE 6-5. Silver has long been considered a precious, useful metal.

Concept Development

Demonstration Put on goggles. To illustrate that glass, a ceramic, can be bent and molded, heat a piece of glass tubing by rotating it over a Bunsen burner. Then quickly bend it. If well heated, the tubing can even be coiled around a cylinder. Ask students what uses the bent glass tubing might have.

Discussion Show students a rusted piece of iron and a stainless steel knife. Ask them to describe the different properties they can see that each item has. Then explain that the iron rusted because iron is very corrosive in the presence of oxygen and water, including moisture in the air. Stainless steel is an alloy, composed of iron, chromium, and nickel. Chromium is very resistant to corrosion and contributes this property to the alloy.

Teacher F.Y.I.

In Japan, ceramic car engines are being tested. These engines are lighter and more heat tolerant than metal and they last five times as long. Ceramic engines also promise greater fuel efficiency and less air pollution. One Japanese car company has test driven a ceramic-engine prototype car over 5,000 kilometers at speeds up to 150 km/h. A radiator, whose purpose is to cool an engine would not be needed because ceramics can withstand temperatures that would melt metal engines. One disadvantage of many ceramics is that they are brittle.

SKILLBUILDER

Sample answers: Ceramics are mixtures of sand and clay; alloys are mixtures of metals. Ceramics are able to withstand higher temperatures, but alloys are less brittle and less likely to shatter on impact. Accept other appropriate answers. L1

EXPLORE!

How is bronze different from copper and tin?

Time needed 10–15 minutes

Materials 10 cm × 10 cm squares of copper, tin, and bronze; triangular files

Thinking Processes Classifying, Comparing and contrasting, Observing and inferring

Purpose To investigate the difference between the properties of an alloy and those of the materials that went into it.

Teaching the Activity

Demonstration If only one set of the metals is available, this can be done as a demonstration and the samples passed around the classroom. L1

Expected Outcomes

Students should find that the bronze is harder than both the tin and the copper and should conclude that an alloy has special properties that its constituents do not have.

Answers to Questions

1. bronze
2. bronze
3. Bronze appears to have about the same shine as the other metals, and its color is similar to that of copper.

a material known as an alloy. An **alloy** is a mixture of a metal with other metals or nonmetals. How is an alloy different from an ordinary metal?

SKILLBUILDER

COMPARE AND CONTRAST

Compare and contrast the properties of alloys and ceramics. If you need help, refer to the **Skill Handbook** on page 653.

EXPLORE!

How is bronze different from copper and tin?

Examine three samples of copper, tin, and bronze, cut into thin 10 cm × 10 cm sheets. Try to bend each sample. Which one is more difficult to shape? Scratch each of the samples with a file. Which one appears the hardest? Compare the color and shine of the three materials. How are they alike?

When you examined bronze in the last activity, you saw that in some ways it was like copper and tin, but that in other ways it was different. Although bronze seems to have the same color and shine of copper or tin, it is stronger and more durable than either of them. Copper and tin are too soft to be made into tools. About 5000 years ago, however, it was discovered that when copper and tin were melted together, a new material was produced that was harder than either metal separately. This material was called bronze. Armor and tools like those in Figure 6-6 were made from it, and that period in history became known as the Bronze Age.

FIGURE 6-6. Humans were working with bronze thousands of years ago.

Alloys have properties that are different from the properties of the materials that went into them. Look at the bracelet shown in Figure 6-7. It appears to be made of pure gold, but it is actually made of an alloy. Pure gold is a soft metal that bends and breaks very easily. Jewelry made from it would not last very long. Copper, on the

OPTIONS

Multicultural Perspectives

Have students research the different methods of metallurgy (preparing metals from their ores) used during the Bronze Age and report their findings to the class.

other hand, is an inexpensive, hard metal that dulls rapidly and turns green when exposed to air or certain substances. Yet when copper and gold are melted together, an alloy is formed that has most of the brilliance of gold and most of the sturdiness of copper. Thus, a new material is formed that is more useful than the individual materials that went into it!

Have you ever had a cavity? If so, you may have an alloy in your mouth right now. These special alloys are known as amalgams (uh MAL gumz). An **amalgam** is an alloy that contains mercury, which is a soft liquid metal. Dental amalgams are mixtures of mercury, silver, and zinc. These metals are used because they are soft and can be kneaded into the cavity, while the chemical reactions that go on in your mouth harden them. These amalgams are more commonly known as fillings.

Table 6-1 shows some common alloys and their compositions. Can you think of other uses for the common alloys that are listed?

You have learned that an alloy consists of two or more metals. But how is an alloy actually made?

FIGURE 6-7. Gold jewelry is made from a gold-copper alloy.

TABLE 6-1. Composition of Some Common Alloys

Name	Composition	Uses
ALNICO	Aluminum, nickel, cobalt	Permanent magnets
Bell metal	Copper, tin	Bells
Brass	Copper, zinc	Hardware, musical instruments
Bronze	Copper, tin, zinc	Castings, statues
Coinage nickel	Copper, nickel	U.S. coins
Coinage silver	Silver, copper	U.S. coins
Coinage gold	Gold, copper	U.S. coins
German silver	Copper, zinc, nickel	Jewelry, silverware
Gold, white	Gold, nickel, zinc, copper	Jewelry
Nichrome	Nickel, iron, chromium, manganese	Heating wire
Pewter	Tin, lead	Household articles
Silver solder	Copper, zinc, silver	Solder
Solder, soft	Tin, lead	Solder
Sterling silver	Silver, copper	Jewelry, silverware

Concept Development

Using the Table Have students look at Table 6-1. Ask them which metal appears most often in the composition of some common alloys. *copper*

Student Text Question Can you think of other uses for the common alloys that are listed? *Lamps or other furniture or plumbing fittings may be uses for brass.*

MAKING CONNECTIONS

Language Arts

Have groups of students write a science fiction story that makes use of a new alloy with unique properties. In the story, have them tell how the alloy is made and what the properties are. An example is the legend surrounding Jim Bowie's knife. It was said to be made from the metal of a meteorite he found. The metal blade was said to be indestructible, and never needed sharpening.

Content Background

Some people believe that galvanized steel is an alloy. In fact, galvanized steel is steel that has been dipped into molten zinc. A thin layer of zinc metal coats the surface and prevents rusting of the iron in the steel. The zinc metal crystals can be seen through a hand lens.

INVESTIGATE!

6-1 MAKING AN ALLOY

Time needed 35–40 minutes

Materials copper penny, 30-mesh zinc, hot plate, dilute nitric acid, dilute sodium hydroxide solution, evaporating dishes, goggles, tongs

Thinking Processes
Observing and inferring

Purpose To observe how metals can combine to form an alloy.

Preparation Have all materials and solutions set out in front of you before beginning. If an old, discolored penny is used, students can better infer the purpose of the nitric acid.

Teaching the Activity

Safety All students should be wearing safety goggles while they watch you perform this experiment. Depending on your class, one student could assist with each step of the procedure. When heating solutions, be sure not to allow them to come to a boil.

Demonstration Have a brass object and another penny available at the end of the experiment for comparison. L1

Expected Outcomes

Students should conclude that the copper in the penny and the zinc combined to form brass.

Answers to Analyze/Conclude and Apply

1. The penny began to turn green.
2. No. Zinc was being deposited on the copper by a chemical reaction.
3. Copper and zinc produce brass.
4. Alloys do not require specific amounts of ingredients to form.
5. For an alloy to form, the materials must be evenly mixed. Heating can melt a metal so this even mixing occurs.

INVESTIGATE!

6-1 MAKING AN ALLOY

In this activity, you will **observe** how an alloy can be made.

PROBLEM

How can two metals be combined into an alloy?

MATERIALS

copper penny
30-mesh zinc
hot plate
dilute nitric acid
dilute sodium hydroxide solution
evaporating dishes
goggles
tongs

PROCEDURE

1. Put on your goggles. **Observe** carefully as your teacher performs Steps 2-7.
2. Carefully pour dilute nitric acid into an evaporating dish to fill halfway. **CAUTION:** *Nitric acid can cause burns. Rinse spills immediately.* Using tongs, grasp the penny and hold it in the acid for about 20 seconds.
3. Remove the penny with the tongs and rinse it in cold tap water.
4. Place one teaspoon of 30-mesh zinc in a second evaporating dish. Carefully add dilute sodium hydroxide to the dish until the liquid is about 2 cm above the zinc. **CAUTION:** *Sodium hydroxide can cause burns. Rinse spills immediately.*
5. Using tongs, carefully place the penny on top of the zinc.
6. Set the evaporating dish on a hot plate and gently heat the contents of the dish until the penny turns a silver color. **CAUTION:** *Do not let the contents come to a boil.*
7. Using tongs, remove the evaporating dish from the hot plate and set it on the counter to cool. Also using tongs, remove the penny from the dish and rinse it.
8. Dry the penny. Hold it in the tongs and place on the hot plate. Heat the penny until it turns a golden color.

ANALYZE

1. Describe the appearance of the penny after it was placed in the nitric acid. How did its appearance change?
2. In Step 6, the penny turned a silver color. Was the penny actually becoming silver? **Determine the cause** of this change in color.
3. What alloy has this procedure produced?

CONCLUDE AND APPLY

4. Can you **infer** why it wasn't necessary to measure out an exact amount of zinc, or to know the exact amount of copper?
5. **Going Further:** Why is heat usually necessary for two metals to combine to form an alloy?

PROGRAM RESOURCES

Teacher Classroom Resources
Activity Masters, pages 25-26, Investigate 6-1

OPTIONS

Enrichment

Demonstration Use an empty aluminum soft-drink can to demonstrate the strength of aluminum. Wearing rubber gloves, twist the can in one direction attempting to tear the can in two pieces. The can should twist but not tear.

From the last activity, you saw that two metals can be combined into an alloy by melting them together. The exact amounts of the metals mixed do not need to be known, as alloys can be formed from different amounts of materials. This means that, like other mixtures you learned about in Chapter 5, alloys do not have a fixed chemical composition.

As you may have guessed by now, most metallic objects are manufactured from alloys. Steel, for example, is an alloy of carbon with other metals. You may have seen advertisements for carving knives with blades of high-carbon steel. The carbon content of this type of alloy varies from 1.0 percent to 1.7 percent. Because this steel is very hard, the knife blades can be made very sharp and will never dull. Steel production is greater than that of any other alloy.

Aluminum alloys are the second largest group of alloys produced. Aluminum alloys are used to manufacture products as different as food wrap and airplanes.

Since the 1980s, aluminum-lithium alloys have become very important. Lithium is the lightest metal known, so alloys of this type are lightweight, yet very strong. In fact, unlike other alloys, aluminum-lithium alloys maintain their strength at very high temperatures. In the future, these alloys may be used to make aircraft that will fly in the upper reaches of Earth's atmosphere.

Alloys and ceramics are only two materials in use today. They share some common properties, yet are different in other ways. In the next section, you will learn about the simpler materials from which both are made.

DID YOU KNOW?

During a three-month period, Americans throw away enough aluminum to rebuild the country's entire commercial airline fleet.

Check Your Understanding

1. Identify each of the following materials as either an alloy or a ceramic: (a) brick, (b) gold ring, (c) dental fillings, (d) glass vase.
2. How are alloys and ceramics alike? How are they different?
3. **APPLY:** Inexpensive gold-colored jewelry sometimes turns green when you wear it. Explain why, using concepts learned in this section.

3 Assess

Check for Understanding

As you discuss the Apply question of Check Your Understanding, ask students to describe what happens to bronze statues and copper roofs after they have been outside for a while. *They turn green as the result of a reaction with substances in the atmosphere just as inexpensive jewelry will react with chemicals in your skin.*

Reteach

Show students a ceramic bathroom tile and a stainless steel knife. Ask them what would happen if the knife were made of ceramic and the tile of stainless steel. Discuss how this would affect their uses. LEP L1

Extension

Have students who have mastered the concepts in this section bring in examples of ceramic and metal objects from home. Then have them spend a few minutes examining one another's objects and write some properties and uses for each. L2

4 Close

Activity

Have students demonstrate their knowledge of ceramics and alloys by identifying each of the following items as a ceramic or alloy and determining how this is related to its function: casserole dish, clay pipe, bathtub, sterling silver or pewter candlestick, stainless steel fork, trombone. L1

Answers to Check Your Understanding

1. a. ceramic b. alloy c. alloy d. ceramic
2. Both alloys and ceramics are mixtures of other materials. Alloys are metal mixtures; ceramics are made from sand or clay. Ceramics are usually able to withstand high temperatures better than alloys, but alloys are less brittle and less likely to shatter on impact.
3. Gold jewelry is really an alloy of pure gold and copper. If too much copper is used in the alloy, the copper can react with air and moisture to turn green.

Section 6-2

PREPARATION

Concepts Developed

In this section, elements, the basic building blocks of matter, are discussed. Elements and mixtures are then related to metals and alloys studied in the previous section. A metal is a material made up of one kind of element. An alloy is a mixture of a metal and one or more other elements. Compounds are also introduced. These substances are composed of more than one kind of element, but unlike mixtures, they cannot be separated by physical means, and the elements do not retain their own properties.

Planning the Lesson

In planning your lesson on elements and compounds, refer to the Chapter Organizer on pages 162A-B for timing suggestions, resources, and additional materials that will help you in your presentation of the lesson concepts. For adequate development of the concepts presented in this section, we recommend that students do the Find Out activities on page 174 and 176.

1 MOTIVATE

Activity This activity will allow students to investigate the component parts of various objects.

Materials needed are foodstuffs such as bread, cereal, cake mix, and potato chips.

Have students identify the simpler materials that make up each item, by looking at the ingredients listed on the packages. Then have students identify the simpler materials that make up objects in your classroom, such as desks, paper, books, and windows. Compare how easy it would be to separate the foodstuffs and the classroom objects into simpler materials. L1

6-2 Elements and Compounds

OBJECTIVES

In this section, you will

- distinguish elements from mixtures;
- state properties of a compound.

KEY SCIENCE TERMS

element

compound

THE BUILDING BLOCKS OF MATTER

What would you get if you took apart your bike? Some of the parts may be made of rubber, plastic, alloys, or metals. The lights may be covered with glass. With the right equipment, you could separate the alloys into the metals from which they are made. The same is true of the rubber, plastic, and other parts. Each is some combination of simpler materials.

Eventually, though, you would reach a point where you couldn't break down the parts into any simpler materials. At that point, you would have a collection of elements. An **element** is a substance that cannot be broken down further into simpler substances by ordinary physical or chemical means.

How can you demonstrate this? Let's do the next activity to find out.

FIND OUT!

How is an element different from a mixture? 

Fill a small test tube about half full of iron powder. Fill another test tube with the same amount of sulfur powder. What is the physical appearance of each? Take a few grains of iron, place the iron on a glass slide, and look at it under the microscope. Make another slide of sulfur particles and examine them under a microscope. How are the iron and sulfur different? Now hold a small magnet near the slide containing the iron. What do you observe? Clean the magnet and hold it near the sulfur particles. What do you observe now?

Empty both test tubes into a mortar. Take a pestle and carefully grind the two substances together until the contents look the same throughout. What have you just made? Take a few grains of this mixture, put it on a glass slide, and look at it under a microscope.

OPTIONS

Meeting Individual Needs

Learning Disabled To complete the Find Out on this page, pair students with more able partners and have them divide the work. The learning disabled students can fill the test tubes, put powder on the slides, grind the substances, and use the magnet. Their partners can record each pair's findings. COOP LEARN

Multicultural Perspectives

One of the earliest attempts to classify matter was made in Greece more than 2,000 years ago. Ancient Greeks believed that all matter was made up of earth, fire, water, and air. Centuries later, scientists used electricity to break apart water into oxygen and hydrogen, showing that water is not an element.

What do you observe? Remove the slide from the microscope and hold a small magnet near it. What happens? Clean the magnet and repeat this step until no more particles are attracted from the slide. Examine the slide once again under the microscope.

Conclude and Apply

1. What do you see now?
2. What can you conclude from your observations?

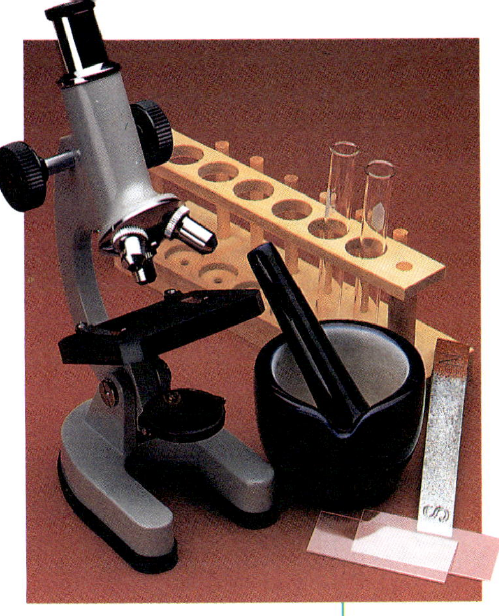

In Chapter 5, you learned that you make a mixture when you combine two or more substances together in such a way that each keeps its own properties. Mixtures can physically be separated into simpler substances. When you mixed together the particles of iron and sulfur in the last activity, you made a mixture. You saw that you could separate the mixture into the simpler substances of iron and sulfur by using a magnet.

Iron particles, however, cannot be broken down any further. Neither can sulfur particles. If you were to continue grinding down samples of each into smaller and smaller particles, you would still be left with particles of iron and sulfur. Nor could they be broken down chemically. Iron and sulfur are already in their simplest forms. Both iron and sulfur are examples of elements. Elements are known as the building blocks of matter.

In the last section, you saw how alloys could be made by melting together two simpler substances. You made brass by heating copper and zinc together. If a sample of brass was heated at a high enough temperature until it began to melt, copper and zinc would separate out. Copper and zinc are also elements.

How do we know?

Elements

The idea that elements are the simplest building blocks of matter is an ancient one. Early Greek philosophers wrote of this idea. Modern scientists have discovered even smaller pieces of matter with extremely powerful microscopes. These pieces, however, no longer possess the properties of an element. Using advanced, modern technology has therefore helped prove an ancient theory.

2 Teach

Tying to Previous Knowledge

Review chemical and physical changes as presented in Chapter 5, Lesson 3. Physical changes occur when mixtures are formed or separated. Chemical changes occur when compounds are formed or broken down.

FIND OUT!

How is an element different from a mixture?

Time needed 15–20 minutes

Materials test tubes, iron powder, sulfur powder, glass slides, microscopes, small magnets, mortar and pestle

Thinking Processes
Observing and inferring, Comparing and contrasting

Purpose To investigate the difference between an element and a mixture.

Preparation If microscopes are unavailable, hand-held magnifying glasses can be used instead.

Teaching the Activity

You will need to instruct students on the use of a microscope. L1

Expected Outcomes

Students should find that, even after they have ground up and mixed the iron and sulfur, they still retain their individual properties.

Answers to Questions

1. Iron powder is gray-black and shiny; solid sulfur is bright yellow and dull.
2. Iron crystals resemble needles; the sulfur powder will have more varied appearances depending on the kind of sulfur used and how it was ground or powdered.
3. Iron particles move toward the magnet.
4. Sulfur particles are not attracted by the magnet.
5. a physical mixture
6. You can still see the separate particles of iron and sulfur.
7. The iron particles in the mixture are attracted to the magnet, while the sulfur particles are not.

Answers to Conclude and Apply

1. Only sulfur particles remain.
2. Iron is magnetic; sulfur is not. Iron particles were separated from the mixture by the magnet.

PROGRAM RESOURCES

Teacher Classroom Resources

Study Guide, page 24

Laboratory Manual, pages 25-26, Mixtures and Compounds L1; pages 27-30, Chromatography 

Take Home Activities, page 13, Stovetop Laboratory L1

Concept Development

Theme Connection A theme that this section supports is energy. By supplying energy to certain elements, they may combine chemically to form a new substance. For example, iron and sulfur can be chemically combined if heated, applying thermal energy. The new substance, iron sulfide, is different from the original iron and sulfur.

FIND OUT!

How can you break down a compound?

Time needed 15–20 minutes

Materials safety goggles, powdered sugar, test tubes and holders, one-hole stoppers with glass tubing, burners, mortar, pestle

Thinking Processes Observing and inferring, Recognizing cause and effect

Purpose Demonstrate that a compound can be broken down into its constituent parts.

Preparation Provide students with stoppers in which you have already inserted the glass tubing.

Teaching the Activity

Point out to students that a majority of known compounds, including powdered sugar, contain carbon. These are called organic compounds which, when burned with adequate oxygen, produce water and carbon dioxide. L2

Expected Outcomes

Students should see water in the tubing and blackened sugar and conclude that the sugar has been changed chemically.

Answers to Questions

1. water
2. It changes in appearance from white crystals to a black lump.

Conclude and Apply

1. no
2. The sugar was broken down into water vapor and carbon.

COMPOUNDS

What would have happened if you had heated the iron and sulfur mixture in the last Find Out activity? You would have made a new substance. This substance would not look like the iron and sulfur mixture, nor would it resemble iron or sulfur by itself. You would have made something totally new!

You have learned that heating can cause chemical changes to occur. When you heat an iron-sulfur mixture, you cause the iron and sulfur to combine chemically into a new substance. This substance is iron sulfide.

Iron sulfide has properties different from those of either iron or sulfur. It is a new substance. A substance whose smallest unit is made up of more than one element is a **compound.** Iron sulfide is an example of a compound. What properties does a compound have that make it different from either an element or a mixture?

FIND OUT!

How can you break down a compound? 

Put on safety goggles and place 10 g of powdered sugar into a test tube. Place a stopper with a long piece of glass tubing into the open end. Using a test-tube holder, carefully heat the test tube over a burner flame.

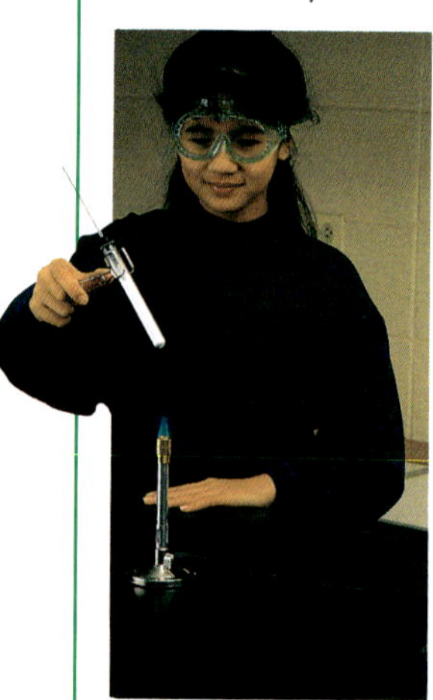

Always keep the stoppered end pointed away from you and away from other people. What do you see collecting at the top of the test tube? What happens to the sugar at the bottom of the test tube?

Remove the test tube and allow it to cool. Scrape out some of the black substance into a mortar. Grind it into a powder with a pestle.

Conclude and Apply

1. Is the substance still sugar?
2. What happened to the sugar?

Sugar is a compound composed of carbon, hydrogen, and oxygen. When you heated the sugar in the last Find Out activity, chemical changes occurred in the sugar. Hydrogen and oxygen left the bottom of the test tube as water vapor. This vapor was the droplets of water you saw collect at the top of the test tube and along the glass tubing. The black clump that remained at the bottom of the test tube was carbon.

How do compounds differ from mixtures? First, compounds cannot be separated by physical means. If you melted water when it was in the form of ice, the hydrogen and oxygen in it would not separate out—you would simply get liquid water.

Second, the substances that make up a compound do not keep their own properties. Carbon is a black solid, whereas hydrogen and oxygen are gases. When you chemically combine carbon, hydrogen, and oxygen, you might get white, solid, sweet-tasting grains of a compound known as sugar. A mixture such as brass, on the other hand, still retains many of the physical properties of the elements that are used to make it—copper and zinc.

Third, the same compound always has the same composition. If you went from store to store buying samples of sugar and then took the time to break each down into its elements, you would always end up with the same amounts of carbon, hydrogen, and oxygen.

How do people decide what materials to put into a mixture or a compound? In the next section, you will learn how certain materials become stronger and more useful when their composition is changed.

DID YOU KNOW?

There are only 92 natural elements, but hundreds of thousands of compounds are made from those elements.

Check Your Understanding

1. How can you distinguish between a piece of copper and a piece of bronze?
2. State three properties of sugar that make it a compound.
3. **APPLY:** A drill containing a high-carbon steel alloy is used so much in a workshop that it overheats. The worker who inspects the drill notices that the tip has turned black and that it has lost its hardness. Propose an explanation for this, using concepts learned in this section.

MAKING CONNECTIONS

Math

One molecule of table sugar, a compound, has 12 atoms of carbon, 22 atoms of hydrogen, and 11 atoms of oxygen. Ask students to find how many atoms of each of these elements three molecules of table sugar has. *36 carbon, 66 hydrogen, 33 oxygen*

3 Assess

Check for Understanding

If available, show students a drill obtained from your school's Industrial Arts Department that shows the effect of use described in the Apply question. LEP

Reteach

Hold up pieces of copper, bronze, and bauxite. Have the class identify each and tell which is an element, a mixture, and a compound. LEP L1

Extension

Materials needed are sand, sugar, a teaspoon, beakers, water, a stirring rod, and a watch glass

Have students mix sand and sugar in a beaker then stir a teaspoonful of the mixture into a beaker of water. They should observe that only the sugar dissolves. Then have students pour some of the sugar water into a watch glass and let the solution evaporate. Sugar crystals will be left. Students should see that sugar and sand formed a mixture that water can separate. Emphasize that if the two materials had formed a compound, they would not have been able to be separated by physical means. L2

4 Close

Demonstration

Show students a beaker filled with salt water. Ask them to identify this solution as a mixture, compound, or element. Then have them identify the compounds. *salt and water* L1

Answers to Check Your Understanding

1. Copper is an element and cannot be broken down into a simpler form. Bronze is a mixture: it can be separated into the elements of copper and tin.
2. Carbon, hydrogen, and oxygen in sugar cannot be separated physically. Sugar does not have the same physical properties as the three elements that make it up. Sugar always has the same chemical composition.
3. High-carbon steel is made up of carbon and other metals in varying amounts. When the drill overheats, the alloy in the tip melts into its simpler substances. The black tip is carbon, separated from the alloy. Alloys usually are harder than the materials they are composed of. After the tip has melted, the drill is no longer the same alloy. It is no longer as hard as the original alloy.

Section 6-3

PREPARATION

Concepts Developed

Throughout this chapter, various materials have been discussed along with their uses in building, pottery, tools, and so on. Plastics, synthetics, and composites are also materials with specific properties that lend themselves to particular uses.

Planning the Lesson

In planning your lesson on modern materials, refer to the Chapter Organizer on pages 162A-B for timing suggestions, resources, and additional materials that will help you in your presentation of the lesson concepts. For adequate development of the concepts presented in this section, we recommend that students do the Investigate activity on page 181.

1 MOTIVATE

Discussion Show students a Styrofoam cup, plastic spoon, ceramic cup, and metal spoon. Discuss how these items are the same and different. Lead students to conclude that unlike the other items, Styrofoam and plastic items are not naturally occurring materials, but are made in a laboratory. Encourage students to also discuss more interesting items such as artificial hearts, fiber optics and materials used in space vehicles. Many large companies produce and advertise new synthetic materials. Have students find examples of these advertisements. L1

SKILLBUILDER

Tables will vary. Most will include empty soft drink or milk containers, packaging, and plastic utensils or dishes. L1

6-3 Modern Materials

OBJECTIVES

In this section, you will

- identify plastics and their uses;
- describe a composite.

KEY SCIENCE TERMS

composite

SKILLBUILDER

MAKING AND INTERPRETING TABLES

Not all plastic materials are the same. Most plastics are assigned recycling numbers so that recycling plants can separate and sort them according to how they should be thrown away. Make a table to show the number and kind of plastic containers your family uses and throws away in a week. Show the number and kind of plastics recycled. If you need help, refer to the **Skill Handbook** on page 648.

PLASTICS

Think how often you and your family use the telephone. Have you ever dropped the receiver or knocked the base onto the floor? Did the telephone break into pieces, or did it still work?

Many telephones are so durable because they are made mostly of plastics. The first plastic was made about a century ago. One hundred years probably seems like a long time. But, if you remember that alloys and ceramics have been used for thousands of years, you will realize that plastics are really modern materials.

You are probably familiar with the rolls of plastic bags that you find in the produce section of the supermarket. These bags are made of polyethylene, one of the world's most widely used and produced plastics. The word *plastic* is given to those materials that can be formed into different shapes, usually through heating. Polyethylene has many uses, including food storage containers, bottles, and banding material for six-pack beverages. Table 6-2 shows other important plastics and their uses.

TABLE 6-2. Common Plastics and Their Uses

Name	Uses
Polypropylene	Rope, protective clothing, textiles, carpet
Polystyrene	Containers, boats, coolers, insulation, furniture, models
Polyvinyl chloride	Rubber substitute, cable covering, tubing, rainwear, gaskets
Polytetrafluorethane	Nonstick cookwear surfaces
Polyvinylidene chloride	Clinging food wraps

PROGRAM RESOURCES

Teacher Classroom Resources

Study Guide, page 25

Transparency Masters, page 25, and **Color Transparency,** number 11, Production of Nylon L1

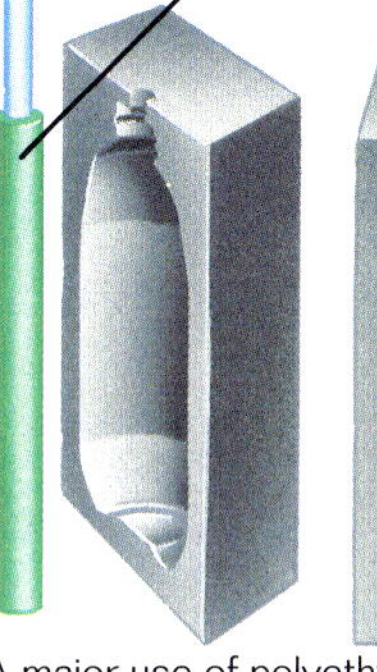
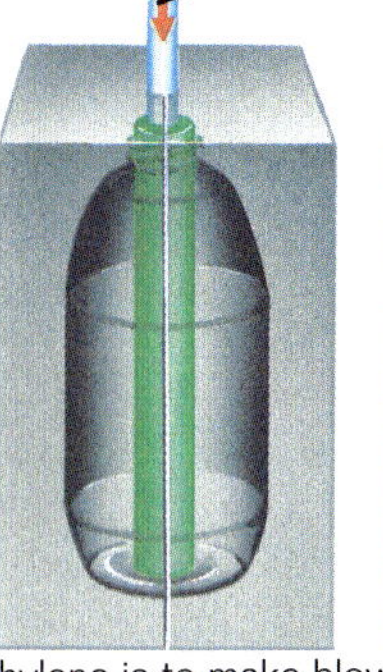
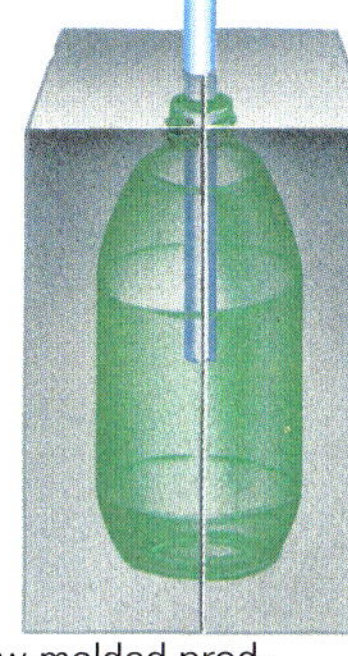

FIGURE 6-8. A major use of polyethylene is to make blow-molded products such as soft-drink containers.

SYNTHETIC MATERIALS

You are probably wearing something made of synthetic materials as you are reading this page. Many of today's fabrics are made from synthetic materials. Permanent-press cottons are a mixture of cotton and synthetic fibers. Such materials do not wrinkle easily because of the strength of the synthetic fibers. Some synthetics have amazing properties. A strand of a fiber called Nomex is so resistant to high temperatures that this synthetic material is used to make protective gloves and clothing for fire fighters, as shown in Figure 6-9.

Do you have indoor-outdoor carpeting in your home? If so, you might be interested in knowing that it is made of a synthetic fiber that resists weather and does not absorb water. Because of their strength, durability, and resistance to stains, synthetic fibers are also used in upholstery materials and automobile seat covers.

Table 6-3 lists the names of several familiar synthetic fibers. Fabrics with new properties are made by weaving natural fibers with synthetic ones. If you look at the label of a permanent-press shirt, you will see the fabric is a mixture of both natural and synthetic fibers. You are most likely to come in contact with these synthetic fibers in clothes and household

FIGURE 6-9. Nomex is an example of a useful synthetic fiber.

2 TEACH

Tying to Previous Knowledge

In the previous lessons, students learned about mixtures and alloys. Composites are similar to alloys in that they too are mixtures of materials. A composite combines the properties of the materials of which it is made. Ask students to describe what an alloy is and how its properties compare to the metals of which it is made.

Concept Development

Theme Connection A theme that this section supports is interactions and systems. The materials that make up a plastic, synthetic, or composite form a system. These materials, working together, form a product that has different applications from each material by itself.

Debate Have students debate the use of plastic or paper bags at the supermarket. Plastic bags require petroleum to produce and many are not recyclable. Paper bags are made from tree products and are definitely recyclable. One solution is to bring a reusable cloth bag to the supermarket to carry your groceries home.

Inquiry Question Synthetic materials are often used in place of natural ones. What are some natural materials that could be replaced by synthetic ones? *Possible answer: Synthetic materials such as rayon and dacron can be used in clothing rather than natural materials such as cotton and wool fibers.*

Activity Have students examine the tags on the insides of their shirts to see what synthetic materials were used to make their clothing. L1

OPTIONS

Enrichment

Research Have teams of students conduct the following interviews and report their findings to the class.

- Interview a salesperson at a local carpet store about the different fibers used in carpet manufacturing. With samples, report the advantages and disadvantages of various carpet fibers.
- Interview a fire prevention officer to determine what dangers there are in curtains, drapes, carpeting, and upholstery made of synthetic fibers. Ask what gaseous products form when various fibers burn. COOP LEARN L2

Concept Development

Activity Have students make a mobile of the different types of plastics listed in Table 6-2 on page 178.

Materials needed are coat hangers, string, and glue or tape.

Have them bring in examples of each plastic or pictures of the examples. The students should label each example with the name of the plastic and tie it to the hanger. Display the mobiles around the classroom. L1

MAKING CONNECTIONS

Physical Education

The strength and flexibility of fiberglass and graphite composites have caught the attention of many athletes. Graphite imbedded in plastic is a composite that is used in sports equipment such as golf clubs, tennis rackets, and fishing rods. Ask a student who has any sports equipment made of graphite to bring it to class and show the other students. Ask a track coach if you can show the class a fiberglass composite pole used in the pole vault event.

Flex Your Brain Use the Flex Your Brain activity to have students explore SYNTHETIC MATERIALS.

Teacher F.Y.I.

Americans use an average of 62 kg of plastic per person per year. Of this, 20 kg goes for packaging.

TABLE 6-3. Synthetic Fibers and Their Uses

Name	Uses
Dacron	Textiles, arterial grafts
Nylon 66	Tire cord, textiles, brush bristles, netting, carpet, athletic turf, sutures
Polyethylene	Tubing, prosthetic devices, packaging materials, kitchen utensils, paper coating
Orlon	Textiles

fabrics. However, some of these synthetic fibers also have important uses in the fields of health and medicine. Because they do not easily react with body fluids and tissues, some synthetics are ideal for skin transplants and sutures, or stitches. Other synthetics can be molded to duplicate legs, arms, toes, and fingers.

COMPOSITES

Have you ever seen a picture of a face made from cut-up photographs of famous people? Or watched a television show where an artist reconstructed the face of a criminal from the descriptions of several witnesses? If so, then you have seen a composite. A **composite** is something that is made of two or more parts.

Some materials are also composites, as shown in Figure 6-10. The sidewalk in front of your home, the bridge on the road, and even the walls in your school are probably composites of two or more materials. Designing composites allows architects to combine the best properties of several different materials into one structure.

FIGURE 6-10. A bridge built with reinforced concrete and an artificial limb are examples of composite materials.

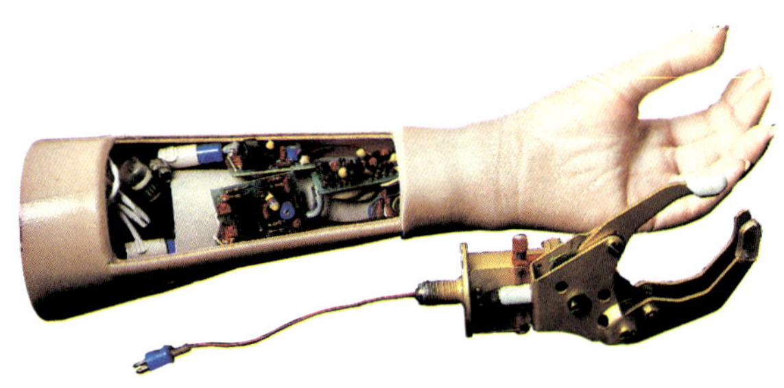

PROGRAM RESOURCES

Teacher Classroom Resources

Critical Thinking/Problem Solving, page 8, Flex Your Brain

Other Resources

Plastics, *The World of Imagination,* video, Modern Talking Picture

Salmen, L. et al. *Composite Systems From Natural & Synthetic Polymers.* Elsevier, NY: Science Publishing Co., Inc. 1986

OPTIONS

Enrichment

Demonstration Ask a student from the local vocational school's body shop to demonstrate for the class how plastics and composites are used to repair damaged metal body panels. L3

I N V E S T I G A T E !

6-2 MAKING A COMPOSITE

In this activity, you will make a composite and then **compare** its properties with a noncomposite.

PROBLEM

How does combining materials make a strong composite?

MATERIALS 

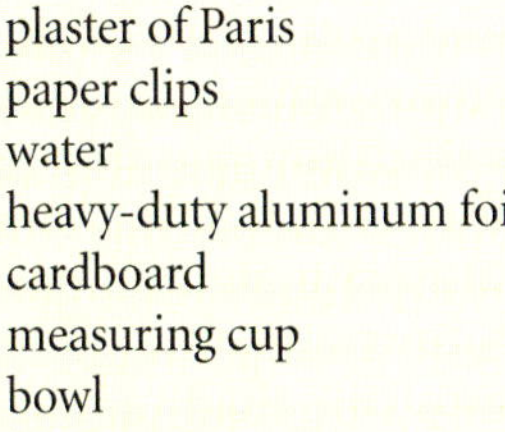

plaster of Paris
paper clips
water
heavy-duty aluminum foil
cardboard
measuring cup
bowl
hammer
paper towels
safety goggles

PROCEDURE

1. Shape the aluminum foil into a rectangular pan (20 cm × 20 cm × 3 cm) with a dividing ridge down the center, as shown in the illustration.
2. **Measure** 2/3 cup of water into a bowl. Then **measure** 1 cup plaster of Paris. Add the plaster slowly to the water.
3. Gently mix the two ingredients and let stand for five minutes.
4. Stir the mixture and pour approximately 1/4 of it into each side of the dividing ridge. Carefully place about 10 paper clips on the surface of the plaster on only one side of the divider.
5. Wait 5 minutes. Pour the rest of the mixture equally into the two compartments. Make sure the paper clips are covered on one side and the other side is at the same depth. Let this set for one full day.
6. After 24 hours, remove the aluminum foil from the blocks of hardened plaster. **Observe** the outward appearance of each block. Wrap each block in a towel.
7. Put on safety goggles. With a hammer, firmly but gently strike each block. If nothing happens, strike the blocks again.

ANALYZE

1. What was the appearance of the hardened blocks before you struck them with a hammer? Did the two blocks look alike?
2. What **effect** did the hammer blow have on each block?

CONCLUDE AND APPLY

3. What can you **infer** about the properties of this composite of plaster and paper clips?
4. **Going Further: Predict** what would happen if you had made this composite with pipe cleaners rather than paper clips.

INVESTIGATE!

6-2 MAKING A COMPOSITE

Time needed 15–20 minutes before drying, 24 hours drying time, 15–20 minutes after drying

Materials plaster of paris, paper clips, water, heavy-duty aluminum foil, cardboard, measuring cup, bowl, hammer, paper towels, safety goggles

Thinking Processes
Observing and inferring, Comparing and contrasting, Recognizing cause and effect

Purpose To compare the properties of a composite with those of a noncomposite.

Preparation If time is short, make several plaster of paris setups yourself and let students complete steps 6 and 7 and examine the results. Rectangular milk cartons can also be cut and used as molds.

Teaching the Activity

Discussion Ask students how their results would have been different if they had used more or fewer clips or placed them differently in the plaster. L2

Expected Outcomes

Students should find that the plaster containing the paper clips is much harder to break apart than the one without the clips.

Answers to Analyze/Conclude and Apply

1. They appeared to be white blocks of hard material, identical on first inspection.
2. The block without the paper clips shattered quite easily. The one with the paper clips probably broke, but into larger pieces, and resisted breaking longer.
3. The composite with paper clips is stronger structurally than the block without.
4. Pipe cleaners are larger reinforcements, so the composite would break into larger pieces.

Meeting Individual Needs

Visually Impaired Assign students to work with fully-sighted students to complete the Investigate. After the fully-sighted students strike the blocks, direct the visually-impaired students to handle pieces from each block and describe any differences they feel. COOP LEARN

PROGRAM RESOURCES

Teacher Classroom Resources

Activity Masters, pages 27-28, Investigate 6-2

3 Assess

Check for Understanding

As students answer the Apply question, have them refer to Figure 6-11.

Reteach

Show students a sample of fiberglass. Tell them it is made of plastic and glass fibers. The glass fibers provide strength and durability, while the plastic provides flexibility. Ask them to explain why this is an example of a composite. Ask them whether this material would be better for boat construction than metal or wood and why. LEP

Extension

Have students make a display of plastic, synthetic, and composite objects. Direct them to prepare a research report on the composition of each object. COOP LEARN

Answers to Check Your Understanding

1. Two possible answers are polyethylene, used in food storage containers, and polytetrafluorethane, used in nonstick pots and pans.
2. Sample answer: Architects use steel reinforcing rods embedded in concrete. The steel supplies strength and the concrete makes it more resistant to weather.
3. Fiberglass might be a good choice because it is strong, lightweight, and resistant to weather and rust.

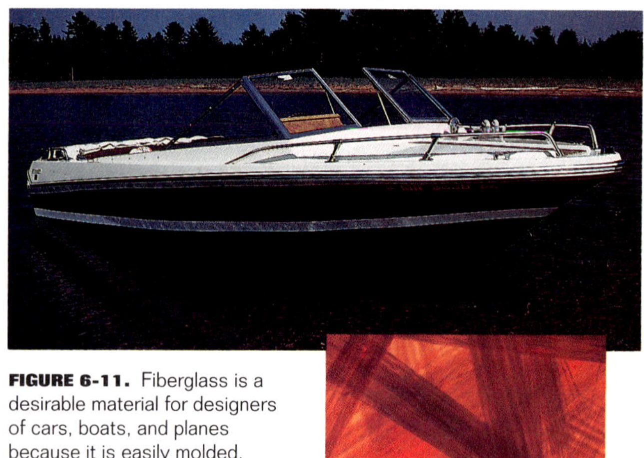

FIGURE 6-11. Fiberglass is a desirable material for designers of cars, boats, and planes because it is easily molded.

Most composites are mixtures of two materials, with one embedded in the other. When you made the composite plaster block in the last activity, what material did you embed in the plaster? The items you added helped make the plaster block stronger and able to withstand more strain from the hammer. Ceramic objects are always much stronger when they are parts of composites.

When a bridge is being built of reinforced concrete, the concrete has long steel rods embedded in it to provide additional strength and support. Reinforced concrete is an example of a composite. Both concrete and steel improve the overall structure and produce a bridge that is better than one made from concrete or steel alone.

Fiberglass is a composite that is a mixture of small threads of glass embedded in a plastic. It is very resistant to weather, is lightweight, and will not dent or rust. It can be easily molded into complex shapes, as shown in Figure 6-11.

Many different composites can be made of various metals, plastics, and ceramics. New composites are being produced every year. In the future, you may be driving a car, working in a building, flying in an airplane, and living in a home that are all made entirely of composites.

Check Your Understanding

1. List two common plastics and discuss their uses.
2. Describe how composites are used in the construction industry.
3. **APPLY:** As a boat designer, you were asked to design a boat for a race from Catalina to Hawaii. What materials might you use? Explain your reasoning.

4 Close

Activity

Provide each student with samples of synthetic and natural clothing fibers, such as swatches of rayon, dacron, nylon, polyester, cotton, and wool. Direct students to compare synthetic and natural fibers by looking at the samples with a hand lens. Have students record and discuss their observations.

EXPANDING YOUR VIEW

CONTENTS

A CLOSER LOOK

ALL THAT GLITTERS IS NOT GOLD

Those gold medals our athletes win in the Olympic Games and that "solid" gold watch your grandfather received when he retired have something in common. In fact, the gold medals and the gold watch aren't pure gold at all. They are made from a gold alloy, most likely 18 parts gold, 3 parts copper, and 3 parts silver.

Pure gold is soft and easily wears away. However, the fact that it does not tarnish, and the fact that it is rare, have made it desirable through the ages. Fortunately, gold retains its color and its resistance to tarnishing when alloyed with more plentiful metals.

Alloys of gold with other metals are measured in terms of karats. Pure gold is described as 24-karat gold. A gold alloy that is by weight 20 parts gold and 4 parts other metals is described as 20-karat gold; 18-karat gold has 18 parts gold to 6 parts other metals, and so on.

Gold used in jewelry is typically alloyed with copper and silver or with a combination of copper and silver. To make the alloy, the metals are melted together, thoroughly stirred, and poured into molds to harden. Most gold jewelry and medals are made from 12-, 14-, and 18-karat gold.

WHAT DO YOU THINK?

The gold jewelry pictured below is from the Moche civilization that existed more than 2000 years ago in present-day Peru. What do you think this gold jewelry tells us about these people?

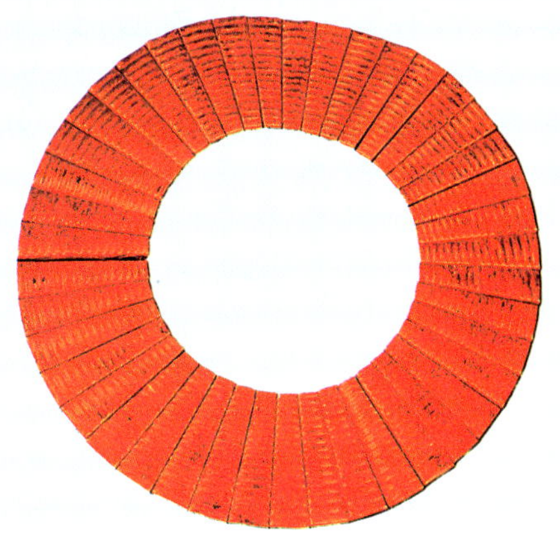

Going Further Working in small groups, have students make lists of objects they know are made of gold. Then have them decide which karat gold would be best for making each particular object. Their lists might include such items as wedding rings, watches, some fillings in teeth, earrings, pins, and statues. Students should realize that gold objects that will be subjected to wear and tear need to be made of less gold and more copper or silver than other gold objects. For example, rings are rarely made of pure, 24-karat gold.

COOP LEARN

You might also have your students work in groups to research different topics about gold, such as the California Gold Rush or the mining and processing of gold.

EXPANDING YOUR VIEW

Using Expanding Your View

Assign one or more of these excursions to expand students' understanding of materials and how they apply to other sciences and other subjects. You might assign these as individual or small group activities.

A CLOSER LOOK

Purpose One of the alloys discussed in Section 6-1 is a gold alloy. A Closer Look explains why a gold alloy is used for jewelry and how it is measured.

Content Background Gold is an element and a mineral that forms from molten material inside Earth. Because of gold's density, it will separate from the molten material it is in and form pure crystals of gold. Gold is a mineral with metallic luster. This means that it reflects light like polished metal and is one of the reasons for gold's popularity in jewelry. There is a copper-bearing mineral called pyrite that looks like gold and was often mistakenly mined for real gold. It was often referred to as fool's gold.

Gold is often found as an ore. An ore is a metal found with impurities mixed in it. The gold ore must go through a process called smelting in order to remove the impurities.

Teaching Strategies Bring in a piece of gold jewelry or several pieces, if possible. Pass these around the class for students to examine. Ask them what makes people so attracted to gold. Then discuss how gold might influence the development of a society or culture.

Answers to

WHAT DO YOU THINK?

Possible answers include that these cultures had the knowledge to mine gold and form alloys and that at least some members of these cultures possessed wealth.

LIFE SCIENCE CONNECTION

Purpose As with other materials described in Section 6-1, the material described in the Life Science Connection, silk, was used in the past and is still used today. The You Try It activity gives students the opportunity to compare silk to some of the synthetic materials mentioned in Section 6-3.

Content Background The history behind the use of the silkworm for producing silk involves the story of a Chinese princess who was drinking tea in her palace one day when the cocoon of a silkworm moth fell from the rafters of the palace roof into the cup of hot tea. The startled princess tried to remove the cocoon from her cup and began to unravel this long thread of silk.

The silkworm feeds on mulberry leaves exclusively and is raised in large numbers to produce silk. Some of the moths are allowed to emerge from their cocoons to mate and lay eggs so a new generation of worms is provided. However, the process of obtaining the silk involves boiling the cocoons before the moths emerge. If the moths are allowed to emerge, they will destroy the cocoon, making it worthless for silk.

Teaching Strategies If possible, order silkworm caterpillars or eggs from a biological supply house. The larva can be raised in class as long as mulberry leaves can be obtained. Mulberry trees are fairly common in most parts of the United States. Students can observe the life cycle of this interesting insect. Other caterpillars could also be used to represent the silkworm life cycle.

Debate Have students debate the use of leather or fur for clothing. Should animals be used to make products for humans? Does the making of silk stir the same emotions as the use of leather or fur?

LIFE SCIENCE CONNECTION

CLOTH FROM WORMS

Do you know what it means when something is described as "silky"? Perhaps you have a silk tie or a silk dress. Can you describe the feel of silk?

Silk, like wool, is a natural animal fiber. Caterpillars spin silk cocoons when they are ready to change into moths or butterflies. The caterpillar of the silk moth, also called the silkworm, produces a long, continuous thread suitable for making fabric.

The silkworm spins a cocoon in much the same way that a spider spins a web. First the silkworm spins a light web of short strands around itself. Then it spins its cocoon in one continuous strand, like thread on a spool. The silkworm cocoons are put through a steaming and drying process. Then the long strands of silk thread can be unraveled and spun into yarn. The thread of silk from a single cocoon might be anywhere from 1000 feet to 2000 feet long. Because the thread from one cocoon is very slender, a single strand of silk used in fabric is usually spun together from the threads of five to eight cocoons.

In China, where much of the world's silk is made, silk thread is still spun by hand. In other silk-producing countries, such as Japan, spinning machines are used. The silk thread is wound onto reels and then into skeins or coils. The skeins are packed into bales and shipped to factories where the silk threads are woven into fabric. The silk may be dyed before or after it is woven into fabric.

Because the demand for silk is greater than the supply, silk is a very expensive fabric. It is often used for fine garments and upholstery. Silk is desirable because of its pleasing texture, because it can be dyed beautiful and brilliant shades, and because the fabric is wrinkle-resistant. Unlike many synthetic fabrics, silk absorbs moisture and is comfortable to wear in hot, humid weather.

YOU TRY IT!

Make a collection of fabric samples. Include natural fibers, such as cotton, linen, wool, and silk. Also include synthetic fibers, such as nylon, Orlon, and Dacron. Accompany each sample with a description of the fabric and the way it is commonly used. Test each sample for wrinkle resistance, tear resistance, and stain resistance. Make a chart that shows the results of the tests.

Going Further Have students work in groups to examine the labels on their shirts and other items of clothing to see what materials they are made of. Have each group share their findings with the class. Then have students make a bar graph to show how many items of clothing worn by class members are made from various synthetic materials and natural fibers. COOP LEARN

Answers to YOU TRY IT

When testing wrinkle resistance, wad the samples up and put a rubber band around the wad. Leave the samples overnight, then observe for wrinkles.

SCIENCE AND SOCIETY

THE THROWAWAY SOCIETY

What if you had a party in your classroom and one person in your class of twenty consumed nearly half the food? You'd probably say that it wasn't fair. Yet the United States, with only five percent of the world's population, uses nearly half of the world's resources! To satisfy the needs of an average United States citizen, about 23,000 kilograms (25 tons) of various chemical resources must be taken from the earth each year. Of equal concern is what happens to all the things produced from these resources after we are finished with them. What happens to the cans and bottles, the batteries and tires, the paper, clothes, and other materials we no longer want?

Today, each person in the United States throws away, on average, nearly 2 kilograms (4 pounds) of unwanted material per day. About half of this is paper and other objects that will burn. The materials discarded by United States citizens would fill the New Orleans Superdome from floor to ceiling twice each day! This doesn't include the much greater amounts of material discarded by manufacturers of the original consumer products.

In the 1970s, people began to be aware of the ever increasing problems of solid waste. Thousands of landfills had been filled. Some highly populated areas in the eastern United States, such as New Jersey, began shipping their waste to the Midwest because they had no more land to use as dumps. A variety of locations were pressed into service, including abandoned rock quarries, wetlands unsuitable for housing, and areas too distant from power and transportation to be suitable for manufacturing. But these landfills often pose a health threat because they contain toxic wastes that can seep into groundwater.

Plans have been developed that allow only certain types and amounts of waste to be discarded. In many areas, the public must pay for the bags they use to throw away their trash. Lawn clippings and yard waste are not allowed. Before tires are accepted, they must be shredded into two-inch pieces. These measures make people think twice about the things they throw away. But even with these plans, it's clear that eventually we will run out of room. Many landfills will be filled in less than 20 years.

One way in which the amount of garbage can be reduced is through recycling. Much research is being done and many creative ideas have been offered for the use of solid waste. The Japanese have suggested that solid waste can be covered with asphalt and used as

EXPANDING YOUR VIEW

SCIENCE AND SOCIETY

Purpose The Science and Society excursion discusses how we dispose of some of the modern materials presented in Section 6-3. It also focuses on how these materials can be recycled.

Content Background When a material is recycled, it is used again. Recycling conserves minerals and living things. For example, recycling paper means that fewer trees need to be cut down. Recycling uses less energy than finding and using new resources.

Teaching Strategies Have students work in small groups to list five things that could be considered problems in their city or town. Students may list such things as pollution, trash pickup, etc. Next to each problem, have them indicate what, if anything, the local government is doing about it. Ask them to decide if each problem they identified will increase or decrease as time progresses. Then have them select from their list one item that they could affect in a positive way. Discuss strategies for doing this. Encourage students, to implement their strategies if possible. They might suggest writing letters to the mayor, petitioning city council, or writing an editorial for the newspaper. COOP LEARN

Answers to

YOU TRY IT

Answers will vary. However, the large volume may surprise students and impress upon them the magnitude of our solid waste problem.

building materials. Crushed glass and shredded rubber can be used in road construction. The United States Bureau of Mines has developed a process that can convert 1000 kilograms of materials high in carbon and hydrogen into 250 kilograms of oil.

The plastic used in beverage containers can be ground, combined with other plastics, and formed into plastic piping suitable for plumbing. Plastic "lumber," such as that shown in the picture, is one of the newest products made from recycled plastics.

There are about 2 billion tires in dumps around the United States, with more than 200 million tires being added each year. In November 1987, a power plant in California demonstrated a process that can burn whole tires to make electricity. The plant is located near the largest tire dump in the United States. This dump contains nearly 35 million tires. The plant can burn 5 million tires a year and generate enough electricity to meet the needs of 15,000 households. The foul-smelling, black smoke that is usually produced when tires are burned is eliminated by the high temperatures at which the plant operates. The pollution control system is designed to remove 99.9 percent of all solid particles in the smoke. The plant even recycles the materials in these solid particles. Plants such as the one in California would go a long way toward eliminating this solid waste problem, while providing much needed energy.

Recycling also uses energy and, in some cases, recycling is not economically feasible. But let's just look at one case. The energy needed to produce one aluminum can from raw materials would keep a 100-watt light bulb going for 19 days. To produce that same can from recycled aluminum requires only 5 percent as much energy. More than 85 billion aluminum cans are produced in the United States each year. Recycling those cans not only saves a tremendous amount of energy, but a tremendous quantity of the raw materials that go into the production of the original cans.

Buying objects made of recycled materials and purchasing products with a minimum amount of packaging are only two of the ways in which we can all help to reduce the amount of solid waste. Clearly, our choices will have long-lasting effects on us and our environment.

YOU TRY IT!

Clean out and bring to school all of the cans or bottles you and your family use in one day. Collect the cans or bottles from the entire class in cardboard boxes. Measure the total volume of the boxes. How much space does this one form of solid waste take up? Measure the volume of your classroom. How many days would it take your class to fill the classroom with cans or bottles? Suggest several ways that you could reduce the space occupied by the cans or bottles.

Going Further Have students work in small groups to list all the things they have had to eat or drink on this or the previous day. Then have them identify the waste that resulted from each item eaten. For example, if they had a sandwich using the last of a loaf of bread, the bread wrapper was the waste produced. This should give students an idea of how much and what types of solid waste they themselves produce in a single day.

Have students research the process of composting. Composting can reduce the amount of organic waste produced by Americans every day, which takes up considerable space in landfills. Depending on the area in which you live and the climate, encourage students to begin their own compost piles at home. For information, have students contact:

Organic Gardening Magazine
33E Minor Street
Emmaus, PA 18098 **COOP LEARN**

Health CONNECTION

ARE AMALGAM FILLINGS SAFE?

An amalgam is a metal alloy of which mercury is an essential part. Dentists use amalgam fillings because they are long-lasting and inexpensive. Ceramic fillings last about the same length of time, but they are more than six times as expensive as amalgam fillings. Composite fillings made from plastic are fairly inexpensive, but they last less than half as long as amalgam fillings. Does your dentist use an amalgam of mercury, silver, and other metals to fill cavities in your teeth? If so, each time you chew or brush your teeth, you release mercury vapor into your mouth. You inhale some of the vapor and convert it in your body into inorganic mercury compounds that may accumulate in your kidneys and other body tissues.

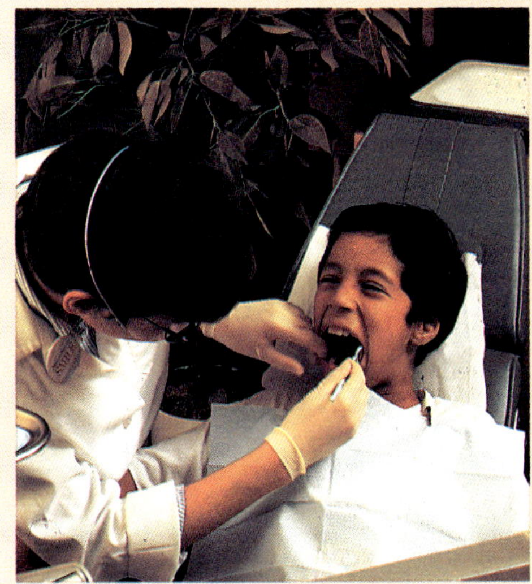

Above a certain level, excesses of mercury in your body can cause tremors, fatigue, memory loss, vision and speech difficulties, and other health problems. Is the level of mercury inhaled by people with amalgam fillings enough to be considered dangerous?

Most members of the American Dental Association believe that amalgam fillings are safe because the level of mercury vapor released by amalgam fillings is far below the toxic level. They point to the studies that show that people with amalgam fillings inhale far less than 20 micrograms of mercury vapor per day. The level inhaled in an industrial setting must be above 300 micrograms per day to be considered toxic. They also note that people who eat certain kinds of fish, such as tuna or swordfish, are exposed to more mercury from their diet than from amalgam fillings in their teeth.

Some scientists, however, feel that more research should be done. They believe there is at least a remote possibility that research might someday show a connection between amalgam fillings and symptoms of mercury poisoning.

WHAT DO YOU THINK?

Is there enough of a possibility of harmful effects from amalgam fillings to warrant their removal? If you need fillings in the future, would you choose amalgam fillings, or would you ask your dentist for an alternative? Why?

EXPANDING YOUR VIEW

HEALTH CONNECTION

Purpose This Health Connection addresses the possibility of mercury poisoning from the amalgams dentists use for fillings. An amalgam which was described in Section 6-1 is an alloy containing mercury, silver, and zinc.

Content Background Various television shows have been aired recently discussing the possibility of mercury poisoning due to amalgam fillings. The CBS show *60 Minutes* aired an especially good documentary on the research and complaints about amalgam fillings.

Research involves studies of people who have complained of various ailments until having their amalgam fillings extracted. After these fillings were extracted and replaced with one of the alternative materials, the symptoms disappeared.

Teaching Strategies Divide the class into two groups, one representing the members of the American Dental Association and the other representing those who believe that amalgam fillings are dangerous. Have each group develop and present arguments that help support their belief. **COOP LEARN**

Answers to WHAT DO YOU THINK?

Answers will vary depending on student's point of view.

Going Further Have students research the latest information available on this topic using science magazines and journals in the library. Students may also research mercury poisoning in general.

EXPANDING YOUR VIEW

TECHNOLOGY CONNECTION

Purpose The Technology Connection introduces polymers and focuses on thermoplastic polymers or plastics, one of the modern materials described in Section 6-3. Elements are presented as the building blocks of matter in Section 6-2. One or more atoms of one or more elements bond together to form molecules. Polymers are formed when smaller molecules bond together to make large molecules.

Content Background The term *polymer* comes from the Greek words *polys,* meaning "many," and *meros,* meaning "parts." The individual units that make up a polymer are called monomers. The type of monomers used and the length and shape of the polymer made determine the physical properties of the polymer. Natural polymers, such as proteins, are made up of monomers called amino acids. Synthetic polymers involve various chemical monomers.

Teaching Strategies Prepare the synthetic fiber nylon, a polymer, in front of the class by using adipyl chloride solution (0.25 M in hexane), hexamethylene diamine solution (0.50 M in 0.50M NaOH), acetone (in alcohol), a paper clip, small beakers, and a graduated cylinder. By pouring 5 mL of the hexamethylene diamine solution into a beaker and slowly adding 5 mL of the adipyl chloride solution, a white film should form where the two solutions meet. Use the paper clip to make a hook with which to lift this white film from the solution. This white film is nylon, which can be rinsed with acetone and allowed to dry.

Answers to YOU TRY IT

Answers will depend on plastic items chosen.

TECHNOLOGY CONNECTION

POLYMERS

It is not much of an exaggeration to say that we live in a world of polymers. Polymers are large molecules made by bonding many small molecules together. Natural polymers are the building blocks of natural rubber, certain protein substances, and plant carbohydrates. In making synthetic polymers, scientists first analyze and then imitate the natural process that produces natural polymers. By controlling the temperature at which polymers form, material with different properties can be obtained. Synthetic polymers are the building blocks of many materials, such as plastics, foam padding, polyester fabrics, paint resins and adhesives, and synthetic rubber.

Thermoplastic polymers are plastics that have insulating properties and are used as protective coatings. If you've ever used an insulated container to keep hot things hot or cold things cold, you've probably used a product made from thermoplastic polymers. The water pipes in your home may be made from thermoplastic polymers. Clear plastic food wrap is also a thermoplastic polymer, as is polyurethane, which is often used as a scratch-resistant coating on gym floors and bowling alleys. Polyurethane foams are used in mattresses and seat cushions.

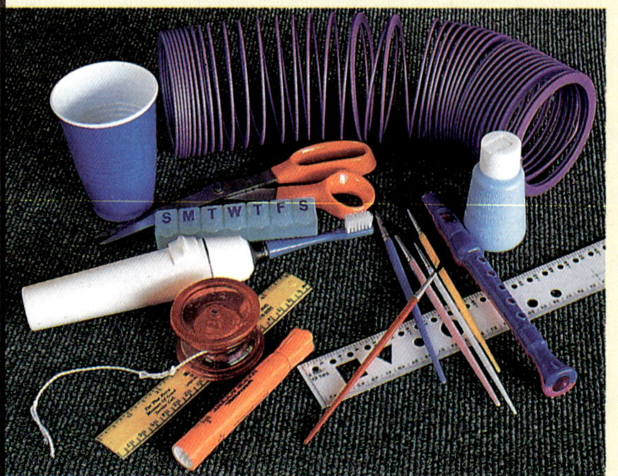

CAREER CONNECTION

A chemist works in a laboratory, often for a private industry, to develop new materials to meet new demands. Courses in mathematics, chemistry, and physics are needed to prepare for a career as a research chemist.

Until recently, it was a nuisance to dispose of polymers in the form of plastic. Now, however, some of these products are being recycled. As a further advance in technology, scientists are developing plastics that dissolve easily and safely and will reduce the daily buildup of solid wastes.

YOU TRY IT!

Make a display of at least ten items found in your home that are made of different kinds of plastic. How were these items made before plastic was discovered? Which items are easier to use — the plastic or the ones made of other material? Which items can be reused frequently? Which can be recycled easily?

Going Further Have students work in small groups. Provide each group with several objects that are made from polymers. Have students examine these products and describe how each material is suitable for the object's function. Then have groups tour the classroom and make lists of all the objects they believe are made of polymers. Have them share their findings with the class.

Students may also research the discovery of various polymers. For example, nylon was discovered in the 1940s and has an interesting story behind it. COOP LEARN

Reviewing Main Ideas

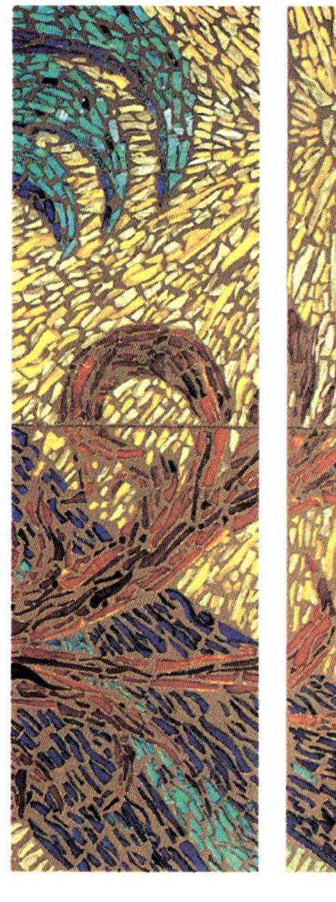

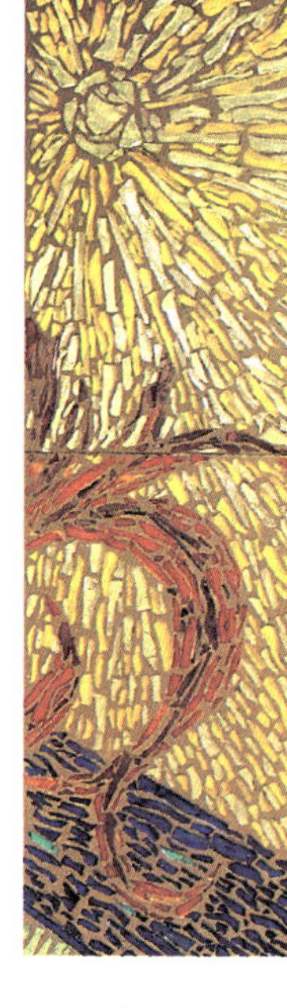

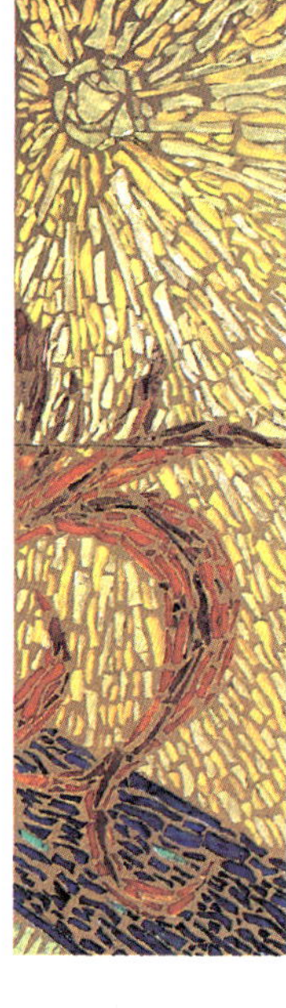

1. Ceramics are mixtures often made from clay or sand. Glass is a common ceramic.

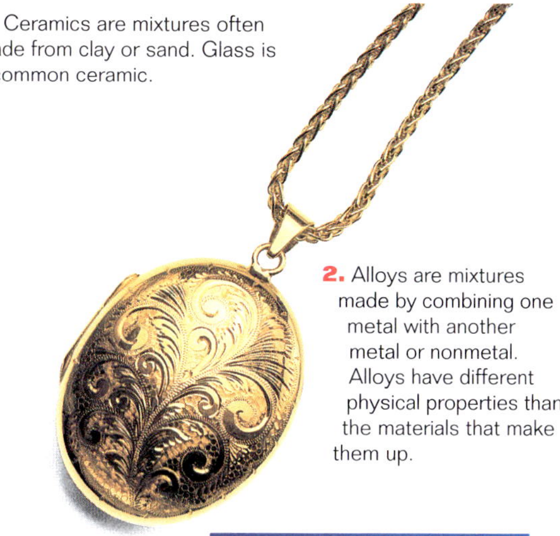

2. Alloys are mixtures made by combining one metal with another metal or nonmetal. Alloys have different physical properties than the materials that make them up.

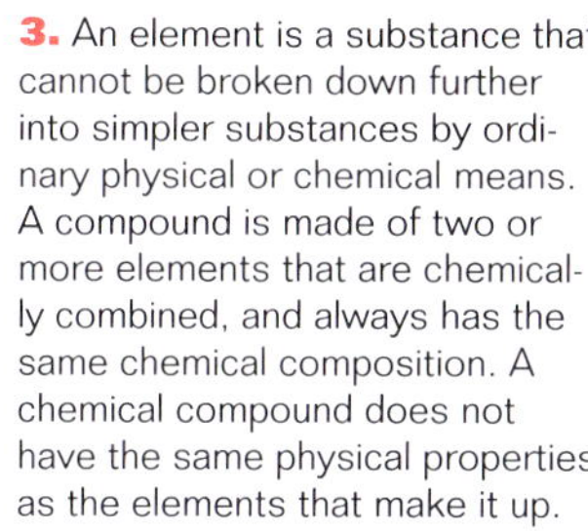

3. An element is a substance that cannot be broken down further into simpler substances by ordinary physical or chemical means. A compound is made of two or more elements that are chemically combined, and always has the same chemical composition. A chemical compound does not have the same physical properties as the elements that make it up.

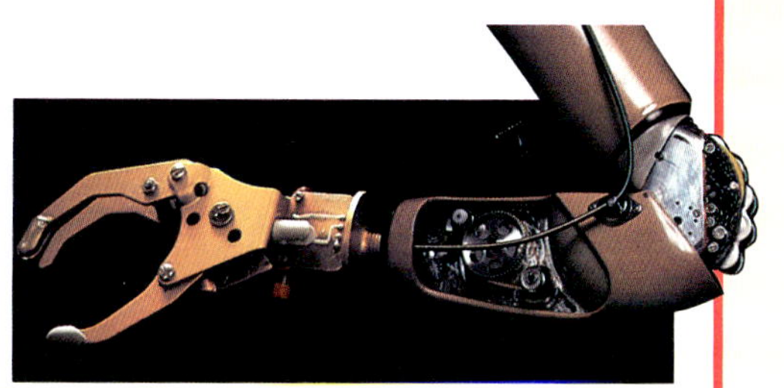

4. Plastics and synthetic fibers are new artificial materials with many uses. Composites are mixtures of two materials, with one embedded in the other.

Chapter 6

Reviewing Main Ideas

Direct the students' attention to the photographs and illustrations. Use them to review the main ideas presented in this chapter. Have students read each statement aloud.

Teaching Strategies

Divide the class into four groups. Assign each group a different quadrant of your classroom. Have each group go on a "materials hunt" within their quadrant, making a list of the materials they find, their composition, and classification as an alloy, metal, ceramic, plastic, synthetic fiber, or composite. Include jewelry or clothing found on students. This activity could be extended out into the hallway as well. You might suggest that the four groups rotate quadrants, and then compare their lists (for materials found in the same quadrant). **COOP LEARN**

Chapter 6

Chapter Review

USING KEY SCIENCE TERMS

Answers

1. compound
2. alloy
3. element
4. amalgam
5. glass
6. composite
7. ceramic

UNDERSTANDING IDEAS

Answers

1. c
2. b
3. c
4. b
5. a
6. d

Chapter Review

USING KEY SCIENCE TERMS

alloy
amalgam
ceramic
composite
compound
element
glass

Each sentence below describes a science term from the list. Write the term that matches each sentence. Use each term one time.

1. Different samples of a substance were collected. In every sample, there was the same amount of carbon and oxygen. What was the substance?
2. Some samples of a material were melted. Each time, the metal separated into two layers when cooled. Different samples, however, gave off different amounts in each layer. What is the material?
3. When scientists try to break this substance down into simpler particles, they cannot do it by ordinary chemical or physical means. What is this substance?
4. You have not been brushing your teeth, and the dentist spots a cavity. After drilling it out, he fills it with a silver-colored material that contains mercury. What is this material an example of?
5. You are walking home from school and spot something on the sidewalk. It is a translucent ceramic with jagged, broken edges. What might this material be?
6. Some workers are repairing a giant pothole on your street. They are placing metal rods in the hole, and are pouring concrete around the rods. What type of material are they using?
7. You are in art class, where you have just made a clay vase. You paint it and put it into an oven to dry. What type of material are you making?

UNDERSTANDING IDEAS

Choose the best answer to complete each sentence.

1. While riding in a boat, you hit a log. The boat didn't dent, but there is a scratch, and you can see threads under the surface. The boat is made of a(n) ____.
   a. alloy **c.** composite
   b. ceramic **d.** element
2. Sugar is a(n) ____.
   a. alloy **c.** ceramic
   b. compound **d.** glass
3. The concrete in highway bridges is a(n) ____.
   a. ceramic **c.** composite
   b. amalgam **d.** alloy
4. Aluminum-lithium alloys are used in aircraft because they ____.
   a. are lighter than air
   b. are lightweight and maintain their strength at high temperatures
   c. can be recycled
   d. are compounds

PROGRAM RESOURCES

Teacher Classroom Resources

Review and Assessment, Chapter Review and Chapter Test pages 25–28

Computer Test Bank, Chapter Test

OPTIONS

Cooperative Learning

Consider using Cooperative Learning in the Understanding Ideas, Critical Thinking, Problem Solving, and Connecting Ideas sections of the Chapter Review. COOP LEARN

5. At the store, you buy a six-pack of soda water with a holder around it. The holder is probably a(n) ____.
   a. plastic c. synthetic fiber
   b. natural fiber d. alloy
6. Oxygen gas is in the air that you breathe. Oxygen gas is an example of a(n) ____.
   a. amalgam c. compound
   b. mixture d. element

CRITICAL THINKING

Use your understanding of the concepts developed in the chapter to answer each of the following questions.

1. An alloy is made of iron, copper, and zinc by heating together sheets of all three in a furnace. No matter how many times the metals are heated, however, the final alloy always has more of the iron located in the middle layers of the alloy than on the surface. Use the information in the table to explain why this happens.

Metal	Density
Iron	7.9 g/cm^3
Copper	8.9 g/cm^3
Zinc	7.1 g/cm^3

2. A railway engineer wants to drill a hole through some hard rock in order to lay down new tracks. He asks you to make a new drill. What kind of materials would you use for the drill? Explain your answer.
3. An architect is asked to design a new coating for a fireplace. Describe the materials she would probably use in her design.
4. Two metals are heated together in a furnace at 50°C for two hours. At the end of that time, they are removed and allowed to cool. The next day, a worker picks up the new alloy and discovers it breaking apart in his hands. What went wrong?

PROBLEM SOLVING

Read the following problem and discuss your answers in a brief paragraph.

You've decided to enter a competition that offers a prize to whoever builds a bicycle with no metal parts.

1. What materials would you use to replace the metal parts of your bicycle? Why?
2. If you wanted to build a racing bike, how would your materials change? Explain.

CONNECTING IDEAS

Discuss each of the following in a brief paragraph.

1. Is the formation of an alloy a chemical or a physical change? Explain.
2. Are most ceramics homogeneous mixtures? Explain why or why not.
3. **A CLOSER LOOK** A jeweler offers to sell you a 16-karat bracelet for $20.00, claiming that it is 80 percent gold. Is the jeweler telling you the truth? Explain your answer.
4. **HEALTH CONNECTION** Mercury vapor escapes when a person with amalgam fillings chews. If a boy's fillings release 15 micrograms of mercury per day, what part of a toxic dose would he be receiving?

CRITICAL THINKING

Answers

1. During melting, all three metals change into liquids. The lightest liquid will rise to the top and the heaviest will sink to the bottom. Iron has a density between these two, and so would naturally be found in the middle of the alloy unless proper mixing occurs.

2. Carbon and steel make the strongest alloys, and would be most suitable for equipment like drills.

3. She would probably use ceramic tiles, which are able to withstand the high temperatures a fireplace would produce.

4. The furnace temperature was too low for the metals to melt together. A true alloy was never formed, and so the material easily fell apart.

PROBLEM SOLVING

Answers

1. Fiberglass would be a good choice because it is lightweight, resistant to weather, easily molded, and will not dent or rust.

2. For a racing bike you would want the lightest materials possible, perhaps a new composite that is sturdy yet lightweight.

CONNECTING IDEAS

Answers

1. It is a physical change, because the two metals still retain their original properties.

2. No. Homogeneous mixtures would have the same composition throughout. Most ceramics have variable compositions. Glass, however, is an example of a homogeneous mixture.

3. No. 16-karat jewelry is 67 percent ($\frac{16}{24} \times 100$) gold, and not 80 percent, as he is claiming.

4. 300 micrograms per day make up a toxic dose. The boy is receiving $\frac{15}{300}$, or $\frac{1}{20}$, of a toxic dose.

CHAPTER ORGANIZER

SECTION	OBJECTIVES	ACTIVITIES/FEATURES
Chapter Opener		**Explore!** What materials seem to disappear in water? p. 193
7-1 Types of Solutions (4 days)	1. **Classify** solutions. 2. **Define and identify** solutes and solvents. 3. **Describe** three factors that affect the rates at which solids and gases dissolve in liquids.	**Find Out!** How can you make cleanser? p. 194 **Find Out!** Can all mixtures be separated by mechanical means? p. 195 **Explore!** What are the properties of a solution? 196 **Investigate 7-1:** Evaporation and Solutions, 199 **Find Out!** Does particle size affect dissolving? 200 **Find Out!** How do stirring (or shaking) and temperature affect dissolving? p. 202 **Skillbuilder:** Comparing and Contrasting, p. 202 **Find Out!** How does temperature affect dissolving of a gas in a liquid? p. 203 **Skillbuilder:** Hypothesizing, p. 204
7-2 Solubility and Concentration (3 days)	1. **Describe** how solubility varies for different solutes and for the same solute at different temperatures. 2. **Interpret** solubility graphs. 3. **Compare and contrast** saturated and unsaturated solutions. 4. **Infer** solution concentrations.	**Explore!** Do sugar and salt dissolve in water in the same amounts? p. 205 **Skillbuilder:** Making and Using Graphs, p. 206 **Investigate 7-2:** Saturating a Solution at Different Temperatures, p. 208
7-3 Colloids and Suspensions (2 days)	1. **Distinguish** between a colloid and a suspension. 2. **Recognize** at least two mixtures that are colloids.	**Explore!** Are all transparent mixtures solutions? p. 211 **Explore!** When is a mixture not a solution or a colloid? p. 213 **Skillbuilder:** Making and Using Tables, p. 214
Expanding Your View	A Closer Look **Can We Change the Freezing Point?** p. 215 Life Science Connection **Keeping the Balance,** p. 216 Science and Society **Cleaning Up the Oceans,** p. 217	Literature Connection **Down to the Sea Again,** p. 219 Sociology Connection **So You Think the Ocean Is Salty?** p. 220

ACTIVITY MATERIALS

EXPLORE!	INVESTIGATE!	FIND OUT!
Page 193 sugar, salt, flour, starch, piece of cotton, 5 glasses, water, stirrer, teaspoon **Page 196** 4 tsp. soft drink mix, water, clear pitcher, flashlight, stirrer, straw **Page 205** 2 400-mL beakers, water, 50 g table salt, 50 g sugar, stirrers **Page 211** gelatin dessert mix, transparent bowl, flashlight **Page 213** glass, muddy water, stirrer	**Page 199** safety goggles, Epsom salt (magnesium sulfate), water, graduated cylinder, large beaker, spoon or stirring rod, 2 small beakers; thick, water-absorbent string **Page 208** distilled water, graduated cylinder, large test tube, table sugar (sucrose), test-tube holder, laboratory balance, thermometer in a two-hole stopper, copper wire stirrer, safety goggles, beaker, water, hot plate, scoop for sugar, oven mitt	**Page 194** 8 g powdered sugar, mortar and pestle, peppermint oil, 3 g castile soap, eye dropper, stirrer, 22 g calcium carbonate, small section of dishcloth, food coloring or fruit juice, corn syrup, old toothbrush, water, scale **Page 195** 2 400-mL beakers, water, 10 g sand, 10 g table salt, 2 rings, 2 funnels, 2 ring stands, 2 filter papers, water, balance **Page 200** distilled water, 2 containers, mortar, pestle, stopwatch, cm graph paper, folded paper, 2 stirrers, 12 sugar cubes **Page 202** 4 glasses; water (hot, iced, and room temp.); stirrer, sugar, teaspoon **Page 203** bottle of chilled soft drink; identical soft drink, unchilled; balloon, tape

Chapter 7
Matter in Solution

TEACHER CLASSROOM RESOURCES	OTHER RESOURCES
Study Guide, p. 26 **Multicultural Activities,** p. 17 **Activity Masters, Investigate 7-1,** pp. 29-30 **Flex Your Brain,** p. 8 **Making Connections: Across the Curriculum,** p. 17 **How It Works,** p. 10 **Concept Mapping,** p. 15 **Making Connections: Technology and Society,** p. 17	**Laboratory Manual,** pp. 31-34, Solutions **Laboratory Manual,** pp. 39-42, Densities of Solutions **Color Transparency and Master 13,** The Solution Process ***STVS:** *Blood Clot Treatment,* Human Biology (Disc 7, Side 1) *Greenhouse Effect,* Ecology (Disc 6, Side 2)
Study Guide, p. 27 **Activity Masters, Investigate 7-2,** pp. 31-32 **Making Connections: Integrating Sciences,** p. 17	**Laboratory Manual,** pp. 35-38, Solubility **Color Transparency and Master 14,** Solubility Graph
Study Guide, p. 28 **Critical Thinking/Problem Solving,** p. 15 **Multicultural Activities,** p. 18 **Take Home Activities,** p. 14 **Review and Assessment,** pp. 29-32	***STVS:** *Arctic Haze,* Ecology (Disc 6, Side 2) **Computer Test Bank** **Spanish Resources** **Cooperative Learning Resource Guide**
	Lab and Safety Skills

***Science and Technology Videodisc Series**

KEY TO TEACHING STRATEGIES

Teaching strategies have been coded for varying learning styles and abilities. As you review teaching strategies in the margin, the following designations will help you decide which activities are appropriate for your students.

L1 Level 1 activities are basic activities and should be within the ability range of all students.

L2 Level 2 activities are average activities and should be within the ability range of the average to above-average student.

L3 Level 3 activities are challenging activities designed for the ability range of above-average students.

LEP LEP activities should be within the ability range of Limited English Proficiency students.

COOP LEARN Cooperative Learning activities are designed for small group work.

ADDITIONAL MATERIALS

SOFTWARE	AUDIOVISUAL
Solubility, EME. *Soluble, Programs for Learning Solutions,* Focus. *Reactions,* J & S Software. *Chemical Reactions,* Compress.	*Mr. Wizard's World: Chemistry in the Kitchen,* video, Macmillan/McGraw-Hill School Division. *Chemical Change All About Us,* film, Coronet/MTI.

Chapter 7

Matter in Solution

THEME DEVELOPMENT

The primary theme of stability and change is illustrated in this chapter by the Find Out activities on pages 200–203. The major differences between solutions and mixtures involve changes that take place when a solute dissolves and how stable those changes are. On a molecular level, the secondary theme of interactions and systems is clearly revealed by the behavior of solutions as systems whose individual particles interact to produce large-scale behavior.

CHAPTER OVERVIEW

Students first consider the qualitative aspects of solutions: how they differ from other mixtures, how they can be separated, and what factors influence solubility. Students also explore quantitative aspects of solubility and its relationship to temperature and the amount and type of solute and solvent. Finally, the differences between true solutions and mixtures, classified as colloids or suspensions, are investigated.

Tying to Previous Knowledge

Present two beakers, one filled with tap water and the other with salt water. First ask students to identify which is which. Can they do it by sight alone? *No, they need some other means, such as taste.* Then have them predict in which solution more salt will be able to be dissolved. Have them justify their predictions with reasoned explanations. Then add known amounts of salt to both beakers until the solutions are saturated. Encourage students to develop an explanation for what happened. *Water can hold only so much salt, so the salt water, being closer to the limit, dissolved less salt.*

DID YOU EVER WONDER . . .

Where the sugar goes when it dissolves in a glass of lemonade?

Why you can add more sugar to a cup of hot tea than to a glass of iced tea?

Why you don't have to shake milk before you drink it?

You'll find the answers to these questions as you read this chapter.

DID YOU EVER WONDER...

Students will explore these questions as they progress through the chapter. Don't spoil their fun and motivation by sharing these answers too early.

- The sugar crystals are broken down to such a small particle size and mixed so evenly in the water that they disappear and become part of a solution. (page 200)
- The solubility of sugar in water increases as the temperature rises, meaning that more sugar will dissolve per unit volume in hot tea than in iced tea. (page 207)
- Milk is a colloid, which is a mixture whose particles do not settle out upon standing. (page 212)

Chapter 7

Matter in Solution

It's a cold morning, and you've just gone into the kitchen for breakfast. Suppose you pour some powdered hot chocolate into your cup, add boiling water, then sit down with a bowl of instant oatmeal and a glass of apple juice.

As you eat, changes are going on. Your oatmeal is getting soggier in your bowl. Bits of powdered hot chocolate settle out in your cup, but they vanish again when you stir them with your spoon. Your apple juice, however, remains the same.

From a scientist's view, you are eating three mixtures. The oatmeal in your bowl, the powdered chocolate in your cup, and the apple juice in your glass all use water. Yet as you have probably guessed by now, not all mixtures look or act the same. Why is your apple juice clear, while your hot chocolate is cloudy? Why doesn't your oatmeal disappear in water like your hot chocolate? This chapter will help you answer questions such as these.

EXPLORE!

What materials seem to disappear in water?

Add a teaspoon of sugar, salt, flour, and cornstarch and some cotton to separate glasses of water. Observe what happens. Stir the contents of each glass and wait for a few minutes more. What happens now? Which of the solids seem to disappear? Which can you still see?

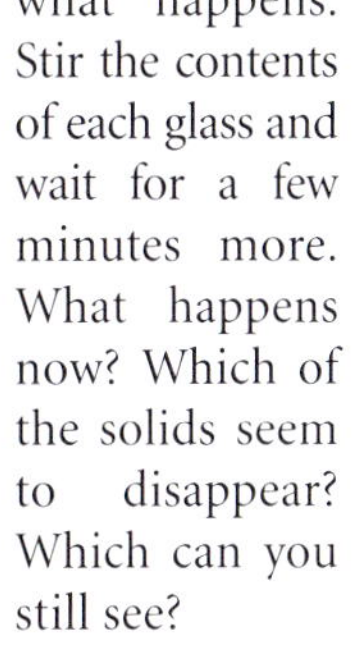

193

Introducing the Chapter

Have students look at the photograph on page 192. Ask students if they can think of any other mixtures that they have eaten.

Uncovering Preconceptions

Students may think that vigorous stirring can cause more of a solute to dissolve in a solvent. Actually, stirring only affects the *rate* of solubility, not how much solute actually dissolves. Demonstrate this with a salt solution, showing that whether you stir slowly or vigorously, the same amount of salt dissolves in either case.

EXPLORE!

What materials seem to disappear in water?

Time needed 15 minutes

Materials teaspoon, sugar, salt, flour, starch, cotton, five glasses of water, stirring rods

Thinking Processes
Thinking critically, Comparing and contrasting, Observing, Practicing scientific methods,

Purpose To compare the solubility of different substances.

Preparation Make sure each glass contains the same amount of water at the same temperature.

Teaching the Activity

Discussion Have students note what is the same and different about the way each substance interacts with water. L1 LEP

Expected Outcomes

Students should find that the sugar and salt disappear, flour and starch turn the water cloudy, and the cotton just gets wet.

Answers to Questions

1. The starch, flour, and cotton start to settle at the bottom.
2. salt and sugar
3. starch, flour, and cotton

Project

Explore whether the particles in a solution will settle out over a long period of time. Prepare an unsaturated sugar-water solution. Cover with a plastic top and allow to sit for a week. Throughout this time, have the class note whether any of the solute settles to the bottom. At the same time, repeat this procedure using a colloid such as gelatin and a suspension such as oil and vinegar salad dressing. Compare the results of each mixture after a week.

Science at Home

Have students prepare samples of colorless soda at temperatures ranging from near-freezing to near-boiling in glasses. Have family members rank the liquids based on how fizzy they appear. Then, have students rank the liquids based on their temperatures. Compare the two rankings. The colder liquids should all rank near the top according to fizziness. They contain more dissolved carbon dioxide gas, which causes the fizziness.

Section 7-1

PREPARATION

Concepts Developed

This section lets students discover qualitative properties of solutions. The distinction between a solution and a mixture is explored.

Planning the Lesson

In planning your lesson on types of solutions, refer to the Chapter Organizer on pages 192A-B for timing suggestions, resources, and additional materials that will help you in your presentation of the lesson concepts. For adequate development of the concepts presented in this section, we recommend that students do the Find Out and Explore activities on pages 194, 196, and 200.

1 MOTIVATE

Demonstration This activity introduces the term *solution* through an environmental problem, acid rain.

You will need two beakers, water, clear acid (white vinegar), pH meter.

Show two beakers, one filled with 100 mL of tap water, the other with a mixture of water and acid. (pH 4) Which water appears more "dangerous?" *They both look the same.* Identify the acidified water as having a similar acid content to acid rain. Explain that acid rain is a *solution* in which acids are dissolved in rainwater. LEP L1

7-1 Types of Solutions

OBJECTIVES

In this section, you will

- classify solutions;
- define and identify solutes and solvents;
- describe three factors that affect the rates at which solids and gases dissolve in liquids.

KEY SCIENCE TERMS

solution
solute
solvent

WHAT IS A SOLUTION?

Think back to the cold-weather breakfast at the beginning of this chapter. The hot chocolate, the oatmeal, and the apple juice were all examples of mixtures, which you read about in Chapter 5. Each was a mixture with water. In the Explore, you saw how sugar and salt seem to disappear in water, while flour, starch, and cotton do not.

Shampoo, toothpaste, and detergent all depend on water to make them work, too. When you clean your hair, teeth, or clothes, you are trying to remove bits of dirt. One way to do this is to mix the dirt with something that will remove it, such as a mixture of soap and water. How can you demonstrate this?

FIND OUT!

How can you make a homemade cleanser?

Place 8 g of powdered sugar in a mortar. Add two drops of peppermint oil and 3 g of castile soap. Mix these together with a pestle. Add 22 g of calcium carbonate, and mix thoroughly. Finally, add corn syrup until a paste is produced. This is now a homemade cleanser.

Carefully stain a small section of a dishcloth with food coloring or fruit juice. Apply some of your homemade cleanser to an old toothbrush, along with a few drops of water. Try scrubbing the stain. What happens?

Conclude and Apply

1. Wash away the cleanser with a little water. What happens now?
2. Why do you think this is happening?

FIND OUT!

How can you make a homemade cleanser?

Time needed 20 minutes

Materials mortar and pestle, scale, scoops, 8 g powdered sugar, 2 drops peppermint oil, 3 g castile soap, 22 g calcium carbonate, corn syrup, food coloring or fruit juice, dish cloth, toothbrush, water, eye dropper

Thinking Process
Observing and inferring

Purpose To observe that the ingredients in a mixture retain their individual properties.

Preparation You may substitute a bowl and stick for a mortar and pestle, and a balance for a scale.

Teaching the Activity

Discussion Focus on the properties of the ingredients. L1

Expected Outcome

The soap retains its cleaning ability.

Answers to Conclude and Apply

1. The stain disappears.
2. Stain dissolves in the mixture.

If you could separate the ingredients from your cleanser, you would still have powdered sugar, peppermint oil, castile soap, calcium carbonate, and corn syrup. Their physical appearance has been changed upon mixing, but not their individual properties. Recall that such a material is a mixture. Toothpastes, most bar soaps, and shampoos such as those in Figure 7-1 are all examples of mixtures.

Mixtures may be separated by mechanical means. Remember in Chapter 5, you separated birdseed by using physical properties. Can all mixtures be separated as easily as this?

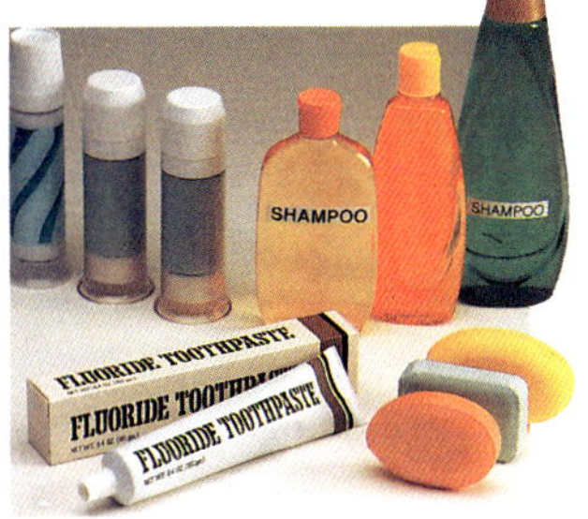

FIGURE 7-1. Some common mixtures are toothpastes, soap bars, and shampoos.

FIND OUT!

Can all mixtures be separated by all mechanical means?

Fill two 400-mL beakers about halfway with water. Add 10 g of sand to the first beaker and 10 g of table salt to the second beaker. Clamp a funnel to each of two ring stands and fold a piece of filter paper to fit in each. Place an empty beaker underneath each funnel. Slowly pour some of your mixture of sand and water into one funnel. Now pour some of your mixture of salt and water into the other funnel. Observe.

Conclude and Apply

1. Which mixture leaves something behind on the filter paper?
2. Which mixture does not?
3. Which mixture can be separated by filtering, a mechanical means?

Sand and salt form mixtures with water, yet they cannot be separated in the same way. While sand can be separated from water by filtering, salt cannot. Why do you think this is?

Certain mixtures, such as salt and water, cannot be separated by all mechanical means. These mixtures are

2 TEACH

Tying to Previous Knowledge

Two factors that affect the rates at which solids and gases dissolve in liquids are temperature and stirring. Ask students to describe how gelatin dessert is made. They should recall that the powder is stirred in boiling water. Ask if they have ever made gelatin dessert when the water was hot enough, but the substances not stirred enough.

FIND OUT!

Can all mixtures be separated by all mechanical means?

Time needed 15 minutes

Materials two 400-mL beakers, water, balance, 10 g sand, 10 g table salt, two ring stands and rings, two funnels, two collecting beakers, filter paper

Thinking Processes Observing and inferring, Comparing and contrasting

Purpose To determine whether all mixtures can be separated by all mechanical means.

Teaching the Activity

Troubleshooting Make sure each mixture is stirred well.

Discussion Have students think of the filter paper as a screen. When sand or salt is dry, will it pass through the filter paper "screen?" *no* How does the situation change when water is introduced? *Salt now passes.* L1

Expected Outcomes

The sand mixture will separate; the salt mixture will not separate. Students may conclude that, when salt dissolves in water, it cannot be separated with a filter.

Answers to Conclude and Apply

1. sand-water mixture
2. salt-water mixture
3. The sand-water mixture can be separated by filtering; the salt-water mixture cannot.

OPTIONS

Meeting Individual Needs

Learning Disabled Students might be unclear about the phrase *mechanical means*. In the Find Out, *mechanical means* refers to a physical, as opposed to a chemical, method of separating mixtures. Filter paper is the mechanical means of separating mixtures in the Find Out activity. LEP

Have students make checklists for the Find Out activity. Before beginning an activity, checklists should require students to:

- obtain all equipment and materials they will need, including "extras" such as labels, pens, scoops, paper towels, etc.
- write the experimental procedure, step by step
- write what they expect the experiment to show
- make tables for collecting data

MAKING CONNECTIONS

Daily Life

Soap is able to clean greasy things in water because it has a "split personality." One end of a soap molecule is water soluble, the other end is oil soluble. The soap molecules break up the oil (grease) into tiny droplets that no longer stick to surfaces. They are thus more easily washed away. L2

EXPLORE!

What are the properties of a solution?

Time needed 15 minutes

Materials 1 package cherry-flavored, unsweetened soft drink mix, 1 quart water in a clear pitcher, flashlight, straw

Thinking Processes
Observing and inferring, Comparing and contrasting

Purpose To investigate the properties of a solution.

Preparation Any flavor of soft drink mix that will produce a clear solution can be used.

Teaching the Activity

Discussion Encourage students to be alert for differences of any type in the soft drink solution. Talk about uniformity. Ask what happened to the crystals. Is there still evidence of their existence?

Expected Outcomes

The crystals will disappear completely; the soft drink left overnight will not change. The particles are evenly mixed and do not separate upon standing.

Answers to Questions

1. no
2. The soft drink is clear; no crystals can be seen.
3. They taste the same.
4. Yes; no particles settled out.

called solutions. Have you ever made instant soft drink on a hot day and watched the crystals disappear in water as you stirred them? Soft drink is an example of a solution. What properties does a solution have that make it different from other kinds of mixtures?

EXPLORE!

What are the properties of a solution?

Add 4 teaspoons of soft drink crystals to a quart of water in a clear pitcher. Stir until all the crystals have disappeared. Look carefully at the soft drink. Do you see any soft drink crystals floating in the pitcher?

Darken the lights in the room and shine a flashlight through the pitcher. What do you observe?

Use a straw to remove a small amount of soft drink from the top of the pitcher. Taste it. Now use the straw to remove a small amount of soft drink from the bottom of the pitcher. Taste it. How do the two samples compare?

Cover the pitcher of soft drink and let it sit undisturbed overnight. Look at the soft drink again tomorrow. Does it look the same?

When you make soft drink, you mix together two kinds of materials. One material is the soft drink crystal, and the other is water. Because they are so small and are mixed evenly throughout the water, you don't see the single particles of soft drink. Also, particles from both materials are evenly mixed throughout the pitcher. A sample from the top will have the same number of dissolved particles as one drawn from the bottom and so will taste as sweet. After waiting, neither material will settle out. Any mixture made up of tiny particles that are evenly mixed and do not settle out is called a **solution**.

A solution is made up of two types of materials, one of which seems to disappear in the other. When you made the soft drink, the soft drink crystal disappeared in the water. Any substance that seems to disappear, or dissolve,

PROGRAM RESOURCES

Teacher Classroom Resources

Study Guide, page 26

Laboratory Manual, pages 31-34, Solutions L3; pages 39-42, Densities of Solutions L3

Multicultural Activities, page 17, Mikhail Tsvet L1

Transparency Masters, page 29, and **Color Transparency,** number 13, The Solution Process

is called a **solute**. The substance in which the solute is dissolved is called a **solvent**. Generally, the substance present in the largest amount is the solvent. In your soft drink, what is the solute? What is the solvent? Because water can dissolve so many different solutes to form solutions, chemists often call it a universal solvent.

DID YOU KNOW?

There is a solution on the surface of your eye that helps you read this page. This solution is slightly salty and is present to keep the eye moist and to trap any dirt particles that might otherwise damage the iris.

TYPES OF SOLUTIONS

Solutions are important to all living things, as shown in Figure 7-2. Water carries dissolved nutrients to all parts of a plant. The ocean is a vast water solution of minerals and dissolved gases from Earth's crust. Medicines are often solutions of different chemicals. Some of your body fluids, such as urine and saliva, are water solutions.

FIGURE 7-2. The fluids that carry nutrients through a plant, the water in the ocean, and liquids that are used in medicines are all examples of solutions.

Concept Development

Discussion Stress the fundamental change that takes place when a solution is formed. Salt is solid and white, yet it disappears when it dissolves. This is a physical change. For all intents and purposes, the salt really *has* disappeared. It is now part of a solution with properties that are not identical to the original sample of salt. L2

Using the Photo Have students name the solute and solvent for each of the solutions shown in Figure 7-2. *Sample answers: solution in plant's vascular system—solvent: water, solutes: nutrients; ocean—solvent: water, solute: salt and other minerals; medicines—solvent: alcohol, solute: active ingredient*

Student Journal In the first Find Out, students should have observed that the cleanser ingredients change appearance but retain other original physical properties. The soap still cleans; the sugar is still sweet; the peppermint oil is still minty. In their journals, have students contrast the cleanser to a solution. *The main difference is that particles are evenly mixed in a solution.*

Teacher F.Y.I.

A glass of chocolate drink left out overnight would settle out. The same drink left out overnight in space, however, would not settle out because there would be no gravity to pull the particles to the bottom of the glass.

OPTIONS

Meeting Individual Needs

Visually Impaired Set up samples of sugar/salt/flour/starch/cotton and water mixtures for examination. Direct visually impaired students to take a pinch of each mixture between thumb and forefinger and test it for texture, viscosity, and uniformity. Encourage them to draw conclusions about the solubility of each substance. The sense of taste may also be employed.

Concept Development

Uncovering Preconceptions Stress that *solute* and *solvent* are useful terms, but they are not exact or absolute. Chemists like to think of two substances being mutually soluble. Practically speaking, it almost always makes sense to have one substance be the solute and the other the solvent. But in some situations—solutions with equal amounts of two substances—the designation of solute and solvent is entirely arbitrary.

MAKING CONNECTIONS

Daily Life

Have students keep track of the liquids they encounter in daily life. For example, on their list they might include milk, soda, vinegar, syrup, liquid medicine, shampoo, cleaning liquid, oils, gasoline, and so on. Discuss which of these liquids are solutions and which are other types of mixtures.

Content Background

The solution on the surface of the eye (see Did You Know? on page 197) is saline, the universal solution of biological systems. It is the fluid that exists around tissues, but outside the circulatory system, in the human body. Saline consists primarily of these salts: potassium chloride, sodium chloride, calcium chloride, magnesium chloride, and a phosphate buffer to keep the pH (acidity) close to neutral. The most highly concentrated salt is sodium chloride. It is interesting that proportions in human saline do not differ greatly from the salt concentrations in ocean water.

Teacher F.Y.I.

Magnesium sulfate can be found in caves in the form of masses of fine fibrous crystals, like those formed during the Investigate experiment.

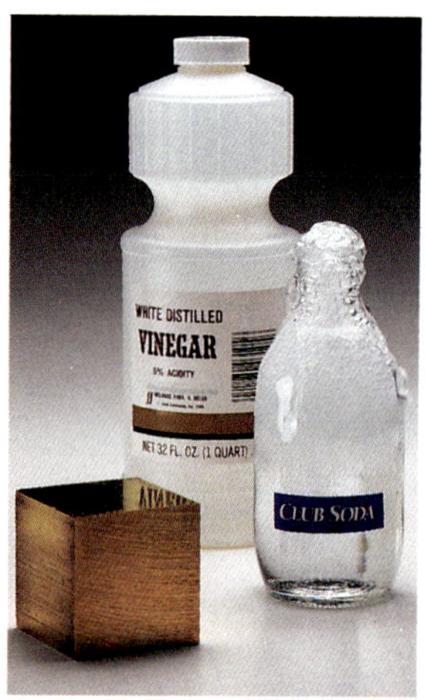

FIGURE 7-3. These are just a few examples of liquid and solid solutions.

Solutions may be mixtures of two or more solids, liquids, or gases, or any one of these in another. Some types of solutions are shown in Table 7-1. Typically, the solute is named first, followed by the solvent. For example, if the solute is a gas and the solvent is a liquid, they form a gas-liquid solution. What type of solution is lemonade that is made with fresh lemons and sugar?

Can you guess what type of solution a bottled soft drink is? If you have ever opened a bottle of soft drink, you may have noticed bubbles coming out of the liquid. These bubbles are carbon dioxide gas particles that have escaped from the soft drink—the carbon dioxide gas has come out of solution. All carbonated beverages have particles of carbon dioxide gas dissolved in them. A soft drink is an example of a gas-liquid solution.

Sterling silver is a solid-solid solution used for jewelry and tableware. Sterling silver is 7.5 percent copper and 92.5 percent silver. Recall your study of metals. Do you remember what solid solutions containing metals are usually called? Vinegar is a liquid-liquid solution, made up of 5 percent acetic acid and 95 percent water. The air you breathe is a gas-gas solution of oxygen and other gases dissolved in nitrogen.

TABLE 7-1. Composition of Solutions

	Type of Solution	Examples
Gas solution	gas-gas	air
Liquid solution	gas-liquid liquid-liquid solid-liquid	club soda vinegar sugar-water
Solid solutions	solid-solid	brass sterling silver

SEPARATING SOLUTIONS

You've separated sand and water by filtering, so you know this mixture is not a solution. Solutions cannot be separated by filtering because the dissolved particles are too small. How can solutions be separated?

OPTIONS

Enrichment

Activity Have students make and use a filtration system to investigate whether dirty (muddy) water is a solution or another type of mixture.

Materials needed are fine gravel, sand, charcoal, Styrofoam cup, dirty water.

Have students poke several holes through the bottom of the cup. Then have them layer fine gravel (1 cm), sand (3 cm), powdered charcoal (1 cm), and fine gravel (1 cm) in the cup. Finally, have them pour dirty water into the cup and compare its appearance before and after the filtering. Students can use this filtering system for other mixtures and solutions.

INVESTIGATE!

7-1 EVAPORATION AND SOLUTIONS

You've seen that solutions cannot be separated by letting them stand or by filtering. In this activity, you'll try to separate a solution using evaporation.

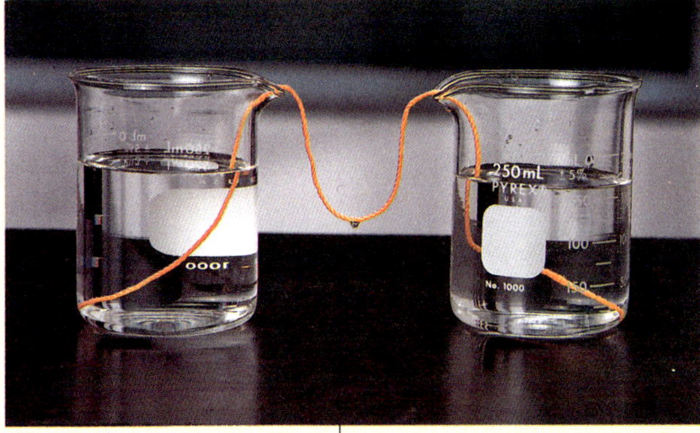

PROBLEM

Can solutions be separated by evaporation?

MATERIALS

safety goggles
Epsom salt (magnesium sulfate)
water
graduated cylinder
large beaker
spoon or stirring rod
2 small beakers
thick, water-absorbent string

PROCEDURE

1. Copy the data table.
2. **Measure** 200 mL of water into a graduated cylinder and then pour this into the large beaker.
3. Put on your safety goggles. Dissolve as much Epsom salt as you can in the water. To do this, slowly add the solute to the water until some of the solute stays undissolved after stirring.
4. Fill the two small beakers with the Epsom-salt solution. Place them side by side about 10 cm apart. Drape the string between the beakers with the ends of the string submerged in the solutions. It should be set up as in the illustration. The string should sag slightly between the beakers. Let the setup stand undisturbed for several days.
5. **Observe** the setup every few days and record your observations in your data table.

DATA AND OBSERVATIONS Sample data

DATE	OBSERVATIONS	
	BEAKERS	STRING
Each day, water level decreases and crystals build up on string in a greater amount		

ANALYZE

1. What happened to the water level in the beakers? Where did the water go?
2. What happened on the string between the beakers?

CONCLUDE AND APPLY

3. **Predict** the effect of the following changes in the outcome of this Investigation.
   a. You dissolved only half as much Epsom salts in the water.
   b. No string was placed between the beakers.
4. Which part of a solid-liquid solution evaporates, the solute or the solvent? Which part is left behind?
5. **Going Further:** Why do you think evaporation can't be used to separate gas-gas solutions?

INVESTIGATE!

7-1 EVAPORATION AND SOLUTIONS

Time needed 20 minutes

Materials safety goggles; Epsom salt (magnesium sulfate); water; graduated cylinder; large beaker; spoon or stirring rod; 2 small beakers; thick, water-absorbent string

Thinking Processes
Observing and inferring, Recognizing cause and effect, Forming a hypothesis

Purpose Determine whether solutions can be separated by evaporation.

Teaching the Activity

Discussion Since the solute and solvent in a solution are "inseparable," students might expect that they will evaporate "together" and neither will be left behind. This is a reasonable, but incorrect, assumption. L3

Troubleshooting Place beakers where they can be observed but not knocked over or disturbed throughout the experiment. Also, assign students to check that the string ends remain submerged as the liquid level goes down.

Expected Outcome

The Epsom salts are left behind. This shows that, while solutions cannot be separated by certain other mechanical means, they can be separated by evaporation.

Answers to Analyze/Conclude and Apply

1. The water level went down. The water evaporated into the air.
2. It dripped liquid and formed a white crust hanging down from the string and building up under it.
3. a. There would be less crust on the string. b. The crust would be left in the beakers.
4. solvent; solute
5. A liquid turns to gas when it evaporates. In a gas-gas solution, the solvent is already gas, so further evaporation cannot occur.

PROGRAM RESOURCES

Teacher Classroom Resources
Activity Masters, pages 29-30, Investigate 7-1

Other Resources
Solubility, software, EME.
Soluble, Programs for Learning Solutions, software, Focus.

PROGRAM RESOURCES

Other Resources
Cohen, I. Bernard. *Theory of Solutions & Stereo-Chemistry.* Salem, NH: Ayer Co. Pub., 1981.

FIND OUT!

How does particle size affect dissolving?

Time needed 10 minutes

Materials two containers, 200 mL distilled water, 12 sugar cubes, grinding instrument (cup), stirring rod, centimeter graph paper, a timing device

Thinking Processes Observing and inferring, Comparing and contrasting

Purpose Observe how the surface area of particles affects the rate of dissolving.

Teaching the Activity

Discussion Talk about surface area. The more area that comes into contact with the solvent, the easier it will be for the solute to dissolve. Note that only the *rate* of dissolving is affected by surface area, not how much sugar ultimately dissolves. L2

Troubleshooting Make sure the sugar is ground adequately. Sugar crystals should be reduced to a fine powder.

Expected Outcomes

The powdered sugar should dissolve more quickly than the sugar cubes. It should also show a much greater surface area than the cubes. Students should conclude that a solute dissolves more quickly when its surface area is increased.

Answers to Questions

1. The cubes took longer to dissolve.
2. Answer depends on size of cubes used.
3. The cubes' surface area is much less than the powder's.

Answers to Conclude and Apply

1. smaller ones
2. smaller ones

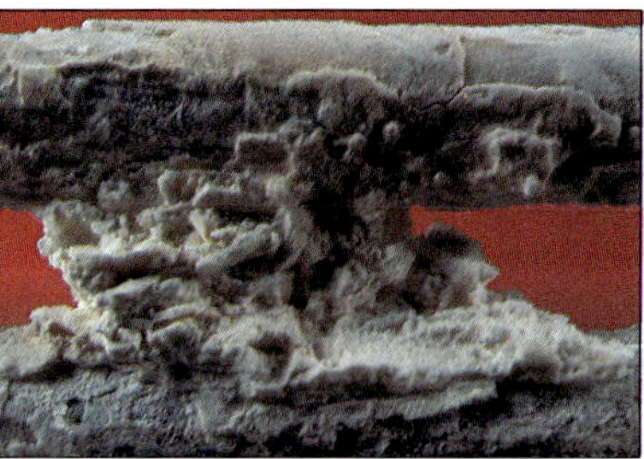

FIGURE 7-4. The material around the pipe was once dissolved in water. What kind of solution was this material in?

In the last activity, you saw that it was possible to separate the solute from a solid-liquid solution by evaporating the liquid solvent. Just how do the particles of solid and liquid mix together in the first place? How does the process of dissolving work?

DISSOLVING

Remember the last Explore activity? When you added the soft drink crystals to water, the crystals seemed to disappear. You can taste the soft drink, so you know the materials from the crystals are still there. Where did they go?

Figure 7-5 shows how dissolving occurs. In a solution, the particles of solute and solvent become evenly mixed. How do you think this happens? Earlier you learned that a solution is made up of tiny particles. Does the particle size of a solid affect how fast it can dissolve in a liquid?

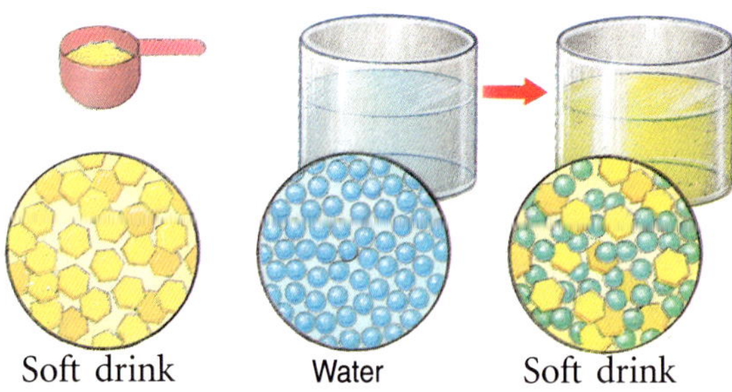

FIGURE 7-5. Soft drink crystals spread evenly throughout the water during dissolving.

FIND OUT!

How does particle size affect dissolving?

Pour 100 mL of distilled water into each of two containers. Grind three sugar cubes into a fine powder. Place this powder on a sheet of folded paper so that you can pour it easily. Have a partner place three whole sugar cubes into one container of water at the exact same time that you add the three powdered cubes to the other container. Immediately start timing. Stir both solutions.

OPTIONS

Enrichment

Activity Materials needed are widemouth 1-gallon jars and distilled water. Have students measure the amount of particulate air pollution in your area. Set jars outside, filled with about 1 inch of distilled water. Leave the jars exposed for 30 days. Then bring the jars in and heat to evaporate the remaining water. Have students calculate the total amount of dustfall per unit area (e.g., square mile). L3

Meeting Individual Needs

Learning Disabled Students might benefit from a more vivid description of the effect of an increase in surface area. Have them visualize and explain situations like these: Which soaks up more butter, an English muffin that was fork split or one that was cut with a sharp knife? (fork split) Which soaks up more paint, a smooth, sanded piece of wood or a rough piece of wood? (rough piece)

Record the times when the powdered sugar has dissolved and when the three cubes have dissolved. Which took longer to dissolve, the powder or the cubes?

Grind up three more sugar cubes. Spread the powder as thinly and as evenly as possible onto a sheet of centimeter graph paper, as shown in the illustration. Count and record how many squares the powder covers. This number is the surface area of the part of the paper that is covered, in square centimeters. The surface area of the powder is six times that of the area covered. What is the surface area of the three whole sugar cubes? How does this number compare with the surface area of the powder?

Conclude and Apply

1. Which particles seem to dissolve faster—smaller or larger ones?
2. Which particles have a greater total surface area—smaller or larger ones?

A larger surface area lets more solid solute come in contact with more solvent. Grinding or breaking up a solid solute increases the surface area of the solute, as you can see in Figure 7-6. Thus, dissolving happens more quickly when a solid solute is broken into smaller pieces. What other factors affect the rate of dissolving?

FIGURE 7-6. Breaking up a solid solute increases its surface area.

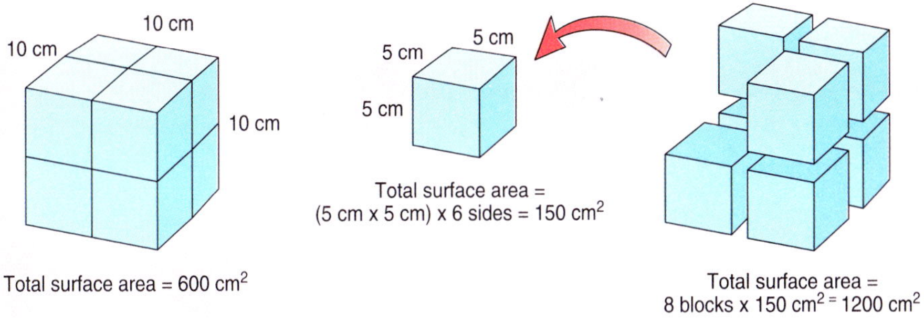

MAKING CONNECTIONS

Math

To visualize how surface area increases when substances are divided into smaller and smaller pieces, as in Figure 7-6, show these diagrams. *Diagram 1:* A single "big" cube with edges measuring 10 cm. Ask students to compute the surface area of the cube. *600 cm^2* *Diagram 2:* The same "big" cube subdivided into "little" cubes with edges measuring 1 cm. Ask: **What is the surface area of each little cube?** *6 cm^2* **How many little cubes are there?** *1,000* **What is the total surface area of all the little cubes?** *1,000 x 6 cm^2 = 6,000 cm^2*

Concept Development

Theme Connection A theme that this section supports is stability and change. The properties of solutions emerge only when they are disturbed. Observation is not enough. Only by making changes such as stirring, heating, filtering, cooling, evaporating, and so on can a true solution be distinguished from a mixture of some other type. For example, in the Find Out activity on page 203, changing the solution by shaking is used to explore the properties of a gas in solution.

Flex Your Brain Use the Flex Your Brain activity to have students explore SOLUTIONS.

Meeting Individual Needs

Learning Disabled Students may find it helpful to keep a vocabulary journal of key terms that they can refer to at all times. Each time they encounter a new word, they should record it in their journal. From this lesson these terms might be recorded: *mixture, solution, solvent, solute, physical, particle,* and *evaporation.*

PROGRAM RESOURCES

Teacher Classroom Resources

Critical Thinking/Problem Solving, page 8, Flex Your Brain

Making Connections: Across the Curriculum, page 17, Surface Area and Rate of Solution L2

SKILLBUILDER

1. Less solid will dissolve in a cool liquid than in a warm liquid.
2. More gas will dissolve in a cool liquid than in a warm liquid. L2

FIND OUT!

How do stirring (or shaking) and temperature affect dissolving?

Time needed 10 minutes

Materials four glasses, table sugar, teaspoon, stirring rod, water, ice, hot water

Thinking Processes
Observing and inferring, Comparing and contrasting, Forming a hypothesis, Recognizing cause and effect

Purpose Observe how motion and temperature affect solubility.

Preparation Make sure that each glass contains the same amount of water. Do not leave ice cubes in the ice water to melt; this will increase the amount of water in the glass.

Teaching the Activity

Discussion The important point to bring out is that stirring affects only the *rate* of dissolving, while temperature affects both the rate and the *amount* that dissolves. Have students predict what will happen before each experiment. L2

Expected Outcomes

Both heat and stirring motion increase the rate of dissolution. Students should recognize that only heat increases the solubility of sugar.

FIND OUT!

How do stirring (or shaking) and temperature affect dissolving?

Fill two glasses with water. Add 3 teaspoons of sugar to the first glass and let it sit. Add 3 teaspoons of sugar to a second glass and stir the contents rapidly. Stop stirring and let the second glass sit. What do you observe?

Fill a third glass with hot water and a fourth one with ice water. Add 3 teaspoons of sugar to each. Do not stir. In which glass does the sugar seem to dissolve more quickly? Now stir the contents of each glass. What do you observe?

Conclude and Apply

1. How does shaking or stirring affect dissolving?
2. How does temperature affect dissolving?

From the Find Out, you have discovered two more factors that affect the rate of dissolving for a solid in a liquid. Figure 7-7 shows how the solute and solvent mix together faster when stirred or shaken. You can also make the sugar dissolve faster by putting it in hot water instead of cold water.

Solids are not the only substances that can be dissolved in liquids. As you already know, a soft drink is an example of a gas dissolved in a liquid. When you shake or stir an opened bottle of soft drink, it spurts out. Why? Stirring or shaking a gas-liquid solution exposes more gas particles to the surface. These gas particles escape freely. Stirring or shaking slows down dissolving for a gas in a liquid, but speeds up dissolving for a solid in a liquid.

Shaking or stirring was only one factor that affected how quickly a gas solute dissolves in a liquid solvent. How does temperature affect the dissolving of a gas in a liquid?

SKILLBUILDER

COMPARING AND CONTRASTING
Compare and contrast the rate of dissolving (1) a solid in a liquid and (2) a gas in a liquid, when one solution is cooled while the other is kept at room temperature. If you need help, refer to the **Skill Handbook** on page 653.

Answers to Conclude and Apply

1. Stirring helps a solute go into solution faster.
2. A hot liquid will dissolve more solid solute than a cold liquid will, and it will dissolve it more quickly than the cold liquid will.

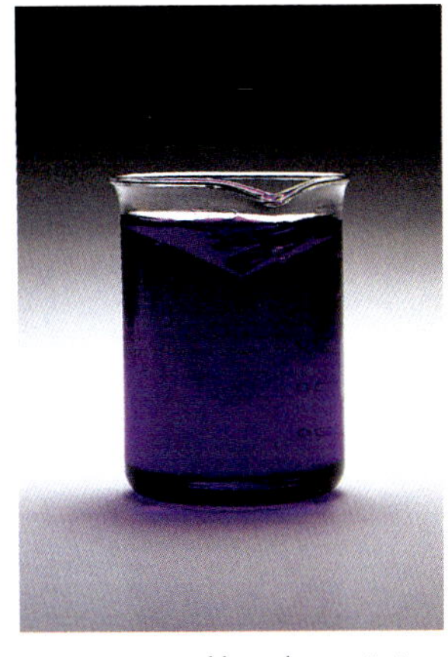

FIGURE 7-7. How does stirring speed the dissolving process?

FIND OUT!

How does temperature affect dissolving of a gas in a liquid?

Carefully open a chilled bottle of soft drink. Cover the opening with a balloon and secure it with tape. Shake the drink. **CAUTION:** *Don't point the bottle at anyone.* What happens? Repeat the procedure with an unchilled bottle of soft drink of the same size, brand, and flavor. Contrast the results from the cold and warm drinks.

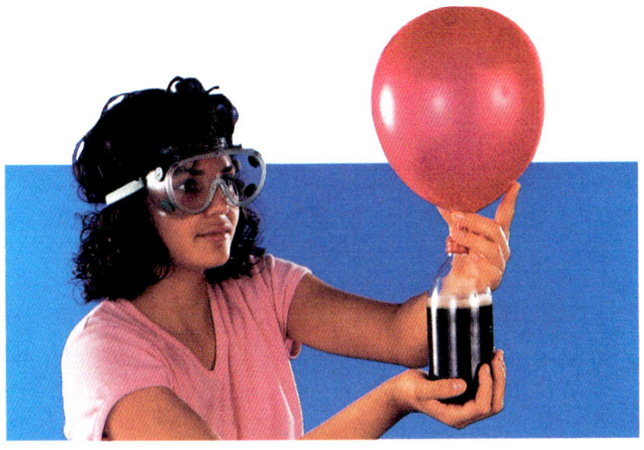

Conclude and Apply

Assuming both bottles had an equal amount of gas before they were opened, which bottle had the greater amount of dissolved gas in it after shaking?

Concept Development

Student Text Question (Figure 7-7) How does stirring speed the dissolving process? *It brings fresh solvent in contact with the solute particles.*

FIND OUT!

How does temperature affect dissolving of a gas in a liquid?

Time needed 10 minutes

Materials chilled soft drink in a bottle, unchilled soft drink in a bottle, balloons, masking or duct tape

Thinking Processes Observing and inferring, Comparing and contrasting, Forming a hypothesis

Purpose Explore the relationship between temperature and solubility of a gas in a liquid.

Preparation Any carbonated liquid in a bottle can be used.

Teaching the Activity

Discussion The undissolved gas in the liquid causes the balloons to inflate. The more undissolved gas there is, the more the balloons will inflate. L1

Troubleshooting Be sure the balloons fit snugly over the bottle openings and they are secured with tape. LEP

Safety To avoid eye injuries, the top of a bottle of carbonated liquid should never be pointed in the direction of anyone's eyes, and goggles should be worn.

Expected Outcomes

The warm liquid had more undissolved gas, so it inflated the balloon to a greater extent. Students should conclude from this that a gas becomes less soluble as the temperature increases.

Answers to Conclude and Apply
the cold soft drink

PROGRAM RESOURCES

Teacher Classroom Resources

How It Works, page 10, How They Put the *Pop* in Pop L1

Concept Mapping, page 15, Solutions L1

Making Connections: Technology and Society, page 17, Smog L1

SKILLBUILDER

The media center is colder because of air conditioning; therefore, the water in the tank will probably be colder and dissolve more oxygen gas for more fish. 

3 Assess

Check for Understanding

Discuss the Apply question with students. Then ask them what the technicians would have found if the bottle contained a solution. *no particles floating in the bottle*

Reteach

Demonstration You will need six glasses, hot and cold vinegar, egg coloring tablets, stirring rod.

Demonstrate the effect of temperature on dissolving by placing egg coloring tablets in glasses of hot and cold vinegar. Demonstrate the effect of stirring by placing egg coloring tablets in two glasses of cold vinegar. Stir the vinegar in one glass. Demonstrate the effect of surface area by placing an egg coloring tablet in a glass of vinegar and a crushed coloring tablet in an equal amount of vinegar. L1

Extension

Have students investigate the effect of boiling and freezing on the separation of a solute from its solvent. L3

4 Close

Discussion

Tell students that chlorine tablets were recently added to a swimming pool. Ask them what type of solution this makes in the pool *solid-liquid* and to identify the solute and the solvent. *chlorine; water* Then ask what would happen to the solution if the pool heater were turned on. *Chlorine dissolves more quickly.* L1

HYPOTHESIZING

You are helping set up one fish bowl in your sunny classroom and another in the air-conditioned media center. Both tanks are the same size and contain the same amount of water. Based on the amount of oxygen that can dissolve in the water, to which tank would you be able to add more fish? Explain why. If you need help, refer to the ***Skill Handbook*** on page 657.

What difference did you notice between opening a bottle of cold soft drink and a bottle of warm soft drink? The warm soft drink inflated the balloon more. This happened because when the bottles were opened and the pressure inside them was released, more gas escaped from the warm soft drink than from the cold soft drink. More carbon dioxide gas can dissolve in cold water than in warm water. The same is true for all gases. More gas can dissolve in cooler solvents.

The amount of a gas in a solvent has a very important consequence to fish and other aquatic animals. As Earth's atmosphere warms, the ocean's surfaces warm as well. What happens to the amount of oxygen dissolved in the water as the water is warmed? What effect might this have on fish, which require oxygen in order to live?

All solutions are mixtures, but not all mixtures are solutions. A solution is made up of tiny particles that are evenly mixed and do not settle out on standing. Unlike other types of mixtures, solutions cannot be separated by mechanical means. Dissolving a solute in a solvent is affected by particle size, stirring or shaking, and temperature. As you have seen, however, gas solutes are affected by these actions differently than solid solutes in the same liquid solvents. In the next section, you'll discover another way in which solutes differ.

Check Your Understanding

1. Air, vinegar, and sterling silver are three solutions. Identify which kind of solution each is. Name the solute and solvents in each.
2. You sprinkle some powdered sugar on a warm, moist, freshly baked cake. A while later you notice that the powdered sugar has disappeared. What happened to it?
3. A soup recipe calls for bouillon powder or bouillon cubes. Use of which ingredient would speed up the making of the soup? Why?
4. **APPLY:** A laboratory receives a bottle of red liquid for analysis. After it sits overnight, bits of red powder are found on the bottom of the bottle. When the lab technicians shine a light through it, the top of the beam appears pink, while the bottom half looks dark red. Small particles are floating throughout the bottle. When the technicians shake the bottle, however, these particles seem to disappear. Does the bottle contain a solution? Explain your answer.

Answers to Check Your Understanding

1. Air—gas-gas solution; oxygen and other gases are solutes; nitrogen is solvent. Vinegar—liquid-liquid solution; acetic acid is solute; water is solvent. Sterling silver—solid-solid solution; copper is solute; silver is solvent.
2. The sugar particles dissolved (or seemed to disappear) in the moisture on top of the cake.
3. Bouillon powder. Smaller solute particles dissolve faster.
4. No. A solution is a mixture of tiny particles that are evenly mixed and will not settle out. The laboratory found that the particles were large enough to be seen with a flashlight, were not evenly mixed, and settled out.

7-2 Solubility and Concentration

REACHING THE LIMIT

Most of the solutions you know about have water as the solvent. Just think of some you've worked with or read about so far in this chapter—lemonade, soft drinks, vinegar, sugar water, and apple juice. Water is the best solvent known. This means that more substances can dissolve in water than in any other liquid. Do you think that two different solutes can dissolve in water in the same amounts?

OBJECTIVES

In this section, you will

- describe how solubility varies for different solutes and for the same solute at different temperatures;
- interpret solubility graphs;
- compare and contrast saturated and unsaturated solutions;
- infer solution concentrations.

KEY SCIENCE TERMS

solubility
saturated
unsaturated
concentrated
dilute

EXPLORE!

Do sugar and salt dissolve in water in the same amounts?

Put in each of two 400-mL beakers 100 mL of water. Add 50 g of table salt to one beaker and 50 g of sugar to the other beaker. Stir both at the same rate. Compare and contrast the results. How much of each solute dissolved?

Not all solutes can dissolve in water in the same amounts. As you have just seen, more sugar than salt can dissolve in the same amount of water. How much more sugar can be dissolved than salt? Look at Figure 7-8. Only 36 g of salt can be dissolved in 100 g of water at room temperature before no more salt will go in, while the same amount of water can dissolve 204 g of sugar!

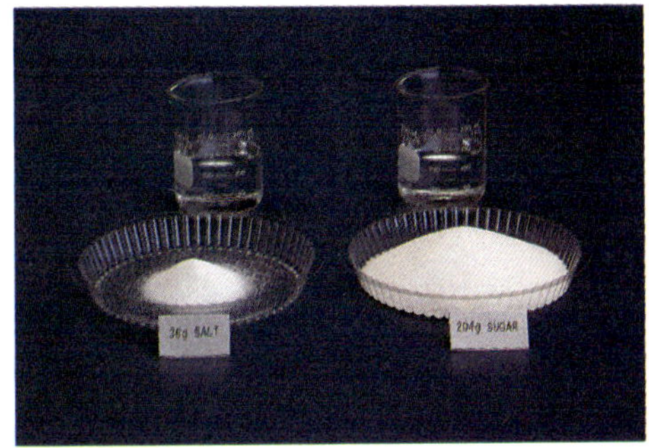

FIGURE 7-8. More sugar than salt can dissolve in the same amount of water at room temperature.

Section 7-2

PREPARATION

Concepts Developed

Students discover solubility in water and temperature's effect. The concepts of concentrated and dilute are also introduced.

Planning the Lesson

In planning your lesson on solubility and concentration, refer to the Chapter Organizer on pages 192A-B for timing suggestions, resources, and additional materials that will help you in your presentation of the lesson concepts. For adequate development of the concepts in this section, we recommend that students do the Explore activity on page 205.

1 MOTIVATE

Demonstrate You will need two large beakers or cups; graduated cylinder; water at room temperature; secret compounds: (see Table 7-2); scale; solubility graph (see Figure 7-10)

Unseen by you, have students slowly add and stir a "secret" compound into 100 mL of water in each beaker until no more will dissolve. Have them label each beaker with the amount of substance (g) dissolved in it. Now announce that you can "magically" identify each secret compound. *The solubility graph on page 207 tells you how much of each compound dissolves at room temperature (20°C).*

EXPLORE!

Do sugar and salt dissolve in water in the same amounts?

Time needed 10 minutes

Materials two 400-mL beakers, 200 mL water, 50 g table salt, 50 g sugar, stirring rod

Thinking Processes Observing and inferring, Comparing and contrasting

Purpose To compare the solubility of substances.

Teaching the Activity

Troubleshooting Stress that students handle and stir both substances in the same manner. L1

Expected Outcome

More sugar than salt dissolves. Students should conclude that only a limited amount of a substance can dissolve in a given medium and solubility is an inherent property of each substance.

Answer to Question

All the sugar dissolved, but some salt settled to the bottom.

2 Teach

Tying to Previous Knowledge

Have students recall the properties of solutions from Section 7-1. Ask them to name the three factors that affect how quickly a solute dissolves in a solvent. *particle size, temperature, and shaking or stirring* A review of the structure of solids, liquids, and gases in Chapter 5 will help students understand how solutes and solvents interact.

Concept Development

Discussion Earlier, students learned that temperature can affect the *rate* at which substances dissolve. Here, stress that temperature increases the *amount* that can be dissolved as well (for the solutes shown). Have students speculate on why some solutes are soluble and why some are insoluble. L1

Activity You will need various solvents such as turpentine, paint thinner, nail polish remover; various solutes such as sugar, salt, and paint.

In a well-ventilated place, have students compare the properties of the various solvents to water. How well do they dissolve each of the solutes? L1

SKILLBUILDER

Salt: 36 g and 36 g
Sugar: 290 g and 487 g L1

TABLE 7-2. Solubility of Various Substances

Substances	Solubility
Barium sulfate (used for X rays)	0.00025 g/100 g water
Calcium carbonate (chalk)	0.0015 g/100 g water
Lithium carbonate (ceramics)	1.3 g/100 g water
Potassium chloride (light salt)	34.0 g/100 g water
Sodium chloride (table salt)	36.0 g/100 g water
Sucrose (sugar)	204.0 g/100 g water

The amount of a substance that can dissolve in 100 g of solvent at a given temperature is called **solubility**. Table 7-2 gives the solubility of various solutes in water at room temperature.

Potassium chloride is the chemical in light table salt for people who want less sodium in their diets. What is the solubility of potassium chloride at room temperature according to Table 7-2? Thirty-four grams of potassium chloride will dissolve in 100 g of water at room temperature before no more will go in. A substance called lithium carbonate is used in making glazes for ceramics. What is its solubility in water at room temperature?

Substances that seem to dissolve in a liquid at a certain temperature to form a solution are said to be soluble. Those that do not seem to dissolve are insoluble. Solubility tables help you decide how much of a solid will dissolve at a given temperature.

In the salt solution that you just made, you started out with 50 g of salt, but not all of it dissolved. According to Table 7-2, only 36 g of the salt dissolved in 100 g of water. What do you think would happen if you poured even more salt into the solution? In solid-liquid solutions, when no more solid solute will dissolve, the extra solute settles out. You can see this happening in Figure 7-9. The solution becomes saturated because no more solute will dissolve. A **saturated** solution is one that has dissolved all the solute it can hold at a given temperature.

What happens to the solubility of a solute if the temperature changes?

MAKING AND USING GRAPHS

Copy the following data table. Using Figure 7-10, estimate the solubility (in grams per 100 g of water) of salt (sodium chloride) and sugar (sucrose) at 50°C and 100°C. Copy your answers in your data table. If you need help, refer to the ***Skill Handbook*** on page 650.

g per 100 g H_2O	50°C	100°C
Table Salt (sodium chloride)		
Sugar (Sucrose)		

OPTIONS

Enrichment  

Activity Materials needed are an oil-based paint, turpentine, a water-based paint, and paint thinner.

Have students investigate the connection between solubility and cleaning ability. Have them test the solubility of both types of paint in both solvents. Then have them apply two samples of each type of paint to a clean, dry surface and let dry. Then have them try to remove the samples with each solvent to find which removes each type of paint better. Have students explain their results. *Each substance was removed more successfully by the solvent with which it was more soluble.* **CAUTION:** *Make sure adequate ventilation is provided and students wear goggles when using these solvents.*

FIGURE 7-9. Saturated solutions cannot hold any more solute.

Solubility graphs can help you compare solubilities of the same substance at different temperatures. For example, look at Figure 7-10. The solubilities of four substances are drawn in this graph. Temperature is plotted on the horizontal axis, and solubility in grams is plotted along the vertical axis.

At any temperature, you can predict how much of a certain substance can be dissolved in 100 g of water. For example, at 60°C about 290 g of sugar (sucrose) can be dissolved in 100 g of water. How much sodium chloride can be dissolved at the same temperature? How much potassium chloride can be dissolved at this temperature? Of the substances shown on the graph, which is the least soluble at 60° C?

Look again at the graph in Figure 7-10. What happens to the solubility of a given solute as the temperature rises? If you raise the temperature of the water, you can add more potassium chloride to the solution.

What do you think would happen to a sugar solution if you heated it? Would more or less sugar solute be able to be dissolved at a higher temperature? The next activity will show you.

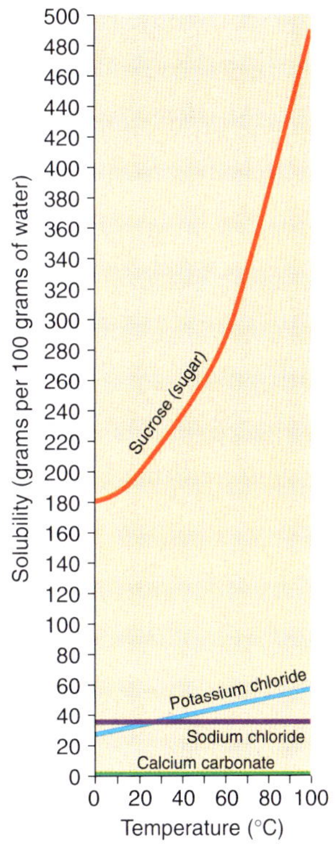

FIGURE 7-10. A solubility graph tells how much of a substance can dissolve at a given temperature.

Concept Development

Using the Diagram Show how a solubility curve forms a boundary between saturated and unsaturated for solutions. For example, at 60°C, 290 g of sucrose dissolve. The point for 60°C, 290 g, lies on the curve for sucrose. At temperatures greater than 60°C, 290 g lies below the curve, indicating that, at temperatures above 60°C, the solution containing 290 g of sucrose is still unsaturated. At temperatures below 60°C, 290 g lies above the curve, indicating saturated solutions.

MAKING CONNECTIONS

Daily Life

In making many types of candy, such as rock candy, the relative solubility of sugar in warm and cold solvents is important. When a warm, saturated sugar solution is cooled, some of the sugar will come out of solution in the form of sugar crystals.

Teacher F.Y.I.

Not all substances become more soluble as temperature increases. Calcium acetate is a substance whose solubility decreases with temperature. This means that its solubility curve will tilt downward in a negative direction. Sodium chloride (Figure 7-10) does not change with temperature, resulting in a flat solubility curve.

Multicultural Perspectives

The Mayas of Central America discovered *cahuchu,* or rubber, as far back as 500 B.C. They made rubber balls, waterproof shoes, and even chewed rubber like gum. The trouble with natural rubber was that it was too soft. It wasn't until the 1800s, when it was dissolved in solvents like turpentine, that a form of "stiff" rubber was finally created. To see how different rubber solutions are used today, examine rubber from sneakers, pencil erasers, rubber cement, foam rubber, rubber bands, and so on. Compare the stiffness and elasticity of each sample.

INVESTIGATE!

7-2 SATURATING A SOLUTION AT DIFFERENT TEMPERATURES

Time needed 30 minutes

Materials distilled water, graduated cylinder, large test tube, table sugar (sucrose), test-tube holder, laboratory balance, thermometer in a two-hole stopper, copper wire stirrer, safety goggles, beaker of water, hot plate, scoop for sugar, oven mitt

Thinking Processes Making and using graphs, Interpreting data, Measuring in SI, Observing and inferring, Recognizing cause and effect

Purpose To observe how temperature affects solubility and to construct a solubility graph.

Teaching the Activity

Troubleshooting Stress *observation* for this activity. Students need to look closely to see when crystals form. Suggest that one student watch for crystals, while a partner keeps track of temperature and recording. COOP LEARN

Discussion Discuss why adding water to the test tube changes the saturation temperature. *It changes the ratio of sugar to water in the test tube, in effect making a "new solution" that has a different saturation temperature.* L1

Expected Outcomes

The amount of sugar that dissolves in water increases with temperature. The precise relationship between temperature and solubility can be represented on a graph. This graph can be used to infer information about solubility at other temperatures.

Answers to Analyze/Conclude and Apply

1. 60°, 40°, 20°
2. 287 g at 60°, 239 g at 40°, 205 g at 20°
3. Temperature decreased.
4. Less sugar could dissolve at lower temperatures.
5. Graphs should approximate the curve for sucrose in Figure 7-10 on page 207.
6. The solubility of sugar increases as the water gets warmer.
7. 179 g, 487 g

I N V E S T I G A T E !

7-2 SATURATING A SOLUTION AT DIFFERENT TEMPERATURES

Solubility graphs predict how much solute can dissolve in a solvent at a given temperature. Solubility curves show the solubility of a solute over a wide temperature range.

PROBLEM

How does the solubility of table sugar in water change at different temperatures?

MATERIALS 

distilled water
graduated cylinder
large test tube
table sugar (sucrose)
test-tube holder
laboratory balance
thermometer in a two-hole stopper
copper wire stirrer
safety goggles
beaker of water
hot plate
scoop for sugar
oven mitt

PROCEDURE

1. Copy the data table.
2. **Measure** 10 mL of distilled water in a graduated cylinder and add it to a large test tube. Weigh 28.7 g of sugar on a balance and add it to the test tube.
3. Obtain a two-hole stopper with a thermometer in one hole. Put the copper wire stirrer in the second hole. Place the stopper in the test tube.
4. Wear safety goggles. Use the wire to stir the contents of the test tube while you heat it slowly to 80°C in a beaker of water. Shut off the heat when all the sugar has dissolved. Remove the test tube with the test-tube holder.
5. **Observe** the solution as it cools. As soon as you see crystals begin to form, record the temperature. This is the saturation temperature.
6. Now add 2 more mL of water to the tube and again repeat Steps 4 and 5.
7. Finally, add another 2 mL of water to the tube. Stir and heat the tube to 80°C until all the sugar has dissolved. Allow the tube to cool until crystals begin to form. Record the saturation temperature.
8. **Calculate** the grams of sugar per 100 g of water at each saturation temperature and volume using this formula:

$$\text{Mass} = \frac{28.7\text{ g}}{x\text{ mL water}} \times 100\text{ mL}$$

Record these masses.

DATA AND OBSERVATIONS Sample data

GRAMS OF SUGAR	ML OF WATER	SATURATION TEMPERATURE (°C)	GRAMS OF SUGAR PER 100 G OF WATER
28.7	10	60°C	287
28.7	12	40°C	239
28.7	14	20°C	205

ANALYZE

1. What were the three saturation temperatures?
2. What was the mass of sugar that dissolved at each saturation temperature?
3. How did the saturation temperature change as more water was added?
4. How did the mass of sugar that dissolved in 100 g of water change as the temperature changed?

CONCLUDE AND APPLY

5. **Graph** the solubility versus temperature for the sugar-water solution.
6. Tell how temperature affects the solubility of sugar in water.
7. **Going Further:** Determine the solubility of sugar at 0°C, the freezing point of water, and at 100°C, the boiling point of water.

208 CHAPTER 7 MATTER IN SOLUTION

PROGRAM RESOURCES

Teacher Classroom Resources

Study Guide, page 27
Laboratory Manual, pages 35-38, Solubility L3
Activity Masters, pages 31-32, Investigate 7-2
Transparency Masters, page 31, and **Color Transparency,** number 14, Solubility Graph L2
Making Connections: Integrating Sciences, page 17, Salt in the Ocean

You have just seen that the solubility of sugar increases with an increase in temperature. A cold solvent will usually hold less solute than a hot solvent will hold. As the temperature of the solvent rises, more solute will dissolve in it.

When you added the 50 g of sugar to water in the Explore, all the sugar dissolved in the water. A solution that can hold more solute at a given temperature is an **unsaturated** solution. An unsaturated solution has room for more solute particles. Each time a saturated solution is heated to a higher temperature, it may become unsaturated. The term *unsaturated* is relative, as an unsaturated solution could contain any amount of solute less than what makes it saturated at that temperature.

Suppose you make a saturated sugar solution at 60°C and then let it cool to room temperature. Part of the solute will become solid again. Why do you think this happens? Most saturated solutions behave in a similar way when cooled.

CONCENTRATION

You've already discovered that solubility is the number of grams of solute that will dissolve in 100 grams of solvent. Sometimes you do not need to know exactly how much solute is dissolved. All you may need to know is that one solution contains more solute than another solution contains.

Suppose you add one spoonful of lemon juice to a cup of water to make lemonade, as in Figure 7-11. A friend adds 4 spoonfuls of lemon juice to a cup of water. You could say that your cup of lemon water is dilute, and your friend's cup of lemon water is concentrated. It has more lemon juice than yours. A

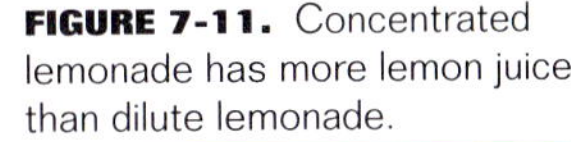

FIGURE 7-11. Concentrated lemonade has more lemon juice than dilute lemonade.

Concept Development

Uncovering Preconceptions To make a solubility graph (as in Investigate) students may ask why they couldn't just keep adding solute to water at a constant temperature until the solution became saturated. This approach would work, but it would be difficult to maintain constant temperature. To get around this difficulty, water is heated so it can hold "extra" solute. As the water cools, students can observe the saturation temperature, the exact temperature at which solute comes out of solution.

Theme Connection The theme this section supports is interactions and systems as it shows that a solution is a system composed of a solute and a solvent. As these interact, the solute continues to dissolve until the solution becomes saturated. These systems can also be described as concentrated or dilute, depending on the amount of solute compared to the amount of solvent.

Inquiry Question Why does air, a solution, feel much more humid on a hot day than on a cool day even if the relative humidity on both days is the same? *On a hot day the air can hold much more water than on a cool day.*

MAKING CONNECTIONS

Math

If students have difficulty understanding the formula on page 208, restate it as a proportion:

$$\frac{\text{dissolved sugar}}{\text{100 mL water}} = \frac{\text{28.7 g sugar}}{\text{10 mL water}}$$

To find the amount of sugar that dissolves in 100 mL, have students solve the proportion for "dissolved sugar."

OPTIONS

Enrichment

Activity You will need two cans of the same type of soda, one at room temperature and the other well chilled.

With the permission of their parents, have students perform a taste test at home to decide which tastes "fizzier" and, therefore, has more carbon dioxide gas in solution. Have students share their findings with the class and relate them to what they have learned about temperature and solubility. *The cold soft drink tastes more fizzy. Therefore, the solubility of a gas must decrease with temperature.*

3 ASSESS

Check for Understanding

A saturated solution contains 75 g of substance X dissolved in 100 g of water at 50°C. Give the answer that is most likely.

- At 60°C, will the solution be saturated or unsaturated? *unsaturated*
- At 60°C, will more substance X dissolve in the solution? *yes*
- At 60°C, how will the concentration of the solution change if more substance X is added? *It will increase.*
- At 40°C, will original solution be saturated or unsaturated? *saturated*

Reteach

Demonstration Show a pictorial version of a solubility graph. In diagram form, show several beakers, all labeled to be saturated solutions and contain 100 g of water. In the first beaker (for example), show 200 g of sugar dissolved in the water at 20°C; in the second beaker, show 220 g dissolved at 30°C. At other temperatures, show separate beakers with different amounts of sugar dissolved. L1

Extension

Have students who have mastered the concepts in this section investigate what happens when two solutes are dissolved in the same solvent. For example, what will happen if you add sugar to a solution that is already saturated with salt? Will the sugar dissolve? How much will dissolve? L3

FIGURE 7-12. Manufacturers use labels to tell you how much juice is in each package.

concentrated solution has a large amount of solute in a solvent. A **dilute** solution has a small amount of solute in a solvent.

Concentrated and *dilute* are relative terms, like *large* and *small.* But there are ways you can describe solution concentrations precisely. One way is to state the percentage of solute by volume of solvent. Have you ever read the label on a juice box to see how much actual juice is in there? Look at Figure 7-12. Suppose that the percentage of juice by volume is 90 percent. The rest is water. The other drink contains 10 percent juice and 90 percent water. Which of these two drinks is more concentrated?

What have you discovered about solubility in this section? The solubility of a solute in a solvent generally increases with temperature. Solubility tables and graphs help you predict how much of a solute will dissolve in a solvent at a given temperature. Solvents that hold as much solute as they can contain are saturated, while those that hold less solute than they can are unsaturated. Concentrated solutions contain more solute in a solvent than equal amounts of dilute solutions.

Are there any other kinds of mixtures that are *not* solutions? Yes, and in the next section you will read about two.

Check Your Understanding

1. Suppose you want to make super-sweet lemonade. You stir 2, 3, 4, or more teaspoons of sugar into a cup of lemonade, and it all disappears. But eventually you add another teaspoon of sugar, and it no longer dissolves. Why?
2. Look back at Figure 7-10. How much sugar would have to be dissolved in 100 g of water at 30°C to form a saturated solution? How much sugar would have to be added to form an unsaturated solution at the same temperature?
3. You add 1 teaspoon of lemon juice to a cup of water, and a friend adds 4 teaspoons of lemon juice to another cup of water. Into whose cup would more spoons of sugar need to be added to make the lemonade sweet? Explain.
4. **APPLY:** A chemist discovers that 5 g of Brand A perfume can dissolve in 50 g of water at room temperature, but 10 g of Brand B perfume can dissolve in 100 g of water at the same temperature. From this, she concludes that Brand B perfume is more soluble in water than Brand A. Do you think she is right? Explain your answer, using concepts learned in this section.

4 CLOSE

Have students summarize their knowledge of solubility by brainstorming how each of these factors affects how a substance dissolves.

- type of solute
- type of solvent
- temperature
- particle size
- color
- stirring
- concentration
- texture L1
- taste

Answers to Check Your Understanding

1. When no more sugar can go into solution, it means that the solubility limit of sugar in lemonade has been reached and the solution has become saturated.
2. 220 g; anything less than 220 g
3. The friend's; it is more concentrated, and would need more sugar to make it sweet.
4. No. Solubility is the number of grams of perfume that can dissolve in 100 g of water at room temperature. Because 5 g of Brand A dissolve in 50 g water, 10 g will dissolve in 100 g water. The solubilities of both brands are the same.

7-3 Colloids and Suspensions

NONSOLUTIONS

OBJECTIVES

In this section, you will

- distinguish between a colloid and a suspension;
- recognize at least two mixtures that are colloids.

KEY SCIENCE TERMS

colloid

suspension

No matter what the concentration of a solution, the particles are always too small to be seen. Because of this, gas solutions and liquid solutions are always transparent. They may be colored, like coffee, tea, or apple juice, but they are always transparent.

Think about things in a kitchen that seem to be transparent. Water, maple syrup, glass, and gelatin desserts come to mind. They are all mixtures, and they all look transparent. Are they all solutions?

EXPLORE!

Are all transparent mixtures solutions?

Make a gelatin dessert by following the package directions. Use a transparent bowl. When the gelatin has set, look at it from the side. Is it transparent? Shine a beam of light from a flashlight through the dessert. Is the gelatin still transparent? Is gelatin a solution?

When you mix water with another material, the combination meets part of the definition of a solution. It is a mixture. You can tell by looking at it whether it also satisfies a second part of the definition. Its particles are too small to see. If you're not sure, shine a light through the mixture, as you did when you made gelatin. True liquid solutions will be clear. Nonsolutions will not.

A solution will not show the path of the beam of light. Think back to when you made lemonade in the first section and shined a flashlight through the transparent pitcher. Did you see any particles? Solution particles are too small to block the light from going straight through.

A nonsolution, however, will show a clearly defined beam of light. Look at Figure 7-13. One container is filled with saltwater. The other container has gelatin dessert.

DID YOU KNOW?

Ketchup is a colloid, consisting of crushed tomatoes, spices, and sugar in water and vinegar.

Section 7-3

PREPARATION

Concepts Developed

This section follows directly from Sections 7-1 and 7-2 that focused on solutions. Here, the differences among solutions, colloids, and suspensions are explored.

Planning the Lesson

In planning your lesson on colloids and suspensions, refer to the Chapter Organizer on pages 192A-B for timing suggestions, resources, and additional materials that will help you in your presentation of the lesson concepts. For adequate development of the concepts presented in this section, we recommend that students do the Explore activities on pages 211 and 213.

1 MOTIVATE

Demonstration You will need a beaker of "clean" pond water, flashlight. Have students describe the appearance of the water in normal room light. *fairly clear* Then shine a flashlight through it and have students describe its appearance. *cloudy* Discuss why this difference occurs. *The water contains particles that are small enough to appear transparent, but large enough to be seen when a light is shined through them.* L1

EXPLORE!

Are all transparent mixtures solutions?

Time needed 15 minutes

Materials gelatin dessert, transparent bowl, flashlight

Thinking Processes

Observing and inferring, Comparing and contrasting

Purpose To investigate the properties of a colloid.

Preparation Prior to class, prepare the gelatin.

Teaching the Activity

Demonstration In contrast, you might want to shine the flashlight through a solution to show that it remains transparent. L1

Expected Outcomes

The gelatin will not be transparent when light is shined through it. Students should conclude that gelatin is not clear like a solution.

Answers to Questions

1. yes
2. no
3. no

2 Teach

Tying to Previous Knowledge

Have students review the properties of a solution and list them on the board. Be sure to include uniformity as a major property as well as transparency and the size of solute particles.

Concept Development

Theme Connection The theme that this section supports is stability and change. The composition of solutions and colloids is stable, but the composition of a suspension will change as the particles settle.

How do we know?

Scientists in the time of Zsigmondy could not explain why colloids didn't settle out like suspensions. Zsigmondy's microscope showed *structural* differences between colloids and other mixtures. This example brings to light a more general concept of chemistry: Microscopic form can be used to explain macroscopic function.

MAKING CONNECTIONS

Health

Homogenized milk is an example of a colloid that consists of tiny droplets of oil dispersed throughout a water solution. This type of colloid easily washes off your skin with water. Another type of colloid consists of tiny droplets of water dispersed throughout an oil. Hand and skin creams are this type of colloid. As such, they add oil or fat content to your surface skin and form a water-repellent surface.

FIGURE 7-13. Gelatin dessert is not a solution because its particles scatter light.

Nonsolution particles are large enough for the light to bounce off. They scatter the light, and so the beam of light can be seen. Saltwater is a solution. Gelatin dessert is not.

You have seen that not all liquid mixtures are solutions. Milk is a mixture of water, fats, proteins, and other substances. It is a mixture but not a solution. Milk is a colloid. A **colloid** is a mixture that, like a solution, does not settle out. Unlike the small particles in a solution, however, the particles in a colloid are large enough to scatter light. That is why milk looks white. Gelatin is a colloid because its particles are also large enough for light to reflect off of.

Dirty air is a colloid, too. Its particles scatter light. You have seen the scattering of light by dust particles when a beam of sunlight shines into a dark room through a slit in the curtain or a partly opened door. The dust particles, many of them too small to be seen, look like bright speckles. You do not see the individual particles. What you see is the light that is scattered by them.

How do we know?

The Ultramicroscope

Richard Zsigmondy [ZHIG mun dee], an Austrian chemist, worked at a glass factory making both clear and colored glass. Colored glass is made when different substances are mixed in melted clear glass. Zsigmondy wanted to study how particles behaved in his glass. In 1902, he developed a device that he called an ultramicroscope, shown in the figure. An ultramicroscope focuses on a colloid at right angles to the light source. The background is dark. Only the light scattered from colloid particles enters the microscope. The colloid particles can be seen not as particles with definite outlines, but as small sparkles. The device enabled Zsigmondy to see that particles in colloids are constantly moving in random, zigzag paths. This is one reason they do not settle out. In 1925, Zsigmondy received a Nobel Prize in chemistry for his work on colloids.

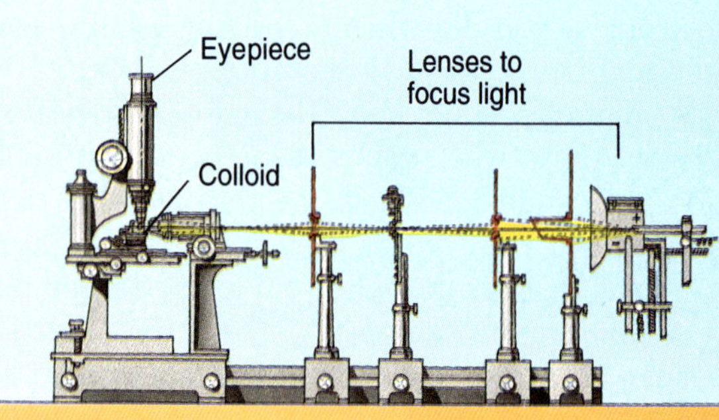

OPTIONS

Meeting Individual Needs

Visually Impaired To help these students understand how a beam of light shining through a colloid is visible when viewed at an angle of 90°, use a box or other simple object that has a right angle. Guide each student's hand along one edge of the box to represent the beam of light. Then use a perpendicular edge to represent the line of sight of the viewer.

Enrichment

Activity You will need colloid samples and a flashlight. Have students perform an experiment to determine the angle at which various colloids scatter the most light by setting up an arrangement as shown above. Have the viewer indicate when the colloid looks cloudiest. Try angles over 90° as well as under.

Some mixtures, such as muddy water, are neither solutions nor colloids. What are they called? How are they different from a solution or a colloid?

EXPLORE!

When is a mixture not a solution or a colloid?

Fill a glass with muddy water. Let the glass sit for a half hour. What do you observe? Stir the contents carefully. What do you see now? Wait a few minutes and then examine the glass again. Is the color the same throughout the glass? Now let the glass sit overnight. What do you observe the next day? Is muddy water a solution?

Muddy water is a suspension. A **suspension** is a mixture containing a liquid in which visible particles settle out. In a suspension, there are particles of solute that are larger than the particles of solvent. The force of gravity causes these particles to settle out.

As in a colloid, the particles in a suspension are not evenly mixed. In the last activity, you noticed that the muddy water turned different shades of brown, even after stirring. A suspension is different from a solution because its particles are not evenly mixed and are large enough to settle out.

How can you tell whether a mixture is a solution, a colloid, or a suspension? Look at Table 7-3. It classifies mixtures according to four basic properties.

Now you've seen how the particles in some mixtures are large enough to interfere with the movement of light through the liquid. These mixtures are not solutions. If the particles in a mixture settle out of the system, the system is a suspension. If particles of a cloudy or light-scattering system do not settle out, the system is a colloid.

EXPLORE!

When is a mixture not a solution or a colloid?

Time needed 30 minutes

Materials muddy water, glass, stirring bar

Thinking Processes
Observing and inferring, Comparing and contrasting

Purpose To investigate the properties of a suspension.

Preparation Chocolate syrup and water could be substituted for muddy water.

Teaching the Activity

Demonstration Put a solution and a colloid next to the muddy water for contrast. Note that they do not settle. Stress the role of gravity in the settling process. L1

Expected Outcome

The muddy water settles over time, proving that it is neither a solution nor a colloid.

Answers to Questions

1. The mud settles out.
2. The water turns cloudy again.
3. no
4. The mud settles out again.
5. no

Flex Your Brain Use the Flex Your Brain activity to have students explore COLLOIDS AND SUSPENSIONS.

PROGRAM RESOURCES

Teacher Classroom Resources

Study Guide, page 28

Critical Thinking/Problem Solving, page 8, Flex Your Brain; page 15, Lead in Paint

Multicultural Activities, page 18, Cheese Making L1

Take Home Activities, page 14, Separating Milk L1

SKILLBUILDER

Gas in solid—marshmallow
Solid in liquid—paint
Solid in gas—smoke
Liquid in gas—fog L1

3 Assess

Check for Understanding

After students complete the Apply question, ask them what they expect would happen to the bits of pulp if the glass of juice was in space and why. *The bits of pulp would not settle because gravity would not pull them down.*

Reteach

Guide students in developing a hierarchy including solutions, colloids, and suspensions based on how well particles "disappear." Solutions are at the top of the hierarchy, because particles appear to vanish completely in them. Colloids are next, since particles seem to disappear in them but can be viewed indirectly when they scatter light. Finally, at the hierarchy's bottom are suspensions, since the particles in them are easy to see as they settle or are separated through a filter. L1

Extension

Materials needed are milk, muddy water, clear water, beakers, heat source, and a thermometer.

Have students who have mastered the concepts in this section investigate a chemical property of colloids and suspensions by testing whether the particles in milk or muddy water make the boiling point of these liquids different from the boiling point of clear water. L3

4 Close

Activity

Have students make a Venn diagram like the one shown at the right, to present the information in Table 7-3. L1

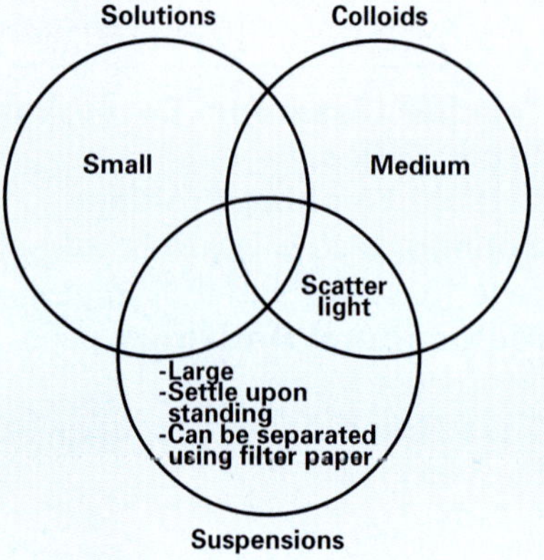

SKILLBUILDER

MAKING AND USING TABLES

Different colloids may involve different states of matter. For example, gelatin is formed from solid particles in a liquid. Copy the following table. Fill in the blanks using the common colloids smoke, marshmallow, fog, and paint. If you need help, refer to the **Skill Handbook** on page 649.

COLLOID	EXAMPLE
Gas in solid	
Solid in liquid	
Solid in gas	
Liquid in gas	

TABLE 7-3. Solutions, Colloids, and Suspensions

Description	Solutions	Colloids	Suspensions
Settle upon standing	No	No	Yes
Can be separated using filter paper	No	No	Yes
Sizes of Particles	Small	Medium	Large
Scatter light	No	Yes	Yes

Homogeneous mixtures make up a large percentage of the materials in your life. The air you breathe, the water you drink, the oceans, and even the blood that flows through your body—each contains a homogeneous mixture. In this chapter, you've explored many of the characteristics of homogeneous mixtures. You've discovered that homogeneous mixtures may be solutions, suspensions, or colloids. You probably now realize that although materials may seem very different, many of them have a great deal in common.

FIGURE 7-14. Not all suspensions occur in water. You've probably seen dust or smog suspended in air.

Check Your Understanding

1. List two examples of colloids.
2. Identify mayonnaise as a colloid or a suspension. Explain your answer.
3. **APPLY:** A glass of orange juice sits on the kitchen counter. After an hour, bits of pulp settle out on the bottom of the glass. What type of mixture does this represent?

Answers to Check Your Understanding

1. Answers may include gelatin dessert, milk, smoke, fog.
2. Colloid. Its particles are too small to be seen and do not settle out.
3. suspension

EXPANDING YOUR VIEW

CONTENTS

A CLOSER LOOK

CAN WE CHANGE THE FREEZING POINT?

Water freezes at 32°F (0°C). However, this doesn't always suit our needs. Ice may be great for hockey, but it can be disaster for someone walking on a frozen sidewalk. So, we alter our environment to suit ourselves.

Antifreeze is one such alteration in our battle against ice. We use it to melt ice on car windshields, and to prevent ice from forming in the water used to cool automobile engines. Water takes up more volume when it freezes. If water freezes in a car engine, it can expand enough to crack the engine!

By adding certain substances to water, we can lower its freezing point. Raoult's law states that the freezing point of a liquid changes with the addition of solutes, such as antifreeze. The law adds that the freezing point also depends upon the amount of substance dissolved in the liquid. So, when you add antifreeze to the water in the radiator of your car, it lowers the freezing point of the water in your radiator. The law also points out that while the freezing point of water drops with the addition of solutes, the boiling point rises.

YOU TRY IT!

Fill three small unbreakable containers with equal amounts of cool tap water. Dissolve two tablespoons of salt in one container and two tablespoons of sugar in another. Add nothing to the third container of water.

Put the three containers of water in your freezer and leave them there. Check them every hour. Which of the contents froze first? second? last? Explain your observations.

When antifreeze is mentioned, most people think of liquids, such as ethylene glycol, poured in radiators to prevent freezing. However, salt is another substance that lowers water's freezing point and is used to melt snow on sidewalks. Like commercial antifreeze, the more salt that is added, the lower the freezing point.

Using Expanding Your View

Assign one or more of these excursions to expand your students' understanding of matter in solutions and how it applies to other sciences and other subjects. You may assign these as small group or individual activities.

A CLOSER LOOK

Purpose A Closer Look reinforces the relation between temperature and solubility presented in Section 7-2 by showing how an antifreeze solute changes the freezing point of water.

Content Background There are several properties of solutions which depend on the concentration of the solute. These are called collective or colligative properties. The four colligative properties are vapor pressure lowering, boiling point elevation, freezing point depression, and osmotic pressure. When added to a solvent, any solute without vapor pressure will lower the solvent's vapor pressure. This is stated in Raoult's law. When the vapor pressure is lowered, two things occur—the boiling point is raised and the freezing point is lowered. Antifreeze added to a vehicle's radiator water accomplishes both these ends.

Demonstration To demonstrate that anti-freeze also affects the boiling point of a liquid, fill two large test tubes with water. Add five or six drops of a commercial antifreeze to one test tube. Heat both test tubes at the same time until one begins to boil. Students should observe that the plain water boils first because the addition of solute raised the boiling point of the other solution.

Going Further Have students work in small groups to explore another property of some liquid-liquid solutions. Have them combine 100 mL of water with another 100 mL of water in a 200 mL graduated cylinder. Then have them combine 100 mL of water with 100 mL of ethanol in another 200 mL graduated cylinder. Compare the results. Students should find that the alcohol-water solution yields a smaller volume (about 5 or 6 mL less) than the water-water solution. This is because the particles fit closer together in the alcohol-water solution. COOP LEARN

Students can research the effects of thermal pollution—environmental temperature change—on fish. What happens to the concentration of oxygen in the heated water released into lakes and rivers by industry? Ask student volunteers to present their findings and hold a class discussion about how these discharges could be changed or reduced so as to be less dangerous to marine life.

Answer to YOU TRY IT

Plain water; sugar water; salt water; substances added to water lower its freezing point, and different substances lower it different amounts.

LIFE SCIENCE CONNECTION

Purpose The Life Science Connection extends Section 7-2 by explaining the importance of a balanced sodium chloride concentration inside and outside of blood cells.

Content Background The process by which a semi-permeable membrane allows solvent molecules from a dilute solution to pass through to a more concentrated solution is called osmosis.

Osmotic pressure is an unbalanced concentration that triggers osmosis. Two solutions of equal concentration, and thus equal pressure, are called isotonic. Where concentrations differ, the more concentrated solution is called hypertonic and the less concentrated, hypotonic. This can be related to fluids in the body's cells. It also applies to processes in nature. When plants lose moisture to the air, their solute concentrations increase. Then, osmotic pressure forces water up through the stems or branches until the concentration is reduced and the osmotic pressure is in balance. The body attempts to balance the sodium chloride concentration within and around the blood cells.

Teaching Strategy Have students consider how the body perspires during exercise. Then show them one or two commercially available products that athletes drink during and after exercise. Read the ingredients label and point out that some of these are solutions or compounds that the body loses through perspiration. Lead students to conclude these products restore proper fluid concentrations by replacing the sodium chloride lost through exercise.

Answer to

WHAT DO YOU THINK?

The cells will become dehydrated as they lose liquid to the surrounding fluid.

LIFE SCIENCE CONNECTION

KEEPING THE BALANCE

When the human body is working properly, the concentration of fluids inside its cells is the same as the concentration of fluids that surround them. For example, sodium chloride makes up slightly less than one percent of blood cells and the fluid around them. If the concentration of sodium chloride is higher outside the cells than inside, fluids ooze out of the cells and into the surrounding fluid and reduce the sodium chloride concentration there. This change could cause the cells to become short of water, or dehydrated.

On the other hand, if the sodium chloride concentration outside the cells is lower than the concentration inside the cells, the cells can become flooded with fluids. This problem can become severe enough to cause cells to burst.

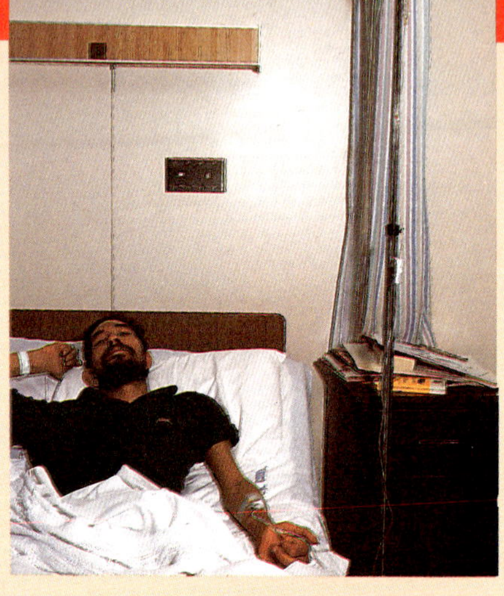

Doctors attempt to balance fluid concentrations by giving patients fluids intravenously. In this procedure, a bag containing the proper fluids is hung above the patient and allowed to drain through a tube into the patient's vein and through the bloodstream. In this way, cells are gathered in fluids containing the proper concentrations of substances.

WHAT DO YOU THINK?

How would a patient's body react if it received too much sodium chloride intravenously?

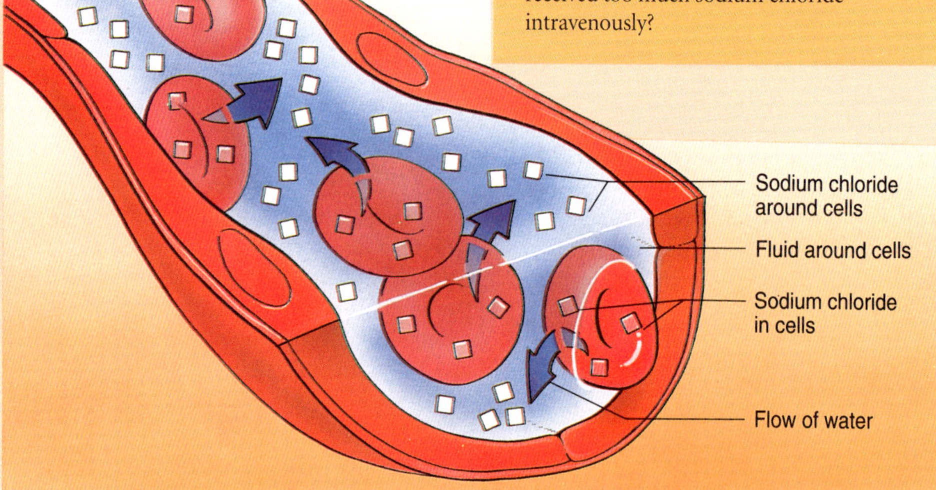

Going Further Have students discuss the role blood plays in transporting oxygen throughout the body. Once the lungs transfer oxygen to the blood, how might body temperature affect the oxygen concentration in the blood? How might breathing polluted air affect the amount of oxygen being transferred to the blood?

Have students work in small groups to research the composition of blood and what happens to fluids in the body during hemorrhaging. How does this relate to concentration levels in the blood? Then have students share their findings, accompanied by diagrams, with the class. COOP LEARN

SCIENCE AND SOCIETY

CLEANING UP THE OCEANS

You already know that the oceans are loaded with salt. But have you ever thought about other substances that are in seawater? Oceanographers and other scientists are very interested in knowing more about the contents of the oceans. Some of these experts are simply curious about the geology or the animal and plant life there. Others want to know more about the vast amounts of chemicals dumped or washed into the oceans from industrial and hospital waste.

For example, some people, including many in the United States, have dumped radioactive hospital wastes — materials from testing procedures and cobalt treatments — into the oceans. Now, concerned citizens want to know what will happen to those wastes. Will they leak from their containers and mix in the seawater? Will they harm sea plants and animals? Will contaminated seawater affect humans? Is there some way to prevent such pollution?

Mercury is another example of a dangerous industrial waste that has been dumped into seawater. In the past, shipbuilders used paint that contained mercury because the mercury prevented the growth of marine plants and animals on the hulls of ships.

Years ago, some people thought mercury could be dumped on the ocean floor without harming anyone. They figured that since the mercury would not dissolve easily in the seawater, it could be safely deposited there.

However, scientists eventually learned that chemical processes in the ocean changed the mercury so that it could get into fish. Then people eating the fish could get mercury poisoning, which can cause very serious health problems. The United States government now prohibits the dumping of wastes that contain mercury, and the use of mercury compounds in paint.

Thinking that a chemical spill or the dumping of small amounts of toxic waste wouldn't make much difference in the vast ocean, people today have made the oceans even more complex by adding such things as sewage, oil, and other pollutants. However, ocean pollution does not go unnoticed, and many countries are trying to control it through their own laws and through agreements with other countries.

In addition to chemicals,

WHAT DO YOU THINK?

You and a partner are in charge of a campaign to clean up the oceans. Think of ways that individuals and organizations can help and explain how you will promote your ideas.

SCIENCE AND SOCIETY

Purpose Science and Society applies concepts of solutes and solvents presented in Sections 7-1 and 7-2 by discussing the concentration of pollutants and trash in the ocean.

Content Background During the last century, people thought ocean resources were limitless and self-sustaining. Today we know this to be false. Numerous forms of pollution are harmful to the ocean's environment. Materials released into the water irresponsibly can interfere with the ecosystems found in the water by settling and forming undesirable deposits. Sometimes thermal pollution occurs. Radioactivity can be released. Also, some materials are broken down naturally, under normal circumstances. When they occur in excessive amounts, they build up to dangerous levels. Agriculture can compound problems by yielding pesticides and other harmful chemicals. Urban areas contribute large amounts of toxic wastes and, often, poorly treated sewage. Methods of controlling ocean pollution include governmental legislation, research into waste treatment and waste recycling, and chemical treatment of water.

Going Further Arrange a field trip to visit a local stream, lake, river, or ocean beach that needs some clean up. Upon arrival, have students note the general appearance of the area. Then have them pick up trash and place it in sacks for proper disposal. After returning, have each student write how they felt about the area when they arrived, as they worked and when they had finished cleaning up. COOP LEARN

Answers to WHAT DO YOU THINK?

Groups can hold fund-raising benefits and use the proceeds for an advertising campaign or donate it to environmental organizations. Individuals and groups can write to members of Congress or ask qualified speakers to educate the public at community meetings.

EXPANDING YOUR VIEW

Teaching Strategy Show students pictures of the Exxon Valdez oil spill and describe various methods used to contain and clean up the oil. Have students share anything they have read about this oil spill. Then discuss whether or not long-term problems will likely result from the spill and, if so, what they might be.

Activity Invite a representative of your local government to discuss water pollution problems in your town, county, or state. Then have students work in small groups and make posters that can be used to make the rest of the school or community aware of these problems and how they can be dealt with. COOP LEARN

tons of solid materials are deposited into the oceans. For example, plastics thrown into oceans pose problems because they do not easily decompose or dissolve in seawater. That means they may clutter the oceans for years, sometimes harming wildlife and frequently destroying the natural beauty of the sea.

One biologist walked 1.5 miles along the beach of a Pacific island to see how much trash he could find. He found hundreds of pieces of garbage, including 74 bottle tops, 25 shoes, 6 light bulbs, toys, cigarette lighters, and a football. The amazing thing about his discoveries was that the island was at least 3000 miles from any continent.

He knew there must be an enormous amount of trash floating in the ocean if he was able to find so much on an uninhabited island. He was so concerned about what he had found there that he wrote to a scientific journal to tell his story.

If the problem of ocean pollution is so severe, what can we do about it? The United States Congress has passed laws to control some dumping of industrial wastes into the oceans. Scientists are trying to develop ways to control environmental damage caused by accidental chemical spills, such as oil spills.

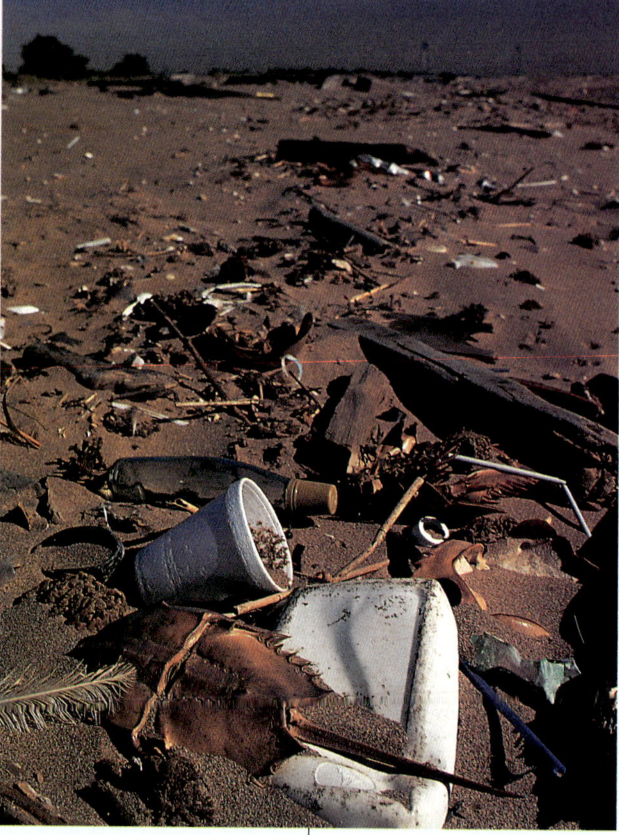

In fact, some researchers have released oil-eating organisms into the ocean to break up oil spills. Others have attempted to contain oil spills by surrounding them with barriers. Increased public concern is just as important as the research and new methods of controlling ocean pollution.

Individuals and organizations everywhere worry that pollution has gotten out of control. They're working to repair the environment by talking to their congressional representatives and even by picking up trash on beaches.

Can you name a few organizations involved in controlling ocean pollution? Do you know of individuals who are concerned about pollution?

Going Further Have students work in groups to research different environmental groups. Discuss what each group represents and how each tries to reach its goals. Do the groups act responsibly? Have groups share their findings with the class and select an organization the class would like to join. If possible, join it!

Possible groups to consider are:
- Greenpeace International
- Earthfirst!
- Sierra Club
- National Geographic Society
- Friends of the Earth
- Cousteau Society
- National Audubon Society

*L*iterature CONNECTION

DOWN TO THE SEA AGAIN

The world's largest solutions—the oceans—have inspired study and exploration throughout recorded history. Scientists and explorers have written volumes filled with ocean facts, and they continue to examine the vast solution that makes up almost three-fourths of Earth's surface.

It's no surprise, then, that the sea fascinates creative writers and storytellers as well. They have passed along their sea legends from generation to generation. Like scientists, they are inspired by the ocean's mysteries. To storytellers, the ocean may be a setting for adventure or a symbol with spiritual meaning, not a scientific problem to be solved.

Herman Melville's *Moby Dick* is one of literature's most famous examples of a story dealing with the seafarer's way of life. Other writers who have used the sea to express themselves include names you may recall: Walt Whitman, Stephen Crane, Wallace Stevens, Samuel Taylor Coleridge, and William Shakespeare.

The poem "Sea-Fever" is yet another example of sea-inspired writing. The poem was written by John Masefield, England's poet laureate from 1930 to 1967, who became a sailor when he was 13 years old. When you read the poem, you'll realize that the poet draws mainly from the visual and emotional parts of his experience.

As you read the poem, think of ways a scientist might talk about the things the poet describes. Do you think of the sea as Earth's vast solution? Or do you see it as a place of romance?

I must go down to the seas again,
To the
lonely sea and the sky,
And all I ask is a tall ship and a star to steer
her by,
And the wheel's kick and the wind's song
and the white sail's shaking,
And a gray mist on the sea's face, and a gray
dawn breaking.

I must go down to the seas again, for the
call of the running tide
Is a wild call and a clear call that may not
be denied;
And all I ask is a windy day with the white
clouds flying,
And the flung spray and the blown spume,
and the sea-gulls crying.

I must go down to the seas again to the
vagrant gypsy life,
To the gull's way and the whale's say where the
wind's like a whetted knife;
And all I ask is a merry yarn from a laughing
fellow-rover,
And quiet sleep and a sweet dream when
the long trick's over.

YOU TRY IT!

Write a short poem about a place that is special to you. Describe the sights, sounds, smells, tastes, and emotions you experienced there.

EXPANDING YOUR VIEW

LITERATURE CONNECTION

Purpose The Literature Connection discusses how the ocean, an enormous solution to scientists, has stimulated creativity in writers and poets.

Content Background Many writers have also spent time at sea as sailors and have used the knowledge gained in their writings. Herman Melville, an American author (1819–1891), not only sailed, but deserted one ship and participated in a mutiny. His sea experiences provided ideas for such books as, *Typee*, *Moby Dick*, and *Redburn*. Jack London, another American author (1876–1910), worked both as a fish patroller and as an oyster pirate. His lifestyle inspired him to become a writer. He is known for many great books such as *The Sea Wolf*. Richard Henry Dana, Jr., an American lawyer (1815–1882), tried sailing to improve his health. His *Two Years Before the Mast* is a classic. John Masefield, an English poet (1878–1967), was a naval cadet officer as a youth. He is best remembered for his collection of sea poems. The word "trick" in the last line of the poem is the time a sailor spends at the pilot's wheel steering the ship.

Teaching Strategy Have each student bring a brief poem or essay relating to the sea to class. Read them in small groups and discuss the emotions they excite. COOP LEARN

Activity Have students list five properties of the ocean that they feel inspired so many writers. Do these properties describe the physical characteristics of a solution? Can any other solution evoke such emotion as the oceans can?

Going Further Have students work in small groups to research sea explorers and their discoveries from one of the following countries: Portugal, Spain, The Netherlands, England, France, and United States. Then have each group prepare journals as if it had accompanied one of the explorers researched. COOP LEARN

Have students locate and share poems, essays, or songs that relate to rivers. Discuss which emotions the authors evoked. Possible authors include Mark Twain, Paul Horgan, Stephen Foster, and John Masefield.

EXPANDING YOUR VIEW

SOCIOLOGY CONNECTION

Purpose The Sociology Connection applies the information about concentrations in Section 7-2 by discussing what happens to a body of water in which the salt concentration is constantly increasing.

Content Background There are several types of salts. Normal salts contain no ions which will cause an acid or base reaction in a solution. Acid salts contain some hydrogen ions, which can act as an acid in a reaction. Basic salts contain hydroxide ions. These salts are called simple salts. So-called double and complex salts in solution will usually yield metal ions.

Salt comprises about two-thirds of the dissolved solids in ocean water, or about 2.8 percent by weight. The composition of the Great Salt Lake is about 15 percent by weight. The concentration of the Dead Sea in the Middle East is double that of the Great Salt Lake. Salt is often found in the form of salt domes on land. Large deposits are found in Louisiana and Texas in the United States and in several European countries. Many other countries produce salt by sea water evaporation.

Teaching Strategy Historically, salt was a common medium of exchange. It was often the main type of tradegood carried on ancient caravan routes. Have students discuss the reasons for the importance and value of salt in early societies. Consider the difficulty of travel and transportation and the location of major sources of production.

Answer to

WHAT DO YOU THINK?

It gets little fresh water while at the same time evaporation continues to cause a higher concentration of salt.

Sociology CONNECTION

SO YOU THINK THE OCEAN IS SALTY!

What do you think happens when rivers flow into a sea that doesn't drain, but instead loses a lot of its water through evaporation?

You may have guessed that the concentration of salt in the sea increases with time.

The Great Salt Lake of Utah is a well-known salt sea that has grown so salty that it has become a tourist attraction and a source of various natural resources.

Business people have sold salt taken from the lake. At first, some of them found dried salt on the shore and hauled it away. The problem with that method, however, was removing the mud gathered along with the salt.

Later, some ambitious folks boiled the salty water in large containers until they were left with salt they could sell. Unfortunately they were also left with other chemicals that had been dissolved in the water. However, salt was not always easy to come by in those days, so slightly contaminated salt was more acceptable then than it would be today.

In some cases, salt is all too easy to collect at the Great Salt Lake. Swimmers, for example, are attracted to the Great Salt Lake because they can float on its surface with little effort. But when they return to shore, the water evaporates from their skin, leaving them covered with salt crystals.

WHAT DO YOU THINK?

Why is the concentration of salt water increasing in the Great Salt Lake?

Going Further Have students work in pairs to research other bodies of water in the world that have high concentrations of salt. In addition, have students compare salt concentrations in the four oceans. **Are there differences? What might account for this?** Students can present their findings in the form of travel posters. **COOP LEARN**

Have students work in small groups to research brackish coastal areas. Have them discuss how these are similar to and different from the ocean. **What life forms and plants exist? How delicate are these areas? What can affect the salt concentrations in these areas?** Ask them to make a poster or diorama of one of these areas. **COOP LEARN**

Chapter 7

Reviewing Main Ideas

1. Solutes dissolve in solvents to form solutions. The particles mix evenly, are too small to be seen, and will not settle out. Solutions may be made up of solids, liquids, and gases.

2. The rate of dissolving a solute in a solvent is affected by particle size, shaking or stirring, and temperature.

3. Solubility of a solution is the amount of solute that can dissolve in 100 g of solvent at a given temperature. Solutions may be concentrated or dilute.

4. Colloids and suspensions are two other types of mixtures. Colloids differ from solutions in their ability to scatter light. Suspensions are different from solutions because they have large particles that will settle out upon standing.

Chapter 7

Reviewing Main Ideas

Direct students' attention to the diagrams. Use the diagrams to review the main ideas presented in the chapter. Have them read each statement aloud.

Teaching Strategies

Have students give a "solute's-eye" view of a solute being dissolved in a solvent. Have them describe the dissolving process from a solute's perspective.

- The solute begins in a "clump" with other solute particles. What happens when they are added to water? *The clump is split up until water surrounds each particle. The solute particles become evenly spaced throughout the water. Individual particles are so small they are invisible to the eye.*
- The solvent is heated. How does heating allow more solute to dissolve? *Heating spreads out the water particles so more solute particles can fit between them. Heating also increases the energy and motion of the water particles, so they move more rapidly to surround solute particles.*
- The solution is stirred. Why does stirring increase the rate of dissolving? *It increases the number of interactions between solute particles and the solvent. Stirring helps to break up solute particles by effectively moving water particles in between solute particles.*
- The solute is ground up into small particles. Why does this increase the rate of dissolving? *It increases surface area to make more solute available to the solvent.*

Chapter Review

USING KEY SCIENCE TERMS

colloid	solute
concentrated	solution
dilute	solvent
saturated	suspension
solubility	unsaturated

For each set of terms below, choose the one term that does not belong and explain why it does not belong.

1. solute, solvent, solution, suspension
2. unsaturated, saturated, concentrated, solution
3. colloid, dilute, solubility, concentrated

UNDERSTANDING IDEAS

Choose the best answer to complete each sentence.

1. To determine the solubility of a substance, you must keep constant the ____.
   a. solvent's temperature
   b. amount of solute
   c. solute's temperature
   d. time of dissolving
2. A mixture that cannot be separated by filtering is a ____.
   a. solution **c.** solute
   b. suspension **d.** solvent
3. The only word that does not refer to concentration is ____.
   a. saturated **c.** dilute
   b. unsaturated **d.** solubility
4. In a solution, the substance present in the greatest amount is the ____.
   a. solute **c.** solvent
   b. colloid **d.** solubility
5. The factor that does not affect the rate of dissolving is ____.
   a. stirring **c.** particle size
   b. solvent temperature **d.** evaporation
6. A substance that can dissolve in a liquid to form a solution is said to be ____.
   a. dilute **c.** concentrated
   b. soluble **d.** saturated
7. The line for sodium chloride stays at the same level across a solubility graph. This means that as the temperature increases, the solubility of sodium chloride ____.
   a. increases **c.** decreases
   b. stays the same **d.** saturates
8. A glass contains a clear liquid, and some solid settled out at the bottom. The glass could contain a/an ____.
   a. colloid
   b. unsaturated solution
   c. suspension
   d. dilute solution

CRITICAL THINKING

Use your understanding of the concepts developed in the chapter to answer each of the following questions.

1. White light shining through a prism separates into a spectrum of colors. Can a colloid act as a prism? Explain.

Chapter 7

Chapter Review

USING KEY SCIENCE TERMS

Answers

1. *Suspension* does not belong because the other three terms involve true solutions and a suspension is not a solution.
2. *Solution* does not belong because it does not refer to the amount of solute in a solvent.
3. *Colloid* is the only term that does not refer to how much solute can dissolve in a solvent.

UNDERSTANDING IDEAS

Answers

1. a	5. d
2. a	6. b
3. d	7. b
4. c	8. c

CRITICAL THINKING

Answers

1. No; light can travel through a prism. A colloid scatters light but does not allow it to travel through its particles.
2. By shaking the two, you make the particles very small so they form a suspension. After a while, the influence of gravity brings the smaller particles into contact and they separate back into oil and vinegar. This is why salad dressings need to be shaken before being used.
3. More gas can dissolve in cold water; cold water may have dissolved air that gets trapped as the water freezes, causing cloudiness. Less gas can dissolve in hot water; any dissolved air was driven out of the hot water as it was heated. Less trapped gas produces clearer ice.
4. The softener in the smaller bottle is probably more concentrated, and less is needed per load.

PROGRAM RESOURCES

Teacher Classroom Resources

Review and Assessment, Chapter Review and Chapter Test, pages 29–32

Computer Test Bank, Chapter Test

OPTIONS

Cooperative Learning

Consider using Cooperative Learning in the Understanding Ideas, Critical Thinking, Problem Solving, and Connecting Ideas sections of the Chapter Review.

COOP LEARN

2. Oil and vinegar do not mix. Yet, when you pour a small amount of each in a bottle and then shake the bottle vigorously, you can make a mixture of salad dressing that will stay together for some time. Explain why you think this is possible, using the concepts learned in this chapter.

3. Gas dissolved in water can make it look cloudy. Which of these ice cubes was probably made with cold water? Which was probably made with hot water? Explain.

PROBLEM SOLVING

Read the following problem and discuss your answers in a brief paragraph.

On a rafting trip, your friend asks you if you want a cracker. Your mouth is dry, but you eat it anyway. The cracker has absolutely no taste, and you struggle to swallow it. Then you take a long, gulping drink of water. Now you eat another cracker, and it tastes delicious!

At home that evening you eat some crispy cookies. They taste okay. With a glass of cold milk, they taste much better.

Oh, no! Broccoli for dinner! You know that if you eat it quickly, you can hardly taste the broccoli. The longer you chew it, the more you can taste it.

Think about the three sets of facts just presented. Try to draw a conclusion from them. Hint: Remember what this chapter is about.

4. A large bottle of fabric softener states it contains enough softener to soften 100 loads of laundry. A different brand in a smaller bottle also states it contains enough to soften 100 loads of laundry. Explain how this can be.

CONNECTING IDEAS

Discuss each of the following in a brief paragraph.

1. Powdered drink mix forms a solution in water. Is this a physical change or a chemical change? Explain.

2. Can an element be a solution? Why or why not?

3. The moon has no water on it. Could there be solutions on the moon? Explain.

4. **A CLOSER LOOK** Salt is cheaper than antifreeze. Why do you suppose we don't put salt in the car radiator, instead of antifreeze?

5. **SOCIOLOGY CONNECTION** Why is the concentration of salt in the Great Salt Lake so high?

PROBLEM SOLVING

Answers

The crackers were tasteless until they mixed with water. The same thing happened with the cookies and milk. The broccoli was deliberately kept out of a liquid, saliva, as much as possible so it would not be tasted. An appropriate conclusion is that the flavor-producing chemicals in food can be tasted only when they are dissolved in a liquid.

CONNECTING IDEAS

Answers

1. This is a physical change because no chemical reaction has taken place, no new substance has been created, and the solute could be recovered if the solvent were evaporated away.

2. No, a solution must be composed of at least two different substances, a solvent and a solute. An element is only one substance, so it alone cannot be a solution.

3. Yes, there could be solid-solid and gas-gas solutions, neither of which involves a liquid. There could also be solid-liquid, liquid-liquid, and gas-liquid solutions that involve some liquid other than water.

4. Salt is corrosive and would destroy a car's radiator.

5. As the Great Salt Lake loses more and more of its water through evaporation, salt is left behind, increasing the concentration in the lake.

CHAPTER ORGANIZER

SECTION	OBJECTIVES	ACTIVITIES/FEATURES
Chapter Opener		**Explore!** Are there rocks deteriorating in your neighborhood? p. 225
8-1 Properties and Uses of Acids (3 days)	1. **Describe** the properties of acids. 2. **Name and compare** some common acids and their uses.	**Find Out!** What effect does a substance known as acid have on rock? p. 226 **Find Out!** How corrosive are acids? p. 228 **Explore!** What are some common acids? p. 229
8-2 Properties and Uses of Bases (3 days)	1. **Describe** the properties of a base. 2. **Name and compare** some common bases and their uses.	**Find Out!** Which materials are bases? p. 232 **Explore!** What bases can you find around you? p. 233 **Find Out!** How can you make an antacid with a base? p. 234 **Investigate 8-1:** Identifying Acids and Bases, p. 235 **Skillbuilder:** Comparing and Contrasting, p. 236
8-3 An Acid or a Base? (2 days)	1. **Analyze** a pH reading and tell what it means. 2. **Explain** what an indicator shows about acids and bases.	**Investigate 8-2:** pH Indicator, p. 239 **Skillbuilder:** Making and Using Graphs, p. 240
8-4 Salts (1 day)	1. **Observe** a neutralization reaction. 2. **Explain** how salts form.	**Find Out!** How does neutralization take place? p. 241
Expanding Your View	A Closer Look **Food Pioneer,** p. 245 Life Science Connection **Oh, My Aching Stomach!** p. 246 Science and Society **Acid Rain,** p. 247	Literature Connection **In Times of Silver Rain,** p. 248 Ecology Connection **Turning Rocks to Soil,** p. 24 Art Connection **Preserving Masterpieces,** p. 250

ACTIVITY MATERIALS

INVESTIGATE!

Page 235
safety goggles, lemon juice, household ammonia, vinegar, cola, baking soda, table salt, 6 test tubes, test-tube rack, 6 stirring rods, graduated cylinder, distilled water, 6 pieces each of red and blue litmus paper, grease pencil

Page 239
safety goggles; apron; 7 test tubes; test-tube rack; 100-mL graduated cylinder; red cabbage juice indicator; grease pencil; 7 dropping bottles with: household ammonia, clear carbonated soft drink; baking soda solution, sodium hydroxide solution, hydrochloric acid solution, distilled water, white vinegar

FIND OUT!

Page 226
5 g marble chips, 250-mL beaker, 50 mL very dilute solution of sulfuric acid (vinegar or soda water will also suffice), laboratory balance (or other exact scale), stirrer, filter paper, sink, towel

Page 228
lemon juice, apple juice, vinegar, aluminum foil, labels

Page 232
baking soda, laundry detergent, cornstarch, sugar, salt, 5 clear plastic cups, 5 pieces of paper, magnifying glass, spoon, labels, beakers, water, stirrer

Page 234
glass jar, water, 1 tsp. Epsom salt, 2 tsp. household ammonia

Page 241
10 mL ammonia, 10 mL white vinegar, 2 test tubes, litmus paper, eyedropper, stirrer

Chapter 8
Acids, Bases, and Salts

TEACHER CLASSROOM RESOURCES	OTHER RESOURCES
Study Guide, p. 29 **Critical Thinking/Problem Solving,** p. 16 **How It Works,** p. 11 **Making Connections: Science and Technology,** p. 19 **Multicultural Activities,** p. 19 **Making Connections: Integrating Sciences,** p. 19	**Color Transparency and Master 16,** Acid Rain ***STVS:** *Research in the Pinelands,* Ecology (Disc 6, Side 1) *Fish and Acid Rain,* Ecology (Disc 6, Side 2)
Study Guide, p. 30 **Activity Masters, Investigate 8-1,** pp. 33-34 **Making Connections: Across the Curriculum,** p. 19	**Laboratory Manual,** pp. 43-46, Acids, Bases, and Indicators
Study Guide, p. 31 **Activity Masters, Investigate 8-2,** pp. 35-36	**Color Transparency and Master 15,** The pH Scale
Study Guide, p. 32 **Multicultural Activities,** p. 20 **Concept Mapping,** p. 16 **Flex Your Brain,** p. 8 **Take Home Activities,** p. 15 **Review and Assessment,** pp. 33-36	**Laboratory Manual,** pp. 47-48, Neutralization ***STVS:** *Salt-Resistant Crops,* Plants and Simple Organisms (Disc 4, Side 2) *Treating Acid Lakes,* Ecology (Disc 6, Side 2) **Computer Test Bank**
	***STVS:** *Acid Rain and Plants,* Ecology (Disc 6, Side 2) **Spanish Resources** **Cooperative Learning Resource Guide** **Lab and Safety Skills**

***Science and Technology Videodisc Series**

KEY TO TEACHING STRATEGIES

Teaching strategies have been coded for varying learning styles and abilities. As you review teaching strategies in the margin, the following designations will help you decide which activities are appropriate for your students.

- **L1** Level 1 activities are basic activities and should be within the ability range of all students.
- **L2** Level 2 activities are average activities and should be within the ability range of the average to above-average student.
- **L3** Level 3 activities are challenging activities designed for the ability range of above-average students.
- **LEP** LEP activities should be within the ability range of Limited English Proficiency students.
- **COOP LEARN** Cooperative Learning activities are designed for small group work.

ADDITIONAL MATERIALS

SOFTWARE

Acid Rain, AIT.
Acids and Bases, COM.
Acid Base Problems, J & S Software.

AUDIOVISUAL

All About Acids and Bases, filmstrip, Science Software.
Acids, Bases and Salts, film, Coronet/MTI Films.
Acid Rain, video, Focus.
Mr. Wizard's World: Chemical Tests, Macmillan/McGraw-Hill School Division.

Chapter 8

Acids, Bases, and Salts

THEME DEVELOPMENT

The acid-base pH system gives chemists a perspective for understanding how acids and bases, some of the most reactive and important compounds on Earth, interact and change in highly predictable ways.

The Investigate activity on page 235 demonstrates the primary theme of interactions and systems by giving students an opportunity to see how acids and bases interact with litmus paper. This interaction provides a means of identifying whether the substance is an acid or a base.

Further, in the Investigate activity on page 239, students observe the change in cabbage juice to determine pH level. This activity illustrates a secondary chapter theme, stability and change.

CHAPTER OVERVIEW

Students are first introduced to acids, their properties, and some of the important functions they have in the world. A similar introduction to bases is also presented. Students then learn how the pH scale and other indicators can be used to identify acids and bases. Finally, students are introduced to neutralization, which occurs when an acid and a base react.

Tying to Previous Knowledge

Put several drops of phenolphthalein in 100 mL of a dilute base solution such as baking soda or ammonia. The solution should turn bright pink. Present this solution to the class. Now add an acid, such as lemon juice or vinegar, drop by drop while stirring. When the solution becomes acidic, it should rapidly change to a colorless solution. Explain that phenolphthalein is an indicator dye that changes color when a solution changes from base to acid.

DID YOU EVER WONDER . . .

Why lemons taste sour?

Why a skull-and-crossbones symbol is on a can of drain cleaner?

How an antacid can settle your upset stomach?

You'll find the answers to these questions as you read this chapter.

DID YOU EVER WONDER...

Students will explore these questions as they progress through the chapter. Don't spoil their fun and motivation by sharing these answers too early.

- A sour taste is one property of an acid. Citrus fruits, including lemons, contain acid.(page 227)
- Drain cleaner contains a very strong base, sodium hydroxide, which reacts vigorously with many things, including human tissue, which it can burn. (page 233)
- The stomach contains hydrochloric acid. An upset stomach is caused by an excess of acid. An antacid is a base that neutralizes the excess acid. (page 234)

Chapter 8

Acids, Bases, and Salts

Have you ever made rubbings of old gravestones? If you place paper against a stone and rub a pencil over the surface, a pattern appears on the paper that shows the words or designs carved on the gravestone. Gravestones have a special value to scientists because they give clues about what has happened in the environment since the gravestones were placed.

You might think that what is written in stone would last forever. But that doesn't happen. Some gravestones, statues, and historical markers are slowly deteriorating. Many famous landmarks in the world are gradually being worn away. How does this happen?

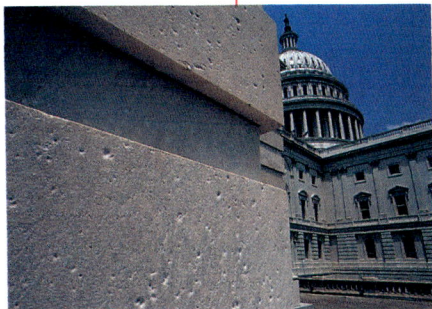

In this chapter, you will find the answer to that question and others as you learn about the chemical substances that make it happen—acids, bases, and salts. Understanding the properties of these chemicals can help you understand the problems of our environment and what some possible solutions are.

EXPLORE!

Are there rocks deteriorating in your neighborhood?

On the next nice day, explore the area around your home or school. Examine structures such as buildings, sidewalks, and streets. Visit a cemetery if one is nearby. Look for examples of deteriorating rock. What do you think could be causing the deterioration?

Introducing the Chapter

Have students look at the photograph on page 224. Have them try to state what the person is doing. *a rubbing of a gravestone* Ask students if they know of any monuments that are weathered.

Uncovering Preconceptions

Students may think rainwater qualifies as "acid rain" if it is at all acidic. Actually, natural rainwater is acidic, measuring as low as pH 5.0 on the pH scale. Acid rain can have a pH as low as 4.0 in some instances, which is ten times more acidic than unpolluted rainwater of pH 5.

EXPLORE!

Are there rocks deteriorating in your neighborhood?

Time needed 90 minutes

Thinking Processes
Thinking critically, Observing and inferring

Purpose To investigate the effects of chemicals in the air on structures made of rock.

Preparation Consult a map before the trip begins. A guidebook to the area might list structures that are old or noteworthy.

Teaching the Activity

Discussion Point out the condition of stone and concrete on some new structures for comparison.

Troubleshooting If there is not time for a field trip, present students with pictures or slides of crumbling stone structures.

Expected Outcomes

Students should observe some degree of deterioration caused by chemicals in the environment.

Answer to Question
Possible answers include acid rain and air pollution.

Project

Have students collect water samples from bodies of water. Use indicator dyes, litmus paper, or a pH meter to test the pH of the samples. Then have students add a base (ammonia) or an acid (vinegar) to the samples to see how much is needed to neutralize them. Have them estimate how much acid or base would be needed to neutralize the body of water from which the sample was taken. Students must estimate the volume of the body of water.

Science at Home

Baking soda is a base that reacts with acid and produces gas to make cakes rise. Prove this by making two small cakes, both using baking soda. Add lemon juice, vinegar, or cream of tartar to ingredients of the first cake. Use water or milk instead of the acid in the second cake. After baking, compare how much each cake rose. The first cake should be much lighter. Do not use baking powder because it already contains an acid ingredient.

Section 8-1

PREPARATION

Concepts Developed

In this section students are shown examples of the role acids play in everyday life and in industry. In addition, properties of acids (including their corrosive effects) are investigated.

Planning the Lesson

In planning your lesson on properties and uses of acids, refer to the Chapter Organizer on pages 224A-B for timing suggestions, resources, and additional materials that will help you in your presentation of the lesson concepts.

For adequate development of the concepts presented, we recommend that students do the Find Out activity on page 228 and the Explore activity on page 229.

1 MOTIVATE

Demonstration Materials needed are dilute hydrochloric acid, a petri dish, magnesium ribbon, dropper, and an overhead projector.

Wearing goggles and a lab apron, put a magnesium strip on the petri dish and place it on the overhead projector. Add a drop of hydrochloric acid. The class will be able to see hydrogen gas bubbles forming. Point out that they are witnessing a chemical reaction between an acid and a metal. L1

8-1 Properties and Uses of Acids

OBJECTIVES

In this section, you will

- describe the properties of acids;
- name and compare some common acids and their uses.

KEY SCIENCE TERMS

acids

ACIDS IN THE ENVIRONMENT

In the chapter opener, you saw how the rock of gravestones and perhaps even structures in your neighborhood can deteriorate. Do this simple activity to discover why rocks wear away.

FIND OUT!

What effect does a substance known as acid have on rock?

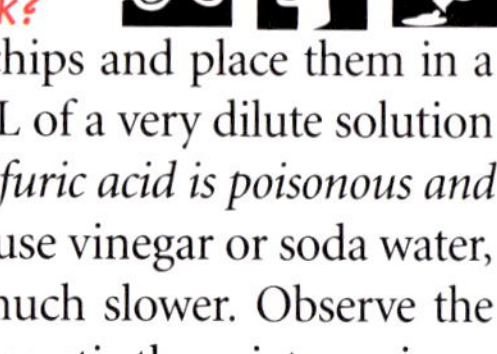

Weigh exactly 5.0 g of marble chips and place them in a 250-mL beaker. Next, add 50 mL of a very dilute solution of sulfuric acid. **CAUTION:** *Sulfuric acid is poisonous and can burn the skin.* You may also use vinegar or soda water, but the reaction time will be much slower. Observe the mixture for several minutes. Then stir the mixture vigorously and let it sit until it stops bubbling. Pour the mixture through a filter paper. Rinse and dry the marble chips and weigh them again. Has their mass changed?

Conclude and Apply

What happened to the mass that was missing from the marble chips?

DID YOU KNOW?

In the late 1800s, gold was discovered in western North America. Mistaken for gold in many areas was a mineral called fool's gold. One way to tell the difference between fool's gold and real gold was to do an acid test. An acid would dissolve the fool's gold but leave the real gold unchanged. Thus, *acid test* came to stand for a test that reveals the genuine article.

You've just discovered that sulfuric acid, or the acid in vinegar, can have a harmful effect on marble. When acids are present in the air, they react with stone and other materials and damage the environment. How do acids get into the air?

FIND OUT!

What effect does a substance known as acid have on rock?

Time needed 20 minutes

Materials 5.0 g of marble chips, 250-mL beaker, 50 mL very dilute sulfuric acid, filter paper, laboratory balance

Thinking Processes

Thinking critically, Observing and inferring, Recognizing cause and effect

Purpose To witness the reactivity of an acid.

Teaching the Activity

Discussion Talk about what the acid might do to the chips. Ask students if they have seen crumbling on buildings. Ask them to suggest the cause of the damage. L3

Expected Outcomes

The marble chips will lose mass. The students may conclude that something in the acid damaged the chips.

Conclude and Apply

The acid causes some of the marble to become part of the solution.

Many industries use coal to provide energy, but coal is impure and contains sulfur. When coal is burned, a chemical change like the kind you learned about in Chapter 5 occurs. The sulfur in the coal combines with oxygen, producing sulfur dioxide and sulfur trioxide. Remember from Chapter 6 that these new substances formed by the reaction between two elements are compounds. Automobile exhaust systems release compounds of sulfur as well as nitrogen. These compounds then combine with the water in the air. The result of all this is acid rain, which can fall hundreds of kilometers away from its source when clouds are carried by the wind.

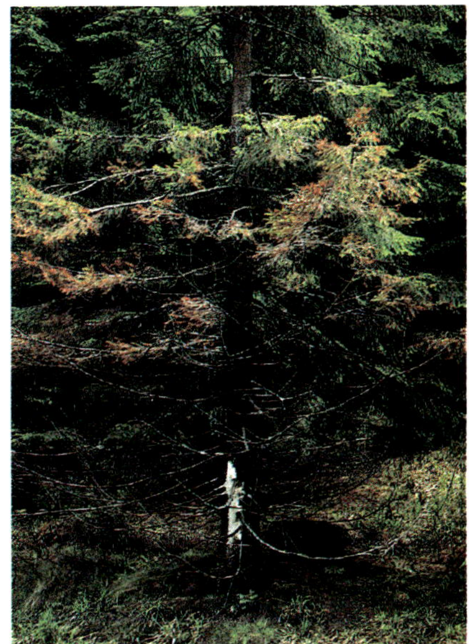

FIGURE 8-1. Acid rain caused the damage to this tree.

Acid rain may make the water in lakes unfit for fish to live. It can harm and kill plants such as the tree in Figure 8-1. In cities where acid rain falls, building materials are affected by the acid. Even hard materials such as marble can be seriously damaged. Normal rainwater does not affect marble. However, in the areas of the world with heavy air pollution, acid rain can react with marble, causing the marble to weaken and crumble over time.

PROPERTIES OF ACIDS

If you had a glass of orange juice this morning, you remember the tart taste in your mouth. A sour or tart taste is one property of an acid. The familiar sour taste of foods such as citrus fruits and tomatoes, shown in Figure 8-2, is due to the presence of weak acids.

FIGURE 8-2. Orange juice and many other foods contain weak acids.

2 TEACH

Tying to Previous Knowledge

Discuss the properties of solutions studied in Chapter 7. Point out that acids are special kinds of solutions that are very reactive. Discuss the concepts of *concentrated* and *dilute* as they relate to acids. **LEP**

Concept Development

Theme Connection Stability and change is an important theme in this chapter. Ask students how acid formed in the atmosphere changes the stability of substances on Earth when it falls as acid rain.

Content Background

Even in the most unpolluted circumstances, natural rainwater is not pure H_2O. As the rain falls through the atmosphere, it dissolves significant quantities of oxygen, nitrogen, and carbon dioxide. Carbon dioxide gives rainwater a slightly acidic character that is not harmful to humans. During electrical storms, lightning can cause oxygen, nitrogen, and water vapor to react to form significant amounts of nitric acid (HNO_3).

OPTIONS

Meeting Individual Needs

Visually Impaired Have students use their sense of touch to identify the effect of the acid on the marble chips. Place well-rinsed and dry acid-treated chips in one hand, and untreated chips in the other. Have the students describe the differences they detect in weight and texture. Place one acid-treated chip into a group of untreated ones. Ask students to locate it by touch.

Multicultural Perspectives

In the 15th and 16th centuries, scurvy was known as the "scourge of the navy," killing sizeable percentages of sailors during long voyages. North American Indians in 1534 successfully treated sick crewmen from a ship captained by Jacques Cartier. Have students research the cause of scurvy, the treatment used by the Indians, and the present treatment for scurvy. Have them identify the role of acids in these treatments.

FIND OUT!

How corrosive are acids?

Time needed 10 minutes and overnight

Materials aluminum foil, lemon juice, apple juice, vinegar

Thinking Processes
Thinking critically, Observing and inferring, Comparing and contrasting

Purpose To compare the corrosive strengths of different acids.

Preparation Make small depressions in the foil so the liquids don't run off. Other acidic liquids such as orange juice, tomato juice, and carbonated soft drink may be substituted for the acids.

Teaching the Activity

Discussion For the purpose of this activity, talk about why aluminum foil is an appropriate material on which to place acidic substances. Then ask what gas might be given off in this experiment.
 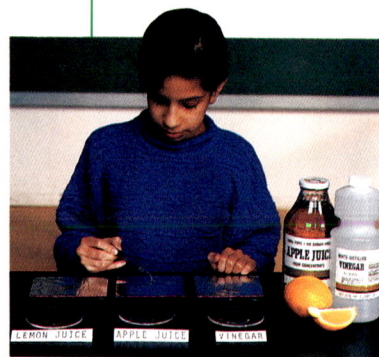

Expected Outcomes

The lemon juice will corrode the most, followed by vinegar and apple juice, respectively. The students should conclude that not all acids have the same corrosive strength.

Conclude and Apply

1. lemon juice
2. apple juice
3. It would quickly corrode the foil.
4. Possible answer: Not all acids have the same corrosive strength.

FIGURE 8-3. Acid can take its toll on a car battery.

Many acids are extremely reactive. By reacting with some metals, these acids seem to eat away, or corrode, the metal. Just look at the car battery in Figure 8-3 for an example. Corrosion is a chemical change that occurs when the acid and the metal come in contact with each other. All acids contain the element hydrogen. An acid reacting with a metal produces a metallic compound and releases hydrogen as a gas. You'll see how corrosive three acid solutions can be in the following activity.

FIND OUT!

How corrosive are acids?

With your teacher's supervision, place samples of lemon juice, apple juice, and vinegar on squares of aluminum foil. Label each square telling what kind of solution is used. Allow the solutions to stand overnight.

Observe the metal surface of each square. What do you notice?

Conclude and Apply

1. Which acid seems to be the most corrosive?
2. Which is the least corrosive?
3. Tell how you think a strong acid such as sulfuric acid would react with aluminum foil.
4. What can you conclude about acid reactions?

In the Find Out, you observed that some acids seem to react more strongly with the aluminum foil than others. You could rank them on the basis of their strength of reaction. You saw that the acids in food are safe to eat. Some other acids, however, are strong and can damage your skin or even corrode metal. That's why taste should never be used as a way to test for their presence. Acids are part of your everyday life. **Acids** are compounds that contain hydrogen, taste sour, and are corrosive.

PROGRAM RESOURCES

Teacher Classroom Resources

Study Guide, page 29

Critical Thinking/Problem Solving, page 16, Is Acid Rain a Threat? L2

Transparency Masters, page 35, and **Color Transparency,** number 16, Acid Rain L2

How It Works, page 11, Invisible Ink L2

Making Connections: Technology and Society, page 19, Cleaning Coal L2

ACIDS AROUND YOU

The acids in acid rain and in citrus fruits are just two examples of the acids around you. There are many others. Some are probably quite familiar to you.

EXPLORE!

What are some common acids?

With an adult's help, look around your home, and you will discover many familiar items that you use every day contain acids. You'll find them in foods such as juices and cottage cheese, in medicines and cosmetics, and in laundry and cleaning agents. You have probably seen or used a few of the acids listed in the table at the right. **CAUTION:** *Never taste any of these unknown acids, do not remove them from the places where they are stored, never transfer them to other containers, and never reuse the containers.* Check ingredients on labels to see if acids are listed.

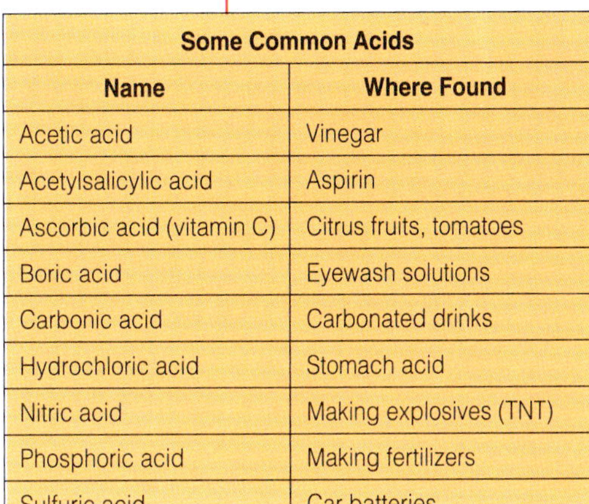

Some Common Acids	
Name	**Where Found**
Acetic acid	Vinegar
Acetylsalicylic acid	Aspirin
Ascorbic acid (vitamin C)	Citrus fruits, tomatoes
Boric acid	Eyewash solutions
Carbonic acid	Carbonated drinks
Hydrochloric acid	Stomach acid
Nitric acid	Making explosives (TNT)
Phosphoric acid	Making fertilizers
Sulfuric acid	Car batteries

With an adult's help, make a list of the kinds of acids that are in your home and how they are used. Bring your list to school and compare it with your classmates' lists. Make a class list of all the products containing acid that are used in the home.

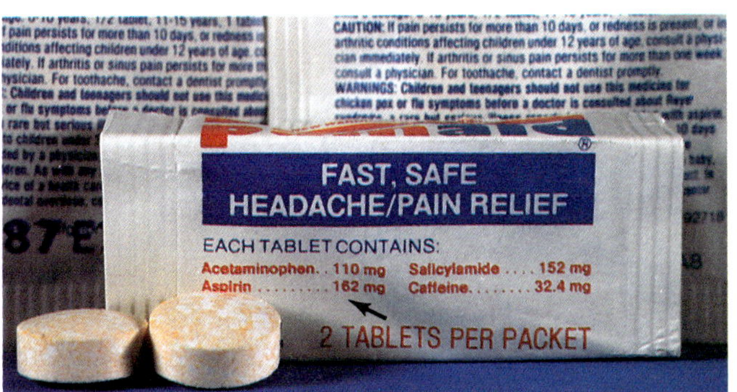

FIGURE 8-4. Labels on foods and medicines are required to list ingredients such as acids.

EXPLORE!

What are some common acids?

Time needed 30 minutes

Materials any household container that has an ingredient list

Thinking Processes Practicing scientific methods, Observing, Organizing information, Making and using tables

Purpose To develop an appreciation for the acids encountered in everyday life.

Preparation Be sure the lids are tightened on any containers that are not empty.

Teaching the Activity

Demonstration Demonstrate how to read an ingredient list (for example, ingredients are listed according to percentage, largest percentage first). Warn students that they will encounter many strange and unfamiliar terms. As an example, point out the ingredient list in Figure 8-4 and tell students that aspirin is a common acid in medicine. L1

Discussion You might encourage students to use reference books to look up the functions of various acids that they find and share them with the class. For example, phosphoric acid adds tartness to soft drinks.

Student Journal Encourage students to write about this activity. They might invent categories such as: "most unlikely substance containing acid" or "acid with most difficult name to pronounce."

OPTIONS

Meeting Individual Needs

Behaviorally Disordered Turn the Explore activity on this page into a game. Give points for each acid students discover on a label.

- 5 points for a "new" acid that hasn't been discovered on any other label
- 3 points for an acid that has already been discovered
- 2 bonus points for an acid that is listed as one of the first five ingredients in a product

Establish a certain number of points as the goal. Any student who reaches the goal can be a winner.

MAKING CONNECTIONS

Health

One of the best known acids is ascorbic acid, vitamin C. Vitamin C plays a role in the formation and breakdown of key body chemicals and the utilization of iron and calcium. Most experts recommend 30-100 mg of vitamin C per day for adults (only 10 mg are needed to prevent scurvy). Nobel winner Linus Pauling's claim that megadoses (500 mg) of vitamin C help prevent cancer is still controversial, but steadily gaining support. Detractors point out that excess vitamin C is excreted unchanged in urine. Supporters, however, point to studies that show the disease-fighting effects of the vitamin.

Concept Development

Activity Have students construct a map of your county, state, or country. On the map, have them shade in forests and bodies of water that are suspected of being damaged by acid rain. To get information on this topic, urge them to contact an environmental group, an elected representative who specializes in environmental issues, or federal, state, or local environmental agencies.

How do we know?

Hydrogen in Acids

One of the key properties of acids is that they contain hydrogen. But no one has ever seen a single acid particle. How do we know acids contain hydrogen? Thousands of reactions of acids have been studied, and in every case hydrogen has either been produced or was a key element in the reaction. In no case has hydrogen not been involved in an acid reaction.

You may have been surprised to learn how many acids you use every day. Besides aspirin, how many acids did you find that are important to your health? Ascorbic acid is often added to packaged foods to help them stay fresh longer. There are some acids that you may depend on that you never use. These industrial acids are used in the manufacture of several important products.

INDUSTRIAL ACIDS

In the last Find Out activity, you saw how some acids react with certain metals. Because of this property, acids play an important role in industry. One acid that is both a common acid and an industrial acid is hydrochloric acid. Industrial-strength hydrochloric acid is a colorless liquid that gives off strong fumes. The fumes not only can burn your skin but can also harm your lungs and eyes. The fumes react with water on the surfaces of these organs, causing severe burns. Impure hydrochloric acid, or muriatic acid as it is commonly called, is used in industry to clean the surfaces of materials such as concrete or steel. Impurities are removed from the metal surfaces by dipping the metals in hydrochloric acid, as shown in Figure 8-5.

You might be surprised to learn that hydrochloric acid also helps you digest the hamburger you may have eaten

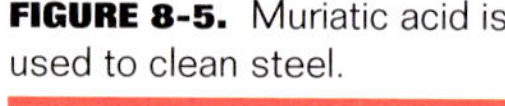

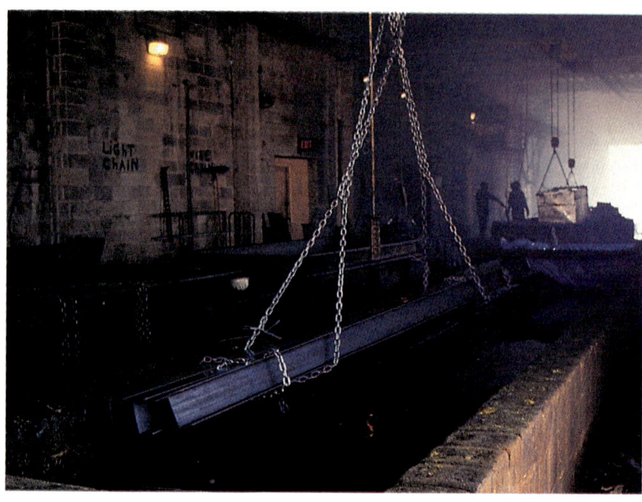

FIGURE 8-5. Muriatic acid is used to clean steel.

OPTIONS

Enrichment

Activity A well-known story states that a dentist placed a tooth in a glass of cola and found that its acid ingredients disintegrated the tooth overnight. While this tale may be apocryphal, students can investigate the "disintegration" properties of soft drinks. Have them place various objects (clay, fingernail clippings, hair, plastic, stone, pencil lead, pencil eraser, bone, and so on) in various soft drinks for various lengths of time. The effect on a piece of raw hamburger is dramatic! Have them write a report on their findings.

Students may wish to compare the effects of different colas as well.

for lunch. Hydrochloric acid in the stomach helps break down food so that it can be further digested. The stomach is protected from this stomach acid by an insoluble coating of mucus. Hydrochloric acid can make a hole in metal or a cotton cloth, yet it does not necessarily harm the lining of your stomach.

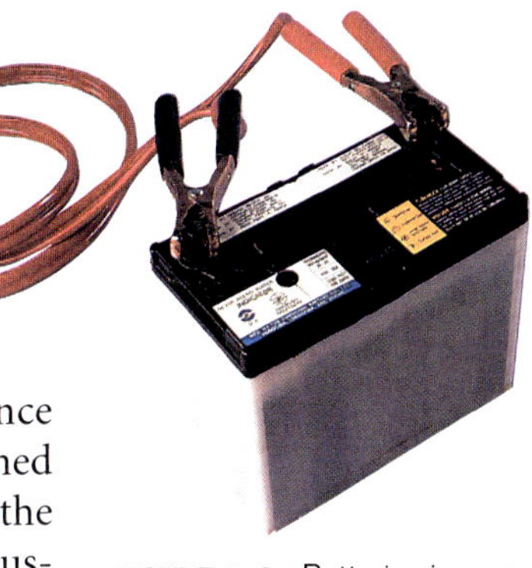

FIGURE 8-6. Batteries in cars and trucks are a major user of sulfuric acid.

Do you remember from Chapter 7 the difference between concentrated and dilute solutions? You learned about the effect of dilute sulfuric acid on marble at the beginning of this chapter. Sulfuric acid is another industrial acid commonly used in automobile batteries and is often called battery acid. Concentrated sulfuric acid is a thick, syrupy liquid that can also cause severe burns. Sulfuric acid is one of the most widely used chemicals in the world. It is used in the production of metals, fertilizers, plastics, paper and petroleum products, as well as thousands of other items. The amount of sulfuric acid a country uses is a measure of how economically advanced the country is. Over 30 billion kilograms of sulfuric acid are produced every year in the United States. Half of it is used by industries in this country, and the rest is exported.

You have seen what a useful group of chemicals acids can be. They are important to your health, but at the same time they can threaten it. Weak acids in food keep you healthy, but acid rain threatens the fish and plants you may eat and the buildings that provide you with shelter. In the next section, you will learn about another group of chemicals that can also affect your environment, but not as dramatically as acids.

Check Your Understanding

1. How are all acids alike? How do acids differ from one another?
2. From the list of acids developed by your class, name the two you use most often and tell how you use them.
3. **APPLY:** You want to store lemon slices in the refrigerator. Will you use a plastic bag or aluminum foil? Explain your answer.

3 Assess

Check for Understanding

1. Have students write *true* or *false* for each statement. If necessary, they should write a sentence or two to explain their answers.

Acids—

- have a sour taste. (T)
- should never be touched. (F)
- are common food ingredients. (T)
- have a distinctive smell. (F)
- exist in your body. (T)
- can be strong or weak. (T)
- are used in batteries. (T)
- can pollute the environment. (T)
- react only with metals. (F)
- have no practical uses. (F)

2. Have students answer questions 1-3 of Check Your Understanding. Refer to the Find Out on page 228 when discussing the Apply question.

Reteach

Some students may not grasp how one acid can destroy metal while the same amount of another acid can be a food ingredient. Compare acid strength to calories in food. Some acids are weak; some are strong. In the same way, an ounce of some foods (for example, chocolate) has more calories than an ounce of other foods (for example, carrots). L1

Extension

Have students who have already mastered the concepts in this section extend the Find Out activity on page 228 to other acids and metals. They might test the corrosiveness of acids such as those in soda pop, dissolved aspirin, and grapefruit juice on such metals as iron, steel, stainless steel, and copper. L2

PROGRAM RESOURCES

Teacher Classroom Resources

Multicultural Activities, page 19, The Sandbox Tree L1

Making Connections: Integrating Sciences, page 19, Stomach Acid L2

Answers to Check Your Understanding

1. Acids all taste sour and contain hydrogen; they differ in reactivity.
2. Sample answer: acetic acid in vinegar and citric acid in juice
3. Plastic bag. The lemon would react with the aluminum foil.

4 Close

Activity

Have students suppose that they are given a mystery substance to identify. They may ask twenty questions to determine whether the substance is an acid. Have them devise questions to arrive at a definitive answer.

Section 8-2

PREPARATION

Concepts Developed

This section introduces the students to bases by exploring their properties and identifying a few common bases. The use of an acid-base indicator is introduced. Industrial applications are pointed out to emphasize the everyday use of bases.

Planning the Lesson

In planning your lesson on properties and uses of bases, refer to the Chapter Organizer on pages 224A-B for timing suggestions, resources, and additional materials that will help you in your presentation of the lesson concepts.

For adequate development of the concepts presented, we recommend that students do the Find Out activity on page 232 and the Explore activity on page 233.

1 MOTIVATE

Demonstration This will allow students to see a base react in water.

Materials needed are sodium bicarbonate antacid, and water.

Place two antacid tablets in the water. Observe the "fizz" of the reaction. Inform students that the bubbles are gaseous carbon dioxide, formed by the reaction of sodium bicarbonate, a base, with citric acid. The resulting solution is a base with the characteristic bitter taste of a base. L1

8-2 Properties and Uses of Bases

OBJECTIVES

In this section, you will

- describe the properties of a base;
- name and compare some common bases and their uses.

KEY SCIENCE TERMS

bases

PROPERTIES OF BASES

You probably think of the word *base* as part of the game played on a baseball diamond. But bases, like acids, are an important group of chemical compounds.

You can find out more about bases by doing the following activity.

FIND OUT!

Which materials are bases? 

Measure 1 tablespoon each of baking soda, laundry detergent, cornstarch, sugar, and salt.

Place each material on a piece of paper. Using a magnifying glass, examine each sample and describe it. Rub each material between your fingers. **CAUTION:** *Do not test any unknown material by touching it.* Label each cup with the name of a material. Add each material to 300 mL of water and stir. Now touch each liquid with your fingertips. Rub your fingers together. Be sure to wash your fingers after touching each liquid.

Conclude and Apply

1. Can you identify each material by looking at it?
2. Can you identify these materials by the way they feel?
3. Do all the liquids feel the same?

Most undissolved bases are solids. When a base is dissolved in water, it feels slippery because it reacts with the oil on your skin. Which of the powders in the Find Out may have been bases? Bases also have a bitter taste, but strong bases, just like strong acids, are very reactive and can burn the skin. *Never* use taste or touch as a way to test for the presence of an unknown base.

FIND OUT!

Which materials are bases?

Time needed 15 minutes

Materials baking soda, laundry detergent, cornstarch, table sugar, table salt, clear plastic cups, tablespoons, magnifying glasses, beakers (300-mL), water

Thinking Processes
Thinking critically, Observing and inferring, Comparing and contrasting

Purpose To investigate tactile properties of bases.

Preparation Be sure to use a white powdered laundry detergent.

Teaching the Activity

Troubleshooting Fingers may remain slippery for other tests if hands are not adequately washed between tests. L1

Expected Outcomes

The baking soda and detergent solutions will feel slippery.

Conclude and Apply

1. Student answers will vary depending on how familiar students are with the products.
2. No, cornstarch and baking soda will feel similar, as will salt and sugar.
3. The baking soda and detergent feel slippery, the others do not.

BASES AROUND YOU

When you washed your face this morning, you probably used a product that has a base in it. Laundry detergents and shampoos are also bases. Bases help clean because of a very interesting property. One end of a soap, detergent, or shampoo particle is soluble in grease or dirt, while the other end is soluble in water. Therefore, the soap can pull the grease or dirt away from your skin, clothes, or hair and then be rinsed away by water. **Bases,** then, are compounds that taste bitter, are usually solids, and feel slippery when dissolved in water. Like acids, bases can be weak and not very reactive, or they can be strong and violently reactive.

You have seen that many products in your home contain acids. Bases can also be found in the many household products shown in Figure 8-7, including the soaps, detergents, and shampoos that you just read about.

FIGURE 8-7. Many household products contain bases.

EXPLORE!

What bases can you find around you?

Some common bases and the ways they are used are listed in the table. Many items in your home contain bases. With the help of an adult, find out what these items are and how they are used. One clue to look for is the word hydroxide in the name of any chemical.

Some Common Bases and Their Uses

Name	Where Found
Aluminum hydroxide	Deodorants, antacids
Ammonium hydroxide	Household cleaner (ammonia water)
Calcium hydroxide	Manufacture of mortar and plaster
Magnesium hydroxide	Laxatives, antacids
Sodium hydroxide	Drain cleaner

2 TEACH

Tying to Previous Knowledge

Discuss the properties of solutions and acids. Introduce bases not as true opposites of acids, but as their counterparts. The reason the two are connected is that (as they will learn in this chapter) acids and bases can be used to neutralize each other.

EXPLORE!

What bases can you find around you?

Time needed 30 minutes

Materials any household container that has an ingredient list

Thinking Processes Practicing scientific methods, Organizing information, Observing, Making and using tables

Purpose To develop an appreciation of the types of bases that are encountered in everyday life.

Teaching the Activity

Troubleshooting Students are more likely to find bases in products that are kept in the garage, under the sink, and in the bathroom; stay away from most edible products unless they are baked goods. L2

Student Journal Just as students wrote about common acids in their journals, have them enter the knowledge gained about common bases in their journals as well.

Expected Outcomes

Students will discover that bases are ingredients in a wide variety of household products.

OPTIONS

Multicultural Perspective

Discussion Concrete is a substance that changed the world. With it, civilizations built bridges, viaducts, roads, and buildings that have stood for thousands of years. The Egyptians were the inventors of this base-containing substance. The formula included calcium carbonate (from limestone), clay, sand and gravel. Later on, the Romans improved on the original Egyptian formula by adding volcanic ash to the mix.

Have students research the composition of concrete used today compared to that of the Egyptians. In addition, have them research the effect concrete had on Egyptian life and how it was first used.

FIND OUT!

How can you make an antacid with a base?

Time needed 15 minutes

Materials glass jar, water, Epsom salts, household ammonia, teaspoons

Thinking Processes
Thinking critically, Observing and inferring, Practicing scientific methods, Forming a hypothesis

Purpose To demonstrate how a common antacid is made.

Preparation Use household ammonia rather than a cleaner that has ammonia as one of its ingredients. L1

Teaching the Activity

Demonstration Have students compare the antacid they made with a commercially-prepared antacid.

Expected Outcomes

The substances will combine to form an antacid as evidenced by the formation of a white solid (precipitate).

Conclude and Apply

1. The solution becomes cloudy.
2. Antacid
3. Because it looks milky

Concept Development

Theme Connection Systems and interactions is an important theme in this chapter. During the Find Out and Explore activities, the interactions of bases in many household products, from cleaning solutions to antacids to fertilizers, with other materials should become evident.

DID YOU KNOW?

Before soap was commercially available, people made laundry soap from animal fats and wood ashes, which contain lye.

BASES AND YOUR HEALTH

As with acids, bases are important to your health and well-being. Blood and many other body fluids are mildly basic; that is, they contain a base. Your body would not function properly without the correct balance of acids and bases. For example, antacid tablets, which are a mild base, will reduce excess stomach acid and also help maintain the acid balance. The Find Out shows you how to make a common antacid.

FIND OUT!

How can you make an antacid with a base?  

Fill a glass jar half full of water. Stir in 1 teaspoon of Epsom salts, a base, into the water. Pour 2 teaspoons of household ammonia into the jar. *Do not stir!* Let this solution stand for five minutes. **CAUTION:** *DO NOT taste this solution. DO NOT let anyone else taste this solution.*

The chemical name for household ammonia is ammonium hydroxide. The chemical name for Epsom salt is magnesium sulfate. When these two bases react, they produce magnesium hydroxide. Magnesium hydroxide is a base found in a product called milk of magnesia.

Conclude and Apply

1. What do you observe happening?
2. What do you think the white milky substance is?
3. Why do you think it is called *milk* of magnesia?

You just read how a base can react with an acid in your stomach. By now, you may have noticed that acids and bases have several characteristics in common. How can you identify which substances are acids and which are bases? The following Investigate will show you.

PROGRAM RESOURCES

Teacher Classroom Resources

Study Guide, page 30

Laboratory Manual, pages 43-46, Acids, Bases, and Indicators L3

Activity Masters, pages 33-34, Investigate 8-1

Making Connections: Across the Curriculum, page 19, Soap 

INVESTIGATE!

8-1 IDENTIFYING ACIDS & BASES

In this activity, you will use litmus paper. Litmus paper turns blue in the presence of a base and red in the presence of an acid.

PROBLEM

How can acids and bases be identified?

MATERIALS   

safety goggles
lemon juice
household ammonia
vinegar
cola
baking soda
table salt
6 test tubes
test-tube rack
6 stirring rods
graduated cylinder
distilled water
6 pieces each of red and blue litmus paper
grease pencil

PROCEDURE

1. Copy the data table.
2. Put on safety goggles.
3. Place 2 mL of each liquid into its labeled test tube in the rack.
4. For each solid, place an amount equal to the size of a pea into the labeled test tubes. Dissolve each solid by adding 2 mL of distilled water and gently stir with stirring rod. Use a different stirring rod for each test tube.
5. Test the lemon juice with a piece of blue litmus paper by dipping a stirring rod into the juice and transferring a drop onto the litmus paper. **Observe** and record the results. Repeat the procedure using a piece of red litmus paper. **Observe** and record the results.Lemon juice is an acid.
6. Test the household ammonia in a similar manner, using red litmus paper first. **Observe** and record the results. Repeat with blue litmus paper. **Observe** and record the results. Ammonia is a base.
7. Test the remaining substances. Use separate pieces of red and blue litmus paper for each test and record your observations.

DATA AND OBSERVATIONS Sample data

	EFFECTS ON LITMUS PAPER		
SUBSTANCE TESTED	RED TO BLUE	BLUE TO RED	NO EFFECT
Lemon juice	none	x	
Ammonia	x	none	
Vinegar	none	x	
Cola	none	x	
Baking soda	x	none	
Table salt	none	none	x

ANALYZE

1. What change did you **observe** in the blue litmus paper in testing the lemon juice? In the red litmus paper?
2. What change did you observe in the red litmus paper in testing the household ammonia? In the blue litmus paper?
3. Which other substances did you **infer** were acids?
4. Which other substances did you **infer** were bases?
5. Were any substances neither acid nor base? If so, list them.

CONCLUDE AND APPLY

6. How can litmus papers be used to identify a substance as an acid or a base?
7. The water in a swimming pool is kept slightly acidic. How could you use litmus paper to check the water?
8. **Going Further: Predict** how acids and bases you identified at home would affect litmus paper.

OPTIONS

Meeting Individual Needs

Learning Disabled Students might benefit from a mnemonic device to help them remember some of the properties of bases. Have students generate a mnemonic of their own.

Bitter
And
Slippery
In
Cleaners

Have them also generate a mnemonic for litmus tests, such as aciD reD

Base
Blue

INVESTIGATE!

8-1 IDENTIFYING ACIDS & BASES

Time needed 20 minutes

Materials safety goggles, lemon juice, household ammonia, vinegar, cola, baking soda, table salt, 6 test tubes and rack, 6 stirring rods, graduated cylinder, distilled water, 6 pieces each of red and blue litmus paper, grease pencil

Thinking Processes
Thinking critically, Observing and inferring, Organizing information, Classifying, Interpreting data, Practicing scientific methods

Purpose To identify acids and bases using litmus paper.

Teaching the Activity

Discussion Have students think of these substances as having three possible "identities:" acid, base, and neutral. The litmus paper allows their true identity to be expressed. 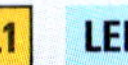 L1 LEP

Troubleshooting Point out that students should check "no effect" only in the event that *neither* color litmus paper changes its color. All acids and bases will fail to change at least one color of litmus paper.

Expected Outcomes

Acids will turn blue litmus paper red and leave red litmus paper unchanged. Bases turn red litmus paper blue and leave blue litmus paper unchanged. Neutral substances leave both papers unchanged.

Answers to Analyze/Conclude and Apply

1. It turned red; no change.
2. It turned blue; no change.
3. Vinegar, cola
4. Baking soda
5. Yes, salt
6. A substance must make one color paper change color while leaving the other unchanged.
7. Blue litmus paper should turn red if the water is acidic.
8. Acids turn bluc litmus paper red. Bases turn red litmus paper blue.

SKILLBUILDER

Similarities: corrosive, cause color changes in indicators (some bases contain hydrogen, too)
Differences: taste, feel, reactions, uses L1

3 Assess

Check for Understanding

Have students answer questions 1-3 of Check Your Understanding. Encourage students to recall the Explore activity on page 233 as they answer the Apply question.

Reteach

Ask students to list four different ways to determine whether a substance is a base. Discuss the reliability and drawbacks of each.

Taste: bitter (Somewhat reliable, but could be poisonous.)

Feel: slippery (Somewhat reliable, but could burn skin.)

Look: crystal (not very reliable)

Test: litmus or indicator (very reliable) L1

Extension

Test a weak acid and a weak base in their ability to dissolve grease. Have students who have mastered the concepts in this section obtain samples of bicycle grease. Place the grease in two dishes. Add washing soda (pH 12) to one dish to make a weak base, and lemon juice (pH 2.3) to the other to make a weak acid. Have students compare the grease-dissolving ability of each liquid. L2

SKILLBUILDER

COMPARING AND CONTRASTING

List ways that acids and bases are similar. Then list the ways in which they are different. If you need help, refer to the **Skill Handbook** on page 653.

INDUSTRIAL BASES

Ammonium hydroxide, the most widely used base, is ammonia gas dissolved in water. Pure ammonia gas has a distinctive and very irritating odor that is also present in ammonium hydroxide. You may know this base as a cleaner commonly called household ammonia. It is especially good for cleaning windows. Ammonium hydroxide is also used to manufacture fertilizers, medicines, plastics, refrigerants, and dyes.

Calcium hydroxide, commonly called lime, is often used on lawns and gardens where the soil is too acidic. Some plants need acidic soil in which to grow. Many others, however, will not grow at all in a soil that has too much acid. Calcium hydroxide reduces the acidity of the soil.

FIGURE 8-8. Household cleaners contain bases that cut grease and dissolve dirt.

Sodium hydroxide, or lye, is a very strong base that reacts rapidly with water and also breaks down grease. It is used as a drain cleaner. Because it is so strong, only a small amount is needed to open a stopped drain. It is also used in oven cleaners. Sodium hydroxide is very dangerous. Anyone using it must wear gloves and eye protection and must avoid inhaling the fumes.

The next time you take an antacid, wash your hands with soap, or use any of the products mentioned in this section, stop and think for a minute. Think about what properties the product has and why it has them.

Check Your Understanding

1. Dishwater feels slippery. What can you infer about the detergent used to wash dishes?
2. How is the structure of a base related to its cleaning properties?
3. **APPLY:** State three different uses for common bases and identify the specific base used.

4 Close

Activity

Tell students their assignment is to design a robot that can automatically test to see if a substance is a base. Have them describe: (a) what tests the robot would need to perform, (b) what materials the robot would need, (c) the sequence of movements the robot would make to perform the tests. L1

Answers to Check Your Understanding

1. It must be a base.
2. For some bases, one end of the molecule is soluble in oils and the other end is soluble in water.
3. Possible answers include household cleaning (ammonium hydroxide), antacids (magnesium hydroxide), and drain cleaner (sodium hydroxide).

OPTIONS

Enrichment

Activity Materials needed are acidic soil, lime, pots, and vegetable or flower seeds.

Have students investigate whether soil in your local area is acidic. Place the soil in two pots. Treat one pot with a recommended amount of lime. Leave the other pot untreated. Plant flower or vegetable seeds in each pot and compare the growth. Have students consult a gardening book on how to use the lime for the seeds. L3

8-3 An Acid or a Base?

THE ACID-BASE BALANCE

You have learned that acids and bases are important in keeping your body functioning properly. For one thing, you could never digest your food without the hydrochloric acid in your stomach. During digestion, the food moves from the stomach to the small intestine. Bile, which is a base made by the liver to help digest food, is then added to the acidic food mixture, making the mixture nonacidic.

On the other hand, blood is basic (that is, it contains a base), and in order for food nutrients to be safely absorbed by the blood, they, too, must be basic. If the acid-base balance in your body becomes unbalanced, you could become seriously ill.

It is important to maintain the balance between acids and bases in swimming pools and in tanks for tropical fish. You need to control the acidity of the water. To control the acidity, you need to adjust the pH by adding either acids or bases.

What is pH? **pH** is a measure that shows the acidity of a solution. The pH scale shown in Figure 8-9 is used to measure pH. Its values range from 0 to 14.

Looking at Figure 8-9, you can see that solutions with a pH value less than 7 are acidic. The lower the value, the more

OBJECTIVES

In this section, you will

- analyze a pH reading and tell what it means;
- explain what an indicator shows about acids and bases.

KEY SCIENCE TERMS

pH
indicator

FIGURE 8-9. A pH scale helps you identify acids, bases, and neutral solutions when you know their pH value.

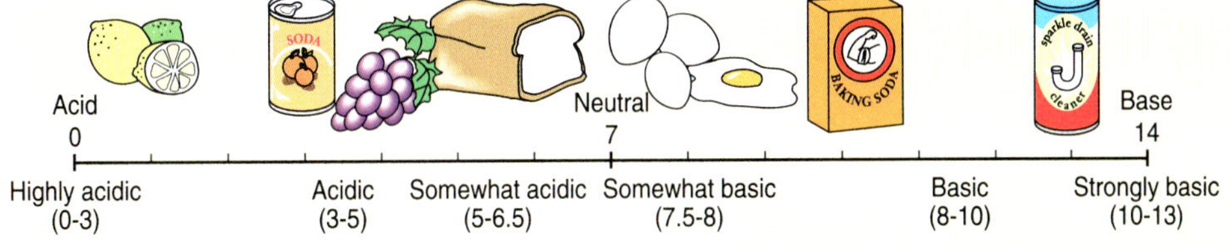

Section 8-3

PREPARATION

Concepts Developed

This section develops the idea of acids and bases as part of a continuum that runs from strong acid to strong base. The pH scale, a numeric way of representing how acidic or basic a substance is, is introduced. A rough way to estimate pH is provided by the use of pH indicators.

Planning the Lesson

In planning your lesson on acids and bases, refer to the Chapter Organizer on pages 224A-B for timing suggestions, resources, and additional materials that will help you in your presentation of the lesson concepts.

1 MOTIVATE

Demonstration Without much lead-in information, this activity will dramatically show students the reaction of an indicator in the presence of an acid and a base.

Materials needed are phenolphthalein, dilute acid, dilute base, and beaker or test tube.

Wearing goggles, put several drops of phenolphthalein in 100 mL of dilute acid. Stir thoroughly. Then begin adding base dropwise to the solution. Suddenly, when the solution reaches the basic pH range, the presence of phenolphthalein will make it turn bright pink, indicating a base is present. Explain that the phenolphthalein color change works much in the same way that litmus paper works. L1

2 TEACH

Tying to Previous Knowledge

Review the properties of acids and bases. Ask students if they think a scale that measures how acidic or basic a solution is would be useful. Then tell them they will learn about such a scale in this section.

Enrichment

Activity Have students fill several small containers with pond water. Add a different dose of ammonia to each container but leave one as a control. Do the same with dilute hydrochloric acid and another set of containers. After several weeks, have students record the growth they observe inside each container. Have them compare algae growth in the set of acidic containers and in the set of basic containers. L3

PROGRAM RESOURCES

Teacher Classroom Resources

Study Guide, page 31

Transparency Masters, page 33, and **Color Transparency,** number 15, The pH Scale L1

Concept Development

Inquiry Question Mia has 100 mL of solution that has a pH of 5. Paul has 100 mL of solution that has a pH of 3. Both solutions have equal amounts of solute dissolved in them. If the solutions are combined, Paul says that the resulting solution will have a pH of 8. Do you agree with him? If not, estimate what the pH of the combined solution will be. *A pH of 8 indicates a very slightly basic solution, but two acids together can't yield a base. The actual pH of the solution would be somewhere between 3 and 5. A pH of 4 would be a good estimate.*

Theme Connection No activity highlights the theme of stability and change more than the indicator tests performed in this section. For example, in the phenolphthalein test in the Motivate section, the transformation from colorless to pink is one of the most dramatic demonstrations in chemistry. Clearly, some real and fundamental barrier has been crossed when the solution changes color (the "base" range of the pH scale).

MAKING CONNECTIONS

Math

The pH scale measures the number of acidic hydrogen ions (H+) in a solution. The scale is set up so that a solution of pH 1 has *10 times* more hydrogen ions than a solution of pH 2, 100 times more hydrogen ions than a solution of pH 3, and so on. Have students complete this table, showing the number of hydrogen ions for a solution at each pH.

pH	H+ ions	pH	H+ ions
6	50	3	50,000
5	500	2	500,000
4	5,000	1	5,000,000

TABLE 8-1. Common pH Values

pH		Substance
Acids	1	stomach contents
	2	lemon
	3	apples
	4	tomato
	5	carrots
	6	milk
Neutral	7	drinking water
Bases	8	eggs
	9	baking soda
	10	milk of magnesia
	11	household ammonia
	12	
	13	
	14	lye

acidic the solution. This means that a solution with a pH value of 1 is very acidic. Solutions with a pH value greater than 7 are basic. The higher the pH number, the more basic the solution. The number 7 on the pH scale represents a neutral solution that is neither acidic nor basic. Pure water has a pH value of 7.

Table 8-1 lists common solutions and substances along with their pH values.

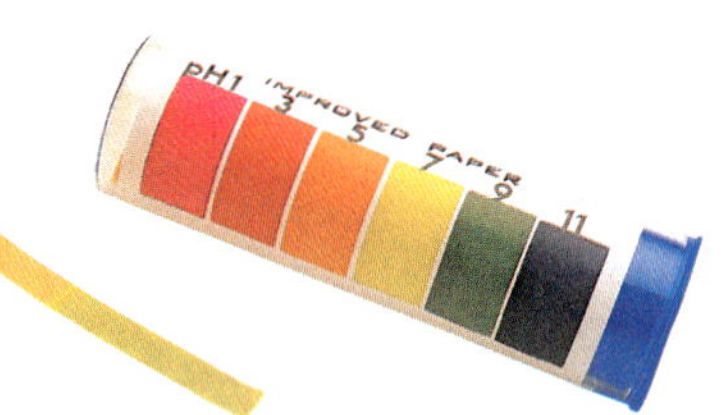

FIGURE 8-10. A color change in an indicator can be a very accurate way to determine the pH of a solution.

HOW TO FIND pH

There are several ways to distinguish between acids and bases. Acids are sour and bases are bitter. Acids corrode metal; bases are slippery. Acids turn blue litmus paper red, and bases turn red litmus paper blue.

Another way to identify acids and bases is to use a pH meter. This meter uses electrical measurements to read out precise pH values on its scale.

Still another way of determining pH is by using an indicator. An **indicator** is a substance that is one color in an acid and another color in a base. To determine pH, you match the change in color to a color chart, as shown in Figure 8-10 (a).

The activity that follows will help you become more familiar with indicators.

OPTIONS

Enrichment

Activity It is interesting to note that human taste buds have the ability to detect four different tastes—sour, bitter, salty, and sweet. Acids and bases account for two of the four tastes. To test tasting abilities of individuals, prepare samples of such things as honey, vinegar, salt solution, lemon juice, unsweetened chocolate, and so on. Blindfold students and present them with the samples. Have them rate each sample as "sour," "bitter," "salty," or "sweet." On the basis of taste, have them predict which foods might contain acids and which ones might contain bases. When they take off the blindfolds, check to see how accurate their ratings were.

Note: Before starting the taste tests, check whether students have food allergies. Also point out that these tests are only safe because common foodstuffs selected by responsible adults are being used.

8-2 pH INDICATOR

A common pH indicator found in nature is red cabbage juice. In this Investigate, you will test the pH of household liquids using red cabbage juice.

PROBLEM

How can cabbage juice indicate the relative pH of acids and bases?

MATERIALS 

safety goggles
apron
7 test tubes
test-tube rack
100-mL graduated cylinder
red cabbage juice indicator
grease pencil
7 dropping bottles with:
household ammonia
clear carbonated soft drink
baking soda solution
sodium hydroxide solution
hydrochloric acid solution
distilled water
white vinegar

PROCEDURE

1. Copy the data table.
2. Wear an apron and goggles. Mark each test tube with the substance name.
3. Fill each test tube with 15 mL of the cabbage juice.
4. Use the following table of colors to **predict** the relative pH of the test solutions. Record these predictions in your table.

INDICATOR COLOR	RELATIVE pH
bright red	strong acid
red	medium acid
reddish purple	weak acid
purple	neutral
blue green	weak base
green	medium base
yellow	strong base

5. Add 5 drops of each test solution to the test tube labeled with its name.

CAUTION: *If you spill any liquids on your skin, rinse the area immediately with water. Alert your teacher if any liquid is spilled in the work area.*

6. **Observe** any color changes of the cabbage-juice indicator. In your data table, record the color and relative pH of each solution.

DATA AND OBSERVATIONS

Sample data

TEST SOLUTION	PREDICTIONS	COLOR OF INDICATOR	RELATIVE pH OF ACID OR BASE
Water		purple	7
Vinegar		red	2-3
Ammonia		green	11
Soft drink		red	2-4
Baking soda		blue/green	9
Sodium hydroxide		yellow	13
Hydrochloric acid		bright red	1

ANALYZE

1. **Classify** which test solutions were acids and which were bases.
2. Which base was weakest?
3. Which acid was strongest ?
4. **Infer** why distilled water didn't change the color of the cabbage juice.

CONCLUDE AND APPLY

5. How do your predictions **compare** with the results?
6. How does cabbage juice indicate the relative strength of acids and bases?
7. **Going Further: Predict** how other substances at home would react with the cabbage juice indicator. Ask an adult to help you use the cabbage juice indicator to test other liquids around your home.

INVESTIGATE!

8-2 PH INDICATOR

Time needed 30 minutes

Materials See student activity.

Thinking Processes
Thinking critically, Observing and inferring, Comparing and contrasting, Representing and applying data, Predicting, Organizing information, Classifying

Purpose To investigate the relative pH of acids and bases.

Preparation To make the indicator, cut red cabbage into quarters and grate into a bowl. Add between one and two cups of water and let stand. When the water turns a deep red remove the cabbage and pour the solution into a glass jar through a strainer.

Teaching the Activity

Troubleshooting With litmus paper, precise shade of color was not important. Here, shade is important. Have students familiarize themselves with the various colors (see table) beforehand so they have a good idea of what to look for. LEP L1

Expected Outcomes

The following substances will turn the indicator the colors indicated: distilled water, purple; white vinegar, red; ammonia, green; soft drink, red; baking soda, blue green; sodium hydroxide, yellow; hydrochloric acid, bright red.

Answers to Analyze/Conclude and Apply

1. Acids: soft drink, hydrochloric acid, vinegar; bases: ammonia, baking soda, sodium hydroxide
2. Baking soda
3. Hydrochloric acid
4. Water is neutral.
5. Answers will vary.
6. The more yellow it turns, the more basic it is; the brighter red it turns, the more acidic it is.
7. Answers will vary.

Meeting Individual Needs

Physically Challenged Preview the Investigate activity on this page with students so they know what kinds of hues to expect from the indicator. When the class does the experiment, they can brief lab partners on what colors to expect from various pH's and how vivid those colors should appear. Have them use crayons to prepare a chart to compare with the test tubes. COOP LEARN

PROGRAM RESOURCES

Teacher Classroom Resources

Activity Masters, pages 35-36, Investigate 8-2

See bar graph below. 

3 Assess

Check for Understanding

As they answer the Apply question, have students think not in terms of which substances are poison, but rather, which substances are harmful if handled or swallowed.

Reteach

Provide students with a copy of the pH organizer shown below, with only the numbers included. Have them fill in the ranges of strong and weak acidity and basicity. L1

ACID							BASE						
1	2	3	4	5	6	7	8	9	10	11	12	13	14
strong		medium		weak			weak	medium			strong		

Extension

Activity Materials needed are lemon juice, beakers, and an acid-base indicator.

Test the pH of different dilutions of a fairly strong acid like lemon juice. With an indicator, find the pH at full strength. Then dilute, with 1 part lemon juice to 1 part water, to 2 parts water, to 3 parts water, and so on. Ask what ratio of dilution will make the solution neutral. Basic? *A very high dilution will make it approach, but not reach, neutral; it is impossible to make it basic using water.* L3

4 Close

Activity

Have students collect water from various sources in the immediate vicinity such as rainwater, different tap waters, river and seawater, pond water, bottled water, and puddle water. Have them use an indicator to test and compare the pH of each sample. L1

SKILLBUILDER

MAKING AND USING GRAPHS

Find the pH of the following materials: rainwater, apples, club soda, seawater, drain cleaner, distilled water, and milk of magnesia. Now use a bar graph to plot the pH of the materials against the pH scale in Figure 8-9. If you need help, refer to the ***Skill Handbook*** on page 650.

INDICATORS AND pH

Acid-base indicators come in two varieties—a solution or an acid-base indicator paper. You used a solution indicator when you tested the pH of solutions in the Investigate activity. The paper can be an indicator itself or treated with an indicator. To use an indicator strip, just place a drop of the solution to be tested on the paper and watch for a color change. You already know about one of the most common indicators—litmus paper. Remember from the Investigate activity in Section 2 that litmus turns blue in the presence of a base and red in the presence of an acid. Would it change color in pure water? Why or why not?

Another common acid-base indicator is a chemical called phenolphthalein (feen ul THAY leen). Phenolphthalein is colorless in the presence of an acid, but it turns bright pink in the presence of a base. Phenolphthalein is also one of the indicators used to treat paper strips.

FIGURE 8-11. Lichens are the source of litmus.

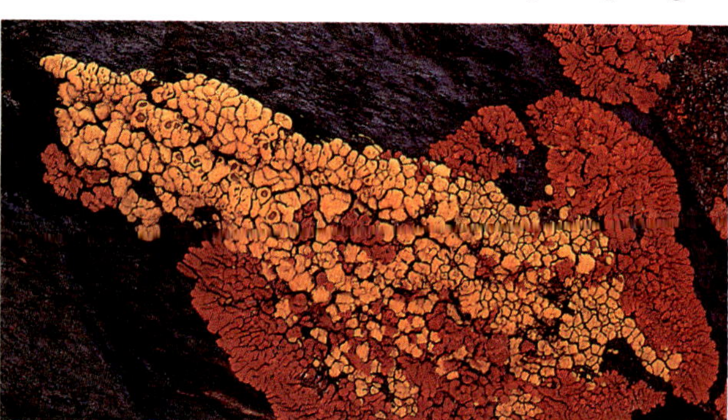

For living things to grow and be healthy, there must be a balance in the acids and bases in their bodies as well as in their environment. In this section, you've learned how to distinguish acids and bases and how to measure the strength of an acid or base. In the next section, you'll discover a way in which acid rain damage might be temporarily repaired.

Check Your Understanding

1. Describe two common acid-base indicators. Which colors will you observe in an acidic solution? In a basic solution?
2. Arrange the following list of solutions in order from most acidic to most basic.
   rainwater, pH 5.8
   club soda, pH 3.0
   seawater, pH 8.9
   drain cleaner, pH 14.0
   distilled water, pH 7.0
3. **APPLY:** Which of the substances mentioned in Question 2 should have a poison symbol on its label? Explain why.

Answers to Check Your Understanding

1. Litmus: An acid will turn blue litmus red, and a base will turn red litmus blue. Phenolphthalein: Colorless in the presence of an acid and pink in the presence of a base.
2. Club soda, rainwater, distilled water, seawater, drain cleaner
3. Drain cleaner; it is such a strong base that it will burn your stomach if swallowed.

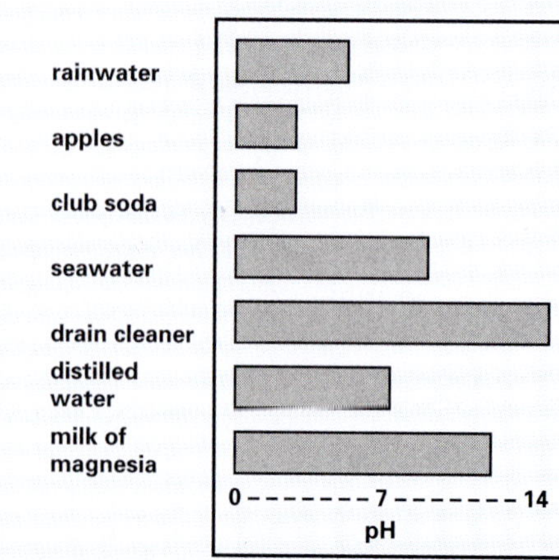

8-4 Salts

NEUTRALIZATION

You've probably heard commercials on television that say, "Are you bothered by an upset stomach? Try our product to neutralize excess stomach acid. You'll feel better fast!"

Would the pH of such a product be less than or greater than 7? For you to feel better, the pH would have to be greater than 7 because only a base can neutralize an acid.

Neutralization is the chemical reaction that occurs between an acid and a base. During neutralization, the acidic and basic properties are canceled, or neutralized. For example, you've read how lime is used to neutralize acid soil and how you can use an antacid to neutralize excess acid in your stomach.

A **salt**, another type of compound, is formed as part of neutralization. Water is also formed. This reaction can be written as follows:

acid plus base produces a salt plus water

The same reaction can also be expressed using the names of specific chemicals

hydrochloric acid plus sodium hydroxide produces sodium chloride plus water

To see how a neutralization takes place, do the following Find Out.

OBJECTIVES

In this section, you will

- observe a neutralization reaction;
- explain how salts form.

KEY SCIENCE TERMS

neutralization

salt

DID YOU KNOW?

Bees and other insects inject a potent acid (formic acid) into their victims when they sting. Bears have been observed rolling in the mud after being stung when they go after honey. That's because the basic soil neutralizes the acid in bee stings.

FIND OUT!

How does neutralization take place?  

Put 10 mL of ammonia in one test tube and 10 mL of white vinegar in another. Test each with litmus paper. What do you observe? Which liquid is the acid? Which liquid is the base? Using an eyedropper, pick up some ammonia and add it drop by drop to the test tube of vinegar, stirring after each drop with a stirring rod. After adding 5 drops, test your solution by touching your stirring rod to litmus paper. Then test with litmus for each additional drop.

Section 8-4

PREPARATION

Concepts Developed

This section develops the concept of neutralization. Students learn that when an acid and base react, they neutralize each other and a salt is formed. Common salts and their uses are listed.

Planning the Lesson

In planning your lesson on salts, refer to the Chapter Organizer on pages 224A-B for timing suggestions, resources, and additional materials that will help you in your presentation of the lesson concepts.

For adequate development of the concepts in this lesson, we recommend that students complete the Find Out activity on page 241.

1 MOTIVATE

Demonstration This activity will allow students to see that a salt is a product of neutralization.

You will need antacid tablets, warm water, a universal indicator, dilute 0.1 M hydrochloric acid, safety goggles, and an eyedropper.

Crush two antacid tablets in warm water. Add a few drops of universal indicator. Add drops of acid until the solution is neutral (see indicator label). Have the class verify that the solution is now neutral. To prove that a salt is formed during neutralization, slowly evaporate the solution in a warm oven overnight. Students should be able to observe the formation of a salt the next day.

PROGRAM RESOURCES

Teacher Classroom Resources

Study Guide, page 32

Laboratory Manual, pages 47-48, Neutralization L3

Multicultural Activities, page 20, Salt

Other Resources

Acids, Bases, and Salts, film, Coronet/MTI Films

FIND OUT!

How does neutralization take place?

Time Needed 10 minutes

Materials

ammonia, white vinegar, graduated cylinder, litmus paper, eyedropper, 2 test tubes, stirring rod

Thinking Processes
Thinking critically, Observing and inferring, Recognizing cause and effect

Purpose To observe the neutralization process.

Teaching the Activity

Discussion Talk about what *neutralize* means. The students know that acids and bases represent opposite ends of the pH scale. Here, they are used to cancel the effect of one another.

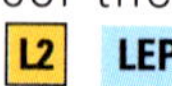

LEP

Troubleshooting Stress that, after the fifth drop of ammonia is added, students must test the solution with litmus paper after *each* additional drop of ammonia is added.

Safety Provide adequate ventilation and warn students that both reactants have strong fumes.

Expected Outcomes

The solution will reach a neutral pH. The students may conclude that a base can be used to make an acidic solution neutral.

Conclude and Apply

1. When neutral, the solution will not change the color of the red or blue litmus paper.
2. Answers will vary.
3. The solution would not change either color of litmus paper.

Conclude and Apply

1. What change do you observe in the litmus?
2. How many drops of ammonia did it take to get a neutral solution?
3. How do you know the solution is neutral?

PARTIAL NEUTRALIZATION

FIGURE 8-12. Copper sulfate and water is the result of a reaction between copper hydroxide, a weak base, and sulfuric acid,a strong acid.

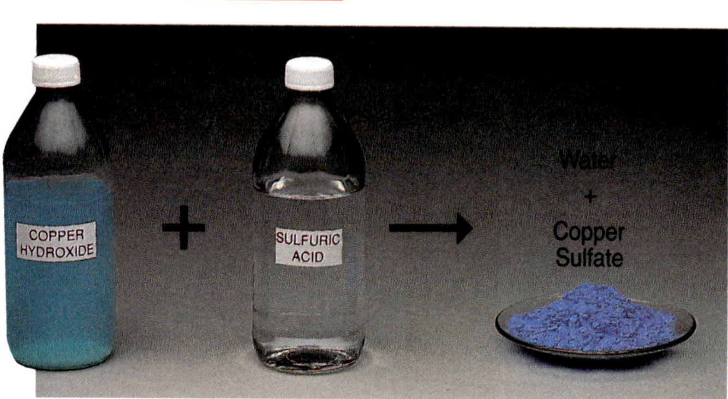

Sometimes, acidic and basic properties are only reduced by a neutralization. An example of this occurs when a strong base reacts with a weak acid, producing a solution that is slightly basic. What would happen when a strong acid reacts with a weak base? Figure 8-12 shows the result of one such reaction.

Partial neutralization also occurs with a massive amount of acid. Acid rain is thought to have contributed to the high acidity of some lakes. A lake might have a pH as low as 3.7. Adding tons of a base, such as lime, to the

2 TEACH

Tying to Previous Knowledge

Review the pH scale and talk about acids and bases in relative terms. Ask the students how they could make an acid solution (a) more or (b) less acidic. (Remind them of the antacid they made in Section 2.) Tell them that in this section they will learn how this is done.

OPTIONS

Multicultural Perspectives

Discussion One of the chief reasons that gunpowder was first developed in China was that that country had an abundance of saltpeter, a salt which is also known as potassium nitrate. The trick to finding saltpeter was knowing how to recognize it. It looked like any other salt, but the Chinese developed a test to identify it: when saltpeter is ignited, the flame is pure violet in color.

TABLE 8-2. Some Common Salts

Name	Common Name	Uses
Sodium chloride	Table salt	Food preparation; Manufacture of chemicals
Sodium hydrogen carbonate	Sodium bicarbonate (Baking soda)	Food preparation; In fire extinguishers
Calcium carbonate	Calcite (chalk)	Manufacture of paint and rubber tires
Potassium nitrate	Salt peter	In fertilizers; Manufacture of explosives
Potassium carbonate	Potash	Manufacture of soap and glass
Potassium chloride	Light salt	Sodium chloride substitute

lake might bring the pH up to around 5. However, acid is constantly being added by rain, so the pH of the lake water may drop back down again.

SALTS

We usually think of salt as just table salt, sodium chloride. Many different salts are formed in neutralization reactions, but not all these salts are edible. You come in contact with some of these salts every day but may not have realized that these compounds are salts. Table 8-2 lists some common salts and tells how they are used.

Like acids and bases, salts are important in industry. For example, table salt is important in food preparation. It's used in the curing of hams and bacon and in the production of lunch meats such as bologna, sausage, and wieners. Salts are also useful as raw materials. Chlorine, a chemical used to purify water, is obtained from sodium chloride. Other salts are used in the production of rubber, water softeners, chemicals, paints, and fertilizers.

Sodium chloride is the product of a very strong acid—hydrochloric acid and a very strong base—sodium hydroxide. When they are of equal strength and combined in equal amounts, the acid and the base are

FIGURE 8-13. Salts are used in the production of common products, such as pool cleaners, paints, meats, erasers, and fertilizers.

Concept Development

Theme Connection The neutralization reaction between an acid and a base is a chemical change. The products of this change are substances that are more stable than either of the two reactants.

Inquiry Question A hospital emergency room patient felt sick because he had taken too many antacid tablets. Can you recommend one treatment that might make him feel better? *Give him some safe, weak dilute acid such as lemon or fruit juice to neutralize his stomach.*

Student Journal Have students write in their journals their impressions of what took place in the Find Out experiment. Have them speculate about the nature of acids and bases. How are they able to transform each other?

MAKING CONNECTIONS

Health/Business

Americans spend over $500 million a year for antacids, chemicals that cause a neutralization reaction in the stomach. Over 800 different brands of antacid are sold in the U.S. The active ingredient in all antacids is one of the following: sodium bicarbonate, aluminum hydroxide, or magnesium hydroxide. Overuse of antacids can cause *alkalosis,* excessive basicity of the blood. Because of their high sodium content, sodium bicarbonate antacids are also not recommended for people with high blood pressure.

Flex Your Brain Have students use the Flex Your Brain activity to explore SALTS.

Meeting Individual Needs

Learning Disabled Model the neutralization process by using red interlocking building set pieces to represent acid components and blue pieces to represent base components. Red and blue pieces locked together represent neutral components. Start with an acid. To "neutralize" it, attach a blue piece to each red piece. Show that the "solution" can be "neutralized" only if there are an equal number of red and blue pieces.

PROGRAM RESOURCES

Teacher Classroom Resources

Concept Mapping, page 16, Acids, Bases, and Salts L1

Critical Thinking/Problem Solving, page 8, Flex Your Brain

Take Home Activities, page 15, Lifting an Ice Cube L1

3 Assess

Check for Understanding

Assign questions 1-3 of Check Your Understanding. After students have completed the Apply question, have them look in a cookbook for cake recipes and locate the acid ingredient in each. Baking powder has acid already in it, usually in the form of tartaric acid, calcium acid phosphate, or sodium aluminum sulfate.

Reteach

To describe a neutralization reaction, use the analogy of balancing a see-saw. You start out unbalanced (i.e. acid), on one end of the see-saw. To balance the see-saw, you must add an equal amount of base to the other side. LEP L1

Extension

Have students give the names of the salts that would form in these neutralizations. (Hint: Two of them appear in Table 8-2.)

a. Nitric acid and potassium hydroxide *Potassium nitrate*

b. Carbonic acid and calcium hydroxide *Calcium carbonate*

c. Hydrochloric acid and ammonium hydroxide *Ammonium chloride* L3

4 Close

Have students imagine they have returned in a time machine to the Middle Ages, a time when salt was a rare and precious commodity. They have bragged to the king that they can manufacture salt. Have them describe what materials and equipment they would need from the local alchemist to perform this feat. L1

FIGURE 8-14. Animals, such as this deer, will travel long distances to get to a salt lick.

neutralized. This neutralization produces a water and sodium chloride (table salt) solution with a pH of 7.

Sodium chloride is important in your diet and the diet of animals. Limited amounts of salt are needed to maintain the body's chemical balance. When salt is lost through perspiration and excretion, it must be replaced if you are to stay healthy. Workers and athletes laboring under hot conditions often take special drinks to replace the salt they perspire away. Some animals will travel miles to get to a salt lick.

In the beginning of this chapter, you read about the damage acid rain causes to monuments, buildings, and the environment. Now you know how these reactions take place.

You also know that acids and bases make it possible for living things to function, grow, and be healthy. The important thing is to keep a balance between these two types of compounds. As you look about your world, be aware of the effects of acids and bases.

Check Your Understanding

1. Hydrochloric acid and baking soda react. Will the resulting solution be basic, acidic, or neutral? Explain your answer.
2. A neutralized solution is slightly basic. What do you infer about the chemicals in the reaction? Explain your answer.
3. **APPLY:** Baking soda is used to make a cake rise, but soda will not react without an acid. Which of these would be a good acid to use: vinegar, hydrochloric acid, lemon juice, or water? Explain your answer.

Answers to Check Your Understanding

1. Acidic; they will not neutralize because hydrochloric acid is a strong acid while baking soda is only a weak base.
2. One chemical must be a strong base and the other a weak acid, since only partial neutralization took place.
3. Lemon juice; it is a strong acid that is not dangerous to eat undiluted and has a better taste for a cake than vinegar.

EXPANDING YOUR VIEW

CONTENTS

A CLOSER LOOK

FOOD PIONEER

You have learned in this chapter that salt is used in the preparation of foods. Pioneering food chemist Dr. Lloyd A. Hall developed new methods of using salts in preparing and preserving foods.

Hall was born in Elgin, Illinois in 1894, and he developed an interest in chemistry during high school. In 1925, Hall became director of research at Griffith Laboratories, where he studied the use of salts in meat curing.

He developed a method of combining sodium with nitrate and nitrite so that the sodium could preserve the meat before the nitrogen-containing salts could penetrate the meat and cause disintigration. The new technique was called flash-drying, and the resulting crystals were more effective than any meat-curing salts used before. Hall's work had a major impact on the meat industry.

Spices had been used for many years to preserve food. Hall found that many spices were actually contaminating the foods they were supposed to preserve. The spices were often infested with molds, yeasts, and bacteria. Hall developed a method to sterilize these spices without ruining their appearance, quality, and flavor. His method was also used for preparing medicines, medical supplies, and cosmetics.

Fats and oils often spoiled, or became rancid, when components of the fat interacted with the oxygen in the air. Many antioxidants, agents that prevent spoiling, would not dissolve in fat, so they could not effectively mix with the product. Hall developed a fat-soluble antioxidant mixture that was 99.64 percent sodium chloride. The remaining ingredients were the key to preserving the fats and oils.

Hall served as a science adviser in two wars. He helped solve the problem of keeping food for the military fresh and healthful. He was the first African-American to be on the board of directors of the American Institute of Chemists.

WHAT DO YOU THINK?

If you've ever gone on a camping or hiking trip, you may have wished you could take along some of your favorite foods. What might a food chemist invent to keep those foods from spoiling along the way?

EXPANDING YOUR VIEW

Using Expanding Your View

Assign one or more of these excursions to expand your students' understanding of the properties of acids, bases, and salts and how they apply to other sciences and subjects. You may assign these as individual or small group activities.

A CLOSER LOOK

Purpose A Closer Look extends the concepts presented in Section 8-4 to the properties and uses of salts in the food industry.

Content Background From ancient times, food preservation required the use of salt. In the Corning process, meat first cured in a brine of salt, sugar and saltpeter. Later the meat was cooked as needed. The Drying process involved rubbing meat with a salt, spice, and sugar mix and then covering it with brine for several weeks. Removed from the brine, the meat hung from a ceiling beam until dried. Pepper rubbed into the meat added flavor and, as a bonus, also acted as an insect repellent.

Teaching Strategy Have students take an inventory at home or at a grocery store and list the various ingredients found in beef jerky and smoked sausage. Have them identify which ingredients act as preservatives. Then have them list food items found in their households that contain these types of preservatives.

Answers to

WHAT DO YOU THINK?

Food preservation techniques might include:

1. Irradiation machines to retard spoilage of foods usually requiring refrigeration.
2. Packages of dried preservatives to coat foods as needed, or to form a brine in which they could be treated prior to leaving home.

Going Further Have students research the issues of the controversy regarding cancer-inducing properties found in the sodium nitrates and sodium nitrites used in meat curing. Have students present their findings to the class. Discuss the tradeoffs between food preservation and health and what this says about current lifestyles. Sources include:

American Cancer Society
1599 Clifton Rd. NE
Atlanta, GA 30329

U.S. Food and Drug Administration
Department of Health and Human Services
370 L'Enfant Promenade SW
Washington, D.C. 20447

American Meat Institute
PO Box 35556
Washington, D.C. 20007

EXPANDING YOUR VIEW

LIFE SCIENCE CONNECTION

Purpose This Life Science Connection applies the concept of neutralization presented in Section 8-4 to explain how antacids relieve many stomach complaints.

Content Background The stomach may "ache" in a variety of ways. "Growling" results from the motions, called peristaltic waves, that the stomach uses to transfer its contents from one end to the other. If the peristaltic waves are strong enough, they may force excess acidic gastric juice upward into the lower portion of the esophagus. When this happens, the common result is called heartburn. An ulcer is another problem that can occur in the stomach. In addition to processing food, hydrochloric acid and digestive juices continually contact the tissue lining of the stomach. When the tissue can't be replaced quickly enough, an open sore called an ulcer may form. High alcohol or aspirin consumption may cause a gastric ulcer. Excessive stomach acid, which can result from stress, may cause an ulcer in the first part of the small intestine called a duodenal ulcer.

Teaching Strategies Have students, with their parents' assistance, make a list of the brand-name antacids found in their homes. Also have them ask their parents what motivated them to buy these products. Then hold a class discussion of how advertising may influence buying decisions.

OH, MY ACHING STOMACH!

If you ever watch TV, you see lots of people complaining of upset stomach, acid stomach, bloating, and other unpleasant stomach complaints. Then you see those same people feeling just great after taking an antacid tablet or liquid. What has happened here?

Everyone's stomach contains acid to help digest food. Sometimes, as a result of overeating, eating the wrong kinds of food, or stress, excess stomach acid can form. As you learned, acids are sour tasting and can be harmful. Sometimes when a person has too much stomach acid, there is a sour taste in the mouth or a feeling of burning in the stomach or throat.

To help solve the problem of too much stomach acid, researchers looked to find a base that would neutralize some of that acid. That is what antacids are. Whether they are a liquid, a capsule, a tablet to be chewed, or something to be dissolved in water, all antacids are bases. They are usually flavored with something pleasant tasting, such as lemon or mint.

Magnesium hydroxide and sodium bicarbonate are bases that you commonly find in antacid medicine. Sodium bicarbonate is the same thing as baking soda. Whatever the content of the medicine, it acts in the same way. Acid in the stomach combines with the base in the medicine to create harmless salts and water in your stomach that help to make you feel better.

YOU TRY IT!

There are many kinds of antacid medicines, all making claims about being "better" or "faster." To find out, dissolve a standard dose of a few different antacid medicines in separate containers of water. To each container, add vinegar, a small amount at a time, until the solution tests acidic with litmus paper. Keep track of how much vinegar you had to add.

What conclusions can you draw about the effectiveness of the antacids you are testing? Does one neutralize acid more quickly than the others? Does one neutralize more acid than the others?

Answers to

YOU TRY IT

Students should conclude that effective antacids are ones that can neutralize several milliliters of acid to a basic pH. More effective antacids will neutralize more acids, and some may do so faster than others.

Going Further Divide students into groups. Direct each group to interview a professional in the field of medicine, pharmacy, or natural healing to get information on stomach ache cures popular in their field or business. Discuss how consumers make their decisions with respect to brand names or choice of cures. Also discuss the validity of folk cures and how they may have influenced medical research. Have students compare their findings. COOP LEARN

Have students find out what stomach ache cures are used in other countries. Determine differences and similarities to cures popular in this country. Sources of information might include:

- Public Library
- Local medical school library
- Foreign embassies and consulates
- Foreign student groups at local colleges
- Missionary organizations
- U.N.E.S.C.O.
- World Health Organization

SCIENCE AND SOCIETY

ACID RAIN

Cars, airplanes, home heaters, most industrial machines, and giant electric generators are all powered by fuel that comes from coal and oil. These fuels have been very important in making our world industrialized and comfortable. But they also produce harmful pollution. When coal and oil are burned for energy, they give off gases into the atmosphere. When these gases combine with water in the clouds, the result is acid rain.

When acid rain falls to Earth, it has a bad effect. Like any acid solution, acid rain affects the substances on which it falls. Fish, crops, forests, and the surfaces of sculptures and buildings (like the Parthenon, built in ancient Greece, pictured on p. 248) can all be damaged by acid rain.

You may be surprised to learn that the term *acid rain* was first used in 1872 by Angus Smith, who wrote about polluted air and rain in and near large cities in England. At that time, all industry in England burned coal, and the thick black smoke released into the air as a result covered everything. It was a century later, though, that people began to regard acid rain as a serious problem. Today acid rain is a problem that all industrialized countries have to consider. The effects of acid rain on the fertile fields of Mexico are just as harmful as the effects of smog on the people of Mexico City, shown in the picture.

There are different kinds of acid rain. Sulfuric acid and nitric acid are produced when sulfur and nitrogen gases combine with rainwater. Even when highly diluted, these acids are harmful to the environment. The more concentrated the acids, the more serious is the problem.

When acid rain falls to Earth, the soil and water become more acidic. Among the first organisms to suffer are plankton. Plankton live in the water and are eaten by small fish, which are eaten by larger fish, and on and on

WHAT DO YOU THINK?

Acid rain is a controversial subject. Some people who earn money from coal and gas production and from the industries that use them claim that acid rain is not a problem. See if you can find more information about acid rain and decide whether it is a serious threat to our environment.

EXPANDING YOUR VIEW

SCIENCE AND SOCIETY

Content Background Acid rain is just one form of acid deposition. Dry acid deposition also occurs on a regular basis. Both depositions have pH values lower than 5.6.

Acid rain results from the release of sulfur dioxides, mostly by coal-fired plants, and from nitrogen oxides in auto emissions. The importance of acid rain stems from being the first global-scale problem caused by burning fossil fuels. Some of our pollution ends up in Canada, and we get some of theirs. Sweden receives emissions from France and Germany. North American, European, and Asian pollution finds its way to the Arctic Circle. Pollution in the South Pacific may derive from East Asia. Controlling acid rain necessitates each country first confronting its own problem and then acting together with others.

Teaching Strategies Have students debate the importance of the acid rain issue. One group should support the position of industry and one group the position of environmentalists. COOP LEARN

Activity Have students make lists of family activities which consume power, such as driving motor vehicles, operating appliances, using lawn mowers, and so on. Have them consider how and to what degree they could reduce the amount of energy they personally consume. Have students share ideas and make a class list of ways students will work to conserve energy. COOP LEARN

Going Further Have students research current positions of different public interest groups and industry-sponsored groups regarding the economic issues behind the acid rain problem. Have each student present his/her group's position in the form of a poster, letter to the editor, or speech to a congressional committee investigating acid rain. Some sources include:

Acid Rain Foundation
1410 Varsity Dr.
Raleigh, NC 27606

Citizens for Sensible Control of Acid Rain
1301 Connecticut Ave. NW, Ste. 700
Washington, D.C. 20036

EXPANDING YOUR VIEW

LITERATURE CONNECTIONS

Purpose This literature Connection, "In Times of Silver Rain", balances the unfavorable effects of acid rain that students learned about in this chapter by presenting one poet's lyric images of rain.

Content Background Langston Hughes (1902-1967) is celebrated as the leader of the "Harlem Renaissance," the 1920 outpouring of music, art, and literature from New York's Harlem section. Hughes was raised by his maternal grandmother in his hometown of Joplin, Missouri. He attended Columbia University for a year in 1921, and then set off to see the world. To this end, he shipped out as a merchant seaman, worked in a Paris nightclub, and bused tables in Washington, DC. His break came when poet Vachel Lindsay ate at the restaurant and Hughes slipped some of his poems under his plate. Impressed, Lindsay helped launch Hughes's career. In addition to poetry, Hughes published biographies, children's stories, song lyrics, and articles.

Teaching strategies To capture the sound of Hughes's imagery, suggest that students read the poem aloud with a partner. Then, student pairs might work together to make collages or paintings that capture the poem's mood and imagery.

Discussion Have students read the poem on their own. Then explain that Hughes was writing in the 1920s, before the effects of acid rain were known. Have students discuss how Hughes' poem might be different if he had written it today.

Answers to

WHAT DO YOU THINK?

Some students may agree with Hughes's life-affirming images of rain, while others may suggest dreary and depressing images to capture rain's less cheerful side.

through the food chain. When the plankton are killed, the fish that depend upon them for food soon die.

Soil and land plants can also suffer from the effects of acid rain. Acid rain can dissolve important mineral nutrients and make the soil highly acidic. Plants deprived of these nutrients do not grow at a normal rate or to a normal size. Thus, crops and forests are damaged or destroyed. Some plants are adapted to normally acid soil, but others are not. These are the ones that suffer from acid rain.

Science and industry are constantly searching for cleaner, more efficient fuels. Harnessing the energy in the sun, the wind, and the atom as an alternative to coal and oil is a major goal. Industry is also hard at work to find ways to use coal and oil without causing harmful by-products.

Literature CONNECTION

IN TIMES OF SILVER RAIN

In this chapter, you've read about acid rain and the unfavorable effects it has on the environment. To get a different view of rain, read the poem, "In Times of Silver Rain" by Langston Hughes (Bontemps, Arna Wendell, ed. *Golden Slippers: An Anthology of Negro Poetry for Young Readers).*

To Langston Hughes, rain is filled with beautiful images that inspire poetry. His image of "silver rain" evokes the idea of a shimmering cascade of raindrops—each like a silvered mirror reflecting the effect of rain on the plants growing on the plain.

WHAT DO YOU THINK?

What images does rain evoke for you?

Going Further Students might enjoy learning more about the Harlem Renaissance. Break the class into three groups. Have one group research the art; another the music, and the third, the literature. Notable artists of the movement include James Chapin and Romare Bearden. Musicians include composers Duke Ellington and Fats Waller, blues singers Ethel Waters and Bessie Smith, and entertainers Josephine Baker, Florence Mills, and Bill Robinson. Some of the writers were Countee Cullen, Claude McKay, Zora Neale Hurston, Jean Toomer, and Arna Bontemps.

Ecology CONNECTION

TURNING ROCKS TO SOIL

Do you remember seeing gray, green, or brownish stuff covering bare rocks or the limbs of trees? This scaly-looking substance is really a group of organisms called lichens (LI kens). Lichens are made up of fungi and algae that have formed a symbiotic relationship—the algae provide food through photosynthesis and the fungi provide protection. Lichens have no stems, roots, or leaves. There are three basic groups of lichen: crusty or flaky, papery or leafy, and stalked or branching.

Some lichens appear to grow out of solid rock. If you look with a microscope, however, you can see that tiny threadlike growths anchor the lichen to the rock surface.

Rock-growing lichens play an important role in converting rocks into soil. Lichens produce a weak acid solution that slowly dissolves the minerals. Soon cracks appear in the rock and the threads of the lichens dig deeper into the rock. The cracks fill with water that freezes and melts, making the cracks bigger.

After a long time, the rocks break apart into smaller pieces, and eventually become soil. Once this process begins, plants can also grow in the cracks and speed up the breakup of the rocks.

YOU TRY IT!

Look around outside for rocks and limbs that have lichens growing on them. You can use lichens just as you use litmus paper to test for acidity or alkalinity. Gather some lichens, then dip one into an acid solution and another into a basic solution. The lichen placed in an acid solution turns red, where as the lichen placed in a basic solution turns blue.

When the rocks break apart, new soil with new minerals forms and more plants begin to grow. Soil that is worn out from over-use or eroded by wind or water is made healthier with the addition of new soil from broken rocks.

In addition to breaking up rocks, lichen acids are also useful ingredients in perfume making. They are used to make all the different ingredients in perfume mingle together to make a pleasant smell. Lichen extracts are also used to manufacture antibiotics, medicines, puddings, and fabric stiffeners.

Going Further Lichens break down rock into soil, but this is not the only means of soil formation. Have students research the various natural ways in which soil is formed. Have them discuss these methods and then consider how the methods might be affected by air pollution. COOP LEARN

Have students check with local and state agencies about the composition and pH of soil in the area. They should find out how local growers treat the soil and with what types of chemicals. Where does the runoff from the land go? Sources of information include:

4-H organizations
County Extension offices
State and Federal Departments of Agriculture
Local growers COOP LEARN

ECOLOGY CONNECTION

Purpose The Ecology Connection extends Section 8-1 about acids by describing how the acid solution produced by lichens starts the process of breaking down rocks into soil. It also adds lichens to the acid-base indicators described in Section 8-3.

Content Background A lichen is a composite organism consisting of 90% fungus and 10% algae. Together, the two organisms form a self-supporting lichen. The alga produces a quantity of organic foods which are then consumed by the fungus. Lichens are considered excellent examples of symbiosis.

Lichens exist in forests, swamps, and tundra. Their acid secretions protect their colonies by reducing the germination of plant forms on the rock. Air pollution inhibits the growth and life of lichen colonies. Therefore, few lichens exist near population centers. Some lichens are used in the manufacture of litmus paper. Some are eaten by invertebrates such as snails and insects and some by caribou and reindeer. The Japanese consider some lichens a gourmet delicacy.

Lichens reduce rock to soil in several ways. The acids secreted by the lichens may dissolve minerals in the rock. This allows water and then larger plants to enter the rock and weather it. Some lichens have a unique way of weathering their rock homes. The lichens expand and attach to the rock when wet. As they dry, the lichens contract, pulling tiny particles off the host rock. Eventually small amounts of soil are formed on the rock. This soil will then support larger plants whose roots will continue the weathering action.

Teaching Strategy Have students examine rocks near their homes and school for lichen colonies. Ask them to compare the different forms and shapes. Have students share their findings with the class.

EXPANDING YOUR VIEW

ART CONNECTION

Purpose The Art Connection extends the activity in Section 8-1 in which students observed the effect of acid on marble by discussing ways in which marble statues and carving can be protected.

Content Background Most discussion about acid rain focuses on the damage to our natural resources. However, damage to our national monuments ultimately erodes our national heritage. Examples include the erosion of facial features at many memorials. What happens chemically during erosion? In one case sugaring occurs. The sulfuric acid in the acid rain reacts with the calcium carbonate found in the stone. The calcium carbonate, which acts like a cement holding the grains of sandstone together, then forms gypsum, the light, powdery coating which looks like confectioner's sugar. This coating is very soluble and less weather resistant then the original stone surface. The powder either washes off, taking away sculptured detail, or forms an unattractive crust. In another type of erosion, acid reactions cause the formation of a soft talc crust on the stone surfaces. Tiny craters then form easily on this softer surface and erosion occurs rapidly. This can be observed on the Capitol Building in Washington, D.C.

Teaching Strategies Invite the maintenance supervisor of an older public building, church, or park with statuary in your area to your class. Ask the supervisor to describe current problems with the building exterior or statues and any preventive maintenance that is done to protect the stone.

Answer to

WHAT DO YOU THINK?

No; acid dissolves marble.

Art CONNECTION

PRESERVING MASTERPIECES

Will the real David please step forward? One of these statues of David was carved by Michelangelo in the 14th century and the other is a more recent copy. You might wonder why copies are made of fine works of art. One of the reasons is that the older sculptures are beginning to fall apart as a result of acid in the atmosphere—including acid rain.

Remember the activity you performed at the beginning of the chapter to see how acid could dissolve marble? Marble statues and marble carvings on buildings are dissolved in the same way. The surfaces soften and crumble so that details of carving are lost, and sometimes noses, fingers, and toes are destroyed.

Marble that has been exposed to acid rain can be partially protected by washing with a solution of some basic compound. Once the marble has been washed and the acid neutralized with a base, the surface can be coated with wax to provide some protection against more acid rain. Making the areas around old marble buildings off limits to cars and machinery that give off pollution can help protect them.

Sculptures can be moved inside where they are protected from acid in the atmosphere, and copies can be made to stand outside where the originals once stood. So the original David is protected indoors at the Academy in Florence, Italy. A copy stands in the courtyard of the Old Palace, where the original first stood. In this way, masterpieces are both protected and left in place for visitors to enjoy.

WHAT DO YOU THINK?

Early restorers of marble statues tried to clean dirt and stains from statues by using solutions containing acid. Just as people today use vinegar to get stubborn stains out of fabric or off glass, they believed that an acid solution would help clean the sculptures. From what you have learned in this chapter, would you agree that acid was a good way to clean marble sculptures? Why or why not?

CAREER CONNECTION

Architects design buildings and the areas around buildings, including where decorative items such as sculptures are placed. Architects have to consider the function of the building and the look they want the building to have. They must also consider the environment's effect on the materials they use to build. When they decide to build a building of rock or metal or marble, they must consider how these materials will stand up to weather, air pollution, and use.

250 CHAPTER 8 ACIDS, BASES, AND SALTS

Going Further Have student groups interview curators at local museums or invite a museum curator or historian knowledgeable in preservation to speak to the class on current restoration projects in your community or state. Find out what problems and opportunities exist with regard to funding or with political, industrial, or social action groups. Discuss how these groups might affect the decision-making process in restoration projects.

COOP LEARN

Select a building, monument or statue in your area that is in need of renovation. Have students debate for and against its renovation. As students plan their arguments, have them consider the various social, economic, and political concerns involved.

COOP LEARN

Reviewing Main Ideas

1. Acids are compounds that taste sour, release hydrogen gas from active metals, and turn blue litmus paper red.

2. Bases taste bitter, feel slippery, and turn red litmus paper blue.

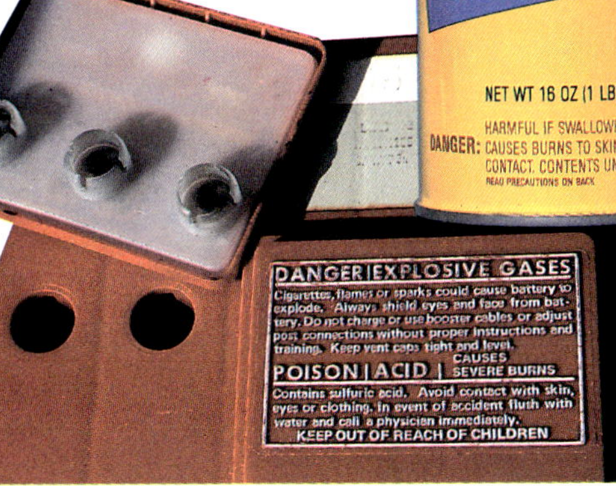

3. Acids and bases can be very reactive.

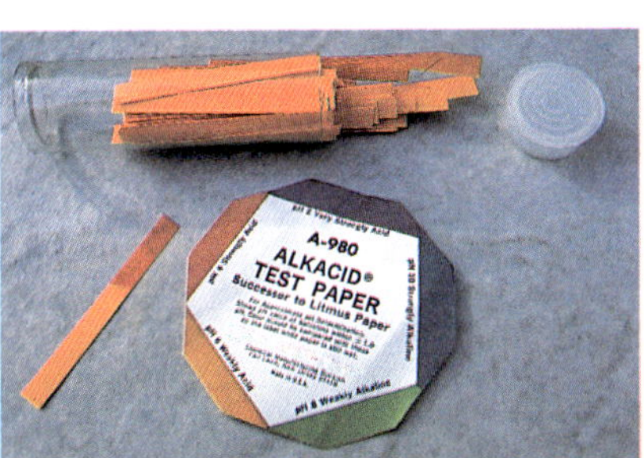

4. Chemical indicators identify acids and bases.

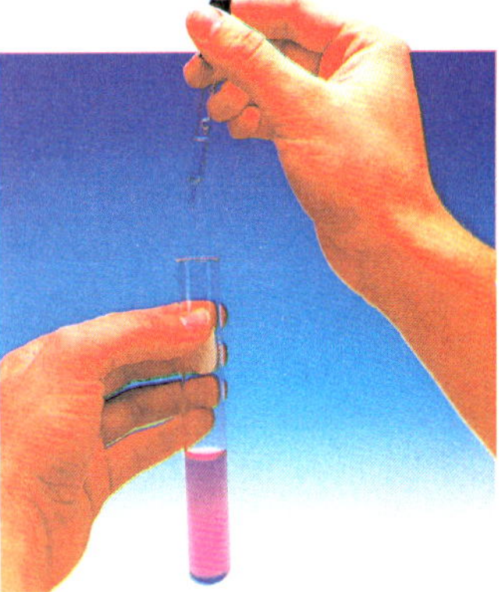

5. In a neutralization reaction, an acid reacts with a base to produce a salt and water.

Chapter 8

Reviewing Main Ideas

Direct students' attention to the diagrams. Use the diagrams to review the main ideas presented in the chapter. Have them read each statement aloud.

Teaching Strategies

Have students use colored paper to make acid and base "profile" cards. The paper color should correspond to the colors of the red cabbage indicator. For example, print *vinegar* on a red card because an acid of vinegar's strength turns the indicator red.

Divide the class up into seven teams: bright red, red, reddish purple, purple, blue green, green, and yellow. Each team should use all available resources to make acid or base cards corresponding to their indicator color. A sample card is shown below.

Profile of a BASE
Name: ANTACID
Active Chemical: Sodium bicarbonate Indicator Color: Green pH: 10.5 Category: Medium Base Feel: Slippery Color: Chalky Taste: Bitter Hazardous to Touch: No Poisonous: No Practical Use: Medicine

Encourage students to find as many examples of acids or bases as they can that match their team color. Substances might include: sulfuric acid (pH 0), washing soda (pH 12), saliva (pH 6.2–7.4), milk (pH 6.3–6.6), cooking oil (pH 7), grapefruit juice (pH 2.5), hydrochloric acid (pH 0), bottled water (pH will vary), and blood (pH 7.35–7.45).

Chapter 8

Chapter Review

USING KEY SCIENCE TERMS

Answers

1. *A base* turns litmus paper blue.
2. *An acid* has a sour taste and reacts with aluminum.
3. An acid and a base react, forming *a salt.*
4. A measure of acidity is called *pH.*
5. A substance used to test for an acid is called an *indicator.*
6. A salt is produced in a *neutralization* reaction.

UNDERSTANDING IDEAS

Answers

1. Food in the stomach needs to be broken down so it can be digested and used by the body. The hydrochloric acid in the stomach is necessary for breaking down this food.
2. Burning coal releases sulfur dioxide, which reacts with water in the atmosphere to form sulfurous acid. This is carried on the wind and falls as acid rain hundreds of miles away, polluting lakes and threatening wildlife.
3. Grapefruit has a sour taste.
4. Answers will vary but may include acetic acid (vinegar), ascorbic acid (lemon juice), sulfuric acid (battery acid), and carbonic and phosphoric acids (in soft drinks).
5. Ammonium hydroxide is used as a cleaning agent and fertilizer.
6. It is a base.
7. Runoff from basic fertilizers used on the park lawn may be making the pond basic. One way to neutralize the base would be to add acid to the water.
8. acid
9. the rock was a base; neutralization.

Chapter Review

USING KEY SCIENCE TERMS

acid	neutralization
base	pH
indicator	salt

Each of the statements below contains a word or words that make it wrong. Replace the words that are wrong with a term that uses the correct science term from above.

1. An acid turns litmus paper blue.
2. A base has a sour taste and reacts with aluminum.
3. An acid and a base react, forming an indicator.
4. A measure of acidity is called neutralization.
5. A substance used to test for an acid is called an acid test.
6. A salt is produced in a displacement reaction.

UNDERSTANDING IDEAS

Answer the following questions.

1. Explain how hydrochloric acid in your body is important to your life and good health.
2. How does the burning of coal in one area of the country affect the environment in another area?
3. What would be a good indication that a grapefruit contains an acid?
4. Name five common acids found in your home and/or school.
5. What is the most commonly used base and what is it used for?
6. A blue liquid has a pH of 8.2. What can you infer about this liquid?
7. The fish are dying in the park pond. You test the water and its pH is 10.2. What might be contributing to the death of the fish? What could be done about it?
8. You buy a can of soft drink at the grocery store and test it with litmus paper. It turns the paper red. Is the soft drink an acid or a base?
9. A pH meter shows that a liquid has a pH of 4.2. You drop a white rock into it, and the meter swings over to 7.1. What was the rock? What kind of reaction went on?

CRITICAL THINKING

Use your understanding of the concepts developed in the chapter to answer each of the following questions.

1. The leaves on the red cabbage in your garden are blue-green in color. What does this indicate about the soil?
2. Despite all your warnings about the danger, your older brother's friend gets battery acid on his best jeans while working on a car. Describe how you could minimize the damage.
3. The inside of a paper carton that your orange juice came in has a silvery color. Explain why it is probably plastic and not aluminum foil.

PROGRAM RESOURCES

Teacher Classroom Resources

Review and Assessment, Chapter Review and Chapter Test, pages 33-36

Computer Test Bank, Chapter Test

OPTIONS

Cooperative Learning

Consider using Cooperative Learning in the Understanding Ideas, Critical Thinking, Problem Solving, and Connecting Ideas sections of the Chapter Review.

COOP LEARN

4. You were in charge of a barbecue and now have to clean up the rib cooker. It is covered with grease. What product would be most effective? Why?
5. You have spilled vinegar all over your mom's new kitchen counter. Give two reasons why soap is the best thing to use to clean it up.
6. The chlorine generator at the pool has gone wild, and the pool's pH is as shown on the meter. Describe what effect this might have on the pool. How would you get the water back to where it is safe to swim?

7. Evergreen trees such as pines, spruces, and firs grow best in slightly acid soil. If you wanted to plant an evergreen, what steps would you take to ensure its healthy growth?

PROBLEM SOLVING

Read the following problem and discuss your answers in a brief paragraph.

Sheila Jones grows beautiful blue hydrangeas. Her neighbor, Manuel Ortiz, wants a root from these plants so that he can grow some just like them. Sheila is delighted to share her plants and gives several roots to Manuel.

Imagine Manuel's surprise when his flowers bloom: they aren't blue, but pink! Because Sheila has only blue hydrangeas, Manuel knows there was no mix-up. Manuel talks to the Green Garden Nursery about these flowers. The person at the nursery tells him to check his soil.

What do you think is the reason that Manuel's blue hydrangeas are pink? Why are Sheila's hydrangeas blue? What should Manuel do to get blue hydrangeas?

CONNECTING IDEAS

Discuss each of the following in a brief paragraph.

1. A recipe for spaghetti sauce states that it must be cooked in a nonaluminum pot. What is the reason for this instruction?

2. Predict the effect of acid rain on various types of landforms.

3. You dissolve sodium hydroxide in water. Is this mixture heterogeneous or homogeneous? Is the mixture a solution?

4. SCIENCE AND SOCIETY What steps can be taken to reduce the amount of acid-producing substances in the air?

5. ART CONNECTION Describe one way of protecting marble from acid rain.

CRITICAL THINKING

Answers

1. The soil is mildly basic.

2. Put a base such as ammonium hydroxide or baking soda on it right away to neutralize the acid.

3. Aluminum would not be a suitable container for orange juice, which contains acid, because metals react with acids.

4. A soap or oven cleaner is a base. It would dissolve the grease and could also be washed away because it is soluble in water.

5. Soap is basic and would neutralize the vinegar, which is an acid. It is also soluble in water, so it can be washed away with water.

6. The acid could react with the mortar in the pool's wall and the metal in the pump and filter. Add a base, such as lime, to the water.

7. Keep it away from chemical fertilizers, which are usually basic. Treat the soil with some very mild acid.

PROBLEM SOLVING

Answer

Hydrangeas must be a natural indicator, like red cabbage juice, that turn color in acidic or basic soil. Manuel and Sheila's soil must be opposite with respect to pH. To get blue hydrangeas, Manuel should adjust his soil so its pH matches that of Sheila's.

CONNECTING IDEAS

Answers

1. Tomato sauce is acidic and could react with aluminum, which would spoil its flavor.

2. Acid rain will damage limestone and marble structures in cities. In forests it will scar, damage, and kill trees.

3. Sodium hydroxide dissolves completely in water. It cannot be separated by filters and will not scatter light. It is a homogeneous mixture, or solution.

4. Possible answers include reducing the amount of coal used to produce electricity and scrubbing sulfur dioxide out of smokestack gases after coal has been burned.

5. Marble can be protected by washing with a basic solution, by coating with wax, or by restricting the area from cars and machinery that give off pollution.

LOOKING BACK

UNIT 2
INTERACTIONS IN THE PHYSICAL WORLD

THEME DEVELOPMENT

The themes developed in Unit 2 were scale and structure, interactions and systems, and stability and change and energy. The theme of scale and structure helped students distinguish between the physical and chemical properties of matter. Comparing the chemical and physical properties of an acid and a base helped students to understand how these two chemicals interact, so that they learned why, for example, hydrochloric acid is dangerous by itself and at the same time is so vital to their digestive system. The more they understand about elements of the world that are stable and those that change, the better they are able to see patterns of change in the environment, and make valid predictions.

Connection to Other Units

Students continued to use their sense to observe and classify, as they learned in Unit 1, while conducting a variety of investigations of the physical world in Unit 2. The investigations of substances and their interactions in Unit 2 will help students understand the more complex interactions explored in Unit 3.

Connecting Ideas

Answers

1. The salt was dissolved in the water. When the water evaporated the salt remained on the skin. The remaining salt appears white and crystalline on the skin.

2. Students suggestions may vary but the brands could be tested with pH paper. If the resultant color was the same, the acidity would be the same.

Exploring Further

Students may check books or pamphlets on safety in the home. A phone call or letter to a local poison control bureau may yield valuable information. First aid manuals also suggest antidotes for household poisons.

LOOKING BACK

UNIT 2 INTERACTIONS IN THE PHYSICAL WORLD

CONTENTS

UNIT FOCUS

In this unit, you investigated how substances on Earth differ. You observed how some materials dissolve in others, forming solutions, while others do not.

You can describe an iron nail using physical properties such as its size and mass, and chemical properties such as its ability to react with oxygen to form rust.

Physical and chemical properties can also be used to identify substances as acids, bases, and salts.

Try the exercises and activity that follow—they will challenge you to use and apply some of the ideas you learned in this unit.

CONNECTING IDEAS

1. Ocean water is very salty. You may have accidentally tasted some while swimming, or noticed that salt crystals formed on your body as you sat in the sun to dry after swimming. How does the salt appear on your skin?
2. **Analyzing Data:** Suppose you are trying to decide which vinegar to buy. One brand is much cheaper than the other brand. You wonder if the cheaper brand has been diluted with water. If this is true, the acidity of the cheaper, diluted vinegar should be lower than the more expensive brand. How could you design an experiment to see if the acidity was the same for both brands?

EXPLORING FURTHER

Make a card file of dangerous materials around your home. Identify acids, bases, and other toxic solutions and materials. Include the danger posed by each substance and the steps to be taken if the material is accidentally spilled or taken into your body. Use this activity to compile a first aid file for the home.

UNIT 3 INTERACTIONS IN THE LIVING WORLD

CONTENTS

UNIT FOCUS

In Unit 2, you investigated materials of the physical world and observed how their physical and chemical properties allow you to identify materials. As you study Unit 3, you'll see how living things survive by interacting with the physical materials of our world. In addition, you will investigate how living organisms on Earth can be classified by their properties just as you classified physical materials in Unit 2. By looking at how plants, animals, and their environment interact, you will learn about the connections that link the biological and physical worlds together.

TRY IT

Look around your classroom. Can you think of ways to group the people in your class? The people in your classroom have many things in common. Everyone breathes, has a heartbeat, and eats. Grouping enables you to classify people based on similar characteristics. You can also observe differences among the people in your class. Perhaps you could group them using hair color or the color of their clothes. People share characteristics with other animals and plants as well. Make a drawing of a cactus plant, a bird, some weeds, and a person about your age. Show on your drawing some of the characteristics that are shared by all of these living things. You might show all of them obtaining energy. Also indicate in your picture some very obvious differences that would enable you to classify them as different organisms. After you've learned more about life forms on Earth, see how accurate your drawing is.

Try It

The purpose of this activity is to recognize similar and different characteristics and use them to classify. Have students prepare a two column table. Mark one column "Similar Characteristics" and the other "Different Characteristics." Ask them to list as many traits or characteristics that they can think of that fit each column for the students in class or some other group. This could also be done as a class project with answers being recorded on the chalkboard. This table may serve as a guide in having the students list similarities and differences found in their drawings of the cactus, bird, weed, and person.

LOOKING AHEAD

UNIT 3
INTERACTIONS IN THE LIVING WORLD

THEME DEVELOPMENT

Interactions and systems is a major theme developed in Unit 3. All living things share the same basic need for food. The relationship among organisms—those that produce food through photosynthesis and those who need to obtain food from other sources is seen. Scale and structure also is a theme in this unit. Students will compare organisms, regardless of size or complexity.

Connections to Other Units

This unit builds on the observations and classification skills developed in previous units. It also provides information that will help students bridge to the next unit. Unit 4 covers concepts dealing with water, erosion, and soil formation. It will directly relate to the identification of those water areas on Earth where specific water life forms may be found. The formation of soil and erosion will explain where minerals present in soil originally came from.

Getting Started

Discussion Some questions you may want to ask your students are:

1. **Define the word "life" without using the words, "living," "alive" or "life" in your definition.** Students may suggest descriptions such as "breathing," "moving" and so on. Most will emphasize familiar animals, neglecting plants and very simple animal forms.
2. **Other than color, how might plants and animals differ? How are they alike?** Students will probably name some similarities and differences but will miss many that will be explored in this unit.
3. **What is the role of the gases in our atmosphere in helping to maintain life on Earth?** Most students will suggest that oxygen is necessary. The answers to these questions will help you establish what misconceptions your students may have.

CHAPTER ORGANIZER

SECTION	OBJECTIVES	ACTIVITIES/FEATURES
Chapter Opener		**Explore!** How would you classify things? p. 257
9-1 What Is the Living World? (3 days)	1. **Determine** the characteristics of living things. 2. **Apply** the characteristics of living things to determine if something is alive or not.	**Find Out!** What are some traits of living and nonliving things? p. 258 **Investigate 9-1:** Is It Living? p. 262
9-2 Why Classify Organisms? (2 days)	1. **Recognize** how a classification system allows scientists to communicate information. 2. **Describe** the levels of the system used to classify organisms. 3. **Explain** the characteristics that make up the five kingdoms of organisms.	**Explore!** How would you name things? p. 264 **Explore!** How do categories help you find what you want? p. 266
9-3 How Organisms Are Classified (4 days)	1. **Demonstrate** that the classification system shows how organisms are related. 2. **Identify** the traits scientists use to classify organisms.	**Find Out!** Compare the classification of a leopard with that of a domestic cat, p. 272 **Explore!** What are useful traits for classifying? p. 273 **Skillbuilder:** Making and Interpreting Graphs, p. 275 **Investigate 9-2:** Identifying Organisms, p. 276
Expanding Your View		A Closer Look **How to Use a Key,** p. 279 Earth Science Connection **Hydrothermal Vents,** p. 280 Science and Society **Endangered Species,** p. 281 History Connection **The History of Plant Classification,** p. 283 Technology Connection **Modern Tools for Classification,** p. 284

ACTIVITY MATERIALS

EXPLORE!	INVESTIGATE!	FIND OUT!
Page 257 envelope containing a variety of objects **Page 264** assorted tree leaves **Page 273** collection of animal pictures	**Page 262** 1 package dry yeast, table sugar, 4 test tubes, water, dropper, microscope, microscope slides, coverslips, flat-ended toothpicks	**Page 258** radish seeds, sand, 2 small flowerpots with soil, water

Describing the Living World

TEACHER CLASSROOM RESOURCES	OTHER RESOURCES
Study Guide, p. 33 **Critical Thinking/Problem Solving,** p. 17 **Multicultural Activities,** p. 21 **Making Connections: Integrating Sciences,** p. 21 **Activity Masters, Investigate 9-1,** pp. 37-38 **Making Connections: Technology and Society,** p. 21	***STVS:** *Aphid Mimic,* Ecology (Disc 6, Side 1) *Sea Turtle Mystery,* Animals (Disc 5, Side 2)
Study Guide, p. 34 **Concept Mapping,** p. 17 **Multicultural Activities,** p. 22 **Making Connections: Across the Curriculum,** p. 21	**Color Transparency and Master 17,** Classification Pyramid **Color Transparency and Master 18,** Life's Five Kingdoms ***STVS:** *Naming Fish,* Animals (Disc 5, Side 2) *Soil Crusts in the Desert,* Plants and Simple Organisms (Disc 4, Side 1) *Fungal Collection for Research,* Plants and Simple Organisms, (Disc 4, Side 1)
Study Guide, p. 35 **Flex Your Brain,** p. 8 **Take Home Activities,** p. 17 **Activity Masters, Investigate 9-2,** pp. 39-40 **Review and Assessment,** pp. 37-40	**Laboratory Manual,** pp. 49-52, Classification ***STVS:** *Nematodes,* Animals (Disc 5, Side 1) **Computer Test Bank**
	***STVS:** *Simple Forms of Life in the Antarctic,* Plants and Simple Organisms (Disc 4, Side 1) *Saving the Spotted Owl,* Ecology (Disc 6, Side 1) **Spanish Resources** **Cooperative Learning Resource Guide** **Lab and Safety Skills**

***Science and Technology Videodisc Series**

KEY TO TEACHING STRATEGIES

Teaching strategies have been coded for varying learning styles and abilities. As you review teaching strategies in the margin, the following designations will help you decide which activities are appropriate for your students.

- **L1** Level 1 activities are basic activities and should be within the ability range of all students.
- **L2** Level 2 activities are average activities and should be within the ability range of the average to above-average student.
- **L3** Level 3 activities are challenging activities designed for the ability range of above-average students.
- **LEP** LEP activities should be within the ability range of Limited English Proficiency students.
- **COOP LEARN** Cooperative Learning activities are designed for small group work.

ADDITIONAL MATERIALS

SOFTWARE	AUDIOVISUAL
Classify—Classification Key Program, Diversified Educational Enterprises. *Taxonomy: Classification and Organization,* IBM. *The Taxonomy Game,* Queue.	*Carolus Linnaeus,* film, EBEC. *Insects: The Little Things That Run the World,* laserdisc, Lumivision. *Classifying Plants and Animals,* film, Coronet/MTI.

Chapter 9

Describing the Living World

THEME DEVELOPMENT

One theme of this chapter is interactions and systems. Students learn a system of classification for living things, based on body structure and interactions with the environment. They learn that this system applies to all organisms regardless of size and scale thus supporting the theme of scale and structure.

CHAPTER OVERVIEW

The chapter defines living things, describes the Linnaean system of binomial nomenclature, and shows students how to classify organisms.

First, students learn six traits that distinguish living from nonliving things and apply the traits to identify living things.

Then, they learn the importance of classification to our understanding of the living world and are introduced to the categories of the Linnaean system. Activities give them practice in the principles of classification.

Finally, students apply their knowledge of classification to specific organisms and use Linnaean categories to understand relatedness among organisms. They identify traits that are useful for classification and use a key to identify species of birds.

Tying to Previous Knowledge

Ask students to name some of the terms and concepts they use to classify parts of Earth, such as mountains and plateaus. Ask them what else is found on Earth. Students should recognize that Earth is full of life. Have them name categories for living things. *Answers may include plants, animals and germs.* Explain that this chapter shows how to describe the living world in order to understand it better.

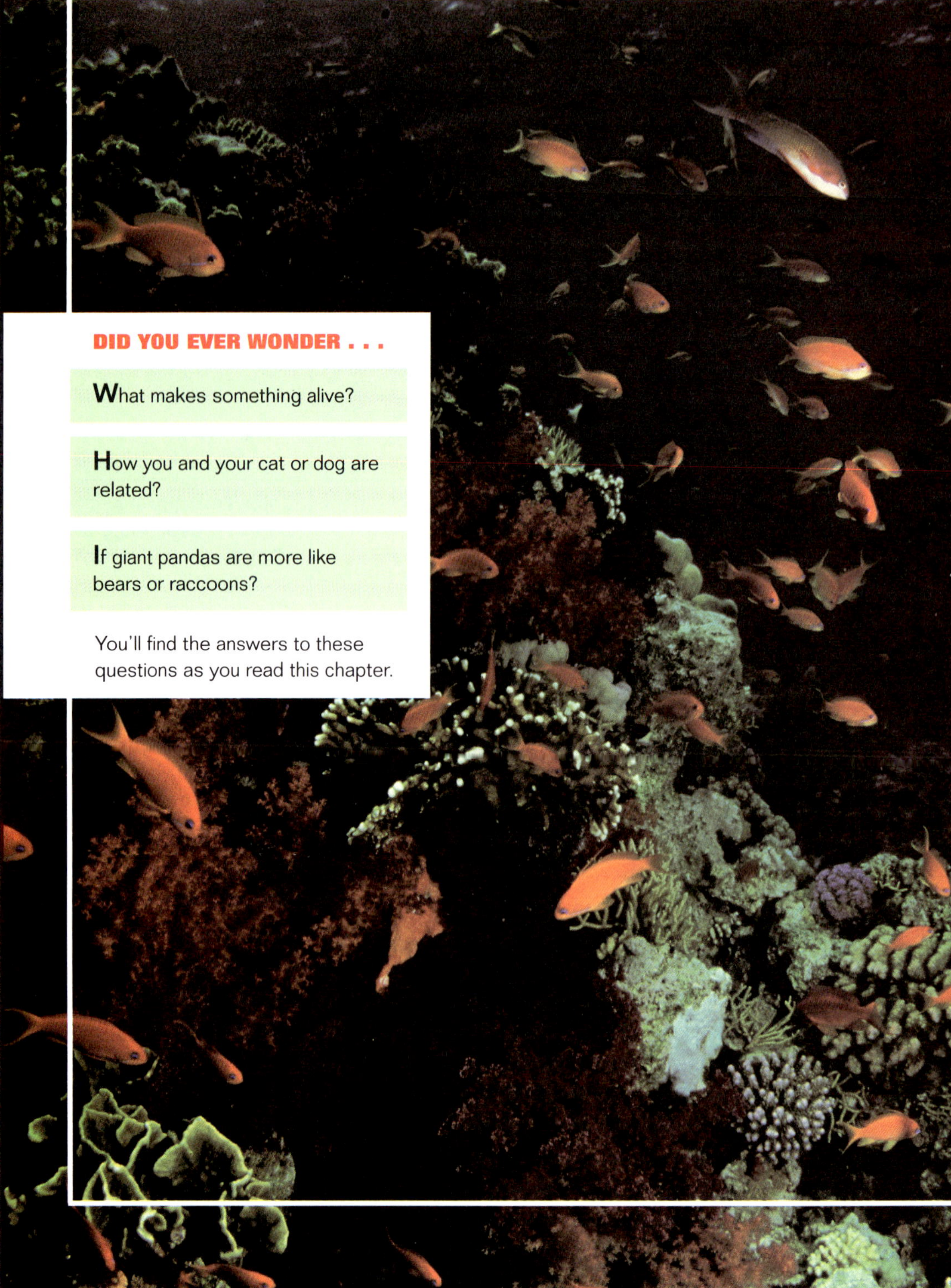

DID YOU EVER WONDER . . .

What makes something alive?

How you and your cat or dog are related?

If giant pandas are more like bears or raccoons?

You'll find the answers to these questions as you read this chapter.

DID YOU EVER WONDER...

Students will explore these questions as they progress through the chapter. Don't spoil their fun and motivation by sharing these answers too early.

- Living things have six traits that nonliving things lack: cellular structure, a need for food and water, growth, reproduction, response to the environment, and adaptation to the environment. (pages 259–260)
- You are both members of the kingdom *Animalia,* the phylum *Chordata,* and the class *Mammalia.* (page 271)
- Giant pandas are more like bears than racoons although they share many traits with raccoons. (page 278)

Chapter 9

Describing the Living World

You rush into the record store, eager to get the latest cassette by your favorite group. You head for the first table of cassettes and begin looking for it. Something must be wrong! There's rock mixed in with reggae, country with classical, rap right next to opera. Nothing is in order!

Record stores would not sell many cassettes if they were this disorganized. Stores make it easy to find what you want by classifying and organizing the cassettes according to musical style and artist. Of course, nature isn't quite as organized as a record store. This coral reef, which is home to an astonishing variety of living things, is proof of that. Yet, classifying living things helps us organize our knowledge and talk about specific animals and plants. When a scientist finds a new kind of creature, it can be classified with other creatures that share many of its characteristics. Classifying living things helps us understand them.

EXPLORE!

How would you classify things?

Get an envelope containing a variety of objects from your teacher. Empty it onto your desk. Take a good look at the objects. Divide the objects into two groups based on one major difference you see among them. Now select another characteristic to divide each of the two groups into two other groups. Note what characteristic you use to make each group. At which stage of classifying did all the objects in each group share the most characteristics?

Introducing the Chapter

Have students examine the chapter opener photo. Lead them in brainstorming a list of all the kinds of things shown in the photo. The list should include fish of several kinds (it is not necessary to identify the kind, but students should note how many different kinds there are), rocks, corals, plants, and water. Tell students that they will be using this information in the first section of the chapter.

Uncovering Preconceptions

Students may think that it is always easy to tell the difference between living and nonliving things. Ask students how they tell the difference. Accept all answers and tell them that this chapter will show them that it can be harder to tell the difference than they might think.

EXPLORE!

How would you classify things?

Time needed 15 minutes

Materials envelope filled with 5–6 small, objects such as a penny, wood chip, key, paper clip, flower petal, nail, leaf and chalk.

Thinking Processes
Organizing information, Classifying

Purpose To introduce classification of objects.

Preparation Envelopes should not all include the same items, but include objects that are examples of living and nonliving things.

Teaching the Activity

Demonstration Show three objects to students: a plant, a pencil and a green marker. Ask students to suggest ways of grouping two of the objects at a time. *Possibilities include the pencil and marker as nonliving; plant and marker as green.* L1

Expected Outcome

Students classify objects into groups at two levels based on shared traits.

Science at Home

Have students select an organism found at home: a pet (other than a cat, which is classified in the text), houseplant, insect, or common household bacteria. Have students observe it closely and write a detailed description of its traits. Have students find the scientific name of the organism by using encyclopedias and field guides at the library.

Project

Have groups of students make a large bulletin board collage of the Linnaean categories, arranging them in order from broadest to narrowest. Have each group select an organism for the species level and illustrate this level with a picture. Have students search old magazines to find pictures of their particular organism. At each higher level, have students add pictures of related organisms to show the broadening of the category.

Section 9-1

PREPARATION

Concepts Developed

Students learn the traits of living organisms that distinguish them from nonliving things.

Planning the Lesson

In planning your lesson on the living world, refer to the Chapter Organizer on pages 256A-B for timing suggestions, resources, and additional materials that will help you in your presentation of the lesson concepts.

For adequate development of the concepts presented in this section, we recommend that students do the Find Out activity on page 258.

1 MOTIVATE

Discussion Have students contrast living versus nonliving things. Obtain a videotape of the classic Boris Karloff *Frankenstein.* Show students the sequence in which Dr. Frankenstein brings his monster to melodramatic life using the electrical power of lightning. (If the film is not available, have students take turns telling the familiar story.) Ask students how the doctor knew his creature lived. *It moved.* Tell students that this section describes six ways that living and nonliving things are different. L1

9-1 What Is the Living World?

OBJECTIVES

In this section, you will

- determine the characteristics of living things;
- apply the characteristics of living things to determine if something is alive or not.

KEY SCIENCE TERMS

organism
reproduction
stimulus
adaptation

IS IT LIVING?

If you visit an aquarium, or if you're ever lucky enough to go snorkeling near a coral reef, you might see a scene like the photograph that opens this chapter. Look again at the picture of the coral reef. If you were face-to-face with a fish, you'd know you were looking at a living thing. But what about the leaf-like objects? Or the coral itself? Are these things living?

Telling the difference between something that is living and something that is nonliving can sometimes be difficult. This next activity will help you identify some characteristics, or traits you can use to distinguish living and nonliving things.

FIND OUT!

What are some traits of living and nonliving things?

Obtain some radish seeds and sand grains from your teacher. Describe how the seeds look. Can you tell if the seeds are living things or nonliving things? Describe how the sand grains look. How do you know grains of sand are not living? Now obtain two small flowerpots with soil from your teacher. Put the radish seeds under 1cm of soil in one pot and put the sand grains under 1cm of soil in the other pot. Water both pots; then put them in indirect sunlight and keep them moist. What do you expect will happen? Observe the two pots for about two weeks. Write down what you see and answer the questions.

Conclude and Apply

1. What observations tell you the seeds are living things?
2. What are the traits the seeds have that the sand grains don't?

FIND OUT!

What are some traits of living and nonliving things?

Time needed 30 minutes, with brief observations weekly for 2 weeks

Materials radish seeds, sand, 2 flowerpots, soil

Thinking Processes
Observing, Forming a hypothesis, Interpreting data

Purpose To identify growth as a trait of living things

Preparation Place the flowerpots where they can obtain sunlight.

Teaching the Activity

Discussion Plant and water the sand and ask students how they know the sand will not grow. Growth is a characteristic only of living things. Encourage students to define *nonliving* as lacking in the traits described in the text. L1

Expected Outcomes

Students will recognize that the seeds are alive but not the sand..

Conclude and Apply

1. They sprout and grow.
2. ability to grow

One trait you probably observed in the Find Out activity is growth. Seeds grow into plants, yet sand doesn't. Growth is one trait that each living thing—each **organism**—shares with all other organisms. What other traits do organisms possess?

FIGURE 9-1. All living things are made up of cells.

ORGANISMS

Organisms, from radish seeds to elephants, generally have six traits that make them different from nonliving things. These six traits are the following:

1. Organisms are made up of cells. Cells are the basic units of all living things. Some organisms, such as bacteria, are made up of just one single cell. You are an organism, along with cats, birds, and trees, made up of billions of cells. Complex organisms like you have many different kinds of cells working together, each performing a different function to keep you alive.

Most cells are microscopic. You can't see the cells in your radish seeds or in yourself without the help of a magnifying device, but they are there.

2. Organisms need water and food to develop and live. Water and food keep life processes going within cells. Growth and movement are processes fueled by food.

Although different kinds of organisms may use different foods, all forms of life that scientists have observed use water to carry on their life processes. Life as we know it would be impossible without water. In fact, every organism is made up of mostly water. For example, your body is about two-thirds water. A human can go without food for about three months but will die in a week without water.

What do you think the radish seeds used for food? What do you use for food?

3. Organisms grow. All organisms increase in size and mass. Puppies, kittens, and saplings grow up to become dogs, cats, and trees. One-celled organisms grow to a certain size and then divide, resulting in two smaller cells.

2 TEACH

Tying to Previous Knowledge

In the previous two chapters, students have classified parts of the physical world. Review briefly the classifications—physical and chemical; elements, alloys, and ceramics—they have studied and then explain that this section describes ways to classify the living world. Have students suggest possible categories for living things.

Concept Development

Activity Have students name any household items that come to mind. As the students name each item, write it on the chalkboard. Then have students put the items into different classifications. For example, the students may name refrigerator, chair, television, sofa, table, and radio. The classifications might be appliances and furniture. L1

Student Journal Have students make an outline in their journals for the six traits that make organisms different from nonliving things, for example:

I. Organisms
  A. Made up of cells
    1. single celled organisms
    2. complex organisms
      a. billions of cells

Students who may have difficulty making an outline can be given the option of making a concept map.

PROGRAM RESOURCES

Teacher Classroom Resources

Study Guide, page 33

Critical Thinking/Problem Solving, page 17, Regeneration L2

Multicultural Activities, page 21, New World Epidemics L1

Making Connections: Integrating Sciences, page 21, The Structure of DNA

Concept Development

Theme Connection The themes that this section supports are interactions and systems and stability and change. Students learn to recognize living things by their interactions with the environment. This theme becomes apparent as the students complete the Investigate activity on page 262.

Demonstration Crumple a piece of paper and place it in a large ashtray, making sure that students can see the paper. Set it on fire with a match and let it burn to ash. Then tell students that they watched fire grow and use and produce energy. Ask students if fire is alive. *no* Ask them if this demonstration suggests why scientists use six traits to tell living from nonliving things. Help them as needed to see that nonliving things may have one or two traits on the list but that only living things have all six. L2

Student Text Question Figure 9-2 Organisms need water and food. They grow and reproduce. How do these dogs exhibit each of these traits? *As they feed on milk from their mother, they will grow and develop.*

MAKING CONNECTIONS

Writing

Have students conduct research into viruses and write an essay describing the controversy over whether viruses are living things.

These organisms grow in the number of individuals rather than in size.

You observed radish seeds grow into seedlings. What evidence do you have that you have changed in size since last year?

4. Organisms can reproduce. **Reproduction** is the process by which organisms make more organisms of the same kind. Humans reproduce and have children. Mosquitoes reproduce and make more mosquitoes. Many plants, like your radish plants, reproduce by making seeds.

5. Organisms respond to their environment. When you hear an unexpected loud noise, you jump. When it gets cold, you shiver. You are responding to what is happening in your environment when you do these things. Anything an organism responds to is a **stimulus**. The stimulus produces a response, a change in the behavior, from the organism.

FIGURE 9-2. Organisms need water and food. They grow and reproduce. How do these dogs exhibit each of these traits?

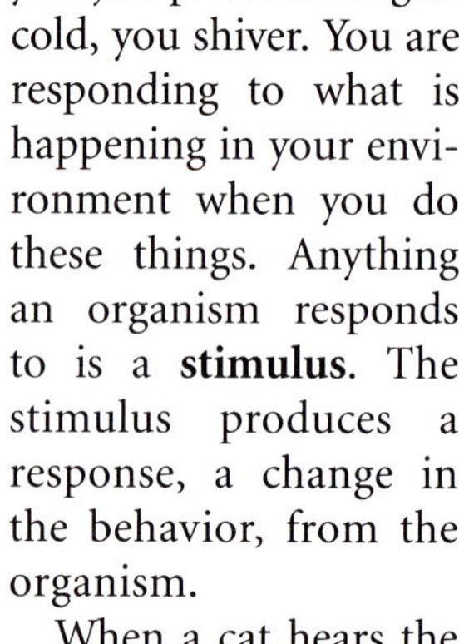

When a cat hears the sound of a can opener, it comes running into the kitchen expecting to be fed. The stimulus is an audible signal to which the cat responds. When a dog sees its owner pick up its leash, it bounds toward the door expecting to be taken for a walk. The leash is a visual stimulus to which the dog responds. Remember the senses you studied in Chapter 4? Each of an organism's senses can deliver a stimulus to which the organism may respond.

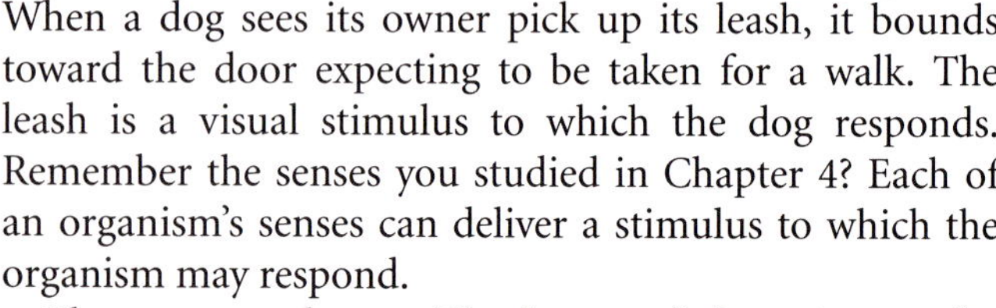

Plants respond, too. The leaves of the mimosa, for example, respond to touch by folding up. You can see this plant response in Figure 9-3. Plants respond to sunlight by growing toward it.

6. Organisms are adapted to their environments. Most penguins are organisms that live in very cold climates.

RROGRAM RESOURCES

Other Resources

Ambrose, E. J. *The Nature and Origin of the Biological World.* Englewood Cliffs, NJ: Prentice Hall, 1982.

OPTIONS

Meeting Individual Needs

Learning Disabled Many learning-disabled students have significant problems with retention even when they have adequate comprehension skills. You may find it useful to make a brief list of the traits in one corner of the chalkboard and leave it there throughout your discussion of this section, so that students can refer to it as needed.

1. Cells 2. Food and water 3. Grow 4. Reproduce 5. Respond 6. Adapt

FIGURE 9-3. Mimosa leaves respond to touch by folding up.

Parrots live in the trees in the hot rain forest. Fish live in water. Cacti survive in the desert. Mangrove trees grow in swamps. Organisms living in different environments often have special traits that enable them to survive in those climates. Any trait of an organism's body or behavior that helps it survive in its environment is called an **adaptation**. The better a plant or animal is adapted to its environment, the better its chances for survival and reproduction.

These six traits of living organisms are not always easy to observe. Look at the barnacles in Figure 9-4, for example. An adult barnacle may live permanently stuck to a rock on the shore. Just observing it won't tell you if it's made up of cells. In fact, its outer shell looks like a rock. You can't see the barnacle eating, growing, reproducing, or reacting to stimuli. It seems adapted to its environment, but then so does a rock on the beach. The barnacle is alive, but you would have to take a much closer look at it to see that it is living. What would you try first? Do the following Investigate to see.

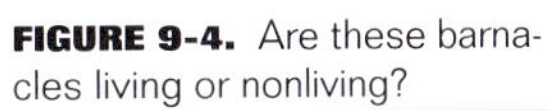

FIGURE 9-4. Are these barnacles living or nonliving?

Concept Development

Activity Have students conduct library research on the *Viking* lander missions to Mars and write an essay describing the experiments that the lander performed to search for signs of life on Mars. The essays should describe when the missions were launched from Earth, when they reached Mars, the experiments conducted, equipment used, and results. L3

Student Text Question Figure 9-4–Are these barnacles living or nonliving? *Living but you would have to watch them over a period of time to determine that they are.*

Content Background

Adaptation occurs through natural selection. In reproduction, random changes occur in the genes of a population that control an organism's growth. Some of these changes, or mutations, produce traits that make an organism more likely to survive and reproduce. Any mutation favoring survival and reproduction is passed on to new generations. In the competition for survival, organisms that lack this new trait are less likely to survive. As these organisms die out, all members of the species finally have the new trait.

Teacher F.Y.I.

Life formed on Earth about 3.5 billion years ago as colonies of one-celled organisms.

Enrichment

Activity Have students perform the Investigate activity on page 262 (but without microscopic examination), using water, vinegar, and baking soda. All test tubes receive 20 drops of water. In addition, test tube B gets 20 drops of vinegar; tube C gets 4 toothpick ends of baking soda; and tube D gets 20 drops of vinegar and 4 toothpick ends of baking soda. Students will observe the bubbling reaction of tube D. Ask them if this indicates that baking soda is alive and, if not, how else they can explain the reaction. *The bubbles are the result of an acid-base chemical reaction.*

Students may need assistance in connecting this activity with materials in Chapter 8 on Acids and Bases.

INVESTIGATE!

9-1 IS IT LIVING?

Time needed 60 minutes

Materials See student activity.

Thinking Processes
Organizing information, Making and using tables, Practicing scientific methods, Observing, Forming a hypothesis, Separating and controlling variables, Interpreting data

Purpose To determine if yeast is living or nonliving.

Preparation This activity may be performed by individuals or pairs of students. COOP LEARN

Teaching the Activity

Demonstration To help students understand the differences among the test tubes, display four test tubes: A (with clear water), B (water with blue food coloring), C (water with red food coloring, and D (water with both blue and red coloring, making purple).

Troubleshooting Divide the class into four groups. Begin work with the first group; after five minutes get the next group started, and so on. Given the need for students to wait 15 minutes between observations, staggering the progress of the groups will allow you to work with all students and ensure that everyone gets access to microscopes when needed. L1

Expected Outcome

Students identify yeast as living because it is cellular, uses food, grows and responds to stimuli.

Answers to Analyze/Conclude and Apply

1. test tube D
2. Tube A is the control, because nothing was added to the water.
3. small, oval-shaped objects
4. It is living. It is cellular, uses food, grows and responds to stimuli.
5. bubbles
6. Bubbles would form as the sugar in grape juice provided food for yeast.

INVESTIGATE!

9-1 IS IT LIVING?

In this activity, you will observe yeast under a microscope to determine if it is living or nonliving.

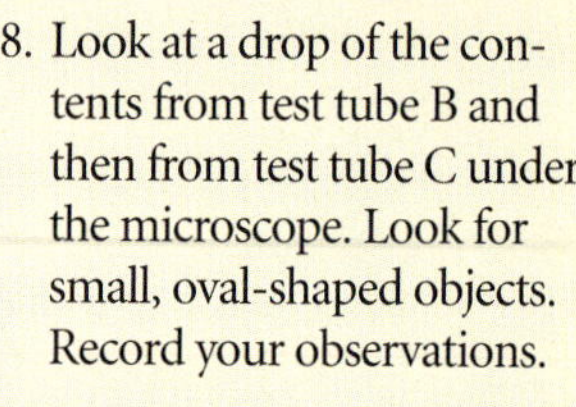

PROBLEM

How can you determine if yeast is an organism?

MATERIALS

1 package dry yeast
table sugar
4 test tubes
water
dropper
microscope
microscope slides
coverslips
flat-ended toothpicks

PROCEDURE

1. Copy the data table.
2. Label the test tubes A, B, C, and D.
3. Add 20 drops of water to each test tube. For the dry ingredients, the amount that will fit on the flat end of a toothpick is considered one toothpick end. For B add 2 toothpick ends of sugar, for C add 2 toothpick ends of yeast; for D add 2 toothpick ends of yeast and 2 toothpick ends of sugar.
4. Carefully swirl each test tube to mix ingredients.
5. **Observe** some of the dry yeast particles with a microscope. Note what you see.
6. After 15 minutes, look at each test tube. Record your observations.
7. After 30 minutes, look at each test tube again. Record your observations.
8. Look at a drop of the contents from test tube B and then from test tube C under the microscope. Look for small, oval-shaped objects. Record your observations.

DATA AND OBSERVATIONS

Sample data

TIME	A	B	C	D
After 15 Minutes	No change	No change	No change	Bubbles
After 30 Minutes	No change	No change	No change	Bubbles
Drawings	YEAST	B	C	

ANALYZE

1. In which test tube(s) did you **observe** a change?
2. **Identify the control** in this experiment. Why was this test tube the control?
3. What did you **observe** in Step 8?

CONCLUDE AND APPLY

4. What conclusion can you draw about whether yeast is living or nonliving? What observation(s) led you to this conclusion?
5. What activity did you **observe** in test tube D?
6. **Going Further: Hypothesize** what would happen if a fifth test tube had a pinch of yeast, 20 drops of water, and 20 drops of grape juice. Explain your suggestion.

PROGRAM RESOURCES

Teacher Classroom Resources

Activity Masters, pages 37-38, Investigate 9-1

Making Connections: Technology and Society, page 21, Environmental Change and Adaptation L1

In the Investigate, you may have observed that the test tube that contained yeast, sugar, and water produced bubbles. Because it is alive, the yeast needs food. The sugar was food for the yeast. The life processes carried out by living things often involve changes in the substances they take in and use. Often, as with the yeast, gases are produced as the organism uses up food and water.

FIGURE 9-5. Plants respond to the stimulus of sunlight.

As you look around your classroom, it may seem fairly easy to determine what is living and what is not. Your classmates may be talking with one another. A plant on your teacher's desk may have turned toward the light from the window. Or maybe the class's pet hamster just had a litter. You've learned, however, that it isn't always easy to see the traits of life.

Observing such life processes and the changes that go with them is one way you can determine whether something is alive. In the next sections, you'll learn why and how traits are used to classify all the things we've determined are alive.

Check Your Understanding

1. Name a trait of living things that each of the following nonliving objects appears to possess. Then explain why they are, nonetheless, not alive.
   a. a gasoline engine
   b. a crystal of salt
   c. a robot
2. Give two examples, other than those mentioned in the text, of an organism responding to a stimulus in its environment.
3. How is an adaptation different from a response to a stimulus?
4. **APPLY**: How does a pigeon pecking at bread crumbs on the ground in the park show the characteristics of living things? Does the pigeon show all the characteristics? If it does not, can you still say it is alive?

3 Assess

Check for Understanding

Materials needed are a fish in tank, a guinea pig, or plant; and a rock.

1. Show students the animal or plant and the rock. Ask them which one is alive. *the animal or plant* Ask students to explain, referring to the six points discussed in the chapter, why they know it is alive. Explain that you will assume a cellular structure even though it is not visible.

2. The questions ask students to apply the list of living traits to specific examples. Use the Apply question to remind students that they can use common sense as well as scientific rules in drawing conclusions about the world.

Reteach

Help students remember the traits of living things by drawing a concept map on the chalkboard, with "living thing" in the center and the six traits in circles around it and connected to it. Lead a discussion on each trait and have students suggest examples of both living and nonliving things that illustrate the trait. L1

Extension

Have students who have mastered the concepts in this section write a science fiction story describing scientists who visit another planet and apply the six traits to try to determine whether or not a green blob is a living thing. L3

4 Close

Discussion

Hold up a piece of paper and ask students to compare it to a tree (the most common source of paper). Why is the piece of paper nonliving while its source, a tree, is living? Ask the same question regarding a cotton ball and a piece of cotton cloth. Ask students if a cotton ball that has been picked is still alive. L1

Answers to Check Your Understanding

1. a. A gasoline engine consumes food but lacks other traits. b. A crystal of salt grows but lacks other traits. c. A robot responds to its environment and may be adapted to it but lacks other traits.
2. Examples may include dogs barking at strangers and trees losing leaves in autumn.
3. Adaptation involves a permanent change in an entire species; responses are individual and not lasting. The ability to perform certain responses, however, is adaptive.
4. Pigeon moves, shows need for food, response to environment, and adaptation to environment. The only thing students may not observe is reproduction, but if numerous pigeons are present, it is obvious that reproduction takes place in the population.

Section 9-2

PREPARATION

Concepts Developed

Students learn the binomial classification system developed by Linnaeus and the types of organisms that belong to the five major kingdoms.

Planning the Lesson

In planning your lesson on classifying organisms, refer to the Chapter Organizer on pages 256A-B for timing suggestions, resources, and additional materials that will help you in your presentation of the lesson concepts.

For adequate development of the concepts presented in this section, we recommend that students do the Explore activity on page 266.

1 MOTIVATE

Activity Ask three volunteers to contribute one object apiece and place them on a table where all students can see them. Objects may be anything students carry with them or select from the room. Ask students to study the objects and then name traits they have in common. Traits may reflect the objects' shape, color, material, or purpose. List students' suggestions on the chalkboard. Then have them suggest ways the objects are different and list these on the chalkboard. Explain that this section uses the same principles to classify the immense number of organisms on Earth. L1

9-2 Why Classify Organisms?

OBJECTIVES

In this section, you will

- recognize how a classification system allows scientists to communicate information;
- describe the levels of the system used to classify organisms;
- explain the characteristics that make up the five kingdoms of organisms.

KEY SCIENCE TERMS

kingdom
phylum
class
order
family
genus
species

WHAT'S IN A NAME?

What kind of bird do you picture when you hear the name *robin*? You probably think of the first bird shown in Figure 9-6. But the name robin means something different to people living in England. They call the second bird robin. And the name means something else again to people in China, who call the third bird robin. You can see that these robins aren't the same bird at all!

People use common names for organisms that they are familiar with. Usually, that's all right because people from the same region are referring to the same organism. But scientists would run into trouble if they used these common names. As in the case of the *robin*, they have to be able to communicate with each other even if they don't speak each other's language. They can't afford to make mistakes in identifying organisms. Therefore, scientists have devised a way to classify and name organisms. By looking closely at the traits of organisms, scientists can classify them in distinct, recognizable groups and give each group a special name. Try this method yourself in the following activity.

EXPLORE!

How would you name things?

Obtain an assortment of tree leaves from your teacher. Work with a partner to determine traits of the leaves that enable you to classify them. After you have classified them, give each group a name that describes one of its most noticeable traits. Tell another pair of classmates the names you've given your groups of leaves. Ask them to match each name with a group. Did they match correctly? Now you and your partner should try to identify the leaf groups your classmates named.

EXPLORE!

How would you name things?

Time needed 15 minutes

Materials 5–6 trees leaves from different plants

Thinking Processes Organizing information, Classifying

Purpose To learn classification and naming of living things

Preparation Sort leaves into envelopes and distribute or make separate piles and have student pairs take one from each pile. COOP LEARN

Teaching the Activity

Encourage students to use words such as *round, oval, long,* and *pointed* to describe leaf shape. Point out other traits that can be used such as leaf edge, vein pattern, color, texture, and shininess. Have students find two traits shared by at least two leaves.

See Meeting Individual needs in the OPTIONS on page 266. L1

Expected Outcomes

Students identify traits by which leaves may be classified and develop names that permit identification.

FIGURE 9-6. These three birds all have the common name "robin." Scientists call the first one *Turdus migratorius*, the second one *Erithacus rubecula*, and the third one *Eopsaltria australis*.

A SCIENTIFIC WAY TO CLASSIFY AND NAME

The classification system that scientists use gives a unique name to each kind of organism known. Although all three birds in Figure 9-6 have the common name *robin*, each one has a different scientific name. This name distinguishes the bird from all other kinds of birds.

This special classification and naming system was developed in the 1700s by a Swedish scientist named Carolus Linnaeus (luh NAY uhs). Linnaeus began by dividing all organisms into two general categories: animals and plants. These categories are called kingdoms. A **kingdom** is the most general and largest group of organisms in the

FIGURE 9-7. Carolus Linnaeus devised the scientific naming system that we still use today.

How do we know?

Linnaeus and the Early History of Classification

Carolus Linnaeus, pictured in Figure 9-7, established the modern system of classification in the 1700s. What influenced Linnaeus to construct such a system? Linnaeus was born in Sweden in 1707. At an early age, his friends and relatives noted his love for the natural world, especially botany (the study of plants). At age 8, he was nicknamed "the little botanist."

In 1728, Linnaeus attended medical school. While in school, he met a famous botanist who persuaded him to continue his botanical studies. Two years later, Linnaeus became a professor of botany, and directed a major scientific expedition to study plant life in the Arctic.

It was from these early studies that Linnaeus got the idea to establish a system of classification. The 1700s were important for the field of botany. Much of the world's vegetation was being described and studied by scientists at this time. Linnaeus established his system to help students of botany quickly put these newly described plants into categories.

2 TEACH

Tying to Previous Knowledge

In the previous section, students distinguished between living and nonliving things by six traits. Ask students how they might distinguish between different kinds of living things by their traits. Encourage them to suggest using such traits as color, shape, size, and habits in order to distinguish among living things. Explain that these traits are the basis of all classification of living things.

Concept Development

Discussion Ask students to brainstorm items that they classify every day—usually without thinking. Suggestions may be hanging shirts in a closet, stacking books to carry to school.

Theme Connection The theme that this section supports is scale and structure. Students learn a classification for living things based on their structure and traits. In the Explore activity on page 264, the students impose their own structure and naming system on a seemingly random pile of leaves.

How do we know?

This feature provides background on Linnaeus and explains the importance of his work. Students interested in more information on him can turn to:

Blunt, Wilfred. *The Compleat Naturalist: Carl Linnaeus.* 1971.

PROGRAM RESOURCES

Teacher Classroom Resources

Study Guide, page 34

Concept Mapping, page 17, Classification of Living Things L1

Multicultural Activities, page 22, Central American Rain Forests L1

Transparency Masters, page 37, and **Color Transparency,** number 17, Classification Pyramid 

EXPLORE!

How do categories help you find what you want?

Time needed 10 minutes

No special materials or preparation are required for this activity, which can be done as an independent assignment.

Thinking Processes

Organizing information, Classifying

Purpose To experiment with classification by groups and subgroups

Teaching the Activity

Demonstration Take students to the school library, where the librarian can explain how the Dewey decimal system organizes nonfiction by groups and subgroups in a fashion similar to the Linnaean system. L1

Discussion You might begin by asking students to discuss their favorite kind of music or their favorite performers. In assigning the activity, lead a brief discussion of categories students might use, such as type of music (jazz, classical, rock), performer or composer, and so on. Suggest a numbered list or outline format for depicting the categories.

Expected Outcome

Students identify levels of categories needed to find the song.

Answers to Questions

Answers may vary but should resemble this pattern:

1. Store
2. Type of music: rock
3. Record, CD, or cassette
4. Name of group
5. Title of album
6. Song

classification system. Today, scientists recognize three additional kingdoms: fungi, protists, and monerans. You'll learn more about these kingdoms later in this section.

Classification doesn't stop with five kingdoms, however. Organisms are classified into smaller and smaller groupings. In fact, there are six levels of groups within each kingdom. Why are so many categories necessary? This next Explore might give you a clue.

EXPLORE!

How do categories help you find what you want?

Pretend you're in a record store—not one in which the music was thrown together any which way, but a more orderly, organized store. How do you find a cassette that has a particular song by your favorite rock group? List the categories of your search from the broadest (the store itself) to the narrowest (the song). How many different levels of categories did you need to work through to locate your favorite?

ORDER OUT OF CONFUSION

The kingdom is still the largest category into which living things are grouped, just as it was in Linnaeus's time.

Kingdoms are divided into subgroups called phyla. (The singular is phylum.) When compared to your search for a song in the record store, a kingdom would be the store itself, and a phylum would be the cassette section within the store.

Each **phylum** is divided into still smaller groups called classes. A class can be compared to the category of music you look under for your song—in this case, rock music. Each **class** is broken down into groups called orders. An order can be likened to the alphabetical sections you find under rock music. Each **order** is divided into families. A family can be compared to all the cassettes of the particular rock group you like.

OPTIONS

Meeting Individual Needs

Visually Impaired Pair visually impaired students with fully sighted students for the leaf classification Explore activity on page 264. The fully sighted student will be able to record such visual traits as color and shininess. Visually impaired students, who are likely to be experienced at learning about objects by touch, may be able to observe far more detail about the texture and shape of leaves than their fully sighted partners. Fully sighted students may wish to experiment by closing their eyes and finding out what they can observe about the leaves with their other senses, including smell and hearing, that their eyes were not able to tell them. COOP LEARN

Each **family** is divided into subgroups called genera. (The singular is genus.) A genus can be compared to the particular cassette that has the song you want. Finally, each **genus** is made up of the smallest categories of all—**species**. A species might be compared to the song itself.

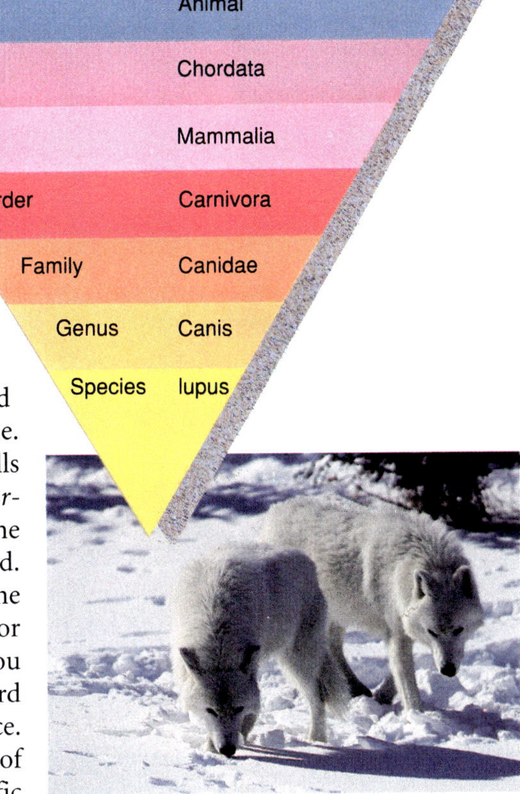

FIGURE 9-8. The classification of the Arctic wolf shows its genus and species to be *Canis lupus*.

Linnaeus completed his seven-level classification system by giving each kind of organism a two-part scientific name. The first part of the scientific name tells the genus of the organism, such as *Turdus* for the bird you know as a robin. The name of a genus is always capitalized. The second part of the scientific name describes the organism specifically. For example, what does *migratorius* tell you about this bird? It tells you that the bird migrates, or moves from place to place. Together, the first and second parts of the scientific name identify a specific organism and only that organism.

Linnaeus used Latin words to name organisms. At the time he worked, no one spoke Latin. However, it was learned and understood by people who attended universities. Most scientists throughout Europe learned to read and write Latin, so Linnaeus used it for his scientific classification system. Scientists still use these Latin names today. All over the world, if you talk about *Turdus migratorius*, scientists know exactly which bird you are referring to. Scientists also use Latin to name new organisms they discover.

Identifying a common bird may not seem very important to you. Imagine, however, that there's a new kind of bacterium causing a deadly disease. Scientists around the world are trying to work together to find a cure. Before they find a cure, they must identify the bacterium. If scientists simply called the disease-causing organism a bacterium,

Concept Development

Using the Diagrams Draw students' attention to the triangular diagram of the Linnaean system. Reproduce it on the chalkboard and ask students questions such as **If two animals belong to different families, what categories might they still share?** *order, class, phylum, and kingdom* This gives them practice with how the system works. You may wish to have students write questions of their own, exchange them, and answer each other's questions. Make sure students understand that kingdom is the most inclusive category, while species is the narrowest or most exclusive.

Multicultural Perspectives

People of different cultures have chosen very different systems of classification. The Navajo of the American Southwest, for example, traditionally divide all beings into those that have speech (human beings) and those that lack speech (animals and plants). Animals are subdivided according to how they move (by running, crawling, or flying) and by their time of greatest activity (day or night). Plants are grouped according to their medicinal value, appearance, and height or size. The nearby Hopi, however, use a different system. They divide the world into directions and associate each with a color; the Northwest is associated with yellow and the Southwest with blue or green. Plants and animals are grouped by color association: the puma, oriole, mariposa lily and yellow corn belong to the Northwest; the bear, bluebird, sagebrush, and blue corn belong to the Southwest.

MAKING CONNECTIONS

Daily Life

Students and their families use informal classification of plants and animals every day. For example, most students quickly learn to recognize poison ivy and poison oak if they live in an area where they are widespread. Similarly, they distinguish among flies, yellowjackets, bees, mosquitoes, horseflies, and deerflies. Students may also be able to classify dogs and cats by breed, a number of birds by sight and song, and food plants by their products.

Content Background

Nearly 2,000 years before Linnaeus began his work, the Greek philosopher Aristotle developed a system to group living things. He divided all organisms into two kingdoms: plants and animals. He then divided the animal kingdom into groups depending on where the animals lived—on land, in water, or in the air. The plant kingdom was also divided into three groups. Eventually, scientists began to criticize this system because it had many exceptions. Frogs spend time on land *and* in water: to which category do they belong? Yet Aristotle's system was used for nearly 2,000 years until it was replaced by the work of Linnaeus.

Teacher F.Y.I.

An animal species consists of animals that can breed together to produce fertile offspring. Horses and donkeys are separate species; the offspring of cross-breeding them is the sterile mule. Mules cannot reproduce themselves; thus, they are not a species.

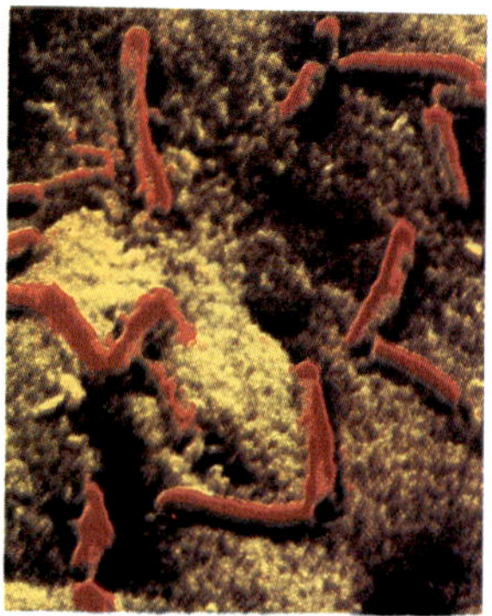

FIGURE 9-9. Monerans are simple-looking, one-celled organisms, such as the bacteria in the top photo and the cyanobacteria in the bottom photo.

they wouldn't get very far in their research. After all, there are thousands of disease-causing bacteria. Scientists must identify the organism precisely according to its traits and give it a name that distinguishes it from all other kinds of bacteria. Only then can scientists around the world know they are studying and communicating about the same organism. Only then can they share their findings and work together to fight the disease.

LIFE'S FIVE KINGDOMS

Linnaeus suggested only two kingdoms into which he grouped all living organisms. As scientists studied the characteristics of more and more different kinds of organisms, they realized that more kingdoms were needed to classify them efficiently. Today, we group living things into five kingdoms.

Moneran Kingdom

The group of one-celled organisms known as monerans has been present on Earth for about 3.5 billion years. The single cell that makes up a moneran has a very simple organization. For example, it doesn't have a central part that controls the cell. There are about 1800 species of monerans, divided into two main groups: bacteria and cyanobacteria. You can see examples of these monerans in Figure 9-9.

Protist Kingdom

Protists have lived on Earth for about one billion years. Today, there are about 38,000 living protist species. The cells of protists are more complex and organized than those of monerans. For example, a protist cell has a central part that controls the cell's activities. Otherwise, protists are a very diverse group. Figure 9-10 shows you some examples. Some protists swim around by moving tiny surface hairs, while other protists have whiplike tails. Some are one-celled, such as amoebas, while others have many cells, such as seaweeds. Some protists, like animals, can't make their own food, while others that are like plants can make their own food. You will learn about animals in the next chapter and about plants in Chapter 11.

DID YOU KNOW?

Whenever you brush with toothpaste, you're using something made with protists! A substance found in one species of protist is used to give both toothpaste and pudding their smooth, creamy texture.

PROGRAM RESOURCES

Other Resources

Starr, Cecie, and Ralph Taggart. *Biology: Concepts and Applications.* Belmont, CA: Wadsworth, 1991

Carolus Linnaeus, film, EBEC

Classify—Classification Key Program, software, Diversified Educational Enterprises

Fungus Kingdom

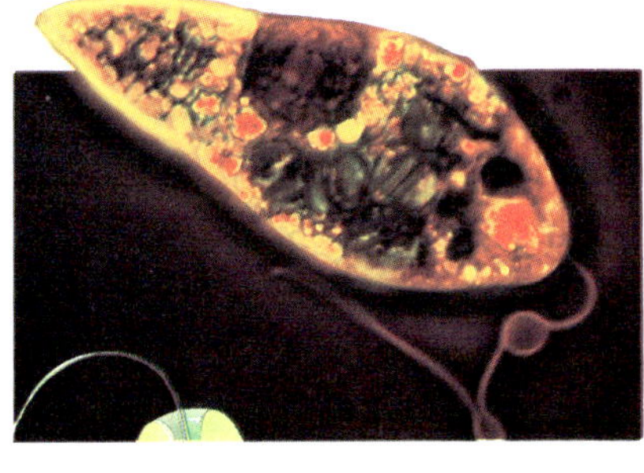

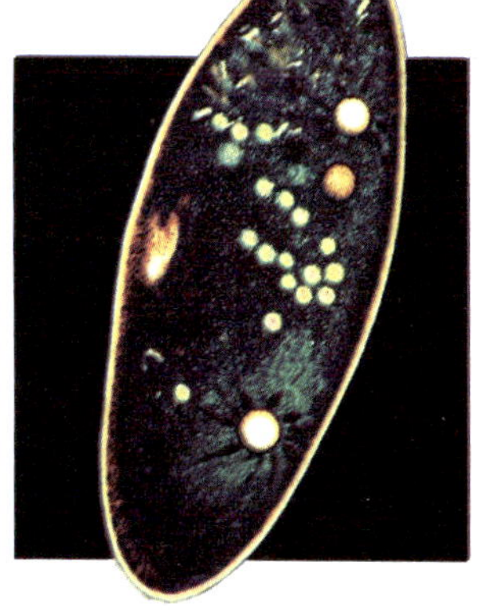

Have you ever eaten mushrooms in a salad or on a pizza? If you have, then you've eaten a member of the fungus kingdom. Fungi can be either one-celled or many-celled. In Chapter 12, you'll learn that fungi obtain food by decomposing other organisms. Fungi cannot move from place to place, and partly for this reason, they were once classified as plants. The fossil record shows that fungi have existed on Earth for over 400 million years. Today, there are about 100,000 known species of fungi. Some fungus species are poisonous.

FIGURE 9-10. Protists are more complex in structure than monerans, but do not appear as complex as plants and animals.

Plant Kingdom

Plants are many-celled organisms. In Chapter 11, you'll learn how plants make their own food by using light from the sun. The ancestors of plants were probably one-celled green algae, members of the protist kingdom. The oldest plant fossils are about 400 million years old. Since these earliest times, plants have developed into a diverse kingdom of some large and long-lived species. There are today at least a quarter of a million known plant species, though scientists suspect that many millions more await discovery in tropical rain forests.

FIGURE 9-11. Most species of fungi have many cells and are major recyclers of nutrients.

FIGURE 9-12. Plants are complex, many-celled organisms that make their own food.

Concept Developments

Uncovering Preconceptions Many students may think there are only two kingdoms: plants and animals. You may wish to spend extra time discussing the other three kingdoms. Monerans are one-celled organisms lacking a nucleus, or central part that controls the cell. Protists can be one-celled or many-celled and have a nucleus. Fungi obtain food by absorbing it from other organisms. Plants are complex, many-celled organisms that make their own food from sunlight. Animals are complex, many-celled organisms that eat other organisms.

Research Have students research to identify the scientific names of a group of related animals. Examples might include several species of monkey, ape, cat, gazelle, or squirrel. Have students list five species and describe the traits that they share and the traits that distinguish them from one another. L3

Activity Write the Linnaean categories on separate sheets of cardboard or stiff paper. Thumbtack them to a bulletin board in jumbled order and have students rearrange them in correct order from kingdom down through species.

PROGRAM RESOURCES

Teacher Classroom Resources

Making Connections: Across the Curriculum, page 21, Classifications L2

Transparency Masters, page 39, and **Color Transparency,** number 18, Life's Five Kingdoms L2

OPTIONS

Enrichment

Discussion Lead a discussion about how misleading the common names of plants and animals can be. For example, starfish are not fish and prairie dogs are more closely related to squirrels than to dogs. Have students suggest other misleading names, such as sea horse and elephant seal.

3 Assess

Check for Understanding

The questions in Check Your Understanding focus on the purpose and principles of Linnaean classification. Use the Apply question to have students explain why Latin names are used, how they fit into the seven Linnaean categories, and why organisms are given the particular Latin names they have.

Reteach

Tell students that scientific names are like their own names. Their last names tell about the family group they belong to, while their first names distinguish them from other family members. In scientific names, it is the first name that tells what group (genus) the organism belongs to and the second name that distinguishes it from other group members so as not to confuse a species with an individual. LEP L1

Extension

Have students work in two or four groups to prepare a matching game. Students should write descriptions of organisms that offer clues about what kingdom they belong to. Have groups exchange descriptions and try to identify the kingdom of each. Or the class can play the game together by dividing into two teams. You read the descriptions written by one team to the other and each correct answer wins one point. The team with the most points at the end wins. COOP LEARN L3

FIGURE 9-13. Armadillos, sponges, and manatees display the amazing variety of animal life.

Animal Kingdom

You, like all humans, are classified as an animal. Animals are many-celled organisms with complex body structures. In Chapter 10, you'll learn how animals must eat other organisms to survive. Animals first appear in the fossil record about 700 million years ago. Today, there are about one million known species. Some animals, such as certain worms, are so tiny they can't be seen without the help of a microscope. Yet the animals known as blue whales are the largest creatures on Earth.

Classifying and naming living things helps reduce confusion about the world around you. The classification system Linnaeus developed is based on traits. You'll learn more about the specific traits used for classifying in the next section.

Check Your Understanding

1. The scientific name for a particular large cat is *Panthera leo.* Why would a scientist want to use this name when communicating about the organism rather than just "large cat"?
2. Which level of classification would hold the largest number of organisms? Which would hold the fewest?
3. Order the kingdoms from oldest to most recent.
4. **APPLY:** Suppose a scientist discovered a new organism and named it *Panthera migratorius.* List everything that the name tells you about the organism.

4 Close

Activity

Ask students to look up the scientific names of common plants and animals in a dictionary. Have each student draw a picture of one plant or animal and label it with its scientific name. Display the drawings around the classroom. LEP L1

Answers to Check Your Understanding

1. "Large cat" could describe many different animals, from lions to leopards, and cause confusion.
2. A kingdom holds the most organisms; a species holds the fewest.
3. moneran, protist, animal, fungus, plant
4. Answers should mention a large cat that migrates.

9-3 How Organisms Are Classified

HOW ORGANISMS ARE RELATED

OBJECTIVES

In this section, you will

- demonstrate that the classification system shows how organisms are related;
- identify the traits scientists use to classify organisms.

You've seen how classifying can help scientists distinguish different species of organisms, like the three different kinds of robin. Yet classifying is important not only to tell organisms apart, but also to show how they are related. For example, if there is a new kind of disease-causing bacterium, it is important to know what it has in common with bacteria we already know about. A treatment or medicine that kills one kind of disease-causing bacteria may also work on a closely related bacterium.

Do you have a domestic cat? If so, the genus name for your tabby is *Felis*, which means cat. The species name is *domestica*, which means tame. The name *Felis domestica* tells you and scientists around the world that you're talking about a domestic cat. If you want to show the complete classification for domestic cats, the scheme would look like Table 9-1.

TABLE 9-1. Classifications for Cats

Group	Group Name	Group Trait
Kingdom	Animalia	many cells; eats food
Phylum	Chordata	backbone
Class	Mammalia	nurses young; has hair
Order	Carnivora	eats flesh; large teeth
Family	Felidae	sharp claws; large eyes
Genus	Felis	small cats
Species	domestica	tame

a

b

c

FIGURE 9-14. Various species of cats include the housecat (a), the cougar (b), and the bobcat (c).

A leopard is often referred to as one of the big cats. How closely related are leopards and domestic cats? What about other animals in the same kingdom? In the Find Out that follows, you will see how these classifications are helpful.

PROGRAM RESOURCES

Teacher Classroom Resources

Study Guide, page 35

Laboratory Manual, pages 49-52, Classification L2

Critical Thinking/Problem Solving, page 8, Flex Your Brain

Take Home Activities, page 17, Classifying Fingerprints 

Section 9-3

PREPARATION

Concepts Developed

Students learn how scientists use traits to classify organisms and determine their relatedness.

Planning the Lesson

In planning your lesson on classifying organisms, refer to the Chapter Organizer on pages 256A-B for timing suggestions, resources, and additional materials that will help you in your presentation of the lesson concepts.

For adequate development of the concepts presented in this section, we recommend that students do the Find Out on page 272 and the Explore on page 273.

1 MOTIVATE

Demonstration Have students identify similar and different traits in two animals.

Materials needed are photographs of a rabbit and a fox. Show the photographs to students and ask them to name traits that the two animals share. Students should note number of legs, existence of fur, and ability to run fast. Then have students name differences; they should note size, weight, color, herbivorous prey versus carnivorous predator, and kind of teeth. Ask students if they think the two animals are closely related. *They should answer no.* L1 LEP

2 TEACH

Tying to Previous Knowledge

In the previous section, students learned the structure of the Linnaean system and what kinds of organisms are grouped in the five kingdoms. Tell students that in this section, they will learn how scientists figure out to what category organisms belong.

FIND OUT!

Compare the classification of a leopard with that of a domestic cat.

Time needed 5 minutes
No special materials or preparation are required for this activity, which can be done as an independent assignment.

Thinking Processes
Organizing information, Classifying, Thinking critically, Comparing and contrasting

Purpose To learn that closely related animals have similar classifications

Teaching the Activity

Discussion Have students discuss the physical similarities and differences among the leopard, domestic cat, and deer. Point out the high degree of similarity between the cat and leopard. L1

Troubleshooting In assigning the activity, ask students to read aloud the category names for each animal and correct their pronunciation as needed. LEP L1

Expected Outcome

Students recognize that the domestic cat and leopard are more closely related than the domestic cat and deer.

Conclude and Apply
1. order, family, genus, and species
2. genus and species
3. domestic cat and leopard
4. family, genus

FIND OUT!

Compare the classification of a leopard with that of a domestic cat:

Group	Domestic Cat	Leopard
Kingdom	Animalia	Animalia
Phylum	Chordata	Chordata
Class	Mammalia	Mammalia
Order	Carnivora	Carnivora
Family	Felidae	Felidae
Genus	Felis	Panthera
Species	domestica	lepardus

What other animals might be related to a domestic cat? You might compare the classification schemes of the domestic cat and a deer:

Group	Domestic Cat	Deer
Kingdom	Animalia	Animalia
Phylum	Chordata	Chordata
Class	Mammalia	Mammalia
Order	Carnivora	Artiodactyla
Family	Felidae	Cervidae
Genus	Felis	Odocoileus
Species	domestica	virginianus

Conclude and Apply
1. At what level are domestic cats and deer different?
2. At what level are domestic cats and big cats different?
3. Which animals are more closely related?
4. Animals closely related to the deer might be found at what levels?

OPTIONS

Meeting Individual Needs

Hearing Impaired If hearing-impaired students have difficulty participating in class discussions, write the main points of the discussion on the board or on an overhead projector. Review students' answers with them on an individual basis, either during or after class. Discussions in which it may be difficult for hearing-impaired students to participate include the Motivate demonstration, Using the Photos, and the Inquiry question. A table could be made of the characteristics listed in the Motivate demonstration for students to complete. The Making Connections activity in the margin on page 275 may be particularly attractive to hearing-impaired students.

The Find Out activity showed you that the more levels two organisms both belong to, the more closely they are related. That is because they share more traits with each other.

SETTING UP CATEGORIES: LEVELS OF SHARED TRAITS

You expect a record store to help you find the music you want by having cassettes organized into understandable categories. In the same way, scientists need a classification system based on useful traits—traits that will help the scientists see how organisms are related. What characteristics do you think would be useful?

EXPLORE!

What are useful traits for classifying?

Obtain a set of animal pictures from your teacher. First, classify the animals according to color. What animals have ended up in the same group? How much do they seem to have in common? Is color a good way to classify animals? Now classify all the animals again. This time, group them according to where they live: for example, in the water, on land, under the ground, and so on. Was this a good characteristic to use? What characteristic, other than color or where an animal lives, would be better for classifying the animals?

You probably decided that color was not a good trait to use by itself when classifying animals. What's wrong with using color? If scientists classified organisms just by color, they'd have to say that black bears, black widow spiders,

EXPLORE!

What are useful traits for classifying?

Time needed 15 minutes

Materials pictures of animals clipped from magazines

Thinking Processes Organizing information, Classifying, Thinking critically, Comparing and contrasting

Purpose To identify traits useful for classification

Preparation This activity may be performed by students working in small groups. If a large number of pictures is available, distribute five to six pictures at random to each group. Otherwise, paste the pictures on a piece of posterboard and display them.

Teaching the Activity

Discussion Discuss with students reasons why color is not an effective grouping for animals. Ask them to give other examples of animals that have the same coloring, but have very little in common, for example, killer whales, penguins, skunks, and zebras. Do the same for animals that live in similar environments, for example, frogs and fish. L1 COOP LEARN

Expected Outcomes

Students recognize that color and habitat are not useful traits for classification.

Answers to Questions

Color and living place are not good ways to classify animals. Better traits include methods of obtaining food, body structure, body covering, size, and methods of reproduction.

Meeting Individual Needs

Visually Impaired Visually impaired students will be able to do the Find Out activity if you or a fully sighted student reads the list of categories to them. Visually impaired students will not, however, be able to do the Explore and Investigate activities as written. To give them practice with classification, have one or more students help you write detailed descriptions of the animals in the pictures. You or a fully sighted student can describe a group of animals to visually impaired students. Have these students suggest characteristics that can be used for classification.

Concept Development

Theme Connection The themes of interactions and systems are supported in this section. Students learn how to apply a system of classification to individual organisms. In the Find Out activity on page 272, students compare classification of various animals. In the Explore activity on page 273, students attempt to find useful traits for a classification system.

Using the Photos Have students examine Figure 9-16 and compare the turtle and tortoise. Have them list similarities, including body shape and shell, and differences, including shape of feet/flippers and habitat. Suggest an example of two animals that live in the same habitat but are unrelated: a shark and a whale. Have students describe the differences between them. *A shark is a fish whereas a whale is a mammal.*

Student Text Question Figure 9-16. What shared traits make them related? *The presence of shells and overall body shape, except for their feet, makes them seem related.*

Content Background

The kingdom *Monera* includes bacteria such as streptococcus, which causes strep throat, and cyanobacteria, one-celled plantlike organisms found in lakes and ponds. Monerans are called prokaryotes, which means "before nucleus." All other organisms are eukaryotes, meaning "true nucleus," and have cells possessing a nucleus and organelles surrounded by membranes.

Teacher F.Y.I.

The phylogeny of an organism is its evolutionary history. It tells scientists what the ancestors of an organism were and helps them classify it. Classification of many organisms today is based on phylogeny.

FIGURE 9-15. Classifying by color only can lead to odd groupings.

and black birds are all similar. Just by looking at Figure 9-15 you can see that's not the case.

What about location? Trying to classify organisms according to where they live might seem reasonable at first. In fact, the Greek philosopher Aristotle attempted to group organisms this way over 2000 years ago. Aristotle saw that there were two main groups of organisms: animals and plants. He divided animals according to where they live and plants according to how they grow (as herbs, trees, or shrubs).

FIGURE 9-16. Can you see how land tortoises and sea turtles are related, even though they live in different places? What shared traits make them seem related?

However, this classification system also groups very different organisms together. For instance, whales and sea turtles would be grouped together because they live in the water, while elephants and tortoises would be related because they both live on land. Yet Figure 9-16 shows you how closely related sea turtles and land tortoises really are.

A CLOSE LOOK AT TRAITS

With seven levels in the classification system we use, how do scientists know which groups an organism belongs to?

OPTIONS

Multicultural Perspectives

Research into classification systems of other cultures has shown that people who live according to ancient, traditional ways often have extremely detailed systems of classifying organisms. The bedouin of North Africa, for example, have nearly 6,000 descriptive words for *camel,* versus perhaps six words used by Europeans or Americans. The Hanunóo of the southern Philippines identify 1,625 different plant forms grouped into 890 categories. A Western botanist would identify the same collection as consisting of 1,100 species and 650 genera. The Hanunóo's classifications identify 600 species as edible and 406 as having medicinal value. The two broadest categories of Hanunóo classification are things that cannot be named and things that can be named. The latter are then divided into two groups.

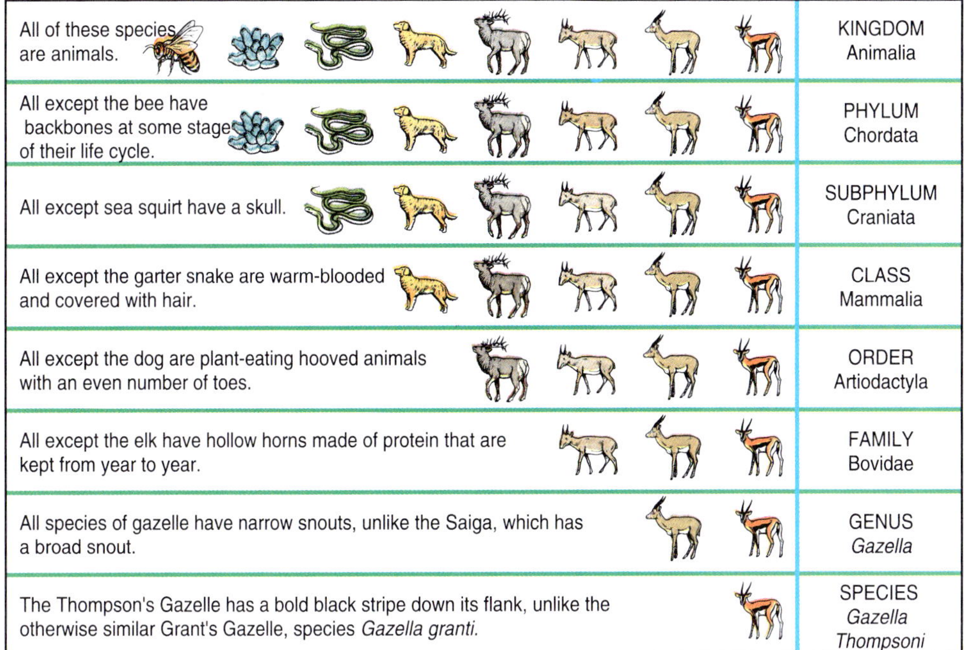

All of these species are animals.	KINGDOM Animalia
All except the bee have backbones at some stage of their life cycle.	PHYLUM Chordata
All except sea squirt have a skull.	SUBPHYLUM Craniata
All except the garter snake are warm-blooded and covered with hair.	CLASS Mammalia
All except the dog are plant-eating hooved animals with an even number of toes.	ORDER Artiodactyla
All except the elk have hollow horns made of protein that are kept from year to year.	FAMILY Bovidae
All species of gazelle have narrow snouts, unlike the Saiga, which has a broad snout.	GENUS *Gazella*
The Thompson's Gazelle has a bold black stripe down its flank, unlike the otherwise similar Grant's Gazelle, species *Gazella granti*.	SPECIES *Gazella Thompsoni*

FIGURE 9-17. Going down the classification levels, the organisms on each level share more and more traits.

First, they must look at all the organism's traits. These include cell structure, methods of reproduction, methods of obtaining food, body structure, body coverings (hair, fur, feathers), color, size, and so on. By examining the traits an organism has in common with others and the traits that make it unique, scientists can place the organism into the appropriate kingdom, phylum, class, order, family, genus, and species.

Figure 9-17 is a diagram showing how one animal, the Thompson's gazelle, is classified scientifically by traits. It shows the traits the Thompson's gazelle has in common with other animals and the traits that are unique to it. Each level is characterized by certain traits, such as body structure or method of getting food.

You can find special keys to help you identify more than a million species living on Earth. There are keys for plants, mushrooms, fish, butterflies, and every other kind of organism. In the following Investigate activity, you'll identify two kinds of bird.

SKILLBUILDER

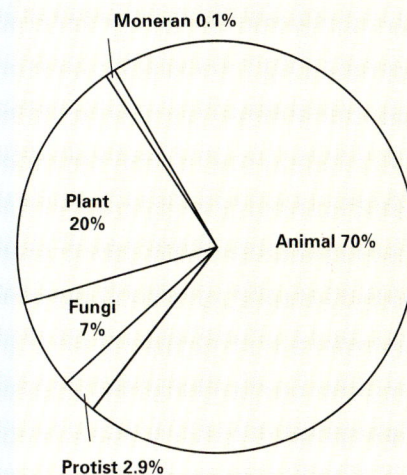

MAKING AND INTERPRETING GRAPHS

Make a pie graph to show the number of species in each kingdom. If you need help, refer to the **Skill Handbook** on page 650.

Kingdom	Number of Species
Moneran	1800
Protist	38.000
Fungi	100,000
Plant	285,000
Animal	1 million

SKILLBUILDER

Moneran 0.1%
Plant 20%
Animal 70%
Fungi 7%
Protist 2.9%

MAKING CONNECTIONS

Fine Arts

Obtain a photograph or model of a reconstructed dinosaur skeleton. Ask students to examine the skeleton and then to draw a portrait of the dinosaur as it may have appeared in life, including all of the features visible in the skeleton. Remind students that no one knows exactly how dinosaurs' bodies were shaped, what color they were, if they had hair or feathers, and the shape and color of their eyes. You may wish to tell students that scientists even disagree about whether dinosaurs were part of the reptile class or are a new class to themselves and whether they were warm-blooded like mammals or cold-blooded like reptiles. Display students' completed work. You may wish to obtain a current book on dinosaurs (published in 1989 or later) and show students some of the widely differing ideas that artists have presented. Possibilities include: Eyewitness Books. *Dinosaur.* New York: Knopt, 1990. Lasky, Kathryn. *Dinosaur Dig.* New York: Morrow, 1990.

INVESTIGATE!

9-2 IDENTIFYING ORGANISMS

Time needed 10 minutes
No special materials or preparation are required for this activity.

Thinking Processes
Organizing information, Making and using tables, Thinking critically, Comparing and contrasting

Purpose To learn the use of a key in classification.

Teaching the Activity

Demonstration To help students understand how the key works, illustrate steps 1–3 on the chalkboard in the form of a flowchart, with the instructions in boxes connected by lines. Each box should contain a question such as **"Crest on head?"** and the words *yes* and *no*. Lines connect *yes* and *no* to the next appropriate box.

Troubleshooting Remind students to study the bird they are identifying as they make their choices. Walk around the room as students work. If they have the wrong answer, direct them to try again and check their choices.

Expected Outcomes

Students use the key to identify the birds and draw conclusions about bird species and genera.

Answers to Analyze/Conclude and Apply

1. Eight different species
2. Five different genera
3. The title of the key specifies that it is a key to the jays of North America.
4. The key identifies jays, not robins.
5. The first pair of descriptions are the most general. The following descriptions are more specific. Correct identification depends on making the correct choice between the first pair of descriptions.

I N V E S T I G A T E !

9-2 IDENTIFYING ORGANISMS

In this activity, you will use a key and your observation skills to identify two jay birds.

PROBLEM

How can a key be used to identify jays?

MATERIALS

paper and pencil

PROCEDURE

1. **Observe** the jays pictured on this page.
2. Begin with Step 1 of the Key to Jays of North America. Use the key to **classify** the bird below labeled A.
3. On your paper, make a data table like the one shown. Write the common name and scientific name for the jay.
4. Use the same procedure to **classify** the species of jay labeled B.

a

b

ANALYZE

1. How many species of jay can you **infer** are in North America?
2. How many genera can be identified with this key?

CONCLUDE AND APPLY

3. How do you know that this key doesn't contain all the species of jays in the world?
4. Why couldn't you be successful in identifying a robin using this key?
5. **Going Further**: Why wouldn't it be a good idea to begin in the middle of a key, instead of with the first step?

KEY TO JAYS OF NORTH AMERICA

1a. If the jay has a crest on the head, go to Step 2.
1b. If the jay has no crest, go to Step 3.
2a. If the jay has white on the tail and wings, it is a blue jay, *Cyanocitta cristata*.
2b. If the jay has a gray or brown crest, it is a stellar's jay, *Cyanocitta stelleri*.
3a. If the jay is mostly blue, go to Step 4.
3b. If the jay has little or no blue, go to Step 6.
4a. If the jay has a white throat, it is a scrub jay, *Aphelocoma coerulescens*.
4b. If the throat is not white, outlined in blue, go to Step 5.
5a. If the jay has a dark eye mask and gray breast, it is a gray-breasted jay, *Aphelocoma ultramarinus*.
5b. If the jay is all steel-blue and has a short tail, it is a pinyon jay, *Gymnorhrinus cyanocephalus*.
6a. If the jay is mostly gray and has black and white head markings, it is a gray jay, *Perisorenus canadensis*.
6b. If the jay is not gray, go to Step 7.
7a. If the jay has a brilliant green body with some blue on the head, it is a green jay, *Cyanocorax yucas*.
7b. If the jay has a plain brown body, it is a brown jay, *Cyanocorax moria*.

DATA AND OBSERVATIONS Sample data

JAY	SCIENTIFIC NAME	COMMON NAME
A	Cyanocitta cristata	blue jay
B	Cyanocorax yucas	green jay

PROGRAM RESOURCES

Teacher Classroom Resources
Activity Masters, pages 39-40, Investigate 9-2

MESSAGES FROM THE PAST

a

b

FIGURE 9-18. Both of these pictures show the snowshoe hare—one in winter, the other in summer. Why is an observable trait like hair color not always a good trait to use when classifying?

In the Investigate activity, you identified two kinds of jay birds by observing their physical traits. There are many traits you can look for when classifying organisms, but what you see is not always the best evidence. Visual traits are often unreliable. For instance, what would happen if you decided to classify humans on their hair color? Today's brunette may be tomorrow's blonde. And if you think humans are the only organisms to change the color of their hair, just look at Figure 9-18. Therefore, observable traits are not always the most useful method of classification.

Scientists also study the traits of the ancestors of the organisms that exist today. They study fossils, the remains of organisms from an earlier time. Fossils have shown scientists how animals that lived in the past, some millions of years ago, are related to animals that live today. For example, fossils have shown that modern horses are probably descended from an animal that was only two feet tall. You can see the resemblance in Figure 9-19. Fossils have also demonstrated that horses and donkeys are more closely related than horses and goats because horses and donkeys have more ancestors in common than do horses and goats. Therefore, the classifications of horses and donkeys have more levels in common than those of horses and goats.

FIGURE 9-19. By studying fossils, scientists can determine what early ancestors of modern organisms might have looked like.

A LOOK INSIDE ORGANISMS

Sometimes the relationship between two different organisms is so close that it is hard to classify them based

Concept Development

Activity Have students perform a nonscientific classification of another classmate. They should start by making a list of identifiable traits for that person. The traits should then be grouped in order from those shared by the most people—age, sex, height, weight, hair color, eye color, etc.—to those that are unique to the person. After producing a list of categories and traits in order from the broadest to the narrowest, students should develop a Latin name for the person based on the most identifiable traits. COOP LEARN

Student Text Question (Figure 9-18) Why is an observable trait like hair color not always a good trait to use when classifying? *Hair color can change as it does on the snowshoe hare in Figure 9-18.*

Inquiry Questions Ask students to think about how scientists classify fossil animals, like that shown in Figure 9-19. What traits of living creatures must these scientists do without? *Answers may include body coverings, color, and methods of reproduction.* What traits do they think scientists use? *Answers may include the shape of bones and how they connect.*

Research Have students research the classification of pandas that is briefly discussed in the text. Students should write a brief essay describing the controversy and explaining why pandas have been reclassified twice. Students can extend this activity by researching the classification of the horseshoe crab, which was once believed to be related to other crabs but has since been shown, through studies of its blood, to be more closely related to spiders than to other crabs. L3

Flex Your Brain Use the Flex Your Brain activity to have students explore ANIMAL CLASSIFICATION.

PROGRAM RESOURCES

Other Resources

Rose, Kenneth J. *Classification of the Animal Kingdom.* New York: David McKay, 1980.

Taxonomy: Classification and Organization, software, IBM.

The Taxonomy Game, software, Queue.

OPTIONS

Enrichment

Research Have students perform library research and write an essay describing how the first dinosaur skeleton was discovered. The essays should discuss where and how it was found, what traits scientists identified, how it changed our view of nature, and who coined the term *dinosaur* and why.

Student Text Question Figure 9-20 What observable traits does a panda share with a bear? *Pandas and bears are similar in size; both have large paws with claws, both are covered with fur.* What observable traits does it share with a racoon? *Both have fur and four legs. Scientists find relationships by studying traits that are not observable such as blood chemistry and DNA.*

3 Assess

Check Your Understanding

Extend question 1 by asking students to name the species and genus for both animals. *Panthera* is the genus they share; *pardus* and *tigris* are their distinct species. Use the Apply question to review with students all of the traits that scientists use in classification.

Reteach

The Investigate activity provides a hands-on application of classification. Demonstrate how to use a key by making a transparency of a key. Show students photographs of an organism that can be identified using the key. Have them go orally through the identification steps. L1

Extension

Have students select four to five common objects and write a key that would allow a person who had never seen them before to identify what they are. The key may be written in list form or as a flowchart. L3

a

b

c

FIGURE 9-20. What observable traits does a panda (a) share with a bear (b)? What observable traits does it share with a raccoon (c)?

on body traits you can see or on fossil evidence alone. In such cases, scientists may look inside organisms and examine the life processes that go on.

The giant panda is a good example of how an organism may be reclassified because of new evidence. Giant pandas were thought to be bears. In the 1980s, pandas were reclassified as raccoons, animals that share some of the panda's physical traits. But later studies of their body parts and processes showed that giant pandas were more closely related to bears. So now they are bears again!

As you can see, classification is not written in stone, so to speak. Scientists continue to develop finer tools for determining the shared and the unique characteristics of organisms. As we learn more, we accept new ways to classify living things.

If you were asked to pick one classmate and describe that student so precisely that the rest of the class could guess who it was immediately, you could probably do it, right? You would probably start with the most general description: sex—male or female. Then you would describe height, weight, hair color, eye color, and the presence of some special trait such as freckles, dimples, or moles. You may have to get down to some particular identifying behavior, if your classmates haven't guessed yet.

That is exactly what Linnaeus and other scientists did to develop a system to identify and classify organisms. The process of identifying traits allows scientists to differentiate all living organisms into five kingdoms and to name and classify these organisms as precisely as possible into phylum, class, order, family, genus, and species.

Check Your Understanding

1. The scientific name for the leopard is *Panthera pardus.* The scientific name for the tiger is *Panthera tigris.* Explain how their names indicate that leopards and tigers are related.
2. Why is height not a good trait to use in classifying trees?
3. **APPLY:** You are given an unknown organism to classify. What might you look at to help? How might you go about identifying and naming it?

4 Close

Activity

Obtain photographs of several plants and animals and learn the classification of each. Refer to an encyclopedia for both photographs and classifications. Then show students the photographs, two at a time, and ask them to guess how many categories, from kingdom through species, the organisms share. L1

Answers to Check Your Understanding

1. The scientific names show that both animals belong to the same genus, which is the closest relationship two different species can have.
2. The height of trees can change with their age.
3. Answers will vary but should cover cell structure, methods of reproduction, methods of obtaining food, body structure, body coverings, color, and size. Once all traits are described, they would compare the traits to those of other organisms, possibly using a key, in order to identify and name it.

CONTENTS

A CLOSER LOOK

HOW TO USE A KEY

Field guides are books that help identify things in nature. Many field guides consist of dichotomous (di KOT uh mus) keys.

A dichotomous key is divided into numbered steps. Each step has two descriptions. At each step, you choose a description that ends with either more directions or the name of a species.

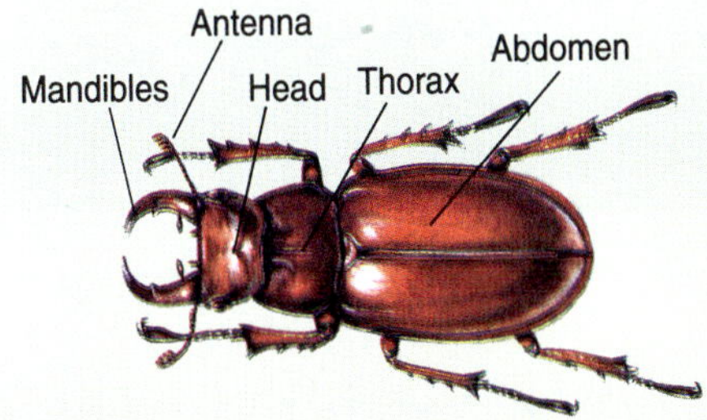

YOU TRY IT!

Using the staghorn beetle key, find the name of the beetle that is 50 mm long, black, and has large, overhanging mandibles.

Staghorn Beetles Of North America

1a If the beetle is longer than 20 mm, go to Step 2.
1b If the beetle is less than 20 mm long, go to Step 5.
2a If it is reddish brown, go to Step 3.
2b If it is dark brown or black, go to Step 4.
3a If the beetle is 22–35 mm long with an oval patch of golden hair on the front legs, it is commonly called a pinching bug, or *Pseudolucanus capreolus.*
3b If the beetle is 20–32 mm long, with silky hairs between segments on the bottom surface, it is also called a pinching bug, *Pseudolucanus placidus.*
4a If it is 20–26 mm long and the mandibles do not overlap, it is commonly called an antelope beetle, *Dorcus parallelus.*
4b If it is 45–60 mm long with large overlapping mandibles, it is commonly called the elephant staghorn beetle, *Lucanus elaphus.*
5a If the head is as wide as the thorax and it is reddish black, it is an oak stag beetle, *Platycerus agassizi.*
5b If the head is much narrower than the thorax with a backward-directed horn, it is a rugose staghorn beetle, *Sinodendron rugosum.*

EXPANDING YOUR VIEW

Using Expanding Your View

Assign one or more of these excursions to expand students' understanding of the living world and how it applies to other sciences and other subjects. You may assign these as individual or small group activities.

A CLOSER LOOK

Purpose A Closer Look gives students additional practice in using dichotomous keys, introduced in Section 9-3 as a system for identifying individual species.

Content Background Beetles belong to the order Coleoptera, which includes more than 250,000 described species, or 40 percent of all known insect species. They are distinguished by thickened or leathery front wings, called elytra, which are not used in flight and normally cover the abdomen and flying wings. Beetle species live on both land and water and eat both plants and animals. Beetle species range from about 0.01 inch to over 8 inches in length. Among the best known are ladybugs and fireflies.

Teaching Strategies Obtain a field guide or other book on insects that includes diagrams or photos of body structure. Show these to students and use them to review the basic body structures common to most insects, including the three-part structure of head, thorax, and abdomen, as well as antenna and legs. Explain that mandibles are large mouth parts that some insects use to catch prey. Then have students perform the You Try It activity.

Going Further Obtain field guides to insects, trees, birds, and other animals from the library (Dewey numbers 590 through 595). Divide the class into groups. Give each group a field guide, and have it develop an identification test for other groups. The group should make a colored tracing of one species from the field guide and develop two or three clues based on the descriptive text. Clues should refer to where the organism is found and what its distinctive habits, or traits, may be. Then have groups exchange their tracings, clues, and field guides and attempt to identify the organisms. Note: Few field guides available at libraries include dichotomous keys. You may need to help the groups identify traits which lead them to a correct classification. COOP LEARN

Answers to YOU TRY IT

The beetle is an elephant staghorn beetle, *Lucannus elaphus.*

EARTH SCIENCE CONNECTION

Purpose One of the traits of an organism described in Section 9-1 is its adaptation to an environment. The Earth Science Connection describes an unusual environment to which living things have become adapted.

Content Background Hydrothermal vents were discovered by the research ship *Knorr,* from Woods Hole Oceanographic Institute. The scientists went to the eastern Pacific Ocean, where a previous team had measured unusually warm water temperatures on the seabed 1.5 miles deep. They surveyed 10 miles of seafloor with a camera-mounted "sled." When photos revealed the warm springs, two scientists descended in the U.S. Navy's *Alvin* submarine. They found up to 2.5 gallons of hot water pouring out of vents every second and a dark "smoke" of minerals in the water. Huge white clams, brown mussels, and white crabs clung to the rocks on the dark bottom.

Teaching Strategies Ask students why scientists were so surprised by the hydrothermal vent communities. Lead students to see that the absence of sunlight means that there is normally little plant or animal life on the bottom.

Answers to YOU TRY IT

Students can check encyclopedias under Oceans, Bathypelagic Zone, and Abyssal Zone and the card catalog under Hydrothermal Vent. Have them present their results in captioned drawings that show the animal's major adaptations and behaviors.

EARTH SCIENCE CONNECTION

HYDROTHERMAL VENTS

Can you imagine strange places at the bottom of the ocean where water comes out of Earth at temperatures of more than 300° F and where many unusual animals thrive? Such places are called hydrothermal vents.

What causes hydrothermal vents? There are many cracks in the ocean floor. Cold water (34°–37° F) sinks down into the cracks, where it comes into contact with hot rocks in Earth that heat the water to great temperatures. The hot water dissolves chemicals found in the rocks and flows back into the ocean through openings in the ocean floor. The vents are most common in the deepest parts of the ocean, as deep as 20,000 feet.

Groups of unusual animals seem to thrive near these vents. Usually, at such depths, lone animals survive on debris from shallower depths or on any prey with which they come in contact. Therefore, scientists were indeed surprised when, in 1977, off the coast of South America, they found a large community of animals living near a hydrothermal vent.

Scientists were even more surprised that such communities could exist when the chemicals flowing from the vents usually would be deadly to most organisms. It since has been discovered that in the bodies of the organisms that live near the vents, bacteria are present that convert the harmful chemicals into food and energy for the larger organisms.

The organisms found in vent communities are unique. They include giant clusters of tube worms that grow to lengths of ten feet, huge white clams, and jellyfish-like animals called siphonophores.

YOU TRY IT!

Find out more about one of the animals discussed in this article or choose another animal found in the deep sea to research. What special adaptations does the animal have for its life in the deep?

Going Further Divide students into groups and assign each to learn about a different aspect of vents: geology, environment, living things, and scientific exploration. Have the groups do library research to obtain information. Tape together sheets of paper to create a large drawing space and have the groups work together to draw a cutaway illustration of a vent community. In addition to showing geology, life, and exploration, students should write information they learned on separate smaller sheets and tape them to an appropriate place on the illustration. For information, students should consult:

Cone, Joseph. *Fire Under the Sea: The Discovery and Exploration of Hot Springs in the Sea Floor.* New York: Morrow, 1991.

Fodor, R. V. *The Strange World of Undersea Vents.* Hillside, NJ: Enslow, 1991.

COOP LEARN

SCIENCE AND SOCIETY

ENDANGERED SPECIES

What do the giant panda, the brown pelican, and the pincushion cactus have in common? They are all endangered species. Endangered species are those organisms that are in danger of becoming extinct. It is estimated that as many as five to ten thousand species become extinct each year.

Many organisms have become extinct during the time of Earth's existence. Usually, extinction is a natural process that may or may not occur over a long period of time. Dinosaurs are probably the most notable extinct animals.

Today, however, most endangered species become endangered as the result of the activities of human beings. Humans kill animals for their fur, tusks, and other body parts as well as for food and sport. Many endangered animals are now protected by laws, but poachers, people who hunt illegally, disobey the laws and kill and trap thousands of endangered species yearly.

The African elephant is an example of an animal that is endangered because of poaching. Poachers illegally kill the elephants for their ivory tusks. It is estimated that in the last ten years, the African elephant population has been slashed from one million to only five hundred thousand.

Besides the demand for products like ivory, another cause for the increasing number of endangered and extinct species is the destruction of the places where organisms live. As the human population increases, so does the need for places for humans to live and farm. The areas where plants and animals live are cleared to make room for housing, industry, roads, and farming. When land is cleared, most of the plants are killed, and those animals that cannot escape die.

As a result of the destruction of land, some species of organisms are becoming extinct before they are even discovered. This is especially true as the largely unexplored rain forests of South America are cleared to make room for ranching and other development.

Pollution also plays a large part in destroying organisms. For example, as water becomes polluted, oxygen and nutrients that are necessary to keep fish, plants, and other

Going Further Organize the class into two teams to debate the issue of the destruction of the rain forests. Explain that the tropical forests are not being cut down without reason. These forests are largely in developing nations where a large proportion of the population lives in extreme poverty. To most of the people in these countries, feeding themselves and their families and making a better life are far more important than the resulting environmental problems that outsiders worry about. Farmers also use farming methods that quickly destroy the ability of the poor tropical forest soil to grow food crops; the only solution is to cut down more forest and plant crops on a new plot of land. COOP LEARN

SCIENCE AND SOCIETY

Purpose Several traits of organisms cited in Section 9-1 include a need for food and water and adaptation to an environment. Reasons cited in this excursion for species becoming endangered include pollution of water and destruction of food sources and environments.

Content Background Extinction is an ongoing process of life. New species evolve and existing species are becoming extinct at a steady rate. In addition, however, there have been mass extinctions of species every 26 to 30 million years since the beginning of the fossil record. The most famous is the extinction of the dinosaur for reasons that are still being debated. The next mass extinction may be caused by humans, unless present trends change. Excessive hunting has been the main cause in nearly all 46 modern extinctions of large land animals and of 88 bird species. The passenger pigeon is one of the most famous examples. In 1850, they represented 40 percent of all birds in North America; only 50 years later, they had vanished. The destruction of habitat has been the cause of fewer extinctions so far, but is of the greatest concern for the future. Tropical forests, for example, support half of Earth's 5 to 10 million species in about 7 percent of the total land area. From one quarter to one third of tropical forests are already gone, and an additional 75,000 square miles are cut down every year. Unless this rate declines, the forests will be gone in 200 years.

Teaching Strategies Obtain photos of the California condor, the woolly spider monkey of South America, the Siberian tiger, the ivory-billed woodpecker, or other endangered species and show them to students. Ask students what these creatures have in common. After students make suggestions, tell them that all of the animals are endangered species. Ask students to explain what this term means. *The species are in danger of becoming extinct.*

Discussion Tell students that the line between being endangered and extinct is a fine one that can be difficult to predict. Once the number of living things in a species reaches a certain critical size—between 10 and 1,000, depending on the species—that species is usually doomed to extinction. Ask students to speculate on why a species cannot survive below this critical number. *The difficulties in finding reproductive partners and in forming the social groups they need to survive are principle causes.* Point out that breeding programs like those for the giant panda are efforts to overcome this critical size limit.

Activity Tell students to start their research in the What Do You Think? activity by checking an encyclopedia or card catalog under Extinct and Endangered Animals. This will provide them with a list of animals that are endangered, which they can then research in more detail.

Answer to

WHAT DO YOU THINK?

Students may choose organisms endangered in their own state. The State Department of Natural Resources would be a source of such information.

inhabitants alive disappear. It doesn't take long before there is no wildlife left in a polluted pond or river.

It is too late to save species that are already extinct, but what is being done to save those that currently are endangered?

National and international laws have been passed to protect endangered species and stop the sale of products from the species. More than 100 nations have signed the Convention on International Trade in Endangered Species (CITES) agreement. Among other things, the agreement makes it illegal to trade furs and skins of endangered species and bans the trading of ivory from elephant tusks. It also regulates the trading of live animals and birds for pets. Many species of parrots, for example, are endangered because they have been so extensively trapped by bird dealers.

To protect endangered species in the United States, the Endangered Species Act was passed in 1973. The act makes it illegal to harm an animal considered an endangered species. Also, the law lets the government label certain areas as critical for wildlife. These are areas that species need in order to survive. The government is not allowed to disturb any lands that are identified as critical for wildlife. Unfortunately, these critical areas are only protected from the government, not from the rest of the population.

Zoos and wildlife preserves are helping to increase the population of many endangered species. Through breeding programs, many of these efforts have been successful. However, in some cases, as with the giant panda, breeding in places other than the animal's natural surroundings is not always easy or successful.

Even with these efforts and more, the fight to save endangered species is far from over. We are likely to see many more species become extinct in our lifetime.

WHAT DO YOU THINK?

The list of endangered animals is getting longer every day. Choose an endangered animal and find out what has caused it to become endangered. Then tell what you think could be done to save the animal from extinction.

Going Further Form two teams to represent opposing sides in a debate: those concerned about the destruction of species and global warming resulting from deforestation, and those who need to cut down the forests to live. Have the teams brainstorm arguments to support their positions, then stage a debate in which three speakers from each team present the arguments and both teams get one chance to rebut the arguments of the other. Close the debate by suggesting that solutions to the problem will require cooperation between the two sides and ask students for suggestions. Suggestions may include grants from wealthy nations to improve farming methods, investment by wealthy nations in enterprises which provide people with other ways to make a living, and the creation of protected national parks in the third world. COOP LEARN

History CONNECTION

THE HISTORY OF PLANT CLASSIFICATION

You know that plant classification is the system that is used to describe and identify the millions of plants in our environment. When did humans first start classifying plants?

Plant classification has been practiced for thousands of years in one form or another. Primitive people first classified plants based on their uses. For example, some plants were used for food, others for making cloth and dyes, and still others for medicine.

Those plants that were used for medicine were carefully gathered and prepared by the medicine person, often the most important member of a primitive tribe. The knowledge and skills of the medicine person were secret and were passed on by word of mouth to only a chosen few.

Around 300 B.C. E., Theophrastus, a Greek, was the first person to devise a system to classify plants. Theophrastus wrote a book in which he identified and described plants. To assist him, he hired a number of traveling students to collect and observe plants in other places. As a result, he was able to include in his book descriptions of 550 species of plants from a large area. This was quite remarkable because the only plants many ancient people had ever seen were in their own back yards.

After Theophrastus, there was little improvement in plant classification for nearly 2000 years. Classification up to this point was still based on how plants could be used, as opposed to how they looked.

Finally, in 1735, Linnaeus published a book called *Systems of Nature.* It was in this book that he described hundreds of plants and gave each a scientific name. Linnaeus was the first to classify plants based on how they looked instead of on how they were used. He is often thought of as the father of modern classification.

CAREER CONNECTION

A botanist is a scientist who studies plants. Botanists raise, identify, and experiment with plants. A botanist might work in a botanical garden, a wholesale greenhouse, a laboratory, or forest preserve.

YOU TRY IT!

Make a book identifying plants commonly found in your area. Draw pictures of the plants and label them with their scientific and common names or make up your own common names. Write a brief description of each plant.

HISTORY CONNECTION

Purpose This excursion provides a history of the development of the system of classifying organisms introduced in Section 9-2.

Content Background Like all the sciences, botany is growing, leading to an increased need for botanists. Careers in botany require a college degree in botany or a related biological field, with many positions also requiring an advanced degree. Botany is divided into many specialities, including plant pathology (death and decay of plants) and paleobotany (botanical fossils). In terms of job opportunities, the largest number of botanists are employed as teachers and researchers. Another large group works for government or international agencies such as the United Nations. Oil and chemical companies also employ botanists to help in the search for oil and in the developemt of fertilizers and herbicides.

Teaching Strategies Show students a sample of coffee beans and of loose tea. Point out that both come from plants and are used to make hot drinks. Ask students if they can assume that the plants are closely related. Explain that although they have almost identical uses, the plants are different. Coffee, known as *Coffea arabica,* of the family Rubiacae, originated in Africa. Tea, known as *Camellia sinensis,* of the family Theaceae, originated in Southeast Asia. The drink coffee is made from the roasted beans of the plant, while tea is made from the dried leaves.

Going Further Divide the class into small groups. Have each group choose a food, object, or medicine found in their homes that they believe is made from plants. Coordinate the groups so that each selects a different object. Have the groups go to the library to find out if their chosen object comes from plants. If not, they should choose a new object and try again. Have each group prepare an oral presentation on the object and bring in one or more samples from home. The presentation should cover the scientific name of the plant, where it grows, and what products are made from it. Have students prepare posters showing the structure of the plant and what parts of it are used ccmmercially. COOP LEARN

Answer to YOU TRY IT

Reports should reflect local plants. A local garden club or herb society would have information on indigenous plants and their common names.

TECHNOLOGY CONNECTION

Purpose The Technology Connection describes how DNA studies are used to determine the relatedness of species more precisely than the consideration of traits discussed in Section 9-3.

Content Background DNA or deoxyribonucleic acid generally consists of two spiral chains of nucleotides intertwined to form a double helix. Four possible nucleotides make up the chain and they are arranged so that one, adenine, in one chain is always paired with thymine in the other, while another, guanine, in one chain is always paired with cytosine in the other. This arrangement lets each chain determine the arrangement of nucleotides in the other, which is how DNA controls reproduction and growth. In cell division, the two chains divide and direct the formation of a new partner chain identical to the old one.

Teaching Strategies Divide the class into six-person teams and each team into two three-person groups. Have each group develop a list of traits for each of the people in the other three-person group in their team. The traits may include color of skin, hair, and eyes; hair style; sex; clothing; and so on. Then have the group decide which two of the three people in the other group are more alike and report their results to the class. COOP LEARN

TECHNOLOGY CONNECTION

MODERN TOOLS FOR CLASSIFICATION

You have learned that the early history of plant classification involved simple observation of the structure of plants. The same is true for the classification of animals. Animal species were classified into groups according to the way they looked. But methods for classification have come a long way since the days of Linnaeus. Today, scientists use a variety of techniques that don't involve observable structures.

One of the more recent advances in animal classification involves studying an animal's genetic material or DNA. All living organisms contain DNA. In simple organisms as well as complex organisms, like humans, dogs, plants, and fish, DNA may be thought of as the instruction booklet for life. It contains a code that determines how an organism will look and act. Because DNA looks different from organism to organism, scientists can use it to help find out how organisms are related.

One recent technique is called DNA hybridization. In this method, DNA taken from the cells of one organism is joined together with DNA from another organism. The more closely related the two organisms are, the better the DNA join together, or match. Your DNA and the DNA of one of your friends would join together almost perfectly. The DNA of a bird would not match very well with your own, however.

Scientists have used DNA hybridization to reclassify certain animals. For example, panda bears were thought to be related to raccoons and not bears, because of some physical similarities. Scientists have determined that pandas really are bears and not related to raccoons.

To refine classifications of some organisms, scientists also use tools that help them look at the microscopic details of organisms. For example, Dr. Roxie Laybourne of the National Museum of Natural History in Washington, D.C., uses a powerful electron microscope for bird classifications.

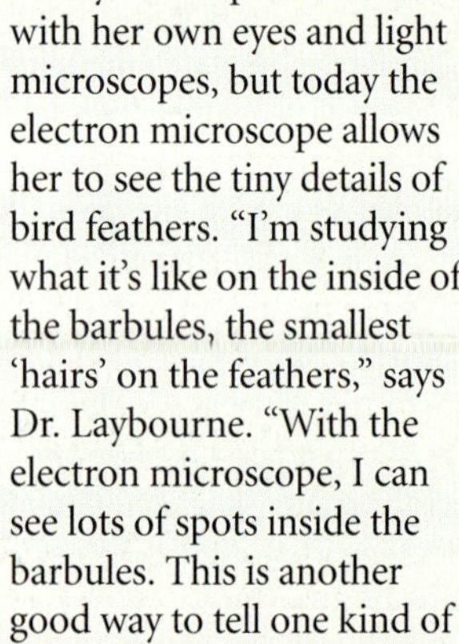

For over 30 years, Dr. Laybourne has been studying the structure, shape, and coloring of bird feathers to find out how birds are related. In the past, Dr. Laybourne had to rely on simple observation with her own eyes and light microscopes, but today the electron microscope allows her to see the tiny details of bird feathers. "I'm studying what it's like on the inside of the barbules, the smallest 'hairs' on the feathers," says Dr. Laybourne. "With the electron microscope, I can see lots of spots inside the barbules. This is another good way to tell one kind of feather from another."

WHAT DO YOU THINK?

How should scientists classify organisms? Which methods should they use? Why should scientists use a combination of classification tools rather than just one tool?

Answers to WHAT DO YOU THINK?

Student answers should probably state a combination of methods mentioned in the article. Make sure student descriptions are accurate.

Going Further Have students work in small groups to create a model of the DNA molecule. Suggest a wide variety of possible materials: paper and marker for drawings or soda straws and clay balls, unbent paper clips and polystyrene balls, or plastic tubing for three-dimensional models. Have each group conduct library research to learn the shape of the molecule and the four nucleotides of which it is composed. Then have them develop their models. Students may wish to use color coding to show the paired relationship of adenine-thymine and guanine-cytosine on which DNA is based. Display the completed models in the classroom. COOP LEARN

Chapter 9

Reviewing Main Ideas

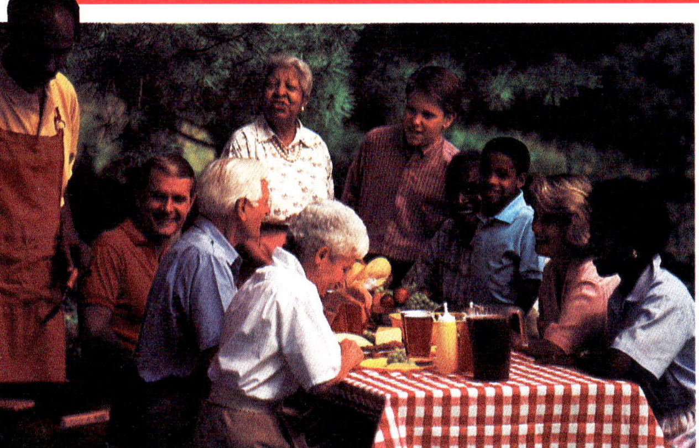

1. Organisms are made of cells, need water and food, grow, reproduce, respond to stimuli, and adapt to their environments.

2. Living things are classified scientifically by kingdom, phylum, class, order, family, genus, and species.

3. Classifying organisms helps scientists understand how organisms are related.

Chapter 9

Reviewing Main Ideas

The suggestions given below will provide students with an opportunity to compare and contrast classification levels used in the Linnaean system.

Teaching Strategies

- Ask students to suggest three tests, based on what they learned in Section 9-1, that they could apply to an object in order to determine if it is living. *Possible answers may include observing it to see if it uses food and water, to see if it grows, to see if it reproduces, or to see if it responds to its environment. Students may also refer to a cellular system and to adaptation, but you may wish to note that these are difficult to observe without special instruments or very long periods of observation.*
- Have students compare the following pairs of kingdoms and describe one or two differences that distinguish them: monerans and protists *monerans have no nucleus, whereas protists do;* fungi and plants *fungi absorb food from other organisms, whereas plants make their own;* plants and animals *plants make their own food, whereas animals eat other organisms;* monerans and plants *monerans are one-celled, whereas plants are many-celled.*
- Ask students a series of questions that test their understanding of how the category levels of the Linnaean system are related. Each question should have the following format: **"Two organisms belong to the same family. Are they part of the same phylum?"** *The answer is yes.* Another example would be **"Two organisms belong to the same class. Does that mean they belong to the same genus?"** *Possibly, but not necessarily.* Develop a list of other questions following this format and test students' understanding of all seven categories.

Chapter 9

Chapter Review

USING KEY SCIENCE TERMS
Answers

1. Stimulus is not a Linnaean category.
2. Organism is not a Linnaean category.
3. Possible answers are loud sounds, cold, and touch.
4. Possible answers are people, cats, plants, bacteria.
5. Possible answers are monerans, protists, fungi, plants, animals.
6. Possible answers are domestic cat, human being, leopard, deer.

UNDERSTANDING IDEAS
Answers

1. d
2. c
3. a
4. d
5. d
6. c
7. a
8. a

CRITICAL THINKING
Answers

1. Meats might be classified as to whether they are red meat or white meat or what animal they come from. Grains could be classified as to whether they are seeds or fruits. Vegetables might be classified as to whether they are leafy or not or by color. Dairy products might be classified by type of product or amount of butterfat.

2. Alphabetizing is the same because it puts each name in order and has levels of order by first letter, second letter, etc. Alphabetizing is different because the groupings do not tell us how names are related.

3. Answers will vary but should note decrease in size of kingdom from animals through monerans; that plants and animals grow largest and have most complex structure whereas monerans and protists are smallest and simplest; and that monerans and protists are oldest.

4. They belong to same genus but are of different species.

Chapter 9

Chapter Review

USING KEY SCIENCE TERMS

adaptation	organism
class	phylum
family	reproduction
genus	species
kingdom	stimulus
order	

For each set of terms below, choose the one term that does not belong and explain why it does not belong.

1. class, order, stimulus
2. phyla, organism, kingdom

Give an example of each of the following.

3. stimulus
4. organism
5. kingdom
6. species

UNDERSTANDING IDEAS

Choose the best answer to complete each sentence.

1. An example of an organism is ____.
   a. a pebble **c.** the moon
   b. water **d.** a bacterium
2. An organism must do all of the following except ____.
   a. require food **c.** move
   b. be able to reproduce **d.** grow
3. When we classify things, we ____.
   a. group them in some order
   b. change their names
   c. give them new traits
   d. limit their use
4. An organism's scientific name is given ____.
   a. in three parts
   b. in English
   c. once and never changed
   d. to one kind of organism only
5. Linnaeus classified animals based on ____.
   a. where they live
   b. their common names
   c. fossil evidence
   d. their body traits
6. The broadest category of scientific classification of organisms is the ____.
   a. order **c.** kingdom
   b. family **d.** species
7. A subcategory of the order is the ____.
   a. family **c.** phylum
   b. class **d.** kingdom
8. Pandas and bears are related because of their similar ____.
   a. body parts and processes
   b. face markings
   c. stimuli
   d. adaptations

CRITICAL THINKING

Use your understanding of the concepts developed in the chapter to answer each of the following questions.

1. Workable classification systems are based on important traits that are alike among the things being classified.

PROGRAM RESOURCES

Teacher Classroom Resources
Review and Assessment, Chapter Review and Chapter Test, pages 37–40
Computer Test Bank, Chapter Test

OPTIONS

Cooperative Learning
Consider using Cooperative Learning in the Understanding Ideas, Critical Thinking, Problem Solving, and Connecting Ideas sections of the Chapter Review.
COOP LEARN

Identify the important traits you would use to classify the following: meats, grains, vegetables, and dairy products.

2. People often use the alphabet as an organizing tool. How is alphabetizing a group of things such as names in a phone book the same as scientific classification and how is it different?
3. Study the pie graph. Then use information from the chapter to write a paragraph comparing the five kingdoms in terms of size, and kind of cell and body structure.

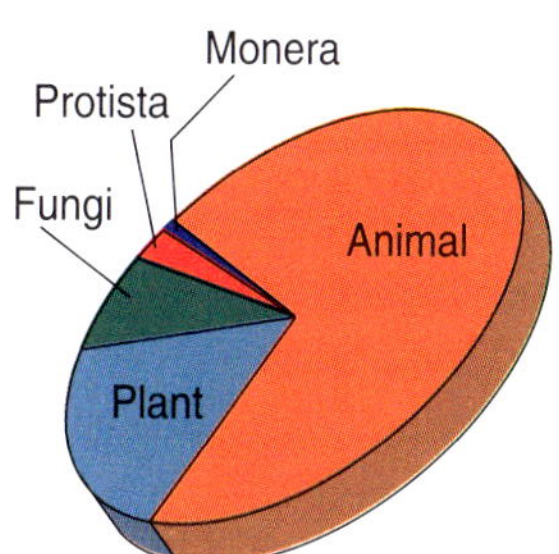

4. The scientific name for present-day humans is *Homo sapiens.* At what level are today's humans related to their ancestors, *Homo habilis*? At what level are we different from *Homo habilis*?

PROBLEM SOLVING

Read the following paragraph and answer the questions.

You are traveling through a rain forest. You see a plant that you believe has never been classified.

1. What could you do to determine if you have discovered a new species?
2. Why is it important to know if the plant is or is not a new species?
3. What traits would you look for in order to identify or classify the plant?

CONNECTING IDEAS

Discuss each of the following in a brief paragraph.

1. Explain how each of our senses brings us information about the physical world in which we live. Give one example of how each sense responds to stimuli from our surroundings.
2. Create a classification system for different landforms or for the different materials that make up Earth.
3. In what ways is a person's two-part name (for example, John Jones) the same and different compared with an organism's scientific name? Would it be possible to name individuals in the same way we name organisms? Why or why not?
4. **EARTH SCIENCE CONNECTION** How can some organisms survive near hydrothermal vents in the ocean?
5. **SCIENCE AND SOCIETY** If there are laws protecting endangered species, why is there still a problem with species becoming extinct?

PROBLEM SOLVING

Answers

1. Observe its traits and compare them to all known species to which it may be related.

2. A new species may offer new and important information about life, or it may be a possible food crop or may even have medicinal uses.

3. size, color, structure, habitat, method of reproduction

CONNECTING IDEAS

Answers

1. Sight gives us information about how things look. A very bright source of light will make us blink our eyes or shade them. Hearing gives us information about the sounds made around us. Our ears let us hear the sound of an approaching car so that we can get out of its way. Taste gives us information about whether things are edible. The sweet taste of fruit tells us that it is good to eat. Smell tells us about objects around us. The smell of rotten eggs lets us know they should not be eaten. Touch tells us about conditions in the world and the positions of our bodies. Touching something very sharp or very hot will result in a reflex that moves the hand, or other body part, away from the source of the sharpness or heat.

2. Answers will vary, but could include items such as land and water, or mountains, plains, valleys, and plateaus.

3. A person's last name, like an organism's genus name, tells what group he or she belongs to. A person's first name identifies him or her as an individual, but the scientific name of an organism does not refer to individual organisms. Scientific names could not work for people because they classify only to the species level; they do not distinguish different members of the same species.

4. They have adapted to conditions near the vent.

5. Many endangered species, some of which are unknown, are not covered by the laws, and the laws can be difficult to enforce.

CHAPTER ORGANIZER

SECTION	OBJECTIVES	ACTIVITIES/FEATURES
Chapter Opener		**Explore!** What do the animals around you do? p. 289
10-1 What Is an Animal? (4 days)	1. **Describe** the characteristics all animals have in common. 2. **Classify** different animals by some of their characteristics.	**Explore!** What are the characteristics of animals? p. 291 **Find Out!** How is a bird's beak useful in getting the kind of food it needs? p. 293 **Investigate 10-1:** Food Choices, p. 295 **Skillbuilder:** Making and Using Graphs, p. 299
10-2 Reproduction and Development (2 days)	1. **Distinguish** between sexual and asexual reproduction. 2. **Trace** the stages of complete and incomplete metamorphosis.	**Explore!** How do you know which animal is the young stage of the adult? p. 300 **Find Out!** What does the metamorphosis of fruit flies look like? p. 303
10-3 Animal Adaptations (3 days)	1. **Explain** how adaptations allow animals to survive on Earth. 2. **Give examples** of some animal adaptations.	**Explore!** Where do people live? p. 306 **Investigate 10-2:** Earthworm Behavior, p. 310
Expanding Your View	A Closer Look **Creature Features,** p. 313 Earth Science Connection **A Natural Disaster,** p. 314 Science and Society **Animal Rights vs. Human Needs,** p. 315 History Connection **Domesticating Animals,** p. 317	Literature Connection **Do Birds Have Knees? Do Lady Bugs Sneeze,** p. 317 Teens in Science **Jessica Knight,** p. 318

ACTIVITY MATERIALS

EXPLORE!	INVESTIGATE!	FIND OUT!
Page 289 paper, pencil, optional tape recorder or camera	**Page 295** 20 mealworms, pan balance, plastic storage box, 20 g bran flakes, 20 g dry oatmeal, 20 g corn flakes, 20 g broken unsalted wheat crackers, cheesecloth, gram masses, hand lens **Page 310** hand lens, toothpick, vinegar, flashlight, live earthworms, covered container, shallow pan, paper towels, beaker, water, cotton swab	**Page 303** vial of food, fruit flies in different stages of metamorphosis

Chapter 10
Animal Life

TEACHER CLASSROOM RESOURCES	OTHER RESOURCES
Study Guide, p. 36 **Multicultural Activities,** p. 23 **Making Connections: Integrating Sciences,** p. 23 **Multicultural Activities,** p. 24 **Making Connections: Across the Curriculum,** p. 23 **Take Home Activities,** p. 19 **Flex Your Brain,** p. 8 **Making Connections: Technology and Society,** p. 23 **Activity Masters, Investigate 10-1,** pp. 41-42	**Laboratory Manual,** pp. 53-54, Vertebrates ***STVS:** *Zooplankton,* Ecology (Disc 6, Side 1)
Study Guide, p. 37 **Concept Mapping,** p. 18 **Critical Thinking/Problem Solving,** p. 18 **How It Works,** p. 12	**Laboratory Manual,** pp. 55-58, Physical Conditions and Behavior **Color Transparency and Master 19,** Frog Life Cycle ***STVS:** *Blood-Fluke Life Cycle,* Animals (Disc 5, Side 1) *Reptilian Sex Change,* Animals (Disc 5, Side 2)
Study Guide, p. 38 **Activity Masters, Investigate 10-2,** pp. 43-44 **Review and Assessment,** pp. 41-44	**Color Transparency and Master 20,** Animal Adaptations ***STVS:** *Temperature Regulation in Dogs,* Animals (Disc 5, Side 2) *Alligator Courtship,* Animals (Disc 5, Side 2) *Kit Fox,* Animals (Disc 5, Side 2) **Computer Test Bank**
	***STVS:** *Sea Skaters,* Animals (Disc 5, Side 1) *Animal Models of Human Physiology,* Animals (Disc 5, Side 2) **Spanish Resources** **Cooperative Learning Resource Guide** **Lab and Safety Skills**

***Science and Technology Videodisc Series**

KEY TO TEACHING STRATEGIES

Teaching strategies have been coded for varying learning styles and abilities. As you review teaching strategies in the margin, the following designations will help you decide which activities are appropriate for your students.

- **L1** Level 1 activities are basic activities and should be within the ability range of all students.
- **L2** Level 2 activities are average activities and should be within the ability range of the average to above-average student.
- **L3** Level 3 activities are challenging activities designed for the ability range of above-average students.
- **LEP** LEP activities should be within the ability range of Limited English Proficiency students.
- **COOP LEARN** Cooperative Learning activities are designed for small group work.

ADDITIONAL MATERIALS

SOFTWARE	AUDIOVISUAL
Animal, Compuware. *The Worm,* Ventura Educational Systems. *Organizing Animals,* Queue. *Animal Reproduction,* J & S Software. *Describing the Behavior of Organisms,* Queue.	*How Animals are Classified,* filmstrip, EBEC. *Animals Without Backbones,* film, Coronet/MTI. *Mammals and Their Characteristics,* film, Coronet/MTI. *Animal Olympians (NOVA),* laserdisc, Image Entertainment. *Beyond Words: Animal Communication,* film, National Geographic.

Chapter 10

Animal Life

THEME DEVELOPMENT

The themes that this chapter supports are interactions and systems and scale and structure. Members of the animal kingdom share common characteristics. Some of these characteristics include methods of obtaining food and how the animal perceives the world around it. All animals are consumers. Thus they have adaptations that enable them to find food. As consumers, all animals interact with their environment and with other living things.

CHAPTER OVERVIEW

This chapter describes certain characteristics that define all members of the animal kingdom, such as methods of obtaining food and movement. Students also learn about sexual and asexual reproduction and animal development.

Finally, students are introduced to adaptations, including behaviors that help different species survive.

Tying to Previous Knowledge

Arrange students in small groups and have them discuss some of the characteristics and behaviors of different kinds of animals with which students are familiar. Use the results of each group discussion to generate a class discussion about the functions, or purposes, of each of the characteristics and behaviors.

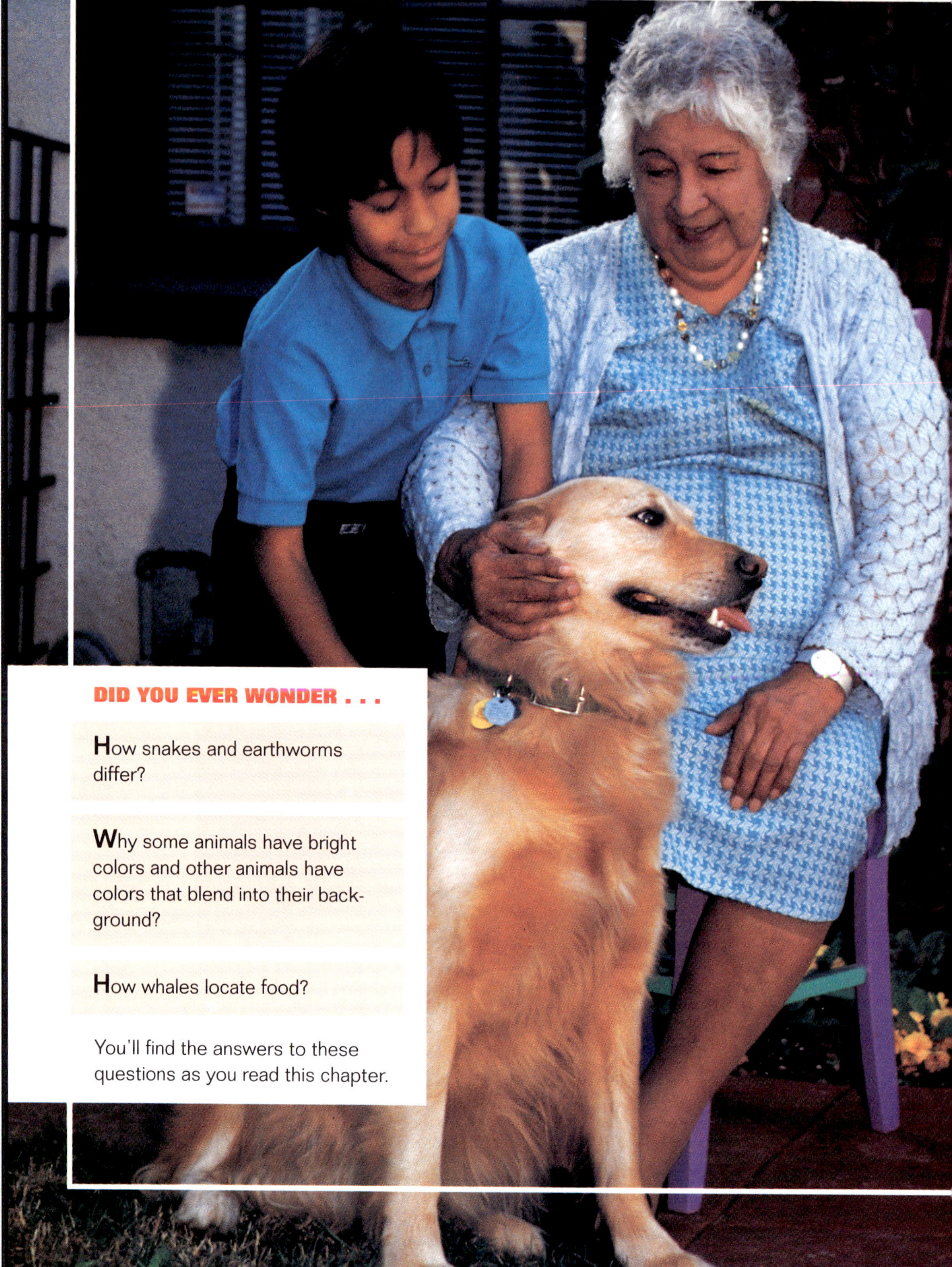

DID YOU EVER WONDER . . .

How snakes and earthworms differ?

Why some animals have bright colors and other animals have colors that blend into their background?

How whales locate food?

You'll find the answers to these questions as you read this chapter.

DID YOU EVER WONDER...

Students will explore these questions as they progress through the chapter. Don't spoil their fun and motivation by sharing these answers too soon.

- Snakes have a backbone; earthworms do not. (pages 296–297)
- Some animals have bright colors to help them attract a mate; some animals have colors that blend into the background to protect them from being seen as they hunt or are being hunted. (pages 311–312)
- Whales use sound to locate their food. (page 294)

Animal Life

If you were given two minutes to list all of the animals that share your life, what examples would you give? Rats and rabbits? Snakes and squirrels? Cats and crickets? Bees, birds, and bats? These animals are found in big cities, small towns, and country farms. You may think raccoons and deer are found only in the woods, yet an amazing number live in backyards or city parks. Countless other animals may live in your home. Termites may chew the wood framing, squirrels may live in the attic, and mice may scamper up the walls. You might say that you are surrounded by animals! And don't forget that people are animals, too. How long is your list now? In this chapter, you will learn about the characteristics of animals—about traits all animals share and traits that make some animals unique. You'll also discover how these characteristics help animals survive.

EXPLORE!

What do the animals around you do?

Choose one animal that lives near you. Observe the animal often for two days and record what you see. Describe what the animal looks like and how it lives. Does it behave differently when people are around? List what it eats and how it gets food. How does it spend most of its time? You might even record any sounds that it makes.

Introducing the Chapter

Have students look at the photograph on page 288. Ask students to brainstorm different types of animals, then discuss which animals would make good pets and which would not. Discuss why some would not be good pets.

Uncovering Preconceptions

Students may think that such familiar organisms as bees, ants, earthworms, snakes, and butterflies belong to classifications that are not part of the animal kingdom. Listen for expressions such as "animals and insects," or "birds and animals," which indicate that students are using the term *animal* in a very narrow sense.

EXPLORE!

What do the animals around you do?

Time needed 2 days

Materials paper, pencil, tape recorder or camera (optional)

Thinking Process
Observing

Purpose To develop a record of animal behavior.

Teaching Strategies

For students who need some structure in an independent assignment, provide data sheets that list the questions asked in this activity. L1

Troubleshooting Emphasize that animals should not be touched, teased, or mistreated in any way. The animals should be observed only.

Expected Outcome

Students should compile a fairly comprehensive record consisting of a description of their animal and its habits and behaviors.

Answers to Questions
All answers will vary, depending on the animal selected.

Project

Have students construct a large poster or chalkboard display that illustrates the concepts developed in this chapter. Have them divide the main heading, *Animals,* into two divisions, *Invertebrates* and *Vertebrates.* Under each subheading, students should include names and pictures of representative animals with descriptions of charactcristics of each.

Science at Home

Have each student watch for different types of animals they see over the course of a weekend. Have them record the names of the animals and where each was seen. As the chapter progresses, have students classify each animal as a vertebrate or invertebrate and describe as many features and characteristics of each animal as possible. You may wish to have students record their observations in their journals.

Section 10-1

PREPARATION

Concepts Developed

Students will discover that all animals have some characteristics in common. For example, they cannot make their own food, so they must eat. These characteristics can be used to classify animals.

Planning the Lesson

In planning your lesson on animal characteristics, refer to the Chapter Organizer on pages 288A–B for timing suggestions, resources, and additional materials that will help you in your presentation of the lesson concepts.

For adequate development of the concepts presented in this section, we recommend that students do the Explore on page 291, and Investigate on page 295.

1 MOTIVATE

Activity Show a general film or filmstrip about animals, like *All Things Animal* (Barr Productions). After the film, have students list characteristics of the animals they saw. Ask students to look for characteristics that animals share. L1

2 TEACH

Tying to Previous Knowledge

Students are familiar with pets such as cats, dogs, birds, or fish. Ask questions about what these animals eat, how they move, and if the animals have learned any behaviors.

Concept Development

Student Text Questions What are some characteristics that all of the organisms in Figure 10-1 share? *They use oxygen, move, eat, and need water.* Into which kingdom would you classify these organisms? *the animal kingdom*

10-1 What Is an Animal?

OBJECTIVES

In this section, you will

- describe the characteristics all animals have in common;
- classify different animals by some of their characteristics.

KEY SCIENCE TERMS

consumer
invertebrate
vertebrate
endoskeleton
exoskeleton

KINGDOM OF ANIMALS

You are a member of many different groups. You are part of a family, a class in school, and a neighborhood. You may belong to an art club, an athletic team, or a youth group. As a member of each group, you have something in common with the other members of the group. For example, you are probably about the same age as the other students in your class and you live in the same city or town. If you belong to an athletic team, you probably share an interest in that sport with the other team members. You may be a fast runner or a good ball thrower. You share some of the same characteristics with other members of the team.

Now look at Figure 10-1. Recall from the previous chapter that scientists classify all organisms into one of five kingdoms. What are some characteristics that all of the organisms in Figure 10-1 share? Into which kingdom would you classify these organisms?

FIGURE 10-1. Animals may look different, but they all share some similar characteristics.

PROGRAM RESOURCES

Teacher Classroom Resources

Study Guide, page 36

Laboratory Manual, pages 53–54, Vertebrates L2

Multicultural Activities, page 23, Horses and Cattle in the New World L1

Making Connections: Integrating Sciences, page 23, Coral Reefs L2

EXPLORE!

What are the characteristics of animals?

Look at the cat. Think about this cat and others you may have seen. List some characteristics that you think describe the cat. Include characteristics of its body, its senses, its movements, and its behavior. Then think about your body, your senses, your behavior. List ways that you and the cat are the same and ways that you differ. What characteristics do you and the cat share? Are you and the cat related in any way?

YOU ARE AN ANIMAL

While doing the last activity, you found that you and the cat share many characteristics. You both have legs for moving, eyes for seeing, ears for hearing, and teeth for chewing. You both sleep, play, and run from danger. Sometimes it's easy to find characteristics that you share with other animals. Sometimes it's not so easy. The animals in Figure 10-2 live in the ocean. Just as you have

FIGURE 10-2. Marine animals include simple mollusks, worms, and mammals.

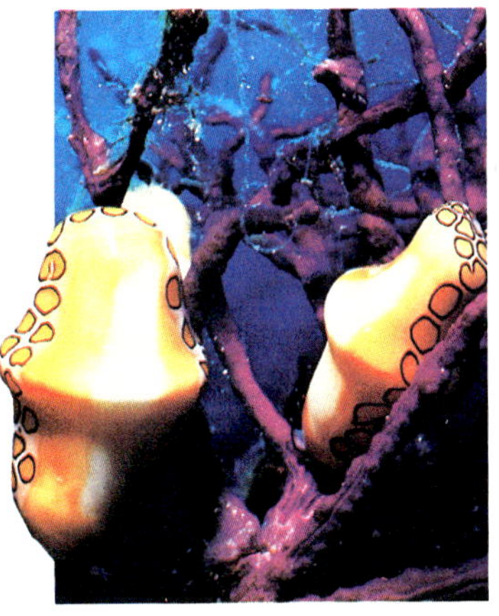

EXPLORE!

What are the characteristics of animals?

Time needed 10 minutes

Materials No special materials or preparation are required for this activity.

Thinking Processes Observing, Comparing and contrasting

Purpose To recognize that humans are both similar to and different from a familiar animal, the cat.

Teaching the Activity

Discussion Give students a few minutes to think about the questions and list some answers. Then write two headings on the chalkboard: *Characteristics we share* and *Ways we differ.* List students' responses under the appropriate heading. Then discuss the question, Are you and the cat related?

Troubleshooting Some students may resist the idea that they are animals. Do not press the issue at this point. As students continue through the section, they will probably conclude that they have the characteristics that define an animal. L1

Expected Outcome

Students will recognize that they share some characteristics with all other members of the animal kingdom.

Answers to Questions

1. Possible answers include: breathing with lungs, having hair or fur, running or walking, eating meat and drinking milk, sleeping, hearing, seeing, and so on.
2. Yes, you and the cat are both animals

OPTIONS

Multicultural Perspectives

Many Native Americans placed great importance on animals. The Mandan, for example, believed that the spirit of the snake was the source of rain and the beaver (also called the "little buffalo") represented food. Members of some tribes believed that the bear, which was hard to kill, was powerful in healing wounds.

Many Pueblo farmers in the parched Southwest thought that the rattlesnake could cause rain to fall. In the spring, the Pueblo captured live rattlers, and during the rain ceremony, stroked the creatures with feathers. After the ceremony, they returned the snakes gently to the ground, where it was hoped they would fulfill their responsibility and bring rain.

Concept Development

Theme Connection All animals share certain characteristics, but the animal kingdom has a broad variety of ways of showing those characteristics. Animal characteristics provide examples of the theme of scale and structure. Ask students to compare the structure of the sponges, shown in Figure 10-3, with that of the fox, shown in Figure 10-4. Ask students how the fox gets its food. *It hunts.* Ask how the sponge gets food—can it hunt? *no* If students cannot figure out how a sponge gets food, tell them that it filters small organisms out of the water.

Discussion

Have students brainstorm other types of animals than those pictured on the page, (soil dwellers, those that are nocturnal, and so on) and the types of foods they conserve to obtain energy.

MAKING CONNECTIONS

Language Arts

Have students look up the prefix *zoo-* and some words that include it. This prefix refers to animals. The branch of biology that deals with the study of animals is called zoology. Those scientists who study animals are zoologists. Ask students what the complete name for a zoo is. *zoological park* L2

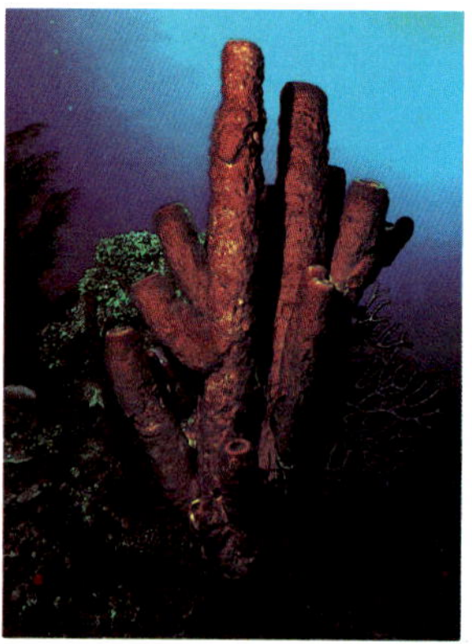

FIGURE 10-3. Some animals, such as sponges, remain attached to rocks during their adult lives.

some common characteristics with the cat, you also have some common characteristics with these animals.

Let's look at some characteristics that you and all other animals have in common.

1. All living things need water and food, but animals *can't* make their own food. Animals depend on other living things for food. Some animals eat plants, some animals eat other animals, and some animals eat both plants and animals.

2. Many animals move from place to place. They move to find food, escape from danger, find shelter, and find mates. Animals that can't move or move slowly have characteristics that allow them to survive. For instance, sponges appear rooted as adults, but move through water in an early reproductive stage.

HOW ANIMALS FIND FOOD

Recall that one characteristic of all animals is that they can't make their own food. Food provides the energy all organisms need to carry out their life processes. Plants have the ability to make their own food. They use water, carbon dioxide, and energy from the sun to produce sugar. You will learn more about this process in the next chapter. Sugar is food for the plants.

Animals must eat or consume other organisms for their energy. Animals are consumers. A **consumer** is an organism that eats other organisms. A consumer gets all of its energy and nutrients from these other organisms.

FIGURE 10-4. Animals like the fox are consumers. They use other organisms for food.

PROGRAM RESOURCES

Teacher Classroom Resources

Multicultural Activities, page 24, The Sami L1

Making Connections: Across the Curriculum, page 23, Cold-Blooded Vertebrates L3

Take Home Activities, page 18, No Thumbs L1

OPTIONS

Enrichment

Activity Have students prepare a bulletin board with pictures of animals representing the various phyla. This can be an ongoing project during the study of the chapter. As students learn more about animal characteristics, reproduction, and adaptive behavior, this new information can be added to the display. Research outside the chapter will be needed for some phyla. L2

FIND OUT!

How is a bird's beak useful in getting the kind of food it needs?

At first glance, birds may seem very much alike. Yet each species is uniquely adapted for getting its specific food. Study the different species of birds shown. Pay close attention to the different beaks. Match the bird to the type of food it eats.

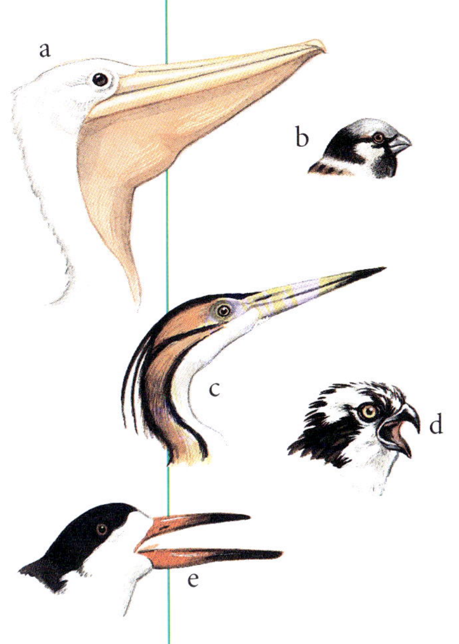

Conclude and Apply

1. This bird has a long, sharply pointed bill for spearing fish.
2. This bird's bill is short and thick for seed eating.
3. This bird's lower bill is longer than the upper so it can scoop food from the water's surface.
4. The powerful, sharp, hooked beak on this bird is for tearing the flesh of animals it kills.
5. This bird has a pouch under its lower jaw so it can collect many fish at once.

BODY PARTS AND SENSES

As you learned in the Find Out activity, animals use different types of body parts to obtain food. Bird beaks are only one example. A giraffe uses its long neck and long tongue to reach leaves on tall trees. An anteater uses its long tongue to pick up ants or termites. A sponge draws water into its body through its many body openings. As the water moves through the openings, food is trapped.

Sometimes an animal's senses are useful for finding food. Think about the last time you found a street vendor or found a food stand at a mall. What senses did you use to find and identify the food being sold? Most people use both sight and smell to locate food. You may think that you have good senses of sight and smell, but this is not really so when compared to other members of the animal kingdom. The expression *eagle-eyed* gives a clue to one type of animal that has a very sharp sense of sight. Eagles

DID YOU KNOW?

A giant anteater's tongue can be as long as 60 centimeters.

FIND OUT!

How is a bird's beak useful in getting the kind of food it needs?

Time needed 15 minutes

Materials No special materials or preparation are required for this activity, which can be done as an independent assignment.

Thinking Process
Observing and inferring

Purpose To learn that birds' beaks are adapted to obtaining the type of food they need.

Teaching the Activity

Birds in the illustration are, top to bottom, left column, pelican, heron, black skimmer; right column, sparrow, osprey.

Troubleshooting Point out that each question has only one right answer, and students will have to make careful observations of details in the drawing. For example, the black skimmer and the heron both have long pointed bills, but only the black skimmer has the lower bill longer than the upper.

Expected Outcomes

Students will recognize that variations in animals' characteristics are related to the way each animal lives.

Conclude and Apply

1. heron
2. sparrow
3. black skimmer
4. osprey
5. pelican

Meeting Individual Needs

Visually Impaired Whenever possible, use real animals, models, or prepared specimens to illustrate the topics under discussion, such as the varieties of birds' beaks. Allow students to handle these objects and answer questions like those in the Find Out activity above.

Enrichment

Activity Have students look at the chart on the evolution of elephants on pages 21–23 of *National Geographic*, May 1991. Have each student select one of the elephants pictured and write a paragraph explaining why the tusks and trunk might have developed in a particular way. They can illustrate their paragraphs to show the adapted features in use. L3

Concept Development

Activity How do snakes hear? Snakes do not have external ears, but they can hear.

Materials needed are a rubber mallet and a tuning fork.

Have students strike a tuning fork with a rubber mallet, then hold it next to their ear. Strike it again and place the stem hard against the chin (do not touch the tines). The sound will be transmitted through the bones of the head to the ear. Tell students that snakes also hear by bone conduction. L2 LEP

Student Text Question
How is this useful for survival? *It is useful to help the whales and dolphins find food, avoid predators, and avoid hitting other objects.*

Flex Your Brain Use the Flex Your Brain activity to have students explore WHALES and DOLPHINS.

Teacher F.Y.I.

- Snakes smell both through their nostrils and their tongues.
- The loudest noise of all is made by the blue whale, which keeps in touch with its companions by using low-frequency sounds that register over 180 decibels, louder than a jet engine would sound if you were standing on the runway when it took off.

Content Background

Large eyes located on the sides of the head in most birds allow birds to see a much wider area than other animals, including people. The eyes focus independently of each other so a bird can see two different images at the same time. Many predator birds such as owls and eagles can focus straight ahead with both eyes focusing on the same image, as humans do. This allows the bird to judge depth and distance and helps it capture prey. Most birds can see in color, which helps them find food.

FIGURE 10-5. Eagles use their keen vision to hunt for food.

DID YOU KNOW?

Biologists shook a tree in the tropical rainforest and caught what fell out. They found over 100 new species of insects. No one knew that these particular animals existed before then.

and hawks look out for their food as they soar high up in the air. For birds that hunt, keen vision is a must for survival.

Visibility is limited under water, so another sense is well developed in many marine animals. You learned in Chapter 3 that sound travels very well through water. Dolphins and whales have a highly developed sense of hearing. They can detect sounds made many kilometers away. They even use sound to locate objects in the water. When they make a sound, they can tell from its echo exactly where the object is. How is this useful for survival?

FIGURE 10-6. Dolphins use echoes to locate objects in the water.

For other animals, the sense of smell is useful for finding food. Hunting animals, such as the coyote or wolf, will often pick up the scent of an animal. They will follow the scent until they find the animal.

Not only do animals use their senses to find food, they also use their senses to find the food they prefer. In the next Investigate, you'll discover what foods meal worms prefer.

PROGRAM RESOURCES

Teacher Classroom Resources
Activity Masters, pages 41–42, Investigate 10-1
Critical Thinking/Problem Solving, page 8, Flex Your Brain
Making Connections: Technology and Society, page 23, Better Ways to Battle Bugs L2

OPTIONS

Enrichment

Debate Have students look into the issue of using animals in scientific research. They can form two groups, with one group trying to find information that gives the point of view of the animal rights groups while the other group searches for the opinion of the researchers. After the information has been gathered, students can conduct a debate on the issue. L3

INVESTIGATE!

10-1 FOOD CHOICES

You may not like to eat spinach. Other members of your family may not like corn. Your dog may prefer to eat your leftover dinner rather than dog food. Many animals have food preferences. In the following activity, you will **observe** how mealworms respond to different kinds of food.

PROBLEM

What food do most mealworms prefer?

MATERIALS

20 mealworms
pan balance
plastic storage box
20 g bran flakes
20 g dry oatmeal
20 g corn flakes
20 g broken unsalted wheat crackers
cheesecloth
gram masses
hand lens

PROCEDURE

1. Copy the data table.
2. Collect mealworms from your teacher.
3. Put each food—bran flakes, oatmeal, corn flakes, and broken crackers—in a separate corner of the plastic box. Moisten the food. Place the mealworms in the center of the box.
4. Cover the box with the cheesecloth and place it in a dimly lit, warm location.
5. **Hypothesize** about which food the mealworms will prefer.
6. The next day, **observe** the locations of the mealworms. Count the number of mealworms that have moved to each corner of the box.
7. Record the number of mealworms that have moved.
8. Return the mealworms to the center of the box. Repeat this procedure each day for three more days.
9. Calculate the total number of mealworms preferring each food.

DATA AND OBSERVATIONS Sample data

TEST FOOD	DAY 1	DAY 2	DAY 3	DAY 4
Oatmeal	7	4	8	5
Corn flakes	Responses of the mealworms			
Wheat crackers	may vary			
Bran flakes				

ANALYZE

1. How did you test your hypothesis?
2. How do mealworms respond to different foods?

CONCLUDE AND APPLY

3. What food would you provide if you wanted to raise mealworms?
4. Was your hypothesis correct? Explain.
5. **Going Further: Predict** whether mealworms might be attracted to dry food. Then test your predictions.

INVESTIGATE!

10-1 FOOD CHOICES

Time needed 20 minutes to set up; several minutes each day for four more days

Materials See student activity.

Thinking Processes
Measuring in SI, Making and using tables, Forming a hypothesis, Separating and controlling variables, Interpreting data

Purpose To conduct a controlled experiment to determine the food preferences of mealworms

Preparation Obtain all materials. Arrange a place in the classroom where each group's experimental box can be kept for several days.

Teaching Strategies

Discussion Ask students to name their favorite and least-liked foods. Then ask if they think mealworms have favorite foods, too. After they set up the experiment, have each group form a hypotheses about which of the available foods the mealworms will prefer.

Student Journal Have students record their hypotheses and results in their journals.

Troubleshooting Remind students to handle the mealworms carefully. Keep the boxes in a warm location.

Expected Outcome

Students will see that mealworms do have food preferences.

Answers to Analyze/Conclude and Apply

1. by exposing the mealworms to various food sources over a period of time
2. Mealworms prefer certain foods, such as oatmeal, over others.
3. the food most mealworms preferred, oatmeal
4. Answers will depend on students' hypotheses.
5. Answers will vary, but students should find that the mealworms are more attracted to moist food.

Enrichment

Activity If you were going to raise mealworms, you would want to provide oatmeal. If you ran a restaurant or cafeteria you would want to provide what your customers preferred. Students can plan an experiment to determine fellow students' food preferences. How do students' food preferences influence what is served in the school lunchroom? Present the results of the research to the school dietician and ask him or her to talk to the class about how lunch menus are determined. 

Concept Development

Activity How can a starfish pry apart a clamshell? Try this to see how it works. Have students work in pairs. One student holds an arm straight out, palm up. The other student places a fairly heavy book on the palm and times how long the first student can hold the arm up with the book on it. The book is the pressure applied by the starfish and the arm is the clam's muscle. Students will notice that the steady pressure quickly overcomes muscle strength. L1 COOP LEARN LEP

Activity Some students will not be comfortable with the touch involved in the "backbone" activity. Allow them to reach behind and feel their own backbones. The backbone is easier to feel if the student leans forward, rounding the back.

Student Text Questions Describe what you feel. What is its name? *Students should feel a long, hard, bumpy set of bones called the backbone or spine.* If you ran your hand along the back of each animal, what would you feel? *You would feel a backbone in the snake but not in the worm.* Which animal's back would feel the same as yours? *the snake* What characteristic do you share with this animal? *both have a backbone*

Content Background

The classification of animals has changed over the years, as more details about animal characteristics are learned. A good source of information on classification is *Five Kingdoms* by Margulis and Schwartz (Freeman, 1988). The book is written at an adult level, but the scenes that place each group into their environment can be used to answer some student questions.

HOW ANIMALS DIGEST FOOD

You know that all animals are consumers. Once they get food, they must be able to break it down into particles small enough for their bodies to use. This is done through the process of digestion. Most animals have a special digestive system. Food enters through a mouth and passes through the system. Enzymes chemically break down the food, and the digested material is passed on through the body for use. Wastes are then expelled through an anus.

The starfish has an unusual method of digesting its food. After prying apart the two shells of a clam, the starfish pushes its stomach out of its mouth and spreads the stomach out over the food. Enzymes secreted by the stomach turn the food into a soupy liquid, which is absorbed by the stomach. Then the starfish pulls its stomach back into its body to continue digestion.

FIGURE 10-7. The starfish begins digesting the mussel outside its body.

HOW SCIENTISTS CLASSIFY ANIMALS

Many different characteristics can be used to place living things into groups. One way to group organisms is by the means they use to get food. Animals are consumers because they can't make their own food. Biologists use another way to further classify all animals. Try this simple activity with a classmate. Take turns running your fingers down the middle of each other's back. Describe what you feel. What is its name?

Now look at Figure 10-8. Which animal's back would feel the same as yours? What characteristic do you share with this animal?

Think about other animals that you see. Decide which ones share this same characteristic with you.

FIGURE 10-8. The earthworm and snake may look similar, but they do not share the characteristic of having a backbone.

OPTIONS

Multicultural Perspectives

The snake is central to ceremonies and legends in many cultures. In Africa, for example, some groups worship pythons; in India, there are cobra cults. The Burmese have long been famous for their snake charming. These snake charmers end their ceremonies by kissing the cobra on the top of its head.

Enrichment

Activity Have students make a mobile of the different animals they have read about thus far in this section. Beneath each animal, students should write the animal's name and the fact they find most interesting about it. When students have finished this section, they might want to rearrange the order of animals on their mobiles to reflect what they have learned about the classification of animals.

When you ran your hand down your classmate's back, you felt a backbone. Biologists use the characteristic of having or not having a backbone as a way to divide all members of the animal kingdom into two groups. Most animals don't have a backbone. These animals belong to the group known as invertebrates. An **invertebrate** is an animal that doesn't have a backbone. Worms, clams, jellyfish, flies, and spiders are some examples of invertebrates.

a b

FIGURE 10-9. Tunicates (a) and lancelets (b) are chordates.

You belong to the smaller group of animals that has a backbone. You are a vertebrate. A **vertebrate** is an animal that has a backbone. Vertebrates belong to the phylum Chordata (kor DAHT uh), as do the tunicates and lancelets, pictured in Figure 10-9.

Figure 10-10 is a chart that shows the different groups of chordates and invertebrates. All chordates have a hollow nerve cord, and gill slits at some time during their life cycles. Fish, amphibians, reptiles, birds, and mammals are all vertebrates. Vertebrates are considered to be more highly developed than invertebrates because of their brains and nervous systems.

FIGURE 10-10. This figure shows several examples of vertebrates and invertebrates in the animal kingdom.

Concept Development

Using the Diagram Have students use Figure 10-10 to answer the following questions. **How many types of cold-blooded vertebrates are shown?** *three: fish, reptiles, amphibians* **What three words from the figure can you use to describe any mammal?** *chordate, vertebrate, warm-blooded* **What do mollusks and worms have in common?** *They are invertebrates.*

Uncovering Preconceptions Many students do not think of invertebrates as animals. Elicit students' help in writing a list of familiar invertebrates on the chalkboard. This will allow you to correct misconceptions. Emphasize that the animals on the list are related by the absence of a structural characteristic—a backbone—rather than the presence of a characteristic.

MAKING CONNECTIONS

Daily Life

Decades ago, many parents and teachers insisted that youngsters adopt a straight-backed posture. It is now widely recognized that the order to "straighten your back" is contrary to nature. The human backbone is not naturally straight, and no effort can ever make it so. As seen from the side, the normal backbone resembles a double S. From under the skull, it moves slightly inward, swoops out at shoulder level, then curves back behind the stomach. At the base of the spine, it turns outward again and then nips back in at the tailbone. What purpose does all this curving serve? *It makes the spine a kind of spring that can absorb shocks that would otherwise travel straight to your brain.*

Enrichment

Activity Current theories of good posture are based on balance. The aim is to stand with your head high, but not pushed back. The shoulders should be held back just far enough to allow ease of breathing. Arrange students in pairs to practice holding their backbones correctly. Tell them to try to imagine that a weighted line hangs down from beside their ears to just in front of their ankles.

Research The most serious complication of a fractured backbone is injury to the spinal column, which can result in paralysis. Have students find out what first aid measures are recommended when it is suspected that a person has fractured his or her backbone. Should the person be moved? If so, in what position? They may wish to contact their local rescue squad for information.

Teacher F.Y.I.

About 80 percent of Americans suffer, off and on, from backaches.

Concept Development

Chordates are classified together because of the presence of a notochord, a rod-shaped structure composed of cells that supports the body of lower chordates. In higher vertebrates, the notochord is present in the embryo but is later replaced by the vertebral column, or spine. *Dorsal* means on or near the back; the opposite of *dorsal* is *ventral.*

Inquiry Question Many sea stars, sea urchins, and sand dollars have pentaradial symmetry. What does *penta-* mean? *It means five.*

Demonstration Students might find the difference between radial symmetry and bilateral symmetry a challenging concept. Hold up a sand dollar to demonstrate radial symmetry. Use a volunteer as a model for bilateral symmetry. Ask students to write a few sentences describing each type of symmetry.

Inquiry Question Which form of symmetry do you think allows an animal to move more efficiently on land? *bilateral* Why? *It allows animals to organize their movement in a straight line.*

Content Background

Most animals are symmetrical in some way. Only a few can be described as asymmetrical. Many asymmetrical animals are sessile (attached at the base, or without any distinct projecting support). Animals with radial symmetry do not move efficiently. Either they are sessile or they float or crawl. Most animals with bilateral symmetry move head first.

FIGURE 10-11. Sand dollars have radial symmetry (a). Butterflies have bilateral symmetry (b), and sponges are asymmetrical (c).

Biologists also look at each animal's basic body plan, or how its body parts are arranged. This body plan is the animal's symmetry. Think about a pie or a bicycle wheel. Both items form a circle. No matter where you divide the pie or the wheel in half, the two halves are always the same. Animals such as hydra and sand dollars have this kind of body arrangement, which is called radial symmetry.

Most animals have a body plan that shows a distinct left and right side. If you draw an imaginary line down the length of an animal's body, its body parts are arranged in the same way on both sides. Animals whose body parts are arranged the same way on both sides have bilateral symmetry. In Latin, the word *bilateral* means "two sides". Humans, dogs, birds, fish, and butterflies have bilateral symmetry. Can you see why this is so?

Some animals are asymmetrical. Animals that are asymmetrical do not have a definite body shape. Figure 10-11 shows examples of the three kinds of symmetry.

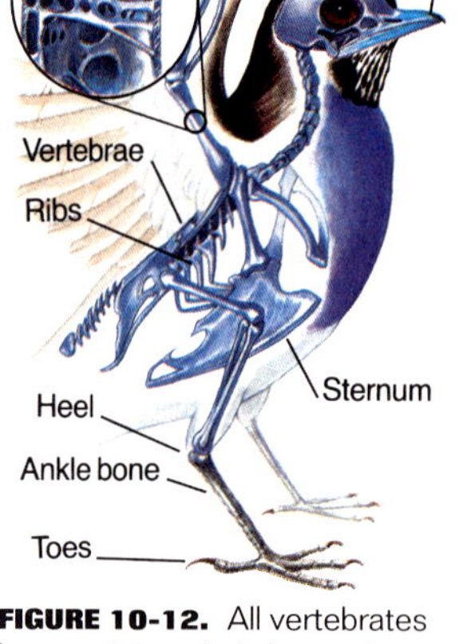

FIGURE 10-12. All vertebrates have an internal skeleton, also called an endoskeleton.

SKELETONS: A MEANS OF SUPPORT

Have you ever watched a tall building being constructed? A system of steel beams provides the support for the walls, floors, and roof. Without the beams, the building would collapse in on itself. Many animals also have a system of support. Remember when you felt your classmate's backbone? The backbone is part of an internal support system called a skeleton. All vertebrates have an internal skeleton. A skeleton that is within an animal's body is, as seen in Figure 10-12, an **endoskeleton**. The endoskeletons of many animals are made of bone, but the skeletons of some, such as skates, rays, and sharks, are made of car-

OPTIONS

Enrichment

Research/Activity Animals, like people, suffer medical problems. Many problems require the attention of an expert in veterinary medicine. Have small groups of students select an animal, such as a pet, and research how it would be treated for medical problems. Students may want to investigate the care required for broken bones, burns, parasites, respiratory infections, insect bites, poisoning, animal bites, choking, frostbite, infections, shock, sprains, wounds, drowning, and heat stroke. L3

FIGURE 10-13. The shell of a crayfish is its exoskeleton.

tilage. Elephant bones are massive to support the weight of these huge animals. Bird bones are light and hollow. This structure provides strength and support, yet makes the bird lightweight and is an advantage for flight.

Unlike vertebrates, some invertebrates have their support systems on the outside of their bodies. They have exoskeletons. An **exoskeleton** is a system of support that is outside of an animal's body. Crayfish, lobsters, shrimp, crabs, ants, bees, and beetles belong to that one phylum of invertebrates known as arthropods. The exoskeleton of arthropods protects their internal organs and supports their bodies. Figure 10-13 shows an example of an exoskeleton.

In this section, you discovered what characteristics separate animals from other living things. You also read about several ways biologists group animals. In the next section you will learn how animals reproduce.

SKILLBUILDER

MAKING AND USING GRAPHS

This bar graph gives you some idea of the relative number of species of invertebrates and vertebrates that biologists have identified. How many species of invertebrates are shown by the graph? Which group of animals is most abundant? Which group has the fewest number? If you need help, refer to the **Skill Handbook** on page 650.

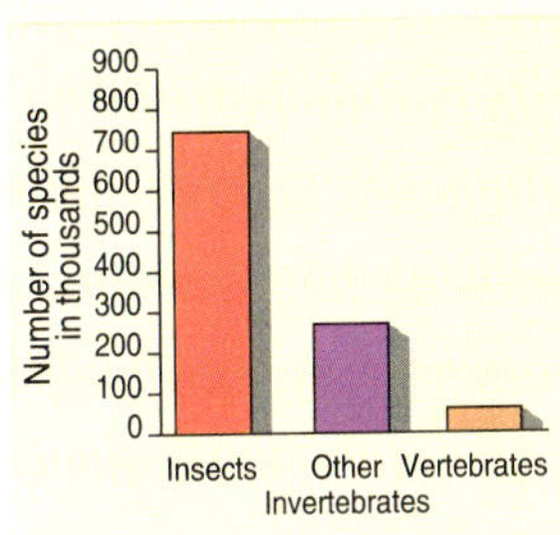

Check Your Understanding

1. A sponge is an animal that doesn't move from place to place. It's attached to one spot on the ocean floor. Why is it still considered an animal?
2. Classify each of the animals listed as vertebrate or invertebrate. Which of the animals has an endoskeleton, and which of them has an exoskeleton?
   bee mouse robin ant deer
3. **APPLY:** If you found a fossil of an organism with a backbone, what characteristics would you know about the organism?

SKILLBUILDER

1. About 1025
2. Insects
3. Vertebrates L1

3 Assess

Check for Understanding

1. Play a game to guess an animal's identity by giving clues about its food-gathering methods, body parts and senses, and classification. Have students comb through this section for animals and clues. They should write the name of the animal on the front of an index card and as many clues as possible on the back. Students can play the game in pairs or teams. COOP LEARN
2. Ask students to make a chart showing how invertebrates are different from vertebrates. Urge them to use this chart as they complete Check Your Understanding.

Reteach

Have students make a concept map showing the steps scientists can use to classify a new animal. *Scientists first determine if the animal is a vertebrate or invertebrate. Next, they determine the animal's symmetry. Last, they compare the animal's characteristics to those of other organisms.* L1

Extension

Discussion In the last 300 years, at least 300 vertebrate animals have become extinct. By comparison, estimates show that dinosaur species died off at the rate of about one per 1,000 years. Have students explain what causes animals to become extinct today and what can be done to help preserve them. L3

4 Close

Have each student draw the outline of a familiar animal. Based on what they learned in this section, what words could they write in the outline to describe the animal? L1

Answers to Check Your Understanding

1. It is an animal because it is a consumer and digests its food.
2. Bee and ant are invertebrates. The rest are vertebrates. All the vertebrates have endoskeletons; the bee and ant have exoskeletons.
3. It is an animal, a consumer, a vertebrate, a chordate, and has an endoskeleton.

Section 10-2

PREPARATION

Concepts Developed

In the previous section, students discovered that all animals share common characteristics, which can be used to classify them. Here, students will learn how animals reproduce. Students will distinguish between sexual and asexual reproduction as well as trace the steps involved in complete and incomplete metamorphosis.

Planning the Lesson

In planning your lesson on animal reproduction and development, refer to the Chapter Organizer on pages 288A–B for timing suggestions, resources, and additional materials that will help you in your presentation of the lesson concepts.

For adequate development of the concepts presented in this section, we recommend that students do the Explore on page 300.

1 MOTIVATE

Discussion Ask volunteers to describe at what age their younger siblings learned various survival skills. When did they learn to walk? *at about a year* Talk? *one–two years.* Have students make a chart showing developmental milestones from birth to 12 years. L1

10-2 Reproduction and Development

OBJECTIVES

In this section, you will

- distinguish between sexual and asexual reproduction;
- trace the stages of complete and incomplete metamorphosis.

KEY SCIENCE TERMS

fertilization

metamorphosis

HOW ANIMALS REPRODUCE

Have you stopped in a pet shop to look at the new, playful puppies and kittens? By the time they get to the store, they're already several weeks old and usually have had the first series of shots that they need to stay healthy. As you laugh at their actions, you probably never really think about the process that took place before these young animals could be born.

Reproduction must take place for a species to survive. Some animals have fairly simple ways to reproduce. Some animals have more complex methods of reproduction.

EXPLORE!

How do you know which animal is the young stage of the adult?

Below are pictures of animals at two different stages in their lives. Match the young with the correct adult. As you choose the pairs, record what clues you used to make the matches. For example, does the young animal look just like the adult? Do you know because you have actually seen the young and adult together? Compare your matches with those of other classmates.

EXPLORE!

How do you know which animal is the young stage of the adult?

Time needed 15 minutes

Materials No special materials or preparation are required for this activity.

Thinking Processes Observing and inferring, Comparing and contrasting

Purpose To see that some young animals resemble their parents, while others do not.

Teaching the Activity

Troubleshooting Students can tackle the obvious pairs before moving to the more difficult matches. L1

Expected Outcome

Students will see that only some young resemble parents.

Answers to Questions

1. Not Always
2. Match two chimps, birds, grass-hoppers; frog and tadpole; the butterfly and caterpillar, jellyfish and polyp.

As you matched the animals in the activity, you found that sometimes young animals look very similar to adults. Yet often, the young do not look like the adults at all. As you read through this section, you will learn that sometimes the different ways animals reproduce might influence how the young appear.

DID YOU KNOW?

A female codfish may lay over 9 million eggs in one mating season!

SEXUAL REPRODUCTION

Sexual reproduction is one way animals reproduce. Most animal species have separate male and female individuals. For reproduction to occur, the male's sperm must unite with the female's egg. **Fertilization** occurs when the sperm and egg unite. Sometimes the sperm and egg unite outside the female's body in a process called external fertilization. External fertilization usually occurs with animals that live in water. For example, the frogs in Figure 10-14 have external fertilization. Sometimes the sperm unites with the egg while it's still within the female's body. This is called internal fertilization. Internal fertilization most often occurs with animals that live on land.

FIGURE 10-14. Frogs use external fertilization to reproduce sexually.

Remember that the result of reproduction is a generation of new individuals. Different animal species may produce one or many new individuals. For starfish, sea urchins, fish, frogs, and other water animals, one method is the production of large numbers of eggs and sperm. During external fertilization, the female releases the eggs into the water. The male then releases the sperm, which swim to the eggs. In this process, the large number of fertilized eggs ensures that some will survive both harsh conditions and animals that eat them.

During internal fertilization, the female produces one or more eggs that stay in the body. The male then deposits the sperm within her body. The sperm swim to and unite with the eggs. Organisms that shelter fertilized eggs in the female's body generally produce smaller numbers of offspring. These organisms appear more able to survive. Another advantage of internal fertilization is that the animals are not restricted to living in or near water.

2 TEACH

Tying to Previous Knowledge

Arrange students in small groups to make posters showing how scientists classify animals, which they learned in the previous section. Tell them to leave about one-quarter of the poster blank. When everyone has finished working, have each group share its poster with the class in a brief oral presentation. Explain to students they will now learn two other ways that animals can be classified, by how they reproduce and how they develop. What animals can you think of that need a lot of care after they are born? *mammals, such as humans, foxes, and kittens, and birds, such as penguins, robins, and cardinals* Which ones are independent very quickly? *Students can cite examples of fish, amphibians, and reptiles.* You can have students complete the posters when they have finished this section. L2 COOP LEARN

Concept Development

Inquiry Questions Why do most amphibians return to the water to lay their eggs? *The eggs lack shells and must be kept moist.* Female fish lay thousands of eggs. Why aren't the waters overcrowded with fish? *Many of the eggs are not fertilized and are eaten by other animals. Some eggs and young fish are eaten by predators.*

Content Background

Once the female emperor penguin lays her single egg, she returns to the sea. The male emperor penguin warms the egg between his feet and his body to incubate it. Huddled together on the pack ice in the darkness of the antarctic winter, the males are unable to feed for the whole of the 64-day incubation period. When the chick hatches, the male feeds it from the secretions in his crop (food store) until the female returns to take care of the chick.

PROGRAM RESOURCES

Teacher Classroom Resources

Study Guide, page 37
Laboratory Manual, pages 55-58, Physical Conditions and Behavior L2
Concept Mapping, page 18, Complete Metamorphosis L1
Critical Thinking/Problem Solving, page 18, Sign Stimuli L2
Transparency Masters, page 41, and **Color Transparency,** number 19, Frog Life Cycle L1

OPTIONS

Enrichment

Research Have students research and report on gestation periods in mammals and the average number of offspring born to different species. Some gestation periods are shown below. L1

hamster	16 days	cow	281 days
mouse	20 days	horse	336 days
rabbit	31 days	camel	406 days
dog	61 days	giraffe	442 days
cat	63 days	whale	450 days

Concept Development

Uncovering Preconceptions Even after reading Section 10-1, some students might not think of sponges as animals because they are sessile. Explain that sponges carry on all the process of life, including reproduction, just as other animals do.

Inquiry Question The hydra was named for a mythical giant water monster with nine heads. Hercules, a Greek hero, was supposed to slay the monster. But each time he cut off one head, Hydra grew two more to take its place. How is the real hydra like the mythical one? *A real hydra can grow new organisms by budding, asexual reproduction.*

Inquiry Question The natural sponge industry has decreased in the last 50 years. Why may this have happened? *Synthetic sponges are less expensive and have replaced natural sponges.*

MAKING CONNECTIONS

Health

Humans undergo a process similar to regeneration in which damaged organs grow larger to compensate for the loss. If three-quarters of the human liver is removed, for example, the remaining portion enlarges to a mass equivalent to the original organ. Recently, surgeons removed part of a mother's liver and transplanted it to her daughter, where it grew large enough to function properly.

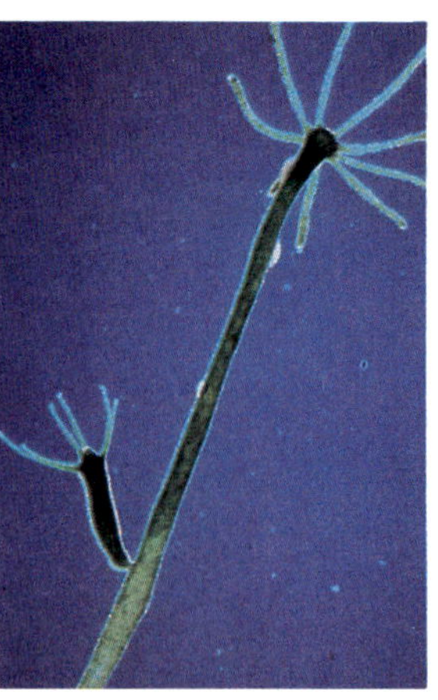

FIGURE 10-15. Budding in hydra is a form of asexual reproduction.

ASEXUAL REPRODUCTION

If you showed a family photograph to some friends, they would probably say that you look like your mother or father. Young animals that develop from sexual reproduction have some characteristics from each parent. This leads to variety within the species because the young are never exactly like either parent. But some animals are exactly like only one parent. These animals are the results of asexual reproduction. Asexual reproduction is the production of a new organism from one parent. Among animals, asexual reproduction occurs in certain invertebrates.

Let's look at two kinds of asexual reproduction. Hydra and sponges can reproduce by budding. During budding, a growth forms on the parent animal. At some point, the growth breaks off from the parent, and a new hydra or sponge is formed. The new animal has the same characteristics as the parent animal.

A few animals can form whole new body parts by regeneration. Regeneration occurs when an animal regrows a missing part. Starfish and sponges may form new animals through regeneration. Sponge growers cut large sponges into smaller pieces and throw the pieces into the ocean. After the pieces have been put back into the ocean, each piece continues to grow into a larger sponge. Figure 10-16 shows that a whole starfish can regenerate from just the arm of a starfish.

FIGURE 10-16. Regeneration, as seen in this starfish, is a form of asexual reproduction.

Teacher F.Y.I.

Virtually all bony fishes can regenerate amputated fins, but cartilaginous fishes (such as sharks and rays) cannot.

PROGRAM RESOURCES

Teacher Classroom Resources

How It Works, page 12, How Birds Fly L1

Other Resources

Mammals and Their Characteristics, film, Coronet/MTI.

Animal Reproduction, software, J & S Software.

OPTIONS

Enrichment

Activity Explain to students that very often there are special names to differentiate young animals from fully grown members of the species. Young dogs are called puppies; young cats, kittens. Have students make a list of animals and the names of their young. To get them started, you might want to write some examples on the board, (kangaroo–joey; deer–fawn; bear–cub; swan–cygnet) L1.

ANIMAL DEVELOPMENT

How often have you heard your parents say, "Wait until you're older!" or "Not until you've grown up!" You are at the age when many changes are occurring to your body. You are growing from a child into a young adult. Your stages of development are similar to the stages of some animals. Other animals have very different stages of development.

Animals such as birds and mammals have young that look very similar to the adults of the species, much like the animals in Figure 10-17. During development, they change gradually, getting bigger and growing feathers or fur until they become adults. You can tell that a kitten will become a cat fairly easily because the kitten has many of the same characteristics that an adult cat has. But many young animals do not look anything like their parent, as you learned in the last Explore. Some change form completely as they grow from egg to adulthood. You know that caterpillars are the young of butterflies. This change in form from young to adult is called **metamorphosis**. *Meta* means "change" and *morpho* means "form." So, metamorphosis is a change in form. What other animals do you know that undergo metamorphosis?

FIGURE 10-17. Many animals have young that look very similar to the adults of the species.

FIND OUT!

What does the metamorphosis of fruit flies look like?

From your teacher, obtain a vial containing food and fruit flies in different stages of metamorphosis. Look at the vial every day for two weeks and record your observations each time.

Conclude and Apply

1. Identify and draw all the stages of metamorphosis you see.
2. In what stages are the flies the most active?

FIND OUT!

What does the metamorphosis of fruit flies look like?

Time needed 15 minutes the first day; a few minutes each day for two weeks

Materials vials containing food and fruit flies in different stages of metamorphosis

Thinking Processes Observing and inferring, Forming a hypothesis, Interpreting data

Purpose To see the states of metamorphosis of the fruit fly.

Preparation Obtain a vial of fruit flies and food for each student group. Arrange for an appropriate place for the vials to be stored during the observation period.

Teaching the Activity

Discussion When the activity begins, students will not know the terms *complete* and *incomplete metamorphosis,* which are covered on the next pages. Distribute the vials and explain that the different-looking creatures are all fruit flies in varying stages of metamorphosis. Have students draw all the different stages they see. After students read pages 304 and 305, have them write their hypotheses about the type of metamorphosis fruit flies undergo. *complete* As the two weeks of observation pass, they may want to revise their hypotheses. L1

Expected Outcome

Students will infer that fruit flies undergo complete metamorphosis.

Conclude and Apply

1. Drawings will reflect stages shown on page 304.
2. The flies are the most active in the larva and adult stages.

Meeting Individual Needs

Visually Impaired Assist visually impaired students to complete the Find Out activity on this page by doing the following. COOP LEARN

- Assign a partner to each visually impaired student.
- Have students together obtain the food and fruit flies from you.
- Give student pairs an enlarged copy of the diagram of fruit fly metamorphosis on this page.
- Direct them to compare what they see on the blowup to what they see in the vial. Allow students to view the insects through a magnifying glass.
- Both students should respond to the questions.

Concept Development

Inquiry Question Many mammals, such as antelopes, deer, elephants, and whales, make their homes out in the open. Do you think their young would be well developed or poorly developed at birth? *well developed* Why? *There is no den or nest for protection.*

Theme Connection All animals develop and grow, but some members of some species change completely as they mature. The different ways that animals develop provide examples of the theme of scale and structure. Ask students to compare the development of the kitten, shown in Figure 10-17, with that of the frog, shown in Figure 10-18. Ask students how the kitten changes as it matures. *It becomes larger.* Ask how the frog changes as it grows up. *It develops from a tadpole—a creature that lives in water, has a long tail, and uses gills to get oxygen—into a frog—a creature that lives on land, breathes air, and eats insects.*

MAKING CONNECTIONS

Language Arts

Ask students to make a list of expressions that draw an analogy between the behavior of an animal and a person. Some examples are: busy as a bee, eats like a bird, quiet as a mouse, busy as a beaver, sly as a fox. L1

Teacher F.Y.I.

- The red kangaroo can weigh up to 375 kilograms, yet its baby weighs less than a gram at birth. The baby stays in the pouch eight months before venturing out on its own.
- Female crocodiles lay 20 to 90 eggs at a time. They bury the eggs in sand or mud. When babies hatch, they call to their mother, who carefully carries them in her mouth to the water's edge.

FIGURE 10-18. Adult frogs develop from tadpoles during metamorphosis.

Figure 10-18 shows a frog metamorphosis. The egg hatches into a larval stage called a tadpole. The tadpole lives in water, has a long tail, and uses gills to get oxygen. As the tadpole grows, legs form, the tail gets smaller, and lungs develop. The mature frog has completely lost its tail, lives on land, breathes air, and eats insects rather than algae.

Insects also undergo metamorphosis, but it is different from frog metamorphosis. There are two kinds of insect metamorphosis, complete and incomplete. Butterflies undergo complete metamorphosis. Butterflies lay eggs that hatch into wormlike larvae called caterpillars. The larvae move around and eat leaves for food. At some point the caterpillars form a shell or case around themselves and change into pupae. During this stage, remarkable changes occur to the animal. At the right time, an adult butterfly emerges from the case. Figure 10-19 shows how completely different the adult form is from the larval stage.

Other animals change form too, but in fewer distinct stages. Incomplete insect metamorphosis involves three stages. Grasshoppers follow this three-stage development. First the egg hatches into a nymph, which looks very similar to an adult grasshopper, only smaller. The nymph grows larger. The grasshopper is mature after its wings develop. Figure 10-20 shows the incomplete metamorphosis of a cricket.

During the stages of metamorphosis, the animal is less able to protect itself than the adult form of its species. The eggs, larvae, and pupae may be eaten by other animals, or they may be destroyed by something in the environment. Animals that develop through metamorphosis tend to produce large numbers of eggs. In contrast, birds

FIGURE 10-19. Moths and butterflies undergo complete metamorphosis.

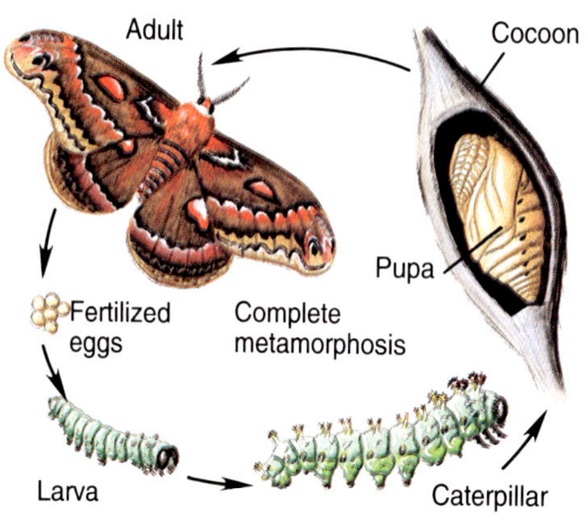

OPTIONS

Multicultural Perspectives

Native-American children traditionally learn their survival skills early and are treated as adults by their early teens. There are specific ceremonies marking this passage.

In some tribes, when a boy is about twelve to fourteen years old, for example, he is taken on his first real hunt. When he kills a buffalo, he is highly praised. The news is announced to the tribe, and if the father is wealthy enough, he gives a horse to a deserving person or has a group of needy people to a feast. Even though he may have a great deal to learn, the boy is now considered a man.

Cheyenne girls go through formal puberty rites, involving unbraiding their hair and having their bodies painted red by older women. They then wrap themselves in robes and sit by fires. Coals from the fires are covered in grass, juniper needles, and white sage, and the fragrant smoke passes around the girls' bodies.

and reptiles produce fewer eggs than frogs and insects. They are adapted with a way to protect the young as they develop outside the female's body. After fertilization, a shell forms around the egg. The shell is an adaptation that protects the egg and helps prevent it from drying out. Figure 10-21 shows an example of a reptile egg.

Most mammals develop within the female's body. Internal development provides protection for the embryo. Nourishment and oxygen are passed to the embryo from the mother's body. Wastes are passed from the embryo to the mother's body where they are eliminated. Each mammal requires a different amount of time for the young to develop. About nine months is the amount of time for a human to develop within the mother's body.

How long has someone been caring for you? Even though some development occurs within the mother's body, most mammals require a lot of care after birth. Young mammals may stay with their parents for months or years. During this time, the parents protect, care for, and teach their young skills that are needed for survival.

Adult
Egg
Incomplete Metamorphosis
Nymph
Nymph

FIGURE 10-20. Grasshoppers, and the crickets shown here, undergo incomplete metamorphosis.

FIGURE 10-21. Shells are adaptations that protect developing young.

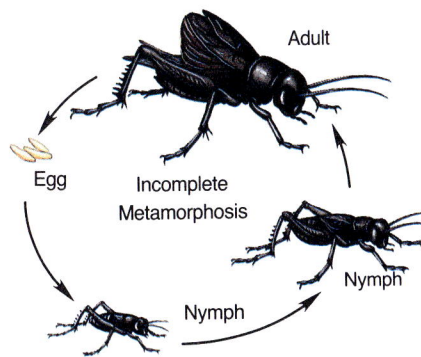

Check Your Understanding

1. What is the difference between sexual and asexual reproduction?
2. List the stages of complete and incomplete metamorphosis.
3. **APPLY:** In what way does an animal that reproduces by internal fertilization differ from one that has external fertilization?

3 Assess

Check for Understanding

Before students answer the Check Your Understanding questions, suggest they make a chart with two columns, headed *Internal Fertilization* and *External Fertilization.* Working in pairs or small groups, have students list as many characteristics of each method of reproduction as they can. Have students use these charts to answer the Apply question. **COOP LEARN** **L2**

Reteach

Activity Bring in a photograph and photo copies of a familiar scene. Have students create their own drawings from the photograph. Display drawings and copies. **How are the copies like asexual reproduction?** *They are identical with the photo, the parent.* **How are the drawings like sexual reproduction?** *Each is similar to the parent yet different.* **L1**

Extension

Have students create a display of Figure 10-19 or 10-20, using pictures, photographs, clay, and other found objects. **L2**

4 Close

Give students pictures of the fertilized eggs, larva, pupa, caterpillar, cocoon, and adult moth or butterfly and have them place the pictures in the correct order to show the cycle of metamorphosis. **L1**

Answers to Check Your Understanding

1. Sexual reproduction occurs if sperm from a male animal unites with an egg from a female animal; asexual reproduction occurs if a new animal is produced from one parent.
2. complete—egg, larva, pupa, adult; incomplete—egg, nymph, adult
3. Female animals that reproduce by internal fertilization release eggs that stay within their bodies, where the male deposits the sperm. These animals generally produce smaller numbers of offspring, which appear more able to survive. In animals that have external fertilization, greater numbers of eggs are produced, but comparatively few survive.

Section 10-3

PREPARATION

Concepts Developed

In Section 10-2, students learned that some animals reproduce sexually; others, asexually. Now students will see how adaptations have enabled animals to survive. For example, they will see how birds' beaks and anteaters' tongues are body structure adaptations that enable each creature to deal more successfully with its environment.

Planning the Lesson

In planning your lesson on animal adaptations, refer to the Chapter Organizer on pages 288A–B for timing suggestions, resources, and additional materials that will help you in your presentation of the lesson concepts.

For adequate development of the concepts presented in this section, we recommend that students do the Investigate on page 310.

1 MOTIVATE

Have students imagine that they had to survive without "modern conveniences" such as housing, running water, or prepared food. What problems would they encounter? Would they be able to solve these problems? Have students describe where they would sleep and how they would get food.

10-3 Animal Adaptations

OBJECTIVES

In this section, you will

- explain how adaptations allow animals to survive on Earth;
- give examples of some animal adaptations.

KEY SCIENCE TERMS

respiration

TAILOR MADE

Would you expect a fish to survive in a forest? Of course not. You already know that a fish has several characteristics that make it better-suited for life in water. Birds, bears, beetles, and butterflies also have characteristics that make each suited for its environment. Each type of animal has characteristics that help it survive in its environment.

EXPLORE!

Where do people live?

Study the pictures showing the different places where people live. Make a chart with the headings *Arctic Tundra, Desert, Grassland,* and *Rain Forest.* Under each heading, write a description of the area from what you see in the pictures. What can you infer from how people are dressed? On a separate sheet of paper, draw the area in which you live. Write a description of how your characteristics help you survive in your area.

EXPLORE!

Where do people live?

Time needed 20 minutes

Materials No special materials or preparation are required for this activity.

Thinking Processes
Observing and inferring, Comparing and contrasting

Purpose To see how people adapt to their environment.

Teaching the Activity

Troubleshooting If students have trouble getting started, prompt them with questions like "Where do they live?" "How are they dressed?" LEP

Expected Outcome

Students will see how people have changed their behavior to survive in their environments.

Answer to Question

Amount and type of clothing give clues to the temperature or climate of each area.

BODY STRUCTURE ADAPTATIONS

The activity shows only four of the many kinds of places on Earth where people live. We are animals that can change our behavior to enable us to survive the conditions around us. For example, people in cold climates change their behavior when they put on warmer clothes, whereas people in tropical climates change their behavior to wear fewer or lighter weight clothes. We also change conditions around us. In hot places, some people might use air conditioning or at least a fan. During frigid winters, we burn fuel to warm our homes, workplaces, and cars. These changes in behavior help us adjust to changing conditions around us.

Remember the Find Out activity you did that involved bird beaks? Each bird's beak was specially adapted to getting the type of food the bird needed to survive. The beak is one adaptation that birds have. Remember that an adaptation is a characteristic that increases the chances of an organism to survive. The activity could have been done using the birds' feet as well. As Figure 10–22 shows, some birds have webbed feet for swimming, or sharp talons for catching rabbits, or long toes for grasping branches.

a

b

The bird's beak is an example of an adaptation that involves the animal's body structure. An anteater's tongue and the teeth of a deer are also body structure adaptations. The beak, teeth, and tongue are all external body structures.

One internal adaptation found in animals is the organ used to obtain oxygen. Most organisms use oxygen for respiration. **Respiration** occurs inside the body when oxygen combines with digested food to release energy from the food. People who live in high mountain areas such as the Andes Mountains of South America are adapted to the lower amounts of oxygen in the atmosphere. They have larger hearts that circulate blood more quickly, and they have more red blood cells to carry oxygen than people who live at sea level.

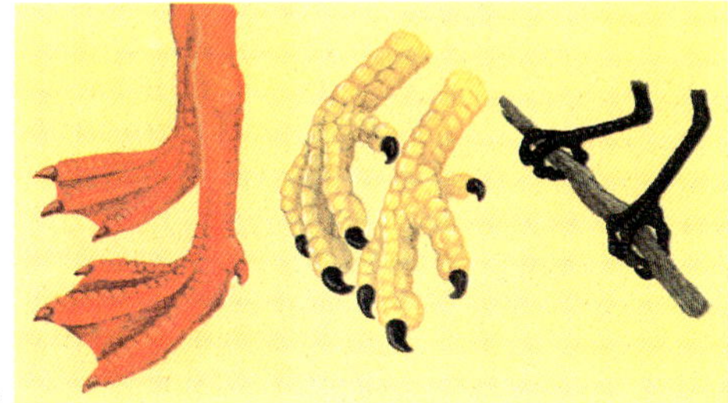

c

FIGURE 10-22. The variety of birds' beaks (a), bears' fur (b), and birds' feet (c) are all examples of an adaptation.

2 TEACH

Tying to Previous Knowledge

Students are familiar with pets' behaviors. Ask them to relate instances of feeding behavior and evidence of communication with other animals and with humans. Ask students to explain what they think causes these behaviors. *Communication, for example, allows animals to find food, defend against enemies, and reproduce successfully.*

Concept Development

Activity Arrange students in pairs. Have one student keep time and count while the other holds his or her arms straight out and flaps. See how many times a person can flap in one minute and how long it takes for the person to tire. Have students switch tasks and repeat the activity. Ask students why our chest muscles would get tired more readily than other muscles, such as those in our legs. *Our leg muscles would be more developed because we use them to walk.* Why would birds have well-developed chest muscles? *They use these muscles for flying.* Why are certain parts of an animal's body adapted in different ways, as with our leg muscles? *Such adaptations in body structure helped the animal to survive better.* L1 COOP LEARN

Inquiry Question Why do you think the sense of smell is not as important to birds as the senses of sight and hearing? *Birds search for food from the air, where scents do not linger.*

Teacher F.Y.I.

Camels have long eyelashes, which help protect their eyes during sandstorms.

PROGRAM RESOURCES

Teacher Classroom Resources

Study Guide, page 38

Transparency Masters, page 43, and **Color Transparency,** number 20, Animal Adaptations L2

OPTIONS

Enrichment

Activity Governments issue special postage stamps to honor famous people, national events, and endangered animals such as the rhino or leopard. Ask students to select one animal from this chapter and design a stamp honoring it. In addition to drawing a picture of the animal, students should include part of its habitat, and the animal's name. Then ask how they could use this stamp to help the animal it depicts. L2

Concept Development

Inquiry Questions Why do you think lions and other cats have retractable claws? *They use their claws to climb and to hold prey. They can be retracted when they are not needed so the animal can walk and run better.* Some mammals, such as elephants and whales, have little body hair. Suggest reasons why this may be an adaptation in these animals. *Elephants have thick skin that insulates the body, and whales have blubber, or fat, that insulates the body.*

Discussions Make sure students understand that respiration is not breathing, that it is a chemical change that takes place in cells. Also, emphasize that metabolism is a broad term, not just referring to the breakdown of food as some students might think. Help students destinguish between warm and cold-blooded animals.

Teacher F.Y.I.

A giraffe's body is ideally suited for obtaining its favorite food, the leaves that grow high in acacia and mimosa trees. Aside from their long necks, giraffes can extend their tongues a foot and a half around a branch to strip it of foliage.

Content Background

Penguins have adapted to life in the antarctic waters. Instead of flying, they swim, using their wings as flippers. The penguin also has a sharp beak for grabbing its fish prey.

A whale's layer of blubber is so efficient at retaining heat that a dead whale may literally start to cook as decomposition sets in, which raises the internal temperature. A healthy whale controls heat buildup by increasing the flow of blood to the surface of the skin.

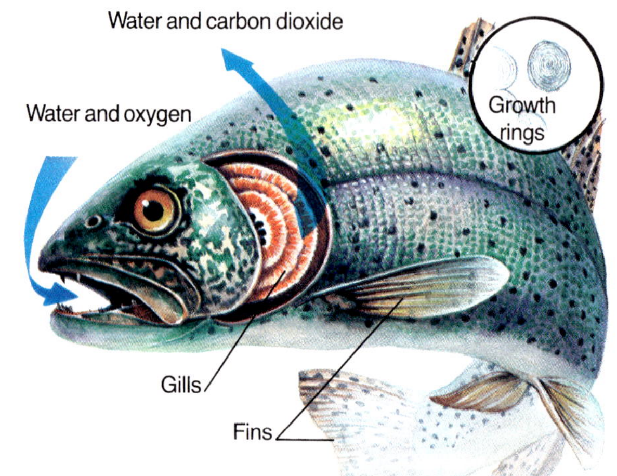

b

FIGURE 10-23. Fish obtain oxygen as water passes from the gills to the circulatory system (a). A bird obtains oxygen as air passes from the lungs to the circulatory system (b).

Fish have gills to get their oxygen. As water passes over the gills, dissolved oxygen is removed and used for respiration. One of the waste products of respiration is carbon dioxide. Carbon dioxide passes from the body back into the water. Insects have small openings along the sides of their bodies for obtaining oxygen. The openings lead to tubes that bring air into and out of the animal's body. Amphibians obtain oxygen through their skin, and most also have lungs. Reptiles, birds, and mammals have lungs. Oxygen passes from small sacs within the lungs to blood cells in the circulatory system. From there, oxygen is carried to all the body cells. Carbon dioxide moves out from the blood into the sacs of the lungs. All of these different methods of obtaining oxygen are adaptations that enable animals to survive in different environments.

In Chapter 5, you learned about chemical changes. Respiration is just one of the chemical changes that goes on in an organism's body. Other chemical changes take place all the time. The combination of all of the chemical changes within an organism is called metabolism. The rate of metabolism will affect the body temperature of an animal. During the chemical change that digests food, heat is released. The faster food is broken down, the more heat is produced.

Cold-blooded animals have body temperatures that are about the same as their surroundings. Cold-blooded animals, such as those in Figure 10-24, can control their body temperature in several ways. Desert reptiles come out in the morning and sit in the sun until their body temperatures reach about 35°C. Once this temperature is reached, they hunt for food, move from place to place, and perform all their life functions. When they begin to cool down, they sit in the sun again to raise their body temperature. Frogs may hibernate in the muddy bottom of a stream or pond. Their activity will be greatly reduced

OPTIONS

Multicultural Perspectives

Beavers played a role in the Dutch settling in America. Native Americans had hunted beavers for food. After the arrival of Europeans, Native Americans hunted beavers for trade, as well as for food. In the seventeenth century, Europeans prized beaver pelts for making hats. For about $24 worth of goods, the Dutch bought Manhattan Island from the Native Americans. No one felt cheated, and the Dutch and Native Americans continued to trade beaver skins. Beavers were also hunted for their strong-smelling oil, which people thought could cure headaches and frostbite. Today we know that beaver oil is largely salicylic acid, the main ingredient in aspirin.

FIGURE 10-24. The cold-blooded turtle suns itself to warm up on a cool morning, whereas the alligator rests in the water to stay cool during the warmest part of the day.

and their metabolism will slow down. Only enough heat to keep the frog alive will be produced.

Birds and mammals are warm-blooded. Their bodies stay at a constant temperature. Their rate of metabolism doesn't change as much as the rate of cold-blooded animals. But mammals such as humans have adaptations to help control body temperature, too. They can sweat when warm or shiver when cold. Each adaptation helps control body temperature.

ANIMAL BEHAVIOR

Animals have many kinds of behavior. Have you ever watched a pet dog bark at people and other animals? The dog has a set of responses it uses when people or other animals come close to the dog's territory. A territory is a specific area that is set aside for hunting, mating, or raising young. In the wild, some animals use their urine to mark their territories. In fact, some dogs mark the corners of their yards in the same way.

You are probably familiar with other kinds of animal behavior. A bird might squawk or shriek if a cat comes too close to its nest. Some bugs quickly skitter away when a light shines on them. These are examples of animal behavior. The set of responses an organism exhibits to changes in its environment is called behavior.

In the Investigate, you will see how an earthworm reacts to several changes in its surroundings.

FIGURE 10-25. Perspiration is one way your body cools.

Concept Development

Uncovering Preconceptions Using anthropomorphic descriptions, many people attribute human feelings and attitudes to animals. This can lead to a misinterpretation of behavior. Animals usually have no motive for their behavior other than being genetically programmed to behave as they do.

Inquiry Question If a hungry rat eats a small amount of poisoned food that makes it ill, the rat will never eat poisoned food again. How can you explain this? *The rat's behavior changes because of the experience.*

MAKING CONNECTIONS

Daily Life

Ask students if they know the meaning of the phrase to "play possum." *to pretend to be dead* Explain that the opossum gave rise to this expression because of the dramatic way it pretends to be dead when threatened by a predator. Its eyes close, its mouth falls open, its breathing seems to stop, and its body becomes paralyzed. Many attackers lose interest if they think their intended victim is dead, as some predators want only live prey. This is because dead prey may be rotten, and make them ill. Have students discuss other ways animals have of defending themselves or tricking their enemies. *Some animals counterattack, skunks use their spray, porcupines threaten with their quills.*

Enrichment

Activity Have students make bird feeders from milk cartons and hang them outside the classroom windows. Place birdseed in the feeders and watch as birds come to eat. Have students record how different birds act when they feed. L1

Research/Activity Have students choose an animal mentioned in the chapter and research it. Students should write a "want ad" for their animal, including the behaviors that would identify it. L2

Teacher F.Y.I.

Some lizards have a special kind of behavior: when the lizard is caught by the tail, the tail drops off! While the predator grapples with the wriggling tail, the lizard makes its escape. The lizard will later grow a new tail. This is called regeneration.

INVESTIGATE!

10-2 EARTHWORM BEHAVIOR

Time needed 30–60 minutes

Materials See student activity.

Thinking Processes
Making and using tables, Observing and inferring, Recognizing cause and effect, Forming a hypothesis, Designing an Experiment to test your hypothesis

Purpose To examine the external structures of the earthworm and note its responses to various stimuli

Preparation Distribute materials before distributing the worms. Caution students to handle the worms gently.

Teaching Strategies

Discussion If the worms are not on top of the soil when students open the container, ask students what might have driven the worms under the soil. *light* Ask students what they might do to get to worms to come to the surface. *Place the container in the dark for a few minutes.* Direct students to consider this when shining the flashlight on the worms. In both cases, the worms will move away from the light. L2

Expected Outcome

Students will see the earthworm has reacted to light, touch, and vinegar in different ways.

Answers to Analyze/Conclude and Apply

1. They move away, under the soil.
2. It moves away, and tries to get free.
3. It avoids the vinegar.
4. Its reaction provides an opportunity for the worm to stay buried in the soil where it won't dry out.
5. The bristles provide traction, which is helpful as the worm moves in the soil.
6. The container with the worms could be placed in a larger bowl with ice cubes on one side of the worm container.

INVESTIGATE!

10-2 EARTHWORM BEHAVIOR

It is possible to **determine the effect** some conditions have on an earthworm. In this activity, you will **observe** some earthworm characteristics and **infer** how they allow the earthworm to survive.

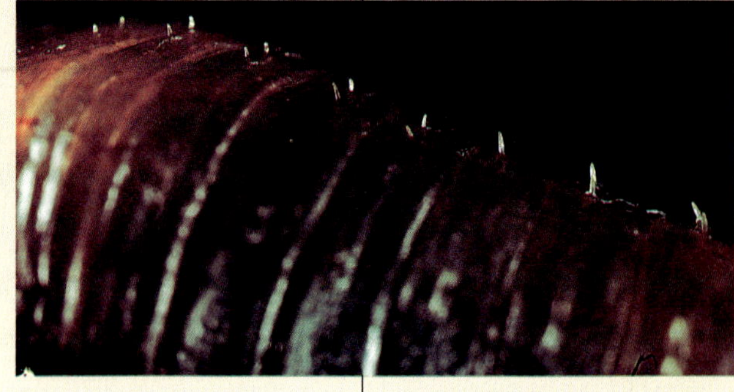

PROBLEM

How is an earthworm adapted to live in soil?

MATERIALS  

hand lens
toothpick
vinegar
flashlight
live earthworms in a covered container
shallow pan
paper towels
beaker of water
cotton swab

PROCEDURE

1. Copy the data table.
2. Open the container to be sure some of the earthworms are on the top of the soil. Shine the flashlight on the worms. Record how the worms react.
3. Wet your hands and remove an earthworm from the container. **CAUTION:** *Use care when working with live animals.* Keep your hands wet while working with the earthworm. Hold the worm gently between your thumb and forefinger. **Observe** its movements and record them in the table.
4. Rub your fingers gently along the body. **Observe** the small, stiff hairs called bristles with a hand lens.
5. With the toothpick, gently touch the worm on the front and back ends. Record your observations.
6. Dip the cotton swab in vinegar. Place it in front of the worm on a wet paper towel. Do not touch the worm with the vinegar. Record your observations.

DATA AND OBSERVATIONS

CONDITION	RESPONSE
Light	
Fingers	
Touch-front	
Touch-back	
Vinegar	

ANALYZE

1. What happens when the light is shined on the earthworms?
2. How does the earthworm react to touch?
3. How does the earthworm react to the vinegar?

CONCLUDE AND APPLY

4. How is the earthworm's reaction to light an adaptation for living in the soil?
5. How are the bristles an adaptation for living in the soil?
6. **Going Further:** How could you change the activity to find out how the earthworm reacts to different temperatures?

PROGRAM RESOURCES

Teacher Classroom Resources
Activity Masters, pages 43-44, Investigate 10–2 L2

a

b

FIGURE 10-26. A peacock spreading its tail feathers (a) and a male frigate bird displaying the expanded air pocket by its throat (b) are two examples of mating behavior to attract mates.

As you review your results from the earthworm activity, you should notice that the bristles are a body structure adaptation. The responses the earthworm made to light, touch, and vinegar are behavioral adaptations. Just as body structure can aid survival, different kinds of behavior can also determine if an organism will survive.

Many animals take part in special activities that attract members of the opposite sex. These activities allow males and females to recognize each other. These behaviors also ensure that both animals are ready to mate at the same time. The peacock spreads his feathers to attract the peahen. Some insects release chemicals that attract members of the opposite sex, whereas other insects rub their legs or wings together to produce sounds that attract mates.

Many of the behavioral adaptations are ways for the animals to communicate. In addition to marking their territory and finding mates, animals communicate to warn of danger, give directions for finding food, and maintain the social order within a group.

Some adaptations protect animals from being seen as they hunt or from being attacked and eaten by other animals. Camouflage is an adaptation that allows an animal to hide by blending into

FIGURE 10-27. Animals use a variety of gestures and actions to communicate with one another.

Concept Development

Activity The oil on birds' feathers helps keep them water-repellant, a very important adaptation. To show how oil waterproofs feathers, cut two 6-cm squares of construction paper. Cover one with petroleum jelly and leave the other one plain. Drop six drops of water on each square. Have students describe what they observe. L1 LEP

Inquiry Question How might territorial displays and aggressive behavior reduce fights and injured animals? *Other animals might be reluctant to challenge stronger animals; fights may end sooner when dominance is demonstrated.*

Teacher F.Y.I.

- Fireflies are attracted to each other on the basis of the intervals between flashes, each species having its own frequency.
- Of all the big cats—lions, tigers, leopards, and jaguars—lions are the only one that are social. They live in family groups called prides, which can include more than 25 members. Males and females can easily be distinguished from each other: males sport a huge fur ruff called a mane. The male grows to 10 feet and weighs up to 500 pounds; the female is somewhat smaller.

Inquiry Question What might be some advantages to animals living together and cooperating with one another? *They can help protect one another and gather food.*

Theme Connection Animals' mating adaptations provide further examples of the theme of scale and structure. Have students study Figure 10-26. **Why might the size of these structures be important in mating?** *They are large to attract the mate's attention.*

Content Background

In territorial species, only individuals with territories mate. This helps ensure an adequate food supply for offspring. It also passes on the genes of the strongest individuals to the next generation.

OPTIONS

Multicultural Perspectives

People in all cultures exhibit courtship rituals. Colombians, for example, have a great number of courtship dances. On the Caribbean coast, people dance the *bullerengue, lumbalu,* and the circular *cumbia.* The national dance, called the *bambuco,* came from the Andean zone. Waving kerchiefs, male and female partners mime a courtship of pursuing and flirting. This same dance is done with a waltz step in southern Colombia.

3 Assess

Check for Understanding

1. Have students create a children's storybook explaining the animal adaptations they learned about in this section. Direct students to include an overview of body structure adaptation and animal behavior and specific examples to illustrate their points. Students can exchange books and write critical reviews of each other's work to assess their understanding. L2
2. To help students answer the Apply question under Check Your Understanding, have them work in small groups to discuss the kinds of information bees would have to communicate to enable other bees to locate a source of nectar. Have groups develop mime skits or dances to convey information about how to locate a special area of the school, such as the library or cafeteria. COOP LEARN L2

Reteach

Have students make a chart with the headings *Territorial Behavior, Courtship Behavior,* and *Social Behavior,* and have them write examples of each of the behaviors under the headings. L1

Extension

Students who have mastered the concepts of this section can research some of the different techniques scientists have used to study the language-learning abilities of primates. Invite them to look into the work teaching chimps Ameslan and the symbol language Yerkish, developed for apes. L3

4 Close

Write the word *communication* on the board. Ask students to brainstorm ways that animals communicate. Then classify these methods as: sounds, visual displays, or chemicals. Have students demonstrate the second method by playing a brief game of charades. L1

How do we know?

Do some animals rely on one another's behavior?

Some animal behaviors can be helpful to more than one species of animal. For example, the frog-eating bats, in parts of Central and South America, hunt frogs at night. Researchers know that the bats use sound to find the frogs. But how do the bats distinguish between poisonous and nonpoisonous frogs? The researchers set up two speakers and a frog-eating bat in a large cage. One speaker played the mating call of a poisonous frog. The second speaker played the mating call of a nonpoisonous frog. The bat always flew toward the sound from the nonpoisonous frog. The researchers concluded that not only did the bats use sound to find the frogs, but the bats used the sound to distinguish poisonous and nonpoisonous frogs. In this example, the bat had a behavior that was dependent on another animal's behavior.

its surroundings. The stripes of a tiger or a zebra are one type of camouflage. A chameleon can turn different shades of green and brown as it moves through vegetation. The speckled fawn of a white-tailed deer can stay safely hidden when it lies motionless on the forest floor, as seen in Figure 10-28.

FIGURE 10-28. The fawn remains safe because it's hidden from enemies by camouflage.

You have learned about several adaptations animals have that allow them to survive in their environment. Some of these adaptations are physical, such as specific beaks, feet, or claws. Other adaptations are behavior changes that help animals communicate or find food. Without these adaptations, animals could not survive.

Check Your Understanding

1. How do these adaptations increase the chance for the animal or the animal's species to survive?
   (a) keen eyesight of an owl
   (b) whiskers of a cat
   (c) courtship dance of a bird
   (d) blending into environment
2. Give an example of an adaptation in body structure.
3. **APPLY:** When a honeybee locates a source of nectar, it flies back to the hive and performs a special dance. What type of adaptation is this and how is it useful for the bees?

Answers to Check Your Understanding

1. **a.** The owl has a better chance of catching food. **b.** The cat's whiskers help it sense narrow spaces in which it might get stuck. **c.** The bird will find a mate and produce young. **d.** can't be seen by predators or prey
2. Possible answers include short, strong beak to crack seeds; large ears to gather sound waves.
3. The dance is a behavioral adaptation that communicates the location of food to the whole hive. It helps maintain an adequate food supply for the hive.

EXPANDING YOUR VIEW

CONTENTS

A CLOSER LOOK

CREATURE FEATURES

Would you believe that building models of animals can help you understand their adaptations? How can you combine serious science with fun arts and crafts? Just ask biomechanics researcher Mimi Koehl from the University of California at Berkeley.

Biomechanics is the field of science that asks how living organisms are affected by the laws of physics. By studying the physical environment an animal lives in, scientists can explain why animals are shaped in a certain way. For example, the shapes of fish and dolphins allow these animals to swim through water smoothly and with little resistance.

But explaining animal structure is not always so easy, especially with live animals.

Recently, Dr. Koehl has been working with biologist Sharon Emerson of the University of Utah to explain the structure of an amazing amphibian—the Malaysian flying frog. Dr. Emerson had been studying this tiny frog for months in its native habitat. Dr. Emerson wanted to know whether this frog's curious adaptations, such as large webbed feet, had anything to do with the frog's gymnastic abilities.

Koehl and Emerson made several realistic models. Also, they made individual legs, hands, and feet of nonflying-frogs, such as the one shown in the photograph.

To investigate whether flying frog shape is related to acrobatic abilities, Koehl and Emerson tested their model frogs in a wind tunnel. The wind tunnel allowed the researchers to investigate how wind resistance affects the frog as it flies through the air. They also replaced parts of the model with the interchangeable nonflying-frog parts to see how these affect wind resistance.

After the experiments, Koehl and Emerson concluded that the flying frog's shape is not related to flying at all. Flying frog shape is related to falling!

YOU TRY IT!

Go to the library and learn about the adaptations of some of your favorite animals. Read about their behaviors in their natural environments. How are your animal's adaptations related to behavior?

Using Expanding Your View

Assign one or more excursions to expand students' understanding of animal adaptations and how they apply to other sciences and subjects. You can assign these to individuals or small groups.

A CLOSER LOOK

Purpose A Closer Look extends Section 10-3's discussion of adaptations by describing how two scientists have used models to study physical adaptations of animals.

Content Background **How can we explain the adaptations of Earth's plant and animal life over millions of years?** In the late 1850s Alfred Wallace and Charles Darwin each proposed a hypothesis called *natural selection.* They said that members of a species of animals, compete for food, energy, shelter, space, and mates. The individuals that succeed in reproducing are those best-adapted to their environment. Thus, their specific traits are passed on to their offspring.

Teaching Strategies Have student pairs present facts on an animal they find interesting. They should collect facts related to the content of this chapter. They should look for adaptations that help the animal move or find food. Students should also look for ways that the animal's eyes, ears, feet, teeth, tail, and body covering are specially adapted for the environment in which the animal lives. COOP LEARN

Answers to

YOU TRY IT

There are many examples of adaptations that are related to behavior. For example, the elaborate tail feathers of a peacock are an adaptation that helps the male attract a mate. It is not just the presence of the feathers, but also the display behavior that attracts the female.

Going Further Have students review the list of animals they came up with at the beginning of this chapter, or allow two minutes for them to create it now. Then have them name at least one adaptation each animal has but the others lack. Ask students why each has its special adaptation: **Does it help the animal move around in its environment, get food, keep warm or cool, or protect itself? Does it help the animal compete with other animals for the same resources? If so, does this have anything to do with how many there are of each species?**

Divide the class into groups. Have each group select an animal from their lists that they think is the most successfully adapted, and tell the class why. Tell them to consider the harshness of its environment, competition for resources, intelligence, size, diet, and so on. COOP LEARN

EXPANDING YOUR VIEW

EARTH SCIENCE CONNECTION

Purpose Earth Science Connection extends the discussion of adaptation in Section 10-3 by looking at what some scientists hypothesize was the fate of the dinosaurs.

Content Background When an environmental change happens, which species survive? If a species' food supply disappears, survival is unlikely. For example, plant-eating dinosaurs probably died out along with their food. If the environment grows too cold, the only survivors will be those with good insulation, a high-energy diet, or ability to travel to a warmer area.

Some environmental changes are temporary, such as drought, flooding, earthquakes, or volcanic eruptions. In these cases, enough members of species usually survive to maintain the species until the ecosystem recovers. If the disruption is local, some species simply move out until the former conditions are reestablished.

Teaching Strategy From the description given here, have student groups draw on the chalkboard the sequence of events that the proposed meteor impact 65 million years ago may have set in motion. Then have them discuss how each event in the sequence affected animals on land, those in the sea, and plants on land.

Answers to WHAT DO YOU THINK?

The bird can fly, so it might find seeds elsewhere. Or it might try gnawing other plant parts, which offer less nutrition; or it might die out. Students may say that the bird could survive on a diet of insects. Point out that this is unlikely, as the seed-eating bird's digestive system is not adapted to digest insects efficiently.

EARTH SCIENCE CONNECTION

A NATURAL DISASTER

Many organisms die as a result of natural catastrophes, such as erupting volcanoes. Evidence seems to support the idea that the dinosaurs vanished about 65 million years ago, probably due to some major environmental catastrophe. Scientists estimate that between 75 to 95 percent of all living creatures were wiped out at that same time.

What happened to cause such a disaster? Many scientists believe the dinosaurs became extinct after a huge meteor—maybe as big as 10 kilometers in diameter—struck Earth around 65 million years ago. The impact would probably have stirred up great clouds of dust that blotted out the sun. This caused temperatures to drop and plants to die. Some scientists suggest that the impact may also have set off volcanic eruptions, which could have further destroyed the dinosaurs and their food supply.

Why do we think a meteor fell? A paleontologist discovered high concentrations of a metal called iridium (ir IHD ee em) in a sample of rock taken from Earth. Meteorites are rich in iridium. When investigators found the same high concentration of iridium at widely spaced places around Earth in rocks of the same age, they began to speculate that a meteorite had fallen. Could it happen again? Yes, unless we learn how to dispose of objects in space before they strike.

No one knows exactly how long it takes for the animals to come back to an area after some destructive natural event. A falling meteor, a huge forest fire, or a flood all change habitats dramatically. Sometimes the change is permanent. Sometimes it is only temporary. How well animals adjust to the changes depends on how generalized or specialized they are. As a group, dinosaurs varied in how specialized they were. They included both meat eaters and plant eaters. Dinosaurs lived all over the world in many habitats.

Evidence suggests that multiple changes must have occurred in the environment to cause all the many different kinds of dinosaurs to die out. One theory is that the plant eaters starved to death first, after fires and molten lava destroyed much of the vegetation. Then, after a while, the meat eaters had no more plant eaters to feast on, so they starved also.

WHAT DO YOU THINK?

What would happen to a seed-eating bird if a widespread drought caused no seeds to be produced in its habitat one year? This bird has a short, strong beak for cracking open and eating seeds and is not accustomed to eating anything else. Would the bird die out? Would it move to another area? Would it find a way to eat something else?

Going Further Scientists keep discovering new facts about dinosaurs that are changing our view of them. Have students research the *Reader's Guide to Periodic Literature* for articles describing current views of dinosaur intelligence, behavior, diet, warm-bloodedness, or body coverings, and write brief reports.

Going Further Some environmental changes are temporary, like the eruption of Mount Saint Helens in 1980. Have student groups use the January 1981 *National Geographic* and other articles to discover how life quickly returned to the mountain. Have students answer these questions: How soon did living things return to the devastated area? What was different about the way plants grew? Did the kind and number of animals change after the eruption?

SCIENCE AND SOCIETY

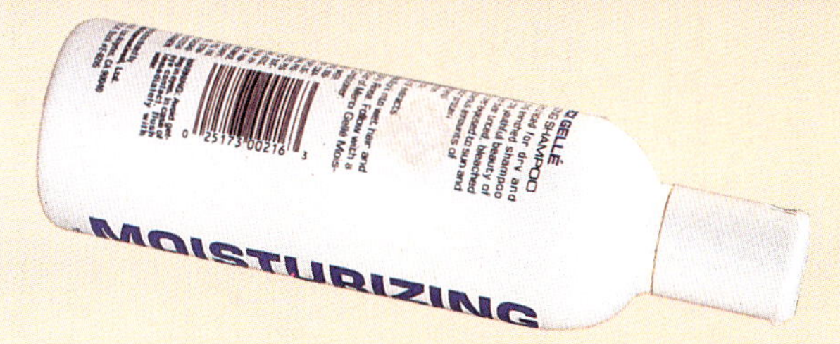

ANIMAL RIGHTS VS. HUMAN NEEDS

Because we are part of the animal kingdom, we share some physical characteristics with everything from mice to elephants. For this reason, scientists regularly use animals to test new drugs and to seek cures for human diseases. Medical schools, hospitals, and drug companies often have laboratories. These drugs can first be tested on animals before they are used on humans. Animals are also used by some companies to test allergic reactions to lipsticks, soaps, shampoos, and other cosmetics. Because animals feel pain, some people believe that humans should never test chemicals or new drugs on animals. The people who believe this point out that animals used for testing are usually kept in laboratory cages instead of being allowed freedom to move around. These people are animal-rights activists who sympathize with the animals. They argue that the end result—safe drugs for use on humans—does not justify causing animals pain, discomfort, and death. Some who favor using animals for medical testing say that animal rights activists want to raise the status of animals to that of human beings.

The term *vivisection* (vih vuh SEK shuhn) used to mean surgery on a living animal for the purposes of research. More recently, it has come to stand for any experimentation using live animals. For years, various humane society members known as *antivivisectionists* have been against such live experimentation. As far back as the 1870s, a strong animal-rights movement in Britain led to the passage of an act to prevent cruelty to animals.

A number of people occupy a middle ground on the use of animals for laboratory tests. They disagree with using animals to test cosmetics or other nonessential products. However, they would allow animal testing to develop drugs that might help save human lives.

In the United States,

EXPANDING YOUR VIEW

SCIENCE AND SOCIETY

Purpose Science and Society explores ethical issues associated with material in Sections 10-1 and 10-2. This feature contrasts the views of animal rights activists, who oppose research using animals, with the views of those who believe animal research is necessary for human well-being.

Content Background **How long have people learned from animals?** Early peoples observed them to locate safe food and water supplies. Famed scientist-artist Leonardo DaVinci (1452–1519) dissected birds to discover how they flew.

Animal testing has been around a long time, but organized opposition has been active only since the mid-1800s. Groups such as the American Society for the Prevention of Cruelty to Animals (ASPCA) actively oppose animal research. Although the concept of species equality is old, supporters of animal research point out that protesters themselves currently enjoy its health benefits. In only a few years your students may be voting on this issue, so encourage them to learn about it.

Teaching Strategies Have students brainstorm a list of controversies arising from animal research, such as medical needs vs. fashion needs; abolishing zoos vs. public education; economic demands vs. animals' rights. Choose one of these controversies and have students form two groups to take sides. Have them focus on the following questions. **In what ways do all humans use animals—food, clothing, benefits from medical testing? How would human life be different without each animal product? Should animals have rights equal to those of humans? Where is compromise possible?**

Going Further Have groups of students interview a doctor, veterinarian, animal-shelter worker, or pet-store owner on the issue of animal rights versus human benefits. Hold a roundtable discussion and have groups compare the viewpoints they heard.

Ask students to contact the local office of the American Society for the Prevention of Cruelty to Animals (ASPCA) or the following organizations for current facts and statistics on animal treatment:

Animal Protection Institute
5894 South Land Park Drive
Sacramento, CA 95822

Animal Welfare Institute
P.O. Box 3719
Washington D.C. 20007

Friends of Animals
11 W. 60 St.
New York, NY 10023

CAREER CONNECTION

Have volunteers locate biology, chemistry, or medical-research labs in the community. These may be found at universities, hospitals, and private firms. Have them find out about the education and experience requirements for new employees and the varieties of jobs available for various degrees or backgrounds. Have students share findings with the class.

Answers to

WHAT DO YOU THINK?

Ask students to write a paragraph answering the questions. Encourage them to imagine someone they know being saved as a result of animal research. At the same time, they should keep in mind that humans and animals are much alike, often depend upon each other, and both feel pain.

voluntary controls exist that govern the use of laboratory animals in experiments. Scientists are urged to ask themselves whether it is necessary to use animals to gather data, or whether that data might be arrived at some other way.

The question of keeping animals in cages, outside their natural environment, raises another issue. Do zoos take unfair advantage of animals? Why should animals be caged and kept in small areas just so people can view them? This is a question the most extreme animal-rights activists sometimes ask.

People who support zoos point out that without them, many species would already have died out. Zoos provide the last refuge for endangered species and allow scientists to study the behavior of animals. Zoos also offer an important educational and entertainment experience for people.

Some animals are trained to provide entertainment. Recently, the government of India took away a man's performing bear out of concern for the bear's well-being. Yet, without the bear, the man had no way to support himself or his family. Whose rights come first—the animal's or the man's?

In recent years, marine parks that keep performing dolphins and killer whales have become popular attractions. Animal-rights activists say it is unfair to these sea creatures to keep them confined. The marine park owners argue that they donate millions of dollars to research and to the conservation of animals. Without the marine parks, they say, this would not be possible.

The question of human needs vs. animal rights is not one that can be easily answered. People on both sides of the issue present both facts and strong emotions.

CAREER CONNECTION

Medical researchers may obtain medical degrees, just as physicians do. However, much medical research is also done by people with advanced degrees in chemistry or biology. Medical researchers work in laboratories. Some discover new drugs by testing the effects of different combinations of chemicals on diseased cells. Medical research is conducted at hospitals, by drug companies, and in universities.

WHAT DO YOU THINK?

What do you think about the use of animals for experiments? What if the experiments save human lives? How would you feel if someone wanted to use your dog or cat? On the other hand, how would you feel if animal experimentation produced a drug that could wipe out cancer?

Going Further We keep animals in zoos, use them in research, and eat some of them for dinner. **What are the benefits to people of using animals for these purposes? What conditions do they live under? Are the animals being treated well?** Divide the class into three groups to research the preceding questions—Group 1 for zoos, Group 2 for research animals, and Group 3 for animals we eat (chickens, cattle, pigs, fish). Then hold a discussion to answer the questions and compare treatment of the three groups of animals. COOP LEARN

History CONNECTION

DOMESTICATING ANIMALS

Paintings in caves show that animals were tamed, or domesticated, many years ago. Once people settled into communities and learned how to plant crops, they also learned to use animals as a source of meat, milk, and wool, and to tame them to perform tasks.

The first animal to be domesticated was the dog. Dogs kept the communities clean by eating garbage, and they protected people from dangerous animals. People bred them for jobs, such as guarding and hunting.

Later, people saw advantages in using tame sheep and goats to supply meat, milk, and wool. Cattle, pigs, and donkeys were soon domesticated, too. The Anasazi, prehistoric Indians of the American Southwest, domesticated turkeys for food and clothing. They used their feathers to make robes and blankets.

WHAT DO YOU THINK?

What can you tell about the people who made the drawings shown in the picture? What can you tell about the animals?

Literature CONNECTION

DO BIRDS HAVE KNEES? DO LADYBUGS SNEEZE?

Sometimes poets use absurd images to convey ideas. Find and read the poem "A Love Song" by poet Raymond Richard Patterson (Adoff, Arnold, ed. *Black Out Loud: An Anthology of Modern Poems by Black Americans).*

What do you think is the answer to the poet's initial question? How did your knowledge of animals help you determine the answer to the question?

YOU TRY IT!

Think of other silly images of animals. Then write and illustrate a picture book to share with a younger child. Use a question like those in the poem on each page of your book.

EXPANDING YOUR VIEW

HISTORY CONNECTION

Purpose History Connection extends the discussion of adaptations in Section 10-3. It focuses upon adaptations that humans find useful in animals, which led to domestication and breeding of certain species.

Teaching Strategies Lead students in a discussion of the evolution of domesticated animals by asking students to think about any "wild" behaviors that remain. Answers may include the startle response; fear reactions; running in fear of loud noises and sudden movement; growling, hissing, and baring of teeth for defense; stalking of prey.

Going Further Have student pairs select an animal and report to the class when it was domesticated, by whom, for what desirable traits, how it has been bred over the years to enhance these traits, and any lost traits or weaknesses that have resulted from this breeding. Have students choose a whole class of animal from this list, or an individual variety: cats, beef cattle, dairy cattle, chickens or turkeys, dogs, horses, fish, sheep, minks, rabbits, or laboratory rats. **COOP LEARN**

Answers to

WHAT DO YOU THINK?

You can tell that the people were farmers and that they had domesticated animals.

LITERATURE CONNECTION

Purpose Literature Connection extends section 10-1, in which students learn about characteristics of animals.

Content Background Although most of the questions can be answered in the negative, two could have "yes" answers. Snakes do not have legs, so one would not expect them to have hips. However, pythons are among the few snakes that have rudimentary pelvic (hip) bones. Penguins do not have arms, but the bones in a bird's wing are similar in many ways to the bones in a person's arms.

Teaching Strategy Ask students to answer the questions in the title of this excursion. Have students give reasons for their answers. Birds have knees, although they do not have kneecaps as humans do. Ladybugs do not sneeze, because a ladybug has no nose.

EXPANDING YOUR VIEW

TEENS IN SCIENCE

Purpose Teens in Science extends Section 10-3, in which students learn about regeneration. This excursion describes Jessica Knights's experiments with regeneration in flatworms.

Content Background Planarians are flatworms, members of phylum Platyhelminthes. Many experiments have been done to investigate regeneration in planarians. When a planarian is cut into pieces, the head end regenerates the rest of the body more quickly than any other piece can.

Teaching Strategies Discuss Jessica's experiments with the class. Some students may wish to try some of these experiments. Point out that the processes described are more complicated than they sound. All equipment must be very clean and scalpels used to make cuts must be very sharp.

Answers to WHAT DO YOU THINK?

Accept all answers that can be supported logically. Students will probably say that the research will be helpful.

TEENS *in* SCIENCE

JESSICA KNIGHT

Jessica Knight, a 16-year-old student at the North Carolina School of Science and Mathematics, wanted to know more about planarians. She knew they are small flatworms that try to avoid light and can regrow missing body parts. She wondered what would happen to planarians if they were exposed to various amounts of light.

By reading about experiments conducted on planarians, Jessica learned that a fragment of planarian about the size of a period on this page could regrow into a complete planarian within two weeks. She also learned that, when exposed to too much light, cancerous cells grow in some planarians. Maybe, she thought, planarians could teach us something about the changes caused in cells by ultraviolet light, an agent which is thought to cause cancer.

For her experiments, Jessica chose *Dugesia tigrina*, a brown planarian that has light receptors on its head and a primitive brain and nervous system.

Jessica placed planarians in petri dishes. Using a dissecting microscope for close observation, she sliced them apart in a variety of ways. She cut off the heads of some and the tails of others. Then she watched how they regenerated missing parts. "Depending on how you cut them," Jessica says, "you can come up with two heads on one end, or a tail on each end, or head on each end, or a head coming out the side."

After weeks of observing and videotaping regeneration in planarians, Jessica is ready to study the effects of various amounts of ultraviolet light on regeneration and cancer growth. She plans to use a light meter and calculations to determine how much light the planarians actually receive.

What levels of light affect regeneration? How does light affect regeneration? What levels cause tumors? How much light kills the planarians? Jessica believes she will have answers to these questions when she has completed her experiment. She believes damage caused by the ultraviolet light will be comparable to damage ultraviolet light does to human skin.

WHAT DO YOU THINK?

Do you think planarian research could someday show scientists how to treat wounds in humans?

Going Further Have students use reference books to find out more about planarians and their structure. Have students relate the simple structure to the worms ability to regenerate.

Reviewing Main Ideas

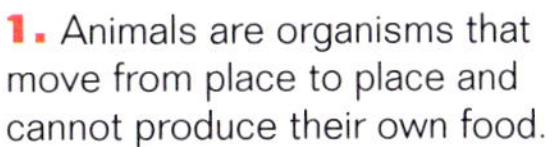

1. Animals are organisms that move from place to place and cannot produce their own food.

2. Some animals have skeletons outside their bodies, but all vertebrates have skeletons inside their bodies.

3. Animals reproduce by sexual and asexual reproduction.

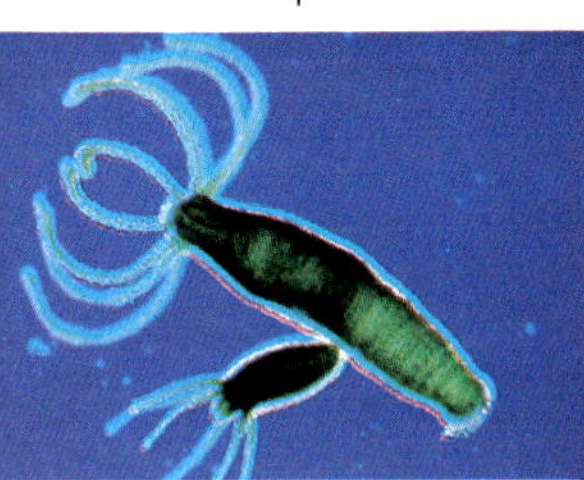

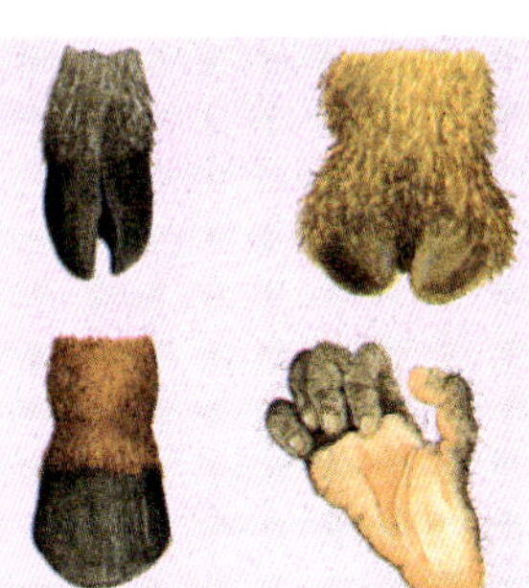

4. Adaptations, such as the structure of the foot, provide a better chance for animals to survive by making them better suited for their environment.

Chapter 10

Reviewing Main Ideas

Have students work in groups to illustrate the main ideas of the chapter.

Teaching Strategies

Divide the class into four groups, and assign one of the main ideas to each group. Have each group make a collection of pictures that illustrate their topic. Students can make drawings and/or cut pictures out of old magazines. Possible illustrations are listed below. COOP LEARN

1. animals running, flying, swimming; animals stalking, chasing, or holding prey; and animals grazing on plants

2. animal bones, drawings of skeletons, pictures of lobsters or crabs, or the exoskeletons of these animals

3. baby animals, including photos that indicate parental care

4. adaptations, such as a giraffe's long neck, an elephant's trunk, a crab's claws, or a grasshopper's long back leg

Have each student select one of the main ideas, and write a short story that illustrates the topic. Encourage students to use their imaginations, but to take care to be scientifically accurate at the same time. Stories can describe how an animal searches for food (Main Idea 1); how the flexible backbone helps a bird preen its feathers or a cat groom itself (Main Idea 2); how animals make nests or dens (Main Idea 3); or how animals use adaptations, such as the long forelimbs of gibbons and other primates (Main Idea 4).

Chapter 10

Chapter Review

USING KEY SCIENCE TERMS

Answers

1. vertebrate
2. adaptation
3. endoskeleton
4. metamorphosis
5. fertilization
6. exoskeleton
7. invertebrate
8. respiration
9. consumer

UNDERSTANDING IDEAS

Answers

1. c
2. a
3. b
4. b
5. a
6. d
7. a

Chapter Review

USING KEY SCIENCE TERMS

consumer	invertebrate
endoskeleton	metamorphosis
exoskeleton	respiration
fertilization	vertebrate

Each phrase below describes a science term from the list. Write the term that matches the phrase describing it.

1. animal with a backbone
2. internal system of support
3. series of body changes as an animal matures
4. uniting of egg and sperm
5. external system of support
6. animal without a backbone
7. oxygen combines with digested food and releases energy
8. organism that eats other organisms

UNDERSTANDING IDEAS

Choose the best answer to complete each sentence.

1. Animals can't ____.
   a. digest food
   b. move
   c. make their own food
   d. get food from other sources
2. One animal that begins digestion while food is outside of its body is a ____.
   a. starfish c. human
   b. horse d. worm
3. Worms, clams, and jellyfish are examples of ____.
   a. fish c. vertebrates
   b. invertebrates d. land animals
4. Hydra and sand dollars have ____.
   a. backbones
   b. radial symmetry
   c. bilateral symmetry
   d. asymmetry
5. Eggs and sperm unite during ____.
   a. fertilization
   b. respiration
   c. metabolism
   d. metamorphosis
6. The stages a tadpole goes through as it grows into an adult is ____.
   a. regeneration
   b. fertilization
   c. metabolism
   d. metamorphosis
7. Of the animals listed, the animal that goes through internal development is a ____.
   a. human c. grasshopper
   b. frog d. butterfly

CRITICAL THINKING

Use your understanding of the concepts developed in each chapter to answer each of the following questions.

PROGRAM RESOURCES

Teacher Classroom Resources

Review and Assessment, Chapter Review and Chapter Test, pages 41–44

Computer Test Bank, Chapter Test

OPTIONS

Cooperative Learning

Consider using Cooperative Learning in the Understanding Ideas, Critical Thinking, Problem Solving, and Connecting Ideas sections of the Chapter Review.

COOP LEARN

1. Compare and contrast the advantages and disadvantages of sexual and asexual reproduction.
2. Why do animals that develop internally produce fewer eggs than those animals that develop externally?
3. Study the picture. What characteristic puts humans in the same group as snakes but in a different group from worms?

4. Give an example of how behavior can increase an animal's chance for survival.
5. Suppose a bird that hatched had a beak that was shaped differently than other birds of the same species. How could this be helpful or harmful?

PROBLEM SOLVING

Read the following problem and discuss your answers in a brief paragraph.

You learned that in species with external fertilization, relatively few animals actually survive to adulthood.

1. Suppose a female fish lays 100,000 eggs in a season. The male's sperm can fertilize 60 percent of the eggs. How many fertilized eggs are there?
2. After fertilization, 90 of every 100 of the fertilized eggs are eaten by other animals. Now how many eggs are left?
3. An additional 20 percent of the remaining eggs are destroyed when the water temperature gets too cold. How many eggs actually hatch?
4. If only half of those fish actually live to be adults, calculate the total number that survive.

CONNECTING IDEAS

Discuss each of the following in a brief paragraph.

1. Explain how a keen sense of sight is an adaptation for survival.
2. How does complete metamorphosis differ from incomplete metamorphosis?
3. Why is a tumbleweed not an animal even though it moves from place to place?
4. EARTH SCIENCE CONNECTION Many scientists don't agree with the meteor theory of dinosaur extinction because not all animals on the planet died 65 million years ago. Pretend that you are a scientist who believes in the meteor theory. How would you explain why not all animals died?
5. SCIENCE AND SOCIETY Do you think that it is acceptable to capture wild animals so they can be displayed in zoos? Why or why not?

CRITICAL THINKING

Answers

1. Sexual reproduction requires two parents, while asexual reproduction requires only one. An advantage of asexual reproduction is that it is faster than sexual reproduction. Sexual reproduction can combine characteristics from both parents, leading to greater variety among the offspring.
2. Fertilized eggs that are developed internally have a better chance to survive and grow to adult organisms.
3. the presence of a backbone
4. Possible answers include a dog barking can deter competitors for food; making loud noises can alert other animals to the presence of a predator and help them to escape.
5. The different shape would be helpful if it enabled the bird to obtain more food or protect itself from enemies. It would be harmful if it prevented the bird from doing these things.

PROBLEM SOLVING

Answers

1. $100{,}000 \times 0.60 = 60{,}000$
2. $60{,}000 - 54{,}000 = 6{,}000$
3. $6{,}000 - 1{,}200 = 4{,}800$
4. $4{,}800 \div 2 = 2{,}400$

CONNECTING IDEAS

Answers

1. Keen sight can help an animal locate food and avoid enemies. Both actions improve chances of survival.
2. Complete metamorphosis takes place in four stages and the larva looks very different from the adult. Incomplete metamorphosis takes place in three stages, and the nymph is very similar in appearance to the adult.
3. A tumbleweed is not a consumer.
4. After the explosion, the effect of the meteor was to darken the skies, thereby lowering temperatures around the world. Plants and animals that were able to adapt to the new conditions survived. Dinosaurs could not adapt and died out.
5. Some students may say that zoos help keep endangered species alive. Other students may say that wild animals should never by captured.

CHAPTER ORGANIZER

SECTION	OBJECTIVES	ACTIVITIES/FEATURES
Chapter Opener		**Explore!** What's for lunch? p. 323
11-1 What Is a Plant? (2 days)	1. **List** the traits of plants. 2. **Describe** the structures and functions of roots, stems, and leaves.	**Explore!** How do you compare with a plant? p. 324 **Explore!** Are all roots, stems, and leaves alike? p. 325
11-2 Classifying Plants (2 days)	1. **Compare and contrast** vascular and nonvascular plants. 2. **Compare and contrast** plants that produce seeds in cones and those that produce seeds in fruits.	**Find Out!** Which tissue is xylem? p. 330 **Explore!** What's in a seed? p. 332
11-3 Plant Reproduction (3 days)	1. **Trace** the stages in the life cycles of a moss, a gymnosperm, and an angiosperm. 2. **Describe** the structure and function of a flower. 3. **List** methods of seed dispersal.	**Find Out!** How can you grow new plants? p. 334 **Find Out!** What are the parts of a flower? p. 337 **Investigate 11-1:** Growth of a Seed, p. 340 **Skillbuilder:** Observing and Inferring, p. 341
11-4 Plant Processes (2 days)	1. **Explain** the role of stomata in gas exchange in plants. 2. **Compare** photosynthesis and respiration.	**Explore!** Where does the water come from? p. 342 **Investigate 11-2:** Stomata, p. 344
Expanding Your View		A Closer Look **Advertising in the Real World,** p. 347 Physics Connection **In Living Color,** p. 348 Science and Society **Green Plants vs. Industrial Growth,** p. 349 How it Works **The Soil-Less Garden,** p. 351 History Connection **Ancient Medicinal Plants,** p. 352 Literature Connection **Sunkissed Flowers,** p. 352

ACTIVITY MATERIALS

EXPLORE!	INVESTIGATE!	FIND OUT!
Page 323 items for salad, such as lettuce, carrots, beans, peppers, cheese, and salad dressing; mixing bowl; paring knife **Page 332** unshelled peanuts **Page 342** 2 plastic bags, with twist-ties or other means to seal; 2 potted seedlings; petroleum jelly; water; label or felt marker	**Page 340** potting soil, water, 2 flowerpots, 6 paper cups, 8 bean seeds, 8 radish seeds, 8 watermelon seeds **Page 344** lettuce, dish, water, coverslip, microscope, microscope slide, salt solution, forceps, paper, pencil	**Page 330** tall jar, water, red food coloring, eye dropper, stirrer, fresh carrot with stems and leaves, scalpel or sharp knife **Page 334** cutting from philodendron plant, glass, water **Page 337** flower, black paper, scalpel, hand lens

TEACHER CLASSROOM RESOURCES	OTHER RESOURCES
Study Guide, p. 39 **Critical Thinking/Problem Solving,** p. 19 **Multicultural Activities,** p. 25 **Making Connections: Across the Curriculum,** p. 25	***STVS:** *Hydrilla Killer,* Ecology (Disc 6, Side 1)
Study Guide, p. 40 **Multicultural Activities,** p. 26 **Making Connections: Integrating Sciences,** p. 25	**Laboratory Manual,** pp. 59-60, Vascular and Nonvascular Plants ***STVS:** *Seed Banks,* Plants and Simple Organisms (Disc 4, Side 2)
Study Guide, p. 41 **Take Home Activities,** p. 19 **Flex Your Brain,** p. 8 **How It Works,** p. 13 **Making Connections: Technology and Society,** pp. 25-26 **Activity Masters, Investigate 11-1,** pp. 45-46	**Color Transparency and Master 21,** Parts of a Flower **Color Transparency and Master 22,** Monocots and Dicots **Laboratory Manual,** pp. 63-64, Plant Growth ***STVS:** *Bats as Pollinators,* Plants and Simple Organisms (Disc 4, Side 2) *Plant Clones,* Plants and Simple Organisms (Disc 4, Side 2)
Study Guide, p. 42 **Concept Mapping,** p. 19 **Activity Masters, Investigate 11-2,** pp. 47-48 **Review and Assessment,** pp. 45-48	**Laboratory Manual,** pp. 61-62, Plant Respiration ***STVS:** *Detecting Climate Changes in Tree Rings,* Plants and Simple Organisms (Disc 4, Side 2) **Computer Test Bank**
	***STVS:** *City Trees,* Plants and Simple Organisms (Disc 4, Side 2) *Plant Chemical Repels Cockroaches,* Plants and Simple Organisms (Disc 4, Side 2) **Spanish Resources** **Cooperative Learning Resource Guide** **Lab and Safety Skills**

***Science and Technology Videodisc Series**

KEY TO TEACHING STRATEGIES

Teaching strategies have been coded for varying learning styles and abilities. As you review teaching strategies in the margin, the following designations will help you decide which activities are appropriate for your students.

- **L1** Level 1 activities are basic activities and should be within the ability range of all students.
- **L2** Level 2 activities are average activities and should be within the ability range of the average to above-average student.
- **L3** Level 3 activities are challenging activities designed for the ability range of above-average students.
- **LEP** LEP activities should be within the ability range of Limited English Proficiency students.
- **COOP LEARN** Cooperative Learning activities are designed for small group work.

ADDITIONAL MATERIALS

SOFTWARE

The Green Machine, Micro-ED.
Pollination and Fertilization, IBM
Plant Growth, Classroom Consortia Media
Green Plants, Educational Activities, Inc.
Reproduction in Plants, J & S Software.

AUDIOVISUAL

Life of a Plant, film, EBEC.
How Plants Are Classified, filmstrip, EBEC.
Flowering Plants and Their Parts, film, EBEC.
Pollination, film, National Geographic.
Green Plants and Sunlight, film, EBEC.
Rain Forest, laserdisc, Image Entertainment.
Photosynthesis, film, EBEC.

Chapter 11

Plant Life

THEME DEVELOPMENT

Students study plant structure in the Explore activities in Section 11-1. Then they learn a system of categories based on plant structure. They explore interactions within plants and between the environment and plants that lead to such changes as the alternation of generations of plants. Students will appreciate the role plants play in affecting stability and change in Earth's environment.

CHAPTER OVERVIEW

The chapter presents plants in terms of structure, reproductive traits, and life processes.

First students review familiar plant traits, and study the structure and function of roots, stems, and leaves.

Then, students learn to classify plants based on the presence or absence of vascular tissue, seeds, cones and flowers.

Next, students focus on reproduction, both asexual and sexual, by spores, cones, and flowers, and study how seeds are formed, dispersed, and germinated.

Finally, students study life processes—transpiration, photosynthesis, and respiration—and the stomata through which gas exchange takes place.

Tying to Previous Knowledge

Divide the class into four groups and assign each a plant type: mosses, ferns, cone-bearing plants, and fruit-bearing or flowering plants. Have each group draw what they think is an illustration of a typical plant in that category and caption it with statements describing what they know of that plant as part of the living world: features, what it needs to grow and live, and what other organisms use it for. Post these illustrations and descriptions. Later as their knowledge develops, have the class critique and change these drawings and captions.

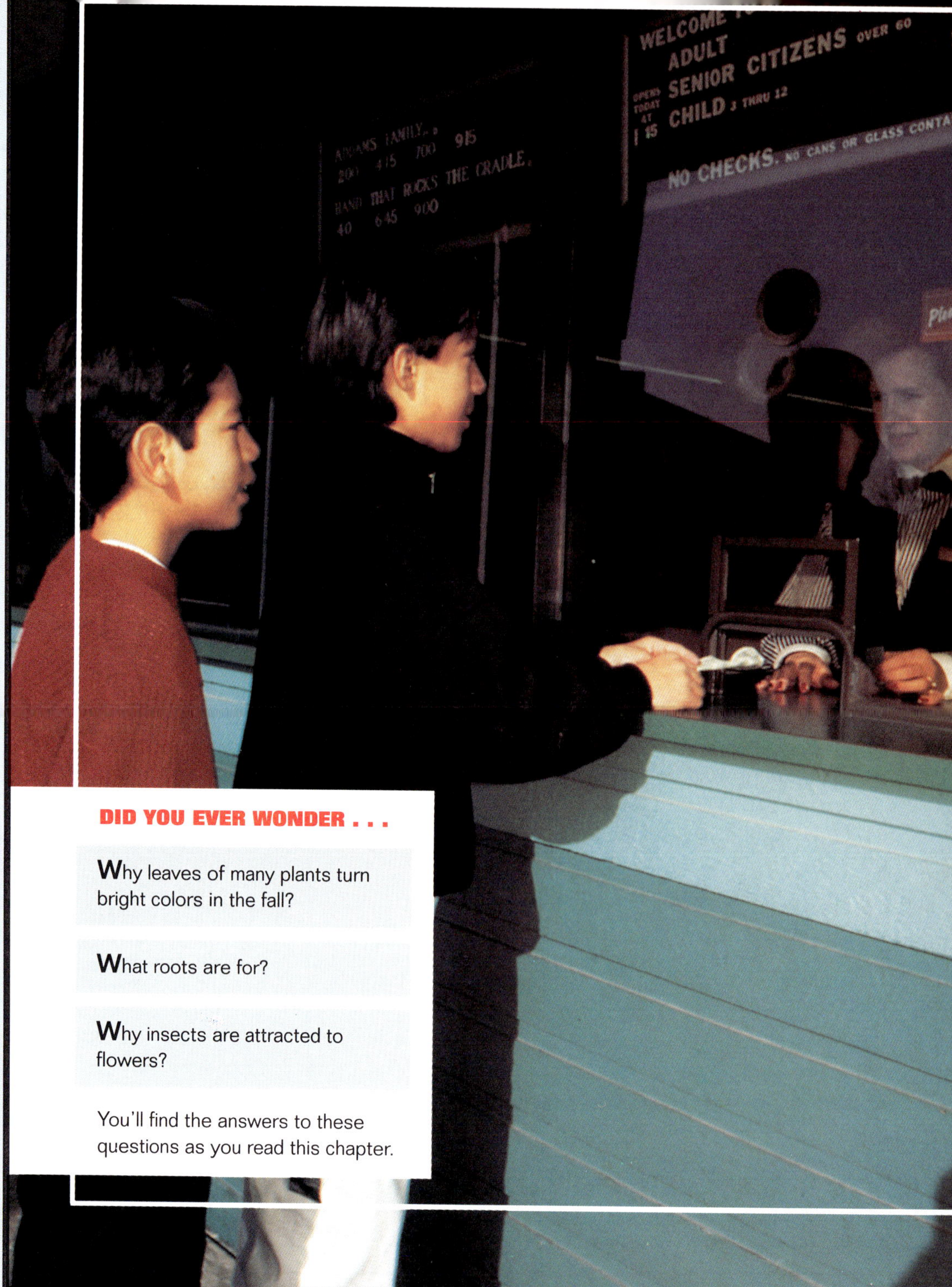

DID YOU EVER WONDER . . .

Why leaves of many plants turn bright colors in the fall?

What roots are for?

Why insects are attracted to flowers?

You'll find the answers to these questions as you read this chapter.

DID YOU EVER WONDER...

Students will explore these questions as they progress through the chapter. Don't spoil their fun and motivation by sharing these answers too early.

- Chlorophyll is a green pigment in plants that traps the light from the sun. Plants are green because chlorophyll reflects green light. Plants produce little or no chlorophyll in cold weather, making other pigments in the leaves visible (page 345).
- All water and minerals used by plants enter through the roots. Roots also anchor the plants in the soil (page 325).
- Insects are attracted by the flowers' color, scent, and nectar (page 338).

Plant Life

When was the last time you and your friends got together for a movie? After reading the newspaper ads, you chose the show. You paid for your ticket, rushed to the concession stand, and then looked for several seats in a row. The lights went out, and you enjoyed two hours of laughter, tears, or thrills.

Unless the movie title was *The Eggplant that Ate Chicago* or *Attack of the Killer Tomatoes*, the last thing on your mind was "plants." But think about all the ways plants were involved. Plants provided the material for the newspaper, ticket, popcorn box, and soft drink cup. The raw materials for all these came from trees. Popcorn is the seed of a plant. The flavoring in your drink came from plant parts. Even your clothes or the seat covers may be made of cotton.

In this chapter, you will find out about plants and their roles in your life.

EXPLORE!

What's for lunch?

With your classmates, bring in items to make a salad. Many different items can be included, such as carrots, lettuce, beans, peppers, and cheese. Before you put the salad together, identify the items in your salad that are plants. What makes them plants? How are they different from foods that aren't plants? List the differences. Were some ingredients in the salad oil or dressing made from plants?

323

Introducing the Chapter

Ask students to study the photograph on page 322 and ask what this picture has to do with plants. Help students see that many of the objects that the two students will encounter, even at a movie theater, come from plants. Have students brainstorm a list of these items.

Uncovering Preconceptions

Students may think that all plants grow from seeds and have leaves, stems and roots. Suggest or ask for examples that refute these ideas: growth from cuttings, runners, and moss.

EXPLORE!

What's for lunch?

Time needed 15 minutes

Materials Salad ingredients and dressing, mixing bowl, plates, paring knife, utensils

Thinking Processes Thinking critically, Comparing and contrasting

Purpose To distinguish plants from nonplant foods.

Preparation Have students bring in a variety of ingredients.

Teaching the Activity

Discussion Encourage students to offer as much information as they can about each plant ingredient. L1

Safety Remind students to cut away from themselves on a hard surface and keep their fingers away from the blade.

Expected Outcomes

Students distinguish plant from nonplant foods and identify differences between them.

Answers to Questions

Students should identify plant foods as growing in the ground, being mostly green, having roots, stems and leaves, etc. Salad oil or dressing contains vegetable oils.

Project

Obtain grass seed, a pot, and potting soil. Have students examine the seed with a hand lens. Fill the pot with soil, plant the seeds and scatter soil very sparingly over them. Place the pot in a sunny spot, watering it daily. Observe the pot daily to see how long the grass takes to germinate. Later, have students unpot the grass and gently wash the soil from the roots in a bucket of water, and examine and identify the parts of the plants.

Science at Home

Have students obtain seeds for an herb or spice that would be useful for cooking at home. Have them plant two herb gardens in large, flat pans or pots according to the directions on the seed package. Students can test the reaction of the herbs to light by placing one garden in direct sunlight and the other in shade and observing the differences in growth.

Section 11-1

PREPARATION

Concepts Developed

Students identify the traits of plants that distinguish them from other living things and make observations of plant structure, including roots, stems, and leaves.

Planning the Lesson

In planning your lesson on plants, refer to the Chapter Organizer on pages 322A-B for timing suggestions, resources, and additional materials that will help you in your presentation of the lesson concepts.

For adequate development of the concepts presented in this section, we recommend that students do the Explore activities on pages 324 and 325.

1 MOTIVATE

Discussion This activity will enable students to identify the importance of plants in their lives.

You will need a pencil, book, cotton garment, fresh vegetable, piece of bread, can of coffee, sneaker, and rubber eraser.

Ask students what these objects have in common. Accept all suggestions while seeking correct answer, which is that all of them come from plants. Help students to identify the plants involved. Lead them to understand that plants are essential to our lives. L1

11-1 What Is a Plant?

OBJECTIVES

In this section, you will

- list the traits of plants;
- describe the structures and functions of roots, stems, and leaves.

KEY SCIENCE TERMS

xylem
phloem

WHAT MAKES A PLANT A PLANT?

Have you ever taken a walk in the woods or in a park with trees and flowers? Maybe someone you know has a garden. Your neighbor may grow herbs in a kitchen window. Most certainly you've seen weeds growing at the sides of roads. Trees, flowers, vegetables, herbs, and weeds are all plants.

All animal life depends on plants. If there were no more plants, animals would not go on living for very long. You know that you are an animal. But do you know what makes you different from a plant? The following activity should help you discover some of the traits that are common to most plants.

EXPLORE!

How do you compare with a plant?

Look at the organisms shown on this page. Describe the traits of each organism. Think about some traits you know about yourself. Tell how you are the same as the organisms in these pictures and how you are different. In which kingdom are you placed? In which kingdom would you put these organisms?

Remember that all organisms can be grouped according to their traits. In the previous chapter, you learned that all animals share certain traits. As you completed the Explore activity, you probably began to realize that plants, too, have common characteristics. These traits separate plants from the other kinds of living things.

EXPLORE!

How do you compare with a plant?

Time needed 5 minutes

There is no special preparation or materials required for this activity.

Thinking Processes

Organizing information, Classifying, Thinking critically, Comparing and contrasting

Purpose To identify traits of plants and compare them with animal traits.

Teaching the Activity

Have students list plant traits and human traits under separate headings. L1

Expected Outcomes

Students compare and contrast plant and animal traits, and identify the kingdoms to which they belong.

Answers to Questions

Plant traits: mostly green; have leaves, roots, and stems; can't move; need water; make own food.Human traits: movement, can't internally produce own food, warm-blooded, etc. Humans and plants are both living, they both need food, they both reproduce, and they both respire. Humans: animal kingdom; plants: plant kingdom.

1. Most plants make their own food. They don't depend on other organisms for their nutrients.

2. Most plants are green.

3. Most plants have roots or rootlike structures that hold them in the ground. Plants usually don't move around.

PLANT STRUCTURE

If you were asked to draw a plant, you'd probably draw one similar to the plants shown in Figure 11-1. Most plants you're familiar with have roots, stems, and leaves. Take a closer look at these special structures in the following activity.

EXPLORE!

Are all roots, stems, and leaves alike?

Look carefully at each of the plants pictured in Figure 11-1. Can you identify the roots of each plant? How are all the roots alike? How are they different? Compare and contrast the stems and leaves of the plants also. Record your observations on paper.

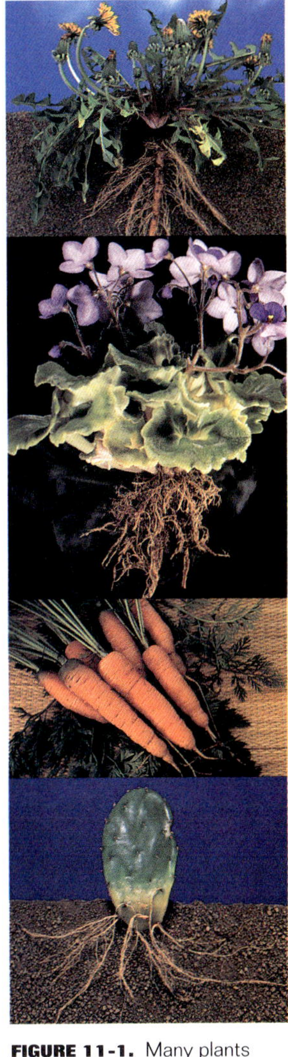

FIGURE 11-1. Many plants have roots, stems, and leaves.

You can see from the Explore activity that roots, stems, and leaves are not all alike. Yet each structure of the plant has a specific function that helps keep the plant alive.

Roots

Suppose you took a walk to observe plants in your neighborhood. You might see trees, potted plants in windows, and dandelions in sidewalk cracks. But you actually saw only about half of each plant! You saw only the parts of the plants that are aboveground. You probably did not see any roots. Most plant roots are below the surface of the ground. The root systems of some plants are as large or larger than the rest of the plant. Why must root systems be so large?

Roots have two important functions. All the water and minerals used by a plant enter through the roots. Roots also anchor the plant in the soil. Without roots, a plant could be blown away by wind or washed away by water.

2 TEACH

Tying to Previous Knowledge

In the previous chapter, students learned about the characteristics of animals. Introduce the lesson by having students suggest three to five ways plants differ from animals.

EXPLORE!

Are all roots, stems, and leaves alike?

Time needed 5 minutes

Thinking Processes
Organizing information, Classifying, Thinking critically, Comparing and contrasting

Purpose To identify plant structural differences.

Preparation Ask students to study Figure 11-1 carefully.

Teaching the Activity

Discussion Ask students to record their observations on three sheets of paper—one each for roots, stems, and leaves—with a column on each sheet for similarities and a column for differences. Discuss students' observations. L1

Expected Outcomes

Students learn that plant structures take many different forms.

Answers to Questions

1. Roots grow at the bottom of plants. Some are systems of long, thin fibers; others are single, thick growths.

2. Stems are generally stiff. Some are thick, some thin, some woody. Most leaves are green, but cacti have spines.

PROGRAM RESOURCES

Teacher Classroom Resources

Study Guide, page 39

Critical Thinking/Problem Solving, page 19, Desert Plants

Concept Development

Theme Connection This section covers the structure of plants, thus supporting the theme of scale and structure. As students examine Figures 11-3 and 11-4, they will see the structure of plant tissue and leaves in detail.

MAKING CONNECTIONS

Daily Life

The healthiest diet for human beings consists of 75 percent plant foods and only 25–30 percent animal foods. This is one reason that the Japanese, who eat mostly rice, tend to live longer than Americans, who eat far more meat.

Teacher F.Y.I.

Rhynia major, about 400 million years old, is the oldest fossil plant known.

DID YOU KNOW?

Most plants can't live in waterlogged soil because they can't get enough oxygen. Those trees that live in very wet soil have roots that grow up into the air. These aerial roots allow the trees to absorb oxygen from the air even when the rest of their root systems are under water.

Recall from Chapter 10 that birds have different kinds of beaks. Each bird has a beak that is useful for getting the type of food it eats. Plants also have different kinds of roots. You know that cacti live where very little rain falls. Some cacti have extensive root systems close to the surface of the ground. These roots quickly absorb water from dew or rain. Some cacti have one large root that grows deep into the ground and reaches stored water. Sometimes roots also store food. When you eat carrots or beets, you are eating roots with stored food.

Stems

Stems carry out several functions for plants. One is to support the aboveground parts of a plant. Some stems, such as potatoes and sugarcane, store food. Stems also allow the movement of materials between the roots and leaves. You learned that roots absorb water and minerals from the soil. These materials move through the plants in special vessels called xylem. **Xylem** (ZI luhm) is made of tubelike vessels that transport water and minerals up from the roots through the stem to the leaves of a plant. You also know that plants make their own food. Most of the food is made in leaves. **Phloem** (FLOH em) is made of tubelike vessels that move food from the leaves to other parts of the plant. Figure 11-3 shows where xylem and phloem are located in a tree.

FIGURE 11-2. A plant's stem supports the aboveground parts and may also store food.

Leaves

Did you notice the different kinds of leaves in the Explore activity? Leaves come in all shapes and sizes. A

PROGRAM RESOURCES

Teacher Classroom Resources

Multicultural Activities, page 25, Earth Medicine L1

Making Connections: Across the Curriculum, page 25, Planning a Vegetarian Meal L2

Other Resources

Fahn, A. *A Plant Anatomy,* 3rd ed., Elmsford, NY: Pergamon, 1982

Life of a Plant, film, EBEC

The Green Machine, software, Micro-ED

cactus has sharp spines, while a holly's leaves are dark, shiny, and prickly. One pine's needles are long and thin, yet another's are short and thick. No matter what shape and size leaves are, they are the plant's organs for trapping sunlight and making food.

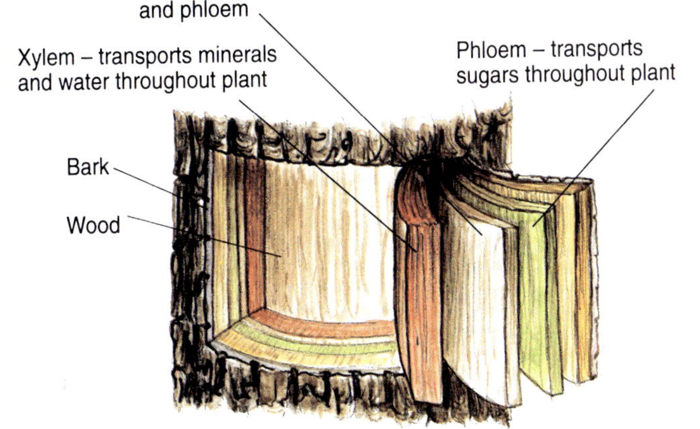

FIGURE 11-3. Xylem and phloem tissues carry water, minerals, and food throughout a plant.

Look at the structure of the leaf in Figure 11-4. A thin layer, called the epidermis, covers and protects the upper and lower surfaces of the leaf. Sometimes a waxy coating called the cuticle covers the epidermis. The cuticle protects the plant from drying out. Materials needed by the plant, such as water, oxygen, and carbon dioxide, pass in and out of the leaf through small openings called stomata (the singular is stoma). Guard cells around the stomata control the size of these openings.

Two different layers are located between the upper and lower layers of the epidermis. The palisade layer is located just below the upper layer of epidermis. Most of the food made by leaves is made in this area. A spongy layer is located between the palisade layer and the lower layer of the epidermis. This layer contains many air spaces as well as the xylem and phloem that transport water, minerals, and food to and from the leaves.

In this section, you read about the traits that set plants apart from other organisms. You've also seen some of the structures many plants have. In the next section, you will find out how to use the structures to group plants.

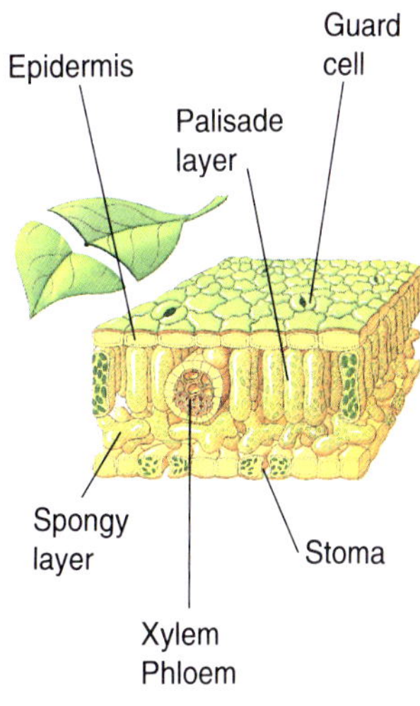

FIGURE 11-4. This shows the internal structure of a leaf.

Check Your Understanding

1. List the traits of plants.
2. What are the main functions of roots, stems, and leaves?
3. Which tissue transports water in a plant?
4. **APPLY:** Why would a cactus usually have a thick, waxy coating covering the stem just like some leaves?

3 Assess

Check for Understanding

Extend the Apply question by asking why cacti must conserve water.

Reteach

Display students' illustration of a fruit or flower-bearing plant completed in the Chapter Opener, Tying to Previous Knowledge. Ask students to identify correct features and features that may be missing. Have students help complete an illustration on the chalkboard showing roots, stems, leaves, xylem, and phloem. L1

Extension

Ask students who have mastered the section concepts to explain how plants get what they need *from* the environment without damaging the environment. Have students write a paper describing how plants use adaptations such as roots, stems, and leaves to solve this problem. L3

Answers to Check Your Understanding

1. They make their own food. They don't depend on other organisms for nutrients. Most plants are green. Most plants have roots, or rootlike fibers, that hold them in the ground. Plants usually don't move from location to location.
2. Roots anchor plants and absorb water and minerals. Stems support the plant, store food, and contain xylem and phloem for transporting materials. Leaves trap light and make food.
3. xylem
4. to prevent water from escaping

4 Close

Demonstration

Have students identify the leaves, roots, and stems of various types of plants and give a one-sentence description of the function of each. Descriptions should reveal students' knowledge of plant structure. L1

OPTIONS

Meeting Individual Needs

Visually Impaired Visually impaired students may use their sense of touch on samples of plants in order to make observations of root, stem, and leaf. Ask a local nursery or flower shop to donate samples for class study. If possible, obtain the same plant varieties as are displayed in Figure 11-1. Pair the students with a fully-sighted student to observe and record their tactile and olfactory observations.

Enrichment

Activity Have students work in groups using the *Guinness Book of World Records* or *Book of Lists* to research the largest prize-winning vegetables on record and other noteworthy plant information, such as the world's largest or oldest tree, harmful plant species, and most common plant in the world. Have them present their findings to the class. COOP LEARN

Section 11-2

Preparation

Concepts Developed

Students learn the purpose of plant vascular tissue (xylem and phloem) and of seeds. They are introduced to plants that lack roots, stems, and leaves, and learn to classify plants as nonvascular, vascular without seeds, or vascular with seeds.

Planning the Lesson

In planning your lesson on classifying plants, refer to the Chapter Organizer on pages 322A-B for timing suggestions, resources, and additional materials that will help you in your presentation of the lesson concepts.

For adequate development of the concepts presented in this section, we recommend that students do the Find Out and Explore activities on pages 330 and 332.

1 Motivate

Discussion Ask students to look closely at their own wrists and describe what they see. Students will see, under the skin, a network of faint blue lines and should be able to identify these as veins, or at least as blood vessels. Ask students what the purpose of these vessels is. Ask students if they think plants have a similar system. *Student responses will vary.* Tell students that they will perform an experiment in this section that will show that although plants may not have veins as many animals do, they do have structures that move water throughout the plant.

11-2 Classifying Plants

OBJECTIVES

In this section, you will

- compare and contrast vascular and nonvascular plants;
- compare and contrast plants that produce seeds in cones and those that produce seeds in fruits.

KEY SCIENCE TERMS

nonvascular plant
vascular plant

PLANT GROUPS

When you went to the movies at the beginning of this chapter, you discovered one way we could classify plants—by their usefulness to us. Scientists, however, determine which groups to place plants in by observing their structures.

NONVASCULAR PLANTS

In the last section, you looked at and described some typical plants. Each had roots, stems, and leaves. You may think that all plants have these structures, but look at the plants in Figure 11-5. They don't have those structures usually associated with plants. The mosses and liverworts in Figure 11-5 belong to a group called nonvascular plants.

Recall from the last section that xylem and phloem are tubelike vessels that carry water, minerals, and food throughout the roots, stems, and leaves of a plant. A **nonvascular plant** is a plant that lacks tubelike vessels to transport water, minerals, and food. Nonvascular plants also

FIGURE 11-5. Mosses and liverworts are nonvascular plants.

PROGRAM RESOURCES

Teacher Classroom Resources

Study Guide, page 40

Laboratory Manual, pages 59-60, Vascular and Nonvascular Plants  L2

Multicultural Activities, page 26, Sumo Indians—Culture at Risk L1

lack roots, stems, and leaves. They do have rootlike fibers, stalks that look like stems, and leaflike green growths.

As you look at the mosses and liverworts in Figure 11-5, you'll notice that these plants do not have flowers or cones. Plants can't produce seeds unless they have flowers or cones. Nonvascular plants use spores to reproduce. You will learn more about this method of plant reproduction later.

Because nonvascular plants aren't able to transport water within their bodies, they must live in moist areas. You often find mosses and liverworts growing on tree trunks, on rocks, or next to streams. The lack of a transport system also means that nonvascular plants can't grow very tall.

Mosses and liverworts are often the first plants to grow in areas that have been ravaged by fire. They also grow on newly formed rocks such as those found in lava beds. As the plants grow, their rootlike fibers move into small cracks in the rocks' surfaces. Mosses release chemicals that actually begin to break down the rocks. As these plants grow and die, the decaying plant material adds nutrients to the newly formed soil. Eventually, other plants are able to survive in the same area. You'll learn more about how plants help change rock into soil in Chapter 16.

DID YOU KNOW?

During World War I, doctors used a type of moss called peat moss as a dressing for soldiers' wounds. The high level of acid of the moss prevented bacteria from growing in the wounds. Thus, there was less chance of infections occurring.

FIGURE 11-6. The growth of mosses and liverworts on lava beds sets the stage for growth of other plants, such as grasses.

Pioneer Plant in Lava

2 TEACH

Tying to Previous Knowledge

Ask students to list ways water is distributed from a reservoir or from a well. Most students will suggest a system of pipes and conduits. Tell students that vascular plants also have systems to distribute water.

Concept Development

Theme Connection Students learn a classification system for plants based on structure. In the Find Out, students learn to identify xylem, which is part of the structure of vascular plants. The theme of scale and structure is supported as students use the structure of seeds for classification.

Inquiry Question What conclusion can you draw about a part of a forest where the ground was thickly covered with moss? *Moss plants are nonvascular, thus they can grow only where water is readily available. Therefore, the ground in the part of the forest where moss plants are found must be very wet most of the time.*

Uncovering Preconceptions Before reading this section, students may think that all plants have roots, stems, leaves, and vascular tissue. Using a clump of moss, you can show them that plants come in many different forms. Letting them gently pull apart moss will enable them to see major differences between large rooted plants and these simpler organisms.

PROGRAM RESOURCES

Other Resources

Dowden, Anne O. *From Flower to Fruit.* New York: Crowell, 1984.

How Plants Are Classified, filmstrip, EBEC.

FIND OUT!

Which tissue is xylem?

Time needed 30 minutes

Materials fresh carrot, tall jar, scalpel or sharp knife

Thinking Processes Thinking critically, Observing and inferring, Comparing and contrasting, Recognizing cause and effect

Purpose To identify xylem and its function

Preparation This activity, which can be performed as a demonstration or by groups, requires two days. The carrot is placed in the food coloring and water mixture on the first day; students see the results 24 hours later. COOP LEARN

Teaching the Activity

Discussion Fill the jar so that the stem, leaves and 5–7 centimeters of the carrot extend above the water. After the carrot has been placed in the jar, ask students to predict what will happen. Record predictions and, before cutting open the carrot, remind students of what they predicted.

Safety Remind students of the importance of safety when using a scalpel or knife. Cut on a hard surface rather than holding the carrot in the hand; hold the scalpel or knife by the handle only; move slowly while holding it; keep fingers away from the blade. L1

Expected Outcomes

Students identify the blue tissue in the carrot as xylem and conclude that water moves up through xylem.

Conclude and Apply

1. The vein structure of the carrot, including the part that was not immersed in water, has taken on the blue color indicating that it is the xylem.
2. Xylem is located in a circle around the center of the root.
3. The blue dye in the stem shows that the water moved from the root to the stem.

SEEDLESS VASCULAR PLANTS

Suppose you are a contestant on a game show. The final question asks you, "If plants without xylem and phloem are called nonvascular, what are plants with these structures called?" You would be correct if your answer was "Vascular." Xylem and phloem make up a plant's vascular system. Thus, a **vascular plant** is a plant with xylem and phloem.

How can you observe the xylem and phloem in a vascular plant? The next activity will show you.

FIND OUT!

Which tissue is xylem? 

Fill a tall jar 3/4 full of water. Add 50 drops of blue food coloring and stir. Place a fresh carrot in the water. Make sure the carrot has its stems and leaves attached. Leave the carrot undisturbed for 48 hours. After this time, remove the carrot from the jar. Use a scalpel or sharp knife to cut horizontally through the center of the carrot. **CAUTION:** *Use care when working with the scalpel.* Observe the sectioned carrot. Then cut lengthwise through the top part of the carrot. Observe the inside of the carrot. Cut the stem both horizontally and lengthwise and observe the inside.

Conclude and Apply

1. How do you know which tissue is xylem?
2. Where is the xylem located?
3. What evidence showed that water moved from the root to the stem?

The activity illustrates why vascular plants can grow taller and thicker than nonvascular plants. The vascular tissues carry water and nutrients to all parts of the plant. Vascular plants can also live in drier areas.

Scientists divide vascular plants into groups according to how they reproduce. Vascular plants without flowers or cones produces spores instead of seeds. These seedless

PROGRAM RESOURCES

Teacher Classroom Resources

Making Connections: Integrating Sciences, page 25, Fossils L2

FIGURE 11-7. Horsetails, club mosses, spike mosses, and ferns are all seedless vascular plants.

vascular plants include club mosses, spike mosses, horsetails, and ferns, which you can see in Figure 11-7. Ferns are the most numerous seedless vascular plants. While some tropical tree ferns may grow to be 5 meters tall, ancient tree ferns that lived about 300 million years ago grew as high as 25 meters, or as tall as a six-story building. These ferns and other plants were the raw materials from which coal and other fossil fuels formed.

SEED PLANTS

By far the largest group of plants on Earth consists of the seed plants. Over 235,000 species of seed plants have been discovered. Seed plants are more complex than the nonvascular plants and the seedless vascular plants. All seed plants have roots, stems, leaves, and vascular tissue. They are different from both nonvascular plants and seedless vascular plants because they grow from seeds. As you do the following Explore activity, you will discover what's in a seed.

FIGURE 11-8. Seed plants are the most plentiful type of plant on Earth.

MAKING CONNECTIONS

Geography

Obtain several field guides to trees, shrubs, and other plants such as the *Golden Guides*, Peterson guides, or Petrides guides. Ask students to look through a guide and select a particular plant. If available, provide students with outline maps of North America or the United States. Have them trace or copy a map of North America or the United States from an atlas if other maps are not available. Help students find the guide's state-by-state (or province-by-province) range information on their plants and have them color in the areas where the plants grow in North America or in the United States.

Content Background

Some mosses have water-conducting cells, but they are not organized as vascular tissue. Mosses, like amphibians, evolved from water-dwelling organisms and still need water for fertilization. Mosses have rhizoids that hold them to the ground but do not conduct water as true roots do.

Teacher F.Y.I.

The jojoba (ho HO bah), a desert plant, produces seeds that are 50 percent oil by weight. This oil has a very high boiling point (398°C) and is valuable for lubricating machinery and for cooking because it has no cholesterol.

OPTIONS

Multicultural Perspectives

Few plants have been as important to the world as the potato, which is a tuber or food storage unit for the plant rather than a root. Potatoes are a gift to the world from South America, where they have grown for at least 13,000 years. The ancient Inca not only grew them, they created a portable, freeze-dried product from them by crushing them to press out the water and then freezing them at night. The Spanish brought the potato to Spain in the 1500s, and from there it spread throughout Europe and to China, Japan, and North America. The potato had a great impact on every place it reached. It gave poor people a nutritious food that was easy to grow. One acre planted in potatoes could feed four times as many people as an acre planted in wheat. This potato became known as the Irish potato.

EXPLORE!

What's in a seed?

Time needed 5 minutes

Materials unshelled peanuts

Thinking Processes
Thinking critically, Observing and inferring

Purpose To identify the parts and purpose of a seed.

Preparation Provide each student with a peanut.

Teaching the Activity

Troubleshooting If students have trouble identifying the seed parts, draw a diagram on the chalkboard. You may also wish to make several hand lenses available for closer inspection of the seed. L1

Expected Outcomes

Students identify the miniature leaves and root or stem in the seed. They also conclude that the rest of the seed is food for the plant.

Answers to Questions
The small bump at one end of the inner part of the seed half is the young plant. The rest of the seed is stored food for the young plant.

Concept Development

Activity Materials needed are a flower, moss, an evergreen cone, an orange, and a fern frond.
Place the materials in front of students and ask which is part of a nonvascular plant. *the moss* Ask students which of the other samples comes from a vascular plant that does not produce seeds. *fern frond* Ask students which of the remaining samples is from a gymnosperm and which is from an angiosperm. *The flower is from an angiosperm and the cone is from a gymnosperm.*

EXPLORE!

What's in a seed?
Use a peanut that's still in its shell. Open the shell and find the seeds. Take the reddish-brown covering off one of the seeds. Carefully pull apart the two halves. Which part of the seed is the young plant? Find the parts that you think would become stem, leaves, or roots. What do you think the rest of the seed is used for?

You just saw that a seed contains a young, undeveloped plant and stored food. Each seed contains everything needed to produce a new plant. While all seeds may have the same function, they are produced by two different groups of plants. Scientists call these groups gymnosperms and angiosperms.

Gymnosperms

Both the oldest trees and the tallest trees alive today are gymnosperms. Gymnosperms are vascular plants that produce their seeds on cones. The word *gymnosperm* means "naked seed" and is very descriptive because the seeds of these plants are not protected.

Figure 11-9 shows the different kinds of gymnosperms. You may know most of these plants by the name evergreen

FIGURE 11-9. Ginkos (a), gnetophytes (b), conifers (c), and cycads (d) are the four types of gymnosperms.

a
b

c

d

OPTIONS

Enrichment

Research Tell students that carrots are edible roots, while peanuts are edible seeds. Have students conduct encyclopedia research to compile a list of roots and seeds that are part of our regular diet. L1

FIGURE 11-10. Most plant species are placed in the flowering plant group.

because they remain green throughout the year. You are probably most familiar with the different types of conifers, such as the pines, firs, and spruces.

Angiosperms

One of the best parts of a summer picnic is biting into a cold, juicy watermelon. Watermelons and many of the other foods you eat are examples of angiosperms. An *angiosperm* is a vascular plant in which the seed is enclosed and protected inside a fruit. You will learn more about how seeds form in both angiosperms and gymnosperms in the next section.

Angiosperms are also known as flowering plants. The variety of flowering plants seems endless. Stately oaks and graceful dogwoods, delicate rice and hearty corn plants, colorful bird-of-paradise and white yucca flowers are a few examples.

You've just read about the major classification of plants into nonvascular, vascular plants that have no seeds, and vascular plants that produce seeds. In the next section, you'll discover how each of these plants reproduces.

Check Your Understanding

1. Explain the differences between a vascular plant and a nonvascular plant.
2. Why is a pine tree placed in a different group from a cherry tree?
3. **APPLY:** You notice some beautiful flowers in a field. What can you tell about the kind of plant they are part of?

3 Assess

Check for Understanding

Use the questions to gauge students' grasp of the traits of vascular and nonvascular plants, and seed-producing and seedless vascular plants. Ask students for additional traits and to explain their answers as appropriate.

Reteach

Ask students to help you make a classification table on the chalkboard. The major headings are *Vascular* and *Nonvascular* plants. Under *Vascular* are the subheadings *seed-producing* and *spore-producing*. Under *seed-producing* are *gymnosperm* and *angiosperm* subsubheadings. Ask students to provide examples of each type. L1

Extension

Have students who have mastered the section concepts repeat the Find Out activity using plants including a stalk of celery, houseplant cuttings, and moss. After 24 hours, students should observe and record any changes in the plant and try to draw conclusions about the plant's structure. L3

4 Close

Demonstration

Have students identify the seeds at the core of a cut apple and classify the apple as coming from a vascular, seed-producing angiosperm. Ask students what purpose the apple serves for the tree. They should be able to tell you that it is the seed, not the apple, that is important to the plant's life cycle. Ask students to suggest how seeds might get from inside the apple to the ground where they can grow. L1

Answers to Check Your Understanding

1. Vascular plants have xylem and phloem tissues to transport water and other materials. Nonvascular plants lack such tissues.
2. Pines produce seeds in cones. Cherry trees are flowering trees that produce seeds protected by fruit.
3. They are angiosperms that have seeds and vascular tissue.

Section 11-3

PREPARATION

Concepts Developed

Students learn about asexual and sexual reproduction in plants, including reproduction by spores, cones, and flowers, and identify the structures used by plants for sexual reproduction. They also explore key factors in seed development and dispersal.

Planning the Lesson

In planning your lesson on plant reproduction, refer to the Chapter Organizer on pages 322A-B for timing suggestions, resources, and additional materials that will help you in your presentation of the lesson concepts.

For adequate development of the concepts presented in this section, we recommend that students do the Find Out activities on pages 334 and 337 and the Investigate activity on page 340.

1 MOTIVATE

Demonstration Bring in a spider plant with baby plants. Ask whether these plants are produced by asexual or sexual reproduction. *asexual* After introducing this term, have students suggest other plants that reproduce in a similar manner. *strawberries by runners, etc.* L1

11-3 Plant Reproduction

OBJECTIVES

In this section, you will

- trace the stages in the life cycles of a moss, a gymnosperm, and an angiosperm;
- describe the structure and function of a flower;
- list methods of seed dispersal.

KEY SCIENCE TERMS

pollination

ASEXUAL AND SEXUAL REPRODUCTION

What is the first picture that comes to mind when you hear the word *nursery*? Most of us usually associate babies or young children with that word. However, sometimes the word is associated with plants. A plant nursery is where you can go to buy plants. In most cases, the plants you buy are young. You might walk through large greenhouses full of young plants as you decide which ones to buy. Where do all the plants come from?

FIND OUT!

How can you grow new plants?

Sometimes new plants can grow from plant parts. Take a cutting from a philodendron plant. Include part of the stem and one or two leaves. Place one end of the stem in water. Observe for a week or two.

Conclude and Apply

1. What happens to the cutting after several weeks?
2. What kind of reproduction do you think has taken place?

ASEXUAL REPRODUCTION

Some angiosperms can reproduce from their roots, stems, or leaves. Reproduction of new plants from roots, stems, or leaves is called vegetative reproduction. The new plants that result are identical to the parent.

The roots of sweet potatoes and blackberries, for example, develop shoots that grow into separate plants.

FIND OUT!

How can you grow new plants?

Time needed 15 minutes

Materials philodendron plant, water, glass

Thinking Processes
Thinking critically, Observing and inferring

Purpose To observe asexual reproduction in plants

Preparation This activity can be performed as a demonstration or by groups. If by groups, you may need several plants to provide enough cuttings. COOP LEARN

Teaching the Activity

Discussion Ask how many "parents" the philodendron cutting has. Students will identify only one. *asexual reproduction.*

Troubleshooting Place cuttings in sunlight to promote rooting.

Expected Outcome

Students see the cutting develop roots in water.

Conclude and Apply

1. It grows roots.
2. asexual reproduction

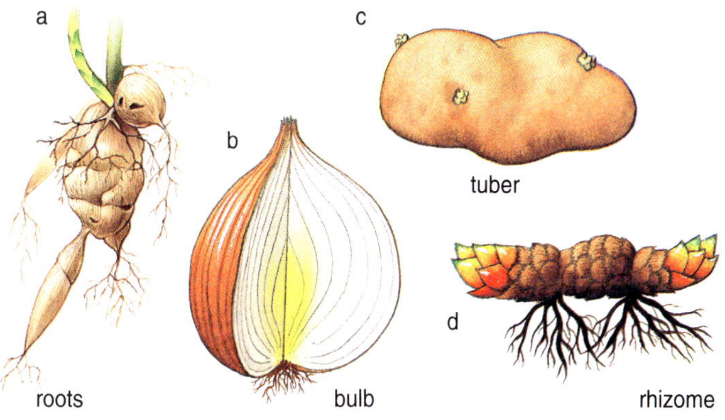

FIGURE 11-11. Roots (a), bulbs (b), tubers (c), and rhizomes (d) can all be used in vegetative reproduction.

An example of a root is shown in Figure 11-11(a). The bulb of an onion, as in Figure 11-11(b), or a daffodil is also part of the stem. The stem of a potato, also called a tuber and shown in Figure 11-11(c), can sprout new plants. The thickened stem is the potato itself.

Some plants, like strawberries, have runners—stems that grow across the top of the soil and touch down at points. New plants grow where the runner touches the ground. Some plants have underground stems called rhizomes, shown in Figure 11-11(d), that push through the ground to become new plants. Lawn grasses can reproduce this way. Some plants, such as philodendrons, grow new plants when their stems or their leaves are put in water.

SEXUAL REPRODUCTION

Recall from Chapter 10 that animals have both sexual and asexual reproduction. In sexual reproduction, the new organism develops from two parents. Sexual reproduction in plants produces spores or seeds.

Reproduction by Spores

Nonvascular plants, such as mosses, and seedless vascular plants, such as ferns, reproduce from spores. Let's follow the life cycle of a moss to see how it reproduces.

Figure 11-12 shows a closeup view of moss. The structures that are sticking up are moss sporophytes. Spores are produced in the capsule on top of the sporophyte. A few days after the spores land on wet soil and sprout,

FIGURE 11-12. Spores form in the capsules of the moss sporophyte.

2 TEACH

Tying to Previous Knowledge

In the previous section, students classified plants partly by their ability to produce seeds. Tell students that in this section, they will learn in detail that plants reproduce by seeds and spores, and asexually.

Concept Development

Theme Connection One theme that this section supports is stability and change. Students learn how interactions with the environment play a role in plant reproduction.

Student Journals Have students record their observations and conclusions in their journals. Suggest that they maintain a list of definitions of the many terms introduced in this chapter. Some students may wish to sketch an illustration of the term, such as a flower part.

PROGRAM RESOURCES

Teacher Classroom Resources

Study Guide, page 41

Transparency Masters, pages 45-48, and **Color Transparency,** number 21, Parts of a Flower L1; number 22, Monocots and Dicots L1

Take Home Activities, page 19, Germination L1

Concept Development

Inquiry Question What are the ways plants depend on the environment to assist with reproduction? *pollination by insects and wind, seed dispersal by wind, water, and other organisms, and the need for water for germination*

Using the Diagrams In order to show that they understand Figures 11-13 and 11-14, ask students to redraw both of them in their own style.

Activity Students may find it hard to master the definitions of many terms presented. To help them, organize a vocabulary activity by writing a definition on one side of a sheet of paper or cardboard and the matching vocabulary word on the other. Show students one definition at a time and have them write the matching vocabulary word (referring to a list of words on the chalkboard, if you wish), then turn over the sheet to show them whether they were correct. LEP

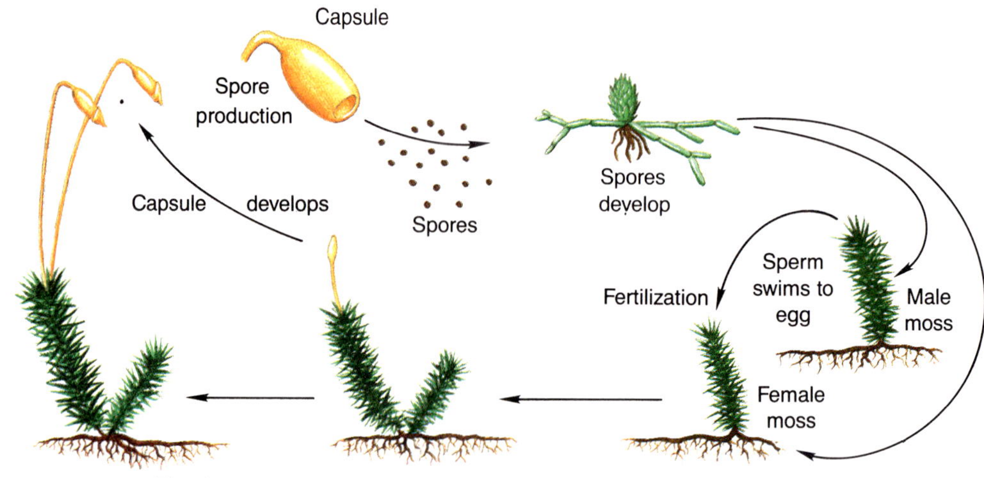

FIGURE 11-13. This diagram shows the life cycle of a moss.

gametophyte moss plants start to grow. These plants produce male sperm and female eggs. After the male sperm fertilizes the female egg, a new sporophyte plant begins to grow. The entire process is shown in Figure 11-13.

Seeds from Cones

Have you ever noticed the many varieties of cones? Some are long and thin; others are short and fat. No matter what their shape, all cones play a part in the reproduction of gymnosperms. Let's look at how a pine tree reproduces. Figure 11-14 will help you picture the process.

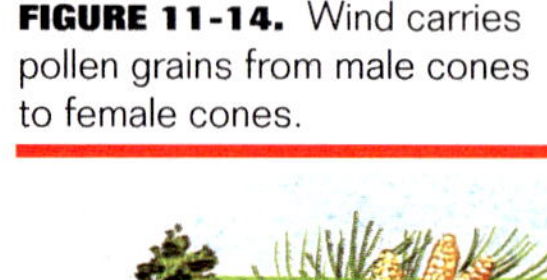

FIGURE 11-14. Wind carries pollen grains from male cones to female cones.

As with most gymnosperms, both male and female cones are produced on the same pine tree. A female cone is made of woody scales. On the top of each scale, two eggs are produced. Pollen grains develop on the smaller, less woody male cones. The pollen grains contain sperm. Wind carries the pollen from the male cones to the female cones, where it becomes caught on a sticky fluid that is located between the scales. A pollen tube grows from the pollen grain to the egg. Then a sperm swims down the tube and fertilizes the egg, after which a seed develops.

PROGRAM RESOURCES

Other Resources

Flowering Plants and Their Parts, film, EBEC.

Pollination, film, National Geographic.

Pollination and Fertilization, software, IBM.

Plant Growth, software, Classroom Consortia Media.

Reproduction in Plants, software, J&S Software.

OPTIONS

Meeting Individual Needs

Visually Impaired Help visually impaired students make the observations of the parts of a flower in Find Out by pairing them with fully sighted students. Have students make close observation by touch of the various structures of the flower, with the fully sighted student naming each one. For the same activity, obtain a pine or other cone and have students examine it carefully for shape, size, texture, and stickiness.

Seeds from Flowers

Flowers are the reproductive organs of angiosperms. Just as you can find a variety of cones, there is also a variety of flowers. Most flowers have certain parts in common.

FIND OUT!

What are the parts of a flower? 

Examine the flower your teacher will give you. Use the illustration to see how the parts are arranged. Remove the outer row of leaflike parts called the sepals.

The leaflike structures inside the sepals are the petals. Remove the petals. Next, locate the stamens, the thin, stalklike structures with the expanded tops, and remove them. Look at one of the stamens with a hand lens. Observe the top part called the anther and the stalk called the filament. Tap the anther against a piece of black paper to knock out the pollen grains.

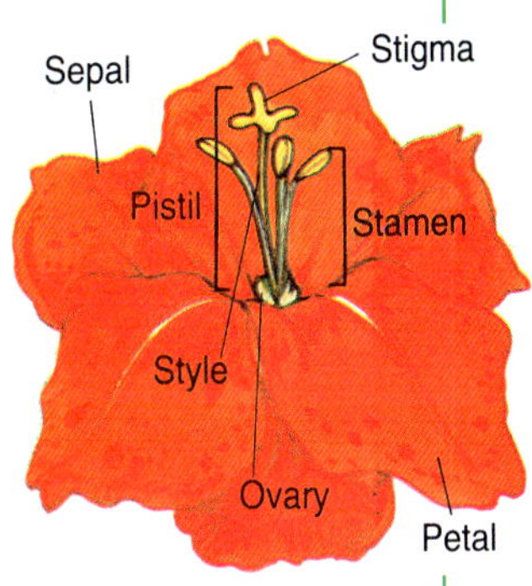

The structure that remains is the pistil. The stigma is at the top. The stalklike part is the style. The ovary is the swollen base of the pistil. Use a scalpel to cut across the ovary. **CAUTION:** *Always be careful with sharp instruments.* Use a hand lens to look at the inside of the ovary.

Conclude and Apply

1. What functions might the petals have?
2. How is the stigma adapted for trapping pollen grains?
3. How might pollen travel to the stigma?

What did you notice when you looked inside the ovary? You should have seen tiny structures that resemble seeds. However, these structures are not seeds, they are ovules. They will become seeds when the eggs inside are fertilized.

FIND OUT!

What are the parts of a flower?

Time needed 15 minutes

Materials large flower with prominent reproductive organs such as an orchid, gladiolus, or day lily; black paper; hand lens; scalpel

Thinking Processes
Thinking critically, Observing and inferring, Comparing and contrasting

Purpose To observe the parts of a flower

Preparation Students may work alone or in pairs. A nursery or flower shop may be willing to donate flowers. Be sure that all structures described in the activity are clearly visible. COOP LEARN

Teaching the Activity

Discussion Encourage students to take time with their observations. When the dissection is completed, reinforce their experience by asking them to name the various parts of a flower and to describe their location and appearance.

Expected Outcome

Students become familiar with the parts of a flower.

Conclude and Apply

1. to attract insects and birds, leading to pollination
2. It is sticky.
3. It could be blown by the wind or carried on the body of an insect or bird.

Teacher F.Y.I.

Seeds can be valuable. One gram of begonia seeds is worth 100 times more than one gram of gold.

Concept Development

Demonstration Obtain a piece of moss, a cone, and a flower. Show students the materials and ask them which one reproduces with spores. *the moss* Ask which of the three materials reproduce using pollen. *the cone and flower* Ask which of these depends primarily on the wind for pollination. *the cone* Ask which of the two contains a pistil and a stamen. *the flower*

Discussion Explain that this section covers three different means of sexual reproduction. In reviewing reproduction by cone and flower, ask students to note similarities and differences. Similarities include use of sperm-carrying pollen and of sticky fluids to trap them. There is less variety in the pollination of conifers. It occurs mainly by the wind. Pollination of flowers occurs by wind, insects and some birds.

Flex Your Brain Use the Flex Your Brain activity to have students explore FLOWERS.

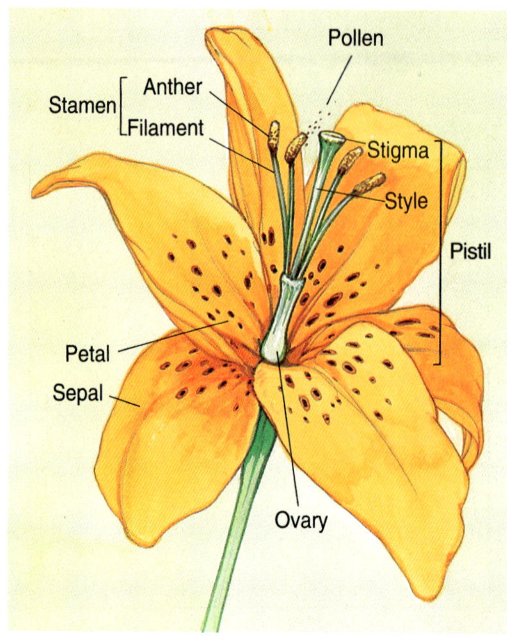

FIGURE 11-15. Parts of a Flower

Figure 11-15 shows the parts of a flower similar to the one you observed in Find Out. The bright yellow parts are the petals. Sepals are leaflike parts that protect a developing flower. The reproductive organs are inside the flower.

Stamens are the male organs. Each stamen has a slender stalk with a thick anther on top. Pollen grains form in the anther. As with gymnosperms, sperm develop in the pollen grains.

The pistil is the female reproductive organ. The pistil includes a sticky stigma, a stalk-like style, and a swollen base called the ovary. In angiosperms, ovules form within the ovary. Eggs develop inside ovules. When seeds grow inside the ovary, it ripens into a fruit.

Seed Development

In gymnosperms seed development begins after wind carries pollen grains to the female cone. In angiosperms, wind, insects, birds, or other animals may transfer pollen from the anther to the stigma. When pollen lands on the stigma, a pollen tube grows down through the style and into the ovule within the ovary. Sperm travel through the tube and unite with the egg in the ovule. The transfer of pollen grains from the stamen to the ovule is called **pollination**.

The shape, size, and color of flowers are important factors in how they are pollinated. For example, large, brightly colored flowers may attract insects that pollinate the flowers. Night-blooming flowers may have strong scents that attract pollinators, such as bats. And

PROGRAM RESOURCES

Teacher Classroom Resources

Laboratory Manual, pages 63-64, Plant Growth L3

How It Works, page 13, Velcro L1

Making Connections: Technology and Society, page 25, Making Paper L2

Critical Thinking/Problem Solving, page 8, Flex Your Brain

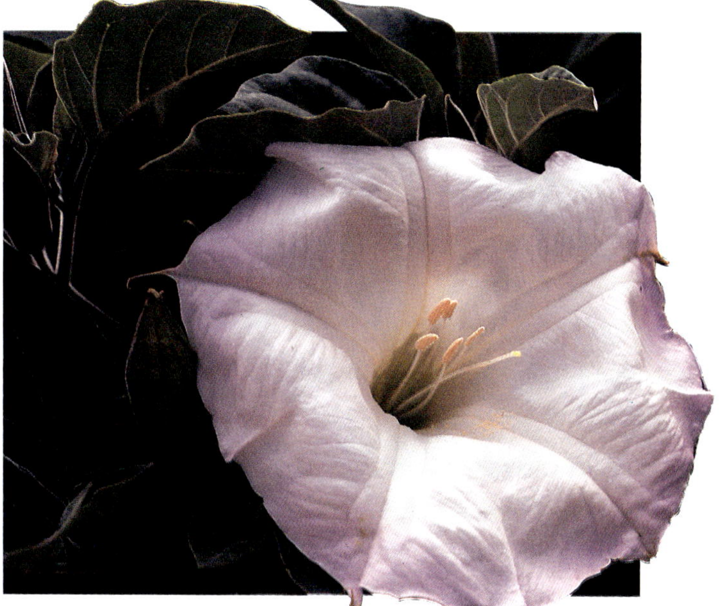

FIGURE 11-16. The night-blooming *Datura* is pollinated by animals that move around at night.

those flowers that are pollinated by the wind may have little color, small petals, or maybe no petals at all.

Figure 11-17 shows the parts of a seed. The embryo plant consists of a root and stem. The seed provides food until the young plant can produce its own. Protection is provided by a seed coat. Remember the peanut you examined earlier in this chapter. You could identify the young plant and its food. In the following activity, you'll investigate the relationship between soaking the seed coat and the time it takes the seed to begin to grow.

FIGURE 11-17. The Parts of a Seed

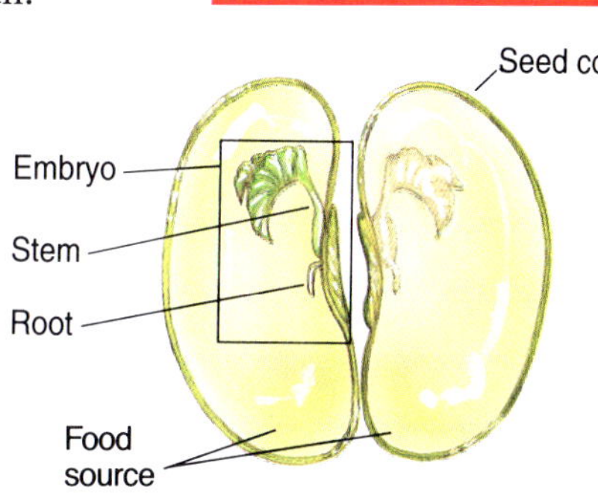

How do we know?

Pollinating Flowers

Scientists used movie cameras to show how pollination happens. They took pictures showing a bumblebee climbing into a flower. As the bee climbs in, you can see an anther full of pollen coming down on its back. As the bee leaves, flecks of pollen grains are sticking to its body. These grains are left on the stigmas of other flowers it visits.

How do we know?

Students gain detailed knowledge of the role of insects in the pollination of flowers. For more information, students can read Hamilton, David. *Flowers*. New York, Arcade, 1990.

MAKING CONNECTIONS

Daily Life

Ask students how they have helped in the dispersal of seeds. *Answers may include blowing the fluff off a dandelion stem, eating a piece of fruit and throwing the core or seeds on the ground, picking burrs off their shoes or socks, and popping the seed pods of jewel weed or touch-me-not plants.*

Content Background

Because plants disperse their spores and seeds widely and at random, they depend on sheer numbers for successful reproduction. A single capsule of a moss sporophyte, for example, can release 50 million spores. A single orchid flower may produce 25,000 seeds. In 1988, after a fire devastated about 230,000 acres of Yellowstone National Park, the first type of trees to produce sprouts was the lodgepole pine. Scientists estimated that the pines produced as many as 11,000 seedlings per acre of burned ground. Most died or were eaten by animals, but enough survived to repopulate the forest.

OPTIONS

Multicultural Perspectives

Rice is the dominant food crop in much of Asia. The average Japanese eats about 84 kg of rice per year, compared to only about 3 kg for Americans. Rice originated in India about 3,000 B.C.E. and spread both east and west, reaching Japan about 250 B.C.E. Rice is an annual grass that grows 4 feet high. Rice seeds are sown in prepared beds; when seedlings are 25–50 days old, they are transplanted into flooded paddies to mature. To the Japanese, rice is more than a staple food. One name for Japan is *Mizuho-no-kuni*, which means Land of the Ripe Rice Ears. Historically, rice has provided the Japanese with food, drink (rice wine), clothing (sandals, rain capes, and rain hats made of rice straw), writing paper, and building materials.

INVESTIGATE!

11-1 GROWTH OF A SEED

Time needed 50 minutes

Materials See student activity.

Thinking Processes Organizing information, Making and using tables, Practicing scientific methods, Observing, Forming a hypothesis, Separating and controlling variables, Interpreting data

Purpose To determine the effect of water on the speed of seed germination.

Preparation Provide a warm space with room for all the flowerpots and paper cups. The activity takes about 25 minutes each during two days of class time, followed by brief, weekly observations for up to three weeks.

Teaching the Activity

Discussion Before students begin the activity, explain that they will be testing the effect of a single variable—the length of time a seed soaks in water—on the sprouting of three different kinds of seeds.

Troubleshooting Obtain illustrations of radish, bean, and watermelon plants to help students identify the plants. You may want to sprout some of these plants beforehand to expedite this activity.

Expected Outcome

Students observe that the seeds soaked longest germinated first.

Answers to Analyze/Conclude and Apply

1. The seeds that were soaked for the longer time began to grow first.
2. to see if length of soaking time affected when a seed would begin to grow
3. Water was absorbed by seed tissues, which swelled and broke the seed coat.
4. yes
5. If students thought soaking the seeds reduced germination time, they were correct.
6. Both tea and lemon juice are acids. They might weaken the seed coats faster than water.

INVESTIGATE!

11-1 GROWTH OF A SEED

You know that seed coats protect seeds. Yet before an embryo plant can grow, this coat must be broken. In this activity, you will determine what effect soaking seeds has on the time it takes them to sprout.

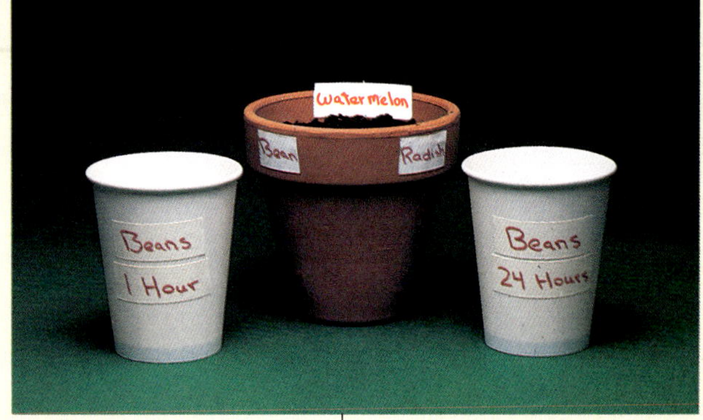

PROBLEM

Will soaking seeds reduce the time it takes them to sprout?

MATERIALS

potting soil
water
2 flowerpots
6 paper cups
8 bean seeds
8 radish seeds
8 watermelon seeds

PROCEDURE

1. Copy the data table.
2. Label one paper cup "Beans—1 hour." Label a second cup "Beans—24 hours."
3. Use the remaining cups and repeat Step 2 for the radish and watermelon seeds.
4. Put 4 of each kind of seed in their 24-hour cups.
5. Cover the seeds with water and set the cups aside.
6. The next day repeat Steps 4 and 5 with the last 4 seeds of each kind and the 1-hour cups.
7. Label the flowerpots "1 hour" and "24 hours." On the side of each pot put labels saying "Radish," "Bean," and "Watermelon."
8. Put the soil in the pots. After one hour, take the seeds from all the cups and plant them in the flowerpots at the same depth. Put all the 24-hour seeds in the 24-hour pots and the 1-hour seeds in the 1-hour pots. Put the pots in a warm area. Add water to keep the soil moist.
9. **Hypothesize** which seeds will begin to grow first.

DATA AND OBSERVATIONS

Sample data

DATE		BEANS		RADISH		WATERMELON	
1 hr	24 hr	1 hr	24 hr	1 hr	24 hr	1 hr	24 hr
Seeds soaked the longest will germinate first.							

ANALYZE

1. Which seeds began to grow first?
2. Why were the seeds soaked for different amounts of time?
3. **Infer** what function the water played in this experiment?

CONCLUDE AND APPLY

4. Does soaking reduce the time it takes for a seed to begin growing?
5. Was your hypothesis correct?
6. **Going Further: Predict** what would happen if you used tea or lemon juice as a soaking solution.

PROGRAM RESOURCES

Teacher Classroom Resources

Activity Masters, pages 45-46, Investigate 11-1

OPTIONS

Enrichment

Discussion In the Investigate activity, students experimented with the seeds of three different plants to determine the effect of soaking on the time of germination of seeds. Ask students to repeat the experiment without soaking the seeds to see if there is a change in sprouting time and which plant sprouts fastest.

FIGURE 11-18. The physical traits of seeds may give clues to the methods of dispersal.

Seed Dispersal

Imagine what would happen if all seeds began to grow close to the parent plant. The young plants would compete with the parent plant, and with each other, for light, water, soil, and nutrients. Seed dispersal helps reduce the competition for these resources and gives each plant a better chance of survival.

Fruits are very important in seed dispersal. Dry fruits, like the peanut you looked at, burst open on their own. Some seeds can be shot several meters away from the plant. Fleshy fruits, like oranges and tomatoes, are filled with water and sugar. Animals are often attracted to them for food. Animals that eat the fruit may spit out the seeds or disperse them in their wastes. Animals usually disperse seeds after traveling away from the parent plant.

Wind and water can disperse seeds. The winged "helicopters" of the maple and silky dandelion seeds are carried away by the gentlest breezes. Tumbleweeds scatter seeds as these plants are blown across the ground.

You—even your pets—disperse seeds. Small seeds may stick to your shoes. Hooked seeds may stick to your dog's fur or to your clothes. In the next section you will learn how plants get the energy they need to produce flowers and seeds.

SKILLBUILDER

OBSERVING AND INFERRING

Figure 11–18 shows three kinds of seeds. Study each seed. Based on its physical traits, decide how it would be dispersed. Wind, water, insects, birds, or mammals are the possible agents of dispersal. If you need help, refer to the **Skill Handbook** on page 652.

Check Your Understanding

1. Trace the life cycle of a moss.
2. How does the seed of an angiosperm develop?
3. What is the function of flowers?
4. List two ways seeds can be dispersed.
5. **APPLY:** Suppose you're eating a piece of watermelon, and you spit out some seeds. What part of the plant are you eating? How are you helping the plant reproduce?

SKILLBUILDER

water, wind, animals 

3 Assess

Check For Understanding

Use the questions in Check Your Understanding to have students describe in detail the reproductive cycles of spore and seed-producing plants. The Apply question helps students explore further their everyday interactions with plants.

Reteach

Help students master the terms and methods of plant reproduction by drawing up to four concept maps on the chalkboard, one each for asexual, spore, gymnosperm, and angiosperm reproduction. Key ideas, such as "flower" or "cone," are drawn in circles surrounding and connected to the appropriate main concept in the center, for example, gymnosperm—cone. L1 LEP

Extension

Have students who have mastered the section concepts make drawings describing their observations in the two Find Out activities. For the first Find Out, have students provide two to three drawings of the philodendron cutting: still on the parent plant, newly placed in the glass of water, and in the glass with roots showing. For the Find Out on page 337, students can draw a cutaway view of the flower and identify its structures with labels. L2

Answers to Check Your Understanding

1. Spores are produced by a sporophyte plant. A gametophyte grows from the spores and produces sperm and eggs. These unite to form a new sporophyte.
2. Pollen grains containing sperm land on the stigma. A pollen tube grows down from the stigma to the ovule. Sperm travel through the pollen tube and unite with the egg in the ovule. An embryo plant then develops within a seed.
3. Flowers are the reproductive organ of flowering seeds.
4. Possible answers include wind blowing seeds to new locations, seeds floating on water, and animals eating seeds and depositing them in their feces.
5. You are eating the fruit, which was once the ovary. You are helping the plant reproduce by dispersing its seeds.

4 Close

Activity

Ask students to prepare an outline of the section using traditional outlining techniques—Roman numerals, capital letters, Arabic numerals, lowercase letters. Remind them that they can use heads from the text, but that they will also have to identify key parts of the text and summarize the material.

Section 11-4

PREPARATION

Concepts Developed

Students will learn about the plant process of transpiration (loss of water through stomata) and the relationship between photosynthesis and respiration.

Planning the Lesson

In planning your lesson on plant processes, refer to the Chapter Organizer on pages 322A-B for timing suggestions, resources, and additional materials that will help you in your presentation of the lesson concepts.

For adequate development of the concepts presented in this section, we recommend that students do the Explore and Investigate activities on pages 342 and 344.

1 MOTIVATE

Discussion Ask students to imagine that they are in a spacecraft that has crash-landed on the moon. Have them help you make a list on the chalkboard of things they will need in order to survive. Students should mention air, food, and water as necessities. Explain that plants have related needs, which they will learn about in this section.

11-4 Plant Processes

OBJECTIVES

In this section, you will

- explain the role of stomata in gas exchange in plants;
- compare photosynthesis and respiration.

KEY SCIENCE TERMS

transpiration
producer
chlorophyll
photosynthesis

TRANSPIRATION

Remember the last time you took part in a physically active game? It may have been aerobics in gym class, a soccer game, or simply chasing your dog around the yard. Think about how your body reacted. Your face was probably flushed, and you breathed hard. You're used to the idea that people and other animals breathe. But the idea that gas exchange also happens in plants may seem a little strange. Did you know that plants release water vapor as part of this exchange? The next activity will give you a clue how.

EXPLORE!

Where does the water come from?

Obtain two plastic bags, two potted seedlings, petroleum jelly, and water from your teacher. Add the same amount of water to both plants. Label one bag "Petroleum jelly" and the other bag "No petroleum jelly." Put one seedling in the bag labeled "No petroleum jelly." Seal the bag and put it in a sunny window. Rub petroleum jelly on the bottom of all the leaves on the second plant. Put this seedling in the other bag. Seal the bag and place it next to the first plant. Wait several hours or until the next day and observe the bags. Water droplets have collected on the sides of which bag?

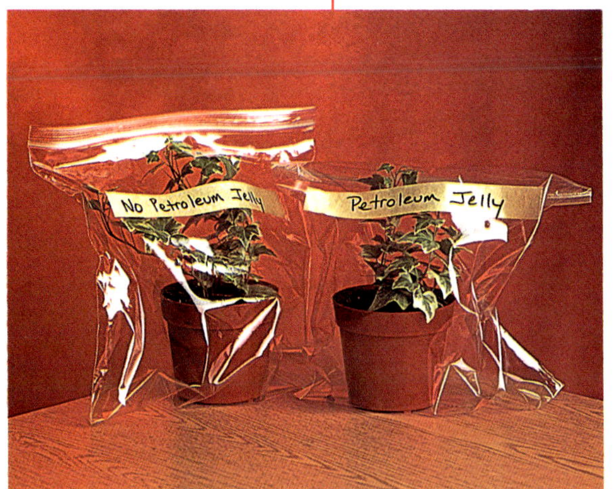

Conclude and Apply

1. Where does the water come from?
2. What does the petroleum jelly prevent from happening?

EXPLORE!

Where does the water come from?

Time needed 50 minutes

Materials two plastic bags, two potted seedlings, petroleum jelly, adhesive-label, measuring cup, water

Thinking Processes
Thinking critically, Observing and inferring, Comparing and contrasting, Recognizing cause and effect

Purpose To identify which part of the plant releases vapor in the air.

Preparation This activity can be performed as a demonstration or by groups of students. COOP LEARN

Teaching the Activity

Rub petroleum jelly on the *bottom* of the leaves where most stomata are. L2

Expected Outcome

Students learn that plants release water vapor through the stomata.

Answers to Questions

In the bag without petroleum jelly.

1. It condenses from water vapor that passes out of the plant.
2. It prevents water vapor from escaping from the plant.

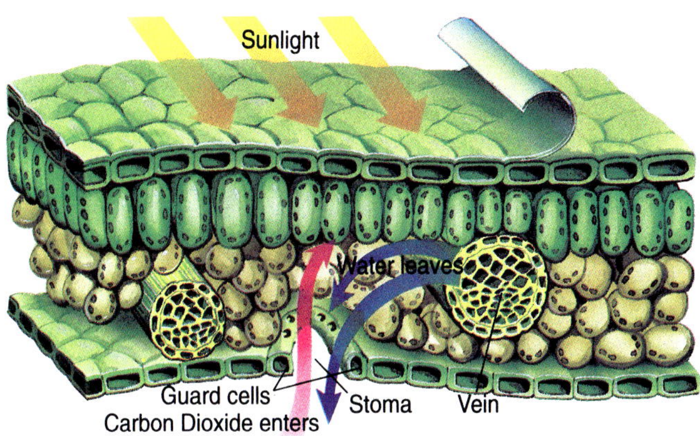

FIGURE 11-19. Water vapor passes out of the leaf through stomata. Carbon dioxide and oxygen also pass through the stomata.

Earlier in this chapter, you learned about the movement of materials throughout vascular plants and the internal structure of some plant parts. These ideas can be put together to explain how gas exchange happens in plants.

You know that water is absorbed by roots and is transfered up to the leaves by xylem vessels. Once in the leaves, some of the water evaporates. The water vapor is released from inside the leaf through the stomata. Remember that stomata are openings that allow water vapor, carbon dioxide, and oxygen to move in and out of leaves. Look at Figure 11-19. Guard cells around the stomata control the size of the openings.

The loss of water vapor through the stomata of a leaf is called **transpiration**. Plants lose large amounts of water every day through the process of transpiration. In fact, plants lose far more water through transpiration than they use in other plant processes.

Think about the Find Out activity you just completed. Water formed inside one bag. It formed when water vapor that transpired from the plant collected on the inside of the bag. The other bag had little or no water. Recall that you rubbed petroleum jelly on the bottom of this plant's leaves. Based on what you know about the structure of a leaf, what did the petroleum jelly do? Where do you think most of the stomata are located on a leaf?

DID YOU KNOW?

A date palm tree may transpire more than 500 liters of water in a single day!

2 Teach

Tying to Previous Knowledge

Remind students of the traits of living things described in Chapter 9. Ask them to suggest other important plant traits besides reproduction. Students should identify cellular structure, growth, needing food and water, response, and adaptation. Explain that this section teaches about basic processes that are characteristic of living plants.

Concept Development

Theme Connection The themes that this section supports are interactions and systems. Students learn about basic plant interactions with their environment through transpiration and photosynthesis. Transpiration is observed when the students perform the Explore activity on page 342.

Discussion Ask students to suggest what purpose the plastic bags and petroleum jelly serve in the Explore activity. Encourage students to see that the plastic bags produce an airtight space, while petroleum jelly prevents gas exchange through stomata.

PROGRAM RESOURCES

Teacher Classroom Resources

Study Guide, page 42

Laboratory Manual, pages 61-62, Plant Respiration L2

Concept Mapping, page 19, Carbon – Oxygen Cycle L1

Other Resources

Kaufman, Peter B. *Plants: Their Biology and Importance.* New York: Harper, 1989.

PROGRAM RESOURCES

Photosynthesis, film, EBEC.

Green Plants, software, Educational Activities, Inc.

INVESTIGATE!

11-2 STOMATA

Time needed 50 minutes

Materials See student activity.

Thinking Processes
Organizing Information, Making and using tables, Thinking critically, Observing and inferring, Comparing and contrasting, Recognizing cause and effect

Purpose To understand the function of stomata

Preparation Soak the lettuce in water for up to an hour before the start of class.

Teaching the Activity

Discussion Ask students whether they can quench their thirst by drinking salt water. Explain that in living tissues, water moves from high-concentration areas to low-concentration areas. Salt water has a lower concentration of water than fresh water because salt has displaced some of the water. Thus, drinking a salt solution tends to draw water from your body's tissues.

Expected Outcome

Students learn that stomata open and close based on how much water plant tissues contain.

Answers to Analyze/Conclude and Apply

1. Guard cells look almost like thick lips.
2. The number of stomata should be about the same.
3. Tissues in the leaf absorbed water.
4. Water diffused *from* guard cells *to* salt solution. They lost water, so they closed.
5. More concentrated salt solutions may cause more stomata to close.

I N V E S T I G A T E !

11-2 STOMATA

You learned that stomata are openings through which oxygen, carbon dioxide, and water pass. In this activity, you will learn what stomata look like and how they work.

PROBLEM

How do stomata work?

MATERIALS

lettuce
dish
water
coverslip
microscope
microscope slide
salt solution
forceps
paper
pencil

PROCEDURE

1. Place the lettuce in a dish of water.

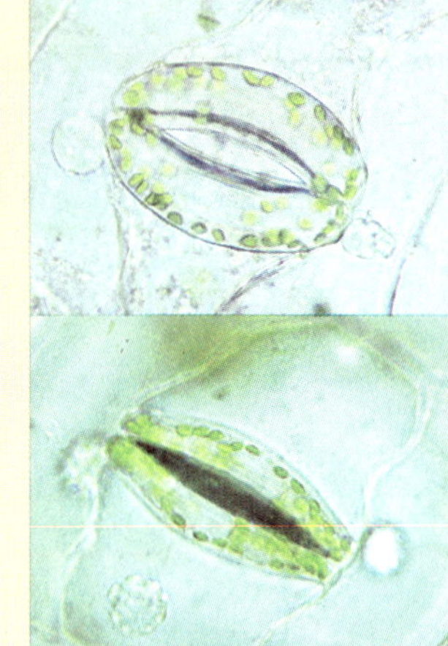

2. Choose a lettuce leaf that is stiff from absorbing the water.
3. Bend the leaf back and use the forceps to strip off some of the transparent tissue covering the leaf. This is the epidermis.
4. Prepare a wet mount of a small section of this tissue.
5. Examine the specimen under low and then high power of the microscope. Draw and label the leaf section in your data table.
6. **Observe** the location and spacing of the stomata. Count how many of the stomata are open.
7. Make a second specimen of the lettuce leaf epidermis. Place a few drops of salt solution on the leaf.
8. Examine the preparation under low and then high power of the microscope. Draw and label the leaf section in your data table.
9. **Observe** the location and spacing of the stomata. Count the number of stomata that are open.

DATA AND OBSERVATIONS

Sample data

	WATER MOUNT	SALT SOLUTION
Number of stomata	number of stomata will vary depending on section	
Spacing of stomata	spacing will vary depending on section	
Drawing of leaf section	stomata open	stomata closed

ANALYZE

1. Describe the guard cells around a stoma.
2. How many stomata did you see in each leaf preparation?

CONCLUDE AND APPLY

3. Can you **infer** why the lettuce leaf became stiff in water?
4. Can you **infer** why more stomata were closed in the salt solution?
5. **Going Further: Predict** what would happen if you soaked the lettuce in a stronger salt solution. Would more or fewer stomata close?

PROGRAM RESOURCES

Teacher Classroom Resources
Activity Masters, pages 47-48, Investigate 11-2

PHOTOSYNTHESIS

FIGURE 11-20. A consumer like this iguana depends on producers like this cactus.

You know that animals are consumers. A consumer gets nutrients by eating other organisms. Almost all consumers depend on plants either directly or indirectly for their food. Plants, on the other hand, produce their own food. Thus, they are called producers. A **producer** is an organism that makes its own food.

Plants produce their food in a series of chemical reactions. The energy for these chemical reactions comes from sunlight. **Photosynthesis** is the process in which plants use light to produce their food. During photosynthesis, plants use sunlight to change water and carbon dioxide into sugar and oxygen.

Chlorophyll is a green pigment in plants that traps the light from the sun. Remember that sunlight is actually a spectrum of colors. Objects absorb some colors and reflect others. Plants are green because chlorophyll absorbs the blue, violet, and red parts of the light spectrum. It reflects green light, so plants appear green to us.

In the fall, however, the leaves of many plants and trees change from green to shades of red, yellow, orange, and brown. This happens because such plants produce little or no chlorophyll in colder weather. The absence of chlorophyll shows us other pigments present in the leaf that we can't normally see.

FIGURE 11-21. Green plants are producers because they use sunlight, carbon dioxide, and water to produce sugar.

Let's look at what happens to the products formed during photosynthesis. Glucose is the sugar formed. Some of it is used by the plant for its own life processes, such as growth. Some of it is stored. When you eat carrots or potatoes, you are eating stored food. Some of the oxygen that forms during photosynthesis passes out of the leaves through the stomata. Plants are important in maintaining the same percentage of gases in our atmosphere. They take up carbon dioxide from the atmosphere and release the oxygen other organisms need to stay alive.

MAKING CONNECTIONS

Daily Life

People worry about the loss of tropical rain forests partly because plants use carbon dioxide, the major gas involved in the "greenhouse effect" that scientists believe will raise global temperatures by 1–5°C over the next 50 years. Use of fossil fuels has resulted in increased levels of carbon dioxide in the atmosphere. Development worldwide has also shrunk forests. One proposed remedy to the loss of tropical rain forests is planting trees to use carbon dioxide and produce more oxygen.

Content Background

In photosynthesis, water splits into hydrogen and oxygen. The oxygen is used for respiration by plant cells, and some also escapes through open stomata. Hydrogen and carbon dioxide join chemically to form glucose.

Teacher F.Y.I.

Photosynthesis produces more than 99 percent of the energy used by living organisms on Earth.

OPTIONS

Meeting Individual Needs

Physically Challenged Standard desks and laboratory tables may be poorly positioned for wheelchair-bound students to use in the Explore and Investigate activities. Provide low tables or a short length of board that can be clamped across the handles of the wheelchair and serve as a workspace.

Visually Impaired You can familiarize visually-impaired students with the structure of stomata by preparing in advance two enlarged models from clay, showing the guard cells in the closed, flattened position and in the open, turgid position. Touching the models will help students understand how the guard cells control the movc ment of gases in and out of the stomata.

3 Assess

Check for Understanding

Use the questions to ask students for complete definitions of transpiration and photosynthesis. Extend the Apply question by asking for examples of producer-consumer dependence.

Reteach

Tell students that stomata can be compared to their own lungs, which take in oxygen and release carbon dioxide. Ask students how they can prove that their lungs release water vapor. Students may mention seeing their breath on a cold day or breathing mist on a mirror. L1

Extension

Remind students who have mastered the section concepts of the large amount of water that plants can lose by transpiration. Ask them to write an explanation of where the water comes from and how it gets to the leaves. Students may consult encyclopedias. L3

Answers to Check Your Understanding

1. Carbon dioxide, oxygen, and water vapor pass in and out of a plant through stomata in leaves.
2. Photosynthesis is the opposite of respiration. Photosynthesis uses carbon dioxide, water, and light energy to form sugar and oxygen. In respiration, organisms break down sugar and oxygen to water, carbon dioxide, and energy.
3. Plants require light for photosynthesis; animals, as consumers, depend on plants either directly or indirectly for food.

4 Close

Discussion

Ask students to imagine that they want to grow plants on the moon. Have them brainstorm the basic necessities the plants will need and explain the purpose of each. L1

TABLE 11-1. Photosynthesis and Respiration

	Energy	Starting Products	End Products
Photosynthesis	stored	light energy, water, carbon dioxide	sugar, oxygen
Respiration	released	sugar, oxygen	water, carbon dioxide, energy

RESPIRATION

Use Table 11-1 to help you compare the processes of photosynthesis and respiration. Notice that respiration is the opposite process of photosynthesis. Some of the oxygen produced by plants during photosynthesis is used by the plant and by other organisms for respiration. The carbon dioxide produced by other organisms during respiration is used by plants to make food during photosynthesis.

FIGURE 11-22. Plants share many characteristics with other living organisims.

In this chapter, you learned about the different classifications of plants. What you learned is that while plants have many traits that are unique to their kingdom, they also share many traits and processes with other organisms on Earth. You now know about the important roles plants play in your life—as producers of the food and oxygen you need to survive. In the next chapter, you'll discover how all organisms on Earth interact with one another.

Check Your Understanding

1. What role do stomata play in gas exchange in plants?
2. Compare photosynthesis with respiration. What are the starting and end products of each?
3. **APPLY:** How is all life on Earth dependent on sunlight?

OPTIONS

Enrichment

Activity Have students pour 25 mL of bromothymol blue into a beaker and note the original color. Then have them place a straw into the solution and blow into it. Students should note the color change to green. Ask students what they have added to the solution by blowing through the straw. *carbon dioxide, to which the solution reacts by turning green* Have students add *Elodea* plants to the beaker and place under a bright light for 15 minutes, observing them every 5 minutes and recording any color change. Ask students to explain their observations. *Students should infer that photosynthesis in the plants removed carbon dioxide from the solutions, changing the color from green back to the original blue.* L3

EXPANDING YOUR VIEW

CONTENTS

A CLOSER LOOK

ADVERTISING IN THE REAL WORLD

Wanted: Insect, bird, bat, or other animal to carry pollen from male to female plant. No experience necessary, but must be able to follow instructions. Benefits competitive.

An ad like this might work for plants if insects and other animals could read. But plants have better ways of attracting willing workers. The color of the blossom may attract a particular pollinator. About 80 percent of all flowers are pollinated by insects, and the rest by wind, birds, and mammals. Which insect or mammal comes to a flower depends on what the flower looks and smells like. For example, hummingbirds are attracted to big, showy, red flowers like the hibiscus for their nectar.

Bees sometimes go to red flowers, too. That's because of the scent they put out, but not because of the red color. Bees see mostly blue, lavender, and yellow colors, so those are the colors of flowers to which bees travel. White attracts flies or night-flying insects and bats, depending on the scent.

Most birds have poorly developed senses of smell. That's why hummingbirds are attracted to color. Bright red flowers are attractive to hummingbirds.

Once a pollinator is attracted to a flower, the appearance of the flower sometimes contributes to the pollination process. On the blossom, there might be a cluster of dots or a converging color pattern visible to insects.

YOU TRY IT!

Design your own flower that would attract a particular type of pollinator. Use color or scent or both. Mark the flower with patterns that might help lead the pollinator to the pollen. Be sure to include the stamen (male) and stigma (female) parts so pollination can take place. You may either draw your flower or make a model flower from colored tissue paper. How might a flower pollinated by the wind differ?

Using Expanding Your View

Assign one or more of these excursions to expand students' understanding of plants and how they apply to other sciences and other subjects. You may assign these as individual or small group activities.

A CLOSER LOOK

Purpose A Closer Look extends the information presented in Section 11-3 on plant reproduction by describing some plant adaptations that promote pollination.

Content Background In evolution, any adaptation that improves an organism's chances of surviving and reproducing will tend to be passed to offspring. Over time, more successful survivors and reproducers prosper in the competition for survival while less successful ones become extinct. An evolutionary relationship that has occurred between specific plants and animals is coevolution. Coevolution occurs when two species of organisms evolve structures and behaviors in response to changes in each other over a long period of time. The pollination of flowers by animals is the most common example of coevolution.

Teaching Strategies Obtain six to eight flower samples. Then ask students to name the animals—bee, hummingbird, or fly—to which individual flowers might be most attractive. Note that some insects will feed on a particular flower based on the flower's structure and the insect's mouth structure.

Going Further Divide the class into small groups and have each group work together to write a story about a day in the life of a bee. Have the groups begin by researching how bees live, with different group members gathering information on different topics: the structure of a hive, the anatomy of the bee, bee communication, nectar and pollen gathering behaviors. Once the research is completed, have students brainstorm a story line for the bee that covers the information they have researched and describes the bee's relationship with flowers. Have one or two members of the group take notes and draft the story, while others provide illustrations to accompany the text. Display the completed 1 to 2 page stories on the bulletin board. COOP LEARN

Answers to

YOU TRY IT

Designs will vary, but students should note that flowers pollinated by wind may not necessarily need showy colors, patterns, or scents.

PHYSICS CONNECTION

Purpose Section 11-3 points out that certain colors attract some pollinators to flowers. This physics connection discusses pigments in plants and gives students the opportunity to test another role of color.

Content Background Scientists have identified ways color influences human emotions. While yellow is thought of as a cheerful color, being in a room painted yellow makes people feel anxious and upset. Blue and pink, on the other hand, make people feel calm. Scientists believe colors influence moods through their effect on the color-sensing cones in the eye. Some of the signals from the cones go to the pituitary gland, which secretes hormones that affect emotions.

Teaching Strategies Review with students the three pigments described in the text and the colors they produce. For example, tomatoes are red because they contain anthocyanin, and bananas are yellow because they contain carotenoid.

Activity For the You Try It activity, point out that the three samples should all be of different colors but, if possible, the same approximate size and ripeness. This activity can be performed by groups of six, with a different type of fruit or vegetable for each. Have students create a data table to record the results for all five volunteers before beginning the tests. COOP LEARN

Physics Connection

IN LIVING COLOR

Color plays a role in how well fruits and vegetables sell in the market. Sometimes a bright red color indicates that an apple is ripe. The Red Delicious variety is the most popular apple in the United States. But ripe apple colors actually range from various shades of red to yellow or green.

Scientists do not yet know if color has any role other than to attract insects, birds, and animals for pollination and for seed dispersal.

Thousands of pigments are found in plants. The basic one is chlorophyll, which is green; then, carotenoid, which is yellow; and the anthocyanins, which range from pale pink to red to a rich purple. A single type of fruit, like an apple, might have different varieties colored by each of the pigments. For example, the Rhode Island Greening (green, chlorophyll), the Golden Delicious (yellow, carotenoid), and the Red Delicious (red, anthocyanin) are all apples. Similar variations can be seen in other fruits and vegetables. Check out the grapes or the squashes the next time you visit the market.

Some of these pigments are so strong that they are able to survive animal digestion. The yellow of an egg yolk and the yellow of butterfat come from yellow plants that were eaten by the chickens and cows.

YOU TRY IT!

Select three fruits or vegetables at the market that are available in more than one color. Among the possible choices will probably be apples, grapes, melons, tomatoes, squash, and onions. Find five people to be your volunteer shoppers and tasters. Line the fruits or vegetables of all one color up in front of your first "shopper." Have each different fruit or vegetable color lettered. Ask the volunteer to list the fruits in order of preference, based on the way they look. Repeat the test using samples of the fruit or vegetable for tasting and touching, but have the volunteer blindfolded. (Note: Be sure to rearrange the fruits or vegetables, so the test subject will not go by order of objects.) Compare the results. Run the same test for all five subjects. Evaluate the results. Was color an important factor? Did color coordinate with taste? What did the test prove, if anything?

Answers to YOU TRY IT

Selections will probably reflect individual tastes.

Going Further Divide the class into groups to design an experiment that tests the effect of color on a herbivore's choice of food. Suggest such herbivores as gerbils, mice, rabbits, goats, cows, and sheep as subjects. Have the groups determine how to isolate the variables so that they can be sure of testing only the animal's color preference, if any, rather than preference for different smells or tastes or appetite levels at different times of day. Have each group record its experiment design in the form of captioned illustrations and a step-by-step numbered set of directions. If animals are easily accessible, interested students may wish to perform their experiment with the supervision of responsible adults, report their results, and discuss any difficulties they met in carrying it out. Students should be reminded that under no circumstances are animals to be fed any harmful foods. COOP LEARN

SCIENCE AND SOCIETY

GREEN PLANTS VS. INDUSTRIAL GROWTH

Like animals, plants can be harmed by the actions of humans. Laws are sometimes used to protect endangered species—animals or plants whose existence is threatened. In what ways are plants threatened, and by whom?

Most people have heard about the threat to tropical rain forests. In Central and South American countries, these diverse forests are being stripped to create new agricultural land for growing populations and to provide lumber.

The photo shows ozone data collected by the NASA satellite Nimbus-7. Ozone in the stratosphere absorbs most of the sun's ultraviolet rays. By shielding Earth, ozone helps to keep temperatures lower. The yellow and orange colors indicate high ozone levels. The blue colors indicate lower ozone levels, and the purple colors indicate the lowest ozone levels. Generally, areas with lower ozone levels to shield them have higher temperatures. An exception to this is a hole in the ozone layer over Antarctica that scientists have recently discovered. They are studying this area now to learn whether this hole was caused by pollutants destroying the ozone. Many scientists believe that the destruction of the rain forests will contribute to global warming because burning to clear land for farming harms the ozone layer.

The loss of rain forests and other forested areas is harmful in other ways, too. You may wonder why it would matter to us if some obscure plant species ceases to exist. It may matter because many of our medicines come from plants. So far, only five percent of the plant species in the world have been analyzed for their potential as medicines. Plants that hold cures for diseases could disappear before we ever get a chance to find them. Rain forests are particularly important because they

EXPANDING YOUR VIEW

SCIENCE AND SOCIETY

Purpose Plants must be able to carry on the processes discussed in Section 11-4 to survive. This excursion focuses on how human activity in industrialized areas interferes with these processes and affects plant survival.

Content Background There are six major kinds of air pollutants: carbon monoxide, suspended particulates, hydrocarbons, sulfur oxides, nitrogen oxides, and ozone and airborne toxic substances such as asbestos and mercury vapor. Vehicles produce 56 percent of the air pollution in the United States. Other sources include electric power and heating plants (22 percent), industrial processes (15 percent), and forest fires, and solvent and solid-waste disposal (7 percent).

Acid rain is rain of higher than normal acidity formed when burning coal, oil, and gas, release sulfur and nitrogen oxides into the air. These compounds combine with water vapor to produce sulfuric acid and nitric acid. They are then carried in wind and deposited in rain and snow. Acid rain, which is most severe in southeastern Canada, the northeastern U.S., and western Europe, has been associated with the death of lake fish and forest trees, changes in soil chemistry, and deterioration of building exteriors. But due to the difficulty of isolating variables in nature, it is not clear to what extent acid rain is responsible for these effects. Many government and industry leaders want stronger evidence before passing laws that will require spending hundreds of millions of dollars on pollution control.

Going Further Divide students into three groups to stage a debate on acid rain. Have one group represent utilities and heavy industries, which generate 37 percent of all air pollution and are alleged to be the major sources of acid rain. Have a second group represent American environmentalists who want to force these companies to spend hundreds of millions of dollars to reduce emissions that they believe cause acid rain. Have a third group represent Canadian fishers who believe that acid rain produced in the United States is polluting Canadian rivers and lakes and killing fish.

EXPANDING YOUR VIEW

Teaching Strategies Ask students to name the ways human activity threatens plant species and the impact that the destruction of plant life has on humans.

Demonstration Construct a simple greenhouse from a cardboard box with a sheet of glass over the top. Cut a hole in the side of the cardboard large enough to let one hand enter the box, and seal it with paper and masking tape. Set the box in sunlight for 30 minutes. Then remove the covering from the hole and have students put their hands inside. They should find that the interior of the box has grown very warm. Explain that the glass acts as a heat trap that lets the light and heat of the sun into the box but does not let the heat leave. Tell students that this is the basis for the greenhouse effect, which a majority of scientists believe is warming the Earth. Air pollutants, including methane and carbon dioxide, trap and reflect the heat of the sun in our atmosphere and are expected to boost average global temperatures 2° to 5C° over the next 50 years, with consequences that are very difficult to predict. You should, in fairness to the scientific community, also point out that not all scientists agree with this hypothesis.

Answers to

YOU TRY IT

Trees are available for free to schools from the Forestry Service.

contain nearly half of the world's species of plants and animals.

Wild plant species face threats in parts of the world that are more highly industrialized. Here threats come from the introduction of exotic species, diseases, insect pests, and water and air pollution. Environmental changes that affect plants usually affect all living creatures. We know that lichens will not grow where air pollution exists. If the air is not good enough for them, is it good enough for us?

Before the Industrial Revolution in England, most peppered moths were white. Their white color enabled them to blend in with the lichen-covered bark of the trees. As the Industrial Revolution came into full swing, soot killed the lichens and blackened the trees. Then black peppered moths became dominant. After Britain passed laws to clean the air, lichens returned, and white peppered moths again became common. The lichen served as an indicator of environmental health. An environmental change sufficient to cause the black peppered moth to be more common must have been both widespread and long-lasting.

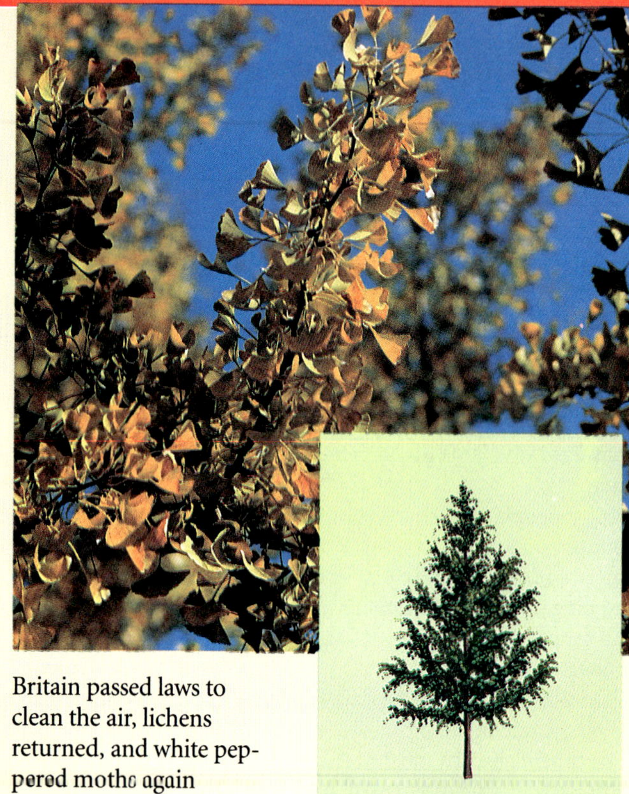

Some people think plants can feel pain and pleasure the way animals can. No scientific evidence exists for this. But plants do send and receive electrical signals within their tissues. Scientists have attached electrodes to leaves and shown that changes in the quality or amount of air, light, or water in a plant's environment make differences within the plant's voltages. Plants are in touch with their environment and are an indicator of the quality of our environment.

CAREER CONNECTION

An urban forester is someone who looks out for the trees in a city. Fighting tree diseases such as oak wilt and educating the public about them are part of the job. An urban forester studies botany and chemistry and attends forestry school. Local, state, and federal governments hire foresters.

YOU TRY IT!

Plant a tree at your school, at home, or in some other place where you have permission to do so. Choose a species that can survive in the environment you have to work with.

Going Further Work with each group to help it develop scientific, economic, and political arguments for their positions. Be sure the fact that consumers ultimately pay higher prices for emission control is presented. For more information, students can check encyclopedias and periodicals or turn to:

Bright, Michael. *Acid Rain.* New York: Gloucester Press, 1991.

Snodgrass, Mary Ellen. *Environmental Awareness—Acid Rain.* Marco, FL: Bancroft-Sage, 1991.

Wilkes, Angela. *My First Green Book.* New York: Knopf, 1991.

After the groups have completed their research, moderate a debate in which each group appoints two representatives to present its arguments and have one chance to rebut the other teams' arguments. Then ask the class to vote on whether legislation should be passed to force business to limit acid rain–causing emissions.

HOW IT WORKS

THE SOIL-LESS GARDEN

Growing plants in nutrient solutions in tanks instead of in soil is called hydroponics (hy droh PAHN iks). It comes from Latin words that mean *to work the water.* Hydroponics was first developed in California in 1929, by Dr. W. F. Gerische.

Growing plants in greenhouses in nutrient solutions has advantages. If soil is unsuitable, or at a premium in an area, or if there are diseases in the soil, hydroponics is a good alternative. It is also a cleaner, more efficient way of growing plants than in the soil. It works with a wide variety of plants, including tomatoes, lettuce, and carnations.

WHAT DO YOU THINK?

Do you think vegetables grown in a hydroponic garden would taste any different from those grown in soil? See if you can find hydroponic tomatoes at your local market. What plants might not be suited to hydroponic growing?

Two methods of hydroponic gardening are commonly used. In the original method, plants grow in a shallow, watertight container, that holds the nutrient solution. Wood fiber, peat, or some other growing medium is supported by a wire framework a few centimeters above the surface of the liquid. Seedlings are set into the growing medium with their roots in the nutrients held in the shallow container. The nutrient solution must have air circulated through it , and must have its pH checked regularly. The solution needs to be completely changed every 10 to 14 days.

A more popular method uses a layer of sand or gravel along with the nutrient solution. The sand or gravel, which is the growing medium, is held in individual pots or in rectangular containers. The nutrient solution may be fed from the top or pumped up from the bottom and allowed to drain back for reuse.

Several other systems that involve recirculation of nutrient solutions are under development. Polyethylene tubing is used with nutrient solution constantly recirculated through it from a storage tank.

The difficulty with hydroponics is that nutrient solutions must be checked and adjusted daily. The nutrients used are essentially the same ones found in fertile soil, or in fertilizers. However, great care must be taken that the nutrients remain in the proper concentration and are aerated so the plants can take them in.

EXPANDING YOUR VIEW

HOW IT WORKS

Purpose In Section 11-1, the typical plant is described as one with roots that anchor it to the soil and absorb nutrients from the soil. This excursion describes how certain plants may grow without soil, using a method known as hydroponics.

Content Background One of the first practical uses of hydroponics was during World War II, when the United States had military bases on Pacific islands that lacked fertile soil or suffered from soil-borne plant diseases. When these islands could not be regularly supplied with fresh vegetables, the soldiers used hydroponics to grow their own. In the future, hydroponics may find a new use in space. For space stations, long-distance spacecraft, and colonies on other planets, hydroponics will offer a means to grow plants that will provide both air and food for human beings.

Teaching Strategies Ask students to identify the labeled parts of the hydroponic system and explain what purposes they serve: the inert compound supports the plant, the plastic mesh supports the inert compound, and the nutrient solution provides nutrients and water for the plant. Then ask students to name the advantages (grow plants in infertile places) and disadvantages (need to control nutrient solution) of hydroponics.

Going Further Divide the class into groups to construct simple hydroponic gardens for the classroom. Have each group select a different plant to grow. Begin by having students research hydroponics.

Bourgeois, Paulette. *The Amazing Dirt Book.* Reading, MA: Addison-Wesley, 1990.

Bridwell, Raymond. *Hydroponic Gardening.* Santa Barbara, CA: Woodbridge Press, 1989.

Johnsen, Jan. *Gardening Without Soil.* Philadelphia: Lippincott, 1979.

Follow the plans in these books or the illustration shown here to build a hydroponic structure in a plastic container. Obtain seedlings of the plants and change the solution every two weeks. **COOP LEARN**

Answers to

WHAT DO YOU THINK?

Plants lacking extensive root systems, such as grass or mosses, might not be suited.

HISTORY CONNECTION

Purpose This history connection expands the Chapter Opener discussion of useful plants by ancient and current uses of medicinal plants.

Content Background For thousands of years, garlic has been eaten to guard against plagues, respiratory problems, colds, inflammations in the mouth, ear infections, and high blood pressure. Herbalists in ancient Rome used marjoram to make people feel calm, relieve bruises, and treat eye diseases. Both Chinese and Native-American traditional medicine use ginseng root to treat senility, diabetes, mental illness, anemia, fever, headache, and stomach ailments. Eucalyptus is used in commercial medicines to clear mucus from the nose and lungs and, in traditional practice, eucalyptus oil is considered an antiseptic, astringent, and stimulant. Chlorophyll or its derivatives are added to gum and mints. Chewing fresh parsley helps cure bad breath.

Teaching Strategies Ask students to suggest how the development of Linnaeus's scientific classifications has helped in the use of medicinal plants.

LITERATURE CONNECTION

Purpose This literature connection expands the concepts presented throughout the chapter through the story "Sunkissed: An Indian Legend."

Content Background Native Americans did not have a written language, although they sometimes recorded legends in pictographs painted on strips of bark or carved into totem poles. To pass on beliefs and values necessary for the survival of the tribe, people learned the tribal legends and communicated them orally to the following generation.

Native Americans believe that each creature in nature has a power by which it maintains itself and affects others. Each tribe has a different name for this power. Many tribes also recognize a primary power that is the source of life and goodness for all living creatures. In this legend, that power is the sun, called "Tonatiuh," the King of Light.

Teaching Strategies After students read the legend on their own, have the class work together to act it out, with some students taking speaking roles, and others handling props, costumes, and scenery. You may wish to invite elementary school children to watch the performance, and videotape it so students can watch themselves later.

Discussion Students can read the legend with partners, and then talk about why the sun would assume the central role in Native American life. Remind students that corn was the primary crop for most tribes, for it could be eaten fresh and be preserved by drying.

History CONNECTION

ANCIENT MEDICINAL PLANTS

Prehistoric people sampled all kinds of plants and found many plants that had special healing powers. Around 4000 years ago, a Chinese emperor put together a book that described more than 300 medicinal plants. Early Sumerians and Egyptians used plants for healing. Later the Greeks and the Romans also provided additional information about medicinal plants.

During the Middle Ages, monks in Europe studied and translated ancient texts about healing herbs. Every monastery had a Physick Garden for growing the herbs. Such gardens later became common at castles, courts, and hospitals.

By the 13th century, there was a system of classifying plants. New books were written giving herbal prescriptions for illnesses. Eventually, scientists learned to isolate the healing ingredient and to make more of it.

Early forms of drugs, such as antibiotics, aspirin, and insulin, can be traced to medicinal plants used by Native Americans. In the 1940s and 1950s, chemist Percy Julian, shown in the photo, developed drugs from chemicals in soybeans. His synthetic cortisone is used by arthritis sufferers today.

Many drugs today can still be traced to natural sources. Digitalis to regulate heartbeat comes from the foxglove plant (see photo). Quinine to treat malaria is from the bark of the cinchona tree.

WHAT DO YOU THINK?

If you were a scientist, how much attention would you pay to ancient beliefs?

Literature CONNECTION

SUNKISSED FLOWERS

You learned that plants need sun in order to live and grow. "Sunkissed: An Indian Legend," as told by Alberto and Patricia de La Fuente (Peña, Sylvia Cavazos, ed. *TUN-TA-CA-TUN*), illustrates the importance of the sun to all living things—especially to the survival of plants.

A legend is a story that has been passed along from earlier times. It may be partly true or simply an imaginative way of explaining some of the things that took place in nature. Obtain a copy of "Sunkissed: An Indian Legend" and read its explanation of how one kind of flower, the Margarita, was changed for all time by a special kiss from the sun.

YOU TRY IT!

Write a short legend that tells why a certain kind of flower is like it is today. Just choose a flower and let your imagination take over!

Reviewing Main Ideas

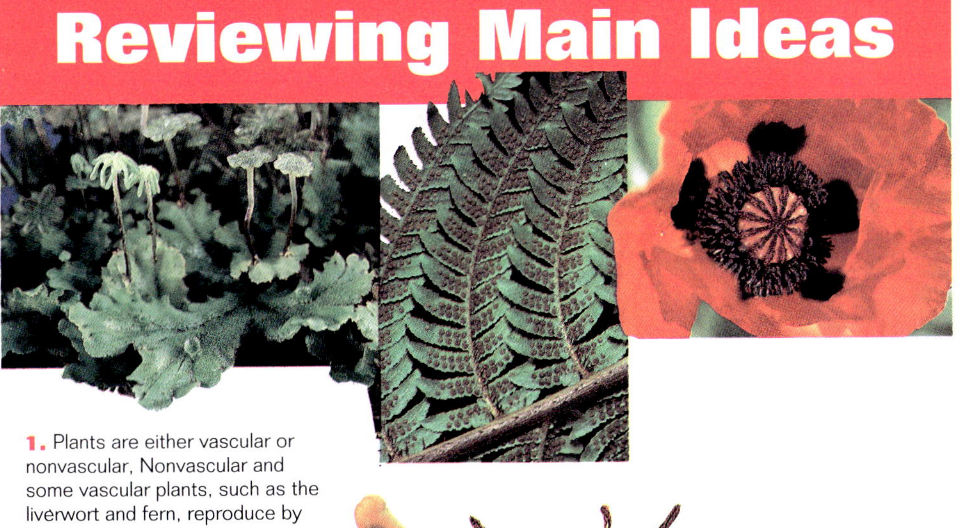

1. Plants are either vascular or nonvascular. Nonvascular and some vascular plants, such as the liverwort and fern, reproduce by spores. Most vascular plants, such as the poppy, reproduce by seeds.

2. Cones are the reproductive organs of gymnosperms. Flowers are the reproductive organs of angiosperms.

	Energy	Starting Products	Ending Products
Respiration	released	sugar oxygen	water carbon dioxide energy
Photo-synthesis	stored	light energy water carbon dioxide	sugar oxygen

3. Transpiration, respiration, and photosynthesis are processes carried on by all plants. Photosynthesis and respiration are plant processes that reduce the food and energy needed for plant growth. Transpiration is water loss from the leaves of plants.

Chapter 11

Reviewing Main Ideas

Ask students to read the page and study the three figures. Then have them organize for review their knowledge of plants by developing a table and by drawing detailed, scientific illustrations of vascular and nonvascular plants and of angiosperms and gymosperms. **LEP**

Teaching Strategies

Referring to Figure 11-1, have students create a table with the two main heads *Vascular* and *Non-vascular* and two subheads under *Vascular, spore-producing* and *seed-producing* plants. Ask students to provide an example for each category. Have students refer to Figures 11-2 and 11-3 and make lists of similarities and differences between cones and flowers. Organize students into groups of 3 or 4. Have them make cutaway drawings of the reproductive organs of an angiosperm or gymnosperm. Students should label all of the important structures, from roots to reproductive organs. If materials are available, students can paste pieces of cone, leaf, flower, root, or other structures to the drawing, identify them with a label, and indicate from what part of the plant they come. Display the finished drawings. Have students come up with some statements that show they understand the differences between gymnosperms and angio-sperms. **COOP LEARN**

Chapter Review

USING KEY SCIENCE TERMS

Answers

1. xylem
2. phloem
3. nonvascular plant
4. vascular plant
5. pollination
6. transpiration
7. producer
8. chlorophyll
9. photosynthesis

UNDERSTANDING IDEAS

Answers

1. Roots
2. asexual
3. seeds
4. transpiration
5. producers
6. Stems
7. gymnosperms
8. spores
9. respiration
10. Photosynthesis

CRITICAL THINKING

Answers

1. Pollen grains from the male cones stick in the fluid produced by the female cones. A pollen tube grows from the pollen grain to the egg.

2. Sporophyte plants grow only after eggs and sperm (which are produced by gametophytes) unite.

3. the waxy cuticle; the stomata

4. Color would not attract animals that are active at night. A strong scent guides animals to the plant.

5. The surface area of the plant with many large leaves is greater and includes more stomata. This plant will lose more water through transpiration.

6. Birds with long, narrow beaks feed from flowers. The beak's shape is an adaptation that enables it to reach nectar.

Chapter Review

USING KEY SCIENCE TERMS

chlorophyll
nonvascular plant
phloem
photosynthesis
pollination
producer
transpiration
vascular plant
xylem

Each phrase below describes a science term from the list. Write the term that matches the phrase describing it.

1. vessels that transport water and minerals throughout a plant
2. vessels that transport food throughout a plant
3. a plant that lacks xylem and phloem
4. a plant with xylem and phloem
5. the process by which pollen grains move from the stamen to the ovules
6. the loss of water vapor through the stomata of a leaf
7. an organism that makes its own food
8. green pigment in plants that traps light
9. the process in which plants use light to produce food

UNDERSTANDING IDEAS

Complete each sentence.

1. ____ absorb water and anchor the plant in the ground.
2. Growing new plants from a cutting is a type of ____ reproduction.
3. Animals, water, and wind are ways that ____ are dispersed.
4. Most water is lost by plants through the process of ____.
5. Plants are ____ because they make their own food.
6. ____ support the above-ground parts of a plant.
7. Plants that produce their seeds in cones are ____.
8. Nonvascular plants reproduce from ____.
9. During ____, plants break down food and release energy.
10. ____ is the opposite of respiration.

CRITICAL THINKING

Use your understanding of the concepts developed in the chapter to answer each of the following questions.

1. What is the function of the sticky fluid that is produced on pine cones?
2. Why are the sporophytes dependent on gametophytes in nonvascular plants?
3. What two features of a leaf help prevent water loss?
4. Why do flowers that are pollinated at night often have a strong scent?
5. Which plant do you think loses more water through transpiration, a plant with few, small leaves, or one with many, larger, leaves? Explain your answer.

PROGRAM RESOURCES

Teacher Classroom Resources

Review and Assessment, Chapter Review and Chapter Test pages 45-48

Computer Test Bank, Chapter Test

OPTIONS

Cooperative Learning

Consider using Cooperative Learning in the Understanding Ideas, Critical Thinking, Problem Solving, and Connecting Ideas sections of the Chapter review. COOP LEARN

6. Some birds pollinate when they feed on nectar from flowers. Look at the birds shown in the picture. Which one probably feeds on nectar? How can you tell?

7. Some plants live in surroundings that are very poor in nutrients, such as bogs. These plants have structures that trap insects . The insects are then used by the plants for food. Would you consider these animal-eating plants—such as the venus fly trap—producers or consumers? Defend your answer.

8. Describe how the size and structure of many seeds help plants reproduce.

PROBLEM SOLVING

Read the following problem and discuss your answers in a brief paragraph.

Dawn went with her grandmother to buy seeds to plant in the garden. She noticed that the package of zinnia seeds she wanted to buy said that the seeds were 95 percent *viable*. Her grandmother explained that viable meant living. She said that 95 out of 100 seeds would sprout and grow.

They purchased the seeds and headed home to plant them around the border of their garden. How could Dawn and her grandmother find out if the seeds they planted were viable? List the steps you would take to determine if a seed is viable.

CONNECTING IDEAS

Discuss each of the following in a brief paragraph.

1. What are some traits and processes that plants share with animals?
2. Why is photosynthesis important for maintaining Earth's present atmosphere?
3. List three ways plants affect your life.
4. **HOW IT WORKS** Compare and contrast two methods of hydroponic gardening.
5. **SCIENCE AND SOCIETY** Why is the preservation of the Amazon rain forest so important?

7. Students' answers may vary. Expect students to consider the animal-eating plants first as consumers. They may revise their thinking as they consider the fact that animals eat these plants thereby making them producers. Some students may suggest the dual role of consumer-producer for these plants.

8. The size of a seed will have an affect on how far it is dispersed. Smaller seeds often travel farther, dispersing new plants over a greater area. Small seeds are adapted with various structures—hooks, stickum, or aerial wings etc. to attach to fur or be carried by wind.

PROBLEM SOLVING

Answers

If the seeds Dawn and her grandmother planted sprout and grow, the seeds are viable. Dawn could soak 100 seeds and count the number that sprout. If 95 or more of the seeds sprout, the statement on the seed package is true.

CONNECTING IDEAS

Answers

1. Both plants and animals have sexual and asexual methods of reproduction. They both use respiration to release energy from food.

2. Photosynthesis uses carbon dioxide from the atmosphere to produce food. In the process, it releases large amounts of oxygen that other living things use.

3. Possible answers: many homes are heated with fossil fuels; you eat plants or plant parts; your oxygen as a product of photosynthesis.

4. One method of hydroponic gardening is the original method in which plants are grown in a shallow, watertight container containing a nutrient solution, and seedlings are set with roots in the solution which must have air circulated through it. The solution needs to be changed every 10 to 14 days. Another more popular method uses a layer of sand or gravel with the nutrient solution. The sand or gravel, which is the growing medium is in individual pots or rectangular containers. The nutrient solution is fed from the top or pumped from the bottom and allowed to drain for reuse.

5. The preservation of the Amazon forest is important to prevent the disappearance of plant species, global warming caused by harm to the ozone layer, and air pollution, which harms all living things.

CHAPTER ORGANIZER

SECTION	OBJECTIVES	ACTIVITIES/FEATURES
Chapter Opener		**Explore!** What would you discover on a neighborhood safari? p. 357
12-1 What Is an Ecosystem? (2 days)	1. **Distinguish** between populations and communities. 2. **Distinguish** between habitats and niches. 3. **Describe** the structure of an ecosystem.	**Explore!** In how many different surroundings do you carry out your everyday activities? p. 358 **Find Out!** Can three different bird species share the same habitat? p. 360
12-2 Organisms in Their Environments (4 days)	1. **Describe** a food chain and its relationship to a food web. 2. **Explain** how natural cycles are important in the environment.	**Explore!** How do organisms get their food? p. 363 **Investigate 12-1:** A Model Ecosystem, p. 365 **Skillbuilder:** Sequencing, p. 369
12-3 How Limiting Factors Affect Organisms (3 days)	1. **Identify** some limiting factors. 2. **Describe** adaptations of organisms to limiting factors.	**Explore!** How do ecosystems differ? p. 371 **Investigate 12-2:** Limiting Factors, p. 373 **Skillbuilder:** Comparing and Contrasting, p. 375
Expanding Your View		A Closer Look **Ecosystems Inside,** p. 379 Chemistry Connection **Oxygen Makers,** p. 380 Science and Society **Saving Chesapeake Bay,** p. 381 Art Connection **Abuelitos Piscando Napolitos,** p. 383 Teens in Science **One for All, and All for Trees,** p. 384

ACTIVITY MATERIALS

EXPLORE!	INVESTIGATE!	FIND OUT!
	Page 365 aquarium with screen lid, small plants (ferns, vines, or other), gravel, soil, water, crickets, oatmeal, charcoal, small stones, anole, warming light, water cup **Page 373** 3 or 4 small marigold plants in each of 3 plastic pots, water, marker, masking tape	**Page 360** ruler, white drawing paper

TEACHER CLASSROOM RESOURCES	OTHER RESOURCES
Study Guide, p. 43 **Concept Mapping,** p. 20 **Take Home Activities,** p. 20 **Multicultural Activities,** p. 27 **Making Connections: Across the Curriculum,** p. 27 **Multicultural Activities,** p. 28 **Making Connections: Technology and Society,** p. 27	**Laboratory Manual,** pp. 65-68, Human Impact on the Environment **Color Transparency and Master 24,** Animal in Wrong Environment ***STVS:** *Preserving Duck Habitats,* Ecology (Disc 6, Side 1)
Study Guide, p. 44 **Critical Thinking/Problem Solving,** p. 20 **Activity Masters, Investigate 12-1,** pp. 49-50 **Flex Your Brain,** p. 8	**Color Transparency and Master 23,** Cycles ***STVS:** *Aquaculture,* Ecology (Disc 6, Side 2) *Energy-Integrated Farm,* Ecology (Disc 6, Side 2) *Diverting Water from the Great Lakes,* Ecology (Disc 6, Side 2)
Study Guide, p. 45 **Making Connections: Integrating Sciences,** p. 27 **Activity Masters, Investigate 12-2,** pp. 51-52 **Review and Assessment,** pp. 49-52	**Laboratory Manual,** pp. 69-72, Living Space **Laboratory Manual,** pp. 73-76, Water Pollution ***STVS:** *Soldier Bug,* Ecology (Disc 6, Side 1) *Resistance to Pesticides in Cockroaches,* Ecology (Disc 6, Side 2) *Bird Sanctuary,* Ecology (Disc 6, Side 1) **Computer Test Bank**
	***STVS:** *Lake Erie Recovery,* Ecology (Disc 6, Side 2) **Spanish Resources** **Cooperative Learning Resource Guide** **Lab and Safety Skills**

***Science and Technology Videodisc Series**

KEY TO TEACHING STRATEGIES

Teaching strategies have been coded for varying learning styles and abilities. As you review teaching strategies in the margin, the following designations will help you decide which activities are appropriate for your students.

- **L1** Level 1 activities are basic activities and should be within the ability range of all students.
- **L2** Level 2 activities are average activities and should be within the ability range of the average to above-average student.
- **L3** Level 3 activities are challenging activities designed for the ability range of above-average students.
- **LEP** LEP activities should be within the ability range of Limited English Proficiency students.
- **COOP LEARN** Cooperative Learning activities are designed for small group work.

ADDITIONAL MATERIALS

SOFTWARE

Food Webs, Diversified Educational Enterprises.

Balance-Predator-Prey Simulation, Diversified Educational Enterprises.

AUDIOVISUAL

Introducing Ecology, film, Coronet/MTI.

Relationships, laserdisc, Syscon Corporation.

Food Cycle and Food Chains, film, Coronet/MTI.

The Ecosystem, Network of Life, film, BFA.

Chapter 12

Ecology

THEME DEVELOPMENT

In an ecosystem, organisms interact with members of their own population and with other members of their community, as well as with the nonliving aspects of the environment. Natural cycles provide an example of systems that maintain a balance of resources in the environment. The theme of energy is evident in the food web in an ecosystem. In this complex system, various organisms either acquire food energy through photosynthesis, by consuming producers, or by decomposition.

CHAPTER OVERVIEW

Students first discover how plants and animals interact with each other as well as with nonliving components in an ecosystem. One type of interaction involves the flow of energy from producers and through consumers to decomposers and is illustrated as simple food chains and as more complex food webs. Not only energy, but other elements and molecules are recycled (water, nitrogen, carbon, and oxygen), ensuring that Earth's limited resources are not wasted.

The chapter concludes with a presentation of the living and nonliving limiting factors that govern the survival of individual organisms and species. The predator-prey relationship is highlighted as well as adaptations that help organisms to survive in extreme environments.

Tying to Previous Knowledge

Ask willing students to describe rooms or shared space at home. Students are already aware of the interactions between living things. In addition, ask students what they ate for dinner last night. A well-balanced meal might consist of meat protein, vegetables, grains, fruit, and milk. Discuss where these foods come from. Which were producers? Which were consumers?

DID YOU EVER WONDER . . .

What's going on when bread gets moldy?

Why our oxygen supply doesn't get used up?

Why penguins don't live in your neighborhood?

You'll find the answers to these questions as you read this chapter.

DID YOU EVER WONDER...

Students will explore these questions as they progress through the chapter. Don't spoil their fun and motivation by sharing these answers too early.

- Molds are decomposers. These multicellular organisms break down dead organic matter such as bread for their food. (page 364)
- Although most animals use up oxygen during respiration, plants produce oxygen as a waste product of photosynthesis. (page 369)
- Penguins are adapted to survive in a habitat that has cold weather. (page 371)

Ecology

Have you been to the zoo recently? If so, you probably received a zoo map as you entered the gate. At a glance, you saw in which areas you could find different kinds of animals. Not too long ago, one zoo building would house all the large cats—the tigers, lions, and panthers. Modern zoos keep the animals in areas that resemble their natural surroundings. Just as it would in nature, the zoo giraffe finds its food in tall trees that grow in a grassland, while zebras and gnus graze on the grass. How can different types of living things survive in the same area?

How do these living things interact with the nonliving world around them? In this chapter, you will learn about ecology—the study of how living things interact with each other and their surroundings.

EXPLORE!

What would you discover on a neighborhood safari?

Go on a safari, or expedition, with two friends. Choose a small area near your school to study local plants and animals. Try to find out where they live, how they get what they need to live, and how they are influenced by the nonliving parts of their surroundings. Write your observations or make drawings of what you see. Compare your findings with those of other groups.

Introducing the Chapter

Have students examine the photograph. Ask them to find examples of producers and consumers in the environment. See if they can name at least two nonliving components. Ask students if there is any benefit to the animals or plants by living together.

Uncovering Preconceptions

Students may believe that any changes to the environment are destructive to all living things. Point out that human-made and natural disasters may actually be beneficial to some organisms. Ask them if they can think of any organisms that might benefit from the clearing of a forest by land development or forest fire. For example, decomposers benefit from the death of animals, while some animals are better adapted to open fields.

EXPLORE!

What would you discover on a neighborhood safari?

Time needed 60–120 minutes

Materials No special materials are needed for this activity.

Thinking Processes Thinking critically, Comparing and contrasting, Practicing scientific methods, Observing

Purpose To make students aware of interactions in an ecosystem.

Preparation This activity is most satisfying to students if conducted in an area and time of the year when animals and plants are abundant.

Teaching the Activity

Troubleshooting If possible students should choose ecosystems with a variety of easily identifiable organisms for a richer experience. L1

Expected Outcomes

Students should be able to identify several populations of animals and plants as well as several nonliving parts in their environment.

Project

Identify an area near the school familiar to all students to study as an ecosystem. On the bulletin board, display pictures of the populations and nonliving features in this ecosystem that can be identified by students. Encourage students to visit the area as often as possible to discover other parts of the ecosystem and add these to the bulletin board. Ask students to find out as much as they can about the animals and plants found there.

Science at Home

Have students write about their role in a food web and illustrate it. Ask them to make note of everything they eat during one 24-hour period. Have them find out where these food products came from. Are they from producers, consumers, or decomposers? What were their native habitats like? In the case of the consumers, from what did they obtain their food?

Section 12-1

Preparation

Concepts Developed

This section teaches students that living and nonliving parts of Earth interact. The knowledge they acquired when studying life in Chapter 7, animal species in Chapter 8, and the plant kingdom in Chapter 9 is integrated into the study of population and communities and the way they influence each other.

The physical world covered in Chapters 1 through 6 is then joined to the living world in a discussion of habitats, niches, and ecosystems.

Planning the Lesson

In planning your lesson on ecosystems, refer to the Chapter Organizer on pages 356A-B for timing suggestions, resources, and additional materials that will help you in your presentation of the lesson concepts.

For adequate development of the concepts presented in this section, we recommend that students do the Explore and Find Out activities on pages 358 and 360.

1 Motivate

Discussion Display pictures of animal and plant populations found in your area on the bulletin board. Discuss how populations interact to make a community. Then point out that communities interact with nonliving things in the environment to form ecosystems. L1

12-1 What Is an Ecosystem?

OBJECTIVES

In this section, you will

- distinguish between populations and communities;
- distinguish between habitats and niches;
- describe the structure of an ecosystem.

KEY SCIENCE TERMS

habitat
population
community
niche
ecosystem

LIVING THINGS AND THEIR NATURAL SURROUNDINGS

You may sometimes move through your daily activities without giving any thought to your surroundings. In school, you spend a large part of your day in rooms interacting with classmates and teachers. After-school activities bring you in contact with different groups of friends and acquaintances. Your location may shift from school to an outdoor playing field, local shopping center, or the busy sidewalk that leads you home. You may not notice the yellow tulips in a pot on a neighbor's porch or the footprints left by a raccoon as it ran through a muddy flowerbed. In your room, a spider's web catches insects. The architect and builder of this trap moves quickly and silently down one wall. Warm air flows out of an air duct and keeps the room at a comfortable temperature. Each day you move into and out of many different surroundings.

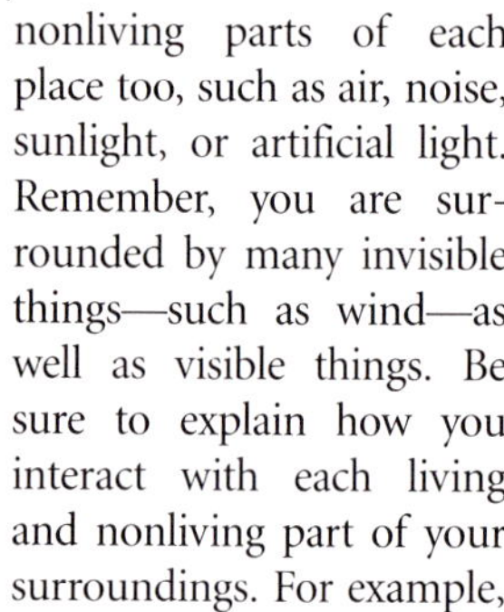

EXPLORE!

In how many different surroundings do you carry out your everyday activities?

For a full day, keep a journal of the different places in which you work, play, and live. Record which plants, animals, or other organisms you interact with. List the nonliving parts of each place too, such as air, noise, sunlight, or artificial light. Remember, you are surrounded by many invisible things—such as wind—as well as visible things. Be sure to explain how you interact with each living and nonliving part of your surroundings. For example,

EXPLORE!

In how many different surroundings do you carry out your everyday activities?

Time needed 20 to 25 minutes

Thinking Processes
Observing and inferring, Recognizing cause and effect

Purpose To recognize how one interacts with one's surroundings.

PROGRAM RESOURCES

Teacher Classroom Resources

Study Guide, page 43
Laboratory Manual, pages 65-68, Human Impact on the Environment L3
Concept Mapping, page 20, Ecosystem L1
Multicultural Activities, page 27, The Yanomami L1; page 28, The Yangtze L1
Take Home Activities, page 20, Dust–The Home Ecosystem L1

PROGRAM RESOURCES

Teacher Classroom Resources

Making Connections: Across the Curriculum, page 27, You and the Environment L3
Making Connections: Technology and Society, page 27, Protecting the Rain Forests L1
Transparency Masters, page 51, and **Color Transparency,** number 24, Animal in Wrong Environment L1

did you drink any water? Eat a piece of fruit? Ride a bicycle? Next, think of how separate places might be related or connected to each other. How might something that happens in one place have an effect on another place?

As you filled out your journal, you became aware of the many different living things that you interact with each day. No matter where you are, you interact with plants, animals, and other organisms. But you also interact with nonliving things. You breathe in oxygen, feel the warmth of the sun, or brace yourself against the force of the wind. You are surrounded by your environment. The environment consists of all the nonliving things around an organism. These nonliving things affect the life of the organism. A person may get goose bumps because a chilly breeze begins to blow. Birds and animals might be poisoned by chemicals used to control insects that are harmful to crops. A plant may grow only so tall because it is wedged in a crack in the sidewalk with little soil beneath.

Think back to the journal you kept. You may have been in several different environments. School, a soccer field, a movie theater, a bus or subway car, a grocery store, or a crowded beach are some examples. Now think of the place where you live. The particular place where an organism lives is its **habitat**. Your habitat might be a house, an apartment, or a trailer. A starfish may live in an underwater cave. A rattlesnake's habitat may be a canyon in the desert.

POPULATIONS, COMMUNITIES, AND NICHES

Figure 12-2 shows some of the animals that were discussed in the chapter opening. These animals live on the grasslands of Africa. In this natural habitat in the wild, large herds of zebra and gnus can be found next to a smaller number of giraffes. Each individual animal within each group is a member of a population. A **population** is a group of individuals of the same species that live in a certain area at a certain time. For example, all the giraffes shown in Figure 12-2 belong to the same population.

DID YOU KNOW?

Your large intestine is the habitat for certain types of bacteria. These organisms produce vitamins that your body needs to survive. Intestinal bacteria can survive only when their environment within your body supplies what they need for life.

FIGURE 12-1. The mallard's habitat is this small pond and the grassy area next to the water's edge.

Teaching the Activity

Student Journal Choose an activity, such as sweeping the sidewalk, and have students write a journal entry about interacting with their surroundings.

Expected Outcomes

Journal entries should indicate a variety of surroundings and parts of each with which students interacted.

Answers to Questions

Answers will vary, but one example is that if you have an especially active day at school, you may want to have more of a snack than usual when you get home.

2 TEACH

Tying to Previous Knowledge

Relate the study of animals in Chapter 8 to that of plants in Chapter 9 in methods of seed dispersal by consumers. For example, in the East African savannah, acacia tree fruit contains a seed which may be eaten and destroyed by beetle larvae. But when the acacia fruit is eaten by grazing animals, the acids of their digestive systems kill the larvae. The seeds pass out of the animals in their feces. Thus the seeds can be spread to germinate elsewhere in the savannah.

Concept Development

Theme Connection As students investigate the surroundings in which they and other organisms carry out their everyday activities, they should develop an appreciation for the way in which living and nonliving parts of the environment interact to form ecosystems. This theme of interaction and systems becomes evident as the students do the Explore activity on pages 358-359.

OPTIONS

Multicultural Perspectives

Have students from different countries identify an environment in their native country. Have them share pictures, photographs or recollections of plant and animal populations that live there. Then have them point out similarities and differences with the environment in which they now live.

Meeting Individual Needs

Gifted Have students research and report on the artificial reefs that have been built to provide habitats for sea plants and animals. Ask students to either construct a model from papier-mache or other materials or draw on paper the major components of these reefs. L2

Concept Development

Student Text Question What are five populations that live and interact with you? Describe the relationships you have with each other. *Possible answers include dogs that you feed and play with, pine trees that shelter your house from the wind, tomato plants that provide you with food, chipmunks that live in your stack of firewood, and birds that eat insects from your lawn.*

FIND OUT!

Can three different bird species share the same habitat?

Time needed 15 to 20 minutes

Thinking Processes Interpreting scientific illustrations

Purpose To illustrate how different species of warblers can feed in the same tree.

Teaching the Activity

Discussion Make sure students understand how the key is to be used. L1

Expected Outcomes

Students should be able to recognize that these three species of birds are able to feed in the same tree because they have different niches.

Conclude and Apply
The different species feed in different parts of the same tree.

FIGURE 12-2 Populations of zebras, giraffes, gazelles, and other organisms live together in this community.

Choose one of your environments. What animal and plant populations live there?

As you study the different populations in Figure 12-2, notice that they interact with each other. Plants such as the grass and animals such as the gazelles are food for other species. When gazelles flee, they warn others of danger. Bushes in such a grassland provide shelter for birds. Together, these populations form a community. A **community** is made up of all the populations that live and interact with each other in an area.

Think of the community in which you live. What are five populations that live and interact with you? Describe the relationships you have with each other.

Can different populations share the same habitat? This next activity will show you.

FIND OUT!

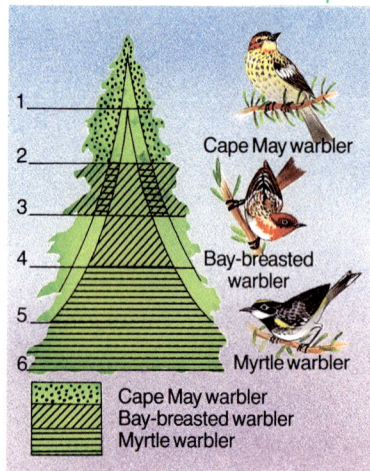

Can three different bird species share the same habitat?

Copy the outline drawing of the tree on a sheet of white drawing paper. Add the two lines to the inside of your drawing. These lines divide the tree into (1) the region nearest the trunk, (2) the middle part of the branches, and (3) the outer region of the branches. Use a ruler to draw lines 1 through 6 representing the six height zones. Make sure that the lines divide the tree into six equal zones. Follow the key for each warbler and fill in your drawing to show where each bird species feeds. In which parts of the tree does each warbler feed? Which birds share the same parts of the tree?

Conclude and Apply
How can three bird species feed in the same tree?

OPTIONS

Enrichment

Activity
Acquire a picture with a large population of a single species of plants or animals that is fairly evenly distributed throughout the picture, a photo of bats on a cave ceiling for example. Make one copy of the picture for each student. Have one group of students individually estimate the number of members of the population contained in the picture. Have students in a second group attempt to count the actual number of members. Tell the students in the third group to divide the photo into a gridwork of squares, count the members in a representative square, and multiply that number by the total number of squares. Have students silently record their numbers and the approximate time it took to obtain them. Then have them compare answers among themselves and with other student groups. COOP LEARN

When you completed the Find Out activity with the three different warblers, you found out that they all shared the same habitat. However, you also saw that they did not share the same areas of the tree. If you observe other communities in nature, you will find the same thing. Many populations live successfully in the same area because each species fills a specific **niche** (nihch) in that area. A niche is the role of an organism within its community. A barn cat, for example, fills a certain role in a farm community by eating mice and rodents. An organism's habitat is part of its niche. What an organism eats, when it eats, and where it eats are also part of its niche. The way an organism reproduces and raises its young are part of its niche, too. In your community, what is the niche of house cats?

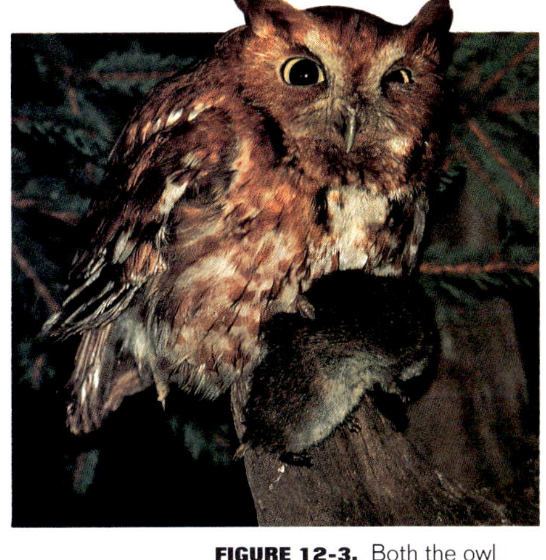

FIGURE 12-3. Both the owl and mouse fill specific roles, or niches, within their community.

Think again about the animals on the African grassland. Giraffes feed on trees, but so do animals like the black rhinoceros and the dik-dik. Each species finds food at a different level of the tree. Hippos spend the hot days in the water and graze on grass at night, while gazelles graze during the day. Oxpecker birds eat insects that live on Cape buffalo. Each type of organism lives in the same habitat, finds food, reproduces, and interacts with other types of organisms. Yet no two types of organism meet their needs in exactly the same way. Each organism fills a particular niche. In this way, organisms can exist together in the same community.

FIGURE 12-4. The rhinoceros lives in the same habitat as the giraffe, but fills a different niche.

ELEMENTS OF AN ECOSYSTEM

You have learned that organisms interact with each other in their community. They also interact with nonliving things—their environment. These relationships form an ecosystem. An **ecosystem** is a community of organisms interacting with one another and with the environment. A rotting tree stump is a small ecosystem.

Concept Development

Discussion Ask students which would be easier to find, the size of a plant population or the size of an animal population. Have them explain their answers. *It would probably be easier to find the size of a plant population because plants don't move.*

Inquiry Question How is the habitat of a squirrel different from its niche? *A squirrel lives in trees in a forest. Its niche involves everything the squirrel does, such as storing nuts to eat.*

Student Text Question In your community, what is the niche of house cats? *Possible answer is to sleep in the sun and eat cat food.*

MAKING CONNECTIONS

Math

Use fish and game magazines to find graphs that show changes in animal population size. Make transparencies of the graphs and show the transparencies on the overhead projector. Have students interpret the graphs and explain trends in the populations.

Content Background

No living things—plant or animal—lives alone. Every living thing depends in some way upon certain other living things.

The word *ecology* comes from the Greek word *oikos* meaning "house" or place to live and *-ology* meaning "the study of." Ecologists study how organisms act together and how they are adapted to their environments.

All parts of Earth where life is found make up the *biosphere*. Ecologists learn about the biosphere by studying smaller and simpler ecological units within it.

Teacher F.Y.I.

The savanna grasslands in Tanzania may seem to be composed of one species but actually contain 55 kinds of guinea grass and 43 species of dropseed alone.

Multicultural Perspectives

Concern about the well-being of Earth's varied ecosystems has increased in recent decades, but the concept is not new. Beginning about 2500 B.C.E. Chinese scientists developed a view of the entire universe as one huge organism. Scientists kept thorough records of natural events, including the weather and star movements. Natural disasters were interpreted as symptoms of the emperor or his officials failing in their duties and thus making the organism ill. Explore with students the current view of the role of humans in environmental disasters facing some ecosystems today. L1

3 Assess

Check for Understanding

Have students answer Check Your Understanding questions 1-4. After students share the niches they named in response to the Apply question, ask them to name their community and ecosystem. *A possible answer is a rural town beside a river in the midwestern plains.*

Reteach

Explain the relationships between population, community, and ecosystem. Point out that populations interact to make a community. Stress that communities and nonliving things make up the ecosystem. L1

Extension

Have students who have mastered the concepts in this section find out how wind and temperature interact to produce the windchill factor. The windchill is an example of how two environmental factors interact. L3

4 Close

Activity

Select a habitat close to the school such as a nearby tree or pond. Have students observe it for several minutes. Ask the class what populations they found there and what niche each species occupied. Discuss the nonliving components of the ecosystem and how the populations affect and are affected by them. L1

a

b

FIGURE 12-5. Ecosystems may be small, like this pond (a), or large, like a city (b).

Here insects, bacteria, and other organisms interact with one another and are affected by sunlight, temperature, wind, water, and soil. Moss, for example, may grow on the cool, dark side of the trunk, while a snake burrows into the soil by the roots. Cities, redwood forests, polar regions, and oceans are examples of larger ecosystems.

In this section, you learned that living and nonliving things interact with each other. You discovered that you and other organisms can be a part of different communities. You began to examine the relationships within communities and ecosystems. In the next section, you'll explore this interaction even more.

Check Your Understanding

1. Give an example of a population of plants.
2. What is the difference between a population and a community?
3. What is the difference between a niche and a habitat?
4. **APPLY:** Describe the niche you fill in your community. Identify how this niche benefits two other populations that share your community.

Answers to Check Your Understanding

1. Sample answers include pine trees in a forest, grass in a field, or dandelions in a yard.
2. A population is a group of individual organisms belonging to the same species and living in the same area at the same time. It is just one part of a community. A community involves different populations of organisms and their interactions.
3. A habitat is just one part of a niche; a niche also involves what an organism eats, how an organism reproduces, and so on.
4. Possible answers may include watering the lawn. The water is used by the grass to grow and by earthworms to keep their skin moist.

12-2 Organisms In Their Environments

FOOD PRODUCERS AND CONSUMERS

You may remember from Chapter 10 that all animals consume other organisms for food. These animals may consume other animals, plants, or plants and animals. You may remember from Chapter 11 that plants produce their own food. Think back to the organisms pictured in the zoo at the beginning of this chapter. Which of the organisms in the picture are consumers? Which are producers? Producing or consuming food is one of the major niches an organism fills. It's one of the major ways in which organisms interact within their environments.

OBJECTIVES

In this section, you will

- describe a food chain and its relationship to a food web;
- explain how natural cycles are important in the environment.

KEY SCIENCE TERMS

decomposer
food chain
food web

EXPLORE!

How do organisms get their food?

Following is a list of organisms that you might find if you took a walk around your school. Study the list and classify the organisms into two groups: those that can make their own food and those that cannot make their own food.

Section 12-2

PREPARATION

Concepts Developed

This section illustrates the cycle of energy from the sun to producers, consumers, and decomposers within ecosystems. Water and nutrient cycles are also presented as nonreplenishable resources that must be used and recycled if organisms are to survive.

Planning the Lesson

In planning your lesson on organisms and their environment, refer to the Chapter Organizer on pages 356A-B for timing suggestions, resources, and additional materials that will help you in your presentation of the lesson concepts.

For adequate development of the concepts presented in this section, we recommend that students do the Explore activity on page 363.

1 MOTIVATE

Discussion Make a bulletin board entitled "Web of Life." Ask the students for their help in connecting pictures of organisms with yarn to illustrate food chains and food webs. Discuss the roles of producers, consumers, and decomposers and how they are interdependent.

EXPLORE!

How do organisms get their food?

Time needed 10 to 15 minutes

Thinking Processes
Classifying

Purpose To recognize organisms as either producers or consumers of food.

Teaching the Activity

Activity You could extend this activity by introducing the terms *herbivore, carnivore,* and *omnivore* and having students further classify the organisms they identified as consumers. L1

PROGRAM RESOURCES

Teacher Classroom Resources

Study Guide, page 44

Critical Thinking/Problem Solving, page 20, Problems of Introducing a Species to a Community L3

cactus	fern	earthworm
gerbil	student	geranium
moss	bird	fish
grass	ant	butterfly
spider	aquarium plant	tree

Which organisms did you classify as producers, or plants? Which did you classify as consumers, or animals?

DID YOU KNOW?

In order to survive, a moose must eat about 35,000 kg of plants per year. This amount equals the weight of about 24 U.S.-made cars.

Now look at the organisms you classified in the Explore as consumers. Some consumers, such as the gerbil, eat only plants. Other consumers, such as the spider, eat only animals. Still other consumers will eat both plants and animals. Which type of consumer are you? Are all humans the same type of consumer?

In the first section, you learned that each organism has its own niche. One kind of consumer, called a decomposer, has a special niche within the community. A **decomposer** is an organism that gets its food by breaking down dead organisms into nutrients. Look at Figure 12-6. Have you ever seen mold on a rotting log or on an old tomato? These organisms, called fungi, are decomposers. Bacteria are decomposers, too. Think of how the world would look if decomposers didn't exist.

Producing, consuming, and decomposing to obtain food are ways organisms interact. Do the next Investigate activity to observe these relationships in an ecosystem you make yourself.

FIGURE 12-6. By breaking down substances in nature, decomposers fill a special niche within a community, whether on food (a) or on a log (b).

a

b

Expected Outcomes

Students should have little trouble distinguishing these organisms as either plants (producers) or animals (consumers).

Answers to Questions

1. Producers: cactus, fern, moss, grass, geranium, tree, aquarium plant
2. Consumers: earthworm, gerbil, student, fish, bird, butterfly, ant, spider

2 TEACH

Tying to Previous Knowledge

In Chapter 8 students studied animals and learned that they were consumers, while in Chapter 9 they found out that plants were producers of food energy. This chapter brings these two kingdoms together by describing the natural cycles with which they are involved.

Concept Development

Student Text Question Are all humans the same type of consumer? *Humans can eat both plants and animals. Vegetarians choose to eat only plants and those foods derived from plants.*

Discussion Ask students to name foods they eat that do not originate with green plants. Help them trace the foods they list back to the producer that began the food chain.

Inquiry Questions Herbivores are called primary consumers, while carnivores are called secondary consumers. Why do you think this is? *Herbivores get food by eating producers directly, while carnivores get their food energy indirectly by eating the herbivores.*

Activity Have students list organisms in or around their homes that are producers and organisms that are consumers. *Producers: green house plants, trees, shrubs; Consumers: people, pets-dogs, cats, fish, gerbils, etc.* L1

OPTIONS

Enrichment

Research Have students research and report on Biosphere II, the ecological project in Arizona. The intent of this project is to produce a self-contained ecosystem capable of sustaining a human crew for two years. Have students create an illustration of the Biosphere identifying and labeling the food chain and natural cycles that the project simulates.

INVESTIGATE!

12-1 A MODEL ECOSYSTEM

In this activity, you will **make a model** of an ecosystem and **observe** the relationships among organisms within it.

PROBLEM

How do organisms interact in an ecosystem?

MATERIALS  

aquarium with screen lid
small plants (ferns, vines, or other)
gravel
soil
water
crickets
oatmeal
charcoal
small stones
anole
warming light
water cup

PROCEDURE

1. Copy the data table.
2. Place the aquarium in a sunny area but not in direct sunlight.
3. Put a layer of gravel and charcoal 2 cm deep in the bottom.
4. Cover the first layer with a layer of soil 3–4 cm deep. Then add the stones.
5. Add the plants in a variety of areas, allowing enough space for growth.
6. Spray water on the plants and soil so they are moist.
7. Add the anole and a small water cup. Add 4 crickets twice a week and 2 flakes of oatmeal once a week. Add water when necessary.
8. Turn on the warming light to provide warmth for the anole. Close the lid.
9. Keep a daily record of the happenings in the ecosystem for two weeks. **Observe** both the living organisms and the nonliving features. Record your observations.

DATA AND OBSERVATIONS

DATE	ORGANISM	OBSERVATIONS

ANALYZE

1. What are the living and nonliving parts of this ecosystem?
2. Which organisms are consumers?
3. Which organisms are producers?
4. Would you **classify** oatmeal as a producer or a consumer? Why?
5. What relationship occurs between the anole and the plants?

CONCLUDE AND APPLY

6. Describe the feeding relationship that exists between the organisms in this ecosystem.
7. **Going Further:** If you wanted to fill more niches in this ecosystem, what could you add to it?

INVESTIGATE!

12-1 A MODEL ECOSYSTEM

Time needed 40 minutes the first day, 5 to 10 minutes per day for two weeks observation and feeding

Materials See student activity.

Thinking Processes Making and using tables, Observing, Making models

Purpose To observe the interaction of organisms in a model ecosystem.

Preparation You may need to use a glass lid if you have small crickets that could get through the screen top. Use a grow lamp if you lack a sunny area for the aquarium.

Teaching the Activity

Discussion Give the students hints as to what they should look for when making observations. L1

Troubleshooting Have access to a second anole if the first should die (or escape).

Expected Outcomes

Students should observe feeding and sheltering relationships between the living parts of the ecosystem.

Answers to Analyze/Conclude and Apply

1. living-anole, crickets, mold (if formed), and plants; non-living-light, soil, charcoal, stones, gravel, water
2. anole, crickets
3. plants
4. Oatmeal is a producer because it is a plant part.
5. The plants shade and shelter the anole. They produce oxygen that the anole breathes. The anole exhales carbon dioxide that the plants need for photosynthesis.
6. Oatmeal (from a producer) is eaten by the crickets, which are eaten by the anole. Mold decomposes the oatmeal.
7. Sample answers include a consumer that would eat the plants and another consumer that would eat the anole.

PROGRAM RESOURCES

Teacher Classroom Resources

Activity Masters, pages 49-50, Investigate 12-1

Concept Development

Theme Connection All living things require energy for maintenance, growth, repair, and reproduction. Feeding relationships within an ecosystem pass this energy from one organism to another. While green plants can absorb light energy, other organisms must acquire energy from producers, either directly, by consuming them, or indirectly, by consuming the consumers that have eaten producers.

Using the Photo Figure 12-7 (b) illustrates a symbiotic relationship between the oxpecker and the water buffalo. The bird is eating insects that feed on the water buffalo. In a symbiotic relationship, food, shelter, support, or transportation is provided for one or both organisms. When both organisms benefit, the relationship is called mutualism. Ask students how the water buffalo benefits from this relationship. *The water buffalo can't reach its back to remove the bothersome insects.*

MAKING CONNECTIONS

Writing

Have students write a short story that illustrates the flow of energy in a food chain. Make sure that the students include a producer capturing sunlight and making sugar during photosynthesis, a plant-eating consumer, a meat-eating consumer, and a decomposer.

ENERGY FLOW IN AN ECOSYSTEM

Whether you observe a small ecosystem, such as your model in the last activity, or a large ecosystem, such as the ocean, you will find feeding relationships among the organisms. Food is required for the life processes of every organism, whether it is a producer, a consumer, or a decomposer. How do producers, consumers, and decomposers interact?

Remember that through the process of photosynthesis, plants use light energy from the sun to make food. This chemical reaction changes water, carbon dioxide, and light into sugar and oxygen. The sugar is food that can be stored and used later by the plants.

When animals—consumers—eat the plants, the energy in the food is passed from the plants to the animals. These animals are then eaten by other animals, which in turn may also be eaten. Each time, food energy passes from one animal to the next. Food is also passed on when decomposers break down dead organisms. Each organism in this relationship is like a link in a chain. A **food chain** is a model of how the energy in food is passed from organism to organism in an ecosystem.

Figure 12-7 shows a simple food chain. Sunlight is used by plants to produce food in the form of sugar. Plants store this food in roots, leaves, and stems. The rabbit eats the plants. Some of the food in the plants is stored in the

FIGURE 12-7. Food passes through each link in a food chain as one organism feeds on another (a), or feeds on food provided by another (b).

OPTIONS

Meeting Individual Needs

Learning Disabled Have students play the parts of a food chain in a community. Have students identify what plants or animals they are and whether they are producers or consumers. L1

rabbit's body, some is changed into heat, and some is used when the rabbit hops, eats, and breathes. The hawk eats the rabbit, stores some of the food from the rabbit, and uses the rest to carry out its life processes. This flow of food energy from one organism to another continues throughout the entire food chain.

FOOD WEBS

A feeding relationship in a single food chain is simple. However, most organisms get their food from more than one source. For example, a bear eats fish, berries, honey, and insects. An owl eats different kinds of rodents and snakes. Grass is eaten by rabbits, cattle, deer, and horses. Thus, an organism can belong to several different food chains. When related food chains are combined, a food web is formed. A **food web** is the combination of all the overlapping food chains in an ecosystem. Figure 12-8 is an

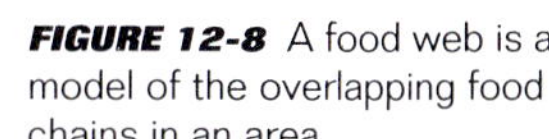

FIGURE 12-8 A food web is a model of the overlapping food chains in an area.

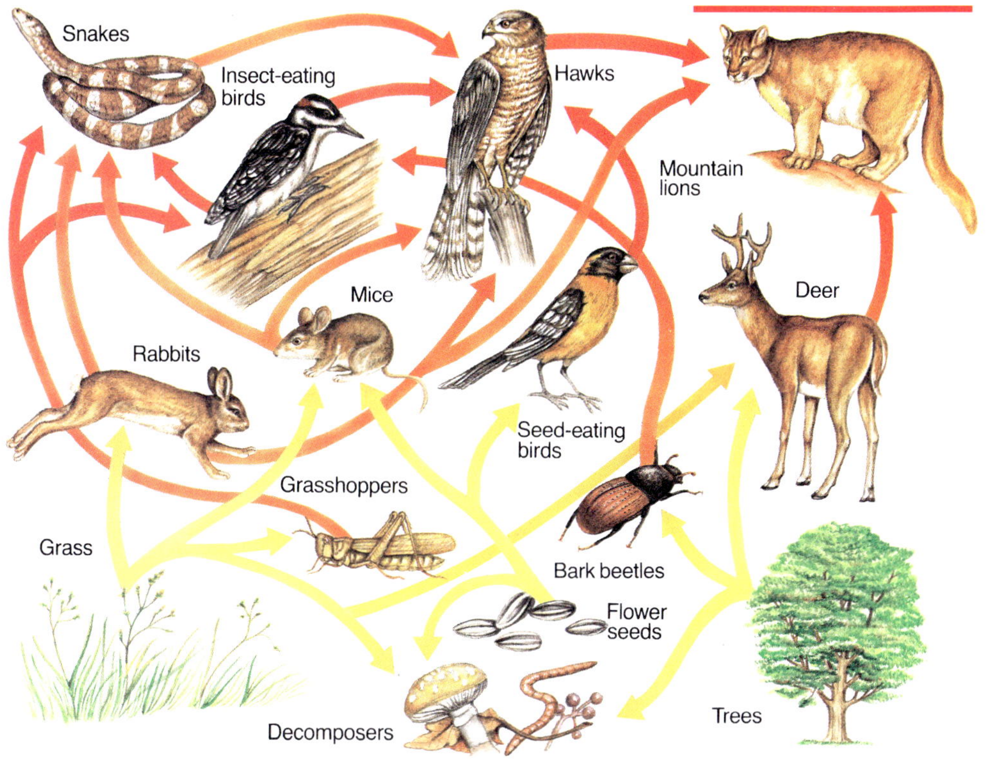

Concept Development

Activity Describe or diagram how organisms may change places in the food chain throughout their lives. *Tadpoles eat plants whereas frogs and toads eat animals. Many insect larvae also eat producers and then become meat-eaters as adults.*

Uncovering Preconceptions The complex interactions of some food webs have been long misunderstood and have led to the misuse of pest control methods over the years. For example, many people, including ranchers, believe the grasshopper to be a voracious pest, destroying crops. Yet at least one grasshopper, the lubber, eats only broad-leaved plants, like the sunflower. This eating habit lets more sunlight and moisture reach the grass roots, which actually improves grazing.

Debate As you move along the food chain from producers to consumers, not all of the energy from plants is being passed on. As the text points out, some of the energy is also used by the organism and some is changed to heat. When the consumer itself is eaten, even more of the original producer's energy is lost. Some agriculturalists have pointed out that we could feed a nutritious diet to Earth's entire present population if we limited food production to crops. But, as long as we continue to feed plants (crops and grain) to livestock for meat production, we will be unable to properly feed everyone.

Form two teams to debate the following: Should efforts be made to eliminate the raising of livestock in order to feed more people on a vegetarian diet? Humanitarian, health, economic, and cultural factors should be taken into consideration by both sides. L3

Multicultural Perspective

Bilingual or multicultural students may have difficulty recognizing the animal and plant populations mentioned and pictured in the text. Whenever possible, encourage them to share information about food chains and ecosystems in their native countries. Relate these producers and consumers to those illustrated in the text. The assistance of a bilingual student or parent may be effective.

Concept Development

Student Text Question In this web can you follow the food chain that an oriole belongs to? *flower seeds → oriole → hawk → mountain lion*

Inquiry Question Can you think of another advantage that consumers of varied diets have over those with limited diets? *A properly varied diet provides a better balance of nutritional elements than a limited diet.*

Activity Make a chart that shows at what ocean depths you would expect to find producers, consumers, and decomposers. Explain your chart.

depth	type
surface	producer, consumer
middle range	consumer
bottom	decomposer, consumer

Producers would most likely be found near the surface where the most sunlight is available for photosynthesis. Consumers could be found at any depth, although plant-eaters would likely feed near the surface. Decomposers could be found near the ocean floor where organic debris settles.

SKILLBUILDER

1. insect larvae
2. crayfish
3. bass
4. person L1

example of a food web. Can you follow the food chains that the seed-eating bird belongs to in this web?

Consumers with varied diets—in other words, those that belong to a fairly large food web—have a better chance of survival than those with limited diets. Can you figure out the reason? If something happens to disturb one supply of food, the consumer can obtain food from another food chain in the web.

NATURE'S CYCLES

A light bulb needs a constant supply of electricity in order to provide light. Organisms also need a constant supply of energy to live. The sun provides the energy that flows through most of the food chains in our world.

Organisms also have other needs for survival, including water and nutrients. These needs are met from a limited supply of Earth's natural resources. Unlike energy from the sun, these resources can't all be continually replaced. Instead, they are constantly being used and recycled. Without the recycling of materials, organisms would quickly run out of the water and nutrients they need.

Water Cycle

Figure 12-9 shows how water is recycled in Earth's ecosystems. Do you recall from Chapter 5 how liquid water can change to gas and back again? Heat from the

FIGURE 12-9. Water is continually recycled for use.

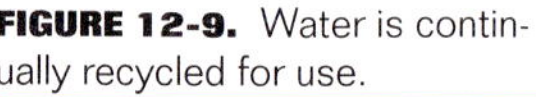

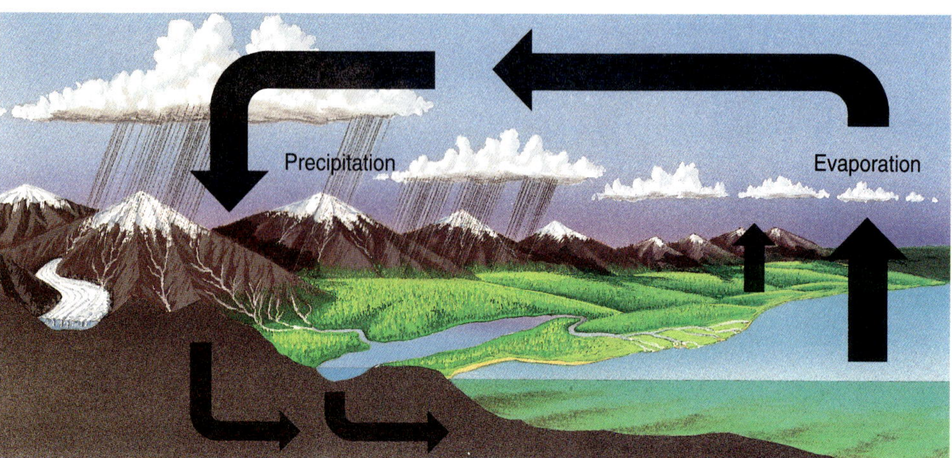

PROGRAM RESOURCES

Teacher Classroom Resources

Transparency Masters, page 49, and **Color Transparency,** number 23, Cycles L2

Critical Thinking/Problem Solving, page 8, Flex Your Brain

OPTIONS

Meeting Individual Needs

Visually Impaired Pair visually-impaired students with fully-sighted students. Have students develop and tell a story with a setting based in a particular ecosystem. The community and the nonliving components should be central to the story. COOP LEARN

sun causes water in Earth's oceans to evaporate. Heated air rises and carries the water vapor up into the cooler atmosphere. Here the water vapor forms clouds. Eventually, the water falls from the clouds as rain or snow.

Most of the rainwater falls back into Earth's oceans. Some of the water moves into the soil. Plants absorb water from the soil through their roots. Animals drink the water or obtain it by eating plants. Both plants and animals use or store some of the water and return the rest of it to the environment. Plants release water through their leaves. Animals release water with waste products. Water evaporates, and the cycle continues.

SKILLBUILDER

SEQUENCING
Study the list of organisms below. Decide in which sequence (or order) they should be placed to make the most likely food chain. If you need help, refer to the **Skill Handbook** on page 648.
bass
insect larvae
person
crayfish

Nitrogen Cycle

Nitrogen is an element used by most organisms to build proteins and other body chemicals. While most of the atmosphere is made of nitrogen, organisms can't directly use this form of the element. Instead, bacteria in the soil and in the roots of bean and pea plants change the gas into a form that can be taken in and used by plants. Animals get their nitrogen by eating either plants or animals that have eaten plants. The nitrogen is returned to the soil when animals release waste products or when dead organisms decay. Figure 12-10 shows this nitrogen cycle.

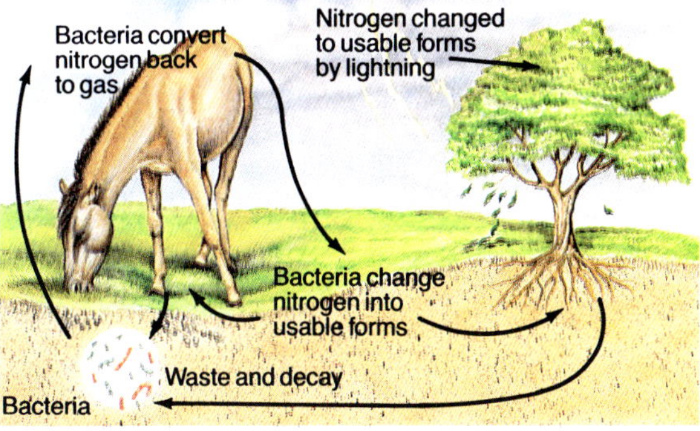

FIGURE 12-10. Nitrogen gas must be changed to another form by bacteria before organisms can use the element to build body proteins.

Oxygen–Carbon Dioxide Cycle

At this very moment, plants, animals, and most other organisms are removing oxygen from the atmosphere. Why hasn't Earth's oxygen supply been used up? The answer is that oxygen is recycled.

Remember from Chapter 11 that during respiration, plants and almost all other organisms take in oxygen and release carbon dioxide. Carbon dioxide also enters the atmosphere when decomposers break down dead organisms. However, during photosynthesis, plants take in carbon dioxide from the air and release oxygen, as shown in Figure 12-11.

Concept Development

Demonstration Demonstrate evaporation and condensation in the water cycle by boiling water in a tea kettle. Hold a cold glass plate over the steam and the steam will condense.

Activity Give students photocopied diagrams of the water, oxygen, carbon dioxide, and nitrogen cycles without labels. Have them fill in the labels.

Content Background

The process by which inorganic materials move from the atmosphere or soil into living organisms and back again is called a biogeochemical cycle.

Oxygen and carbon make up much of the body's carbohydrates, proteins, and fats. They are also involved in many chemical reactions. The oxygen-carbon dioxide cycle is driven by photosynthesis and respiration.

The nitrogen cycle includes four major processes: nitrogen fixation, ammonification, nitrification, and denitrification. In nitrogen fixation, bacteria that live on the roots of legumes (alfalfa, clover, peas, and beans) convert nitrogen into ammonium compounds. Lightning also plays a role in nitrogen fixation. In ammonification, bacteria break down nitrogen-containing amino acids from animal wastes and dead organisms. Chemosynthetic bacteria oxidize ammonia compounds to produce nitrites and nitrates in nitrification. In denitrification, bacteria break down nitrates, releasing nitrogen gas back into the atmosphere.

Flex Your Brain
Have students use the Flex Your Brain activity to Explore ECOSYSTEMS

Teacher F.Y.I.

Less than 3 percent of the water on Earth is fresh. Most of this water is frozen in the polar ice caps. Only a very small amount of all water is available to land organisms for metabolism.

3 Assess

Check for Understanding

1. Have students diagram a food web for organisms in your area. Discuss the importance of food webs and how human activities or natural disasters disrupt food webs.
2. Have students share the food chains they constructed for the Apply question. Identify the producer(s) which appeared most often.

Reteach

Play the food web game. List producers, consumers, and decomposers in a food web on separate index cards. Give a card to each student. Give each producer a ball of colored yarn. Have producers roll the ball to their primary consumers, who roll it to each subsequent consumer until each chain is complete. This creates a food web. This will help students understand the interrelationships among organisms in food chains. L1

Extension

Have students who have mastered the concepts in this section construct a food web by choosing an animal and then using field guides and reference books to find out what the animal eats and what eats the animal. L3

4 Close

Activity

Use the classroom terrarium as an ecosystem. Have students identify producers (mosses and liverworts) and consumers (salamanders, turtles, lizards). Point out that the decomposers are bacteria and fungi. L1

FIGURE 12-11. Because of photosynthesis and respiration, oxygen and carbon dioxide are continually recycled.

Lately, many people have become concerned with another way in which carbon dioxide is released. Sometimes dead organisms do not decay. After millions of years, they turn into fossil fuels such as coal. When the fossil fuels are burned, carbon dioxide is released. The use of fossil fuels has greatly increased since the 1800s. Thus, the amount of carbon dioxide in the atmosphere has also increased. The increase of this gas in the atmosphere has caused a rise in the temperature of the air. Continued high use of fossil fuels is changing the delicate balance of Earth.

In the last chapter, you read about another human activity that can affect the oxygen-carbon dioxide cycle. Cutting down large sections of Earth's rain forests can result in less oxygen being produced and released into the air because there are fewer plants to carry out photosynthesis.

You have learned that all organisms interact with the living and nonliving parts of their environment in order to meet the basic needs for survival. Some of the materials they need are recycled continuously. The natural recycling program of Earth ensures that living things will be able to obtain the materials needed for life.

Check Your Understanding

1. Explain the relationship between a food chain and a food web.
2. Is it possible to find a food chain that includes only a producer and decomposer? Explain your answer.
3. Describe what might happen if the water cycle was interrupted.
4. **APPLY:** Identify a meat or fish product that you have recently eaten. Construct a food chain that shows the feeding relationships that preceded your eating the product. Place yourself at one end of the food chain.

Answers to Check Your Understanding

1. A food chain is one line of food transfer from organism to organism. A food web consists of all the food chains that overlap in an ecosystem.
2. Yes, a producer may die from a disease and decay.
3. Eventually all of the water would be used. Oceans and rivers would dry out. All organisms would die.
4. Possible answer may look like: sun → aquatic plant → fish → student.

12-3 How Limiting Factors Affect Organisms

LIMITING FACTORS

At the zoo, you'll notice that animals are displayed in different environments. Some animals, such as penguins, are housed behind glass, where the temperatures can be kept cool during hot weather. Others, such as rattlesnakes, are found in hot, dry display areas. Still others, such as bats, are literally kept in the dark. Why do all these different animals have such different requirements?

OBJECTIVES

In this section, you will

- identify some limiting factors;
- describe adaptations of organisms to limiting factors.

KEY SCIENCE TERMS

limiting factor

EXPLORE!

How do ecosystems differ?

Suppose your class wants to have an aquarium. You are a member of the committee that has been chosen to plan, purchase the materials, and set up the aquarium. Some members of the committee want a freshwater aquarium, while others want a saltwater aquarium. Visit a pet shop or use resource materials to find out what factors need to be considered when setting up each kind of ecosystem. Pay careful attention to the mineral content of the water, temperature, types and sizes of organisms that can be placed together, and the number of organisms. Then decide which ecosystem you would rather maintain and why.

Section 12-3

PREPARATION

Concepts Developed

Now that the students understand relationships between living and nonliving members of an ecosystem, they are introduced to limiting factors. These factors are the conditions that determine the survival of an organism, population, or species in its environment. Biotic and abiotic limits are shown, as well as adaptations that some plants and animals have made in order to survive.

Planning the Lesson

In planning your lesson on how limiting factors affect organisms, refer to the Chapter Organizer on pages 356A-B for timing suggestions, resources, and additional materials that will help you in your presentation of the lesson concepts.

For adequate development of the concepts presented in this section, we recommend that students do the Explore activity on page 371.

1 MOTIVATE

Discussion Discuss the area in which you live and the limiting factors there. Talk about climate, geography, and soil. Ask the students how the plants and animals in your region have adapted to your environment.

EXPLORE!

How do ecosystems differ?

Time needed 25 to 30 minutes

Thinking Processes

Comparing and contrasting

Purpose To select an ecosystem to maintain by considering the requirements of freshwater and saltwater aquariums.

Teaching the Activity

Activity You may want to organize a field trip to a pet shop or invite an employee of a pet shop to visit your class. L1

Expected Outcomes

Students should be able to support their choice of a freshwater or saltwater aquarium.

Answer to Question

Choices will vary. Saltwater aquariums are usually thought to be more difficult to maintain. Saltwater fish are more colorful, however.

2 TEACH

Tying to Previous Knowledge

Review the characteristics and requirements of life from Chapter 7, with particular emphasis on adaptation. Regardless of the area in which you live, there are limiting factors which should be recognizable by students. Mountainous or desert conditions provide obvious examples, but bird migration or hibernation in winter or competition from human encroachment into natural habitats are other possible factors.

Concept Development

Theme Connection The stability of many plant and animal populations is maintained only within a certain range of conditions. Rattlesnakes, sharks, marigolds and cactus are each adapted to a particular environment and will die if there is a sudden change in the living or nonliving components.

Activity Different kinds of grasses grow well in different regions of North America. Have students visit a local nursery or lawn care center to find out the variety of grass most suited for lawns in your area. Have them find out the soil conditions, watering practices, and fertilization requirements particular to that variety of grass.

FIGURE 12-12. Temperature is a limiting factor for most organisms. Neither the penguins nor the rattlesnake would survive in each other's habitat because of the difference in temperature.

As you worked on the Explore activity, you quickly found out that freshwater and saltwater aquariums are very different ecosystems. Factors such as size, water temperature, amount of light, and type of minerals dissolved in the water vary. Organisms within the aquarium survive only if all the conditions they need to live and grow are met. The plants and animals from a freshwater aquarium probably would die if put into the saltwater aquarium.

The environment determines whether an organism can live in it. Think about a shark. Will that shark survive in the ocean or a lake? Of course, you know that sharks live in the ocean. The shark is a saltwater organism, and most species of sharks can't survive in a freshwater lake. Now think about plants. Cacti grow in the desert. Too much water will kill them. A **limiting factor** is any condition that influences the growth or survival of an organism or species.

FIGURE 12-13. Water is a limiting factor for the shark, and too much water is a limiting factor for the cactus.

Limiting factors can be nonliving, environmental conditions, such as temperature, wind, chemicals in the soil, amounts of light and water, as well as pollution in the water or air. Limiting factors can also be the relationships between living organisms in a community. You will see what kinds of relationships can be limiting as you continue to read the chapter. But first, do the next Investigate activity to determine some nonliving limiting factors for plants.

PROGRAM RESOURCES

Teacher Classroom Resources

Study Guide, page 45

Other Resources

Balance-Predator-Prey Simulation. software, Diversified Educational Enterprises

Odum, Eugene P. *Ecology and Our Endangered Life-Support Systems.* Sunderland, MA: Sinauer Associates, Inc., 1989

OPTIONS

Enrichment

Research Ask students to use the library and research the introduction of Russian thistle, starlings, English sparrows, gypsy moths, and kudzu into the United States; or have students read and report on the work of John Garcia, who studies the interactions of animals and their environment in California.

I N V E S T I G A T E !

12-2 LIMITING FACTORS

You have learned that certain factors will influence how well an organism will live and grow in an environment. Now, assume that you are a gardener trying to produce the healthiest marigolds possible. You will **observe** plants under different watering conditions to **infer** if the conditions limit the growth of marigolds.

PROBLEM

Does amount of water limit plant growth?

MATERIALS

3 or 4 small marigold plants in each of 3 plastic pots
water
marker
masking tape

PROCEDURE

1. Copy the data table.
2. Use masking tape to label the pots 1, 2, and 3.

3. Place the pots in a location that receives a lot of light, but not direct sunlight.
4. Water pot 1 just often enough to keep the soil moist but not wet.
5. Water pot 2 daily so that the soil is always wet.
6. Water pot 3 once every ten days. Make sure the soil is completely dry before watering.
7. **Hypothesize** how the amount of water will affect the appearance of the plants over time.
8. Take care of the plants daily for three weeks and record your observations at the end of each week. **Measure** and record the heights of the plants.

ANALYZE

1. **Compare and contrast** the appearances of the plants in the three pots.
2. How does your hypothesis compare with the results of the activity?
3. **Identify the variable** in this experiment.

CONCLUDE AND APPLY

4. What was the limiting factor in the activity?
5. **Going Further:** Design an experiment that would investigate the effect of temperature on plants.

DATA AND OBSERVATIONS

Sample data

PLANTS	WEEK 1		WEEK 2		WEEK 3	
	APPEARANCE	HEIGHT (CM)	APPEARANCE	HEIGHT (CM)	APPEARANCE	HEIGHT (CM)
1	Healthy Growth					
2	Healthy, but yellowing leaves					
3	Some wilting of leaves					

INVESTIGATE!

12-2 LIMITING FACTORS

Time needed 15 to 20 minutes to set up and 5 minutes per day for three weeks

Materials 3 or 4 small marigold plants in each of 3 plastic pots, water, marker, masking tape

Thinking Processes
Observing and inferring, Forming a hypothesis, Separating and controlling variables, Designing an experiment to test your hypothesis

Purpose To investigate the effect of different watering conditions on marigold plant growth.

Preparation You can either use small plants or start with seeds. If you start from seed, sprouts should appear in a few days as long as the soil is warm. Use sterile potting soil to minimize danger from harmful organisms in garden soil.

Teaching the Activity

Discussion Tell students the proper way to water the plants. They should water around the entire surface and pour until water comes out of the drainage holes.

Troubleshooting Avoid south and west sunlight which may burn the plants. If this is unavoidable, set plants back from windows or moderate the sunlight with thin curtains. Keep plants away from hot air registers which lower humidity.

Expected Outcomes

The healthiest plants should be in pot 1.

Answers to Analyze/Conclude and Apply

1. The plant in pot 1 looked healthy; the plant in pot 2 is yellow; and the plant in pot 3 is brown or dead.
2. Answers will vary depending on the hypothesis made.
3. the amount of water
4. too much or too little water
5. A possible experiment might have one plant near an air conditioner, one near a heater, and one where it is not affected by either appliance.

PROGRAM RESOURCES

Teacher Classroom Resources

Activity Masters, pages 51-52, Investigate 12-2

Concept Development

Inquiry Questions How do animals endure the heat in some deserts? *They stay in their burrows during the day and come out at night.*

Why do most tropical rain forest animals live in trees? *More food sources are available in the lighted area of the canopy.*

Discussion Have students explore whether any place on the rain forest floor would ever have thick vegetation. *Any place where sunlight reaches the forest floor, such as a clearing, an area where a tree has fallen, or along a river bank, might have thick vegetation.*

MAKING CONNECTIONS

Geography

Have students find out about the nonliving limiting factors in the area in which they live. Direct them to use a globe or world map to determine the latitude, longitude, and altitude of their school. Have them research the climate, including the length, amount of rainfall, and average temperature of each of the seasons and the number of days of sunshine, as well as soil conditions, pollutants, erosion, and human land development and use.

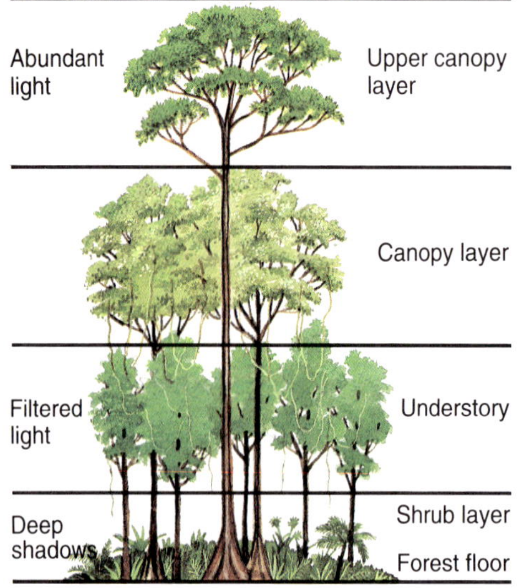

FIGURE 12-14. In a rain forest, most organisms live in the layers above the forest floor.

NONLIVING LIMITING FACTORS

The Investigate activity showed you that plants need a certain amount of water to grow. Although plants that receive too little or too much water may not die, they certainly don't look healthy.

Surviving within a Range

Every organism has a best set of conditions in which it thrives. But often that specific set of conditions isn't available in its environment. Think about temperature for instance. Most organisms are able to survive if the temperature in an environment falls within a certain range. For example, some fish in a freshwater aquarium are comfortable and carry on their life processes in water that is room temperature (22°C). They can live in water that is 5.5 degrees warmer or colder. If the water's temperature goes beyond that 11-degree range for too long, the fish die. Tropical fish have a different temperature range within which they can survive. All organisms have a temperature range in which they can live.

The amount of direct sunlight an ecosystem receives is another limiting factor. Go to a greenhouse or a store that sells plants. A tag with instructions for proper care is often included with each plant. Bright, direct light kills some plants. Other plants thrive in it.

FIGURE 12-15. The rain forest floor has fewer plants and animals than the top layer.

A rain forest is a good example of how the amount of sunlight influences plant growth. Look at Figure 12-14. Most of the forest's plants and animals live in the upper layers, where sunlight is abundant. As you travel down the layers into the areas of filtered light and shade, the number of plants and animals becomes smaller.

How often have you listened to a news report about the effects of a drought on an area? The amount of rainfall in an environment is also a limiting factor. Generally, each ecosystem has an average level of rainfall.

PROGRAM RESOURCES

Teacher Classroom Resources

Laboratory Manual, pages 69-72, Living Space [L2]; pages 73-76, Water Pollution [L3]

Making Connections: Integrating Sciences, page 27, Searching for Life on Other Planets

FIGURE 12-16. What do you think has been happening to the numbers of wild animals in this area?

SKILLBUILDER

COMPARING AND CONTRASTING

Look below at the list of topics presented in this chapter. Decide how the topics in each pair are similar by comparing them. Then decide how the topics are different by contrasting them. Explain your answers to the class. If you need help, refer to the **Skill Handbook** on page 653.

habitat — environment
food chain — food web
predator — prey

Many factors work together to determine that level. If rainfall doesn't meet that level over a long period of time, plants die. Can you infer what happens to the animals, including humans, in the ecosystem?

OTHER ORGANISMS AS LIMITING FACTORS

You have just learned about some nonliving limiting factors. Now you will find out how relationships between living organisms can also be limiting factors.

Recall that in Section 12-1 you learned that each organism fills a certain niche in its community. Competition results when two organisms try to fill the same niche. The ecosystem can't supply enough to meet the needs of both organisms. The organisms will compete for food, shelter, water, and other needs until one organism is forced to leave the area or dies.

The most obvious example of this limiting factor is what happens to

FIGURE 12-17. Many times lions will invade each other's territory in search of food.

Concept Development

Using the Photo The photograph in Figure 12-16 shows the bulldozing of forest land to make way for housing. The destruction of their habitat will drive many animals away. Some other animals may actually benefit from the change, depending on whether the land is paved over or planted with grass seed, for example.

SKILLBUILDER

1. Both terms relate to the surroundings of living things. The particular place where an organism lives is its habitat. The environment consists of all the nonliving things around an organism.
2. Both terms describe the feeding relationships among organisms in the same community. A food chain shows how food energy flows through a community, while a food web is the combination of all the interlocking food chains in the community.
3. Both describe animals in the same community and their part in the food chain. Predators are animals that catch and eat other animals. The animals they eat are called prey. L1

Student Text Questions (Figure 12-16) What do you think has been happening to the numbers of wild animals in this area? *The development of homes is forcing wild animals to leave the area.* Can you infer what happens to the animals, including humans, in the ecosystem? *Besides the disruption to the natural cycles, when plants are removed from the ecosystem, the producers are removed from the food web. Animals, including humans, would have trouble finding enough to eat, even if they could find an alternate water supply.*

Concept Development

Uncovering Preconceptions Students may believe that the decrease in the population of predators is solely due to the death of those that cannot find enough food to eat. Actually, some organisms vary their number of offspring depending on limiting factors.

Inquiry Questions What happens to the animals in an area when the plants in the area change due to man-made or natural causes? *Animals adapted to the new conditions move in.*

Why can people live in so many different environments? *They can control the conditions necessary to live almost anywhere on Earth.*

Activity One of the limiting factors for organisms is space. Have students do this simple activity to find out how much space each person has in the classroom. Have them find the area of the classroom in square meters by using a meterstick to measure the length and width and multiplying the two measurements. Divide the result by the number of individuals in the class. Have students discuss whether this factor influences their ability to learn.

Student Text Question What do you think will happen next to the size of each population? *With fewer predators, the mice population will increase. Then the number of owls will also increase.*

Demonstration Take apart an owl pellet to see what the owl eats. The pellets consist largely of unwanted parts of the animals the owls eat; they are coughed up twice a day. Soak the pellet in water for a few hours. Then, using tweezers, separate the bones, teeth, claws, beaks, heads, insect wings, and fur to aid in identification. L3

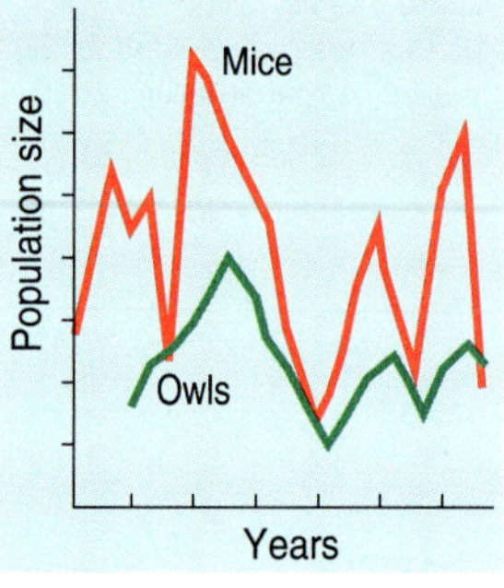

FIGURE 12-18. In a predator-prey relationship, the size of each population rises and falls in related cycles.

wildlife as humans move into an area. As shown in Figure 12-16, humans build houses, cut down trees, pave roads, and carry on other activities that greatly change the environment. Many wild animals are forced to live elsewhere.

A close look at a food chain can provide a clue to another behavior-linked limiting factor. Animals that catch and eat other animals are called predators. The animals they eat are called prey. The predator-prey relationship has an effect on the size of populations of both predators and prey. Usually the numbers of predators and prey within a community will stay about the same. But look at what happens when the size of one population changes. Figure 12-18 shows how the populations of mice and owls change over several years. You'll notice that as the mice (prey) population rises, the number of owls (predator) also rises. At some point the large owl population will eat so many mice that only a few will be left. Without enough mice to eat, the owl population will then decrease. What do you think will happen next to the size of each population?

HOW ORGANISMS ARE ADAPTED

The success of an organism within its environment depends on how well it is adapted to that environment. Remember that an adaptation is a characteristic that increases the chance of an organism to survive in its environment. Look at how some organisms meet their needs in spite of the limiting factors in their environment.

FIGURE 12-19. This epiphyte, or "air plant," is adapted to life above the ground in a rain forest.

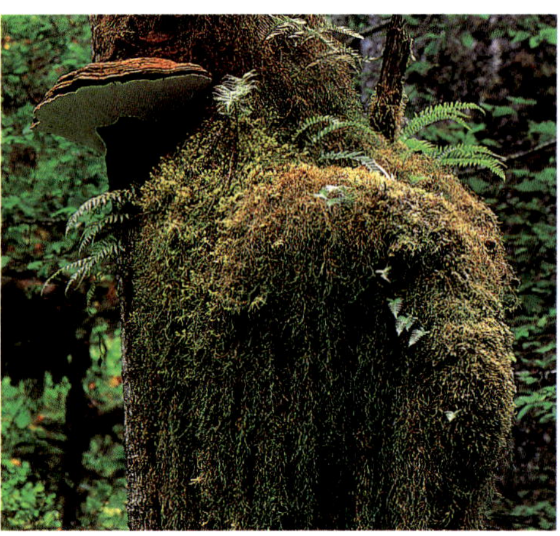

Lack of rainfall in a desert is a limiting factor for many types of plants. Why, then, do cacti grow successfully in a desert environment? You'll recall from Chapter 11 that a cactus plant is adapted in two ways. First, its extensive root system quickly absorbs any water that may fall during a rainstorm. Second, its stems and leaves prevent the loss of water. The waxy covering called the cuticle prevents water loss through the stem. The leaves of the cactus are long, sharp spines. Because

OPTIONS

Multicultural Perspectives

George Washington Carver (1864-1943) conducted important research to extend and diversify the food chain. He found hundreds of new ways to use peanuts, sweet potatoes, and pecans. Peanuts have nodules on their roots in which nitrogen-fixing bacteria can operate. These bacteria help replenish the soil by returning nitrogen to it. Born a slave in Missouri, Carver attended school in Iowa and taught at Iowa State University. Then for 47 years, he served as director of agricultural research at Tuskegee Institute in Alabama. Carver's work reduced the South's reliance on soil-depleting cotton. His efforts provided farmers with an incentive to rotate crops and to plant crops that replenish soil. Although honored as a member of the US National Inventors Hall of Fame, Carver never took out patents on his discoveries, saying "God gave them to me, how can I sell them to someone else?"

FIGURE 12-20. This alpaca is adapted to cold temperatures and less oxygen in the air.

there is less leaf surface area, less water is lost through the spines than would be with other types of leaves.

Plants in rain forests are adapted to different limiting factors. The lower levels of the rain forest receive very little light. Any nutrients in the topsoil are quickly absorbed by the roots of tall trees, so the soil has few nutrients. Plants called epiphytes (EHP uh fites) grow high up on the branches of the taller trees. They grow in the top layers of the forest and get water from the air and nutrients from decaying plant matter near their roots. Figure 12-19 shows you what an epiphyte looks like.

How do we know?

Earth's Warming

Scientists agree that average temperatures on Earth have risen 0.5°C over the last 100 years. They also agree that the amount of carbon dioxide in the atmosphere has increased over the last century. Measurements and observations have given us this information. However, scientists don't agree on how much this increase will affect Earth's climate or, if so, how soon a climate change will occur.

Models of climate changes can be made by computers. Scientists input data on past climate conditions. They also add data such as wind speed, air and water temperatures, land features, and precipitation patterns. All this information is analyzed by the computers, and models of climate changes are produced. Sometimes the models don't agree. You might ask why. Think about how often your local weather forecasts don't agree about tomorrow's weather. Now try to predict the climate for the next century.

Concept Development

Discussion Have students discuss and give examples of the kinds of adaptations different organisms have made to the ecosystems in which they live.

Content Background

The biosphere of Earth is divided into biomes, which are large geographic areas that have similar climates and climax communities. The major biomes are the tundra, northern coniferous forests, deciduous forests, grasslands, tropical rain forests, and desert. Succession is a gradual change in a community over time. Succession involves replacement of the dominant species in a given area by other species. The most important cause of succession is the altering of the physical environment by the community itself. Communities tend to alter the area in which they live in such a way as to make it less favorable for themselves and more favorable for other communities. There are two main types of competition. Intraspecific competition occurs between organisms of the same species. Interspecific competition occurs between organisms of different species.

Teacher F.Y.I.

Owls hunt mainly at night. In the dark, they can see from 10 to 100 times better than humans. They also have superb hearing.

Enrichment

Activity Have student groups research and record the ways in which the peanut can be used as a food, such as cooking oil and peanut butter. Then have the groups share their findings and develop a list combining the lists of each group. **COOP LEARN**

3 Assess

Check for Understanding

Assign Check Your Understanding questions 1-4. As an introduction to the Apply question, ask students if they have ever gone on an overnight camping trip. Ask those who have what they brought with them. Discuss how these items protected them from nonliving and living limiting factors.

Reteach

Review common human activities with the students and ask them to identify limiting factors in them. Breathing, eating, drinking, and wearing clothes are a few behaviors that reveal limiting factors. L1

Extension

Have students who have mastered the concepts in this section plant a cactus dish garden, paying particular attention to how requirements for soil, water, and light differ from those of other plants. L3

4 Close

Discussion

Talk about living and nonliving limiting factors that apply to the students in the class. Include factors such as the amount of food they require, the temperature range within which they can live, etc. Ask them how they could survive in areas that they are not adapted to, such as the polar regions, the ocean, and the desert. L1

FIGURE 12-21. Earth is made up of a variety of ecosystems.

Just as plants are adapted to various environments, animals are also adapted. Some humans live in the very high mountain areas of the world. Animals that live in this environment have adaptations to several limiting factors. For example, as you climb to higher elevations, the temperature drops, and the amount of oxygen in the atmosphere decreases. Humans who live in this environment breathe more deeply, and they have enlarged hearts that circulate oxygen-carrying blood more rapidly. They also have more red blood cells to carry oxygen throughout their bodies. Animals that live in this environment, such as the alpaca in Figure 12-20, are protected against the cold by their thick coats of wool. Their bodies are adapted to the thinner air because their blood is also very efficient at carrying oxygen.

If you were an astronaut orbiting Earth, you would be able to see the white areas of the polar caps, the blue oceans, the brown deserts, and the green grasslands. Even at that distance you could recognize that Earth is home to a variety of ecosystems. But only a closer look shows you how much the characteristics of each ecosystem influence the lives of the organisms that live there. It may be easy to study how plants and animals adapt or react to one limiting factor. It is more difficult to determine how they adapt to a variety of limiting factors.

Check Your Understanding

1. What effect would placing a plant in a box have on its growth? What limiting factor(s) is involved?
2. Why would competition among organisms increase when resources are limited?
3. Would the adaptations of a cactus help or harm the plant if it were placed in a wet environment?
4. **APPLY:** Limiting factors exist for humans as well as other organisms. Suppose you were going on a camping trip in a desert. Make a list of the limiting factors you would need to deal with. Then identify the equipment you would need to protect yourself from these limiting factors.

Answers to Check Your Understanding

1. The plant's growth would be slowed or stopped. Light and possibly temperature are the limiting factors.
2. The same number of organisms would be competing for a smaller supply of resources.
3. These adaptations would harm the plant since they are designed to help the plant get more water.
4. Possible limiting factors include little water, cold nights, and hot days. Possible equipment includes canteens, blanket, water, and an umbrella to shade out the sun.

EXPANDING YOUR VIEW

CONTENTS

A CLOSER LOOK

ECOSYSTEMS INSIDE

Ecosystems are not just outside of you. You are part of an ecosystem that you can't see. This ecosystem, inside your intestines, plays a role in keeping you healthy. At birth, your digestive system is free of bacteria. Early on, however, bacteria—some of it carried on the food you eat—begin to live and reproduce in your intestines. Some types, such as *Escherichia coli*, help you digest your food by "eating" some of the large molecules your body is unable to break down. In this way, your internal ecosystem is formed. You provide food for the bacteria, and the bacteria help you to digest it, providing you with additional nutrients.

Usually your immune system keeps this ecosystem in balance by preventing either too many bacteria, or the wrong types of bacteria, from growing. Occasionally, however, this ecosystem gets out of balance, and you get sick.

Besides digestion, bacteria have other important functions in your body, such as making vitamins. For instance, a normal diet does not contain as much vitamin K as your body needs. Fortunately, the bacteria in your

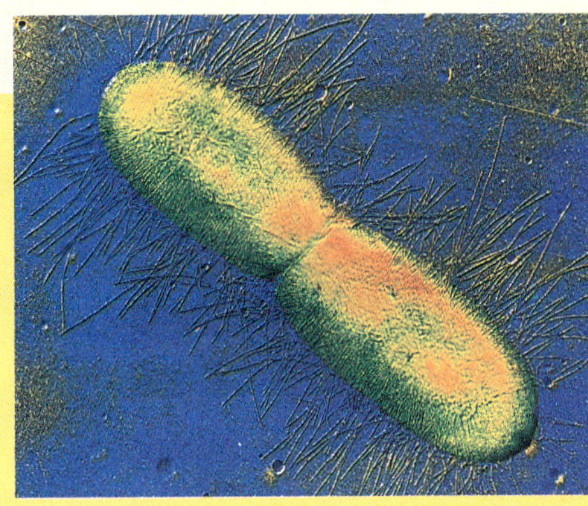

intestines make extra vitamin K for you. Without enough vitamin K, your body couldn't form blood clots to stop you from bleeding when you cut yourself. Vitamin B_{12} is also made by bacteria. Your body uses it to make red blood cells. If you didn't have enough vitamin B_{12}, you might suffer from anemia. Maintenance of your internal ecosystem, then, is important for keeping you healthy.

WHAT DO YOU THINK?

Antibiotics are used to treat bacterial infections. What do you think happens to the bacteria normally found in your intestines when you have to take antibiotics for a long period of time? What do you think would happen if the antibiotic killed only your normal bacteria and not the bacteria making you ill?

EXPANDING YOUR VIEW

Using Expanding Your View

Assign one or more of these excursions to expand students' understanding of the principles of ecology and how they apply to other sciences and other subjects. You may assign these as individual or small group activities.

A CLOSER LOOK

Purpose A Closer Look reinforces the discussion of feeding relationships in Section 12-2 by explaining how bacteria break down food in their ecosystem, the human digestive system.

Content Background

Teaching Strategies Infectious bacteria can develop strains immune to the effect of a certain type of antibiotic when they are constantly exposed to it. Some antibiotics have been fed to cattle to enable them to gain weight faster. Ask students if they can see any danger in this practice.

Answers to WHAT DO YOU THINK?

1. If the antibiotic is specific enough, the infectious bacteria should be controlled while the beneficial bacteria are left alone. Otherwise, both types of bacteria would be destroyed, leaving you free from infection but unable to digest your food properly.
2. The infectious bacteria might very well spread unchecked, while you would be further weakened by your body's inability to obtain the nutrients needed for good health.

Going Further Divide the class into groups to research the benefits to humans of other bacteria and organisms. Each group should identify the name of the bacteria or organism, the state of the food (for example, fresh or spoiled) that they eat, and the useful by-product that they leave. Assign from the following: bacteria used in the production of cheese, wine and vinegar, penicillin, vitamin B_{12}, vitamin K, bread dough; bacteria used in soil enrichment; and those used to decompose organic waste in septic tanks. Have groups share their findings with the class. COOP LEARN

CHEMISTRY CONNECTION

Purpose The Chemistry Connection extends the discussion of the role of plants in the oxygen-carbon dioxide cycle, which is presented in Section 12-2. Students also have the opportunity to observe the production of oxygen by plants as a by-product of photosynthesis.

Content Background The simplified equation for photosynthesis is:

$$6CO_2 + 12H_2O + \text{light energy} \rightarrow C_6H_{12}O_6 + 6O_2 + 6H_2O$$

Whereas land plants utilize the free oxygen in the atmosphere, aquatic plants use carbon dioxide dissolved as a gas or as carbonates in the water. The rate of photosynthesis in land plants is greater when there is an increase in the amount of carbon dioxide. Earth's early atmosphere, therefore, may have allowed plants to grow faster, and produce even more oxygen, than they do today.

Teaching Strategies Have students examine the effects of sunlight on the amount of oxygen produced. Place one setup in bright sunlight, one setup in a shaded area, and cover one with a box to eliminate any sunlight. After several hours, compare the pockets of air in the top of the containers.

Chemistry Connection

OXYGEN MAKERS

The Earth's atmosphere—what we commonly think of as air—is an almost transparent blanket of gases and tiny particles. It provides several essential ingredients for life: oxygen, carbon dioxide, nitrogen, and water vapor. The atmospheric blanket shields us from the sun's deadly ultraviolet rays and, at the same time, lets the sun's more beneficial rays shine through. The atmosphere also helps regulate Earth's temperature. Without an atmosphere, life as we know it could not exist!

However, Earth's early atmosphere was probably much less hospitable to life. Most scientists believe Earth's original atmosphere was produced by a buildup of volcanic gases: ammonia, carbon dioxide, carbon monoxide, hydrogen, methane, nitrogen, sulfur dioxide, and water vapor. Earth's early atmosphere probably contained very little oxygen, but its current atmosphere is about 21 percent oxygen. So where did all the oxygen come from?

You learned that oxygen is the product of photosynthesis—the process by which plants and some bacteria and algae absorb carbon dioxide from the air, combine it with sunlight and water to convert it to starch and sugar, and then release oxygen into the air. It appears that the oxygen content of Earth's atmosphere began to increase about 3½ billion years ago, when cyanobacteria and algae started growing in the ocean. In a way, we owe our very existence to bacteria and algae.

The ability of plants to convert carbon dioxide into oxygen is one reason why people are so concerned about our vanishing forests. So far, scientists have not found a way to make photosynthesis occur outside living organisms.

YOU TRY IT!

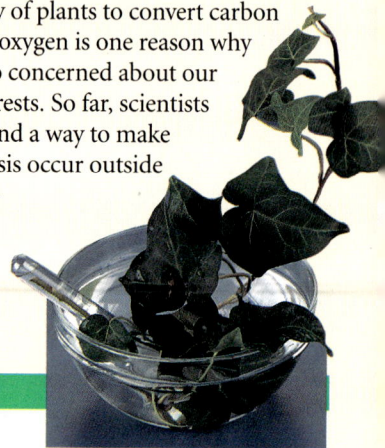

You can observe the results of photosynthesis in action.

Materials

- small live plant with a growing vine or runner
- deep basin or pan
- tall, narrow glass container or test tube
- water hose or a bucket full of water

Procedure

1. Take all of your materials outside to a sunny location.
2. Fill the basin with water.
3. Fill the glass container or test tube to its very brim.
4. Completely cover the open end of the container or test tube with your thumb or the palm of your hand.
5. Place the container upside down in the basin and carefully remove your hand, without letting any air inside.
6. Thread a vine or runner of the plant inside the container while keeping the open end of the container completely submerged. Do not cut the runner from the plant when you do so!
7. Leave the entire setup in the sun for several hours.

When you return, a pocket of air will have formed at the top of the container. Through photosynthesis, the plant will have released oxygen through its leaves inside the container.

Going Further Ask students to write a story from the viewpoint of one of the nonliving components of an ecosystem, air. Have them include the exchange of gases, the presence of sunshine, and the protection afforded by the ozone layer. Suggestions include how they feel when rain forests are chopped down, what the destruction of the ozone layer would do to them, and how they feel different during the day and at night.

SCIENCE AND SOCIETY

SAVING CHESAPEAKE BAY

You may have studied estuaries (ES chyew war ees) in geography or in a science class. An *estuary* forms where a river or other body of water enters the sea, creating a mixture of fresh water and salt water. Chesapeake Bay is the largest estuary in the United States. The bay stretches 185 miles from the north where the Susquehanna River enters, to the south between Cape Charles and Cape Henry in southeastern Virginia. Chesapeake Bay is probably best known for the massive number of crabs and oysters pulled from its shallow waters. In fact, *Chesapeake* is an Indian word that means *Great Shellfish Bay*.

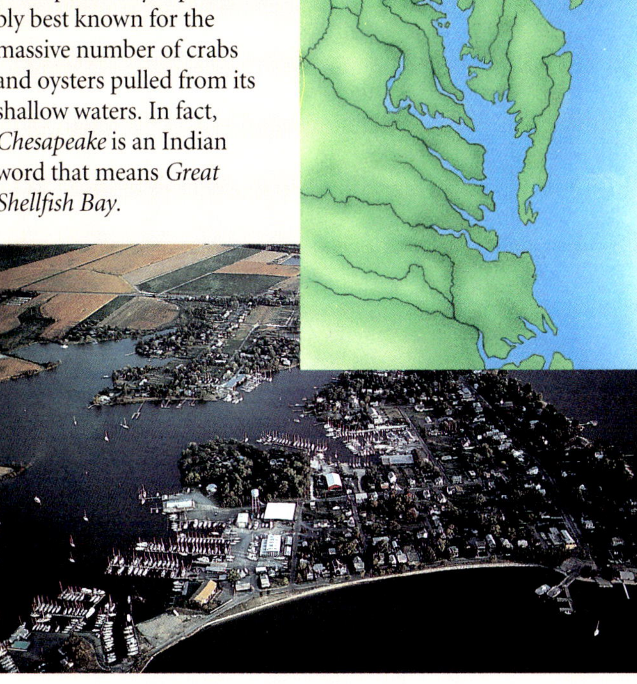

The bay and its 7000 miles of shoreline are also home to many water birds, including Canadian geese, green-backed heron, snowy egrets, and the largest population of ospreys found in the United States.

Forty-six major rivers and hundreds of small tributaries carry fresh water to mix with the salty sea in Chesapeake Bay. But the "fresh" water is really far from fresh. It is full of chemical runoff (contaminated water) from farms, factories, and sewage plants. These chemicals cause diseases in the fish and shellfish—sometimes severe enough to make the people who eat them sick.

But that is only one of the problems. Where water circulation is low—in narrow parts of rivers and estuaries—an overabundance of plant nutrients can cause problems, too. When runoff contains nitrates and phosphates, such as those found in fertilizers, the algae in the water feed on them and reproduce more rapidly. Curtains of these plantlike protists have been known to grow as much as three feet thick! This keeps the sun from reaching any oxygen-producing plants below.

EXPANDING YOUR VIEW

SCIENCE AND SOCIETY

Purpose Section 12-2 explains food chains and food webs. This Science and Society describes how changes in Chesapeake Bay caused by pollution affected the food web in this ecosystem.

Content Background Chesapeake Bay was settled by English colonists in the seventeenth century and fishers, crabbers, and oyster hunters have made their living there ever since. It is estimated that 70 percent of the fish of the Atlantic coastal waters of North America spend at least part of their lives there.

The state of Virginia harvested 693 million pounds of fish in 1990 from Chesapeake Bay—the largest catch of any state in the continental United States.

- The decaying of the algae that form the thick curtains that block sunlight from reaching submerged grasses is caused by bacteria that then consume even more oxygen than the algae. In spite of this, some species have actually flourished in this changed environment—bluefish and menhaden, for example.
- Every piece of land that is cleared near the bay results in four tons of sediment being deposited in the water.
- DDT and other chlorinated hydrocarbons have been replaced by insecticides containing compounds that break down more quickly into nontoxic forms. Biological control agents, or predator insects, may prove to be a better long-term substitute as pests become resistant to insecticides.

EXPANDING YOUR VIEW

Teaching Strategies Fill a large clear glass baking dish with water about halfway to the top. Mix food coloring into a heavily salted (4–6 teaspoons) cup of water. Pour the salt water gently into one end of the dish. Students should see that the salt water sinks to the bottom of the dish. Explain that in an estuary, the mixture of salt and fresh water is not uniform. The force of the river flow and the tides of the ocean produce regions of varying salinity. Most freshwater fish can live only in fresh water. Contamination of this water may not be cleansed rapidly by the ocean tides.

Answers to

WHAT DO YOU THINK?

1. The area may be vulnerable due to pollution from the surrounding population, industry, or farmlands.
2. Careful control of runoff, sewage, and other spills into the estuary could be legislated.

When the nutrients in the water have been used up, the algae die and begin to decay. Rather than solving the problem, the decomposing algae make the situation even worse. The decaying process uses up the oxygen in the water, and the lack of oxygen makes it hard for fish and other aquatic organisms to survive.

Polluted waters take a toll on water birds, too. From the 1950s to the early 1970s, runoff containing the pesticide DDT caused widespread contamination. Organisms have no way of eliminating DDT from their systems. This means the chemical becomes more concentrated in their body tissues with each step up the food chain.

Here's how DDT moved through one food chain in Chesapeake Bay. The runoff contaminated plants and organisms in the water. The fish ate these plants and organisms, or absorbed DDT directly through their skins. Then the birds ate the contaminated fish. When the ospreys ate fish containing DDT, they produced eggs with shells so thin that the chicks were crushed beneath their nesting parents. Because of this, the osprey's breeding population fell to only about 1000 pairs. However, since the United States banned DDT in 1972, the osprey population in the bay has doubled.

Efforts by the states of Maryland, Virginia, and Pennsylvania to clean up the bay have concentrated mainly on wastewater treatment and regulation of development near its waters. Treating sewage more thoroughly than required by law, limiting construction and the use of concrete and asphalt, and finding ways to keep farmers' soil and chemicals on their land and out of the water will all go far to help save the bay.

WHAT DO YOU THINK?

On a map of your state, locate the areas that would be most likely to face problems similiar to those of Chesapeake Bay. Why do you think these areas might be vulnerable? What types of laws or changes could be made to protect them in the future?

Going Further Estuaries, besides often containing large quantities of fish, make good harbors. Major port cities such as New York, London, Hong Kong, and Calcutta are situated on estuaries. On a world map, identify estuaries and major cities that are located on them. Divide the class into small groups and assign each group one of the cities or estuaries. Have students research any destruction to the ecosystem that has occurred there as well as any efforts that are being made to clean it up. Students may find that many of these areas have more fish in them today than they did ten or twenty years ago, while others are getting worse. Have the groups compare notes to see what factors seem to work in cleaning up this fragile type of ecosystem in different areas of the world. **COOP LEARN**

Art CONNECTION

ABUELITOS PISCANDO NAPOLITOS

The painting, *Abuelitos Piscando Napolitos*, shows the harvest of prickly pear cactus fruits, which are used in southwestern cooking. The artist, Carmen Lomas Garza, grew up in Kingsville, Texas. The painting is one of several works that represent Garza's response to the Latino movement. The artist wanted to show Chicano culture "in fine art form."

One thing important to any culture, of course, is the food people eat. The prickly pear cactus the southwestern Latinos use in their cooking is well-adapted to its desert environment.

Spines on a cactus take the place of leaves and help to discourage predators. The fleshy pads that make up the prickly pear and other cacti are actually stems whose spongy tissues hold moisture. In the brief rainy season, these stems expand quickly as the cactus' shallow, but extensive, roots absorb the rainfall.

A number of desert animals use the spiny cacti to protect themselves. The jumping cholla (CHOY yuh) cactus has stems that break off at the slightest touch. Large animals find it very unpleasant. But cactus wrens prefer to nest in chollas because they use the cholla stems to protect the entrance to their burrows.

So you see that the cacti of the desert play an important role in the local ecology. Carmen Garza wished to portray things that her culture finds important, beautiful, and moving.

Carmen Garza probably inherited her talent from her grandmother, who was a skilled needleworker, and from her mother, a self-taught artist. As a teenager, Carmen decided to become an artist. She persued her interest in art in college and received masters degrees in both art and education.

WHAT DO YOU THINK?

1. From the painting, what can you tell about the climate of the southwestern United States?
2. What are some of the things that are important or beautiful to the Chicano culture, as revealed in this painting?
3. How do you think the artist, Carmen Lomas Garza, feels about nature?

EXPANDING YOUR VIEW

ART CONNECTION

Purpose This Art Connection reinforces Section 12-2 by showing how organisms interact within a particular environment.

Content Background Carmen Lomas Garza was born in Kingsville, Texas in 1948. Her mother's family has lived in Texas for many generations, working as ranch hands and on the railroads. Carmen Garza graduated from Texas Arts and Industries University in Kingsville in 1972 with a B.S. in art education. She continued her education at the Juarez-Lincoln Campus of Antioch Graduate School in Austin, where she earned a master's degree in education in 1973. She then went on to Washington State University at Pullman, where she received a master's degree in art in 1979. Her work has been exhibited in galleries in Texas, Pennsylvania, and New York.

Teaching Strategies Have each student choose a particular ecological area such as the desert, rain forest, tundra, coast, etc. Have them research the ways in which the ecology of an area may influence the culture of its people. Have selected students present their findings to the rest of the class for discussion.

Activity Have groups of students research Southwestern cooking. Have them locate recipes that use the fruit of the prickly pear cactus. If possible, obtain some prickly pears from your local market. **COOP LEARN**

Going Further Have students work in pairs to research other artists who painted landscapes or other works that depict a natural setting. Have each pair select one other work and write a short report comparing it to the painting of Carmen Garza. Students should attempt to understand the way that the painting reflects the artist's feelings about nature. Artists may be chosen from almost any school or time. Possibilities include prehistoric cave paintings, Far Eastern silk paintings, or works of the Romanticists, Impressionists, Realists, Postimpressionists, and so on. **COOP LEARN**

Answers to WHAT DO YOU THINK?

1. The climate appears to be dry and sunny due to the lack of grass.
2. Family, as different generations of a family are shown working together; hard work, as the harvesting of crops in the desert is a difficult task.
3. That nature provides for individuals if they are willing to work for it.

TEENS IN SCIENCE

Purpose Teens in Science extends the discussion of limiting factors in Section 12-3 by showing how these can be changed by planting trees.

Content Background Trees are defined as perennial woody plants with a single main stem from which branches and stems extend to form a crown. If they have broad leaves that are shed at the end of the growing season, they are called *deciduous. Coniferous* trees have needles that are shed less frequently. Trees are a source of wood, food, resins, rubber, quinine, turpentine, and cellulose. Tree rings can be used to measure the age of a tree, and often, they reflect climatic conditions of the past. Narrow rings can be an indication of drought or low temperature, while broad rings indicate years of favorable growing conditions.

Teaching Strategies Have students tie bags around leaves in parts of the tree that are not exposed to strong sunlight and compare the amount of moisture that collects with that from the sunny part. Try the experiment with other plants such as evergreens and cacti.

Discussions Ask students the name of your official state tree. Discuss whether there are any of these trees in your community today or if there were any of them in the past.

TEENS *in* SCIENCE

ONE FOR ALL, AND ALL FOR TREES

Have you heard about The Tree Musketeers? No, they don't carry swords or fight bad guys. But in their home town of El Segundo, California, these young people are real heroes.

The Tree Musketeers began when several girls met in a Brownie Girl Scout troop. "We were studying ecology," explains one of the founding members, 13-year-old Sabrina Alimahomed. "We learned how trees help clean the air and create rain. Since our state has an air quality problem and a drought, we felt that we could help by planting some trees." That was more than five years ago. Many of the original members are still active today. Sabrina explains how the organization works.

"The Tree Musketeers teaches people how to plant and care for trees," she says. "We got started by planting one tree, and the organization just grew from there. It's been very positive for us. When we first heard about pollution, many of us felt frightened. We'd all assumed that because we were children, we didn't have to worry about things like the environment yet. But now we know that children need to care about the planet, too. Grown-ups always tell us that we can do anything if we set our minds to it. So we decided to save the world."

There is no doubt about how valuable trees are to the environment. Trees not only produce the oxygen we breathe, they also prevent soil erosion, help control noise pollution by absorbing sound, and help create rain by releasing moisture into the air.

Over the years, more than 300 children have participated in The Tree Musketeers. Hundreds of trees have been planted.

Sabrina continued,"We hope that our work in The Tree Musketeers will continue to help both children and adults realize that when it comes to saving our planet, every person makes a difference."

YOU TRY IT!

This experiment will show how much moisture is released by trees. Gather a clear plastic bag and some string. On a hot, sunny day, tie a small plastic bag around a few leaves hanging on a low tree branch. Leave the bag for a few hours. Now measure the amount of moisture that has collected on the inside of the bag.

Going Further Have students get involved in a tree planting project in the community, if appropriate. Decide where the need is greatest in your area—whether to control soil erosion or noise pollution, produce more oxygen or rain, provide a habitat for local wildlife, or generally improve the beauty of the community. They might consider writing to The Tree Musketeers or any other national or local environmental group for more information on how to get started.

Reviewing Main Ideas

1. A community of organisms interacting with the nonliving environment is an ecosystem.

2. A food chain shows how food energy flows through an ecosystem.

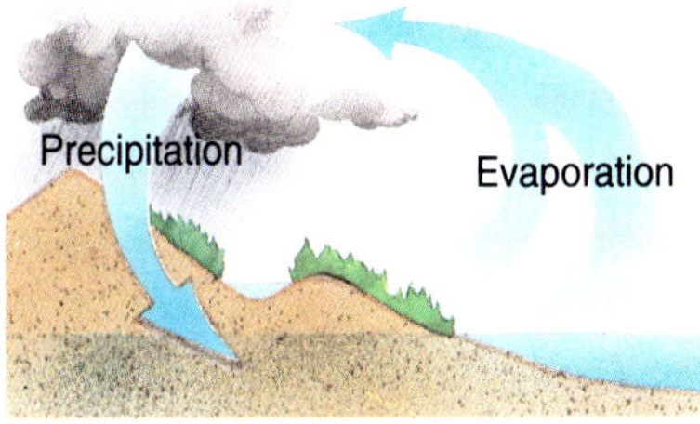

3. Many materials, such as water, oxygen, carbon dioxide, and nitrogen, are constantly being recycled through the environment.

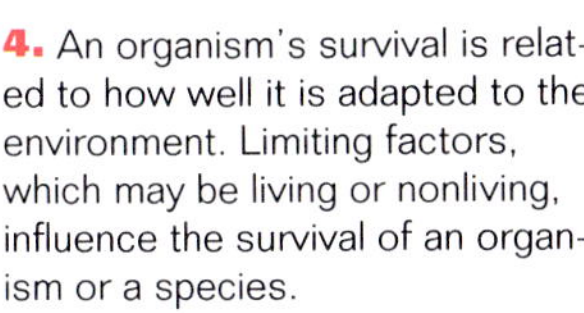

4. An organism's survival is related to how well it is adapted to the environment. Limiting factors, which may be living or nonliving, influence the survival of an organism or a species.

Reviewing Main Ideas

Have students look at the four illustrations on this page. Ask them to describe details that support the main ideas of the chapter found in the captions for each illustration.

Teaching Strategies

Divide the class into four equal groups. Assign each group one of the illustrations. Building on the picture or diagram, have students construct and label a three-dimensional model that incorporates the scene and highlights a main idea of the chapter as stated in the caption. Ideas for the four models include:

1. Use various materials to re-create this woodlands scene inside a cardboard box. Include producers such as the grass and trees, and consumers such as the deer and raccoon. Nonliving components of the scene could include a stream of water and soil. A rotting log could be included to show the work of decomposers in an ecosystem.

2. Construct a model of a food chain. Predator-prey relationships, producers, consumers, and decomposers can be included in a more complex food web.

3. Although this diagram shows the water cycle, this group should attempt to model one of the other natural cycles described in the text and explain it.

4. Re-create a desert environment, adding consumers and nonliving factors to the cacti shown in the illustration. Students should concentrate on limiting factors and the adaptations that plants and animals have made in order to survive under desert conditions.

The groups should share their findings with the class.

Chapter 12

Chapter Review

USING KEY SCIENCE TERMS

Answers

1. Niche is the role an organism fills in a community and includes what it eats and where it lives. Habitat is its home and, therefore, part of its niche.
2. Population is the total number of individuals of a species in an area; community is all of the populations that interact with each other in that area.
3. Decomposers cause the decay of dead organisms; they are part of a food chain, often considered the "end" of the chain.
4. A food chain shows how food energy flows through a community; a food web is the combination of all the interlocking food chains in the community.
5. A limiting factor is a condition within an ecosystem—either living or nonliving—that influences the growth or survival of an organism or species.

UNDERSTANDING IDEAS

Answers

1. producers
2. Prey
3. decomposers
4. niche
5. limiting factor
6. recycled
7. energy
8. habitat
9. photosynthesis
10. adaptations

CRITICAL THINKING

Answers

1. Accept all reasonable answers. One possible answer: Marigolds will turn yellow and die if too much water is provided. They will also die if not enough water is available.

2. Earth has a limited supply of resources, such as water, oxygen, carbon dioxide, and nitrogen. If they were not recycled, we would run out of these resources.

Chapter Review

USING KEY SCIENCE TERMS

community	habitat
decomposer	limiting factor
ecosystem	niche
food chain	population
food web	

For each set of terms below, explain the relationship that exists.

1. niche—habitat
2. population—community
3. food chain—decomposer
4. food chain—food web
5. limiting factor—ecosystem

UNDERSTANDING IDEAS

Complete each sentence.

1. All food chains must include organisms that are____.
2. ____ is food for a predator.

3. Dead organisms are broken down by ____.
4. Two organisms cannot occupy the same ____ at the same time.
5. Lack of rain is a ____ for some organisms.
6. Oxygen, carbon dioxide, and water are continually ____ in the environment.
7. The sun is the source of ____ for most food chains.
8. An underground burrow is the ____ of a prairie dog.
9. In the process of ____, plants use light energy to make their own food.
10. The sharp spines of a cactus are ____ to the desert environment.

CRITICAL THINKING

Use your understanding of the concepts developed in the chapter to answer each of the following questions.

1. Give examples of situations when too much and too little of a material become limiting factors.
2. Explain why natural cycles are important in the environment.
3. Explain why two species cannot occupy the same niche at the same time.
4. Suggest a niche for a
   a. honeybee
   b. cow

PROGRAM RESOURCES

Teacher Classroom Resources

Review and Assessment, Chapter Review and Chapter Test, pages 49-52

Computer Test Bank, Chapter Test

OPTIONS

Cooperative Learning

Consider using Cooperative Learning in the Understanding Ideas, Critical Thinking, Problem Solving, and Connecting Ideas sections of the Chapter Review. COOP LEARN

5. What effect would humans have if they tried to kill all the bark beetles in this community with a chemical?

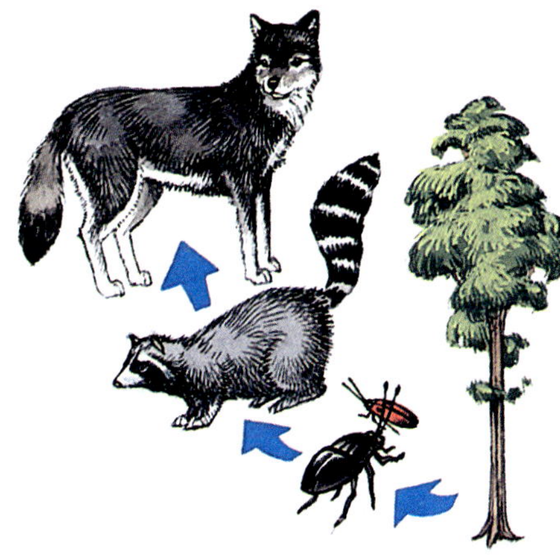

PROBLEM SOLVING

Read the following problem and discuss your answers in a brief paragraph.

Large areas of the rain forest are being destroyed each year. This loss of habitat means fewer animals can live in the remaining area. You are a biologist trying to predict how long the habitat can support three animal populations.

1. Animal A currently has a population of 100. Each year its population doubles. How large will its population be after 1 year, 2 years, 3 years, and 4 years?
2. Animal B has a population of 50. Each year its population triples. How large will its population be after 1 year, 2 years, 3 years, and 4 years?
3. Animal C has a population of 25. Each year its population quadruples. What is its population after 1 year, 2 years, 3 years, and 4 years?
4. Right now the area in the rain forest that you are studying can provide food for 10,000 animals. Because of continued habitat destruction, that number is reduced by 10 percent a year. Find out how many animals the habitat can feed after 1 year, 2 years, 3 years, and 4 years.
5. What can you do to find out how long the habitat can support the three populations?
6. In which year will the total population outstrip the food supply?

CONNECTING IDEAS

Discuss each of the following in a brief paragraph.

1. What effect might cutting down large areas of forest have on the temperature of Earth? Explain your answer.
2. How does a food web show the relationship between organisms in an ecosystem?
3. What role does sunlight play in an ecosystem on Earth?
4. **A CLOSER LOOK** Describe some ecosystems that you are a part of. How are they alike and how are they different?
5. **SCIENCE AND SOCIETY** How are food webs related to the spread of poisonous chemicals and other pollutants in an ecosystem?

3. If two organisms try to occupy the same niche at the same time, they compete with each other for the exact same role and resources. There would not be enough to meet the needs of each species.

4. a. an area near flowers from which the bees can gather nectar

b. an area with plenty of grazing lands

5. Accept all reasonable answers. Students should recognize that the removal of bark beetles from the food chain will have some effect, such as a decline in the raccoon population (due to lost food) or an increase in the tree population.

PROBLEM SOLVING

Answers

1. present population of Animal A—100; first year—200; second year—400; third year—800; fourth year—1,600
2. present population of Animal B—50; first year—150; second year—450; third year—1,350; fourth year—4,050
3. present population of Animal C—25; first year—100; second year—400; third year—1,600; fourth year—6,400
4. at present can support 10,000 animals; after first year—9,000; second year—8,100; third year—7,290; fourth year—6,561
5. Find the total of the three populations for each year. When the total population for one year is greater than the answer you got in problem 4 for that year, you have found the correct year.
6. in the fourth year

CONNECTING IDEAS

Answers

1. If large numbers of plants were killed, more carbon dioxide would remain in the atmosphere. Therefore, temperatures would rise.
2. A food web shows the feeding relationships between organisms.
3. Sunlight supplies the energy producers in the ecosystem use to make food.
4. All of the ecosystems described must provide food, water, and a survivable climate. They will differ in the types of plants and animals.
5. Poisonous chemicals and pollutants enter the body of an organism that is consumed by other animals, endangering their health as well.

LOOKING BACK

UNIT 3
INTERACTIONS IN THE LIVING WORLD

THEME DEVELOPMENT

All living things are structurally similar in terms of cellular organization and chemical reactions occurring within them. They also are similar in terms of their basic life qualities and needs such as food, energy, reproduction, and response to the environment. These concepts were developed in this unit as students were introduced to the variety of living things present on Earth and the technique used for classifying them.

Connections to Other Units

All living things are composed of chemicals. As a consequence of this, living things have many similarities with non-living forms of matter. Thus, living and non-living matter is composed of atoms, molecules, and compounds. The behavior and characteristics of solutions and the presence of acids, bases, and salts are as apparent in living matter as they are in non-living materials. Thus Unit 3 is closely related to Unit 2. The relationship between living things and the systems moving on Earth's surface are explored in the following unit, Unit 4.

Connecting Ideas

Answers

1. Intake of water from the soil takes place via root hairs using osmosis as the process. Water loss from the leaf occurs through the stomates when they are open. Students must be aware of the water cycle and how the different states of water are involved. For example, water as a gas is released from plant leaves and then condenses into clouds.

2. A clue to the difference between living (or once living) and nonliving would be the microscopic organization (cellular organization) of each item.

LOOKING BACK

UNIT 3 INTERACTIONS IN THE LIVING WORLD

CONTENTS

UNIT FOCUS

In this unit, you classified organisms as plants or animals using characteristics such as the ability to move about freely and search for food and water.

You learned how plants can manufacture their own food using sunlight and that animals then rely on this stored food in plants to survive. You also saw how plants and animals form an important part of the oxygen-carbon dioxide cycle.

Try the exercises and activity that follow—they will challenge you to use and apply some of the ideas you learned in this unit.

CONNECTING IDEAS

1. Trace the pathway of water from soil, through a vascular plant to its leaves, and back again to the soil. Explain what processes occurred in which plant parts both inside and outside the plant. Relate the processes inside and outside the plant to their effects on the ecology of the plant's habitat.
2. Obtain samples of a wide variety of objects from your teacher. Design a classification scheme that will enable you to classify living and nonliving things. Decide if other groupings are needed to further classify the living things and the nonliving things.

EXPLORING FURTHER

Design an experiment that will determine if radish seedlings will grow in salt. Be sure to keep all factors except the amount of salt constant. The amount of salt given to the plants will be the only variable in your experiment.

Exploring Further

Radish seedlings will sprout in about 3-4 days after seeds are soaked in water overnight. Use sand or vermiculite in plastic cups as the material for planting the seedlings. Provide a different concentration of saltwater to be used in watering each cup of plants. Mark all plant cups with the saltwater concentration being used. Make sure that all plants receive the same volume of saltwater each time watering takes place. Describe how each plant grows.

TRY IT

Erosion by running water can occur at a very slow rate. But it can also occur very rapidly. What are some of the factors that can affect how rapidly water will erode Earth's surface? Place a layer of small rocks in the bottom of one pan and a layer of sand in the bottom of another. Fill a pitcher full of water. Tilt each of the pans at a 10 degree angle and slowly pour the contents of the pitcher into the raised end of the pan. Predict what will happen to the rocks in the pan. Test your prediction. Now predict what will happen to the sand in the other pan. Test your prediction. Set up both pans again, but this time pour the water in very rapidly. Predict what will happen to the rocks and sand in the pans and test your predictions. Be sure to set a large container under the pans to collect overflow. After you've learned more about erosion of Earth's surface, try to explain your observations.

UNIT 4 SYSTEMS IN MOTION

CONTENTS

UNIT FOCUS

In Unit 3, you learned about the ecology of Earth by investigating the interactions between plants, animals, and the physical world. As you study Unit 4, you'll see how motion affects you and the physical world around you. You'll see how the motion of water, wind, and ice changes Earth's physical appearance and can change the overall ecology of the planet.

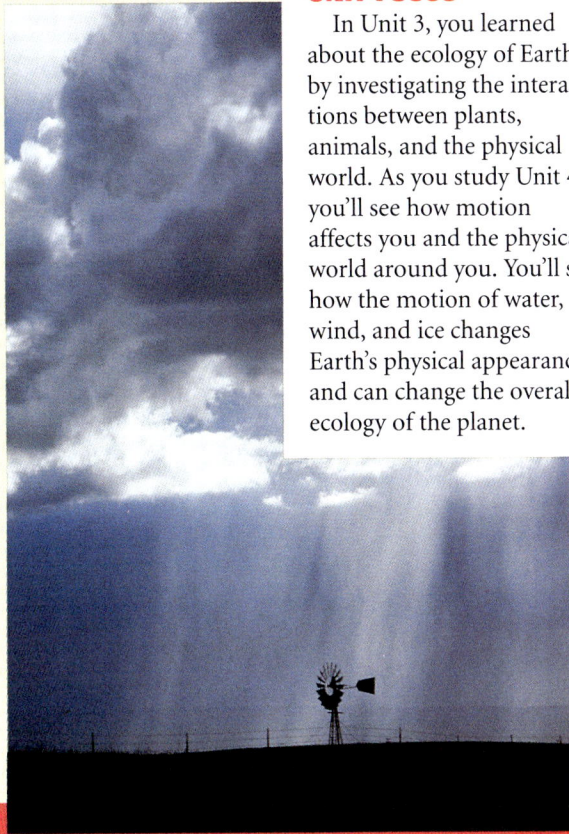

LOOKING AHEAD

UNIT 4
SYSTEMS IN MOTION

THEME DEVELOPMENT

Themes developed in Unit 4 are energy, stability and change, and interactions and systems. How time, distance and displacement are related provides the basis for understanding the changes that take place when motion occurs. Another important focus of this unit is how mechanical and chemical energy interact with matter to weather and erode the surfaces of Earth, and thus create changes in the environment. The importance of soil, a basic element of the biological environment, and how it is formed through the interaction of rock fragments, living things, and erosion processes is also presented.

Connections to Other Units

The concept of motion, both on and near Earth, is strongly related to the next unit. In Unit 5, movement of Earth and Earth materials during earthquakes and volcanoes is described. Also, movement of the moon as part of the Earth-moon system and the effect of this motion on Earth's oceans is explained.

Getting Started

Discussion Some questions you may want to ask your students are:

1. **In which direction does the moon move around Earth?** Students who answer other than east to west, are holding misconceptions.
2. **What force causes water to flow down a mountainside into a valley?** Gravity is the correct answer. Some students may show misconceptions by answering "slope or steepness."
3. **Which Earth material, very important to farmers and gardeners, forms from the weathering of rock?** Some students may not be able to identify the material as soil.

The answers to these questions will help you establish what misconceptions your students may have.

Try It

There are two purposes for this activity. One is to show students that the rate of erosion is dependent on the type of material being eroded. The other purpose is to show students that the speed at which the agent of erosion is applied also affects the rate of erosion. Obtain rocks of about the same size for the pan with rocks. Be sure the depth of the rocks and sand in the two pans is the same. Students should observe that the sand will erode quicker than the rocks when the water flow is slow. The sand will also erode quicker when the water flow is rapid, but additional erosion will occur in the rocks as well, compared to when the water flow is slow.

CHAPTER ORGANIZER

SECTION	OBJECTIVES	ACTIVITIES/FEATURES
Chapter Opener		**Explore!** How would you tell someone where you are? p. 391
13-1 Position, Time, and Speed (3 days)	1. **Specify** the position of an object. 2. **Find** the distance along a path. 3. **Determine** the average speed of a moving object.	**Explore!** How can you use a map to help describe motion? p. 393 **Find Out!** How can you use your pulse as a clock? p. 395 **Investigate 13-1:** Average Speed, p. 397
13-2 Velocity Along a Straight Line (2 days)	1. **Distinguish** between displacement and distance. 2. **Find** the average velocity of a moving object. 3. **Distinguish** between velocity and speed. 4. **Use** the concept of relative velocity.	**Skillbuilder:** Making and Using Graphs, p. 400 **Explore!** What is relative velocity? p. 401
13-3 Acceleration (2 days)	1. **Distinguish** between velocity and acceleration. 2. **Determine** acceleration from velocity change and time.	**Investigate 13-2:** Instantaneous Acceleration, p. 405
13-4 Motion Along Curves (2 days)	1. **Distinguish** between a displacement and a distance along a curved path. 2. **Find** the average velocity for motion along a curved path. 3. **Recognize** situations for which there is an acceleration, called centripetal acceleration, even when the speed is constant.	**Find Out!** How is displacement along a curved path measured? p. 407 **Explore!** What is the direction of acceleration of an object moving along a circular path? p. 409
Expanding Your View	A Closer Look **Around and Around We Go,** p. 411 Life Science Connection **How Fast Do Animals Move?** p. 412 History Connection **History of Time,** p. 413	Technology Connection, **The Technology of Thrills,** p. 415 Art Connection **How Do You Paint Motion?,** p. 416

ACTIVITY MATERIALS

EXPLORE!	INVESTIGATE!	FIND OUT!
Page 391 lined, graph, and blank paper; pencil **Page 393** overhead projector, transparency of House of Terror map; copies of transparency for students **Page 401** battery-powered toy car, paper **Page 409** test tube with stopper, water, record turntable, masking tape	**Page 397** meterstick, stopwatch, masking tape **Page 405** protractor, 10 to 12-cm length of string, button	**Page 407** protractor, metric ruler

Chapter 13
Motion

TEACHER CLASSROOM RESOURCES	OTHER RESOURCES
Study Guide, p. 46 **Critical Thinking/Problem Solving,** p. 21 **Take Home Activities,** p. 22 **How It Works,** p. 14 **Making Connections: Integrating Sciences,** p. 29, **Activity Masters, Investigate 13-1,** pp. 53-54 **Flex Your Brain,** p. 8	**Color Transparency and Master 26,** Distance-Time Graph ***STVS:** *New Skid Control,* Physics (Disc 1, Side 1)
Study Guide, p. 47 **Concept Mapping,** p. 21 **Flex Your Brain,** p. 8 **Making Connections: Across the Curriculum,** p. 29 **Making Connections: Technology and Society,** p. 29	**Color Transparency and Master 25,** Displacement Map ***STVS:** *Mars Ball,* Physics (Disc 1, Side 2) *Wind Engineering,* Physics (Disc 1, Side 2)
Study Guide, p. 48 **Activity Masters, Investigate 13-2,** pp. 54-55 **Multicultural Activities,** p. 30	**Laboratory Manual,** pp. 77-80, Speed and Acceleration
Study Guide, p. 49 **Multicultural Activities,** p. 29 **Review and Assessment,** pp. 53-56	***STVS:** *Safer Roads,* Physics (Disc 1, Side 1) **Computer Test Bank**
	Spanish Resources **Cooperative Learning Resource Guide** **Lab and Safety Skills**

***Science and Technology Videodisc Series**

KEY TO TEACHING STRATEGIES

Teaching strategies have been coded for varying learning styles and abilities. As you review teaching strategies in the margin, the following designations will help you decide which activities are appropriate for your students.

- **L1** Level 1 activities are basic activities and should be within the ability range of all students.
- **L2** Level 2 activities are average activities and should be within the ability range of the average to above-average student.
- **L3** Level 3 activities are challenging activities designed for the ability range of above-average students.
- **LEP** LEP activities should be within the ability range of Limited English Proficiency students.
- **COOP LEARN** Cooperative Learning activities are designed for small group work.

ADDITIONAL MATERIALS

SOFTWARE

Motion and Energy: Physical Science Simulations, Focus.

Motion: A Microcomputer Based Lab, Queue.

Fall Guy: Investigations of Falling Objects, Queue.

Investigating Gravitational Force, IBM.

AUDIOVISUAL

Attraction of Gravity, film, BFA.

Black Holes of Gravity, film, Time-Life Films.

Mr. Wizard's World: Inertia, video, *Gravity,* video, Macmillan/McGraw-Hill School Division.

Chapter 13

Motion

THEME DEVELOPMENT

One theme that this chapter supports is stability and change. The term *motion* itself implies change. The position of an object and the change in its position over time are described in this chapter.

The theme of systems and interactions is illustrated by looking at objects and their motion from different viewpoints. For example, relative velocity involves motion determined by the frame of reference of another object.

CHAPTER OVERVIEW

Students learn to specify the position of an object through the use of a reference point and to calculate the average speed of an object.

Next, the direction and change in initial position are taken into account, causing *distance* to be replaced by the term *displacement* and *speed* by the term *velocity.* Relative velocity is also introduced.

Types of acceleration, or change in velocity, are described, along with techniques for determining them.

The chapter concludes by measuring and defining motion along a curved path.

Tying to Previous Knowledge

Have students look around and point out any motion that they can see. They might notice the motion of a wall clock, the movement of a classmate, or activities taking place outside the window. Ask them about motion that was implied from other chapters such as the revolution of the moon, the movement of light through a prism, the traveling of sound waves, the blinking of the eyes, the dispersal of seeds, etc.

DID YOU EVER WONDER . . .

Why you have a sensation of movement as you sit in a car while one next to you is pulling away from a traffic light?

Why your stomach feels funny when you're on a roller coaster?

How your bicycle speeds up as you go downhill?

You'll find the answers to these questions as you read this chapter.

DID YOU EVER WONDER...

Students will explore these questions as they progress through the chapter.

- The relative velocity of an object is determined from the frame of reference of another object. Even though your car is not moving, you think you are moving in the opposite direction relative to the other car. (page 401)
- Your body senses motion more when you accelerate than when you move at a constant velocity. A roller coaster accelerates as it suddenly speeds up, slows down, and turns sharply, causing the funny feeling in your stomach. (page 403)
- As your bicycle moves downhill, your speed is constantly increasing. This change in velocity at each instant is called instantaneous acceleration. (page 406)

Motion

The first visit to the amusement park each summer is the best. The rides seem more thrilling, and the hot dogs tastier. New rides every year add to the excitement. When you were younger, the merry-go-round was the most fun. This year, the high point of the visit is the new ride—the sky ride that goes from one end of the park to the other and back again. Did you notice that as the chairs of the sky ride start forward, you feel pushed backward into your seat? Did you also notice that as the ride stopped for new passengers, you slid forward a little? Do you remember how the roller coaster went faster and faster as it went downhill? These are some of the effects of motion that we'll be exploring in this chapter.

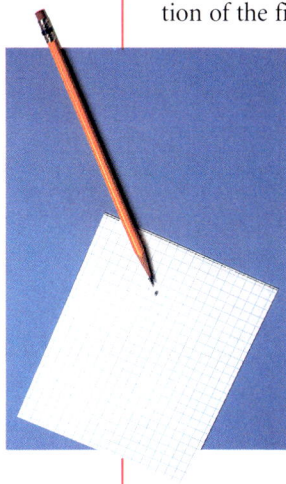

EXPLORE!

How would you tell someone where you are?

With your pencil, make a dot somewhere along the top edge of a sheet of paper. How would you describe the location of the dot on your paper to someone else? What are some ways you could make your description clearer to another person? Put a second dot on the same sheet of paper. How would you describe its position? How would you compare the location of the first dot with the second? What could you say or do so that a friend could draw a dot in the exact spot on an identical sheet of paper? Try repeating this exercise with lined paper and then with graph paper. Does your ability to tell someone where you are improve each time? Why do you think this is so?

Introducing the Chapter

Have students look at the picture of the amusement park on page 390 and identify the objects that show or imply motion. Ask students to describe other motion they saw when they last went to a fair. Some of the rides in this photo will be used to illustrate motion in this chapter.

Uncovering Preconceptions

Many people use the terms *speed* and *velocity* interchangeably. Draw a large circle on the chalkboard as you count slowly. The average speed that you drew the circle could be measured as the circumference divided by the time interval. But inform students that the average velocity was zero, since the displacement was zero.

EXPLORE!

How would you tell someone where you are?

Time needed 5–10 minutes

Materials pencil; paper: unruled, ruled, and graph

Thinking Processes
Thinking critically, Observing and inferring, Comparing and contrasting

Purpose To explore the value of reference points in describing position.

Expected Outcome

Students should find it easier to describe position when they refer more precisely to other objects.

Answers to Questions

Possible answers

1. halfway across the top
2. measure exactly from one side
3. 2 inches from the top and 4 inches from the left side
4. 1 inch below the first dot
5. Be as precise as possible in describing your dot's position.
6. yes
7. Reference points become more precise, from paper edges, to horizontal lines to graph paper squares.

Project

Ask students to collect newspaper and magazine headlines and photos that describe motion. The sports page should be a good source of materials, as will science pages and weather reports. Build a collage of the pictures and headlines. Build a second collage of headlines that use the terms of motion but do not imply physical movement, such as changes in attitude, rise and fall of the stock market, and acceleration of negotiations. **LEP**

Science at Home

Have students use the accelerometer created in the Investigate activity on page 405 to measure and log the change in velocity they experience as they ride in various vehicles. Ask them if the acceleration is about the same at each point in their ride to school from day to day. For example, does the vehicle accelerate the same amount when it stops at a particular stop sign or traffic light?

Section 13-1

PREPARATION

Concepts Developed

In this section, students learn how objects can be described in terms of their position, direction of movement, and speed. They are taught how to locate an object, measure the distance it travels, and find its average speed.

Planning the Lesson

In planning your lesson on position, time, and speed, refer to the Chapter Organizer on pages 390A-B for timing suggestions, resources, and additional materials that will help you in your presentation of the lesson concepts. For adequate development of the concepts presented in this section, we recommend that students do the Explore and Find Out activities on pages 393 and 395.

1 MOTIVATE

Demonstrate Ask one student to walk, hop, or run from one side of the classroom to the other. Then ask the other students to describe in as many ways as they can the motion they just saw taking place. Answers may include the type of motion, such as walking or running; the speed of the motion, such as fast or slow; and the direction of the motion, such as north or across the room. L1 LEP

13-1 Position, Time, and Speed

OBJECTIVES

In this section, you will

- specify the position of an object;
- find the distance along a path;
- determine the average speed of a moving object.

KEY SCIENCE TERMS

position
distance
time
average speed

POSITION AND MOTION

One of the best things about going to an amusement park is going there with friends. Sometimes, however, not everyone can arrive together—you need to decide where and when people are to gather so that no one gets left out. As an example, you might specify at 2:00 P.M. by the front gate, or perhaps by the merry-go-round at noon.

In the Explore activity, you tried to explain the location or position of a dot on a sheet of paper. If you described the position of the dot by saying how far it was from the top and side edges of the paper, you were using the edges of the paper as reference points. The **position** of an object must always be described by comparing it to a reference point. By the time you did the exercise with graph paper, all you had to do to describe your position to a friend was to say something like "over five squares from the edge and down six squares from the top."

Where you are located is your position compared to a reference point. A reference point might be the base of a Ferris wheel during your trip to the amusement park. A reference point could also be in front of a certain store in a mall or by the door of a particular building on a farm.

FIGURE 13-1. How can you be sure everyone will be at the same place at the same time?

PROGRAM RESOURCES

Teacher Classroom Resources
Study Guide, page 46

The main thing is that everyone needs to know what the particular reference point is in order to locate his or her position. What if you walk from the water slide to the tilt-a-whirl? Doesn't your position change? When you change your position you experience motion. You could describe your change in position to a friend in terms of the number of steps you took walking from the water slide to the tilt-a-whirl. For your friend to be able to take the same walk, however, you would also have to say in what direction you walked. For example, you could say that you walked 75 steps north and then 100 steps west. The direction of motion can be described using compass directions or using the number of degrees in a circle. Let's explore how you might describe both the direction and distance of motion by using just a map.

EXPLORE!

How can you use a map to help describe motion?

Using the figure shown, what distance and in what direction must you travel to go from the Tunnel of Love to the House of Terror? What direction describes the path you would take when moving from the Ferris wheel to the Tunnel of Love? Where do you end up if you travel directly west 50 meters from the Ferris wheel?

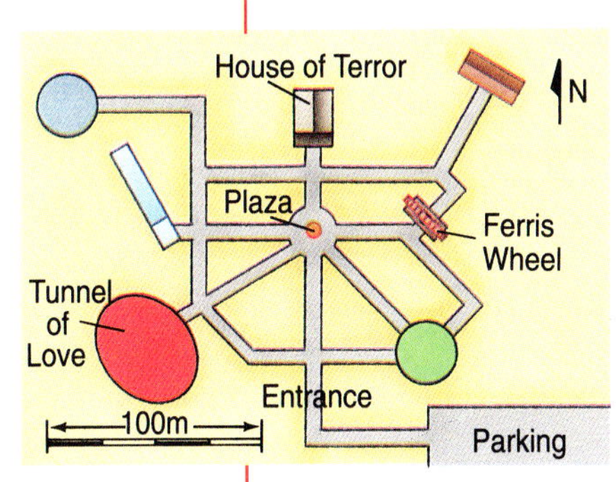

DISTANCE ALONG A PATH

When you walk through the amusement park, you change your position with every step you take. In doing so, you travel a certain distance. **Distance** is how far you travel along a path while you change your position. You've seen that a distance can be measured using just about any units—the number of steps, or the number of city blocks, for example. In science, we usually use SI units. The SI unit for measuring distance is the meter, abbreviated m. Walkers and joggers wear a small device to

2 TEACH

Tying to Previous Knowledge

Motion is a big part of everyday life. Ask students for examples of activities they or other organisms perform that involve motion. *getting out of bed, walking from the classroom to the cafeteria, running, and flying, for example* Inanimate objects show motion as well. Have students name such objects. *cars, buses, ocean waves*

EXPLORE!

How can you use a map to describe motion?

Time needed 10 to 15 minutes

Materials overhead projector, transparency of House of Terror map; copies of transparency for students

Thinking Processes Thinking critically, Observing and inferring, Measuring in SI

Purpose To describe motion using distance and direction.

Preparation If you do not have access to an overhead projector or you cannot make a transparency, sketch the map on the chalkboard.

Teaching the Activity

Demonstration Before assigning students to work in pairs, ask a volunteer to trace the path from the Tunnel of Love to the House of Terror. Then review with students how to use the map scale to find actual distance. COOP LEARN

Expected Outcome

Using the map, students should be able to describe the distance and direction of motion needed to get from one place to another.

Answers to Questions From Tunnel of Love to House of Terror go 100 m northeast then 38 m north. From the Ferris Wheel to the Tunnel of Love you would travel southwest. If you travel 50 m west from the Ferris Wheel you would end up at the plaza.

Concept Development

Theme Connection When you change your position, motion occurs. Distance is how far you travel as you change your position. Your average speed tells how fast you move as you change your position. All motion concepts include the ideas of stability (for example, a reference point) and change.

Activity Have students close their eyes while you or a volunteer moves something in the classroom. Have students open their eyes and see if they can tell what was moved. Ask them what clues they used. If they can figure out what was moved, ask if they can measure how far it was moved. Ask them what means of measurement they would use and provide a metric ruler or meterstick. If they measure the distance in a straight line, ask them what other possible ways the object could have been moved. LEP L1

Flex Your Brain Have students use the Flex Your Brain activity to explore MOTION.

Teacher F.Y.I.

In the 100-m dash at the 1988 Olympics, Carl Lewis and Ben Johnson covered one 10-meter section in 0.83 second.

record the distance that they travel. If you wanted a snack at the amusement park, you might walk 225 m from the merry-go-round to the snack bar. Walking back along the same route, you would travel another 225 m to return to your starting point. The distance along the path between those two points is 225 m, the total distance to the snack bar and back is 450 m.

CLOCK READINGS AND TIME INTERVALS

DID YOU KNOW?

Before the invention of mechanical clocks, sundials were often used to tell time. Hands on modern clocks run in the clockwise direction to copy the natural motion of the shadow across the face of the sundial.

Whenever motion takes place, time must pass as well. Therefore, motion involves both distance and time. But what exactly is time? For hundreds of years, scientists have studied the nature of time. For everyday purposes, **time** can be simply defined as a quantity that is measured with a clock. Over the years, people have devised many ways to measure time. Thousands of years ago, people used the movement of the moon, sun, and planets to keep time. Then came clocks that used dripping water, burning candles, and trickling sand. Later yet, more accurate mechanical clocks, driven and controlled by springs and pendulums, were developed. Today, atomic clocks are used for our most accurate timekeeping.

Time can be measured using many very different kinds of devices, even your own body. Can you think of a way to use your own body to measure time?

FIGURE 13-2. These watches all depend on wheels turned by springs.

PROGRAM RESOURCES

Teacher Classroom Resources

Critical Thinking/Problem Solving, page 8, Flex Your Brain

How it Works, page 14, Speedometers L2

Making Connections: Integrating Sciences, page 29, The Peregrine Falcon L2

FIND OUT!

How can you use your pulse as a clock?

As shown in the photograph, you are going to use your own pulse as a timing device. Your teacher will help you find a place on your wrist where your pulse is strong enough so that you can feel it. Your teacher will read a passage from your science book. Start counting your pulse beats when you hear the first word. Stop counting when the teacher closes the book. Record your pulse count. Your teacher will then read a second passage. Again count how many pulse beats it takes.

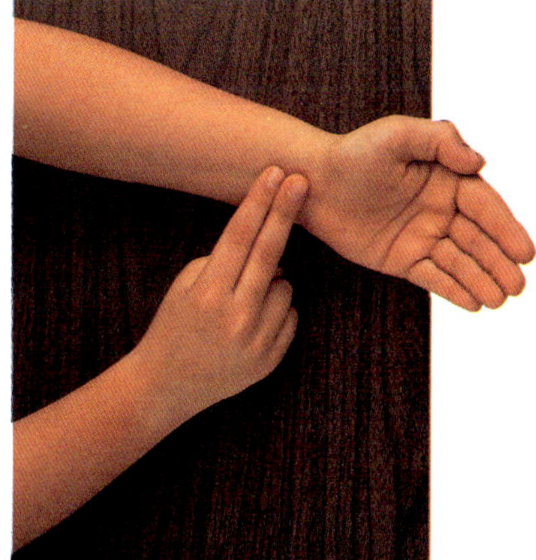

Conclude and Apply

1. Divide your pulse beat measurement for the second reading by the pulse beat measurement for the first reading. Do this for each set of student measurements. What is the result? How can you explain this?
2. Think of two other ways in which you could measure time without using a clock.

Although each of you has a pulse rate that is different, comparing the values after division gives the same number. For instance, if you had pulse readings of 240 and 120, you would find that $240/120 = 2$. Another person might find that his or her readings were 120 and 60, and $120/60 = 2$. The fact that the ratios of time intervals are the same is the basis of all time measurements. **Time** is the interval between two events. A clock is designed to mark off equal time intervals. A count of its ticks is a standard that we all agree to use.

A grandfather clock uses the swing of the pendulum as its unit of measurement. In quartz watches, the time required for the quartz crystal to vibrate once back and forth is the unit of time measurement. Clocks may use many different mechanisms for counting equal time intervals but they all work to give you the same reading of the time. A clock reading tells you a point in time. The difference between two clock readings tells you how long something takes and is called a time interval.

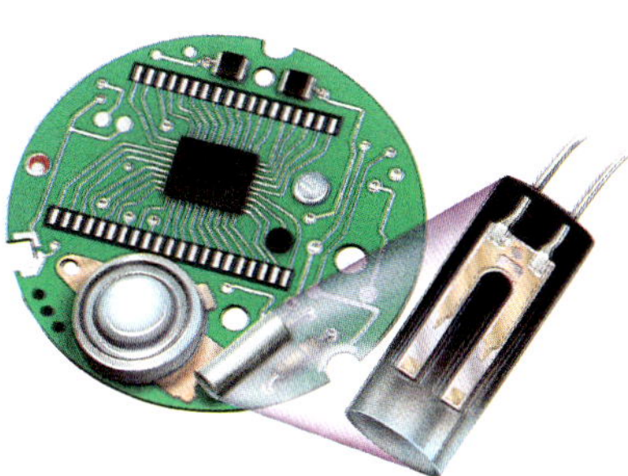

FIGURE 13-3. The vibration, or "pulse" of the quartz crystal is used to measure time.

FIND OUT!

How can you use your pulse as a clock?

Time needed 10 minutes

Thinking Processes Thinking critically, Observing and inferring, Practicing scientific methods, Interpreting data

Purpose To investigate a method for measuring time without using a clock.

Preparation Select two passages from this section of the student text. The first passage should be two or three times longer than the second. Make sure students know how to take their pulses. Use the photo on this page. If students have trouble finding their pulses on their wrists, have them find their pulses on their necks, just below the back of their jaws.

Teaching the Activity

Troubleshooting Close the book noticeably so students will know exactly when you are finished. Don't read sections with numbers that might confuse the counting. Go around the room and ask for the results from each student. Double-check the arithmetic of any answer that is very different from the majority of the class's answers. Students should not feel intimidated if their data do not match that of most of the class. Discuss why this might be so. It may be a function of their arithmetic. L1

Expected Outcomes

The answers to the division should be similar for all students. This implies that pulse rates for an individual are relatively stable even though the rates may vary among students. Knowing this, students should see that they can use pulse to measure the passage of time.

PROGRAM RESOURCES

Teacher Classroom Resources

Transparency Masters, page 55, and **Color Transparency,** number 26, Distance-Time Graph L1

Take Home Activities, page 22, Homemade Hourglass L1

Conclude and Apply

1. Results will vary, but should be similar. because each person's pulse rate is relatively stable.
2. Use anything that occurs often and at a steady pace, such as a dripping faucet, a metronome, and counting at a steady pace, e.g., "One, Mississippi, two, Mississippi . . ."

Concept Development

Inquiry Question How could you measure the average speed of a car you are traveling in if all you had was a watch and no odometer? Since you would have no way to determine the distance covered in SI units, you would have to divide a measurement such as the number of city blocks traveled or telephone poles passed per minute or hour by the number of minutes or hours traveled.

MAKING CONNECTIONS

Fine Arts

Using drawing materials, have students depict motion. A single drawing could reflect action or movement by its subject or contents (a dancer or a basketball player dunking the ball) or by a series of sketches showing a sequence in which motion takes place.

Daily Life

Have students monitor TV and newspaper articles on sports events and collect verbs and adjectives used to describe the action. Have students monitor TV and newspapers to find measurements of motion. Have them categorize the types of motion and the units used to measure the motion.

Content Background

Speed is the rate of change in position. Instantaneous speed is the speed by which an object changes position in a given instant and can be measured by a speedometer or radar gun, which aims microwave pulses at a moving object. Average speed requires less sophisticated equipment since you must measure only the total distance the object traveled and the total time it took.

Standard time intervals are measured in seconds. Suppose that you want to know how long it takes for the train to travel around the amusement park. You might record the starting time. Once the train completed the trip around the park, you might record the time again. If you subtract the first reading from the second reading, you'll find the amount of time it takes to circle the park.

HOW FAST IS FAST?

Perhaps one of the most exciting rides you recall from your trip to the amusement park is the roller coaster. Up, down, around—first fast, then slow, then really fast. It's not too surprising that some people scream, especially when racing down the tracks toward what looks like a crash landing.

One of the things that changes the most on a roller coaster is the speed. *Speed* is the distance traveled by an object during a given time interval. For instance, some roller coasters may travel 30 meters per second. In other words, the roller coaster covers a distance of 30 meters for every second it travels. Walking around the amusement park might give you a speed of around 1 meter per second, if you're not in much of a hurry.

Does a roller coaster maintain a speed of 30 meters per second for a long time? No. Like the roller coaster, most objects don't travel with constant speed. They speed up, slow down, and sometimes stop. Suppose that in one hour, while walking around the amusement park, you run to catch up with some friends, stop to talk, buy some cotton candy, and watch the reptile show. Like most moving things, you do not maintain a constant speed during your walk. Even when your motion isn't constant, it is possible to find your average speed.

FIGURE 13-4. During a roller coaster ride, you travel at many different speeds.

The **average speed** is found by dividing the total distance traveled by the total time required to travel the distance. That is,

$$\text{average speed} = \frac{\text{total distance}}{\text{time interval}}$$

In the next activity, you will find your average walking speed.

OPTIONS

Meeting Individual Needs

Visually Impaired Discuss ways motion can be determined through non-visual means. Include hearing objects move, the sensation of movement, feeling objects such as a mosquito move on you, and so on. Then move a sandpaper-covered block along a strip of sandpaper. Have students locate the starting place and put their fingers on it. Have them begin counting seconds (you may need to work with them on timing), or let them count ticks on a metronome while you move the block. Direct them to stop counting when they hear the movement stop. Stop moving the block when it is one meter away. Let students locate the block and measure the distance with a meterstick. They should then be able to determine the average speed of the object.

I N V E S T I G A T E !

13-1 AVERAGE SPEED

Have you ever wondered what your average speed is when you walk? Do the Investigate to find your average walking speed.

PROBLEM

What is your average speed when walking?

MATERIALS

meterstick
stopwatch
masking tape

PROCEDURE

1. Copy the data table.
2. Use the meterstick to **measure** a distance of 10 m. Mark the beginning and end points of the 10 m with strips of masking tape.
3. Use the stopwatch to time how long it takes for you and the others in your group to (a) walk, (b) run, (c) walk backward, and (d) hop on one leg the 10 m distance. Each partner should take a turn being the timer. As you perform each event, record your data in the table.
4. **Calculate** the average speed for each event for each group member. Use the equation:

$$\text{average speed} = \frac{\text{total distance}}{\text{time interval}}$$

5. **Calculate** the average of the average speeds for each event by adding all the individual average speeds together. Then divide by the number of group members.

DATA AND OBSERVATIONS

Sample data

STUDENT'S NAME	DISTANCE (meters)	TIME REQUIRED (seconds)	SPEED (m/s)
Jose	10m	9.0	1.1 m/s
Sally	10m	6.7	1.5 m/s
Ginger	10m	7.7	1.3 m/s

ANALYZE

1. During which event did you have the greatest average speed?
2. What units did you use for average speed?
3. Does the average speed describe how you moved at each moment during the event? Why or why not?
4. Why could you only calculate your average speed?

CONCLUDE AND APPLY

5. If you had stopped for a while when performing any of the events, **predict** your average speed for that event.
6. **Going Further:** How would the average speed results change if the markers were placed 5 m apart?

INVESTIGATE!

13-1 AVERAGE SPEED

Time needed 20–25 minutes

Materials meterstick, stopwatch, masking tape

Thinking Processes Organizing information, Making and using tables, Practicing scientific methods, Interpreting data

Purpose To learn a method for determining a person's average speed

Preparation Clear classroom space. Divide the class into groups. If necessary, provide instruction on using a stopwatch.

Teaching the Activity

Troubleshooting Students who are having difficulty with the division required can use a calculator or work cooperatively. COOP LEARN

Expected Outcomes

Average speeds are likely to vary for each person for each event. Students learn to calculate average speed once total distance and time are known.

Answers to Analyze/Conclude and Apply

1. Answers will vary. The most probable answer is running.
2. meters per second
3. No, it is a measure based on total distance and time.
4. During each event, you likely speeded up and slowed down. The equipment you were using was not able to measure these variations in speed. It could only measure speed over the entire event.
5. Since the time interval would increase and distance stay the same, your average speed would decrease.
6. The average speed would not change. You could probably move half the distance in half the time.

Enrichment

Activity Have each student find the average speed of a pet or a neighbor's pet using the method learned in Investigate 13-1. Then have students research the average speeds of other animals such as ants, turtles, horses, and ostriches. Have students organize their findings in a bar graph.

PROGRAM RESOURCES

Teacher Classroom Resources

Activity Masters, pages 53-54, Investigate 13-1

Concept Development

Student Text Questions Figure 13-5: Which object has the greatest instantaneous speed? *cheetah* Which animal had the faster average speed? How do you know? *the tortoise; it won the race*

3 ASSESS

Check for Understanding

Compare the Apply question with the Investigate activity and results. Since the distance is twenty times more, have students imagine how fast she was going compared to their running speeds.

Reteach

Materials meterstick, windup or battery-powered toy car, clock with second hand or stopwatch

Have students find the average speed of the car using the meterstick and clock or stopwatch

Extension

Have students investigate or measure the speeds at which various animals move.

4 CLOSE

Demonstration

This activity will allow students to see motion in the movement of a ball.

Drop the ball onto a desk and catch it on the rebound. Then toss the ball into the air and catch it. Discuss distance, position, and average speed in relation to the movement of the ball. Finally, ask students where the ball went when you dropped it and when you tossed it, relative to where it started.

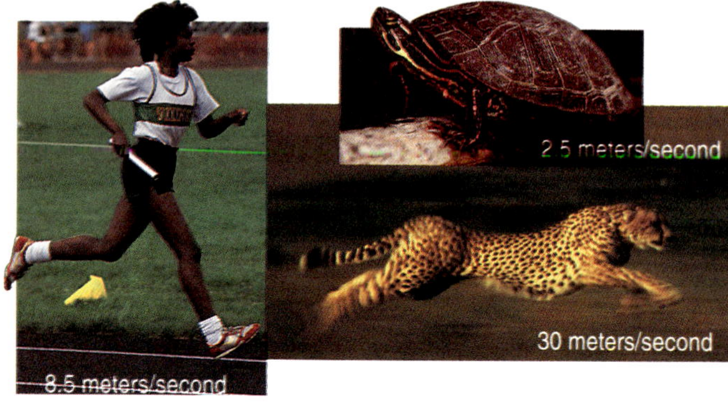

FIGURE 13-5. Which object has the greatest instantaneous speed?

As you saw in the Investigate, the speed of an object at any one instant may not be the same as the object's average speed. Instantaneous speed is the rate of motion at any given instant. Figure 13-5 gives the speed of each object at the instant the photo was taken—the instantaneous speed. A car's speedometer shows instantaneous speed. In the fable of the tortoise and the hare, the hare's instantaneous speed could be much greater than the tortoise's speed. Which animal had the faster average speed? How do you know?

Walking around an amusement park, riding a roller coaster, driving a car, riding a skateboard, even orbiting planets—all involve a motion during an interval of time. For each motion, we can determine the object's average speed over the path taken by dividing the total distance traveled by the time interval.

The average speed of a moving object tells you how rapidly it travels but it does not tell which way the object goes. In the next section, you will learn how to combine speed and direction to describe an object's motion.

DID YOU KNOW?

The fastest roller coaster has often been subject to dispute. Speeds are frequently exaggerated for commercial reasons, but one of the fastest is the Magnum XL-200 at Cedar Point Park, Sandusky, Ohio. It has a vertical drop of nearly 59 m and attains a speed of 32 m/s.

Check Your Understanding

1. In your own words, describe what is meant by (a) position and (b) distance.
2. Explain how a time interval can be measured with a clock.
3. How could you measure the distance of your path from home to school?
4. List the information you need to calculate the average speed of a car traveling from your house to school.
5. **APPLY:** Florence Griffith Joyner set a world record by running 200 m in 21.34 s. What was her average speed?

Answers to Check Your Understanding

1. (a) Position is your location compared to a reference point. (b) Distance is how far you travel when you change position.
2. Record the time at the beginning and end of the interval. Then find the difference between these times.
3. Possible answers: in a car with an odometer, use a pedometer, count blocks
4. total distance car traveled; total time trip took
5. 9.37 m/s

13-2 Velocity Along a Straight Line

DISPLACEMENT

Have you ever ridden on a merry-go-round or carousel? Usually, a ride on the carousel involves 15 or 20 turns in a circular path. You may ride for three or four minutes, but you get on and off at the same place. Despite all of the trips around in a circle, you really haven't gone anywhere at all.

Here's another example. You need milk. You walk three blocks to the store and walk the three blocks home again. When you return home, how will your position have changed for the entire trip? The answer, as with the carousel, is not at all. You have traveled six blocks, but your position did not change at all.

Displacement is the change in position of an object. The round trip to the store, like the round trips on the carousel, produced a displacement of zero because you ended up where you started.

Displacement is described by both a length and a direction. Distance is described only by length. To say that you live 16 kilometers from the amusement park is not necessarily helpful to another person. Sixteen kilometers could be anywhere in a circle of radius 16 kilometers from the amusement park. To make it more understandable and useful to others, you need to specify which way. As shown by the map, home is 16 kilometers south of the amusement park.

Suppose, instead of walking, you drove to and from the amusement park. What would the odometer in your family's car measure? An odometer measures the distance the car has moved. As with walking, the round trip to and from the amusement park measures a distance of 32 kilometers. Your displacement is still zero. Is there a way to describe motion that takes displacement into account?

OBJECTIVES

In this section, you will

- distinguish between displacement and distance;
- find the average velocity of a moving object;
- distinguish between velocity and speed;
- use the concept of relative velocity.

KEY SCIENCE TERMS

displacement
average velocity
relative velocity

FIGURE 13-6. How can you be sure you get home if you walk 16 kilometers from the park?

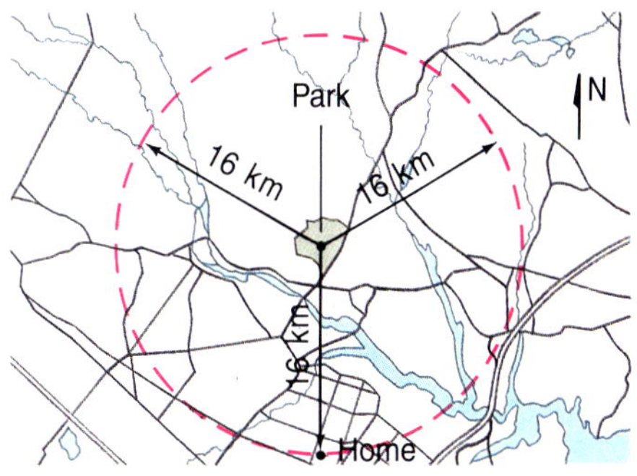

Section 13-2

PREPARATION

Concepts Developed

This lesson contrasts average speed with average velocity and distance with displacement. It then introduces the concept of relative velocity, in which an object's apparent velocity depends on the observer's frame of reference.

Planning the Lesson

In planning your lesson on velocity along a straight line, refer to the Chapter Organizer on pages 390A-B for timing suggestions, resources, and additional materials that will help you in your presentation of the lesson concepts. For adequate development of the concepts presented in this section, we recommend that students complete the Explore activity on page 401.

1 MOTIVATE

Discussion To introduce the concept of relative velocity, have students imagine that they are flying in an airplane traveling at 800 km/h, and one of them gets up and walks toward the front of the airplane at 1 m/s. Ask how fast that person would appear to be moving to the other passengers on the plane. *1 m/s* Then ask how fast that person would appear to be moving if he or she could be seen by an observer on the ground. *(at the speed of the plane plus 1 m/s)* Discuss what might account for this difference. L1

PROGRAM RESOURCES

Teacher Classroom Resources

Study Guide, page 47
Concept Mapping, page 21, Motion L1
Critical Thinking/Problem Solving, page 21, Radar Detectors and Speeding L3
Transparency Masters, page 53, and **Color Transparency,** number 25, Displacement Map L1

2 TEACH

Tying to Previous Knowledge

In the previous section, students learned about position, distance, and average speed. If they were riding in a car, they could use the odometer to measure the distance and the speedometer to measure speed. But these readings would not help them to know the direction in which they were traveling or how far they were from their starting point. Displacement and average velocity, concepts presented in this section, would help them determine this information.

Concept Development

Theme Connection The development of the theme of systems and interactions is introduced when the students study the velocity of one object relative to another.

Demonstration This activity will determine relative velocity.

You will need a globe and masking tape. Put a small piece of masking tape somewhere on the equator. Have students imagine that the tape is a person. Spin the globe. Ask students how fast the person would think he or she was going. Since Earth is the frame of reference for the person, that person would not think he or she was moving at all. Compare this to how rapidly the person seems, to the students, to be spinning around in a circle. Stop the spinning globe in the same position it was in when you started. Ask students what the displacement of the person was. The answer is 0, since the starting and ending points are the same. This should be contrasted with the distance traveled, which was several rotations of Earth.

Flex Your Brain Use the Flex Your Brain Activity to have students explore VELOCITY.

Braking distance increases 4.6 m.

a

b

FIGURE 13-7. Wind socks measure wind direction (a) and anamometers measure wind speed (b).

A measure of motion that tells you how fast and which way an object moves is velocity. Wind is usually described in terms of a velocity. The velocity of wind is especially important to know because wind from the north usually brings colder weather. When the weather forecaster speaks of 10 mi/h breezes from the northwest, you can be sure that he or she is speaking of a velocity, not of a speed. You learned in Section 1 that the average speed of an object depends on the distance traveled within a certain time. Now that you know the difference between distance and displacement, do you think there could also be a measure of how fast an object moved over a certain displacement? There is! The measure of such motion is called **average velocity**.

Calculating an average velocity is similar to calculating an average speed. We are concerned here with the total displacement rather than the total distance traveled. To find average velocity:

$$\text{Average Velocity} = \frac{\text{total displacement}}{\text{time interval}}$$

To see the difference between average speed and average velocity, consider the following example.

Suppose you walk 10 m due north and then reverse your direction and walk 2 m due south. If this to-and-from motion requires a total of 12 seconds, what is (a) your average speed and (b) your average velocity?

$$\text{(a) average speed} = \frac{\text{total distance}}{\text{time interval}} = \frac{12\text{ m}}{12\text{ s}} = 1.0\text{ m/s}$$

$$\text{(b) }\begin{matrix}\text{average}\\\text{velocity}\end{matrix} = \frac{\text{total displacement}}{\text{time interval}} = \frac{8\text{ m}}{12\text{ s}} = 0.67\text{ m/s north}$$

As your calculations show, the average speed is not the same as the average velocity! Notice that the direction is given with the average velocity, because displacement includes direction.

SKILLBUILDER

MAKING AND USING GRAPHS

The table gives the stopping distances for different speeds. Graph the points with the speed in m/s along the horizontal axis and the stopping distance in m along the vertical axis. Connect the points with a smooth line.

Using the graph, determine how much braking distance increases when the speed increases from 4 m/s to 8 m/s. If you need help, refer to the ***Skill Handbook*** on page 650.

SPEED (m/s)	BRAKING DISTANCE (m)
2	1.0
4	2.3
6	4.2
8	6.9
10	10.0

PROGRAM RESOURCES

Teacher Classroom Resources

Critical Thinking/Problem Solving, page 8, Flex Your Brain

Other Resources

Lightman, Alan P. et al. *Problem Book in Relativity and Gravitation.* Princeton, NJ: Princeton University Press, 1975.

OPTIONS

Multicultural Perspectives

Benjamin Banneker (1731-1806), an African-American inventor, mathematician, and astronomer, is credited with building the first clock made in America. In 1761 he constructed a highly accurate wooden "striking" clock. His invention kept time so well that it struck each hour without fail for over twenty years. His understanding of time, motion, and astronomy permitted him to predict a solar eclipse in 1789.

RELATIVE VELOCITY

Have you ever sat in a car at a traffic light and felt you were moving backward? When you looked at other objects outside the car you realized, much to your relief, that it was the car next to you moving forward.

The same effect can happen at the amusement park on a double roller coaster with a double track. While waiting for your car to move, the car in the roller coaster next to yours starts moving. You think that you are moving in the opposite direction.

This is an example of relative velocity. **Relative velocity** is the velocity of one object determined from the view, or frame of reference, of another object. Either one or both of the objects may be moving relative to some third object.

EXPLORE!

What is relative velocity?

Send a battery-powered toy car along the length of a sheet of paper. Observe the velocity of the car. Can you predict what will happen if you send the car along the paper while a friend pulls the paper on the table in the direction of the motion of the car? Try it! Describe the car's velocity. Now observe the velocity of the car when the sheet is moved in the direction opposite to the car's motion. What do you see?

In the Explore, the car moved over the paper and over your desk top. The car's motion over both the paper and desk top was the same as long as the paper didn't move. As soon as you made the paper move, however, the car's motion over the desk top was not the same as its motion over the paper. When you describe the motion of the car or any object, you have to compare it to something else—in this case, either the desk top or the paper. The motion that you describe depends on your frame of reference, or what you are comparing the car's motion to. We usually use Earth as our frame of reference. For example, you speak of your motion to and from school in terms of the distance and direction you travel on the surface of Earth.

EXPLORE!

What Is relative velocity?

Time needed 10–15 minutes

Materials battery-powered toy car, sheet of paper

Thinking Processes
Thinking critically, Observing and inferring, Recognizing cause and effect

Purpose To observe the difference between an object's speed and its relative velocity.

Preparation Make sure the car is slow and small enough that it takes several seconds to cross the length of the paper. Some wind-up cars work just as well. If the car moves slowly enough, have students use a stopwatch and time how long it takes for the car to travel the length of the paper in each situation.

Teaching the Activity

Troubleshooting Don't jerk the paper or the car may fall off. Pull the paper slowly and steadily.

Expected Outcomes

The car will take the same amount of time to travel the length of the paper whichever way it is pulled. To the observer, however, the car will seem to be moving faster in the first case than in the second.

Answers to Questions

1. It appears to move faster.
2. It appears to move slower.

Enrichment

Research Have students research the term *escape velocity,* the speed necessary for an object to escape Earth's gravitational pull. Ask what would happen to a rocket that did not reach the escape velocity shortly after takeoff.

PROGRAM RESOURCES

Teacher Classroom Resources

Making Connections: Across the Curriculum, page 29, Reading Maps L2

Making Connections: Technology and Society, page 29, Should School Buses Have Seat Belts? L2

3 Assess

Check for Understanding

To answer the Apply question, it is important that students realize that moving in the same direction and at the same speed as another object will make the relative velocity 0.

Reteach

Have a student walk to make a complete circle. Then ask the student to run in the same circle. Ask him or her whether walking or running produced a greater average speed. Then ask which produced the greater average velocity. Lead students to see that the average speed was greater when running because the same distance was covered in a shorter time. But the average velocity was the same because the displacement was zero each time. LEP

Extension

Ask students who have already mastered the section concepts to find and compare the speed and velocity of Earth and the moon as each completes one orbit. L3

4 Close

Activity

Students will determine average velocity of a partially filled balloon. Materials needed are a meterstick, a stopwatch, and a balloon. Blow up the balloon but do not tie the end. Let the balloon go. Have a student time the interval from when the balloon is released until it comes to rest. Have students measure the distance along a straight line from the point that the balloon was let go to the spot that it landed. Divide the balloon's displacement by the time elapsed to determine its average velocity. COOP LEARN

FIGURE 13-8. The velocity of the astronaut depends on the frame of reference.

We don't always use Earth as our frame of reference, however. An astronaut working outside a space shuttle would use the shuttle as his or her frame of reference, rather than Earth. If the astronaut and shuttle are moving in orbit around Earth at the same orbit speed, then their relative velocity would be zero. In this case, the astronaut would say that he or she is motionless compared to the space shuttle. On the ground, however, NASA controllers would describe both the astronaut's and the shuttle's orbit speed as about 40,000 kilometers per hour, using Earth as their frame of reference.

Walking through an amusement park exposes you to a great deal of fun, and to a great number of moving objects. Are you surprised that your legs are tired from walking so far, but that by the time you leave through the gate you entered, your displacement is zero? Can you describe what happens to your speed on the roller coaster? The next time you're at an amusement park try to compare your relative velocity while walking to the velocity of the sky ride or the roller coaster. You may be able to see and do a lot more if you take your own motion into account, both inside and out of an amusement park!

Check Your Understanding

1. A man walks 2 km due west, then turns around and walks 3 km due east. What distance does the man walk? What is the man's displacement?
2. Explain whether it is possible for a car's average velocity to be zero even if the car traveled a distance of 200 km.
3. An airplane flying toward the west has a speed of 200 km/h. What is the plane's velocity?
4. A student decides to have some fun on a moving walkway at the airport. The walkway moves to the north with a speed of 2 m/s, and the student walks at the same speed in the same direction. What velocity would a person standing next to the walkway measure?
5. **APPLY:** If the same student sees a friend standing next to the walkway and wants to remain at rest relative to that friend, at what velocity (speed and direction) should he or she walk?

Answers to Check Your Understanding

1. 5 km; 1 km due east
2. Yes; the average velocity of a car is its displacement divided by time. If the car traveled from point A to B and then back to A, its displacement is 0, and $\frac{0}{\text{time}} = 0$.
3. 200 km/h west.
4. 4 m/s
5. 2 m/s opposite to the direction of the walkway's motion

13-3 Acceleration

CHANGING VELOCITY

Have you ever enjoyed an absolutely smooth ride? Surely not at the amusement park, where half of the fun comes from sharp turns, moving up and down, and spinning around in circles. Some airliners can sometimes provide an absolutely smooth ride. If it were not for the sound of the engines, you might be able to convince yourself that you were standing on the ground.

A smooth flight occurs only when the plane is flying with a constant velocity. Normally, planes do not move with constant velocity. Turbulence, air pockets, or even changes in course cause the velocity of the plane to change, letting you know you're not on the ground.

When the velocity of an object changes, the object accelerates. You often do not sense your motion when you are moving at a constant velocity. You do, however, sense motion when you accelerate. Anyone who has ridden on a roller coaster knows about acceleration. When the car takes off quickly from rest, you feel as though you are being pushed back in your seat. When the car's brakes are suddenly applied, you may feel as if you are moving forward. Even in the family car, you move

OBJECTIVES

In this section, you will

- distinguish between velocity and acceleration;
- determine acceleration from velocity change and time.

KEY SCIENCE TERMS

acceleration

average acceleration

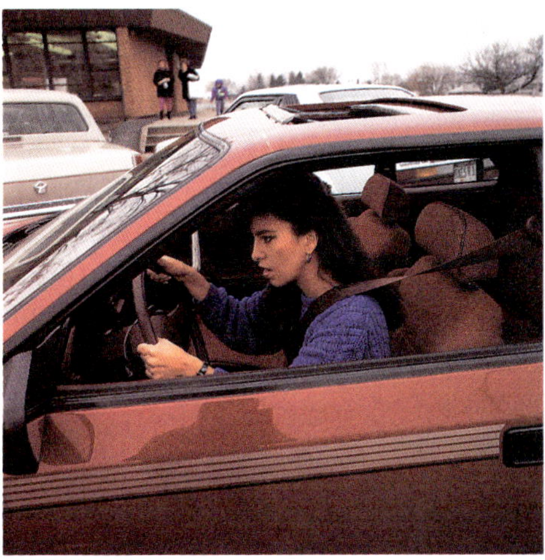

FIGURE 13-9. Seat belts keep you from moving through the car's windshield when the car stops suddenly.

Section 13-3

PREPARATION

Concepts Developed

So far the chapter has primarily dealt with average or constant speed and velocity. Acceleration occurs whenever the velocity of an object changes. The change can involve either a difference in speed or in direction of the object. The measurement of average acceleration must take into account how much the velocity of the object changed during a given time interval.

Planning the Lesson

In planning your lesson on acceleration, refer to the Chapter Organizer on pages 390A-B for timing suggestions, resources, and additional materials that will help you in your presentation of the lesson concepts. For adequate development of the concepts presented in this section, we recommend that students do the Investigate activity on page 405.

1 MOTIVATE

Demonstrate This activity will show students how an object's velocity can change.

You will need a windup toy car.

Wind up the car and place it on a desktop or the floor. Ask students to note the points at which the car accelerates. While most will note that the car speeds up until it reaches a constant speed, not all will be aware that the car also accelerates as it slows down.

PROGRAM RESOURCES

Teacher Classroom Resources

Study Guide, page 48

Laboratory Manual, pages 77-80, Speed and Acceleration L3

Multicultural Activities, page 30, Ellison Onizuka 

2 Teach

Tying to Previous Knowledge

Ask students how they know that they are moving when they are traveling in a car or elevator at a constant velocity (same speed and direction). What clues do they use to note a change in velocity? *They may use visual hints to see their relative velocity, comparing their movement to that of objects moving faster or slower than themselves. Or they may just feel the change, such as the upward or downward movement of an elevator.*

Concept Development

Theme Connection The theme that this section supports is stability and change. From the time an object starts moving until it stops, it does not maintain a constant velocity. Acceleration, another facet of stability and change, is a change in velocity that occurs when an object changes its speed or direction.

Student Text Question (Figure 13-10) In what other way does he accelerate? *The boy accelerates as he slows down when entering the water. He also accelerates when his direction changes as the slide curves upward or downward.*

MAKING CONNECTIONS

Health and Safety

When a car traveling about 50 km/h collides head-on with something solid, the car suddenly slows down. Any passenger not wearing a seat belt continues to move forward at the same speed the car was traveling, slamming into the dashboard or front seat at 50 km/h. A person wearing a seat belt becomes part of the car. As the car slows down, so does the passenger. It takes about 14 times a person's weight to slow him or her down fast enough to prevent injury. Have students calculate the force necessary to slow them down in the event of a head-on crash at this speed.

DID YOU KNOW?

The driver of a car actually controls three accelerators: the gas pedal, the brakes, and the steering wheel. The steering wheel is an accelerator because it changes the direction of the car.

forward if the car stops suddenly. This is an everyday example of acceleration.

You sense your motion when you are moving along in one direction at a constant speed, but then turn quickly to the right or left. This is another example of acceleration. Since velocity involves both speed and direction, to change your velocity requires that you change either one or the other. Thus, acceleration can be produced by changing your speed (how much) or by changing your direction of travel (which way), or both.

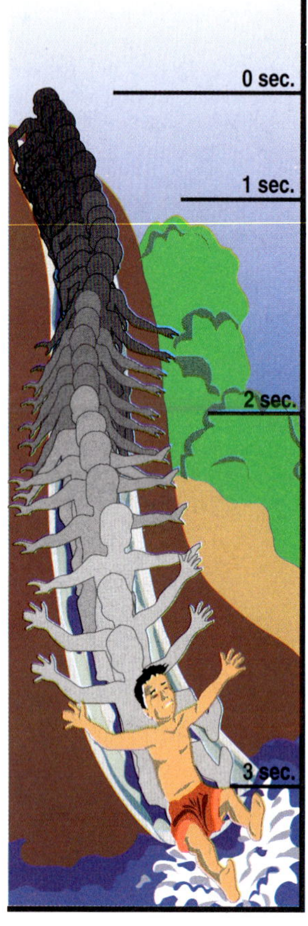

FIGURE 13-10. This boy accelerates as his speed increases. In what other way does he accelerate?

You often use the word *acceleration* in conversation when you speak of something speeding up. Did you know you would be equally correct to refer to an object that is slowing down as accelerating? Astronauts undergo large accelerations when they take off from Earth. This is due to their large change in velocity as they move from Earth to their position in orbit around Earth. For this reason, astronauts have comfortably padded seats to absorb the force. When the shuttle and the astronauts return to Earth, they need to slow down by an equal amount. This slowdown is referred to as a negative acceleration.

Think of **acceleration** as the rate at which one's velocity is changing. For an example, suppose you are on a water slide and speeding up as you move. Your speed changes by 1 meter per second for every second that you move. We would say that your acceleration is 1 meter per second per second, or 1 m/s/s. If you were on a steeper slide and were gaining speed more rapidly—say 2 meters per second for every second that you slide down—your acceleration would be 2 m/s/s.

On the water slide, you may be thinking about what is happening to your acceleration at each instant. You may be moving faster at the end of the slide than you were at the beginning. At each instant on the slide your acceleration changed. Your velocity and your acceleration change every time you go over a bump. The acceleration at each instant is called the instantaneous acceleration. An instrument called an accelerometer is used to measure the acceleration at any given instant. Let's investigate one way to measure instantaneous acceleration.

OPTIONS

Meeting Individual Needs

Physically Challenged Adapt the Investigate activity in one of these ways so that students in wheelchairs can participate.

1. The student can hold the accelerometer in one hand while another student pushes the chair.
2. Attach a meterstick to the wheelchair so that it protrudes forward. Attach the protractor to the stick so the string hangs down at eye level, thus freeing both hands to achieve greater acceleration.

INVESTIGATE!

13-2 INSTANTANEOUS ACCELERATION

An accelerometer will allow you to measure the instantaneous acceleration of moving objects.

PROBLEM

How can you measure instantaneous acceleration?

MATERIALS

protractor
10 to 12 cm length of string
button

PROCEDURE

1. Copy the data table.
2. Assemble the materials as shown in the picture.
3. Hold the protractor upside down. The string should line up with the 90-degree mark on the protractor. When taking a reading, hold the protractor level.
4. Hold the accelerometer at arm's length in front of your face with the numbers facing you. Quickly move the accelerometer to one side. **Observe** the angle of the string measured by the protractor. In what direction does the string move? What can you **infer** about the direction of acceleration? Try moving the accelerometer to the other side. What does this tell you?
5. Use the conversion chart to convert the angle reading on the accelerometer to an acceleration in meters per second per second.
6. Hold the accelerometer level and begin to run. Have a friend run with you and read the angle. Enter this data in the table.

DATA AND OBSERVATIONS Sample data

MOVING OBJECT	ACCELERATION M/S/S
75°	2.63
50°	8.22

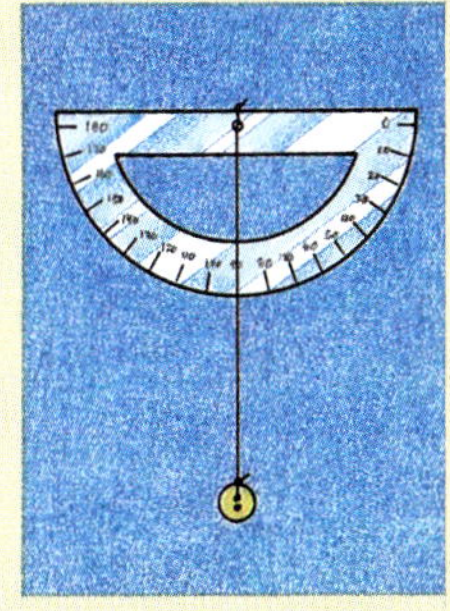

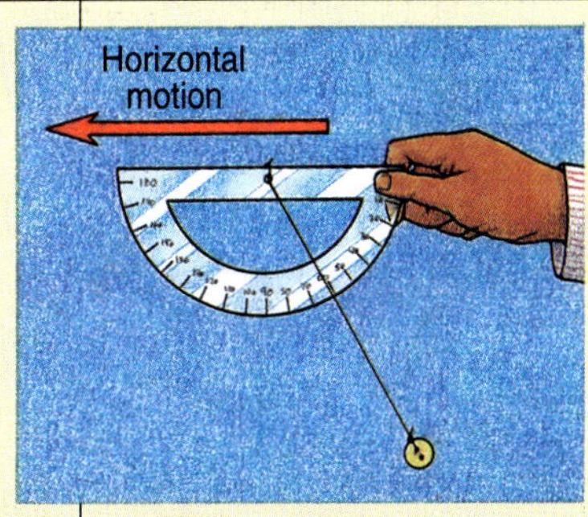

ANALYZE

1. In what direction does the string move in comparison with the direction you move when you speed up? Describe.
2. How did the string behave as you slowed down?

CONVERSION CHART

MOVING OBJECT	ACCELERATION M/S/S
90°	0
80°	1.73
70°	3.57
60°	5.66
50°	8.22
45°	9.8
40°	11.7
30°	17.0
20°	26.9
10°	55.6
0°	—

CONCLUDE AND APPLY

3. Describe the position of the string while you were moving with constant velocity.
4. **Going Further: Predict** whether or not loose objects in a car would tend to move in the same direction of the string, or in the opposite direction.

INVESTIGATE!

13-2 INSTANTANEOUS ACCELERATION

Time needed 15–20 minutes

Materials protractor, string 10–12 cm long, button

Thinking Processes
Organizing information, Making and using tables, Practicing scientific methods, Observing and inferring, Predicting

Purpose To investigate one way to measure instantaneous acceleration.

Preparation Make sure that the object used to weigh down the string is heavy enough to pull the string taut and that the string is thin and smooth to allow it to move freely as it swings alongside the protractor. You may find that a key or $\frac{1}{2}''$ or $\frac{5}{8}''$ washer works better than a button on some types of string.

Teaching the Activity

Troubleshooting Depending on the protractors your students use, they may find that a 25–30 cm-long string works better.

Have students do this activity in pairs, one to hold the protractor and one to read the angle. Tell students that the angle should be read as quickly as possible during their partners' movements, as students will quickly reach relatively constant velocities.

Expected Outcomes

The acceleration measurements will likely vary widely, although increases should be seen from walking to running to riding in a car. Students should find that the string swings away from the direction of motion as they speed up and toward the direction of motion as they slow down.

Teacher F.Y.I.

The moon is not rotating around Earth at a constant speed. It is actually accelerating at an increase of about 20 seconds per century.

PROGRAM RESOURCES

Teacher Classroom Resources
Activity Masters, pages 55-56, Investigate 13-2

Answers to Analyze/Conclude and Apply

1. The string moves in the opposite direction: away from the direction of motion.
2. The string moved toward the direction of motion.
3. The string hangs straight down.
4. They would move in the same direction as the accelerometer string.

3 Assess

Check for Understanding

Ask students to explain what their answer to the Apply question means. *The car's speed increases by 1.6 m/s every second that it accelerates.*

Reteach

Direct a volunteer to begin walking at a constant velocity. Have the other students, one at a time, call out a different command that, when followed, will accelerate the volunteer's motion. These should include commands to change speed and direction. The type of commands students call out should indicate their understanding of the different ways acceleration can occur to change velocity.

Extension

Attach a hard-boiled egg to the center of a skateboard with a small piece of clay. Thrust the skateboard against a wall about 2 m away. Secure another egg with rubber bands and repeat the crash. Put the third egg in an egg carton and crash one more time. Have students compare the acceleration of the skateboard and the egg and its effect on the egg during each trial. LEP

4 Close

Demonstration

Throw a ball up into the air and catch it. Ask students to analyze the ways the ball accelerated. *Some possible answers: It increased velocity when it was tossed; it slowed down as it reached its highest point; it changed direction when it started to fall; it speeded up as it fell; it decreased velocity when you caught it.*

DID YOU KNOW?

Your inner ears contain organs which act just like accelerometers. They tell you exactly how much your head moves and in what direction. You may not be aware of what these accelerometers are sensing, but signals from them help you to adjust the movements of your eyes as you move your head. This allows you to keep your eyes fixed on what you want to look at while your head moves.

Calculating average acceleration is similar to finding average velocity. **Average acceleration** is the change in the velocity divided by the time interval during which the change occurs:

$$\text{Average acceleration} = \frac{\text{change in velocity}}{\text{time interval}}$$

For example, if a toy car speeds up from 0 to 3 m/s in 8 seconds, the toy car's average acceleration is:

$$\text{Average acceleration} = \text{change in velocity/time interval}$$

$$= \frac{(3\text{/m/s} - 0\text{ m/s})}{8\text{ s}}$$

$$= 0.375\text{ m/s/s}$$

Again, just like average speed and average velocity, average acceleration does not say anything about what happens to the acceleration at each instant.

Every day of your life, you move in a variety of different ways and experience acceleration of some kind. Whenever you slow down, speed up, turn a corner, or move in a circle, you are accelerating. You are experiencing either a change in your direction of motion or your speed in a particular direction. Smooth rides at a constant velocity in cars, planes, trains, or roller coasters can be interrupted by a change in velocity. When observing the different motions around you, try to describe them in terms of position, distance, displacement, velocity, and acceleration. Don't forget that velocity, but not acceleration, may be different for different frames of reference.

FIGURE 13-11. The second you begin to change your direction you begin to accelerate.

Check Your Understanding

1. A car moves with a constant velocity of 15 m/s north. What is the car's acceleration?
2. What must happen to the velocity of an object when the object is accelerating?
3. Explain how it is possible for an object to be accelerating if it is moving with constant speed.
4. **APPLY:** Calculate the average acceleration of a car that increases its velocity along a straight line from 10 m/s to 21 m/s in 7 seconds.

Answers to Check Your Understanding

1. 0 m/s/s
2. Its velocity must change.
3. Its direction must be changing.
4. 1.6 m/s/s

OPTIONS

Enrichment

Activity Make a gently sloping ramp by propping a board on a textbook. Mark off a 5-m distance from the bottom of the ramp. Measure the length of the ramp. Let a marble roll down from the top of the ramp to the bottom, and time it. Roll the marble again and measure its travel time to the 5-m mark. Calculate the average velocity in each case. Compute the difference in average velocity between the two cases.

13-4 Motion Along Curves

CHANGES IN POSITION: DISPLACEMENT

When you look at a long roller coaster, it has many curves and bends. Obviously, if you were in a hurry to get from one place to another, a path like the one described by the tracks of the roller coaster would not be the quickest way to go! You can easily see that a straight line is a shorter route. Recall that you find displacement along a straight line by subtracting the starting position from the finishing position and noting direction. But how do you find displacement between two points along a curved road, for example?

OBJECTIVES

In this section, you will

- distinguish between a displacement and a distance along a curved path;
- find the average velocity for motion along a curved path;
- recognize situations for which there is an acceleration, called the centripetal acceleration, even when the speed is constant.

KEY SCIENCE TERMS

centripetal acceleration

FIND OUT!

How is displacement along a curved path measured?

Look closely at the drawing. It shows both the actual path and the displacement of a train along an amusement park track. What is the train's displacement for this trip? To describe completely the train's displacement, both the distance and direction of the straight line between the end points must be given.

Use the scale at the bottom of the diagram to determine the length of the displacement. Use a protractor to measure the direction. If you have measured correctly, you will find that the distance is 9 km and the angle is 30 degrees north of east. The displacement, therefore, is 9 km north of east.

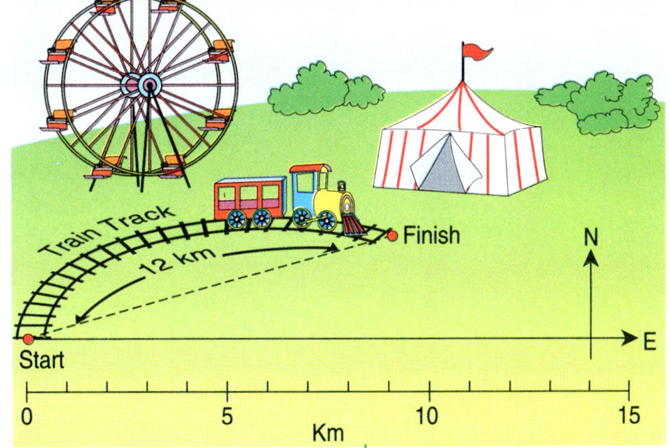

Section 13-4

PREPARATION

Concepts Developed

The previous sections in this chapter assumed that objects move in a straight line. This section describes motion along curves, which always involves acceleration. The knowledge gained in this lesson is not only applicable to physics on Earth, but is especially useful in understanding the orbits of satellites and planets.

Planning the Lesson

In planning your lesson on motion along curves, refer to the Chapter Organizer on pages 390A-B for timing suggestions, resources, and additional materials that will help you in your presentation of the lesson concepts. For adequate development of the concepts presented in this section, we recommend that students do both the Find Out on page 407 and the Explore activity on page 409.

1 MOTIVATE

Activity This activity will allow students to observe an indication of acceleration by changing direction.

You will need small rubber balls.

Direct students to put the balls in the open palms of their hands. Tell them to run forward. The balls should roll toward them since the direction of acceleration is forward. Have them repeat the experiment, this time walking forward and turning left. The balls should roll off their hands to the right.

FIND OUT!

How is displacement along a curved path measured?

Time needed 5–10 minutes

Materials metric ruler, protractor

Thinking Processes
Thinking critically, Measuring in SI

PROGRAM RESOURCES

Teacher Classroom Resources

Study Guide, page 49

Multicultural Activities, page 29, Carousels L1

Other Resources

Walker, Jearl. "Thinking about physics while scared to death (on a falling roller coaster)." *Scientific American,* Oct. 1983, pp. 162–169.

Purpose To learn how to determine the displacement and average velocity along a curved path.

Preparation Students may notice that the scale of the diagram is 1 cm = 1 km. Just measuring the displacement allows them quickly to find the actual length by changing centimeters to kilometers.

Teaching the Activity

Troubleshooting Some students may need help in properly placing the protractor on the diagram to measure the direction.

Expected Outcomes

Students should be able to use distance and direction to describe displacement along a curved path.

Answers to Conclude and Apply

1. 3 km/h, 30 degrees north of east
2. yes.

2 TEACH

Tying to Previous Knowledge

In the study of acceleration in a straight line illustrated in the previous section, students were reminded that they were forced backward when a car accelerated forward. They should also be familiar with how their bodies are thrown to the left when the car turns to the right, and vice versa. Since the direction of the acceleration is inward when moving along a curved path, they should not be surprised by this phenomenon.

Concept Development

Theme Connection The motion of an object along a curved path involves stability and change. Even if it is maintaining a constant speed, it is undergoing a change, centripetal acceleration.

Conclude and Apply

1. What is the average velocity of the 9-km displacement if the train completes the trip in 3 hours? Divide the total displacement by the time interval: average velocity = total displacement/total time. For this instance, the train's average velocity is 9 km/3h, 30 degrees north of east, which equals 3 km/h, 30 degrees north of east.
2. Is the distance along a curved path always greater than the displacement between the start and end points?

CENTRIPETAL ACCELERATION

You learned in the Find Out that displacement along a curved path is measured along a straight line connecting the start and end points. If you travel on a curved road from one town to another, your displacement will be the distance, measured along a straight line, between the two towns. The actual distance you traveled along the curved road will be greater than the displacement. If you were traveling on a curve, in which direction would you accelerate? In the next exercise you will explore the direction of acceleration along a curved path.

FIGURE 13-12. In this ride, the centripetal acceleration keeps the carriage moving in a circle.

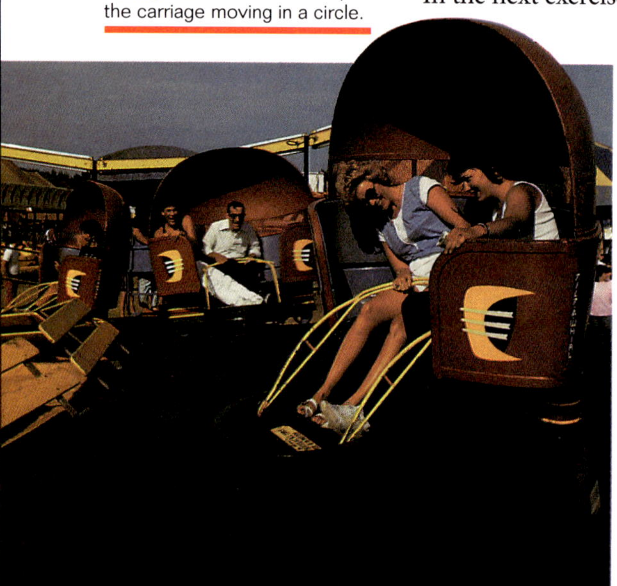

One of the rides at the amusement park is the tilt-a-whirl. In it, you spin around in a small circular path. At the same time, your small cart is sweeping in a larger circular path. At times, you find yourself flung against the side of the cart. This is the result of an acceleration, it happens because you are changing direction. If you carried an accelerometer with you on the ride, you would see the string move outward. Since the direction of the acceleration is always opposite the movement of the string, you know that the acceleration is directed toward the center of the circular path you are following.

PROGRAM RESOURCES

Other Resources

Moreki, A. *Biomechanics of Motion.* New York: Springer Verlag, 1981.

Henry, Ed, and Sherri Miller, "Air Bags vs. Seat Belts: Why You Should Care." *Changing Times,* March 1988, pp. 67–70.

Radetsky, Peter, "The Man Who Mastered Motion." *Science 86,* May 1986, pp. 52–60.

OPTIONS

Meeting Individual Needs

Learning Disabled Encourage these students to act as volunteers. The forces involved in acceleration can be felt and experienced and will supplement the more intellectual concepts described in the text and class discussions. Also pair these students with peer helpers to complete any necessary calculations. LEP

You are already familiar with the effects of acceleration. When the car speeds forward, you feel pushed backward. As an elevator moves upward, you feel pushed downward. By experience you know you are accelerating in a direction opposite to the push. Therefore, in a circular case, since the push feels outward, acceleration must be inward. A device that shows direction inward when moving in a circle is the bubble accelerometer. The next activity will help you see how this works.

EXPLORE!

What is the direction of acceleration of an object moving along a circular path?

Fill a test tube with water. There should be 1 cm air space at the top after a stopper has been inserted into the test tube. When you turn the test tube on its side, you will have a bubble accelerometer. If you move the test tube quickly to the right, the bubble will move in the direction of the acceleration. Try it. Lay the test tube on the radius of a record turntable. After attaching the test tube securely with masking tape, start the turntable rotating at its slowest speed. Which way does the bubble move? Could you use this bubble accelerometer to measure other objects that can move in circular paths?

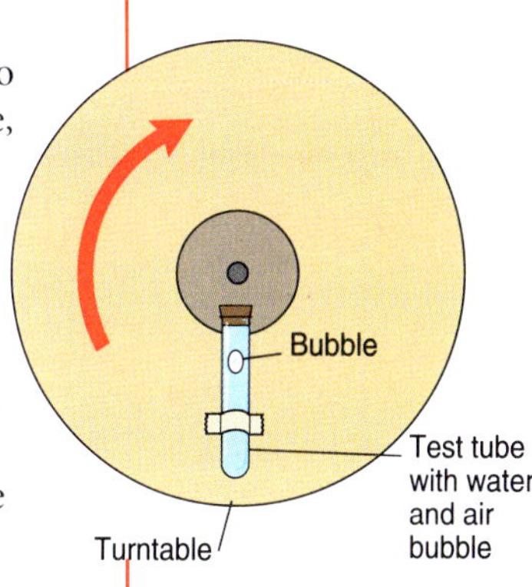

In the Explore, the inward motion of the bubble shows that the acceleration is directed toward the center of the turntable. The direction of the acceleration of an object moving along a circular path is toward the center of the circle and is called **centripetal acceleration.**

You've had a busy day at the amusement park. You have learned some amazing things about objects that travel in circular paths. Now you're hungry. You've really worked up an appetite. To get to the ice cream stand as quickly as possible, you would take the straightest path. You had a chance to take measurements yourself and prove that the straight line distance from one point to another in a certain direction, or the displacement, is indeed the shorter route. You calculate the displacement in the same way, whether the path traveled is straight or

EXPLORE!

What is the direction of acceleration of an object moving along a circular path?

Time needed 10–15 minutes

Materials test tube with stopper, water, masking tape, record turntable

Thinking Processes
Practicing scientific methods, Observing

Purpose To make and use an instrument to identify the direction of acceleration of an object traveling in a circular path.

Preparation Any wheel that can spin when lying flat can be substituted for the turntable.

Teaching the Activity

Discussion Ask students to predict the direction of acceleration before you spin the turntable.

Troubleshooting If the test tube is not full enough, the bubble will be too large for the experiment to be successful. Be prepared for spills.

Expected Outcomes

Students should observe that the bubble moves toward the center of the turntable.

Answers to Questions

1. The bubble moves toward the center of the turntable.
2. Yes; if they were traveling in a bus or car, the bubble accelerometer would show the direction of acceleration as they speeded up, slowed down, or turned.

Multicultural Perspectives

Measuring and computing motion, including acceleration, requires the use of mathematics. Our modern system of mathematics owes a great deal to Islamic mathematicians. They developed the "Arabic numerals" by building upon Hindu mathematics. By the sixteenth century, Arabic numerals had replaced Roman numerals in the West. One Islamic scholar, Abu Jafar al-Khwarizmi, invented algebra (from the Arabic word "al-jabr") during the 9th century AD. One of his contemporaries, Abu al-Battani, developed trigonometry. Thus the modern mathematical tools that we use to study and record motion date back more than one thousand years.

Content Background

As the moon orbits Earth, and Earth orbits the sun at very high velocities, students may wonder what keeps this huge centripetal acceleration from flinging them into space in the opposite direction of the acceleration. An equal force of gravity is what prevents this from happening.

3 Assess

Check for Understanding

To answer the Apply question, students must understand how the bubble accelerometer worked in the Explore activity.

Reteach

When a ball is thrown straight ahead, it eventually follows a curved path as it falls to the ground while still traveling forward. Ask students to draw a diagram of the ball's path and indicate the different types of acceleration that occur.

Extension

Have students use the turntable from the Explore activity. Place a small object on the turntable and spin it at the slow speed. The object will fall off the edge of the turntable. Ask students to predict what would happen if the turntable were rotated at a higher speed. Then repeat the activity using a higher speed. The object should fall off with a greater velocity. This shows that the faster the velocity around a curved path, the greater is the centripetal acceleration. LEP

4 Close

Activity

You will need a 2-m length of string, wooden bead (or any object heavy enough to weigh down the string).

Tie the bead on the end of the string and swing in a circular motion. **CAUTION:** *Be sure object is firmly attached to the string and that students are wearing goggles and are not close to other students while doing this activity.* Ask students in which direction the centripetal acceleration is. They should guess that it is directed along the string toward your hand. Swing the string faster. Ask them if the acceleration increased.

FIGURE 13-13. The distance the car travels is far greater than the displacement from the bottom to the top of the hill.

curved. Remember that displacement and not the distance along any path traveled is used to calculate average velocity. If you ride in a roller coaster at a constant speed on a curved track, you are constantly undergoing centripetal acceleration. You are always accelerating toward the center of the curve or circle that you are traveling around.

As a satellite or space shuttle travels in its orbit around Earth, even when it has a constant speed, it is accelerating toward Earth. You will find out what the source of this acceleration is in the next chapter.

Check Your Understanding

1. If you travel on a curved road from one town to another, your displacement is always different from your actual distance traveled. One is always greater. Explain how you would measure each and why one is greater. Draw a diagram to help you with your explanation.
2. Explain what you would need to know to find the average velocity for motion along a curved path.
3. Why is an object accelerating when it is moving in a circle at constant speed?
4. **APPLY:** Could you use a bubble accelerometer to study the centripetal acceleration of a moving car? Explain how you would do it.

Answers to Check Your Understanding

1. The shortest distance between two points is a straight line. This is also the displacement. Since the road is curved, your travel distance is greater.
2. total displacement and total time
3. Acceleration involves both speed and direction. When an object moves in a circle, its direction is constantly changing, so it is accelerating.
4. Yes. Tape the bubble accelerometer to a flat place in the car; watch the direction in which the bubble moves. The bubble moves in the direction of centipetal acceleration.

EXPANDING YOUR VIEW

CONTENTS

A CLOSER LOOK

AROUND AND AROUND WE GO

Although we generally express our velocity relative to Earth, we can get some interesting information if we consider our velocity relative to other locations. For example, you know that Earth rotates once every 24 hours. When you stand still, your velocity relative to Earth is zero, yet you are moving as Earth rotates. If a friend were suspended above the North Pole in a spaceship and looking down at Earth, what would your friend observe your velocity to be?

The circumference of Earth at the equator is about 25,000 miles (40,000 km). This means that if you were standing at a point on the equator, you would move 25,000 miles in 24 hours as Earth rotates. That's about 1040 mi/hr (1667 km/hr). Your friend in the spaceship would observe you moving in a circle at that velocity.

What is the velocity of Earth as it revolves around the sun? Let's find out!

YOU TRY IT!

Use your math skills to figure out how fast Earth would appear to be moving if you observed it from the sun. Although Earth's path or orbit around the sun is not a perfect circle, we can get a rough idea of our velocity by assuming that it is.

1. The circumference of a circle can be calculated using the equation $c=2\pi r$ where c=circumference, r=the radius of the circle and π=3.14. The average distance from Earth to the sun is about 93,000,000 miles (148,800,000 km). This is the radius of the circle or orbit that Earth travels around the sun. Calculate the circumference of the circle.
2. Earth travels this distance, c, in one year (365 days). How far does Earth travel in one day?
3. What is the velocity of Earth in miles/hour?
4. Why do you think it might become more important to use relative velocity as we increase our travel in space?

Using Expanding Your View

Assign one or more of these excursions to expand your students' understanding of motion and how it applies to other sciences and other subjects. You may assign these as individual or small group activities.

A CLOSER LOOK

Purpose A Closer Look reinforces Section 13-2 by having students consider the velocity of Earth relative to different frames of reference. This excursion also gives students the opportunity to apply the formula for average speed introduced in Section 13-1.

Content Background Because Earth is not a perfect sphere, the text uses the circumference of Earth at the equator. The polar radius is about 19 km less than the equatorial one.

Earth actually takes 365.26 days to complete one orbit around the sun, which is why we add one day to the calendar every four years.

Teaching Strategies Use a world globe to illustrate the concept of relative velocity. Put a piece of tape on the globe and spin it to show that the tape moves with the same velocity as the globe. Students can then observe how their movement would appear to someone in a spaceship.

Going Further Have students work in pairs to calculate speeds and distances traveled by other bodies in the solar system. The moon has a radius of about 1,086 miles and rotates once every 27.32 days. Have students use this information to determine the circumference of the moon and its rotational velocity in miles per hour. *About 6,796 miles; about 10 miles/hour*

The moon has a mean distance from Earth of 240,250 miles and takes 27.32 days to complete its orbit. Ask students to calculate the circumference of Moon's orbit, the distance it travels in one day, and the velocity of the orbit in miles per hour. *About 1,508,770 miles; about 55,222 miles; about 2,301 miles/hour* Use mean distances from the sun and periods of revolution of other planets in the solar system to assign other problems. This data can be found in any good almanac, encyclopedia, or book on the solar system. COOP LEARN

Answers to YOU TRY IT

1. about 584,040,000 miles (934,464,000 km)
2. about 1,600,110 miles (2,560,175 km)
3. about 66,671 miles/hour
4. The rotation of Earth, the revolution of Earth around the sun, and even the speed at which the entire solar system is moving is necessary in order to determine where an object will be when you are traveling great distances over a long period of time through space.

EXPANDING YOUR VIEW

LIFE SCIENCE CONNECTION

Purpose This Life Science Connection reinforces concepts of speed discussed in Section 13-1 by having students compare data presented in a table of fastest animal speeds. The relationship of speed to different animal sizes and habitats is also explored.

Content Background Larger animals tend to have faster average speeds due to increased size in their skeletal and muscular systems resulting in greater strength and stride. For example, a horse can cover about 7.6 m in one stride, an ostrich about 4.6 m, and the cheetah can travel up to 6.1 m.

The cheetah's long stride for its size is largely due to its flexible spine which allows its hind legs to reach ahead of its front legs while running. A cheetah can reach a speed of 72 k/h in two seconds from a standing start. This incredible acceleration (more than most cars) allows it to outrun its prey over short distances.

Teaching Strategy Have students check with their physical education teachers for school records. These teachers may also be able to give them current age-group records for the state, country, and world. Then conduct a 50 or 100-meter dash competition for your class or school. Have the students carefully measure the distance to be run and time the event.

Answers to WHAT DO YOU THINK?

1. Cheetah
2. Snail
3. 4
4. Answers will vary with schools and individuals.

LIFE SCIENCE CONNECTION

HOW FAST DO ANIMALS MOVE?

All animals have specialized structures that allow them to move in different ways and at different speeds.

Animals can move on land, on water, under water, and through the air. They can move their whole bodies or just some of their parts. Animals can walk, run, leap, jump, climb, and dig. Most birds can run, walk, fly, glide, soar, swim, or waddle on land. Snakes can slither. Squids and scallops can move by jet propulsion.

For vertebrates, animals with backbones, movement requires muscles attached to movable bones, and energy. The faster an animal moves, the more energy it uses. For invertebrates, animals without backbones, movement requires other very specialized structures, such as waving hairs, wings, siphons, and sometimes many legs.

Does it surprise you that, generally, the larger the animal, the faster it can move? Does it also surprise you that swimming is the most energy efficient way for an animal to move? Flying requires more energy, because the bird must overcome gravity.

Speed is a measure of the distance traveled in a given amount of time. What animals do you think can move with the highest speeds?

The chart provides the fastest speeds ever measured for a variety of animals. Keep in mind that the greatest speed that an animal is capable of can only last a short amount of time. For every animal, there is a preferred speed that is usually far less than its top speed.

Speeds of Animals

Animal	Speed
Mammals	
cheetah	26.7 m/s
racehorse	19.1 m/s
blue whale	18.0 m/s
dog	16.0 m/s
human	11.0 m/s
cat	10.0 m/s
rabbit	8.0 m/s
squirrel	2.0 m/s
Birds	
vulture	17.0 m/s
ostrich (running)	9.5 m/s
penguin (swimming)	3.5 m/s
duck (swimming)	0.7 m/s
Reptiles	
lizard	6.7 m/s
turtle	2.0 m/s
Amphibians	
frog	1.5 m/s
Fish	
tunny	20.0 m/s
flying fish	10.0 m/s
salmon	3.0 m/s
Invertebrates	
locust	4.5 m/s
dragonfly	3.0 m/s
ant	0.03 m/s
snail	0.0025 m/s

WHAT DO YOU THINK?

Which animal has the fastest top speed? Which animal has the slowest? How many times around a circular track could a rabbit run for every one circuit of a turtle?

What is your school record for the 50 and 100 meter dash? What is this speed in meters per second? How does this compare with the human top speed? What is your best speed in the 50 or 100 meter dash? How does this compare with the fastest human and with your school record?

Going Further Ask students to work in pairs to find the fastest men's and women's times for running events. Have them make a double line graph of their findings by plotting the distance on the horizontal axis and the speed on the vertical axis. One line should represent men and the other women. Ask students to identify any trends shown in their graphs and possible reason for them. COOP LEARN

Going Further Have students work in small groups to research other speeds. Topics could include the speeds of other animals such as the frigate bird and the diving speed of the peregrine falcon and events and speed records set in the special and handicapped olympics. Ask each group to present their findings to the class. COOP LEARN

History CONNECTION

HISTORY OF TIME

Ask a friend, "What time is it?" and she will look at her watch or at the clock on the wall. Watches make it easy for you to know exactly what time it is. This is important to us too, because our days are so full of classes, games, bus rides, TV shows, and other events that start right "on time."

How accurately did people know the time before watches and electric clocks were invented? How did people organize their days before agreeing on a system?

When people first began to farm and build towns, about 10,000 years ago, the most important times to know were the seasons of the year. These were easy to measure by counting the days since the sun was highest in the sky in summer, or since the river flooded in the spring. People soon realized that the seasons repeated themselves about every 365 days.

As life in towns required cooperation among many different people, it became important to know the time of day. The position of the sun in the sky gave a clue, and this could be measured using the first clock, a shadow clock or sundial as shown in the figure. About 3000 years ago in Egypt, the first shadow clock was a post in the ground. If you stood looking at the post toward north, the post would cast a shadow toward the west, to your left, as the sun rose in the morning. At sundown, the shadow would be cast toward the east, to your right, as the sun set in the west. At any point in the day, the shadow would fall on a different position on the ground. This position told the time. During the day, the shadow's tip would move from left to right in an arc to the north. We now call this kind of motion "clockwise," and all clocks are made to move their hands this same way.

The shadow clock was only useful during the day, and people began to invent new clocks that would work at night too. One of these was the water clock. If you made a water jug with a small hole in the bottom, the water would slowly leak out and the water level would go down. The level of the water in the jug would tell you how much time had passed since the jug was filled.

The water clock worked fine during the summer, but not when water froze during winter. This problem was solved by substituting fine sand for water. By about the year 800, the sand clock became the hourglass, a bottle with two compartments separated by a partition with a small hole in it. When the sand all fell through the hole to the bottom compartment, someone quickly turned it over so that the sand would flow the other way. You may

EXPANDING YOUR VIEW

HISTORY CONNECTION

Purpose The History Connection extends Section 13-1 by presenting methods of measuring time that relied on the regular motion of various objects.

Content Background The piece of metal which stands in the center of a sundial is called a gnomon or style. The face of the sundial is called the dial face or plane. The earliest description of a sundial was written by a Chaldean astronomer named Berossus, in about 300 B.C. Daylight was divided into twelve equal sections called temporary hours because they changed with the seasons. A standard length for an hour didn't come until clocks were invented.

Clocks require a stable mechanical oscillator for their operation. The earliest clocks used a heavy weight attached to a string and were first built in the 9th century. Christiann Huygens, a Dutch scientist, built the first pendulum clock about 1656. Around 1500 coiled springs were introduced into clock making allowing for lighter-weight timepieces.

Electric clocks were built in the late 19th century. They have an electric motor synchronized with the frequency of alternating current.

Quartz clocks use the vibrations of a quartz crystal for more precise time keeping and were introduced in 1929. Atomic clocks which measure time by the oscillations of atoms or molecules were first built in 1948.

Going Further Have students work in small groups to build sand or water clocks. Have them use two plastic, wide-mouth containers for each clock. To make a sand clock, students should fasten the containers together at their bottoms and put a small hole through the bottoms. To make a water clock, students should stack the containers and put a small hole in the bottom of the top container and a matching hole in the top of the bottom container. Holes should be small so sand water can drip at a slow but steady rate. Depending on the size of the containers, have students mark the level of sand or water at regular intervals. COOP LEARN

Teaching Strategies Discuss the advantages and disadvantages that digital clocks have over analog clocks. Students may feel that digital clocks are more precise, easier to read, and quicker to learn. On the other hand, analog clocks may show the passage of time better. Talk about common terms such as a quarter or half hour and how they relate to digital clocks.

Activity To complete the You Try It! activity, have small groups set up shadow clocks in the school yard. If that is not possible, have students make a class shadow clock by securing the stick to the floor close to a south-facing window using masking tape.

Answers to YOU TRY IT

1. The shadow clock times require an estimation because only the hours are marked.
2. The shadow clock time could easily be off by 5 to 10 minutes from the actual time.
3. The shadow tips will not match with the stones after a few weeks. The changing position of the sun will cause the shadow to shorten or lengthen and to move at a different rate.

have one of these in your home for measuring cooking times or you may have them in some of your games.

The water and sand clocks were inconvenient because someone always had to be there to refill the water or turn the hourglass over.

By the 1300s, accurate mechanical clocks were invented using a falling weight that turned an axle, indicating the time in hours. These were used in towns to ring bells so that everyone would know what hour it was. It was not until the 1600s that accurate portable clocks using springs were used on sailing ships to help in navigation. These ships' clocks were later made much smaller so that everyone could carry an accurate watch.

As clocks became more accurate and as more people carried watches, the pace of modern life, with all the appointments that fill our days, began to speed up.

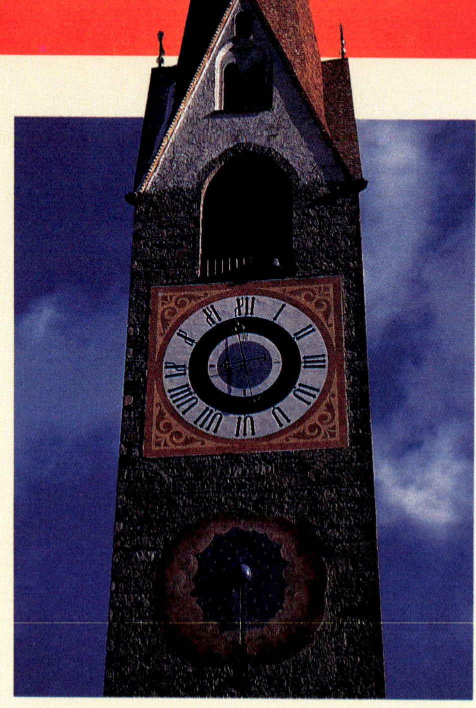

YOU TRY IT!

Build a shadow clock and measure its accuracy. Place a straight stick in the ground. At 8:00 A.M., place a small stone at the tip of the stick's shadow. At every hour after 8:00, place another stone on the shadow's tip.

On another day, choose five times during the day and use your shadow clock to measure the time as accurately as possible. Compare the shadow clock times with the actual time measured with a clock. What are the differences between the shadow clock times and the actual times? How much error would you make in estimating the time using the shadow clock?

Check your shadow clock a few times for the next few weeks. Do the shadow tips still match perfectly with your stones at selected times? Explain why.

TECHNOLOGY CONNECTION

THE TECHNOLOGY OF THRILLS

Ron Toomer gets motion sickness and hates to ride on roller coasters. He especially hates to ride on the Magnum XL-200 in Sandusky, Ohio, the world's largest roller coaster. The Magnum reaches a speed of 75 miles per hour and drops 210 feet on one of its downhill runs. When the cars reach the bottom, the riders are pressed into their seats with about as much force as astronauts taking off in the space shuttle. Ron Toomer is the engineer who designed the Magnum and 80 other roller coasters all over the world. He and the other engineers who design roller coasters have two important thoughts in mind when they begin to plan a new ride — how to make it safe for the riders, and how to produce as many thrills as possible. The first wooden roller coasters built over 100 years ago were rickety and unsafe, and the thrill for some of the riders was the real danger that an accident might happen.

Some coasters are still made of wood, but most are now built from thick steel tubes. A team of engineers uses computers to calculate how strong the track has to be to stand up to the weight, speed, and forces of the cars as they climb, coast down, and go into loops upside down. For every foot of track, the computers calculate the car's velocity and its forces upward, downward, and sideways. New coaster cars are made with wheels above, below, and inside the tracks to keep the car from flying off into space when it goes upside down through corkscrew loops. After the roller coaster is built, computers monitor the speed of each car and apply several different brakes if the car begins to move too fast. The steel tracks and supports are checked for cracks with X ray machines, and padded steel lap bars and belts keep the riders safely in their seats.

For every new thrill the designers build into a roller coaster, new safety features are added.

If Ron Toomer thinks of a new loop or twist that he would find terrifying, he knows that it will be popular with the public and his own kids. His fun comes from using his knowledge of mechanical engineering to create the most terrifying but safest roller coaster rides he can think of.

WHAT DO YOU THINK?

Take a survey of your classmates and friends to find out how many have ridden on a roller coaster, and how many of them would ride on one again. Ask what the roller coaster fans like about the rides and why the others would rather just watch.

TECHNOLOGY CONNECTION

Purpose The Technology Connection extends Sections 13-3 and 13-4 by describing how the concepts of acceleration and motion along curves is used to design roller coasters.

Content Background Mechanical engineering is the study of design, construction, operation, and maintenance of machines for industry and everyday life.

Motion sickness is characterized by nausea, vomiting, and dizziness and can be caused by movement in a car, boat, airplane, etc.

Teaching Strategies Use straight and curved track from a model railroad or race car track to demonstrate the design necessary to keep a roller coaster car from flying off the track. Build a straight section of track that ends in a sharp curve. Push a car so that it travels the length of the track. Raise the straight end of the track slightly and repeat. Keep raising the track slightly until the car flies off the track. Then if possible, bank the curved section so that the outside edge is higher than the inside edge and repeat the raising of the straight end of track.

Answers to WHAT DO YOU THINK?

Students who like the ride will say that it is fun or exciting. Students who do not like the ride will say that it is frightening or that it makes them sick.

Going Further Discuss other rides that students may have experienced at an amusement park or county fair. Have them describe the motion of the rides in terms of acceleration, velocity, and movement around curves. Then ask pairs of students to design and sketch the most frightening ride they can imagine.
COOP LEARN

Going Further Have groups of students research the history of the roller coaster and present their findings in an oral presentation to the class or as a poster.
COOP LEARN

EXPANDING YOUR VIEW

ART CONNECTION

Purpose The Art Connection reinforces Section 13-1 by presenting a style of painting that portrays motion.

Content Background The Futurist movement was not just an artistic period, but a philosophy of life. It was begun in 1908 in Italy by the poet Emilio Marinetti who wanted to destroy the culture of the past and replace it with a new art form and poetry based on dynamic movement and modern urban living. The Futurist movement grew out of the more famous Cubist school of art. Besides Balla, other Futurist painters included Umberto Boccioni, Joseph Stella, and Raymond Duchamp-Villon and his brother Marcel Duchamp.

Dynamism of a Dog on a Leash was inspired by the multiple-exposure photographs of movement by Eadweard Muybridge.

Teaching Strategies Have pairs of students produce a series of pictures which can be flipped through to illustrate motion. One student can pose for the pictures while the other draws simple stick figures. Have students decide upon a movement to draw. It can be a simple dance step or a sports activity. Students may choose to show this same movement in one picture as they complete the What Do You Think activity. Then have the students change roles and create a second series of sketches. COOP LEARN

Art CONNECTION

HOW DO YOU PAINT MOTION?

Italian painter Giacomo Balla painted *Dynamism of a Dog on a Leash* in 1912. He and his artistic friends at the time called themselves "futurists." They were tired of paintings that only showed objects and people at one instant in time like a snapshot. They believed that the future of the modern world would be full of machines in motion and they wanted a new way to paint moving objects that showed the excitement of their motion.

In this painting, which is shown below, the dachshund dog and its fashionable lady are shown with their feet in all possible positions as the dog trots down the street on its daily walk. Looking at the picture, you may get the idea that motion produces a blur to the eye. Single instants of time blend into one another because the eye and the brain cannot keep up with rapidly changing positions.

This painting was probably inspired by the first primitive movies that were made a few years earlier. These were a series of photographs of moving animals and people taken quickly, one after the other. Looking at one picture and then the next by flipping through the photographs lets you imagine the motion taking place. Balla painted the moving dog as if many of these photographs were added together in one place. The effect is to show changing positions over time in a single painting. This kind of painting was very unusual in 1912.

WHAT DO YOU THINK?

Do you think Balla was successful in capturing the rapid motions of the dachshund in this painting? Can you think of other ways that a painting or drawing can show motion? Draw a picture using one of these ideas.

Answers to

WHAT DO YOU THINK?

1. Students may feel that the drawing is just a blur and does not show the dog covering any distance. Others may feel that the drawing looks just as if the dachshund and lady are walking.
2. One possible way to imply motion is to draw something in the picture that is known by the viewer to be moving, such as a bird in the air.

Going Further Have students work in small groups to study paintings of other periods and see the way movement was shown in them. Include paintings by the Cubists and Expressionists. Have the groups explore other art forms, such as sculpture and architecture, that were created during those periods. If possible, take your students on a field trip to an art museum. Then have each student select one piece of art that he or she sees as having movement. Ask students to write short reports explaining how the artists depicted motion in these works.

Reviewing Main Ideas

1. Average speed is the total distance traveled divided by the total time required to travel the distance. This cyclist's instantaneous speed will vary, but he will win the race if he has the greatest average speed.

2. Average velocity is a quantity giving both the average speed and the direction of motion. These sailboats must take the average speed of the wind and the direction in which the wind is blowing into account in order to win a race.

3. Acceleration is a change in velocity that occurs over time. This space shuttle will accelerate from 0 to 700 miles per hour in the 50 seconds after liftoff. Its acceleration is tremendous.

4. While traveling along a curved path at a constant speed, the direction of motion is constantly changing. Objects traveling a curved path experience centripetal acceleration.

Reviewing Main Ideas

Students will participate in a contest to find the fastest attainable speeds and greatest acceleration for animals, humans, and machines. They research and write a short report about one of the other main ideas.

Teaching Strategies

Create a contest to see which student can find the fastest recorded speeds and accelerations in various categories. You can either have students pick one of the categories or assign all of them. The categories for the contest can include:

1. Fastest average speed for men and women in various races, such as the 100 meter, 200 meter, 400 meter, 1,500 meter, 3,000 meter, and marathons.

2. Fastest average speed for nonhuman animals. You can subdivide this category into land, air, and marine animals.

3. Fastest average speed for machines. You can also subdivide this category into land, air, and water speeds.

Students must be able to verify their answers by quoting the source of their information. In a separate activity, students should write a short report about one of the other main ideas. If they elect to cover average velocity, they could write about the way sailboats achieve an average velocity.

A report on the main idea of acceleration might include information about the astronauts aboard the space shuttle. Have students research and write about the training and simulations to prepare for takeoffs.

A report on centripetal acceleration could have students research the curved tracks used for roller coasters or race cars. Have them find out how either of these must be designed in order to keep the cars on the track rather than flying off in a straight line.

Chapter 13

Chapter Review

USING KEY SCIENCE TERMS
Answers
1. acceleration
2. average acceleration
3. displacement
4. average acceleration
5. average velocity or relative velocity
6. acceleration; centripetal acceleration
7. position

UNDERSTANDING IDEAS
Answers
1. Divide the total distance by the total time interval.
2. Speed is a measure of distance over time; velocity requires the direction of motion or displacement and is measured as total displacement over total time interval.
3. Displacement is a measure of distance and direction from your starting point. If you travel two km north and two km south, for example, your distance traveled is four km but your displacement is zero.
4. Determine if it is changing position.
5. Distance is a measurement of length; displacement involves both length and direction from starting position.
6. total distance
7. One cyclist increases speed or accelerates more rapidly than the other.
8. Average acceleration is measured as the change in velocity over the time interval.
9. how fast an object is moving in relation to the frame of reference
10. Toward the center of the circle; in centripetal acceleration, the direction of the acceleration of an object along a circular path is toward the center of the circle.

Chapter Review

USING KEY SCIENCE TERMS
acceleration
average acceleration
average speed
average velocity
centripetal acceleration
displacement
distance
position
relative velocity
time

Use one of the key science terms to complete each sentence.

1. A change in speed or direction is a(n) ____.
2. Dividing the total velocity change by the total time gives ____.
3. A round trip that takes 20 minutes has zero ____.
4. Ten miles per hour is a description of ____.
5. Ten miles per hour south could be a description of ____ or of ____.
6. If you drive along a curved road the ____ toward the center of the curve is ____.
7. Where you sit in the classroom compared to the location of the front desk is your ____.

UNDERSTANDING IDEAS
Answer the following questions.

1. How is average speed determined?
2. How do speed and velocity differ?
3. How can the amount of your displacement be less than the distance you travel?
4. How can you determine if an object is moving?
5. How do distance and displacement differ?
6. What does an odometer measure?
7. What does it mean to say that one cyclist speeds up faster than another?
8. How do you determine average acceleration?
9. What do you need to know to determine relative velocity?
10. In centripetal acceleration, does the object moving in a circular path accelerate toward or away from the center of the circle? Explain your answer.

CRITICAL THINKING
Use your understanding of the concepts developed in the chapter to answer each of the following questions.

1. Does the distance along a path ever equal the displacement?
2. If two friends riding bicycles together both have the same velocity relative to Earth, what is their velocity relative to each other?

PROGRAM RESOURCES
Teacher Classroom Resources
Review and Assessment, Chapter Review and Chapter Test, pages 53-56
Computer Test Bank, Chapter Test

OPTIONS

Cooperative Learning
Consider using Cooperative Learning in the Understanding Ideas, Critical Thinking, Problem Solving, and Connecting Ideas sections of the Chapter Review.
COOP LEARN

Breaking distance needed for specific car speeds

Car speed in meters/second ⟶

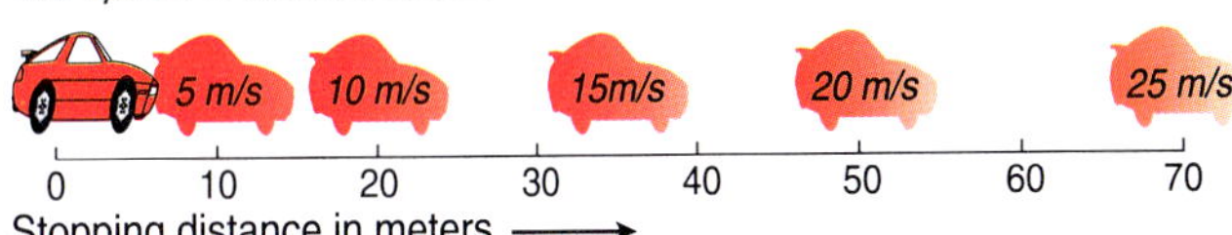

Stopping distance in meters ⟶

3. The data in this illustration give the stopping distances for different car speeds. Plot these points on a graph with the speed in m/s along the horizontal axis and the stopping distance in meters along the vertical axis. Connect the points with a smooth line. Using your graph, determine how much the breaking distance increases when the speed increases from 15 m/s to 30 m/s.
4. Cruise control in a car keeps the car's speed constant. Does it also necessarily keep the car's velocity constant?
5. If you are on a train or a plane with the window shades down, how do you know that you are moving? What could you do to find out if you are moving or not?
6. When you enter some tollways, you are given a toll card that tells the location and time you entered. When you exit, the time on the toll card can be checked. Could a driver ever be issued a speeding ticket with this information? Explain.

PROBLEM SOLVING

Read the following problem and discuss your answers in a brief paragraph.

Your friend lives in another city in your state and wants to visit you. Your friend just called and wants to know the shortest highway route between your two cities. All you have is your state map and a piece of string. Can you determine the shortest route with just the map and the string? Can you determine the displacement? Try it.

Obtain a map of your state and select another city on the map. Using a piece of string, how could you find the shortest highway route from your city to the one you picked? How would you determine the displacement involved?

CONNECTING IDEAS

Discuss each of the following in a brief paragraph.

1. Draw a diagram that shows some of the possible paths of a bicyclist who has a displacement of 3 km to the northeast from his or her home. Make sure you mark the distance of each path.
2. How might you determine the speed of your car if the speedometer broke?
3. **A CLOSER LOOK** Sometimes, as you wait in a car at a stoplight, you feel as though you are moving backward. Give two examples that could explain your feeling.
4. **HISTORY CONNECTION** Compare and contrast three different methods of measuring time. What are the advantages and the disadvantages of each method?
5. **TECHNOLOGY CONNECTION** In which position(s) on a roller coaster track do you experience centripetal acceleration?

CRITICAL THINKING

Answers

1. Yes, if the path traveled is in one direction in an exact straight line. Example: Your distance and displacement would both be 10 km if you traveled 10 km due north.
2. zero
3. by 15 m
4. No, you could be changing direction all the time.
5. You could not really be sure if you were moving unless you experienced a change in velocity. You have no other frame of reference. You could pull up the window shade and look for relative motion of plane/train compared to trees, clouds, etc.
6. Yes, if you know the total distance and the total time interval and there is a given speed limit, it is easy to determine if you traveled faster than the existing speed limit. Example: If your total distance is 100 miles and your total time is 1 1/2 hours, your average speed is 100 ÷ 1.5, or 67, mph. If the speed limit is 55 mph, you are traveling 12 mph over the limit and could be issued a ticket.

PROBLEM SOLVING

Answers

Yes; for each route, place the string along the highway(s) between the two cities, exactly following all curves. Mark the length of each route on the string and compare to determine the shortest route. To determine displacement, place the string in a straight line connecting the two cities.

CONNECTING IDEAS

Answers

1.

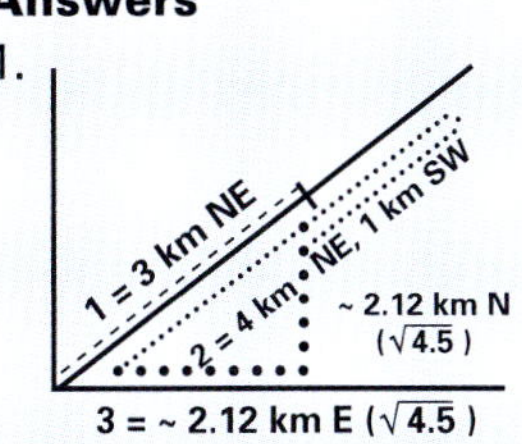

2. Use the odometer and a watch. Find the time it takes to travel one mile. Divide distance by time to determine the speed of your car.
3. moving backward or standing still and a car beside you moves forward; moving forward slowly, and a car beside you moving forward rapidly
4. Examples: clock, hourglass, water clock, and movement of sun, moon, and stars. Advantages and disadvantages are degree of accuracy, precision, convenience, consistency.
5. at any point where the track is curved

CHAPTER ORGANIZER

SECTION	OBJECTIVES	ACTIVITIES/FEATURES
Chapter Opener		**Explore!** How do things fall? p. 421
14-1 Falling Bodies (3 days)	1. **Calculate** the acceleration of a falling object given measurements of its position at various times. 2. **Explain** how strobe photography is useful for analyzing motion. 3. **Describe** the motion of an object as it falls freely toward Earth.	**Find Out!** Do heavier objects fall more quickly? p. 422 **Investigate 14-1:** Acceleration of Falling Objects, p. 425 **Skillbuilder:** Making and Using Graphs, p. 427
14-2 Projectile Motion (1 day)	1. **Describe** the horizontal motion of a projectile. 2. **Describe** the vertical motion of a projectile. 3. **Explain** how vertical and horizontal motions of projectiles are independent.	**Find Out!** Does forward motion affect falling speed? p. 429
14-3 Circular Orbits of Satellites (2 days)	1. **Describe** how a satellite is a projectile in free-fall. 2. **Connect** weightlessness to free-fall. 3. **Explain** certain satellite motion in terms of relative velocity.	**Find Out!** How did *Sputnik I* stay in orbit? p. 433
14-4 The Motion of a Pendulum (3 days)	1. **Define** the period of a pendulum. 2. **Define** frequency, as it relates to periodic motion. 3. **Describe** the relationship between the period of a pendulum, the mass of a bob, the length of the pendulum, and the amplitude of the motion.	**Investigate 14-2:** The Period of a Pendulum, p. 439
Expanding Your View	A Closer Look **Terminal Velocity: Falling in Air,** p. 441 Life Science Connection **Biological Effects of Weightlessness,** p. 442	Science and Society **Weather Satellites,** p. 443 How It Works **The Metronome,** p. 445 History Connection **Galileo,** p. 446

ACTIVITY MATERIALS

EXPLORE!	INVESTIGATE!	FIND OUT!
Page 421 modeling clay, pencil	**Page 425** paper, pencil **Page 439** 80-cm piece of string, 8 metal washers, masking tape, ruler, meterstick, seconds timer	**Page 422** string; heavy bolt or nut, or another object of that size; light piece of wood **Page 429** meterstick, 2 coins

Chapter 14
Motion near Earth

TEACHER CLASSROOM RESOURCES	OTHER RESOURCES
Study Guide, p. 50 **Concept Mapping,** p. 22 **Multicultural Activities,** p. 31 **Making Connections: Across the Curriculum,** p. 31 **Making Connections: Technology and Society,** p. 31 **Activity Masters, Investigate 14-1,** pp. 57-58	**Laboratory Manual,** pp. 81-82, Speed of Falling Objects **Color Transparency and Master 27,** Strobe of Ball Falling ***STVS:** *Reducing Hail Damage,* Earth and Space (Disc 3, Side 1)
Study Guide, p. 51	**Laboratory Manual,** pp. 83-86, Projectile Motion **Color Transparency and Master 28,** Projectile Motion ***STVS:** *VTOL Airliners,* Physics (Disc 1, Side 2) *Shock Impact Gun,* Chemistry (Disc 2, Side 1)
Study Guide, p. 52 **Critical Thinking/Problem Solving,** p. 22 **Multicultural Activities,** p. 32 **Take Home Activities,** p. 23 **How It Works,** p. 15 **Making Connections: Integrating Sciences,** p. 31 **Flex Your Brain,** p. 8	***STVS:** *Balloons in Science,* Earth and Space (Disc 3, Side 2)
Study Guide, p. 53 **Activity Masters, Investigate 14-2,** pp. 59-60 **Review and Assessment,** pp. 57-60	**Computer Test Bank**
	***STVS:** *Growing Plants in Space,* Plants and Simple Organisms (Disc 4, Side 2) **Spanish Resources** **Cooperative Learning Resource Guide Lab and Safety Skills**

***Science and Technology Videodisc Series**

KEY TO TEACHING STRATEGIES

Teaching strategies have been coded for varying learning styles and abilities. As you review teaching strategies in the margin, the following designations will help you decide which activities are appropriate for your students.

- **L1** Level 1 activities are basic activities and should be within the ability range of all students.
- **L2** Level 2 activities are average activities and should be within the ability range of the average to above-average student.
- **L3** Level 3 activities are challenging activities designed for the ability range of above-average students.
- **LEP** LEP activities should be within the ability range of Limited English Proficiency students.
- **COOP LEARN** Cooperative Learning activities are designed for small group work.

ADDITIONAL MATERIALS

	AUDIOVISUAL
Free Fall, Educational Coursewear. *Newton's Laws,* J&S Software. *Investigating Gravitational Force,* IBM.	*Projectile Motion,* film, EME. *Let's Move It: Newton's Laws of Motion,* video, Focus.

Chapter 14

Motion Near Earth

THEME DEVELOPMENT

One theme of this chapter is interaction and systems. In the Find Out activity on page 422 and the Investigate activity on page 425, students analyze the interaction between gravity and falling objects that produces acceleration in the gravitational system of Earth. The theme of stability and change becomes evident as students learn how a projectile moving at the right speed can enter a stable orbit around Earth. In the Investigate activity on page 439, students learn what factors change the motion of a pendulum.

CHAPTER OVERVIEW

The chapter covers gravitational acceleration and its effect on stationary and moving objects.

Students calculate the acceleration of gravity based on strobe photos of falling objects and learn that this acceleration is less on the moon.

Then students learn that the motion of a projectile consists of independent vertical and horizontal components.

Next, students extend the idea of projectile motion to explain the orbits of satellites, weightlessness, and orbits in which satellites appear to remain motionless over Earth.

Finally, students study the motion of a pendulum and prove that only pendulum length and amplitude—not bob weight—determine its frequency.

Tying to Previous Knowledge

Tell students that in the last chapter they learned about both velocity and acceleration. Ask if a moving object's velocity tends to remain the same. Students will recall that, friction excepted, a moving object tends to keep moving at the same velocity. Tell them that in the next chapter they will learn about a situation in which moving objects accelerate rather than maintain velocity.

DID YOU EVER WONDER . . .

Whether heavy objects and light objects hit the ground at the same time when they fall?

How satellites can stay in orbit?

Why astronauts float around in the space shuttle?

You'll find the answers to these questions as you read this chapter.

DID YOU EVER WONDER...

Students will explore these questions as they progress through the chapter. Don't spoil their fun and motivation by sharing these answers too early.

- Heavy and light objects hit the ground at the same time if released at the same time, assuming no air resistance. (pages 422–423)
- Satellites stay in orbit because their combined forward and falling motions make a path that matches the curvature of Earth.
- Because they are freely falling around Earth, they are weightless. (page 434)

Motion near Earth

Humans live only on Earth. We seldom stray far from its surface. You may have flown in an airplane, but that's still close to Earth. Some humans have gone to the moon. That may seem a long way from Earth, but compared with the distance to the other planets or the stars, it's not far at all.

Because we have spent nearly all of our time on Earth's surface, almost all our experience with motion has to do with the way objects move near or on Earth. When you shoot a basketball at a basket, you know the ball will fall back down. When you run down a basketball court, you know you are continually pushing off Earth and dropping back to it with each step.

How does motion close to Earth differ from what it would be in space? In this chapter, you'll explore motion on Earth and get an idea of how you would move elsewhere.

EXPLORE!

How do things fall?

Make two balls out of modeling clay. Make one about 1.5 cm in diameter and the other 4 cm. You now have one light object and one heavy object. Hold them in your hand. Which do you think will fall more quickly when dropped? Drop them at the same time from the same height. Which hits first? Do they hit at the same time? Now, attach one clay ball to each end of a pencil. You now have an object with a light end and a heavy end. Hold this object high and drop it! Does one side seem to hit before the other? Drop the object several more times, each time turning it in a different position before dropping. What change do you notice?

Introducing the Chapter

Have students study the photo on page 420 and describe what will happen next. Students should note the falling of players and the ball. Tell students that this chapter explains why and exactly how falling objects fall.

Uncovering Preconceptions

Students may believe that a heavier object falls faster than a light object. You may wish to ask them about it before they do the Explore activity.

EXPLORE!

How do things fall?

Time needed 15 minutes

Materials modeling clay, pencil

Thinking Processes Thinking critically, Observing and inferring, Comparing and contrasting

Purpose To determine whether a heavier object falls faster than a lighter object.

Preparation Have students work in pairs, taking turns dropping and observing from near floor level. COOP LEARN

Teaching the Activity

Troubleshooting The clay balls will tend to fly off the pencil and will need to be retrieved and replaced before each drop. L1

Expected Outcome

Students observe that objects fall at the same rate regardless of their weight.

Answers to Questions

Both balls hit at the same time when dropped together. When attached to a pencil, they still fall at the same rate; the pencil does not change orientation during the fall.

Project

Have students build a kinetic sculpture in which a rolling marble tips balances, rings bells, spins "water wheels," and leaps over gaps to demonstrate gravity's acceleration. Pathways can be built from cardboard bent into U-shaped channels, taped together, and mounted on cardboard legs. Students may wish to compete in groups to build the most interesting sculpture and explain the forces involved.

Science at Home

Students can study pendulum motion by poking a small hole in a plastic bottle, filling it with sand, and using it as a pendulum bob. Caution students to spread taped-together newspapers beneath the pendulum to catch the sand for reuse. The trail of sand will show the pendulum path. Students can try both back-and-forth and circular movements to see what patterns result.

Section 14-1

Preparation

Concepts Developed

The previous chapter discussed motion and its characteristics. In the first section of this chapter, students learn about motion caused by the acceleration of gravity both on Earth and on the moon. In two activities, students analyze the behavior of a pendulum and of two freely falling objects, and draw conclusions about gravity.

Planning the Lesson

In planning your lesson on falling bodies, refer to the Chapter Organizer on pages 420A-B for timing suggestions, resources, and additional materials that will help you in your presentation of the lesson concepts.

For adequate development of the concepts presented in this section, we recommend that students do the Find Out activity on page 422.

1 Motivate

Demonstration Fill a small balloon with water and tie it. Hold the balloon 2 centimeters above a tabletop and ask students what will happen when you let go. Students should say that it will fall. Ask students to raise their hands if they think the balloon will break, then drop the balloon, which will not break. Then hold the balloon a meter above the tabletop. Ask students if they think the balloon will break when dropped from this height. Most students should believe that the balloon will break. Ask them why they thought the balloon would break when dropped from a higher point. Students should say that the balloon will be going faster and will hit the tabletop harder. As is the case with most demonstrations, you should test this before doing it in front of the class. L1

14-1 Falling Bodies

OBJECTIVES

In this section, you will

- calculate the acceleration of a falling object given measurements of its position at various times;
- explain how strobe photography is useful for analyzing motion;
- describe the motion of an object as it falls freely toward Earth.

KEY SCIENCE TERMS

acceleration due to gravity

DESCRIBING HOW THINGS FALL

You experience falling objects every day. On the way to school, raindrops or snowflakes may have fallen on you, and you may have seen leaves, seeds, or twigs fall from trees. You have probably fallen down yourself in gym class or in other activities. When you jump, you always come back to Earth. Falling to Earth is usually harmless when you jump from the ground, but you know that falling from a greater height may be dangerous. What always brings you back to Earth when you jump? In this section, you will describe the motion of falling objects and learn that there is something similar about the motions of all falling objects, including yourself.

FIGURE 14-1. The beauty of a gymnast's routine is the athlete's ability to keep from falling to Earth.

FIND OUT!

Do heavier objects fall more quickly?

There are several ways to find out whether heavy objects fall more quickly than light objects. One way is to construct something called a pendulum. Try the following activity. Tie a string to a heavy bolt or nut or another object of that size. Hold the end of the string with one hand while you pull the nut, which we call the pendulum

PROGRAM RESOURCES

Teacher Classroom Resources

Study Guide, page 50

Laboratory Manual, pages 81-82, Speed of Falling Objects L2

Concept Mapping, page 22, Acceleration L1

Multicultural Activities, page 31, Moon Lore L1

Transparency Masters, page 57, and **Color Transparency,** number 27, Strobe of Ball Falling L2

bob, to one side with the other hand. Let the bob go and observe it closely. Notice that it doesn't come to a complete stop immediately. When the bob reaches the bottom of the swing, it continues on, swinging back up, almost to its original position, then it reverses and starts to fall again. Observe the swing closely. If heavy objects fall more quickly than light ones, you would expect a heavy pendulum bob to reach the bottom of a pendulum swing more quickly than a lighter object. Construct another pendulum using a light piece of wood as a bob. With a partner holding one pendulum and you holding the other, start the pendulums swinging at the same time. Make sure the strings are the same length.

Conclude and Apply

1. What happened?
2. Did the heavy bob reach the bottom first, or did both pendulums arrive at the same time?

More than 2300 years ago, the Greek philosopher Aristotle was interested in the same question—do heavy objects fall at the same speed as lighter objects? At that time, people didn't do experiments to learn things. Instead, they used reasoning based on their beliefs about nature. Aristotle, like others of his time, believed that Earth was the center of the universe and that objects containing more mass would naturally rush more quickly to the center of the universe. Aristotle would have said that a large stone would fall faster than a small pebble.

In the early 1600s, the Italian scientist Galileo used experimentation to answer the question about falling objects. According to legend, Galileo dropped objects of different weights from the top of the Leaning Tower of Pisa to find out which would hit the ground first. His experiment is illustrated in Figure 14-2. Galileo concluded that all objects will fall from the same height in the same time. Galileo, however, had the same problems

FIGURE 14-2. Galileo did an experiment to see how objects of different weights fell.

FIND OUT!

Do heavier objects fall more quickly?

Time needed 15 minutes

Materials for each group of students, two 3-foot lengths of string, a bolt or nut or another heavy object, and a light object such as a small piece of wood

Thinking Processes
Observing and inferring, Comparing and contrasting, Recognizing cause and effect

Purpose To learn that the swing of a pendulum is independent of the bob's weight.

Preparation This can be a better demonstration if the first pendulum has one bolt for a bob and the second pendulum has two bolts. Students can see more clearly that the mass at the end of the string is doubled. Some students actually think that the material of a bob makes a difference.

Teaching the Activity

Troubleshooting Caution students holding the upper end of the string to keep it as still as possible. Have students pull the pendulum bob only 1 foot to the side and release it; raising it farther disturbs the swing.

Caution students to pull the same distance each time they try this. COOP LEARN L1

Expected Outcomes

Students learn that a pendulum set in motion continues to swing, and that the weight of the bob makes no difference in its speed.

Conclude and Apply

1. The light and heavy bobs swung at the same speed.
2. Both pendulums arrived at the same time.

OPTIONS

Multicultural Perspectives

An Italian doctor named Santorio Santorio developed the first accurate way to measure the human pulse. In an age before accurate timekeeping—before the pendulum was used to regulate clocks—Santorio applied the pendulum principle discovered by his friend Galileo to create a device he called the pulsiloge. It consisted of a string with a weight on one end, which was wound around a drum. The physician turned the drum to shorten or lengthen the string until the swing of the pendulum exactly matched the pulse rate of the patient. A pointer on the drum indicated this rate on a dial.

2 TEACH

Tying to Previous Knowledge

In the previous chapter, students learned to distinguish between velocity and acceleration. Begin this section by asking students to review the differences between velocity and acceleration. In this section, they will use both concepts to analyze how gravity affects objects motion.

Concept Development

Theme Connection The theme of interactions and systems is supported as students explore the interaction of objects with gravity. This interaction becomes evident as students perform the Find Out and Investigate activities.

Demonstration This activity will show the constant acceleration of gravity. Materials needed are 2-m lengths of string and metal washers.

Securely attach a metal washer at each of the following positions along a 2-m length of string: 0 cm, 5 cm, 20 cm, 80 cm, 125 cm, and 180 cm. Hold the string by the end nearest to the 180 cm position over a metal wastebasket or pie plate. Ask students to predict what they will hear when the string is dropped. Release the string. Students should hear regular intervals between the clicks of the washers striking metal. Ask students to explain how this activity demonstrates the constant acceleration of gravity. *The constant time interval between clicks indicates that each washer, which had to fall a longer distance than the one beneath it, covered that distance in the same time, due to the constant acceleration of gravity.*

Content Background

The acceleration of gravity varies with location on Earth. Its pull is slightly stronger in northern latitudes and is weaker at the peaks of mountains than at sea level. The variation is not more than 0.3 percent.

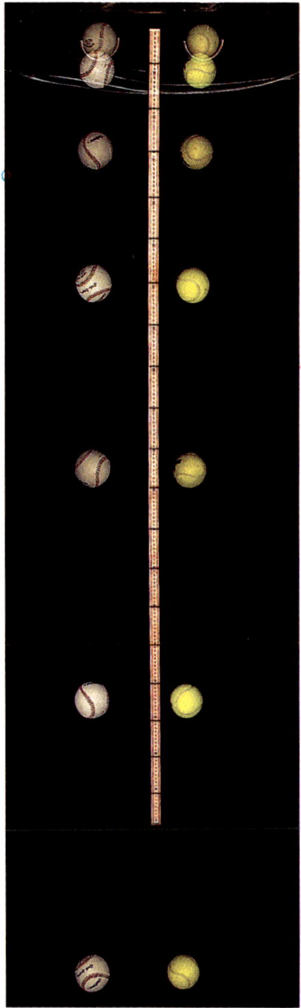

FIGURE 14-3. Photography can show that two objects of different mass reach the ground at the same time when dropped from the same height.

you may have had in the last activity. He couldn't really be certain whether the objects reached the ground at the same time or not because they were moving too quickly.

After swinging the light and heavy pendulum bobs at the same time, it probably seemed to you that they reached the bottom of their swings at the same time. But, like Galileo, how can you be sure?

If you stood in the middle of a basketball court and threw a real basketball and foam ball into the air at the same time and observed them closely, do you think you could tell which ball falls more quickly? Probably not. Like Galileo's objects and your pendulums in the last activity, the balls would be moving too quickly for you to see precisely how they moved. What you would need is something that could allow you to see exactly where the balls were at certain instants of time.

A method of photography called strobe photography allows you to take several photographs of moving objects only fractions of a second apart. In a way, strobe photography stops the motion of objects at specific and consistent time intervals. This allows us to see the motion more easily and accurately.

An example of strobe photography is shown in Figure 14-3. The figure shows a baseball and a tennis ball that have been dropped from the same height. Each image that you see is a photograph of a ball taken every $1/10$ second. If the first photo was taken at $1/10$ second, the next was taken at $2/10$, and the one after that was taken at $3/10$ second, and so on. From the figure, you can see that both balls are falling in unison even though they don't have the same mass.

In the background of the photograph is a two-meter measuring stick. If you look at each ball carefully, you can tell that as the ball falls, there seems to be more distance between each succeeding image. You can test this by using a ruler. You learned in Chapter 13 that distance traveled in a given time is a measure of speed. Therefore, if the balls are moving greater distances in the same period of time, as is shown in Figure 14-3, they are speeding up or accelerating. In the following activity, you will use Figure 14-3 to discover the acceleration of these two falling objects.

OPTIONS

Meeting Individual Needs

Learning Disabled Learning-disabled students may have trouble with the mathematics required by the Investigate activity but may be able to make accurate measurements of position. Team learning-disabled students with one or more other students, with the learning-disabled student responsible for measurements. You may also wish to spend additional time with learning-disabled students, reviewing the fundamental concepts of velocity and acceleration and using the example of a car or bicycle's motion, with which they will be familiar, to explain the difference. COOP LEARN

INVESTIGATE!

14-1 ACCELERATION OF FALLING OBJECTS

The photograph in Figure 14-3 gives you the opportunity to measure how quickly objects fall.

PROBLEM

What is the acceleration of falling objects?

PROCEDURE

1. Copy the data table. Using the metric ruler in the background of Figure 14-3, record the position of the first image of one ball after it has been dropped. Always **measure** the ball position from the same point on the ball.
2. Record the position of the second image.
3. **Calculate** the distance from the first to the second image by subtracting the position of the first image from the position of the second image. Record this distance in the table under Image 2.
4. The images were taken 1/10 of a second apart. Use this information to calculate the average velocity of the balls between the first and second image in centimeters per second by dividing the distance fallen by 1/10 second.
5. Record the position of the rest of the images. Make sure you always measure to the same place on the ball.
6. Find the distance between each pair of images and the average velocity. Fill these in for the rest of the images.
7. The last column of the table shows the exact time the balls' velocity reached the average velocity. To calculate these times, we assumed the clock started at the time of the first image and that the ball reached average velocity halfway between any two images.

DATA AND OBSERVATIONS

Sample data

ACCELERATION OF FALLING OBJECTS

IMAGE	POSITION (CM)	DISTANCE FALLEN (CM)	AVERAGE VELOCITY (M/S)	TIME (S)
1				
2	10	10	1	0.05
3	28	18	1.8	0.15
4	60	32	3.2	0.25
5	115	55	5.5	0.35
6	167.5	52.5	5.25	0.45

ANALYZE

1. Did the velocity of the ball change as it fell? How do you know?

CONCLUDE AND APPLY

2. How much did the average velocity increase between the second and third images? Between the third and the fourth images?
3. **Going Further:** You can determine the ball's acceleration by dividing the velocity change by the time it takes for the velocity to change.

   How much did the velocity increase between the image at 0.05 s, and the image at 0.35 s? Find the acceleration by dividing the increase in velocity by the time interval in seconds. What was your result?

INVESTIGATE!

14-1 ACCELERATION OF FALLING OBJECTS

Time needed 20 minutes

Thinking Processes
Organizing information, Making and using tables, Practicing scientific methods, Observing, Interpreting data

Purpose To determine the acceleration of gravity.

Preparation Before starting, confirm that students copied the data table correctly. LEP

Teaching the Activity

Troubleshooting Guide students as they complete the data table by going over the following information. The *Position* column gives the position of the ball as shown by the metric ruler. The *Distance Fallen* column shows the *change* in position: current position subtracted from the position in the previous image. *Average Velocity* is the distance fallen divided by 0.1 second. L1

Expected Outcomes

Students learn that gravity accelerates objects at 9.8 m/s^2.

Answers to Analyze/Conclude and Apply

1. Yes; the average velocity increased from Image 2 to 5. There was more space between images.
2. 0.98 m/s between the second and third and 2.4 m/s between the third and fourth images
3. As measured in the sample data: The velocity increased 4.5 m/s between 0.05 and 0.35. The acceleration was $\frac{4.5 \text{ m/s}}{0.30 \text{ s}}$ =15m/s^2.

Content Background

The acceleration of gravity varies with location on Earth. Its pull is slightly stronger in northern latitudes and is weaker at the peaks of mountains than at sea level. The variation is not more than 0.3 percent.

PROGRAM RESOURCES

Teacher Classroom Resources

Activity Masters, pages 57-58, Investigate 14-1

Making Connections: Across the Curriculum, page 31, Gravity L2

Making Connections: Technology and Society, page 31, Space Law L2

MAKING CONNECTIONS

Math

Ads for sports cars often say how long the car takes to accelerate from 0 to 60 miles per hour. Ask students if they can name the time for their favorite car; otherwise, use 10 seconds. Ask students if the car accelerates faster or slower than gravity. Lead students in converting miles per hour into meters per second: 60 mph × 1.61 = 96.6 km/h × 1,000 = 96,600 m/h ÷ 3,600 = 26.8 m/s. Have students use the formula in the Going Further question in Investigate to calculate the car's average acceleration. *26.8 divided by 10, or 2.68 m/s^2—over three times less than gravity.* L3

Concept Development

Demonstration Take two identical sheets of paper, crumple one of them up into a ball, and hold them up in front of you. Ask students to predict whether they will hit the ground at the same time when dropped. Drop both pieces of paper to confirm the prediction. Ask students to explain why the flat sheet of paper takes longer to fall. Air resistance opposes a falling object and slows it down; the paper ball encounters less air resistance because of its round, compact shape. L1

SKILLBUILDER

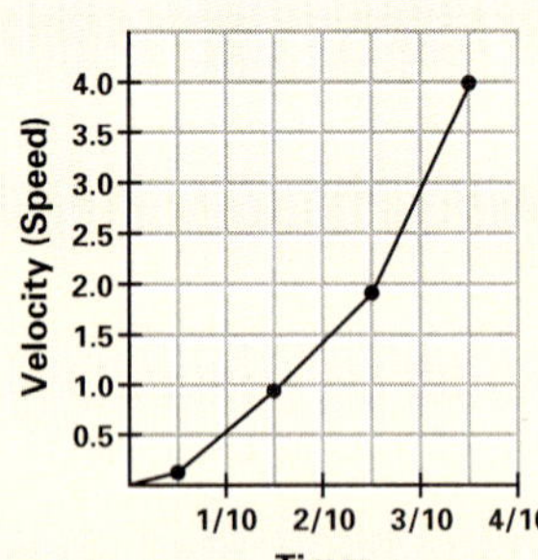

Student descriptions should note that as the time increases, the velocity of the falling objects also increased. L1

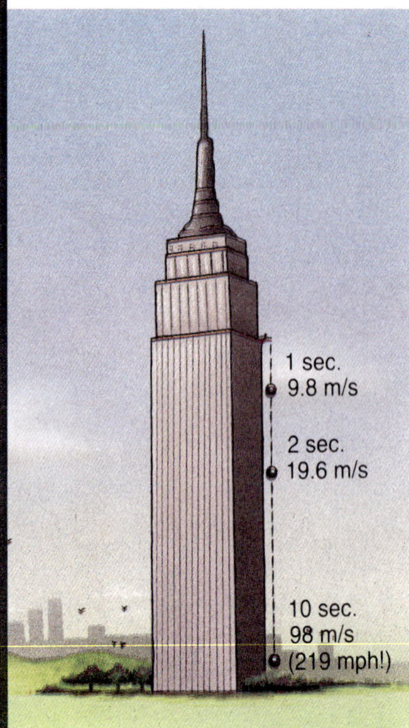

FIGURE 14-4. A falling bowling ball could be dangerous, not just because of its weight but because of its velocity.

FIGURE 14-5. The acceleration due to gravity is less on the moon than Earth, so it's easier to jump high on the moon.

You're probably familiar with the acceleration of a car. When a car changes speed or direction, we say that the car is accelerating. A car can speed up when you give it energy by pressing on the accelerator. What causes the balls in the Investigate to speed up? As you will learn later, acceleration requires forces. The force that produces this acceleration has been given the name gravity.

In the Investigate, when you measured the **acceleration due to gravity**, the result was 980 cm/s/s, which can be written as 9.8 m/s^2. You saw that the acceleration was the same for two different objects of different size and mass. The acceleration due to gravity, which is given the symbol g, is the same for any free falling objects. A basketball falling through the air will accelerate at 9.8 m/s^2, and a two-ton truck, if dropped from a building, would accelerate toward Earth at 9.8 m/s^2. Thus we say:

$$g = 9.8\ m/s^2$$

When you sit back and think about this number, you begin to realize that free falling objects accelerate very quickly. Imagine if you climbed up to the top of a large building and dropped a bowling ball off the roof!

Look at Figure 14-4. When you first let go of a bowling ball, its velocity would be zero. After one second, it would be falling at 9.8 meters per second, or 9.8 m/s. A second later, the ball would pick up another 9.8 m/s, and it would be falling at 19.6 m/s. If the bowling ball were still in the air after 10 seconds, it would be falling at about 98 m/s. That's about 353 kilometers per hour! Have you ever moved that fast?

ACCELERATION ON THE MOON

Have you ever seen films of astronauts on the moon? If you have, you may have wondered why the astronauts were able to jump so high off the ground. You can see an astronaut jumping on the moon in Figure 14-5. How are they able to do that?

OPTIONS

Enrichment

Activity Students can have a parachute-making contest. Let students experiment with a variety of materials, sizes, and shapes for their parachutes. Have them determine which parachutes will stay aloft the longest and which ones will support the most weight.

Astronauts are able to jump so high on the moon because the acceleration of gravity on the moon is less than the acceleration of gravity on Earth. Jumping astronauts on the moon can reach a greater height before the acceleration of gravity slows them to a stop and causes them to fall back to the surface.

Objects of different masses on the moon still accelerate downward at the same rate, but that rate is less than 9.8 m/s^2. On the moon, the acceleration due to gravity is about 1.6 m/s^2.

If you had the opportunity to play basketball on the moon, even Michael Jordan would be amazed at what you could do. Slam-dunking the ball would be simple because the lower acceleration due to gravity on the moon would allow you to jump higher.

We experience *g* in our everyday activities. Gravity is important even as you walk or run. It determines how far forward you lean, how hard you must push off the ground, and how your body and feet feel as you transfer your weight from one foot to the other.

Heavy objects, light objects, and objects in between all fall with an acceleration equal to *g*. You now know at what rate of acceleration dropped objects fall at or near Earth's surface. What about when something is actually thrown, like when you throw a ball to the catcher to get a player out at home plate? Does this motion affect the way the object falls? In the next section, you will explore the kinds of motion that occur when an object is thrown.

SKILLBUILDER

MAKING AND USING GRAPHS

Plot a graph of the results of Investigate 14-1. Put the average velocity of the ball on the vertical axis. Put the times that the ball actually fell at this velocity on the horizontal axis. Connect the points on the graph with a smooth line that goes all the way to the horizontal axis. Describe this line in words using the variables in your experiment (time and average velocity) in your description. If you need help, refer to the **Skill Handbook** on page 650.

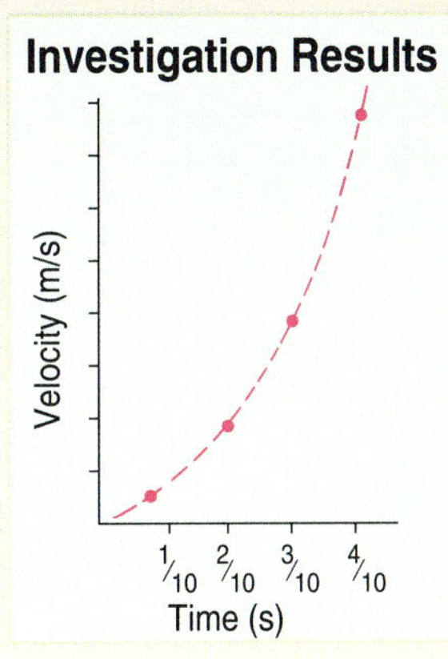

Check Your Understanding

1. Calculate the speed of an object, in meters per second, that has been falling from a building for eight seconds.
2. Explain in your own words how falling objects accelerate.
3. How could you show that the acceleration due to gravity of an object is a constant?
4. **APPLY:** Suppose an astronaut on the moon dropped a piece of rock from a height of 2 m and measured the time it took to fall to the ground. Explain why a rock dropped from the same height on Earth would reach the ground more quickly.

3 Assess

Check for Understanding

The Apply question calls for students to recognize that gravity is constant on the moon but is less powerful than on Earth.

Reteach

Have students imagine catching a baseball that had fallen from the second story of a house. Then have them contrast this with the feel of catching a ball that had fallen from the roof of a five-story building. Ask students which ball would hit harder and why.

Lead students to see that the second ball will hit harder because it is moving faster. L1

Extension

Ask students to imagine a gun shooting a bullet straight up. The bullet leaves the gun at 805 km/h. Have students calculate how many seconds it takes the bullet to come to a stop. You may need to remind students that a rising object slows down at the same rate at which a falling object speeds up. The answer is 805 km/h × 1,000 = 805,000 m/h ÷ 3,600 = 223.6 m/s ÷ 9.8 m/s = 22.8 seconds. L3

4 Close

Activity

Students learned that the acceleration of gravity on the moon is only 1.6 m/s^2 versus 9.8 m/s^2 on Earth. Ask students to use these numbers to calculate how much a 1,500-pound car would weigh on the moon's surface. Suggest that students determine the ratio of moon gravity to Earth gravity. *1.6 ÷ 9.8 = 16%* Then to calculate what something would weigh on the moon, students can multiply its Earth weight by 0.16. Therefore, a car that weighs 1,500 pounds on Earth would weigh only about 245 pounds on the moon. L1

Answers to Check Your Understanding

1. 8 × 9.8 m/s = 78.4 meters/second
2. Gravity exerts a constant force on the object, making its velocity constantly increase.
3. Measure the velocity at two different intervals and compare the two velocities.
4. Earth's gravity accelerates the rock at a higher rate than the moon's gravity, that is, force of gravity is greater.

Section 14-2

PREPARATION

Concepts Developed

In the previous lesson, students analyzed the effects of gravity on falling objects. In this lesson, students learn about the motion of projectiles. They learn that projectile motion has both a vertical (falling) component and a horizontal (forward travel) component that act independently of each other, so that a projectile falls at the same rate as an object that is not moving forward while falling.

Planning the Lesson

In planning your lesson on projectile motion, refer to the Chapter Organizer on pages 420A-B for timing suggestions, resources, and additional materials that will help you in your presentation of the lesson concepts. For adequate development of the concepts presented in this section, we recommend that students do the Find Out activity on page 429.

1 MOTIVATE

Demonstration Show students a small rubber ball. Hold it up in one hand and release it so that it falls straight down into your other hand. Then have one student catch the ball when you toss it to him or her. Ask students to describe the two motions. Lead students to see that you first dropped the ball vertically and then threw the ball horizontally. Ask students if they think the ball was falling in both cases. Students should conclude that a thrown ball is still falling as it is moving forward. L1

14-2 Projectile Motion

OBJECTIVES

In this section, you will

- describe the horizontal motion of a projectile;
- describe the vertical motion of a projectile;
- explain how vertical and horizontal motions of projectiles are independent.

KEY SCIENCE TERMS

projectile motion
horizontal component
vertical component

THE MOTION OF PROJECTILES

Everyone has, at one time or another, experienced projectile motion. What happens when you throw a stone or ball? The object will follow some curve through the air until it falls back down to Earth. Objects that are launched forward into the air, such as rockets, bullets, and satellites, are called projectiles. But even common objects, such as the soccer ball or baseball shown in Figure 14-6(a), are also projectiles. This type of motion is called **projectile motion**. How does such a thrown object move?

Imagine that you're back on the basketball court where the floor is perfectly flat. Standing at one end of the court and holding a basketball up to your chest, you fire the ball horizontally as hard as you can. The ball goes speeding off your fingertips. At the exact moment that you let go of the ball, a friend drops a coin from the same height as your chest, as shown in Figure 14-6(b). Which will hit the ground first, the basketball or the coin? The basketball in this example has forward motion at the same time that it is falling to Earth. Does the forward motion affect its falling speed?

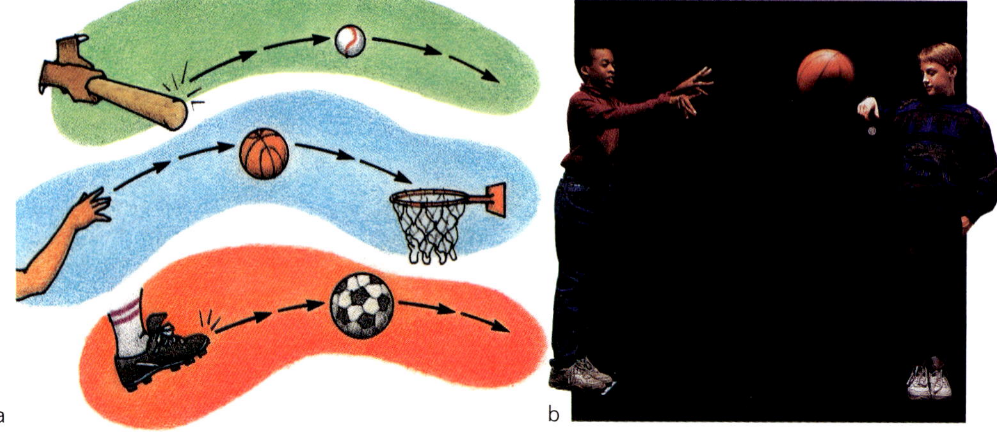

FIGURE 14-6. Projectile motion occurs whenever objects are launched forward (a). Does projectile motion affect falling speed (b)?

PROGRAM RESOURCES

Teacher Classroom Resources

Study Guide, page 51
Laboratory Manual, pages 83-86, Projectile Motion COOP LEARN
Transparency Masters, page 59, and **Color Transparency,** number 28, Projectile Motion L1

FIND OUT!

Does forward motion affect falling speed?

You can investigate the motion of projectiles by doing the following activity. Lay a meterstick across the edge of a table. Place one coin between the meterstick and the table's edge. It should be right on the edge and just a few millimeters from the stick. Place a second coin 15 to 20 cm further up the meterstick. It, too, should be just a few millimeters from the stick. While making sure that the meterstick stays in contact with the table, quickly swing the meterstick so that it pivots at the table's edge, as shown in the figure. It should push both coins off the table at the same time.

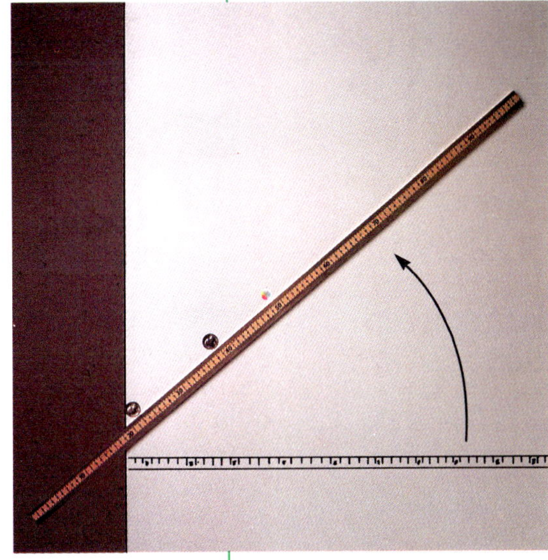

Conclude and Apply

1. Does the coin further up the meterstick fly off the table faster or more slowly than the one placed at the table's edge?
2. Does one coin hit the floor before the other?

In this Find Out, the motion of the coins may have been too quick to let you analyze exactly what is happening. A strobe photograph can take pictures as objects fall. Later, looking at the photographs we can see what actually happened as the objects fell. Figure 14-7 shows a photograph of a similar experiment done with two golf balls. One ball has been propelled to the right, and the other has been dropped. Both were put into motion at the same instant.

You can see that, even though one ball is moving to the right, it's falling at the same rate as the one that's been dropped. This means that a basketball fired from your hands horizontally will hit the ground at the same time as a coin dropped by your friend. Is that what you would expect? How do we explain this?

FIGURE 14-7. The ball on the right is moving horizontally and vertically the same time.

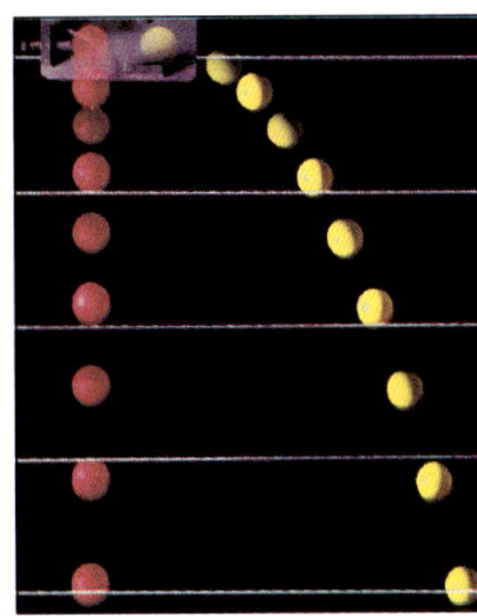

2 TEACH

Tying to Previous Knowledge

This section divides the motion of projectiles into horizontal and vertical components. You may wish to point out to students that in the previous section they learned about the vertical component caused by the gravity.

FIND OUT!

Does forward motion affect falling speed?

Time needed 15 minutes

Materials Meterstick and two coins per student or group

Thinking Processes Observing and inferring, Comparing and contrasting

Purpose To learn that objects moving horizontally fall at the same rate as objects dropped vertically.

Preparation This activity can be performed by groups. Designate one student in each group to place the coins, one to handle the meterstick, and one or more to observe the motion of the coins. COOP LEARN

Teaching the Activity

Troubleshooting The meterstick is pivoted with a finger on it at the point where it crosses the table.

Discussion Have students perform the activity two or three times. Then ask them to describe the motion of the two coins.

Expected Outcomes

Students should observe that the coin nearest the edge falls nearly vertically while the other coin moves in an arc, but that both coins hit the floor at the same time.

Conclude and Apply

1. It flies off faster.
2. no

PROGRAM RESOURCES

Other Resources

Projectile Motion, film, EME.

Newton's Laws, software, J & S Software.

OPTIONS

Meeting Individual Needs

Visually Impaired Visually impaired students can interpret the results of the Find Out activity by listening for the sounds of the coins hitting the floor. Students with normal vision may also find it interesting to perform the activity once with eyes closed in order to hear whether the coins make two separate clicks or one combined click as they reach the floor.

Concept Development

Theme Connection Projectile motion results from the interaction of two factors: gravity and the energy imparted to the object when it is launched. This supports the theme of interactions and systems. Students observe the interaction of these two factors through strobe photographs of experiments with golf balls. In this experiment one ball is propelled to the right and the other has been dropped.

Student Text Question Figure 14-8 Did the basketball's forward motion affect the time it takes to fall? *no*

Activity Have students make a line graph of the velocity of the ball in Figure 14-9. The vertical axis of the graph should indicate velocity and the horizontal access should indicate duration. Students will see that the line graph is the same as the path of the ball through the air. L3

MAKING CONNECTIONS

History

The world's first general-purpose computer was the 1945 ENIAC, which weighed over 30 tons and was built to calculate the paths of artillery projectiles. It took 20 hours to calculate a projectile's path by hand; ENIAC did it in 30 seconds.

Content Background

Physicists measure force in newtons. A newton is the amount of force needed to give a mass of 1 kg an acceleration of 1 m/s^2.

FIGURE 14-8. Did the basketball's forward motion affect the time it takes to fall?

DID YOU KNOW?

The pull of gravity differs from place to place on Earth. In the U.S., gravity is greatest in Minot, North Dakota, and smallest in Key West, Florida.

Look at the golf balls in Figure 14-7 again. One golf ball in the photo was fired horizontally. There was nothing to speed it up or slow it down, so for the short time shown in the photo, the ball moved horizontally at a constant speed.

The golf ball that was dropped accelerated downward just like the baseball and tennis ball you studied in the Investigate. It accelerated down at 9.8 m/s^2. The golf ball hit the ground at the same time as the horizontally-fired golf ball. This means that the ball fired horizontally also is falling down, even though it is moving forward horizontally during the same time. The same is true for the basketball and the coin dropped from chest height by your friend.

HORIZONTAL AND VERTICAL COMPONENTS

We've been talking about projectile motion almost as if it were two separate motions. There's motion across the ground that we've been calling horizontal motion, and there's falling motion that we've been calling vertical motion.

The horizontal part of a velocity is the **horizontal component**. Similarly, the vertical part of a velocity is

OPTIONS

Enrichment

Activity Ask students to make a ramp from a plastic rule or half a cardboard tube from a roll of paper towels. Have them set up the ramp at the edge of a table and experiment with setting the ramp at different angles and rolling marbles down it and onto the floor. Ask students to assume that it takes 0.5 seconds for the marbles to reach the floor from the top of the table. For each position of the ramp, have students measure from the edge of the table to the point of impact and then calculate the speed at which the marble was moving when it left the table. The speed is calculated by dividing the distance by 0.5 seconds.

Concept Development

Theme Connection Students learn how the interaction of horizontal and vertical motion can create a stable orbit around Earth. This supports the theme of interactions and systems. The nature of the interaction becomes clear as students study the equation for calculating the speed a projectile must travel for its path to match the curve of Earth.

Discussion Students may need help distinguishing clearly among the acceleration of gravity, the final velocity of an object after falling for one second, and its average velocity during that second. Remind students that an object dropped on Earth reaches a speed of 9.8 m/s at the end of one second. Ask students how far the object falls in that time. Many students may think the object falls 9.8 m. Explain that this could be so only if it fell at an average speed of 9.8 m/s from the moment it was released. Instead, the object starts at 0 m/s and reaches 9.8 m/s one second later. We can calculate its average speed by adding together its starting speed (0 m/s) and its final speed (9.8 m/s) during that second and dividing by 2. Have students perform the arithmetic; the answer is 4.9 m/s. Ask students how far an object falls in 1 second. *4.9 m*

MAKING CONNECTIONS

Geography

Ask students how many of them have seen a satellite dish for receiving TV signals. Ask them to describe the angle at which the dish points; high into the sky or low near the horizon. Explain that this angle depends on how far from the Equator they live; the farther north, the lower the angle. Explain that communication satellites circle Earth in a ring 22,300 miles above the Equator, where their forward speed matches Earth's rotation.

In the Find Out, *Sputnik 1* was able to stay in orbit at an altitude of 516 km only by traveling at a velocity of 7.6 km/s. Satellites can travel in orbits at many different altitudes from Earth. At each altitude, however, a certain velocity is required for the satellite to stay in its orbit. The higher the altitude, the lower the velocity required because the acceleration due to gravity is less the further away from Earth you are. The space shuttle is a satellite that has carried astronauts in orbit around Earth. Perhaps you've seen pictures of astronauts floating weightless inside a space shuttle. Why does this happen?

WEIGHTLESSNESS

Why do we say that astronauts are weightless when in orbit? Have you ever jumped on a trampoline? Even if you haven't, you have probably ridden in an elevator, in a car, or on an amusement park ride. Have you felt lighter at some point on any of these rides?

In an elevator that starts downward rapidly, you may have a tickle in your stomach and a feeling that you suddenly weigh less. The floor of the elevator does not seem to push on your feet. At the amusement park, when the roller coaster just goes over the top of the hill at high speed, you feel lifted up and floating free—weightless.

FIGURE 14-12. You don't need to travel to the moon to experience weightlessness.

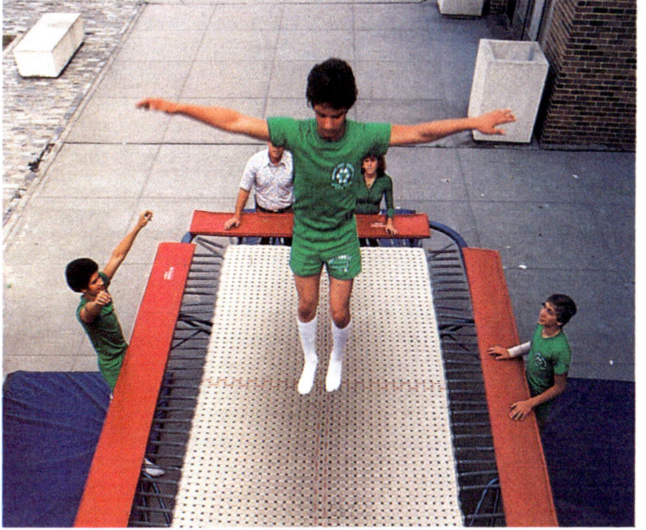

All of these experiences occur when you are falling freely. Whatever the direction of your velocity, you are experiencing acceleration toward Earth in a free-fall. This is what we mean by **weightlessness**. If you could stand on a bathroom scale during this time, it would register less than your actual weight.

The satellites in orbit around Earth are in free-fall and that is why every-

OPTIONS

Multicultural Perspectives

The development of orbiting satellites is based on advances with roots in many cultures. The Chinese are credited with the first development of rockets. In 1232, the Mongols laid siege to the city of K'ai-feng Fu, in Honan province, and the Chinese defenders used "flying arrows of fire" to fight them off. These are believed to have been rockets consisting of a tube of gunpowder mounted on an arrow.

Meeting Individual Needs

Learning Disabled Ask a student to come to the front of the room. Walk around the student in a circle, having the student turn to face you at all times. Ask students how this demonstration explains the ability of satellites to seem motionless in the sky overhead. **LEP**

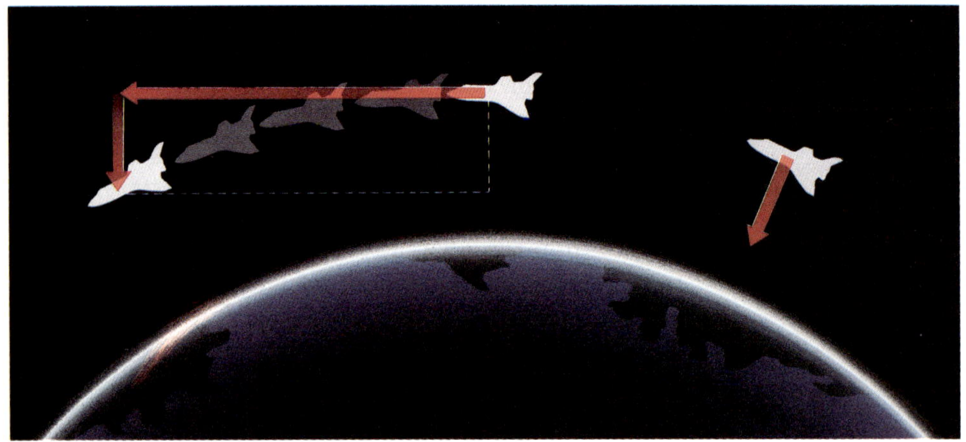

FIGURE 14-11. Once in orbit, the *Challenger* space shuttle moves through space horizontally, and it is attracted by Earth and falls vertically.

will be moving at 9.8 m/s at the end of 1 second. Its average downward velocity for that second is 9.8 m/s divided by 2 = 4.9 m/s. The bullet will fall 4.9 m during that second.

Scientists have calculated that a projectile must travel 7.9 km horizontally in that second for its path to match the curve of Earth. Since there are 3600 seconds in one hour, this velocity is equal to

$$\frac{7.9 \text{ km}}{\text{s}} \times \frac{3600 \text{ s}}{1 \text{ h}} = \frac{28{,}440 \text{ km}}{\text{h}}$$

This is the speed a satellite must travel around the equator very close to Earth in order for it to stay in orbit.

FIND OUT!

How did Sputnik I stay in orbit?

Sputnik I traveled in an orbit about 516 km above the surface of Earth. At that altitude, the satellite traveled at a horizontal velocity of 7.6 km/s. In the 7.6 km it travels in its orbit in one second, it must fall toward Earth a distance of 4.18 m to stay in its orbit. What is its average velocity of free-fall toward Earth in that second? What must be its final velocity of free fall in that second?

Conclude and Apply

From this result, what is the acceleration due to gravity at this altitude?

OPTIONS

Meeting Individual Needs

Learning Disabled Understanding the orbits of satellites requires a fairly high level of abstract thinking. Learning-disabled students may be aided by using physical objects to model projectile motion leading into orbit. Obtain a globe of Earth and small toy cannon. Placing the cannon on top of the globe, use your finger to trace the path of a projectile fired with normal force and falling to Earth. Then tell students to imagine firing a bigger and bigger cannon with more and more force and use your finger to trace the path of the projectiles, showing how the impact point eventually moves beyond the curve of Earth, leading into orbit. L1

2 TEACH

Tying to Previous Knowledge

In the previous section, students learned about projectile motion. In this section, students learn that putting a satellite into orbit is an extension of projectile motion. Ask students to describe their experiences with observing launches on TV. Perhaps some students have been fortunate enough to have seen a launch at Cape Canaveral in person.

FIND OUT!

How did Sputnik 1 stay in orbit?

Time needed 5 minutes

Thinking Processes
Thinking critically, Comparing and contrasting, Recognizing cause and effect

Purpose To calculate varying acceleration of gravity at different altitudes.

Preparation Draw a diagram like Figure 14-11 on the chalkboard to help students visualize the problem. L3

Teaching the Activity

- Write on the chalkboard the formula for gravity's acceleration and velocity on Earth's surface as given in the text:

Acceleration = 9.8 m/s^2
Velocity after 1 second = 9.8 m/s
Average velocity = $\frac{9.8 \text{ m/s}}{2}$ = 4.9 m/s
Distance fallen = 4.9 m/s
Ask students to apply this formula to the problem.

Expected Outcomes

Students should calculate the average and final earthward velocity of *Sputnik* during one second of orbit and the acceleration of gravity at an altitude of 516 km.

Answers to Questions

1. 4.18 m/s
2. 2 × 4.18 m/s = 8.36 m/s.
3. 8.36 m/s^2

Section 14-3

PREPARATION

Concepts Developed

This section shows how projectile motion can be used to explain the motion of satellites in orbit, why orbiting objects are weightless, and how satellites are able to remain stationary over Earth.

Planning the Lesson

In planning your lesson on circular orbits of satellites, refer to the Chapter Organizer on pages 420A-B for timing suggestions, resources, and additional materials that will help you in your presentation of the lesson concepts. For adequate development of the concepts presented in this section, we recommend that students do the Find Out activity on page 433.

1 MOTIVATE

Discussion Obtain photos of astronauts aboard a space shuttle in orbit. Show them to students and ask students to name the one thing shown by the photos that proves they were not taken on Earth. Students should identify weightlessness as the key. Ask students to suggest reasons why people might be weightless in space. Tell students that this section reveals the secret of weightlessness. L1

14-3 Circular Orbits of Satellites

OBJECTIVES

In this section, you will

- describe how a satellite is a projectile in free-fall;
- connect weightlessness to free-fall;
- explain certain satellite motion in terms of relative velocity.

KEY SCIENCE TERMS

weightlessness

stationary satellite

NEWTON'S PREDICTION OF SATELLITE MOTION

Isaac Newton was born in England on Christmas day, in 1642. This was the same year that Galileo died. Newton discussed many of the physical laws we still use, and to do so, he also invented the mathematics called calculus. Newton was one of the first scientists to develop our understanding of projectile motion, and he described, even back then, how a satellite could be put into orbit. It took another 270 years before people actually had the technology to send an artificial satellite into orbit. This satellite was the famous *Sputnik I*, sent up by the Soviet Union on October 4, 1957. It circled Earth once every 95 minutes, traveling at about 27,420 km/h.

Imagine Earth as perfectly round with no mountains or hills or air to stop or slow a projectile down. Now, suppose you horizontally fire a projectile, perhaps a rifle bullet. For bullets, like baseballs, the projectile moves horizontally and falls to the ground. But Newton asked an interesting question. Suppose you throw something, or fire it, with enough velocity that it travels many kilometers. Imagine that it travels so far that as it falls, it falls just enough to follow the curvature of Earth. It would keep falling, always toward Earth, but Earth's curvature would just match the projectile's fall so that the projectile would never hit Earth. This is shown in Figure 14-10. It would fall until it went all the way around Earth. It would keep on falling like this, staying in orbit around Earth forever.

FIGURE 14-10. If an object travels at least 7.9 km/s, its path will follow the curve of Earth, and it will stay in orbit.

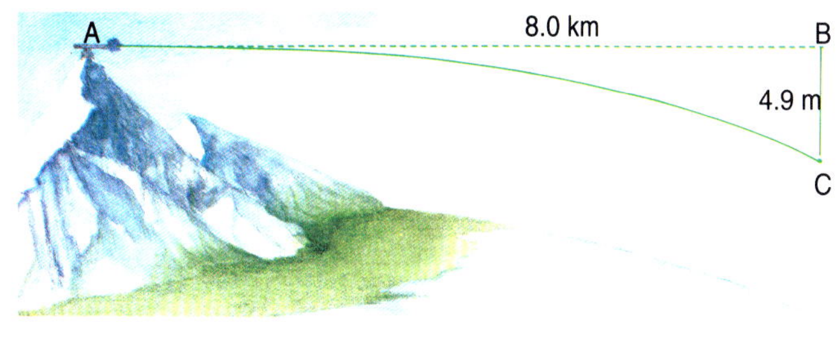

How fast would the projectile have to travel to continuously fall around Earth without hitting it? If the projectile begins its vertical movement with a velocity of 0 m/sec and accelerates downward at 9.8 m/s², it

PROGRAM RESOURCES

Teacher Classroom Resources

Study Guide, page 52

Critical Thinking/Problem Solving, page 22, Studying the Effects of Space Travel L2

Multicultural Activities, page 32, Japanese Technology L1

Take Home Activities, page 23, Weightlessness L1

called the **vertical component**. Every motion has both horizontal and vertical components, but each component acts as if the other were not present. We say that the vertical motion is independent of the horizontal motion. The vertical component has an acceleration equal to 9.8m/s^2. The horizontal component has a constant velocity.

So far, you've only looked at the motion of projectiles fired horizontally. However, most projectiles that you are familiar with are actually launched up into the air at an angle.

Figure 14-9 shows a ball that's been thrown upward at an angle. Notice that the ball slows down as it rises and then speeds up as it falls from its highest point. You can see the images remain the same distance apart horizontally. This means that the ball is not speeding up or slowing down in the horizontal direction. In short, the vertical and horizontal components are still independent.

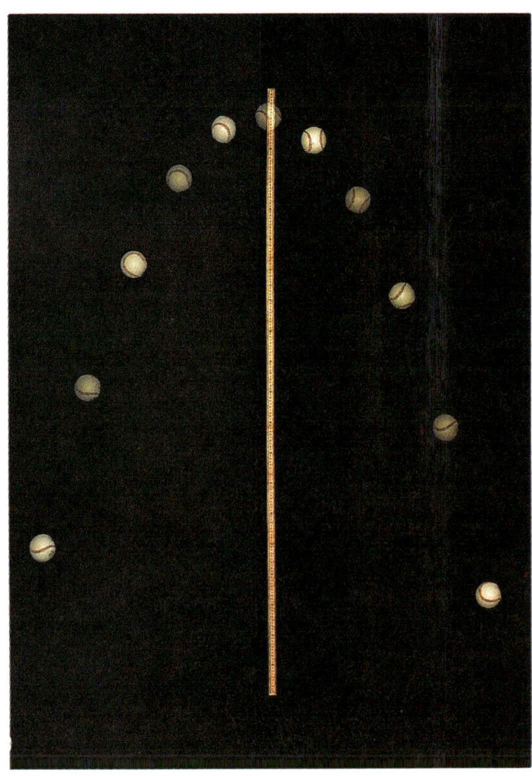

FIGURE 14-9. A ball thrown up in the air changes its velocity on its way up and on its way down.

Understanding the motion of projectiles was an important step in our quest to put objects into orbit around Earth. In the next section, you'll learn more about these objects and how they stay in orbit.

Check Your Understanding

1. Provide three examples of a projectile not mentioned in this section.
2. Which object would hit the ground first, a baseball launched perfectly horizontally off the bat of a professional baseball player or a baseball dropped from the same height as the player's bat?
3. Explain how the motion of a basketball after a jump shot can be separated into vertical and horizontal components.
4. **APPLY:** Draw a diagram to show why a dart player has to aim above the target to hit the bull's-eye. Show the dart's path and the two kinds of motion involved.

3 Assess

Check for Understanding

For the Apply question, have students draw diagrams showing the path of a horizontally thrown dart and the path for hitting the target.

Reteach

Rest a marble or steel ball bearing at the edge of a table. Make a ramp from half a cardboard paper towel tube. Roll a second ball down the ramp so that it strikes the first ball. Have students observe that both balls hit the floor at the same time regardless of the paths they take. Ask students, why this happens. LEP L1

Extension

Activity Have students demonstrate the variations in the paths taken by a projectile. Materials needed are 1.5-meter flexible hose and 30-cm stick.

Tie an end section of the hose to the stick so that the stick holds it straight and rigid. Have students prop up the stick, hold the other end of the hose high, and drop a marble into the high end. The marble will accelerate down the length of the hose and come out the other end at an upward angle. Students can try different heights for the upper end and different angles for the stick, keeping a table of height, angle, and marble's impact point. L3

4 Close

Give three students who are about the same height identical rubber balls. Ask one to drop the ball from shoulder height, one to throw the ball horizontally, and one to throw the ball upward, all simultaneously. Ask the class to describe the motion of the three balls. *The balls dropped and thrown horizontally should hit the floor together; the ball thrown upward should hit later.* Ask students to explain the motion of the three balls. LEP L1

Answers to Check Your Understanding

1. Examples may include a baseball, basketball, arrow, bullet, etc.
2. Both land at the same time.
3. The basketball moves both horizontally and vertically; a strobe photo would show both movements.
4. Diagrams should show the dart falling during horizontal travel.

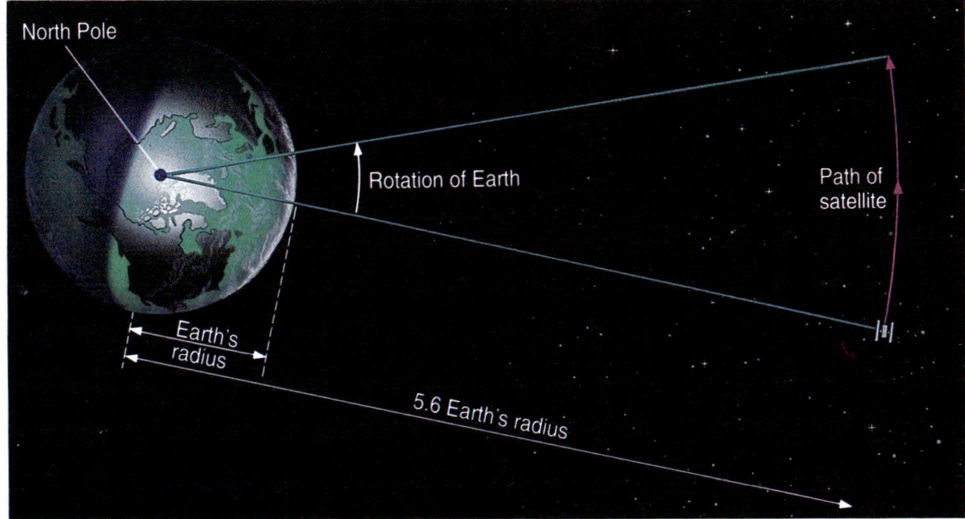

FIGURE 14-13. Some satellites move along with Earth and stay above the same place on the Earth.

thing appears to be weightless aboard a satellite. The satellite and everything in it, including the astronauts, are all falling toward Earth with exactly the same acceleration. Satellites fall toward Earth and never really escape Earth's gravitational pull. The acceleration due to gravity is smaller for higher orbits. But such satellites still fall toward Earth with some acceleration, even though it is less than 9.8 m/s^2. Have you ever looked up at the sky on a clear night and seen a bright spot moving across the sky? This may have been a satellite. Some satellites appear to move across the sky, and others do not. Why do some satellites appear to remain stationary?

THE STATIONARY SATELLITE

Imagine a satellite placed in orbit around Earth at just the right altitude and just the right velocity so that it moves around its orbit once per day. Suppose that it is moving in the same direction as Earth is rotating. What motion would this satellite have relative to Earth? It would appear stopped!

Relative to a person on Earth, this satellite has no motion. We would call it a **stationary satellite**. It would

Concept Development

Activity Have students attach a small weight to a short length of string and twirl the string in a circle, weight outward. Make sure students are standing a safe distance apart. Ask them to describe what they feel. Students will feel a pull on the string that increases with the speed of the whirling. Ask students to explain the forces involved. Ask them what would happen if the weight were released. *The weight would move away from them in a straight line. It is unable to do so because of the string.* Ask students to explain why this activity is a good model of the force acting on a satellite in orbit. L3

Content Background

Isaac Newton (1642–1727) was an English mathematician and physicist. He is best known for his laws of motion, published in 1686–87, which described the properties of moving objects. The laws are a remarkable achievement, partly because Newton saw past the forces of friction and gravity, which limit motion on Earth, and envisioned motion as human beings would not experience it until they traveled into space. In addition to motion, Newton did major work in the properties of light, astronomy, and mathematics, to which he contributed calculus.

Flex Your Brain Use the Flex Your Brain activity to have students explore SATELLITE MOTION

Enrichment

Research Have students research what it is like to live aboard an orbiting spacecraft. Both encyclopedias and numerous books provide detailed information about life aboard Skylab and a space shuttle, including working, eating, exercising, and sleeping in free-fall.

PROGRAM RESOURCES

Teacher Classroom Resources

Critical Thinking/Problem Solving, page 8, Flex Your Brain

How It Works, page 15, Training for Weightlessness L1

Making Connections: Integrating Sciences, page 31, Living in Space L2

3 Assess

Check for Understanding

Use the questions to review the major points of the section: how projectile motion explains orbits; weight and free-fall; and the motion of satellites. Use the Apply question to let students apply their knowledge of free-fall to new areas. You may wish to have students speculate on other things astronauts are not able to do while weightless.

Reteach

Students may find it hard to grasp how projectile motion can lead to orbital motion. Draw a circle on the chalkboard representing Earth. At the top of the circle, draw a cannon firing. Show the path of projectiles fired with increasing force: the path becomes flatter and the impact points move away from the cannon until the curve matches Earth's curve. LEP L1

Extension

Have students calculate the acceleration of gravity experienced by an object that stays in orbit by falling 3.64 m toward Earth in 1 second. *7.28 m/s²* L3

4 Close

Activity

Have students turn to Figure 14-9 in the previous section showing the path of a projectile. Note that the projectile accelerates as it falls toward Earth. Remind students that an object in orbit falls toward Earth and ask them if this means an orbiting object speeds up. Have students debate the question, then explain that the object does not increase in speed.

move in its orbit with Earth's rotation and above the equator always appear at the same point in the sky. Stationary satellites are often used as communication satellites to relay radio messages from one city to others. For example, a stationary satellite placed over Chicago could receive radio communications from Boston and relay them to Los Angeles. Stationary satellites are used to beam television transmissions of events—as they happen—across the world.

You have learned in this section that satellites are constantly falling toward Earth as they orbit. You will find that the study of other falling bodies, such as a swinging pendulum, will help you understand much more about motion in many different areas of science.

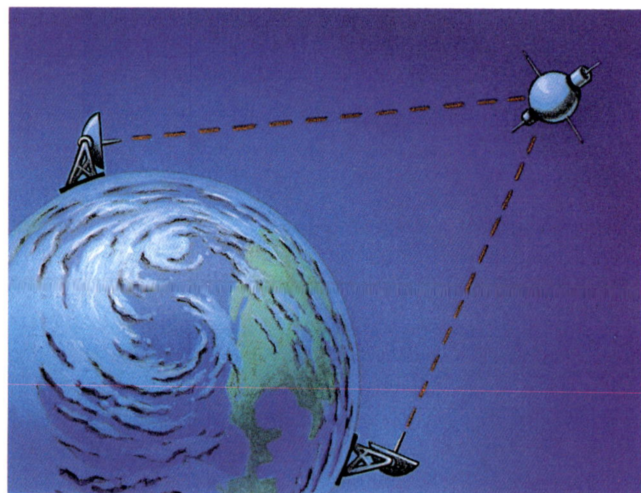

FIGURE 14-14. Stationary satellites allow us to view football games and revolutions as they happen.

Check Your Understanding

1. Explain how a satellite stays in orbit.
2. If you brought a bathroom scale into an elevator and stood on it as you went down, what would you predict would happen to the weight it registers for you when the elevator first starts to move? Explain your answer.
3. Why would a stationary satellite appear stopped to you if you could see it from Earth?
4. **APPLY:** Could an astronaut in the space shuttle exercise by lifting weights? Explain.

Answers to Check Your Understanding

1. The satellite's horizontal velocity must be just great enough so that, in one second, it falls toward Earth the same distance as Earth's curvature deviates from the horizontal.
2. It would show less weight because you and the elevator are both accelerating toward Earth.
3. Both the satellite and the Earth's surface, where you are standing, are moving in the same direction at the same relative velocity.
4. No, the weights would be weightless in free-fall.

14-4 The Motion of a Pendulum

PERIODIC MOTION

Galileo is said to have first thought about falling bodies while in church one day. He watched a chandelier slowly moving back and forth. It was behaving like a pendulum. He began to see that a pendulum's behavior would tell him something about how things fall on Earth. You used a pendulum earlier in this chapter. You used it to slow down falling motion so you could study it more closely. You found that whatever material you used for the pendulum bob, it all fell and reached the bottom of its swing in the same time. The way a pendulum behaves turns out to be related to many other motions that are important to you in everyday life. You will find examples of pendulum motion over and over again as you learn about heat, light, sound, and the back-and-forth motions, or oscillations, of other bodies. Repeated motions such as these are called periodic motions.

OBJECTIVES

In this section, you will

- define the period of a pendulum;
- define frequency, as it relates to periodic motion;
- describe the relationship between the period of a pendulum, the mass of a bob, the length of the pendulum, and the amplitude of the motion.

KEY SCIENCE TERMS

period

Period

Let's begin to study the periodic motion of a pendulum by first observing and then defining the experimental variables. Obtain one of the masses to be used as a pendulum bob from your teacher, tape a 40-cm length of string to it, and tape the free end of the string to a ruler. Then tape the ruler to the edge of a table as shown in Figure 14-15. Carefully pull back the weight a short distance.

Now let the bob go. How does it move? It moves past the bottom and back up again to a position where it briefly stops. Then it reverses direction and swings back over to where you had let it go in the first place. The pendulum continues to swing back and forth. How long does it take for the pendulum to swing over and back again once? Since it happens pretty fast, you can let it swing 10 times, and use a clock or watch second hand to time the motion. Divide the total time by 10 to obtain the time for one swing over and back. The time for the pendulum bob

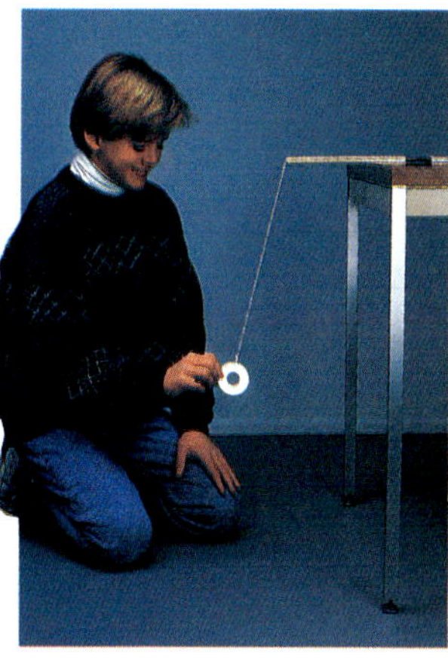

FIGURE 14-15. You can make a pendulum with a string and a weight.

Section 14-4

PREPARATION

Concepts Developed

Students learn to define the motion of a pendulum by period and frequency. Students determine by experiment the factors that affect a pendulum's period.

Planning the Lesson

In planning your lesson on the motion of a pendulum, refer to the Chapter Organizer on pages 420A-B for timing suggestions, resources, and additional materials that will help you in your presentation of the lesson concepts. For adequate development of the concepts presented in this section, we recommend that students do the Investigate activity on page 439.

1 MOTIVATE

Demonstration Make two pendulums from string and small objects; one should be half the length of the other and have a heavier bob.

Set both pendulums swinging. Ask students how they are different. *Responses should include string length, object size, and speed of swing.* Tell students that they will learn what makes pendulums behave as they do. L1

2 TEACH

Tying to Previous Knowledge

In Section 14-1, students used a pendulum to explore gravity's acceleration. Ask students to draw on this knowledge while completing section 14-4, where they will learn what determines a pendulum's frequency. You might begin this lesson by asking students to describe pendulums they have seen, for example, on grandfather clocks.

PROGRAM RESOURCES

Teacher Classroom Resources

Study Guide, page 53

Other Resources

Brehmer, Steven. "Driving Home the Laws of Motion." *The Science Teacher,* Dec. 1981, pp. 14–15.

Let's Move It: Newton's Laws of Motion, video, Focus.

Concept Development

Theme Connection The theme of stability and change is supported in this section by the factors that affect the swing of a pendulum: period, frequency, and amplitude. For example, changing the length of the pendulum changes the time for swings and the pendulum period.

Using the Diagram Point out that Figure 14-16 shows how amplitude is measured: horizontally from the bob's starting point to a vertical line at the bottom of the swing.

Student Text Questions What is the frequency of a playground swing that swings back and forth once every $\frac{1}{10}$ second? *= 10 Hz* What is the frequency of a swinging door that swings back and forth once every four seconds? *$\frac{1}{4}$= 0.25 Hz*

MAKING CONNECTIONS

History

Pendulums revolutionized timekeeping. Within 30 years after Galileo died, pendulums reduced the average error of the best timepieces from 15 minutes to 10 seconds per day.

Content Background

Nineteen-year-old Galileo Galilei (1564–1642) was attending the Cathedral of Pisa when he noticed the altar lamp swinging. He used his pulse to time it and concluded that it completed every swing in the same amount of time. He wrote that this observation made him give up medicine, which his father wanted him to study, and take up mathematics and physics.

DID YOU KNOW?

If you take a grandfather clock that keeps perfect time at sea level to the top of a mountain, it will run slow. Can you figure out why?

to swing over and back once is called the **period** of the pendulum. Because the pendulum swings back and forth repeating its motion again and again with the same period, its motion is termed periodic.

Frequency

It is sometimes easier to use the number of times an object moves back and forth in each second, rather than how long it takes for one motion over and back. The number of times an object moves back and forth in 1 second is called frequency. We talked about the frequency of sound in Chapter 3. The process of moving over and back once is called a cycle. Frequency then is measured in cycles per second. Recall that a cycle per second is given the name hertz, abbreviated Hz, for cycles per second. What is the frequency of a playground swing that swings back and forth once every $^{1}/_{10}$ second? What is the frequency of a swinging door that swings back and forth once every 4 seconds? You have learned how to define the frequency of a pendulum as the number of swings it makes in 1 second. Now, can you define how far the pendulum bob travels as it swings?

Amplitude

Pull back the pendulum bob once again and release it. As the pendulum moves toward its lowest point, note the distance the pendulum bob has traveled from the starting point to the bottom of the swing. This distance is called the amplitude. Figure 14-16 illustrates several different amplitudes. You can see that the farther you pull back the bob before you release it, the greater the pendulum's amplitude will be.

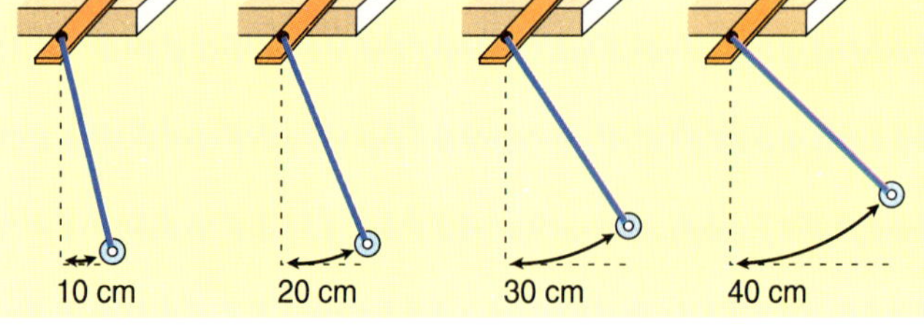

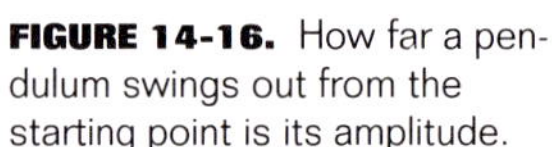

FIGURE 14-16. How far a pendulum swings out from the starting point is its amplitude.

OPTIONS

Meeting Individual Needs

Visually Impaired Visually impaired students who have difficulty observing pendulum motion can draw conclusions about pendulums from a metronome. Metronomes are upside-down pendulums powered by clockwork, in which the speed of the swing is controlled by the distance of the bob from the pivot. Have visually impaired students compare the period of the metronome at various positions of the bob (measured relatively rather than numerically), with a fully sighted student timing 10-second intervals. Students will find that the farther the bob is from the pivot, the longer the period. **COOP LEARN**

INVESTIGATE!

14-2 THE PERIOD OF A PENDULUM

In the following activity you will manipulate amplitude, mass, and pendulum length to find which of them can affect the pendulum's motion.

PROBLEM

What affects the period of a pendulum?

MATERIALS

1 80-cm piece of string
8 metal washers
masking tape
ruler
meterstick
seconds timer

PROCEDURE

1. Tape a ruler to the top of a table so it extends from the edge by 5 cm.
2. Tie one end of the string to a pendulum bob made of one washer.
3. Tape the other end to the ruler so that the distance from the ruler to the center of the bob is 50 cm.
4. Holding the bob, pull the pendulum 10 cm to one side and release it.
5. **Measure** the time it takes for the bob to swing back

and forth 10 times. Calculate and record one period of the pendulum.

6. Repeat Steps 4 through 6 pulling back the bob 20 cm, 30 cm, and 40 cm.
7. Repeat Steps 3 through 5 three more times using 2 washers, 4 washers, and 8 washers. Keep the amplitude 10 cm.
8. Change the length of the pendulum to 60 cm by retaping the string.
9. Pull the pendulum 10 cm to one side and release it.
10. Determine the period and record your data.
11. Repeat Steps 9 through 10 two more times using string lengths of 40 and 30 cm. Keep the pullback distance 10 cm.

ANALYZE

1. Describe the effect of the pendulum bob's mass on the pendulum's period.
2. Describe the effect of the amplitude on the period.
3. Describe the effect of the pendulum's length on the pendulum's period.

CONCLUDE AND APPLY

4. **Draw a graph** plotting the pendulum's period for the different string lengths. Connect the points. Is the line straight or curved? Does the period get shorter or longer as the string increases in length?
5. Using your graph, **predict** the pendulum's period for a string of 100 cm. **Predict** the period for a 20-cm length.
6. In this experiment, you held two variables constant and changed a third variable. **Identify which variables** were held constant and which were varied.
7. **Going Further:** If you were building a pendulum clock, what would you adjust so that the clock would be as accurate as possible?

INVESTIGATE!

14-2 THE PERIOD OF A PENDULUM

Time needed 50 minutes

Materials 80-cm piece of string, 8 metal washers, masking tape, ruler, meterstick, seconds timer

Thinking Processes Making and using tables, Observing, Separating and controlling variables, Interpreting data

Purpose To identify the factors that determine the period of a pendulum.

Preparation Provide tables or racks at least three feet high to which rulers can be taped.

Teaching the Activity

Before starting, have students copy the following data tables. LEP L1

a LENGTH = 50 cm WEIGHT ____

PULLBACK DISTANCE (cm)	TIME FOR 10 SWINGS (s)	PENDULUM PERIOD (s)
10	14	1.4
20	14	1.4
30	14	1.4
40	14	1.4

b AMPLITUDE = 10 cm LENGTH = 50 cm

PENDULUM BOB WEIGHT (NUMBER OF WASHERS)	TIME FOR 10 SWINGS (s)	PENDULUM PERIOD (s)
1	14	1.4
2	14	1.4
4	14	1.4
8	14	1.4

c AMPLITUDE ____ WEIGHT ____

PENDULUM LENGTH (cm)	TIME FOR 10 SWINGS (s)	PENDULUM PERIOD (s)
30	11	1.1
40	12	1.2
60	15	1.5

Expected Outcomes

Students prove that length is the only factor affecting period, and that the period increases with length.

Answers to Analyze/Conclude and Apply

1. no effect on period
2. no effect on period unless the amplitude is too great
3. Period changed as length of pendulum changed.
4. curved, longer
5. Answers will vary depending on graphs; longer string has longer period.
6. First: length and weight constant, amplitude varies. Second: length and amplitude constant, weight varies. Third: weight and amplitude constant, length varies. Testing one variable at a time permits determination of its effect.
7. pendulum length

PROGRAM RESOURCES

Teacher Classroom Resources

Activity Masters, pages 59-60, Investigate 14-2

Other Resources

Morecki, A. *Biomechanics of Motion.* New York: Springer-Verlag, 1981.

Investigating Gravitational Force, software, IBM.

3 Assess

Check for Understanding

Use the Check for Understanding questions to make sure students understand the difference between period and frequency and that pendulum length affects both. Accept all reasonable answers to the Apply question.

Reteach

Use Data Tables a–c from the Investigate activity on page 439. Fill in the *Time for 10 Swings* column from the Sample Data. Have students divide each number by 10 and fill in the *Pendulum Period* column. For each data table, ask students if all of the numbers in the *Pendulum Period* column are the same or different. Only Table c contains different numbers, indicating that only length affects the period. Ask students what this means. LEP L1

Extension

Have students use the apparatus from Investigate 14-2 to determine the pendulum length that produces a 0.5-second and 1-second period. L2

4 Close

Demonstration

Repeat the demonstration in Motivate with which you began the lesson: swinging unequal pendulums. Ask students to apply the knowledge they gained in Investigate 14-2 to identify the key difference between pendulums that affects how they act. *the length of string* L1

FIGURE 14-17. What would happen to the amplitude of the swinging cat's tail if the tail were longer?

In the Investigate, you studied the effects of mass, amplitude, and length on the period of a pendulum. These three factors that you tested are called independent variables. The factor that depended on the value of the independent variable, the period, is called the dependent variable. An experiment is a procedure in which you hold all variables constant except one. For example, in the first experiment you held the length of the pendulum and the amplitude constant while you varied mass to see how it affected the period.

Changing one independent variable at a time allows you to draw conclusions about the effect of that variable on what you're measuring, the dependent variable. For example, if you varied both length and mass at the same time and found that the period of the pendulum had changed, you would not know whether the change in period was caused by the change in mass or the change in length.

Experiments like these are used by scientists to discover the causes of the behavior of things you observe. The relation between pendulum length and its period that you plotted in your graph will help you understand more about the back-and-forth movements of many other objects.

There are many other kinds of oscillations and vibrations that you will learn about later in this book. What you now know about the pendulum will help you understand their periods, frequencies, and amplitudes.

Check Your Understanding

1. What's the difference between the frequency and the period of a pendulum?
2. Explain how you measure the frequency of the periodic motion of a pendulum. What units is frequency measured in?
3. If you wanted to change the period of a pendulum, which of the three variables you tested would you change?
4. **APPLY:** Give three examples of other objects or events that undergo periodic motion. How might you go about testing what affects the periodic motion of a guitar string?

Answers to Check Your Understanding

1. Frequency is number of swings per second; period is time needed for one complete swing.
2. Number of swings per second is measured in cycles per second or Hertz (Hz).
3. length of string
4. Guitar strings, earthquakes, water waves. Fret string to change its length and listen to pitch.

OPTIONS

Enrichment

Discussion Ask students why they think the weight and amplitude of a pendulum make no difference to its period. *Accept all reasonable suggestions. An object's weight does not affect its acceleration by gravity. The greater the amplitude, however, the faster the bob returns to center.* Students can think of amplitude as a ramp: a small amplitude as a low ramp, and a large amplitude as a steep one.

EXPANDING YOUR VIEW

CONTENTS

A CLOSER LOOK

TERMINAL VELOCITY: FALLING IN AIR

The term *free fall* means that the only force acting on the falling body is gravity. An object in free fall is accelerating at a rate of 9.8 meters per second squared. However, for objects falling near Earth, air resistance increases the faster the object goes.

If you were to put your hand out of a car window with your palm forward when the car is moving slowly, the force of air would not be very great. When the car is moving faster, the force would be much greater.

How does air resistance affect a falling object? Not much if the object falls only a short way. But in a long fall, the effect can be very great.

For example, when sky divers fall toward the ground, they are falling through air, not a vacuum. The faster they fall, the greater the air resistance. When the divers' speed reaches about 280 kilometers per hour, air resistance pushing up against them is equal to the force of gravity pulling them down. This means the forces acting on the diver are balanced. As you have seen in this chapter, if forces are balanced, then there is no acceleration. The direction and speed of the diver remain con-

stant. This constant velocity is called terminal velocity. Terminal velocity is not the same for all objects—it depends on the speed, size, and shape of the falling object. The larger the object, the greater the amount of air resistance on it. This is why, after a parachute opens, a diver falls at a velocity that is slow enough to allow a safe landing.

YOU TRY IT!

Show that the terminal velocity is not the same for all objects. Drop different objects — such as a flat sheet of notebook paper, a sheet of notebook paper folded in quarters, and a sheet of notebook paper crumpled into a small ball — from a height of about two meters. Do they fall at the same rate? If not, which falls fastest? Slowest? How can you explain your observations?

Using Expanding Your View

Assign one or more of these excursions to expand students' understanding of motion near Earth and how it applies to other sciences and other subjects. You may assign these as individual or small group activities.

A CLOSER LOOK

Purpose A Closer Look extends the discussion of the motion of a falling object in Section 14-1 by explaining the effect of air resistance.

Content Background Air resistance is important in daily life. Automotive designers boost gas mileage by giving cars a shape with less air resistance. Some trucks have curved plastic shields to guide air around the trailer. Air resistance is also important in space flight. The space shuttle relies on air resistance to slow down from orbital speed to landing speed. Missions to Mars are being planned that involve diving into the Martian atmosphere to slow down enough to enter Mars orbit.

Teaching Strategies Ask students what the text means by "the forces acting on the diver are balanced." Have students describe the forces (gravity and air resistance) and why air resistance increases. *the faster you go, the more air friction there is.* Have students look at the picture and explain how these skydivers are using terminal velocity. *This is accomplished by maneuvering the body position to increase velocity until all divers reach the same altitude. Then they adjust themselves to the same position to maintain the same velocity.*

Going Further Have students work in small groups to experiment with parachutes, air resistance, and falling rate. Cut cloth into three or four different-sized squares. Provide each group with one of each size piece of cloth, string, and a small weight. Have the groups design and conduct an experiment to determine the relation between the area of the cloth in square inches and the time it takes the parachute to fall six feet. Each experiment should include measuring the squares of cloth, building the parachutes, dropping them from a fixed height, and timing the fall. Suggest that students time three drops for each parachute and average the times. Ask each group to display its data in a table and a line graph. Have groups compare results and discuss any differences. **COOP LEARN**

Answers to

YOU TRY IT

1. no
2. the crumpled ball of paper
3. the flat sheet of paper
4. Larger objects have more air resistance on them.

LIFE SCIENCE CONNECTION

Purpose Section 14-3 describes what weightlessness is and when people experience it. This life science connection describes the effect of weightlessness on people and the concern this creates for astronauts.

Content Background When the body first becomes weightless, the fluid in the inner ear, which provides our sense of balance, is no longer held down by gravity and sloshes around, producing dizziness and nausea. The impact is short-lived, however, because the body's supply of blood, lymph, and other fluids rapidly redistributes upward from the lower body where gravity normally concentrates it. The higher fluid pressure overwhelms the inner ear's ability to sense motion changes. Astronauts also see their faces become noticeably puffy and many report feeling stuffed-up as though with a cold.

Teaching Strategies Have students work in small groups to develop a table listing the effects of weightlessness mentioned in the text and, for each effect, one or two possible remedies described in the text or based on their own ideas. Compare the tables in a class discussion and then have students name body functions that are not affected by weightlessness. List their suggestions on the chalkboard. COOP LEARN

LIFE SCIENCE CONNECTION

BIOLOGICAL EFFECTS OF WEIGHTLESSNESS

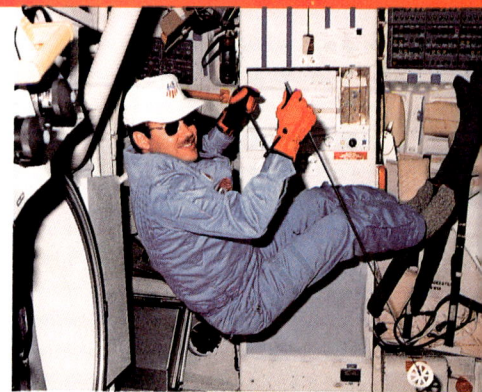

Here on Earth, the force of gravity acts on everyone and everything. We call this downward force weight. In the eons that people have lived on Earth, the human body has adapted to this gravity environment. For example, the circulatory system must move blood from the heart to all parts of the body. Our muscles and skeleton continually work against gravity. Even our sense of balance has developed in a gravity environment.

In contrast, astronauts in an orbiting satellite are in a condition of weightlessness. How does the body respond to long periods of weightlessness? What happens when the person comes back to Earth, where gravity is present?

One area of concern was whether astronauts would become disoriented in orbit. After all, our sense of balance depends upon gravity. Luckily, becoming disoriented has not become a major problem. Some astronauts did experience brief periods of nausea or disorientation, but these effects were short-lived.

Medical factors such as pulse rate, breathing rate, body temperature, and blood pressure are all carefully watched. In addition, body wastes are collected, and once returned to Earth, are carefully analyzed. Of these factors, the only one that has shown a significant change is the pulse rate, which often increases during lift-off and space walks. In all cases, however, the rate has returned to normal in a very short time. Upon return to Earth, there has been a tendency toward faintness when the astronauts first stand up after leaving the spacecraft. Some Soviet cosmonauts—the Soviet term for space travelers—found it difficult to adjust to gravity after 17 days in orbit. For several days after their return, their arms, legs, and head felt as if they were very heavy. These same cosmonauts also seemed to have less blood—doctors called it loss of blood volume—and some changes in the walls of their veins. The reasons are not yet clearly understood.

Another observed effect that may be important is the loss of calcium in the bones. On very long trips, such as to another planet, this could be serious. Weight loss is another effect. So far, astronauts have quickly regained lost weight after returning to Earth.

With every returning space flight crew, doctors are learning more and more about how the human body reacts to long periods of weightlessness.

WHAT DO YOU THINK?

After several months in space, the heart, muscles, and bones will adapt to a lower gravity environment. What problems could arise for astronauts when they return to Earth after several months in space?

Answers to WHAT DO YOU THINK?

Without gravity, muscles and bones rapidly lose strength. Returning astronauts could be too weak to move, their hearts too weak to pump blood, and their bones too brittle to support them on Earth.

Going Further Divide the class into small groups and have each group conduct research on how human beings may live in space without suffering ill effects. Have each group focus on a specific activity in space: a flight to Mars, living in a colony on the moon, or living in a space station. Have the groups prepare oral presentations, illustrated on the chalkboard or on posterboard, describing the problems life in space presents and how we hope to solve them.

For information, students can write to
NASA Headquarters
Washington, DC 20546
Students can also read
Bernards, Neal. *Living in Space.* San Diego: Greenhaven Press, 1990.
Fradin, Dennis. *Space Colonies.* Chicago: Children's Press, 1985.
Rickard, Graham. *Homes in Space.* Minneapolis: Lerner, 1989. COOP LEARN

SCIENCE AND SOCIETY

WEATHER SATELLITES

Can you think of any natural occurrence that affects people's lives as much as the weather does? Farmers depend on the weather for good crops. Floods, hurricanes, and tornadoes cause terrible damage and loss of life. Not as tragic, but very frustrating, are parades, picnics, ball games, and other events that get spoiled by nasty weather. Snowstorms cause traffic problems. Can you think of other ways in which the weather not only affects day-to-day activities, but also causes long-term and widespread problems?

It's no wonder, then, that much time, effort, and money is put into trying to forecast, or predict, what the weather will be like.

Accurate forecasts could mean that problems caused by the weather would be less frustrating, damaging, and deadly.

Meteorologists, people who study the weather, have many tools and instruments such as those shown in the picture to help them. To make predictions about the weather, meteorologists need to have a complete picture of conditions in the atmosphere. These conditions include wind speed and direction, air pressure and how it is changing, temperature, precipitation, and humidity. Observations of these conditions are made regularly from land stations, from ships and buoys at sea, and from airplanes and balloons in the sky. As you can imagine, gathering all the data from all parts of the world presents a big problem.

Since 1960, there has been a new high-tech aid in observing the weather. At that time, the United States government put into orbit *Tiros I*, the first artificial satellite equipped to take pictures of Earth's weather in detail. *Tiros III*, launched in 1961, was the first satellite to discover a hurricane over the Atlantic Ocean.

More recent developments include an advanced series of satellites called the *Tiros-N* (shown in photo below). Besides observing weather conditions, these satellites collect data about infrared radiation in Earth's atmosphere.

There are two kinds of weather

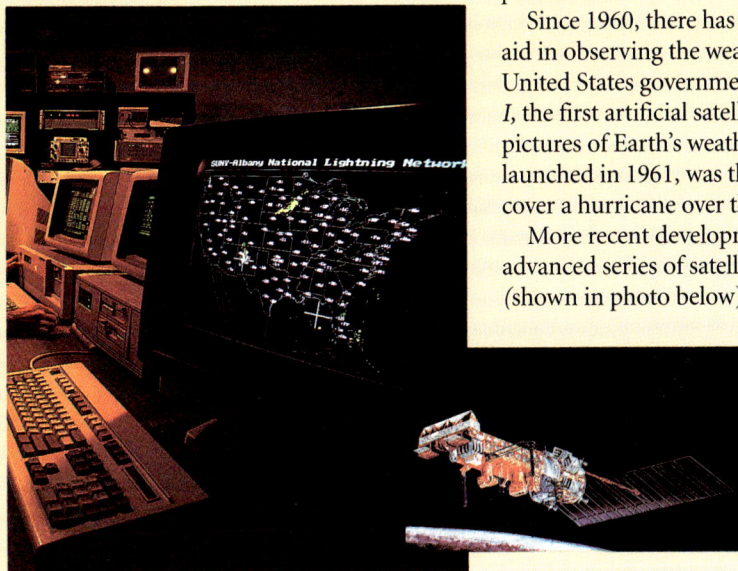

EXPANDING YOUR VIEW

SCIENCE AND SOCIETY

Purpose The role of satellites in studying and predicting Earth's weather is one application of satellites, which are discussed in Section 14-3.

Content Background Weather is a complex phenomenon that involves five basic elements. The first, air pressure, is caused by the weight of the atmosphere above Earth. Air pressure varies widely, resulting in high- and low-pressure areas. The second element is temperature, which averages 15°C (59°F) globally. The third element is wind, measured in knots (1.15 miles) per hour. Moisture, the amount of water vapor mixed with air, is the fourth element. The higher the temperature of the air, the more water vapor it can hold. Relative humidity is the ratio of the amount of water vapor in the air to the maximum amount the air can hold at that temperature. Clouds are direct evidence of atmospheric moisture. The fifth element is precipitation, which occurs when a change in temperature and/or pressure decreases the air's ability to hold moisture. The basis of weather is the unequal heating of the atmosphere-ocean system of Earth. The tropical regions near the equator receive more heat from the sun than the polar regions. Heated air circulates upward and toward the poles. The cold air pushes warm, less dense air from the poles toward the equator.

Going Further Divide students into five-member groups to create weather maps showing the change in weather over a one-week period. Distribute eight copies of a black-and-white political map of your region or the U.S. (without state names, if possible) to each group. Make each member of the group responsible for watching one day's televised weather report or obtaining a printed weather map from a daily newspaper. Based on that resource, each student should draw his own weather map for that day, showing high- and low-pressure areas, areas of cloudiness and precipitation, and temperature readings at various standard locations. COOP LEARN

EXPANDING YOUR VIEW

Teaching Strategies Obtain a weather map from a daily newspaper and use an overhead projector to project it for the class. Point out the major features of the map, such as high- and low-pressure areas, cloudiness, precipitation, and temperature readings. Ask students to explain each of the features and what they think it means. Point out that weather forecasting is based on identifying systems of weather, such as cloudless high-pressure areas or rainy low-pressure areas, measuring the direction and speed at which they are moving across Earth's surface, and predicting when the weather system will reach a given area.

Discussion Ask students to explain why weather satellites are put into two different orbits. Explain as needed that low, polar orbits allow satellites to make in-depth studies of constantly changing portions of Earth's surface, while geostationary satellites give forecasters a stable view of larger weather systems and groups of systems. Have students refer to the article and name the kinds of data that satellites gather. List their answers on the chalkboard, including major weather patterns, cloud formations, ocean surface temperature, and data transmitted by ground stations.

Activity Have students research the history of weather satellites, including the current shortage of satellites due to constrictions in launch capacity following the *Challenger* disaster.

satellites. One kind orbits Earth in a low orbit — 800 to 1400 kilometers — that passes over the poles. Because Earth rotates, low-orbit satellites pass over a different area on each orbit. The other kind of satellite has a very high orbit — 40,000 kilometers.

At this height, the satellite goes around Earth in the same time it takes Earth to make one turn on its axis. In other words, the satellite is always over the same spot. Such satellites are so high, the pictures they take cover a large part of Earth's surface.

What kind of information can satellites gather? One thing that satellites do very well is to keep track of worldwide weather patterns. Weather patterns for big storms, such as hurricanes, can be identified and tracked so people in the storm's path can be warned.

Worldwide conditions such as snow and ice cover are easy to see on photos taken by satellites. Satellites also take pictures of the cloud patterns that occur during storms. The photo above shows one such cloud pattern. Besides taking pictures, satellites continually monitor the temperature of the water near the surface of the oceans by measuring the infrared radiation in Earth's atmosphere.

Satellites collect information from their own instruments and relay it to ground stations for analysis. But they do more. The satellites also collect information from the thousands of land stations on Earth's surface. Instruments at these land stations operate automatically, and the data they collect are transmitted by radio signal to a satellite. From there, the information is relayed to ground stations and analyzed by computers.

With this data-collecting system and high-speed computers to analyze the data, scientists continue to learn about the interaction of the air with land and the oceans. Researchers also learn about how the atmosphere gains and loses heat by radiation. Patterns of weather behavior will be better understood, and long-range weather prediction will continue to become more and more reliable.

YOU TRY IT!

In many cities, people interested in weather have formed clubs. These clubs are usually associated with the American Meteorological Society. Such groups meet regularly to learn about recent developments in weather forecasting or to discuss different types of weather phenomena.

Find out about such a group and what topics they plan to discuss. Tell which topic interests you and why.

Going Further Once all members of the group have created their weather maps, have the groups meet to develop a set of maps showing the change in weather systems over the five-day period. The groups should create three maps: one showing the movement of high- and low-pressure areas across the map, a second showing the movement of cloud masses and storms across the map, and a third showing the movement of zones of common temperature across the map. Have the groups develop a system of symbols and colors to represent the positions of pressure, clouds, and temperature zones on Day 1, Day 2, Day 3, and so on. Display the completed maps on the bulletin board or wall. COOP LEARN

HOW IT WORKS

THE METRONOME

A metronome is a device that can be used to beat exact time for a musician. It works on the principle of the pendulum, which you have learned swings back and forth at a regular rate.

A metronome consists of a steel rod mounted on a pin, or pivot, on which the rod can swing to and fro in a wooden case. Below the pivot is a small weight that holds the rod straight up and down when it is not working. Above the pivot is a weight that can be moved up and down along the rod. The rod is set in motion by a spring inside the case.

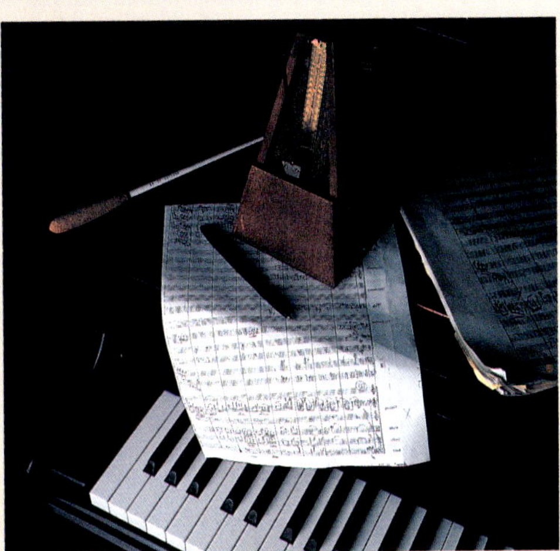

As the rod goes back and forth, it makes a ticking sound. The tempo, or rate of ticking, is adjusted by sliding the movable weight up or down the rod. Moving the weight away from the pivot produces a slower tempo. Moving the weight closer to the pivot produces a faster tempo. How is this similar to the rate of a pendulum?

A scale on the rod, or behind it, shows the number of swings per minute. For example, if you want one tick per second, you set the movable weight at 60. Where would you set it to get two ticks per second? How many ticks per second would you get if it were set at 90?

The first metronome was probably made in 1815 in Amsterdam by an inventor named Dietrich Winkel. However, he did not get a patent for the device. In 1816, a German mechanic, Johann Maelzel, patented a similar device. Winkel went to court to get the patent rights. He won the court battle, but Maelzel's device was already widely used. In fact, many pieces of printed music have a notation, such as MM120, to indicate the tempo at which the composer wanted the music to be played. The MM stands for *Maelzel metronome,* and the 120 indicates the number of beats per minute.

YOU TRY IT!

Listen to several pieces of music. Using a second hand on a watch or a clock, determine at which number a metronome would have been set when these musical selections were played.

HOW IT WORKS

Purpose A metronome is a device that is used to beat exact time in music. Its operation is based on the principle of the pendulum, which is discussed in Section 14-4.

Content Background A metronome is a pendulum that swings, not from its end, but from a point several inches in from the end. A heavier, fixed weight swings at the short end of the rod, while a lighter movable weight is positioned on the longer end to regulate the speed of the swing. Energy from a tightened coil spring is fed to the swinging rod by the kind of toothed escapement found in all mechanical clocks. The escapement also produces the loud ticking sound that makes the metronome useful. In addition to mechanical metronomes, musicians now use electronic ones that can be set digitally to produce an exact number of ticks per second.

Teaching Strategies Obtain a mechanical and digital metronome from the music program or as a loan from a local music store. Demonstrate both for students, showing how the number of ticks per second is set.

Discussion Ask students why musicians use metronomes. Explain as needed that a metronome allows composers to tell musicians exactly how slow or fast a piece of music is to be played rather than letting each musician determine his or her own speed. Both music students and professional musicians also use metronomes as they practice, to improve their ability to keep a steady beat.

Going Further Have students work in small groups to build a pusiloge, a device invented by Santorio Santorio, a friend of Galileo, to measure pulse rate. Each group will need a cardboard paper towel tube, a laboratory stand with a clamp at right angles to it, a piece of string, small weight, paper, pencil, and tape. Have students attach one end of the string to the weight and one end to the middle of the tube. Place the tube over the laboratory clamp so that it is parallel to the table. Turn the tube so that it winds up the string and lifts the weight. Have students start the weight swinging. By winding the weight up and down, they can change the period of the pendulum's swing. Play a recording of music and have students adjust their pendulums so that the pendulum's swing is the same as the beat of the music. **COOP LEARN**

EXPANDING YOUR VIEW

HISTORY CONNECTION

Purpose The history connection provides further information about Galileo's influence on the study of motion and the advancement of science, which are mentioned in Sections 14-1 and 14-4.

Content Background Galileo's early interest was in the science of motion. Hearing about the Dutch invention of the telescope, however, Galileo improved on it, creating a 30-power telescope he used to discover the mountains on the moon, new stars, four of Jupiter's moons, sunspots, and the rings of Saturn. Galileo's troubles with the Vatican began in 1615, when he publicly defended Copernicus. His problems culminated in 1632, after he published a book presenting arguments for the Copernican model; Galileo was imprisoned and the book burned. Under house arrest, Galileo secretly wrote another book on motion and astronomy, which was smuggled out of Italy. In 1638, Galileo became blind, possibly due to his observations of sunspots.

Teaching Strategies Ask students why they think the religious authorities of his day condemned Galileo's ideas about the sun-centered model of the universe. Explain as needed that, until that time, people believed that a motionless Earth was at the center of the universe, that the sun, moon, and stars revolved around it, and that heaven lay beyond the stars. Galileo's work and Copernicus's model denied this idea and, thus, seemed to attack the church.

History CONNECTION

GALILEO

Galileo Galilei (1564–1642) began his career as a medical student, but soon gave up medicine for mathematics and the physical sciences. Early in his career, he studied and wrote about the motion of falling objects. His interests changed, though, when he heard about the invention of the telescope. He made one of his own and used it to study objects in the sky. These studies led to many new observations. He observed the cratered surface of the moon, the rings of Saturn, the moons of Jupiter, the phases of Venus, and many stars that had not been seen before.

It seemed to Galileo that everywhere he looked, he found evidence that supported the Copernican (sun-centered) model of the solar system and thus cast doubt on the Ptolemaic (Earth-centered) model.

He published his observations and conclusions. Because his ideas went against the teachings of his religion at that time, he was arrested and forced to deny his ideas.

Despite these setbacks, he continued his studies on motion. The results of his studies were published in a book entitled *Dialogues Concerning Two New Sciences.*

Galileo's studies of falling bodies, motion on an inclined plane, and projectile motion all helped give a better understanding of motion. Even though he seemed to understand what is now called inertia, his writings never included the idea of inertia. The same is true of acceleration. He wrote about it but didn't connect it with forces. It was Newton, born in the year Galileo died, who tied together many of the ideas of motion. Newton's three laws include inertia, acceleration, and forces. Newton freely admitted, however, that without the work of Galileo and others, he could not have achieved all the works credited to him.

YOU TRY IT!

Galileo wanted to study the motion of falling objects, but they moved too fast. So he slowed the motion by allowing marbles to roll down an incline instead of falling freely.

On a smooth, level floor, prop one end of a 30-cm ruler up about 2 cm. Let a marble roll down the ruler. After it gets to the floor, see how far it rolls in two seconds. Do this three times and find the average distance. Then use $v = d/t$ to find the average velocity. Change the slant of the ruler and repeat. What is the velocity now? How would you explain the difference, if any?

Answers to

YOU TRY IT

The steeper the slant, the higher the average velocity, because the steeper slant provides an acceleration closer to that of a freefall.

Going Further Obtain a copy of Bertolt Brecht's *Galileo,* his play describing the work of Galileo and its importance, his conflict with the church, and his old age. Copies may be available at your library (Dewey number 832.912):

Brecht, Bertolt. *Seven Plays.* New York: Grove Press, 1961.

_____. *Galileo.* New York: Grove Press, 1966.

Select short scenes from the play that convey the action, and divide the class into groups. Assign each group a scene to read, including characters and stage directions. Have the groups read the scenes aloud in the proper sequence. When the reading is finished, ask students for their comments and reactions. COOP LEARN

Reviewing Main Ideas

1. On or near Earth the acceleration due to gravity is a constant 9.8 m/s^2. An elephant and a mouse falling freely off a high wire would reach the net at the same time.

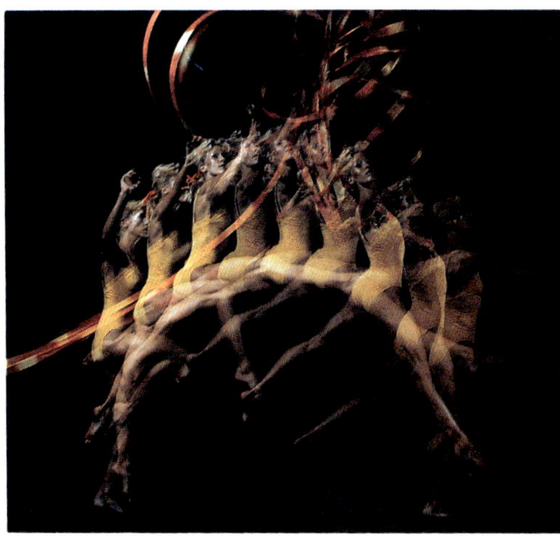

2. Projectiles, such as hurled basketballs, gymnasts, and divers all move forward and downward at the same time. These objects move independently horizontally forward at a constant velocity and vertically downward at an increasing velocity because of the acceleration due to gravity.

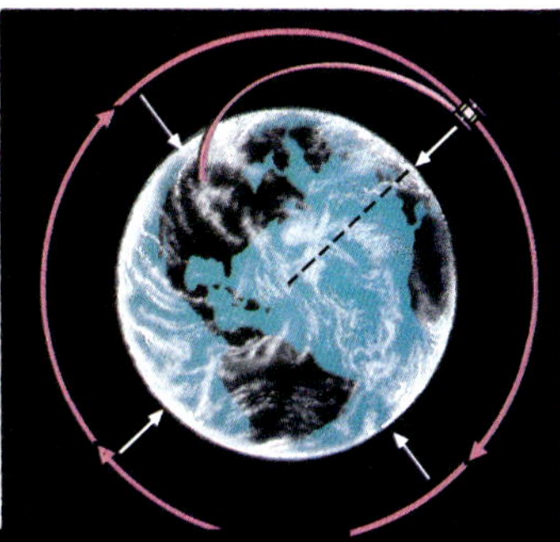

3. Satellites stay in orbit around Earth because of their horizontal velocity and the acceleration due to gravity.

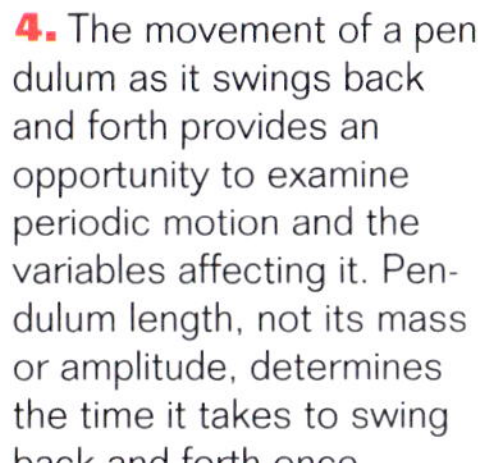

4. The movement of a pendulum as it swings back and forth provides an opportunity to examine periodic motion and the variables affecting it. Pendulum length, not its mass or amplitude, determines the time it takes to swing back and forth once.

Chapter 14

Reviewing Main Ideas

The strategies below ask students to recall how they calculated the acceleration of gravity; to compare gravitational acceleration to the tendency of an object to move at a continuous velocity; and to make predictions based on their knowledge of motion near Earth. Have students study the photographs and illustrations on this page.

Teaching Strategies

Have students describe the method they used to determine the acceleration of gravity. Help them recall the measurement of velocity between points, the calculation of average velocity, and the calculation of velocity change between each interval, leading to the measurement of gravity's acceleration. Tell students that one of the laws of motion developed by Isaac Newton states that an object in motion tends to remain in motion at the same velocity unless acted on by some force. Ask how they can explain the fact that falling objects move faster with each passing second. Students should recognize that gravity is a force acting on objects to accelerate them.

Test students' understanding of the chapter by asking the following questions. What would happen if a satellite was fired into orbit at a speed greater than that needed to maintain the orbit? *It would move outward from Earth, following a curved path.* Are astronauts in space still weightless when they fire their rocket to move them around? *No, the rocket accelerates them, creating weight.* How would a pendulum behave in orbit? *There can be no pendulum motion in orbit because of weightlessness.* If gravity gets weaker the farther you are from Earth's center, would a pendulum on top of the world's highest mountain swing faster or more slowly than one at sea level? *more slowly*

Chapter 14

Chapter Review

USING KEY SCIENCE TERMS

Answers

1. projectile motion
2. acceleration due to gravity
3. period
4. vertical component
5. vertical component, horizontal component

UNDERSTANDING IDEAS

Answers

1. c
2. a
3. b
4. d
5. a
6. b
7. b

CRITICAL THINKING

Answers

1. $9.8 \text{ m/s}^2 \times 3 = 29.4 \text{ m/s}$
2. The tennis ball thrown upward will be moving faster because it started falling from a greater height.
3. At position 2, the rocket has enough velocity to match the acceleration due to gravity, so it goes into orbit. At position 3, the rocket gains velocity from rocket firing and possibly an auxillary rocket booster, and moves away from Earth.

PROBLEM SOLVING

Answer

Materials: camera, strobe light, meterstick, object to drop. To record object's fall, open shutter of camera in darkness and drop object in camera's view next to meterstick while strobe light is firing every $\frac{1}{10}$ second. On developed photo, measure distance traveled between intervals and calculate average velocity, then subtract average velocity in first interval from average velocity in second interval to get change of velocity or acceleration. Divide by number of seconds between flashes to get acceleration in units of second per second.

Chapter Review

USING KEY SCIENCE TERMS

acceleration due to gravity
horizontal component
period
projectile motion
stationary satellite
vertical component
weightlessness

An analogy is a relationship between two pairs of words generally written in the following manner: a:b::c:d. The symbol : is read "is to," and the symbol :: is read "as." For example, cat:animal::rose:plant is read "cat is to animal as rose is to plant." In the analogies that follow, a word is missing. Complete each analogy by providing the missing word from the list above.

1. dropping:free-fall motion::throwing :____
2. seconds:period::m/sec^2:____
3. cycles per second:frequency::seconds per cycle:____
4. forward:horizontal component::downward motion:____
5. horizontal component:one dimension:: ____:two dimensions

UNDERSTANDING IDEAS

Choose the best answer to complete each sentence.

1. Acceleration due to gravity near Earth's surface is _____.
   a. greater for heavy objects
   b. greater for light objects
   c. a constant
   d. less for heavy objects
2. The velocity of an object moving at constant acceleration ____.
   a. increases or decreases uniformly
   b. remains the same
   c. decreases
   d. is zero
3. Projectiles fired horizontally accelerate ____.
   a. forward only
   b. downward only
   c. away from Earth only
   d. both forward and downward
4. You would most likely experience weightlessness ____.
   a. climbing stairs
   b. riding your bicycle
   c. going up in an elevator
   d. riding downhill in a roller coaster
5. If you saw a stationary satellite directly above your house at noon, where would you see it at midnight?
   a. directly above your house
   b. could not be seen
   c. on the horizon
   d. halfway between your house and the horizon

PROGRAM RESOURCES

Teacher Classroom Resources

Review and Assessment, Chapter Review and Chapter Test, pages 57–60

Computer Test Bank, Chapter Test

OPTIONS

Cooperative Learning

Consider using Cooperative Learning in the Understanding Ideas, Critical Thinking, Problem Solving, and Connecting Ideas sections of the Chapter Review.

COOP LEARN

6. Increasing a pendulum's length ____.
   a. shortens its period
   b. lengthens its period
   c. does not change its period
   d. increases its amplitude
7. A satellite stays in orbit because of ____.
   a. its shape
   b. acceleration due to gravity
   c. mass
   d. its period

CRITICAL THINKING

Use your understanding of the concepts developed in the chapter to answer each of the following questions.

1. A flower pot falls from the balcony of a twelfth-floor apartment. It smashes on the ground 3 seconds later. What is its velocity just before it hits the ground?
2. You have two tennis balls. You allow one to drop straight to the ground. The other you toss 5 meters straight into the air and then let it fall to the ground. Which ball is moving faster when it hits the ground? Why?
3. In the diagram, a rocket is fired from Earth in position 1. Describe what happens to its velocity in position 2. What do you think has to happen for it to go into position 3?

PROBLEM SOLVING

Read the following problem and discuss your answers in a brief paragraph.

You are an astronaut who has just landed on a planet. You would like to know what the acceleration due to gravity is on this planet. Explain the materials you would need and steps you would take to determine this.

CONNECTING IDEAS

Discuss each of the following in a brief paragraph.

1. Why can some animals on Earth jump higher than humans, even though they are affected by the same gravity?
2. Do you think an accelerometer would work on a space shuttle? How do you think the accelerometer readings would change during and after lift-off, and finally in orbit?
3. **HOW IT WORKS** You and a friend are comparing metronomes. Yours has a sliding weight made of copper. Your friend's has a brass sliding weight. How does this affect the periods of the metronomes?
4. **SCIENCE AND SOCIETY** How do weather satellites help weather forecasters?
5. **A CLOSER LOOK** What is the relationship between a falling object's size, shape, and mass and the object's terminal velocity?

CONNECTING IDEAS

Answers

1. Some animals have greater muscular strength compared to body weight than human beings and therefore can jump higher.
2. Yes; during liftoff, it would increase as the acceleration of the shuttle was added to gravity's acceleration. When the rocket switched off and the shuttle went into orbit, the acceleration would fall to zero.
3. Students' answers will vary but should center on the concept that the weight of a pendulum bob makes no difference in the period of a pendulum. Therefore, the weight of the sliding bob on a metronome would not affect the period of the metronome. It would not make a difference if one metronome had a copper weight and the other had a brass weight.
4. Students' responses will vary but should include the information that the stationary satellite can take pictures of large areas of Earth and so weather patterns over a great portion of Earth can be seen. Photos from these satellites can also show cloud patterns that occur during storms. This information as well as the storm path, can be used by weather forecasters to know what weather to expect.
5. Students' responses will vary but should include the information that larger objects encounter more air resistance as they fall. They fall more slowly and reach terminal velocity more quickly than do smaller objects. A streamlined object can be large but its shape would reduce the amount of air resistance acting on it and so it would fall faster than a bulky object. The mass of an object is less important in considering terminal velocity than is the size or shape of the object.

CHAPTER ORGANIZER

SECTION	OBJECTIVES	ACTIVITIES/FEATURES
Chapter Opener		**Explore!** How do Earth's surfaces affect what happens to water? p. 451
15-1 Water Recycling (2 days)	1. **Describe** how water moves through the hydrologic cycle. 2. **Identify** the processes involved in the hydrologic cycle. 3. **Demonstrate** runoff.	**Find Out!** How does water cycle through the environment? p. 452 **Skillbuilder:** Sequencing, p. 454
15-2 Streams and Rivers (3 days)	1. **Describe** how and why streams form. 2. **Discuss** characteristics of streams on steeply sloped land and streams on gently sloped land.	**Explore!** What happens to rainwater that runs off? p. 456 **Investigate 15-1:** Differences in Streams, p. 458
15-3 Groundwater in Action (4 days)	1. **Explain** how soil and rocks can be porous and permeable. 2. **Describe** groundwater, aquifers, and the water table. 3. **Explain** how groundwater is obtained from a well.	**Explore!** How can the water level in the ground be changed? p. 461 **Investigate 15-2:** Ground Permeability, p. 463 **Skillbuilder:** Recognizing Cause and Effect, p. 466
Expanding Your View		A Closer Look **Hot Springs and Geysers,** p. 467 Chemistry Connection **Caves, Sinkholes, and Stalactites,** p. 468 Science and Society **Water Wars,** p. 469 How It Works **Waterwheels,** p. 470 Technology Connection **Flood Control,** p. 471 Teens in Science **The Clean Stream Team,** p. 472

ACTIVITY MATERIALS

EXPLORE!	INVESTIGATE!	FIND OUT!
Page 451 waxed paper, cardboard, water, paper towels **Page 456** sand, stream table, 2 or 3-cm block of wood, water, sprinkling can, metric ruler **Page 461** sand, tub or stream table, water	**Page 458** 2 pails, plastic hose, 2 screw clamps, stream table, sand, blocks of wood **Page 463** 3 coffee cans open at both ends, watch with second hand, 500-mL. beaker, water, spade, metric ruler, permanent marker	**Page 452** large beaker, small beaker, water, plastic wrap, marble, lamp, or several hours of direct sunlight, rubber band

Chapter 15
Moving Water

TEACHER CLASSROOM RESOURCES	OTHER RESOURCES
Study Guide, p. 54 **Concept Mapping,** p. 23 **Multicultural Activities,** p. 34 **Take Home Activities,** p. 24 **How It Works,** p. 16 **Making Connections: Integrating Sciences,** p. 33	**Laboratory Manual,** pp. 87-88, The Hydrologic Cycle **Color Transparency and Master 29,** Water Cycle ***STVS:** *Cloud Chemistry,* Chemistry (Disc 2, Side 1) *Bacteria in the Clouds,* Plants and Simple Organisms (Disc 4, Side 1) *Global Weather Forecasting,* Earth and Space (Disc 3, Side 2)
Study Guide, p. 55 **Multicultural Activities,** p. 33 **Activity Masters, Investigate 15-1,** pp. 61-62 **Making Connections: Across the Curriculum,** p. 33	**Laboratory Manual,** pp. 89-92, Stream Patterns **Color Transparency and Master 30,** Distribution of Water on Earth ***STVS:** *Frazil Ice,* Earth and Space (Disc 3, Side 2) *Hydroelectric Power,* Chemistry (Disc 2, Side 2) *Mini-Hydroelectic Power Plants,* Chemistry (Disc 2, Side 2)
Study Guide, p. 56 **Activity Masters, Investigate 15-2,** pp. 63-64 **Critical Thinking/Problem Solving,** p. 23 **Making Connections: Technology and Society,** p. 33 **Flex Your Brain,** p. 8 **Review and Assessment,** pp. 61-64	**Laboratory Manual,** pp. 93-96, Permeability **Computer Test Bank**
	Spanish Resources **Cooperative Learning Resource Guide** **Lab and Safety Skills**

***Science and Technology Videodisc Series**

KEY TO TEACHING STRATEGIES

Teaching strategies have been coded for varying learning styles and abilities. As you review teaching strategies in the margin, the following designations will help you decide which activities are appropriate for your students.

L1 Level 1 activities are basic activities and should be within the ability range of all students.

L2 Level 2 activities are average activities and should be within the ability range of the average to above-average student.

L3 Level 3 activities are challenging activities designed for the ability range of above-average students.

LEP LEP activities should be within the ability range of Limited English Proficiency students.

COOP LEARN Cooperative Learning activities are designed for small group work.

ADDITIONAL MATERIALS

SOFTWARE	AUDIOVISUAL
Hydrologic Cycle, IBM. *Streams and Rivers,* Aquarius. *Stream Erosion,* Computer Software. *GroundWater,* IBM.	*The Earth and its Wonders: The Story of Rivers,* filmstrip/cassette, EBEC. *Water Below,* film, USGS.

Chapter 15

Moving Water

THEME DEVELOPMENT

Using the theme of systems and interactions, students learn how the various forms of water are linked in a hydrologic system that recycles the moisture of Earth. The theme of stability and change is used to describe how streams and rivers are formed and the differences in their strength and flow. Students also learn about groundwater, how it forms and how it is used. Students will use diagrams to discover how the continuous change in the form of water creates a stable overall system.

CHAPTER OVERVIEW

Students learn the basic processes of the water cycle and how runoff functions in the cycle.

Then students trace the development of rivers and streams from runoff. They will also see how the shape of the land affects and is affected by running water.

Finally, the idea of an aquifer is introduced. Students learn how water collects underground.

Tying to Previous Knowledge

Ask students if they think of water as in motion or as standing still. Students will probably be divided on this. Explain that, because of gravity, water is almost constantly in motion. Also ask what examples for water in motion they can think of. They may name rivers. Point out that there are many ways water travels on, above, and under Earth's surface.

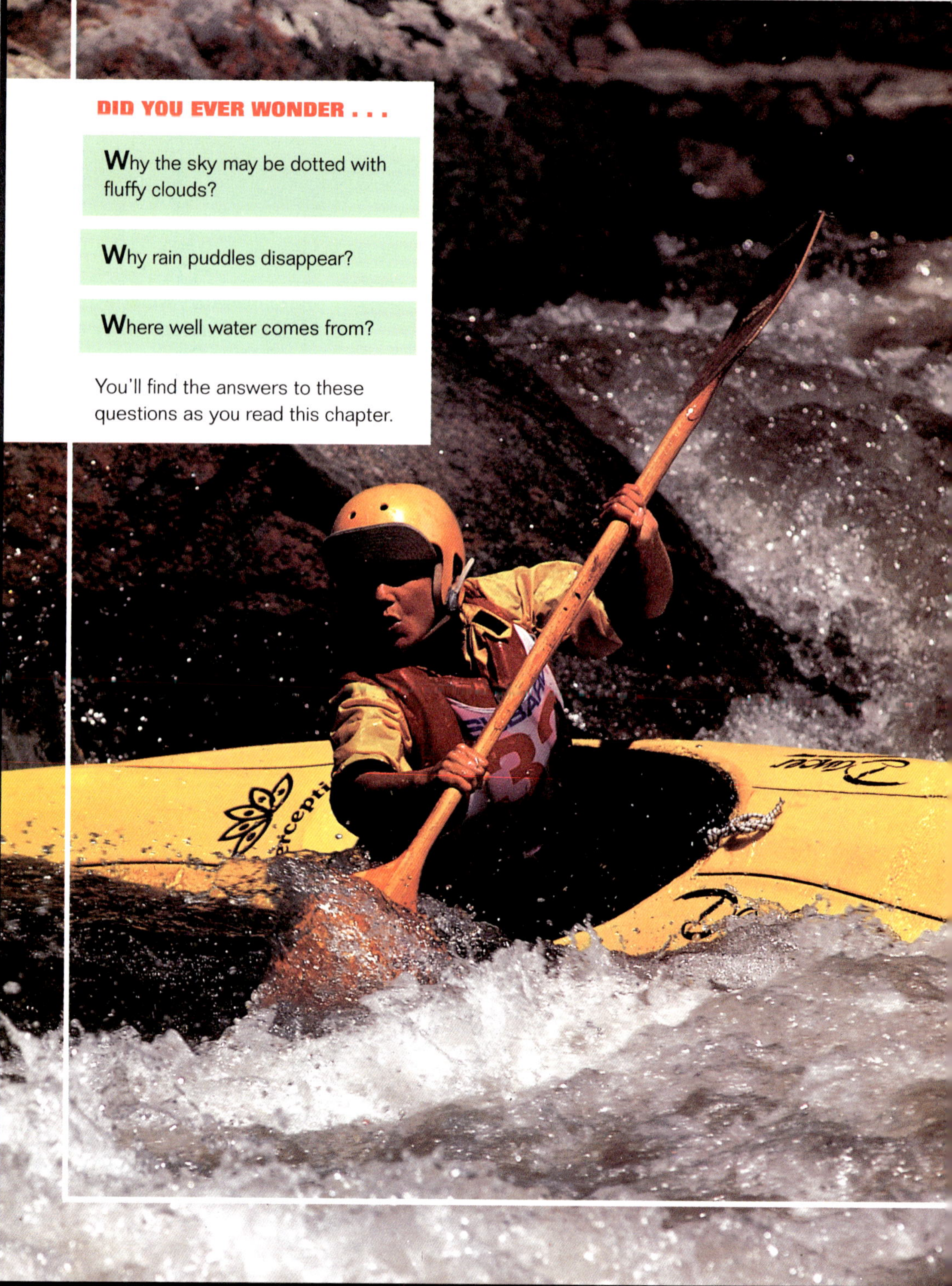

DID YOU EVER WONDER . . .
Why the sky may be dotted with fluffy clouds?
Why rain puddles disappear?
Where well water comes from?
You'll find the answers to these questions as you read this chapter.

DID YOU EVER WONDER...

Students will explore these questions as they progress through the chapter. Don't spoil their fun and motivation by sharing these answers too early.

- As water evaporates, it rises. As it cools, it condenses into cloud formations. (page 453)
- Puddles disappear because they evaporate under the heat of the sun. (page 453)
- Well water comes from groundwater trapped in layers of soil and rock. (page 465)

Moving Water

Have you ever seen a raging, roaring stream like the one shown in the picture? Its rushing waters could take you on the most exciting ride of your life!

What if you could follow a tiny droplet of water? You might race with it down a swift stream, while it crashes, tumbles, and foams as it goes downstream. After a while, the drop might splash onto a low tree branch or settle on a sunny rock. Or you could follow a droplet as it lazily drifts down a gentle, quiet river. Eventually you might follow the droplet as it soaks into the ground. You might even find the droplet has made its way to a lake or in the ocean.

Have you ever wondered why water flows the way it does? What happens to the rainwater that falls on grassy areas compared to the rainwater that falls on a parking lot? Try the Explore activity to see how surfaces on Earth can affect what happens to water.

EXPLORE!

How do Earth's surfaces affect what happens to water?

Put waxed paper over some cardboard. Slowly pour some water onto the paper and tilt the cardboard. Repeat the procedure, this time using paper towels. What happens to the water in each case? How do the surfaces act differently?

Introducing the Chapter

Have students look at the photograph on page 450 and discuss what kind of water they see. Invite students to discuss similar bodies of water they have seen. Also ask them where they might expect to find this kind of water. Use the background of the photo as a hint.

Uncovering Preconceptions

Many people take the availability of drinkable water for granted. Some think that there is an endless supply. But water resources depend on both the amount of rainfall in the area and the type and size of porous soil. Droughts can cause shortages of available fresh water.

EXPLORE!

How do Earth's surfaces affect what happens to water?

Time needed 10 minutes

Materials water, cardboard, waxed paper, paper towel

Thinking Processes
Critical thinking, Observing and inferring

Purpose To show that surfaces have an effect on the flow of water.

Teaching the Activity

Discussion Have students discuss how the activity relates to flowing water in their area such as after a rainstorm. L1

Expected Outcomes

Students will notice that water runs off the waxed paper quickly and easily, but the paper towels absorb some of the water. Students should realize that different surfaces affect water differently.

Answers to Questions

1. The water ran off the waxed paper very rapidly but some of it soaked into the paper towel.
2. The waxed paper allowed water to flow freely. The paper towel absorbed some of the water.

Project

Have students discover what their major source of water is by contacting the local water company. Then students should either build a model or make a poster series showing how the hydrologic cycle and the water company contribute to the delivery of water to homes. The model or posters can be displayed in the hall showcase.

Science at Home

Ask students to identify the places in their homes where evaporation and condensation take place. After they have made a list of these places, have students think of ways to conserve water by taking advantage of these processes. For example, water evaporated from boiling eggs could be collected and used to water plants.

Section 15-1

PREPARATION

Concepts Developed

In this chapter, students will learn that water moves through several processes.

Planning the Lesson

In planning your lesson on water recycling, refer to the Chapter Organizer on pages 450A-B for timing suggestions, resources, and additional materials that will help you in your presentation of the lesson concepts. For adequate development of the concepts presented in this section, we recommend that students do the Find Out activity on page 452.

1 MOTIVATE

Discussion Tell students that worldwide, about 517,000 cubic kilometers of water evaporates every year. A cubic kilometer is a cube that measures one kilometer on each side. Of this amount, about 108,000 cubic kilometers fall as precipitation on land. Ask students to discuss what happens to the water Earth receives. They should conclude that some is absorbed by plants, some filters into the soil, some fills ponds and lakes, but most is runoff that eventually flows to the ocean. L1

15-1 Water Recycling

OBJECTIVES

In this section, you will

- describe how water moves through the hydrologic cycle;
- identify the processes involved in the hydrologic cycle;
- demonstrate runoff.

KEY SCIENCE TERMS

hydrologic cycle
runoff

WATER CYCLE

Gray clouds roll in from the horizon, lightning flashes, thunder booms, and there you are—drenched by a sudden summer downpour. An hour later, the clouds have rolled past, the sky is bright blue, and puddles of rainwater are shimmering in the sunlight. Wait several hours more, and the puddles have disappeared. Where did the water go? The following activity will help you find out.

FIND OUT!

How does water cycle through the environment?

Although you can't see water when it's a vapor, you can show that water can become a vapor. Obtain a large beaker, a small beaker, some plastic wrap, a marble, a rubber band, and a lamp. Pour 2 cm of water into the large beaker. Then place the small beaker upright in the center of the large beaker. Cover the opening of the large beaker loosely with plastic wrap. Seal the wrap with the rubber band. Put the marble in the middle of the plastic wrap. Place the beaker under the lamp or in direct sunlight for several hours.

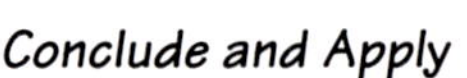

Conclude and Apply

1. Describe what occurred after several hours.
2. How does this activity help show what happens to water on Earth?

The liquid water went into the air as water vapor, a gas. You learned about liquids and gases in Chapter 5. Did you see the water become a vapor? How do you know it did? Eventually, the water vapor collected on the sides of the beaker and on the plastic wrap. The vapor then condensed and formed droplets of liquid water.

FIND OUT!

How does water cycle through the environment?

Time needed 5 minutes to prepare, several hours until effect

Materials large beaker, small beaker, plastic wrap, marble, rubber band, lamp

Thinking Processes Thinking critically, Observing and inferring

Purpose To show how water evaporates under heat and then condenses to form precipitation

Preparation You can use a large bowl or jar for the large beaker.

Teaching the Activity

Troubleshooting Be sure the rubber band fits snugly around all edges of the plastic wrap. L1

Expected Outcomes

The water in the large container evaporates, condenses on the plastic wrap, and should fall into the smaller container.

Conclude and Apply

1. See expected outcomes.
2. It shows the hydrologic cycle.

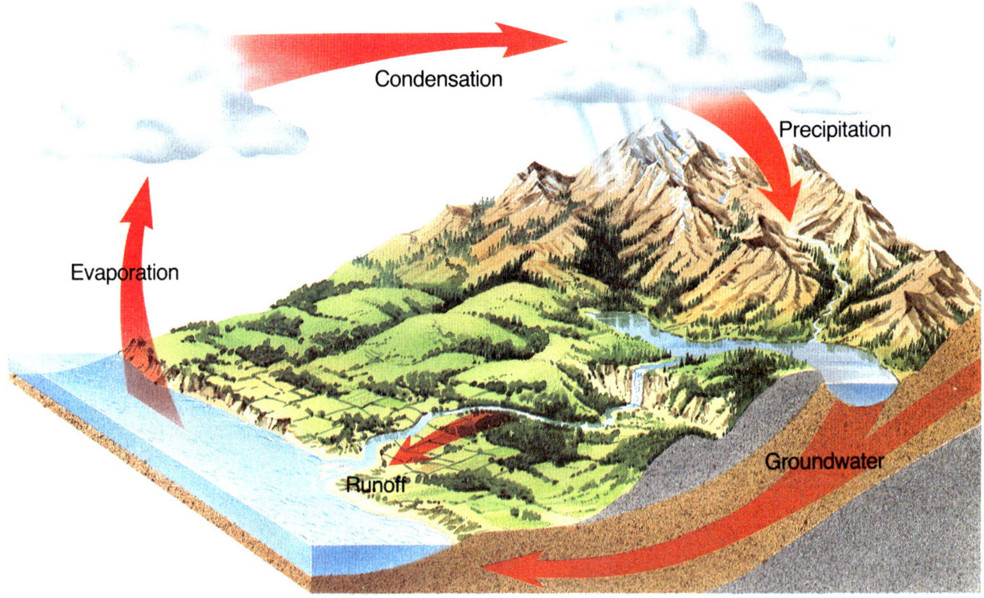

FIGURE 15-1. Water moves from Earth to the atmosphere and back to Earth again in the hydrologic cycle.

Rainwater in puddles does the same thing. Let's follow what happens to a drop of water as it moves in a cycle from being vapor in the air to being liquid on Earth and from Earth back into the air. You can see this cycle in Figure 15-1. It is called the **hydrologic cycle**.

How does water move from Earth to the air? This movement requires heat, which is provided by the sun. The sun's heat causes water to change into water vapor. This process is called *evaporation*. Water evaporates from lakes, streams, rivers, and oceans, and even from the land. What do you think happens next?

After evaporation, water vapor rises into the atmosphere. Usually, this water vapor will eventually turn back into a liquid. This process is called *condensation*. The tiny particles of water formed from condensation make up the clouds you see in the sky. Water particles in clouds often join together to become drops of water. When the drops get large and heavy enough, the cloud can no longer hold them, and they fall to Earth as rain or snow. If the drops freeze, they may fall to Earth as hail. Rain, snow, and hail are the part of the hydrologic cycle that concerns most people. Why do you suppose this is so?

DID YOU KNOW?

Because the oceans cover about three-fourths of Earth's surface, most water vapor comes from the oceans.

2 TEACH

Tying to Previous Knowledge

Have students name the three most common states of matter. *solid, liquid, gas* Explain that water circulating through Earth's water cycle exists in each of these states.

Concept Development

Theme Connection The interaction of the hydrologic cycle between Earth and its atmosphere is one of Earth's important systems. This system interacts with and greatly influences our weather.

Using the Drawing Point out that Figure 15-1 shows that evaporation tends to occur at lower levels. Ask students where condensation is most likely to occur.

Student Text Question Rain, snow, and hail are part of the hydrologic cycle that concerns most people. Why do you suppose this is so? *Precipitation is a component of weather conditions that affect people's activities.*

PROGRAM RESOURCES

Teacher Classroom Resources

Study Guide, page 54

Laboratory Manual, pages 87-88, The Hydrologic Cycle L2

Concept Mapping, page 23, Precipitation L1

Multicultural Activities, page 34, Summer Monsoons L1

Transparency Masters, page 61, and **Color Transparency,** number 29, Water Cycle L1

OPTIONS

Enrichment

Activity Divide the class into groups. Have each group make a list of places in their homes where evaporation or condensation takes place. They may name steam coming from boiling water or the frost that forms in a freezer. Have students try to explain why these things happen. COOP LEARN

SKILLBUILDER

Rain falls to Earth. Water evaporates. Water vapor is forced upward and condenses. Condensation forms clouds. Water falls again as rain, snow, or hail. L1

Concept Development

Inquiry Question What do you think will happen to the amount of runoff from an area when an asphalt parking lot is built on top of the soil? *Runoff increases because the asphalt cannot absorb water.*

Discussion Grasses have many shallow roots that spread laterally across soil. A pine tree has a few long roots. Ask students to describe which plants would better reduce runoff and help prevent soil erosion. *They should conclude that grass roots can soak up more surface water and thus better prevent erosion.* L2

MAKING CONNECTIONS

Daily Life

Tell students that they have probably seen an example of using plants to prevent erosion. Have them recall what covers the slopes that border highways. It is usually grass or ground cover. This vegetation prevents excessive runoff from the slopes onto the highway.

Content Background

Evaporated water condenses as the air cools. When the air near the ground cools, tiny droplets of water can form. Instead of falling to the ground, the droplets float. The result is fog.

SKILLBUILDER

SEQUENCING

Sequence the events in the hydrologic cycle beginning with rain falling to Earth. If you need help, refer to the **Skill Handbook** on page 648.

One of three things will happen to a drop of water after it falls to Earth. The water could evaporate again, it could flow along the ground to someplace else, or it could soak into the ground. Let's next explore what happens to water that flows along the ground.

RUNOFF

Most people have spilled a glass of water or milk. You probably have, too. Picture it in your mind. You accidentally hit the glass with your hand or elbow. The glass topples over, and the water spills. The water then runs off the table to the floor. If the water falls on a carpet, it quickly soaks in. If it spills on a tile or linoleum floor, it forms a puddle. If the floor is uneven, the liquid soon flows toward the lowest spot on the floor. Isn't this similar to what happened in the Explore activity at the beginning of this chapter? The water soaked into the paper towel but ran off the waxed paper. This is also what happens to rainwater on Earth. Water soaks into the ground in some places but flows on the top of other surfaces. Water that flows and does not soak in is called **runoff**. Water that runs off will move along the ground and will eventually enter a stream.

FIGURE 15-2. After a heavy rain, this water didn't soak into the ground and became runoff.

What determines whether rainwater soaks into the ground or runs off? One factor is the ground itself. If the land is hard and smooth, like the waxed paper in your experiment or like rock in the real world, water will likely run off.

What other factors affect whether rain soaks in or runs off? You know from experience that sometimes rains are fast, hard driving, and heavy. At other times, they are little more than slow, soft drizzles. Figure 15-2 will give you an idea of what happens when rain is fast and heavy. Light rain falling over several hours will probably have time to soak into the ground. However, heavy rain falling for about an hour may run off because it doesn't have time to soak in.

OPTIONS

Meeting Individual Needs

Learning Disabled You will need a sheet of waxed paper, lumpy sponge or string dishwashing brush, bucket. Some students may have difficulty understanding how plants help to decrease runoff. Have them imagine the sponge or dish brush as the roots of a plant. Have two students hold the waxed paper at an angle over the bucket. This is Earth's surface. Have one student hold the brush or sponge gently on the waxed paper. Pour some water over the waxed paper so that it passes through the "roots." Students will see that some of the water is absorbed. LEP

Another factor that affects the amount of runoff is the slope of the land. You probably know that water flows downhill. This downward flow is due to Earth's gravity, which you learned about in Chapter 14. Gently rolling slopes and flat areas usually hold water in place until it can evaporate or sink into the ground. Steep slopes, however, do not hold the water, and it runs off. Therefore, slope of the land has an effect on whether water soaks in or runs off.

Study Figure 15-3. Do you think plants can affect runoff? Just like water running off a table, water on Earth tends to run off smooth surfaces. However, plants and their roots act like a sponge to soak up and hold water.

As you have read, there are many factors that affect runoff. A hard rain that falls on sloping, barren ground will probably run off. But a slow steady rain that falls on a level, grass-covered lawn will probably soak in and not become runoff. In the following sections, you'll learn what happens to water that soaks into the ground.

a 

b 

FIGURE 15-3. Runoff is less likely to occur where there is vegetation (a). Runoff is more likely to occur where there is little or no vegetation (b).

Check Your Understanding

1. What supplies the heat for the hydrologic cycle?
2. What processes are involved in the hydrologic cycle?
3. How can runoff be decreased?
4. **APPLY:** Use the hydrologic cycle to explain why water can be described as recycled.

PROGRAM RESOURCES

Teacher Classroom Resources

Take Home Activities, page 24, Evaporation in a Jar L1

How It Works, page 16, A City Water System L2

Making Connections, Integrating Sciences, page 33, El Niño L2

Other Resources

Hydrologic Cycle, software, IBM.

Answers to Check Your Understanding

1. the sun
2. precipitation, evaporation, condensation, precipitation
3. Vegetation helps to decrease runoff.
4. The form of water is changed in the hydrologic cycle so that the water is continually reused.

3 Assess

Check for Understanding

1. Ask students what they think would have happened if they had not used the marble in the Find Out. They should conclude that water vapor would have condensed more evenly on the plastic. The "precipitation" would not have funneled directly into the smaller container.
2. To answer the Apply question, be sure students know the meaning of the word *recycle*. It means a process that uses a material over and over again.

Reteach

Materials needed are a paint tray half full of soil, a piece of cardboard, a clump of grass, and a beaker of water.

Have students work in groups to see how different surfaces affect runoff. Have them design and execute an experiment using the cardboard to simulate a paved street and the clump of grass to simulate a field. LEP COOP LEARN

Extension

Have students who have mastered the concepts in this section find out what happens to runoff in their community. To do so, they should contact the community public works department. If appropriate data are made available to them, students can prepare a map showing the location of storm sewer drains in the area of their school. L3

4 Close

Discussion

Ask students what might cause droplets of water to form on the outside of a cold soda can. Explain that the cooler temperature of the soda cools the air right next to the can. The water vapor in the air next to the can condenses and forms small drops of water. L1

Section 15-2

PREPARATION

Concepts Developed

Students learned about runoff in the previous section. This section explores where much of that water goes. Students will learn how streams and rivers are formed and the characteristics of different types of streams and rivers. They will see how sloped land affects the flow of streams and rivers.

Planning the Lesson

In planning your lesson on streams and rivers, refer to the Chapter Organizer on pages 450A-B for timing suggestions, resources, and additional materials that will help you in your presentation of the lesson concepts. For adequate development of the concepts presented in this section, we recommend that students do the Explore on page 456.

1 MOTIVATE

Discussion Use a map of the United States and Figure 15-4. Have students find the Mississippi drainage basin on the map. Have them find and name some of the tributaries of the Mississippi. L1

15-2 Streams and Rivers

OBJECTIVES

In this section, you will

- describe how and why streams form;
- discuss characteristics of streams on steeply sloped land and streams on gently sloped land.

KEY SCIENCE TERMS

drainage basin
meander

STREAM DEVELOPMENT

Remember the storm you were caught in at the beginning of the last section? You never imagined that one storm could bring so much rain in so little time. Not all the rain collected in puddles, however. Where did all the rest of the water go? Doing the Explore activity will help you discover what happens to some runoff.

EXPLORE!

What happens to rainwater that runs off?

Put sand in a stream table to a depth of 4 cm, but leave one end of the table empty. Put a block under the end of the table that is full of sand so that it is lifted 2 or 3 cm. Use a sprinkling can to sprinkle water in the sand on the upper side of the stream table. The sprinkled water will be like rain falling on Earth. Observe what happens.

In the activity, did streams of water form in the sand? Did the water settle in the lower part of the stream table? Runoff does the same thing on the surface of Earth.

As you saw in the activity, water particles tend to stay together when they move. Because of gravity, water also flows downhill until it reaches the lowest point possible. Water flowing within a smaller channel is generally called a stream. Water in a larger channel is generally called a river.

Small streams eventually join together to form a larger stream. That larger stream will join with other large streams to form a river.

DID YOU KNOW?

The longest river in the world is the Nile in Africa. The largest river in water capacity is the Amazon River in South America.

EXPLORE!

What happens to rainwater that runs off?

Time needed 5 minutes

Materials stream table (see illustration on page 458), sand, block of wood, watering can

Thinking Processes
Thinking critically, Observing and inferring, Representing and applying data, Making models

Purpose To show how streams form from runoff

Preparation Use the illustration on page 458 as a guideline. Set up the stream table ahead of time. You can substitute bricks for wood blocks. Test the process to see how much water to sprinkle.

Teaching the Activity

Demonstration Before using the stream table, tilt a cookie sheet over a sink and sprinkle water on the uplifted end. Students can see the water's path.

Expected Outcomes

The sprinkled water will tend to form into channels that run down to the lower end of the table.

DRAINING THE LAND

The water in streams and rivers comes from rain or melted snow—that is, runoff. The land area from which a stream gets its water is like a bathtub. The water that was collected in a bathtub flows toward the drain when the drain is open. Likewise, all the water in a land area eventually flows down, or drains, into one stream. The area that a stream drains is called a **drainage basin**. Each stream has its own drainage basin.

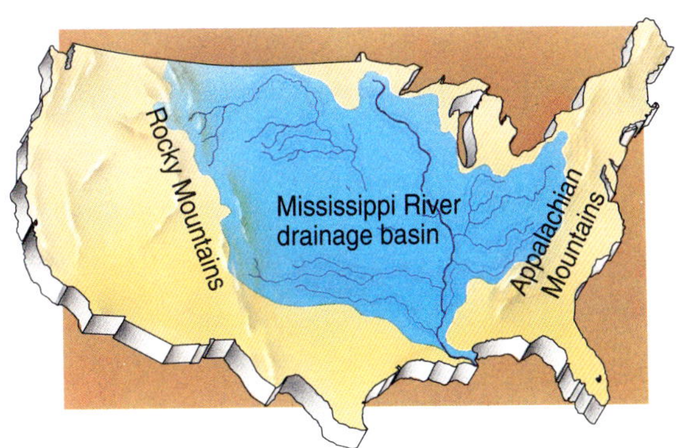

FIGURE 15-4. The Mississippi River has one of the largest drainage basins on Earth.

The drainage basin of a large river usually includes the drainage basins of smaller rivers and streams. The largest drainage basin in the United States is the Mississippi River drainage basin, shown in Figure 15-4. Most of the rain that falls between the Rocky Mountains and the Appalachian Mountains drains into small streams and rivers that eventually drain into the Missouri or Ohio rivers. In turn, these large rivers and other streams and rivers, flow into the Mississippi River. All the streams and rivers in a major drainage basin form a river system. As you can see, the Mississippi River system drains about one-third of the United States.

FIGURE 15-5. This stream in Arkansas flows through a cave.

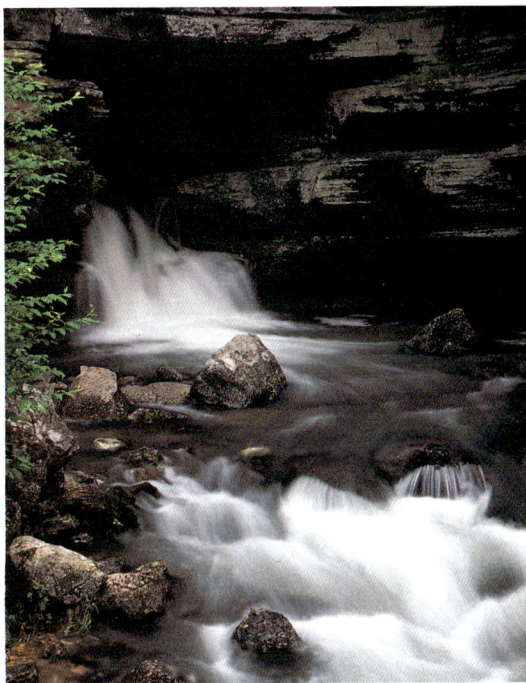

STREAMS OF EVERY KIND

Think of streams that flow near your home or streams you may have visited. Some streams are narrow and noisy, have steep sides, and flow swiftly. These streams may form white-water rapids or waterfalls, as shown in Figure 15-5. Other streams are wide and slow-moving. Why are streams different? Doing the next Investigate activity will help you answer this question.

2 TEACH

Tying to Previous Knowledge

Ask students to describe any brooks, streams, or rivers they have seen. Encourage them to comment on the size of the feature, the color of the water, and the slope of the surrounding land.

Concept Development

Theme Connection The theme that this section supports is interactions and systems. Streams and rivers form systems within the hydrologic cycle. People use these interconnected waterways for travel, fresh drinking water, and irrigation.

MAKING CONNECTIONS

Literature

The great Mississippi River formed the background for many of Mark Twain's stories. Have students read the chapter called "Sounding" in *Life on the Mississippi.* Have students discuss how the chapter relates to what they have learned about rivers.

Content Background

Streams are classified as young, mature, or old. These names come from what geologists call the geomorphologic age of the land on which a stream flows. This is based on the geologic principle that mountains wear down over time. Thus, steep land becomes less steep over time, as water wears down land. Mountainous areas are generally geomorphologically young, so streams flowing on them are labeled young. Rapidly flowing streams on steep slopes have a high degree of energy and erode the stream bottom more than the sides. A mature stream curves down a gradual slope and erodes its sides. It flows less swiftly through its valley. This stream will begin to meander. An old stream flows very slowly through the flood plain it has carved. The erosion of the sides causes major changes in its meander.

PROGRAM RESOURCES

Teacher Classroom Resources

Study Guide, page 55
Laboratory Manual, pages 89-92, Stream Patterns L2
Activity Masters, pages 61-62, Investigate 15-1
Multicultural Activities, page 33, The Panama Canal L1

INVESTIGATE!

15-1 DIFFERENCES IN STREAMS

Time needed 10–15 minutes

Materials 2 pails, plastic hose, 2 screw clamps, stream table, sand, blocks of wood

Thinking Processes
Thinking critically, Observing and inferring, Comparing and contrasting, Recognizing cause and effect, Representing and applying data, Making models, Predicting

Purpose To show that slope affects the flow of a stream

Preparation Have the stream table and materials set up in advance (see illustration below). You may want to have a large spoon or spatula ready to smooth out the damp sand.

Teaching the Activity

Troubleshooting Be sure the tube from the supply pail is secure. The tube that carries excess water out of the stream channel may become clogged with sand. To prevent this, be sure the stream channel is deep enough near the tube opening that the tube is above the sand. But also be sure the water is able to reach the tube. L1

Expected Outcomes

Stream patterns will form. The steeper the slope, the narrower and faster the stream.

Answers to Analyze/Conclude and Apply

1. by loosening the screw clamp
2. by tightening the screw clamp
3. narrow and swift
4. broad and slow
5. The channel formed when the sand end was high was narrower and swifter than the channel formed when sand end was lower.
6. The difference is caused by the change in slope.
7. Broad channels form on plains. Narrow channels form in mountainous areas.

INVESTIGATE!

15-1 DIFFERENCES IN STREAMS

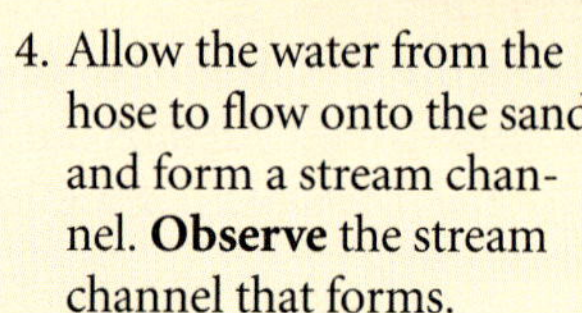

To discover why streams have different characteristics, make your own model streams.

PROBLEM

Does slope affect a stream?

MATERIALS

2 pails
plastic hose
2 screw clamps
stream table
sand
blocks of wood

PROCEDURE

1. Set up the stream table. Place the sand about 4 cm deep at one end of the stream table. Smooth out the sand and slope it down toward the other end of the stream table, which will be a reservoir.
2. Place several blocks of wood under the stream table at the end where the sand is deepest.
3. By using the screw clamp on the supply hose, adjust the flow of water to about the amount from a slow-running faucet.
4. Allow the water from the hose to flow onto the sand and form a stream channel. **Observe** the stream channel that forms.
5. Stop the flow of water and remove the blocks that you had placed under one end in the previous step. Note: Do not make the reservoir end higher than the other end of the stream table. Smooth out the sloping sand from the previous stream channel. Allow the same amount of water to flow onto the sand and form a stream channel as you did before. **Observe** the stream channel that forms.

ANALYZE

1. How could the flow of water be increased?
2. How could the flow of water from the supply pail be slowed down?
3. Describe the channel that was formed when the sand end was high.
4. Describe the channel that was formed when the sand end was lower.

CONCLUDE AND APPLY

5. **Compare and contrast** the two types of stream channels.
6. **Determine the cause** of the differences between the two channels you made.
7. **Going Further:** What kind of stream channels would you expect to form on plains? What kind form in mountainous areas?

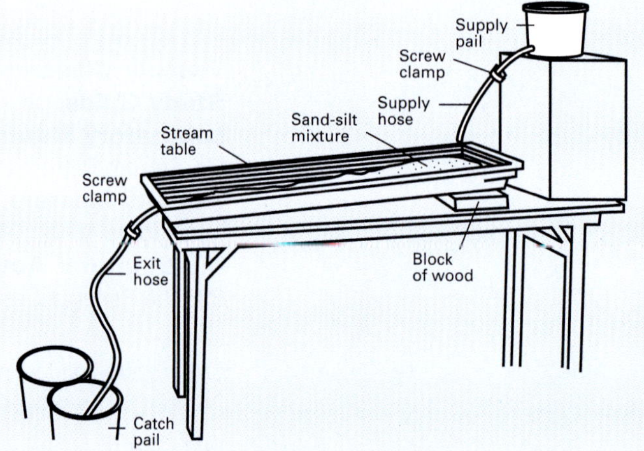

Streams have different characteristics for several reasons. You discovered one—slope—in the Investigate activity.

Streams that flow through steeply sloped areas run swiftly downhill. Such a stream may carve a narrow, steep, V-shaped valley because the running water wears away the stream bottom more than its sides. You can see an example of such a stream in Figure 15-6. Streams on steep slopes may also form areas of white-water rapids or tumble over waterfalls.

A stream from a steep slope may eventually reach land that slopes very little. Or a stream may begin in such an area. A stream moving along a gradual slope flows much more slowly. Its valley is wide and low. Most of the rocks in the streambed associated with white water or waterfalls have been worn away. Instead, the water has started to wear away the sides of the streambed, developing curves and bends in its path.

The curves in a river form because the speed of the water varies depending on the width of the stream channel. Water in wide, shallow areas of a stream is slowed down by the friction created with the bottom of the river. In deep areas, less of the water comes in contact with the bottom, so less friction is created. Therefore, deep water can flow faster.

FIGURE 15-6. Streams on steep slopes flow swiftly and fairly straight.

MAKING CONNECTIONS

History

The changing path of the lower portion of the Rio Grande has, in the past, created an international problem between the United States and Mexico. The international boundary between Mexico and the United States was originally defined as the main channel of the river; however, over the years it has become harder and harder to define the main channel of the river. In order to avoid continued problems, the border between the United States and Mexico was defined by a series of fixed points, on the basis of latitude and longitude. Ask students to research the Treaty of Guadalupe Hidalgo, which ended the Mexican War, to find out more about U.S./Mexican border problems affected by rivers.

Daily Life The effect of slope and width of water flow can be seen in city streets during or after a heavy rain. Water flows faster in gutters than on the rest of the street. As water approaches the downward slope into a drain,

Content Background

Because of its age, the Mississippi River has carved out a flood plain that covers over 39,000 square kilometers. Flood waters can rise as much as 15 to 17 meters above the river's lowest stage. When floods occur on the Ohio and Missouri, heavy floods also happen along the Mississippi. This is because both rivers drain into the Mississippi.

PROGRAM RESOURCES

Teacher Classroom Resources

Transparency Masters, page 63, and **Color Transparency,** number 30, Distribution of Water on Earth L1

Making Connections: Across the Curriculum, page 33, River Communities L2

Other Resources

Stream Erosion, software, Computer Software.

Teacher F.Y.I.

The Mississippi erodes about 268,000,000 cubic meters of topsoil a year. If this soil were spread in a 2.5-centimeter-thick layer, it would cover an area almost as large as the state of Connecticut.

It has taken the Colorado River 10 to 15 million years to carve the Grand Canyon, which ranges from 6 to 29 kilometers wide and is more than $1\frac{1}{2}$ kilometers deep.

3 Assess

Check for Understanding

To help students with the Apply question, remind them that fast-flowing water tends to run in a fairly straight path. Ask students where fast-flowing water is usually found. *steep slopes*

Reteach

Have students write a description of what they think the bed of a mountain stream looks like. They should picture it as narrow, with rocks and pebbles at its bottom.

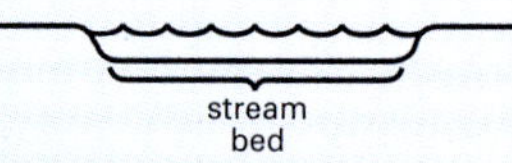

Have students then write a description of the bed of a large river. The image should be of a wide bed with a sandy or muddy bottom, the result of wearing away of both bottom and sides. L1

Extension

To understand another very important use of rivers, have students who have mastered this section research the names of some of Earth's rivers that form boundaries between states and countries. Ask students to make a table listing the name of the river and the states and/or countries that it divides. L3

4 Close

Activity

Have students draw an imaginary river system. They should link several fast-flowing streams from mountains to two or three slower, meandering rivers. These should flow into a large, highly curved river on a plain. Have students label the types of slopes and the types of rivers. L1

FIGURE 15-7. Streams on gentle slopes or broad, flat plains flow slowly around bends and curves.

You can see that the river gently turns and curves as it moves along the gentle slope. This faster-moving water wears away the sides of the streambed where it flows more quickly, forming curves. A curve that forms in this way is called a **meander**. Figure 15-7 shows what a meandering stream looks like from the air.

The broad, flat valley formed by a river on a gentle slope is called a floodplain. When the stream floods because of heavy runoff, it often covers part or all of its floodplain.

What about the water that does not drain into streams, water that is not runoff? It soaks into the ground. In the next section, you'll learn more about this process.

Check Your Understanding

1. What causes streams to form and flow downhill?
2. Where are slow-moving streams most likely to be found?
3. **APPLY:** Why don't meanders form in streams on steep slopes?

Answers to Check Your Understanding

1. Streams are formed by runoff water and run downhill because of the force of gravity.
2. Slow-moving streams are most likely to be found in valleys and plains.
3. The water in a stream on a steep slope is flowing too quickly to form gentle curves.

OPTIONS

Multicultural Perspectives

Ancient Egyptians made good use of the flood plain created by the Nile River. The Nile rose every year to flood stage. It left behind a deposit of rich soil that enabled the residents along the river to get two or three harvests a year. The regular annual flood also gave birth to the idea of a 365-day year. This was based on the average period between rises over fifty years.

15-3 Groundwater in Action

INTO THE GROUND

Just as spilled water may soak into a carpet, some rainwater that falls on Earth soaks into the ground. What happens then? Do the following activity to help you find out.

EXPLORE!

How can the water level in the ground be changed?

Fill a tub or stream table with sand and level it out. Pour water into the tub until the water is almost to the top of the sand. Make a shallow hole in the sand so that you can see the water at the bottom of the hole. Think of the water in the hole as a pond or lake. Now add more water to the sand. What happens to the level of the water in the hole? How could you make the level of the water go down?

As you have observed, water that enters the sand moves from one place to another. There must be a lot of space between the fragments of sand. A drop of water that soaks into such ground would just seem to disappear because the ground has so much space within it.

Just watering a plant shows you how quickly water may soak into soil. Like most soils, the soil in which most houseplants are potted is made up of many tiny rock fragments. Some fragments may be sand-sized, some larger, and others smaller. The spaces among the fragments are called pores.

OBJECTIVES

In this section, you will

- explain how soil and rocks can be porous and permeable;
- describe groundwater, aquifers, and the water table;
- explain how groundwater is obtained from a well.

KEY SCIENCE TERMS

groundwater
aquifer
water table

Section 15-3

PREPARATION

Concepts Developed

Students have read about one main part of the hydrologic cycle. A second water system involves groundwater. Students will learn how water enters soil and rock layers and forms groundwater reserves. Water accumulates underground and forms the water table. Students will also learn about other sources of water, such as aquifers and springs. They will learn how wells are used to get water from an aquifer.

Planning the Lesson

In planning your lesson on groundwater, refer to the Chapter Organizer on pages 450A-B for timing suggestions, resources, and additional materials that will help you in your presentation of the lesson concepts. For adequate development of the concepts presented in this section, we recommend that students do the Explore activity on page 461.

1 MOTIVATE

Discussion Ask students to imagine that they are building a house in an uninhabited wilderness area. The problem is that the spot they chose to build on is far from streams and rivers. Have students think of what they can do to provide themselves with water. L1

EXPLORE!

How can the water level in the ground be changed?

Time needed 5 minutes

Materials tub, sand, water

Thinking Processes Representing and applying data, Making models, Predicting

Purpose To show how groundwater levels change

Preparation Set up the sand and water ahead of time.

Teaching the Activity

Troubleshooting When adding more water to the sand, try not to disturb the hole you made. You may have to firm the sides of the hole. L1 LEP

Expected Outcome

The water level in the hole rises when more water is poured into the sand.

Answer to Question

The water level rises. The water level would go down if more sand were added.

2 TEACH

Tying to Previous Knowledge

Ask students where they get water in their homes. They will probably say from the faucet. Then ask where the water from the faucet originates. If they say the water company, ask where the water company gets it. Continue to query students until they see that the water they drink comes from one of Earth's many supplies of fresh water: rivers, lakes, reservoirs, aquifers, and springs.

Concept Development

Theme Connection The water we drink and use for washing comes from a system connected to the entire hydrologic cycle. Other parts of the cycle involve the movement and interaction of water through the air and over the land. The groundwater system is the movement of water through Earth.

Demonstration This will show how water reacts to an impermeable material. You will need a piece of slate or a ceramic plate.

Pour some water onto the slate or plate. Ask students what happens to the water. *It does not go anywhere.* Have students contrast what happened to the water in the sand from Explore and the water on the plate.

Inquiry Question What do you think happens to water that is soaking into the ground when it meets a layer of impermeable material? *It flows along the material rather than soaking through it.*

FIGURE 15-8. Water disappears into soil because the soil has air spaces within it.

DID YOU KNOW?

The amount of water in the ground may be ten times more than the amount of water in streams, rivers, and lakes at the surface.

Water that soaks into the ground collects in the pores and becomes part of what is called **groundwater**. In fact, it becomes part of a groundwater system, just as the water that stays above the ground becomes part of a river system. The groundwater system is similar to a river system. However, instead of having stream channels that connect different parts of a drainage basin, a groundwater system may have connecting pores that water can move through.

Soil or rock that has many connecting pores is said to be permeable. Water can pass through such ground materials easily. Soil or rock that has few or very small pores is less permeable. Water can't pass through it as easily. Some materials, such as clay, shale, and slate, have very small pores or no pores at all. Because water can't pass through these materials, they are said to be impermeable.

How quickly water seeps into the ground depends on the permeability of that ground. Do you think water would seep quickly into hard-packed soil? Find out by doing the following activity.

MAKING CONNECTIONS

Daily Life

After a normal rain, puddles form on concrete or other hard surfaces. But the water is absorbed by grassy areas and ordinary soil.

OPTIONS

Meeting Individual Needs

Learning Disabled You will need a large jar or beaker, water, pebbles and rocks. Some students may have difficulty understanding the idea of permeability. Fill the beaker with pebbles and rocks. Have students note the spaces in between; these are pores. Slowly fill the jar with water. Have students observe how the water flows around the rocks and pebbles and fills the spaces in between. LEP

PROGRAM RESOURCES

Teacher Classroom Resources

Study Guide, page 56

Laboratory Manual, pages 93-96, Permeability L3

Activity Masters, pages 63-64, Investigate 15-2

INVESTIGATE!

15-2 GROUND PERMEABILITY

There are many different kinds of soils. Why does water seep into some soils better than it seeps into others? This test can help you compare how fast water seeps into soil.

PROBLEM

How can you compare the permeability of different soils?

MATERIALS

3 coffee cans open at both ends
watch with second hand
500-mL beaker
water
spade
metric ruler
permanent marker

PROCEDURE

1. Copy the data table.
2. Use the metric ruler and permanent marker to **measure** and mark the outside of each coffee can 3 cm from one end.
3. Obtain permission to test three different locations on the school grounds. List each in the data table.
4. Use the spade to dig a small hole about 20 cm deep in each location.
5. **Observe** and record the texture and color of the ground at each location. Are the particles small and fine or large and coarse?
6. **Predict** the permeability of the soil in each location. Write your predictions in the data table.
7. Use your foot to press a can into the ground up to the 3 cm mark at each location. Press the can in where the soil has not been disturbed.
8. Fill the 500-mL beaker with water and then pour it into a can. Repeat this procedure for the other cans.
9. Use the watch to determine how much time it takes for all the water in each can to sink into the soil. Record the amount of time for each location in the data table.

DATA AND OBSERVATIONS

Sample data

LOCATION	OBSERVATIONS OF SOIL	PREDICTION	AMOUNT OF TIME TO SINK IN
Next to flagpole	pale brown, gritty, no organisms, no clay but mostly sand	most permeable soil sample	1 minute 23 seconds

ANALYZE

1. Which of the locations had the most permeable soil? How can you tell that the soil was more permeable at this location?
2. Which of the locations had the least permeable soil? How can you tell that the soil was less permeable at this location?
3. Which sample did you **predict** would be the most permeable? The least permeable?
4. **Determine the controls** that you used in this experiment.

CONCLUDE AND APPLY

5. How can you explain the differences in permeability of the soil samples?
6. What **conclusions** about groundwater can you draw from this activity?
7. How can you **compare** the permeability of soil in different locations?
8. **Going Further**: Explain how permeability might affect runoff.

INVESTIGATE!

15-2 GROUND PERMEABILITY

Time needed 1 hour or more

Materials See student text page.

Thinking Processes
Thinking critically, Observing and inferring, Comparing and contrasting, Recognizing cause and effect

Purpose To show that some soil is more permeable than others

Preparation If you have several available locations on the school grounds, ask for permission. You may need to find locations around the neighborhood instead. Any standard measure can be substituted for the beaker. This activity should be conducted as a group rather than individual project.

Teaching the Activity

Discussion Divide the class into groups and assign prelocated spots to each group. Have each group state a reason why they think their spot is more or less permeable. Encourage other groups to challenge them. COOP LEARN

Troubleshooting Students probably will need to make a much larger version of the data table than is pictured. To avoid confusion, assign soil sampling to groups or individuals. LEP L2

Expected Outcomes

Rockier soil samples will be more permeable than sandy or hard-packed soils.

Answers to Analyze/Conclude and Apply

1. Answers will vary. Water soaked into the ground the fastest at this location.
2. Answers will vary. Water took the longest time to soak into the ground at this location.
3. Answers will vary.
4. The control for this experiment is the 500 mL of water used at each location.
5. Less permeable soils may have smaller pores or they might contain more clay, or they might be more compacted. More permeable soils may have larger pore spaces and be less compacted.
6. Water that falls on Earth's surface can become groundwater quicker in some places, depending on the permeability of the ground.
7. Soils from different locations, composed of different materials may have different levels of permeability.
8. Water will soak into permeable soils, thus reducing the amount of runoff.

Concept Development

Theme Connection The theme that this chapter supports is interactions and systems. The groundwater system is more than just a part of the hydrologic cycle. It interacts with the systems of living things, providing a necessary resource for plants and animals.

Using the Diagram Ask students to look at Figure 15-9. Ask them to explain the differences between these three types of rocks. They should discuss the spaces and arrangement of the spaces.

Demonstration Show students how pore space can be measured.

Materials needed are two 250-mL beakers, a graduated cylinder, and enough sand and gravel to fill two beakers to the 100 mL mark respectively.

Fill one beaker to the 100 mL mark with sand, and fill the other beaker to the 100 mL mark with gravel. Fill a graduated cylinder with 100 mL of water. Pour the water slowly into the gravel and stop when the water just covers the gravel. Record the volume of water used. Repeat the procedure with the sand.

Be sure the sand and gravel grains are dry. Ask students to predict which material will allow more water before being filled to capacity. Which substance has more pore space? Why? *It takes about the same amount of water for each material. The two substances will be about equal in total amount of pore space. Although the individual pore spaces are larger between gravel grains, there are fewer of them compared to the smaller but more numerous pore spaces of the sand grains.* L2

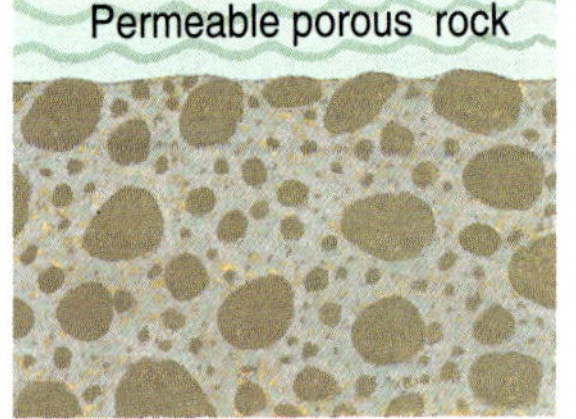

FIGURE 15-9. A permeable, porous rock allows water to pass through (a). An impermeable, porous rock does not allow water to pass through (b). A rock that is not porous or permeable does not allow water to seep in (c).

All the ground you tested was probably permeable to some degree. But what about soils or layers of rock that are impermeable? How do they affect groundwater? To understand how impermeable materials affect groundwater, think about a raincoat. You know that a raincoat is designed to keep rainwater from getting through. So the raincoat is impermeable to water. But other kinds of clothing might let some or all of the rainwater through.

Look at Figure 15-9 (b). Some soils and rock materials are porous but are not porous. If the pores in a material are not connected, water cannot move freely through the material. Sandstone is a common permeable rock. Yet some sandstone is porous material that is not permeable.

How deep into the ground do you suppose groundwater can go? That depends on the permeability of the soil and rock. Groundwater will keep going down to lower levels until it reaches pores that are already filled with water. This water is resting on a layer of impermeable rock, such as the rock in Figure 15-9 (c). When this happens, the impermeable rock acts like a dam, and the water can't move down any deeper. So the water begins to fill up the pores in the rocks above the impermeable rock. See Figure 15-10. A layer of permeable soil or rock that allows water to move in and out freely is called an **aquifer.** Soils that contain sand or gravel and rocks like sandstones and limestones are often aquifers.

Why do you suppose aquifers are important to people? Aquifers are sources of water for many communities. In fact, if you do not live near a large river or a large fresh-

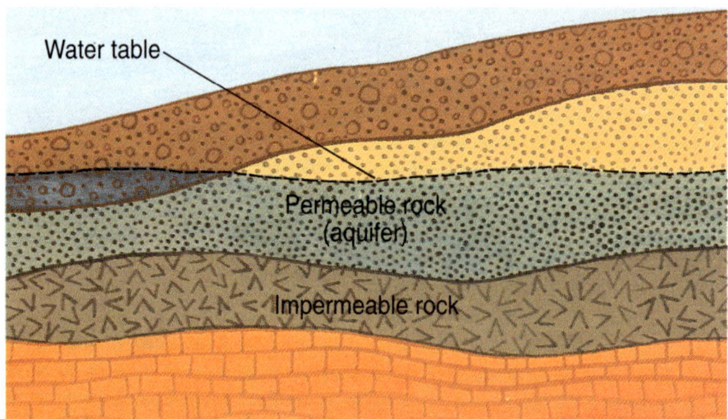

FIGURE 15-10. An aquifer is a layer of sand, gravel, or other materials that are permeable.

PROGRAM RESOURCES

Teacher Classroom Resources

Critical Thinking/Problem Solving, page 8, Flex Your Brain; page 23, Groundwater Pollution L2

Making Connections: Technology and Society, page 33, Protecting an Aquifer L2

OPTIONS

Enrichment

Research There have been water wars in the United States for over one hundred years. The arguments over water continue. According to the U.S. Water Council, by the year 2000, there will be insufficient water in 17 of the nation's 106 water supply regions. Have students research aspects of disputes over water distribution.

water lake, the chances are good that you get your water from an aquifer. Where does the water that you drink come from?

WELLS AND SPRINGS

The water level in an aquifer may change from season to season. Recall the Explore activity you did at the beginning of this section. You discovered you could change the level of water in the aquifer you made. Knowing the level of water in the ground is important to many people because they get their drinking water from groundwater. They drill water wells down into the aquifers. Water from an aquifer flows into a well and then is pumped back up to the surface.

A well must go down past the water table to reach water. What is the water table? The diagram shown in Figure 15-11 will give you an idea of what it is. The **water table** is the top of the level where groundwater has collected in the ground. If the well is far enough below the water table, the well should provide a reliable source of cool drinking water in every season of the year.

During dry seasons, a well might dry up because the water table drops. The water table may also drop if too

FIGURE 15-11. A stream's surface is the level of the water table in that area. Ponds and lakes are often part of the water table at the surface, too.

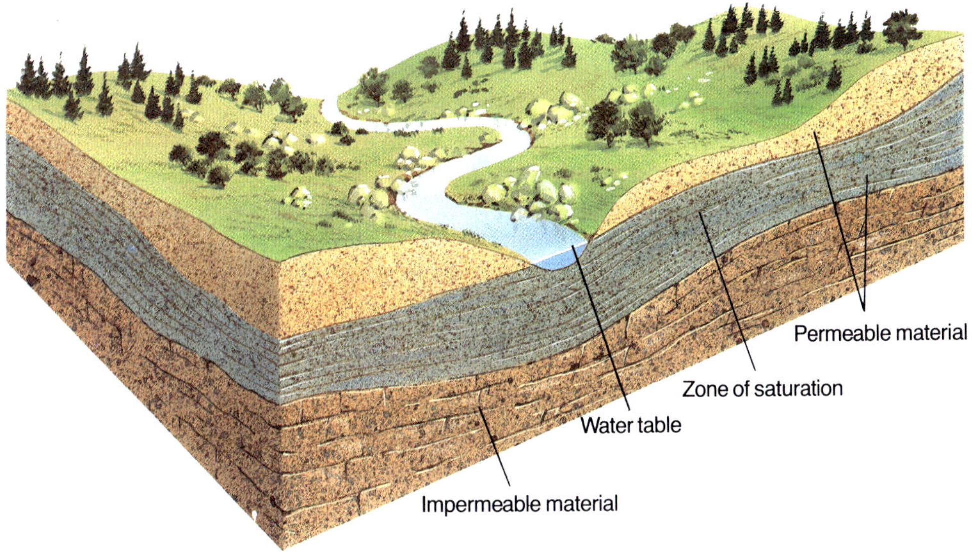

MAKING CONNECTIONS

Math

Tell students that in an experiment, they find that a beaker filled to the 100 mL mark with gravel (Total Volume) can hold 31 mL of water (Volume of pore spaces, VPS). Have them calculate the percentage of pore space (porosity) using the following formula.

$$\frac{\text{VPS}}{\text{Total Volume}} \times 100 = \text{\% Porosity}$$

$$= 31\%$$

Concept Development

Discussion In the past, wells had to be dug. As technology improved, wells could be drilled to deeper levels. Ask students to discuss why wells now need to be drilled to depths of thousands of feet. L2

Research Have students look up artesian wells and how they work. Some students might like to describe the wells. Others might want to make a model of how an artesian well works. L3

Flex Your Brain Use the Flex Your Brain activity to have students explore AQUIFERS.

Teacher F.Y.I.

Only about three fifths of 1 percent of the world's water is underground. Yet this is Earth's most important resource for drinking water.

PROGRAM RESOURCES

Other Resources

Patrick, Ruth, et al. *Groundwater Contamination in the United States.* Philadelphia, PA: University of Pennsylvania Press, 1987.

Ground Water, software, IBM.

Water Below, film, USGS.

SKILLBUILDER

The added amount of water being drawn from the wells causes the water table to drop. Nature's remedy would be enough rain to replenish the water table. L1

3 Assess

Check for Understanding

To help students answer the Apply question, lead them to see that groundwater, aquifers, and the water table are interdependent. Ask them how an aquifer is dependent on groundwater. Then ask how the water table is dependent on the aquifer.

Reteach

Use a sponge to help students understand the porous nature of an aquifer. Point out the holes, or pores, in the sponge that contain water. Explain that the fibers of the sponge are not so much absorbing as trapping water. LEP L1

Extension

Have students who have mastered this section do research on how groundwater in limestone can create caves. L3

4 Close

Remind students that water picks up minerals and other materials as it travels through layers of permeable soil. Have students describe the water from a well that has been drilled through layers of iron-laden soil and limestone. L1

FIGURE 15-12. Springs may flow wherever the water table is exposed at Earth's surface.

many wells are drilled in an area. In this instance, more water is taken out of the ground than can be replaced by rain. Unlike wells, most streams and rivers do not run dry in dry weather. One reason streams and rivers usually have water is that the water table meets the surface at those places. Another reason is that streams and rivers are usually lower in elevation than the surrounding land.

In some places, the water table meets Earth's surface. Groundwater simply flows out of the rock or soil at these places. Springs can be found on hillsides or any other place where the water table is exposed at the surface. As you might expect, springs can often be used as a source of water.

You have taken a long journey through the hydrologic cycle. As part of that cycle, rainwater can evaporate, run off, or seep into the ground to become groundwater. It can collect in aquifers and perhaps be pumped back up to the surface, where it once again moves through the cycle.

SKILLBUILDER

RECOGNIZING CAUSE AND EFFECT

Suppose you live in a town in which the population stays the same for many years. Then a number of new houses are built, and the population grows. The people in the town notice that the wells show signs of drying up. What could be the cause? What would be nature's remedy? If you need help, refer to the **Skill Handbook** on page 653.

Check Your Understanding

1. How does rainwater enter the groundwater system?
2. How can rocks be porous and permeable?
3. How can a well go dry? How can the well be made useful again?
4. **APPLY:** Explain how groundwater, aquifers, and the water table are related.

Answers to Check Your Understanding

1. Rainwater soaks through permeable soil into the groundwater system.
2. Some rocks have pores through which water can travel.
3. A well can go dry when the water table drops too far. More rainwater is required to make the well useful again. Also, the well could be drilled deeper.
4. Groundwater supplies the water to fill aquifers. The upper boundary of the aquifer is the water table.

EXPANDING YOUR VIEW

CONTENTS

A CLOSER LOOK

HOT SPRINGS AND GEYSERS

In some locations beneath Earth's surface, underground water comes in contact with hot rock. When that happens, the water heats up. If the water then makes its way to the surface, a hot spring is formed. Usually, hot springs bubble gently and are only a few degrees warmer than the surrounding air.

In some cases, however, the underground water heats up so that it bursts violently through Earth's surface. These hot springs are called geysers.

Geysers exist in locations where there are vast underground passageways for the water to travel through. Usually, all of these connecting tunnels, as shown in the illustration, lead to a single opening on the surface.

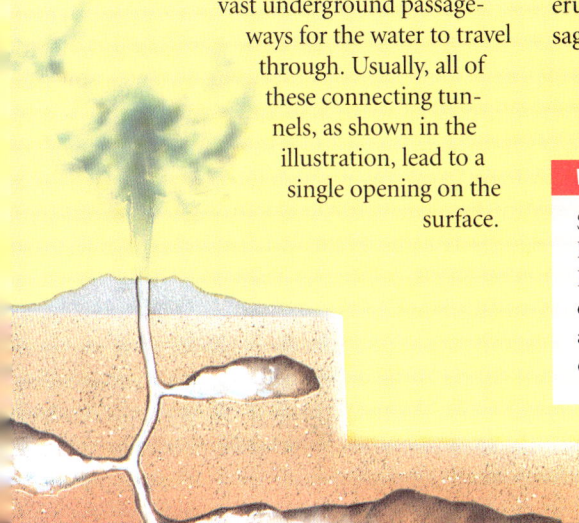

The groundwater, from its contact with hot, underground rock, is heated to very high temperatures, causing it to expand to fill these tunnels. This expanding water forces some of the water on top out of the ground, taking the pressure off the remaining water. The remaining water boils quickly, with much of it turning to steam. The steam shoots out of the opening like steam out of a teakettle, forcing the remaining water out with it. Once the geyser erupts, groundwater begins to refill the passageways, and the process begins again.

WHAT DO YOU THINK?

Some geysers follow a regular schedule. Old Faithful Geyser in Yellowstone National Park, for instance, erupts an average of once every 65 minutes. The geyser has not missed a single eruption for over 80 years. Can you explain why this happens?

EXPANDING YOUR VIEW

Using Expanding Your View Assign one or more of these excursions to expand your students' understanding of moving water and how it applies to other sciences and other subjects. You may assign these as individual or small group activities.

A CLOSER LOOK

Purpose A Closer Look extends Section 15-3 by showing what can happen to groundwater that becomes heated, forming geysers.

Content Background The thermal energy that heats underground water comes from pockets of magma close to Earth's surface. Yellowstone National Park has several types of features resulting from heated groundwater. Steam and other gases forced up through cracks in the rocks are called fumaroles. Sometimes the emerging stream brings acids with it to form a mud pot. The acids dissolve rock around the fissure and make a pool of bubbling mud. A hot spring's groundwater has unrestricted flow to the surface. A geyser forms when water is heated in a complex maze of underground passageways. When pressure in the passageways is reduced because the water has expanded and flowed out of the opening, the water boils rapidly and much of it turns to steam. Water and steam are forced upwards in a sudden surge.

Answers to WHAT DO YOU THINK?

The supply of water and heat to this geyser system has been consistent for over 80 years. After the geyser erupts, it takes 65 minutes for new water to seep back into the system, become heated, and erupt again.

Going Further Students can work in small groups to further research hot springs. Health spas all over the world have grown up around hot spring areas. Have students act as though they are trying to attract tourists to such a hot spring. Have students write a brochure explaining why people should visit a hot springs resort. COOP LEARN

Have students find pictures of geysers and hot springs in magazines and books. Ask what they notice about the colors and formations in the area. What is responsible? Also ask if they think that life exists in these hotwater systems. *Algae, bacteria, and even some insects live in many hot springs. The life in hot springs and the minerals that surface through the action of the water cause bright colors and rock formations.* Students can write to:

Yellowstone Library and Museum Association
Yellowstone Park, WY 82910

EXPANDING YOUR VIEW

CHEMISTRY CONNECTION

Purpose The Chemistry Connection reinforces Section 15-3 by describing how groundwater interacts with rock beneath Earth's surface.

Content Background Another common feature associated with cave formation is a sinkhole. Like caves, sinkholes are created by the action of carbonic acid on limestone. Sinkholes are depressions in the ground visible at the surface that are caused when groundwater dissolves limestone beneath the depression, causing the ground to collapse. Some large sinkholes are caused by the collapse of cave ceilings. These large holes can collect runoff water and become lakes. Sinkholes are common in areas where there are large limestone deposits. In Europe, sinkholes are called karsts. This term is also used in the United States to describe topography containing caves and sinkholes. Sinkholes are common in Florida, Kentucky, Tennessee, Virginia, and Indiana. Highway 26 in northeastern Indiana is sometimes impassable because of sinkholes. Farmers in the area are concerned about where they build because the underground limestone can collapse without warning.

Teaching Strategy Ask if any students have been in a cave. Have students discuss how they felt when they were underground or how they imagine they would feel.

Answers to WHAT DO YOU THINK?

1. The drip from a stalactite leaves more deposit at the top than at the bottom.
2. The colors are caused by deposits of various minerals in the water.

Chemistry Connection

CAVES, SINKHOLES, AND STALACTITES

You have learned some of the ways in which water has the power to shape Earth. But not all of the features caused by the action of water can be explained by the force of its motions.

You may recall from studying about solutions that water is the most effective solvent known. This property of water can create an amazing change on portions of Earth. It can bring about a chemical reaction that results in the formation of limestone caves.

A limestone cave or cavern is a type of cave known as a solution cave. It forms when underground water slowly dissolves the rock.

This process begins when rainwater falls to the ground. Carbon dioxide, which is a gas, is absorbed from the surrounding air into a solution with the water. This type of solution—a gas into a liquid—is also found in soft drinks.

When carbon dioxide mixes with water, it forms a chemical compound called carbonic acid. This acid is very weak, but it can dissolve certain types of rock, notably limestone.

Some areas of Earth have huge deposits of limestone underground. The main ingredient in limestone is calcite, a mineral form of calcium carbonate, a material found in the shells of many sea creatures. Many regions that have large deposits of limestone were once under the sea, where these shells accumulated and eventually turned into stone.

Carbonic acid reacts with calcium carbonate. When rainwater soaks into the soil, it sometimes flows into cracks within the limestone. The carbonic acid slowly dissolves the surrounding rock, creating underground holes. After many years, these holes grow so large that people can actually walk around inside them. Sometimes the ground above caves in, creating a sinkhole.

Have you ever visited one of these caverns? If so, you have probably seen rock formations hanging from the ceiling that look almost like giant icicles. These rock formations are called stalactites. Stalagmites are rock formations that rise from the floor.

A single stalactite may take thousands of years to form. When underground water dissolves limestone, it absorbs calcite. The stalactite begins as a single drop of water clinging to the roof of the cave. As the drop of water evaporates, it loses some carbon dioxide. When that happens, calcite is deposited on the end of the stalactite. The stalactite grows as other drops of water cling to the outside of the stalactite.

Every so often, a drop of water will fall on the ground, depositing some calcite on the cave floor. After many years, the calcite will form a stalagmite, which looks like an upside-down stalactite.

WHAT DO YOU THINK?

Stalactites look like giant icicles. Why? Stalactites and stalagmites may show shades of different colors. Can you think why?

Going Further Students can work in small groups to discuss why people are so fascinated by caves. Have students who have been in a cave make a list of what they saw. Have other students make a list of what they would expect to see in a cave. Then have students compare and contrast both lists to what they see on Earth's surface. COOP LEARN

The power of water is quite impressive. Ask students how large they think underground caves get. Most students will probably guess room- or house-size. Then tell students that Mammoth Cave in Kentucky has over 200 miles of passageways. The deepest cave known is Pierre St.-Martin Cavern in France. Its lowest passageway is 4,364 ft deep. In Spain, Carlista Cavern has one chamber whose floor covers 20 acres and whose ceiling is 400 feet high.

SCIENCE AND SOCIETY

WATER WARS

Water is an essential part of our everyday lives. In a single day, the average person in the United States uses 227 liters of water—that's enough liquid to fill up 678 soft drink cans. We use water every time we take a shower, brush our teeth, or wash our clothes. We also use a lot of water indirectly. Many industries rely upon water to manufacture products such as paper and plastic. Farmers need water to irrigate the crops that produce the fruit and vegetables that we eat.

Where does all of this water come from? Some towns and cities get their water from nearby rivers, lakes, or underground wells. However, not everyone lives next to a source of fresh water, especially in the desert regions of our country. In many parts of the United States, communities are forced to get their water from other locations. Dams and pipelines are constructed to carry water from rivers that might be hundreds of kilometers away. Changing the natural flow of water in such a way is called water diversion.

There is, however, a problem with water diversion. When you take water away from a distant river, you leave less water for people who are living near the river. In some parts of the country, individuals, towns, and even states have gone to court to fight over water rights.

For many years, California has been involved in a water dispute. More than two-thirds of California's fresh water is supplied by the Sacramento River in the northern part of the state. Southern California, on the other hand, provides less than 20 percent of the state's fresh water.

Despite the fact that Southern California produces only a small amount of water, it consumes 85 percent of the water available in the entire state. Most of this water is used by farmers to irrigate their crops. Meanwhile, city dwellers in Northern California are facing severe water shortages. They want the government to pass laws that will restrict the amount of water used by the farmers.

In some parts of the world, water wars are on the verge of becoming full-scale wars. In the late 1980s, Turkey built a massive dam across the Euphrates River. The water in the dam's reservoir is used to irrigate crops and to generate electricity for almost half of the country. But Syria —Turkey's neighbor to the south — also depends upon water from the Euphrates. Syria has argued that the dam is stealing water away from its farmers. The dam has created tremendous tension between the two countries.

WHAT DO YOU THINK?

Some people say that if cities made a concerted effort not to waste so much water, there would be plenty of water available for everyone. Do you agree? Can you think of a few simple things that you can do around your own home that will help conserve our supply of water?

EXPANDING YOUR VIEW

SCIENCE AND SOCIETY

Purpose Science and Society develops Sections 15-2 and 15-3 by examining how water sources are an integral part of human life.

Content Background Water disputes are not new. Many of the range wars between the sheep herders and cattle ranchers in the old West were over water rights as well as grazing rights. The problem is not so much the amount of water available as the location. In fact, experts estimate that the average runoff of annual rainfall in the United States is about 8.7 inches. The average annual amount needed to supply all residential, agricultural, and industrial needs is about 1.5 inches. To solve the current problem, two approaches will have to be considered. One will be a political evaluation of fair distribution. But that is less important in the long run than conservation. Several ideas being considered are reducing the amount of evaporation and flooding in existing reservoirs, setting up a universal metering system, and devising more efficient systems of crop irrigation.

Teaching Strategies Divide students into four groups. Assign two groups to study urban water needs and two to study agricultural needs. Set up debate teams based on their research.

Discussion Tell students that their average water usage has been reduced by ten gallons a day. In what ways will they arrange their water consumption? Remind students that all basic needs must be taken care of.

Going Further Students can work in pairs to explore the question of water rights. Have students decide if water can really be owned. Students should consider whether one group of people has more right to a water source than another group. They should keep in mind that water is a basic need of all life on Earth. COOP LEARN

Have students write individual letters to either local or state governments explaining the importance of cooperation in water distribution. For example, the state department of agriculture would be a good place to start. Have students suggest ways to settle arguments about which areas or groups should have special water rights. Students could also write letters of inquiry about local or state policy on water distribution.

Answers to WHAT DO YOU THINK?

Answers will vary. Some students will want to avoid taking baths. More practical suggestions may be to avoid letting water run while washing dishes or brushing their teeth.

EXPANDING YOUR VIEW

HOW IT WORKS

Purpose How It Works explains how people have used the flow of rivers and streams, the subject of Section 15-2, as a source of power.

Content Background Waterwheels are still in use in the United States to power some small gristmills and sawmills. In gristmills the waterwheels turn big stone wheels used to grind grain. Overshot water wheels have an efficiency rating of 85 percent. Breast wheels are about 75 percent efficient. Undershot wheels are only about 35 percent efficient.

Teaching Strategies Have small groups of students design each of the three types of waterwheel. Their results can take the form of drawings, diagrams, or models. COOP LEARN

Activity Have pairs of students write a short essay explaining the historical value of preserving some existing waterwheels.

Answers to

WHAT DO YOU THINK?

The power supplied by waterwheels made production of many materials such as ground corn and iron quicker and easier. Without this power, many industries, such as the iron and paper industries, could not have developed.

EXPANDING YOUR VIEW

HOW IT WORKS

WATERWHEELS

Waterwheels are devices that can convert flowing water into mechanical energy. The earliest mention of waterwheels dates back to the first century B.C.E., when the Greeks constructed simple mills to grind corn into flour. Medieval Europeans improved on the design of the waterwheel and used it for a variety of industrial purposes, including sawing wood, polishing metals, pumping water, and preparing cloth.

WHAT DO YOU THINK?

The waterwheel was one of the world's first labor saving devices. In ancient times, grinding grain into flour by hand was much harder, slower work. A single waterwheel could do the job all by itself. How do you think the invention of the waterwheel changed society?

There are three basic waterwheel designs: the undershot, the overshot, and the breast. The undershot wheel is fitted with paddles. Water flows beneath the undershot, pushing against the paddles and turning the wheel.

The overshot wheel does not have paddles but a series of containers, commonly referred to as buckets. Water passes above the overshot and flows down into the buckets, where the weight of the water turns the wheel.

The breast waterwheel combines the undershot and the overshot designs. A stream of water hits the breast wheel at mid-level,

and then flows down beneath the wheel.

When a waterwheel turns, it spins an axle. The axle is connected to a series of gears, which operate machinery. Waterwheels were used throughout America and Europe until the middle of the nineteenth century, when they were replaced with steam engines.

Going Further Students can work in small groups to expand the idea of using natural forces to make life easier. Have students make a list of all the natural forces they can think of. Then have them write down how they make life easier. Write a class list on the board. Then ask students what new uses these natural forces might have in the future. COOP LEARN

Ask students to imagine that they are the inventors of the waterwheel. Ask them what gave them the idea. Have students describe why their invention works.

TECHNOLOGY CONNECTION

FLOOD CONTROL

Many cities are built near rivers, where there is a constant supply of fresh water. But living next to a river also poses a constant threat. In times of heavy rainfall, a river might overflow, covering a city with water. In 1913, for instance, the Miami River flooded, sending a wall of water crashing down into Dayton, Ohio. More than 400 people were killed.

For centuries, people have struggled to find ways to prevent rivers from flooding. One of the oldest methods for controlling an overflowing river is to construct a levee. A levee is simply a wall built alongside a riverbank. The ancient Chinese built levees by piling dirt along the Hwang Ho River. Today, levees are constructed either with earth or with reinforced concrete.

A levee might not always be enough to hold an overflowing river. The dirt walls built by the Chinese did not prevent the Hwang Ho from flooding in 1887 and drowning nearly one million people.

The most effective way to control a flood is to construct a dam. A dam is a barrier built across a river. Large amounts of water gather behind the dam, creating an artificial lake known as a reservoir. Dams usually have huge gates that open and close, making it possible to regulate the level of water in the reservoir. In this way, a dam can control the amount of water that flows into the river. During a period of heavy rainfall, a dam would completely close its gates and hold all of the water in the reservoir to prevent the river from flooding.

The water that is stored in the reservoir can be used to irrigate crops or to provide drinking water for a nearby city. Also, as water is drained from the reservoir, the force of the falling water can turn giant turbines that generate electricity.

YOU TRY IT!

Building dams can have broad effects on the economy of a region. Divide your class into small groups. Have one person represent local farmers. Someone else can represent industry. Have a third person represent the viewpoint of environmentalists. Then debate whether a dam should be constructed across a river in your area. Who do you think will be concerned with power generation? With lands being flooded? Can you think of other economic effects of a dam? As representatives, give reasons for your opinions, for or against.

CAREER CONNECTION

Civil engineers design and build structures such as dams, tunnels, bridges, and water pipelines. They study engineering and geology.

Going Further Have students work in small groups to discuss the importance of flood control. Ask students to make a list of the damages that can be caused by a flood. They may want to read newspaper and magazine reports of major flooding such as the floods in southern Texas of 1992. Then have students use their lists to develop a list of ways that individuals can prepare for floods. COOP LEARN

Dams have to be very strong structures because of the intense pressure and weight of the water behind them. Have students research the feats of engineering that go into building modern dams. Several examples of 20th century dams are:

The Coolidge Dam in Arizona
The Hoover Dam on the Colorado River
The Cabora Bassa Dam in Mozambique
Itaipu Dam on the Parana River between Brazil and Paraguay

TECHNOLOGY CONNECTION

Purpose Technology Connection should help students better understand Section 15-2 by describing what can happen in flood plains. It also explains how a portion of the hydrologic cycle can be partially controlled by levees and dams.

Content Background Flood control is most important in areas where heavy or extended rainfall is an annual occurrence. The amount of normal rainfall before a major storm can increase the possibility of flooding. Soil can absorb only so much water before surface runoff begins. Soil saturation can be caused by one-half inch of rain during a 24-hour period. If a major storm happens within ten days, nearby rivers and streams are likely to flood. Heavy spring rains combined with melting snow also increase the possibility of flooding. In winter and spring, soil tends to frost or freeze. So water from a heavy rain is more likely to run off. Open, bare field soil freezes more easily than wooded areas. So low-lying agricultural areas near rivers also contribute to the extent of floods.

Teaching Strategies After reading the selection, have a class discussion on where flooding occurs in your area, when and why it occurs, and what method is used to control it.

Have students work in groups to create a survey that could be handed out to local residents seeking their opinions on the economic and environmental results of a dam in a particular location.

Answers to YOU TRY IT

1. Industry
2. Farmers and Environmentalists
3. Recreation

TEENS IN SCIENCE

Purpose Teens in Science should help students better understand Sections 15-1 and 15-2 by describing how pollutants poured into just one part of a runoff system can affect rivers and streams.

Content Background Although they certainly add to the problem, water pollution is also caused by more serious things than small amounts of hazardous wastes dumped from individual households. A little over 9 percent of river pollution comes from industrial toxic wastes. Companies that have feeder pipes emptying contaminated waste into waterways can be located and heavily fined. But about 65 percent of water pollution comes from agriculture. The pollutants are more difficult to detect and control. Chemicals, mostly pesticides, are sprayed daily over hundreds of thousands of acres of farmland. Salts, nitrate fertilizers, sediments and other materials wash into the overall runoff system and are absorbed by the soil. Pollutants then filter into the groundwater system and can damage fresh water in aquifers, wells, and lakes. Because groundwater is the source for over fifty percent of the United States' drinking water, water pollution is a major concern.

Teaching Strategies To show how every little bit of pollutants hurts, you will need several household cleaners, motor oil, and garden herbicides and pesticides. Have student volunteers read aloud the ingredients lists on each product. Then put a few drops of each into a glass of water. Ask students if they would want to drink that water. Then have other student volunteers read any directions on the products regarding their disposal. Encourage students to tell their parents how to dispose of hazardous household waste.

TEENS *in* SCIENCE

THE CLEAN STREAM TEAM

How would you describe the city or town where you live? For 14-year-old JoAnna Gott, the answer is simple. "My town is beautiful. And that's the way we want to keep it."

JoAnna lives in Strafford, Missouri. The many nearby lakes, rivers, and streams are a large part of why people love to live in Strafford. So, it was only natural for JoAnna to get involved in a recent Urban Streams Festival held in her town.

"The festival was created to remind people to take care of our water. Right now we're lucky. Our water is clean. And that is a good reason to celebrate."

During the festival, residents of Strafford were encouraged to do more than think about water. They were urged to get involved in protecting this important resource. JoAnna's 4-H club accepted the challenge.

"We went to a park in town and painted a warning on all the storm drains. The storm drains are located along a road that runs through the park. Sometimes people have disposed of hazardous waste by pouring it down the storm drains."

To help people understand the dangers of this type of pollution, JoAnna and her group stenciled this message on each drain: "Dump No Waste. Drains to Stream."

"People need to know what happens if they are careless. A person might think that a little old paint or household cleaner can't make that much difference in a big stream. But if the person actually thought about that poison running into their favorite stream, I don't think they would do it. Maybe this sounds silly, but I wish more people would think about how they would like it if they were a fish or some other animal that lives in the stream. I'd feel bad if someone dumped paint thinner down our chimney at home."

WHAT DO YOU THINK?

JoAnna loves her town. How about you? Make a list of the best and worst things about the city or town you live in.

Using your "best and worst" list as a guide, write a brief description of one thing that you could do to make your city or town a better place to live.

Going Further Have students work in small groups to promote awareness of water pollution. Each group should identify a special problem around the school or community. Then encourage each group to make a poster illustrating the problem. Arrange to have posters put up around the school or in public buildings. **COOP LEARN**

Students might think that throwing out poisonous wastes is better than pouring them down the drain. Ask students how seepage from landfills might cause water contamination. Lead them to discuss the types of trash that could cause water pollution. Some students might want to find out about local landfills. Suggest that they ask about state standards for landfill safety. Have students discover how those standards help to prevent water pollution.

Reviewing Main Ideas

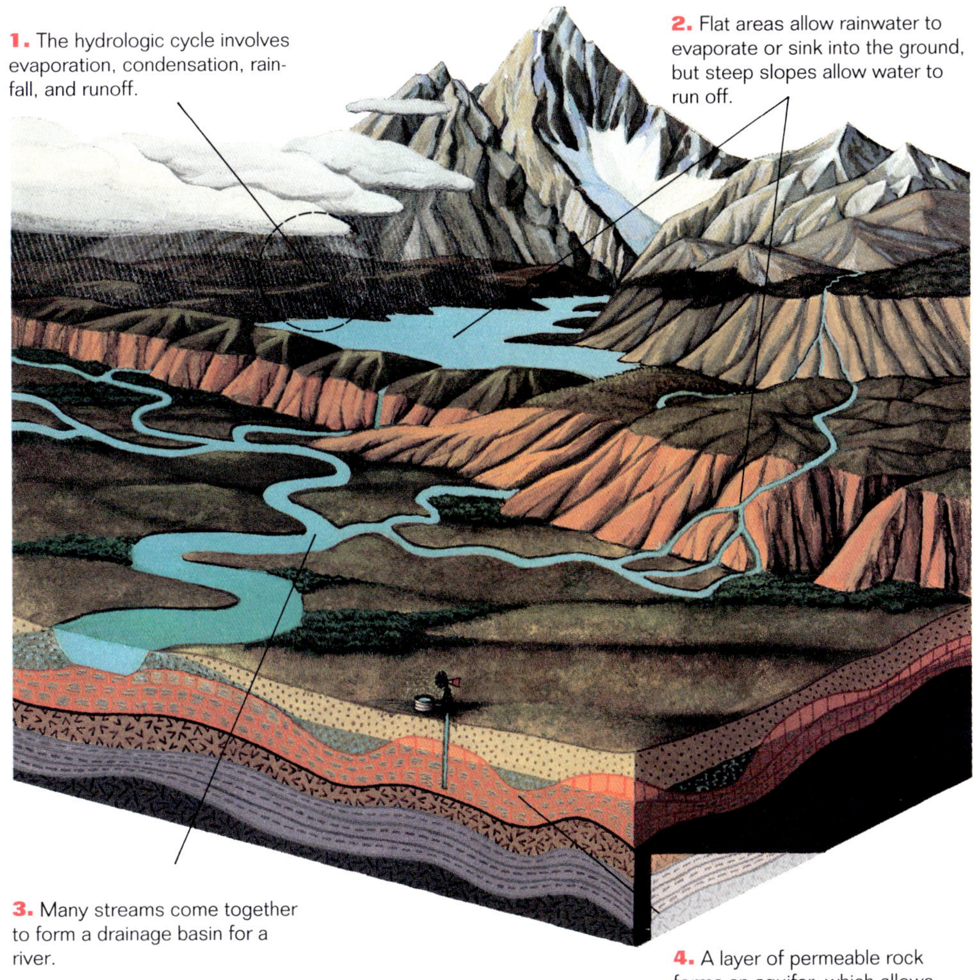

1. The hydrologic cycle involves evaporation, condensation, rainfall, and runoff.
2. Flat areas allow rainwater to evaporate or sink into the ground, but steep slopes allow water to run off.
3. Many streams come together to form a drainage basin for a river.
4. A layer of permeable rock forms an aquifer, which allows water to move freely.

Chapter 15

Reviewing Main Ideas

Have students look at the diagram on this page. Direct them to read the four captions to review the main ideas of this chapter.

Teaching Strategies

Divide the class into four groups. Assign one of the four sections of the diagram to each group. Have the first group make a poster showing each phase of the hydrologic cycle according to caption 1. They should look in old magazines for pictures that could be used on their poster. Encourage students to include their own diagrams and drawings, especially to represent condensation and evaporation. Be sure each major section of the poster is labeled.

Have the next group read caption 2 and make a poster or bulletin board illustrating flat areas that allow rainwater to evaporate and steep slopes that allow runoff. Have the students find pictures in old magazines. The bulletin board should be divided into two sections so the contrast in land areas can be readily seen.

Have the third group look for photographs of streams forming a drainage basin for rivers (caption 3). Encourage the students to find as many different examples of this as possible. Have the group create a poster using the photos they find. Make sure the students label each photo indicating the geographic location of each area.

Have the fourth group do research to find out about the aquifer (caption 4) under the Great Plains region of the United States. During the course of their research, have students find examples in the form of illustrations of how the aquifer benefits the people of this region.

Chapter 15

Chapter Review

USING KEY SCIENCE TERMS

Answers

1. Runoff is a part of the hydrologic cycle.
2. An aquifer is a reservoir of groundwater.
3. The area into which runoff flows is called a drainage basin.
4. The water table is the top of the groundwater level.
5. A river or stream meanders when it reaches the flat area of a drainage basin.

UNDERSTANDING IDEAS

Answers

1. a
2. b
3. d
4. a
5. c
6. c
7. a
8. a
9. c

CRITICAL THINKING

Answers

1. The water table will vary depending on the amount of rainfall in the area.
2. The river will increase in volume and speed and might flood.
3. A groundwater system flows underground and is replenished by absorption of water by the ground. A drainage basin system exists aboveground and is fed by the runoff of streams and rivers.
4. The nonporous surfaces will cause heavy runoff and, perhaps, flooding if structures such as storm drains are absent or inefficient.
5. Both a drilled well and a spring are fed by groundwater. However, a well collects water that must be brought to the surface, while spring water naturally flows out of the ground.

Chapter Review

USING KEY SCIENCE TERMS

aquifer
drainage basin
groundwater
hydrologic cycle
meander
runoff
water table

For each set of terms below, explain the relationship that exists.

1. hydrologic cycle, runoff
2. groundwater, aquifer
3. runoff, drainage basin
4. water table, groundwater
5. meander, drainage basin

UNDERSTANDING IDEAS

Choose the best answer to complete each sentence.

1. Water in lakes is evaporated by ____.
   a. heat from the sun **c.** rainfall
   b. condensation **d.** runoff
2. Slow-moving streams are likely to be found ____.
   a. in the mountains
   b. on flat land
   c. on hills and slopes
   d. near aquifers
3. Rainwater enters the groundwater system by ____.
   a. runoff
   b. evaporation
   c. condensation
   d. soaking into the ground
4. A rock that cannot let water pass through it is ____.
   a. impermeable **c.** permeable
   b. porous **d.** an aquifer
5. The entire length of a stream or river is a part of its ____.
   a. slope **c.** drainage basin
   b. aquifer **d.** runoff
6. A flat surface with plants may prevent ____.
   a. evaporation **c.** runoff
   b. condensation **d.** groundwater
7. Streams on hills or mountains have ____.
   a. a high speed **c.** muddy water
   b. wide, shallow areas **d.** many curves

8. A well must be deep enough to reach ____.
   a. the water table **c.** a spring
   b. runoff **d.** impermeable rock
9. A wide stream is known as a ____.
   a. creek **c.** river
   b. runoff **d.** drainage basin

PROGRAM RESOURCES

Teacher Classroom Resources

Review and Assessment, Chapter Review and Chapter Test, pages 61–64

Computer Test Bank, Chapter Test

OPTIONS

Cooperative Learning

Consider using Cooperative Learning in the Understanding Ideas, Critical Thinking, Problem Solving, and Connecting Ideas sections of the Chapter Review.

COOP LEARN

CRITICAL THINKING

Use your understanding of the concepts developed in the chapter to answer each of the following questions.

1. How can the level of the water table vary even when the groundwater is not disturbed by people?
2. Study the illustration. If a spring thaw suddenly melts a great deal of snow in the region labeled A, what do you think will happen to the river in the region that is labeled B? Explain your answer.
3. Compare a groundwater system with a drainage basin system.

4. How can sidewalks, streets, and highways affect what happens to rainfall?
5. What are the similarities and differences between a drilled well and a spring?

PROBLEM SOLVING

Read the following problem and discuss your answers in a brief paragraph.

One way to test the permeability of different kinds of soil materials is to see how much time it takes water to flow through them. Suppose you had some water, a watch, some funnels lined with filter paper, some beakers, a graduated cylinder, and equal amounts of potting soil, marbles, and clay.

1. How could you set up an experiment to determine which material was the most permeable and which was the least permeable?
2. Predict which material would be the most permeable.
3. Predict which material would be the least permeable.

CONNECTING IDEAS

Discuss each of the following in a brief paragraph.

1. What factors affect whether water will run off, evaporate, or soak into the ground at a certain location?
2. Earth has often been called a water planet. Based on what you've learned in this chapter, would you agree? Explain.
3. What is the relationship between the largest drainage basin in the United States and the kind of landform that is dominant in that region?
4. **A CLOSER LOOK** What role does groundwater play in the formation and eruption of a geyser?
5. **TECHNOLOGY CONNECTION** Would a fast-moving stream or a slow-moving one be more likely to be dammed? Explain your answer.

PROBLEM SOLVING

Answers

1. Arrange each material to the same depth in the funnels. Pour equal amounts of water on each material. Measure the time it takes for water to flow through the filter for each material.
2. The marbles would be the most permeable.
3. The clay would be the least permeable.

CONNECTING IDEAS

Answers

1. temperature, the slope and porosity of the land, the amount of rainfall, vegetation
2. Yes; most of Earth's surface is covered with water.
3. The Mississippi drainage system consists of a large gently sloping valley. This creates a drainage system made up of many slowly flowing and meandering rivers and streams.
4. Geysers are fed by groundwater that is heated underground.
5. A fast-moving stream would be dammed in order to produce energy. A slow-moving stream might be dammed in order to divert water or to form a reservoir. The likelihood of damming either would depend on the needs of the community and the consideration of environmental factors.

CHAPTER ORGANIZER

SECTION	OBJECTIVES	ACTIVITIES/FEATURES
Chapter Opener		**Explore!** What does a close examination of soil reveal? p. 477
16-1 Looking at Soil (4 days)	1. **Compare and contrast** soils from different places. 2. **Describe** a soil profile and the leaching process. 3. **Explain** the relationship between humus and plant life.	**Find Out!** What is a recipe for making soil? p. 478 **Investigate 16-1:** Soil Traits, p. 481 **Skillbuilder:** Observing and Inferring, p. 482
16-2 From Rock to Soil (5 days)	1. **Examine** how physical weathering and chemical weathering break rocks into fragments. 2. **Explain** the factors that affect the rate of weathering. 3. **Describe** soil formation.	**Investigate 16-2:** Breaking Down Rocks, p. 488 **Explore!** Can you find signs of physical weathering? p. 490 **Explore!** How can steel be changed? p. 491 **Skillbuilder:** Recognizing Cause and Effect, p. 492
Expanding Your View		A Closer Look **Frost Action,** p. 495 Life Science Connection **George Washington Carver–Peanut Pioneer,** p. 496 Science and Society **Save Our Soil,** p. 497 Art Connection **She Paints with Dirt,** p. 499 Teens in Science **Growing a Future,** p. 500

ACTIVITY MATERIALS

EXPLORE!	INVESTIGATE!	FIND OUT!
Page 477 handful of fertile soil, magnifying glass **Page 491** steel wool, shallow dish or bowl, water	**Page 481** soil sample, 3 plastic lids from coffee cans, sand, cheesecloth squares, clay, rubber bands, gravel, pencil, magnifier, 3 250-mL beakers, water, thumbtack, graduated cylinder, paper, watch, 3 large paper cups, scissors **Page 488** 100 g limestone or shale chips, pan balance, plastic bottle with cap, water, wire strainer, small piece of sandstone, freezer	**Page 478** 2 pieces of soft rock (such as limestone, sandstone, or shale), peat moss, dried insects, small amount of fertilizer, pinch of dried fish food, bean seeds, water, paper cups, spoons, safety goggles

Soil and Weathering

TEACHER CLASSROOM RESOURCES	OTHER RESOURCES
Study Guide, p. 57 **Flex Your Brain,** p. 8 **Multicultural Activities,** p. 35 **Making Connections: Technology and Society,** p. 35 **Activity Masters, Investigate 16-1,** pp. 65-66 **Critical Thinking/Problem Solving,** p. 24 **Making Connections: Integrating Sciences,** p. 35	**Color Transparency and Master 31,** Soil Profile ***STVS:** *Pollution Record in Lake Sediments,* Ecology (Disc 6, Side 2)
Study Guide, p. 58 **Concept Mapping,** p. 24 **Take Home Activities,** p. 25 **How It Works,** p. 17 **Making Connections: Across the Curriculum,** p. 35 **Activity Masters, Investigate 16-2,** pp. 67-68 **Multicultural Activities,** p. 36 **Review and Assessment,** pp. 65-68	**Color Transparency and Master 32,** Soil Evolution **Laboratory Manual,** pp. 97-98, Chemical Weathering **Laboratory Manual,** pp. 99-100, Carbon Dioxide and Limestone ***STVS:** *Eliminating Potholes,* Physics (Disc 1, Side 1) *Bacterial Waste Treatment,* Plants and Simple Organisms (Disc 4, Side 1) *New Uses for Algae,* Plants and Simple Organisms (Disc 4, Side 1) **Computer Test Bank**
	Spanish Resources **Cooperative Learning Resource Guide** **Lab and Safety Skills**

***Science and Technology Videodisc Series**

KEY TO TEACHING STRATEGIES

Teaching strategies have been coded for varying learning styles and abilities. As you review teaching strategies in the margin, the following designations will help you decide which activities are appropriate for your students.

- **L1** Level 1 activities are basic activities and should be within the ability range of all students.
- **L2** Level 2 activities are average activities and should be within the ability range of the average to above-average student.
- **L3** Level 3 activities are challenging activities designed for the ability range of above-average students.
- **LEP** LEP activities should be within the ability range of Limited English Proficiency students.
- **COOP LEARN** Cooperative Learning activities are designed for small group work.

ADDITIONAL MATERIALS

SOFTWARE	AUDIOVISUAL
Weathering and Erosion, Queue.	*Soils: An Introduction,* film, BFA. *Erosion and Weathering,* film, EBEC. *The Changing Land,* filmstrip, National Geographic.

Chapter 16

Soil and Weathering

THEME DEVELOPMENT

The themes that are supported by this chapter are stability and change and energy. Students will see that soil forms as rocks are changed into small particles. As students learn about weathering, they will see that this process requires energy. The energy of moving water, air, and rock particles contributes to the weathering process.

CHAPTER OVERVIEW

This chapter is concerned with soil and how it is formed. Soil is a mixture that contains rock particles as well as decaying matter from living things. Soil is formed by the weathering of rock matter. Weathering can be caused by chemical action, such as the breaking down of limestone by acids, or by physical action, such as the splitting of rock material by freezing water.

Tying to Previous Knowledge

Demonstration Have students classify physical and chemical changes, which were covered in Chapter 5.

Materials needed are a small piece of sandstone, old towel, a hammer, a small piece of limestone, beaker, and vinegar.

Wrap the sandstone in the towel and hit it with a hammer. Show students the pieces that form. This is a physical change. Then place the piece of limestone in a beaker containing vinegar. Students will see that bubbles form and identify this as a chemical change. Point out that students will see both chemical and physical changes as they learn about the formation of soil.

DID YOU EVER WONDER . . .

Where dirt—or soil—comes from?

How far down is "rock bottom"?

Why sidewalks and roads crack?

You'll find the answers to these questions as you read this chapter.

DID YOU EVER WONDER...

Students will explore these questions as they progress through the chapter. Don't spoil their fun and motivation by sharing these answers too early.

- Soil comes from a combination of decayed organic matter and rock, which is broken down by physical and chemical weathering. (page 487)
- "Rock bottom" refers to the solid rock layer that exists below the three horizons, or layers, of soil. The depth at which this layer is found varies from place to place on Earth. (pages 483–484)
- Sidewalks and roads crack because of physical weathering. The two most common causes are ice wedging and the forces exerted by tree roots. (pages 489–490)

Chapter 16

Soil and Weathering

Have you ever played football or soccer on a wet, rainy day? If so, you know how it feels to have your clothes covered with muddy streaks, your fingernails stained by globs of dirt, and your face and arms splattered with cold, muddy splashes.

When your hand squishes into the ground as you make a play, how does the soil feel between your fingers? What color is it? Do you want to hurry to a sink to wash away the dirt? How does the muddy mess change as it slides off your hands and disappears down the drain?

Being dirty may feel uncomfortable sometimes, but after reading this chapter and learning about where soil comes from, you may think about dirt in a different way. You'll discover that dirt is actually very important. Without it, life on Earth would not be the same. Grass and trees wouldn't grow, flowers wouldn't bloom, and beans wouldn't sprout. And you wouldn't have a place to play football or soccer.

EXPLORE!

What does a close examination of soil reveal?

Obtain a handful of fertile soil and look at it closely. Can you guess what the soil is made of? Rub some between your fingers. Describe how the soil feels and how it smells. Then look at some of the soil under a magnifying glass. What can you observe? Do you see anything that looks like bits of rock or sand? Can you detect the remains of living things?

477

Introducing the Chapter

Have students look at the photograph on page 476 and describe what they see. Ask students if there is a difference between *dirt* and *soil*. *The difference is one of semantics. Generally, soil is part of Earth. Dirt is what we call soil when it gets on our clothing.*

Uncovering Preconceptions

Ask students to define the term *soil*. Accept all reasonable answers at this time, but be alert to common misconceptions. Students often think that soil is simply ground-up rock, with no organic matter in it. Do not address this misconception now, but return to students' initial definitions when you discuss humus, the organic matter in soil.

EXPLORE!

What does a close examination of soil reveal?

Time needed 10 minutes

Materials soil sample, magnifying glass

Thinking Process
Observing

Purpose To investigate the components of a soil sample.

Preparation Obtain soil from a garden, or use commercial potting soil.

Teaching the Activity

Discussion Ask students if they think all soils are the same. Then have them guess where the sample used in this activity came from. L1

Expected Outcome

Students will see that soil contains a mixture of rock particles and materials from living things.

Answer to Question
Students will probably see bits of rock. They may see bits of leaves or other remains of living things.

Project

Have students use nursery or seed catalogs or gardening books from home or the school library to identify a kind of plant they would like to grow. Have students find out about the needs of the plant. What should the soil texture be like? How much organic material is needed? Have students draw a picture of the plant and list its requirements. Arrange these items on a bulletin board.

Science at Home

Have students plant bean seeds in one or more samples of soil taken from local sources. Also have students plant seeds in commercial potting soil. Students should observe the plants for two weeks and compare the growth of the groups of plants. Students should be sure that all plants receive the same amount of water and sunlight. The only difference between groups of plants should be the soil in which they are planted.

Section 16-1

PREPARATION

Concepts Developed

Soil varies from one location to another. There are variations in the type and amount of rock, the type and amount of organic material, soil particle size, and the thickness of the layers, called soil horizons. These variations are due to climate, underlying rock layers, and other local conditions.

Planning the Lesson

In planning your lesson on soil variation refer to the Chapter Organizer on pages 476 A-B for timing suggestions, resources, and additional materials that will help you in your presentation of the lesson concepts.

For adequate development of the concepts presented in this section, we recommend that students do the Investigate activity on page 481.

1 MOTIVATE

Activity Have students work in small groups. Give each group a small sample of soil. The samples should be from at least three different local sources, and each sample should be given to two groups. Have groups take about five minutes to list characteristics that describe the soil in the sample. Have a volunteer from each group read the description of the sample and ask if any other groups recognize it.

COOP LEARN L1

16-1 Looking at Soil

OBJECTIVES

In this section, you will

- compare and contrast soils from different places;
- describe a soil profile and the leaching process;
- explain the relationship between humus and plant life.

KEY SCIENCE TERMS

humus
horizon
soil profile
leaching

SOIL MATERIALS

You know what soil looks and smells like, and you know how it feels. What were some of the things you discovered in the soil that you examined in the Explore activity? You may have seen some evidence of things that were once alive. You may also have seen some living things. But there are rock materials in soil, too. Perhaps you saw some. What is in soil? Make some soil of your own to see.

FIND OUT!

What is a recipe for making soil?

Rub together two pieces of a soft rock, such as limestone, sandstone, or shale, to create some small bits of powdered rock. Add some peat moss, some dried insects, a small amount of fertilizer, and a pinch of dried fish food to the powdered rock. Mix all these ingredients together thoroughly. This completes the soil recipe. To test your soil recipe, plant a bean seed in your soil and add a little water to it. Keep the soil in a warm place and wait approximately one week to see what happens.

Conclude and Apply

1. What once-living things did you put into your soil?
2. What nonliving things went into it?
3. What do you think will happen after a week?

FIND OUT!

What is a recipe for making soil?

Time needed 30 minutes, plus a few minutes one week later

Materials safety goggles, pieces of soft rock (limestone, sandstone, or shale), peat moss, fertilizer, dried insects, dried fish food, paper cups, spoons, bean seeds, water

Thinking Processes
Predicting, Observing and inferring

Purpose To discover that soil is a mixture of many materials.

Preparation Some fish foods contain dry insects. Dry beans (soaked overnight) can be used, but soaked planting beans work better. L1 COOP LEARN

Teaching the Activity

Safety Wear safety goggles while pieces of rock are being rubbed.

Expected Outcomes

The seed should sprout in a week. Students will conclude that a mixture of rock and other particles is a soil recipe.

Conclude and Apply

1. once-living: dried insects, fish food, peat moss, fertilizer
2. non-living: rock particles
3. Most will expect the seed to sprout.

Did you notice the color of the soil you stirred up in your recipe? It probably didn't look much like the soil you picked up outdoors and examined in the Explore activity at the beginning of this chapter. But you could still call the outcome of your recipe soil. And if your bean seed grows, you know without a doubt that you formed soil. Soil is that upper covering of Earth's land surface in which green plants grow.

TYPES OF SOIL

Soils across the country differ greatly from one place to another. If you've done any traveling, you know that the colors of soils you can see in road cuts and farming areas may be quite different from place to place.

For example, one sixth-grade student traveled with his family from Ohio to Florida by car. He was amazed at the red soils he saw in Georgia because back home in Ohio the soil was dark brown. Figure 16-1 shows you the different soils the student saw on his trip. What color is the soil where you live?

Some areas with similar soils stretch for hundreds of square kilometers. Other areas have different types of soil within just a few blocks of each other. The soil you examined under the magnifying glass differs from the soils that students in many other schools in your state will look at. What makes soil different?

a

b

FIGURE 16-1. Many factors such as composition and climate determine how a soil looks. Compare Ohio soil (a) with the red clay dirt of this roadbed in Georgia (b).

2 TEACH

Tying to Previous Knowledge

Students should recall from Chapter 15 that water moves through porous soil and dissolves some of the materials in the soil. Have students think about the soil samples they saw in the Motivate activity. Which of these samples is the most porous? How would this characteristic affect the way water moves through the soil?

Concept Development

Flex Your Brain Use the Flex Your Brain activity to have students explore SOIL AS A MIXTURE.

Using the Photograph Have students look at the soils shown in Figure 16-1. Ask students to identify some differences in the soils. Color is the most obvious difference, but students should also see that the Ohio soil looks loose, and the Georgia soil looks compacted. Ask students to suggest reasons for this difference. They will probably recognize that the Ohio soil is on a farm, and is loosened when it is plowed. Students should recognize that a roadbed is subject to pressures that push the soil particles together.

Content Background

Soils that look red generally contain large amounts of clay particles. These particles are rich in a red-colored compound of iron called hematite. Its name comes from the Greek word meaning blood.

PROGRAM RESOURCES

Teacher Classroom Resources

Study Guide, page 57

Critical Thinking/Problem Solving, page 8, Flex Your Brain

Multicultural Activities, page 35, Drip Irrigation L1

Transparency Masters, page 65, and **Color Transparency,** number 31, Soil Profile L1

Making Connections: Technology and Society, page 35, No-Till Farming L2

Concept Development

Student Text Question How do the particles of loam soil appear to differ from both the sand and the clay? *There are particles of many different things in the loam.*

Discussion Ask students what soil would be like without organic matter. Encourage students to think about color, texture, and other physical characteristics, as well as the ability to support plant life.

Student Text Question Which of the soils in Figure 16-2 has the most humus? *loam*

Demonstration Before class time, obtain a brick, wrap it in paper towels, and hit it with a hammer to break off some pieces. Show the brick and the pieces to the class. Tell them that bricks are made of soil that has been pressed together and baked at a high temperature. Ask students what kind of soil was used to make the brick. *Clay* Ask students to give a reason for their answers. *The brick is made up of fine particles and clay has fine particles.*

For one thing, soils differ in the size of their particles. All soils, just like the soil you made, are composed of small particles of different substances. The particles can range from tiny and smooth to large and coarse. Sand particles, for instance, are larger than clay particles. Look at the three different soil samples pictured in Figure 16-2. How do the particles of loam soil (c) appear to differ from both the clay (a) and the sand (b) particles? Loam soils contain a mixture of sand, silt, and clay.

You already know that the soils of much of Ohio are dark brown, while some soils in Georgia are red. Color certainly makes soils differ. What could be responsible for the varying colors of soils? Remember the dried insects and dried fish food you used in your soil recipe. These were humus ingredients in your soil. **Humus** is the decaying organic material made of the remains of plants and animals. Soils rich in humus are dark brown to black. These are also the most fertile soils, where plants find the most nutrients. You learned in Chapter 9 how plants need nutrients for growth. Which of the soils in Figure 16-2 has the most humus?

Your soil recipe also called for peat moss and some small pieces of rock. One is a soft, spongy ingredient, while the other is hard and compact. Can you imagine what they may have contributed to your mixture? Do the following Investigate to find out.

FIGURE 16-2. Magnified views of a clay soil (a), a sandy soil (b), and a loam soil (c) are pictured.

a

b

c
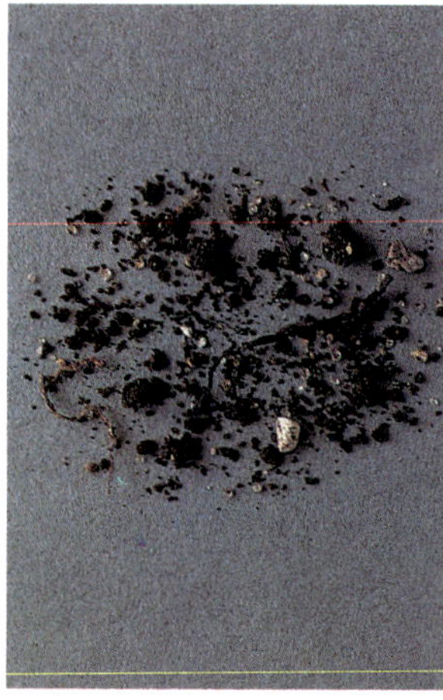

PROGRAM RESOURCES

Teacher Classroom Resources

Critical Thinking/Problem Solving, page 24, Growing Plants without Soil L2

Making Connections: Integrating Sciences, page 35, Lichens L2

Other Resources

Soils: An Introduction, film, BFA.

OPTIONS

Meeting Individual Needs

Visually Impaired During the Investigate activity, have visually impaired students compare the textures of the soil samples. Provide large magnifying glasses so that students can see the particles in the samples. Severely impaired students can estimate the relative amount of water released by the soil by lifting each beaker of water. Be sure that these students are working with three identical beakers.

I N V E S T I G A T E !

16-1 SOIL TRAITS

The particles of humus and rock in soil come in all shapes and sizes and help create other important characteristics. You will discover some of them now.

PROBLEM

What are the characteristics of soil?

MATERIALS 

soil sample
3 plastic lids from coffee cans
sand
cheesecloth squares
clay
rubber bands
gravel
pencil
magnifier
3 250-mL beakers
water
thumbtack
paper
graduated cylinder
watch
3 large paper cups
scissors

PROCEDURE

1. Describe the color of the soil sample.
2. Spread some of the soil on the paper and **observe** it with a magnifier. Name or describe some of the different particles you see.
3. Rub a small amount of the soil between your fingers. Describe the texture.
4. Use a thumbtack to punch the same number of holes in the bottom and around the lower part of each paper cup.
5. Cover the holes in each cup with a cheesecloth square. Secure each cloth with a rubber band.
6. Cut a hole in each plastic lid; fit the cups inside the holes.
7. Place each lid over a beaker.
8. Label the cups A, B, and C.
9. Fill Cup A half full of sand. Fill Cup B half full of clay. Half fill Cup C with an equal mixture of sand, gravel, and clay.
10. Use the graduated cylinder to pour 100 mL of water into each cup. Record the time when the water is first poured into each cup and when the water first drips from each cup.
11. Allow the water to drip for 25 minutes. Then **measure** and record the amount of water in each beaker.

ANALYZE

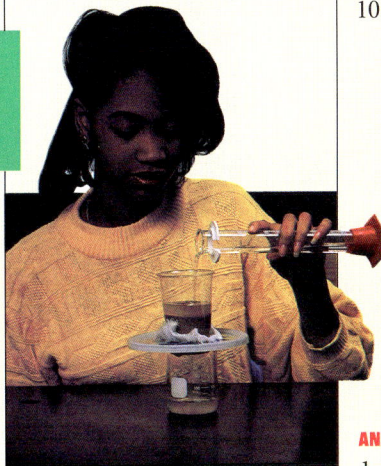

1. Based on your examination of the soil sample in Steps 1–3, describe your soil in as much detail as possible.
2. Recall that permeability refers to the ability of soil to allow water to pass through it. **Compare** the substances that you tested in Steps 9 –11. Which substance is most permeable? Which is least permeable?

CONCLUDE AND APPLY

3. What can you **infer** about how the addition of gravel affects the permeability of clay?
4. What are three characteristics of soil?
5. **Going Further:** Why do you think many plant pots are made of clay?

I N V E S T I G A T E !

16-1 SOIL TRAITS

Time needed two class periods

Materials See student activity.

Thinking Processes
Observing and inferring, Classifying, Interpreting data

Purpose To compare the characteristics of several soil samples.

Preparation Have a bucket of fresh soil for students to use in this activity. The soil should be evenly moist. If binocular microscopes are available, allow students to use these in place of hand lenses.

Teaching the Activity

Discussion All three cups should have the same number and distribution of holes. This is an opportunity to discuss the importance of controlling variables in an experiment.

Troubleshooting Have students check to be sure that the cheesecloth is securely fastened to the bottom of the cups before adding soil.

Student Journal Encourage students to record their observations in their journals. Some students may wish to make a sketch of the particles in each sample. L1

Expected Outcomes

Students should conclude that different soils retain different amounts of water.

Answers to Analyze/Conclude and Apply

1. Answers will vary by soil samples used. Characteristics should include color, types and percentages of particles, organisms, texture, and drainage.
2. The sand was the most permeable material; the clay was the least permeable material.
3. It makes the clay more permeable.
4. color, texture, and permeability.
5. A clay pot will hold much of the water you pour into the soil.

PROGRAM RESOURCES

Teacher Classroom Resources
Activity Masters, pages 65-66, Investigate 16-1

Other Resources
Weathering and Erosion, software, Queue.

SKILLBUILDER

The sand-rich soils have the greater permeability. L1

MAKING CONNECTIONS

Daily Life

Students may have seen bags of topsoil for sale at a garden center, or they may have seen "Topsoil Wanted" signs at a construction site. Topsoil is soil from horizon A. This layer of soil is often lost because of erosion during construction, and so it must be replaced if gardens or a lawn are part of the construction plan.

Concept Development

Using the Photo Have students study Figure 16-3. Ask them to list differences between horizon A and the lower horizons. Students should notice that horizon A has darker soil and that rock layers are clearly visible in lower horizons.

Uncovering Preconceptions

Many students may assume that soil characteristics in any location are the same at all depths until you dig down to rock layers below the soil. Experiences working in gardens may foster this. Well-worked garden soil is a homogeneous mixture. Students would have no reason to doubt that soil near the surface is the same as soil near underlying rock.

SKILLBUILDER

OBSERVING AND INFERRING

After a heavy rainfall, you observe that large puddles have formed in some areas but not in others. You investigate and find that the areas with clay-rich soils have large puddles and the areas with sand-rich soils have no puddles. Which soils have a greater permeability, clay-rich soils or sand-rich soils? If you need help, refer to the ***Skill Handbook*** on page 652.

If you make a mental list of soil characteristics now, you'll use such words as color, texture, earthy odor, and permeability. Which ingredients in your soil recipe do you think helped most to give your soil its permeability? If you feel that powdered rock is the answer, you are correct. Soil must have some degree of permeability if water is to reach the roots of plants growing in it. As you know from Chapter 15, however, the movement of water in soil goes deeper than the roots of most plants.

DOWN TO NEW SOIL HORIZONS

Dandelion roots can be quite long. Suppose you were an ant crawling into the hole left by the root of a dandelion. As you travel down to the point where the root had ended, the soil you see would probably all look the same. But suppose you could keep on going, deeper and deeper into the soil. You would soon reach a point where you notice a change. You would have arrived at a new horizon in the soil profile.

Figure 16-3 shows soil layers called **horizons.** Stacked together, the layers make up the **soil profile.** Most profiles

FIGURE 16-3. A soil profile is made of layers called horizons. Horizons A, B, and C are identified below.

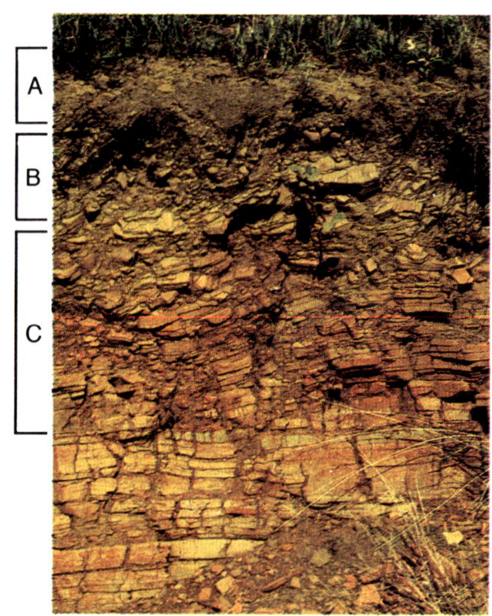

OPTIONS

Multicultural Perspective

The traditional dwellings of the Hopi, Native Americans of the Southwest, are made of adobe. Adobe are bricks made from clay, which are sundried, not fired in a kiln. Show students pictures of a pueblo, a village of such buildings.

Students may be surprised that clay can be hardened into bricks without the use of a kiln. Look around the school grounds for a place where people have walked across a grassy area and worn a hard path in it. The constant compacting of the soil can produce a brick-like hardness. If your soil contains large amounts of clay, have students experiment with making clay bricks and drying them in the sun.

have three horizons known as A, B, and C. Find the top and bottom horizons in the figure and identify their labels.

Horizon A is the layer where most of the humus and plant life exist. It is also home to ants and worms, which create tiny tunnels that allow air to mix with the soil. And when it rains, horizon A is the first layer that the water runs through. Some of this water becomes the groundwater that you read about in Chapter 15.

Have you ever watched a coffeemaker like the one in Figure 16-4? As water moves through the coffee grounds, it picks up substances that give it the flavor, aroma, and color of coffee. Water running through soil's horizon A involves a similar process, called leaching. **Leaching** occurs when seeping groundwater picks up some of the soil materials and carries them to lower horizons.

Look for a moment at those lower horizons in Figure 16-3. How do you know that there is less humus in horizon B than in horizon A? Horizon C, the lowest layer, contains fragments of broken rock. Below this layer, solid rock begins. What do you think happens to soil's permeability in horizon C?

FIGURE 16-4. A coffeemaker makes coffee the same way that rainwater leaches materials from horizon A.

DIFFERENT PLACES: DIFFERENT SOIL CONTENTS AND PROFILES

You're still an ant. How far down the hole would you have to travel before reaching the soil's horizon B? The depth would depend on the geographic area. If you were in a prairie farming region of the United States, as shown in Figure 16-1, chances are you would have to travel about 30 centimeters. You might have to go another 60 or 70 centimeters to get to horizon C. You could possibly go just as far before you reached rock bottom—the layer where solid rock begins. The same trip could be longer or shorter in other regions. In other words, soil profiles can differ from place to place as much as the soil content differs. Behind all these differences are at least five natural factors: the number of plants and animals in the area; the climate; the type of rock in the soil; the time it took the soil to form; and the slope of the land.

Concept Development

Student Text Questions How do you know that there is less humus in horizon B than in horizon A? *It is lighter in color.* What do you think happens to the soil's permeability in horizon C? *The soil becomes less permeable.*

Inquiry Question Why is the soil in horizon A fertile? *It contains humus, which is full of nutrients.* How can chemicals, such as fertilizers, dumped onto the soil pollute groundwater? *The chemicals are leached by water that moves through the soil and enters the groundwater supply.*

Demonstration To demonstrate leaching, show how a colored substance moves through the particles in soil.

Materials needed for this demonstration are sand, fine-mesh strainer, large beaker, powdered dye (must dissolve in cold water).

Place a layer of sand in the strainer and place the strainer in the beaker. Sprinkle the dye on the sand. Pour a small amount of water on the sand and let it trickle through. Continue adding small amounts of water until the color is seen in the water that leaves the strainer. Have students compare this to periods of rain on soil that has been contaminated by chemical spills or other pollutants. Have students think back to the Investigate activity. Through which of their soil samples would contaminants move most quickly?

Enrichment

Research Have students prepare an oral presentation about different kinds of soils in your area or in your state. Students might contact a local university geology department or the state's Department of Agriculture. Many states have extension services that will test soil samples for pH (acidity) as well as some nutrients. Have interested students contact an extension service and make arrangements to have a soil sample tested.

The Plant-and-Animal Factor

The number and kind of plants and animals living in a particular soil area determine the amount of humus the soil has. When these organisms die, their remains decay and become part of the soil. Living plants also drop leaves, broken stems, and other debris to the ground. These too break down and become part of the soil, releasing nutrients into it. Even small amounts of organic material increase the soil's ability to support life. The more organic material that enters the soil, the more humus it has. The dark, thick loam soil in Figure 16-2(c) has a great deal of humus. A desert soil has little humus because few plants grow there.

The Climate Factor

Remember the rock rubbings you made as part of your soil recipe? All soils have particles of rock in them. But soil in an area where there is little rainfall is very different from soil in an area where there is a lot of rainfall. In a climate where little moisture falls, the natural processes that grind down rocks take place slowly. As a result, soil profiles are thin, like that of the tundra in Figure 16-5(a). Deserts also have thin soil profiles. But notice the thicker

FIGURE 16-5. Soils in cold, dry climates have thin horizons (a). Soils in warm, humid climates have well-developed horizons (b).

a

b

Concept Development

Theme Connection Scale and structure is a major theme in science. As students compare the two soil profiles shown in Figure 16-5, the difference in thickness of the layers will be obvious. Have students look for similarities in the structure of the layers. Students should see that the layers differ in scale, but are similar in structure.

Demonstration Find the mass of a sample of peat moss. Place the peat moss in a bowl and add water. After 30 minutes, drain the peat moss and find the mass again. Discuss with students the gain in mass. Peat moss is very absorbent and is added to porous soils to improve water retention.

Teacher F.Y.I.

In one kilogram of soil, there are more than one hundred billion living things. Billions of them are bacteria.

Content Background

Earthworms are very important as aerators of the soil. As earthworms burrow, they produce tunnels through which oxygen enters the soil. Much of this oxygen is used by many of the bacteria that serve as decomposers in the soil. Decomposers break down matter from living things and add nutrients to the soil.

Content Background

The tundra is a cold, dry region in the far northern areas of North America, Europe, and Asia. The soil layer is thin and is frozen for much of the year. During the short summer season, only the upper part of the soil defrosts. The lower layer of soil remains frozen, and is called permafrost.

OPTIONS

Enrichment

Activity Have students plant bean seeds in samples of soil taken from local sources. Students should spend two weeks observing and comparing the growth of the plants in local soil and the growth of the plants in the soil mixed in the Find Out activity. Students should plan their procedures so that variables such as light and water are controlled. The only difference between groups of plants is the soil in which they are planted. L2

FIGURE 16-6. The white cliffs of Dover, on England's southeastern coast, are composed of chalk.

horizons for the forest area in Figure 16-5(b). The climate there brings frequent rains, so, rocks break down into soil particles more readily. Higher temperatures and humidity also speed up the decay of organic materials in the soil. Now compare the forest and tundra soils for the amount of humus in their A horizons.

DID YOU KNOW?

Depending on the location, the rate of new soil formation varies from several meters per century to less than two centimeters in 10,000 years.

The Rock Factor

The kind of rock particle in any kind of soil is usually the same as the kind of rock that lies beneath it. Shale rock, for instance, breaks down into clay particles, so the soil above it will be clay. What kind of soil would you expect to find above a layer of solid sandstone? What color and texture of soil would you find above rocks like those shown in Figure 16-6?

The Time Factor

When you made your soil, it took you only a few minutes. Soil formation in nature moves much more slowly. The actual rate depends on several other factors, especially

Concept Development

Student Text Questions What kind of soil would you expect to find above a layer of solid sandstone? *sandy soil* What color and texture soil would you find above rocks like those shown in Figure 16-6? *white, chalky soil*

Discussion Ask students to distinguish between the rock component of soil and the humus component. Then ask which soil characteristic does the rock component determine, how porous the soil is, or how fertile it is. Have students give a reason for their answers. *The porosity of soil depends on the spaces between the rock particles, which depends mostly on the size of the rock particles in the soil.*

Content Background

The white cliffs shown in Figure 16-6 are made of chalk, which is a fine-grained form of limestone. Limestone is made of calcite, also called calcium carbonate. The fine texture of chalk is due to the tiny size of its particles, which are actually the remains of microscopic marine organisms.

Enrichment

Activity Have groups of students investigate the movement of water through soil by capillary action. Capillary action is the movement of water into small spaces, such as the spaces between soil particles. It is the cause of lateral movement of water through soil.

Materials needed for this activity are thumbtack, plastic cups (transparent or translucent), soil samples, tray or shallow pan, water.

Students should use a thumbtack to make holes in the bottom of plastic cups, then place different soil samples into the cups. Place the cups into a shallow tray of water. Look through the sides of the cups to see how high the water rises in each sample. Generally, the smaller the spaces between particles, the higher the water will rise, or the farther the water will move laterally. **LEP**

Concept Development

Student Text Questions Which soil in Figure 16-5 would have formed more quickly? *the soil from the warm, humid climate* Which kind of slope would be more likely to have a fully developed soil—a steep hill or a gently sloping hill? *the gently sloping hill*

3 Assess

Check for Understanding

Ask questions 1–3 and the Apply Question in Check Your Understanding. Have students discuss their answers to the Apply Question. Ask students to compare this effect with the effect of a moderate amount of irrigation, in which leaching would carry fertilizers applied to the surface just far enough to reach the roots.

Reteach

Ask students to describe what is in their favorite sandwich. Then have students make a sketch of the sandwich, as seen from the side. Have students compare their sketches. Students should see that the general components of most sandwiches (bread, filling) are similar, just as the general components of soil profiles (three horizons) are similar. For example, horizon A always contains humus, although the thickness of the layer may vary.

Extension

Research Have students interview a landscape gardener to find out what kind of soil is best for growing shrubs or flowers. Or have students look up this information in garden books in the local library.

4 Close

Ask students to explain the following statement: Soil is made of materials that come from above and below the soil layer.

FIGURE 16-7. Steep slopes have few plants growing on them. Gentle slopes have many plants growing on them.

climate. A soil will form extremely slowly in a cold climate; it can form more quickly in a mild, rainy climate. Which soil in Figure 16-5 would have formed more quickly?

The Slope Factor

The slope of the land has a great deal to do with soil formation, too. Look at the photographs in Figure 16-7. Rainwater would tend to wash the soil off a steep hill if the soil was not held in place by plants. Which kind of slope would be more likely to have fully-developed soil—a steep hill or a gently sloping hill?

Now that you know the factors involved in forming a soil type, how does rock first get broken up to begin to form soil? If you could look at the same rock over a long period of time, you would see that the solid rock would be worn down and changed. But what causes this change to take place? That is the topic of the next section.

Check Your Understanding

1. What part does leaching play in forming a soil profile?
2. Why might soils from two different places differ?
3. If a soil is very dark, what would you expect its humus content to be—low or high? Why?
4. **APPLY:** What problem might farmers have with soil if they irrigate their crops too often?

Answers to Check Your Understanding

1. A soil profile is the layers of soil in the ground. Leaching causes material in horizon A to be carried down to B.
2. Soils from two different places might differ in the amount of humus, the climate under which the soil was formed, the type of rock below the soil, the time it took to form the soil, and the slope of the land under which the soil was formed.
3. It would be high because a great deal of organic material has decayed and become a part of the soil, making it dark in color.
4. Leaching would occur each time irrigation took place. In time, too much of the valuable materials in horizon A would be leached down into horizon B. As a result, the annual yield from the farmer's crops would decrease.

16-2 From Rock to Soil

PHYSICAL WEATHERING

You've probably heard people say that something of value and lasting quality is solid as a rock. Rocks are indeed quite solid, as the climber in Figure 16-8 is discovering. But they don't really last forever. Just think of the mud on the soccer field in the opening picture of this chapter. It was actually part of rock at one time.

Over time, rocks become part of the soil. Before this can happen, however, the solid rock must crack into chunks and then break into smaller, and smaller, and smaller fragments.

When you followed the Find Out recipe in the last section to create soil, you scraped and rubbed two small rocks together to produce the powdery bits you needed. No one has ever heard any scraping or hammering going on in nature as rocks break apart. Yet even rocks as big as the one the climber is scaling and the solid rock layer lying somewhere beneath your feet can crack and crumble over time. So what's happening to the rock? You'll find out as you do the following Investigate.

OBJECTIVES

In this section, you will

- examine how physical weathering and chemical weathering break rocks into fragments;
- explain the factors that affect the rate of weathering;
- describe soil formation.

KEY SCIENCE TERMS

physical weathering
ice wedging
chemical weathering
oxidation

FIGURE 16-8. A mountain climber has to pound hard with a hammer to drive pitons into the rock.

Section 16-2

PREPARATION

Concepts Developed

Students have seen that particles of rock make up part of the mixture that is soil. These particles are produced when larger rocks are broken down by wind, water, ice, and the actions of humans. Some of the particles that are produced become part of the soil in that location. This aspect of rock particles is the focus of this lesson. In the next chapter, students will learn what happens as rock particles are carried from one place to another.

Planning the Lesson

For adequate development of the concepts presented in this section, we recommend that students do the Investigate and Explore activities on pages 488 and 491.

1 MOTIVATE

Discussion Ask students to describe objects that they have seen deteriorating. Students may mention bridges, sidewalks, buildings, roads, or other structures. Ask students to suggest reasons for the deterioration. Lead students to realize that several factors may be involved in the breakdown of a single structure. Explain that many of the same agents are at work weathering Earth's rocks.

2 TEACH

Tying to Previous Knowledge

In Chapter 5, students learned about physical and chemical changes. Review the differences between these kinds of changes before teaching this lesson. In Chapter 8, students learned about acids and bases. In this lesson, students will see how acids affect rocks. Ask students to predict what effects acids might have on rocks.

PROGRAM RESOURCES

Teacher Classroom Resources

Study Guide, page 58
Concept Mapping, page 24, Weathering L1
Transparency Masters, page 67, and **Color Transparency,** number 32, Soil Evolution L2
Take Home Activities, page 25, Weathering Concrete L1
How It Works, page 17, Sandblasting L1

INVESTIGATE!

16-2 BREAKING DOWN ROCKS

Time needed 10 minutes on the first day to soak the rock, 60 minutes on the second day, and 15 minutes on the third day

Materials See student activity.

Thinking Processes
Observing and inferring, Recognizing cause and effect, Controlling variables

Purpose To identify factors that contribute to the weathering process.

Preparation Use fresh limestone chips for this activity. The shaking process causes the limestone pieces to become rounded, which reduces the abrasive effect they have on one another.

Teaching the Activity

Discussion Presoaking the chips is important, because dry chips will absorb some water. Ask students what might happen if they did not control this variable, but did the activity with dry chips. There would be a gain in mass due to the water absorbed, so the loss of mass due to abrasion would be offset by the mass of the water. L1 COOP LEARN

Expected Outcomes

The rock chips should decrease in mass each time they are shaken. Students should conclude that the repeated collisions between pieces of rock cause particles to break off.

Answers to Analyze/Conclude and Apply

1. Answers will vary, but the mass should be lower each time that a measurement is taken.
2. Answers will vary, but the mass should be lower at the end of the shaking.
3. The sand at the surface should come off easily.
4. The rough-and-tumble action in a fast-moving stream could break off many small pieces.
5. The freezing and thawing in winter in a northern climate could cause the breakdown.
6. City streets and sidewalks will break down because of freezing and thawing and the rubbing by vehicle tires and pedestrians.

I N V E S T I G A T E !

16-2 BREAKING DOWN ROCKS

You could probably break rocks into small pieces with a hammer. But this process would not be a natural one. You will now **observe** how breaking rocks can take place in nature.

PROBLEM

How can rocks be broken without a hammer?

MATERIALS 

100 g limestone or shale chips
pan balance
plastic bottle with cap
water
wire strainer
small piece of sandstone
freezer

PROCEDURE

1. Copy the data table.
2. Soak the chips and the sandstone overnight.
3. **Measure** the mass of the chips with the pan balance.
4. Place the chips into the plastic bottle and add enough water to fill it about halfway. Then seal the bottle with the cap.
5. Shake the bottle vigorously for two minutes. Uncap the bottle and pour the water and rock chips into the strainer. Rinse the chips and again **measure** the mass of the chips. Record this measurement in your data table.
6. Repeat Steps 4 and 5 until 20 minutes of shaking time have passed. Stop the shaking every two minutes and record the original mass and the final mass of the chips for each two-minute period.
7. Place the water-soaked sandstone in the freezer. After 24 hours, remove it and allow it to thaw.
8. Examine the sandstone.

ANALYZE

1. How did the mass of the rock chips change after each shaking?
2. How did the total mass of the rock chips change from start to finish?
3. How did the sandstone change after thawing?

CONCLUDE AND APPLY

4. **Hypothesize** how the breakdown of the chips could occur in a natural setting.
5. How could the breakdown of the sandstone occur in a natural setting?
6. **Going Further: Predict** where you might see the breakdown of rocklike materials in a city. Why?

DATA AND OBSERVATIONS — Sample data

SHAKING TIME	2 MIN.	4 MIN.	6 MIN.	8 MIN.	10 MIN.	12 MIN.	14 MIN.	16 MIN.	18 MIN.	20 MIN.
Original mass	100	98	96	95	94.2	93.6	93.2	93	92.9	92.8
Final mass	98	96	95	94.2	93.6	93.2	93	92.9	92.8	92.7
Change in mass	2	2	1	0.8	0.6	0.4	0.2	0.1	0.1	0.1

PROGRAM RESOURCES

Teacher Classroom Resources

Laboratory Manual, pages 97-98, Chemical Weathering L2; pages 99-100, Carbon Dioxide and Limestone L3

Activity Masters, pages 67-68, Investigate 16-2

Multicultural Activities, page 36, Pollution in Switzerland L1

Suppose someone from another class had walked in while you were doing the Investigate activity and asked what you were doing. You probably would have replied, "Breaking down rocks." You could also have correctly said, "Weathering rocks. Physical weathering, to be precise." When a rock undergoes **physical weathering,** it breaks down into smaller pieces of the same kind of rock. In other words, the rock pieces change in size, but they do not change in composition. Physical weathering is an example of a physical change you studied in Chapter 5. It occurs in nature in several different ways.

Have you ever noticed that rocks in or on the banks of a stream are rounded? How did they get this way? You could say that the water polishes the rocks. As the water speeds over the rocks, it lifts them up and churns them about so that they collide with one another. Tiny bits of rock are broken off with each and every little bump. The collisions happen again and again so that the rocks become smooth. Given enough time, the rocky bottom of the streambed could change to a soft, muddy one.

Have you ever tried to skate down an old tree-lined sidewalk like the one in Figure 16-9? If so, you've run into a second way in which physical weathering occurs. Tree roots can grow under and around rocks just as they do near concrete sidewalks. The roots enlarge as the tree grows and eventually break the rocks just as they break up a sidewalk.

FIGURE 16-9. Tree roots break up naturally formed rocks the same way that they break up sidewalks.

MAKING CONNECTIONS

Math

Have students express the loss of mass of the rocks in the Investigate activity as a percentage of loss. To find the percentage of mass lost, use the following equation:

$$\text{\% of mass lost} = \frac{\text{change in mass}}{\text{original mass}} \times 100$$

Concept Development

Theme Connection The themes of Energy, and Stability and Change should be evident as students do the Investigate activity. The energy of moving water carries rock particles and causes them to strike each other. As a result, rock particles are changed in size as physical weathering takes place.

Inquiry Questions How does wind cause mechanical weathering? *Wind picks up sand and other particles and hurls them against buildings and rock surfaces. Small pieces of the buildings and rocks break off or become scratched and pitted due to this type of weathering.* Why do people sandblast building exteriors made of stones or brick? *Sandblasting "weathers away" the dirty outer surfaces of the rocks, exposing a clean surface.*

Discussion Ask students to identify ways water can cause physical weathering of rocks. Students will probably say that water moves rocks around, causing them to collide. Ask how this is an example of a physical change. The size and surface texture of the particles is changed in the process.

OPTIONS

Meeting Individual Needs

Behaviorally Disordered In the Investigate activity, it is important that the shaking process be as uniform as possible. Have all students in the group watch the person who does the shaking to see that he or she continues at a steady rate and with a steady force. For students with a short attention span, this responsibility should help them stay focused on the activity.

Enrichment

Activity Have interested students try other variables in the Investigate activity. Repeat the experiment with a few marble or quartz chips added to the limestone chips. The marble or quartz chips will increase the loss of mass by the limestone chips.

L2 COOP LEARN

Concept Development

Discussion Most students have probably placed a canned soft drink in the freezer to make it extra cold. Ask students what happens when the can is left in the freezer for too long. Compare this expansion with what happens in ice wedging.

Demonstration Demonstrate what happens to a patched pothole. Use sand and modeling clay to simulate pavement. Place some of the clay in a pan and sprinkle a thin layer of sand on the surface. Make a depression in the clay and then "patch" it with more clay. Pour water on the surface of the "pavement" and place the pan overnight in the freezer. The patch should become loosened by ice wedging.

Inquiry Question What would happen if you didn't empty a concrete birdbath of its water before the temperature dropped to freezing? *When water freezes, it expands and can break concrete.*

EXPLORE!

Can you find signs of physical weathering?

No special materials or preparation are required for this activity, which can be done as an independent assignment.

Thinking Process
Observing and inferring

Purpose To identify agents of weathering in their environment.

Teaching the Activity

For students who need more structure, this activity could be done during a walk around the school grounds. L1

Expected Outcomes

Specific observations will vary, depending on the places students notice. Potholes in roads, cracked sidewalks, and worn-down steps are likely observations.

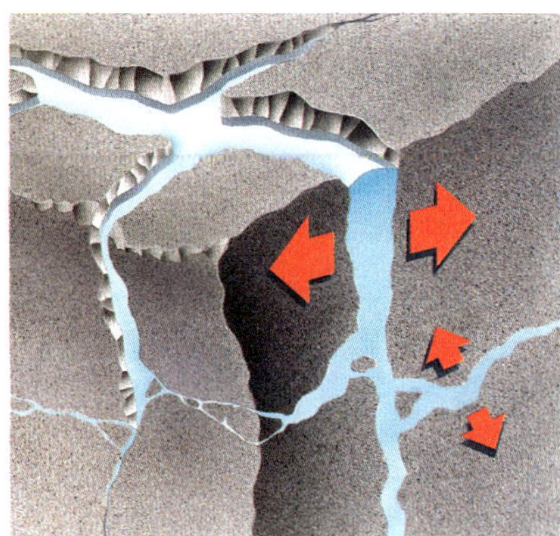

FIGURE 16-10. When water gets into cracks in a rock and freezes, it expands and forces the rock apart.

If summers are warm and winters are freezing cold where you live, you have probably seen drivers trying to dodge potholes in paved streets. Potholes result from a third type of physical weathering. Look at Figure 16-10. When water seeps into cracks in rocks and then freezes with falling temperatures, it expands and forces the rocks to break into smaller parts. Thus, **ice wedging** occurs. The process can be repeated many times throughout a season of freezing and thawing temperatures—and the freezing water and thawing ice they bring. Rocks are no different from city streets in this regard. Mountain peaks are weathered rapidly by ice wedging because they are exposed to warm temperatures during the day and freezing temperatures at night.

EXPLORE!

Can you find signs of physical weathering?

Be on the lookout for signs of physical weathering around you for several days. Check buildings, streets, sidewalks, and other structures. Keep a list of your observations. What do you think caused the physical weathering that you observed?

CHEMICAL WEATHERING

Do you ever see rusty old cars or vans like the one in Figure 16-11? Why does this happen?

FIGURE 16-11. Deterioration of the steel surface of this van is due to chemical weathering.

OPTIONS

Enrichment

Discussion Contact the Department of Public Works in your community, county, or state. The Department of Public Works is responsible for maintaining roads. Find out if there is a way to keep roads from developing potholes, or how the department decides which roads to repair. Ask students how they would decide which roads to repair. Would they patch potholes or repave entire streets?

Enrichment

Demonstration The jewelry industry uses physical weathering. Gemstones are worn smooth in a tumbler, a turning cylinder in which stones strike one another and become smooth. This is a common hobby. Find out if any of the students have ever had a rock tumbler, or know someone who does. Borrow a tumbler or some tumbled stones to show the class how the stones are smoothed.

EXPLORE!

How can steel be changed?

Place a piece of steel wool in a shallow dish or bowl containing about 2 mL of water. Observe the steel wool for several days. Note what happens to it.

You should have noticed changes in the steel wool. Was it weathering? Yes, but this time it was chemical rather than physical weathering. **Chemical weathering** occurs when water, air, and other materials react with rocks, often changing the substances that make up the rocks. Chemical weathering is an example of the chemical change you studied in Chapter 5.

Water is the main cause of chemical weathering. You saw that when you placed steel wool in a small amount of water and watched it rust. In this instance, oxygen reacted with iron in a process called oxidation. During **oxidation,** oxygen combines with a metal to form a new material. Paint usually protects iron and keeps it from oxidizing, but rust forms if the iron under the paint gets exposed to oxygen and water. Some rocks contain iron and so will oxidize just like the steel wool or an unprotected car. The rock in Figure 16-12 is an example.

Now think of the last time you made lemonade. If you did not use a sweetened mix, you put sugar into it. But what happened to the sugar? You'll remember from Chapter 7 that the water in the lemonade dissolved it. Water does the same thing with some rocks. It dissolves

FIGURE 16-12. Rocks that contain iron oxidize, giving them a reddish color.

EXPLORE!

How can steel be changed?

Time needed 10 minutes on the first day, 5 minutes each day for three more days

Materials steel wool pads, without soap; shallow dish; water

Thinking Process
Observing

Purpose To observe a chemical change that is an example of chemical weathering.

Preparation Wear protective gloves and gently tear the steel wool pads into small pieces.

Teaching the Activity

Discussion After students have completed the activity, discuss the chemical change that they observed. Then ask students which type of weathering—chemical or physical—takes place more quickly. Students should recall that the physical weathering of the limestone chips in the Investigate activity took place more quickly than this chemical weathering. L2

Expected Outcomes

The steel wool will become rusty. From this, students should conclude that chemical weathering has taken place.

Concept Development

Discussion Ask students if they have ever seen chalking paint on a house or a fence. Perhaps they have brushed against a fence and had the paint rub off on their clothing. Point out that the paint was not chalky when it was first put on the fence or house. What might have happened to the minerals in the paint? *They have been chemically weathered.*

PROGRAM RESOURCES

Teacher Classroom Resources

Making Connections: Across the Curriculum, page 35, The Statue of Liberty L2

Other Resources

Erosion and Weathering, film, EBEC.

The Changing Land, filmstrip, National Geographic.

"Saving Face; Mount Rushmore National Memorial". *Life,* February 1990, pages 50-52.

SKILLBUILDER

1. The chemical weathering by acid rain was the cause. The effect on the statue was a discoloration.
2. The tree roots may have caused the cracks. Or the cracks may have formed due to other types of weathering, thus exposing the roots.
3. Carbonic acid may have caused the chemical weathering. The effect of the chemical weathering is the appearance of the rock. L1

Concept Development

Discussion Ask students to suggest definitions of the term *pioneer. someone who settles in a place where people did not live before* Botanists, scientists who study plants, refer to mosses and other small plants that live on rocks as pioneers. Ask students why this is appropriate. Students should see that just as other people move in after pioneers have settled a new region, other plants move in after the mosses have begun to weather the rock into soil.

MAKING CONNECTIONS

Social Studies/Art

Many historians use the inscriptions on gravestones as a source of information. Weathering often makes it difficult to read old limestone gravestones, and photographs usually cannot capture much of the detail. Historians often make "rubbings" of gravestones. To make a rubbing, place a sheet of paper over the stone and rub a soft crayon over the paper. If there are any commemorative plaques in the school, obtain permission to have your class make some rubbings. Making rubbings has been a popular activity of amateur historians for some time. Some old cemeteries no longer permit rubbings because this activity, too, wears away bits of the stone.

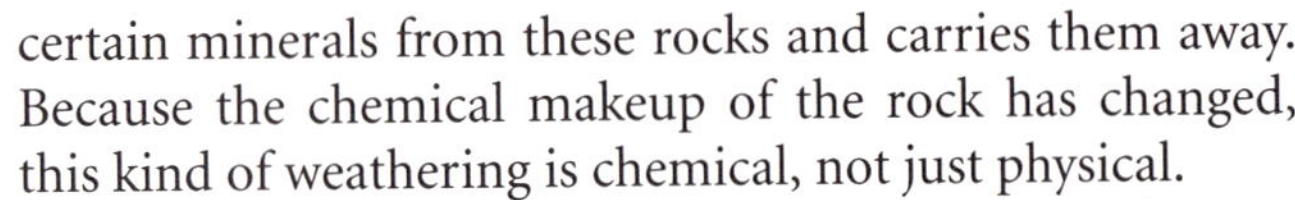

SKILLBUILDER

RECOGNIZING CAUSE AND EFFECT

Identify the cause and effect in each of the examples of weathering below. If you need help, refer to the ***Skill Handbook*** on pages 653-654.

1. Acid rain has turned a bronze statue green.
2. Tree roots are exposed in cracks in your sidewalk.
3. A piece of limestone has a honeycomb appearance.

certain minerals from these rocks and carries them away. Because the chemical makeup of the rock has changed, this kind of weathering is chemical, not just physical.

Compounds in the air sometimes combine with rainwater. You've already learned in Chapter 8 how acid rain can form and fall to the ground, eating away at rock structures such as statues, gravestones, and buildings.

When rainwater mixes with carbon dioxide in the air, a very weak acid called carbonic acid forms. When this acid comes in contact with certain materials in rocks, chemical reactions form new materials. For example, carbonic acid will react with rocks that have the material feldspar in them to form clays.

Chemical weathering also occurs when carbonic acid comes in contact with limestone rocks. You can see the results of this contact in Figure 16-13. Carbonic acid dissolves limestone. Over thousands of years, the acid can dissolve enough limestone to form caves.

FIGURE 16-13. Carbonic acid and water cause limestone rocks to dissolve, forming caves.

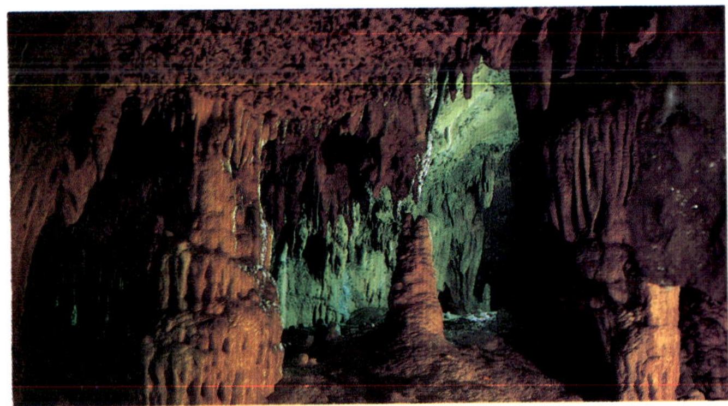

The next time you find a moss-covered rock like the one in Figure 16-14, peel back the moss and examine the small pits you see in the rock's surface. Acids from the moss caused the pits. A number of other living as well as some decaying plants also give off acids. When the acids come in contact with rocks, they dissolve some of the substances in the rocks. Thus, chemical weathering weakens the rocks and eventually causes them to break up.

WEATHERING: HOW FAST AND WHY

Think back to your last soft drink with ice cubes. If you were watching, you would have noticed that a large ice cube takes longer to melt than two small ice cubes. That is because the two smaller ice cubes together have a greater surface area than one large ice cube. Recall from

OPTIONS

Meeting Individual Needs

Learning Disabled To help students grasp the concept of surface area, assemble a large cube out of smaller ones, such as small blocks or boxes. Mark every exposed surface square with a stick-on dot. Premark the bottom cubes before you assemble the rest of the large cube. After the entire surface has been marked, gently knock it over, so that students can see the previously unexposed surfaces. Have students compare the number of marked squares with the number of unmarked squares. Ask students to imagine that the cubes are rocks. Would weathering be faster if the rock were left whole or if it were broken into pieces?

Chapter 7 that surface area helps determine how fast a material will dissolve. It also affects how fast a material melts. So, the smaller cubes tend to melt faster.

A similar process happens with rocks. Lots of small rocks undergo weathering faster than one large rock because the small rocks have more surface exposed to the weather.

A rock's makeup also affects the rate of weathering. Granite, for example, is more resistant to chemical weathering than marble or limestone because granite is not very soluble.

FIGURE 16-14. This moss is breaking down the rock on which it grows.

Do you live in a dry region like Arizona, in a coastal area like San Francisco, or in a place that has both hot and cold weather? Weathering happens at different rates depending on the climate of the area. Ice wedging in climates with big temperature differences can cause rapid physical weathering. Ice wedging could create the damaged pavement in Figure 16-15 in just a few winter months.

If you lived in the desert of Saudi Arabia, with its short period of cold temperatures and scant rainfall, it would take centuries for your community to undergo chemical weathering or physical weathering, except for weathering by the wind. If you lived in a South American rain forest, you would see physical weathering only in streams and rivers. But chemical weathering would be all around you. Daily rainfalls and steamy temperatures mean that water and acids are constantly dissolving and eating away rocky substances. Chemical weathering is always most rapid in warm, rainy climates.

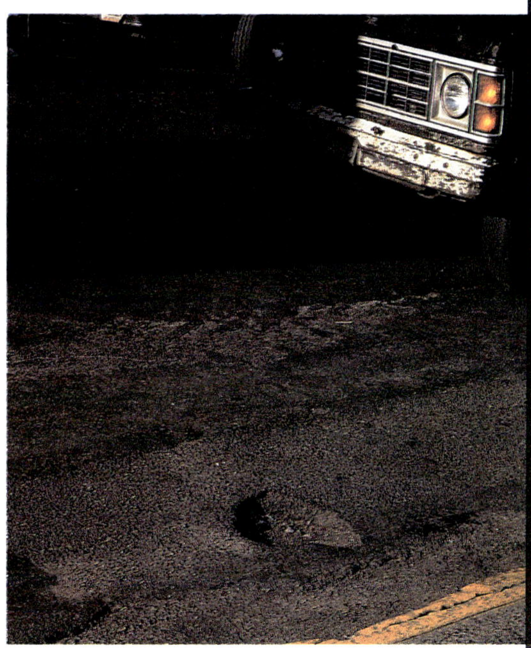

FIGURE 16-15. Potholes and cracks can be caused by freezing and thawing in just one winter.

SOIL FORMATION

As rock weathers into smaller and smaller fragments, plants begin to grow in the weathered rock. Then worms, insects, bacteria, and fungi begin living among the plant roots. These organisms don't just live in the weathered rock; they help it develop into soil by adding humus to it. When the plants and animals that live in the soil eventually

Concept Development

Discussion Provide a world map (see Appendix F, pages 638-639) and have volunteers locate the places mentioned in the text. Also ask students to identify areas similar to those discussed in the text. Students might mention the deserts of the southwestern United States and the cold regions of Canada and Alaska. Point out the northwestern United States, and tell students that this area receives a large amount of rainfall but is not as warm as a tropical rain forest. What kind of weathering would be most common here? Would it be fast or slow? *Weathering would be mostly chemical, but not as fast as in the tropics.*

Content Background

The rate of a chemical reaction depends on temperature. The chemical reactions that cause weathering occur faster at higher temperatures. This is one reason that chemical weathering is so fast in tropical rain forests. Another reason is that most reactions take place in a water-based solution. The daily rainfall provides plenty of water in which the reactions can take place.

Multicultural Perspective

In the rain forests, the soil layer is very thin and is constantly replenished by decay of leaves that fall from trees. The people who live in the forest traditionally farmed beneath the canopy of trees, and the soil remained rich enough to support crops. The more modern technique of clearing all trees for farming removes the source of humus, and the soil becomes exhausted in a few years.

3 Assess

Check for Understanding

1. Have students look at the shape of the red rocks shown in Figure 16-12 and identify evidence of various kinds of weathering. The red color is due to chemical weathering. The large rocks on the ground were probably broken off by physical weathering. Some of the rocks on the ground have rounded edges, probably due to physical weathering from windblown sand.
2. Ask questions 1–4 and the Apply question in Check Your Understanding. Discuss students' answers to the Apply question. Challenge students to give evidence to support their answers.

Reteach

Demonstration Show students a lump of brown sugar that you have left out for a few days. Discuss ways to get this hard lump of sugar mixed into a recipe. Compare these methods with physical weathering (break up the lump or rub it against something) and chemical weathering (dissolve it).

Extension

Have students research the chemical makeup of limestone and granite and use this information to explain why the chemical weathering of granite is slower than that of limestone.

4 Close

Discussion

At the base of a waterfall, the water is often much deeper than it is just a few meters downstream. Ask students what causes this difference. *It is due to the physical weathering of the rock by the force of the falling water.*

FIGURE 16-16. Chemical weathering is very rapid in rain forest areas.

FIGURE 16-17. Soil forms from weathered rock as well as organic material such as leaves, twigs, and insects.

die, they break down in a process called decay. As worms and insects burrow through the soil, they mix the humus with the fragments of rock. Weathered rock is constantly changing into soil.

Most soil is made up of about 50 percent rock and mineral fragments and 50 percent air, water, and humus. Soil can take hundreds of years to form and can range in thickness from 60 meters in some areas to just a few centimeters in others.

In the next chapter, you will see how other processes move around the rock fragments created by weathering. These processes work in an even larger cycle that keeps Earth's materials constantly on the go.

Check Your Understanding

1. How are rocks broken by physical weathering in nature?
2. What is the main cause of the chemical weathering of rocks in most parts of the world? Explain.
3. What factors affect the rate of weathering?
4. How does soil develop after physical and chemical weathering have taken place to form tiny rock fragments?
5. **APPLY:** How do you think the weathering of rock under a forest soil differs from the weathering of rock on a mountain peak?

Answers to Check Your Understanding

1. Rocks can be broken by other rocks hitting them in a stream, by tree roots growing near rocks, and by ice wedging.
2. Water is the main cause. Oxidation occurs when a metal is exposed to oxygen and water. Water itself dissolves some materials in rocks and carries them away. Water will also combine with carbon dioxide in the air to form an acid that causes new materials to form from rocks. Carbonic acid will dissolve limestone so that caves are formed.
3. The climate of a region, the size of rocks, and the makeup of rocks
4. Humus is added to the soil by plants and animals and the soil is mixed together by worms and insects.
5. Weathering of rock under a forest soil is chiefly chemical weathering; on a mountain peak, it is physical weathering.

EXPANDING YOUR VIEW

CONTENTS

A CLOSER LOOK

FROST ACTION

If you live in an area with cold winters, check the condition of the local roads. Frost action probably damaged them by creating holes or bumps. Over time, frost action breaks apart roads the same way it breaks apart rocks, because roads are mostly made of rocks and soil.

A typical asphalt road is built on the base of natural soil that is left when the ground is cleared of plants along the road's path. A mixture of asphalt and crushed stone is then poured on top of the soil base. About 90 percent of the mixture is crushed rock. The other 10 percent is asphalt that holds the rocks together.

During warm winter days, the sun heats the ground and the air—and any water around. The temperature is above freezing and melted snow seeps around the rocks in the asphalt and into the soil of the roadbed under the asphalt.

At night when the temperature drops, water freezes. Groundwater freezes in the roadbed under the road.

As freezing groundwater expands, it pushes up sections of the road, breaking the asphalt apart and creating a bump. This process is called frost heaving, and it can eventually push apart large sections of road.

Water also freezes in and around the rocks in the asphalt. In a rock crevice, freezing water becomes an ice wedge that can eventually shatter the rock. When the rocks in the asphalt are broken into smaller pieces, the pieces get free from the asphalt, which damages the road.

WHAT DO YOU THINK?

Could we make roads stronger than frost action? Is there any way to keep water from seeping into the ground under a road? What could we mix with asphalt that could not be broken apart by freezing water?

EXPANDING YOUR VIEW

Assign one or more of these excursions to expand students' understanding of soil formation and weathering processes. You may assign them as small group or individual activities.

A CLOSER LOOK

Purpose A Closer Look reveals the process of physical weathering in action on a typical asphalt road. It shows how the forces described in Section 16-2 create bumps, potholes, and other damage to road surfaces. These weathering processes keep road crews at work maintaining roads and highways.

Content Background Water is perhaps the chief problem in road maintenance. The oldest paved road in Europe leads to the palace of Knossos on the Greek island of Crete (circa 2000 B.C.). The road's excellent drainage system probably contributed to its longevity. The later Appian Way and other Roman roads (circa 300 B.C.) were laid on a bed 3 to 4 feet deep, with successively finer layers of stone set in mortar. The surface was paved over with stone blocks. "Crowning" a road, or building it with a slightly raised level in the center, promoted water runoff and proved easier than digging drainage ditches on each side.

Teaching Strategies Ask students for examples of small forces that have tremendous effects similar to that of water on a road, for example, tree roots cracking rock or erosion slowly destroying a region.

Going Further After sharing some of the Content Background with students, ask them to find out and write briefly about a great water-control or major drainage project either from history or contemporary news. Examples might include the Fayum in Egypt, the Roman Forum, the Zuider Zee, or the Aswan Dam.

Going Further Have groups of students research and report to the class on advances in the art of road building. Some might report on the characteristics of Daniel Boone's "Wilderness Road" or Germany's Autobahn of the 1930s. Other students might research how a weigh station works and protects a road or biographical facts on John L. McAdam, for whom modern macadam surfaces are named.

COOP LEARN

Answers to WHAT DO YOU THINK?

Students should deduce from Section 16-2 that impermeable surfaces would prevent potholes, since water and ice wedging most damage roads. Students should realize though that making surfaces impermeable reduces friction. Ask students to speak with local engineers about this problem.

EXPANDING YOUR VIEW

LIFE SCIENCE CONNECTION

Purpose Life Science Connection expands on the information presented in Section 16-1. Students learn that nutrients are constantly taken from and replaced in soils.

Content Background Legumes are plants that bear fruit in the form of pods or shells, which contain one or more seeds. The pods of the peanut plant, unlike those of most legumes, develop underground.

Carver's initial research was on fungi. It wasn't until 1914 that he became interested in peanuts. In addition to his work with peanuts, Carver produced 118 products and many recipes that used sweet potatoes.

Teaching Strategies Provide peanuts still in their shells. Have students shell a few of the nuts, examine the shells, and brainstorm to come up with a list of uses for the shell of the peanut. Responses might include abrasives, gardening or wallboard.

Discussion Discuss the nitrogen cycle with the class. Explain that certain plants have bacteria in their roots that add usable nitrogen to the soil. Then, discuss how nitrogen returns to the soil.

Answers to WHAT DO YOU THINK?

1. Plants need minerals to grow and to produce fruits and seeds.
2. Carver's experiments largely consisted of processing peanuts in a variety of ways, such as cooking, to find out what sort of products would result.
3. Farmers were probably skeptical about growing peanuts and sweet potatoes. They may have been afraid that no one would buy these crops.

LIFE SCIENCE CONNECTION

GEORGE WASHINGTON CARVER—PEANUT PIONEER

George Washington Carver (1864–1943), an agricultural pioneer, helped the Southern United States overcome its dependence on the cotton crop. Carver, a professor at Alabama's Tuskegee Institute, introduced the idea of crop rotation to the South. At the turn of the century, farmers in Alabama and across the South had been planting only cotton for over one hundred years. The planting of only one crop (cotton) eliminated minerals from the soil, producing low-quality cotton. Because mineral-rich soil is vital to growing strong, healthy crops, Carver restored the mineral content of the Southern soil by planting nitrogen-producing legumes. He discovered that sweet potatoes and peanuts (both legumes) yielded very productive crops in the Southern soil. He encouraged farmers across the South to diversify their crops by planting different crops every few years (crop rotation).

Carver is perhaps best-known for discovering over 300 by-products of the peanut. After encouraging farmers to produce peanut crops, Carver realized that more uses for the peanut needed to be found to make sure that farmers could sell their crops. Through creative experimentation, Carver discovered that peanuts could be used as essential ingredients in inks, dyes, plastics, cheese, milk, coffee, wood stains, soap, shoe polish, and cosmetics. Carver gained respect for his experiments and agricultural knowledge and was often invited to speak to groups of scientists. He published many books and pamphlets about his work, and the results of his research became known throughout the world. In 1973, he was elected to the Hall of Fame for Great Americans.

WHAT DO YOU THINK?

1. Why are minerals in the soil so important to producing healthy crops?
2. How do you think Carver came up with so many uses for the peanut? What kinds of experiments do you think he used to discover these uses?
3. How do you think people first reacted to his news about the different uses for peanuts?

Going Further Have students use a world soil map to determine the soil type(s) present in your area. Then have students find out the main crops grown in the region and explain which nutrients are removed from the soil by these crops and what is done to replace these essential minerals. If you live in a region that is heavily farmed, have students form small groups and have each group report on a specific crop.

Going Further Have students gather various food items, baked goods, candies, margarines, salad dressings, breads, sauces, and so on and read the labels to find out whether or not the items contain peanuts and/or peanut oil.

SCIENCE AND SOCIETY

SAVE OUR SOIL

Think of the soil as your friend, for it gives you many things. The book you are reading was once a tree growing in the soil. The tree was cut down, ground up, and made into paper for your book. The sweet grapes you ate for lunch grew on a vine. Your cotton shirt came from a bush growing in soil. The bush grew a cotton boll that was gathered and spun into cotton thread for your shirt.

Because soil is so important to our lives, you'd think people would take care of it. But they haven't always. Sometimes people have made mistakes that caused the soil to dry up and blow away.

Farming mistakes created the Dust Bowl in the 1930s, when the soil on about 50 million acres near the center of the United States dried up and blew around—and away!

Farmers in the Dust Bowl region had made the mistake of using several poor farming practices. First, they overgrazed their land, letting animals eat nearly all the plants. There were not enough plant roots to hold down the soil. New soil could not develop because old plants were not being recycled into the soil. After several years without rain, the soil dried out. Strong winds picked it up and blew clouds of dust hundreds of miles away. Thousands of tons of valuable topsoil were lost. Roads and houses were buried by the soil deposited from the windstorms. People wore masks so they wouldn't breathe in the dust, and many of them moved away. The famous writer John Steinbeck wrote about this problem and the suffering it caused Oklahoma farmers in

WHAT DO YOU THINK?

Do you think the government should allow ranchers to overgraze the public lands they rent? Remember that the lower the costs to the rancher, the lower the costs to the consumers. Would you pay more to be sure the public lands were not overgrazed? What do you think will happen to the overgrazed lands?

Going Further If possible, have students read or watch portions of Steinbeck's *The Grapes of Wrath* to get a better idea of the relationship between soil and humans, and of how the fortunes of one can affect the other. **What other nonscientific ideas of interrelationships can they find?** Groups might wish to share passages from Chief Seattle's writings, lyrics to old songs of farming and agricultural communities throughout the world, or details of customs from planting and harvesting festivals that suggest these relationships. **How do they each relate to modern scientific views?** COOP LEARN

EXPANDING YOUR VIEW

SCIENCE AND SOCIETY

Purpose Science and Society shows both the vital value and the great fragility of soils produced by the processes discussed in Section 16-2. The article examines what happened to soil and, thus, to humans, in the 1930s in the southwestern United States after decades of unwise farming and land use. It also lists solutions that were discovered for these problems of soil loss and soil-quality degradation.

Content Background The disastrous effects of overgrazing became obvious in the 1930s, as Science and Society suggests. But another leading cause of soil destruction—overuse with single kinds of crops—has continued to challenge scientific remedial techniques. For thousands of years humans have added animal waste called manure and compost directly to fields; they now usually plant either cover crops or green-manure crops as part of the modern rotation system. Cover crops, such as legumes, protect soil during winter months and fix nitrogen; they also bring farmers some extra income. Green-manure crops can be of almost any variety, since their purpose is served when they are merely plowed under and enrich the soil. Such crops may seem to yield nothing, until their nutrients add to the bounty of the next season's crop of corn, wheat, or other foodstuffs.

Answers to WHAT DO YOU THINK?

As students debate these issues, have them concretely relate their position to their own habits of dress, eating, and so on. That is, **can students who wish to stop the rancher from overgrazing do so without a governmental law to assist them?** Introduce the idea of boycotts. **Can supporters of overgrazing find any other way to keep food prices down?**

EXPANDING YOUR VIEW

Teaching Strategy Ask volunteers to link aspects of their daily life to the soil. Challenge them to detail the process backward to the soil. Can they name anything that does not originate there?

CAREER CONNECTION

Have students write to agriculture/animal husbandry departments at major universities for publications and details on how to combine farming know-how with writing and journalism skills. Local reporters who do daily farm prices reports may be able to offer facts on internships at local TV and radio stations.

his moving novel *The Grapes of Wrath.*

Years later, rain quieted the dust, and farmers learned better ways to take care of their land. They planted more and didn't allow the animals to overgraze.

But the mistake of overgrazing is still being made today in some parts of the world. Animals are allowed to graze one area until it is barren before being moved to another.

In the United States, overgrazing still happens, even on public land. The government owns millions of acres of public land that people can use for different purposes. Many ranchers rent it to graze their cattle. Putting cattle on public land costs ranchers about half what it would cost them to rent private land. Sometimes, ranchers allow their cattle to overgraze the public land.

Another mistake the Dust Bowl farmers made was to grow the same crops on the same land every year. This is a poor farming method that wears out the soil by using all the nutrients. Once the soil is worn out, it cannot be revived for a long time. It takes between 10 to 30 years for 1 millimeter of soil to evolve!

This mistake is easy to avoid by using crop rotation. Healthy soil can be maintained by planting a different crop each year and by sometimes plowing under a crop to help enrich the soil.

If an area is already short of rain and the land is overgrazed, it can become a desert. Some places in the United States, Africa, and China are becoming deserts because of overgrazing.

CAREER CONNECTION

Agricultural journalists might write stories for farm magazines. They also create radio and television shows about farming and farmers. An agricultural journalist has an educational background in both agriculture and journalism.

Art CONNECTION

SHE PAINTS WITH DIRT

Artist Daryl Howard paints with dirt. In a studio closet, she stores 133 different colors of dirt from around the world, and her collection is growing.

Howard's first dirt came from the Hopi Indians. She spent eight weeks on their reservation one summer, working on her art. When she left, they gave her five bottles of dirt.

"An Indian's gift from Earth is quite spiritual," she says. "At first, I didn't know what to do with my present. About six months later, I realized I was supposed to paint with the dirt!"

Howard grinds and sifts her dirt, which she calls Earth pigment. Then she mixes it with an acrylic polymer medium, a liquid plastic. Sometimes she mixes several dirt colors together or layers one color over another.

Earth pigment is only one part of Howard's landscape art. She starts by painting a museum board with a thin layer of metal that comes from Earth: gold, silver, or copper.

On top of the metal base, she glues strips of handmade paper torn to represent hills, clouds, or trees. Then she applies Earth pigment, building it up in layers. Using tweezers, Howard completes each collage with gemstones, such as uncut diamonds, rubies, sapphires, and garnets."I use precious Earth," she says.

The very first paint was made from dirt. "I am painting with dirt and for me it's new," Howard says. "But I know for a fact it's really old. Prehistoric people mixed dirt with animal fat to make the pigment they used to paint the walls of their caves."

YOU TRY IT!

Make your own Earth pigments. Collect dirt, break it up into tiny grains, sift out leaves and clods, mix it with glue, and paint it on paper.

EXPANDING YOUR VIEW

ART CONNECTION

Purpose The Art Connection profiles Daryl Howard and her ancient art of sand painting. With this article students can see one of the cultural benefits of weathering processes outlined in Section 16-2. Both physical and chemical weathering produce the different shades of colored soil Howard and other artists have used for centuries.

Content Background Some of the earliest known artistic uses of Earth pigment can be seen in the caves of Altamira, Lascaux, and other Stone Age sites, where animal fat and other added substances were mixed with colored soils to help keep them stuck to surfaces. Ancient artists often "signed" their works by blowing red ochre (iron oxide pigment) over their hands to leave palmprints on the walls. You may refer students to the October 1988 issue of *National Geographic* for photographs.

Teaching Strategies Ask students what they think Howard means when she says that the Indians' gift from Earth is "spiritual." What is soil to them?

Demonstration Ask volunteers to bring in/demonstrate examples of art that represents or employs natural substances or objects, such as Georgia O'Keeffe's paintings of skulls and flowers.

Going Further Ask students to look around in their daily activities and find at least one example of weathering that makes an object look as if it has been artistically developed. Have them tell or demonstrate how this came about. Examples might include the patterns on a rock that come from wind and water action, the smooth edges of a streambed or contours of a piece of driftwood, or the rock towers of Monument Valley.

Answers to YOU TRY IT

Students may wish to try and compare two techniques of sand painting: spreading sand premixed with glue over a pattern or by sprinkling loose sand over a glued surface.

EXPANDING YOUR VIEW

TEENS IN SCIENCE

Purpose Teens in Science shows how a student like Mia Balko can make use of information about soil and weathering, such as concepts presented in Sections 16-1 and 16-2. Her early success in soil-judging competitons is probably due to careful study of physical and chemical weathering processes that produce various soils. Knowing where a soil came from tells her what will and will not grow in it.

Content Background Future Farmers of America is an organization of young people who learn about agriculture and farm economics. Affiliated with the Extension Service of the U.S. Department of Agriculture, these organizations boast over 2 million members. Their efforts not only fund extension projects such as Mia Balko describes, but also award hundreds of thousands of dollars in financial aid for students pursuing degrees in related fields.

Teaching Strategies Ask volunteers to describe experiences they have had with soil or rocks. **Can they imagine themselves in a career related to these topics?** Why or why not?

Student Writing Have students write a short paragraph on how their career plans relate in some way to Earth and its processes. Future restaurateurs, for example, will be getting their food supplies from farms. Encourage students to use their imaginations to find similar links between work and nature.

TEENS *in* SCIENCE

GROWING A FUTURE

Mia Balko is growing a future from her crops.

Mia is a teenager who has won many high school awards for her crops and the hogs she has raised. Today, she is in college studying to be an agriculture teacher. Her tuition is paid by a full college scholarship she won for her high school agriculture work. The Balko family lives on a farm outside Banquete, a small Texas farming community. They moved there when Mia was six years old.

When she started high school, Mia did not plan to go into agriculture. "My ag teacher was a good friend of the family," she says. "I thought I would like him for a teacher." She did.

As a freshman, Mia started in the soil-judging competition. During the next three years she expanded into crops, learning to keep good records and studying yield per acre. She also learned about chemicals used as fertilizers and how to control insects and weeds.

Through the years, Mia has earned area grand championships and reserve grand championships in corn, grain, and cotton. As a junior, she was second in the state of Texas. As a senior, she was named Nontraditional Student of the year.

Mia competes as a member of the Texas Association of Future Farmers of America (FFA), which she joined as a high school freshman. Now a college freshman, she has applied for the group's highest honor, the American FFA Degree in the area of diversified crop production. If she wins, she'll receive another scholarship.

For two summers, Mia worked at the grain elevator near her home. "I worked in the scale room, weighing trucks and taking samples," she says. "I took a probe and stuck it way down in the grain and opened it up to let the probe fill up. It helped me learn about the crops and where our family income is coming from."

YOU TRY IT!

Plant some seeds or small plants in two different containers of soil. Use fertilizer on one and no fertilizer on the other. Keep track of the growth of the plants. What differences in growth do you observe? How is this similar to what Mia Balko did with her crops?

Answers to YOU TRY IT

Plants that were given fertilizer will probably grow faster. Mia's experiments with soil included a study of fertilizers.

Going Further If they wish, volunteers can look into the facts on "alternative crops" that farmers and others are turning to as both income supplements and energy sources. **What kinds of crops are involved in the process of making gasahol and other alternative fuels? What kinds of research careers may be available?**

Have groups of students each write a letter to the Department of Agriculture (at the local or federal level) to learn more about career opportunities in a farming-related activity. They should then compare responses and information and see if they can discern the major trends of the coming decade. They can write to:

Department of Agriculture
Small Community & Rural Development Office
The Mall
12th and 14th Sts.
Washington, DC 20250 COOP LEARN

Reviewing Main Ideas

1. There are usually three horizons in a soil profile—A, B, and C. The A horizon is the layer in which humus, plants, and animals are found.

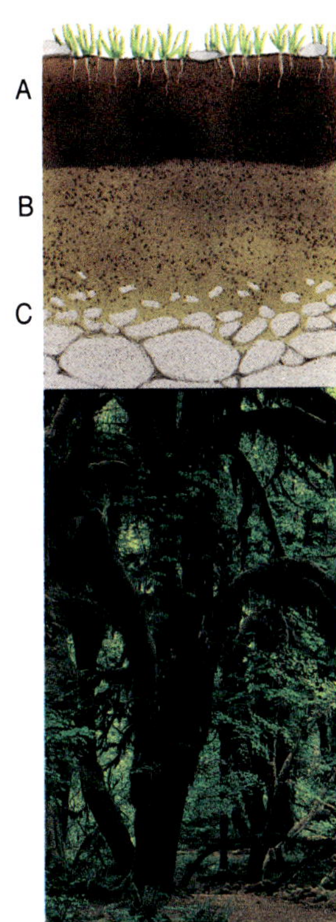

2. The soils of cold, dry climates have thin horizons, but the soils of warm, humid climates have thick horizons.

3. A cracked sidewalk and a pothole are examples of physical weathering. A limestone tombstone that has been worn away is an example of chemical weathering.

5. Soil develops as organic matter is added to weathered rock.

4. The climate of a region—along with rock size and rock composition—determines how fast weathering takes place.

Chapter 16

Reviewing Main Ideas

Students will review the main ideas of the chapter and develop alternate illustrations for these ideas.

Teaching Strategies

Divide the class into five groups. Assign each group one of the main ideas. Each group should study the photograph or drawing that accompanies the main idea. Have students brainstorm other examples that illustrate the main idea. Each group should produce a drawing that shows its main idea. Have a representative of each group explain the group's drawing to the class.

Chapter 16

Chapter Review

USING KEY SCIENCE TERMS

Answers

1. soil profile; the other terms describe weathering
2. humus; oxidation is a form of chemical weathering
3. oxidation; a horizon is part of a soil profile
4. horizon; leaching and ice wedging are forms of weathering
5. soil profile; the other terms are kinds of weathering

UNDERSTANDING IDEAS

Answers

1. b	5. b
2. a	6. d
3. d	7. b
4. c	8. d

CRITICAL THINKING

Answers

1. Water increases the rate of chemical weathering, so a desert area would have slow weathering. Temperature affects the rate of weathering. In a polar region, the low temperature would slow chemical weathering.

2. The soil is relatively young. Older soil with plant life would have abundant humus.

3. Each soil contains sand, silt, and clay particles. Loam has little clay, and large amounts of silt and sand.

Chapter Review

USING KEY SCIENCE TERMS

chemical weathering	leaching
horizon	oxidation
humus	ice wedging
physical weathering	soil profile

For each set of terms below, choose the one that does not belong and explain why it does not belong.

1. physical weathering, ice wedging, soil profile
2. chemical weathering, humus, oxidation
3. soil profile, oxidation, horizon
4. horizon, leaching, ice wedging
5. physical weathering, chemical weathering, soil profile

UNDERSTANDING IDEAS

Choose the best answer to complete each sentence.

1. The kind of soil that will trap water in puddles at the surface is ____.
   a. sandy **c.** gravel
   b. clay **d.** loam
2. If soil has a great deal of humus in it, it is probably ____.
   a. dark **c.** in a dry climate
   b. light **d.** in a cold climate
3. A desert soil has very little ____.
   a. sand **c.** rock
   b. gravel **d.** humus
4. A soil will form very slowly in a climate that is ____.
   a. humid **c.** dry
   b. snowy **d.** rainy
5. Rocks may be forced apart by ____.
   a. dissolving
   b. ice wedging
   c. carbonic acid
   d. chemical weathering

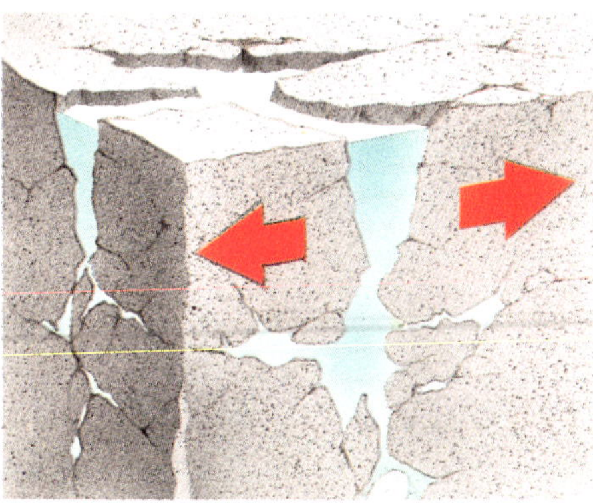

6. The rate of weathering is affected by ____.
   a. ice wedging **c.** the soil horizon
   b. leaching **d.** the size of the rocks
7. Chemical weathering may form caves when carbonic acid comes in contact with ____.
   a. sandstone **c.** shale
   b. limestone **d.** granite
8. How fast weathering takes place is really determined by ____.
   a. limestone **c.** acids
   b. ice wedging **d.** climate

PROGRAM RESOURCES

Teacher Classroom Resources

Review and Assessment, Chapter Review and Chapter Test, pages 65-68

Computer Test Bank, Chapter Test

OPTIONS

Cooperative Learning

Consider using Cooperative Learning in the Understanding Ideas, Critical Thinking, Problem Solving, and Connecting Ideas sections of the Chapter Review.

COOP LEARN

CRITICAL THINKING

Use your understanding of the concepts developed in the chapter to answer each of the following questions.

1. Explain why desert and polar areas have a slower rate of chemical weathering than a forest region with much rainfall.
2. Suppose a soil has little humus in it. Also suppose that it has plant life and receives sufficient rainfall. What might you conclude about the age of the soil? Why?
3. The graphs show the kinds and amounts of particles found in three common soil types. What three kinds of particles does each soil type have? What kinds of particles are most abundant in loam?

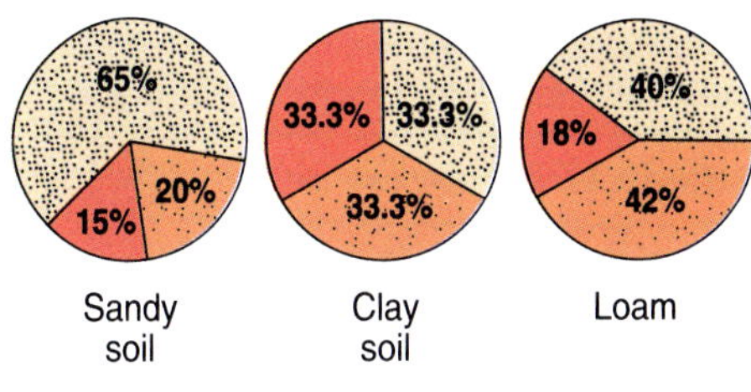

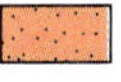 Sand (coarse particles)

 Silt (medium-sized particles)

Clay (fine particles)

4. Which area would be more likely to be missing the A horizon—a gently sloping area or a steep hill? Why?
5. If you find well-rounded rocks in a stream, what can you assume about what happened to the rocks?
6. What might be a soil problem for a farmer in an area that floods for two months each spring? Explain.

PROBLEM SOLVING

Read the following problem and discuss your answers in a brief paragraph.

Suppose you want to grow a garden in an area that has not had a garden before.

1. After you start digging, you should find out if the soil is rich in humus or not. What do you do to find out if it is rich in humus? What might you do to the soil if it is not rich in humus?
2. Your soil may form puddles after a rain. What could you do to make the soil more permeable?
3. If your soil has too much sand in it, what might you have to add to the soil to help it hold water for a longer time?

CONNECTING IDEAS

Discuss each of the following in a brief paragraph.

1. What does chemical weathering do to rocks that physical weathering does not do?

2. Would rocks be more likely to break down in a small, swiftly moving stream or in a large, slow-moving river? Explain.

3. Some soils have too much acid in them. Lime is often added to such soils. What do you think the lime does to these soils?

4. SCIENCE AND SOCIETY Name three different practices that farmers can use to prevent another Dust Bowl.

5. LIFE SCIENCE CONNECTION Explain why the peanut is a good crop to rotate. How does it affect soil quality?

4. A steep hill would be likely to miss the A horizon because this layer is likely to wash off a steep hill when it rains.

5. The rocks were weathered by the action of the moving water.

6. The floodwaters might leach out much of the nutrients that the farmer's crops will need.

PROBLEM SOLVING

Answers

1. Check the color of the soil. Soil rich in humus is dark in color. If the soil is rich in humus, you may not have to add anything to it. If the soil has little humus, you may have to add some peat moss or compost to the soil.

2. The soil probably contains mostly clay particles. Mix in some sand, which would separate the clay particles and increase the porosity of the soil.

3. Add peat moss or other absorbent organic material.

CONNECTING IDEAS

Answers

1. Only chemical weathering changes the chemical makeup of the rock materials.

2. They would break down more in the swiftly moving stream, because the faster water moves, the more rock particles it can carry. More moving rock particles would increase the rate of weathering.

3. The lime reacts chemically with the soils, reducing the acidity.

4. contour plowing, crop rotation, planting trees as windbreaks, planting ground cover when soil is not being used

5. The peanut is a good crop to rotate because it is a legume. This group of plants adds nitrogen to the soil.

CHAPTER ORGANIZER

SECTION	OBJECTIVES	ACTIVITIES/FEATURES
Chapter Opener		**Explore!** How can sediments move from one location to another? p. 505
17-1 Gravity (1 day)	1. **Distinguish** between erosion and deposition. 2. **Identify** creep and slump as erosion caused by gravity. 3. **Describe** rockslides and mudflows.	
17-2 Running Water (3 days)	1. **Explain** how streams carry sediment. 2. **Compare** the relationship between amount of sediment and rate of stream flow. 3. **Explain** how streams and rivers shape the land.	**Explore!** How can streams carry away rock and soil? p. 510 **Investigate 17-1:** Stream Erosion and Deposition, p. 512 **Skillbuilder:** Observing and Inferring, p. 513
17-3 Glaciers (3 days)	1. **Describe** how a glacier is formed. 2. **Differentiate** between the two major types of glaciers. 3. **Describe** how glaciers erode the land.	**Investigate 17-2:** How Do Glaciers Change the Land? p. 517 **Find Out!** How can glaciers make grooves in rocks? p. 518 **Skillbuilder:** Testing a Hypothesis, p. 520
17-4 Wind Erosion (2 days)	1. **Describe** how wind erodes and deposits sediment. 2. **Describe** how a dune is formed and how it moves. 3. **Identify** two factors that can decrease wind erosion.	**Explore!** Which particles can be readily carried by the wind? p. 521 **Find Out!** How do dunes move? p. 522 **Skillbuilder:** Observing and Inferring, p. 523
Expanding Your View		A Closer Look **Controlling Soil Erosion,** p. 525 Physics Connection **Eyes on the Planet,** p. 526 Science and Society **Developing the Land,** p. 527 History Connection **Puzzle Solved!** p. 529 Technology Connection **Cameras in Orbit,** p. 530

ACTIVITY MATERIALS

EXPLORE!	INVESTIGATE!	FIND OUT!
Page 505 waxed paper, sand, gravel, safety goggles **Page 510** instant coffee grains, salt, rice, paper plates, spray bottles, water **Page 521** aluminum foil, scissors	**Page 512** stream table, sand, pails, water, plastic hose, block of wood, screw clamps **Page 517** ice block containing sand, clay, and gravel; stream table; sand; lamp with reflector; ruler	**Page 518** sand and other small particles of soil, rocks, or gravel; container; water; ice cube trays; freezer; small piece of wood; safety goggles **Page 522** covered shoebox, scissors, flour, spoon, metric ruler, towel

Chapter 17

Shaping the Land

TEACHER CLASSROOM RESOURCES	OTHER RESOURCES
Study Guide, p. 59 **Critical Thinking/Problem Solving,** p. 25 **Multicultural Activities,** p. 37 **Take Home Activities,** p. 26 **Making Connections: Integrating Sciences,** p. 37 **Making Connections: Technology and Society,** p. 37 **Multicultural Activities,** p. 38	***STVS:** *Indian Pompeii,* Earth and Space (Disc 3, Side 2)
Study Guide, p. 60 **Making Connections: Across the Curriculum,** p. 37 **Activity Masters, Investigate 17-1,** p. 69-70 **How It Works,** p. 18	**Laboratory Manual,** pp. 101-102, Rivers **Laboratory Manual,** pp. 103-104, Transporting Soil Materials by Runoff ***STVS:** *Cutting Water,* Physics (Disc 1, Side 2) *Unusual Estuary,* Ecology (Disc 6, Side 1)
Study Guide, p. 61 **Activity Masters, Investigate 17-2,** p. 71-72	**Color Transparency and Master 33,** Glacial Erosional Features **Color Transparency and Master 34,** Glacial Depositional Features **Laboratory Manual,** pp. 105-108, Glaciation and Sea Level ***STVS:** *Meteorites in the Antarctic,* Earth Science (Disc 3, Side 1)
Study Guide, p. 62 **Concept Mapping,** p. 25 **Flex Your Brain,** p. 8 **Review and Assessment,** pp. 69-72	***STVS:** *Sand Blasting with Dry Ice,* Chemistry (Disc 2, Side 1) *Home Grown Tornadoes,* Earth and Space (Disc 3, Side 1) **Computer Test Bank**
	Spanish Resources **Cooperative Learning Resource Guide** **Lab and Safety Skills**

***Science and Technology Videodisc Series**

KEY TO TEACHING STRATEGIES

Teaching strategies have been coded for varying learning styles and abilities. As you review teaching strategies in the margin, the following designations will help you decide which activities are appropriate for your students.

- **L1** Level 1 activities are basic activities and should be within the ability range of all students.
- **L2** Level 2 activities are average activities and should be within the ability range of the average to above-average student.
- **L3** Level 3 activities are challenging activities designed for the ability range of above-average students.
- **LEP** LEP activities should be within the ability range of Limited English Proficiency students.
- **COOP LEARN** Cooperative Learning activities are designed for small group work.

ADDITIONAL MATERIALS

SOFTWARE	AUDIOVISUAL
Surface Water, IBM. *Glacial Landforms,* IBM. *Glaciers,* Compress.	*Erosion—Each Moving Grain,* film, UEVA. *Evidence for the Ice Ages,* film, EBEC.

Chapter 17

Shaping the Land

THEME DEVELOPMENT

The major theme of this chapter is stability and change. In each section, a different agent of erosion (gravity, water, ice, or wind) is described, along with the changes it makes in the landscape. The physical interaction between each of these agents and land results in erosion or deposition. The other theme of this chapter is energy. The agents of erosion are moving, so they have energy. This energy enables each agent to change the landscape.

CHAPTER OVERVIEW

In this chapter, students learn the basic concepts of erosion and deposition. They also learn about different types of erosion and deposition caused by gravity.

The effect of stream flow on erosion is presented. Students see how flowing water deposits sediments.

Students learn about continental and valley glaciers. How glaciers erode land is also presented.

Finally, students learn how wind forms dunes and causes soil erosion.

Tying to Previous Knowledge

Ask students to summarize quickly what they have learned in Chapter 16 about the effect of weathering on rock. Explain that erosion is a process of wearing away substances by something that is moving. Ask students to brainstorm some possible forces in nature that can cause erosion. Write their ideas and display them as students preview the section headings in this chapter to check their predictions.

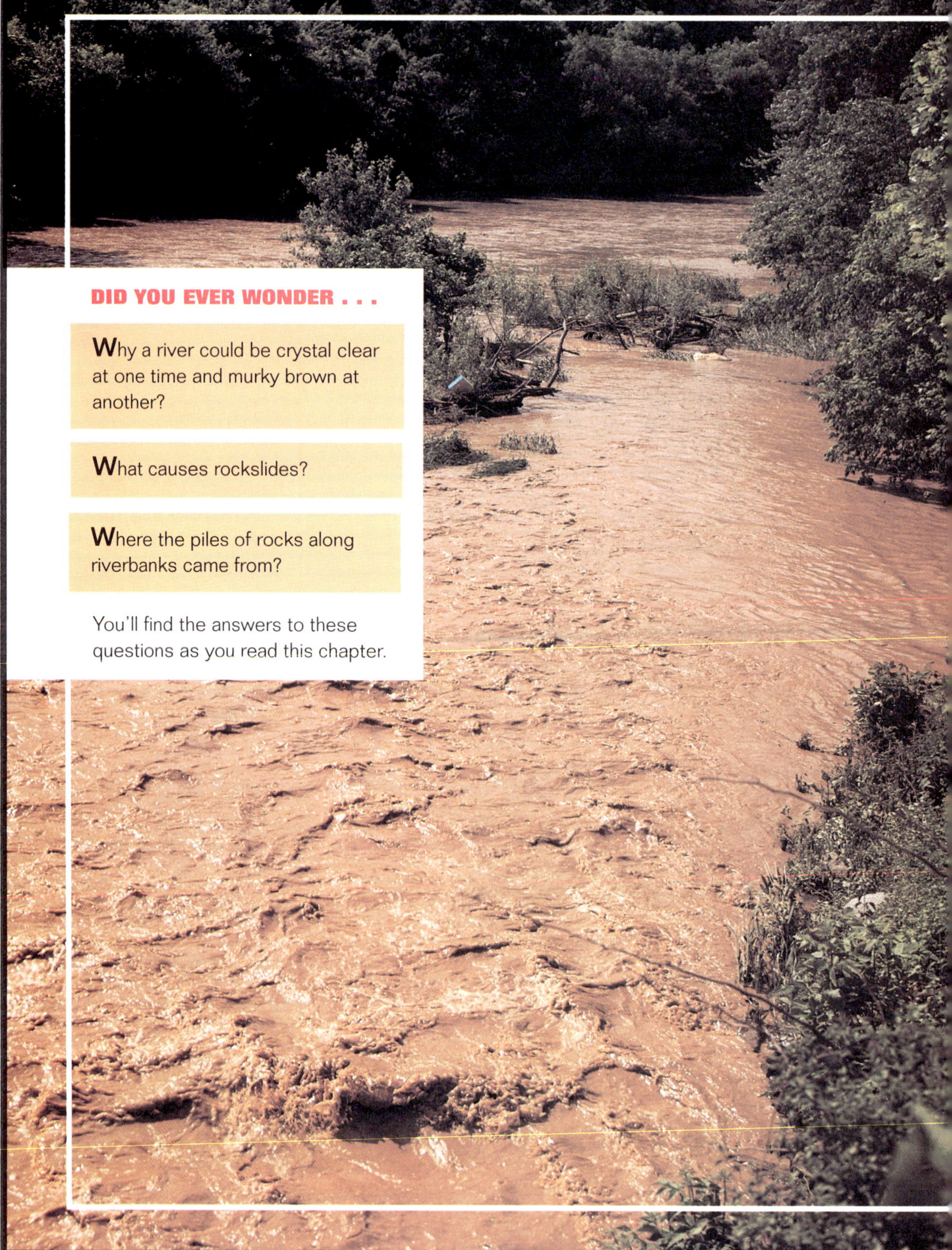

DID YOU EVER WONDER . . .

Why a river could be crystal clear at one time and murky brown at another?

What causes rockslides?

Where the piles of rocks along riverbanks came from?

You'll find the answers to these questions as you read this chapter.

DID YOU EVER WONDER...

Students will explore these questions as they progress through the chapter. Don't spoil their fun and motivation by sharing these answers too early.

- A river could be clear at one time and muddy at another because a heavy rainstorm might erode soil along the riverbank. The sediment would make the water appear muddy. (page 511)
- Gravity acting on a steep slope may combine with rain or an earthquake to cause a rockslide. (page 508)
- Weathering processes break large rocks into smaller rocks. Rocks move downslope by gravity or water and end up in streambeds. Rivers themselves also erode rock chunks and deposit them in piles along riverbanks. (page 513)

Chapter 17

Shaping the Land

Only two days ago, the river near Toshiko's house sparkled crystal clear. That was before the storms came and all the rain fell. Now the rock bridge she and her friends use to cross the river has disappeared beneath murky, chocolate-colored waters. Toshiko also notices that some of the river's bank has been swallowed up as well.

What caused the river to darken? What will happen to the rock bridge? Will the riverbank look the same after the water subsides?

You have already learned that rain, ice, and wind can change Earth through weathering. They can break up the largest, hardest rocks into small, fine particles of soil and other sediments. In this chapter, you will learn how the forces in nature such as water and wind not only can change but can actually carry away parts of Earth. You'll find out how human activities can have both destructive and constructive effects.

EXPLORE!

How can sediments move from one location to another?

Put a piece of waxed paper on a desk or table and place a small pile of sand and gravel on the paper. Devise ways of moving the sand from one place to another without touching it. How many different ways can you move the mixture? Do you think nature could move these sediments in the same way?

Introducing the Chapter

Ask students if they have ever observed a river undergo changes in depth, width, or color. Ask if they know the source of a nearby river.

Uncovering Preconceptions

Students may think that erosion is a process that only takes place over long periods of time, such as the action of glaciers. The following Explore activity will demonstrate that erosion can also occur rapidly.

EXPLORE!

How can sediments move from one location to another?

Time needed 15 minutes

Materials wax paper, sand, gravel, safety goggles

Thinking Process Making models

Purpose To model forces that cause erosion.

Preparation Have students wear safety goggles during this activity. Instruct them not to move the sand or gravel beyond the edges of the wax paper.

Teaching Strategies Provide water and materials such as drinking straws for students to experiment with. Do not provide specific suggestions about how to move the sand unless some students need assistance.

Discussion Have students identify the methods they used for moving the sand and gravel, such as flushing it with water, blowing on it, tilting the surface on which it is lying, or taking another object and pushing it.

Expected Outcomes

Students will begin to generalize air, water, and gravity as forces that contribute to erosion.

Answers to Questions

1. Students will devise a number of different ways to move the mixture.
2. Nature could also use air, water, and gravity to move sand.

Project

Divide students into teams to create a three-dimensional model of a valley or continental glacier and the landforms underneath them. Students might use materials such as clay or papier-mâché for this project. COOP LEARN

Science at Home

To observe the layers of material in a glacier, students can fill a milk carton with ice cubes, sand, dirt, gravel, and water. Have students freeze this mixture. Then they can observe it periodically as it melts in a dishpan tilted slightly on one end. Students should notice what happens to the sediment as the water runs off.

Section 17-1

PREPARATION

Concepts Developed

In the previous chapter, students explored the process of weathering. In this section, students will learn to distinguish between erosion and deposition and understand how gravity contributes to both processes. They will learn about the role of gravity and other conditions that lead to the development of slump and creep. They will also understand the nature of rockslides and mudflows.

Planning the Lesson

In planning your lesson on gravity, refer to the Chapter Organizer pages 504A-B for timing suggestions, resources, and additional materials that will help you in your presentation of the lesson concepts.

1 MOTIVATE

Activity Take students on a walk around the school grounds to search for sediments that have been transported, such as grit on curbs and dust on windowsills. Ask them to think about the sources of the sediments and how they were transported to the present location. Discuss the types of agents, such as wind or water, that could carry sediments away from one location and deposit them elsewhere.

17-1 Gravity

OBJECTIVES

In this section, you will

- distinguish between erosion and deposition;
- identify creep and slump as erosion caused by gravity;
- describe rockslides and mudflows.

KEY SCIENCE TERMS

erosion
deposition
creep
slump
rockslide
mudflow

THE JOURNEY BEGINS

In the Explore activity, you may have tilted the wax paper because you realized that sediment can move by itself from a higher to a lower place. Now, think about sliding down a hill on skis in the winter or on roller blades in the summer. Gravity helps you overcome the force of friction, and you slip down the slope with very little effort.

Recall that solid rock can be broken down into smaller pieces and changed into other materials as a result of weathering. When weathering occurs on hills and slopes, the resulting broken rocks can slide downhill just as you can. The movement of the products of weathering from where they formed to a different location is **erosion**. The four major causes of erosion are gravity, running water, glaciers, and wind. These are also known as agents of erosion. Throughout this chapter, you will discover how gravity, water, ice, and wind help erosion occur.

Eventually, your skis or roller blades come to a stop. In the same way, sediments will stop moving and pile up, or accumulate. This accumulation of eroded sediments is called **deposition**.

Figure 17-1 shows a good example of the erosion and deposition of land.

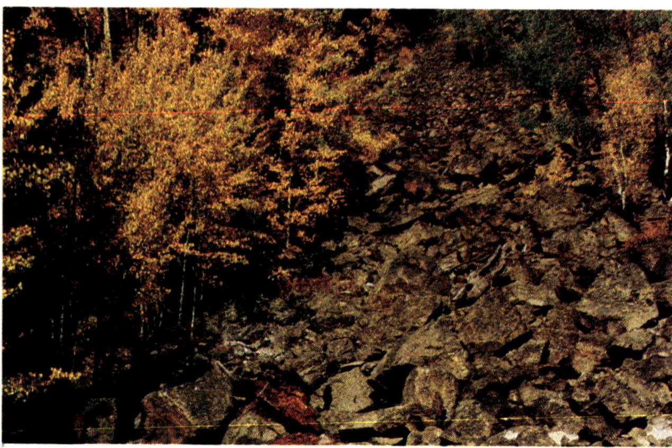

FIGURE 17-1. Gravity can cause large amounts of rocks and soil to move down a slope.

PROGRAM RESOURCES

Teacher Classroom Resources

Study Guide, page 59

Critical Thinking/Problem Solving, page 25, A Disappearing Civilization L2

Multicultural Activities, page 37, Aswan Dam L1; page 38, Disaster in Puerto Rico L1

Take Home Activities, page 26, Soil Erosion L1

PROGRAM RESOURCES

Teacher Classroom Resources

Making Connections: Integrating Sciences, page 37, Avalanches L2

Making Connections: Technology and Society, page 37, Shoreline Erosion L2

Other Resources

Erosion—Each Moving Grain, film, UEVA.

a

b

Gravel or large rocks may stop moving, while the soil continues moving beyond them. Can you explain why greater erosion occurs in more steeply sloped areas?

Now look at the photographs in Figure 17-2. You can see slopes and loose materials in each. Although gravity is the main cause of both cases of erosion shown, the rates of erosion are different.

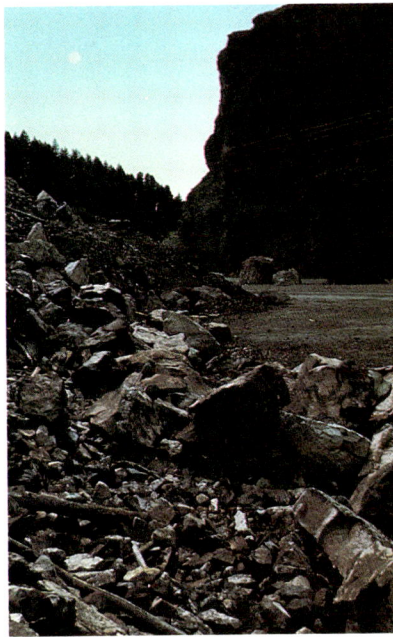

FIGURE 17-2. Movement of soil and rocks downslope can be slow (a) or rapid (b).

SLOW EROSION

The next time you travel by car or bus, look along the roadway for trees, utility poles, fenceposts, or other objects leaning downhill as in Figure 17-3. The tilt of these objects indicates that movement is happening. Trees and poles leaning downhill are especially common in areas where freezing and thawing occur. As the ground freezes, small soil particles are pushed up by ice expanding in the soil. Then, when the soil thaws, it falls downslope, often less than a millimeter at a time. Several years of soil moving downslope very slowly can cause objects such as utility poles and fenceposts to lean. This slow movement of soil downhill is called **creep**. Creep gets its name from the way soil slowly creeps down a hill.

FIGURE 17-3. Objects tilting in the same direction indicate that creep is occurring.

Sometimes one large mass of loose material or rock layers slips down

2 TEACH

Tying to Previous Knowledge

Remind students that they learned in Chapter 15 that water runs downhill due to gravity. Also review with them the ways that weathering breaks down soil, as they learned in Chapter 16. Be sure they understand that once weathering has broken rocks down into smaller pieces, they are more easily moved.

Concept Development

Theme Connection The theme that is supported by this section is stability and change. Point out to students that gravity, streams, glaciers, and wind are all forces that upset stability and change the form of land on Earth.

Inquiry Question Suppose you were purchasing property at the bottom of a hill. Why should you examine the bottom of the hill for sediments? *Sediment piled at the bottom would show that there have been previous landslides, and that there may be more.*

MAKING CONNECTIONS

Daily Life

Point out to students that there are examples of erosion or deposition in their daily lives. Ask if any of them have observed snowdrifts or sand dunes and ask what caused each. Ask whether each can cause erosion and under what conditions. *Sand blown by wind can scour the land. When snow melts it can form fast-moving streams that erode the land.*

OPTIONS

Meeting Individual Needs

Visually Impaired Allow students to use a variety of materials, such as sand, clay, pebbles, and talcum powder, to create models of different types of erosion discussed in the chapter. Students can vary the speed of flowing water and then feel the medium through which the water has flowed.

Enrichment

Discussion Invite an engineer to speak to the class about innovations in technology that are used to control erosion. Prior to this activity, have students suggest their own solution, the merits of which the engineer can discuss.

Concept Development

Using the Photos Ask students how the deposit from a mudflow differs from deposits made by slump, creep, and rockslides. Refer them to figures 17-3, 17-4, 17-5, and 17-6 in particular. *Mudflows spread out more.*

MAKING CONNECTIONS

Language Arts

Have students use dictionaries to look up the meanings of *slump* and *creep*. Have them demonstrate the verb forms and then relate them to the technical meanings used here to refer to erosion.

Discussion Ask students what slump, creep, rockslides and mudflows have in common. *All are examples of erosion on sloped surfaces.* Ask how these kinds of erosion differ. *Slump and creep are slow. Rockslides and mudflows are fast.*

FIGURE 17-4. Slump occurs when material slips downslope as one large mass, leaving a curved scar.

a steep slope but doesn't travel very far. This slow mass movement is called **slump**. Slump occurs because the material under the slumped material weakened. It could no longer support the material over it, so the overlying material slipped down the slope, as shown in Figure 17-4.

Although such movements are slow, over time they can reshape the lay of the land. Valleys may gradually widen by the slipping of soil down their sides, and the hills lining the valleys become more rounded and less steep.

FAST EROSION

How would you describe the slope shown in Figure 17-5? On a really steep slope like this, large blocks of rock can break loose and tumble quickly to the bottom. As they fall, these rocks crash into other rocks, and they too break loose. The mass movement of falling rocks is called a **rockslide**. Rockslides can be dangerous.

FIGURE 17-5. In a rockslide, erosion occurs quickly.

Where would you expect to find rockslides? If you think back about the landforms you studied in Chapter 1, you'll likely say mountains. Mountains are most likely to have steep, rocky slopes where this sudden mass movement could occur. You may have seen signs along the road warning you to beware of falling rocks. Rockslides happen most often after heavy rains or during earthquakes, but they can happen on any rocky slope at any time without warning. At the bottom of the cliff, piles of broken rock accumulate. This is a sign that a rockslide has occurred in the past and may occur in the future.

Have you ever molded a sand castle from a thick mixture of sand and water? Now

OPTIONS

Enrichment

Research Have students research and present oral reports on how creep, slump, rockslides, and mudflows can be prevented. Have each student select one of these topics.

Meeting Individual Needs

Gifted Ask students to create a crossword puzzle using the new science words presented in this chapter. Have students exchange puzzles to test each other's work.

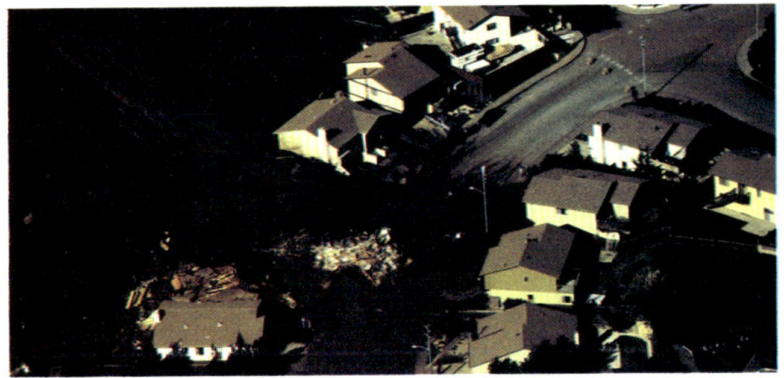

FIGURE 17-6. Here, a mudflow has destroyed at least one house and parts of others.

imagine a relatively dry area where weathering forms thick layers of dry sediments. When heavy rains fall in this area, the water mixes with the sediments and forms a thick, pasty substance that is like the wet sand you used to make your sand castle. A similar thick mixture forms when ash from an erupting volcano combines with water in a stream. Masses of such wet, heavy material will easily slide downhill in a **mudflow**. The flowing mud can move almost anything in its path, including cars and houses.

As a mudflow reaches the bottom of a slope, it slows down, eventually comes to rest, and deposits all the sediment and debris it has been carrying. Can you see in Figure 17-6 why mudflows are considered to be highly destructive?

Mudflows, rockslides, creep, and slump all occur on slopes. These types of erosion depend on gravity. Regardless of the type of movement, erosion will occur more often after a heavy rain because the water adds mass and allows the sediments to flow. What part do people play in causing erosion by gravity to occur?

FIGURE 17-7. Building on steep slopes can have severe consequences.

Check Your Understanding

1. How is erosion related to weathering?
2. Where is the deposition of sediment most likely to occur?
3. How can you identify creep and slump?
4. Why can rockslides and mudflows be dangerous?
5. **APPLY:** How might cutting into hillsides to build houses or roads affect erosion?

Concept Development

Student Text Questions Can you see in Figure 17-6 why mudflows are considered to be highly destructive? *The mudflow shown in Figure 17-6 has demolished at least one house and possibly parts of others.* What part do people play in causing erosion by gravity to occur? *By building structures on hillsides, naturally stable slopes are disturbed. This can lead to landslides.*

3 Assess

Check for Understanding

Ask students questions 1 through 4. Have students discuss the Apply question. Point out that some communities now restrict building on hillsides.

Reteach

Have students use the information in the text to make a table relating speed to the movement of slump, creep, rockslides, and mudflows.

Extension

Have students explore the connection between weathering and erosion as they relate to rockslides. Students should infer that materials on a slope do not fall if they are in a single mass. A solid rock cliff is fragmented by weathering processes. Chemical and mechanical weathering processes break the rock into small, unconsolidated pieces. Gravity causes the pieces of rock to fall.

4 Close

Discussion

Have students identify two major differences between fast and slow erosion. *speed of movement and mass of material moved*

Answers to Check Your Understanding

1. Erosion moves material from one place to another after it has been broken down by weathering.
2. Sediment is most likely to be deposited at the bottom of a steep slope.
3. You can identify creep by the tilted appearance of trees or posts on the surface of a slope. Slump can be identified by large cracks or scars where material has broken away.
4. They have the power to bury or move anything in their path.
5. Cutting steepens the angle of the slope, which increases erosion by gravity.

17-2 Running Water

OBJECTIVES

In this section, you will

- explain how streams carry sediment;
- explore the relationship between amount of sediment and rate of stream flow;
- explain how streams and rivers shape the land.

KEY SCIENCE TERMS

delta

STREAMS ERODE

You know that the force of gravity can erode rock and soil material from slopes and deposit it at lower places. Can anything else erode and deposit sediments? What factors cause loose material to travel down a slope?

EXPLORE!

How can streams carry away rock and soil?

Sprinkle some instant coffee grains, salt, and rice on a paper plate to represent loose soil and rock material.

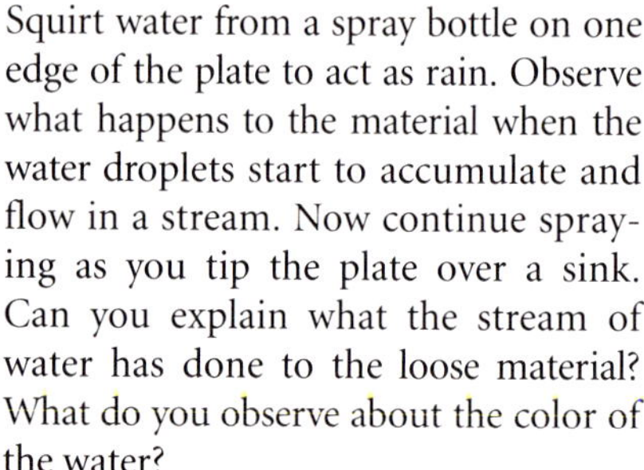

Squirt water from a spray bottle on one edge of the plate to act as rain. Observe what happens to the material when the water droplets start to accumulate and flow in a stream. Now continue spraying as you tip the plate over a sink. Can you explain what the stream of water has done to the loose material? What do you observe about the color of the water?

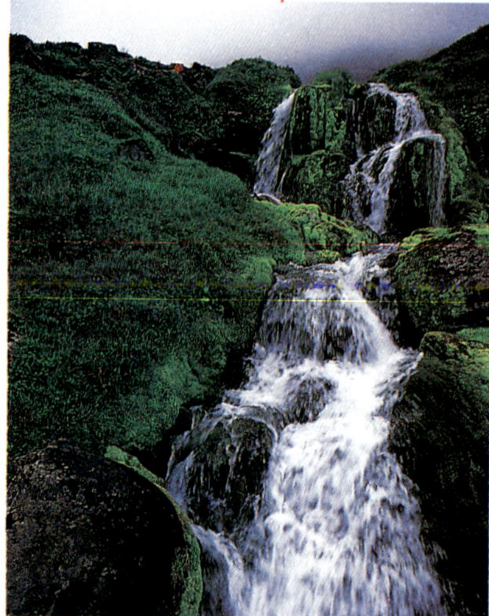

As you observed in the Explore activity, some loose material dissolves in water, while other material floats. As the water moves in a stream, loose material is carried away with it.

Now imagine following one small rock that landed in a creek at the bottom of a cliff after a rockslide. A heavy rain starts to fall. Soon the runoff begins to flow downhill in the creek and picks up speed. The small rock is lifted and carried along with the flowing water. This is one way that weathered rock particles get eroded. Water can move them.

The water in the creek is flowing quickly from a higher to a lower elevation. The rock and other sediments in the

Section 17-2

PREPARATION

Concepts Developed

In the previous section, students learned about how gravity contributes to fast and slow erosion. In this section, they will discover the combined effect of gravity and water on erosion, including how streams carry sediment, factors affecting the rate of flow in streams, and the relationship between load and rate of stream flow. Students will also study the effect of streams and rivers on shaping the land, forming alluvial fans and deltas.

Planning the Lesson

In planning your lesson on the effects of running water, refer to the Chapter Organizer on pages 504A-B for timing suggestions, resources, and additional materials that will help you in your presentation of the lesson concepts.

For adequate development of the concepts presented in this section, we recommend that students do the Investigate activity and Skillbuilder on pages 512 and 513.

1 MOTIVATE

Activity Take students outside to look for evidence of water erosion around the school grounds. They might find small channels on the sides of slopes or low, flat areas where fine sediments have been deposited.

EXPLORE!

How can streams carry away rock and soil?

Time needed 15 minutes

Materials clothing protection, instant coffee, salt, rice, paper plates, spray bottles with water

Thinking Process
Observing and inferring

PROGRAM RESOURCES

Teacher Classroom Resources

Study Guide, page 60

Laboratory Manual, pages 101-102, Rivers L1; pages 103-104, Transporting Soil Materials by Runoff L2

Making Connections: Across the Curriculum, page 37, Floods L2

OPTIONS

Meeting Individual Needs

Learning Disabled Have students make a picture dictionary of erosion terminology discussed in the chapter. Pictures may be cut from old magazines or students may prefer to make their own drawings.

water roll and scrape against the sides and bottom of the stream channel, knocking loose even more sediments. Therefore, water in streams and rivers not only carries sediment, but it also creates sediment.

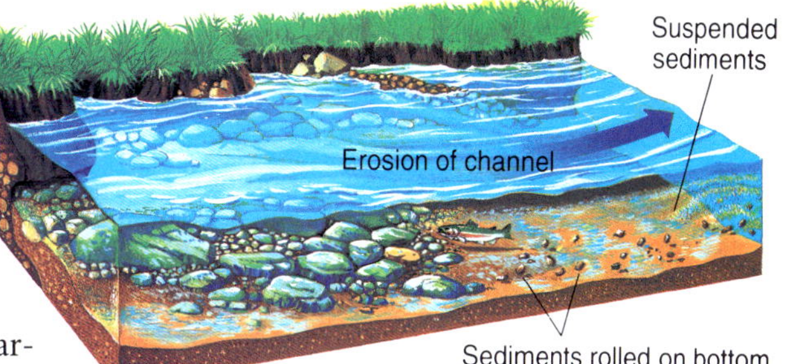

FIGURE 17-8. This cross section of a stream channel shows how a stream erodes.

Now more bits of rock and particles are eroded away by the water and the tumbling, scraping rocks it carries. The swiftly flowing water you see in Figure 17-8 shows the great eroding ability of a stream. The water in a stream is able to carry a great amount of sediment. As it erodes rock and soil along its bottom and sides, the stream cuts a deeper and wider channel.

Water in a stream flows faster when the slope of the stream is increased. It also flows faster when the volume of water is increased. When more water is added to a stream as it combines with other streams, it speeds up. As you can see in Figure 17-9, an increase in runoff from rainfall can have the same effect.

You may remember from Chapter 15 that streams flowing swiftly down a steep hill may eventually reach less sloping ground and flow less swiftly. As the rate of flow slows, it changes the way that a stream erodes. Investigate to find out how.

FIGURE 17-9. The same stream is shown before (a) and after (b) a heavy rain. Note how swiftly the rain-swollen river moves.

a 

b  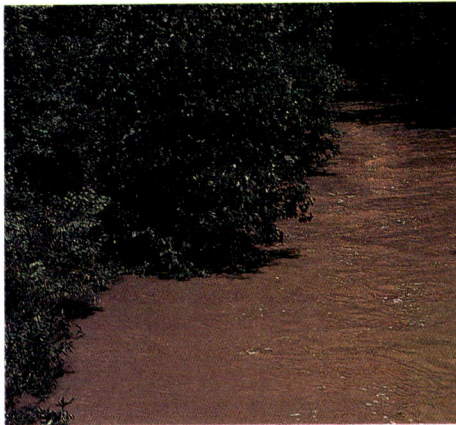

Purpose To discover that streams can dissolve and erode sediments.

Preparation Have students work in teams, assigning the following tasks to individuals: set up, sprayer, observer, cleanup. COOP LEARN

Teaching Strategies

Provide waste cans for discarding coffee grains and rice to avoid clogging the sink.

Expected Outcomes

Students will observe that some of the sediment is dissolved (salt); some is partly dissolved (coffee); and other sediment is carried away (rice).

Answers to Questions

1. Material has been moved "downhill" and/or dissolved.
2. One "sediment," coffee, changed the color of the water.

2 Teach

Tying to Previous Knowledge

Have students recall the importance of water in weathering sediments. In this section, they will learn that once weathered, sediments can also be eroded by water.

Concept Development

Theme Connection The theme supported by this section is stability and change, since running water as a force of erosion is an agent of change. Discuss with students the ways the theme of energy is also related to the topic of water erosion, in particular the effects of the energy transferred by running water.

Using the Photos Discuss with students the differences in the river shown in the photographs in Figure 17-9. Point out that after the rain, the river looks muddy, since it carrics more sediments.

Multicultural Perspectives

Tell students that ancient cities developed along the Nile River in Egypt and in Mesopotamia between the Tigris and Euphrates rivers. In both places, the fertile river floodplains led to the development of highly advanced cultures. In ancient Egypt, the calendar was based on the agricultural cycle. The first of their three seasons was called Inundation, and the first day of the year was the day when the river could be expected to flood. The flood left behind rich deposits, in which seeds were sown. The second season was called Sprouting, and the third was called Harvest.

INVESTIGATE!

17-1 STREAM EROSION AND DEPOSITION

Time needed 30–40 minutes

Materials plastic hose, pails with water, block of wood, stream table, sand, screw clamps

Thinking Processes
Separating and controlling variables, Recognizing cause and effect

Purpose To discover how the rate of flow affects erosion and deposition of sediments.

Preparation If time is limited, you may wish to set up the materials before class.

Teaching Strategies

Discussion Begin the activity by having students predict how the meanders in the stream might be affected by the water flow. List these predictions on the chalkboard for comparison after the experiment.

Student Journal You may prefer to have students record their predictions in their journals. Students should also record their data and observations in their journals.

Expected Outcome

Students will discover how streams erode and deposit sediments.

Answers to Analyze/Conclude and Apply

1. In the first trial, the meanders grew slightly as they were eroded by water. In the second trial, erosion and widening of the meanders were much faster as water flow was increased.
2. Sediments that had been carried by the flowing water were deposited.
3. The increased water flow caused an increase in the rate of erosion. This caused the meanders to enlarge faster.
4. It was deposited on the inside of the next meander.
5. The water moves more slowly at this point.
6. The water moves more slowly in the lake, and cannot carry much sediment.
7. near the point where it enters the sea

I N V E S T I G A T E !

17-1 STREAM EROSION AND DEPOSITION

You learned in Chapter 15 that streams are affected by the land's slope. Slope also affects the way a stream erodes and deposits sediments. You will **observe** the erosion and deposition of a stream on a gradual slope that flows into a large body of water.

PROBLEM

How do streams erode and deposit sediments?

MATERIALS 

stream table
sand
pails with water
plastic hose
block of wood
screw clamps

PROCEDURE

1. Set up a stream table and other materials as shown.
2. Smooth out sand at the upper end of the stream table. The lower part of the stream table will be the lake that your stream will flow into.
3. In the sand, use a block of wood to carve out a stream channel for a stream of water to flow through. Put some slight meanders in the channel.
4. Start water flowing in the stream. **Predict** what will happen to the stream channel, especially at the meanders. **Observe** and record the results.
5. Increase the water flow into the stream. **Observe** and record what happens to the stream channel. Also **observe** what has happened where the stream flows into the lake at the lower end of the stream table.

ANALYZE

1. Describe what happened to the meanders in your two trials.
2. What happened where the water entered the lake?
3. **Determine the effect** that increasing the amount of water flow had.

CONCLUDE AND APPLY

4. What happened to the sand that was eroded from one part of a meander?
5. Why was sand deposited there?
6. Why do you think sand accumulated where the stream flowed into the lake?
7. **Going Further**: Where might the greatest amount of sediment be found along a river's course—at its beginning, along its middle , or near the point where it empties into the sea?

FIGURE 17-10. A meandering river erodes and widens its valley, depositing sediments on its floodplain at times of floods.

The Investigate activity demonstrated how moving water on a gentle slope erodes the outside curves of a river instead of cutting downward into the streambed. If the river continues to meander in snakelike bends, it will erode its valley walls and widen the valley. If the volume of water in the river increases, the erosion increases.

STREAMS DEPOSIT SEDIMENT

Look at the river curving across the valley floor in Figure 17-10. What happens when this river floods? You know that runoff from heavy rains can cause a river to overflow its banks. During floods, a river carries a larger than normal amount of sediment. Bulky, heavy sediments are dropped along the banks of the river, forming ridges. Finer, lighter sediments travel out beyond the river channel onto the floodplain. Because these light sediments contain minerals and rich topsoil, they make the floodplain a fertile area for planting.

Moving water deposits sediments even when the volume of water in the river is not increased. As a river starts to slow down, it eventually does not flow fast enough to continue carrying heavier, bulkier sediments. So, the river begins to deposit them. Slow-moving water is still able to carry fine, light sediments, however. Often sediments are deposited when the river empties into a body of water, such as a bay or lake. The deposited sediments may form a triangular-shaped land area called a **delta**.

SKILLBUILDER

OBSERVING AND INFERRING

Imagine you are at the bottom of a canyon. You observe that its walls consist of reddish brown sandstone. You also observe that the water in the river has a similar reddish brown color. How would you use your observations to explain the formation of this canyon? If you need help, refer to the **Skill Handbook** on page 652.

SKILLBUILDER

Students should infer that the water contains sediments of eroded sandstone from the canyon wall. They should assume that the canyon was formed by the river's erosion over thousands of years.

Concept Development

Discussion The relationship between rate of speed and amount of deposition might be likened to a blizzard. When winds are very high, snow travels almost horizontally and little is deposited until the wind hits an obstruction such as a house, a tree, or a hill. In a sense, the wind stops and great drifts of snow form. However, if the same amount of snow were to fall on a windless day, the deposition would be uniform across the land.

MAKING CONNECTIONS

Language Arts

Have students use a dictionary to find out how deltas got their name. They will discover that both the Greek capital letter and the sediment deposit have a triangular shape.

Teacher F.Y.I.

Approximately 12 percent of the population of the United States lives on land that floods periodically.

PROGRAM RESOURCES

Teacher Classroom Resources

Activity Masters, pages 69-70, Investigate 17-1

How It Works, page 18, Locks

L2

Other Resources

Surface Water, software, IBM

OPTIONS

Enrichment

Activity Discuss with students places in the community where they have observed evidence of water erosion. Encourage interested students to take photographs or make drawings of some of these places, showing the effect of water erosion.

3 Assess

Check for Understanding

Ask students questions 1 through 4. Have students discuss the Apply question. Encourage them to think about how this construction might affect farmland in the delta area.

Reteach

Demonstration Pour water into the deep end of a paint tray and cover the top of the tray with fine soil. Gently pour water from a beaker onto the soil at the top of the tray. Students will observe the formation of a delta.

Extension

Have students write a short report on the evolution of the Mississippi Delta, emphasizing the relationship between sediment size and distance from the source.

4 Close

Activity

Discuss why people would be likely to build farms in or near a flood plain although the area is likely to flood on a regular basis. Guide students to understand that the sediment deposited there helps create rich topsoil, which is excellent for farming.

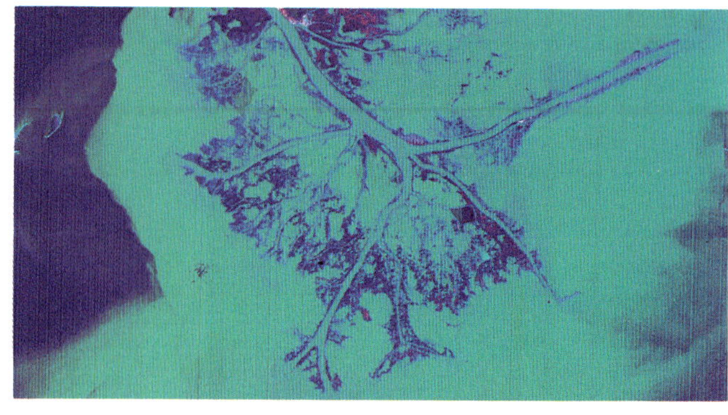

FIGURE 17-11. A satellite image of the Mississippi River Delta shows how the river's sediments accumulate where it enters a gulf. Sediments of the delta appear pink in this image.

THE MIGHTY MISSISSIPPI

Let's use the Mississippi River system to review how rivers erode Earth's surface. Thousands of smaller streams flow quickly from higher elevations into larger streams and rivers. These small, swift-moving streams erode sediments from the bottoms of their channels. As the larger streams and rivers reach gradually sloping ground, they slow down. When they finally reach the Mississippi River, they are flowing on flatter areas and beginning to meander.

The Mississippi River itself cuts into its banks, widens its valley, and picks up more sediment. As you can see in Figure 17-12, the slow-moving Mississippi carries a great volume of water and large amounts of sediment. Eventually, at the Gulf of Mexico, it loses most of its sediment and forms a delta on the Louisiana coast. This is the delta pictured in Figure 17-11.

FIGURE 17-12. An old-fashioned riverboat is shown here on the broad, slow-moving Mississippi River.

Check Your Understanding

1. How do rivers cause erosion?
2. How does slope affect the amount of sediment the stream can carry?
3. How do rivers shape valleys and deltas?
4. **APPLY:** How could the construction of a dam upriver affect a delta?

Answers to Check Your Understanding

1. The flowing water in rivers picks up and carries sediment.
2. An increase in slope increases the rate of stream flow, which enables it to carry a larger load of sediment.
3. Streams on steep slopes erode downward, carving deep, straight valleys. Slow-moving streams widen valleys. Streams deposit sediments when they enter larger bodies of water, forming deltas.
4. A dam would change the river's rate of flow and affect the river's ability to carry sediments. The delta would eventually wear away because sediments could not be replaced.

17-3 Glaciers

WHAT ARE GLACIERS?

What would it be like to live at a time when every winter is longer and colder than the one before? Every summer would be shorter and cooler—until eventually there would be almost no summer at all. This is what the climate was like over a million years ago, during the last ice age. Then ice covered much of the land.

An ice age is a period of time when ice and snow cover much of Earth's surface. There have been a number of ice ages in Earth's history. The last ice age ended about 10,000 years ago. Yet huge masses of moving snow and ice called glaciers still cover parts of Earth. In fact, glaciers cover about one-tenth of Earth's land. Moving glaciers make enormous changes in Earth's surface. Melting glaciers provide much of the water that flows into rivers. These rivers, in turn, erode and change the land. In addition, many people depend on this melted ice for their water supply.

OBJECTIVES

In this section, you will

- describe how a glacier is formed;
- differentiate between the two major types of glaciers;
- describe how glaciers erode the land.

KEY SCIENCE TERMS

continental glaciers
valley glaciers

How Do Glaciers Form?

Have you ever seen ice build up on the freezer walls of an old refrigerator? The same thing can happen in nature where there is snow year-round. If the snow doesn't melt during the summer, it begins to pile up just as frost can pile up in a freezer. As the snow accumulates, the weight of the top layers of snow becomes great enough to compress the bottom layers into ice. When the accumulated snow is about 50 or 60 meters high, the bottom layers partially melt, and the whole mass begins to flow slowly downhill.

FIGURE 17-13. This map shows the extent of glaciers in North America during the last ice age.

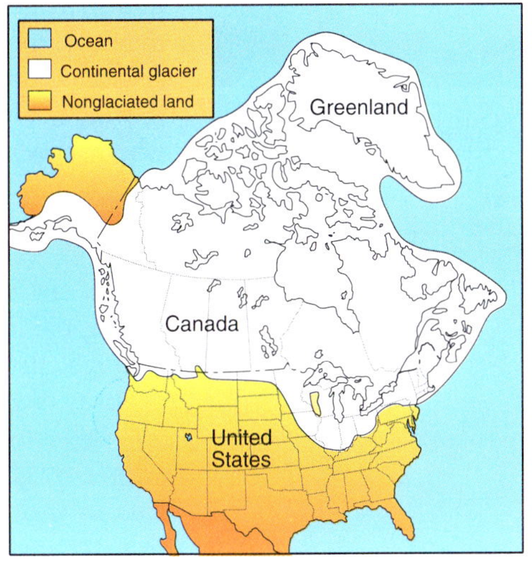

Types of Glaciers

Masses of ice and snow that cover large land areas near Earth's polar regions are called **continental glaciers**. Today, continental glaciers, like the one shown in

Section 17-3

PREPARATION

Concepts Developed

In this section, students learn about glaciers, another important agent of erosion that has extensively shaped Earth's topography. Students will learn the characteristics of continental and valley glaciers and discover how Earth is affected by their movement.

Planning the Lesson

In planning your lesson on glaciers, refer to the Chapter Organizer on pages 504A-B for timing suggestions, resources, and additional materials that will help you in your presentation of the lesson concepts.

For adequate development of the concepts presented in this section, we recommend that students do the Investigate and Find Out activities on pages 517 and 518.

1 MOTIVATE

Discussion Ask students who have ice-skated if they have noticed that the ice gets scratched and grooved when skaters have been on it. Explain that this is the result of the skaters' weight on the skate blades causing pressure that makes the ice melt under the blades, forming grooves in the ice. The thin layer of water that results acts as a lubricant and helps skaters glide across the ice. This is similar to the phenomenon that enables glaciers to move.

2 TEACH

Tying to Previous Knowledge

Have students recall that water can exist in three states (solid, liquid, and gas). For the most part, a glacier is a solid, but its bottom layers flow and are deformed by the pressure of the overlying ice.

PROGRAM RESOURCES

Teacher Classroom Resources

Study Guide, page 61

Transparency Masters, pages 69-72, and **Color Transparency** number 33, Glacial Erosional Features L2; number 34, Glacial Depositional Features L2

OPTIONS

Enrichment

Student Journals Have students write in their journals about what it might have been like to live during the Ice Age. Encourage creativity, but insist that the scientific content of the stories is accurate.

Concept Development

Uncovering Preconceptions Ask students to guess how much the average world temperature would need to drop before Earth would undergo another ice age. They are likely to guess a large number of degrees. In reality, an average 2.3° C drop in the ocean and a 6.5° C average drop on the land temperature would be enough to produce a new ice age.

Theme Connection The actions of glaciers should provide students with evidence of the theme of stability and change. You might have students preview the illustrations in this section as you tell them that the movement of glaciers affects the evolution of land surfaces, changing surface and structure of landmasses. The activities in this section give students experience with models of change due to glacial action.

MAKING CONNECTIONS

Social Studies

Explain to students that scientists have hypothesized that during the last ice age, people traveled from Asia to North America across a land bridge. Have students locate the Bering Strait on a map. Then ask them to suggest why there is no bridge today. *During the ice age, much of Earth's water was frozen in glaciers, leaving more land exposed. Today the land bridge across the Bering Strait is below sea level.*

FIGURE 17-14. Antarctica is covered by continental glaciers.

FIGURE 17-15. Valley glaciers form between mountain peaks in areas where snow accumulates each year.

Figure 17-14, are found only in Greenland and in Antarctica. They make up about 96 percent of glacial ice.

Glaciers can also be found at high elevations in mountain regions. That's because the climate gets colder as elevation increases. Notice how the glacier in Figure 17-15 is different from the continental glacier in Figure 17-14. This glacier occupies a single valley between mountains. Huge, moving masses of ice and snow that form at high elevations where snow stays year after year are called **valley glaciers**.

GLACIAL EROSION

You saw how glaciers covered large portions of land during the last ice age. As they moved, these glaciers cut through mountains, eroded the land, and left large deposits of ground-up rock. As the glaciers melted, rivers and lakes formed. Much of Earth's landscape has been shaped by glacial ice. You learned in the last chapter how ice can weather hard rock. Now investigate how erosion by ice changes the land.

OPTIONS

Multicultural Perspectives

Cape Cod, a hook-shaped peninsula in Massachusetts, was formed by a glacier. A storm in 1991 eroded a beach there, uncovering a Native American site that was inhabited about 8,000 years before the Pilgrims landed nearby. Evidence of buildings was found there, but other coastal storms eroded some of the site before it was completely excavated.

Enrichment

Research Have students find photographs of the Palisades, a set of sheer cliffs along the Hudson River near New York City. Ask them to find out how the river valley and cliffs were formed.

I N V E S T I G A T E !

17-2 HOW DO GLACIERS CHANGE THE LAND?

Glaciers erode the land and can change it a great deal. In this activity, you'll **observe** how glaciers change the land as they erode Earth's surface.

PROBLEM

How do valley glaciers affect Earth's surface?

MATERIALS

ice block containing sand, clay, and gravel
stream table with sand
lamp with reflector
ruler

PROCEDURE  

1. Copy the data table. Then set up the stream table and lamp as shown.
2. Make a V-shaped river channel. **Measure** and record its width and depth. Draw a sketch that includes these measurements.
3. Place the ice block at the upper end of the stream table.
4. Gently push the glacier along the river channel until it's under the light, halfway between the top and bottom of the stream table.
5. Turn on the light and allow the ice to melt. **Observe** and record what happens.
6. **Measure** and record the width and depth of the glacial channel. Draw a sketch of the channel and include these measurements.

DATA AND OBSERVATIONS

	WIDTH	DEPTH	OBSERVATION
River			
Glacier			

ANALYZE

1. How can you **infer** the direction from which a glacier traveled?
2. How can you tell how far down the valley the glacier traveled?

CONCLUDE AND APPLY

3. **Determine the effect** valley glaciers have on the surface over which they move.
4. **Going Further**: How can you identify land that was once covered by a glacier?

PROGRAM RESOURCES

Teacher Classroom Resources

Laboratory Manual, pages 105-108, Glaciation and Sea Level L2

Activity Masters, pages 71-72, Investigate 17-2 

INVESTIGATE!

17-2 HOW DO GLACIERS CHANGE THE LAND?

Time needed 30–40 minutes

Materials eye and clothing protection; ice block of sand, gravel, and clay; stream table with sand; ruler; lamp with reflector; pail

Thinking Processes
Observing and inferring, Making and interpreting tables

Purpose To observe how valley glaciers erode the surface of Earth.

Preparation Prepare the trays of ice a day ahead.

Teaching the Activity

Student Journal Suggest that students record the data in a table in their journals.

Troubleshooting Set up the reflector lamp so that it provides enough energy to melt the ice, but so that students will not get burned by it.

Expected Outcome

Students will observe that the model glacier left deposits and eroded the stream channel.

Answers to Analyze/Conclude and Apply

1. The area where the glacier has been will probably be smoother and have steeper sides than the section it has not eroded.
2. The channel will be U-shaped to the point where the glacier stopped, and V-shaped past that point. Small hills of deposits will be left at the end of the glacier.
3. Valley glaciers erode the surface like a bulldozer, leaving a U-shaped valley with steep sides and a flat bottom.
4. Glaciers leave behind characteristic deposits and patterns of erosion.

FIND OUT!

How can glaciers make grooves in rocks?

Time needed overnight for ice to freeze; 15 minutes in class

Materials eye and clothing protection, ice trays, water, sand, wood, gravel

Thinking Process
Observing and inferring

Purpose To observe how glaciers can erode soil and rock.

Preparation Prepare ice trays a day ahead.

Teaching the Activity

Troubleshooting Tell students to avoid scraping the ice cubes against other surfaces such as desktops, which may get scratched.

Expected Outcome

Students will observe how rough matter trapped in the model glaciers can scratch the surfaces they rub against.

Conclude and Apply

1. The ice cubes left scratches in the wood's surface.
2. Sediment along the bottom of the glacier scratches the soil and rock it moves over.

FIGURE 17-16. The brown streaks in this glacier in Canada are long ridges of sediment being deposited as the glacier recedes.

As you saw in the Investigate, a glacier acts like a bulldozer as it moves over land, pushing loose materials out of its path. These eroded sediments are added to the mass of the glacier or are piled up along its sides. Figure 17-16 shows ridges that formed when a glacier receded and deposited rocks and sediments. You can see hills or ridges like this in places that were once the sides or ends of a glacier.

Glaciers do more than just move sediments. They also weather and erode rock and soil that aren't loose. Glacial ice melts, and the water flows down into cracks in rocks. Later, the water refreezes in these cracks and expands. The freezing water breaks the rock into pieces. The rock fragments then move along with the glacial ice. This process results in boulders, gravel, and sand being added to the bottom and sides of a glacier. Find out how this matter frozen in glacial ice can cause further erosion.

DID YOU KNOW?

The Great Lakes were formed by glacial ice that covered the area from about 250,000 to 11,000 years ago.

FIND OUT!

How can glaciers make grooves in rocks?

Mix sand and other small particles of soil, rocks, or gravel in a container of water. Pour the mixture into an ice cube tray and place the tray in a freezer. Let each frozen cube represent a glacier.

Remove the cubes from the freezer. After leaving the cubes at room temperature for a few moments, feel their texture. You should feel the grains of sand and small particles. Rub the cubes over a small piece of wood.

OPTIONS

Meeting Individual Needs

Visually Impaired Visually impaired students should be able to participate fully in this activity because setup and observation of results are tactile rather than visual.

Enrichment

Activity Have students work in groups to prepare a chart showing types of glaciers, the kind of erosion they are likely to cause, where they might occur, and when they were commonly found on Earth. COOP LEARN

Conclude and Apply

1. What do you observe in the wood's surface?
2. Can you now explain how glaciers make similar grooves in rocks?

In the Find Out activity, you saw how particles frozen in ice scratched a piece of wood. In the same way, materials at the base of a glacier scrape the soil and bedrock over which the glacier moves. The loose particles can cause even more erosion than the ice and snow alone. When bedrock is gouged by rock fragments, grooves like the ones you see in Figure 17-17 may be left behind. Usually these scratches are long, parallel scars like the grooves shown in the photograph.

In the Investigate activity, you discovered that valley glaciers erode land and deposit sediments as they move down mountain slopes. Valleys eroded by glaciers are a different shape from valleys eroded by streams. You learned in Chapter 15 that stream-eroded valleys are normally V-shaped because the water in a stream erodes downward into its channel. Glacier-eroded valleys like the

DID YOU KNOW?

85 percent of all the fresh water on Earth is in the form of glaciers and ice sheets such as the one that covers Antarctica.

FIGURE 17-17. These grooves gouged into bedrock at Kelleys Island, Ohio, are 10 m wide and 5 m deep.

Concept Development

Discussion Glaciers leave behind deposits of rock materials that have been carried for great distances. Ask students how they might decide if rock debris had been left behind by a glacier. *If the loose rock is different from local types of rock, it has been brought from another area. This could have been caused by a glacier. If it is similar to local rock it was probably weathered from local rocks.*

MAKING CONNECTIONS

Fine Arts

The cave paintings in Altimira, Spain, and Lascaux, France, were painted by Ice Age hunters. During the Ice Age, glaciation was widespread. Photos of cave paintings can be found in an encyclopedia or anthropology book. Ask students what they believe the paintings mean. Anthropologists believe that the paintings were created to bring good hunting.

Content Background

When continental glaciers recede they leave large chunks of ice, similar to icebergs. Sediment from the glacier is deposited around the ice chunks. When the ice chunks melt, the water fills in the holes in the surrounding sediment, creating lakes. These are called kettle lakes because of their shape.

Teacher F.Y.I.

In 1991, a well-preserved human body was discovered in a glacier between Italy and Austria. Because the ice had preserved the body so well, anthropologists could see that the 4,600-year-old man had stuffed his leather boots with straw for insulation. Found with the man were a bow and arrows, as well as flint and copper tools.

PROGRAM RESOURCES

Other Resources

Evidence for the Ice Ages, film, EBEC

Walker, Sally M. *Glaciers: Ice on the Move.* Minneapolis, MN: Carolrhoda Books, Inc., 1990

SKILLBUILDER

Students might try freezing blocks of ice of different thicknesses and comparing the amount of erosion they cause by pushing them along in sand on a stream table.

3 Assess

Check for Understanding

Ask students questions 1 through 3. Have them discuss the Apply question. Use the U.S. map in Appendix G on page 640-641 to help students locate the Great Lakes.

Reteach

Activity Have individual students push an ice cube into a pile of sand. Have them note what happens to the sand that was in the path of the ice. Relate this form of erosion to the action of a glacier as it erodes layers of soil in its way.

Extension

Have students use a map or globe to predict what the future shoreline of North America might be if global warming caused the ice caps in Greenland and Antarctica to melt. Have them draw diagrams that show the new shoreline. The sketches should show much of the East and Gulf coasts of the United States under water.

4 Close

Display a map of the Finger Lakes region of New York State. Use a road map of the state or a map in an atlas. Tell students that the land in the area was once covered by a continental glacier. Ask how that information helps explain the formation of the elongated lakes in the area.

FIGURE 17-18. A U-shaped valley formed by a glacier differs from the V-shaped valleys formed by water erosion.

one you see in Figure 17-18 are usually U-shaped. They have this shape because glaciers pick up and drag soil and rock fragments along their sides as well as on their bottoms. Also, glaciers tend to erode downward into underlying rock less than streams do.

You had to imagine what life on Earth was like long ago when much of it was covered by ice and snow, but you don't have to imagine the changes that were made. Many of the U-shaped valleys, rivers, and hills that were formed when ice age glaciers eroded the land and deposited sediments still exist today. The huge amounts of frozen snow and ice that remain in today's continental glaciers and valley glaciers provide us with a supply of fresh water.

SKILLBUILDER

TESTING A HYPOTHESIS
Do all glaciers erode in the same way? Do thicker glaciers erode more than less thick glaciers? Devise an experiment that would test the effect the thickness of a glacier would have on erosion. If you need help, refer to the **Skill Handbook** on page 657.

Check Your Understanding

1. How can snowfall lead to the formation of a glacier?
2. How can valley glaciers form in places where continental glaciers could not?
3. How do scientists know which areas were once covered by glaciers during the ice age?
4. **APPLY:** Explain how the Great Lakes could have been formed by a glacier.

Answers to Check Your Understanding

1. In areas where the snow does not melt completely it piles up, forming a heavy layer. The weight of the top snow exerts pressure on the layers below, hardening them into ice.
2. Valley glaciers generally form at higher elevations. Although the sea level temperature at a particular latitude may be too warm for a continental glacier, winter snow may not completely melt during the summer at high elevations.
3. They can observe the glacial deposits and landforms.
4. As a continental glacier pushed south, it could have gouged out the depressions that are now the Great Lakes. Then melting glacial ice could have filled the depressions with fresh water.

17-4 Wind Erosion

UP, UP, AND AWAY!

Trying to eat a picnic lunch on the beach can be a challenge. Light items like napkins, plastic sandwich bags, paper cups, and potato chips blow away easily if the wind is strong. You may try to recover them as they bounce or roll away, only to find them useless because they are covered with sand. Can the same wind that blows your lunch away cause erosion? Find out the answer to this question.

OBJECTIVES

In this section, you will

- describe how wind erodes and deposits sediment;
- describe how a dune is formed and how it moves;
- identify two factors that can decrease wind erosion.

KEY SCIENCE TERMS

dune

EXPLORE!

Which particles can be readily carried by the wind?

Cut a sheet of aluminum foil into a variety of large and small sizes. Then form the pieces into assorted shapes. Crumble some of the pieces of foil into loose balls, some into tight balls, and leave other pieces flat. Put the assortment of aluminum shapes on a table and blow at them. Which pieces move more readily? How do the size and shape of materials affect their ability to be transported by the moving air?

As you saw in the Explore activity, moving air can move loose particles. Particles that were too heavy to lift were dragged along the surface of the table. Others were light enough to be picked up and carried by the air. Wind can move sand, clay, silt, and other loose sediments in the same ways.

WIND CHANGES THE LAND

When wind erodes loose sediments by blowing them away, it eventually deposits the sediments when it stops blowing. This deposition can create new features on the land. For example, sand or loose sediment may be blown by the wind into a formation called a **dune.** Look at the

Section 17-4

PREPARATION

Concepts Developed

In this section, students learn about wind erosion. They will study how the wind moves particles of sediment and deposits them, as well as how the abrasive action of particles in wind erodes objects. The section describes how sand dunes move and identifies techniques for controlling wind erosion.

Planning the Lesson

In planning your lesson on erosion caused by wind, refer to the Chapter Organizer on pages 504A-B for timing suggestions, resources, and additional materials that will help you in your presentation of the lesson concepts.

For adequate development of the concepts presented in this lesson, we recommend that students do the Find Out activity on page 522.

1 MOTIVATE

Activity Take students outside to observe the direction from which the wind is blowing and what materials are being carried by the wind. Ask students how wind speed affects the amount and kind of material that the wind is able to transport. To make this observation more visible, toss a handful of flour into the air and have students observe as it is dispersed.

EXPLORE!

Which particles can be readily carried by the wind?

Time needed 15 minutes

Materials sheets of aluminum foil

Thinking Processes
Observing and inferring

Purpose To relate particle size and shape to the ability to be transported by wind.

Preparation To avoid using a lot of aluminum foil, a nonrenewable resource, have students work in pairs or teams of four. COOP LEARN

Teaching the Activity

Suggest that students test variables such as blocking the wind or joining pieces to make them larger.

Expected Outcomes

Lighter, smaller foil particles will be lifted by wind. Larger, heavier particles will not move or may be dragged along the surface.

Answers to Questions

1. the lighter and flatter pieces
2. The larger the object, the less likely it will be moved.

2 Teach

Tying to Previous Knowledge

Remind students that other agents of erosion they have studied, in particular water and glaciers, erode land by scraping the land surface smooth or by breaking the land into smaller particles, which are then carried away. Explain that wind may cause erosion in similar ways.

Concepts Developed

Discussion Any mechanical force, whether it is moving water, particles, or air, can erode the land.

FIND OUT!

How do dunes move?

Time needed 15 minutes

Materials shoe box, flour, knife or scissors, spoon, towel

Thinking Processes Observing and inferring, Recognizing cause and effect

Purpose To discover how dunes form and move.

Preparation You might wish to cut the openings in the shoe boxes in advance.

Expected Outcomes

Students will observe a hill piling up, falling down, and drifting.

Conclude and Apply

1. The side you are blowing on forms a hill.
2. Eventually the flour piles up so high that it falls down on the other side.
3. As you continue blowing air into the box, the pile of flour moves farther and farther.

Flex Your Brain Use the Flex Your Brain activity to have students explore SAND DUNES.

FIGURE 17-19. A sand dune typically has a gentle slope on one side and a steep slope on the other.

sand in Figure 17-19. You might find a dune on a beach or in a desert. Can you tell how these dunes formed? Remember that the lightweight particles in the Explore activity stopped when you stopped blowing or when something got in their way. The sand particles that formed these dunes were deposited in a similar way.

The dunes shown in the photograph are a result of erosion and deposition. The sand particles were eroded from one location and deposited here to form dunes. Not only can the sand particles in a dune move, but amazingly, the dune itself can move. Try the following activity to find out how dunes travel.

FIND OUT!

How do dunes move? 

Get a covered shoebox and cut a 5-cm-square opening in one end. Spoon flour into the box toward the open end to form a layer about 2.5 cm deep. Cover the box and put it on a level surface. *Gently* blow air into the box through the open end. Be sure to have a towel handy to wipe off any flour that gets on your face. Occasionally lift the lid and observe what is happening to the layer of flour.

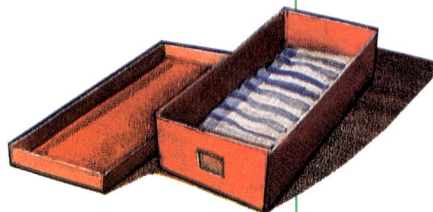

Conclude and Apply

1. What happens to the flour on the side that you are blowing air?
2. What happens on the other side?
3. What happens to the little piles of flour as you continue blowing air into the box?

PROGRAM RESOURCES

Teacher Classroom Resources

Study Guide, page 62

Concept Mapping, page 25, Erosion L1

Critical Thinking/Problem Solving, page 8, Flex Your Brain

OPTIONS

Meeting Individual Needs

Behaviorally Disordered Pair students with responsible partners. Caution the students not to blow into the box as they are lifting the lid or while it is open.

The Find Out activity helped you understand how dunes form and move. Sand builds up a gentle slope on the side facing the wind. The sand continues to build up until it falls down a steeper slope on the other side. As the wind continues to blow, this process is repeated over and over. Eventually, the dune moves to a different location unless something stops the wind or the dune.

The roots of growing plants like beach grass or sage brush help anchor the sand on some beaches and in some deserts. This helps keep the sand from blowing away. Along some coasts, dunes provide a barrier to the lake or ocean waves, protecting the nearby land and wildlife.

SKILLBUILDER

OBSERVING AND INFERRING

While driving across the desert of the southwestern United States, you notice that large rocks have been piled up along the bases of some utility poles. You also notice sand dunes forming on parts of the highway. However, where fences have been built along the highways, no sand dunes have formed. Why have people piled rocks and put up fences in the desert? If you need help, refer to the **Skill Handbook** on page 652.

WIND EROSION

Not only does wind create deposits such as sand dunes, but it also erodes Earth's surface. Look how wind has smoothed the surface of the sculpture in Figure 17-20. It does this primarily by a process that is similar to sandblasting. Wind picks up small sand-sized particles and moves them. When these particles come in contact

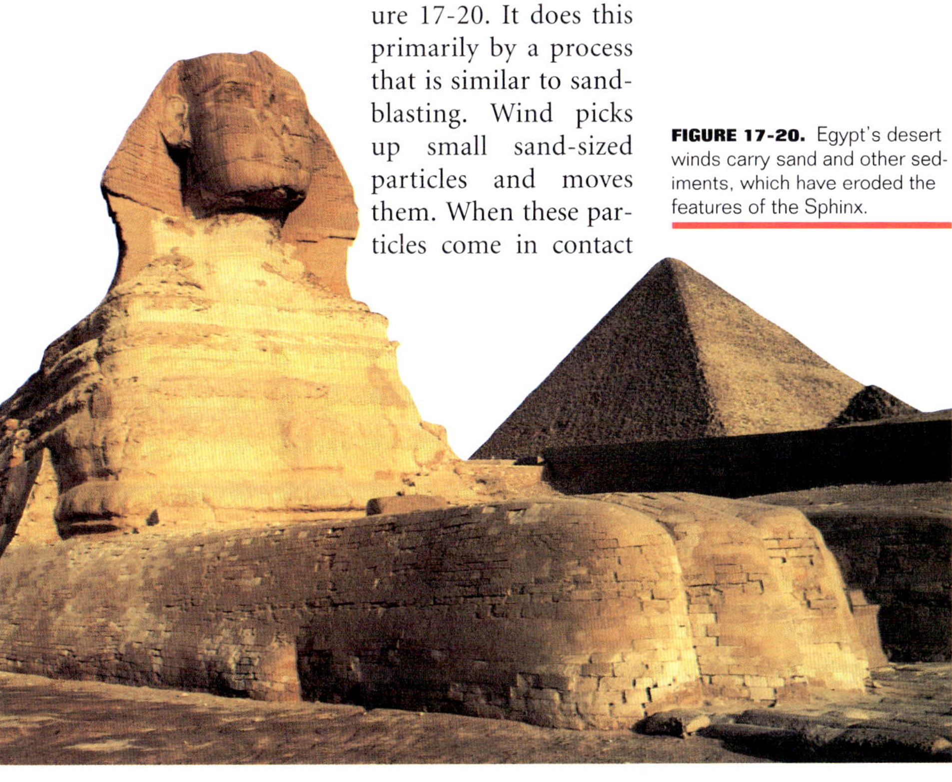

FIGURE 17-20. Egypt's desert winds carry sand and other sediments, which have eroded the features of the Sphinx.

SKILLBUILDER

The rock piles keep the sand and soil from eroding at the base of the poles. The fences act as windbreaks and encourage the formation of dunes to keep the sand from blowing over the highway.

Concept Development

Theme Connection As students read this section, they will see examples of the theme of energy. Wind is generated by heat energy from the sun. The secondary effects of that energy create patterns of change in the land.

MAKING CONNECTIONS

Language Arts

The effects of the wind have been described in almost countless works of literature. Some references include allusions to the erosive effects of wind. Have students peruse the entries under "wind" and "winds" in the index of John Bartlett's *Familiar Quotations*. Students should identify quotations that refer to wind erosion and bring in and recite the appropriate poem or excerpt.

Teacher F.Y.I.

Extended drought conditions in California produced a dust storm in 1991 that reduced visibility on a highway to near zero at one point during the storm, causing a pileup of over 100 vehicles.

Multicultural Perspectives

Some winds that cause erosion and other problems occur so regularly that they have names. Each spring, a khamsin blows the sand across the Sahara Desert for fifty days. In southern California, Santa Ana winds are known for contributing to devastating forest fires at the end of each rainless summer.

Enrichment

Have students read the poem "Ozymandias" by Percy Bysshe Shelley. Discuss the theme that humans have little power over time and nature, in particular the force of wind erosion in the desert.

Student Text Questions What other areas on Earth have dry, loose material on the surface and very little rainfall? *deserts* Why do you think the shape of desert landscapes is always shifting? *There are very few plants to anchor the sand, and it is exposed to strong winds.*

3 Assess

Check for Understanding

Ask students questions 1 through 4. Have them discuss their answers to the Apply question and ask what other methods could be used to control erosion near the corners of a house.

Reteach

Help students develop a concept map showing types of wind erosion and examples of each.

Extension

Discuss with students why off-road vehicles are damaging to beaches and desert soil. Be sure they understand that the vehicles destroy vegetation, which keeps sand and soil anchored and also acts as a wind block.

4 Close

Discuss what a family could do to save their beach-front property from being eroded by wind and water. Some possible solutions might be to put in a structure to encourage a dune to form and plant beach grass; plant bushes as a windbreak; cover the sand with a rock wall.

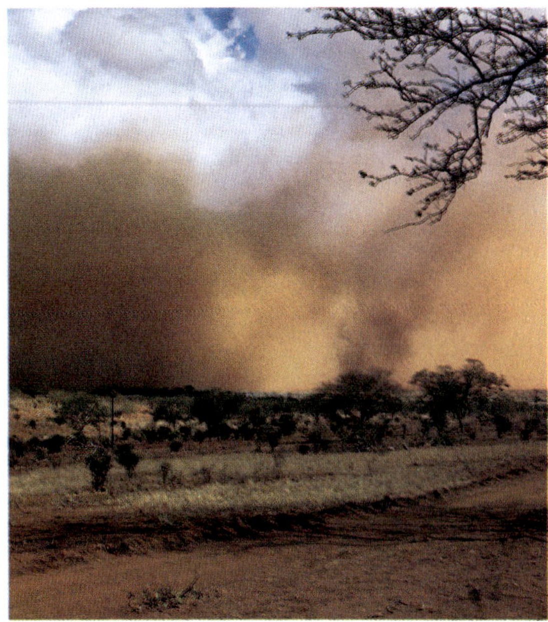

FIGURE 17-21. Wind easily picks up and moves small sediments.

with objects such as the sculpture, they erode them. Windblown materials like sand grind away whatever they hit.

Land can be eroded more easily during a drought. The soil gets very dry, and the plants in it dry up and die. Then wind can easily erode the soil. This happened in the central plains of the United States in the 1930s. The area became known as the Dust Bowl because as the soil was carried away by the wind, it created great swirling bowls of dust. Farmers today use planting and watering techniques that prevent this type of soil erosion.

What other areas on Earth have dry, loose material on the surface and very little rainfall? Why do you think the shape of desert landscapes is always shifting?

You can see the ability of the wind to carry and move sediments in Figure 17-21. Yet erosion by wind is much less than that of water and ice. Water is a more effective mover of sediments than wind. While wind can move materials, it does not have the ability that running water does.

Wind, like gravity, running water, and glaciers, shapes the land as it erodes. But the new landforms created by these agents of erosion are themselves being eroded. Erosion and deposition are part of a cycle of change that constantly shapes and reshapes the land around you.

Check Your Understanding

1. Explain how wind changes the landscape at beaches and in deserts.
2. In what ways are dunes constantly changing?
3. Describe at least two steps a farmer might take to decrease soil erosion.
4. **APPLY:** Explain how trees planted near the corners of a house can help keep the land from changing.

Answers to Check Your Understanding

1. The wind constantly moves loose sediment and deposits it to form dunes and move them to new locations. Windblown sediment also erodes the surface of material it hits.
2. New dunes are constantly being formed as the wind carries and deposits sediments. Sediment from existing dunes is constantly being carried away by the wind and redeposited to new locations.
3. A farmer could grow ground cover in fields that are not being used to cut down on the chance of soil blowing away. Also, irrigation might be used to keep soil moist to prevent loose particles of dry dust from being blown away.
4. They can break the wind and protect the soil from being blown away. Also, trees hold the soil in place to prevent it from being washed away by water.

EXPANDING YOUR VIEW

CONTENTS

A CLOSER LOOK

CONTROLLING SOIL EROSION

Farmers have developed methods to help them grow crops on land that otherwise might just erode away. Most of these methods are ways to keep water and soil from running downhill.

One method is to create terraces around steep inclines or mountains. The terraces are flat fields where crops can be grown. Steep inclines separate the terraces from each other. Rainwater runs down the inclines to soak the terraces below them. It's a good way to save water in dry climates.

A similar method is to create a terrace that coils around and up a mountain. In this case the fields are not flat, but gently rise, winding around and around the mountain.

On gentle slopes, farmers catch water by plowing across the slopes rather than up and down. This is called contour plowing. As the water travels downward, the plowed rows catch and slow it. Some of the water soaks in before the rest continues flowing downhill.

If land is prone to erosion, the use of good farming practices is especially important. Plowing a crop back into the ground helps it resist erosion. In windy areas, sandy soil can be protected by planting coarse grasses to help hold the soil in place.

People cannot control the causes of erosion, but they can do some things to keep erosion from destroying farm land.

CAREER CONNECTION

Agriculture extension agents help farmers prevent erosion. In college, extension agents study the science of erosion prevention. Then they show farmers how to prevent erosion on their own property.

WHAT DO YOU THINK?

Walk around your neighborhood or town, looking for examples of eroded land. How could that land be improved? Is there anything you can do to prevent further erosion?

Assign one or more of these excursions to expand students' understanding of earth science and how it applies to other sciences and other subjects. You may assign these as individual or small group activities.

A CLOSER LOOK

Purpose A Closer Look reinforces Section 17-2 by explaining farming practices that are used to control soil erosion.

Content Background In the early 1930s, the U.S. Department of Agriculture provided funds for research on soil conservation. Much of the funds were used to employ people to terrace land so that runoff would not wash away rich topsoil. But soon another destructive force began to erode the soil of Oklahoma and nearby states. These were the great dust storms of the Depression. To block the effects of this wind-caused erosion, agriculture specialists developed additional farming techniques including contour plowing, strip-cropping (planting rows at right angles to prevailing winds), and planting rows of trees as windbreaks.

Teaching Strategies Terraces and contour plowing may best be understood by having students make models of them. If students construct the models using soil, they can then perform experiments to determine how these techniques control water and wind erosion.

Answers to WHAT DO YOU THINK?

Responses to these questions will reflect students' observations of land erosion in their community. Some suggestions for improvements might include planting grasses or shrubs to decrease wind and soil erosion and constructing rock walls to control erosion by a river or sea.

Going Further If possible, invite an agriculture extension agent to speak to the class on erosion prevention. Have students prepare a list of questions before the speaker's presentation.

Going Further Have students collect and display photographs that depict anti-erosion techniques used in various countries and regions. Students should focus on mountainous regions such as those in China, Tibet, and South America.

PHYSICS CONNECTION

Purpose The Physics Connection reinforces Section 17-1 by explaining how satellites are used to monitor soil conditions around the world. This excursion also shows how the information from the satellites has revealed how the soil has changed through erosion caused by wind. It has revealed that this process can be reversed and stabilized by changing grazing methods.

Content Background Vast areas of agricultural land in Africa have been lost due to overgrazing, rangeland burning, and excessive wood gathering. This has resulted in desertification—the expansion of arid desert lands into areas once agriculturally productive.

Teaching Strategies To show students how great the impact of soil erosion can be, have them research famine in Africa in the recent past. They can examine microfiche of newspaper articles or news magazines and share their findings with classmates.

Answers to

WHAT DO YOU THINK?

Since these questions involve subjective ethical decisions, accept any responses that students can defend. You may wish to have students respond to these questions in the form of a debate.

Physics Connection

EYES ON THE PLANET

United States Landsat satellites are watching soil conditions and crops all over the world. These observation satellites are machines just a little bigger than a car. They're built tough to work in Earth's orbit, which can be a harsh environment. Landsat satellites orbit Earth 14 times a day at a height 400 miles above the ground.

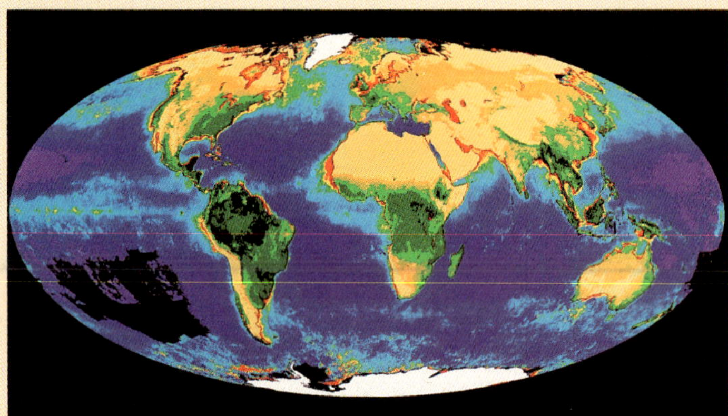

The Landsat satellites are filled with machines that gather information. Among them is the Landsat Thematic Mapper, which has 100 different detectors. As the satellite circles Earth, the machines take pictures of Earth. Their sensors can tell the difference between land and water, city and country, wheat and corn. They work even when Earth is covered with clouds, fog, storms, or darkness.

Scientists on Earth collect the Landsat information and pass it on to people who need it. Sometimes the information helps save lives.

For example, information from one Landsat orbit showed a massive erosion problem in Africa. Huge numbers of people in Africa were starving, but the exact reason had been unclear. Conditions there were similar to the dust bowl the United States experienced in the 1930s. Back then, there was no satellite information to show the problem.

But 50 years later, pictures from the Landsat satellites clearly identified the problem in Africa. Pictures showed that people had allowed animals to overgraze a large area of grassland. Years of overgrazing followed by no rain had created desert conditions. Wind blew the dry soil away. With no grasses to eat, the animals starved, leaving the people with no food.

Because of the Landsat satellite information, the African people can prevent future problems by changing their animals' grazing methods.

WHAT DO YOU THINK?

Should satellite information collected by the United States be available to all countries on Earth? What if the satellite information could prevent massive starvation in a country that was our political enemy? Should we help our enemies avoid starvation?

Going Further Have students explore the effect of erosion in a historical context. Ask them to research the relationship between the Dust Bowl and the Great Depression in the United States in the 1930s. You may then wish to tie in the evolution of the New Deal to show a positive response to this natural disaster.

SCIENCE AND SOCIETY

DEVELOPING THE LAND

Have you noticed that many people live in houses and apartments beside rivers and lakes and on the sides of hills and mountains? If you ask real-estate agents, they'll tell you that people like to live where there's a good view. People like to look down on a valley or watch boats sail along a river. However, when you think of the effects of gravity and water, do you think steep slopes and river banks are good places for people to live? Perhaps not.

When people settle in these locations, they must constantly battle erosion problems. They have to deal not only with erosion that occurs naturally, but sometimes with additional problems they create themselves. When people make a slope steeper or remove vegetation, they are speeding up the erosion process.

Once an area that has a natural slope is developed by clearing the land, building asphalt roads and parking lots, and putting up buildings, several effects may follow. Because there is less vegetation to absorb the water from heavy rainfalls, water runoff can increase in volume. This rapidly flowing water may sweep loose soil particles down the hill. The resulting increase in erosion may, over a period of time, actually make the slope of the hill steeper. And the steeper the slope, the more rapidly the water runoff flows, and the more erosion there is. Furthermore, the loss of topsoil may make it harder for any plants to grow and help in stabilizing the remaining soil.

There are a variety of things that people can do to reduce erosion. Planting vegetation is one of the best

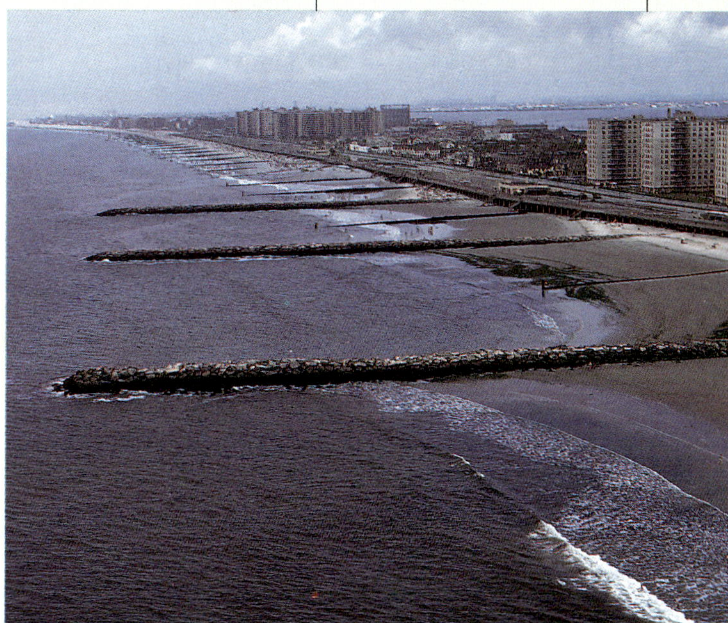

EXPANDING YOUR VIEW

SCIENCE AND SOCIETY

Purpose Science and Society reinforces Sections 17-1 and 17-2 by explaining how gravity and water contribute to erosion around building sites. This excursion also shows landscaping techniques that can minimize erosion on slopes and near bodies of water.

Content Background Erosion is a factor in land use that has political impact at the local and national levels. Some communities now restrict building on steep slopes to control erosion. Wetlands are being redefined. Zoning decisions about building on or near wetlands may affect runoff and drainage in many areas. Storm damage in coastal areas may result in extensive erosion, threatening existing dwellings. The prevention, or limitation, of such damage has become a political issue in many coastal regions of the United States.

Teaching Strategies Suggest that students attend local zoning meetings at which erosion-related problems are to be discussed.

Going Further Encourage students to apply their experience and knowledge on erosion-related issues by writing letters to local newspapers or legislators to support their views concerning land development.

EXPANDING YOUR VIEW

Activity You may wish to have students respond to the What Do You Think questions by role-playing. Have students take the roles of mayor, citizens, and zoning board members to discuss the issues described. Local libraries may contain vertical files with current information on local land use for student reference.

Answers to

WHAT DO YOU THINK?

Since these questions are subjective, accept all reasonable and well-supported answers.

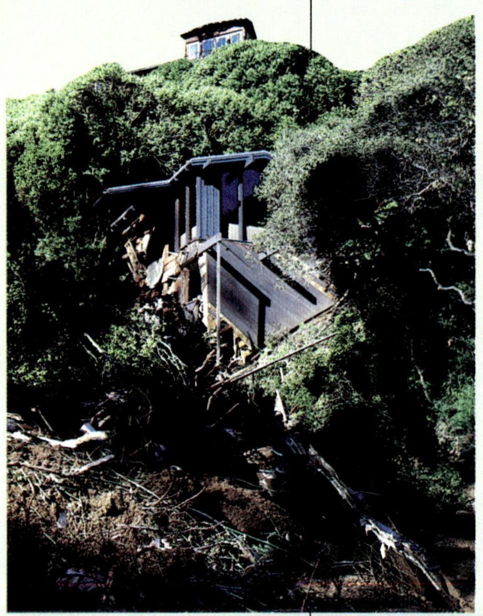

WHAT DO YOU THINK?

Suppose you live beside a river. You love it there. It's beautiful, and there's so much to do. The only problem is that the river frequently floods. Several times your family has been evacuated to higher ground. One day, the mayor informs your family that you must move. She tells you that living along the river is not only dangerous, but it costs the city too much money each time you're evacuated. Do you think this is fair? Should communities be able to control where people live?

Also, people often want to rebuild their homes in the same place after their original homes were destroyed by natural erosion. Do you think that federal disaster funds should be available for homeowners who choose to live in a region that is often threatened by mudslides or river floods?

ways because not only do roots hold soil, but plants absorb a lot of water. A person living on a steep slope might also build terraces or retaining walls.

You already know that terraces are broad, steplike cuts made into the side of a slope. When water flows onto a terrace, it is slowed down, so it can't erode as much.

Retaining walls are often made of concrete, stones, wood, or railroad ties. Their purpose is to keep soil and rocks from sliding downhill. These walls can also be built along stream channels, lakes, or ocean beaches to reduce erosion caused by flooding, running water, or waves.

People who live in areas with erosion problems spend a lot of time and money trying to preserve their land. Sometimes they're successful in slowing down erosion, but they can never eliminate it. Eventually, cliffs cave in, streams overflow their banks, and soil and rocks are pulled downhill.

Sediments constantly move from place to place, changing the shape of the land forever. Erosion is all part of Earth's natural dynamic processes.

History CONNECTION

PUZZLE SOLVED!

Long ago, scientists had a problem—they couldn't figure out how the first people got from Africa and Europe to North and South America. Water separates these two continents from all other continents. Early humans didn't have the sailing or boat-making skills to cross large oceans from Europe or Africa.

Scientists discovered that glaciers were responsible. Glaciers dominated much of Earth during the Ice Age, which ended about 10,000 years ago.

When more glaciers were created, the level of water in the world's oceans dropped. As the oceans shrank, more land was exposed. It's like being at the beach and seeing the tide go out, giving you more beach to play on.

When the water level in the oceans went down, a land bridge was exposed near the Arctic Circle. Look at a map to see where Asia and North America nearly touch. It is the land to the north of the Bering Sea. Several times in the last two million years those pieces of land did connect with each other, and early human beings migrated—slowly—to North America. That piece of land, which is now under water, is called the Bering Land Bridge.

Scientists believe early people migrated across this land bridge at different times 10,000 to 30,000 years ago. The land at that time was covered with Arctic vegetation similar to dry grasslands. Marshes and forests supported animals such as reindeer, horses, mammoths, mastodons, birds, and fish. There was enough food for people to eat.

WHAT DO YOU THINK?

What would life be like at the edge of a melting glacier? Would it be cold? Where would people get water? Can plants grow there? What would people eat? How would it sound near the glacier?

HISTORY CONNECTION

Purpose The History Connection reinforces Section 17-3 by explaining how a land bridge appeared across the Bering Sea during various ice ages. This excursion also shows how the buildup of glaciers lowered the water level of the oceans, revealing the natural structure that people used as a bridge to North America.

Content Background The Bering land bridge allowed movement of animals from Asia to North America long before the land bridge was used by humans. What effect did this movement have on human migration? Many scientists think it is likely that some of the earliest human travelers across this bridge were hunters in search of meat.

Teaching Strategies Use a relief map or globe to look at the Bering Strait and other areas that might have been exposed during the Ice Age.

Discussion If possible, display photographs of that area or other arctic regions using sources such as *National Geographic Magazine* to stimulate a discussion of students' responses to You Try It.

Going Further If possible, have students write to other students who live and attend school near a glacier. Students should ask about living conditions near a glacier. Do the sounds bother the people? What's it like to walk on a glacier? Is it safe to do this? What kinds of animals live on or near a glacier? How fast does the glacier move? How does it affect the land around it? How tall and wide is it?

Answers to YOU TRY IT

The climate near a melting glacier would most likely be cold all year long. Much fresh water would come from streams of melting ice. The vegetation would probably be similar to that found in cold areas of the world today—grasses and low bushes. People's diets would consist mostly of meat and fish. Some sounds near a glacier would include the noise of meltwater streams and booming cracks as chunks of glaciers thaw, shift, and break off.

TECHNOLOGY CONNECTION

Purpose The Technology Connection reinforces Sections 17-2 and 17-3 by explaining how photomapping is used to monitor river and glacier erosion and deposition.

Content Background Photographs taken in daylight detect sunlight reflected off clouds, landmasses, and bodies of water. These images reveal such things as cloud cover and masses of ice that might be blocking shipping lanes in such places as the Great Lakes and polar regions.

Infrared images, taken day or night, reveal patterns of heat released from objects on Earth's surface. The hottest of these appear white and the coldest appear black.

Teaching Strategies Have students watch a weather channel to observe the results of global photomapping. Have them identify on the weather map the part of the world in which they live and interpret the data on the map for their region.

Answers to WHAT DO YOU THINK?

Responses to these questions are highly subjective and will vary.

EXPANDING YOUR VIEW

TECHNOLOGY CONNECTION

CAMERAS IN ORBIT

High above Earth, satellites like the one shown below are photographing everything in sight—and much that would not be within sight of a human being.

Satellite television cameras located 500 to 1500 miles above Earth take moving pictures with a satellite camera that has a vidicon tube. A transparent plate in the tube is covered with a complex compound of selenium, a photoconductive material. The selenium has high electrical resistance in the dark, but low electrical resistance to the light. Light from the image is admitted to the tube for 1/25 of a second.

During that time, the light and dark areas are passed through the selenium layer and the resulting image is scanned by an electron beam. The beam scans 800 lines every 200 seconds.

Every 208 seconds, one complete picture is scanned and transmitted to receiving transmitters on Earth.

Until the late 1980s, only 35 percent of Earth's surface had been photomapped from low-flying aircraft. Today, the entire planet is photographed at least once daily. In addition to the vidicon system, Earth is

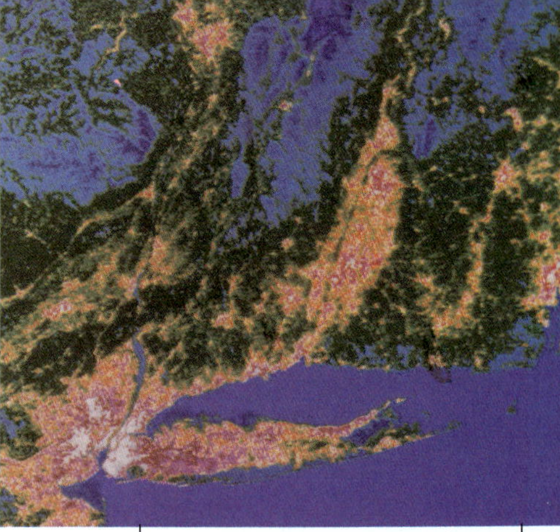

photographed using infrared equipment, which allows night photography and reveals landform variations in temperature, like those shown above. Temperature-based cameras also record temperatures around the world—over the ocean as well as the land.

Using satellite photomapping, scientists can track glaciers, identify expanding alluvial fans, and track river changes.

WHAT DO YOU THINK?

As satellite cameras improve, spying on individual people will become easier. What will happen to personal privacy? What laws could protect individuals from their own government? From other governments?

Going Further Have groups of students work together to draft a law that they think would adequately protect an individual's right to privacy in a world in which satellites can detect objects as small as a person. Organize the class into groups of four and designate roles for group members to select. Roles may include a Facilitator to keep the discussion moving, a Summarizer to review the important points of the discussion, a Recorder to make notes on the discussion, and a Presenter to present and explain the drafted law to the class.

Students should address constitutional questions involving the right to privacy. They might wish to cite Supreme Court decisions that support their law. You might want to make this an interdisciplinary activity by inviting a social studies teacher to join you. COOP LEARN

Reviewing Main Ideas

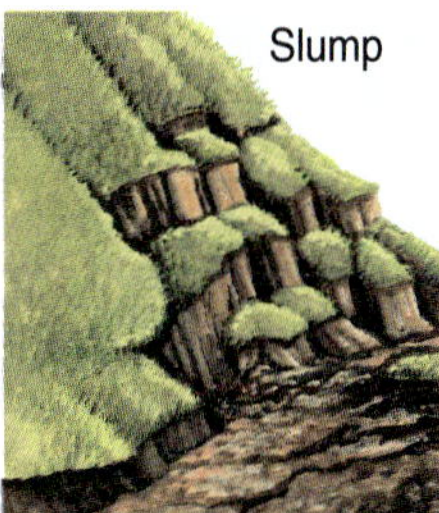

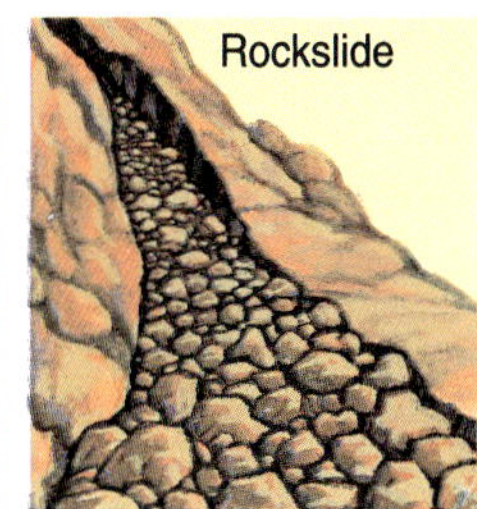

1. Erosion by gravity can be slow, as in slump and creep, or fast, as in mudflows and rockslides.

2. Streams erode and deposit sediments. Fast streams erode more than slow streams. As streams slow down, they deposit more sediments.

3. Glaciers form U-shaped valleys as they push and carry loose materials and scrape against rock surfaces.

4. Wind can carry loose particles great distances, as well as erode rock surfaces.

Chapter 17

Reviewing Main Ideas

In this activity, students will trace in sequence the path of part of a mountain that is weathered by the four agents of erosion until it is a speck of dust.

Teaching Strategy

To review the main concepts of this chapter, ask students to trace in sequence the path of a bit of dirt, from its beginning as a part of a mountain. Tell them that on its way to becoming a bit of dust, the substance undergoes erosion by gravity, a glacier, water, and wind. Have various students diagram the changes the substance might go through in sequence, labeling the agents that cause it to erode or be deposited.

Chapter 21

Chapter Review

USING KEY SCIENCE TERMS

Answers

1. deposition (not a type of erosion)
2. rockslide (not slow erosion)
3. erosion (not a feature of deposition)
4. slump (not a type of glacier)

UNDERSTANDING IDEAS

Answers

1. a
2. d
3. a
4. c
5. a
6. b
7. b
8. a
9. d
10. b

CRITICAL THINKING

Answers

1. Slope is one factor that affects erosion. Rate is another, such as rate of flow of water, or speed of wind.

2. River valleys are flat. Generally, large amounts of sediment are deposited on the floodplain. Often the sediment contains rich organic materials and minerals. This makes the land very fertile. The river flows slowly because it flows across gently sloping land.

3. Rainfall increases erosion by gravity on steep slopes. It makes sediments heavier and allows them to slide downslope easier. Rainfall decreases erosion by wind on level land. Rain tends to hold down wet sediments, making them more difficult for wind to move.

4. Valley glaciers form between mountain peaks at high elevations where snow does not melt completely. Continental glaciers are larger, covering large landmasses.

5. Each process of erosion loosens a substance where it occurs, moves the substance, and deposits it elsewhere.

Chapter 17

Chapter Review

USING KEY SCIENCE TERMS

continental glacier	erosion
creep	mudflow
delta	rockslide
deposition	slump
dune	valley glacier

For each set of terms below, choose the one term that does not belong and explain why it does not belong.

1. mudflow, creep, deposition
2. rockslide, creep, slump
3. erosion, dune, delta
4. continental glacier, valley glacier, slump

UNDERSTANDING IDEAS

Choose the best answer to complete each sentence.

1. Erosion may be caused by ____.
   a. gravity **c.** deltas
   b. deposition **d.** dunes
2. A stream's rate of flow is affected by ____.
   a. rainfall **c.** its slope
   b. sediments **d.** all of these
3. An example of slow erosion is ____.
   a. creep **c.** a mudflow
   b. a rockslide **d.** a delta
4. Glaciers do not change the land by ____.
   a. scraping **c.** mudflow
   b. deposition **d.** erosion
5. Streams joining to form a river can increase ____.
   a. flow rate **c.** slopes
   b. mudflow **d.** deposition
6. Deposition occurs when a stream or river flows ____.
   a. in rapids **c.** swiftly
   b. slowly **d.** over a waterfall
7. Examples of deposition by wind include ____.
   a. rockslides **c.** creep
   b. dunes **d.** deltas

8. Masses of moving ice and snow near the South Pole are called ____.
   a. continental glaciers
   b. deposition
   c. valley glaciers
   d. erosion
9. Wind erodes ____.
   a. rocks **c.** soil
   b. plants **d.** all of these
10. Valley glaciers erode valleys in a ____.
    a. V shape **c.** canyon shape
    b. U shape **d.** triangular shape

PROGRAM RESOURCES

Teacher Classroom Resources

Review and Assessment

Chapter Review and Chapter Test, pages 69-72

Computer Test Bank, Chapter Test

OPTIONS

Cooperative Learning

Consider using Cooperative Learning in the Understanding Ideas, Critical Thinking, Problem Solving, and Connecting Ideas sections of the Chapter Review.

COOP LEARN

CRITICAL THINKING

Use your understanding of the concepts developed in the chapter to answer each of the following questions.

1. What factors can increase the rate of erosion?
2. Study the photograph. Then explain why farmland is common in river valleys. Do you think this river flows fairly quickly or fairly slowly? Why?

3. How does rainfall affect erosion by gravity on a steep slope? How does it affect erosion by wind on level land?
4. How do continental glaciers differ from valley glaciers?
5. How are the processes of erosion by gravity, wind, streams, and glaciers similar?

PROBLEM SOLVING

Read the following problem and discuss your answers in a brief paragraph.

Imagine that you live in a hilly area. Your family is planning on building a new home.

1. What should they be concerned about when looking for a lot on which to build?
2. What steps should they take to prevent erosion if they build on the side of a slope?
3. How might landscaping with plants help prevent erosion?

CONNECTING IDEAS

Discuss each of the following in a brief paragraph.

1. Explain how rocks from an inland mountain might become sediments in the ocean.
2. How do glaciers affect stream erosion?
3. How can erosion explain the formation of various landforms on a map?
4. **A CLOSER LOOK** How does the building of terraces control soil erosion?
5. **PHYSICS CONNECTION** Explain how United States Landsat information helped explain the cause of dusty conditions in Africa.

PROBLEM SOLVING

Answers

1. They should avoid sites that have a potential to creep or slump. They should also avoid very steep slopes, which could be subject to landslides.

2. A retaining wall might be built to help prevent rocks or soil from sliding down the hill onto the building site. They should ensure that the foundation is being built on solid bedrock.

3. Landscaping with plants will cause plant roots to keep water and wind from eroding topsoil. The stems and leaves will act as a windbreak. The roots will hold particles of soil together.

CONNECTING IDEAS

Answers

1. Rocks on a mountain might be eroded by a glacier and carried along as sediment when the glacial ice melts and joins a stream. This sediment may then be moved along through tributaries until a river deposits it in an ocean.

2. Melting ice contributes water to river systems. Increases in the amount of water in a stream cause the stream to move faster and carry more sediment.

3. Landforms like an alluvial fan or delta are a result of deposition of sediments that have been eroded. Valleys are generally caused by river or glacial erosion.

4. Terraces break a sloped surface into a series of flat surfaces. Since slope, an important factor in erosion, is removed, there is less erosion.

5. LandSat satellite photographs have enabled scientists to identify locations and the extent of desert expansion in Africa.

LOOKING BACK

UNIT 4
SYSTEMS IN MOTION

THEME DEVELOPMENT

The themes developed in Unit 4 were energy, stability and change, and interactions and systems. Motion is considered a change in position. Objects undergo change in their positions when forces act on them. Speed is an expression of how much time it takes for that change to occur. Energy in the form of physical weathering such as ice wedging is seen as a force that weathers rock, leading to soil development. Weathering and erosion show that parts of Earth are not stable and do undergo great change. The motion of moving water causes the change of unstable Earth materials through weathering, erosion, and deposition, illustrating how the motion, energy and change work together to sculpt Earth's surface.

Connections to Other Units

The view of Earth and objects near Earth in space, as presented in Unit 1, can be related to how these objects move. In Unit 2, the physical world and its materials are presented. These materials work to weather rocks, forming soil, which can then be moved by the process of erosion. Animals and plants, covered in Unit 3, affect weathering and erosion of Earth's surface materials and Earth's ecology is affected by motion within Earth's water systems.

Connecting Ideas

Answers

1. As the rock fragments fall they hit other rocks causing them to weather as well. The smaller weathered rock fragments can then be moved by other agents of erosion.

2. As the speed of the water slows, the larger rock particles settle out first. As the speed of the water slows more, the smaller particles of rock will settle out. This process builds up layers of sorted sediments along the path of deposition at the bottom of the stream bed.

Exploring Further

The purpose of this activity is two-fold. First, it will help students realize the importance of controlling variables when conducting an experiment. Second, it will help students realize that varying types of soil will affect the growth of plants differently. Students should observe that soil that is rich in organic material is usually best for plant growth. The plants use the organic material in the soil as food for growth.

LOOKING BACK

UNIT 4 SYSTEMS IN MOTION

CONTENTS

UNIT FOCUS

In this unit, you investigated motion and how it affected you, Earth, and objects near Earth.

You also learned that movement of water, wind, and ice on Earth's surface can have slow but ever-changing effects on features of the land. There may be shaping of the land through erosion and deposition. The "finger lakes" in New York State, for example, were formed from grooves left by retreating glaciers thousands of years ago.

Try the exercises and activity that follow—they will challenge you to use and apply some of the ideas you learned in this unit.

CONNECTING IDEAS

1. As rocks on a cliff weather, fragments fall to the base of the cliff due to gravity. How does this motion caused by acceleration due to gravity affect weathering and erosion on Earth's surface?
2. Explain what happens to various sized particles of rock that are carried by a stream as the water in the stream empties into a larger body of water. What do these particles form?

EXPLORING FURTHER

Obtain soil samples from three different areas near your home or school. Compare and contrast the samples looking at color, texture, composition, and number of organisms present. Plant a small plant of the same type in each of the soil types and provide the same amount of light, water, and food to each plant. Determine which soil is best for growing this particular plant. Use your knowledge of plants to suggest why.

LOOKING AHEAD

TRY IT

Mechanical waves are all around you. You see a mechanical wave when you watch a flag wave in the wind. You may have felt a mechanical wave when you laid in a raft in a wave pool or in the ocean. You have even heard mechanical waves when your teacher tells you the next day's assignment. What causes a wave to form? Why does it move the way that it does? What happens to an object when a wave passes it by? Obtain a tuning fork from your teacher. Gently tap the tuning fork against the edge of a book and observe the motion produced. Hold the tuning fork up near your ear. What do you notice? How do you think the tuning fork is affecting your eardrum? After you've learned more about waves and the motion of objects affected by waves, see how accurate your explanation was.

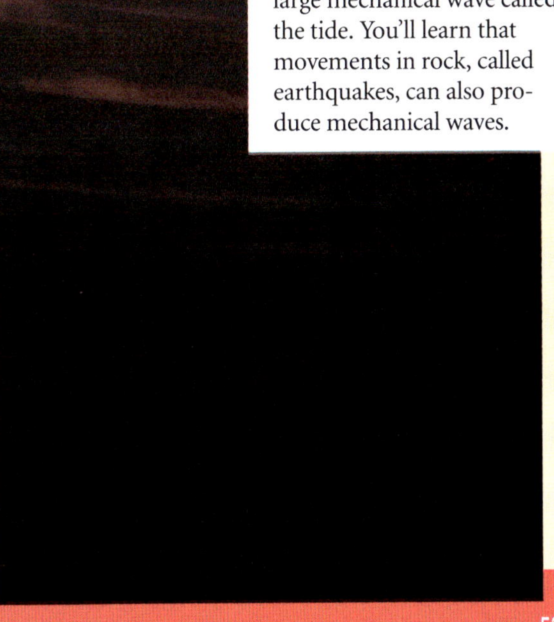

UNIT 5 WAVE MOTION

CONTENTS

UNIT FOCUS

In Unit 4, you learned about motion and how you, Earth, and objects near Earth are affected by it. As you study Unit 5, you'll see how the motion of an object can produce waves. You'll also learn how the interaction of Earth and the moon causes a large mechanical wave called the tide. You'll learn that movements in rock, called earthquakes, can also produce mechanical waves.

Try It

The purpose of this activity is to enable students to realize mechanical waves exist in many forms. They will learn the concept that waves seen in a flag as it moves in the wind, water waves, and sound waves have similar characteristics. Students will observe and hear the effects of a passing mechanical wave. Students will observe the very rapid back and forth motion of the tuning fork. When they hold it near their ear, they will hear a sound caused as sound waves, generated by the back and forth motion of the tuning fork, strike their eardrum. For your hearing impaired students, hold the tuning fork near a glass of water so they can observe the effects of the wave on the water. As the mechanical wave passes through air, it causes it to vibrate. This vibration is transmitted to the student's eardrum, causing it to vibrate as well.

LOOKING AHEAD

UNIT 5
WAVE MOTION

THEME DEVELOPMENT

The themes developed in Unit 5 are scale and structure, energy, stability and change, and interactions and systems. The two themes that work to interconnect all three chapters are energy and interactions and systems. Mechanical waves are produced by releases of energy. As they move through various types of material, mechanical waves interact with this material to change Earth's surface.

Connections to Other Units

The concepts of this unit can be related to Unit 1 where light and sound were explored as forms of energy, as both are transmitted by waves. The concepts in this unit also related to landforms described in Unit 1 and the movements of the Earth-moon system.

Getting Started

Discussion Some questions you may want to ask your students are:

1. **In what way or ways are all waves, regardless of type, related?** Some students may not recognize waves basic similarities. All waves move energy through a system.
2. **If tides on Earth are caused by the gravitational pull of the moon and the sun, when would their combined effect be greatest?** Many students will not know about the relationships among the moon, sun and tides. The greatest effect on Earth's oceans would occur when the two objects are either pulling in together or pulling in opposite directions. The first occurs at new moon and the latter at full moon.
3. **Do areas that have many volcanoes also experience large numbers of earthquakes?** This relationship may be unclear. Many of the volcano belts around Earth also are known as earthquake belts.

The answers to these questions may help you establish misconceptions your students may have.

CHAPTER ORGANIZER

SECTION	OBJECTIVES	ACTIVITIES/FEATURES
Chapter Opener		**Explore!** Can you make a wave on a rope? p. 537
18-1 Waves and Vibrations (3 days)	1. **Describe** how waves are produced. 2. **Identify** transverse and longitudinal waves.	**Find Out!** Can you observe the effects of a longitudinal wave? p. 540 **Investigate 18-1:** Waves on a Coiled Spring, p. 541
18-2 Wave Characteristics (3 days)	1. **Draw** a wave. 2. **Identify** the wavelength, amplitude, crest, and trough of a wave. 3. **Explain** the relationship among frequency, wavelength, and speed in a wave.	**Find Out!** What are wave crests and troughs? p. 543 **Investigate 18-2:** Ripples, p. 546 **Skillbuilder:** Hypothesizing, p. 548
18-3 Adding Waves (2 days)	1. **Explain** how waves add together. 2. **Describe** two examples of wave interference. 3. **Demonstrate** a standing wave.	**Find Out!** How can you make a standing wave? p. 549 **Find Out!** What happens when waves pass? p. 550
18-4 Sound as Waves (1 day)	1. **Demonstrate** sound as a wave. 2. **Explain** the Doppler effect.	**Find Out!** Can you see sound? p. 554
Expanding Your View		A Closer Look **How Does That Sound Look?** p. 559 Earth Science Connection **Seismic Prospecting,** p. 560 Science and Society **Sounds Dangerous,** p. 561 Technology Connection **Wave Power,** p. 563 Teens in Science **Riding a Musical Wave,** p. 564

ACTIVITY MATERIALS

EXPLORE!	INVESTIGATE!	FIND OUT!
Page 537 4-m rope	**Page 541** coiled spring, goggles, small piece of colored thread **Page 546** clear glass dish (approximately 30-cm square), strips of plastic foam, overhead light, tape, water, pencil or pen, piece of blank white paper, ruler	**Page 540** portable radio with round speaker, metal can or other container with same or slightly larger diameter than that of the speaker, can opener, plastic wrap, rubber band, dry rice grains **Page 543** 4-m rope, 5-m white string, pencil, paper, meterstick **Page 549** 4-m rope **Page 550** clear dish, water, overhead light, 2 pencils, paper **Page 554** coffee can with 2 open ends, balloon, scissors, rubber band, flashlight or sunlight, small mirror, glue

TEACHER CLASSROOM RESOURCES	OTHER RESOURCES
Study Guide, p. 63 **Activity Masters, Investigate 18-1,** pp. 73-74 **Making Connections: Integrating Sciences,** p. 39 **Making Connections: Across the Curriculum,** p. 39 **Making Connections: Technology and Society,** p. 39	***STVS:** *Artificial Waves,* Earth and Space (Disc 3, Side 2)
Study Guide, p. 64 **Concept Mapping,** p. 26 **Multicultural Activities,** p. 39 **Activity Masters, Investigate 18-2,** pp. 75-76 **Flex Your Brain,** p. 8 **Multicultural Activities,** p. 40	**Laboratory Manual,** pp. 109-112, Velocity of a Wave **Color Transparency and Master 36,** Wave Properties
Study Guide, p. 65 **Take Home Activities,** p. 28	**Color Transparency and Master 35,** Constructive/Destructive Interference
Study Guide, p. 66 **Critical Thinking/Problem Solving,** p. 26 **Review and Assessment,** pp. 73-76	***STVS:** *Detecting Flaws in Machine Parts,* Physics (Disc 1, Side 1) *Tornado Detectors,* Physics (Disc 1, Side 1) **Computer Test Bank**
	Spanish Resources **Cooperative Learning Resource Guide** **Lab and Safety Skills**

***Science and Technology Videodisc Series**

KEY TO TEACHING STRATEGIES

Teaching strategies have been coded for varying learning styles and abilities. As you review teaching strategies in the margin, the following designations will help you decide which activities are appropriate for your students.

- **L1** Level 1 activities are basic activities and should be within the ability range of all students.
- **L2** Level 2 activities are average activities and should be within the ability range of the average to above-average student.
- **L3** Level 3 activities are challenging activities designed for the ability range of above-average students.
- **LEP** LEP activities should be within the ability range of Limited English Proficiency students.
- **COOP LEARN** Cooperative Learning activities are designed for small group work.

ADDITIONAL MATERIALS

SOFTWARE	AUDIOVISUAL
Waves and Sound Energy, Focus. *Sound Waves,* J&S Software. *Sound: A Microcomputer Based Lab,* Queue.	*What is a Wave?,* video, Focus. *The World of Sound Energy,* video, Focus. *Noise Pollution,* video, LCAD.

Chapter 18

Waves

THEME DEVELOPMENT

The themes this chapter supports are energy and interactions and systems. Waves are produced by energy. They transmit that energy from a source, through a medium, to a destination. When waves meet, the interaction can be constructive (the waves add together) or destructive (the waves cancel each other). The Doppler effect explains how waves interact with the environment under specific conditions. All wave behavior is systematic and predictable.

CHAPTER OVERVIEW

This chapter is concerned with the characteristics and behavior of waves. First, students will learn how waves are produced. They will also study the characteristics of transverse and longitudinal waves. Students will also learn how to describe a wave, using several terms—*wavelength, amplitude, crest,* and *trough.* They will examine the relationships among frequency, wavelength, and speed in a wave.

Students will investigate wave interference and examine standing waves. Finally, students will investigate the characteristics of sound waves. They will also learn what causes the Doppler effect.

Tying to Previous Knowledge

Ask students to picture waves rolling in on a beach. Have them describe the characteristics of the waves. They should mention that each wave has a high point and a low point, that a wave covers a certain distance, and that the characteristics of individual waves vary. Students will be familiar with sound from their study of Chapter 3, although they have not studied sound as a wave phenomenon. Tell students that sounds are caused by waves. Explain that in this chapter, they will learn about sound waves.

DID YOU EVER WONDER . . .

Why sometimes the waves in a swimming pool get so big?

Why a horn on a train seems to change pitch as it passes you?

How a radio speaker produces sound?

You'll find the answers to these questions as you read this chapter.

DID YOU EVER WONDER...

Students will explore these questions as they progress through the chapter. Don't spoil their fun and motivation by sharing those answers too early.

- Waves are constantly being produced in a swimming pool by people diving or just moving about. When the crest of one wave meets the crest of another, the two waves add together, making one wave twice as large. (page 551)
- As an object approaches, the sound waves it produces are pushed closer together, causing the pitch to sound higher. As it moves away, the waves are spread farther apart, causing the pitch to sound lower. This is called the Doppler effect. (page 557)
- The speaker vibrates, producing compressions and rarefactions in the air. (page 554)

Chapter 18

Waves

It's a beautiful day, and you're at the local pool. You are in the water with your friend Ladonna, who is basking on a float. Out of the corner of your eye you see Louie, the bodybuilder, launch himself off the diving board. SPLASH! Suddenly you are under the water, Ladonna bobs straight up, and water bursts over the sides of the pool. Louie has made a large wave in the pool.

After you get your hair out of your eyes, you think about what just happened. If someone had told you the wave was coming, you would have assumed it would knock you down. But the wave just flowed over and around you. You probably would have predicted that Ladonna would be thrown against the edge of the pool. But she simply bobbed up and down and ended up right back beside you. Later in this chapter, you will think back to these observations and be able to explain them.

EXPLORE!

Can you make a wave on a rope?

Tie one end of a 4-m rope to a desk or a doorknob, as shown in the picture. Holding onto the other end of the rope with your hand, shake the rope up and down once. Observe the pulse, a single disturbance, as it travels away from your hand. Shake the rope up and down slowly and at a steady rate. This will form a wave—a continuous series of disturbances. Describe the motion of the wave on the rope. Does the wave seem to move from one end of the rope to the other?

Introducing the Chapter

Have students look at the chapter opening photo. Ask them if they have ever been in the water when someone did a "cannonball" off the diving board. Based on their own experiences, have them suggest what effect the waves the diver created will have on the girl on the float.

Uncovering Preconceptions

Because waves crashing in on the seashore will carry objects in with them, students may have trouble accepting that, in general, waves pass through matter. The activities in this chapter will help clarify this. Also, students may be so familiar with water waves that they have difficulty picturing other types of waves, such as longitudinal waves. Experimenting with a Slinky should help this problem. Sections 18-1 and 18-2 contain such activities.

EXPLORE!

Can you make a wave on a rope?

Time needed 10 minutes

Materials a rope about 4 meters long

Thinking Processes Observing and inferring, Recognizing cause and effect

Purpose To see the motion of a transverse mechanical wave.

Teaching the Activity

Demonstration Shake the rope up and down once and explain that a single disturbance, or wave, is described as a pulse. Be sure that students see that one pulse is produced for each movement of your hand. L1

Expected Outcome

Students will learn to recognize the characteristic up-and-down curve of a transverse wave.

Answer to Question

Yes, the wave moves along the rope.

Project

Ask students to collect newspaper and magazine articles about waves. These articles could range from reports about earthquake or tsunami detection, research on new types of hearing aids, or scientific study of wave characteristics. Display the articles in the classroom and refer to them as appropriate during classroom discussions.

Science at Home

Ask students to experiment with waves in their bathtub or a basin of water. Have them try to produce and measure waves of differing amplitude and frequency. They should place various floating objects in the water and observe the effect the waves have on those objects. They should also attempt to produce constructive and destructive interference. Have students record their results in their journals and share their observations with the class.

Section 18-1

Preparation

Concepts Developed

In this chapter, students will study a particular type of motion—the wave. A wave is a rhythmic disturbance that transfers energy. In this section, students will learn the difference between transverse and longitudinal waves.

Planning the Lesson

In planning your lesson on waves and vibrations, refer to the Chapter Organizer on pages 536A–B for timing suggestions, resources, and additional materials that will help you in your presentation of the lesson concepts.

For adequate development of the concepts presented in this section, we recommend that students do the Find Out activity on page 540 and the Investigate activity on page 541.

1 Motivate

Discussion Ask students to brainstorm all the different types of waves they can think of. Their list may include waves at the seashore, a stadium wave, microwaves, or sound waves. Ask students whether any characteristic is common to all waves. Try to lead students to realize that a similar, repeated type of motion is involved in each case.

2 Teach

Tying to Previous Knowledge

Ask students to recall their study of earthquakes in Chapter 1. The vibrations of an earthquake move through Earth in the form of waves. From Chapter 3, ask students to recall the properties of sound. Review the terms *compression* and *rarefaction* as they apply to sound waves.

18-1 Waves and Vibrations

OBJECTIVES

In this section, you will

- describe how waves are produced;
- identify transverse and longitudinal waves.

KEY SCIENCE TERMS

transverse waves
longitudinal waves

WAVES AROUND YOU

What do you think of when you hear the word *wave*? Perhaps you think of a friendly greeting, the ocean, the beach, or people in a stadium performing a "wave."

What exactly is a wave? Think about Louie's wave. He converted his dive into a large disturbance as he pushed the water aside. That disturbance traveled out across the pool in the form of a wave.

Louie's wave certainly disturbed Ladonna and you, to say nothing of the water in the pool. Now try to think of some more everyday experiences you've had with waves.

Think back to the Explore activity. Do you remember how you made the rope wave? You disturbed the rope by shaking it. This made the rope vibrate. You saw these vibrations as the up-and-down movement of the rope. But the wave you created didn't stay in one place. It moved along the rope, hit the doorknob, and came back. Thus the wave was a vibration traveling along the rope, influencing everything that it touched—the rope, the air around the rope, even your ears if the wave made a sound.

FIGURE 18-1. Some kinds of waves are familiar.

Concept Development

Theme Connection In this section of the chapter, you can explore the themes of energy and systems and interactions. Emphasize to students that waves transmit energy from a source to a destination in a systematic and predictable manner.

Inquiry Question Waves can move through solids, liquids or gases. We've demonstrated how to produce a wave in a solid (the rope) and a liquid. Can you suggest a way to produce a wave in a gas? *Air is a gas and any sound will produce waves that travel through the air.*

TYPES OF WAVES

One type of wave is a mechanical wave. A mechanical wave is a wave that travels through matter. For now, think of matter as anything that takes up space. You saw one example of a mechanical wave when Louie landed in the water. Waves in the rope and sound waves in the air are also mechanical waves. In Chapter 3, you learned that air was the medium that carried sound from the source to your ear. In any mechanical wave, the matter through which the waves move is called the medium. A mechanical wave can be described as a continuous disturbance in a medium.

Once again, think back to the opening Explore activity. In the wave you made on the rope, the rope was the medium. The rope moved up and down or side to side. This was at right angles to the direction of the wave itself, which moved away from the source of the disturbance—in this case, you. The wave you produced with the rope was a transverse wave. As shown in Figure 18-2(a), **transverse waves** are waves in which the wave disturbance moves at right angles to the direction of the wave itself. There are transverse waves, such as light, that travel without a medium. However, in this chapter we will use mechanical transverse waves, such as the waves that travel along the rope or through water, as models for light waves. It is easier to see the wave travel along the rope or through water.

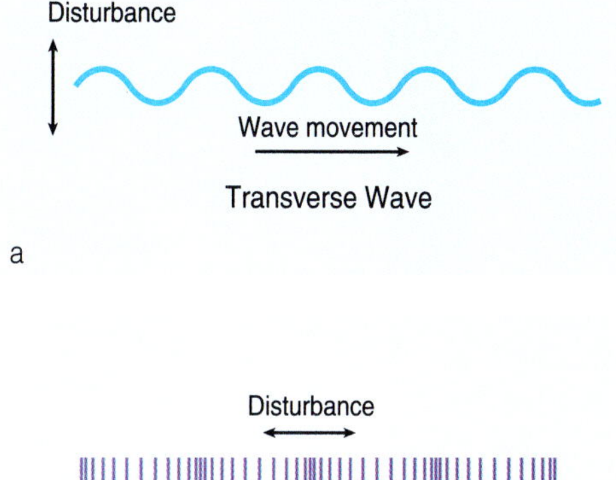

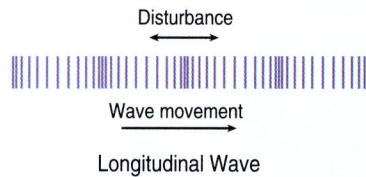

FIGURE 18-2. In a transverse wave (a), the disturbance moves at right angles to the direction the wave travels. In a longitudinal wave (b), the disturbance is in the same direction that the wave travels.

In Chapter 3, you learned that sound traveled through the air in a series of compressions and rarefactions—a bunching up and spreading out of the air that carried the sound from the source to you. This type of wave is called a longitudinal wave. In a **longitudinal wave,** as shown in Figure 18-2(b), the medium vibrates in the same direction as the wave itself travels. You can't directly observe longitudinal waves in air. However, you can find out more about them by seeing how they affect other substances.

Concept Development

Demonstration The movement of transverse waves in water can also be observed by dropping golf balls in a large tub of water.

Materials needed are a large tub, water, golf balls, and a cork.

Fill a large tub about half full of water. Let students take turns dropping golf balls into the center of the tub. Have students observe the waves. Put the cork in the water and watch the movement of the cork when balls are again dropped in. Ask why the cork does not move to the side of the tub. *The water, or medium, is not moving to the side. It is just going up and down. Only the energy from the disturbance moves to the side of the tub.* L1

MAKING CONNECTIONS

Language Arts

Before writing became widespread, people used oral storytelling, often using poetry. It is still a good memory device—and a lot of fun. Have students make up poems to help them remember the terms *transverse, longitudinal, compression,* and *rarefaction.* They could use haiku, limerick, free verse, rap, or a traditional rhyming verse.

Examples:

Transverse waves move at right angles;
they swerve with an up-and-down curve.
But longitudinal waves move all in one direction;
they bunch and they spread, I've heard.

or:

Compression is a bunching up, tight as tight can be.
Rarefaction means spreading out, footloose and fancy free.

PROGRAM RESOURCES

Teacher Classroom Resources

Study Guide, page 63

Making Connections: Technology and Society, page 39, Weather Forecasting with Radar L2

Other Resources

Waves and Sound Energy, software, Focus.

What is a Wave?, video, Focus.

OPTIONS

Meeting Individual Needs

Behaviorally Disordered Get students with a short attention span physically involved in distinguishing between transverse and longitudinal waves. Have them use their hands to mimic the up-and-down motion of a transverse wave. Then ask them to move their arms forward alternately making a fist and then spreading out their fingers, mimicking the motion of a longitudinal wave. L1 LEP

Content Background

Waves that require a medium to pass through, such as sound and water, are called mechanical waves. Waves that do not require a medium, such as radio, light, and X rays, are electromagnetic waves.

FIND OUT!

Can you observe the effects of a longitudinal wave?

Time needed 15 minutes

Materials portable radio with a round speaker, metal container with a diameter slightly larger than the radio speaker, plastic wrap, large rubber band, dry rice

Thinking Processes Observing and inferring, Comparing and contrasting, Recognizing cause and effect

Purpose To enable students to observe a longitudinal wave.

Preparation Students should assemble the radio and metal container ahead of time in the manner described in the text.

Teaching the Activity

Review with students the form sound waves take. Use the terms *longitudinal waves, compression,* and *rarefaction* as you review. After the music has left a pattern on the plastic wrap with the rice, ask students to describe what they see. L2

Troubleshooting Make sure plastic wrap is tight around the can.

Expected Outcomes

Students should be able to see a pattern of compression and rarefaction in the rice and identify the pattern as that of a longitudinal wave.

Conclude and Apply

1. The rice is moving into a pattern of compression and rarefaction.
2. Sound waves from the speaker. The plastic is vibrating because of the sound waves that are striking it.
3. The amplitude of the sound waves increases, modifying the pattern of the rice.
4. Yes. By vibrating back and forth. These are longitudinal waves. Waves on a rope are transverse waves.

FIND OUT!

Can you observe the effects of a longitudinal wave?

Get a portable radio with a round speaker. Now find a metal can or some other container with the same or slightly larger diameter than that of the speaker. Cut out the bottom of the can with a can opener so that both ends are open. Stretch a piece of plastic wrap across one end of the can and secure it with a rubber band.

Now place the radio so that its speakers are pointing up. Place the open end of the can over the speaker and sprinkle some dry rice grains on the plastic. Tune the radio to a song with a "heavy beat" and observe. Put your fingertips lightly on the plastic. What do you feel? Turn up the volume.

Conclude and Apply

1. What do you see happening?
2. What is causing it? What do you feel?
3. What happens when you turn up the volume?
4. If it isn't covered, take a close look at the paper cone of the radio speaker. Is it moving? How does it make waves in the air? Compare and contrast these waves with the waves on a rope.

FIGURE 18-3. A vibrating speaker produces compressions and rarefactions in the air.

The waves you observed in the preceding Find Out were produced by the speaker vibrating back and forth. As shown in Figure 18-3, as the speaker moved out, it pushed the air in front of it. Then, as the speaker moved back, the air suddenly expanded, becoming more rarefied. Thus, the speaker produces a series of compressions and rarefactions. These move out from the speaker. Therefore, they behave like the compressions and rarefactions on the coiled spring in Chapter 3. We can therefore say that sound behaves like a longitudinal wave.

To better understand the difference between transverse and longitudinal waves, let's once again investigate waves in a coiled spring.

PROGRAM RESOURCES

Teacher Classroom Resources

Activity Masters, pages 73-74, Investigate 18-1

Making Connections: Integrating Sciences, page 39, How Animals Use Waves L2

Making Connections: Across the Curriculum, page 39, Crushing Stones with Waves L2

OPTIONS

Meeting Individual Needs

Visually Impaired/Hearing Impaired If you have a visually impaired or hearing-impaired student in the class, ask him or her to share with the class how he or she uses the vibrations caused by sound waves as cues to the nature of objects or events in the environment. For example, to get the attention of a hearing impaired person, family members may stamp their feet on the floor to cause a vibration.

INVESTIGATE!

18-1 WAVES ON A COILED SPRING

A mechanical wave is the motion of a disturbance that travels through a medium such as water, a rope, or air. Waves can be either transverse or longitudinal. In this activity, you'll be creating and observing the behavior of transverse and longitudinal waves in a coiled spring.

PROBLEM

How do waves behave on a coiled spring?

MATERIALS 

coiled spring
goggles
small piece of colored thread

PROCEDURE

1. **CAUTION**: *Wear goggles to avoid eye injury.* Have two people hold the coiled spring, one at each end. Stretch the coiled spring 3 m on a smooth floor. Tie the thread to a coil near the middle of the spring.
2. Have one person, the source, slowly shake his or her hand back and forth once on the floor, about 30 cm in each direction. This will send a pulse down the spring.
3. Diagram the pulse as it moves down the spring.
4. **Observe** the reflected pulse. Diagram the pulse that was sent and the reflected pulse that returns to the source. With an arrow, show the direction of movement of the string.
5. Have an end person squeeze together about 15 cm of the coiled spring, creating a compression.
6. Release the compression and **observe** the wave as it travels down the spring. Repeat Steps 3 and 4 for this pulse.

ANALYZE

1. In Step 4, was the reflected pulse on the same or opposite side as the original?
2. What type of wave pulse was produced in Step 2? How do you know?
3. What type of wave pulse was produced in Step 6? How do you know?

CONCLUDE AND APPLY

4. Would you **infer** that a water wave is mostly transverse or longitudinal?
5. Would you **infer** that the sound wave from a radio is transverse or longitudinal?
6. **Going Further:** A neighbor likes to play a stereo very loud. **Sequence** the media through which the sound waves pass as they travel from the stereo to your ears.

INVESTIGATE!

18-1 WAVES ON A COILED SPRING

Time needed 20 minutes

Materials coiled spring, goggles, small piece of colored thread

Thinking Processes
Observing and inferring, Comparing and contrasting, Recognizing cause and effect

Purpose To observe both transverse and longitudinal waves in a coiled spring.

Preparation Have a clear area large enough so the spring will not contact surrounding objects.

Teaching the Activity

Discussion Before beginning the activity, ask students to suggest what they might do to produce transverse and longitudinal waves with the coiled spring. L1

Student Journal As each wave is produced, ask students to make a diagram in their journals of the wave pattern. LEP

Safety Be sure students wear their goggles.

Expected Outcomes

Students should understand that transverse waves move at right angles to the source of the disturbance, while longitudinal waves move in the same direction as the vibrating medium, alternately compressed and rarefied.

Answers to Analyze/Conclude and Apply

1. opposite
2. Transverse; the medium moved at right angles to the pulse itself.
3. Longitudinal; the medium moved in the same direction as the wave.
4. transverse
5. longitudinal
6. Waves may pass through the air, through the wall (or a glass window), through the air, to your ears.

Enrichment

Activity The popular children's toy Slinky is excellent for experimenting with different types of waves. If possible, get a Slinky for each member of the class. Have students hold one end in each hand and produce transverse waves of varying lengths. Ask students to describe how they are producing a wave and ask them to predict what will happen if they move their hands faster or slower. Using stacks of books, have Slinky go downstairs. Ask students to describe how this action resembles a longitudinal wave. Then start a longitudinal wave by compressing one end and letting the pulse move through the coils. L1 LEP

3 Assess

Check for Understanding

Assign questions 1 and 2 and the Apply question under Check Your Understanding. If possible, borrow a drum from the music teacher and allow students to check their answers by trying the activity.

Reteach

Activity Have all the members of the class join hands in a circle. Beginning at one point, have students raise and lower their arms, mimicking the motion of a wave. Try changing the speed or height of the wave. Apply the terms learned in the chapter to the wave patterns that emerge. L1

Extension

Activity Bring in a variety of common materials to serve as media: a scarf, a metal pipe or rod, a stringed instrument are examples. Ask students to produce waves in these media. Discuss the types of waves that can be produced. L2

Answers to Check Your Understanding

1. A wave is a continuous, rhythmic disturbance that transmits energy. Examples include: shake a rope, drop rocks in water, and shout.
2. See Figure 18-2. Diagrams should include movement of medium and direction of wave motion.
3. The rice would arrange itself into a pattern of compression and rarefaction; longitudinal.

4 Close

Demonstration

Draw half a dozen different waves on the chalkboard. Vary amplitude and wavelength, but make sure each wave can be identified as transverse or longitudinal. Ask students to make that identification.

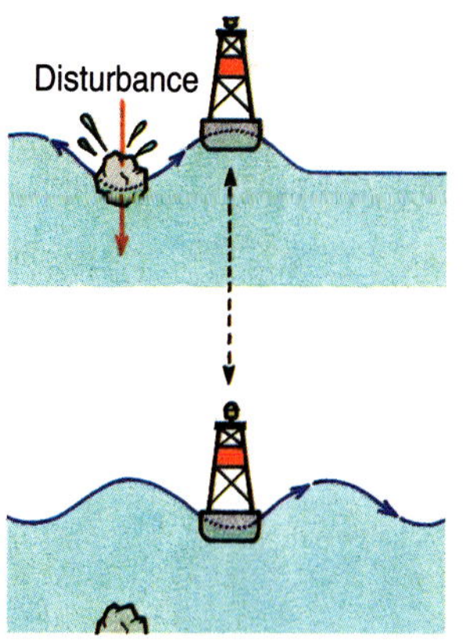

FIGURE 18-4. Water moves up and down as the wave moves away from the disturbance.

You saw in the Investigate that in a transverse wave, as the wave moved away from the source, the string moved back and forth at right angles to the spring.

Figure 18-4 shows a transverse wave in water. Notice that the water moves almost straight up and down. The medium moves up and down, but the disturbance—the wave—moves away from the source at right angles to the motion of the medium. You may also have noticed that an object, such as a buoy or boat floating in the waves, will stay in one place unless it is moved by the wind or a water current.

When you made a longitudinal wave in the Investigate, the compressions moved away from the source, and the thread vibrated back and forth in the same direction. Notice in Figure 18-5 that a longitudinal wave is disturbed along the direction the wave travels, while in transverse waves the disturbance occurs at right angles to the direction of wave motion. This is just one difference between transverse and longitudinal waves. You will find others later.

FIGURE 18-5. In a longitudinal wave, the spring moves back and forth as the wave moves away from the disturbance.

Waves are all around you, and your life is influenced by them every day. People talking, music on the radio, waves in the pool, and surf at the beach are just a few of the waves you encounter. In the next section, you will learn more about wave characteristics. You'll find out what the hills and valleys of waves are actually called, as well as what wavelength and frequency mean.

Check Your Understanding

1. Define a wave. List three examples of ways in which a mechanical wave may be produced.
2. Draw diagrams of a transverse wave and a longitudinal wave. Through labeling and brief descriptions, compare and contrast their properties.
3. **APPLY:** If you were to sprinkle dry rice onto the head of a drum and strike the drumhead at the edge with a drumstick, what would you observe? What type of wave is this?

OPTIONS

Meeting Individual Needs

Hearing Impaired Invite a physician, nurse or audiologist to visit your class and discuss hearing disorders. If you have a hearing impaired student who is willing to discuss his or her situation, provide time for this student to talk to the class. Ask the guest speaker to explain how sound waves produce sound we can understand and what can go wrong so that some people do not sense those sounds. Ask the speaker to distinguish among various causes of hearing impairment, such as nerve damage, a damaged eardrum, or damaged bones in the middle ear. Ask him or her how these disorders are detected and how they can be treated.

18-2 Wave Characteristics

PROPERTIES OF WAVES

The wave you produced earlier with the rope can be described by its properties. When you quickly moved the rope up and down, you may have noticed high and low points—hills and valleys. These low points, the valleys, are called **troughs.** The high points, the hills, are called **crests.**

In the following Find Out activity, you will observe these parts of a wave again.

OBJECTIVES

In this section, you will

- draw a wave;
- identify the wavelength, amplitude, crest, and trough of a wave;
- explain the relationship among frequency, wavelength, and speed in a wave.

KEY SCIENCE TERMS

crest
trough
wavelength
amplitude

FIND OUT!

What are wave crests and troughs?

Use your 4-m rope again and tie it to a doorknob. Take a 5-m piece of white string and tie it at the same height, but about 30 cm in front of the rope. Stretch out the rope level while one classmate stretches out the string parallel to the rope. Have a third classmate stand with a pencil, a piece of paper, and a meterstick at the center of the rope about 30 cm away from the string. The three of you should be positioned as shown.

Now start humming your favorite song or rap with a good rhythm and move the rope up and down in time with the song. This should set up a series of waves on your rope. If it doesn't, adjust your rhythm. Have the classmate with the meter stick make a quick sketch of your wave using the string as a reference. Then have your classmate measure how high above the string the highest point on the wave is.

Section 18-2

PREPARATION

Concepts Developed

In this section, students will continue their study of waves, learning the properties of a wave (crest, trough, wavelength, and amplitude) and the relationship among frequency, wavelength, and speed.

Planning the Lesson

In planning your lesson on wave characteristics, refer to the Chapter Organizer on pages 536A-B for timing suggestions, resources, and additional materials that will help you in your presentation of the lesson concepts. For adequate development of the concepts presented in this section, we recommend that students do the Find Out activity on page 543 and the Investigate activity on page 546.

1 MOTIVATE

Demonstration Students will observe waves of varying properties. Materials needed are a large tub half filled with water, rocks of varying sizes.

Drop a series of rocks into the tub of water, producing waves of different properties. Ask students to describe the differences they observe. L1

FIND OUT!

What are wave crests and troughs?

Time needed 25 minutes

Materials 4-m rope, 5-m piece of white string, meterstick

Thinking Processes Observing and inferring, Comparing and contrasting, Measuring in SI, Interpreting data

Purpose Students will learn to identify wave crests and troughs.

PROGRAM RESOURCES

Teacher Classroom Resources

Study Guide, page 64
Laboratory Manual, pages 109-112, Velocity of a Wave L3
Concept Mapping, page 26, Waves L1
Multicultural Activities, page 39, The Alphorn L1
Transparency Masters, page 75, and **Color Transparency,** number 36, Wave Properties L2

Teaching the Activity

Ask the student who will produce the waves to begin by slowly moving the rope. You may want to have the student who is sketching the wave to put his or her drawing on the chalkboard rather than on paper. When the first drawing has been completed, identify the "hill" as the wave crest and the "valley" as the wave trough. Draw a line across the top of the wave crests and another where the white string is (the rest position, about halfway between the crest and trough). Measure this distance between the rest position and either the crest or the trough and identify this distance as the amplitude of the wave. Draw perpendicular lines down the middle of two neighboring crests or troughs. Measure the distance between these two lines and identify it as the wavelength. Repeat the exercise several times, drawing waves with different amplitudes and wavelengths. L2 COOP LEARN

Troubleshooting Make sure the rope doesn't get tangled up in the string.

Expected Outcomes

Students will be able to identify wave crests, troughs, amplitudes, and wavelengths.

Conclude and Apply

1. Yes; sometimes it was shorter and sometimes it was longer.
2. The faster the beat, the shorter the distance between the crests.

Student Text Questions How might you measure the wave length using other points on the wave? *Any point on one wave to the same point on the next wave can be used to measure wave length.* What other wave properties can you describe? *Properties of transverse waves such as direction of motion vs direction of disturbance.*

The next measurement should be how far it is from the top of one wave to the top of the next.

By now you're probably pretty tired, so trade off duties until each member of the team has done each job. Use songs with different rhythms.

Compare your drawings. Remember, the crest of a wave is its highest point. Label the crest on your drawing. A wave trough is its lowest point. Label the troughs of your wave.

Conclude and Apply

1. Did the distance between the wave crests change as your team went from one song to another?
2. What was the relationship between the distance from wave to wave and the rate of the beat?

Wavelength

In the Find Out, you measured one property of waves by measuring the distance between one wave crest and the next. The property you measured is called the **wavelength**. For instance, you could measure the distance between one crest and the next, as shown in Figure 18-6(a). How might you measure the wavelength using other points on the wave? What other wave properties can you describe?

Amplitude

Let's imagine that you want to know how high the crests of Louie's wave were. The normal level at the deep end of the pool is 3 meters. But when Louie jumped in, the level rose 30 centimeters because of the wave he made. Thus the crest of Louie's wave was 30 centimeters higher than the normal level of the pool. This was the amplitude

FIGURE 18-6. The distance between one crest on a wave and another is called *wavelength* (a). The distance from the crest of a wave to the rest position of the medium is called the *amplitude* of a wave (b).

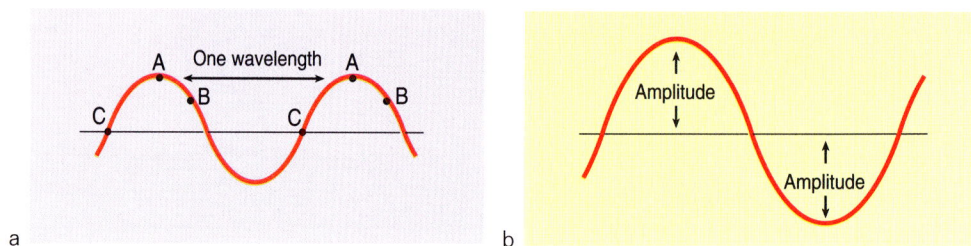

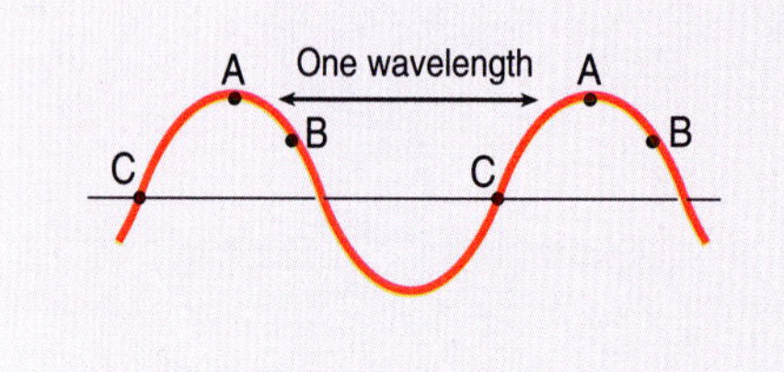

a

Amplitude
Amplitude

b

OPTIONS

Enrichment

Discussion A tsunami is a gigantic ocean wave usually generated by an earthquake or volcanic eruption on the ocean floor. If these waves hit a coastal area where people live, they can cause great destruction and take many lives. The largest tsunami may have occurred in 1470 in the Aegean Sea. Scientists have found evidence suggesting that a wave 90 meters high struck there. A tsunami hit southeastern Bangladesh in the spring of 1991. Waves described "as high as mountains" struck the country's coast, leaving 100,000 dead and 9 million homeless.

Scientists are researching ways to predict tsunamis. Ask students what patterns they think the scientists should look for. Then have them research and report on the Tsunami Warning System based in the Hawaiian Islands.

of his wave. **Amplitude** is the distance from the crest or the trough of the wave to the level of calm water.

Study Figure 18-6(b) to see how amplitude is measured. The disturbance that Louie made in the pool was greater than the disturbance made by the wind blowing the pool's surface. You know this because the wave Louie made piled up far more water than the wind could. Now think back to the measurements you made during the Find Out activity. Which measurement gave you the amplitude of your rope wave? Was the amplitude of your wave different from the amplitude of your partner's? If it was, hypothesize why.

DID YOU KNOW?

The largest wind-driven wave ever measured had an amplitude of over 34 meters. It was created by winds of over 100 kilometers per hour blowing across the ocean for thousands of kilometers.

Frequency

What else changed from person to person in your Find Out activity? You found that the person who used a song with the fastest beat created more crests and troughs on the rope. You could say that this person shook the rope more frequently than the others. In fact, the wave property you would be describing is called a wave's frequency. The frequency of a wave is the number of crests or troughs that pass a given point in one second. Figure 18-7 shows two waves. The blue wave has twice the frequency of the red wave.

In the following activity, you will be able to study the relationship between wavelength and frequency.

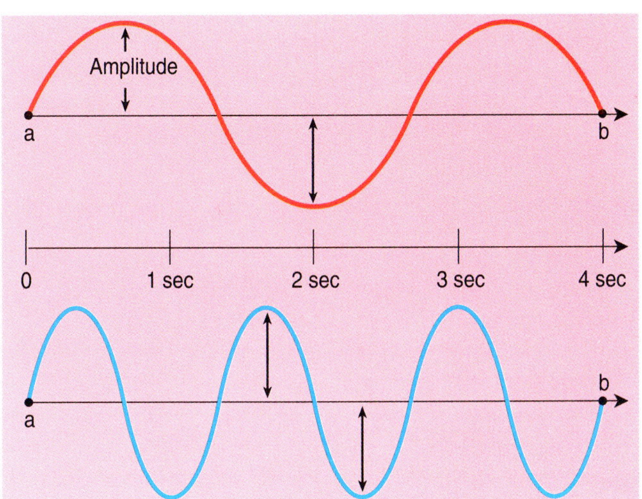

FIGURE 18-7. These waves have different frequencies. Which one has the higher frequency?

2 TEACH

Tying to Previous Knowledge

Ask student to recall their study of pendulum movement in Chapter 14, reviewing the terms *period* and *amplitude*. Explain that the movement of waves can be described in a similar manner.

Concept Development

Theme Connection As they learn to identify the properties of a wave, students will better understand the wave system. In this section, the relationship between wavelength and amplitude is an example of interactions between two factors that affect a system.

Student Text Questions Which measurement gave you the amplitude of your rope wave? *the measurement from the crest to the highest point* Was the amplitude of your wave different from your partner's? *Probably—It would depend on the range of motion of the hand shaking the wave.*

Using the Diagrams Discuss Figures 18-6, 18-7, and 18-8 simultaneously. In each diagram, ask students to identify the wave crests and the wave troughs. Note how the wavelength is measured from point A to point A, point B to point B, or point C to point C in diagram 18-6. Have students arrive at the generalization that a wavelength is the distance between points on the same parts of neighboring waves. Ask students to measure the wavelengths in Figures 18-7 and 18-8. Note how amplitude is measured in Figure 18-7. Use that method to measure amplitude in the other diagrams. Note how frequency is measured in Figure 18-8. Use that method to measure the frequency in the other diagrams.

Multicultural Perspectives

Countries and islands that have coastlines in the Pacific and Indian oceans have been struck by devastating tsunamis. One of the most famous occurred in the summer of 1883, when a volcano erupted on a small island of Krakatoa, just off Indonesia. The enormous explosion destroyed two-thirds of the island. Worse than that, though, the energy from the explosion started a tsunami. The tsunami was as tall as a twelve-story building and traveled at 560 km.p.h. When it hit the coast of Java, it destroyed 300 villages and killed 36,000 people. Other tsunamis have struck Hawaii and South American countries such as Chile. Have students research legends that different cultures have, explaining tsunamis.

INVESTIGATE!

18-2 RIPPLES

Time needed 20 minutes

Materials clear glass dish approximately 30 cm square, strips of plastic foam, tape, water, pencil or pen, overhead light, piece of white paper, ruler

Thinking Processes
Observing and inferring, Comparing and contrasting, Interpreting data

Purpose Students will learn how changing the frequency of a wave affects the wavelength.

Preparation Collect materials for each group of students and place at appropriate workstations.

Teaching the Activity

Discussion As each wave is produced in the dish, ask students to describe what they see. Then ask a student to draw the shapes of the waves on the chalkboard. Have students identify the wave crests and troughs, then measure the amplitude and wavelength for each set of waves. Compare the results of the various groups. L1

Troubleshooting Sketches should be drawn similar in size so relative measurements will be valid.

Expected Outcomes

Students will be able to see that as the frequency of a wave is increased, its wavelength decreases. Likewise, they will see that as the frequency of a wave is decreased, its wavelength increases.

Answers to Analyze/Conclude and Apply

1. Increasing the frequency causes the wavelength to decrease.
2. The wave goes in the opposite direction.
3. Wavelength and frequency are inversely proportional (as one increases, the other decreases).
4. Examples might include waves produced in any enclosure such as a sink or bathtub.

INVESTIGATE!

18-2 RIPPLES

While a water wave may not be as simple as a wave on a coiled spring, it should be familiar to you. On a bright sunny day, you may have noticed the continuously moving, zig-zagging, bright lines on the bottom of a swimming pool. These lines are sunlight focused on the pool bottom by wave crests. Wave troughs produce dark lines compared with the normal bottom appearance. In the following ripple-tank activity, you'll use this observation to study the relationship of frequency, wavelength, and speed.

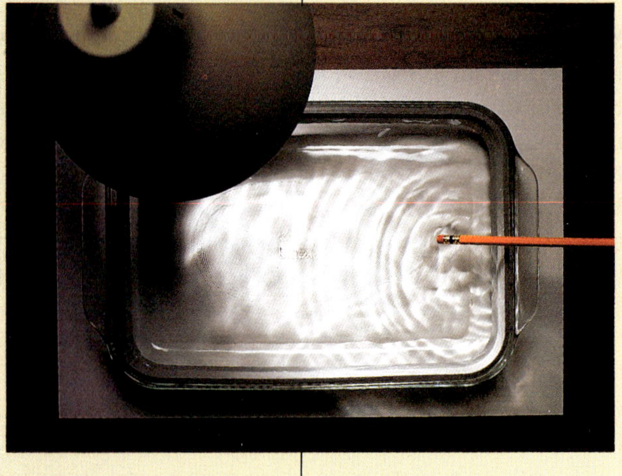

PROBLEM

How are a wave's frequency and wavelength related?

MATERIALS

clear glass dish approximately 30-cm square
strips of plastic foam
tape
water
pencil or pen
overhead light
1 piece of blank white paper
ruler

PROCEDURE

1. Tape strips of plastic foam to the inner edges of the dish. Then fill the clear glass dish with about 3 cm of water. Set it on a piece of blank white paper under an overhead light source.
2. Tap the water with the end of your pencil or pen. **Observe** the wave by looking at the paper. Draw the shape of the wave. **Compare** the speed of the wave in all directions.
3. Now tap the water again, producing a series of waves. Increase the frequency by tapping the water faster and **observe** the change in wavelength. Draw an example of low and high frequency waves being produced.
4. Lay your pen or pencil flat and tap the water. Draw the shape of the wave. **Observe** what happens when the wave strikes the sides of the dish.

ANALYZE

1. What **effect** does increasing the frequency have on the wavelength of the waves produced in Step 3?
2. As the wave strikes the sides of the dish, or barrier, what is the new direction of the wave?

CONCLUDE AND APPLY

3. What is the relationship between wavelength and frequency in water waves?
4. **Going Further:** Give two other examples of reflected waves from your own observations.

PROGRAM RESOURCES

Teacher Classroom Resources
Activity Masters, pages 75-76, Ripples
Critical Thinking/Problem Solving, page 8, Flex Your Brain
Multicultural Activities, page 40, Water Drums L1

In the Investigate, you found that as you increased the frequency of the wave, the wavelength got smaller.

Think back to the Find Out. If one of your group used a song with a faster rhythm, his or her drawing should have shown a shorter distance between wave crests. This happened because the classmate shook the rope up and down faster, and more crests were created each second. In this way, he or she increased the frequency of the wave. What do you think will happen to the wavelength when the frequency of a wave decreases? Yes, it will increase.

SPEED

As you have just seen, the wavelength decreases as frequency increases. But what about the water waves in the dish? Did they seem to speed up or slow down?

The speed of a mechanical wave depends only on the medium through which it travels. You learned in Chapter 13 that speed is the total distance traveled in a given amount of time. Look at Figure 18-8. The two waves are both in water. They have the same amplitude and speed, but one has two times the frequency and one half the wavelength of the other. Notice that the distance traveled by each wave is the same, as represented by the horizontal

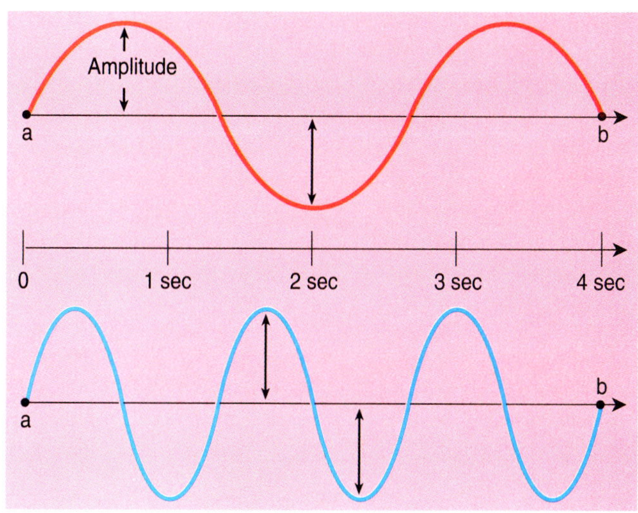

FIGURE 18-8. The wavelength and the frequency of a wave are related. As the wavelength decreases, the frequency increases. Notice that the amplitude remains the same.

MAKING CONNECTIONS

Math

Scientists use a simple formula to determine how fast a wave is traveling: velocity = wavelength × frequency. Give students several problems to solve. For example: A wave moving along a rope has a wavelength of 1.2 m/wave and a frequency of 4.5 waves/s. How fast is the wave traveling along the rope? *1.2 m/wave × 4.5 waves/s = 5.4 m/s.* A wave in the ocean is 3.2 m long and its frequency is 0.6 waves/s. What is the velocity of the wave? *3.2 m/wave × 0.6 waves/s = 1.92 m/s* When students are comfortable with the formula in this order, turn it around and give them velocity and wavelength and ask them to find frequency. Example: An earthquake can produce a wave traveling 5000 m/s with a wavelength of 417 m. What would be the frequency of that wave? L3

$$\text{frequency} = \frac{\text{velocity}}{\text{wavelength}}.$$

$$\frac{5{,}000 \text{ m/s}}{417 \text{ m/wave}} = 12 \text{ waves/s}.$$

Inquiry Question How could the terms *crest, trough, wavelength,* and *amplitude* be applied to longitudinal waves? *The crest of a longitudinal wave is the point of maximum compression. The trough is the point of maximum rarefaction. The wavelength can be measured from one crest to the same spot on the next crest, or one trough to the next. The amplitude can be measured from a crest to a point about halfway between two crests.*

Flex Your Brain Use the Flex Your Brain activity to have students explore RADIO WAVES.

OPTIONS

Meeting Individual Needs

Learning Disabled/Behaviorally Disordered Be sure learning disabled and behaviorally disordered students are actively involved in this activity. Allow them to tap the water, producing the waves. Ask them to draw the pictures of the waves produced.

You may want to assign partners, teaming mainstreamed students with other students, to discuss the results. Peer teaching provides concentrated individual attention. It also helps students gain a deeper understanding of the concept, because they have to understand it to explain it to another student. COOP LEARN LEP

SKILLBUILDER

Students are probably aware that air at high altitudes is "thin," or of low density. Accept hypotheses that relate slower speeds to lower densities. L1

3 Assess

Check for Understanding

1. Draw two transverse waves of differing frequencies on the chalkboard. Ask students to identify the wave crests, wave troughs, amplitude, wavelength, and frequency of the waves.
2. Assign questions 1 and 2 and the Apply question from Check Your Understanding. Have students discuss their answers to the Apply question. Ask students if they have ever tried surfing or watched surfing, either in person or on television. Point out that the surfer does not ride the crest, but slides down the slope of the wave, ahead of the crest.

Reteach

Activity Give each student a piece of string about one meter long. Have students shape the string into a wave and glue it to a piece of paper. Have students label the wave crests, wave troughs, amplitude, and wavelength. If students are having difficulty with amplitude, have them glue a straight piece of string across the wave, representing the string at rest. L1

Extension

Activity Let students experiment making waves in a tub of water. Mark the level of the water at rest on the side of the tub. Then drop items into the water, creating waves. Students can mark the height of the wave crest on the side of the tub and calculate amplitude and wavelength. You may also want to provide a stopwatch so that frequency can also be determined. L3

FIGURE 18-9. The waves in this pool are of equal wavelength and amplitude.

SKILLBUILDER

HYPOTHESIZING
Sound travels slower in air at high altitudes than at low altitudes. State a hypothesis to explain this observation. If you need help, refer to the **Skill Handbook** on page 657.

arrow. The time it took each wave to travel that distance is also the same. Therefore, the speed is the same. As long as the waves are traveling through the same medium, their speed is unaffected by a change in wavelength or frequency because as one increases, the other decreases.

Think back to the wave Louie made in the opening of this chapter. The crest of Louie's wave is what lifted Ladonna, and the amplitude was how high she was lifted. The wavelength in Figure 18-8 is the distance between the crests or troughs, and the frequency is how many crests or troughs flow by you in one second. What happens when waves run into one another? You'll find out in the next section.

Check Your Understanding

1. Sketch a transverse wave. Label a crest, a trough, a wavelength, and the amplitude.
2. What is the relationship among the frequency, wavelength and speed of a wave?
3. **APPLY:** What characteristic of a wave would be most important to a surfer?

4 Close

Activity

Draw a wave with several crests on the chalkboard. To the side of the first wave, draw a different wave. Have students use the properties of waves to compare the two waves. L1

Answers to Check Your Understanding

1. Sketches should resemble Figures 18-6, 18-7, and 18-8.
2. Speed is determined by the medium only. Wavelength and frequency are inversely proportional (as one increases, the other decreases).
3. the amplitude

18-3 Adding Waves

STANDING WAVES

In the previous section, you and your team made some waves on a rope. Because the rope was fixed on one end, you may have created an important kind of wave without realizing it. In the following activity, you are going to make these waves on purpose.

OBJECTIVES

In this section, you will

- explain how waves add together;
- describe two examples of wave interference;
- demonstrate a standing wave.

KEY SCIENCE TERMS

interference

FIND OUT!

How can you make a standing wave?

Using a 4-m rope, tie it to the same spot as you did earlier. Shake the loose end up and down until waves begin to form. Now increase or decrease the frequency until you get a wave like one of those shown. If you can't do it, try changing the length of rope you are shaking.

Once you get a wave like one of those shown, see if you can produce the other two waves shown by varying the rope's frequency and/or length. Now make the wave with a single depression, as in the middle example. Have one of the non-shaking members of your team carefully place a finger just above the rope at the trough.

Conclude and Apply

1. Does the rope touch the finger?
2. Why or why not?

What you have made is called a standing wave because it does not travel down the rope. It vibrates in place. If the wind is blowing just right, a standing wave may form in a clothesline. The line will start to vibrate, giving off a hum. When the clothesline does this, observe it closely, and you will see a wave in it. The whole line may be vibrating with a single crest, or you may see several crests. If you can safely reach the clothesline, see what effect trying to stop it has.

Section 18-3

PREPARATION

Concepts Developed

In this section, students will discover what happens when two sets of waves meet. They will learn that when two crests meet, the waves add together; when a crest and a trough meet, the waves cancel each other. This is called wave interference.

Planning the Lesson

In planning your lesson on wave interference, refer to the Chapter Organizer on pages 536A-B for timing suggestions, resources, and additional materials that will help you in your presentation of the lesson concepts.

For adequate development of the concepts presented in this section, we recommend that students do the Find Out activities on page 549 and 550.

1 MOTIVATE

Discussion Ask students if they have ever pushed someone on a swing. **What happens if your pushes are timed correctly?** *The swing's amplitude increases.* **What happens if your pushes are not timed correctly?** *The swing's amplitude decreases.* Point out that when two waves interact, the timing of their interactions affects the results.

FIND OUT!

How can you make a standing wave?

Time needed 10 minutes

Materials 4-meter rope

Thinking Processes
Observing and inferring, Recognizing cause and effect

Purpose To learn how standing waves are produced.

Troubleshooting Keep the immediate area around the rope clear of objects and students.

Teaching the Activity

Make sure students have their textbooks open to Figure 18-13. Choose a volunteer to produce the wave. Then ask another volunteer to hold his or her finger over the rope as described in the text.

Expected Outcome

Students will see that they can produce a wave in which the crest and trough remain in the same locations along the rope.

Conclude and Apply

1. no
2. When the crest of one wave met the trough of the other, the two canceled.

2 Teach

Tying to Previous Knowledge

In Chapter 14, students learned that an object in motion changes its motion when it reaches the ground or collides with another object. This can be contrasted with waves, which add together or cancel each other out when they collide and can pass through each other without being affected themselves.

FIND OUT!

What happens when waves pass?

Time needed 10 minutes

Materials clear glass dish approximately 30 cm square, water, overhead light, piece of white paper, two pencils

Thinking Processes Observing and inferring, Comparing and contrasting, Recognizing cause and effect

Purpose Students will observe the effects when waves meet.

Preparation Prepare dish just as you did for the Investigate in section 18-2. Place over piece of paper and fill half full of water.

Teaching the Activity

When a student taps with both pencils, he or she should tap once with each, so that each produces a single wave.

Expected Outcomes

Students should see that when two waves meet, they either increase in size or cancel each other out.

Conclude and Apply Allow students to speculate. As they read on, they will learn that when the crest of one wave meets the trough of another, the two cancel, producing a calm point on the water's surface.

In the rest of this section, you will learn what causes standing waves and where they can be found in your environment.

INTERFERENCE

Before you can explain a standing wave, you need to understand how waves can interact. Imagine you are on the edge of a pond or pool. Now suppose you drop two rocks into the water about 30 centimeters apart. The ripples created by each rock move out in circles, as shown in Figure 18-10. Notice that they quickly run into each other.

FIGURE 18-10. Water ripples move right through each other.

If you have seen these kinds of ripples, you know that the waves don't bounce off each other. Instead, they seem to pass through each other. Thus, it appears as if the waves from both rocks are able to exist in the same place at the same time.

FIND OUT!

What happens when waves pass?

Using the clear dish, water, and light from Investigate 18-2, tap the surface of the water with the tip of one pencil. Notice the brightness of the crests and troughs. Now tap the surface with the tips of two pencils about 10 cm apart. Observe the bright and dark patterns on the paper.

Conclude and Apply

What do you think causes the lines where there appear to be no crests or troughs?

OPTIONS

Meeting Individual Needs

Behaviorally Disordered Make sure students with a short attention span are actively involved in both Find Out activities. Ask them to hold a hand over the calm part of the rope or tap the water to produce the waves. To help students understand how the waves are changing, measure the amplitude of a single wave, then measure the amplitude of a standing wave and compare the two. The concrete numbers are easier for students to follow.

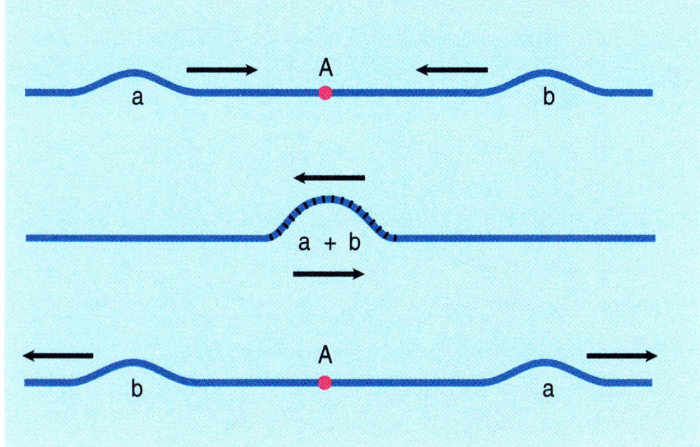

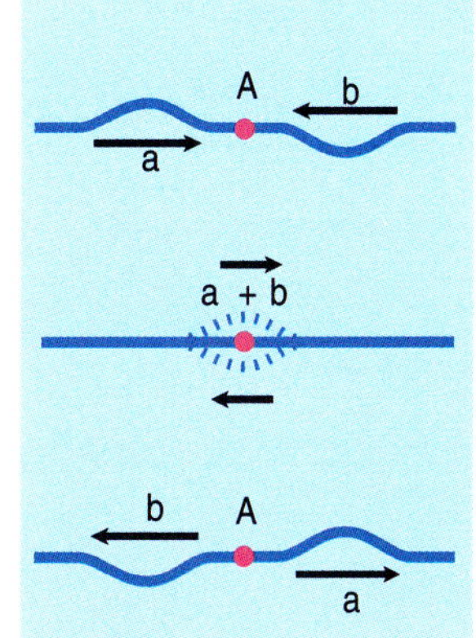

FIGURE 18-11. When two crests pass through each other, they add together (a). What happens when the crest of one wave passes through the trough of another (b)?

As the waves pass through each other, they interact in one of two ways. If two crests pass through each other, they briefly form a new wave that is equal to the sum of the amplitudes of the two waves, as shown in Figure 18-11(a).

Because the waves in Figure 18-11(a) "interfere" with each other, this situation is called interference. **Interference** is the action of two or more waves at one point. When two or more waves add together, it is called constructive interference.

But what would happen if a trough of one wave passed through the crest of another? Look at Figure 18-11(b). What happened?

You might say that one wave destroyed the other. This would be a good observation because what you just saw is called destructive interference. The waves, however, are not really destroyed because they will emerge on the other side unchanged.

In Figure 18-12, you see a display from a ripple tank. It is a more sophisticated version of what you used in the Investigate. Notice that two overlapping water waves have been produced by two sources hitting the water at the same time. Locate a crest and a trough close to a source. How did you identify each of them?

Now locate the areas where two wave crests have added, producing a larger crest. Look for very bright bands of light. How can you tell that constructive interference is going on? Now find areas where destructive interference is going on. How can you tell that waves are canceling each other?

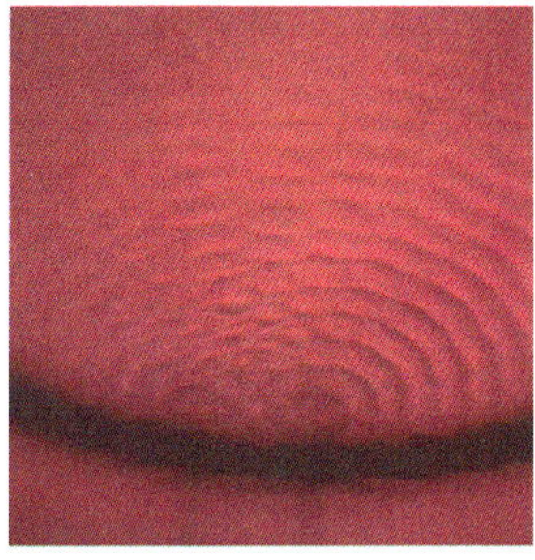

FIGURE 18-12. In the ripple tank, you can observe constructive and destructive interference.

Concept Development

Demonstration Take your class to the gymnasium or some other large, empty room. Ask a volunteer to go to the center of the room while the rest of the class stays together near the edge of the room. Ask the volunteer to clap his or her hands together loudly. Is there an echo? Why? *With nothing in its way, one sound wave hits the wall and is reflected back.* Then ask the class to group itself around the individual in the center of the room. Ask him or her to clap again. Is there an echo this time? Why not? *The sound waves bounce off all the different people standing in the way, setting up many reflected waves that interfere with one another.* Move the students to different locations, such as all in the front of the volunteer, all behind, and in a circle around him or her. Ask students to describe any differences these changes make in the sound. L2

Enrichment

Discussion Ask students to brainstorm a list of places where it would be useful to design a room or building so that sound waves interfere with one another. How would the needs of a basketball gymnasium differ from the needs of a theater? What about the needs of a cafeteria versus the needs of a classroom? What would you be trying to accomplish in each of these different places?

PROGRAM RESOURCES

Teacher Classroom Resources

Study Guide, page 65

Transparency Masters, page 73, and **Color Transparency,** number 35, Constructive/Destructive Interference L2

Take Home Activities, page 29, Wave Interference L1

Concept Development

Theme Connection By studying what happens when waves meet, students should be able to better understand the theme of interaction within a system of waves. After doing the Find Out activity on page 550, students will be aware that waves act on each other in a systematic and predictable manner.

MAKING CONNECTIONS

Language Arts

Have students write a science fiction short story set on a water planet with two opposing societies, one in which the inhabitants wish always to live on the crests of the waves, one that wishes to live in the troughs. Encourage the students to remember scientific principles in resolving the conflict.

Content Background

In a standing wave, the points on the wave where there is no displacement of the medium are called nodes. The crests and troughs between the nodes are called antinodes. A standing wave can be compared to a ship that is rolling in heavy seas. As the ship rolls back and forth, the center of the ship is not displaced and is like the node. The edges of the ship are greatly displaced in an up-and-down motion and are like antinodes.

Have you noticed what happens when one boat crosses behind another? Where the wakes of the two boats cross, the water looks "mixed up." This is the result of constructive and destructive interference from the two sets of waves. If you happen to be unfortunate enough to be water skiing through that area, hold on tight! Part of it will be very rough, and part of it will be very smooth.

INTERFERENCE AND STANDING WAVES

But what about the wave you created on the rope? What does it have to do with interference? Interference is what causes standing waves. Here's how.

When you created a wave on the rope, it traveled down the rope and reflected back, as shown in Figure 18-13. As you continued making waves, you had them traveling in two directions—waves going down the rope, and reflections coming back. These waves were of the same frequency and amplitude. So when a trough of a wave going one way met a crest of a wave going the other, the amplitudes of the trough and the crest canceled, as shown in Figure 18-11(b). Remember when you put your finger next to the rope. What did you feel? You didn't feel anything because the rope was not moving up and down at that point. Yet, on both sides of that spot, the rope was moving rapidly. This is strong evidence of the effects of interference.

FIGURE 18-13. A standing wave is produced when the reflected wave interferes with the original wave.

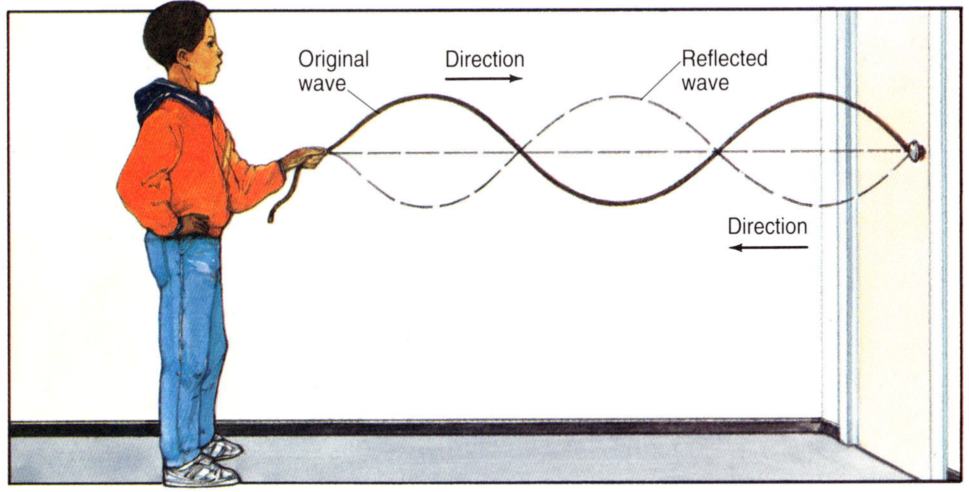

OPTIONS

Enrichment

Discussion Ask students to choose a room in the school and describe its design. They should describe the placement of walls, ceiling, and any permanent fixtures. If furniture is present, describe its type and placement. Describe the type of material used to cover the ceiling, the floor, and the walls. Limiting the discussion to the effect these features have on sound waves, ask students to describe why each feature is designed as it is. Why do gymnasiums have such high ceilings? Why is a theater shaped like a V? What difference does it make if a floor is carpeted or left bare? How does adding or removing furniture change the way sound travels in the room? L3

Recently, interference has been put to use protecting human hearing. In the past, people working in noisy environments have damaged their hearing. One example includes pilots of small planes. The pilots could not shut out all noise. They had to be able to hear the instructions from the air traffic controllers. Now pilots can wear special ear protection that not only protects their hearing, but allows them to hear normal conversation.

These special earphones have circuits in them that produce sound that destructively interferes with the damaging engine noise but allows conversation to be heard and understood. Figure 18-14 shows an example of these new earphones. Because sounds of low or high frequency are equally damaging to the ears, these new earphones can be made to interfere with frequency of specific industrial noises. People who work in a factory environment and those who use tools such as jackhammers also wear protective ear covers. Can you think of other occupations that could benefit from similar coverings?

FIGURE 18-14. These earphones use destructive interference to cancel noise that could injure a pilot's ears.

In this section, you learned how waves interact by producing standing waves. If you were really lucky, you could do the same thing with Louie's wave. If Louie's identical twin, Roberto, dived into the other end of the pool a little later than Louie, Louie's and Roberto's waves would be opposite in terms of where their crests and troughs were located. Then the two waves would meet in the center, and destructive interference would produce a calm area. However, if Roberto jumped in at the same time as Louie, constructive interference would give Ladonna a real ride! What other effects can waves have on you? You'll find out in the next section.

Check Your Understanding

1. Compare and contrast constructive and destructive interference.
2. Explain how it is possible for one wave to cancel another with a resulting amplitude of zero. Use a diagram in your answer if you like.
3. Explain how to create a standing wave and what causes it.
4. **APPLY:** In some theaters, you may find that there are certain areas where the sound is either much softer or muffled in some way. What do you think causes this?

3 Assess

Check for Understanding

Assign questions 1–3 and the Apply question from Check Your Understanding. To help students understand the Apply question, take the class to the school's auditorium, and have them try to find any "dead" spots where sounds are muffled. If your school has a combination auditorium/gymnasium, try to find an auditorium that is more acoustically sound.

Reteach

Activity Seat a long line of students across the front of the classroom. Beginning at both ends, ask students to raise and lower their arms in a stadium wave. When the waves meet in the middle, the students there should stand if two crests (arms raised) arrive at the same time, representing a wave that is twice as big. If a crest and a trough hit at the same time, the students in the middle should keep their arms level to indicate that one canceled the other. Have observers describe what is happening in terms of waves. L1 COOP LEARN LEP

Extension

Allow students to experiment with golf balls and a large tub of water. Have students stand on either side of the tub and drop balls in, producing waves. Ask them to describe what happens when the waves meet. Have them try deliberately to produce constructive and destructive interference. Have a mop and bucket handy. L3

4 Close

Ask students to look again at Figure 18-11. Recall that wave interference can be used to reduce the impact of sound. Ask students to discuss the different ways sound in their environment affects them.

Answers to Check Your Understanding

1. Constructive interference occurs when two crests meet. It results in one crest equal in height to both the original crests added together. Destructive interference occurs when the crest of one wave meets the trough of another. It results in the two waves canceling each other out.
2. Suggest that students express this in mathematical terms. If the crest of the wave is a positive number (indicating distance above the medium at rest) and the trough is a negative (indicating distance below), the two numbers cancel each other when added together.
3. A standing wave is produced by interference between an original wave and a reflected wave.
4. Destructive interference as sound reflects from walls, ceiling, and floor.

Section 18-4

PREPARATION

Concepts Developed

In this section, students will investigate sound waves. They will learn about the Doppler effect, why sound seems to change in pitch as you draw closer or move farther from the source of the sound.

Planning the Lesson

In planning your lesson on sound waves, refer to the Chapter Organizer on pages 536A-B for timing suggestions, resources, and additional materials that will help you in your presentation of the lesson concepts.

For adequate development of the concepts presented in this section, we recommend that students do the Find Out activity on pages 554-555.

1 MOTIVATE

Demonstration Bring a radio to class and turn it on. Switch stations several times. Explain to the class that the radio stations are broadcasting sound on different frequencies. Next, turn the volume up and down. Explain that this changes the amplitude of the sound waves coming from the radio. In this section, students will learn how varying sound waves affects people. L1

FIND OUT!

Can you see sound?

Time needed 15 minutes

Materials oatmeal or coffee container with both ends cut out, large balloon, scissors, large rubber band, glue, small mirror, flashlight, loudspeaker

Thinking Processes
Observing and inferring, Comparing and contrasting, Recognizing cause and effect

18-4 Sound as Waves

OBJECTIVES

In this section, you will

- demonstrate sound as a wave;
- explain the Doppler effect.

KEY SCIENCE TERMS

Doppler effect

LOOKING AT SOUND

Have you ever felt a vibrating loudspeaker on your stereo? If you are able to touch the cone of the speaker, you will feel it move in and out in time with the music. You also felt these vibrations in the Find Out in the first section. When a loud, low-frequency sound such as a drum is heard, you can even see the cone move in and out. This in-and-out movement creates the compressions and rarefactions in the air that are characteristic of compression waves. Under normal conditions you can't see sound. However, the following Find Out activity will allow you to see some of its effects.

FIND OUT!

Can you see sound?

Use the same container or coffee can that you used in the Find Out in Section 18-1. Make sure both ends are open. Now cut a piece of balloon large enough to fit over one end. Stretch the balloon over the end and hold it in place with a rubber band, as shown. Next, glue a small mirror slightly off the center of the balloon.

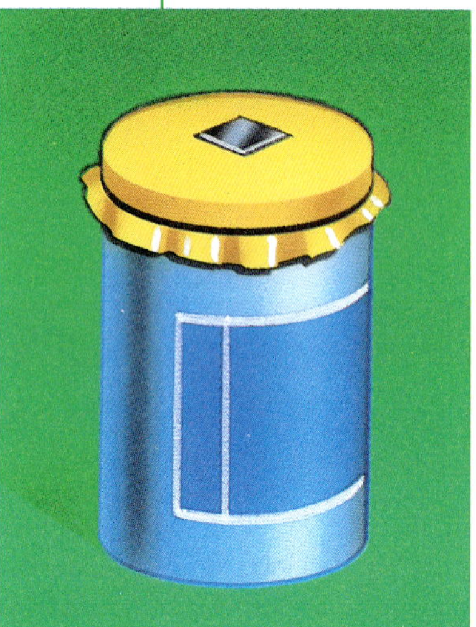

After the glue has dried, hold the open end of the container to your mouth or a loudspeaker. Have a classmate reflect a flashlight beam or sunlight off the mirror to a wall or other flat surface. Explore the effect of sounds on the patterns produced on the wall. Make a low-pitched hum, talk, or play music into the open end of the container.

PROGRAM RESOURCES

Teacher Classroom Resources

Study Guide, page 66

Critical Thinking/Problem Solving, page 26, Sonic Booms L2

Other Resources

Sound Waves, software, J & S Software.

Sound: A Microcomputer Based Lab, software, Queue.

Noise Pollution, video, LCAD.

OPTIONS

Meeting Individual Needs

Hearing Impaired/Visually Impaired
Allow hearing or visually impaired students to feel the sound waves created in the Find Out activity. Ask them to place their fingertips on the cover of the container when the loudspeaker is on. They will be able to feel the vibrations produced by the sound waves. Ask them to describe any difference they feel when the volume of the music changed.

Conclude and Apply

1. Draw the patterns and label them. What happened to the reflected spot on the wall when a loud sound went into the container?
2. How did the reflections change as you changed the sounds?

DID YOU KNOW?

The housefly buzzes at a frequency equivalent to the middle octave F on the piano.

The patterns you observed were produced by the compressions and rarefactions of air moving the balloon. As the compressions caused the balloon to bulge, the mirror was tilted, and the light reflected in one direction. Then, when the rarefactions were behind the balloon, the mirror was tilted the other way, and the reflection moved in another direction. Thus, the pattern traced on the wall was a rough picture of the sound waves.

PROPERTIES OF SOUND

Recall your earlier experience with sound and vibrations. Sound is produced by alternating compression and rarefaction of the air. The distance from one compression to the next compression is one wavelength of that sound. The frequency of a sound is the number of compressions that pass a point in one second. A low sound will have a frequency from about 20 to about 200 hertz whereas the highest sounds you can hear are about 15,000 to 20,000 hertz. You would hear a frequency of 20 hertz as a low rumble, such as thunder or a truck passing by. In music, middle C has a frequency of 264 hertz. Most musical sounds are less than 4,000 hertz but certain effects of music are much higher and add richness to the tone. The hearing champion of the animal world is the bat, which uses sound of over 80,000 hertz to locate its prey.

FIGURE 18-15. A piano produces sound as its strings are hit with small hammers.

The louder the sound, the greater the amplitude of the wave. In fact, some sounds can hurt you. Some rock concerts are so loud that the musicians have damaged their hearing. Even the spectators should be careful, as overexposure to loud noise can destroy their hearing.

Purpose Students will observe and compare the patterns created by sound waves.

Preparation Before class, cover the end of the container with the balloon piece and attach the mirror. If you wish, students may do these things themselves the day before.

Teaching the Activity

Ask volunteers to hold the container over the loudspeaker and to shine the flashlight. Make sure they hold them steadily so that any change in the light pattern is a result of the sound and not their movement. You may want to direct the light reflected from the mirror onto a large sheet of white paper taped to the wall. This will enable you to sketch the waves directly. Be sure to vary the volume and pitch of the sound to produce different patterns. L2

Expected Outcomes

Students will observe differing up-and-down patterns of light, representing the pattern of the sound waves produced.

Conclude and Apply

1. The patterns would be an up and down line. The sound from the speaker caused the balloon to vibrate.
2. Amplitude and wavelength varied.

2 TEACH

Tying to Previous Knowledge

In Chapter 3, students learned many of the characteristics of sound waves: compression, rarefaction, frequency, pitch, and loudness. This section expands their understanding of these characteristics by helping students visualize sound as a wave and by explaining how high amplitude sound waves (loud sounds) can damage hearing. Invite students to describe experiences they have had with loud sounds. Ask if they felt, as well as heard, the vibrations.

Multicultural Perspectives

Most cultures have a musical sound unique to that culture. The world of popular music is just discovering the richness and diversity of these sounds. It's called the "world beat," and an increasing number of pop artists are seeking to incorporate it into their music. Artists are experimenting with calypso beats from Jamaica, rhythms from Africa, chants from India, and many other sounds. For example, a group called Simple Minds combined bagpipes and African drums, for an "Afro-Celtic" sound. Suggest to students that they research one of these types of music. Ask them to determine what sound characteristics define the type of music they chose. Then have students bring in samples of the music they have researched and share what they learned of its characteristics.

Concept Development

Theme Connection As students learn about the properties of sound waves, they should be reminded that waves transmit energy away from a source. Discuss with students the damage that can be caused by high-amplitude (high-energy) waves.

How do we know?

Further information on this subject can be found in "How Noise Can Make You Sick," by Linda Troiano, *Good Housekeeping,* May 1991, p. 207 and "Turn It Down (effects of personal stereos on hearing)" by Lisa Davis, Deborah Franklin, Katherine Griffin, and Mary Hossfeld, *In Health,* May-June 1990, p. 10.

Content Background

Sounds that have frequencies above the range of human hearing are described as ultrasonic. Some alarm systems that are used in stores are ultrasonic. These alarms use a beam of sound, much like the "electric eye" that opens an automatic door. If the sound beam is broken by an intruder, it sets off an alarm. The frequencies used in these alarms are not very far above the average range of human sensitivity. Some people, whose ranges of sensitivity are a bit higher than average, can hear these sounds. They often describe the sensation as a pressure in the ear rather than a sound or recognizable pitch.

How do we know?

Loud Sounds Damage Hearing

People sometimes doubt that loud concerts or machines can damage their hearing. This is because the damage doesn't show up immediately, and the ear seems to recover from temporary deafness. However, long-term studies have shown that overexposure to loud sounds can permanently damage hearing in several ways.

Sometimes people doubt this because the loss of hearing may not show up for many years.

High amplitude compressions can force your eardrum beyond its limits, causing it to rupture. When scar tissue grows over the split, the eardrum can no longer reproduce sound accurately. It is like mending a drumhead with tape.

Secondly, inside your ear are tiny nerve fibers surrounded by fluid. When a compression caused by a loud sound travels through the fluid in your ear, it can damage or destroy the nerve fibers. If enough fibers are destroyed, hearing is permanently damaged because the nerves do not grow back.

FIGURE 18-16. Workers in loud environments protect their hearing with special equipment.

Machinery, such as air compressors and jet engines, are also very loud, and it is important that workers using them wear ear protection. It is the loudness or amplitude that creates the large compressions. Sounds of low or high frequency are equally damaging.

THE DOPPLER EFFECT

You've probably been at a railroad crossing when a train passed by. Did you notice that the train's horn

OPTIONS

Enrichment

Demonstration Borrow a model or large diagram of the human ear. Explain how sound waves cause the eardrum and nearby nerves to vibrate. Show how too intense a vibration can cause damage by rupturing the eardrum or damaging the nerves. Ask students to suggest ways that this kind of damage can be prevented. Students should suggest reducing the amount of noise, erecting sound wave barriers, and using equal and opposite sound waves to create destructive wave interference.

seemed to be higher in pitch as it approached and then was lower as it went away? Pitch is how the ear recognizes frequency. This situation is so noticeable that it has been given its own name. It is called the **Doppler effect.**

If you are on the train, you wouldn't hear the Doppler effect. To people on the train, the horn would seem to have the same pitch at all times. How can two people listening to the same horn hear different notes?

The motion of the train as it moves toward you causes the sound waves to be emitted closer together. Imagine that the frequency of the sound is 100 hertz or 100 vibrations per second. Now imagine that the train is moving at 20 meters per second. That means that five compressions are sent out from the horn every meter that the train moves. But as each compression is sent out, the train moves closer, and the next compression gets a head start. Thus, the compressions get closer and closer together, as shown in Figure 18-17. This causes a higher frequency to reach your ear. What do you think happens as the train passes you? Think about it.

FIGURE 18-17. What do you notice about the sound of a train's horn as it approaches and then passes you?

Concept Development

Inquiry Question If you were standing on the sidewalk when a fire truck raced past with its sirens blaring, you would hear the pitch rise and fall as the truck approached and departed. How would it be possible for you not to observe the Doppler effect? *If you were on the fire truck or moving in the same direction, at the same speed, you would not hear it.*

MAKING CONNECTIONS

History/Health

When an object travels faster than the speed of sound, it overtakes the sound waves it produces, generating a loud "crack" called a sonic boom. This boom can damage people's hearing and even damage property. On October 14, 1947, Captain Charles E. Yeager became the first person to break the sound barrier. Ask students to research this historic flight. You may also want them to research what is now being done to protect people from the damage caused by sonic booms.

Teacher F.Y.I.

The Doppler effect is named for Christian Johann Doppler, an Austrian who first explained the effect in terms of frequency in 1842.

Enrichment

Activity Cut a small hole in a Nerf ball or other soft foam ball. Put a piezoelectric buzzer connected to a battery into the hole. You may need to secure it with tape. Hold the ball and buzzer in one place and ask students to describe the noise they hear. Be sure to get a description of the pitch. Then ask for two volunteers. Have one stand in the front of the room and the other stand in the back. Ask them to toss the ball gently back and forth a few times. Then ask the class to describe any differences in the sound they hear. They should be able to hear an increase and decrease in pitch caused by the Doppler effect. Review with students that this effect is caused by sound wave compression: as the source of a sound wave moves closer, the waves are compressed and the pitch becomes higher; as it moves away, the waves are spread out and the pitch becomes lower.

3 Assess

Check for Understanding

Assign questions 1 and 2 and the Apply question from Check Your Understanding. To help students with the Apply question, have them look at Figure 18-17. Ask students what conditions cause a sound to seem higher than its true pitch. *The sound and listener are approaching each other.*

Reteach

Bring a drum to class (a child's toy drum or a covered container such as the one you used in the Find Out will do). Sprinkle chalk dust evenly over the top of the drum and then strike it with a stick. Observe the wave pattern created in the dust. Explain to students that this pattern represents the sound waves created by striking the drum. L1

Extension

Activity Ask students to keep a record for a day or over a weekend of all the waves they encounter. They should record in their journals the source of the energy that produced the wave, the medium it traveled through, characteristics of the wave, and any unusual effect they notice, such as the Doppler effect. Share in class the observations students made and note how many different kinds of waves they observed. L2

4 Close

Draw a transverse and a longitudinal wave on the chalkboard. Ask students to identify the characteristics of each wave and to suggest where they might experience each different wave in the course of their daily lives. L1

FIGURE 18-18. Police radar uses the Doppler effect to determine how fast a car is moving.

What about the operator and passengers on the train? Do they hear the Doppler effect? No, they hear the same frequency all the time because they and the sound are moving together.

The Doppler effect is more than just an interesting phenomenon. Most radar (*ra*dio *d*etection *a*nd *r*anging) depends on the effect to locate and determine the speed of objects. One use you are probably familiar with is the Doppler radar that police use to identify speeding motorists.

If a wave of a specific frequency is aimed at a stationary automobile, a wave of the same frequency bounces back. If the automobile is moving, the wave that returns to the police equipment will be of a different frequency. The greater the difference in frequency between outgoing and incoming wave, the greater the speed of the automobile.

As you've seen in this chapter, there's a lot more to waves than water splashing up on the beach. From the waves in the pool, to the concert hall, to standing on the street as a train goes by, understanding the science of waves is one key to understanding what is happening around you every day. As you go to school or just walk around the neighborhood, identify the waves you observe and how they affect your life.

Check Your Understanding

1. How can you demonstrate that sound is a wave?
2. When will the pitch of a racing car engine be the highest— approaching you, going away, or directly opposite you? Explain your answer.
3. **APPLY:** You are talking to your friend on the schoolbus when you hear a car theft alarm going off. The pitch is getting higher. Should you look in front of or behind the bus to see the car? Explain.

Answers to Check Your Understanding

1. Students may describe the Find Out activity on pages 554-555. They may note that sound waves have the wave characteristics of wavelength and frequency that are inversely related.
2. Just as it comes opposite you. As an object approaches you, the sound waves it produces are emitted closer together, causing the pitch to sound higher. As it moves away, the waves become farther apart, causing the pitch to sound as if it is lower. This is called the Doppler effect.
3. In front of the bus. You are moving toward the sound source so the sound waves are crowded together and have a higher frequency.

EXPANDING YOUR VIEW

CONTENTS

A CLOSER LOOK

HOW DOES THAT SOUND LOOK?

Symphony Hall in Boston, built in 1898, was designed by a professor of physics who had studied acoustics. It is considered one of the greatest music halls of all time.

Acoustics, the science of sound, is used in designing buildings such as concert halls and recording studios. Imagine sound waves coming out of your stereo speaker, like rings in the water where you've tossed in a pebble. When sound waves strike a surface such as a wall, floor, or ceiling, some of the sound is absorbed, and some is reflected. A hard surface reflects more sound. Soft materials, such as drapes or a carpet, absorb more sound.

A room that absorbs too much sound is acoustically dead. The sound in a room with some reflections is more pleasing to the ear. As people also absorb sound, a large audience reduces reflections.

Have you ever shouted when you were in a tunnel? You hear many echoes or sound reflections. Sometimes the echoes last for almost a second. The echoing sound is called reverberation. The time it takes for the sound to die out is called reverberation time.

An auditorium or concert hall must be carefully designed to have the proper reverberation time. Many concert halls built in the 19th century have better acoustics than modern halls. The halls were usually long and narrow. In a narrow hall, you hear the sound coming from the source first, and then reflected off the walls. The reverberation was correct for music played by an orchestra. The halls were smaller, too. With a smaller audience, less sound was absorbed.

Modern halls are built to hold more people. They are usually built wide to provide more emergency exits. Ceilings are lower, which also affects the sound. In the older halls, the reverberation builds up, so you seem to be surrounded by sound. Acoustic experts today are taking their cues from the older builders.

YOU TRY IT!

Turn stereo speakers so that the sound reflects off the ceiling, then off the opposing walls. Describe the differences.

EXPANDING YOUR VIEW

Using Expanding Your View

Assign one or more of these excursions to expand your students understanding of the properties of waves. You may assign them as small group or individual activities.

A CLOSER LOOK

Purpose A Closer Look familiarizes students with basic principles of acoustics, the science of controlling sound waves within a particular environment. The characteristics and behavior of single and multiple waves, treated in Sections 18-2 and 18-3, strongly influence the design of concert halls.

Content Background Acoustic experts, architects and engineers, look at ancient halls and theaters for efficient properties of design. In the Classical Greek world, outdoor theaters were carved into hillsides in semicircular shape, creating a curved and "terraced" sound-reflector out of the hill and the audience itself, which maximized amplification of sounds from the stage. At Athens, Halicarnassus, Delphi, Epidauros and other sites, performances continue today.

Teaching Strategies Have students analyze details in the article's 5th and 6th paragraphs. Does a good hall depend on constructive or destructive interference, as defined in Section 18-3? *Constructive, because wave crests meet crests and troughs meet troughs. The reverberations build up around listeners, rather than neutralize each other as in destructive interference.*

Going Further Have volunteers describe a place they know of that has good reverberations: a room, a hall, perhaps a stairwell; and they should see what architectural traits these places share. Ask them to relate these traits to details in the chapter on sound waves.

Answers to YOU TRY IT

Students will probably find that the stereo speakers, when levelled at opposite walls, fill the room with more sound than when they bounce their sounds off ceilings and floors.

EXPANDING YOUR VIEW

EARTH SCIENCE CONNECTION

Purpose Earth Science Connection brings together concepts from Sections 18-1, 18-3 and 18-4 to show how the properties of waves—in this case, seismic waves—can be used as a tool to locate hidden mineral resources.

Content Background Seismology is a relatively new science born of 20th-century technology. The Richter scale, developed in 1935, and other units of seismic measurement are still being refined in the light of advancing knowledge. Nevertheless, the rapid accumulation of data on the properties of both and of the *media* (rock, earth, water, and the like) through which waves pass, has made seismic prospecting a highly successful endeavor. Precise seismic studies of the conditions in which lodes of valuable materials are often found make the acquisition of resources easier—and thus reduce their cost in the marketplace.

Teaching Strategies Ask students to discuss the magnitude and usefulness of waves including, perhaps, those generated by earthquakes or explosions; those of radar screens and radar speed detectors; radio waves, and ocean waves.

Discussion Have volunteers list the kind of data that a seismic prospector might use to determine a given land-area's subsurface structures before deciding whether actual drilling should be done. For example, how do wave-*energy, time* of passage through a *medium,* and *distance* from the wave-source affect the judgment?

Answers to

WHAT DO YOU THINK?

Encourage students to become as objectively informed as possible before forming an opinion.

EARTH SCIENCE CONNECTION

SEISMIC PROSPECTING

Seismic waves are the shock waves, or energy waves, produced by an earthquake. Scientists measure seismic waves in order to study earthquakes. Seismic waves are studied for other reasons as well. One reason involves the search for mineral deposits. This method, called seismic prospecting, is used to search for oil, coal, and other mineral deposits. More oil has been found with the seismic method than by any other method.

Seismic prospecting begins with the creation of an artificial earthquake. Artificial earthquakes are created by setting off explosives in a small hole in the ground. Vibrator trucks that can violently shake the ground are also used. The artificial earthquake sends seismic waves thousands of feet into the ground. Waves then bounce off the rock formations and are reflected back. Acoustic receivers, called geophones, placed at different distances from the explosion, pick up the seismic waves and send signals to a truck outfitted with recording equipment. There, the seismic waves are amplified and recorded on tape.

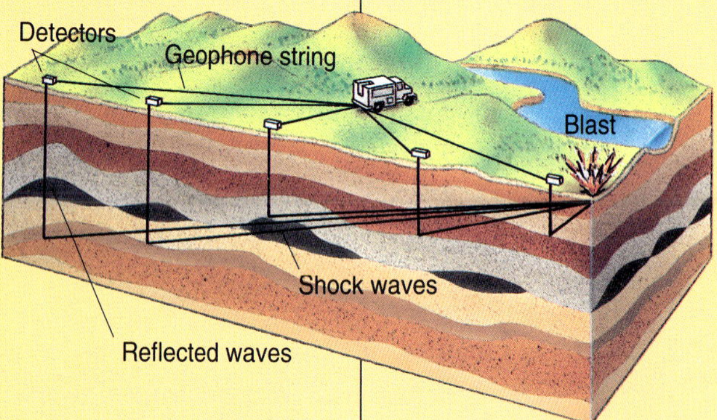

The tapes are processed on a computer, and a printout is produced. This process is called seismic mapping. By analyzing the amplitudes of the seismic waves, and the time it takes them to bounce off rocks, scientists can get an idea of the nature of rock layers, and the depths and locations of mineral deposits. This is a much less expensive way of deciding where to drill for mineral deposits, than prospecting by drilling a number of deep holes. More and more industries that rely on mineral deposits, such as coal and oil, are using the artificial earthquake and seismic waves to show them the way.

WHAT DO YOU THINK?

Many environmentalists are opposed to the idea of seismic prospecting because of possible damage to the environment.

The explosions used could destroy trees and other plant life. This could lead to the erosion of soil and a decrease in food for the animals in the area.

What do you think? Is finding oil important enough to prospect in untouched regions of the world?

Going Further Have volunteers consult local records in the town hall, library, or historical society to discover what early settlers of the area considered to be its subsurface, mineral or other "hidden" wealth. Were their predictions and estimates borne out by later scientific studies and commercial activities? What "evidence" led the early settlers to reach their conclusions?

Going Further Have groups of students find other examples of the use of waves by people and/or in nature. Examples might include the songs of humpback whales; the science of earthquake-prediction; finding water in desert regions; the details of seismic prospecting; and the use of waves in archaeological research. COOP LEARN

SCIENCE AND SOCIETY

SOUNDS DANGEROUS

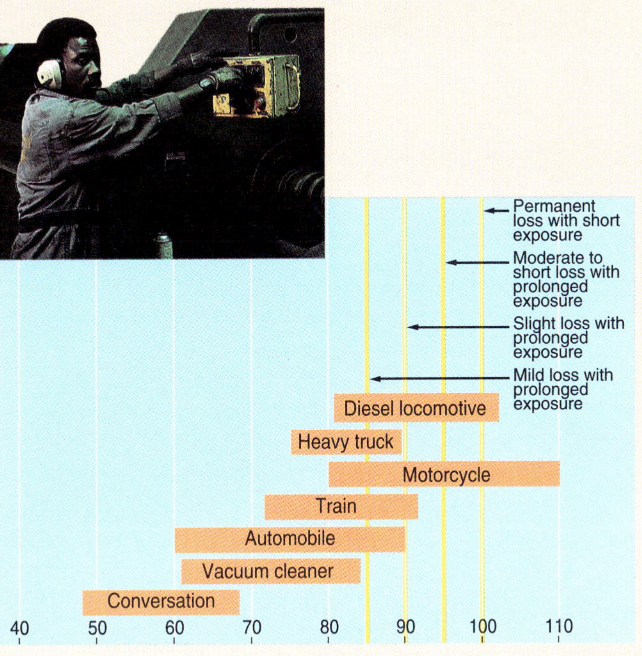

You get up in the morning and turn on the radio. You travel in busy traffic. At school, the halls are noisy, and loud bells ring. After school, you play your stereo or mix a milkshake in the blender. It's just an average day for your eardrums. Noise pollution is so much a part of our everyday lives, we hardly notice it's there.

To understand how sound waves can be hazardous to your health, remember that sound is produced when something vibrates. The vibration squeezes together molecules in the air, creating sound waves that move through the air.

When sound waves reach the ear, the air pressure pushes against the eardrum. The vibration is passed to microscopic nerve cells, and then to the brain where it is interpreted as sound. The loudness of sound depends on the size of the pressure vibrations. The loudness is measured in decibels. The louder the sound, the higher the decibel level. For example, the sound level of a quiet library is 30 decibels, while that of loud rock music might be 110 decibels.

Many people become deaf from long exposure to loud noise. Nearly 10 million employees in the United States work in places with constant loud noise. They may not know the noise is harmful because they adapt, or get used to, the sound. Over time, the loud noise damages the tiny cells in the ears that transmit the sound waves to the brain. The graph above shows the average sound levels for several common items. The graph also shows what kind of hearing damage is caused by exposure to high sound levels.

The way noise affects people's behavior may be as important as the damage it does to hearing. Acoustical sociologists and other experts who specialize in hearing study noise to see how it influences physical and mental health. Noise pollution is all around us. We may adapt, but our bodies and minds still

CAREER CONNECTION

Acoustical physicists study the production, reflection, and absorption of sound. Many are employed by the auto industries and other transportation companies. They study ways to improve or control noise, sounds, and vibration.

EXPANDING YOUR VIEW

SCIENCE AND SOCIETY

Purpose On this and the next page, Science and Society treats some of the less useful or more hazardous effects of wave properties explored in Sections 18-3 and 18-4. The physical and behavioral consequences of extremely noisy environments in daily life, work, and play have resulted in various government and private efforts to reduce noise. Many citizens have banded together to recapture some quiet in their communities. The human environment is literally filled with soundwaves, but only in recent decades has this become a health and safety issue.

Content Background Details in the article—such as the effect of noise on people's appetite, emotions, health, and ability to think—suggest the serious problems associated with noise pollution. The recognition of these problems have led to attempts to regulate and/or reduce noise in the human environment. Beginning in the 1970s and 1980s, and continuing into the 1990s, the need (or at least the debate on the need) for regulations has increased. As implied by the Acoustical Society of America's study, at issue is often the familiar prevention-vs-treatment factor—whether it is more efficient to reduce noise (as from airports), or to find cures for the ailments which high-amplitude sound waves are believed to create. If airlines and other major noise sources comply with limits set for the year 2001, follow-up studies may show reductions in connected ailments. Without such results, the government may be asked to step in once more.

Teaching Strategies Ask students to list their most hated and most liked noises. Ask what effect each has on them.

Going Further Have two or three groups research in more detail how the human ear works in relation to sound waves, how hearing-loss comes about, and what remedies have been and are being used to reduce the threat to hearing by noise pollution. A fourth and fifth group might explore how "close-captioned" TV shows for the hearing-impaired work; and how "signing" came into being to allow the deaf to communicate with one another and with people who can hear.

Discussion Tally up the responses to the above and have students discuss measures that might be instituted to modify the "sound environment" so it more closely conforms to student likes and dislikes.

Debate How do students feel about the government's deregulation of noise pollution? Why did the government do so? *Is* there a problem?

CAREER CONNECTION

Have students discuss precisely what kinds of physics people in these job-fields study. Students should also do research to find out what kind of education is required to become an accoustical physicist.

Answers to YOU TRY IT

Encourage students to notice small noise-oriented details of their environment as they answer (for example, posted regulations at parks or beaches about radio-playing; "Quiet" signs at libraries, and automobile-muffler requirements.) Which if any of these regulations were approved of by the local population? Which were legislated? Which were executive or administrative orders? Which do students or their friends generally abide by?

experience stress from the extreme noise.

People often may react physically to noise pollution. The Acoustical Society of America released a study that said people who live near airports are more likely to suffer from physical problems such as heart disease or high blood pressure. People may react emotionally or mentally to noise. People who live in noisy neighborhoods complain of increased anxiety and sleeplessness. When too many sound waves assault the eardrums, the brain cannot process all the information at once. This may explain why people in noisy environments say they are unable to think. Studies on noise pollution have shown that in noisy neighborhoods, people feel more isolated and afraid. A person's appetite may be lowered when there is a lot of noise, which may be why it is harder to enjoy a meal in the school cafeteria. There are also more traffic accidents at very noisy intersections.

The Environmental Protection Agency (EPA) established the Office of Noise Abatement and granted it powers to regulate sources of noise pollution by passing the Noise Control Act in 1972. However, the Office of Noise Abatement was closed in1982 due to government budget cuts. Most experts agree that passing laws on noise control is the most important step toward controlling noise pollution. In recent years, most noise laws have been passed at the local level of government. But that may be changing.

The U.S. Department of Transportation and the Federal Aviation Administration recently released new policy guidelines to control airport noise. The policy requires airlines to replace older aircraft with newer, quieter models. The policy also restricts local communities from imposing their own noise control laws. The airlines have until the year 2001 to comply with the new regulations, so local areas may have to live with the noisier aircraft until then.

Noise pollution activists are not happy with the new policy. With government offices getting involved in noise pollution again, noise control may be the next big wave for environmentalists.

YOU TRY IT!

Are you breaking any local laws against noise pollution? Is there a local law in your area about playing music in public, such as on a bus or on the beach? Find out by writing to your local health department or the mayor's office and ask about local ordinances against noise.

Going Further Have students act on the results of the class lists of favorite and most-hated noises by interviewing or polling people in the community on the same question. Correlate the findings to determine whether the class is representative of the larger population, and determine whether any remedial actions would be possible with the community's help. COOP LEARN

TECHNOLOGY CONNECTION

WAVE POWER

The first wave-powered electricity generating station powered by the ocean was opened in the mid-1980s on the coast of Norway. Since then, other power stations have opened in England and Scotland. The technology of ocean wave power may be one answer to the world's energy crisis.

The amplitude of a wave determines how much energy it can produce. The energy contained in waves comes from the wind. How hard the wind blows, how long the wind blows, and the distance it blows across the water all help determine wave amplitude. Waves grow taller as they absorb more of the wind's energy. Every time waves double in height, their energy is quadrupled in strength.

One well-known wave-powered device is called the Salter duck, named for its inventor, Dr. Stephen Salter of Scotland. The device looks like a duck bobbing on the water. It uses a hydraulic pump that moves on the action of the waves, pumping fluid into a turbine-driven generator that produces electricity. Salter has built duck models, but estimates indicate that at least five million pounds of concrete would have to be poured for a full-scale generating plant. Salter is working on the problem of size.

The oscillating water column (OWC) also uses wave power. The device traps a column of water inside a chamber that is moved up and down by wave action. It compresses air at the top of the chamber and forces the air into a turbine, which turns a generator. The OWC must be built on a huge scale to produce a substantial amount of electricity.

Scientists estimate that wave-powered stations could provide at least ten percent of the world's energy needs. Inventors and investors will continue to pursue the power of the ocean wave.

WHAT DO YOU THINK?

How do you think this emerging technology will change the world? Tell what you think are the advantages and disadvantages.

TECHNOLOGY CONNECTION

Purpose Like the examples and activities in Sections 18-1 and 18-2, **Technology Connection** demonstrates the energy in waves and human attempts to use that energy. The Salter duck and the oscillating water column show students two proposals for turning ocean wave energy into electric energy.

Content Background The Salter duck and the oscillating water column are two of the latest approaches to a familiar mechanical problem. Like more traditional systems that derive energy from fossil fuels, steam, wind, and water, these new devices depend on their power-sources' turning a turbine to generate electricity. The first crude turbines were in fact nonelectric water-driven machines for grinding grain while today's colossal turbines generate electric current. Of all these power-sources, only solar or photo-voltaic cell systems dispense with the turbine and generate electricity directly.

Teaching Strategies Show students photos of devices, or actual devices, that use alternative energy sources to function. Examples may include wind-wheels, geothermal power plants, tidal power plants, solar panels on roofs, or solar-powered calculators and wristwatches.

Discussion Have students discuss ideas of their own for generating electric energy from unusual sources. What types—burning refuse, harnessing wind and water, nuclear fusion—do they most favor developing? Why?

Answers to WHAT DO YOU THINK?

Advantages may include reduced pollution and renewability; disadvantages may include expense of development and transmission of electricity to inland areas.

Going Further Have students consult almanac statistics and other sources to find out what three countries use the most fossil fuels, and what three countries lead the way in using or developing alternative energy-sources. How do weather and climate play a role in determining the answers? For example, why do Mediterranean countries use more solar power than other nations?

Going Further Have research teams find out where the most constant and energetic conditions exist for the possible construction of a Salter duck or oscillating water column plant. Remind them to take into account factors such as hospitability to humans and closeness to population-centers which will use the resultant energy, as they seek out the places with the most energetic and constant wave-producing conditions. COOP LEARN

EXPANDING YOUR VIEW

TEENS IN SCIENCE

Purpose Teens in Science shows how a person such as Jason Cobb can turn characteristics of waves, which were discussed in Sections 18-3 and 18-4, into music and art. Computers, synthesizers and their display screens allow people to "see" music as they create it.

Content Background Drum machines, computers that provide full-orchestra accompaniment to solo musicians, and variations on the original 1970s MOOG music synthesizer, which can reproduce sounds ranging from tropical rain forests to train wrecks, are mainstays of modern music. Their sounds can be heard on radio, on television, and in the recording studio. Some artists such as Paul Winter ("Wolf Eyes" and other naturalistic recordings) have pioneered the use of these systems musically. Other people find careers as sound technicians, working behind the scenes of film, TV, radio and theater productions.

Teaching Strategies Students should discuss their favorite sound-artists. They should address questions such as: Do these people or groups use electronic or accoustical instrumentation? In what ways do electronic effects add to listening pleasure?

Debate Is high-tech music destroying musicians' careers? How have machines come to replace many studio musicians and other performers and technicians? What are students' views on this trend? Can technology make a star out of someone with little talent?

Answers to YOU TRY IT

Some students may say that there is something too mechanical about computer-generated music—too little natural variation in pitch or tempo.

TEENS in SCIENCE

RIDING A MUSICAL WAVE

Jason Cobb always loved computers. When he moved from Montana to Austin, Texas, in the seventh grade, he had his first science lesson on sound. For his class project, Jason wrote a computer program about how sound works. Thus began his adventure as a computer music composer.

After his first sound project, Jason studied programming languages on his own. Now nineteen, he is an intense young man whose conversation is peppered with computer music lingo. Jason composes music on a personal computer with a keyboard, mouse, synthesizer, and stereo system.

Jason writes music in the language of sound waves. Each key he presses on the keyboard represents a different musical sound. The sounds appear as graphic pictures, called waveforms, on his computer screen. The waveforms let him "see what the music looks like." Jason edits sounds and puts together simple waveforms into complex compositions. He stores his compositions on a disc until he's ready to convert them to audio tape.

The technical wizardry is in the synthesizer, a musical instrument that produces sounds electronically.

Playing the synthesizer allows Jason to determine the loudness, pitch, and tone of the sounds. The synthesizer uses Musical Instrument Digital Interface (MIDI.) MIDI is a standard language that connects computers to electronic instruments. MIDI converts the waveforms into forms that the instruments can use to produce sound. With MIDI and a synthesizer, Jason can change the pitch, tempo, or tone of a variety of musical sounds.

For all his technical mastery, what Jason produces is melodic music. His dream is to be an electronic musician, creating computerized compositions that the public and other electronic artists will appreciate. Does he have an equipment wish list? "Are you kidding?" he asks. "Of course, but what I really want costs a million dollars, so I'll have to wait awhile to buy it."

YOU TRY IT!

Can you tell the difference between music that is computer-generated and music from traditional instruments? Next time you're listening to the radio, see if you can identify each type of music.

Going Further Ask volunteers to seek out examples of both "naturally" produced and electronic music and to write a brief magazine-style review of them, contrasting and comparing them on various points on which the student feels strongly. For example, why is one more or less "listenable" than the other, or why does one reveal or cover up the artists' talents or lack of talent.

Going Further Have groups of students create a history of natural and synthetic music by finding examples of each which they can play for the class, either performing themselves or by using tapes. For example, in "Peter and the Wolf," how do various instruments play the parts of characters and animals? What kinds of noises, tones and so on in the everyday environment now appear in synthesized electronic "space music" and other genres?

Reviewing Main Ideas

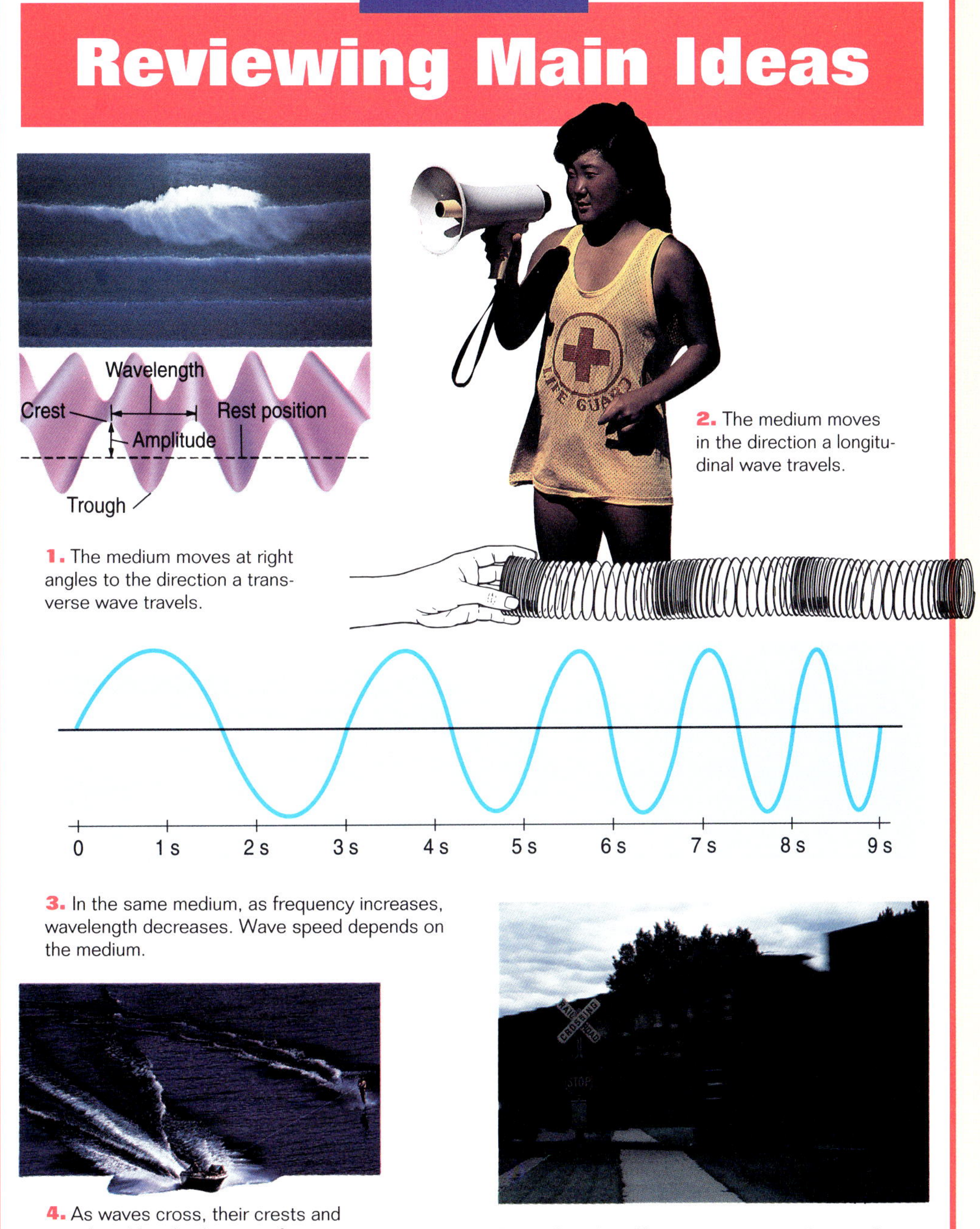

1. The medium moves at right angles to the direction a transverse wave travels.

2. The medium moves in the direction a longitudinal wave travels.

3. In the same medium, as frequency increases, wavelength decreases. Wave speed depends on the medium.

4. As waves cross, their crests and troughs add and subtract to form constructive and destructive interference patterns.

5. The Doppler effect is an apparent change of frequency and pitch of a sound as an object moves with respect to another.

Reviewing Main Ideas

The following activity will help students review the main ideas of the chapter through repetition of the important facts discussed in the chapter. It will be necessary for students to have internalized these facts in order to discriminate between true and false statements.

Teaching Strategy

Rewrite each of the review statements in the student text into sentences containing only one idea. For example: *The highest point of a wave is the crest. The lowest point of a wave is the trough. The distance between one wave crest and the next is the wavelength. When two crests meet, the waves add together in constructive interference,* etc. Write each statement on a separate piece of paper. For each statement, think of two false statements. For example: *As frequency increases, wavelength also increases. Longitudinal waves travel at right angles to the medium. The Doppler effect is the result of destructive interference,* etc. Put each of these statements on a piece of paper and then fold all the papers and put them into a hat. Divide the class into two teams and have team members choose one piece of paper at a time. The student should read the statement and say if it is true or false. You may also wish to require students to provide the correct statement if they choose a false statement and an additional fact if they choose a correct statement. Keep track of which team correctly identifies the most statements.

Chapter 18

Chapter Review

USING KEY SCIENCE TERMS
Answers

1. *Interference* does not belong. Each of the other terms refers to an individual wave property.
2. *Doppler effect* does not belong. Each of the other terms refers to characteristics involved in interference.
3. *Transverse waves* does not belong. Each of the other terms refers to characteristics related to sound or longitudinal waves.
4. *Compression waves* does not belong. Each of the other terms refers to transverse waves.

UNDERSTANDING IDEAS
Answers

1. amplitude
2. Doppler effect
3. transverse, or mechanical, wave
4. Preferred answer is standing wave. Can also accept transverse wave.
5. longitudinal waves
6. destructive interference
7. should indicate a place where the waves cross and form a point
8. No, the surfer is moving at a right angle to the wave disturbance.

CRITICAL THINKING
Answers

1. Answers will vary, but they should include the following: frequency, amplitude, longitudinal waves, constructive interference, and destructive interference.
2. Unit 2; it reproduces all frequencies within human hearing.

Chapter 18

Chapter Review

USING KEY SCIENCE TERMS

amplitude
crest
Doppler effect
interference
longitudinal waves
transverse waves
trough
wavelength

For each set of terms below, choose the one term that does not belong and explain why it does not belong.

1. amplitude, interference, wavelength, crest
2. crests, troughs, Doppler effect, interference
3. rarefaction, transverse waves, compression, longitudinal waves
4. water waves, transverse waves, compression waves, crests

UNDERSTANDING IDEAS

Answer the following questions.

1. The highest wave ever measured on the open ocean was over 34 meters high. What characteristic of the wave is this a measurement of?
2. Lying in your room at night you hear a large truck out on the freeway. It approaches from a distance, passes your home, and goes on. The changing pitch of the truck's sound is an example of what?
3. The wave that Louie made in the pool is an example of what type of wave?
4. At certain wind speeds, the clothesline outside your window begins to hum. You look outside and the whole line is vibrating up and down in a single unit. What kind of wave is it?
5. You are listening to your favorite rap tape. What kind of waves are transmitting the sound to your ears?
6. When the crest of one wave passes through a trough of another, what happens?
7. Draw a standing wave and show where the medium is not moving.
8. Does a surfer move in the same direction as the wave disturbance? Explain.

CRITICAL THINKING

Use your understanding of the concepts developed in the chapter to answer each of the following questions.

1. Write a brief paragraph that explains how your knowledge of waves might make you a better musician.
2. You want to buy a new stereo unit to play your tapes. In the store you see three units that are attractive. Unit 1 costs $500.00 and reproduces frequencies from 10 to 30,000 Hz. Unit 2 costs $300.00 and reproduces frequencies from 20 to 20,000 Hz. Unit 3 costs $250.00 and reproduces frequencies from 50 to 10,000 Hz. Which unit would be the best value for playing all kinds of music?

PROGRAM RESOURCES

Teacher Classroom Resources

Review and Assessment, Chapter Review and Chapter Test, pages 73-76

Computer Test Bank, Chapter Test

OPTIONS

Cooperative Learning

Consider using Cooperative Learning in the Understanding Ideas, Critical Thinking, Problem Solving, and Connecting Ideas sections of the Chapter Review.

COOP LEARN

3. The graph shows the noise level of several situations. Hearing damage is caused by extended exposure to sound over 85 decibels. Which of the sounds on the graph could damage your hearing?

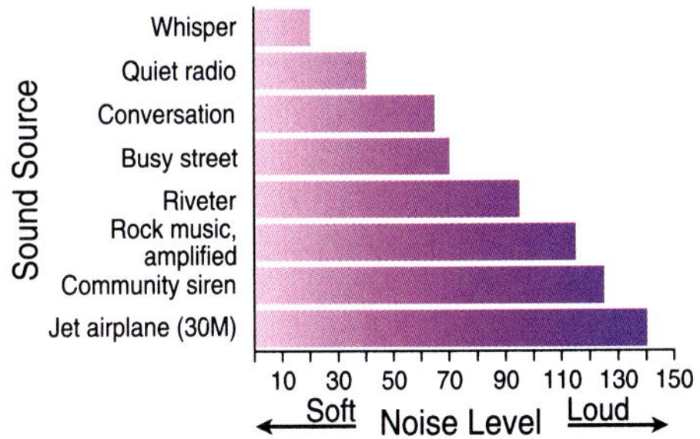

4. A bus driver is rounding a curve approaching a railroad crossing. She hears a train's whistle and then hears the whistle's pitch become lower. What assumption can she make about what she will see when she rounds the curve and looks at the crossing?

PROBLEM SOLVING

Read the following problem and discuss your answers in a brief paragraph.

You've just been given a new stereo system for your birthday, and you want to set it up in your room to get the best possible sound.

1. Draw and discuss three separate setups for the speakers, showing the direction of the sound from each speaker, how to get the best stereo effect, and possibilities for destructive interference—dead spots. Keep in mind that sound will also be reflected from the walls.
2. Your baby sister's crib is against the wall in the room next to yours. How would that affect the placement of your speakers?

CONNECTING IDEAS

Discuss each of the following in a brief paragraph.

1. You find a barrel in an empty lot on the way home from school. The barrel is empty and when you yell into it, the sound makes the barrel vibrate. Write a paragraph on what is probably happening.
2. People living near airports sometimes report that their windows rattle as a plane passes overhead. Explain what happens in these cases.
3. **SCIENCE AND SOCIETY** There are tapes available of sounds such as babbling brooks, gentle rain, and bird calls. Why would these tapes help calm people who live in urban areas?
4. **A CLOSER LOOK** You're in charge of converting a gymnasium to a lecture hall. What can you do to be sure the audience noises do not drown out the lecturer?
5. **EARTH SCIENCE CONNECTION** If a seismic wave in one area is reflected back in less time than in another, what might be true of the density in the first area compared to the the second?

3. jet airplane, community siren, rock music, riveter
4. The train will have already passed the crossing.

PROBLEM SOLVING

Answers

1. Answers will vary but should include some description of interference in waves as they emerge from speakers and are reflected.
2. Answers should include the idea that sound travels through the walls better than through the air.

CONNECTING IDEAS

Answers

1. Answers will vary but should include longitudinal waves, compression, sound, energy, and resonance.
2. The sound waves from the airplanes are vibrating the walls and windows.
3. The sounds on the tapes interfere destructively with the sounds from the streets, thus reducing or eliminating irritating noises.
4. Arrange walls and furniture so that they will interact destructively with noise coming from the audience area.
5. The first area would be more dense than the second area.

CHAPTER ORGANIZER

SECTION	OBJECTIVES	ACTIVITIES/FEATURES
Chapter Opener		**Explore!** How can you experience an earthquake? p. 569
19-1 Earthquakes, Volcanoes, and You (4 days)	1. **Explain** how waves at Earth's surface generated by earthquakes cause structures to collapse. 2. **Make** models of volcanic cones and describe the types of eruptions that produce them.	**Explore!** How do vibrations travel through a material? p. 570 **Investigate 19-1:** Earth's Hot Interior, p. 573 **Find Out!** What are two types of volcanic shapes? p. 574
19-2 Earthquake and Volcano Destruction (2 days)	1. **Determine** four factors that influence the amount of damage caused by an earthquake. 2. **Describe** the types of damage caused by earthquakes. 3. **Describe** the types of damage caused by volcanoes.	**Explore!** What makes an earthquake destructive? p. 576 **Find Out!** What may happen when an earthquake strikes offshore? p. 578
19-3 Measuring Earthquakes (3 days)	1. **Demonstrate** how a seismograph measures an earthquake's strength. 2. **Explain** how the Richter scale is used to indicate earthquake magnitude.	**Investigate 19-2:** Making a Model Seismograph, p. 584 **Skillbuilder:** Making and Using Tables, p. 586
Expanding Your View		A Closer Look **The Great San Francisco Earthquake and Fire,** p. 587 Physics Connection **The Terror of the Tsunami,** p. 588 Science and Society **Earthquake Prediction,** p. 589 Technology Connection **Earthquake-Proof Construction,** p. 591 Teens in Science **Shake, Rattle, and Roll,** p. 592

ACTIVITY MATERIALS

EXPLORE!	INVESTIGATE!	FIND OUT!
Page 569 blindfold **Page 570** rectangular pan, water, ping pong ball, pencil **Page 576** rectangular pan, sand or fine soil, 2 large books	**Page 573** metric ruler, circle compass, paper, pencil **Page 584** ring stand with ring, wire hook from coat hanger, piece of string, 2 rubber bands, fine-tip marker, metric ruler, masking tape, sheet of paper	**Page 574** 1 cup sugar or sand, 2 paper plates, 1 cup plaster of Paris, metric ruler, water, protractor **Page 578** 1 or 2 books, cake pan, water, sand, plastic lid, hole puncher, 20-cm string, metric ruler, optional: small houses from a board game, scissors

Chapter 19
Earthquakes and Volcanoes

TEACHER CLASSROOM RESOURCES	OTHER RESOURCES
Study Guide, p. 67 **Concept Mapping,** p. 27 **Making Connections: Integrating Sciences,** p. 41 **Activity Masters, Investigate 19-1,** pp. 77-78 **Critical Thinking/Problem Solving,** p. 27 **Take Home Activities,** p. 29	**Laboratory Manual,** pp. 113-116, Earthquakes **Laboratory Manual,** pp. 117-118, Pumice **Color Transparency and Master 37,** Forms of Volcanoes ***STVS:** *Moving Continents,* Earth and Space (Disc 3, Side 2) *Miniature Volcanoes,* Earth and Space (Disc 3, Side 2) *Deep Hole Research,* Earth and Space (Disc 3, Side 2) *Geothermal Wells,* Chemistry (Disc 2, Side 2)
Study Guide, p. 68 **Multicultural Activities,** p. 42 **Making Connections: Across the Curriculum,** p. 41 **Flex Your Brain,** p. 8	**Color Transparency and Master 38,** Earthquake-Safe Construction
Study Guide, p. 69 **Multicultural Activities,** p. 41 **Activity Masters, Investigate 19-2,** pp. 79-80 **Making Connections: Technology and Society,** p. 41 **Review and Assessment,** pp. 77-80	**Computer Test Bank**
	***STVS:** *Underwater Seismograph,* Earth and Space (Disc 3, Side 2) *Seismic Simulator,* Earth and Space (Disc 3, Side 2) **Spanish Resources** **Cooperative Learning Resource Guide** **Lab and Safety Skills**

***Science and Technology Videodisc Series**

KEY TO TEACHING STRATEGIES

Teaching strategies have been coded for varying learning styles and abilities. As you review teaching strategies in the margin, the following designations will help you decide which activities are appropriate for your students.

L1 Level 1 activities are basic activities and should be within the ability range of all students.

L2 Level 2 activities are average activities and should be within the ability range of the average to above-average student.

L3 Level 3 activities are challenging activities designed for the ability range of above-average students.

LEP LEP activities should be within the ability range of Limited English Proficiency students.

COOP LEARN Cooperative Learning activities are designed for small group work.

ADDITIONAL MATERIALS

SOFTWARE	AUDIOVISUAL
Quakes, MECC.	*The Earthquake* Simulator, Focus. *Earthquakes,* Aquarius. *Predictable Disaster (Nova),* laserdisc, Image Entertainment.

Chapter 19

Earthquakes and Volcanoes

THEME DEVELOPMENT

The two themes of energy and stability and change are integral to this chapter. The energy released by earthquakes and volcanoes changes Earth in many ways. These changes are often sudden, powerful, and frightening, and can destroy the stability of affected areas. This chapter deals with how the energy generated by earthquakes and volcanoes causes different types of destruction. It also describes ways to measure an earthquake's strength.

CHAPTER OVERVIEW

This chapter focuses on the causes and effects of earthquakes and volcanoes. Surface waves generated by earthquakes can cause the collapse of structures. The three different types of volcanoes—shield, cinder cone and composite—are also described and the distinctions among them are identified.

Students learn that the damage done by an earthquake depends on the earthquake's strength, its location relative to population centers, the design of structures in the area, and the type of ground on which the structures are built. The damage done by volcanoes is described. Lava can start fires, and ash and cinders kill plant life near the volcano.

Finally, students will learn how a seismograph measures an earthquake's strength. They will be introduced to the Richter scale, used to indicate the magnitude of an earthquake.

Tying to Previous Knowledge

Most students will have some knowledge of both earthquakes and volcanoes. You may wish to have students think about how landforms as viewed in Chapter 1 can change because of earthquakes and volcanic eruptions. Wave motion, described in Chapter 18, is relevant to the destruction caused by earthquakes.

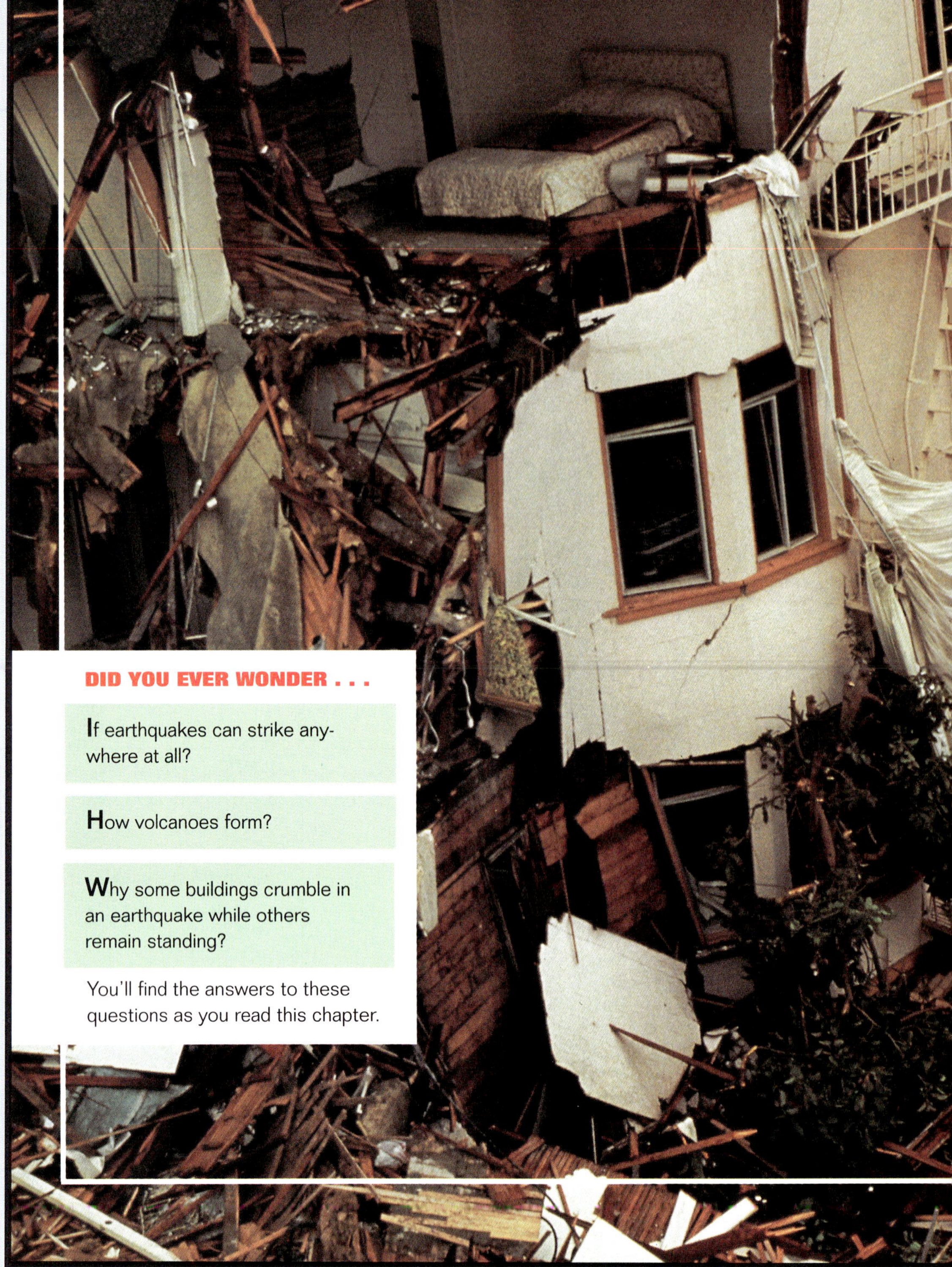

DID YOU EVER WONDER . . .

If earthquakes can strike anywhere at all?

How volcanoes form?

Why some buildings crumble in an earthquake while others remain standing?

You'll find the answers to these questions as you read this chapter.

DID YOU EVER WONDER...

Students will explore these questions as they progress through the chapter. Don't spoil their fun and motivation by sharing these answers too early.

- Earthquakes can strike anywhere there is a shifting of rock in the solid earth below the surface. (page 583)
- Volcanoes form when hot, melted rock material rises from inside Earth to the surface. The material can flow out as lava and form shield volcanoes. Violent explosions can form cone volcanoes. Composite volcanoes can form when alternating quiet and explosive eruptions occur. (pages 574–575)
- Whether or not a building collapses during an earthquake depends on the type of materials which the building is made of and the type of soil on which it is built. (page 578)

Earthquakes and Volcanoes

Change is always taking place on Earth. The sun appears to change position in the sky. Seasons change. The weather changes. Some changes, such as the carving of a canyon by a river, take place so slowly that you may not notice the change in your lifetime. Other changes, however, are sudden and dramatic, catching everyone's attention.

Among the most powerful and frightening types of change that take place on Earth are earthquakes and volcanic eruptions. They occur suddenly and can cause tremendous amounts of destruction. Earthquakes move the very ground you walk on. The vibrations make the ground shift, causing buildings to tremble and sometimes collapse. Volcanoes can blast tons of rock and smoke into the air. Because earthquakes and erupting volcanoes are powerful and unpredictable, it is important for you to understand these violent changes. This chapter will explain why these fascinating and destructive changes occur.

EXPLORE!

How can you experience an earthquake?

Join your classmates in a trip to some nearby bleachers or a room with a wooden floor. Take turns lying down blindfolded while the rest of the students pound their feet as hard as they can. Listen to the noise and feel the vibrations. How do you think this experience is like a real earthquake?

Introducing the Chapter

Have students look at the photograph on page 568 and speculate on what the building looked like before this change took place. Have students identify an earthquake as the agent of change. Have students describe what it would have felt like to be sleeping on the bed shown in the photograph.

Uncovering Preconceptions

Students may believe that earthquakes can strike only in places such as California or Mexico. Although earthquakes are more frequent in some areas, they can strike anywhere.

Students may not be concerned with volcanic activity if they live far from a volcano. Inform students that volcanic eruptions can change climates globally as ash and dust are added to the atmosphere.

EXPLORE!

How can you experience an earthquake?

Time needed 30 minutes

Materials bleachers or room with wooden floor, blindfolds

Thinking Processes Recognizing cause and effect, Observing and inferring, Making models

Purpose To simulate the noise and vibrations that occur during an earthquake

Preparation Suggest that students wear casual clothes for this activity.

Teaching the Activity

Discussion After doing the activity, have students discuss their results. Point out that the vibrations of an earthquake can be much more powerful and can cause great damage. L1 LEP

Expected Outcome

The blindfolded students should hear noise and feel vibrations.

Answer to Question

A real earthquake also produces noise and vibrations.

Project

Have students work together to research and diagram procedures for strapping a hot water heater to avoid earthquake damage. Have students explain why this procedure would decrease potential damage from an earthquake. A good resource is *Home Earthquake Preparedness Guide,* published by the Bay Area Regional Earthquake Preparedness Project, Metrocenter, 101 8 St., Suite 152, Oakland, CA 94007-4756.

Science at Home

Have students inspect their homes or school and identify measures that might be taken to prevent earthquake damage. For areas that are not particularly earthquake-prone, the discussion will be more theoretical. Many states and localities offer useful earthquake preparedness information or kits for both homes and school. The Bay Area Regional Earthquake Preparedness Project offers a free kit.

Section 19-1

PREPARATION

Concepts Developed

In this section students will learn that surface waves generated by earthquakes can cause the collapse of buildings and other structures. In this section, students will also learn about mountains that are formed by volcanoes.

Planning the Lesson

In planning your lesson on earthquakes and volcanoes, refer to the Chapter Organizer pages 568A-B for timing suggestions, resources, and additional materials that will help you in your presentation of the lesson concepts. For adequate development of the concepts presented in this section, we recommend that students do the Explore activity on page 570 and the Investigate activity on page 573.

1 MOTIVATE

Discussion Show pictures, slides, or videotapes of the October 16, 1989, Loma Prieta earthquake in the San Francisco Bay area. If any students in your class experienced that quake or any other firsthand, have them share their observations with the class. A set of slides entitled *Loma Prieta I, Overview* is available from Earthquake Engineering Research Institute, 6431 Fairmount Avenue, Suite 7, El Cerrito, CA 94530. L1

19-1 Earthquakes, Volcanoes, and You

OBJECTIVES

In this section, you will

- explain how waves at Earth's surface generated by earthquakes cause structures to collapse;
- make models of volcanic cones and describe the types of eruptions that produce them.

KEY SCIENCE TERMS

magma
lava

VIBRATIONS IN EARTH

Have you ever felt the earth quake beneath your feet? Or seen the fiery eruption of a volcano? You've probably seen pictures of the destruction caused by earthquakes in magazines or watched volcanic eruptions on television.

People have long wondered about earthquakes and volcanoes. What happens when unseen events inside Earth unleash such tremendous amounts of energy that the very ground vibrates? In the following activity, you will construct a model and observe material when it vibrates.

EXPLORE!

How do vibrations travel through a material?

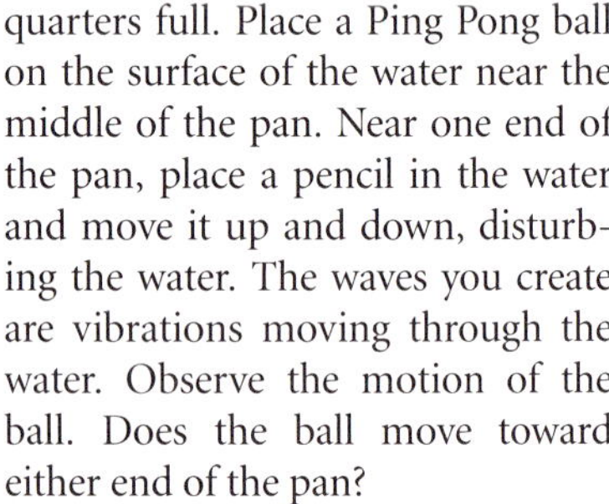

Pour water into a rectangular pan until it is about three-quarters full. Place a Ping Pong ball on the surface of the water near the middle of the pan. Near one end of the pan, place a pencil in the water and move it up and down, disturbing the water. The waves you create are vibrations moving through the water. Observe the motion of the ball. Does the ball move toward either end of the pan?

The waves you produced in the activity are similar to the transverse waves you learned about in Chapter 18. They are also very similar to waves generated by an earthquake. However, earthquake waves move through the solid earth.

What would happen to a building if the ground beneath it moved in a way similar to the water? Keep this

EXPLORE!

How do vibrations travel through a material?

Time needed 15 minutes

Materials rectangular shallow pan, water, pencil, Ping Pong ball

Thinking Processes
Observing and inferring, Recognizing cause and effect, Making models

Purpose To show how waves affect materials through which they move.

Teaching the Activity

Troubleshooting If students have difficulty observing the motion of the ball, place a colored dot sticker or a colored pencil mark on the ball. Be sure students hold the pencil horizontally in the water. L1

Expected Outcome

Students should see that waves cause the motion of the ball and realize that this motion is caused by waves moving through the water.

Answer to Question
The ball moves up and down, but not across the pan.

picture in your mind as you learn what it is like to experience an earthquake.

EXPERIENCING AN EARTHQUAKE

An earthquake occurs when part of the solid earth below the surface suddenly shifts. This action produces waves like the ones you caused when you made waves in the pan of water. The sudden shifting in Earth causes rocks and soil at the surface to vibrate. These vibrations travel out in all directions from this surface spot, as in Figure 19-1. They create movement similar to the water waves. Buildings and other structures on Earth then move like the ball in the activity. When the waves pass through them, the structures vibrate. This movement can cause buildings to crumble and fall.

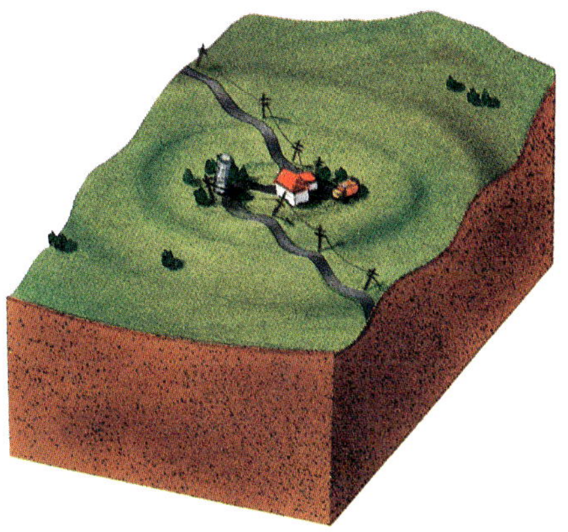

FIGURE 19-1. When rocks below Earth's surface shift suddenly, waves are generated. They travel to the surface, where they spread out in circles, the way water ripples outward from a disturbance.

Earthquakes can cause a great deal of destruction. Look at the picture of Mexico City in Figure 19-2 to get an idea of this destruction. Mexico City was dramatically rocked by an earthquake in 1985. When the earthquake hit, vibrations moved through the city in a series of waves that could be seen moving up and down, much like waves in the ocean. Standing in a building in Mexico City during the quake would have been like standing in a rowboat on a stormy sea. If you had been there, you would have heard a sound like hundreds of locomotives rushing through the city. Many of the buildings and other structures could not withstand the strain, and they crumbled, killing thousands of people and injuring many others.

FIGURE 19-2. Earthquake-generated vibrations moving through Mexico City in 1985 caused extensive death and destruction.

Think about what would happen to your school if an earthquake similar to the Mexico City quake struck nearby. With the arrival of the first wave, first one side of the building would be lifted, then the other. Your school would be put in motion similar to that of the ball in the Explore activity. What would happen to books and other

2 TEACH

Tying to Previous Knowledge

The vibrations generated by an earthquake are a form of mechanical wave. Help students recall what they learned about mechanical waves in Chapter 18. For example, the speed of a mechanical wave varies according to the medium through which it travels.

MAKING CONNECTIONS

Math

The National Oceanic and Atmospheric Administration defines a major earthquake as one having a Richter magnitude of at least 7.0 (see SE page 585) and/or resulting in property damage of at least $1 million. Have students draw a line graph for the data below to show the number of major earthquakes in the United States for each decade from 1900 to 1990. Have students place the decade on the horizontal, or *x*-, axis and the numbers from 0 to 16 on the vertical, or *y*-, axis.

Decade	Number of major earthquakes
1900–1909	10
1910–1919	3
1920–1929	7
1930–1939	4
1940–1949	9
1950–1959	11
1960–1969	7
1970–1979	7
1980–1989	15

Answer

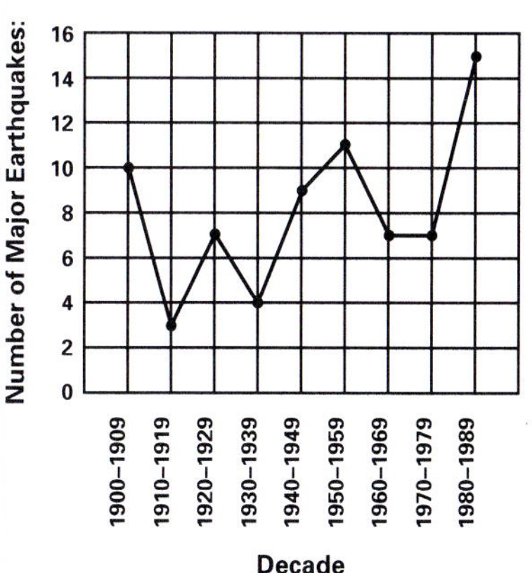

PROGRAM RESOURCES

Teacher Classroom Resources

Study Guide, page 67

Concept Mapping, page 27, Volcanoes L1

Making Connections: Integrating Sciences, page 41, Plant Nutrients L2

Laboratory Manual, pages 113-116, Earthquakes L2

OPTIONS

Meeting Individual Needs

Learning Disabled Have students with learning disabilities use musical instruments to feel vibrations. Students can beat drums and feel the vibrations of the membrane with their fingers. They can pluck the strings of guitars or ukeleles and feel the vibrations. You may wish to use other musical instruments available in the classroom. Have volunteers describe or draw a diagram of how a vibration feels to them. LEP

Concept Development

Demonstration Make a model of a volcano to show students what an erupting volcano looks like.

Materials needed are modeling clay, baking soda, red food coloring, vinegar, and safety goggles.

Use clay to make a small model volcano with a crater at the top. Place about a teaspoon of baking soda and a drop of red food coloring in the crater. Put on safety goggles to protect your eyes. Then add about a tablespoon of vinegar to the baking soda in the crater and have students observe what happens. Have students describe how your model eruption is similar to a real volcanic eruption and how it differs. *The model eruption shows how liquid overflows the "crater" and flows down the sides of the volcano. However, the lava that flows from a real volcano is composed of melted rock material and is much hotter than the product of the chemical reaction in this experiment.* L2

Debate Have students form two teams to debate whether they think the eruption of the Parícutin volcano in the middle of a corn field was beneficial or detrimental to the farmer and to his village. Have students consider possible dangers, economic implications, and scientific fame. L3

Theme Connection In this section, students will see evidence of the themes of energy and change and stability. Energy produced by changes within Earth is evident in volcanic eruptions and earthquakes. Energy is released during an earthquake in the form of seismic waves. Energy is also involved in the change from solid rock to magma and the rise of magma to Earth's surface in a volcano. These two kinds of occurrences provide very visible evidence of the energy produced by changes in Earth.

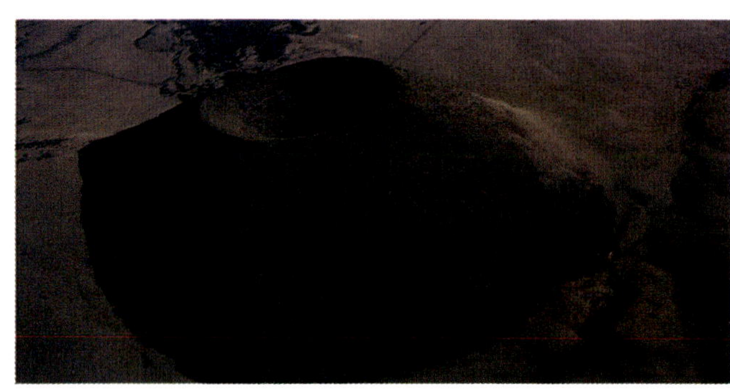

FIGURE 19-3. Parícutin erupted from a farmer's field in Mexico, emitting ash and cinders that formed this steep-sided, cinder cone volcano.

objects on shelves inside the building? What would happen to the building itself?

DID YOU KNOW?

Although earthquakes tend to occur in specific areas, they can happen almost anywhere. Some of the most powerful earthquakes ever to occur in the United States took place in New Madrid, Missouri, in late 1811 and early 1812.

OBSERVING VOLCANOES

Are there any volcanoes near where you live? If not, how would you feel if one suddenly began forming in your neighborhood? Probably like the farmer in Mexico who went out to work in his cornfield one day in 1943. He discovered hot smoke and ash rising from an opening in the ground that had formed in his field.

The Mexican farmer was witnessing the birth of a volcano. In less than 24 hours, a hill 40 meters high stood where the land had once been flat. By the end of a week, the hill was more than 160 meters high and still forming. The volcano, called Parícutin, eventually reached a height of 412 meters, and its base covered an area larger than 16,000 football fields. But almost nine years from that day in 1943, Parícutin stopped erupting. The volcano, pictured in Figure 19-3, has been inactive ever since.

Like Parícutin, all volcanoes originate when hot, melted rock material rises to Earth's surface from deep underground. This molten rock material beneath Earth's surface is called **magma**. Once it reaches the surface, it is called **lava.** Figure 19-4 shows how magma from Earth's interior forms a volcano near its surface. How does this rock material become melted in the first place? Investigate 19-1 will help you answer this question.

FIGURE 19-4. Hot magma rises from Earth's interior to form a volcano.

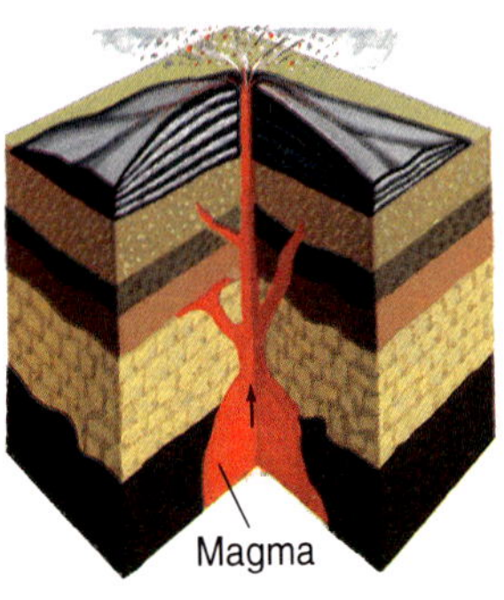

OPTIONS

Multicultural Perspectives

Encourage students to examine how different cultures have explained earthquakes through folktales and legends. Tales from Southeast Asia suggest that Earth was supported by a water buffalo. When the water buffalo shifted its weight, an earthquake resulted. Some Native American legends tell of a giant tortoise that supported Earth and whose movements caused earthquakes.

Meeting Individual Needs

Learning Disabled Some students may need help reading the graph on page 573. To find the temperature at a given depth, students should move a finger along the horizontal, or *x*-, axis to the depth they are looking for and then move their finger up to the graph line. Next they should move their finger straight left to the vertical, or *y*-, axis and read the temperature. L1

19-1 EARTH'S HOT INTERIOR

As you have learned, all volcanoes consist of hot, melted rock material rising to the surface from deep underground. In this activity, you will make and **interpret a scientific illustration** to show what this melted material indicates about temperatures in Earth's interior.

PROBLEM

How does the heat change as you go deeper into Earth's interior?

MATERIALS 

metric ruler
circle compass
paper and pencil

PROCEDURE

1. The distance from Earth's surface to its center is almost 6400 kilometers. Using a scale of 1 cm = 1000 km, draw a circle representing Earth.
2. Inside your large circle, draw a series of concentric circles with the following radii: 5.4 cm, 4.4 cm, 3.4 cm, 2.4 cm, and 1.4 cm.
3. Using the scale of 1 cm = 1000 km, write the depth below the surface of each circle on your drawing.
4. **Interpret the temperature-depth graph** shown here and write the approximate temperature at each depth on your model of Earth.
5. Most rock materials melt at temperatures around 900°C. Plot this point on your model Earth.

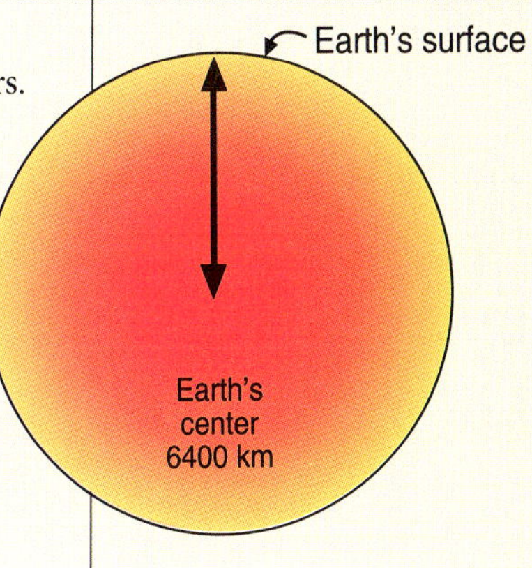

ANALYZE

1. What happens to the temperature of materials as you go further into Earth's interior?
2. Within what interval does temperature rise most rapidly?
3. What is the temperature at 2000 km? 4000 km? 6000 km?
4. What is the approximate depth of the point at which rock materials will melt?

CONCLUDE AND APPLY

5. Can you **infer** the depths at which magma may be found?
6. **Going Further**: What would be some reasons we cannot drill down to the depths where magma is found?

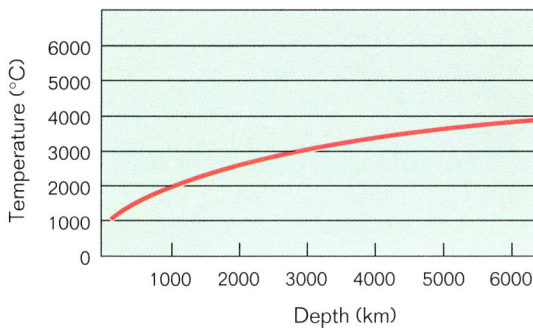

Temperature (°C): 0, 1000, 2000, 3000, 4000, 5000, 6000
Depth (km): 1000, 2000, 3000, 4000, 5000, 6000

INVESTIGATE!

19-1 EARTH'S HOT INTERIOR

Time needed 30 minutes

Materials metric ruler, circle compass, paper and pencil

Thinking Processes
Observing and inferring, Making and using graphs, Making models, Measuring in SI, Interpreting data, Forming a hypothesis

Purpose To find Earth's temperature at different depths from the surface and relate this knowledge to the formation of magma.

Teaching the Activity

Have students note that the difference between the radii of adjacent concentric circles in their drawings will be 1 cm. Be sure students understand the scale 1 cm = 1,000 km and how to calculate the radius of the large circle. Dividing 6,400 by 1,000 would result in 6.4 cm for the radius.

Troubleshooting Remind students to label Earth's surface zero and that numbers will increase as they approach the center of Earth.

Expected Outcomes

Students should notice that the temperature of Earth increases with depth below the surface. They should relate this to the melting of rock material.

Answers to Analyze/Conclude and Apply

1. The temperature increases.
2. The temperature increases most rapidly between 0 and 300 km beneath Earth's surface.
3. 2700°C, 3300°C, 3800°C
4. 200 km
5. Since rock becomes molten at about 900°C and this temperature is reached about 200 km below Earth's surface, students may infer that magma may be found at and below this depth.
6. We don't have the technology to drill as deep as most magma. Also, metal in well drills might melt.

Multicultural Perspectives

Volcanoes hold a unique place in the folklore of many countries. The Greeks explained the activity of Mount Etna by telling the tale of Typho and Zeus. Typho was a 100-headed monster who was the mortal enemy of the god Zeus. Zeus struck Typho with a thunderbolt and then flung Mount Etna on top of him to help hold him down. According to the legend, Typho still vomits out flame, smoke and destruction.

PROGRAM RESOURCES

Teacher Classroom Resources
Activity Masters, pages 77-78, Investigate 19-1

Concept Development

Uncovering Preconceptions Students may think that volcanic eruptions occur only at the summit of volcanic mountains. Inform students that the initial eruption of Mount St. Helens in 1980 originated several hundred meters below the summit. Show students some photographs of this eruption. Tremendous amounts of debris were forced laterally from the volcano. L1

FIND OUT!

What are two types of volcanic shapes?

Time needed 30 minutes

Materials 1 cup of sand or sugar, 2 paper plates, about 1 cup of a thick mixture of plaster of paris, protractor

Thinking Processes Making models, Observing and inferring

Purpose To make models of two volcanoes.

Preparation Adjust the amount of water called for to make sure that the plaster of paris is thick.

Teaching the Activity

Troubleshooting Be sure students pour the materials gently and carefully so that volcanic shapes are formed by pouring rather than by splattering.

Demonstration Some students may need help reading a protractor. You may need to show them how to read the correct angle for the slope. LEP L1

Expected Outcomes

The granular material produces a "volcano" with steep sides. The plaster of paris produces a "volcano" with a more gradual slope.

Answers to Conclude and Apply

1. Lava forms gentle slopes.
2. Gases, dust, ash, and rock form steep slopes.

FIGURE 19-5. In a quiet eruption, lava oozes onto the surface of Earth and flows downhill, often quite slowly, as in the figure to the left. In an explosive eruption, lava, gas, dust, ash, and rocks may be sent forcefully into the air, as in the figure to the right.

Any time volcanic material reaches the surface of Earth, we call the event an eruption. However, not all volcanic eruptions are the same. They range from quiet lava flows to violent explosions that send lava, gases, rock, ash, and dust several kilometers into the atmosphere. The figure on the left in Figure 19-5 shows a quiet eruption in which lava is flowing slowly onto Earth's surface and downhill. The figure on the right in Figure 19-5 shows the explosive eruption of a volcano.

Different kinds of eruptions produce differently shaped volcanoes. Do the following Find Out activity to discover two of these shapes.

FIND OUT!

What are two types of volcanic shapes?

Create models of two volcanoes. First, pour 1 cup of a substance like sand or sugar into the center of a paper plate from a height of about 50 cm. Then prepare a thick mixture of plaster of paris and water and pour it into the center of a second paper plate from a height of about 20 cm. Compare the shapes of your volcano models. Use a protractor to measure the slope angles of the sides of the two models. What are the differences in the two forms of models produced?

Conclude and Apply

1. Of the materials that erupt from volcanoes—lava, gases, dust, ash, and rock—which do you think form volcanoes with gentle slopes?
2. Which materials probably form volcanoes with steep slopes?

Shield Volcanoes

In a quiet eruption, dense lava flows onto Earth's surface and spreads out over a large area in fairly flat layers. Over

PROGRAM RESOURCES

Teacher Classroom Resources

Laboratory Manual, pages 117-118, Pumice L2

Critical Thinking/Problem Solving, page 27, Magma Heats Water L2

Transparency Masters, page 77, and **Color Transparency,** number 37, Forms of Volcanoes L2

Take Home Activities, page 29, Homemade Volcano L1

OPTIONS

Multicultural Perspectives

Obsidian is a glasslike volcanic rock frequently used in jewelry. There is a cliff made of obsidian, called Obsidian Cliff, in Yellowstone National Park. At one time Native Americans near Yellowstone used obsidian for knives, arrowheads, and spearheads. Have students observe a piece of obsidian in class and discuss what properties make it useful for jewelry or tools. Then have students design a tool or piece of jewelry that incorporates obsidian.

time, these layers build up to form a broad mountain with gently sloping sides called a shield volcano. Mauna Loa in Hawaii, shown in Figure 19-6, is the largest active shield volcano in the world. It rises from the Pacific Ocean floor to an altitude of 4 kilometers above the ocean's surface. How do you think shield volcanoes differ from volcanoes formed by explosive eruptions?

FIGURE 19-6. Quiet eruptions of lava form shield volcanoes such as this one on a Hawaiian island.

Cinder Cones

In an explosive eruption, gases and rock fragments may be hurled many kilometers into the air before the rock falls back to Earth. These rock fragments range in size from powdery volcanic dust and rice-sized particles of volcanic ash to cinders and large lumps of lava called bombs. The rock fragments fall to the ground to form a steep-sided, loosely packed mountain called a cinder cone. Parícutin, the Mexican volcano shown in Figure 19-3, is a cinder cone.

Composite Volcanoes

Some volcanoes, called composite volcanoes, are produced by alternating quiet and explosive eruptions. The sides of composite volcanoes are made up of alternating layers of lava and layers of ash and cinders. Mount Saint Helens is a composite volcano. Compare the shape of this volcano, shown in Figure 19-7, with the volcanoes in Figures 19-3 and 19-6.

Powerful and potentially dangerous earthquakes and volcanic eruptions originate deep below Earth's surface. In the next section, you'll discover some of the effects they have on us at the surface.

FIGURE 19-7. A composite volcano is made up of alternating layers of lava and rock, cinders, and ash.

Check Your Understanding

1. Explain why buildings and other structures crumble during earthquakes.
2. Name and describe the three forms of volcanoes and the type of eruption associated with each.
3. **APPLY:** Why might a building made of flexible material like wood withstand an earthquake better than a building made of a rigid material like brick?

Answers to Check Your Understanding

1. The vibrations travel in waves that pass through structures and produce up-and-down movements, causing structures to crumble.
2. Shield volcanoes are broad with gently sloping sides, formed by quiet eruptions. Cinder cone volcanoes are steep, caused by explosive eruptions. A composite volcanoe's shape is in between that of a shield and a cinder cone, caused by alternating quiet and explosive eruptions.
3. Flexible materials can more easily bend and withstand the movement and vibration of surface waves than can rigid materials.

3 Assess

Check for Understanding

1. Have students compare and contrast what they might observe during an earthquake with what they might observe during a volcanic eruption.
2. Have students answer questions 1 and 2 of Check Your Understanding individually. Then have them work with partners to discuss question 3. Suggest that students begin their discussions by comparing brick structures and wooden structures. COOP LEARN

Reteach

Demonstration Use a set of building blocks to make a wall or a simple building. Hit the side of the desk to make it vibrate. Have students watch the blocks as you increase the force of the vibrations. Students should note that weak vibrations may shift or otherwise disturb the wall, and stronger vibrations may make it collapse. L1 LEP

Extension

Have students who do not need the Reteach activity reread the description of the earthquake in Mexico City on page 571. Then have students make a drawing that portrays the wave motion, chaos, and destruction that took place. COOP LEARN LEP

4 Close

Activity

On the chalkboard, have students draw the outline of the classic shapes of a shield volcano (gently sloping sides) and a cone volcano (steep sides).

If possible, bring in photos of volcanoes that show the differences in shape between shield and cinder cone volcanoes. (Suggested sources: encyclopedia; book on volcanoes; illustrated book about a particular region where there is a well-known volcano, for example, Washington State or Sicily.)

Section 19-2

PREPARATION

Concepts Developed

Students continue their exploration of earthquakes and volcanoes, with emphasis on the factors causing differences in earthquake damage. The role of earthquakes in the production of tsunamis and the damage caused by these tsunamis are described. The damage caused by volcanic eruptions is also discussed.

Planning the Lesson

In planning your lesson on earthquake and volcano damage, refer to the Chapter Organizer pages 568A-B for timing suggestions, resources, and additional materials that will help you in your presentation of the lesson concepts.

For adequate development of the concepts presented in this section, we recommend that students do the Find Out activity on page 578.

1 MOTIVATE

Discussion Ask students what they would do if an earthquake were predicted to occur near their city tomorrow. What information could scientists provide to help them prepare for the earthquake? Are there particular buildings or areas that they think would be safer than others? L1

19-2 Earthquake and Volcano Destruction

OBJECTIVES

In this section, you will

- determine four factors that influence the amount of damage caused by an earthquake;
- describe the types of damage caused by earthquakes;
- describe the types of damage caused by volcanoes.

KEY SCIENCE TERMS

tsunami

EARTHQUAKE DAMAGE

How would you feel if your home collapsed during an earthquake? Your first concern would probably be your family's safety. Once you knew everyone was safe, you'd survey your home. Your clothes, furniture, television, and other belongings—all would be buried under rubble. Fire would be a possible hazard because natural gas lines are often split open by a quake, and sparks may ignite the escaping gas.

From time to time, people face this kind of damage after an earthquake has hit. Actually, very few earthquakes are destructive. Earthquakes vary in strength, and most quakes are so weak that people don't even notice them. This next activity will show you how the strength of an earthquake, plus one other earthquake characteristic, can determine the amount of damage it will cause.

EXPLORE!

What makes an earthquake destructive?

Take a rectangular pan and fill it halfway with sand or fine soil. Place its ends on two large books so that you can reach your hand underneath. Pound lightly on the underside of the pan. Observe how much sand or soil moves in the pan. Now pound harder, then harder still. Note how much more sand or soil shifts the harder you hit the bottom of the pan. Imagine what would happen to a building on the surface of the sand or soil after a particularly hard pound.

Now vary the place where you strike the pan. First pound in the middle and note where most of the sand or soil shifts. Is it directly over

EXPLORE!

What makes an earthquake destructive?

Time needed 15 minutes

Materials rectangular pan, sand or fine soil, two large books

Thinking Processes
Observing and inferring, Determining cause and effect, Making models, Hypothesizing

Purpose To model the damage an earthquake might cause.

Teaching the Activity

Troubleshooting Be sure students fill the pan only half full. L1

Expected Outcomes

The greatest movement of sand or soil occurs when the pounding is hardest.

Answers to Questions

1. When the pan is struck in the middle, the soil or sand falls evenly to either side.
2. Pounding shifts the soil or sand to the side of the pan resting on the table.
3. A building might crumble and fall.
4. A building farther away might be damaged but remain standing.

the spot where you strike the pan, or off to the side? Move the pan so that one side extends over the edge of the table and pound under this side. Where does most of the sand or soil shift? What could happen to a building directly above such an underground disturbance? What would happen to a building on the other side of the pan?

Strength and distance from inhabited areas are two factors that affect the amount of destruction an earthquake will cause. To gain a better understanding of how two other factors can influence the damaging effects of earthquakes, consider the destruction caused by three major earthquakes of about the same strength.

In 1988, entire villages were destroyed and more than 45,000 people were killed when an earthquake struck Armenia. In 1989, an earthquake struck the San Francisco Bay area, damaging some older structures and killing 67 people. In 1990, an earthquake in Iran destroyed hundreds of structures and killed more than 50,000 people.

FIGURE 19-8. Earthquakes have caused extensive loss of life because of damage to buildings.

As you can see, the amount of structural damage and the number of deaths were much greater in Armenia and Iran than they were in San Francisco. One reason for this great difference is that many structures in San Francisco were designed to better withstand the effects of earthquakes. The structures in the other locations were not. As a result, many structures in Armenia and Iran collapsed, trapping and killing the people inside.

You read about a major earthquake in Mexico City earlier in this chapter. Most of Mexico City was built on loosely packed sediments. The quake shifted and vibrated these loose materials easily, causing the collapse of about 250 structures and killing more than 7000 people.

Therefore, when considering the threat of an earthquake, you must consider four factors: the strength of the

2 Teach

Tying to Previous Knowledge

Students have learned that surface waves of an earthquake cause damage and that different types of eruptions form different shapes of volcanoes. In this section they will learn about factors that affect the amount of damage done. Start with a discussion of a disaster such as a fire, flood, or storm that students are familiar with. Have students discuss factors that increase or decrease the damage done.

Concept Development

Discussion Have students discuss the validity of this statement: *Earthquakes don't kill. Falling structures do.*

Lead students in a discussion of how earthquakes result indirectly in fatalities. Include the collapse of buildings, broken gas lines, downed power lines, and water contamination. Some students may be able to relate the statement to the fact that the collapse of Highway 880 in Oakland, California, caused most deaths in the 1989 San Francisco bay area earthquake.

Uncovering Preconceptions Some students may think that all earthquakes begin at Earth's surface. Explain that earthquakes may originate near Earth's surface or deep under Earth's crust.

Content Background

The point at which the earthquake waves originate is called the *focus*. The point on Earth's surface directly above the focus is called the earthquake's *epicenter*. The energy generated by the earthquake travels outward from the epicenter like ripples on a pond. The earthquake's energy is strongest at its epicenter.

PROGRAM RESOURCES

Teacher Classroom Resources

Study Guide, page 68

Multicultural Activities, page 42, Mount Pinatubo L1

Transparency Masters, page 79, and **Color Transparency,** number 38, Earthquake-Safe Construction L2

Other Resources

Quakes, software, MECC.

OPTIONS

Multicultural Perspectives

The eruption of Nevado del Ruiz in Colombia in November 1985 caused almost 23,000 deaths. However, most of these deaths resulted from mud flows. The volcano was covered with glaciers and snow that melted and mixed with ash and soil and then flowed rapidly downhill.

Concept Development

Discussion Have students describe ways waves can cause damage at a seashore or at a large lake. Then have them imagine the kind of damage a wave over 30 meters in height could cause. To help them envision the height of a crest of a tsunami, tell students that because they are all under two meters tall, the crest of a tsunami can be higher than 15 students standing on top of one another. If possible, help students locate some neighborhood buildings that are about 30 meters tall (approximately 9 stories high).

Activity Have students draw a diagram showing the height of their school in relation to the height of a wave crest of a tsunami. L3

FIND OUT!

What may happen when an earthquake strikes offshore?

Time needed 30 minutes

Materials books, rectangular baking pans, water, sand, scissors, 20 cm of string, circular plastic lids

Thinking Processes Making models, Observing and inferring, Recognizing cause and effect

Purpose To simulate the effects of an offshore earthquake on a seashore.

Preparation Use a circular lid with a diameter less than the width of the rectangular pan. Be sure students place the lid in the pan gently to avoid waves before they simulate an earthquake. Provide students with plastic "houses" or "hotels" from a board game. LEP

Teaching the Activity

Discussion Be sure students understand that an offshore earthquake causes an abrupt movement of the ocean floor. This movement pushes against the water much like the plastic lid does in the activity.

earthquake, its location relative to populated areas, the design of buildings, and the type of ground on which these structures are built. While people can't do anything about the first two factors, they do have some control over the other two. They can design and construct buildings that will withstand many earthquakes, and they can build these structures on solid ground.

For people living along the seashore, the threat of an earthquake presents an additional problem. Can you think what this concern might be? You'll learn about it next.

TSUNAMIS

If you lived at the seashore in an area where earthquakes occurred fairly often, what major concerns would you have? You might worry about the sandy soil on which your house is built. You know from the Mexico City example and from your own Explore activity that loose material like sand becomes unstable when earthquake waves travel through it. But there is another problem you may face at your seashore home.

FIND OUT!

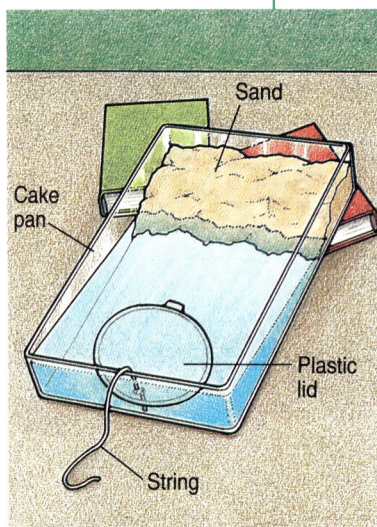

What may happen when an earthquake strikes offshore? 

In this activity, you will build a model of a seashore to demonstrate the special earthquake-related problems faced by people living in such a location. First use one or two books to tilt a cake pan at a 20-degree angle. Pour water into the lower end of the pan. Leave about one-third of the pan at the upper end dry.

Create a coastline by packing a layer of damp sand 2–3 cm thick at the dry end of the pan. Use your hands to build dunes and low areas. Create roads parallel to the shoreline. You might even place small houses from a board game on the shore. Punch a hole near the rim of a plastic lid and thread a piece of string about 20 cm long through the hole.

OPTIONS

Enrichment

Debate Have students form two teams to debate the advisability of living in an area where earthquakes are common. Have teams consider such items as earthquake-resistant construction, earthquake insurance, climate, and economic factors that keep people from moving away. Some team members may point out negative features of other areas as they build a case for living in an earthquake-prone area. Do not expect the class to reach a unanimous decision but rather to present a balanced picture. L2

Tie a knot near the end of the string to keep it from slipping back out. Carefully place the lid on the bottom of the pan at the low end. Avoid splashing the water. The short end of the string should be beneath the lid near the end of the pan. The long end should hang over the end of the pan. Use your fingers to hold the edge of the plastic lid near the upper end of the pan firmly against the bottom of the pan. While holding this edge of the lid down, pull the string straight up with one rapid movement. This action simulates an underwater earthquake. Observe what happens.

Conclude and Apply

1. What do you think happens to the water when an earthquake strikes under the ocean?
2. What happens to land near the water?

Expected Outcome

Students should see that the motion of the lid generates a wave that travels to the surface. The wave will most likely cause destruction along the students' shorelines.

Answers to Conclude and Apply

1. The water forms a wave that increases dramatically as it approaches the shore.
2. Land near the water is washed away.

As you learned in the Find Out activity, an underwater earthquake can send a huge, rapidly moving water wave crashing onto the shore.

When an earthquake occurs under the ocean, the movement of the ocean floor pushes against the water, creating a powerful wave that reaches all the way to the ocean surface. These enormous water waves may travel thousands of kilometers in all directions. Recall what you learned in Chapter 18 about wavelengths and crests. Far from shore, where the water is deep, the wavelengths of earthquake-related waves can be hundreds of kilometers long. But when one of these waves nears a coastline, the water piles up and forms a towering wave crest that can exceed 30 meters in height.

Such a tremendous ocean wave generated by an earthquake is called a **tsunami** (soo NAHM ee). Figure 19-9 shows how a tsunami is formed. When the tsunami crashes into a shoreline, it can engulf entire towns, causing

FIGURE 19-9. A tsunami begins over the site of an earthquake. The wave's height increases dramatically near the shore.

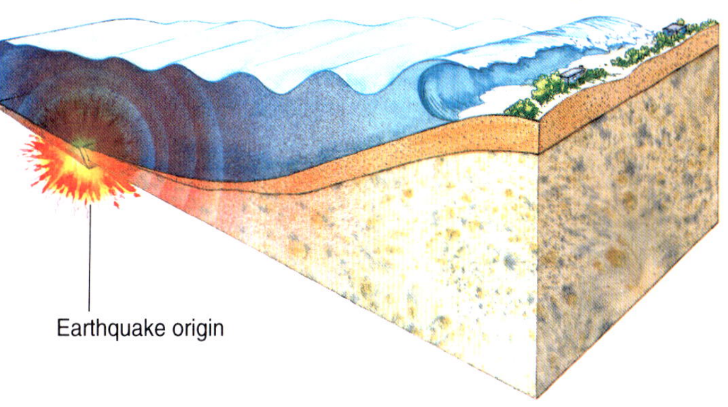

Concept Development

Uncovering Preconceptions

Many people mistakenly call a tsunami a "tidal wave." Some students may confuse waves associated with earthquakes with waves associated with tides. Although both kinds of waves can do great damage, their causes are different. Another misconception is that *all* offshore earthquakes produce tsunamis, which is not the case.

Theme Connection The theme supported by this section is energy. Energy from an earthquake is released at the earthquake's focus. Seismic waves are produced and travel outward from the focus. The point on Earth's surface directly above the focus is called the epicenter. Energy that reaches Earth's surface radiates from the epicenter in the form of surface waves.

Teacher F.Y.I.

An earthquake on November 1, 1775, near Lisbon, Portugal, was described by Voltaire in his novel *Candide.* In this earthquake, about 60,000 people died because of the collapse of buildings and the action of a tsunami generated by the earthquake.

Multicultural Perspectives

Tsunami is a Japanese word that means "storm or harbor wave." Tsunamis have been depicted by Japanese woodcutters such as Katushika Hokusai and Utagawa Kuniyoshi. Have students use a medium such as watercolors, pastels, or ink to portray the power and danger of a tsunami.

MAKING CONNECTIONS

Social Studies

In 1964 a tsunami caused more than $100 million worth of damage to Valdez, Alaska. On March 24, 1989, an oil spill of about 10,080,000 tons also caused a great deal of damage to this coastal town. Have students research, compare, and contrast the damage caused by each occurrence, keeping in mind human, environmental, and economic concerns. Have students find photographs to illustrate their research, if possible. Some students may wish to describe recovery and cleanup efforts.

Concept Development

Demonstration Show slides or photographs of the damage caused by the recent volcanic eruption of Mount Pinatubo in the Philippines and Mount Unzen in Japan. Discuss the fact that mudslides and widespread flooding are major causes of damage. Point out that although loss of human life from volcanic explosions has decreased due to better methods of warning people and other precautions, death, injury, and destruction can still be harsh realities in areas of volcanic eruptions.

Activity Have students write letters to friends describing the sudden eruption of a volcano near their homes. Encourage creativity, but have students maintain scientific accuracy. Be sure students differentiate between the types of volcanic eruptions—quiet, explosive, or a combination—and their results. Indirect results such as flooding and mudslides can be addressed. Some students may wish to include drawings with their letters. L2

How do we know?

The average wavelength of a tide is 10,000 km.

How do we know?

Wavelengths of Tsunamis Far from Shore

Tide stations have been set up to detect waves with very long wavelengths. At these tide stations, gauges filter out normal tides and waves caused by wind. Any waves with long wavelengths that are not filtered out are assumed to be the result of earthquakes.

enormous destruction and taking many lives. In 1964, an earthquake in Alaska produced a tsunami that reached a height of 52 meters in the town of Valdez. This huge wave killed more than 100 people and caused more than 100 million dollars in damage.

VOLCANO DAMAGE

Can you imagine red-hot lava oozing toward your home? People in Hawaii—and elsewhere on Earth—have had to watch just such a scene.

Early in Earth's history, volcanic activity was more widespread than it is today. Most of the volcanoes on Earth today are dormant, which means that they are not currently active. An active volcano is one that shows evidence of releasing materials, ranging from occasional smoke and gases to constant spewing of dust, ash, cinders, and lava. Currently, more than 600 volcanoes on Earth are classified as active.

The most active volcano in the world at the present time is Kilauea (kil uh WAY uh) in Hawaii. It has been quietly erupting off and on for centuries. The most recent series of eruptions began in January 1983 and continued into the 1990s. Although the eruptions consisted of quiet

FIGURE 19-10. Homes can be destroyed when they lie in the path of lava.

OPTIONS

Enrichment

Discussion To provide some balance to the negative aspects of volcanic activity, point out that geothermal energy from volcanoes can generate electricity. It is used in Iceland, Hawaii, California, Italy, Mexico, New Zealand, and Japan. Have students discuss benefits and drawbacks of this energy source. They may need to research the topic to understand how geothermal energy is related to volcanic activity and how electricity is produced from geothermal energy. *Possible benefits include decreased use of fossil fuels and reduced air pollution. Possible drawbacks include damage to the environment in tapping this energy and the release of harmful gases.* L3

lava flows, Figure 19-10 shows how homes have been destroyed by the lava released by this volcano. A large number of homes were destroyed when the town of Kalapana was completely buried by lava in May 1990.

Another volcano you may have heard about is Mount Saint Helens in the state of Washington. The explosive eruption of this volcano in 1980 was one of the largest recent eruptions in North America. On May 18, 1980, Mount Saint Helens hurled over 275 trillion tons of ash and rock into the air, killing nearly every living thing in a fan-shaped area extending as far as 90 kilometers from the mountain. Heat from the eruption melted snow, and the meltwater caused widespread flooding and mudslides. Look at Figure 19-11—one photo showing the region before the eruption and the other showing it afterward—to see the destruction this volcano caused. Because of early warnings, few people were in the area of Mount Saint Helens when it erupted. Still, about 60 human lives were lost.

Perhaps the best known volcanic eruption in the world is that of Italy's Mount Vesuvius in the year 79. Ash and cinders from the eruption buried the nearby cities of Pompeii and Herculaneum. They were not unearthed for more than 1500 years.

The most recent eruption of Vesuvius occurred in 1944. No one thinks it will be the last. Yet many thousands of people live in the area around Vesuvius. They choose to live in the shadow of this potentially dangerous

FIGURE 19-11. Compare these photographs of the region around Mount Saint Helens before (a) and soon after (b) its 1980 eruption. What effect did the explosive eruption have?

a

b

Concept Development

Discussion Have students find articles about or drawings of the eruption of Vesuvius in A.D. 79. Books and scientific journals have many fascinating reports on the unearthing of artifacts from this eruption. Have students read aloud to the class from the articles they find.

MAKING CONNECTIONS

Life Science

Although Mount Saint Helens may still look bleak and barren, life is beginning anew on the slopes. Scientists see this as a unique opportunity to study recovery and succession. But they had better do it quickly because geologists predict a 50 percent chance of another eruption within the next 20 or so years. In the meantime, a video camera is in place, recording any activity in the crater. Interested students may want to write to the U.S. Forest Service's National Volcanic Monument, Mount Saint Helens, for information on the return of life to the approximately 110,000 acres that were devastated by the volcano in 1980.

Flex Your Brain Have students use the Flex Your Brain master to explore ENERGY PRODUCED WITHIN THE EARTH.

Enrichment

Research As recently as the summer of 1991, eight more bodies were found in the ruins of Pompeii. The volcanic ash mummified these bodies. Have students find articles about and pictures of the lifelike casts archaeologists have created of Vesuvius's victims by using plaster to fill the cavities left in volcanic ash by people killed over 1,900 years ago. LEP L2 COOP LEARN

PROGRAM RESOURCES

Teacher Classroom Resources

Making Connections: Across the Curriculum, page 41, Deadly Earthquakes L2

Critical Thinking/Problem Solving, page 8, Flex Your Brain

Other Resources

Predictable Disaster (NOVA), laserdisc, Image Entertainment

3 Assess

Check for Understanding

Have students work individually or with partners to answer questions 1–3 of Check Your Understanding. Have students work in small groups to hypothesize about question 4. COOP LEARN

Reteach

Have students draw concept maps to summarize factors that affect the amount of damage done by an earthquake, kinds of damage done by earthquakes, and kinds of damage done by volcanoes. L1

Extension

Have students choose an earthquake, tsunami, or volcanic eruption that is not covered in this textbook and find out more about it. Students should look for information on geologic events leading to the eruption or quake, as well as information on the damage and loss of life it caused. L3

4 Close

Activity

Have students draw a simple picture of damage resulting from either a volcanic eruption or an earthquake and tell how some of the damage might have been avoided. L1

DID YOU KNOW?

One of the most destructive volcanic eruptions known to humans occurred in Indonesia in 1883. Krakatoa, a volcano that had been dormant for more than 200 years, blew apart in a spectacular eruption. Much of the island on which it stood, also called Krakatoa, collapsed into the sea, producing tsunamis as high as 12-story buildings. More than 96,000 people were killed as a result of the eruption and the waves.

volcano because the climate is mild, the harbor is good, and the fine, volcanic soil is very fertile.

In 1815, Mount Tambora in Indonesia erupted in a series of explosions, the loudest of which was heard over 600 kilometers away. More than 10,000 people were killed as a direct result of the eruption, and at least 82,000 more died of starvation and disease caused by the terrible conditions produced by the eruption.

In addition to this death and destruction, the eruption of Tambora produced another startling effect. The explosive strength of this eruption sent particles of volcanic dust as high as 100 kilometers into the atmosphere. This dust circled the globe for months and reduced the amount of sunlight that reached Earth's surface. Average temperatures in the Northern Hemisphere were lowered by about 0.5°C. The year following Tambora's eruption was called "the year without a summer" in some regions of the world. Places such as England and the East Coast of the United States experienced snow in July and August of 1816. The summer months were so cold and overcast that many crops could not grow, and many people went hungry.

You have explored the types of damage that can be caused by earthquakes and volcanoes. You know that the amount of damage that can occur depends partly on how big or how strong a volcano or an earthquake is. In the next section, you will discover how the strength of an earthquake is measured.

Check Your Understanding

1. List four factors that affect the amount of damage caused by an earthquake.
2. What kind of damage occurs when an earthquake strikes on land? When an earthquake strikes the ocean floor?
3. What are some of the dangers faced by people living near an active volcano?
4. **APPLY:** Some scientists have hypothesized that high levels of volcanic activity may have occurred about 65 million years ago. This time is the same period during which the dinosaurs became extinct. If many volcanoes were spewing ash and dust into the atmosphere, how might the climate of Earth have changed? How would a climate change have affected plant and animal life at that time?

Answers to Check Your Understanding

1. Four factors are the strength of the earthquake, its location relative to populated areas, the design of structures in its path, and the type of ground on which these structures are built.
2. When an earthquake strikes on land, buildings and structures may crumble, causing loss of life and property damage. When an earthquake strikes the ocean floor, tsunamis may be formed. These waves crash into shorelines, causing widespread destruction and loss of life.
3. Dangers include oozing hot lava; dust, cinders, ash, and rocks spewed in the air; flooding and mudslides.
4. It is possible that ash and dust blocked out much of the sunlight, making the climate cooler and destroying the plant life necessary for dinosaur survival.

19-3 Measuring Earthquakes

RECORDING VIBRATIONS

OBJECTIVES

In this section, you will

- demonstrate how a seismograph measures an earthquake's strength;
- explain how the Richter scale is used to indicate earthquake magnitude.

KEY SCIENCE TERMS

seismograph
magnitude

Just as the severity of volcanic eruptions varies from one to the next, the strength of earthquakes varies as well. Recall that an earthquake is caused by a shifting of rock in the solid earth below the surface. Many earthquakes are not even felt at the surface. Earthquakes that are felt range in strength. At one end, they may be only a mild shaking of the ground, similar to the vibrations you felt when your classmates pounded the floor or bleacher in the Explore activity at the beginning of this chapter. At the other end, they may be a violent trembling.

Whether or not they are felt at Earth's surface, earthquakes produce vibrations in rocks and soil. The strength of an earthquake is determined by recording and measuring its vibrations.

A scientist who studies earthquakes is called a seismologist (siz MAHL uh jihst). Seismologists use an instrument called a **seismograph** to record earthquake vibrations. A seismograph works on the following principle. The roll of paper is held firmly in the frame of the seismograph, while the pen moves freely. When the ground vibrates, the frame of the seismograph and the roll of paper also vibrate, but the pen does not. As the roll of paper turns, the pen traces a record of the vibrations on the paper. This record appears as a wavy line. The height of the peaks of the wavy line indicates the earthquake's magnitude. The **magnitude** of an earthquake is a measure of the earthquake's strength.

In the next Investigate activity, you will make your own seismograph and measure magnitudes with it.

FIGURE 19-12. This seismograph measures the magnitude of earthquake vibrations.

Section 19-3

PREPARATION

Concepts Developed

In Section 19-2, students learned that the strength of an earthquake is a factor in the amount of damage it can do. In this section, students will learn how this strength is measured by a seismograph and how the magnitude of an earthquake is expressed numerically.

Planning the Lesson

In planning your lesson on measuring earthquakes, refer to the Chapter Organizer pages 568A-B for timing suggestions, resources, and additional materials that will help you in your presentation of the lesson concepts.

For adequate development of the concepts presented in this section, we recommend that students do the Investigate activity on page 584.

1 MOTIVATE

Discussion Ask students whether they think it is important to measure the strength of an earthquake. Then focus on the idea that measuring the strength of an earthquake *is* important. Ask students why. *Answers may include to learn more about earthquakes, to be able to compare earthquakes in different places, possibly to be able to predict earthquakes, to help in the design of more earthquake-proof buildings.* L1

2 TEACH

Tying to Previous Knowledge

Ask students for examples of instruments used to measure scientific data. *Possibilities include thermometers to measure temperature, metric rulers to measure length, and clocks to measure time.* Ask students what aspects of an earthquake they might want to measure. *its strength*

PROGRAM RESOURCES

Teacher Classroom Resources

Study Guide, page 69

Multicultural Activities, page 41, Earthquakes in Mexico L1

Activity Masters, pages 79-80, Investigate 19-2

Making Connections: Technology and Society, page 41, Measuring Earth Movements with Lasers L2

INVESTIGATE!

19-2 MAKING A MODEL SEISMOGRAPH

Time needed 50 minutes

Materials See student edition materials.

Thinking Processes Observing and inferring, Recognizing cause and effect, Measuring in SI, Forming a hypothesis, Separating and controlling variables, Making models

Purpose To make a model of a seismograph and measure the magnitude of vibrations.

Preparation Be sure students tape the ring stand down carefully so that they can accurately observe the effects of different forces acting on the table.

Teaching the Activity

Demonstration Before beginning the activity, have students work in pairs, one student holding a fine-tip marker steady and the other pulling a sheet of paper under it. Have students observe what sort of line is created. *a straight line* COOP LEARN L2

Troubleshooting Encourage students to pull the paper evenly with a smooth, slow motion to avoid distorting the results. Be sure that students hit the table from the sides so the line is wavy, not straight.

Expected Outcomes

Students should observe that the amplitude of the waves is greater when the table is hit with greater strength. Students should recognize that the same relationship exists between the strength of waves generated by an earthquake and their amplitude waves.

INVESTIGATE!

19-2 MAKING A MODEL SEISMOGRAPH

In this activity, you will make a model seismograph and record some vibrations.

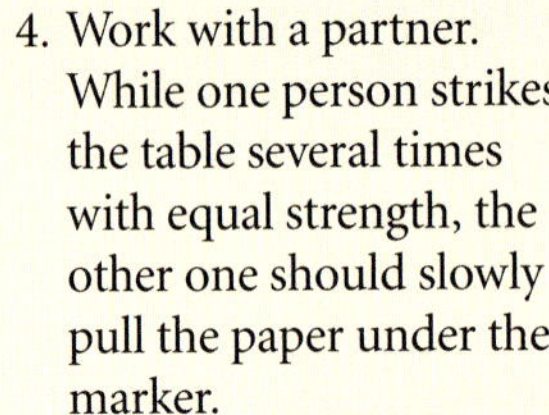

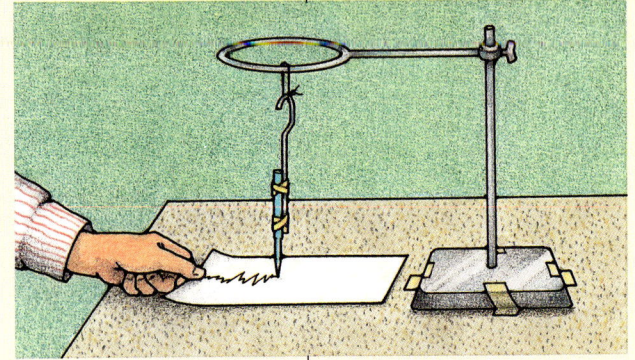

PROBLEM

How can you measure the magnitude of vibrations?

MATERIALS

ring stand with ring
wire hook from coat hanger
piece of string
2 rubber bands
fine-tip marker
masking tape
metric ruler
sheet of paper

PROCEDURE

1. Copy the data table.
2. Set up your seismograph using the illustration as a guide.
3. Place a sheet of paper under the ring. Adjust the position of the marker so that its tip just touches near the end of the paper.
4. Work with a partner. While one person strikes the table several times with equal strength, the other one should slowly pull the paper under the marker.
5. Recall from Chapter 18 that amplitude is half the height of a wave from crest to trough. **Measure** the amplitude marked on your paper. Record your measurements and observations as Trial 1.
6. **Hypothesize** about the effect of the magnitude of the vibrations on the amplitude of the peaks.
7. Repeat Steps 3 and 4, hitting the table with less strength for Trial 2 and more strength for Trial 3. Record your measurements and observations.

ANALYZE

1. Which trial resulted in the greatest amplitudes recorded on the wavy line?
2. How did the movement of the marker **compare** with the movement of the frame of the seismograph?

CONCLUDE AND APPLY

3. How does your hypothesis compare with the results of the activity?
4. Determine the effect the magnitude of vibrations had on the amplitude of the wave peaks.
5. **Going Further:** What difference would you expect there to be between the amplitudes generated by a strong earthquake and those generated by a weaker one?

DATA AND OBSERVATIONS Sample data

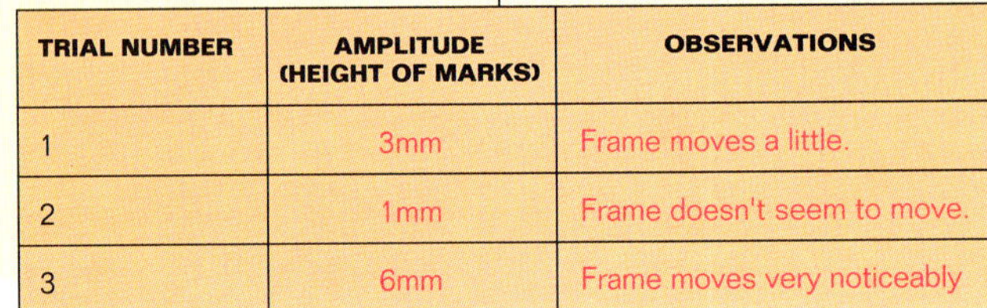

TRIAL NUMBER	AMPLITUDE (HEIGHT OF MARKS)	OBSERVATIONS
1	3mm	Frame moves a little.
2	1mm	Frame doesn't seem to move.
3	6mm	Frame moves very noticeably

Answers to Analyze/Conclude and Apply

1. trial 3
2. In a real seismograph, the pen would remain stationary while the frame moved with the vibrations. Students' models don't do this because the pen is not isolated from the motion of the frame.
3. Responses will vary depending on students' hypotheses.
4. As the magnitude of the vibrations increased, the amplitude of the wave peaks increased.
5. Strong earthquakes should generate greater amplitudes.

TABLE 19-1. Earthquake Occurrences

Richter Magnitude	Number Expected Per Year
1.0 to 3.9	100,000
4.0 to 4.9	6200
5.0 to 5.9	800
6.0 to 6.9	120
7.0 to 7.9	20
8.0 to 8.9	<1

Seismologists use a special scale called the Richter (RIHK tur) scale to describe the earthquake magnitudes they measure. The numbers on the scale relate to the amounts of energy released by the earthquakes. Each number on the scale represents an earthquake about 30 times stronger than the previous lower number on the scale.

For example, an earthquake measuring 6.5 on the Richter scale is 30 times stronger than an earthquake that measures 5.5 on the scale. How much stronger would an earthquake measuring 7.5 on the Richter scale be than one measuring 5.5? Because there is a difference of 2.0 on the scale, you would multiply 30 times 30. The stronger earthquake would be 900 times stronger than the weaker one.

Study Table 19-1 to see how many earthquakes at each magnitude are expected each year. What happens to the number of occurrences as the magnitude increases? How many earthquakes are predicted to occur with a Richter value between 1.0 and 3.9? How would you account for the fact that you hear about only a few earthquakes each year?

Which do you think is more destructive—an earthquake measuring 8.5 that occurs in a desolate, unpopulated part of the world or one measuring 6.5 that occurs near a densely populated area? Although the stronger quake releases much more energy, the second quake may cause much more damage. The magnitude of an earthquake does not tell you all you need to know about an earthquake.

How do we know?

The Richter Scale

The Richter scale was devised by Charles Richter in 1935. How do we determine the magnitudes of earthquakes that occurred before the scale was devised? The Richter values for earthquakes that occurred before 1935 are based on records of damage caused by the earthquakes. The Richter values of these quakes are estimates.

Concept Development

Uncovering Preconceptions Many students may think that there are only a very few earthquakes each year since only those with high Richter values or those that cause significant damage are reported in the news. There are actually more than 100,000 earthquakes each year.

Theme Connection The theme that is supported by this section is energy. The height of the lines a seismograph makes is a measure of the energy released by an earthquake. The energy released by an earthquake is called its magnitude. The Richter scale describes how much energy is released by an earthquake.

Student Text Questions What happens to the number of occurrences as the magnitude increases? *It decreases.* How many earthquakes occur at the low end of the scale? *100,000* How would you account for the fact that you hear about only a few earthquakes each year? *Many earthquakes are slight and do not cause much, if any, damage. Earthquakes that are stronger, or occur in heavily populated areas, have a greater impact on people's lives, so they are reported by the news media.*

MAKING CONNECTIONS

Social Studies

Draw a horizontal time line showing the dates of the major earthquakes shown in Table 19-2. Use the scale 1 inch = 100 years. Ask: In which century were the most major earthquakes recorded? Why do you think this is true? *The most earthquakes were recorded in the twentieth century. It is possible that there were actually more earthquakes or simply that recording methods and communications were better in the twentieth century than in previous centuries.*

OPTIONS

Meeting Individual Needs

Learning Disabled Help students understand the idea of 30 times greater by asking what objects in their school might be 30 times longer than the average new pencil. *The average new pencil is about 18 cm long, so the objects suggested should be between 5 and 7 m long.* LEP

Enrichment

Research Have students work in small groups to research the benefits of volcanoes to surrounding areas. Some possibilities for students to explore include the fertile soil produced and the dramatic scenery which brings tourists to places such as Etna, Stromboli, and Vesuvius. COOP LEARN

SKILLBUILDER

1. 1556 in Shensi, China—most deaths. 1811–12 in New Madrid, MO—fewest deaths.
2. 1755 in Lisbon, Portugal
3. The quake may have occurred in a less populated area, the ground may have been more solid, there may have been fewer structures. L1

3 ASSESS

Check for Understanding

Have students review their work on the Investigate activity on page 584 before answering question 3 of Check Your Understanding.

Reteach

Have students work in pairs. One student tries to write while the other pounds on the desk. Have students relate the force of the pounding to the effect on the handwriting. COOP LEARN L1

Extension

Have students make line graphs to show Richter values of earthquakes of the twentieth century as shown in Table 19-2. Then ask students if their graphs give a good picture of the fact that the San Francisco earthquake of 1906 was more than 30 times greater than the San Francisco earthquake of 1989. L3

4 CLOSE

Activity

Have students explain how quake A and quake B had the characteristics described in this table.

	Richter Value	Deaths	Damage
A	7.1	800	$1 million
B	7.5	300	$0.5 million

Quake A was closer to a heavily populated area where structures were not seismically safe. L1

SKILLBUILDER

MAKING AND USING TABLES

Use Table 19-2 to answer the following questions:

1. Which earthquake resulted in the greatest number of deaths? The fewest?
2. Which quake had the greatest magnitude?
3. Hypothesize why the 1920 China quake resulted in fewer deaths than the 1976 quake.

If you need help, refer to the **Skill Handbook** on page 649.

TABLE 19-2. Major Earthquakes

Year	Location	Richter Value	Deaths
1556	Shensi, China	?	830,000
1737	Calcutta, India	?	300,000
1755	Lisbon, Portugal	8.8	60,000
1811–12	New Madrid, MO	8.3	few
1886	Charleston, SC	?	60
1906	San Francisco, CA	8.3	700
1920	Kansu, China	8.5	180,000
1923	Tokyo, Japan	8.3	143,000
1939	Concepcion, Chile	8.3	30,000
1964	Prince William Sound, AK	8.5	117
1970	Peru	7.8	66,000
1976	Tangshan, China	7.6	240,000
1985	Mexico City, Mexico	8.1	7000
1988	Armenia	6.9	45,000
1989	San Francisco Bay, CA	7.1	67
1990	Iran	7.7	50,000
1991	Costa Rica	7.4	100

Table 19-2 shows some strong earthquakes that have occurred in the past 400 years. Can you see that loss of life is not always related directly to earthquake magnitude? Do you live in an area where earthquakes are common? Can you think of ways to reduce your risk of being injured in an earthquake?

Check Your Understanding

1. How is earthquake magnitude measured?
2. Using Table 19-2, what would be the magnitude of an earthquake that is 30 times stronger than the 1988 quake in Armenia?
3. **APPLY:** Suppose you studied seismograph readings from two earthquakes, A and B. What would you infer from the fact that the amplitude of the peaks produced by quake B were much higher than those produced by quake A?

Answers to Check Your Understanding

1. Earthquake magnitude is measured by the Richter scale, which describes the relative amounts of energy released by earthquakes.
2. An earthquake 30 times the magnitude of the 1988 Armenian quake (6.9) would have a Richter value of 7.9.
3. If the amplitude of the peaks produced by quake B were much greater than those produced by quake A, you would infer that quake B was stronger, released more energy, and had a higher Richter value.

EXPANDING YOUR VIEW

CONTENTS

A CLOSER LOOK

THE GREAT SAN FRANCISCO EARTHQUAKE AND FIRE

When powerful earthquakes strike, they can break gas lines, short-circuit electrical wires, overturn stoves, and crack chimneys. Any of these problems may lead to a fire. When a gas line is broken, all it takes is a spark to start a fire.

One of the worst earthquakes of the twentieth century struck San Francisco on April 18, 1906. About 80 percent of the damage was caused by the fires that followed the earthquake, and only 20 percent by the earthquake itself.

The violent tremors that had shifted the ground—as much as 20 feet in places—had broken many water mains (huge pipes) for the city's 80-million-gallon reservoir system. This left fire fighters nearly powerless to stop the blaze that roared through the city for three days and nights.

After trying one fire hydrant after another, the city's desperate fire fighters finally found just enough water to help tame the leaping flames—but not until several hundred people had lost their lives.

The 1906 earthquake and fire destroyed most of the city's business district and a number of residential areas.

WHAT DO YOU THINK?

If you were in an earthquake in which the water mains were broken, where might you look for safe water to use until the pipes could be repaired?

EXPANDING YOUR VIEW

Using Expanding Your View

Assign one or more of these excursions to expand your students' understanding of earthquakes and volcanoes and how they apply to other sciences and other subjects. You may assign these as small group or individual activities.

A CLOSER LOOK

Purpose A Closer Look demonstrates the tremendous damage to cities that can result from seismic waves like those described in Section 19-2. With many details of the 1906 San Francisco earthquake, the article narrates one of the most destructive quakes in North American history.

Content Background An earthquake is the sudden release of built-up pressure in Earth's crust. When the crust breaks and moves as a result of waves emanating from the focus a fault is formed. The place in Earth's interior where an earthquake begins is called the *focus*. The point on Earth's surface directly above the focus is the *epicenter*. However, an earthquake usually occurs along a line rather than at a point. The shock waves radiate outward not in perfect circles but in ellipses.

Teaching Strategies Have students tell of their own or another person's experience with seismic waves and/or earthquakes. Was the person in any danger or called upon to help others? What happened?

Going Further How have the layout and construction of San Francisco changed since the 1906 earthquake? Have structures been relocated to more seismically safe areas of the city, or have they simply been reinforced or rebuilt on the same disaster-site? Students might create a "Then and Now" portrait of this or another hard-hit city to show how humans have—or haven't—changed their building and planning habits.

Answers to WHAT DO YOU THINK?

Answers will vary, but may include buying bottled water or using local lake or river water.

EXPANDING YOUR VIEW

PHYSICS CONNECTION

Purpose The Physics Connection describes how tsunamis are produced, how they travel, and what consequences they can have for coastal areas. This ties to the discussion of tsunamis in Section 19-2.

Content Background Earthquakes and tsunamis also plaqued the ancient world, and one of the worst such catastrophes ever known took place in approximately 1500 B.C. in the Aegean Sea near Greece. When a huge volcano on the island of Thera collapsed inward on itself, cold seawater rushed into the crater which was filled with magma. The resulting explosion and tremors created a tsunami believed to have reached 80 meters in height and over 200 mph in speed—devastating islands and shore zones in a vast circular region of the eastern Mediterranean Sea. This disaster may have brought to an end the civilization of ancient Crete, and may be at the root of myths about the lost city of Atlantis.

Teaching Strategies Have volunteers plot the path of the Alaskan tsunami on a map of North America so that the class can clearly see the wave's far-reaching effects.

Discussion What thoughts and feelings do the words 'earthquake' and 'tsunami' evoke in students? Do such movies about these natural disasters help people to understand the dangers they face from these phenomena? Do these movies help people understand what to do in a disaster? Have students discuss their reactions to movies about natural disasters.

Answers to

WHAT DO YOU THINK?

Cities that have U- or V-shaped harbors or shallow waters offshore are at greatest risk because these conditions amplify, or heighten, the wave.

Physics Connection

THE TERROR OF THE TSUNAMI

Earlier you read about tsunamis—giant waves caused by earthquakes beneath the ocean floor or by underwater landslides or volcanic eruptions in the sea. How do the characteristics of tsunamis compare with the waves you studied in Chapter 18?

Let's assume that the tsunami in question is produced by an earthquake. You know that an earthquake produces a series of vibrations in Earth's crust. The frequency of the tsunami is dependent on the frequency of the earthquake vibrations.

Because tsunamis move massive amounts of water, the resultant wavelength of a tsunami is very long, compared to the waves you produced in the Find Out activity in this chapter. In fact, when tsunamis are produced in deep water, their wavelengths may be greater than 200 kilometers.

The powerful wave of a tsunami can travel as rapidly as a jet plane. As the wave moves away from the spot of its origin, it may travel at a speed of more than 700 kilometers per hour. At this rate, a tsunami produced near the Hawaiian Islands could reach Seattle, Washington, in less than six hours.

The amplitude of a tsunami may not look any greater than a normal ocean wave when it is in deep water. As it reaches shallower depths, however, the water begins to pile up, dramatically forming a wall of water by the time the tsunami reaches the shallow waters near the shore. The shallower the water, the taller the wave becomes. Some tsunamis have been measured at over 50 meters in height. Tons of water crash onto coastal areas, doing tremendous damage.

In 1964, a powerful earthquake shook Prince William Sound on the Alaskan coastline. Anchorage was hit hardest by the earthquake itself. Valdez, Seward, Whittier, and Kodiak suffered much damage, mostly due to the tsunamis that followed. The tsunami that struck Kodiak, a town of about 4000 people, towered more than 10 meters high and left the town almost completely destroyed. Valdez, a coastal town on an inlet, also suffered tremendous damage. When the survivors decided to rebuild the town, they did so 8 kilometers away from its original site.

Waves from this earthquake reached as far as Hawaii and Japan. A tsunami flooded a 50-block section of Crescent City, California, 2260 kilometers away from its beginning.

WHAT DO YOU THINK?

Why might the damage to a coastal town on a U- or V- shaped inlet be greater than to a coastal town on a straight shoreline?

Going Further The 1883 eruption and subsequent earthquakes on the island of Krakatoa in the Java Sea caused some of the worst tsunami damage ever recorded. Reaching from Australia to India to Madagascar, the waves took the lives of over 30,000 people in over 300 seaside localities. Have groups of students report on aspects of this dramatic disaster, including photographs and readings from eyewitnesses' journals available in libraries. COOP LEARN

Going Further Have one or more students report on what they can learn of plans in the local community for what would be done in the event of a massive earthquake or tsunami. How would health care, water, food and shelter be administered? What skills would be in greatest demand if power and communications were cut off? Have students share findings with the class.

SCIENCE
AND
SOCIETY

EARTHQUAKE PREDICTION

Earthquakes rarely strike without warning. Often, the ground will vibrate days or even months before a major earthquake hits. Animals often act quite strangely just before an earthquake. Scientists believe that animals can sense the changes inside Earth or smell the gases that are often released by the shifting ground.

Measuring even the slightest shifts in Earth can therefore help scientists predict an impending earthquake. Seismologists obtain data about movements within Earth from instruments that register changes in Earth's crust. You already know about seismographs. Let's examine some other seismic measurement devices.

An extensometer has a long quartz tube threaded through a row of posts in the ground. Look at the picture of the extensometer. One end of the tube is anchored firmly inside the first post. The other end of the tube moves freely inside the last post. The additional posts help support the quartz tube. Extensometers can be more than 300 feet long.

When an earthquake occurs, the free end of the tube moves farther into or out of the last post. By reading a scale on the free end of the tube, scientists can measure the tremors.

Tiltmeters set up near faults in Earth's surface help detect changes in the slope of the ground. A change in the tilt of the ground may indicate that one side of a fault is being forced upward or downward in relation to the other side of the fault.

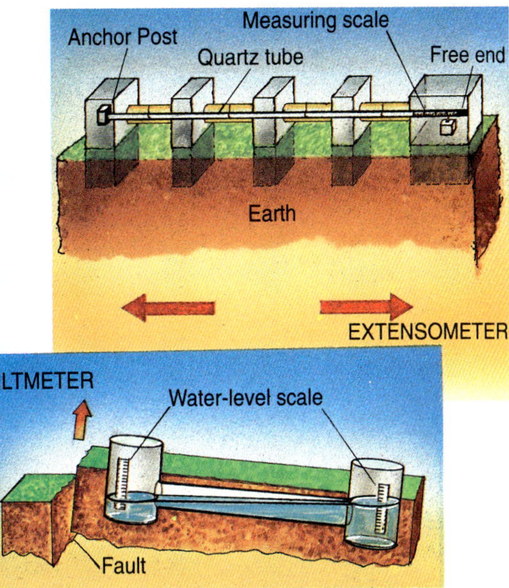

CAREER CONNECTION

Seismologists study faults and earthquakes to learn more about Earth's interior, to predict earthquakes, and to provide advice about construction sites and building materials in earthquake-prone areas. They often work for the government or for petroleum or mining companies.

Have you ever seen a carpenter's level? A tiltmeter works the same way. It has a tube connected to two water-filled containers. When the ground near one of the containers

Going Further What are some of the accompanying destructive events that follow earthquakes and volcanic disasters? Groups of students might choose a particular event such as the 1964 Alaskan earthquake or the 1883 eruption of Krakatoa to study for these subsidiary effects. Students should look for information about damage caused by ash, both locally, and down wind. Students should also look for evidence of changes in climate due to increased ash and dust in the atmosphere.

SCIENCE AND SOCIETY

Purpose Science and Society explores some of the many ways in which people try to predict earthquakes. Analysis of the patterns in seismic events, such as those described in Sections 19-1 and 19-2, is clearly linked to the saving of lives. With techniques ranging from the observation of animal behavior to high-tech, long-term studies of shifts in Earth's crust, the effort to understand and predict earthquakes is a worldwide, slowly advancing science. The benefits of the science are most dramatically clear in the recent cases of Liaoning and Tangshan, China, where success can be measured in tens of thousands of lives saved.

Content Background While animals and some humans can be sensitive to the magnetic and chemical changes that precede earthquakes, technological devices such as the extensometer and tiltmeter give seismologists more objective sources of information. Tiltmeters on the slopes of Mt. St. Helens, for example, on May 18, 1980, recorded a telltale "bulge" over 300 feet high on the mountain's north slope. Its growth of five feet per day alerted scientists to the danger of a potential eruption, and many people evacuated the area just in time. Other tiltmeters around the mountain helped indicate in which direction the eruption would occur, saving more lives by helping to avoid widespread panic.

Teaching Strategies Have students share what they know of the various methods of earthquake prediction, be they animal or technological. What are the particular strengths and weaknesses of each method?

EXPANDING YOUR VIEW

Discussion How vulnerable do students feel their own community is to seismic disaster of any kind? What evidence (geographical location, history, etc.) supports each student's opinion? Ask them to describe any evidence of major geological activity in the surrounding landscape, and explain why they think a seismic disaster may or may not occur in their community in the future.

CAREER CONNECTION

Encourage interested students to contact local university research centers and/or government or local agencies for facts on degree and work-experience requirements for careers in seismological fields.

Answers to WHAT DO YOU THINK?

Answers will vary, but students are likely to point out that premature warnings can lead to unnecessary concern and possibly, panic. Also, too many early warnings that are not followed by an earthquake may lead people to disregard earthquake warnings. Other students may say that warnings may be annoying, but may save lives eventually.

shifts upward, the water level in that container drops, while the water level in the other, lower container rises. Tiltmeters are usually about 30 feet long.

Seismologists use laser distance-ranging devices to help detect small horizontal shifts in Earth's surface along fault lines. As shown in the picture, these devices aim a narrow laser beam from one side of a fault toward a reflector on the other side of the fault, and time how long the beam takes to return.

Do you remember that light travels at 299,792 kilometers per second? Because light moves so fast, laser distance-ranging devices must use special clocks that measure billionths of a second. When the beam's return time is longer or shorter than previous readings and no other conditions exist that might explain the change, the variation in return time may indicate an earthquake is on its way. Because we know the speed at which light travels, if the beam takes less time or more time to return, we know that the distance it is traveling has changed. This change in distance may indicate a shift in Earth's crust—a sign that an earthquake may be on its way.

We may not be able to prevent earthquakes, but if we learn to predict them accurately and if we're well prepared, we may save many lives. To demonstrate the difference a warning can make, let's compare two earthquakes that occurred in China and were of approximately the same magnitude.

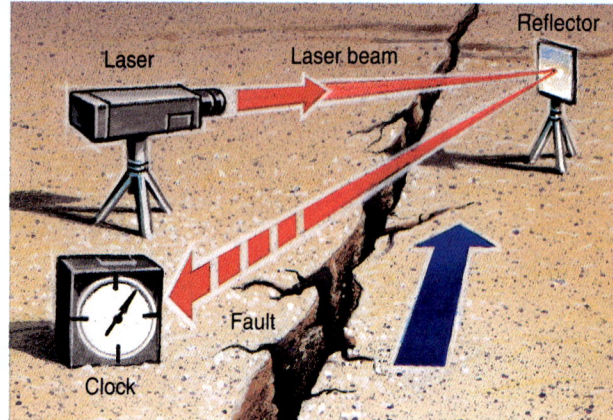

The earthquake in the Liaoning Province of China in February 1975 took very few lives because people knew it was coming. Days before, the ground had shifted, and minor tremors had been felt. People had noticed that well waters were bubbling, and that pond waters were muddy and strong smelling.

The day before the earthquake struck, government officials told people to stay outside their homes so they would not be crushed if their homes collapsed. Even with the warning, 300 lives were lost. Had the people not been warned, 10,000 more might have died!

The following year, an earthquake hit Tangshan, China. The people had no warning. As many as 240,000 people were killed—about one-sixth of Tangshan's population at the time! Little was left of the city except piles of bricks and twisted steel.

WHAT DO YOU THINK?

It's hard to pinpoint precisely when an earthquake will hit. What problems might occur if officials warn people about an earthquake too early? Should officials wait to inform people until they are more certain about when an earthquake will strike? Why?

Going Further Have groups of students explore how an area changes after volcanic activity ends. Plant and animal life gradually return to the area. Students should find out which life forms are the first to return, and which ones follow later. COOP LEARN

TECHNOLOGY CONNECTION

EARTHQUAKE-PROOF CONSTRUCTION

What makes some structures withstand earthquakes, while others are damaged or destroyed?

The geological foundation is perhaps the most important factor. Buildings built on solid rock near an earthquake's center—where vibrations are the strongest—may hold up better than buildings built on softer ground farther away. Densely packed soil moves less during an earthquake than sand and loose soil, which tend to separate and shift. For this reason, old swamps and ravines that have been filled with dirt and other loose materials make poor foundations during earthquakes.

Extending a building's foundation well below ground level can help a building withstand an earthquake because the building will be less likely to lean or tip. Structural reinforcement also helps. Buildings may be reinforced by beams that cross at different angles or with steel that's been embedded in concrete.

Because buildings with a lot of glass often lack support, steel-framed buildings and concrete buildings with few doors or windows hold up better than some other types of structures. Brick buildings tend to buckle during earthquakes. This happens when earthquake vibrations turn the mortar between bricks to powder and the bricks come loose.

The objective in earthquake-proof construction is to build structures that will move as a unit during an earthquake, rather than as individual, unrelated parts. Engineers accomplish this by placing rollers, jacks, springs, bearings, or special plastic sheets under the bases of buildings.

Architects are experimenting with shock absorbers for buildings and bridges. With these shock absorbers, energy from Earth's movements will be absorbed, while the building above moves as a whole.

Even if you are in a building with earthquake-proof construction, during an earthquake it is important that you follow these safety measures:

- Keep away from windows.
- Avoid standing where objects might fall on you.
- Do not go near fallen power lines.
- Stay clear of rubble that could contain sharp edges or broken gas lines.

YOU TRY IT!

Start with photos or drawings of three different structures. Examine the structures carefully. For each structure, mark on the picture of each structure or describe on paper three areas where damage from an earthquake is most likely to occur. Explain why. Next, indicate how and where these structures might be reinforced to prevent or minimize damage from an earthquake. Explain why.

EXPANDING YOUR VIEW

TECHNOLOGY CONNECTION

Purpose The Technology Connection lists some specifics of the ongoing effort to create safer buildings and other structures. Features of the latest buildings described herein are designed to resist the often-devastating forces students learned about in Sections 19-1 and 19-2. Safety tips for people in even the most earthquake-proof structures conclude the selection.

Content Background Early versions of the well known Labyrinth of Cnossos on the Greek island of Crete (circa 2000 B.C.E. had solid brick walls. After damage caused by several major earthquakes, the ancient Cretans learned to lay wooden beams within the walls so that they could sway slightly with seismic waves. The result was a building complex that endured not only 3500 years of time but also the worst seismic disaster ever known—the explosion of the island-volcano of Thera. Reconstructed in places with reinforced concrete, the Labyrinth today still withstands the seismic activity of the region.

Teaching Strategies What local buildings do students feel would remain standing the longest if a serious earthquake struck? Have them base their answers on both details of that building and statements as to why it satisfies one of the general construction rules in the article. For example, what kind of ground is it built on? What special reinforcements does it have?

Going Further Have groups of students consult leading journals and magazines of Earth science and seismology to get an idea of technological and architectural advances with regard to earthquakes. Exactly what kinds of shock absorbers and other devices are in use? Where have they been tested with actual earthquakes—and what happened? How, also, do these new architectural sciences affect the look of new buildings? COOP LEARN

Answers to YOU TRY IT

Answers will vary, depending on the structures chosen. Students should look for details, such as the size and placement of windows and doors.

TEENS IN SCIENCE

Purpose Deena Stroham's experiment in Teens and Science show how the forces described in Section 19-1 can affect buildings and other human structures.

Content Background Decades of patient statistical analysis and experimentation with building materials have resulted in still-evolving building codes, designed to maximize human safety during seismic disturbances. California's and other states' building codes reflect increased knowledge of how structures "behave" under stress: a ceiling beam placed at the wrong angle, or the placement of a house foundation only a few feet to the left or right of the most solid ground may cost lives later when the earth beneath them shakes. Because seismology is a young science, great controversy still exists as to what the most effective building traits are. However, a bedrock foundation is known to be essential to safety, as Stroham's demonstration shows.

Teaching Strategies Have students visualize the experiment in the article and predict what the result will be. Have them support their answers with facts from the chapter.

Discussion What kind of demonstration of any principle in the chapter can students design to show how that principle works? For example, how would passing water through a narrowing channel (as when a tsunami enters a narrow harbor) accelerate and raise the level of the water? What principle does this reveal at work? **COOP LEARN**

Answers to YOU TRY IT

As students perform the experiment, remind them to carefully apply the same amount of "earthquake-force" to each model.

TEENS *in* SCIENCE

SHAKE, RATTLE, AND ROLL

The floor is moving under your feet. A lamp swings from side to side over your head. Can you guess why? It's an earthquake!

Seventeen-year-old Deena Stroham knows a lot about earthquakes. As part of a 4-H project, Deena teaches younger students what she has learned. "I try to help kids know what to expect. But the lessons are fun."

Although Deena lives in earthquake-prone California, she has never actually felt one. "But that's the neat part about science. Learning why things happen means you don't have to experience them firsthand."

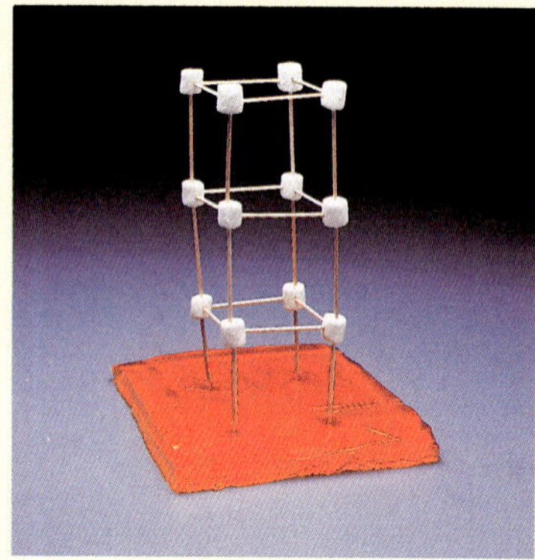

YOU TRY IT!

Deena uses this experiment to show how earthquakes affect houses built on two different types of earth. The gelatin dessert represents landfill. The clay represents bedrock.

Materials

- 1 package of gelatin dessert
- 1 package unflavored gelatin
- boiling water
- firm clay
- 48 toothpicks
- 24 marshmallows
- 6-in by 6-in by 1-in container

Procedure

1. Mix the powdered gelatin dessert and unflavored gelatin together. Follow the directions on the back of the dessert package. Pour the mixture into a container that is at least 6 inches by 6 inches and 1 inch deep. Refrigerate. When firm, cut the gelatin dessert into a 6-inch by 6-inch square.
2. Make a 6-inch by 6-inch square at least 1 inch thick out of clay.
3. Now build a house from the toothpicks and marshmallows. Make the vertical corners first. Press a marshmallow on the end of a toothpick. Push the other end of the toothpick into the gelatin square. Space each of the four corners a toothpick's length apart. Next, connect the four marshmallows with horizontal toothpicks. This is the first story of your house. Add two more. Follow the same steps with the clay square.
4. Shake each square to simulate an earthquake. Which house stood longer? Is it safer to build on landfill or bedrock?

Going Further Have groups of students relate recent space program activities, such as moon landings or Space Shuttle observations, to seismic research. For example, how did laser reflectors placed on the moon by astronauts affect the science of earthquake prediction, if at all? How have satellites and other NASA-spawned technologies contributed to Earth sciences in the last 30 years? Students can look in science and technology reference books. The *Readers Guide to Periodic Literature* or computer information search system at a local library can help students find magazine articles on these topics. **COOP LEARN**

Reviewing Main Ideas

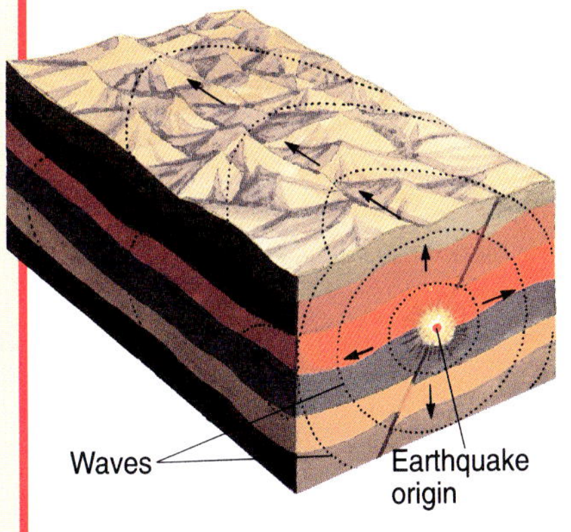

1. An earthquake is caused by vibrations set in motion when part of the solid earth below the surface suddenly shifts.

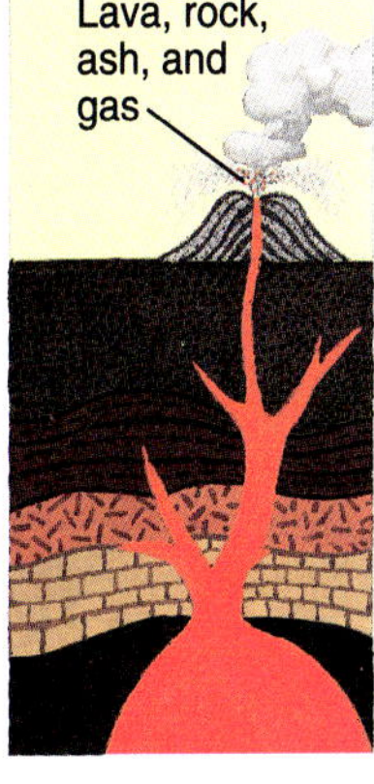

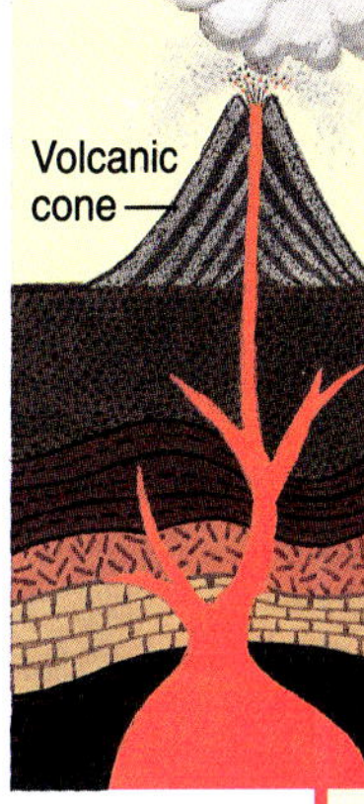

2. A volcano builds as magma reaches Earth's surface and material from eruptions accumulates over time.

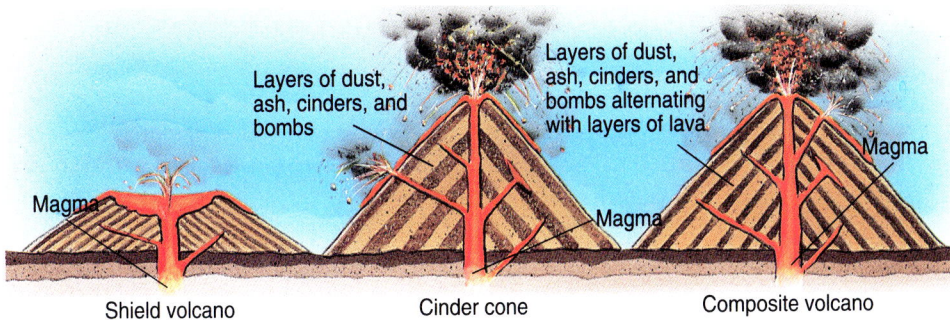

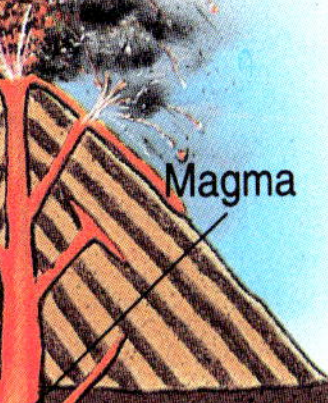

3. The shape of a volcano depends on the material it's made of and whether the eruptions are quiet or explosive.

4. The amount of damage caused by an earthquake depends on the strength of the quake, its distance from inhabited areas, the design of buildings, and the type of ground on which the buildings are found.

Reviewing Main Ideas

Have students observe the illustrations and discuss the energy released by each occurrence. Have them discuss similarities and differences for each photograph. Be sure they understand that both earthquakes and volcanoes occur because of changes below the surface of Earth.

Teaching Strategies

Ask students to choose one of the illustrations and explain how they might safely observe the occurrence.

Divide the class into four groups. Have each group use an illustration as the center of a concept web. Ask each group to provide additional information that is related to the illustration. Allow students to review the chapter while doing this activity. Have groups present their webs to the class.

Chapter 19

Chapter Review

USING SCIENCE TERMS

Answers

1. seismograph
2. magma
3. tsunami
4. lava

UNDERSTANDING IDEAS

Answers

1. c
2. b
3. a
4. c
5. b
6. d
7. b

CRITICAL THINKING

Answers

1. Parkfield; North Coast
2. An explosive volcanic eruption can spew tons of dust and ash into the air. This dust and ash can be carried by the wind to other parts of the world, where they may block some of the sun's radiation, causing weather to be colder than usual.
3. If a building is made from flexible materials or with a flexible design, it is better able to move with the surface waves produced by an earthquake. Rigid structures are more likely to break apart.
4. When an earthquake strikes below the ocean, the tsunamis that are generated can cause destruction hundreds of kilometers away, when they hit the shore.

Chapter Review

USING KEY SCIENCE TERMS

lava
magma
magnitude
seismograph
tsunami

An analogy is a relationship between two pairs of words generally written in the following manner: a:b::c:d. The symbol : is read "is to," and the symbol :: is read "as." For example, cat:animal::rose:plant is read "cat is to animal as rose is to plant." In the analogies that follow, a word is missing. Complete each analogy by providing the missing word from the list above.

1. air temperature:thermometer::earthquake magnitude:____
2. geyser:groundwater::volcano:____
3. air:sound::ocean water:____
4. ice cream:chocolate syrup::Earth's surface:____

UNDERSTANDING IDEAS

Choose the best answer to complete each sentence.

1. All of these factors affect the amount of damage caused by an earthquake except ____.
   a. magnitude
   b. structure design
   c. altitude
   d. type of ground on which structures are built
2. The amplitude of the wavy line of a seismograph reading is an indication of an earthquake's ____.
   a. location
   b. strength
   c. depth below the surface
   d. length in time
3. Material associated with a quiet volcanic eruption is ____.
   a. lava **c.** cinders
   b. ash **d.** dust

4. The type of eruption that produces a volcano with steep sides and a narrow base is ____.
   a. alternating **c.** explosive
   b. quiet **d.** composite
5. A sudden shift in part of the solid earth below the surface of a continent causes ____.
   a. a quiet eruption
   b. an earthquake
   c. an explosive eruption
   d. a tsunami
6. The hot, melted rock material below Earth's surface is ____.
   a. cinder **c.** ash
   b. lava **d.** magma

PROGRAM RESOURCES

Teacher Classroom Resources

Review and Assessment, Chapter Review and Chapter Test, pages 77-80

Computer Test Bank, Chapter Test

OPTIONS

Cooperative Learning

Consider using Cooperative Learning in the Understanding Ideas, Critical Thinking, Problem Solving, and Connecting Ideas sections of the Chapter Review.

COOP LEARN

7. According to Table 19-1, earthquakes with a magnitude of less than 4.0 on the Richter scale are likely to occur______.
   - a. one million times a year
   - b. more than 100,000 times a year
   - c. about 6000 times a year
   - d. less than once a year

CRITICAL THINKING

Use your understanding of the concepts developed in the chapter to answer each of the following questions.

1. The table shows the chances that an earthquake of a specified magnitude will strike five selected locations in California within the next 30 years. Which location is most likely to be struck by an earthquake? Which location is likely to experience the strongest earthquake?

Location	Richter Scale Magnitude		
	8^+	7-7.9	6-6.9
North Coast	10%		
San Francisco		20%	
Parkfield			90%
Mojave		30%	
Coachella Valley		40%	

2. Explain how the climate effects of an explosive volcanic eruption on an island in the Pacific Ocean can be felt months later at locations on the other side of the world.
3. Why is flexibility an important factor in designing an earthquake-safe structure?
4. On land, the closer a spot is to the source of an earthquake, the more damage may occur. How does this situation compare with what happens when an earthquake occurs below the ocean?

PROBLEM SOLVING

Read the following problem and discuss your answers in a brief paragraph.

Suppose you live in an area where earthquakes are common, and you want to set up a seismograph at home.

1. Describe how a seismograph that uses a beam of light and photographic film might work.
2. Can you think of another way to set up a seismograph using common objects? Explain.

CONNECTING IDEAS

Discuss each of the following in a brief paragraph.

1. Name two ways in which earthquake waves are similar to sound waves.
2. How does gravity affect the motion of lava?
3. How are earthquakes and volcanoes alike? How are they different?
4. **TECHNOLOGY CONNECTION** What areas of interest do seismologists and building engineers have in common?
5. **PHYSICS CONNECTION** Suppose a tsunami strikes two towns the same distance from the site of an underwater earthquake. Which town would probably have more damage—the one along a straight coastline or the one at the inland end of a narrow bay? Explain your answer.

PROBLEM SOLVING

Answers

1. The photographic film would move with the vibrations, while the source of light (a dangling flashlight, perhaps) would not. In this way, the film would capture the vibrations as a wavy line.

2. Answers will vary. Sample answer: A screwdriver or other long, pointed object can be suspended over loose materials, such as sand. When the container with the material moves, the screwdriver would produce a seismograph-type line.

CONNECTING IDEAS

Answers

1. Both have the properties of waves—peaks or crests, and troughs. Both travel through a medium. Earthquake waves travel through the ground, water, and buildings. Sound waves can also travel through these materials.

2. Gravity causes lava to flow down the slopes of volcanoes.

3. Both earthquakes and volcanoes have their origins below Earth's surface. Both are powerful and unpredictable and can cause tremendous destruction. Earthquakes send vibrations through the ground. Volcanoes blast rock, ash, dust, and lava into the air or send lava flowing along the ground.

4. Both seismologists and building engineers try to decrease potential destruction from earthquakes.

5. The town at the inland end of a narrow bay would probably have more damage because the tsunami would increase greatly in height as it moved through the narrow bay.

CHAPTER ORGANIZER

SECTION	OBJECTIVES	ACTIVITIES/FEATURES
Chapter Opener		**Explore!** What if Earth were shaped like a pizza box? p. 597
20-1 Earth's Shape and Movements (4 days)	1. **Demonstrate** evidence that shows Earth's shape. 2. **Describe** the cause of day and night. 3. **Explain** what causes the seasons on Earth.	**Find Out!** How does Earth's shape affect what you see? p. 598 **Find Out!** What causes the changing seasons? p. 601 **Investigate 20-1:** Tilt and Temperature, p. 603 **Explore!** Where are Earth's warm spots? p. 604 **Skillbuilder:** Observing and Inferring, p. 606
20-2 Motions of the Moon (3 days)	1. **Recognize** that the moon's phases are caused by the relative positions of the sun, the moon, and Earth. 2. **Demonstrate** the arrangement of the sun, the moon, and Earth during solar and lunar eclipses.	**Find Out!** What are two ways in which the moon moves? p. 607 **Explore!** How is your perception of an object's size affected by its distance from you? p. 610 **Skillbuilder:** Measuring in SI, p. 610 **Investigate 20-2:** Eclipses and Moon Phases, p. 613
20-3 Tides (2 days)	1. **Describe** the changes you might observe along a coastline during high and low tides. 2. **Diagram** the relative positions of the sun, the moon, and Earth during the highest tides.	**Find Out!** What is the relationship between the height of tides and the position of the moon? p. 616
Expanding Your View		A Closer Look **The Moon's Surface,** p. 619 Life Science Connection **Life in an Intertidal Zone,** p. 620 Science and Society **Spin-offs from the Space Program,** p. 621 Technology Connection **Electricity from Tides,** p. 623 Teens in Science **Reaching for the Stars,** p. 624

ACTIVITY MATERIALS

EXPLORE!	INVESTIGATE!	FIND OUT!
Page 597 atlas, small pizza delivery box, sheet of paper, glue **Page 604** globe or world map, encyclopedia	**Page 603** tape, black construction paper, gooseneck lamp with 75-watt bulb, Celsius thermometer, watch, protractor **Page 613** pencil, polystyrene ball, globe, unshaded light source	**Page 598** strip of cardboard 5 cm × 20 cm, and decorated with colorful stripes lengthwise; scissors, tape, basketball, metric ruler **Page 601** lamp without a shade, globe **Page 607** basketball, tape **Page 616** paper and pencil

Chapter 20
The Earth-Moon System

TEACHER CLASSROOM RESOURCES	OTHER RESOURCES
Study Guide, p. 70 **Concept Mapping,** p. 28 **Multicultural Activities,** p. 43 **Take Home Activities,** p. 30 **Activity Masters, Investigate 20-1,** pp. 81-82 **Multicultural Activities,** p. 44	**Laboratory Manual,** pp. 119-120, Earth's Spin ***STVS:** *Indian Medicine Wheels,* Earth and Space (Disc 3, Side 1)
Study Guide, p. 71 **Flex Your Brain,** p. 8 **How It Works,** p. 19 **Making Connections: Integrating Sciences,** p. 43 **Making Connections: Across the Curriculum,** p. 43 **Activity Masters, Investigate 20-2,** pp. 83-84 **Critical Thinking/Problem Solving,** p. 28	**Laboratory Manual,** pp. 121-122, Moon Phases **Color Transparency and Master 39,** Moon Phases **Color Transparency and Master 40,** Meteorite Impact ***STVS:** *Effects of the Solar Eclipses,* Earth and Space (Disc 3, Side 1)
Study Guide, p. 72 **Making Connections: Technology and Society,** p. 43 **Review and Assessment,** pp. 81-84	***STVS:** *Monitoring the Sun,* Earth and Space (Disc 3, Side 1) **Computer Test Bank**
	Spanish Resources **Cooperative Learning Resource Guide** **Lab and Safety Skills**

***Science and Technology Videodisc Series**

KEY TO TEACHING STRATEGIES

Teaching strategies have been coded for varying learning styles and abilities. As you review teaching strategies in the margin, the following designations will help you decide which activities are appropriate for your students.

- **L1** Level 1 activities are basic activities and should be within the ability range of all students.
- **L2** Level 2 activities are average activities and should be within the ability range of the average to above-average student.
- **L3** Level 3 activities are challenging activities designed for the ability range of above-average students.
- **LEP** LEP activities should be within the ability range of Limited English Proficiency students.
- **COOP LEARN** Cooperative Learning activities are designed for small group work.

ADDITIONAL MATERIALS

SOFTWARE	AUDIOVISUAL
The Earth and the Moon Simulator, Focus.	*How We Know the Earth Moves,* film, BFA. *The Earth in Motion,* film, EBEC.

Chapter 20

The Earth-Moon System

THEME DEVELOPMENT

One theme supported by this chapter is interactions and systems. Earth, the moon, and the sun interact within our solar system, causing day and night, seasons, moon phases, eclipses, and tides. Scale and structure is also evident in this chapter, as students learn how the size of Earth and its position with relation to the sun and the moon help explain the occurrence of eclipses and tides.

CHAPTER OVERVIEW

Evidence is first presented that Earth is a sphere, and students learn why day and night and the seasons occur.

The motions of the moon are then explored. Students will learn that the moon, like Earth, has a period of revolution and rotation. The position of Earth, the moon, and the sun during moon phases and eclipses is also discussed. Finally, the relationship between tides and the relative positions of Earth, the moon, and the sun are discussed.

Tying to Previous Knowledge

Place a large ball or globe in the center of the classroom. Shine a concentrated beam of light from a flashlight at the globe from one side. Ask students in different parts of the room to describe what they see. *Answers will vary depending on the position of the student with respect to the illuminated sphere. Students should realize that much of what we see depends on the viewer's position.*

DID YOU EVER WONDER . . .

Why it's cooler in winter and warmer in summer?

What the far side of the moon is?

Why sometimes a beach is narrower than it was just a few hours earlier?

You'll find the answers to these questions as you read this chapter.

DID YOU EVER WONDER...

Students will explore these questions as they progress through the chapter. Don't spoil their fun and motivation by sharing these answers too early.

- The amount and angle of light shining on a surface is directly related to the temperature of the surface. During the winter, the rays of the sun striking Earth are not as direct as they are in the summer. They also strike the surface at one location for fewer hours per day. (page 604)
- Because the moon rotates on its axis once as it revolves around Earth, we always see the same side of the moon. The side we do not see is referred to as the far side of the moon. (page 608)
- A beach becomes narrower during high tide. The gravitational attraction among the sun, the moon, and Earth causes the tides. (page 618)

The Earth-Moon System

Do you like to travel? Let's hope so, because you're on a journey right now—around the sun. You'll travel 940 million kilometers and never leave town. You'll complete your trip in one year without missing school. You'll need nothing special, but you'll take everything you own. Your vehicle? You are riding planet Earth, and the moon will be coming right along on this trip.

As you ride Earth on this 940-million-kilometer trip, it is spinning like a top. The moon is also spinning and is traveling around Earth. As this pair travels around the sun, we observe the seasons, the cycle of day and night, and the changes in the shape and location of the moon.

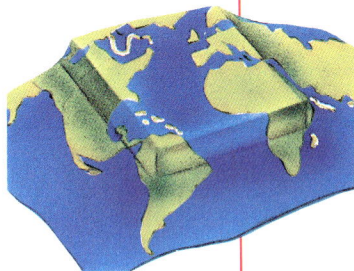

At certain times, Earth blocks out sunlight to the moon, casting a coppery-red shadow on it. At other times, the moon blocks out sunlight to Earth, and we can be in total darkness during the middle of the day.

This chapter will explore the relationship between Earth and the moon. Let's begin our trip. We'll be traveling through space at more than 107,000 kilometers per hour!

EXPLORE!

What if Earth were shaped like a pizza box?

Using an atlas, trace the continents on a sheet of paper. Then glue the sheet onto the top of a small pizza delivery box. Fold the map around the edges of the box. What places are now at the edge of the world? What effect would this shape have on people's lives?

Introducing the Chapter

The photograph on page 596 is a view of Earth from the moon. Ask students why only a portion of Earth can be seen. *From space, Earth has phases like the moon.* Ask students what similarity between Earth and the moon this photo suggests. *Like the moon, Earth experiences phases.*

Uncovering Preconceptions

Students might think that in order to understand the motions of Earth, the moon, and the sun, one needs to be in outer space to watch these events. Remind them that they are all familiar with how the sun and the moon appear to change positions in the sky. Tell them that their observations of these changes along with models they can make can be used to understand the motions of Earth, the moon, and the sun.

EXPLORE!

What if Earth were shaped like a pizza box?

Time needed 20–30 minutes

Materials atlas, sheet of paper, paste, small pizza box

Thinking Processes
Thinking critically, Recognizing cause and effect

Purpose To investigate what Earth might be like if it were flat.

Preparation If pizza boxes are unavailable, any rectangular, shallow boxes will do.

Teaching the Activity

If time constraints exist, photocopy a map and have students paste copies on the boxes.

Expected Outcomes

Depending on placement of continents on the boxes, various continents should overlap the edges.

Answers to Questions

1. Answers depend on size of the box and position of continents.
2. Possible answers: seasons and cycles of day and night would change significantly based on a person's location on the box.

Project

Have a group of students measure the angle of the shadow the school flagpole throws at five different times during a five-day period. Have another group chart the phases of the moon each night. If available in your location, have a third group use newspapers or other sources to chart the times of high and low tides each day at one location.

Have each group display their findings on a poster. **COOP LEARN**

Science at Home

Have students collect calendars, newspapers, magazines, or other materials that provide predictions of moon phases, sun positions, and tides. Students can bring whatever they find into class for a discussion of why predicting these Earth-sun-moon motions is important to us.

Section 20-1

PREPARATION

Concepts Developed

This section discusses how Earth's motions are related to day and night, the seasons, and temperatures.

Planning the Lesson

In planning your lesson on Earth's shape and movement, refer to the Chapter Organizer on pages 596A-B for timing suggestions, resources, and additional materials that will help you in your presentation of the lesson concepts.

For adequate development of the concepts presented in this section, we recommend that students do the Find Out activity on page 601 and the Explore activity on page 604.

1 MOTIVATE

Discussion Ask students to speculate why people long ago thought Earth was flat. Lead students to discuss that Earth is so big relative to our viewpoint that it seems to stretch out in all directions. In addition, people long ago did not have the sophisticated technology we have today to see the shape of Earth. As an example, show students photographs of Earth from space, pointing out that it is shaped like a sphere. L1

FIND OUT!

How does Earth's shape affect what you see?

Time needed 15–20 minutes

Materials cardboard, colored markers or crayons, scissors, tape, basketball, metric ruler

Thinking Processes Thinking critically, Observing and inferring, Recognizing cause and effect

Purpose To observe evidence that Earth's surface is curved.

20-1 Earth's Shape and Movements

OBJECTIVES

In this section, you will

- demonstrate evidence that shows Earth's shape;
- describe the cause of day and night;
- explain what causes the seasons on Earth.

KEY SCIENCE TERMS

sphere
rotation
revolution
equinox
solstice

EVIDENCE OF EARTH'S SHAPE

In the very first Explore in this book, you looked all about you and drew what you observed. How far away could you see? On a clear day, across open country, you can see about 32 kilometers. If you turn full circle, the world you can actually see is about 64 kilometers from edge to edge. From what you can personally observe, Earth might as well be a flat circle 64 kilometers in diameter.

For thousands of years, people decided how big the world was based on how far they could see or travel. As you know, the Italian explorer Christopher Columbus thought there was more to see. He planned an ocean voyage to test his hypothesis. In the following Find Out, you will observe the type of evidence that suggested to many people that Earth was not flat.

FIND OUT!

How does Earth's shape affect what you see? 

Cut a strip of cardboard 5 cm by 20 cm and decorate it with colorful stripes across its 5-cm width. Fold this strip widthwise at 2 cm. Tape the narrow 2-cm section to a basketball so that the remaining 18 cm are sticking straight up from the surface of the ball. Now set the basketball on a table so that the strip is sticking out horizontally, parallel to the table, with the stripes facing up. Kneel down on the other side of the ball so that you are eye level with it. Look at the top of the ball; think of this curve as a horizon.

PROGRAM RESOURCES

Teacher Classroom Resources

Study Guide, page 70

Laboratory Manual, pages 119-120, Earth's Spin L2

Concept Mapping, page 28, Solstices L1

Multicultural Activities, page 43, George Washington Carver L1

Take Home Activities, page 30, Making a Sundial L1

Now roll the ball toward you very slowly so that the stripes come into view over the top curve of the ball. Stop when you can see the entire length of the paper.

Conclude and Apply

What effect did the shape of the basketball have on your view of the approaching stripes?

FIGURE 20-1. Imagine you are a sailor of long ago, seeing these views from your ship as it approaches a distant island. What would you conclude about the shape of Earth?

Ancient Greek scientists were the first to suggest that Earth was shaped like a ball. Sailors noticed that as they approached an island, it seemed to rise from the horizon. Figure 20-1 shows what these ancient sailors were seeing. They also noticed that as another ship approached, they would first see the top of its mast, then the sails, and finally the hull. This experience is similar to yours as you observed the strip of paper coming toward you with the roll of the basketball. The sequence of mast-sail-hull suggested to the sailors that the ship was approaching over a curved surface.

Earth is sphere-shaped. A **sphere** is a round, three-dimensional object whose surface at all points is the same distance from its center. You have probably played with a basketball, beachball, or volleyball. These balls are all spheres. In reality, however, Earth bulges slightly at the equator and is somewhat flattened at the poles, as shown in Figure 20-2. You could make this shape by sitting on a basketball.

FIGURE 20-2. The diameter of Earth at the equator is about 42 kilometers wider than the diameter at the poles.

Preparation Any large ball can be substituted for the basketball.

Teaching the Activity

Discussion Ask students if they have ever been out on the ocean on a boat. Ask them if they have ever noticed that the sails of an approaching boat will appear first over the horizon and then the rest of the boat as it draws nearer.

Troubleshooting Help students get their eye level correct to observe the cardboard. L1

Expected Outcomes

As the ball rolls toward them, students should notice that the free end of the cardboard becomes visible at first and then the rest of the strip gradually comes into view.

Conclude and Apply

Because the surface of the ball is curved, only a small portion of its surface can be viewed at eye level at once. The cardboard was placed beyond the "horizon" at the beginning of the activity so it was not visible until the ball was rolled and the horizon changed.

2 TEACH

Tying to Previous Knowledge

Review motion along a curved path and motion of satellites presented in Chapters 13 and 14. Ask students to apply their knowledge of this motion to explain the movement of Earth around the sun. Ask students to recall from Chapter 14 the motion of a satellite near Earth. Point out that in a sense, Earth is a satellite of the sun. Earth is held in place around the sun by the sun's gravity. Earth's forward motion keeps it from crashing into the sun.

OPTIONS

Meeting Individual Needs

Visually Impaired To help students with the concept of an object appearing gradually over the horizon, use modeling clay to fasten an unsharpened pencil straight up from the surface of a basketball. Have students place their hands perpendicular to the surface of the ball. Turn the ball and slide the pencil up between their fingers. They will feel the pencil rising higher and higher as the ball turns.

Concept Development

Theme Connection In this section, students model the Earth-sun system and find that the interactions of Earth and the sun are responsible for day and night and seasons on Earth.

Demonstration This demonstration will show how night and day are caused by Earth's rotation.

Materials needed are a globe, a lamp, paper, and tape.

On a table, set up a lamp and a globe about 0.5 m apart and turn out the classroom lights. Tell students that the lamp represents the sun and the globe represents Earth. Turn on the lamp so that it shines on the globe and casts a shadow. Ask students what they see. Point out that half the globe is lit and the other half is cast in shadow. Have a student write an X on a small slip of paper and tape it to the globe. Then begin turning the globe counterclockwise. Ask students what happens to the X as the globe makes one complete turn. *It passes from light into dark and back into light.*

EARTH KEEPS SPINNING, DAY AND NIGHT

Picture yourself on an average day. You wake up after sunrise. During breakfast and into the morning, you begin to feel the sun's heat and to notice its movement across the sky. Back in Chapter 1, you observed the sun and its changing position throughout the day. But is the sun really moving? Or are you?

People have always talked about the sun moving across the sky. Today, we know that the change in its position is actually caused by motion of Earth, not the sun. Earth spins in space. This spinning motion is called **rotation**.

Look at Figure 20-3. It shows how Earth rotates around an imaginary line running through its poles. This line is called Earth's axis. As Earth rotates around its axis, the sun comes into view over the horizon as a location begins to face the sun. Although we call this approach to the sun sunrise, we know that the sun is not *rising* from anywhere.

As Earth continues to rotate, the sun appears to be moving across the sky. You observe it move from east to west until it goes below Earth's horizon. We refer to the last minutes before the sun disappears from the horizon as sunset.

During the next several hours, you experience the growing darkness of night, and then the sunrise-sunset cycle begins again. In reality, a spot on Earth spins toward the sun and away from the sun. However, people commonly refer to the sunrise-sunset cycle as though it is the sun that moves.

FIGURE 20-3. Earth rotates once about every 24 hours. This motion creates day and night.

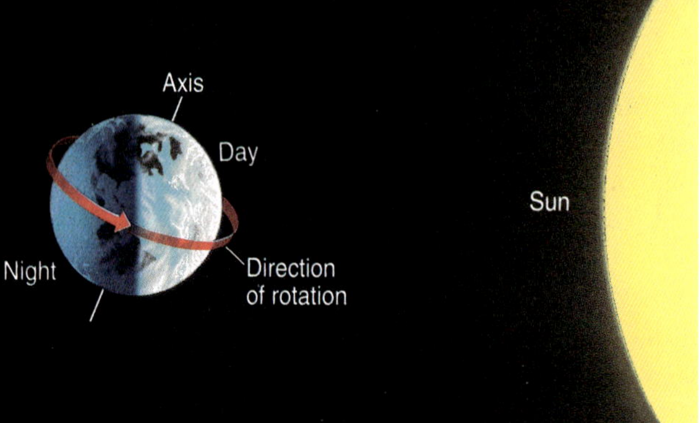

THE REASON FOR SEASONS

You have learned that Earth's rotation causes day and night. Earth is also in motion on a yearly trip around the sun. A

OPTIONS

Multicultural Perspectives

Artifacts that show evidence of interest in astronomical objects have been found all across the North American continent. These drawings and other artifacts were left by early Native Americans. Native Americans from what is now California drew pictures on rocks showing celestial patterns. Other Native Americans recorded a picture of a supernova that appeared in the year A.D. 1054. Native Americans also constructed observatories in New Mexico to observe the solstices. This information was used in many instances for agricultural and religious purposes.

complete **revolution,** or trip, takes about $365\frac{1}{4}$ days or one year. It's during the course of one revolution that we experience the change of seasons.

If Earth's revolution followed a perfectly circular path around the sun, Earth would maintain a constant distance from the sun. However, this isn't the case. Earth's revolution around the sun is in the shape of an ellipse, a closed curve that looks somewhat like a flattened circle. The sun is a bit off center of the ellipse, as you can see in Figure 20-4. Therefore, the distance between Earth and the sun changes during Earth's year-long journey.

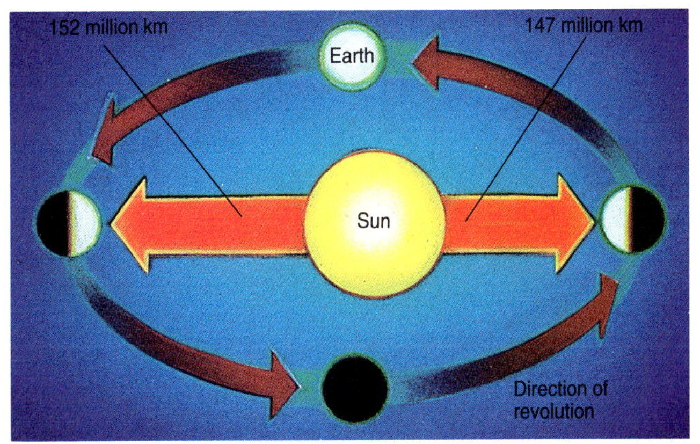

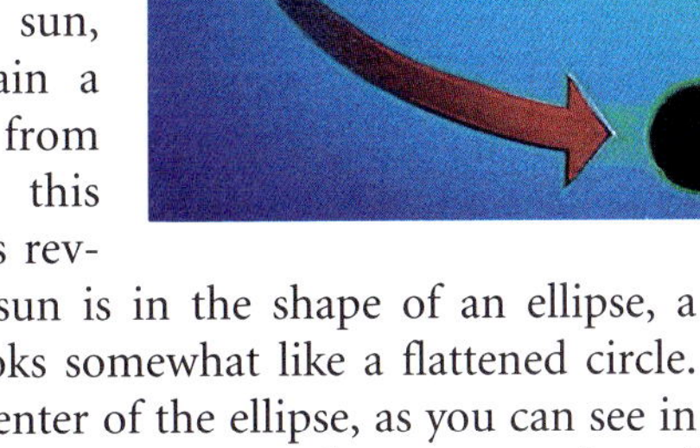

FIGURE 20-4. Earth's revolution around the sun follows an elliptical shape, with the sun positioned off center.

Earth travels closest to the sun—about 147 million kilometers away—in January. Earth is farthest from the sun—about 152 million kilometers away—in July. Is this elliptical path causing the changing temperatures and changing seasons on Earth? If it were, you would expect the warmest days to occur in January. But you know from experience that this isn't the case in the Northern Hemisphere. Something else is causing the seasons to change. The following Find Out activity will show you the cause.

FIND OUT!

What causes the changing seasons?

Use a lamp without a shade to represent the sun and use a globe to represent Earth. With the lamp on, hold the globe about 2 m away. Tilt the globe slightly so that the northern half points toward the lamp. Where on the globe is the light striking most directly? Now walk the globe around the lamp, keeping it tilted at the same angle and pointed in the same direction as when you started. What do you notice about this tilt and the area receiving the most direct light?

Concept Development

Inquiry Questions If Earth's axis were straight up and down, how would the amount of sunlight received by the North Pole compare with the amount received by the South Pole? *Both poles would receive the same amount of sunlight.*

Content Background

Even though Earth's orbit is in the shape of an ellipse, this has virtually no effect on the seasons. Earth is actually closest to the sun (at its *perihelion*) during the winter in the Northern Hemisphere and is farthest from the sun during the summer (its *aphelion*). These differences in distance are so slight that they have no appreciable effect on the intensity of sunlight Earth receives. Also, Earth's elliptical orbit around the sun is so slight that it is almost circular.

FIND OUT!

What causes the changing seasons?

Time needed 10–15 minutes

Materials globe, lamp

Thinking Processes
Thinking critically, Observing and inferring, Recognizing cause and effect

Purpose To observe the effect Earth's position with respect to the sun has on the changing seasons.

Preparation Balls can be used instead of globes.

Enrichment

Activity Have students keep a record of times for sunset and sunrise for a month. This information is usually provided daily in newspapers or on television news. Then have students graph the change in minutes from day to day. Ask them to find out why times for sunrise and sunset change daily.

Teaching the Activity

Troubleshooting If students have difficulty determining exactly where the direct rays of the light source are striking on the surface of the globe, show them that the pole pointing toward the sun at any one time will receive more direct sunlight than the pole pointing away.

Demonstration Ask students where summer is occurring when we are experiencing winter in the Northern Hemisphere. Ask a volunteer to use the globe and lamp to demonstrate why this reversal of seasons exists between the northern and southern halves of the world. L2 LEP

Expected Outcomes

Students should be able to tell when the globe is in a position that represents summer and winter in both hemispheres. The light strikes most directly on the part of the Northern Hemisphere facing the lamp when the northern half of the globe points to the lamp. The area tilted toward the lamp gets the most direct light as students walk the globe around the lamp.

Conclude and Apply
When the Northern Hemisphere is tilted away from the lamp.

DID YOU KNOW?

A stationary object at Earth's equator is actually traveling about 1670 kilometers per hour as it spins with its location.

Conclude and Apply
At what point in your walk around the lamp do you think winter would occur in the northern half of this globe?

In the activity, you tilted the globe because Earth's axis is tilted at a $23^1/2°$ angle. You demonstrated how the amount of direct sunlight striking Earth varies from one hemisphere to the other because of this tilt. Figure 20-5 illustrates this idea. As Earth revolves around the sun, the half of Earth tilted toward the sun receives direct rays from the sun. In the next activity, you'll see how the angle at which the light strikes a surface affects the amount of heat absorbed by that surface.

FIGURE 20-5. When the Northern Hemisphere is tilted toward the sun, it receives the sun's most direct rays and therefore experiences summer. Meanwhile, the Southern Hemisphere is tilted away from the sun, receiving less direct rays and experiencing winter. When the Northern Hemisphere is tilted away from the sun, it experiences winter, and the Southern Hemisphere experiences summer.

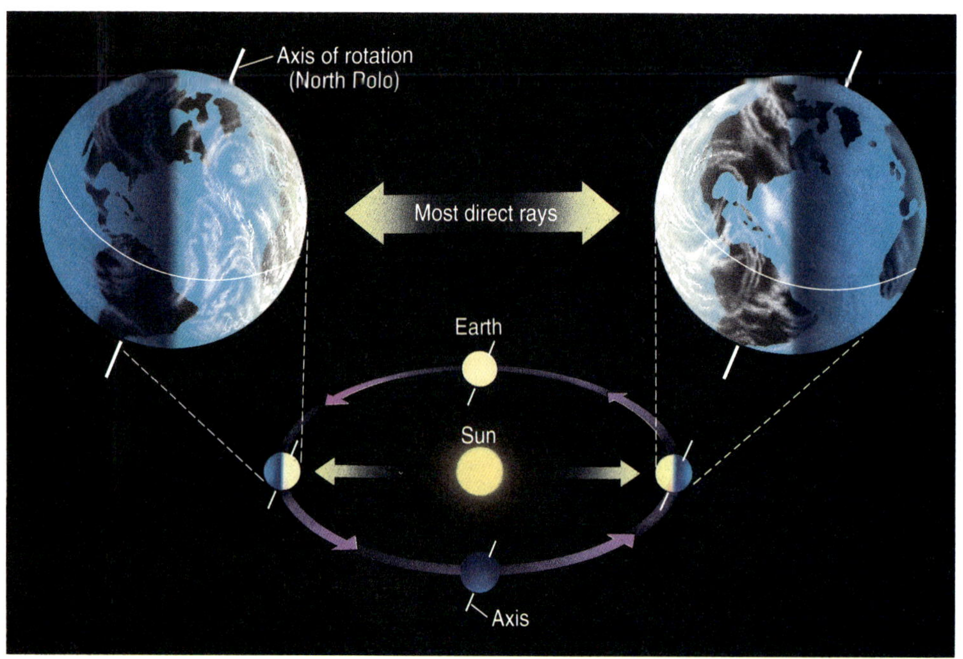

OPTIONS

Meeting Individual Needs

Learning Disabled, Behaviorally Disordered Demonstrate the relationship of the sun and Earth in the Find Out activity by using a circular light bulb and a globe. Have one student hold the light stationary to represent the sun. Walk around that light, tilting the globe to represent spring, summer, winter, and fall in the Northern Hemisphere. L1

INVESTIGATE!

20-1 TILT AND TEMPERATURE

In this activity, you will demonstrate that the angle at which the sun's rays hit an area determines the amount of heat received by the area.

PROBLEM

How does the angle of light affect temperature?

MATERIALS 

tape
black construction paper
gooseneck lamp with 75-watt bulb
Celsius thermometer
watch
protractor

PROCEDURE

1. Copy the data table.
2. Fold a piece of notebook-sized black construction paper in half lengthwise. Tape the short edges together to form an envelope.
3. Adjust the gooseneck lamp so that it will shine straight down. Then make sure the lamp is turned off.

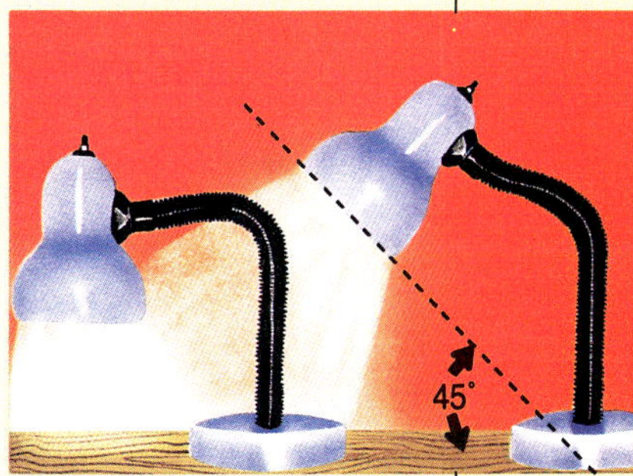

4. Read the thermometer and record the room temperature on the data table.
5. Place the thermometer in the black envelope and place the envelope directly under the lamp. **Hypothesize** what effect the light will have on the envelope and its contents.
6. Turn on the lamp. Every three minutes, record the temperature.
7. After three readings, turn off the lamp. **CAUTION:** *The shade will be very hot.*
8. Remove the thermometer and allow it and the lamp to cool.
9. When both objects are at room temperature, use the protractor to adjust the lamp so that its light will be shining at a 45° angle to the tabletop.
10. With the thermometer back in the envelope, place the envelope so that it will now receive light at a 45° angle. **Hypothesize** how this new angle will affect the temperature in the envelope.
11. Repeat Steps 6, 7, and 8.

DATA AND OBSERVATIONS

Sample data

TEMPERATURE AT	START	3 MIN	6 MIN	9 MIN
Direct light	27°	33°	34.5°	35°
Angled light	27°	31°	32°	33°

ANALYZE

1. Did the temperature in the envelope continue to rise at the same rate every three minutes?
2. **Identify the variables** in your experiment: What was the independent variable? What was the dependent variable?
3. Did the envelope absorb more heat from the direct light or the angled light?

CONCLUDE AND APPLY

4. How does the angle of light affect temperature?
5. **Going Further**: **Predict** how the absorption of heat would be affected if the lamp shade were tilted at an angle greater than 45°, then at an angle less than 45°.

PROGRAM RESOURCES

Teacher Classroom Resource
Activity Masters, pages 81-82, Investigate 20-1

INVESTIGATE!

20-1 TILT AND TEMPERATURE

Time needed 20–25 minutes

Materials tape, black construction paper, gooseneck lamp with 75-watt bulb, Celsius thermometer, watch, protractor

Thinking Processes
Making and using tables, Observing and inferring, Recognizing cause and effect, Measuring in SI, Forming a hypothesis, Separating and controlling variables, Interpreting data, Making models, Predicting

Purpose To observe how the angle at which light strikes a surface affects the temperature of that surface.

Preparation If a gooseneck lamp is not available, have students use a fixed-neck lamp and fasten the black paper and thermometer to the cover of their textbooks with masking tape. The angle of the surface can be changed by propping open the book cover to various angles.

Teaching Strategies

Discussion Ask students at what time of day a blacktop driveway would probably heat the most. Ask them to describe the position of the sun at this time of day. *During the middle of the day when the sun is at its highest position* L1

Expected Outcome

Students should see that the rate of increase in temperature was greater when the light was striking the surface directly rather than at a 45° angle.

Answers to Analyze/Conclude and Apply

1. no
2. angle of light; temperature
3. from the direct light
4. When light is angled, temperature increases more slowly.
5. Less heat would be absorbed; more heat would be absorbed.

EXPLORE!

Where are Earth's warm spots?
Time needed 20–25 minutes

Materials world map, encyclopedia

Thinking Processes
Thinking critically, Observing and inferring, Comparing and contrasting

Purpose To observe that the areas between the Tropic of Cancer and the Tropic of Capricorn are generally the warmest places on Earth.

Preparation You may wish to take students to the library to conduct their research.

Teaching Strategies

Discussion Relate the latitudes of the Tropic of Cancer and Tropic of Capricorn (23.5° north and south) to Earth's tilt of 23.5°. The sun appears directly overhead at some point during the year at all latitudes between the Tropic of Cancer and the Tropic of Capricorn. Nowhere else on Earth do the sun's rays strike directly.

Expected Outcomes

Students should find that the mean annual temperatures of cities between the Tropic of Cancer and Tropic of Capricorn are higher than those of cities outside this region.

Answers to Questions

1. 23.5°
2. Answers will vary, less.

As the Investigate activity shows, the more directly light falls on a surface, the more heat that surface absorbs and the higher the temperature of the surface becomes. This principle explains the change of seasons. The hemisphere that is tilted toward the sun receives more direct sunlight. It becomes warmer. As you observed in the Investigate activity, the amount of time an area is exposed to light is also important. The number of daylight hours an area has contributes to the warmth of the area. Therefore, the number of daylight hours and the angle of the sunlight cause the change in season, not the distance of Earth from the sun.

EXPLORE!

Where are Earth's warm spots?

On a globe or world map, locate the Tropic of Cancer and the Tropic of Capricorn. They should be clearly marked latitudes above and below the equator. Recall from Chapter 1 that lines of latitude measure distance north and south of the equator. At what degree north and south do the tropic lines lie? The area between these lines of latitude is often referred to as the tropics. Now select a city that lies within the tropics and use an encyclopedia to find its mean annual temperature. Select two other cities, one from each hemisphere, that lie outside the tropics. What are their mean temperatures? Are they more or less than the temperature of the city in the tropics?

EQUINOXES AND SOLSTICES

You now know that the tilt of Earth as it revolves around the sun causes the change in seasons. Because of this tilt, the sun's position relative to Earth's equator changes, too. Most of the time, the sun's most direct rays fall north or south of the equator. Two times during the year, however, the sun is directly over the equator. Each of these times is called an **equinox.**

PROGRAM RESOURCES

Teacher Classroom Resources
Multicultural Activities, page 44, Dr. Chang-Diaz L1

OPTIONS

Enrichment

Activity Have groups of students conduct an ongoing experiment by placing a pole or some other object that will cast a good shadow out in the middle of a field. At different times throughout the school year, have students measure the length, direction, and angle of this shadow at the same time of day to see how the shadow changes according to the season. COOP LEARN

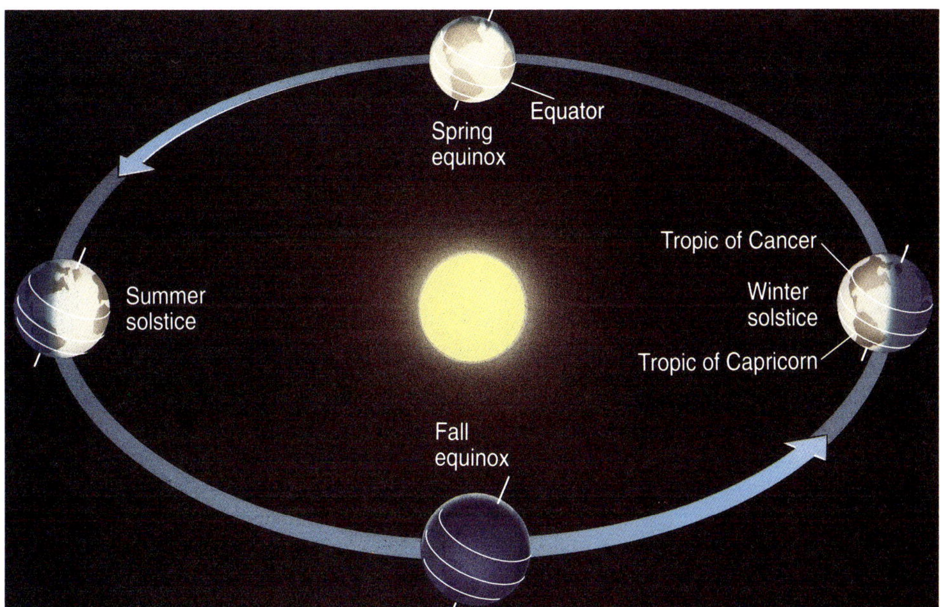

FIGURE 20-6. At an equinox, neither hemisphere is tilted toward the sun, and every place on Earth has about 12 hours of daylight and 12 hours of darkness. At a solstice, the sun is directly over either the Tropic of Cancer or the Tropic of Capricorn, and the seasons of summer and winter are beginning on Earth.

When the sun reaches an equinox, night and day are the same length all over the world. Neither the Northern nor the Southern Hemisphere is tilted toward the sun. Figure 20-6 shows you how this can happen. An equinox is reached on March 20 or 21 and again on September 22 or 23. In the Northern Hemisphere, we call these days the beginning of spring and fall. In the Southern Hemisphere, these seasons are reversed.

A solstice also occurs two times each year. At the time of a **solstice**, the sun is directly over the north or the south edge of the tropics. Figure 20-6 shows you how this happens.

The sun is never directly overhead in regions outside the tropics. The sun is directly over the northernmost point—the Tropic of Cancer—on June 21 or 22. This day marks the beginning of summer in the Northern Hemisphere and the beginning of winter in the Southern Hemisphere. During this June solstice (called the summer solstice by people in the Northern Hemisphere), the north is getting sunlight at its most direct angle. As you can conclude from your Investigate

MAKING CONNECTIONS

Math

Have students calculate how many times Earth spins on its axis in two trips around the sun. *2 × 365.25 = 730.5*

Daily Life

Discuss with students how the changing seasons and changing of day to night affect their lives. Include changing types of clothes, activities, holidays, and even the foods we eat.

Concept Development

Discussion Ask students to describe the position of the sun and Earth at the time of the winter solstice and the summer solstice in the Northern Hemisphere. Then, ask them what is occurring in the Southern Hemisphere at these times. Finally, ask them to describe a place on Earth where people enjoy a summerlike climate all year round.

Student Journal Have students record their observations and conclusions from the Find Out, Explore, and Investigate activities in their journals.

Meeting Individual Needs

Visually Impaired, Learning Disabled

When discussing the tilt of Earth and its effect on seasons, hold a globe so that the northern axis is pointed toward an intense light source about 2 m away. Allow students to feel the surface of the globe. Students should be able to feel greater warmth where direct rays hit the globe than where indirect rays hit. Explain to them that this occurs during summer in the Northern Hemisphere.

SKILLBUILDER

Unless viewed from south of the Tropic of Cancer, the sun will never be in the *north* sky. L1

3 Assess

Check for Understanding

Have students answer questions 1–3 in Check Your Understanding. Have a globe available for students as they complete the Apply question.

Reteach

Use two students to represent the sun and Earth. Have the student representing the sun stand still. Have the other student walk around the "sun" while spinning. At various points, ask the class which side of the "Earth" student is experiencing night and day. Then have "Earth" tilt toward the "sun" while spinning and walking. Ask the class to identify which part of "Earth" is experiencing summer and winter. L1

Extension

Have students make a simple sundial for use outside throughout the school day. Have them place a pole or meterstick in the middle of the area where they will make their dial. At hourly intervals, have students use chalk or a stick to mark the shadow cast by the upright pole or meterstick. Then have them check the accuracy of their dial over several days. L3

4 Close

Discussion

Ask students how the length of a day and year on a planet that turns slower but completes its orbit faster than Earth would compare to our day and year. *longer day; shorter year* Have them explain their reasoning. L1

SKILLBUILDER

OBSERVING AND INFERRING

On a globe, locate a point closest to your city or town. Use your knowledge of solstices to determine whether there is a compass direction (N, S, E, or W) in which you will *never* see the sun from your position. If you need help, refer to the **Skill Handbook** on page 652.

experiment and from your own experience, the June solstice also begins the hottest season of the year for people in the Northern Hemisphere. In the Southern Hemisphere, people experience winter beginning in June because they receive less direct sunlight at this time.

The sun is directly over the southernmost point—the Tropic of Capricorn—on December 21 or 22. People in the Northern Hemisphere consider this time the first day of winter and therefore call it the winter solstice. The sun appears low in the southern sky during winter in the Northern Hemisphere. For people in the Southern Hemisphere, however, the December solstice marks the beginning of summer because the sun is more directly over them. If you measured the number of daylight hours each day for one year, you would find that the day of the winter solstice has the fewest daylight hours in the Northern Hemisphere. This fact demonstrates what you've already learned: when sunlight is at a less direct angle for less time, the temperature will be lower than if the sunlight is direct and shines for a longer time.

As you've seen, the motions of Earth affect you a great deal. The rotation of Earth causes day and night, and the revolution of Earth around the sun on a tilted axis is responsible for the change in seasons. However, Earth is just one of the many bodies traveling around the sun. In the next section, you will learn how Earth's neighbor, the moon, is also moving through space. You will learn the effects of this movement and observe its consequences.

Check Your Understanding

1. What observable evidence do we have of Earth's shape?
2. There is not truly a sunrise or sunset in the usual sense of the terms *rise* and *set.* How can you explain the apparent movement of the sun across the sky?
3. Based on what you have learned about Earth's tilt and the effect of direct sunlight, how do these factors affect the temperature of Earth's polar regions?
4. **APPLY:** Consider yourself manager of the United States ski team. The team needs year-round practice to be the best. Around the time of the summer solstice in the United States, to what region of the world would you take the team for practice? What factors influenced your decision?

Answers to Check Your Understanding

1. the gradual appearance of objects over the horizon; pictures of Earth from space; we can sail around the world and not fall off
2. As Earth rotates, places on Earth pass in and out of the sun's light.
3. Earth's polar regions never receive direct light from the sun and are, therefore, generally colder than other areas on Earth.
4. You would take them to the Southern Hemisphere where they are experiencing winter because the tilt of Earth results in opposite seasons.

20-2 Motions of the Moon

MOON'S ROTATION AND REVOLUTION

Remember the satellites mentioned in Chapter 14? Humans have built and sent satellites into space, but Earth also has its own natural satellite—the moon. Do you also remember the moon journal you started in Chapter 1? You recorded how the moon's shape appears to change from day to day. Sometimes, just after sunset, you can see a bright, round moon low in the sky. At other times, only a small portion of moon is visible, and it is high in the sky at sunset. These phases of the moon are due to changes in the position of its lighted side in relation to Earth. How does this satellite moon move to change its position? The following activity will show you.

OBJECTIVES

In this section, you will

- recognize that the moon's phases are caused by the relative positions of the sun, the moon, and Earth;
- demonstrate the arrangement of the sun, the moon, and Earth during solar and lunar eclipses.

KEY SCIENCE TERMS

solar eclipse
lunar eclipse

FIND OUT!

What are two ways in which the moon moves?

Work with several classmates to perform this activity. Tape an X on a basketball. One person should stand facing another, holding the ball at head level with the X toward the other person. Now, as the rest of the group watches, the person with the ball should move in a circle around his or her partner while keeping the X toward him or her.

Conclude and Apply

After the person with the ball has made one trip around, discuss whether the other group members were able to see all sides of the ball from where they were viewing.

1. How does this compare with what the partner was able to see as he or she followed the X?
2. How many revolutions did the ball make around the partner?
3. How many times did the ball itself rotate?

Section 20-2

PREPARATION

Concepts Developed

Students learned in Section 1 that Earth rotates and revolves around the sun, causing Earth to experience day and night and seasons. The moon, Earth's only natural satellite, revolves around Earth as Earth revolves around the sun. The various phases of the moon, as seen from Earth, are caused by the relative positions of Earth, the sun, and the moon. Occasionally, Earth, the moon, and the sun are lined up in such a way that an eclipse occurs.

Planning the Lesson

In planning your lesson on motions of the moon, refer to the Chapter Organizer on pages 596A-B for timing suggestions, resources, and additional materials that will help you in your presentation of the lesson concepts.

For adequate development of the concepts presented in this section, we recommend that students do the Find Out activity on page 607.

1 MOTIVATE

Discussion Ask students if they have ever witnessed a solar or lunar eclipse. Have them describe it. Check your local planetarium for schedules of past and upcoming eclipses (partial or total).

FIND OUT!

What are two ways in which the moon moves?

Time needed 10–15 minutes

Materials basketball, tape

Thinking Processes

Thinking critically, Observing and inferring

Purpose To observe two motions of the moon.

Teaching the Activity

Any large ball or balloon can be used instead of a basketball. This activity can be done with small groups. COOP LEARN

Expected Outcomes

Students should see that the moon makes one revolution around Earth so we always see the same side of the moon.

Conclude and Apply

1. The partner saw the same side. The onlookers saw different sides.
2. one
3. once

2 Teach

Tying to Previous Knowledge

In Chapter 1, students were introduced to the phases of the moon. Ask them to describe the pattern of these phases. In this section, they will learn that the moon's phases are dependent on the relative positions of the moon, the sun, and Earth. Before considering these three bodies as a system, review the relative positions of the sun and Earth.

Concept Development

Theme Connection The theme of interactions and systems becomes evident as the students perform the Investigate activity on page 613 in which they will demonstrate how the interaction of the components of the sun-moon-Earth system cause the phases of the moon as well as lunar and solar eclipses.

Discussion Ask students to compare what a person might see of another person who is riding a merry-go-round as the observer runs alongside as the merry-go-round turns. Students should realize that the observer will always see the same side of the rider. Point out that our view of the moon is similar to the view of the person running.

FIGURE 20-7. People associate the moon with night, but it is often visible during the day.

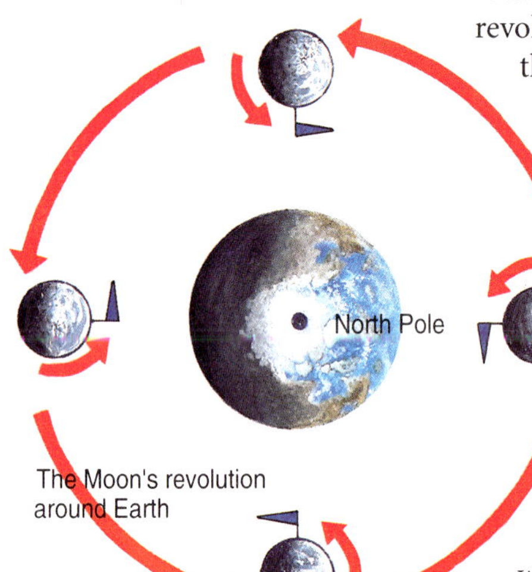

FIGURE 20-8. The same side of the moon always faces Earth.

Just as the ball rotated once on its axis while making one revolution around the partner, so does the moon rotate once on its axis each time it makes one complete revolution around Earth. Because these two motions of the moon take the same amount of time, the same side of the moon always faces Earth. The other side is never turned toward us, and therefore we cannot see it from Earth. Figure 20-8 shows how this happens. We refer to the side of the moon that we cannot see as the far side.

But if the same side of the moon is always facing Earth, why does the moon's appearance seem to change from one night or day to the next? Why does it change from a large, full disc to a small sliver in the sky before disappearing entirely from view?

The appearance of the moon changes because we see different parts of its surface lighted by the sun. We see the lighted side from different angles because the moon is revolving around Earth. The phase you see on a particular night or day depends on the position of the moon in relation to both Earth and the sun.

Look at Figure 20-9. A new moon occurs when the moon is between Earth and the sun. During the new moon phase, the lighted half of the moon is facing the sun. The side that isn't lighted is facing Earth. As the moon continues to revolve around Earth, more and more of its lighted side becomes visible from Earth. Approximately 24 hours after a new moon, you can see a

PROGRAM RESOURCES

Teacher Classroom Resources

Study Guide, page 71

Laboratory Manual, pages 121-122, Moon Phases L2

Critical Thinking/Problem Solving, page 28, The Origin of the Moon L2, page 8, Flex Your Brain

Transparency Masters, page 81, and **Color Transparency,** number 39, Moon Phases L2

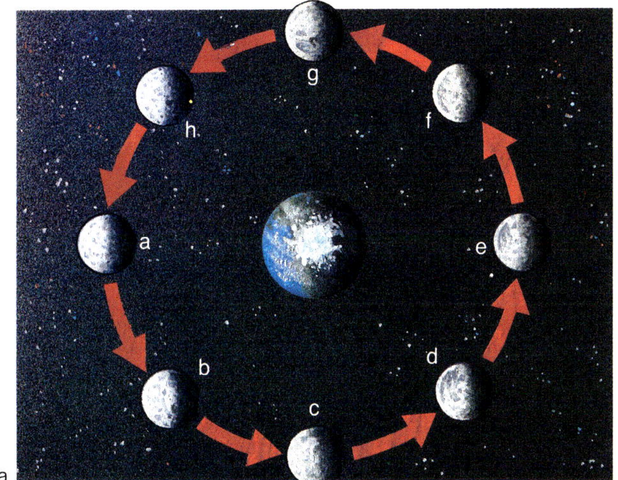

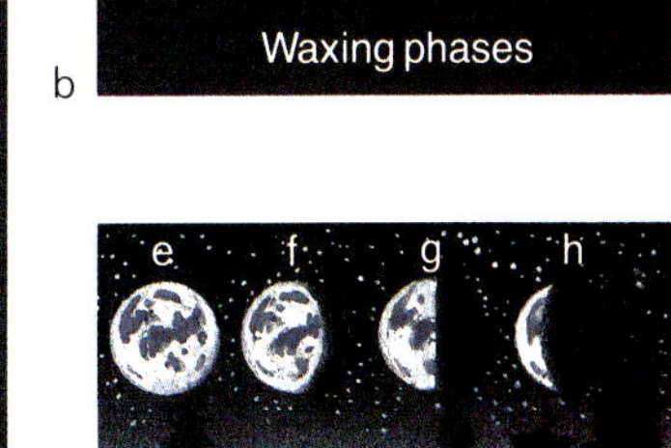

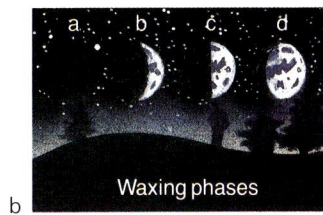

FIGURE 20-9. The phases of the moon are the new moon (a), crescent (b), first quarter (c), gibbous (d), full moon (e), gibbous (f), third quarter (g), crescent (h).

thin slice of the lighted side. This phase is called a crescent phase. About a week later, you can see half of the lighted side, or one quarter of the moon's surface. This phase is called first quarter.

Over the next few days, you can see more and more of the lighted side of the moon. When you see more than one quarter but less than half of the lighted side, the moon is said to be in its gibbous phase. Full moon occurs when the whole lighted half of the moon is visible from Earth. After becoming full, the portion of visible moon shrinks, with the moon passing through gibbous, quarter, and crescent phases. The cycle of moon phases takes about 29 1/2 days, or one month, to complete.

The moon's revolution around Earth causes more than just moon phases. The next section examines spectacular and, for some people, terrifying events that occur whenever the moon moves into a line with the sun and Earth.

ECLIPSES

What do you think can happen when one member of the sun-moon-Earth system moves between the other two? Your view of this occurrence is affected by the size and distance of the sun and moon.

Concept Development

Discussion Discuss with students the fact that the moon does not generate any light of its own. It is simply reflecting light emitted by the sun.

Inquiry Question How would our perception of the moon change if the moon completed one revolution around Earth in 24 hours? *Only one area on Earth would ever see the moon since it would be revolving at the same rate Earth rotates.*

Flex Your Brain Use the Flex Your Brain activity to have students explore an ECLIPSE.

Teacher FYI

The actual period of the moon's revolution around Earth is 27.3 days. The time from one phase until the same phase occurs again is 29.5 days. This discrepancy of nearly two days is due to the fact that as the moon orbits Earth, Earth and the moon are also orbiting the sun. Although the moon may have made a complete orbit of Earth, it has not returned to its original position directly between Earth and the sun. The complete return to original position takes almost two more days.

Meeting Individual Needs

Learning Disabled Show students the photographs in Figure 20-9 that show the various phases of the moon. Explain that each phase is related to the position of Earth, the moon, and the sun. Explain to students that the sun does not move, so the movement of Earth and the moon cause the phases. Have students work in groups of three. Give one student a flashlight, give one student a globe, and give the last student a smaller ball to represent the moon. As you discuss each phase of the moon, position students to represent that phase. Continue this activity, one phase at a time, until students can position themselves without help. COOP LEARN

EXPLORE!

How is your perception of an object's size affected by its distance from you?

Time needed 5–10 minutes

Thinking Processes Thinking critically, Observing and inferring

Purpose To observe how small, close objects can appear larger than large, distant objects.

Preparation Student pairs should be taken outside or out in a hallway for this activity. COOP LEARN

Teaching the Activity

Demonstration If this activity must be done in the classroom, stand in the front of the room and ask students to close one eye and line up their thumbs so that they block out your head. Then direct students to bring their thumbs closer to their eyes to block out your entire body. Discuss why this is possible. L1

Expected Outcome

Students should see that a small, close object can block their view of a larger object that is farther away.

Answers to Questions

1. Answers may vary. They may still see part of the object.
2. no part.

SKILLBUILDER

13,904 km; 1,390,400 km 

EXPLORE!

How is your perception of an object's size affected by its distance from you?

With a partner, choose an object in the distance that you know is larger than you are, for example, a car or a house. Have your partner stand directly between you and this object. Stand far enough apart so that your view of the object is partially blocked. Describe to your partner what you can see. Next, ask your partner to move closer. Can you still see the object? Finally, ask your partner to stand as close as 0.5 m from you. Now what part of the object can you still see?

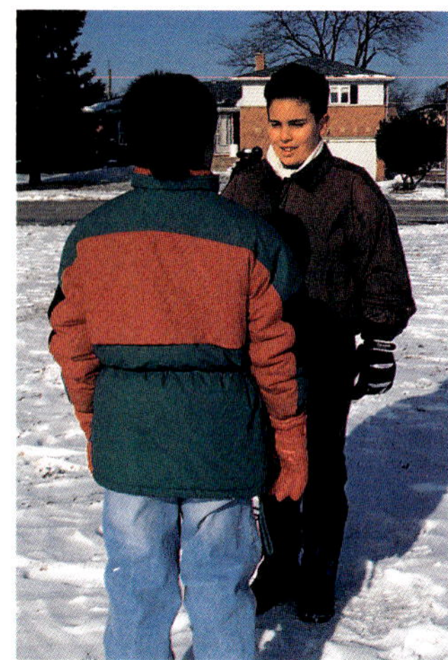

In this simple demonstration, you observed how a small, close object can appear to be as big or bigger than an object that is far away and known to be much bigger. This same principle causes the sun and the moon to appear equal in size. Even though the sun's diameter is 400 times greater than the moon's, the moon is about 400 times closer to Earth than the sun. Therefore, the sun and the moon appear to us to be about the same size.

The Explore demonstration also showed how a smaller object can totally block your view of a larger object. When the moon blocks our view of the sun, as your partner blocked your view of a distant object, we call the event a solar eclipse.

SKILLBUILDER

MEASURING IN SI

The moon's diameter is about 3476 kilometers. This measure is about a fourth of the diameter of Earth and about 400 times smaller than the diameter of the sun. Calculate the diameters of Earth and the sun. If you need help, refer to the **Skill Handbook** on page 654.

Solar Eclipses

Around 600 B.C.E., warriors from ancient Media, in what is now northern Iran, launched an early-morning attack on the neighboring country of Lydia, in present-day Turkey.

PROGRAM RESOURCES

Teacher Classroom Resources

How It Works, page 19, Viewing an Eclipse COOP LEARN

Making Connections: Integrating Sciences, page 43, Lunar-Day Rhythms L2

Making Connections: Across the Curriculum, page 43, Stonehenge L2

Transparency Masters, page 83, **Color Transparency,** number 40, Meteorite Impact L1

OPTIONS

Enrichment

Activity Have students construct a year-long calendar based only on the phases of the moon. Students can be creative with this, so accept any rendering of this theme. Have students note problems with using a calendar of this nature. Display their calendars in class.

After several hours of battle, the clear, blue sky darkened, and all color seemed to drain from the landscape. The air became cool, and within minutes the day was as black as night. The planets and stars were visible. The soldiers were stunned. But after several minutes, the stars began to fade, daylight replaced darkness, and the sun reappeared. The soldiers were so frightened that they dropped their weapons and fled the battlefield. They were certain that the end of the world was near.

FIGURE 20-10. This total solar eclipse was seen on July 11, 1991, over Baja California.

The soldiers had experienced a solar eclipse. You can see what a total solar eclipse looks like in Figure 20-10. It is a rare but natural event that leaves observers standing in the shadow of the moon. Recall from Chapter 2 how shadows are formed. A **solar eclipse** occurs when the moon passes directly between Earth and the sun. The moon blocks out some of the sun's light, casting a shadow on Earth.

Look at Figure 20-11 to help you understand how a solar eclipse occurs. In areas of total solar eclipse, the only portion of the sun that is visible is part of its atmosphere. This appears as a white glow around the edge of the eclipsing moon.

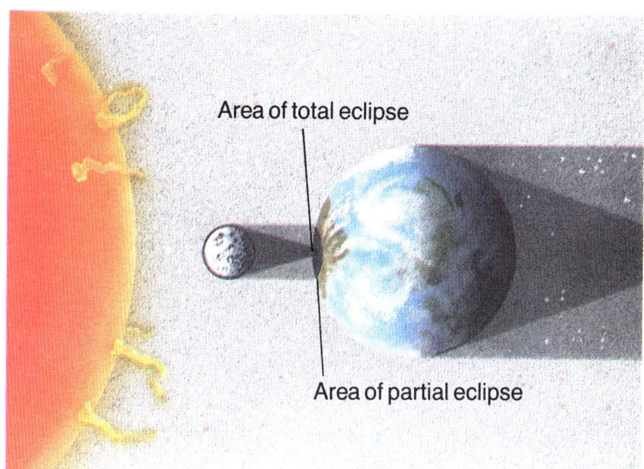

FIGURE 20-11. Only a small area of Earth experiences a total solar eclipse during the eclipse event. Only the outer portion of the sun's atmosphere is visible during a total solar eclipse.

Concept Development

Using the Photo Ask students to describe the position of the sun, the moon, and Earth when the photograph in Figure 20-10 of a total solar eclipse was taken. *The moon was passing directly between Earth and the sun.*

Using the Diagram Have students refer to Figure 20-11 to explain why the entire Earth cannot witness a total solar eclipse at the same time. They should see from the diagram that the shadow produced by the moon falls on only a very small portion of Earth's surface.

Discussion Explain the meaning of the terms waxing and waning in Figure 20-9. After passing full moon, the amount of the lighted side of the moon that can be seen becomes smaller. The phases are said to be *waning*. Shortly after a new moon, more and more of its lighted side becomes visible. These phases are *waxing*. Present several examples of moon phases and have the students determine if the moon is waxing or waning. For example, the moon moves from the new-moon phase to first quarter (thus is waxing because more of the lighted side becomes visible).

Enrichment

Research Have students research a historical event that was affected by a solar eclipse such as the event described on pages 610-611. As an alternative, students can research the myths and stories used to explain solar eclipses. For example, several Chinese cultures thought that solar eclipses happened when a dragon in the sky tried to swallow the sun.

Concept Development

Demonstration This demonstration will show students the various phases of the moon.

You will need one overhead projector in the front of the room aimed toward the back at an angle above the students' heads. Have students cluster at the center of the room. Tell the students that the projector represents the sun and that they are on Earth. Holding a ball, revolve around the students, telling them that the ball represents the moon. Be sure to hold the same side of the ball facing them. Have students identify each phase as you revolve around them.

MAKING CONNECTIONS

Math

Ask students to determine when the next full moon will occur. Give them the date of the last full moon. Students should recall that it takes 29.5 days for the moon to complete one cycle of its phases.

Content Background

The moon revolves around Earth in an elliptical path similar to the way Earth revolves around the sun. The moon appears to move west across the sky. Actually, the moon is moving east, but because of the motion of Earth, it appears to be moving west.

FIGURE 20-12. In areas of partial solar eclipse, only part of the sun is blocked by the moon.

A partial eclipse occurs on Earth when the moon covers only part of the sun. See Figure 20-12. As the moon slides in front of the sun, it may look as though a sliver has been cut out of the edge of the sun.

Although a rare and dramatic event, a solar eclipse can be dangerous to careless observers. You should never look directly at the sun, particularly during a solar eclipse. The sun's radiation can damage your eyes and cause blindness. A solar eclipse should be viewed firsthand only with the help of special viewing devices. If you can't witness the event firsthand, you now have the option of live and taped video coverage of such events.

Solar eclipses do not happen every time the moon travels around Earth, however. This is because the path of the moon's revolution is tilted at about a 5° angle to Earth's path around the sun. Because of this difference, the moon usually passes above or below the sun and not directly in front of it.

While between two and five solar eclipses occur every year, they can be seen in only a few areas on Earth at any one time. A total solar eclipse can be seen only once every 360 years from any one location. Often, solar eclipses occur in remote regions such as Siberia and the middle of the Atlantic Ocean. So unless you are able to travel, and depending on the weather once you get there, your chances of seeing a total eclipse are not very good.

If you do the following Investigate, however, you will see exactly how solar eclipses—as well as moon phases—occur.

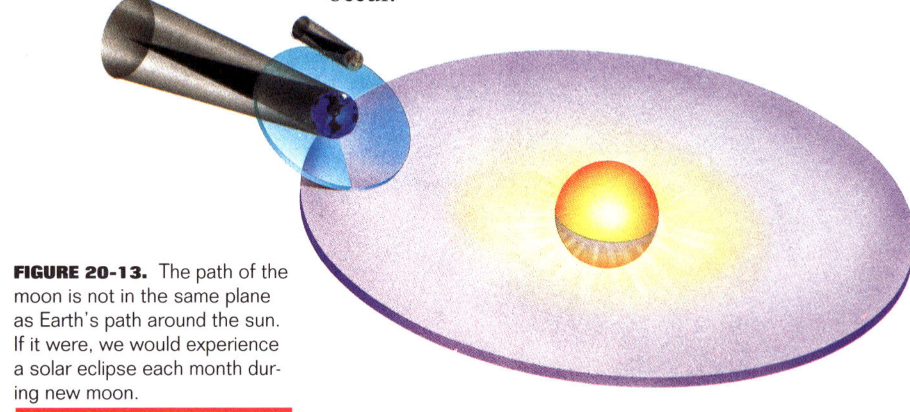

FIGURE 20-13. The path of the moon is not in the same plane as Earth's path around the sun. If it were, we would experience a solar eclipse each month during new moon.

OPTIONS

Enrichment

Activity Have students research the meaning and origin of the phrase "once in a blue moon." Have them present their information to the class.

I N V E S T I G A T E !

20-2 ECLIPSES AND MOON PHASES

You know that moon phases and solar eclipses result from the relative positions of the sun, the moon, and Earth. In this activity, you will demonstrate the positions of these bodies during certain phases and eclipses. You will also see why only a very small portion of Earth sees a total solar eclipse.

PROBLEM

How can you demonstrate moon phases and solar eclipses?

MATERIALS 

pencil
polystyrene ball
Figures 20-9 and 20-11
globe
unshaded light source

PROCEDURE

1. Copy the data table.
2. Stick the pencil into the polystyrene ball, making a model moon with a handle.
3. Study the positions of the sun, the moon, and Earth as shown in Figure 20-11 when they line up to produce an eclipse.
4. Set the globe and the lamp on a table about 0.5 m apart and turn on the light.
5. Holding the model moon by its pencil handle, move it around the globe to duplicate the position that will cause a solar eclipse.
6. Study Figure 20-9. Then hold the moon at each of the following phases: new moon, first quarter, full moon, and third quarter. **Predict** during which phase(s) of the moon a solar eclipse could occur. **Observe** and record your data.
7. Again place the moon at the location where a solar eclipse could occur. Move it slightly toward and then away from Earth. **Observe** if there is any change in the size of the shadow resulting from this eclipse. Record this information.

DATA AND OBSERVATIONS

Sample data

MOON PHASE	OBSERVATIONS
New	Solar eclipse
First quarter	No eclipse
Full	No eclipse
Third quarter	No eclipse

ANALYZE

1. During which phase(s) of the moon is it possible for a solar eclipse to occur?
2. **Determine the effect** that a small change in the distance between Earth and the moon would have on the size of the shadow during an eclipse.
3. As seen from Earth, how does the apparent size of the moon compare with the apparent size of the sun? How can an eclipse be used to confirm this?

CONCLUDE AND APPLY

4. Why doesn't a solar eclipse occur every month? Explain your answer.
5. Suppose you wanted to make a more accurate model of the movement of the moon around Earth. How might you adjust the distance between the light source and the globe? How would you adjust the size of the moon model in comparison with the globe you are using?
6. **Going Further: Hypothesize** what would happen if the sun, the moon, and Earth were lined up with Earth directly in between the sun and moon.

INVESTIGATE!

20-2 ECLIPSES AND MOON PHASES

Time needed 20–25 minutes

Materials pencil, polystyrene ball, globe, unshaded light source, FIgures 20-9 and 20-11

Thinking Processes
Thinking critically, Observing and inferring

Purpose To demonstrate the position of the sun, the moon, and Earth during moon phases and eclipses.

Preparation Overhead lights should be off while students are conducting this investigation.

Teaching Strategies

Troubleshooting Students may have trouble lining up the moon, the sun, and Earth to produce the phases as seen from Earth. Ask students to pretend that they are standing on Earth looking out or up at the moon. L2

Expected Outcomes

Students should be able to position their "moons" in order to produce a lunar and a solar eclipse as well as the four major phases of the moon.

Answers to Analyze/Conclude and Apply

1. new moon phase
2. The smaller the distance between Earth and the moon, the larger the shadow.
3. The apparent size of the moon is the same as the apparent size of the sun. This can be demonstrated during a solar eclipse because the moon appears to completely cover the sun.
4. because the orbit of the moon is not in the same plane as Earth's orbit around the sun.
5. Move the light source farther away. Use a smaller ball.
6. Earth would cast a shadow on the moon.

PROGRAM RESOURCES

Teacher Classroom Resources

Activity Masters, pages 83-84, Investigate 20-2

3 Assess

Check for Understanding

1. Set up a light source, globe, and polystyrene ball to represent the moon, the sun, and Earth. Model different phases of the moon, a solar eclipse, and a lunar eclipse. Ask students to identify what phase or eclipse is being modeled. Then show students photographs of various phases of the moon and eclipses and ask them to arrange the light source, globe, and ball to model the events shown in the photos. LEP
2. Have students verify their answer to the Apply question using the lamp-globe-ball model of the sun-Earth-moon system.

Reteach

Activity Obtain calendars that indicate the various phases of the moon. Have students find the next phase of the moon that will occur after the present date. Then have them locate this phase in Figure 20-9. Continue until students have identified the dates for all of the phases. L1

Extension

Have students who have mastered the concepts in this section research the dates of total solar eclipses that will occur in the remainder of this decade and where they can best be viewed. L3

4 Close

Activity

Have students describe in writing the positions of Earth, the moon, and the sun during a lunar and solar eclipse as well as their positions during full and new moon phases as seen from Earth. L1

FIGURE 20-14. During a total lunar eclipse, Earth blocks light coming from the sun.

In the Investigate activity, did you conclude that a shadow can also be cast on the moon? Such a shadow is called a lunar eclipse.

Lunar Eclipses

You know that the solar eclipse that the Medians and the Lydians found so terrifying was nothing more than the shadow of the moon on Earth. When positions are right, Earth can also cast a shadow on the moon.

Earth casts a shadow on the side facing away from the sun. Once every 29 days, in its revolution around Earth, the moon moves near this shadow. Usually it passes above or below the shadow. When the moon does pass through Earth's shadow, we see a **lunar eclipse.** At this time, Earth is directly between the sun and the moon. Figure 20-14 will help you understand how a lunar eclipse occurs.

During a lunar eclipse, the moon becomes darker as it moves into the curved shadow of Earth. A lunar eclipse can last up to one hour and forty minutes. During this time, the moon may reflect a dark, coppery red light. Unless clouds hide the view, everyone on the nighttime side of Earth can see it.

In this section, you learned that moon phases and eclipses are a result of the way Earth, the sun, and the moon line up. In the following section, you'll discover one more interesting effect their positions can produce.

Check Your Understanding

1. Draw the relative positions of the sun, the moon, and Earth during a full moon phase.
2. Which type of eclipse can occur during a full moon?
3. **APPLY:** Why does only a small percentage of Earth's population witness a solar eclipse, while people on the entire nighttime side of Earth can see a lunar eclipse?

Answers to Check Your Understanding

1. Drawings should show the moon on the opposite side of Earth from the sun.
2. lunar eclipse
3. The moon is much smaller than Earth so it casts a small shadow on Earth during a solar eclipse. Only people located within this shadow observe the total solar eclipse. Because Earth's shadow is larger than the moon, the entire moon is cast in shadow during a lunar eclipse. This event is visible anywhere the moon can normally be seen—the entire night side of Earth.

20-3 Tides

EARTH, MOON, AND OCEAN

Have you ever been to an ocean beach? Many people unfamiliar with the ocean will place their towels and sandals at what seems a safe distance from the water and then return to find them floating away. What happened? The lifeguard on duty will tell you that the tide came in.

Do you remember what you learned about waves and wavelengths in Chapter 18? **Tides** are slow-moving water waves with long wavelengths. They produce an alternate rise and fall of the surface level of the oceans. When the tide comes in, the water level rises, and the waves break farther and farther inland. At high tide, the surface level of the ocean is at its highest point. Once this high point has been reached, the level then begins to drop. Over a period of several hours, the water recedes, and more and more land is exposed. At low tide, the surface of the ocean has reached its lowest level.

OBJECTIVES

In this section, you will

- describe the changes you might observe along a coastline during high and low tides;
- diagram the relative positions of the sun, the moon, and Earth during the highest tides.

KEY SCIENCE TERMS

tides

FIGURE 20-15. When high tide comes in, a beach becomes narrower as waves break farther and farther inland.

Section 20-3

PREPARATION

Concepts Developed

Students learned in Section 2 that the position of the moon with respect to the sun and Earth causes the various moon phases and eclipses. The position of the moon also affects the tides that occur in Earth's oceans. Earth and the moon exert a gravitational pull on each other. It is this gravitational attraction that causes oceans to bulge away from Earth and cause the tides.

Planning the Lesson

In planning your lesson on tides, refer to the Chapter Organizer on pages 596A-B for timing suggestions, resources, and additional materials that will help you in your presentation of the lesson concepts.

For adequate development of the concepts presented in this section, we recommend that students do the Find Out activity on pages 616-617.

1 MOTIVATE

Discussion Ask students if they have ever been to an ocean beach. Ask them to describe how the shoreline changed over a period of hours. If none of the students has ever been to an ocean beach, ask if they think an ocean shoreline remains the same throughout the day. Show students pictures of the same beach at high tide and low tide. Students may be surprised at the difference. Ask them to speculate on why this happens and write their responses on the board. L1

OPTIONS

Enrichment

Activity Have students make mobiles of the sun, the moon, and Earth and representing the various phases of the moon. Polystyrene balls of different sizes, coat hangers, and string can be used to accomplish this. Parts of the polystyrene balls could be darkened to help represent the phases as seen from Earth.

2 TEACH

Tying to Previous Knowledge

A discussion of waves and wavelengths from Chapter 18 might be useful to remind students how waves form and travel. Emphasize that tides are actually slow-moving waves with long wavelengths. The smaller waves breaking on a shoreline are usually the result of wind action and have smaller, shorter wavelengths. Have students recall the relative positions and motion of Earth, the sun, and the moon. Remind them that the moon is exerting a measure of gravitational force on Earth. This force is evident through our tides as the moon literally pulls the water slightly away from Earth's surface.

FIND OUT!

What is the relationship between the height of tides and the position of the moon?

Time needed 15–20 minutes

Thinking Process
Making and using tables

Purpose To identify the relationship between moon phases and tides.

Preparation Make sure students know how to read the table.

Teaching the Activity

Discussion Discuss the methods for finding tide differences. Students may not realize that they must add to find the tide difference when a negative height is involved. For example, the difference between a high tide of 1.8 m and a low tide of -0.1 m is 1.8 + 0.1, or 1.9 m. L2

Expected Outcome

Students should see a correlation between the phases of the moon and the heights of tides.

TABLE 20-1. Tide Chart for Boston Harbor, October 6–19

TIDES
Boston October, 1991

Date	Morning	Afternoon	Date	Morning	Afternoon
SUNDAY **6**	High 9:28 height 10.8 Low 3:12 height -0.3 Sunrise 5:44	High 9:52 height 10.8 Low 3:38 height -0.5 Sunrise 5:21	SUNDAY **13**	High 2:33 height 8.9 Low 8:26 height 1.6 Sunrise 5:52	High 2:39 height 9.7 Low 9:05 height 0.9 Sunrise 5:09
MONDAY **7** NEW MOON	High 10:15 height 11.1 Low 4:00 height -0.4 Sunrise 5:45	High 10:42 height 10.7 Low 4:28 height -0.8 Sunrise 5:19	MONDAY **14**	High 3:24 height 8.5 Low 9:16 height 2.0 Sunrise 5:53	High 3:32 height 9.3 Low 9:58 height 1.3 Sunrise 5:08
TUESDAY **8**	High 10:59 height 11.2 Low 4:45 height -0.3 Sunrise 5:47	High 11:29 height 10.5 Low 5:15 height -0.9 Sunrise 5:18	TUESDAY **15** FIRST QUARTER	High 4:16 height 8.2 Low 10:11 height 2.3 Sunrise 5:54	High 4:27 height 9.0 Low 10:54 height 1.6 Sunrise 5:06
WEDNESDAY **9**	High 11:41 height 11.2 Low 5:29 height -0.1 Sunrise 5:48	High – height – Low 6:00 height -0.8 Sunrise 5:16	WEDNESDAY **16**	High 5:13 height 8.1 Low 11:09 height 2.4 Sunrise 5.56	High 5:25 height 8.9 Low 11:50 height 1.7 Sunrise 5.04
THURSDAY **10**	High 12:14 height 10.2 Low 6:11 height 0.3 Sunrise 5:49	High 12:24 height 11.0 Low 6:45 height -0.5 Sunrise 5:14	THURSDAY **17**	High 6:09 height 8.3 Low – height – Sunrise 5:57	High 6:24 height 8.9 Low 12:05 height 2.2 Sunrise 5:03
FRIDAY **11**	High 12:57 height 9.8 Low 6:56 height 0.7 Sunrise 5:50	High 1:06 height 10.6 Low 7.29 height 0.0 Sunrise 5:13	FRIDAY **18**	High 7:02 height 8.6 Low 12:43 height 1.6 Sunrise 5:58	High 7:16 height 9.1 Low 1:02 height 1.9 Sunrise 5:01
SATURDAY **12**	High 1:43 height 9.3 Low 7:41 height 1.2 Sunrise 5:51	High 1:52 height 10.2 Low 8:15 height 0.5 Sunrise 5:11	SATURDAY **19**	High 7:50 height 9.0 Low 1:31 height 1.3 Sunrise 5:59	High 8:05 height 9.3 Low 1:53 height 1.4 Sunrise 5:00

Eastern Standard Time – Add 1 Hour For Daylight Savings Time

Eastern Standard Time – Add 1 Hour For Daylight Savings Time

Examine the tide chart in Table 20-1. Notice that a high tide occurs about every $12\frac{1}{2}$ hours. A low tide occurs about $6\frac{1}{4}$ hours after every high tide. In other words, there are two high tides and two low tides every day. High and low tides occur about six hours apart along much of the East Coast of the United States.

You may be asking yourself, "What do tides have to do with this chapter? After all, I'm studying about the moon now." This next activity will show you.

FIND OUT!

What is the relationship between the height of tides and the position of the moon?

Study Table 20-2, a chart that lists the range of tidal heights for a month and also the observed moon phases for this same time period. Identify the two times during this month that the tide difference was the greatest. What phases of the moon correspond to these two dates?

OPTIONS

Enrichment

Research Have students research how the tides affect marine life. For example, the reproductive cycles of many fish, marine turtles, and mammals are timed according to the tides. L3

Multicultural Perspectives

Discuss with students how the Japanese rely heavily on the ocean for their food. Sampling some Japanese cuisine might be useful and fun to show the different products from the oceans that are used for food. Have students look up aquaculture practices in Japan or how the Japanese diet is related to their health.

Conclude and Apply

1. Sketch the way the sun, the moon, and Earth are positioned when the tide difference was greatest.
2. How would you change the sketch for dates when the tidal difference was the lowest?
3. What relation do you see between tide movement and moon position?

TABLE 20-2. Tides in San Diego for a One-Month Period

Date	Height of high tide (meters)	Height of low tide (meters)
1	1.4	0.5
2	1.5	0.4
3	1.7	0.2
4	1.8	–0.1
5	2.1	–0.3
6	2.2	–0.5
7	2.3	–0.6
8	2.3	–0.6
9	2.3	–0.6
10	2.1	–0.5
11	1.9	–0.2
12	1.6	–0.1
13	1.6	0.2
14	1.6	0.4
15	1.6	0.4
16	1.6	0.2
17	1.7	0.1
18	1.7	–0.1
19	1.8	–0.2
20	1.9	–0.2
21	1.9	–0.2
22	1.9	–0.2
23	1.9	–0.2
24	1.8	–0.2
25	1.7	–0.1
26	1.6	0.0
27	1.4	0.1
28	1.3	0.3
29	1.5	0.4
30	1.5	0.5

DID YOU KNOW?

Tides also occur on the land surface of Earth as well as in the air. That's because the moon's gravity pulls on soil and air just as it pulls on water. However, the tidal effect on land and air is so slight that only very sensitive scientific instruments can detect it.

Conclude and Apply

1. The sketch should show that during the new moon tide, the moon is positioned between the sun and Earth. During the full moon tide, Earth is positioned between the sun and the moon.
2. Moon, sun, and Earth would be at right angles to one another.
3. When the moon is aligned with the sun and Earth, the difference in tides is the greatest.

Concept Development

Theme Connection By studying a table of moon phases and high and low tides for a month, students will see how the interaction of components of the sun-moon-Earth system affects the tides.

Demonstration To model the bulging of ocean water that causes tides, partially fill a basketball with air.

Squeeze the ball between your hands and ask students to identify where on the ball a high tide and low tide are occurring.

Inquiry Question Does the gravitational force of the moon affect the solid part of the Earth as well as the water? Explain your answer. *The moon's gravity does create a slight bulge in the solid parts of Earth, but it has a greater, more noticeable effect on the water.*

Content Background

The moon's gravitational force affects all bodies of water on Earth. However, it is only where large bodies of water meet the land that it is noticeable. The effect on small, inland bodies of water like lakes, ponds, and streams is so small that it is not noticeable.

PROGRAM RESOURCES

Teacher Classroom Resources

Study Guide, page 72

Making Connections: Technology and Society, page 43, Mariculture in the Bay of Fundy

MAKING CONNECTIONS

Math

Ask students to figure out how many high tides will occur in one month. *two times the number of days*

3 Assess

Check for Understanding

1. Using a globe, polystyrene ball, and flashlight in various positions to represent Earth, the moon and the sun, ask students to identify specific regions on the globe that are experiencing high and low tides.
2. Assign questions 1-3 of Check Your Understanding. While discussing the Apply question, ask students to share any shell collecting experiences.

Reteach

Discussion Remind students that the moon has a gravitational pull about one-sixth that of Earth's gravitational pull, so it pulls weakly at Earth. Ask students if this gravitational pull has an effect on Earth even though it is weak. *yes* Then ask what kind of an effect it has. *It causes a bulge in Earth's oceans.* L1

Extension

Have students try to map the movement of a high tide as it moves over the surface of one of Earth's oceans. They can do this with various resources from the library or just experimenting on their own with Earth and moon models. L3

4 Close

Discussion

Have students discuss how people who live near the coastline have adapted to tides. *For example, Fishers rely on tides to determine the best time for fishing or to navigate channels.* The discussion should include how tidal information is obtained, such as from local newspapers and television news reports. Also, if your area has cable television, it may carry the Weather channel, which provides nationwide as well as local reports. L1

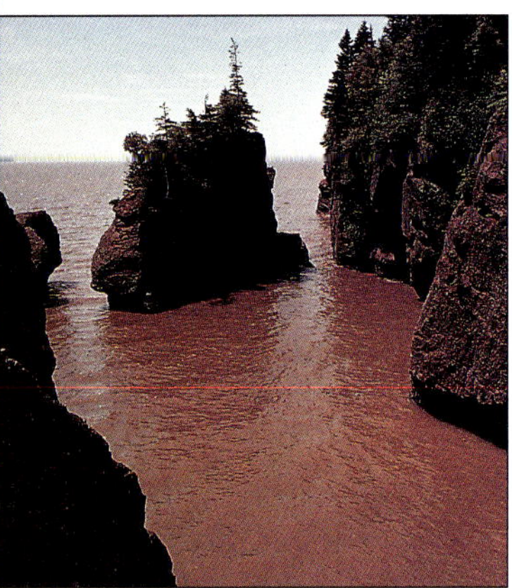

FIGURE 20-16. High tide (pictured at left) and low tide (pictured at right) in the Bay of Fundy in New Brunswick, Canada, are largely the result of the moon's gravitational pull on Earth's oceans.

Recall from Chapter 14 that the sun, the moon, and Earth have gravitational forces acting between them. These gravitational forces actually pull on Earth's oceans. The bulges of seawater that result form the tides.

As you could see from the Find Out, the moon has a great effect on tides. That's because it is much closer to Earth than the sun. It's distance from Earth ranges from about 357,000 kilometers to 407,000 kilometers. That is 400 times closer than the sun is to Earth.

What effect might tides have on people living along an ocean coast? What other people might make use of our knowledge of tides? People who fish rely heavily on tides and tide charts to help them decide what time of day is best for fishing. Fishermen have discovered that the best time to fish is when the ocean tides are about to turn: about one hour before and after both high tide and low tide. The fish seem to feed most at this time.

Other mariners rely on the tide charts to navigate channels. Shallow, rocky passageways must be avoided at low tide.

Now you know why you've studied tides with the moon. Tides aren't caused by the moon's phases, but the highest tides of the month occur when the moon, the sun, and Earth are lined up.

Check Your Understanding

1. Compare and contrast a beach at high tide and a beach at low tide.
2. Diagram the relative positions of the sun, the moon, and Earth during the highest tides of the month.
3. **APPLY:** Suppose you want to search for shells along a beach. How would a knowledge of tides help you in your search?

Answers to Check Your Understanding

1. At high tide, the waves reach far onto the shore and may cover the beach. At low tide, the waves break farther from shore and more beach is exposed.
2. Diagrams should show Earth, the moon, and the sun lined up.
3. Looking for shells at low tide would be easier, after the tide has left them behind and a great deal of beach is exposed.

EXPANDING YOUR VIEW

CONTENTS

A CLOSER LOOK

THE MOON'S SURFACE

Scientists studying the 380 kilograms of moon rock brought back by *Apollo* astronauts have concluded that the moon is about the same age as Earth—about 4.6 billion years old. For the first 1.5 billion years, the moon was struck by thousands of huge, rocky objects called meteorites. Also, during these early years, numerous volcanoes erupted, flooding moon basins with lava.

In Chapter 1, you learned that the moon has large, flat areas called maria (singular mare, pronounced MAR ay). Remember, mare means *sea,* although there is no water on the moon. Scientists believe that maria were formed during the lava flows mentioned earlier.

The low-lying maria have fewer craters than other areas. The indentations in the maria (visible through a telescope) were formed by the impact of interplanetary rocks since the time of the lava flows. The moon's largest mare is called Oceanus Procellarum. Some of the other moon features have been named lacus (lake) and palus (marsh), while edge inlets are called sinus (bays), all despite the fact that—once again—there is no water on the moon.

Other regions, called highlands, are covered with craters. Some of these craters, measuring hundreds of kilometers across, have central peaks. Explosive bombardment of meteorites formed the round craters.

Their peaks, too, were a result of these crashes.

The moon has mountain ranges and smaller rows or peaks known simply as ridges. Some valleys, called rilles, curve and wind great distances across the moon's surface.

YOU TRY IT!

Make a model of a portion of the moon's surface, using photographs from a book on the *Apollo* missions. Write a description of your creation, explaining how the formations occurred.

Going Further Have students work in small groups to simulate the formation of craters by filling a shoebox a third of the way with a very thick mixture of plaster of paris. Have them drop small rocks of different sizes from different heights into the hardening plaster. Have students record the diameter of each rock and the height from which it is dropped. Remove the rocks before plaster craters harden. Explain that when rocky objects from space impact the moon's surface, the objects usually break apart explosively and are ejected from the craters they form. When hardened, have students measure the diameter of the craters. Then have them look for any relationships between the size of the rock, the height it is dropped from, and the size of the crater. COOP LEARN

EXPANDING YOUR VIEW

Using Expanding Your View
Assign one or more of these excursions to expand your students' understanding of the Earth-moon system and how it applies to other sciences and other subjects. You may assign these as individual or small group activities.

A CLOSER LOOK

Purpose Section 20-2 describes the motions of the moon and what we see when we look at the moon with the naked eye. A Closer Look reinforces this section by describing the surface features that are visible through a telescope or in pictures taken during space missions.

Content Background On July 20, 1969, astronauts took their first steps on the surface of the moon. Since then, many interesting facts about the moon's geography have been uncovered. Some of the mountain highlands on the moon reach 8000 meters above the surrounding plains. One large well-defined crater on the moon's surface is called Copernicus after the scientist Nicolaus Copernicus. This crater is approximately 91 kilometers in diameter. Scientists have discovered that the moon experiences seismic activity called moonquakes. Astronauts measured this activity on the moon's surface and found that there are approximately 3000 moonquakes per year. From this moonquake data, scientists know that the moon's crust is thicker than the Earth's. It is about 60 kilometers thick on the side facing Earth and 100 kilometers thick on the side that faces away from Earth.

Teaching Strategies Discuss with your students that the moon is a dry, airless, barren place. Noonday temperatures may be in excess of 127°C. At night the temperature can drop to −173°C. The moon has no atmosphere, so there are no weather conditions. Ask students what type of erosion likely occurs on the moon that could change its surface features.

LIFE SCIENCE CONNECTION

Purpose This Life Science Connection reinforces the discussion of tides in Section 20-3 by describing how tides affect the lives of organisms in an intertidal zone.

Content Background In the intertidal zone, complex food webs occur. Sponges, clams, mussels, and oysters filter algae and other microscopic forms of life from the water. Sea urchins, shrimp, copepods, and small fish feed on floating or attached plants. Many carnivorous animals also use this area for feeding. Large fish, herons, raccoons, and octopus come to feed on the smaller fish and shellfish.

The tides also create tidal marshes which are important breeding grounds for many species of fish. The adult fish lay their eggs in the marsh's quiet, warm waters. The young fish hatch, spend some time in the protective marsh, and then make their way out to the ocean to mature.

Teaching Strategies Try to bring in some seashells for the students to examine. Ask them if they can explain how the shell might help the animal survive in the intertidal zone.

Answers to WHAT DO YOU THINK?

1. The organisms of the intertidal zone have ways to deal with fast moving water such as burrowing in the sand or attaching themselves to objects. They can also deal with changes in the amount of water by closing their shells, burying in the sand, or moving with the tides.
2. Possible answer: Amphibians and reptiles are cold-blooded and can adapt to changes in temperature.

LIFE SCIENCE CONNECTION

LIFE IN AN INTERTIDAL ZONE

As you learned in the chapter, the gravitational pull of the moon causes tides in the oceans of Earth. You know that tides can affect the daily activities of people who fish and other peoples who rely on the sea. But did you also know that tides affect the activities of some of the many organisms that inhabit Earth's oceans?

If you were on a boat in the middle of the ocean, you would not be able to see the effects of tides. However, if you were on shore, you would see the changes in water level due to tides. The area near shore that is alternately covered and uncovered by tides is known as the intertidal zone, and it is home to a variety of organisms.

The continuously changing environment of the intertidal zone presents quite a challenge to the many organisms that live there. One of the toughest tasks for the many tiny animals living in intertidal zones is dealing with the intermittent rush of water and waves. Many of these animals, such as barnacles and mussels, survive by attaching themselves to large rocks. Other animals, such as crabs, lugworms, and shelled mollusks, avoid crashing waves by burrowing into the ground.

Another challenge in an intertidal zone is the dry condition of the zone when the tide is out. Many marine organisms require a moist environment to survive. Seaweeds often attach to cracks and crevices in large beach rocks where water collects. The barnacle, shown here, can close its shell, sealing in moisture and protecting itself from predators and the sun's rays.

Feeding habits of animals are also affected by tides. Barnacles close up during low tide, but as soon as the sea covers them again, their shells open, and out pop their arms, which they use for feeding. Another animal, the limpet, while fixed to one spot during low tide, is known to travel long distances when the tide is in. As the tide goes out, limpets travel back to their original rock homes.

WHAT DO YOU THINK?

The intertidal zone represents one example of how physical factors affect living organisms. How are the organisms of the intertidal zone adapted to their changing environment? Can you think of other animals or plants that are adapted to continuously changing environmental conditions?

Going Further Have students work in groups to develop an Intertidal Corner in your classroom. One group could be responsible for preparing drawings of the various plants and animals living in an intertidal zone. Another group could work with you in setting up a saltwater aquarium for animals such as crabs, starfish, anemones, minnows, and urchins. Your local aquarium shop would be a helpful resource. If a beach is nearby, organize a field trip or ask a third group to be responsible for collecting organisms or shells that represent an intertidal zone. COOP LEARN

SCIENCE AND SOCIETY

SPIN-OFFS FROM THE SPACE PROGRAM

From the beginning of space exploration, some people have wondered why so much time and money have been devoted to the pursuit of knowledge about space. Aren't there more important concerns than learning about space? Wouldn't money be better spent on improving the quality of life on Earth?

The space program has benefited many people right here on Earth. Much of the technology developed for space exploration is adapted and used to make our lives better. These technologies are called spin-offs. Let's look at some of the spin-offs from the United States space program.

Medical science has gained much from space research. Patients with internal bleeding may wear astronaut-type pressure suits that temporarily alter blood flow to promote healing. Heart attack victims benefit from heart monitoring techniques, as pictured here, while NASA's sonar (sound tracing) machines make early detection of heart irregularities possible. Pacemakers, which help to regulate the heartbeats of some heart patients, use tiny batteries first developed for spacecraft.

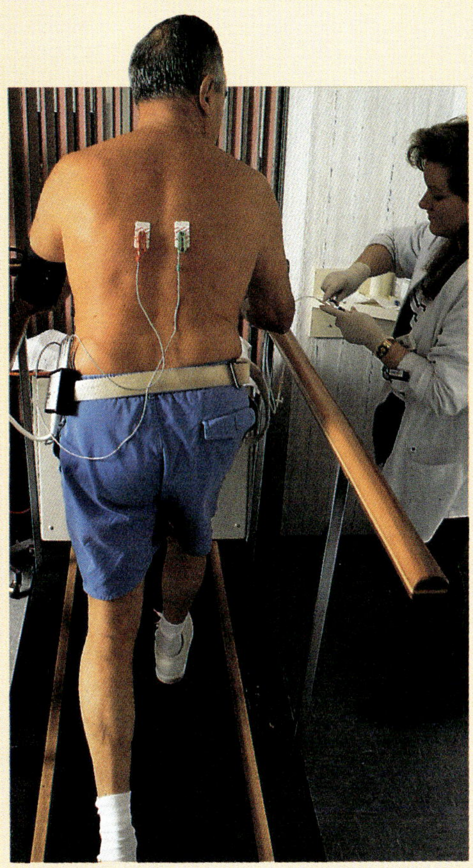

Movable artificial limbs, designed for NASA's robots, are available for use by amputees and victims of paralysis of the legs (paraplegics) or of all four limbs (quadriplegics). Lasers, used as an improved "vision" for spacecraft by NASA, provide an alternative method of performing delicate eye and brain surgery.

Fire fighters have also benefited from space technology. Fire-resistant clothing now worn by many fire fighters, such as the suit shown on p. 622, was first designed to be worn by astronauts. A lightweight breathing apparatus, first designed for use by astronauts, gives fire fighters better visibility and allows them to store more air in their air tanks than did earlier breathing equipment.

SCIENCE AND SOCIETY

Purpose Our knowledge of the Earth-moon system has increased as a result of space exploration. But, as this Science and Society excursion points out, space exploration has also resulted in numerous technologies which make our lives better.

Content Background Artificial satellites as well as other space technology products have improved the lives of people on Earth. Satellites developed and monitored by the space program provide us with important things in our every day lives. Communication satellites allow us to view television, listen to the radio, and talk long distance on the telephone. Weather satellites allow us to track weather patterns and receive advanced warning of storms, tornadoes, and hurricanes. Navigational satellites help planes and ships head in the right directions, safely delivering millions of people annually to their destinations.

Teaching Strategies Discuss the tragic accident involving the space shuttle *Challenger* on January 28, 1986. Seven astronauts were killed trying to learn more about space. Other astronauts have also lost their lives in pursuit of knowledge regarding space. Ask students to express their feelings about the human risks involved in space travel and exploration.

Also discuss with your students the possibilities of developing large space colonies for people to live in as Earth becomes more crowded.

Answers to

WHAT DO YOU THINK?

Have students focus on how large a portion of the population the space program benefits as they determine whether the program is worth it.

New homes and offices are often built with fire-resistant and fire-retardant materials developed through NASA's research. Highway crash barriers have been designed similar to cushions used to protect astronauts from flight turbulence. Antifogging substances created for the visors of space helmets now help keep car windshields and numerous types of protective eye and head gear free from fog.

Many of our clothes are made from fabrics originally created for astronauts. These fabrics provide maximum flexibility and warmth without a lot of bulk. Our digital clocks evolved from NASA's timepieces. We can wear sunglasses that change tint with changes in the light around us. These lenses were first developed for space pioneers.

Even in the kitchen, we can find cookware coated with heat-resistant substances, plastic film and aluminum foil for preserving food, and freeze-dried foods—all originally developed for the space program.

Space laboratories also benefit biologists' study of plant and animal growth. On Earth, all plants and animals are affected by the force of gravity, the changes of day and night, and other Earth forces. Space laboratories allow biologists to study the development of living things that aren't influenced by Earth's various forces.

WHAT DO YOU THINK?

Considering the amount and types of spin-offs from the space program, is all the time and money devoted to the program worth it? Write a few paragraphs giving your opinions.

Going Further Have students work in groups of two or three to research the specific contributions the space program has made to the medical, safety, and building industries. Then ask each group to design a presentation for the class, including how the technique or device was developed, how it was or still is used in space, and how it is used by today's society. Students can utilize drawings, photographs, or slides to help with their presentations.

Students may want to contact:

Johnson Space Center
National Aeronautics and Space Administration
Houston, TX 77058 **COOP LEARN**

TECHNOLOGY CONNECTION

ELECTRICITY FROM TIDES

Half the fun of building a sand castle is watching the tide come in, fill the moat, and then knock the castle down. The same tide you see leveling your sand castle is capable of generating a great amount of energy.

The use of tidal energy can be traced back to the ancient Romans, who built tide mills that ran simple mechanisms for grinding corn and other grains. These mills were so successful that over the next several centuries similar mills were built all along the European coast. Unfortunately, the use of tidal energy was governed by the flow of the tides. A miller's working hours depended on when the tides occurred. With the development of the steam engine in 1698, however, many mills combined steam power with tidal power for a more consistent flow of energy.

Tidal power dams are often built across the mouths of bays. When the tide comes in, the water flows through gates in the dam to the bay. This flow of water moves the engine's turbines, like the blades on a fan, until high tide is reached. Then, gates temporarily close off the bay. When the tide goes out, the gates are opened, which allows water to flow back to the sea. As the water flows out through the doors in the dam, the force of the flow spins the turbines again. The amount of power generated depends upon the range from low to high tide.

The world's first tidal power plant was opened in the mid-1960s at the mouth of the Rance River, on the northern coast of France. Every year it produces 625 million kilowatt hours of electricity.

Canada's Bay of Fundy, located north of the coast of Maine, has the greatest range of tides on Earth (16 meters). The power of the incoming tide at the Bay of Fundy has been calculated to have more power than 8000 freight locomotives or 25 million horses. At high tide, the water is kept in the bay by the force of the incoming tide. Then at low tide, the water slowly returns to the sea.

The Canadian government is building a dam at this site with large gates to let water enter the bay at each high tide. The gates will be closed when the tide is in, and water will be stored behind the dam. As the tide goes out, the receding water will pass over turbines, turning a generator to produce electricity. When complete, the plant will provide relatively low-cost electrical power to cities in Canada and the United States.

YOU TRY IT!

Find out how much tidal power costs consumers compared to how much other types of energy, such as natural gas or coal, cost. Discuss with your class the costs of the different forms of energy, and the advantages and disadvantages of each form.

EXPANDING YOUR VIEW

TECHNOLOGY CONNECTION

Purpose The Technology Connection describes how the phenomenon of tides explained in Section 20-3 can be utilized to provide energy for humans.

Content Background The tidal power plant built on the Rance River, an estuary of the English Channel in Brittany, was completed in 1968 with a dam nearly 2,500 feet long. The dam channels the water into 24 turbines, each capable of generating 10 megawatts, or enough power to light a town of about 40,000 people.

Passamaquoddy Bay, an arm of the Bay of Fundy, has been contemplated as a site for a tidal power plant since the 1920s. The flow of the tide is more than ten times that of the Rance estuary. Plans were drawn to build the dam in the 1930's but the project was too ambitious for its time. Economic support collapsed in 1937, when a Works Project Administration (WPA) plan was blocked by the Congress. After World War II, a joint United States-Canadian commission again attacked the problem. At that time, considerations included the immense cost, possible ecological damage, and the opposition of private interests to a public power program.

Teaching Strategies Show students how moving water can generate energy. Pour water over a wheel attached to an axle to show that this will cause the wheel to turn. Explain to students that, in earlier times, the running water of streams was used to turn water wheels in mills. The turning water wheel caused a rod to turn which caused a heavy stone to grind grain to make flour. Use this to lead into a discussion regarding the use of water today to turn turbines to generate electricity.

Going Further Invite students to work in small groups to study the possible ecological damage caused by the installation of a tidal power plant or dam at the Bay of Fundy or any other suitable site. Students can consider the impact to animals, birds, insects, and plants, as well as to aquatic organisms.

For additional information, students can write to:

Environmental Protection Agency
Public Affairs
401 M Street
Washington, DC 20460

Energy Department
1000 Independence Avenue, SW
Washington, DC 20585 **COOP LEARN**

TEENS IN SCIENCE

Purpose Teens in Science extends Section 20-2, in which eclipses are described. This excursion tells how 14 year-old Natalie Sanchez was inspired by a solar eclipse to investigate a career in astronomy. To that end, she did extensive library research.

Content Background Natalie Sanchez is far from the first to be awestruck by a solar eclipse. A total eclipse of the sun once blacked out the sky over Mesopotamia during a savage battle between Lydians, people from what is now Turkey, and Medes, people from what is now Iran. Terrified by what they took to be an omen, the armies put down their weapons and made peace on the spot. Because solar eclipses are now known to fall at predictable intervals, modern astronomers have pinpointed the day as May 28, 585 B.C.E. The battle is the earliest historical event for which a precise date is known.

The ancient Chinese, Lapps, and Persians believed that an eclipse was caused by a monster devouring the sun or moon. Ancient Mexicans believed eclipses were caused by the sun and moon quarreling.

Teaching Strategies Students can read the selection with a partner, each reading paragraphs in turn. Invite students to then make a picture showing what they think Natalie saw. Remind students to make their illustrations capture the majesty of the sight.

Debate After students read the selection, have them debate whether or not they think there are other solar systems in the universe.

Answers to

WHAT DO YOU THINK?

1. Suggest that students who have not yet overcome an obstacle describe one they might encounter in the future. Remind students that obstacles can be psychological as well as physical.

TEENS *in* SCIENCE

REACHING FOR THE STARS

Have you ever experienced a solar eclipse? If so, you might remember that as the moon passed in front of the sun, darkness fell on Earth—even though the eclipse happened during the day.

Some people describe eclipses as being eerie or strange. But 14-year-old Natalie Sanchez, a freshman at Valley High School in Albuquerque, New Mexico, describes a recent eclipse in a completely different way.

"I was on a field trip with the Math and Engineering Club at school," Natalie said. "We had gone to the observatory to watch the eclipse. The staff had given us really good glasses to protect our eyes. I thought it was the most beautiful thing I have ever seen. As it grew dark, everyone started cheering. But I was very quiet. I was completely in awe. On the bus ride home, I made up my mind that I want to be an astronomer."

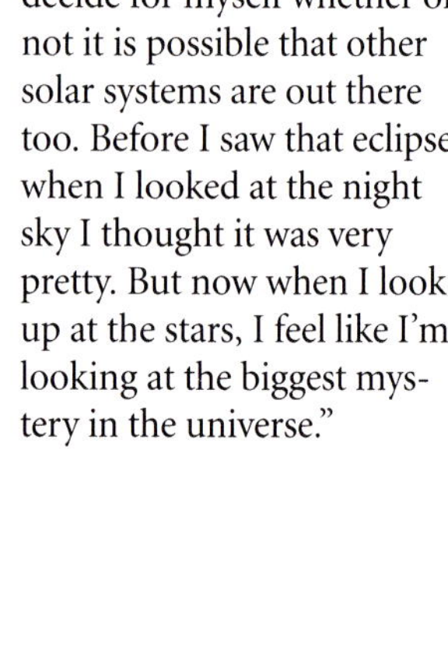

Natalie soon discovered that her school does not offer any in-depth classes about astronomy. But she has not let that stop her from finding out more about her new hobby.

"After school, I spend a lot of time doing research at the library," Natalie explained. "I read everything about astronomy that I can get my hands on—and that's a lot. But the more I read, the more I want to know. Sure, I'm curious about our solar system. But I'm also trying to decide for myself whether or not it is possible that other solar systems are out there too. Before I saw that eclipse, when I looked at the night sky I thought it was very pretty. But now when I look up at the stars, I feel like I'm looking at the biggest mystery in the universe."

WHAT DO YOU THINK?

Observing the eclipse changed the course of Natalie Sanchez's life. Have you ever had an experience that affected your plans for the future?

When Natalie found out that her school didn't offer astronomy classes, she overcame the obstacle by doing her own research in the library. Write a paragraph describing an obstacle that you have overcome.

Going Further During the 20th century, 375 eclipses have or will take place: 228 solar eclipses and 147 lunar eclipses. Divide the class in half. Have one team research the lunar and solar eclipses that have occurred in this century. Which are the most important or notable? Why? Have the other team find out about the eclipses that have yet to occur. Where will the best vantage points be?

For information, students can contact:

American Astronomical Society
211 FitzRandolph Road
Princeton, NH 08540

Hale Observatories
813 Santa Barbara Street
Pasadena, CA 91101

Reviewing Main Ideas

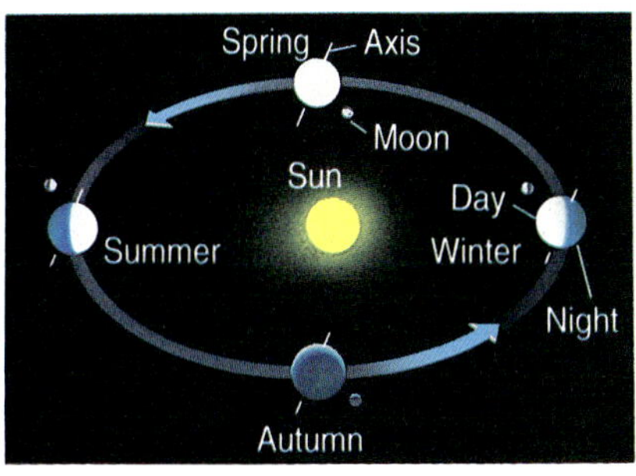

1. The motions and relative positions of Earth, the moon, and the sun are responsible for night and day, the change of seasons, the phases of the moon, eclipses, and tides. Night and day are caused by the rotation of Earth on its axis. The change of seasons is caused by the tilt of Earth as it revolves around the sun.

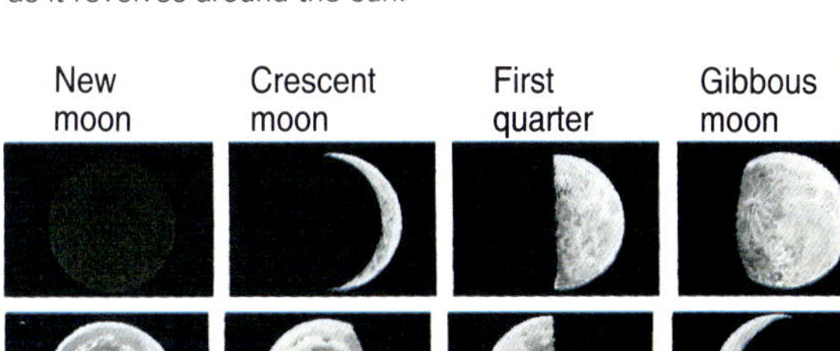

2. The moon rotates once during its month-long revolution around Earth. We see different portions of the moon's lighted side during its revolution.

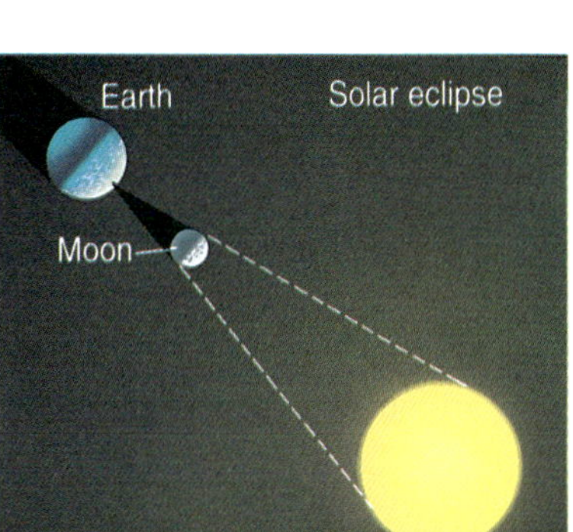

3. During a solar eclipse, the moon passes between the sun and Earth and casts a shadow on Earth. During a lunar eclipse, Earth passes between the sun and moon, casting a curved shadow on the moon.

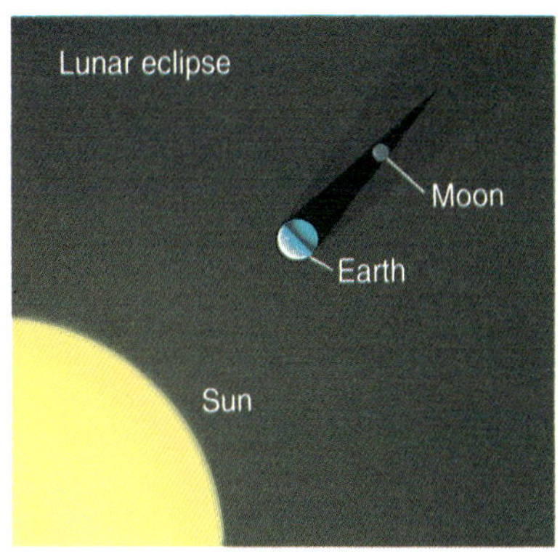

4. Tides are the alternate rise and fall of the surface level of the oceans and are directly related to the gravitational force of the moon and the sun on Earth.

Chapter 20

Reviewing Main Ideas

Have students look at the four diagrams on this page. Direct them to read the statements to review the main ideas of the chapter.

Teaching Strategies

Divide the class into four groups. Assign each group a diagram and one of the accompanying statements. Have each group prepare a presentation for the class by constructing a poster that depicts the statement and writing a paragraph explaining how the event occurs. You may want to provide groups with some of the demonstration materials you used during the teaching of this chapter. Then ask each group to use its poster, paragraph, and the demonstration materials to convey its ideas to the class. Encourage other students to ask the presenting group questions. COOP LEARN

Chapter Review

USING KEY SCIENCE TERMS
Answers

Answers may vary. Possible answers are given below.

1. Equinox and solstice refer to events that occur at regular intervals every year. A lunar eclipse occurs only when the moon, the sun, and Earth are aligned.
2. Equinox is not a type of motion.
3. Tides are affected by the rotation of Earth and the moon: the highest tides of the month occur when the moon, the sun, and Earth are lined up. The fact that Earth is a sphere does not affect the height of tides.
4. Both types of eclipses occur as a result of the revolutions made by Earth and the moon. Rotation has nothing to do with eclipses except that it affects what part of Earth experiences an eclipse.
5. Tides and lunar eclipses are directly related to the position of the moon with relation to the sun and Earth. An equinox is dependent only on the relative positions of the sun and Earth.
6. revolution
7. rotation
8. solstice

UNDERSTANDING IDEAS
Answers

1. b
2. d
3. b
4. a
5. c
6. d
7. b

Chapter Review

USING KEY SCIENCE TERMS

equinox	solar eclipse
lunar eclipse	solstice
revolution	sphere
rotation	tides

For each set of terms below, choose the one term that does not belong and explain why it does not belong.

1. equinox, lunar eclipse, solstice
2. revolution, rotation, equinox
3. sphere, rotation, tides
4. solar eclipse, lunar eclipse, rotation
5. lunar eclipse, tides, equinox

Use one of the terms to complete each sentence.

6. Earth's movement around the sun is called a ____.
7. Earth's spinning on its axis is called ____.
8. In the Northern Hemisphere, the summer ____ occurs on June 21 or 22, when the North Pole is tilted toward the sun.

UNDERSTANDING IDEAS

Choose the best answer to complete each sentence.

1. The shape of Earth is ____.
   - **a.** a perfect sphere
   - **b.** flatter at the poles, slightly bulging at the equator
   - **c.** a round, flat disc
   - **d.** slightly narrower at the equator, bulging at the poles
2. Night and day are caused by ____.
   - **a.** the rotation of the moon
   - **b.** the sun's revolution around Earth
   - **c.** the tilt of Earth's axis
   - **d.** the rotation of Earth
3. The seasons result from ____.
   - **a.** Earth being closer to the sun at times
   - **b.** the tilt of Earth's axis
   - **c.** Earth's rotation
   - **d.** Earth's closeness to the moon
4. At the new moon phase, an observer on Earth ____.
   - **a.** cannot see the moon
   - **b.** sees a round disc
   - **c.** sees half of the moon
   - **d.** sees a crescent
5. The highest tides occur ____.
   - **a.** every day at noon
   - **b.** during an equinox
   - **c.** when Earth, the moon, and the sun are in a line
   - **d.** during a solstice
6. A lunar eclipse occurs when ____.
   - **a.** the sun passes between Earth and the moon
   - **b.** Earth, the moon, and the sun form a right triangle
   - **c.** the moon passes between Earth and the sun
   - **d.** Earth passes between the sun and the moon
7. The moon is a natural satellite of Earth because it ____.
   - **a.** rotates around Earth
   - **b.** revolves around Earth
   - **c.** has a gravitational pull on Earth
   - **d.** appears in different phases to us on

PROGRAM RESOURCES

Teacher Classroom Resources

Review and Assessment, Chapter Review and Chapter Test, pages 81-84

Computer Test Bank, Chapter test

OPTIONS

Cooperative Learning

Consider using Cooperative Learning in the Understanding Ideas, Critical Thinking, Problem Solving, and Connecting Ideas sections of the Chapter Review.

COOP LEARN

c. has a gravitational pull on Earth
d. appears in different phases to us on Earth

CRITICAL THINKING

Use your understanding of the concepts developed in the chapter to answer each of the following questions.

1. Why do the sun and moon appear to move westward in the sky? Include in your answer why the terms *sunrise* and *sunset* are misleading.

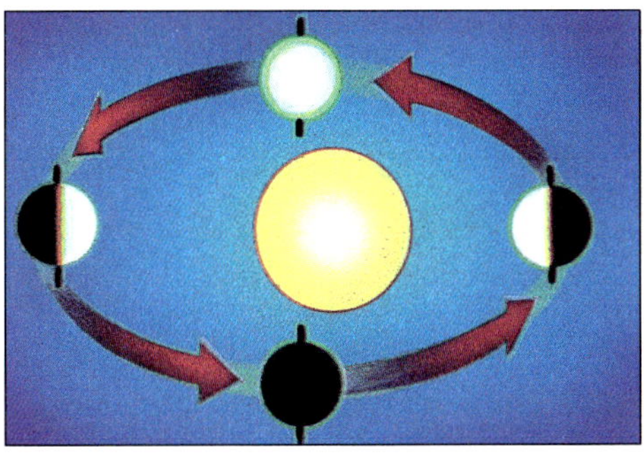

2. Imagine that Earth is not tilted on its axis, as shown in the illustration. What effect would this have on the number of hours of daylight and darkness throughout the year? What effect would this have on seasons?
3. Earth is actually closest to the sun during the Northern Hemisphere's winter. Explain how this can be so.
4. Why do you think this chapter was titled "Earth-Moon System"?

PROBLEM SOLVING

Read the following problem and discuss your answers in a brief paragraph.

You are being given a great opportunity. You and your friends will be spending the coming year traveling throughout the world! Because you don't like cold weather, you will want to arrange a schedule allowing you always to be someplace warm.

Using a globe, describe the route you and your friends would take to make sure that over the course of the year you are always someplace on Earth that is experiencing the summer season. Be specific. Give dates and locations and reasons that you chose the course you did.

CONNECTING IDEAS

Discuss each of the following in a brief paragraph.

1. Explain the moon's revolution around Earth in terms of a satellite's motion. What force holds the moon in its path around Earth? What keeps it from crashing into Earth?
2. Explain why a lunar eclipse can occur only during a full moon phase.
3. If the moon were transparent instead of opaque, what effect would this have on the occurrence of solar eclipses? What if it were translucent?
4. **SCIENCE AND SOCIETY** Summarize the technological benefits we have received from the space exploration program.
5. **A CLOSER LOOK** At which phase of the moon do you think you can best see the maria and craters from Earth?

CRITICAL THINKING

Answers

1. The sun and the moon appear to move westward through the sky because Earth rotates from west to east. Sunrise and sunset are misleading terms because the sun only appears to rise in the east and set in the west as a spot on Earth rotates toward and away from the sun.

2. For a certain spot on Earth, the number of hours of daylight and darkness would be the same every day throughout the year. There would also be no change in seasons because one hemisphere would not be tilted toward the sun at one time and away from it at another.

3. Distance to the sun does not determine whether a hemisphere is experiencing winter. It is the tilt of Earth on its axis that causes seasons.

4. The chapter's title is "The Earth-Moon System" because it describes the relationship between the motions and positions of the moon and Earth.

PROBLEM SOLVING

Answer

Answers will vary but should name locations in the Northern Hemisphere from June to September and in the Southern Hemisphere from December to March. For other months of the year, students should name locations near the equator to make sure they are experiencing warm, summerlike weather.

CONNECTING IDEAS

Answers

1. The moon is the natural satellite of Earth. Acceleration due to gravity holds the moon in its path around Earth. Its horizontal velocity keeps it from crashing into Earth.

2. Only during a full moon phase is Earth in between the moon and the sun. This position is also necessary for a lunar eclipse to occur.

3. If the moon were transparent, a solar eclipse could not occur because sunlight could pass through it. If the moon were translucent, it could only partially block sunlight from Earth.

4. Answers will vary but may include benefits to medicine, fire fighting, construction materials, clothing, kitchen appliances, and food preservatives.

5. These features can be observed whenever a portion of the moon's lighted surface is visible. However, the best time to observe the moon is during first and third quarter.

LOOKING BACK

UNIT 5
WAVE MOTION

THEME DEVELOPMENT

The key themes developed in Unit 5 were energy and interactions and systems. The interaction of the gravity of the sun with that of the moon and Earth, within the Earth-moon system, produce a large-scale, planet-wide ocean wave on Earth called tides. Mechanical waves produced by earthquakes and volcanoes interact with Earth materials at the surface causing change in many Earth systems. Faults and earthquake or volcanic damage may result. The energy of waves is shown in examples such as water waves, and earthquakes. This relationship between energy and waves is developed using examples of sound waves and earthquake waves.

Connections to Other Units

In Unit 5, Earth movement and the movement of Earth materials during earthquakes and volcanoes was connected to the general processes of motion described in Unit 4. In addition to this, movement of the moon as part of the Earth-moon system and the effect of this motion on Earth's oceans was explained. Movement of Earth's oceans as large waves called tides is caused by the interaction of the motions of Earth, the moon, and the sun. Motions near Earth as described in Unit 4 were used as a basis for explaining the causes of tides on Earth.

Connecting Ideas

Answers

1. No, the water is not rigid. If the water particles were moved to one side, they would not rebound and thus a transverse wave would not be generated. The waves would stop.

2. As the waves move through Earth's surface and the buildings at the surface, the particles of the building try to move in different directions. Particles of rock move upward and downward with some forward and backward motion similar to waves in water.

Exploring Further

The purpose of this activity is to help students clear up any misconceptions they may have about the cause of eclipses. It will show them that eclipses are caused by the shadow of one object, Earth or the moon, falling on the other object. Students should demonstrate that solar eclipses occur when the moon passes directly between Earth and the sun. The moon's shadow falls on Earth's surface. They should also demonstrate that lunar eclipses occur when Earth is directly between the sun and the moon. The moon is passing through Earth's shadow.

LOOKING BACK

UNIT 5 WAVE MOTION

CONTENTS

UNIT FOCUS

In this unit, you investigated mechanical waves and found that they may be longitudinal, depending on how particles within a wave move.

You also learned that movements of Earth and the moon cause tides, moon phases, and lunar and solar eclipses to occur. In addition to this, you learned how humans are affected by the motion caused by earthquakes and volcanoes.

Try the exercises and activity that follow—they will challenge you to use and apply some of the ideas you learned in this unit.

CONNECTING IDEAS

1. Do you think that a transverse wave can pass through water? When you send a transverse wave through rope, the particles of rope move side to side. Would water particles move side to side to allow a transverse wave to pass? What do you think would happen to transverse waves generated by earthquakes when they encountered liquid rock material inside Earth?
2. How do waves at Earth's surface cause buildings to crumble during an earthquake? In what way are these waves similar to waves generated in water?

EXPLORING FURTHER

Design and construct a moving model that demonstrates the cause of eclipses. Demonstrate it for the class.

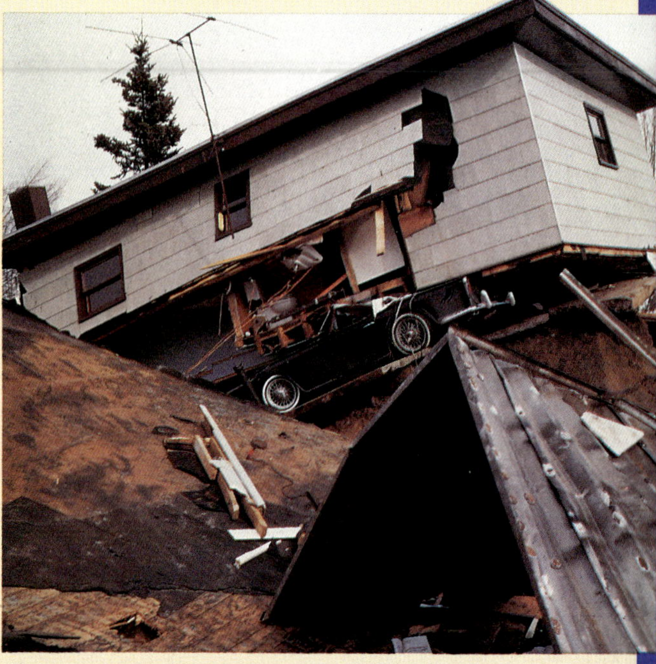

Appendices
Table of Contents

APPENDICES 629

Appendix A

INTERNATIONAL SYSTEM OF UNITS

The International System (SI) of Measurement is accepted as the standard for measurement throughout most of the world. Three base units in SI are the meter, kilogram, and second. Frequently used SI units are listed below.

TABLE A-1

FREQUENTLY USED SI UNITS	
LENGTH	1 millimeter (mm) = 1000 micrometers (µm) 1 centimeter (cm) = 10 millimeters (mm) 1 meter (m) = 100 centimeters (cm) 1 kilometer (km) = 1000 meters (m) 1 light-year = 9,460,000,000,000 kilometers (km)
AREA	1 square meter (m^2) = 10,000 square centimeters (cm^2) 1 square kilometer (km^2) = 1,000,000 square meters (m^2)
VOLUME	1 milliliter (mL) = 1 cubic centimeter (cm^3) 1 liter (L) = 1000 milliliters (mL)
MASS	1 gram (g) = 1000 milligrams (mg) 1 kilogram (kg) = 1000 grams (g) 1 metric ton = 1000 kilograms (kg)
TIME	1 s = 1 second

Temperature measurements in SI are often made in degrees Celsius. Celsius temperature is a supplementary unit derived from the base unit kelvin. The Celsius scale (°C) has 100 equal graduations between the freezing temperature (0°C) and the boiling temperature of water (100°C). The following relationship exists between the Celsius and kelvin temperature scales:

$$K = °C + 273$$

Several other supplementary SI units are listed below.

TABLE A-2

SUPPLEMENTARY SI UNITS			
MEASUREMENT	**UNIT**	**SYMBOL**	**EXPRESSED IN BASE UNITS**
Energy	Joule	J	$kg \bullet m^2/s^2$ ($N \bullet m$)
Force	Newton	N	$kg \bullet m/s^2$
Power	Watt	W	$kg \bullet m^2/s^3$ (J/s)
Pressure	Pascal	Pa	$kg/m \bullet s^2$ (N/m^2)

Appendix B

TABLE B-1

SI/METRIC TO ENGLISH CONVERSIONS			
	WHEN YOU WANT TO CONVERT:	**MULTIPLY BY:**	**TO FIND:**
LENGTH	inches	2.54	centimeters
	centimeters	0.39	inches
	feet	0.30	meters
	meters	3.28	feet
	yards	0.91	meters
	meters	1.09	yards
	miles	1.61	kilometers
	kilometers	0.62	miles
MASS AND WEIGHT*	ounces	28.41	grams
	grams	0.04	ounces
	pounds	0.45	kilograms
	kilograms	2.2	pounds
	tons	0.91	tonnes (metric tons)
	tonnes (metric tons)	1.10	tons
	pounds	4.45	newtons
	newtons	0.23	pounds
VOLUME	cubic inches	16.39	cubic centimeters
	cubic centimeters	0.06	cubic inches
	cubic feet	0.02	cubic meters
	cubic meters	35.3	cubic feet
	liters	1.06	quarts
	liters	0.26	gallons
	gallons	3.78	liters
AREA	square inches	6.45	square centimeters
	square centimeters	0.16	square inches
	square feet	0.09	square meters
	square meters	10.76	square feet
	square miles	2.59	square kilometers
	square kilometers	0.39	square miles
	hectares	2.47	acres
	acres	0.40	hectares
TEMPERATURE	Fahrenheit	5/9 (°F – 32)	Celsius
	Celsius	9/5 °C + 32	Fahrenheit

*Weight as measured in standard Earth gravity

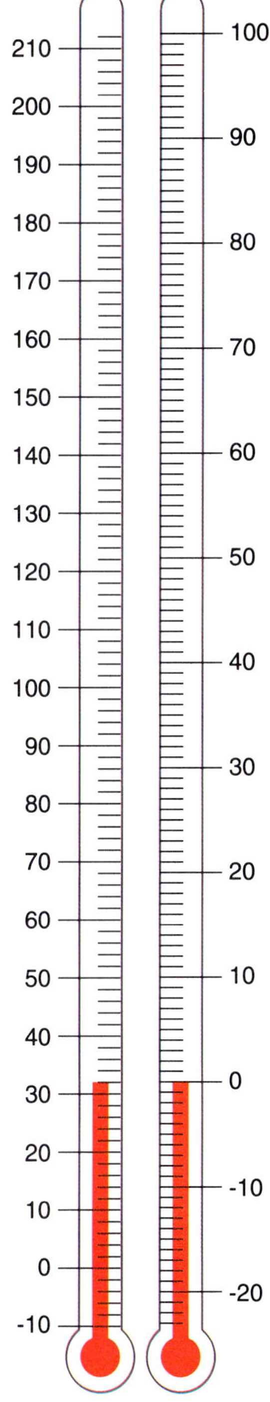

Appendix C

SAFETY IN THE SCIENCE CLASSROOM

1. Always obtain your teacher's permission to begin an investigation.
2. Study the procedure. If you have questions, ask your teacher. Understand any safety symbols shown on the page.
3. Use the safety equipment provided for you. Goggles and a safety apron should be worn when any investigation calls for using chemicals.
4. Always slant test tubes away from yourself and others when heating them.
5. Never eat or drink in the lab, and never use lab glassware as food or drink containers. Never inhale chemicals. Do not taste any substances or draw any material into a tube with your mouth.
6. If you spill any chemical, wash it off immediately with water. Report the spill immediately to your teacher.
7. Know the location and proper use of the fire extinguisher, safety shower, fire blanket, first aid kit, and fire alarm.
8. Keep materials away from flames. Tie back hair and loose clothing.
9. If a fire should break out in the classroom, or if your clothing should catch fire, smother it with the fire blanket or a coat, or get under a safety shower. **NEVER RUN.**
10. Report any accident or injury, no matter how small, to your teacher.

Follow these procedures as you clean up your work area.

1. Turn off the water and gas. Disconnect electrical devices.
2. Return all materials to their proper places.
3. Dispose of chemicals and other materials as directed by your teacher. Place broken glass and solid substances in the proper containers. Never discard materials in the sink.
4. Clean your work area.
5. Wash your hands thoroughly after working in the laboratory.

TABLE C-1

FIRST AID	
INJURY	**SAFE RESPONSE**
Burns	Apply cold water. Call your teacher immediately.
Cuts and bruises	Stop any bleeding by applying direct pressure. Cover cuts with a clean dressing. Apply cold compresses to bruises. Call your teacher immediately.
Fainting	Leave the person lying down. Loosen any tight clothing and keep crowds away. Call your teacher immediately.
Foreign matter in eye	Flush with plenty of water. Use eyewash bottle or fountain.
Poisoning	Note the suspected poisoning agent and call your teacher immediately.
Any spills on skin	Flush with large amounts of water or use safety shower. Call your teacher immediately.

Appendix D

SAFETY SYMBOLS

TABLE D-1

	**DISPOSAL ALERT** This symbol appears when care must be taken to dispose of materials properly.		**ANIMAL SAFETY** This symbol appears whenever live animals are studied and the safety of the animals and the students must be ensured.
	**BIOLOGICAL HAZARD** This symbol appears when there is danger involving bacteria, fungi, or protists.		**RADIOACTIVE SAFETY** This symbol appears when radioactive materials are used.
	**OPEN FLAME ALERT** This symbol appears when use of an open flame could cause a fire or an explosion.		**CLOTHING PROTECTION SAFETY** This symbol appears when substances used could stain or burn clothing.
	**THERMAL SAFETY** This symbol appears as a reminder to use caution when handling hot objects.		**FIRE SAFETY** This symbol appears when care should be taken around open flames.
	**SHARP OBJECT SAFETY** This symbol appears when a danger of cuts or punctures caused by the use of sharp objects exists.		**EXPLOSION SAFETY** This symbol appears when the misuse of chemicals could cause an explosion.
	**FUME SAFETY** This symbol appears when chemicals or chemical reactions could cause dangerous fumes.		**EYE SAFETY** This symbol appears when a danger to the eyes exists. Safety goggles should be worn when this symbol appears.
	**ELECTRICAL SAFETY** This symbol appears when care should be taken when using electrical equipment.		**POISON SAFETY** This symbol appears when poisonous substances are used.
	**PLANT SAFETY** This symbol appears when poisonous plants or plants with thorns are handled.		**CHEMICAL SAFETY** This symbol appears when chemicals used can cause burns or are poisonous if absorbed through the skin.

Appendix E

CLASSIFICATION OF PLANTS AND ANIMALS

PLANT KINGDOM

Spore Plants

Division Bryophyta: nonvascular plants that reproduce by spores produced in capsules; many-celled; green; grow in moist land environments; mosses and liverworts

Liverwort

Division Lycophyta: many-celled vascular plants; spores produced in cones; live on land; club mosses

Division Sphenophyta: vascular plants with ribbed and jointed stems; scalelike leaves; spores produced in cones; horsetails

Division Pterophyta: vascular plants with feathery leaves called fronds; spores produced in clusters of sporangia called sori; live on land or in water; ferns

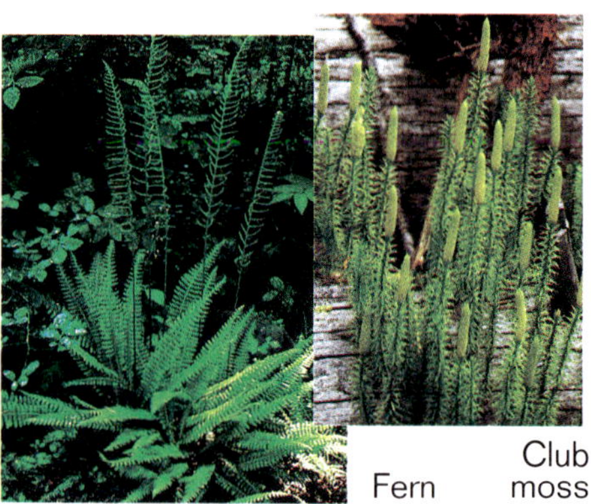

Fern Club moss

Seed Plants

Division Ginkgophyta: deciduous gymnosperms; only one living species called the maiden hair tree; fan-shaped leaves with branching veins; reproduces with seeds; ginkgos

Division Cycadophyta: palmlike gymnosperms; large compound leaves; produce seeds in cones; cycads

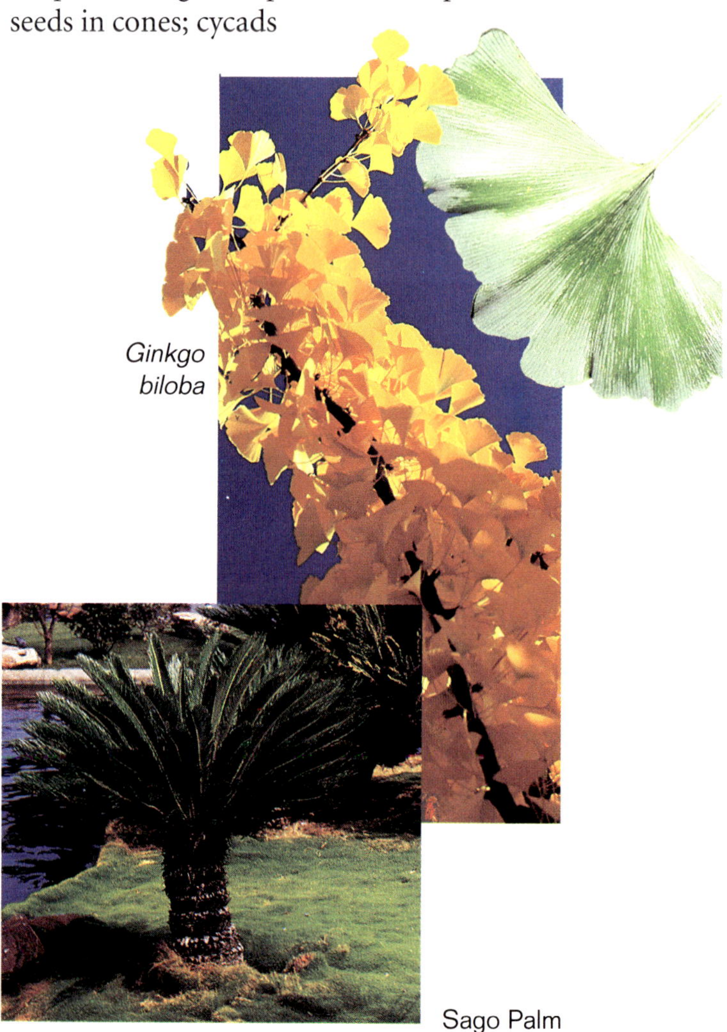

Ginkgo biloba

Sago Palm

Division Coniferophyta: deciduous or evergreen gymnosperms; trees or shrubs; needlelike or scalelike leaves; seeds produced in cones; conifers

Slash Pine Cones

Pine forest, North Yukon, Canada

Division Gnetophyta: shrubs or woody vines; seeds produced in cones; division contains only three genera; gnetum

Welwitchia mirabilis

Cranberries and blueberries

Purple Cornflower

Oranges and blossoms

Division Anthophyta: dominant group of plants; ovules protected at fertilization by an ovary; sperm carried to ovules by pollen tube; produce flowers and seeds in fruits; flowering plants

Blue Columbine

Blind Prickly Pear

ANIMAL KINGDOM

Phylum Porifera: aquatic organisms that lack true tissues and organs; asymmetrical and sessile; sponges

Phylum Cnidaria: radially symmetrical organisms with a digestive cavity with one opening; most have tentacles armed with stinging cells; live in aquatic environments singly or in colonies; includes jellyfish, corals, hydra, and sea anemones

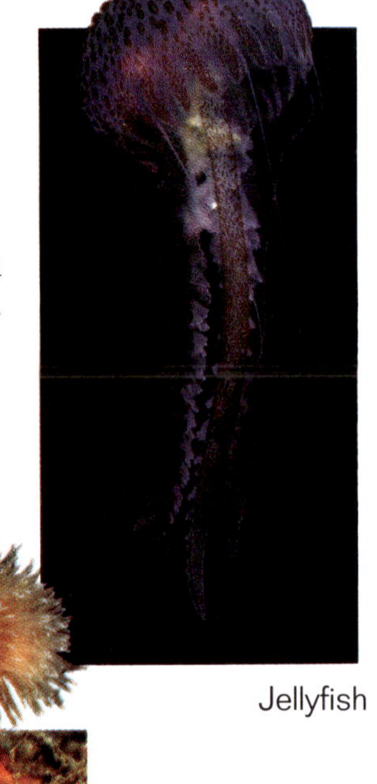

Jellyfish

Frilled Anemone

Phylum Platyhelminthes: bilaterally symmetrical worms with flattened bodies; digestive system has one opening; parasitic and free-living species; flatworms

Flatworm

Phylum Nematoda: round bilaterally symmetrical body; digestive system with two openings; some free-living forms but mostly parasitic; roundworms

Phylum Mollusca: soft-bodied animals, many with a hard shell; a mantle covers the soft body; aquatic and terrestrial species; includes clams, snails, squid, and octopuses

Snail

Spanish Shawl Nudibranch

Phylum Annelida: bilaterally symmetrical worms with round segmented bodies; terrestrial and aquatic species; well-developed body systems; includes earthworms, leeches, and marine polychaetes

Christmas Tree worm

Phylum Arthropoda: very large phylum of organisms that have segmented bodies with pairs of jointed appendages, and a hard exoskeleton; terrestrial and aquatic species; includes insects, crustaceans, spiders, and horseshoe crabs

Swallowtail butterfly

Sally Light-foot crab

Jumping spider

Seahorse

Toucan

Phylum Chordata: organisms with internal skeletons and specialized body systems; all at some time have a notochord, dorsal nerve cord, gill slits, and a tail; include fish, amphibians, reptiles, birds, and mammals

Phylum Echinodermata: saltwater organisms with spiny or leathery skin; water-vascular system with tube feet; radial symmetry; includes starfish, sand dollars, and sea urchins

Brittle stars

Peninsula turtles

Mare and foal

Appendix F

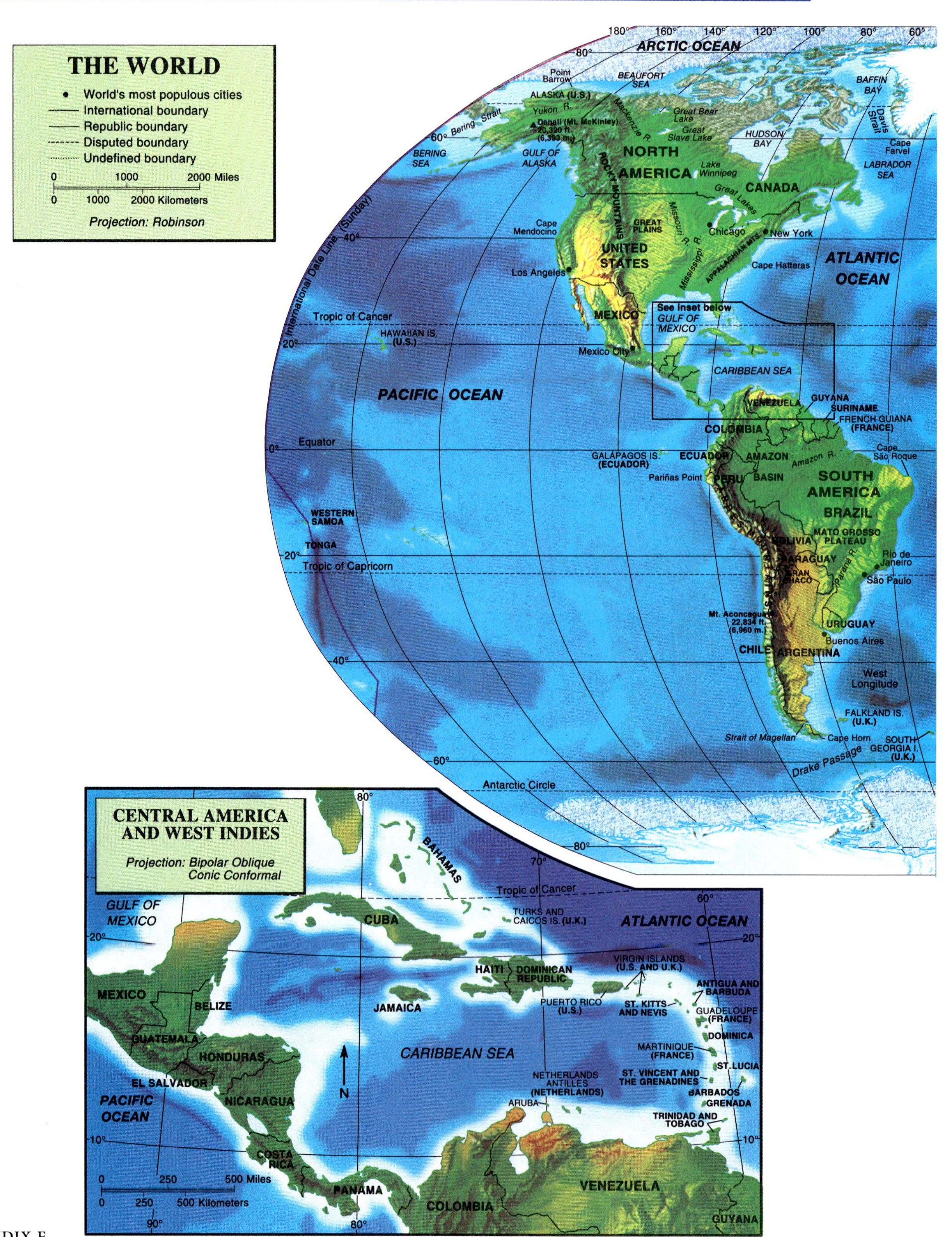
THE WORLD
World's most populous cities
International boundary
Republic boundary
Disputed boundary
Undefined boundary
0 1000 2000 Miles
0 1000 2000 Kilometers
Projection: Robinson
ARCTIC OCEAN
BEAUFORT SEA
BAFFIN BAY
Point Barrow
ALASKA (U.S.)
Bering Strait
Yukon R.
Denali (Mt. McKinley) 20,320 ft. (6,193 m.)
Great Bear Lake
Great Slave Lake
Mackenzie R.
HUDSON BAY
Davis Strait
Cape Farvel
BERING SEA
GULF OF ALASKA
NORTH AMERICA
ROCKY MOUNTAINS
Lake Winnipeg
LABRADOR SEA
CANADA
Great Lakes
Cape Mendocino
GREAT PLAINS
Missouri R.
Chicago
New York
UNITED STATES
APPALACHIAN MTS.
Mississippi R.
Los Angeles
Cape Hatteras
ATLANTIC OCEAN
International Date Line (Sunday)
See inset below
GULF OF MEXICO
MEXICO
Tropic of Cancer
HAWAIIAN IS. (U.S.)
Mexico City
CARIBBEAN SEA
PACIFIC OCEAN
VENEZUELA
GUYANA
SURINAME
FRENCH GUIANA (FRANCE)
COLOMBIA
Equator
GALÁPAGOS IS. (ECUADOR)
ECUADOR
AMAZON BASIN
Amazon R.
Cape São Roque
Pariñas Point
PERU
SOUTH AMERICA
BRAZIL
WESTERN SAMOA
MATO GROSSO PLATEAU
BOLIVIA
TONGA
PARAGUAY
Tropic of Capricorn
Rio de Janeiro
São Paulo
Mt. Aconcagua 22,834 ft. (6,960 m.)
URUGUAY
Buenos Aires
CHILE
ARGENTINA
West Longitude
FALKLAND IS. (U.K.)
Strait of Magellan
Cape Horn
SOUTH GEORGIA I. (U.K.)
Drake Passage
Antarctic Circle
CENTRAL AMERICA AND WEST INDIES
Projection: Bipolar Oblique Conic Conformal
BAHAMAS
Tropic of Cancer
GULF OF MEXICO
CUBA
TURKS AND CAICOS IS. (U.K.)
ATLANTIC OCEAN
VIRGIN ISLANDS (U.S. AND U.K.)
HAITI
DOMINICAN REPUBLIC
ANTIGUA AND BARBUDA
MEXICO
BELIZE
JAMAICA
PUERTO RICO (U.S.)
ST. KITTS AND NEVIS
GUADELOUPE (FRANCE)
DOMINICA
GUATEMALA
MARTINIQUE (FRANCE)
HONDURAS
CARIBBEAN SEA
ST. LUCIA
EL SALVADOR
NETHERLANDS ANTILLES (NETHERLANDS)
ST. VINCENT AND THE GRENADINES
PACIFIC OCEAN
NICARAGUA
N
BARBADOS
GRENADA
ARUBA
TRINIDAD AND TOBAGO
COSTA RICA
0 250 500 Miles
0 250 500 Kilometers
PANAMA
VENEZUELA
COLOMBIA
GUYANA

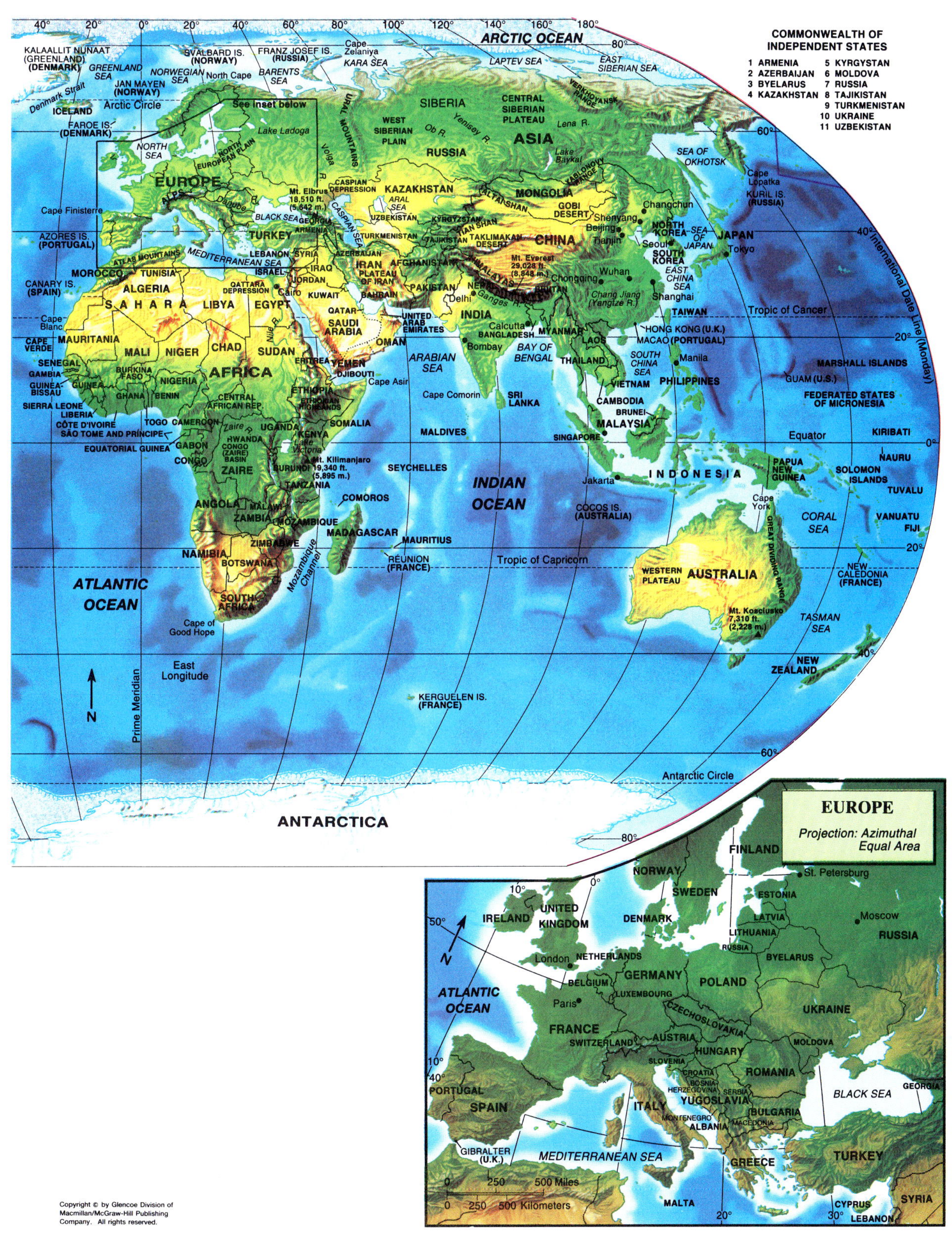
ARCTIC OCEAN
COMMONWEALTH OF INDEPENDENT STATES
1 ARMENIA
2 AZERBAIJAN
3 BYELARUS
4 KAZAKHSTAN
5 KYRGYSTAN
6 MOLDOVA
7 RUSSIA
8 TAJIKISTAN
9 TURKMENISTAN
10 UKRAINE
11 UZBEKISTAN
SIBERIA
ASIA
EUROPE
AFRICA
INDIAN OCEAN
ATLANTIC OCEAN
AUSTRALIA
ANTARCTICA
Arctic Circle
Tropic of Cancer
Equator
Tropic of Capricorn
Antarctic Circle
International Date Line (Monday)
Prime Meridian
East Longitude
EUROPE
Projection: Azimuthal Equal Area
0 250 500 Miles
0 250 500 Kilometers
639

Juan de Fuca Strait
Puget Sound
Seattle
Tacoma
Olympia
F.D. Roosevelt Lake
COLUMBIA PLATEAU
Spokane
Mt. Rainier 14,410 ft. (4,392 m.)
WASHINGTON
Portland
Columbia River
Salem
Corvallis
Eugene
Mt. Hood 11,235 ft. (3,424 m.)
CASCADE
COAST RANGES
OREGON
Medford
Mt. Shasta 14,162 ft. (4,316 m.)
Goose Lake
Eureka
Cape Mendocino
Sacramento River
Pyramid Lake
Reno
Lake Tahoe
Carson City
Sacramento
SIERRA NEVADA
San Francisco
Oakland
Stockton
San Jose
San Joaquin
Fresno
Mt. Whitney 14,494 ft. (4,418 m.)
Mono Lake
CALIFORNIA
Bakersfield
Point Conception
MOJAVE DESERT
Los Angeles
San Bernardino
Riverside
Long Beach
Salton Sea
San Diego
PACIFIC OCEAN
GREAT BASIN
NEVADA
Death Valley −282 ft. (−86 m.)
Las Vegas
Lake Mead
Colorado River
Yuma
Pend Oreille Lake
Flathead Lake
Lewiston
BITTERROOT RANGE
ROCKY MOUNTAINS
Missouri River
Great Falls
Helena
Butte
Fort Peck Lake
MONTANA
Yellowstone R.
Billings
BIGHORN MTS.
IDAHO
Borah Peak 12,662 ft. (3,859 m.)
Boise
Grand Teton Peak 13,770 ft. (4,197 m.)
Idaho Falls
Snake River
Twin Falls
Pocatello
Great Salt Lake
GREAT SALT LAKE DESERT
Ogden
Salt Lake City
Orem
Provo
Utah Lake
WASATCH RANGE
UTAH
Green River
Lake Powell
COLORADO PLATEAU
PAINTED DESERT
Grand Canyon
Flagstaff
ARIZONA
Glendale
Phoenix
Mesa
Gila River
Tucson
GULF OF CALIFORNIA
WYOMING
Casper
Powder River
Continental Divide
Rock Springs
Laramie
Cheyenne
Fort Collins
Boulder
Denver
Mt. Elbert 14,433 ft. (4,399 m.)
Colorado Springs
Pueblo
COLORADO
Arkansas River
SANGRE DE CRISTO
Santa Fe
Albuquerque
Rio Grande
NEW MEXICO
Roswell
Las Cruces
El Paso
Minot
Lake Sakakawea
Grand Forks
NORTH DAKOTA
Bismarck
Fargo
Lake Oahe
Aberdeen
SOUTH DAKOTA
Pierre
BLACK HILLS
Rapid City
Sioux Falls
GREAT PLAINS
NEBRASKA
North Platte River
North Platte
Grand Island
South Platte River
Platte
Lincoln
Republican River
KANSAS
Salina
Hutchinson
Wichita
Enid
OKLAHOMA
Canadian River
Amarillo
Oklahoma City
Norman
Lawton
Red River
Lake Texoma
LLANO ESTACADO
Lubbock
Brazos River
Dallas
Fort Worth
TEXAS
Pecos River
EDWARDS PLATEAU
Austin
San Antonio
Rio Grande
Corpus Christi
Brownsville
MEXICO
CANADA
HAWAII
PACIFIC OCEAN
Kauai Channel
Honolulu
Kailua
Alenuihaha Channel
Mauna Kea 13,796 ft. (4,205 m.)
Hilo
0 100 Miles
0 100 Kilometers
ALASKA
Pt. Barrow
BROOKS RANGE
Arctic Circle
U.S.S.R.
Bering Strait
SEWARD PEN.
Yukon River
Fairbanks
Tanana
Denali (Mt. McKinley) 20,320 ft. (6,193 m.)
ALASKA RANGE
Bethel
Anchorage
Iliamna Lake
BERING SEA
BRISTOL BAY
ALASKA PENINSULA
Shelikof Str.
Kodiak
GULF OF ALASKA
Juneau
Sitka
ALEUTIAN ISLANDS
0 250 500 Miles
0 250 500 Kilometers
640 APPENDIX G

Appendix G

UNITED STATES
National capital
State capital
Major city
Other city
International boundary
State boundary
0 100 200 Miles
0 100 200 Kilometers
Projection: Albers Equal Area
ATLANTIC OCEAN
GULF OF MEXICO
Strait of Florida
THE BAHAMAS
Lake of the Woods
Red Lake
Lake Superior
Lake Michigan
Lake Huron
Lake Erie
Lake Ontario
St. Lawrence
Moosehead Lake
Lake Champlain
DELAWARE BAY
CHESAPEAKE BAY
Cape Cod
Cape Hatteras
Cape Canaveral
Cape Sable
Lake Okeechobee
Lake Pontchartrain
Sam Rayburn Reservoir
Toledo Bend Res.
Harry S. Truman Res.
R.S. Kerr Res.
Lake Eufaula
MINNESOTA
WISCONSIN
MICHIGAN
IOWA
ILLINOIS
INDIANA
OHIO
PENNSYLVANIA
NEW YORK
VT.
N.H.
MAINE
MASS.
R.I.
CONN.
N.J.
MD.
DEL.
D.C.
WEST VIRGINIA
VIRGINIA
KENTUCKY
TENNESSEE
NORTH CAROLINA
SOUTH CAROLINA
GEORGIA
FLORIDA
ALABAMA
MISSISSIPPI
LOUISIANA
ARKANSAS
MISSOURI
CENTRAL LOWLAND
COASTAL PLAIN
OZARK PLATEAU
CUMBERLAND PLATEAU
APPALACHIAN MOUNTAINS
ADIRONDACK MTS.
Mt. Washington 6,288 ft. (1,917 m.)
Mt. Mitchell 6,684 ft. (2,037 m.)
Mississippi River
Ohio River
Wabash R.
Cumberland River
Tennessee River
Susquehanna River
Hudson
Roanoke River
Chattahoochee R.
Alabama R.
Duluth
Minneapolis
St. Paul
Rochester
Green Bay
Appleton
Milwaukee
Madison
Racine
Rockford
Chicago
Aurora
Joliet
Gary
Hammond
South Bend
Grand Rapids
Lansing
Flint
Detroit
Ann Arbor
Toledo
Fort Wayne
Dubuque
Cedar Rapids
Davenport
Des Moines
Sioux City
Omaha
Council Bluffs
Peoria
Springfield
Decatur
Muncie
Indianapolis
Dayton
Columbus
Cincinnati
Cleveland
Akron
Canton
Youngstown
Erie
Buffalo
Niagara Falls
Rochester
Syracuse
Utica
Binghamton
Albany
Burlington
Montpelier
Concord
Manchester
Augusta
Bangor
Lewiston
Portland
Boston
Worcester
Springfield
Providence
Hartford
New Haven
Yonkers
New York
Newark
Allentown
Trenton
Philadelphia
Camden
Wilmington
Dover
Harrisburg
Pittsburgh
Wheeling
Parkersburg
Baltimore
Annapolis
Washington
Arlington
Charleston
Huntington
Richmond
Newport News
Norfolk
Roanoke
Greensboro
Winston-Salem
Durham
Raleigh
Charlotte
Spartanburg
Greenville
Columbia
Charleston
Augusta
Savannah
Atlanta
Macon
Columbus
Albany
Frankfort
Lexington
Louisville
Owensboro
Evansville
Knoxville
Nashville
Chattanooga
Memphis
Huntsville
Birmingham
Tuscaloosa
Montgomery
Mobile
Pensacola
Tallahassee
Jacksonville
Orlando
Tampa
St. Petersburg
Palm Beach
Miami Beach
Miami
Key West
Kansas City
Topeka
Lawrence
Kansas City
Independence
Jefferson City
St. Louis
East St. Louis
Springfield
Tulsa
Fort Smith
North Little Rock
Little Rock
Hot Springs
Pine Bluff
Greenville
Meridian
Jackson
Hattiesburg
Biloxi
Shreveport
Baton Rouge
Lafayette
Lake Charles
New Orleans
Houston
45°
40°
35°
30°
25°
70°
75°
80°
85°
90°
95°
N
APPENDIX G 641

Appendix H

TOPOGRAPHIC MAP SYMBOLS

Primary highway, hard surface

Secondary highway, hard surface

Light-duty road, hard or improved surface

Unimproved road

Railroad: single track and multiple track

Railroads in juxtaposition

Buildings

School, church, and cemetery — cem

Buildings (barn, warehouse, etc.)

Wells other than water (labeled as to type) — o oil o gas

Tanks: oil, water, etc. (labeled only if water) — water

Located or landmark object; windmill

Open pit, mine, or quarry; prospect

Marsh (swamp)

Wooded marsh

Woods or brushwood

Vineyard

Land subject to controlled inundation

Submerged marsh

Mangrove

Orchard

Scrub

Urban area

Spot elevation — ×7369

Water elevation — 670

Index contour

Supplementary contour

Intermediate contour

Depression contours

Boundaries: National

State

County, parish, municipio

Civil township, precinct, town, barrio

Incorporated city, village, town, hamlet

Reservation, National or State

Small park, cemetery, airport, etc.

Land grant

Township or range line, United States land survey

Township or range line, approximate location

Perennial streams

Elevated aqueduct

Water well and spring

Small rapids

Large rapids

Intermittent lake

Intermittent streams

Aqueduct tunnel

Glacier

Small falls

Large falls

Dry lake bed

Appendix I

SOLAR SYSTEM INFORMATION

Planet	Mercury	Venus	Earth	Mars	Jupiter	Saturn	Uranus	Neptune	Pluto
Diameter (km)	4878	12104	12756	6794	142796	120660	51118	49528	2290
Diameter (E = 1.0)*	0.38	0.95	1.00	0.53	11.19	9.46	4.01	3.88	0.18
Mass (E = 1.0)*	0.06	0.82	1.00	0.11	317.83	95.15	14.54	17.23	0.002
Density (g/cm^3)	5.42	5.24	5.50	3.94	1.31	0.70	1.30	1.66	2.03
Period of Rotation days / hours / minutes; R = retrograde	58 / 15 / 28	243 / 00 / 14_R	00 / 23 / 56	00 / 24 / 37	00 / 09 / 55	00 / 10 / 39	00 / 17 / 14_R	00 / 16 / 03	06 / 09 / 17
Surface gravity (E = 1.0)*	0.38	0.90	1.00	0.38	2.53	1.07	0.92	1.12	0.06
Average distance to sun (AU)	0.387	0.723	1.000	1.524	5.203	9.529	19.191	30.061	39.529
Period of revolution	87.97d	224.70d	365.26d	686.98d	11.86y	29.46y	84.04y	164.79y	248.53y
Eccentricity of orbit	0.206	0.007	0.017	0.093	0.048	0.056	0.046	0.010	0.248
Average orbital speed (km/s)	47.89	35.03	29.79	24.13	13.06	9.64	6.81	5.43	4.74
Number of known satellites	0	0	1	2	16	18	15	8	1
Known rings	0	0	0	0	1	thou-sands	11	4	0

*Earth = 1.0

Appendix J

STAR CHARTS

Shown here are star charts for viewing stars in the Northern Hemisphere during the four different seasons. These charts are drawn from the night sky at about 35° north latitude, but they can be used for most locations in the Northern Hemisphere. The lines on the charts outline major constellations. The dense band of stars is the Milky Way. To use, hold the chart vertically, with the direction you are facing at the bottom of the map.

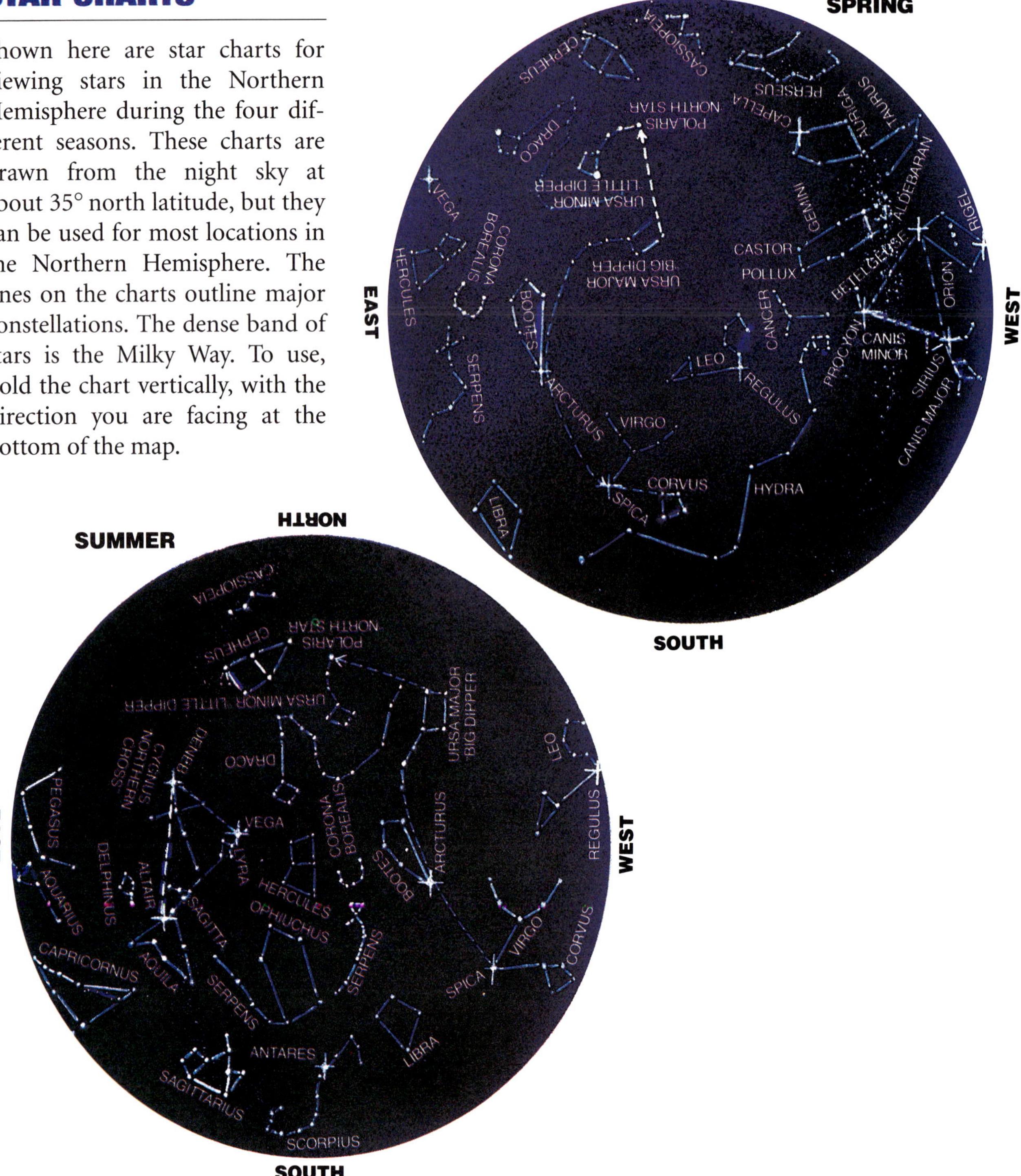

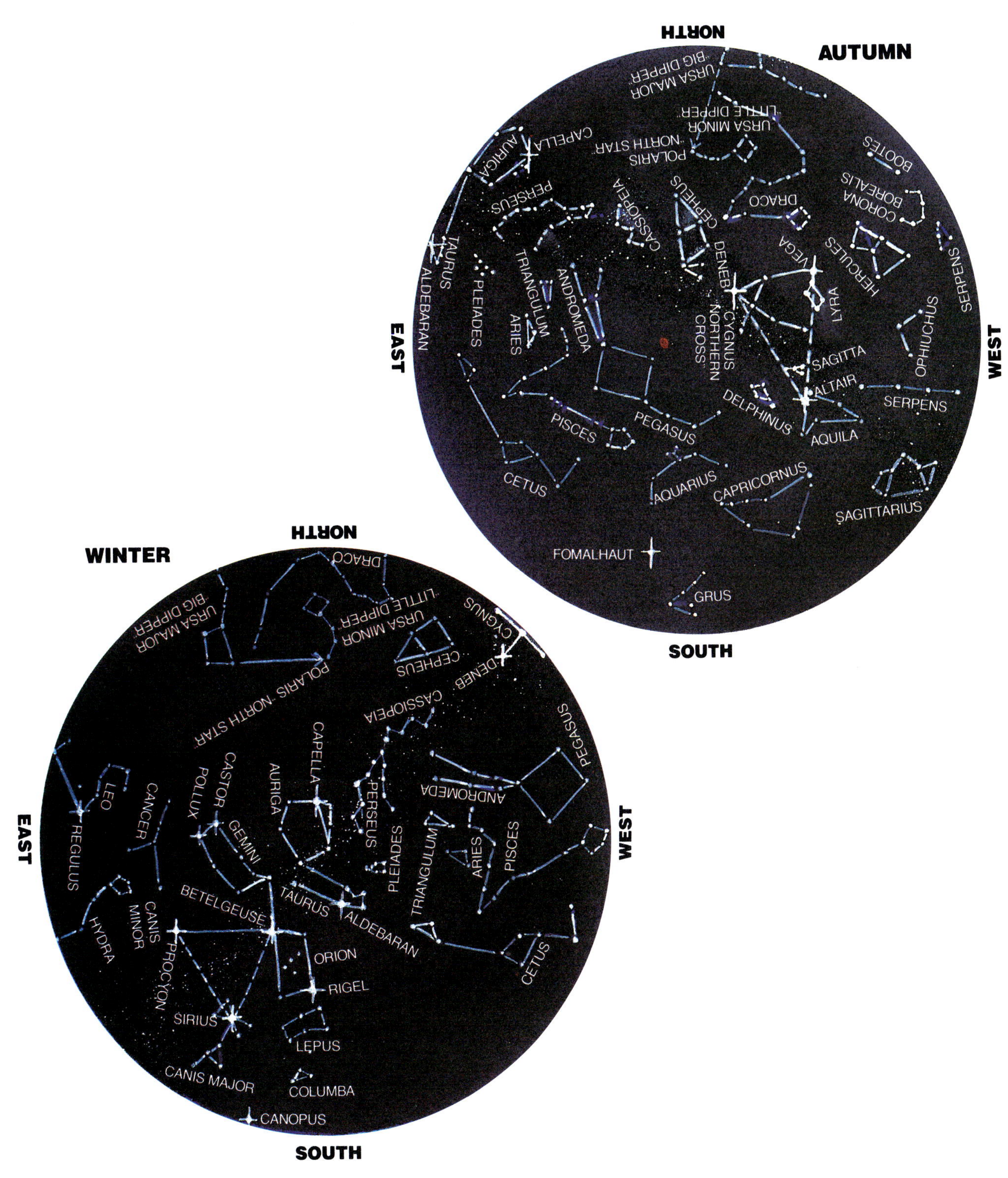
AUTUMN
NORTH
EAST
WEST
SOUTH
URSA MAJOR "BIG DIPPER"
URSA MINOR "LITTLE DIPPER"
POLARIS "NORTH STAR"
CAPELLA
AURIGA
PERSEUS
CASSIOPEIA
CEPHEUS
DRACO
BOOTES
CORONA BOREALIS
HERCULES
VEGA
LYRA
DENEB
CYGNUS "NORTHERN CROSS"
TAURUS
ALDEBARAN
PLEIADES
TRIANGULUM
ARIES
ANDROMEDA
SAGITTA
OPHIUCHUS
SERPENS
ALTAIR
DELPHINUS
AQUILA
PISCES
PEGASUS
CETUS
AQUARIUS
CAPRICORNUS
SAGITTARIUS
FOMALHAUT
GRUS
WINTER
NORTH
EAST
WEST
SOUTH
DRACO
URSA MAJOR "BIG DIPPER"
URSA MINOR "LITTLE DIPPER"
CEPHEUS
CYGNUS
DENEB
POLARIS "NORTH STAR"
CASSIOPEIA
CAPELLA
AURIGA
CASTOR
POLLUX
CANCER
LEO
REGULUS
GEMINI
PERSEUS
ANDROMEDA
PEGASUS
PLEIADES
TRIANGULUM
ARIES
PISCES
BETELGEUSE
TAURUS
ALDEBARAN
CANIS MINOR
HYDRA
PROCYON
ORION
RIGEL
SIRIUS
LEPUS
CANIS MAJOR
COLUMBA
CANOPUS
CETUS

Appendix K

CARE AND USE OF A MICROSCOPE

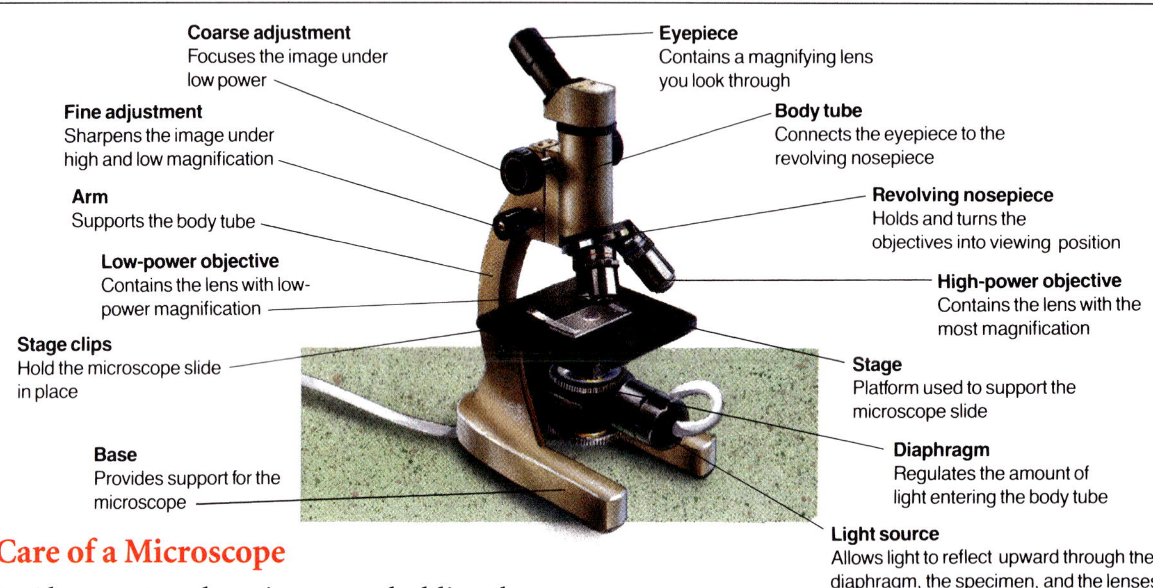

Coarse adjustment
Focuses the image under low power
Fine adjustment
Sharpens the image under high and low magnification
Arm
Supports the body tube
Low-power objective
Contains the lens with low-power magnification
Stage clips
Hold the microscope slide in place
Base
Provides support for the microscope
Eyepiece
Contains a magnifying lens you look through
Body tube
Connects the eyepiece to the revolving nosepiece
Revolving nosepiece
Holds and turns the objectives into viewing position
High-power objective
Contains the lens with the most magnification
Stage
Platform used to support the microscope slide
Diaphragm
Regulates the amount of light entering the body tube
Light source
Allows light to reflect upward through the diaphragm, the specimen, and the lenses

Care of a Microscope

1. Always carry the microscope holding the arm with one hand and supporting the base with the other hand.
2. Don't touch the lenses with your finger.
3. Never lower the coarse adjustment knob when looking through the eyepiece lens.
4. Always focus first with the low-power objective.
5. Don't use the coarse adjustment knob when the high-power objective is in place.
6. Store the microscope covered.

Using a Microscope

1. Place the microscope on a flat surface that is clear of objects. The arm should be toward you.
2. Look through the eyepiece. Adjust the diaphragm so that light comes through the opening in the stage.
3. Place a slide on the stage so that the specimen is in the field of view. Hold it firmly in place by using the stage clips.
4. Always focus first with the coarse adjustment and the low-power objective lens. Once the object is in focus on low power, turn the nosepiece until the high-power objective is in place. Use ONLY the fine adjustment to focus with this lens.

Making a Wet Mount Slide

1. Carefully place the item you want to look at in the center of a clean glass slide. Make sure the sample is thin enough for light to pass through.
2. Use a dropper to place one or two drops of water on the sample.
3. Hold a clean coverslip by the edges and place it at one edge of the drop of water. Slowly lower the coverslip onto the drop of water until it lies flat.
   If you have too much water or a lot of air bubbles, touch the edge of a paper towel to the edge of the coverslip to draw off extra water and force air out.

Skill Handbook
Table of Contents

ORGANIZING INFORMATION

THINKING CRITICALLY

PRACTICING SCIENTIFIC METHODS

REPRESENTING AND APPLYING DATA

SKILL HANDBOOK 647

Skill Handbook

ORGANIZING INFORMATION

CLASSIFYING

You may not realize it, but you make things orderly in the world around you. If your shirts hang in the closet together, your socks take up a particular corner of a dresser drawer, or your favorite cassette tapes are stacked together, you have used the skill of classifying.

Classifying is the process of sorting objects or events into groups based on their common features. When classifying, you first make observations of the objects or events to be classified. Then, you select one feature that is shared by some members in the group but not by others. Those members that share the feature are placed in a subgroup. You can classify members into smaller and smaller subgroups based on characteristics.

How would you classify a collection of cassette tapes? You might classify cassettes you like to dance to in one subgroup and cassettes you like to listen to in another. The cassettes you like to dance to could be subdivided into a rap subgroup and a rock subgroup. Note that for each feature selected, each cassette only fits into one subgroup. Keep selecting features until all the cassettes are classified. The concept map in the next column shows one possible classification.

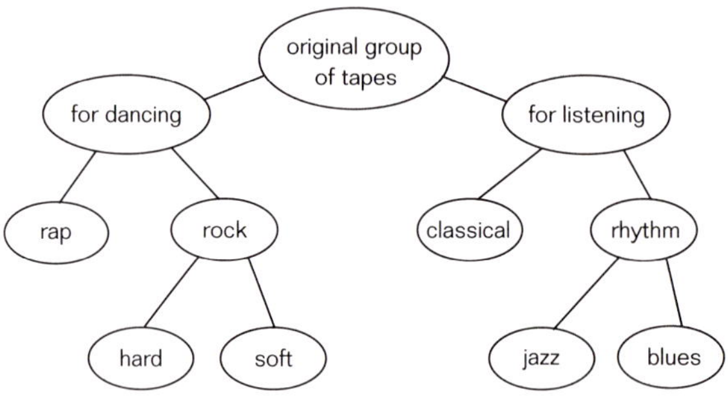

Remember when you classify, you are grouping objects or events for a purpose. Select common features to form groups and subgroups with your purpose in mind.

SEQUENCING

A sequence is an arrangement of things or events in a particular order. A sequence with which you are familiar is sitting in alphabetical order in a class. Another example of sequence would be the steps in a recipe. Think about baking chocolate chip cookies. The steps in the recipe have to be followed in order for the cookies to turn out right.

648 SKILL HANDBOOK

When you are asked to sequence objects or events, identify what comes first, then what should come second. Continue to choose objects or events until they are all in order. Then, go back over the sequence to make sure each thing or event in your sequence logically leads to the next.

Suppose you wanted to watch a movie that just came out on videotape. What sequence of events would you have to follow to watch the movie? You would first turn the television set to Channel 3 or 4. Then you would turn the videotape player on and insert the tape. Once the tape started playing, you would adjust the sound and picture. When the movie was over, you would rewind the tape and return it to the store.

MAKING AND USING TABLES

Browse through your textbook, and you will notice many tables both in the text and in the activities. Tables arrange data or information in such a way that makes it easier for you to understand. Activity tables help organize the data you collect during an activity so that results can be interpreted more easily.

Most tables have a title that tells what the table is about. The table then is divided into columns and rows. The first column lists items to be compared. In the table in the next column, different magnitudes of force are being compared. The rows across the top list the specific characteristics being compared. Within the grid of the table, the collected data is recorded. Look at the features in the following table.

EARTHQUAKE MAGNITUDE

MAGNITUDE AT FOCUS	DISTANCE FROM EPICENTERS THAT TREMORS ARE FELT	AVERAGE NUMBER EXPECTED PER YEAR
1.0 to 3.9	24 km	> 100 000
4.0 to 4.9	48 km	6 200
5.0 to 5.9	112 km	800
6.0 to 6.9	200 km	120
7.0 to 7.9	400 km	20
8.0 to 8.9	720 km	< 1

What is the title of this table? The title is "Earthquake Magnitude." What is being compared? The distance away from the epicenter that tremors are felt and the average number of earthquakes expected per year are being compared for different magnitudes on the Richter scale.

What is the average number of earthquakes expected per year for an earthquake with a magnitude of 5.5 at the focus? Locate the column labeled "Average number expected per year" and the row "5.0 to 5.9." The data in the box where the column and row intersect is the answer. Did you answer "800"? What is the distance away from the epicenter for an earthquake with a magnitude of 8.1? If you answered "720 km," you understand how to use the table.

To make a table, you simply list the items compared in columns and the characteristics compared in rows. Make a table and record the data comparing the mass of recycled materials collected by a class. On Monday, students turned in 4 kg of paper, 2 kg of aluminum, and 0.5 kg of plastic. Wednesday, they turned

SKILL HANDBOOK 649

in 3.5 kg of paper, 1.5 kg of aluminum, and 0.5 kg of plastic. On Friday, the totals were 3 kg of paper, 1 kg of aluminum, and 1.5 kg of plastic. If your table looks like the one shown, you should be able to make tables to organize data.

RECYCLED MATERIALS			
DAY OF WEEK	PAPER (KG)	ALUMINUM (KG)	PLASTIC (KG)
Mon.	4	2	0.5
Wed.	3.5	1.5	0.5
Fri.	3	1	1.5

MAKING AND USING GRAPHS

After scientists organize data in tables, they may display the data in a graph. A graph is a diagram that shows how variables compare. A graph makes interpretation and analysis of data easier. There are three basic types of graphs used in science, the line graph, bar graph, and pie graph.

A line graph is used to show the relationship between two variables. The variables being compared go on two axes of the graph. The independent variable always goes on the horizontal axis, called the *x*-axis. The dependent variable always goes on the vertical axis or *y*-axis.

Suppose a school started a peer study program with a class of students to see how science grades were affected.

AVERAGE GRADES OF STUDENTS IN STUDY PROGRAM	
GRADING PERIOD	AVERAGE SCIENCE GRADE
First	81
Second	85
Third	86
Fourth	89

You could make a graph of the grades of students in the program over the four grading periods of the school year. The grading period is the independent variable and is placed on the *x*-axis of your graph. The average grade of the students in the program is the dependent variable and would go on the *y*-axis.

After drawing your axes, you would label each axis with a scale. The *x*-axis simply lists the four grading periods. To make a scale of grades on the *y*-axis, you must look at the data values. Since the lowest grade was 81 and the highest was 89, you know that you will have to start numbering at least at 81 and go through 89. You decide to start numbering at 80 and number by twos through 90.

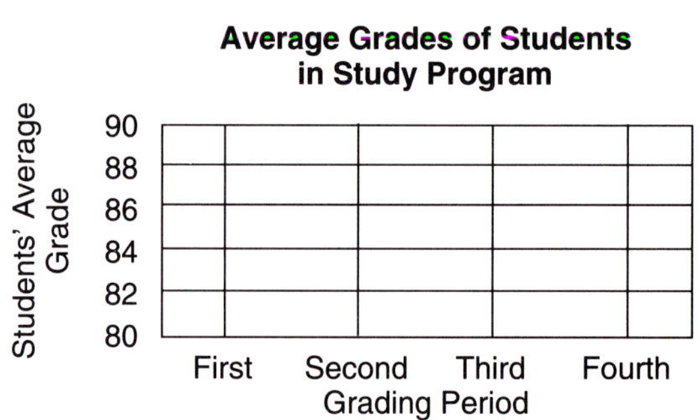

Next, you must plot the data points. The first pair of data you want to plot is the first grading period and 81. Locate "First" on the *x*-axis and locate "81" on the *y*-axis. Where an imaginary vertical line from the *x*-axis and an imaginary horizontal line from the *y*-axis would meet, place the first data point. Place the other data points the same way. After all the points are plotted, connect them with straight lines.

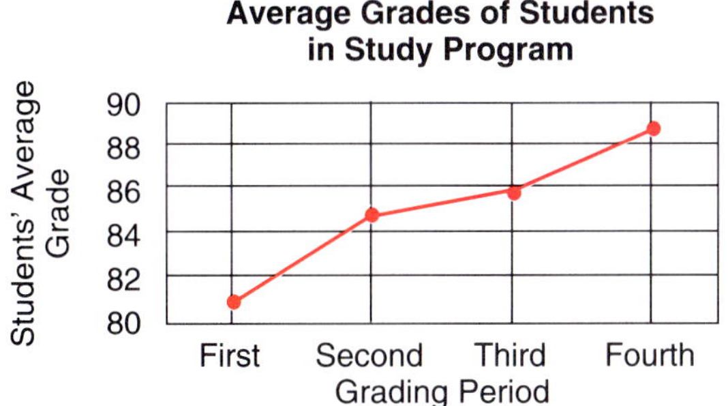

Bar graphs are similar to line graphs, except they compare or display data that do not continuously change. In a bar graph, thick bars show the relationships among data rather than data points.

To make a bar graph, set up the *x*-axis and *y*-axis as you did for the line graph. The data is plotted by drawing thick bars from the *x*-axis up to a point where the *y*-axis would intersect the bar if it was extended.

Look at the bar graph comparing the masses lifted by an electromagnet with different numbers of dry cell batteries. The *x*-axis is the number of dry cell batteries, and the *y*-axis is the mass lifted. The lifting power of the electromagnet as it changed with different numbers of dry cell batteries is being compared.

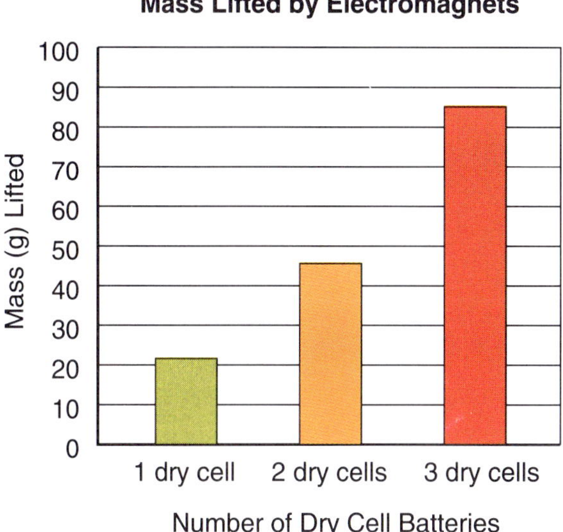

A pie graph uses a circle divided into sections to display data. Each section represents part of the whole. All the sections together equal 100 percent.

Suppose you wanted to make a pie graph to show the number of seeds that germinated in a package. You would have to count the total number of seeds and the number of seeds that germinated out of the total. You find that there are 143 seeds in the package. This represents 100 percent, the whole pie.

You plant the seeds, and 129 seeds germinate. The seeds that germinated will make up one section of the pie graph, and the seeds that did not germinate will make up the remaining section.

To find out how much of the pie each section should take, divide the number of seeds in each section by the total number of seeds. Then multiply your answer by 360, the number of degrees in a circle, and round to the nearest whole number. The number of seeds germinated as a measure of degrees is shown on the following page.

SKILL HANDBOOK 651

$$\frac{143}{129} \times 360 = 324.75 \text{ or } 325 \text{ degrees}$$

Plot this group on the pie graph, with a compass and a protractor. Use the compass to draw a circle. Then, draw a straight line from the center to the edge of the circle. Place your protractor on this line and use it to mark a point on the edge of the circle at 325 degrees. Connect this point with a straight line to the center of the circle. This is the section for the group of seeds that germinated. The other section represents the group of seeds that did not germinate. Label the sections of your graph and give the graph a title.

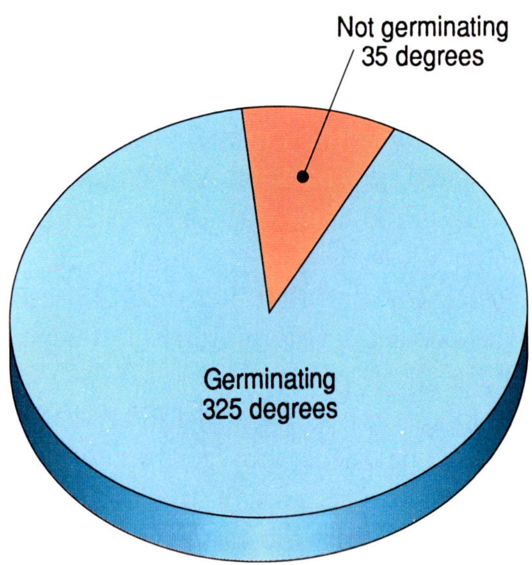

THINKING CRITICALLY

OBSERVING AND INFERRING

Imagine that you have just finished a volleyball game. At home, you open the refrigerator and see a jug of orange juice on the back of the top shelf. The jug feels cold as you grasp it. "Ah, just what I need," you think. When you drink the juice, you smell the oranges and enjoy the tart taste in your mouth.

As you imagined yourself in the story, you used your senses to make observations. You used your sense of sight to find the jug in the refrigerator, your sense of touch to feel the coldness of the jug, your sense of hearing to listen as the liquid filled the glass, and your senses of smell and taste to enjoy the odor and tartness of the juice. The basis of all scientific investigation is observation.

Scientists try to make careful and accurate observations. When possible, they use instruments, like microscopes, to extend their senses. Other instruments, such as a thermometer or a pan balance, measure observations. Measurements provide numerical data, a concrete means of comparing collected data that can be checked and repeated.

When you make observations in science, you may find it helpful first to examine the entire object or situation. Then, look carefully for details. Write down everything you see before using other senses to make additional observations.

Scientists often make inferences based on their observations. An inference is an attempt to explain or interpret observations or to say what caused what you observed. For example, if you observed a CLOSED sign in a store window around noon, you might infer the owner is taking a lunch break. But, it's possible that the owner has a doctor's appointment or has taken the day off to go fishing. The only way to be sure your inference is correct is to investigate further.

When making an inference, be certain to make use of accurate data and observations. Analyze all of the data that you've collected. Then, based on everything you know, try to explain or interpret what you've observed. If possible, investigate further to determine if your inference is correct. What is there in the photo that you could use to check your inference?

COMPARING AND CONTRASTING

Observations can be analyzed by noting the similarities and differences between two or more objects or events that you observed. When you examine objects or events to see how they are similar, you are comparing them. Contrasting is looking for differences in similar objects or events.

Suppose you were asked to compare and contrast the planets Venus and Earth. You would start by looking at what is known about these planets. Then make two columns on a piece of paper. List ways the planets are similar in one column and ways they are different in the other. Then, report your findings in a table or in a paragraph.

COMPARISON OF VENUS AND EARTH

PROPERTIES	EARTH	VENUS
Diameter (km)	12 742	12 112
Average density (g/cm^3)	5.5	5.3
Percentage of sunlight reflected	39	76
Daytime surface temperature	300	750
Number of satellites	1	0

Similarities you might point out are that both are similar in size, shape, and mass. Differences include Venus having hotter surface temperatures, a dense cloudy atmosphere, and an intense greenhouse effect.

RECOGNIZING CAUSE AND EFFECT

Have you ever watched something happen and then tried to figure out why

SKILL HANDBOOK 653

or how it happened? If so, you have observed an event and inferred a reason for its occurrence. The event is an effect, and the reason for the event is the cause.

Suppose that every time your teacher fed fish in a classroom aquarium, she or he tapped the food container on the edge of the aquarium. Then, one day your teacher just happened to tap the edge of the aquarium with a pencil while making a point about an ecology lesson. You observed the fish swim to the surface of the aquarium to feed. What is the effect, and what would you infer to be the cause? The effect is the fish swimming to the surface of the aquarium. You might infer the cause to be the teacher tapping on the edge of the aquarium. In determining cause and effect, you have made a logical inference based on your observations.

Perhaps the fish swam to the surface because they reacted to the teacher's waving hand or for some other reason. When scientists are unsure of the cause for a certain event, they design controlled experiments to determine what caused the event. Although you have made a logical conclusion about the fish's behavior, you would have to perform an experiment to be certain that it was the tapping that caused the effect you observed.

MEASURING IN SI

You're probably somewhat familiar with the metric system of measurement. The metric system is a system of measurement developed by a group of scientists in 1795. The development of the metric system helped scientists avoid problems by providing an international standard of comparison for measurements that all scientists around the world could understand. A modern form of the metric system called the International System, or SI, was adopted for worldwide use in 1960.

Your text uses metric units in many measurements. In the activities and experiments you will be doing, you will frequently use the metric system of measurement.

The metric system is convenient because it has a systematic way of naming units and a decimal base. For example, meter is a unit for measuring length, gram for measuring mass, and liter for measuring volume. Unit sizes vary by multiples of ten. When changing from smaller units to larger, you divide by ten. When changing from larger units to smaller, you multiply by ten. Prefixes are used to name units. Look at the following table for some common metric prefixes and their meanings.

654 SKILL HANDBOOK

METRIC PREFIXES			
PREFIX	SYMBOL	MEANING	
kilo-	k	1000	thousand
hecto-	h	100	hundred
deka-	da	10	ten
deci-	d	0.1	tenth
centi-	c	0.01	hundreth
milli-	m	0.001	thousandth

Do you see how the prefix kilo- attached to the unit gram is kilogram, or 1000 grams? The prefix deci- attached to the unit meter is decimeter, or one-tenth (0.1) of a meter.

You have probably measured distance many times. The meter is the SI unit used to measure distance. To visualize the length of a meter, think of a baseball bat. A baseball bat is about one meter long. When measuring smaller distances, the meter is divided into smaller units called centimeters and millimeters. A centimeter is one-hundredth (0.01) of a meter, which is about the size of the width of the fingernail on your ring finger. A millimeter is one-thousandth of a meter (0.001), about the thickness of a dime.

Most metric rulers have lines indicating centimeters and millimeters. The centimeter lines are the longer numbered lines, and the shorter lines are millimeter lines.

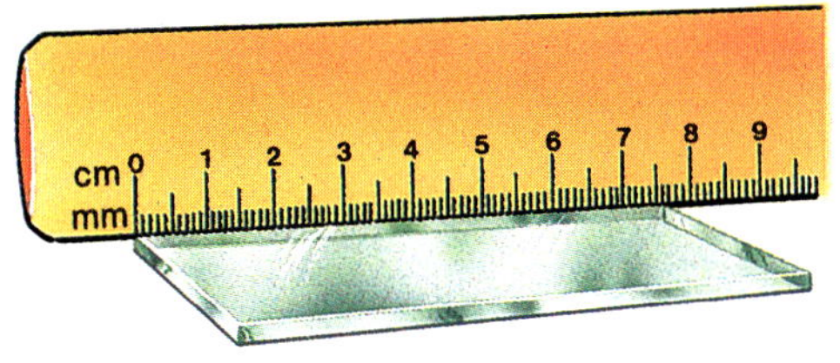

When using a metric ruler, first decide on a unit of measurement. You then line up the zero centimeter mark with the end of the object being measured and read the number where the object ends.

Units of length are also used to measure surface area. The standard unit of area is the square meter (m^2). A square that's one meter long on each side has a surface area of one square meter. Similarly, a square centimeter (cm^2) is a square one centimeter long on each side. The surface area of an object is determined by multiplying the number of units in length times the number of units in width.

The volume of rectangular solids is also calculated using units of length. The cubic meter (m^3) is the standard SI unit of volume. A cubic meter is a cube one meter on a side. You can determine the volume of rectangular solids by multiplying length times width times height.

Liquid volume is measured using a unit called a liter. A liter has the volume of 1000 cubic centimeters. Since the prefix milli- means thousandth (0.001), a milliliter equals one cubic centimeter. One milliliter of liquid would completely fill a cube measuring one centimeter on each side.

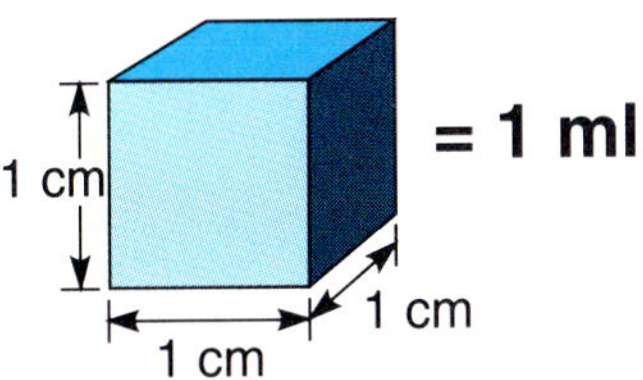

During science activities, you will measure liquids using beakers and graduated cylinders marked in milliliters. A graduated cylinder is a tall cylindrical container marked with lines from bottom to top.

SKILL HANDBOOK 655

Scientists use a balance to find the mass of an object in grams. You will likely use a beam balance similar to the one illustrated. Notice that on one side of the beam balance is a pan and on the other side is a set of beams. Each beam has an object of a known mass called a rider that slides on the beam.

Before you find the mass of an object, set the balance to zero by sliding all the riders back to zero point. Check the pointer on the right to make sure it swings an equal distance above and below the zero point on the scale. If the swing is unequal, find and turn the adjusting screw until you have an equal swing.

You are now ready to use the balance to find the mass of the object. Place the object on the pan. Slide the rider with the largest mass along its beam until the pointer drops below the zero point. Then move it back one notch. Repeat the process on each beam until the pointer swings an equal distance above and below the zero point. Read the masses indicated on each beam. The sum of these masses is the mass of the object.

You should never place a hot object or pour chemicals directly on the pan. Instead, find the mass of a clean container, such as a beaker or a glass jar. Place into the container the dry or liquid chemicals you want to measure. Next, you need to find the combined mass of the container and the chemicals. Calculate the mass of the chemicals by subtracting the mass of the empty container from the combined mass.

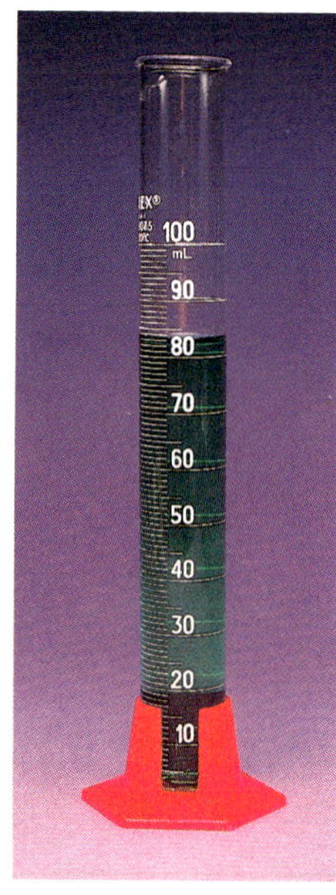

PRACTICING SCIENTIFIC METHODS

You might say that the work of a scientist is to solve problems. But when you decide how to dress on a particular day, you are doing problem solving, too. You may observe what the weather looks like through a window. You may go outside and see if what you are wearing is warm or cool enough.

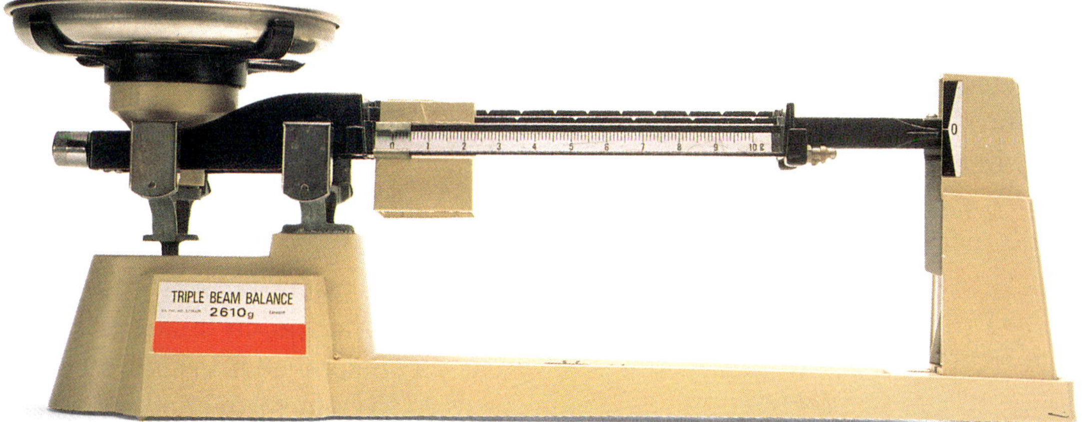

656 SKILL HANDBOOK

Scientists use an orderly approach to learn new information and to solve problems. The methods scientists use include observing, forming a hypothesis, testing a hypothesis, separating and controlling variables, and interpreting data.

OBSERVING

You observe all the time. Anytime you smell wood burning, touch a pet, see lightning, taste food, or hear your favorite music, you are observing. Observation gives you information about events or things. Scientists must try to observe as much as possible about the things and events they study.

Some observations describe something using only words. These observations are called qualitative observations. If you were making qualitative observations of a dog, you might use words such as cute, furry, brown, short-haired, or short-eared.

Other observations describe how much of something there is. These are quantitative observations and use numbers as well as words in the description. Tools or equipment are used to measure the characteristic being described. Quantitative observations of a dog might include a mass of 459 g, a height of 27 cm, ear length of 14 mm, and an age of 283 days.

FORMING A HYPOTHESIS

Suppose you wanted to make a perfect score on a spelling test. You think of several ways to accomplish a perfect score. You base these possibilities on past observations. If you put these possibilities into a sentence using the words *if* and *then*, you have formed a hypothesis. All of the following are hypotheses you might consider to explain how you could score 100% on your test:

If the test is easy, then I will get a good grade.

If I am intelligent, then I will get a good grade.

If I study hard, then I will get a good grade.

Scientists use hypotheses that they can test to explain the observations they have made. Perhaps a scientist has observed that plants that receive fertilizer grow taller than plants that do not. A scientist may form a hypothesis that says: If you fertilize plants, their growth will increase.

DESIGNING AN EXPERIMENT TO TEST A HYPOTHESIS

Once you have stated a hypothesis, you probably want to find out if it explains an event or an observation or not. This requires a test. A hypothesis *must* be something you can test. To test a hypothesis, you have to design and carry out an experiment. An experiment involves planning and materials. Let's figure out how you would conduct an experiment to test the hypothesis stated before about the effects of fertilizer on plants.

SKILL HANDBOOK 657

First, you need to lay out a procedure. A procedure is the plan that you will follow in your experiment. A procedure tells you what materials to use and how you will use them. In this experiment, your plan may involve using ten bean plants that are 15-cm tall in two groups, Groups A and B. You will water the five bean plants in Group A with 200 mL of plain water and no fertilizer once a week for three weeks. You will treat the five bean plants in Group B with 200 mL of fertilizer solution once a week for three weeks.

You will need to measure all the plants in both groups at the beginning of the experiment and again at the end of the three-week test period. These measurements will be the data that you record in a table. For instance, look at the data in the table for this experiment. From the data you recorded, you will draw a conclusion and make a statement about your results. If your conclusion supports your hypothesis, then you can say that your hypothesis is reliable. If it did not support your hypothesis, then you would have to make new observations and state a new hypothesis, one that you could also test.

GROWING BEAN PLANTS

PLANTS	TREATMENT	HEIGHT 3 WEEKS LATER
Group A	no fertilizer added to soil	17 cm
Group B	3 g fertilizer added to soil	31 cm

SEPARATING AND CONTROLLING VARIABLES

In the experiment above with the bean plants, you made everything the same except for treating one group (Group B) with fertilizer. By doing so, you've controlled as many things as possible. The type of plants, their beginning heights, the soil, the frequency with which you watered them—all these things were kept the same, or constant. By doing this, you made sure that at the end of three weeks any change you saw depended on whether or not the plants had been fertilized. The only thing that you changed, or varied, was the use of fertilizer. The one factor that you change in an experiment—in this case, the fertilizer—is called the *independent* variable. The factor that changes as a result of the independent variable is called the *dependent* variable—in this case, growth. Always make sure that there is only one independent variable. If you allow more than one, you will not know what causes any change you observe in the dependent variable.

Experiments also need a control, a treatment that you can compare with the results of your experiment. In this case, Group A was the control because it was not treated with fertilizer. Group B was

658 SKILL HANDBOOK

the test group. At the end of three weeks, you were able to compare Group A with Group B and draw a conclusion.

INTERPRETING DATA

The word *interpret* means to explain the meaning of something. Information, or data, needs to mean something. Look at the problem originally being explored and find out what the data is trying to show. Perhaps you are looking at a table from an experiment designed to answer the question: does fertilizer affect plant growth and leaf color? Look back to the table showing the results of the bean plant experiment.

Identify the control group and the experimental group so you can see whether or not the variable has had an effect. In this example, Group A was the control and Group B was the experimental group. Now you need to check differences between the control and experimental groups. These differences may be qualitative or quantitative. A qualitative difference would be if the leaf colors of plants in Groups A and B were different. A quantitative difference would be the difference in number of centimeters of height among the plants in each group. Group B was in fact taller than Group A after three weeks.

If there are differences, the variable being tested may have had an effect. If there is no difference between the control and the experimental groups, the variable being tested probably had no effect. From the data table in this experiment, it appears that fertilizer does have an effect on plant growth.

REPRESENTING AND APPLYING DATA

INTERPRETING SCIENTIFIC ILLUSTRATIONS

Most of the textbooks you use in school have illustrations. Illustrations help you to understand what you read. As you read this textbook, you will see many drawings, diagrams, and photographs. Some are included to help you understand an idea that you can't see by yourself. For instance, we can't see atoms, but we can look at a diagram of an atom and that helps us to understand what atoms are and how they work. Seeing something often helps you remember more easily. The text may describe the surface of Jupiter in detail, but seeing a photograph of it may help you to remember that it has cloud bands. Illustrations also provide examples that clarify something you have read or give additional information about the topic you are

SKILL HANDBOOK 659

studying. Maps, for example, help you to locate places that may be described in the text.

Most illustrations have captions. A caption is a brief comment that identifies or explains the illustration. Diagrams often have labels to identify parts of the item shown or the order of steps in a process.

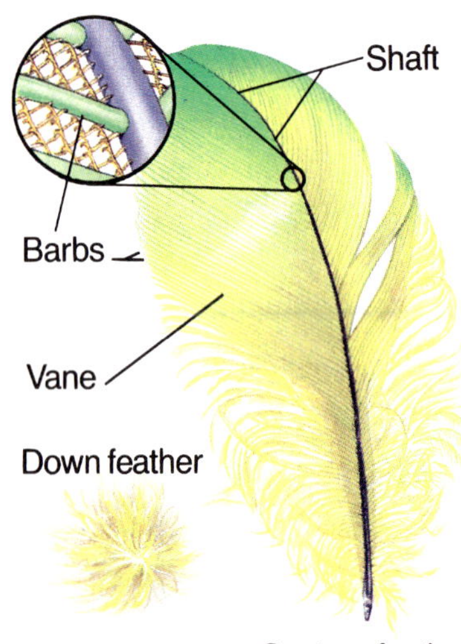

An illustration of an organism shows that organism from a particular view or orientation. In order to understand the illustration, you need to identify the front (anterior) end, tail (posterior) end, the underside (ventral), and the back (dorsal) side of the organism shown.

You might also check for symmetry so you know how many sides the organism has. A shark has bilateral symmetry. This means that drawing an imaginary line through the center of the animal from the anterior to posterior end forms two mirror images. If you can draw a second imaginary line at right angles to the first and divide the organism into four equal parts, the organism has radial symmetry.

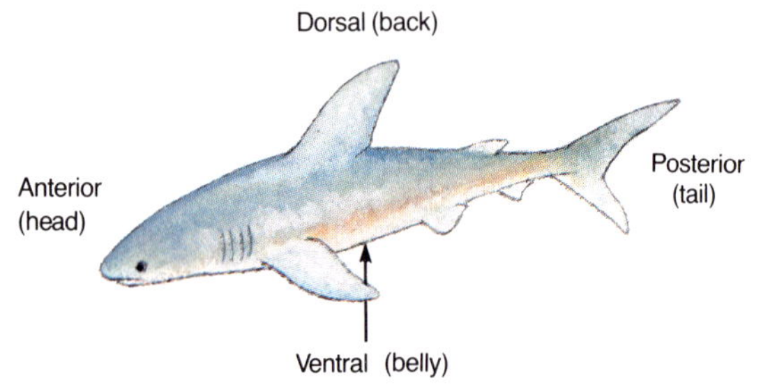

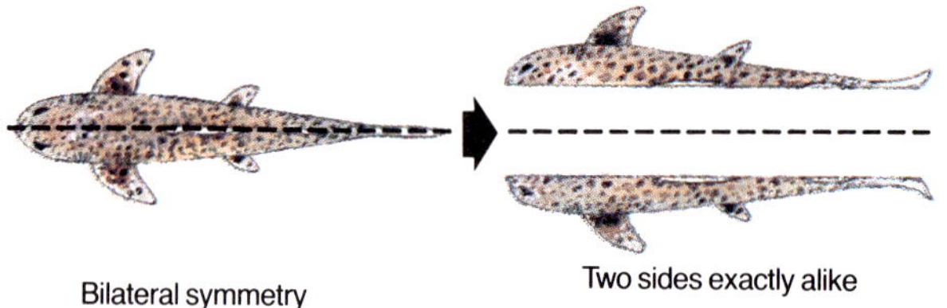

Some illustrations give an internal view of an organism or object. These illustrations are called sections.

Look at all illustrations carefully and read captions and labels so that you understand exactly what the illustration is showing you.

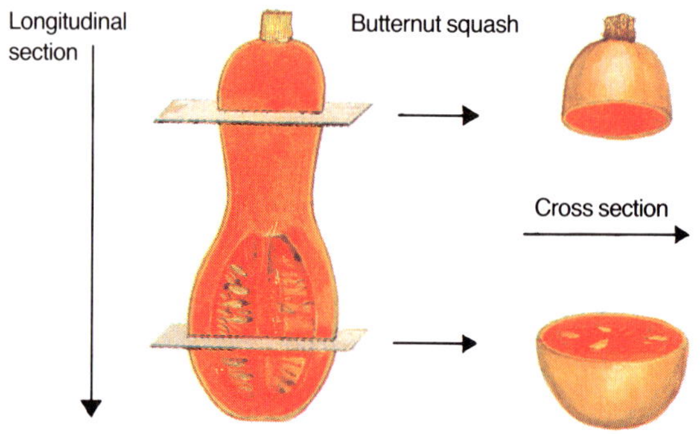

MAKING MODELS

You or your friends may have worked on a model car or plane or rocket. These models look, and sometimes work, just like the real thing, but they are usually much smaller than the real thing. In science, models are used to help simplify processes or structures that may be difficult to understand.

660 SKILL HANDBOOK

Often, everyday objects are used to make scientific principles and ideas simpler.

In order to make a model, you first have to learn about the structure or process involved. You decide to make a model showing the differences in size of arteries, veins, and capillaries. First, you must read about these structures. All three are hollow tubes. Arteries are round and thick. Veins are flat and thinner than arteries. Capillaries are very small.

Now you will need to decide what you can use for your model. Different kinds and sizes of pasta might work. Different sizes of rubber tubing might do just as well. Cut and glue the different noodles or tubing onto thick paper so the openings can be seen. Then label each. Now you have a model showing the differences in size of arteries, veins, and capillaries.

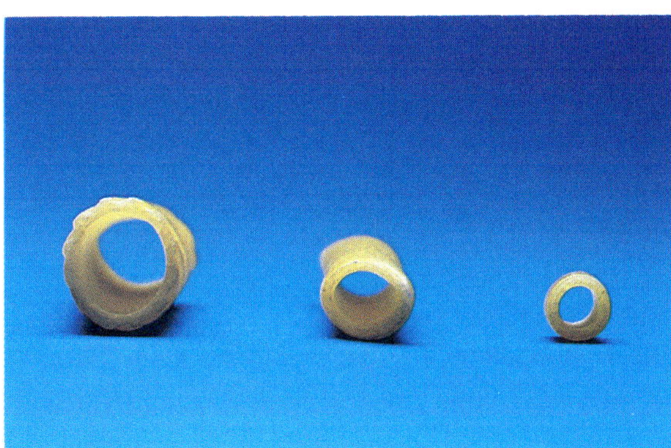

What other scientific ideas might a model help you to understand? A model of a compound can be made from gumdrops (using different colors for the different elements present) and toothpicks (to show different chemical bonds). A working model of a volcano can be made from clay, a small amount of baking soda, vinegar, and a bottle cap.

PREDICTING

When you apply a hypothesis, or general explanation, to a specific situation, you predict something about that situation. First, you must identify which hypothesis fits the situation you are considering. Maybe you want to predict whether or not eating a chocolate candy bar will increase your pulse rate. You've read that chocolate contains caffeine. So you could hypothesize that: if you consume caffeine in some form, then your pulse rate will increase. Next, you must figure out how the hypothesis affects the question you are asking. Since chocolate candy bars have caffeine and you think caffeine increases your pulse rate, you would predict that eating a chocolate candy bar would make your pulse rate faster.

We use predicting to make everyday decisions. Based on your previous observations and experiences, you may form a hypothesis that if it is wintertime, then temperatures will be lower. You may then use this hypothesis to predict specific temperatures and weather for four or five days in advance. You may use these predictions to plan what your activities will be for that time period.

SKILL HANDBOOK 661

Glossary

This glossary defines each key term that appears in **bold type** in the text. It also shows the page number where you can find the word used.

A

acceleration: rate at which velocity is changing (404)

acceleration due to gravity: for any free-falling object, $g = 9.8\ m/s^2$ on Earth's surface (426)

acids: compounds that contain hydrogen, taste sour, and are corrosive (228)

adaptation: any variation in an organism's body or behavior that helps it survive in its environment (261)

alloy: mixture of a metal with other metals or nonmetals (170)

amalgam: alloy that contains mercury (171)

amplitude: distance from the crest or the trough of a wave to the level of the medium when it is calm (545)

aquifer: layer of permeable soil or rock that allows water to move in and out freely (464)

average acceleration: change in the velocity divided by the time interval during which the change occurs (406)

average speed: total distance traveled divided by the total time required to travel the distance (396)

average velocity: total displacement divided by total time (400)

B

bases: compounds that taste bitter, are usually solids, and feel slippery when dissolved in water (233)

C

centripetal acceleration: center-directed acceleration of an object moving along a circular path (409)

ceramic: material made from dried clay or clay-like mixtures (165)

chemical change: change during which one of the substances in a material changes into a different substance (146)

chemical property: any characteristic that gives a substance the ability to undergo a chemical change (146)

chemical weathering: reaction between rocks and water, air, and other materials, often changing the substances that make up the rocks (491)

chlorophyll: green pigment in plants that traps the light from the sun (345)

class: group of related organisms below the phylum and above the order levels of classification (266)

cochlea: fluid-filled space in your skull bone that contains thousands of tiny receptor hairs (107)

colloid: a mixture that scatters light and whose particles do not settle out over time (212)

community: all populations that live and interact with each other in an area (360)

composite: something made of two or more parts (180)

compound: substance whose smallest unit is made up of more than one element (176)

compression: dense area in a longitudinal wave (68)

concentrated: solution with a relatively large amount of solute in a solvent (210)

cones: receptors in the retina that are sensitive to all the colors in the visible spectrum of light (98)

constellation: a pattern formed by a group of stars (22)

consumer: organism that eats other organisms to obtain food (292)

continental glaciers: masses of ice and snow that cover large land areas near Earth's polar regions (515)

contour lines: lines on a topographic map that connect points of equal elevation (11)

creep: slow movement of soil downhill (507)

crest: high point in a wave (543)

D

decomposer: organism that gets its food by breaking down dead organisms (364)

delta: triangular-shaped land area that may form when a river deposits sediment as it enters a body of water (513)

density: amount of mass an object or a material has compared to its volume (141)

662 GLOSSARY

deposition: accumulation of eroded sediments (506)
dilute: solution with a relatively small amount of solute in a solvent (210)
displacement: change in position of an object (399)
distance: measure of how far you travel along a path while you change your position (393)
Doppler effect: situation when a noise gets higher in pitch as the source of the sound approaches and lower in pitch as the source goes away (557)
drainage basin: area that a stream drains (457)
dune: a formation of wind-blown sand or loose sediment (521)

E

eardrum: thin tissue stretched across the ear canal that vibrates in response to sound waves (107)
ecosystem: community of organisms interacting with one another and with the environment (361)
element: substance that cannot be broken down further into simpler substances by ordinary physical or chemical means (174)
elevation: height above or depth below sea level (11)
endoskeleton: skeletal system within an animal's body (298)
equinox: one of two times during the year when the sun is directly over the equator (604)
erosion: movement of the products of weathering from where they formed to a different location (506)
exoskeleton: support system and protective covering outside an animal's body (299)

F

family: group of related organisms below the order and above the genus levels of classification (267)
fertilization: uniting of sperm and egg during reproduction (301)
food chain: model of how the energy in food is passed from organism to organism in an ecosystem (366)
food web: combination of all the overlapping food chains in an ecosystem (367)
frequency: number of cycles of any periodic motion in one second (74)

G

genus: group of related organisms below the family and above the species levels of classification (267)
glass: ceramic that is usually transparent or translucent (168)
groundwater: water that soaks into the ground and collects in the pores of the soil (462)

H

habitat: particular place where an organism lives (359)
hertz: unit of frequency; one cycle per second (74)
heterogeneous mixture: mixture in which the different substances are distributed unevenly (132)
homogeneous mixture: mixture in which the different substances are distributed evenly throughout (132)
horizons: soil layers (482)
horizontal component: horizontal part of a projectile's velocity or acceleration (430)
humus: in soil, decaying organic material made of the remains of plants and animals (480)
hydrologic cycle: the movement of water from Earth to atmosphere and back to Earth again (453)

I

ice wedging: process that occurs when water seeps into cracks in rocks and freezes, forcing the rocks to break apart (490)
indicator: substance that is one color in an acid and another color in a base (238)
interference: action of two or more waves passing through the same point (551)
invertebrate: an animal that does not have a backbone (297)

K

kingdom: most general and largest group of organisms in the classification system (265)

L

landforms: surface features of land, such as mountains, plains, and plateaus (4)
latitude: distance in degrees either north or south of the equator (15)
lava: molten rock material that has reached the surface of Earth (572)

GLOSSARY 663

leaching: process that occurs when seeping groundwater picks up some of the soil materials and carries them to lower horizons (483)
limiting factor: any condition that influences the growth or survival of an organism or species (372)
longitude: distance in degrees either east or west of the prime meridian (16)
longitudinal wave: wave in which the medium vibrates in the same direction as the wave is traveling (539)
lunar eclipse: event that occurs when the moon passes through Earth's shadow, because Earth is directly between the sun and the moon (614)

M

magma: molten rock material beneath Earth's surface (572)
magnitude: measure of an earthquake's strength (583)
meander: curve formed from faster-moving water wearing away the side of a stream bed (460)
medium: substance that carries the pattern of waves such as sound waves (71)
metamorphosis: change in form from young to adult (303)
mixture: any material made of two or more substances (131)
mudflow: downslope movement of a mass of mud (509)

N

neutralization: chemical reaction that occurs between an acid and a base (241)
niche: role of an organism within its community (361)
nonvascular plant: plant that lacks xylem and phloem tissue (328)

O

opaque: allowing no light to pass through (42)
order: group of related organisms below the class and above the family levels of classification (266)
organism: a living thing made of one or more cells, uses energy, moves, responds to its environment, adapts and has a life span (259)
oxidation: reaction during which oxygen combines with a metal to form a new material (491)

P

period: time for any periodic motion to complete one cycle (438)
pH: measure that shows the acidity of a solution (237)
phase: in reference to the moon, the changes in appearance of the moon as it orbits Earth (22)
phloem: tubelike vessels that transport food from the leaves to other parts of the plant (326)
photosynthesis: process in which plants use light energy to produce their food (345)
phototaxis: movement of an animal in relation to light (104)
phylum: second-highest level of classification of living organisms (266)
physical change: changes in physical properties of a substance, where the kind of substance remains the same (145)
physical property: any characteristic of a material that can be observed or measured (135)
physical weathering: process that breaks down rock into smaller pieces of the same kind of rock (489)
pitch: highness or lowness of the sound heard (75)
pollination: transfer of pollen grains from the stamen to the stigma of flowering plants (338)
population: group of organisms of the same species that live in a certain area at a certain time (359)
position: place where a thing is, described by comparing it to a reference point (392)
producer: organism that makes its own food through the process of photosynthesis (345)
projectile motion: motion of an object with an initial horizontal velocity that then moves only under the force of gravity (428)

R

rarefaction: less dense area in a longitudinal wave (68)
receptors: light-sensitive structures in the retina (98)
reflection: light bouncing off a surface (36)
refraction: bending of light when it passes from one medium to another (53)
relative velocity: velocity of one object determined from the view, or frame of reference, of another object (401)
reproduction: process by which organisms make more organisms of the same kind (260)
resonance: tendency for an object to vibrate at the same frequency as another object (82)
respiration: chemical process in which glucose is broken down, in the presence of oxygen, to release the energy needed to carry out life processes (307)

664 GLOSSARY

retina: tissue in the eye that is sensitive to light (97)

revolution: complete trip of Earth around the sun (601)

rockslide: quick, mass movement of falling rocks (508)

rods: receptors in the retina that are sensitive to light and dark (98)

rotation: spinning motion of an object around its axis (600)

runoff: water that flows over the ground and does not soak in (454)

S

salt: type of compound formed as part of neutralization (241)

saturated: solution that has dissolved all the solute it can hold at a given temperature (206)

seismograph: instrument used to record earthquake vibrations (583)

semicircular canals: half-circle shaped channels in the ear that control the sense of balance (108)

slump: slow mass movement of Earth material downslope (508)

soil profile: a vertical section of soil layers (horizons) (482)

solar eclipse: event that occurs when the moon passes directly between Earth and the sun, casting a shadow on Earth (611)

solstice: the two times each year that Earth's tilt results in the sun being directly overhead at the northernmost or southernmost point from the equator; marks the start of summer or winter (605)

solubility: amount of a substance that can dissolve in 100 grams of solvent at a given temperature (206)

solute: any substance that dissolves in a solution (197)

solution: mixture made up of tiny particles that are evenly mixed and do not settle out (196)

solvent: in a solution, substance in which the solute is dissolved (197)

species: smallest group of related organisms (267)

spectrum: band of colors formed as a beam of light passes through a prism (40)

sphere: round, three-dimensional object whose surface at all points is the same distance from its center (599)

stationary satellite: satellite that moves around its orbit once per day and always appears at the same point in the sky (435)

stimulus: anything an organism responds to (260)

substance: anything that contains only one kind of material (131)

suspension: mixture containing a liquid in which visible particles settle out (213)

T

taste buds: sense receptors located on the tongue (113)

tides: the periodic change in the surface level of the oceans due to the gravitational force of the sun and moon on Earth (615)

time: quantity that is measured with a clock (394)

translucent: allowing some light to pass through; not easily seen through (42)

transparent: allowing light to pass through; easily seen through (42)

transpiration: loss of water vapor through stomata of a leaf (343)

transverse wave: wave in which the wave disturbance moves at right angles to the direction of the wave itself (539)

trough: low point in a wave (543)

tsunami: tremendous ocean wave generated by an earthquake (579)

U, V, W, X

unsaturated: solution that can hold more solute particles at a given temperature (209)

valley glaciers: huge, moving masses of ice and snow that form at high elevations where snow stays year after year (516)

vascular plant: plant with xylem and phloem tissue (330)

vertebrate: an animal that has a backbone (297)

vertical component: vertical part of a projectile's velocity or acceleration (431)

water table: the top of the zone of saturation; the area where all of the pores in the ground are completely filled with water (465)

wavelength: distance between one wave crest and the next (544)

weightlessness: a condition experienced during free-fall (434)

xylem : tubelike vessels that transport water and minerals from the roots through the stem to the leaves of a plant (326)

GLOSSARY 665

Index

The Index for *Science Interactions* will help you locate major topics in the book quickly and easily. Each entry in the Index is followed by the numbers of the pages on which the entry is discussed. A page number given in **boldface type** indicates the page on which that entry is defined. A page number given in *italic type* indicates a page on which the entry is used in an illustration or photograph. The abbreviation *act.* indicates a page on which the entry is used in an activity.

A

B

666 INDEX

C

INDEX 667

F

G

668 INDEX

H

I

INDEX 669

N

O

670 INDEX

P

INDEX 671

S

672 INDEX

INDEX 673

674 INDEX

Photo Credits

xx, Mak 1; **xxi,** Matt Meadows; **xxii,** (t) Matt Meadows, (c) Raymond G. Barnes/TSW, (b) Lennart Nilsson, BEHOLD MAN, Little Brown & Company; **xxiii,** (t) Earth Scenes/John L. Pontier, (b) Leo de Wys/Marie Ueda; **xxiv,** Nick Pavloff/The Image Bank; **1,** Greg Vaughn/Tom Stack & Associates; **2,** Mike Surowiak/Tony Stone Worldwide; **3,** Tony Freeman/PhotoEdit; **4,** Kenji Kerins; **5,** William Felger/Grant Heilman; **6,** (t) Comstock/Cameron Davidson, (b) Grant Heilman; **7,** (tl) DRK Photo Source/Tom Till, (tr) Earth Scenes/Jim Tuten, (bl) ©Michael Giannenchini/Photo Researchers, (br) ©Craig Aurness/Westlight; **8,** DRK Photo Source/Peter French; **9,** ©Chuck O'Rear/Westlight; **12,** Ken Ferguson; **13,** Doug Martin; **14,** (t) DOI/USGS, (b) Kenji Kerins; **19,** (t) Steve Satushek, (b) NASA; **20,** Ralph Brunke; **24,** ©Keith Kent/Peter Arnold, Inc.; **25,** ©Earl Roberge/Photo Researchers; **26,** (t) Mark Richards/PhotoEdit, (b) H. Wendler/The Image Bank; **27,** ©Ray Pfortner/Peter Arnold, Inc.; **28,** (t) ©Alex S. McLean/Peter Arnold, Inc., (b)Doug Martin; **29,** NASA; **30,** Courtesy of Jessica Flintoft; **31,** USGS; **34,** Kenji Kerins; **35,** Ralph Brunke; **36,** Kenji Kerins; **37,** K S Studios; **38,** Ralph Brunke; **40,** ©David Parker/Photo Researchers; **42,** Ralph Brunke; **43,** Kenji Kerins; **44,** Ken Ferguson; **45,** ©J & L Weber/Peter Arnold, Inc.; **48,** Ken Ferguson; **49,** Courtesy of the Lyric Opera of Chicago; **50, 52,** Kenji Kerins; **53,** Comstock/Russ Kinne; **54,** Eric Lessing/Magnum; **56,** (t) ©Richard Weiss/Peter Arnold, Inc., (b) Stanley Scheonberger/Grant Heilman; **57,** (tl) ©Alfred Wolf/Photo Researchers, (tr) W. Rosin Malecki/PhotoEdit, (b) Tony Freeman/PhotoEdit; **58,** Tony Freeman/PhotoEdit; **59,** SuperStock; **60,** JPL; **61,** (l) Courtesy of Kodak, (r) Ken Ferguson; **62,** David Schaefer/PhotoEdit; **63,** Kenji Kerins; **64,** ©Rafael Macia/Photo Researchers; **65, 67,** Kenji Kerins; **68,** ©James H. Karales/Peter Arnold, Inc.; **70,** (t) NASA, (b) Kenji Kerins; **71,** Ralph Brunke; **74,** Studiohio; **75,** Runk/Schoenberger/Grant Heilman; **76,** (l) ©Will McIntyre/Photo Researchers, (r) ©Susan McCartney/Photo Researchers; **77,** Ken Ferguson; **79, 81,** Ralph Brunke; **82,** Myrleen Ferguson/PhotoEdit; **84,** H. Armstrong Roberts; **86,** Kenji Kerins; **87,** (l) Custom Medical Stock Photo, (r) ©Ed Lettau/Peter Arnold, Inc.; **88,** David R. Frazier Photolibrary; **89,** ICM Artists, Ltd.; **90,** Courtesy of Torey Verts; **91,** (t) Ken Ferguson, (b) Tony Freeman/PhotoEdit; **92,** Studiohio; **93,** (t) Tim Courlas, (b) Kenji Kerins; **94,** Enrico Ferorelli; **96,** (l) Ron Dahlquist/SuperStock, (r) ©Rafael Macia/Photo Researchers; **97,** (t) David R. Frazier Photolibrary, (b) ©Ralph C. Eagle, M.D./Photo Researchers; **98,** (t) ©Petit Format/Photo Researchers, (b) Kurt Scholz/SuperStock; **100,** ©Bill Ross/Westlight; **101,** (t) Animals Animals/Z. Leszczynski, (b) ©Georg Buchold/Photo Researchers; **102,** (t) Comstock/T. P. Dickinson, (bl,br) ©M.W.F. Tweedie/Photo Researchers; **103,** (t) ©Charles E. Mohr/Photo Researchers, (cl) ©Joseph T. Collins/Photo Researchers, (cr) ©T. Davidson/Photo Researchers, (bl,br) Ken Ferguson; **104,** ©Manfred Kage/Peter Arnold, Inc.; **105,** Ken Ferguson; **106,** ©Charles Campbell/Westlight; **107,** Mia & Klaus/SuperStock; **108,** Robert Llewellyn/SuperStock; **109,** (tl) Buff & Gerald Corsi/Tom Stack & Associates, (tr) Runk/Schoenberger/Grant Heilman, (c) Comstock/Dever Bryan, (bl) Gary Milburn/Tom Stack & Associates, (br) Medford Taylor/SuperStock; **110,** Brian Parker/Tom Stack & Associates; **111,** Ralph Brunke; **112,** (t) Zao Grimberg/The Image Bank, (b) Rivera Collection/SuperStock; **113,** (l) Bruce Iverson, (r) Lennart Nilsson/ *Behold Man*/Little, Brown & Company; **115,** (t) Myrleen Ferguson/PhotoEdit, (b) Comstock/Russ Kinne; **116,** Comstock/Franklin Viola; **117,** Thomas McAvoy/Courtesy of Time/Life Inc.; **118,** Brian Parker/Tom Stack & Associates; **119,** David R. Frazier Photolibrary; **120,** Comstock/Michael Stuckey; **123,** ©Richard Hutchings/Photo Researchers; **124,** H. Armstrong Roberts/Rauschenbach/Zefa; **125,** (tl) David M. Dennis/Tom Stack & Associates, (tr) ©Karl & Stephen Maslowski/Photo Researchers, (br) H. Armstrong Roberts, (bl) John Warde/SuperStock; **126,** Jane Grushow/Grant Heilman; **127,** Kenji Kerins; **128,** M. Richards/PhotoEdit; **129,** Kenji Kerins; **130,** Ken Ferguson; **131,** (t) Kenji Kerins, (bl,br) Ken Ferguson; **132,** (l) E. R. Degginger/Color-Pic., (r) Latent Image; **133,** Ken Ferguson; **134,** H. Armstrong Roberts/M. Spector; **135,** Studiohio; **136,** Ralph Brunke; **137,** Kenji Kerins; **138,** Ralph Brunke; **139,** Doug Martin; **140, 141,** Ralph Brunke; **142,** Ken Ferguson; **143,** Ralph Brunke; **144,** Kenji Kerins; **145,** (t) Barry L. Runk/Grant Heilman, (b) Kenji Kerins; **146,** (t) Tony Freeman/PhotoEdit, (b) NASA; **148,** Ralph Brunke; **149,** (t) Ralph Brunke, (b) ©Paolo Loch/Photo Researchers; **150,** Kenji Kerins; **151,** Ken Ferguson; **153,** Kenji Kerins; **154,** NASA; **155,** (tl,tr) Tony Freeman/PhotoEdit, (b) Don & Pat Valenti/Tom Stack & Associates; **157,** (t) Deborah Davis/PhotoEdit, (b) ©Leonard Lessin/Peter Arnold, Inc.; **158,** Art Resource; **159,** (tl) ©Charles Falco/Photo Researchers, (tr) ©Leonard Lessin/Peter Arnold, Inc., (b) Tony Freeman/PhotoEdit; **160,** Tony Freeman/PhotoEdit; **162,** David R. Frazier Photolibrary; **164,** Matt Meadows; **165,** (t) Smithsonian Institute; **165,** (bc) BLT Productions, (bl,br) Ken Frick; **166,** NASA; **167,** Kenji Kerins; **168,** Ken Ferguson; **169,** Runk/Schoenberger/Grant Heilman; **170,** (t) Ralph Brunke, (bl,br) C. M. Dixon Colour Photo Library; **171, 172,** Doug Martin; **175, 176,** Kenji Kerins; **179,** Grant V. Faint/The Image Bank; **180,** (l) Doug Martin, (r) Dan McCoy/Rainbow; **181,** Doug Martin; **182,** (t) Tom Stack & Associates, (b) Runk/Schoenberger/Grant Heilman; **183,** ©Heinz Plenge/Peter Arnold, Inc.; **184,** ©Martha Cooper/Peter Arnold, Inc.; **185,** Thomas Kitchin/Tom Stack & Associates; **186,** (l) Greg Vaughn/Tom Stack & Associates, (r) David Young-Wolff/PhotoEdit; **187,** Bill Aron/PhotoEdit; **188,** Tony Freeman/PhotoEdit; **189,** (tl,tr,cr) Doug Martin, (cl) Studiohio, (bl,bc) Ken Frick, (br) Dan McCoy/Rainbow; **190,** Billy E. Barnes/Tony Stone Worldwide; **192,** Ralph Brunke; **193,** Kenji Kerins; **194,** Ken Ferguson; **195,** (t) Kenji Kerins, (b) Ralph Brunke; **196,** Matt Meadows; **197,** (tl) H. Armstrong Roberts, (tr) Garneau & Prevost/SuperStock, (bl) Comstock, (br) Ken Ferguson; **198,** Ken Ferguson; **199,** Ralph Brunke; **200,** Barry L. Runk/Grant Heilman; **201,** Aaron Haupt; **202,** Kenji Kerins; **203,** (t) Ken Ferguson, (b) K S Studios ; **205,** (t) Ken Ferguson, (b) Ralph Brunke; **207,** Ralph Brunke; **209,** Kenji Kerins; **210,** Ralph Brunke; **212, 213,** Kenji Kerins; **214,** Al Cook Photography; **215,** Thomas Hovland/Grant Heilman; **216,** Mary Kate Denny/PhotoEdit; **217,** (l) ©Tom Myers/Photo Researchers, (r) Larry Lefever/Grant Heilman; **218,** ©Ray Pfortner/Peter Arnold, Inc.; **219,** ©Richard Divald/Photo Researchers; **220,** Grant Heilman; **221,** (tl,tc,tr,br) Ralph Brunke, (rc) Matt Meadows, (bl) Matt Meadows; **223, 224,** Kenji Kerins; **225,** Runk/Schoenberger/Grant Heilman; **226,** Ralph Brunke; **227,** (t) ©Tom McHugh/Photo Researchers, (b) Ken Ferguson; **228,** (t) Tony Freeman/PhotoEdit, (b) Ralph Brunke; **229,** Runk/Schoenberger/Grant Heilman; **230,** First Image; **231,** Gary Russ/The Image Bank; **232,** Kenji Kerins; **233,** Ken Frick; **234,** Kenji Kerins; **236,** Ken Frick; **238,** (t) Doug Martin, (b) Chip Clark; **240,** Robert Lee/Photo Researchers; **242,** (t) Matt Meadows; **243,** Ken Ferguson; **244,** Leonard Lee Rue III/Photo Researchers; **246,** Roberto Valladares/The Image Bank; **247,** David R. Frazier Photolibrary; **248,** (t) ©Roland Blake/Peter Arnold, Inc., (b) Pictoral Parade; **249,** ©Stephan L. Krasemann/Peter Arnold, Inc.; **250,** (t) ©Jack & Letha Pier/Peter Arnold, Inc., (b) ©Tom Pix/Peter Arnold, Inc.; **251,** (tr) H. Armstrong Roberts, (lc) Runk/Schoenberger/Grant Heilman, (bl) Tony Freeman/PhotoEdit, (tl) Studiohio, (rc) ©Leonard Lessin/Peter Arnold, Inc., (br) Doug Martin; **253,** (l) Matt Meadows, (r) Grant Heilman; **254,** Barry L. Runk/Grant Heilman; **255,** H. Armstrong Roberts; **256,** Unlimited Collection/SuperStock; **257,** Kenji Kerins; **258,** Ken Ferguson; **259,** (tl) ©Jerome Wexler/Photo Researchers, (tr) ©Ralph A. Clevenger/Westlight, (bl) Sharon M. Kurgis, (br) Jim Strawser/Grant Heilman; **260,** ©SIU/Photo Researchers; **261,** (tl,tr) Earth Scenes/John L. Pontier, (b) Stuart Westmorland/Tom Stack & Associates; **262,** Kenji Kerins; **263,** Tony Freeman/PhotoEdit; **264,** Roderick Chen/SuperStock; **265,** (tl) Steven Holt/Academy of Natural Sciences VIREO, (tc) B. Gadsby/Academy of Natural Sciences VIREO, (tr) C.H. Greenholt Academy of Natural Sciences VIREO, (b) Bettmann Archives; **266,** David R. Frazier Photolibrary; **267,** Lynn M. Stone; **268,** (t) ©SPL/Photo Researchers, (b) ©Tom E. Adams/Peter Arnold, Inc.; **269,** (tl) ©Biophoto Associates/Photo Researchers, (tr) ©Eric Gray/Photo Researchers, (c) David M. Dennis, (b) E.R. Degginger/Color-Pic.; **270,** (l) Jeff Foott/Tom Stack & Associates, (c) Brian Parker/Tom Stack & Associates, (r) Animals Animals/Greg Brown; **271,** (t) Jean Wentworth, (c,b) E.R. Degginger; **273,** (tl) Ron & Valerie Taylor/Bruce Coleman, (tr) H. Armstrong Roberts/K. Scholz, (bl) Erwin & Peggy Bauer/Bruce Coleman, (br) E.R. Degginger/Bruce Coleman; **274,** (l) Anna E. Zuckerman/PhotoEdit, (r) David B. Fleetham/Tom Stack & Associates; **276,** (l) Animals Animals/Robert A. Lubeck, (r) ©Leonard Lee Rue III/Photo Researchers; **277,** (tl) H. Armstrong Roberts/Leonard Lee Rue III, (tr) Don & Esther Phillips/Tom Stack & Associates, (b) ©Tom McHugh/Photo Researchers; **278,** (t) ©Stan Wayman/Photo Researchers, (c) ©Pat & Tom Lesson/Photo Researchers, (b) John Shaw/Tom Stack & Associates; **280,** ©Peter Ryan/Photo Researchers; **281,** (t) John Cancalosi/Tom Stack & Associates, (b) Tony Freeman/PhotoEdit; **282,** ©Tom McHugh/Photo Researchers; **283,** (t) ©W.H. Hodge/Peter Arnold, Inc., (l) F. Stuart Westmorland/Tom Stack & Associates, (r) ©Clyde H. Smith/Peter Arnold, Inc.; **284,** (l) ©Vic Cox/Peter Arnold, Inc., (r) ©Clyde H. Smith/Peter Arnold, Inc.; **285,** (bl,br) Earth Scenes/Henry Ausloos, (t) Comstock, (c) ©G.G. Dimijian/Photo Research-ers; **288,** Lawrence Migdale; **289,** ©Stephen Dalton/Photo Researchers; **291,** (t) ©Harvey Lloyd/Peter Arnold, Inc., (bl,bc) Geri Murphy; (br) ©Francois Gohier/Photo Researchers; **292,** (t) Comstock/Franklin Viola, (b) John Warden/SuperStock; **294,** (t) Alan Carey, (b) F. Stuart Westmorland/Tom Stack & Associates; **295,** Ken Ferguson; **296,** (t) Runk/Schoenberger/Grant Heilman, (bl) Rod Planck/Tom Stack & Associates, (br) Runk/Schoenberger/Grant Heilman; **297,** (l) Al Grotell, (r) Animals Animals/Oxford Scientific Films; **299,** E.R. Degginger/Color-Pic.; **301,** Grant Heilman; **302,** (t) ©Biophoto Associates/Photo Researchers, (b) ©Fred Bavendam/Peter Arnold,

Inc.; **303,** ©H. Reinhard/Photo Researchers; **305,** Animals Animals/Zig Leszczynski; **307,** (t) Larry Lipskey/Tom Stack & Associates, (c) Greg Vaughn/Tom Stack & Associates, (bl) H. Armstrong Roberts/T. Ulrich, (br) Jeff Foott /Tom Stack & Associates; **309,** (tl) ©Gregory K. Scott/Photo Researchers, (tr) Richard Heinzen/ SuperStock, (b) Nick Pavloff/The Image Bank; **310,** ©Hans Pfletschinger/Peter Arnold, Inc.; **311,** (tl) Paul Brown, (tr) Animals Animals/Leonard Lee Rue III, (b) ©Tom McHugh/Photo Researchers; **312,** (t) ©Merlin D. Tuttle/Photo Researchers, (b) ©Leonard Lee Rue III/Photo Researchers; **313,** Animals Animals/C.W Schwartz; **315,** (t) Michael Newman/PhotoEdit, (b) Bianalberto Cigolini/The Image Bank; **316,** Robert Brenner/PhotoEdit; **317,** Jack Baker/The Image Bank; **318,** Courtesy of Jessica Knight; **319,** (t) Dominique Brand/Tom Stack & Associates, (c) ©Elizabeth Weiland/Photo Researchers, (b) ©Biophoto Associates/Photo Researchers; **322,** David R. Frazier Photolibrary; **323,** Rivera Collection/ SuperStock; **325,** (t,tc,b) Runk/Schoenberger/Grant Heilman, (bc) ©Brian Furner/Photo Researchers; **328,** (l) E.R. Degginger/Color-Pic., (r) Robert & Linda Mitchell/ Mitchell Photography; **329,** Earth Scenes/Brent P. Kent; **330,** Ken Ferguson; **331,** John Shaw/Tom Stack & Associates; **332,** (t) Mary Lou Uttermohlen, (bl) Robert & Linda Mitchell/Mitchell Photography, (c,bc,br) E.R. Degginger/Color-Pic.; **333,** (l) Charles Gupton/Tony Stone Worldwide, (r) Lefever/Grushow/Grant Heilman, (cl) ©Doug Peebles/Westlight, (c) Bobbi Lane/Tony Stone Worldwide, (cr) Comstock/George Lepp; **335,** E.R. Degginger/Color-Pic.; **339,** Larry Minden/Minden Pictures; **340,** Ken Ferguson; **341,** (l) Earth Scenes/C.C. Lockwood, (c) Dwight R. Kuhn, (r) Comstock/ Russ Kinne; **342,** Kenji Kerins; **344,** Dwight R. Kuhn; **345,** (t) Wolfgang Kaehler, (b) Aaron Haupt; **346,** Tom Algine/SuperStock; **347,** Charles Mahaux/The Image Bank; **348,** (t) ©Michel Viard/Peter Arnold, Inc., (b) Kenji Kerins; **349,** (l) NASA, (r) Chip & Jill Isenhart/Tom Stack & Associates; **350,** Tony Freeman/PhotoEdit; **352,** (l) ©Ed Reschke/Peter Arnold, Inc., (r) Courtesy of the DuSable Museum of African American History; **353,** (tl,bl,br) Runk/Schoenberger/Grant Heilman, (c) Comstock/M. & C. Werner, (tr) Peter Pearson/Tony Stone Worldwide; **355,** (tl) H. Armstrong Roberts/T. Ulrich, (tc) Comstock/George Lepp, (c) Tony Stone Worldwide, (b) Eric Carle/SuperStock; **356,** Animals Animals/Bradley Smith; **357,** Lawrence Migdale; **358,** (l) Richard Hutchings/PhotoEdit, (r) Stephan McBrady/ PhotoEdit; **359,** David R. Frazier Photolibrary; **360,** Comstock/P. Greenberg; **361,** (t) H. Armstrong Roberts, (b) Joe McDonald/Tom Stack & Associates; **362,** (l) ©Peter Aitken/Photo Researchers, (r) ©Margot Granitsas/Photo Researchers; **363,** Lawrence Migdale; **364,** (l) Michael Newman/PhotoEdit, (r) David M. Dennis/ Tom Stack & Associates; **365,** Ken Ferguson; **366,** E.R. Degginger/Color-Pic.; **371,** Tony Freeman/PhotoEdit; **372,** (tl) ©George Holton/Photo Researchers, (tr) ©John Cancalosi/Peter Arnold, Inc., (bl) Charles Seaborne/Tony Stone Worldwide, (br) John Shaw/Tom Stack & Associates; **374,** ©Gregory G. Dimijian/Photo Researchers; **375,** (t) Larry Lefever/Grant Heilman, (b) ©Mitch Reardon/Photo Researchers; **376,** Raymond Barnes/Tony Stone Worldwide; **377,** ©George Holton/ Photo Researchers; **378,** NASA; **379,** ©CNRI, Science Photo Library/Photo Researchers; **380,** Ralph Brunke; **381,** Steve Dunwell/The Image Bank; **382,** (tl) Animals Animals/Leonard Lee Rue III, (tr) Animals Animals/Fred Whitehead, (b) ©Lowell Georgia/Photo Researchers; **383,** Courtesy of Carmen Lomas Garza; **384,** Aaron Haupt; **386,** R.S. Virdee/Grant Heilman; **388,** Larry Lefever/Grant Heilman; **389,** H. Armstrong Roberts; **390,** H. Armstrong Roberts/ R.J. Bennett; **391,** Ken Ferguson; **392,** Lawrence Migdale; **394,** David Spindel/ SuperStock; **395,** Kenji Kerins; **396,** Daniel L. Feicht/Courtesy of Cedar Point; **398,** (l) Aaron Haupt/David R. Frazier Photolibrary, (tr) Christopher Crowley/Tom Stack & Associates, (br) ©Gunter Ziesler/Peter Arnold, Inc.; **400,** (l) Tony Freeman/PhotoEdit, (r) ©Jules Bucher/Photo Researchers; **401,** Ken Ferguson; **402,** NASA; **403,** Kenji Kerins; **406,** William Hamilton/SuperStock; **408,** Cathlyn Melloan/Tony Stone Worldwide; **410,** Carl Purcell/ Photo Researchers; **411,** NASA/ Grant Heilman; **412,** Jack Swenson/Tom Stack & Associates; **414,** (t) ©Horst Schafer/Peter Arnold, Inc., (b) Robert Brenner/PhotoEdit; **415,** Chad Slattery Photography; **416,** Albright-Knox Art Gallery; **417,** (t) ©James Steinberg/ Photo Researchers, (cl) Zao Grimberg/The Image Bank, (cr) NASA, (b) Mike Howell/SuperStock; **418,** Bud Fowle; **420,** Robert E. Daemmrich/Tony Stone Worldwide; **421,** Kenji Kerins; **422,** ©Jerry Wachter/Photo Researchers; **423, 424,** Ken Ferguson; **426,** NASA; **428,** Ken Ferguson; **429,** (t) Ralph Brunke, (b) Richard Megna/Fundamental Photographers; **430,** K S Studios; **431,** Ken Ferguson; **433,** UPI/Bettmann; **434,** ©Richard Hutchings/Photo Researchers; **437, 439, 440,** Ken Ferguson/Used by permission of The California Clock Co.; **441,** Heinz Fischer/The Image Bank; **442,** NASA; **443,** (l) Dr. Richard Orville/The Image Bank, (r) NASA; **444,** NASA; **445,** Alfred Gescheidt/The Image Bank; **446,** (l) Courtsey of Royal Society of London, (r) Bettmann Archives; **447,** (t) ©Bruce Curtis/Peter Arnold, Inc., (bl) NASA, (br) Barry L. Runk/Grant Heilman; **448,** NASA; **450,** Doug Lee/Tom Stack & Associates; **451, 452,** Ken Ferguson; **454,** Grant Heilman; **455,** (l) Doug Martin, (r) Lindsay Gerard/Glencoe; **456,** Ralph Brunke; **457,** H. Armstrong Roberts/H. Abernathy; **458,** Doug Martin; **459,** Pictures Unlimited; **460,** Larry Hammill; **461,** Ralph Brunke; **462,** Studiohio; **466,** Earth Scenes/Ken Cole; **467,** Dale Jorgenson/ Tom Stack & Associates; **468,** (t) ©Mike Lewis/Peter Arnold, Inc., (b) Stewart M. Green/Tom Stack & Associates; **469,** David R. Frazier Photolibrary; **470,** Larry Lipsky/Tom Stack & Associates; **471,** Brian Parker/Tom Stack & Associates; **472,** Courtesy of JoAnna Gott; **474,** Bettmann Archives; **476,** ©James H. Karales/Peter Arnold, Inc.; **477, 478,** Ken Ferguson; **479,** (l) Terry Donnelly/Tony Stone Worldwide, (r) Comstock/Russ Kinne; **480,** Ken Ferguson; **481,** Doug Martin; **482,** W. E. Ferguson; **483,** Ralph Brunke; **484,** (l) Roger K. Burnard, (r) James Westwater; **485,** Joanna McCarthy/The Image Bank; **486,** (l) Glenn Frank/PhotoEdit, (r) Dale Jorgenson/Tom Stack & Associates; **487,** ©Pat & Tom Leeson/ Photo Researchers; **488,** Doug Martin; **489,** Studiohio; **490,** Tony Freeman/PhotoEdit; **491,** (t) Ralph Brunke, (b) Tom Bean; **492,** Weldon King/FPG International; **493,** (t) Index Stock Photography, (b) ©Leonard Lessin/Peter Arnold, Inc.; **494,** (t) ©Gregory G. Dimijian/Photo Researchers, (b) Studiohio; **495,** John Colwell/ Grant Heilman; **496,** Bettmann Archives; **497,** Courtesy of Library of Congress; **498,** ©G. Carleton Ray/Photo Researchers; **499,** Courtesy of Daryl Howard; **500,** Courtesy of Mia Balko; **501,** (tl) David R. Frazier Photolibrary, (cl) ©Elaine Braithwaite/Peter Arnold, Inc., (r) H. Armstrong Roberts/D. Muench, (bl) Kevin Schafer/Tom Stack & Associates; **504,** Grant Heilman/Grant Heilman Photography; **505,** Studiohio; **506,** Grant Heilman; **507,** (tl) Walt Anderson/Tom Stack & Associates, (tr) James Westwater, (b) Earth Scenes/Raymond A. Mendez; **508,** (t) Thomas G. Rampton/Grant Heilman, (b) Jeff Foott/Tom Stack & Associates; **509,** (t) Lawrence S. Burr/Sygma, (b) SuperStock; **510,** Kevin Schafer/Tom Stack & Associates; **511,** Aaron Haupt/David R. Frazier Photolibrary; **512,** Ralph Brunke; **513,** Wendy Shattil & Bob Rozinski/ Tom Stack & Associates; **514,** (t) NASA, (b) Bert Vogel/SuperStock; **516,** (t) Wolfgang Kaehler, (r) Roger K. Burnard; **517,** Doug Martin; **518,** ©S.J. Krasemann/ Peter Arnold, Inc.; **519,** James Westwater; **520,** John Barger; **521,** Ken Ferguson; **522,** Steve Lissau; **523,** Floyd Holdman/The Stock Solution; **524,** Earth Scenes/M. J. Coe; **525,** Larry Lefever/Grant Heilman; **526,** (t) UPI/Bettmann, (b) NASA; **527,** Comstock/Russ Kinne; **528,** Mark E. Gibson; **529,** Mark Newman/Tom Stack & Associates; **530,** NASA; **531,** Anne Gransden/SuperStock; **532,** Bill Hickey/The Image Bank; **533,** ©Mike Yamashita/ Westlight; **534,** ©James Simon/Photo Researchers; **535,** Larry Lefever/Grant Heilman; **536,** Beermann/SuperStock; **537,** Ken Ferguson; **538,** Juan Alvarez/The Image Bank; **541,** Kenji Kerins; **546,** Ken Ferguson; **548,** Adventure Island, Tampa, 1991; **549,** Kodansha; **550,** Ken Ferguson; **551,** Kenji Kerins; **553,** Juan-Pablo Lira/The Image Bank; **555,** Tony Freeman/PhotoEdit; **556,** Thomas Browne/PhotoEdit; **559,** Bettmann Archives; **561,** Richard Hutchings/PhotoEdit; **562,** (tl) David R. Frazier Photolibrary, (tr) Richard Cash/PhotoEdit, (bl) Brian Parker/ Tom Stack & Associates, (br) Greg Vaughn/ Tom Stack & Associates; **563,** Earth Scenes/Stefan Meyer; **564,** Courtesy of Jason Cobb; **565,** (tl) Kaz Mori/The Image Bank, (tr) David R. Frazier Photolibrary, (bl) Grant Heilman, (br) ©Bjorn Bolstad/Peter Arnold, Inc.; **568,** Gordon L. Kallio/ The Image Bank; **570,** Ken Ferguson; **571,** ©Wesley Bocxe/Photo Researchers; **572,** DRK Photo Source/Tom Bean; **574,** (l) Greg Vaughn/Tom Stack & Associates, (r) Tony Stone Worldwide; **575,** (t) Earth Scenes/Breck P. Kent, (b) Noriyuki Yoshida/SuperStock; **576,** Ken Ferguson; **577,** ©Bruce Brander/Photo Researchers; **580,** ©Douglas Peebles/Westlight; **581,** (l) ©Pat & Tom Leeson/Photo Researchers, (r) H. Armstrong Roberts; **583,** Andrew Rafkind/Tony Stone Worldwide; **587,** Alexandra Avakian/Woodfin Camp & Associates; **588,** Bettmann Archives; **591,** Mary Kate Denny/PhotoEdit; **592,** (t) Courtesy of Deena Strohman, (b) Ken Ferguson; **593,** ©Francois Gohier/Photo Researchers; **594,** Manfred Gottschalk/Tom Stack & Associates; **596,** NASA; **598,** Ken Ferguson; **599,** NASA; **601,** Kenji Kerins; **604,** Tim Courlas; **607,** Ralph Brunke; **608,** H. Armstrong Roberts; **610,** Kenji Kerins; **611,** ©Francois Gohier/ Photo Researchers; **612,** ©Dennis di Cicco/Peter Arnold, Inc.; **615,** Richard H. Thom/Tom Stack & Associates; **618,** ©Gregory G. Dimijian, M.D./Photo Researchers; **619,** NASA; **620,** (l) Jeff Foott/Tom Stack & Associates, (tr,br) F. Stuart Westmorland/Tom Stack & Associates; **621,** Martin/ Custom Medical Stock Photo; **622,** (t) Ken Ferguson, (b) Comstock/Thomas Wear; **623,** Cameramann International; **624,** Courtesy of Natalie Sanchez; **628,** H. Armstrong Roberts/Zefa; **634,** (tl) Alton Biggs, (c) David Dennis, (br,tr) Unicorn Photos, (bl) E.R. Degginger/Color-Pic.; **635,** (tl) SuperStock, (tr) Johnny Jonson, (cl) James Westwater, (cc) File Photo, (cr) Al Staffan, (bl) ©Roger Caras/Photo Researchers, (bc) Gwen Fidler, (br) Sean Warren; **636,** (tl) ©Bill Curtsinger/Photo Researchers, (tr) Gene Frazier, (cl) Breck Kent, (cr) Norbert Wu, (bl) ©Roger Caras/Photo Researchers, (br) Joey Jacques; **637,** (tl) Hutchins, (tc) Jim Rorabaugh, (tr) Al Grotell, (lc,bc) Lynn Stone, (c) Wolfgang Kaehler, (bl) Kjell Sandved, (br) Jean Wentworth; **648, 650, 652,** Ken Frick; **653,** Lloyd Lemmermann; **654,** Janet L. Adams; **656,** Doug Martin; **657,** ©Keith Kent/Photo Researchers; **659,** NASA; **661,** (l) Ken Ferguson, (r) ©Bill Bachman/Photo Researchers

676